W9-CHE-905

GENERAL INSURANCE

THE IRWIN SERIES IN RISK AND INSURANCE

ATHEARN *General Insurance Agency Management*

BLACK, KEIR, & SURREY *Cases in Life Insurance*

BRAINARD *Automobile Insurance*

DICKERSON *Health Insurance* Revised Edition

DONALDSON *Casualty Claim Practice*

EILERS & CROWE *Group Insurance Handbook*

FOLLMANN *Medical Care and Health Insurance: A Study in Social Progress*

FRAINE *Valuation of Securities Holdings of Life Insurance Companies*

GOSHAY *Information Technology in the Insurance Industry*

GREGG *Life and Health Insurance Handbook* Second Edition

GREIDER & BEADLES *Law and the Life Insurance Contract*

HABER & COHEN *Social Security: Programs, Problems, and Policies*

HABER & MURRAY *Unemployment Insurance in the American Economy*

LONG & GREGG *Property and Liability Insurance Handbook*

MAGEE *Life Insurance* Third Edition

MAGEE *Property Insurance* Third Edition

MAGEE & BICKELHAUPT *General Insurance* Seventh Edition

MCGILL *Legal Aspects of Life Insurance*

MCGILL *Life Insurance* Revised Edition

MEHR & CAMMACK *Principles of Insurance* Fourth Edition

MEHR & HEDGES *Risk Management in the Business Enterprise*

MELONE & ALLEN *Pension Planning: Pensions, Profit Sharing, and Other Deferred Compensation Plans*

MYERS *Social Insurance and Allied Government Programs*

REDEKER & REID *Life Insurance Settlement Options* Revised Edition

SNIDER *Readings in Property and Casualty Insurance*

STALNAKER *Life Insurance Agency Financial Management* Revised Edition

General
INSURANCE

By JOHN H. MAGEE

Late Director for Maine of the Federal Housing Administration and Assistant Professor of Economics and Sociology, University of Maine

and DAVID L. BICKELHAUPT

Professor of Insurance
College of Commerce and Administration
The Ohio State University

SEVENTH EDITION
1964
RICHARD D. IRWIN, INC.
HOMEWOOD, ILLINOIS

SEVENTH EDITION

First Printing, August, 1964

Second Printing, April, 1965

Third Printing, April, 1966

Fourth Printing, March, 1967

Library of Congress Catalog Card No. 64-21030

PRINTED IN THE UNITED STATES OF AMERICA

To

All Who Have "Shared the Risk" (of Me), and

Especially to

MY PARENTS

And

MY FAMILY

—David L. Bickelhaupt

PREFACE

MANY years ago it was said that "the beginning is the most important part of the work."[1] To this might be added that the completion is next in importance, followed closely by what comes between start and finish!

The Seventh Edition of this book began nearly thirty years ago with the fine work of John H. Magee. It progressed in successive revisions which kept pace with the rapidly changing field of insurance. Probably more than a quarter of a million students and businessmen have used this text to increase their understanding of risk and insurance.

Tremendous needs continue to exist for the further study of insurance. No society, business firm, family or individual can reasonably ignore the widespread uses, benefits and effects of insurance today. Its unusual interrelationship with many business subjects is fully recognized only when one sees its universal place as: (1) a separate business function, (2) a major economic factor in our society, (3) a significant item in both personal and public finance, (4) one of the most common legal contracts, and (5) a business institution with challenging opportunities for marketing and managerial decision making.

As an established text for many basic college courses on risk and insurance, the objective of this revision has been a blending of several alternative approaches. Just as no single teaching technique is "best," the beginning student of insurance needs an understanding of each perspective from which to evaluate the subject of insurance. The student using this text needs a "consumer-oriented" viewpoint, including the newer "risk management" approach as introduced in Part One. He also needs a "functional" understanding of the structure and operations of the insurance business, as used in Part Two. The "society" approach as emphasized in Part Three, concerning the relationship of insurance and government, is also essential. For greater depth of knowledge, the more traditional "line" approach is used in Parts Four and Five, permitting intensified study of each of the fundamental areas of property, liability, life, and health insurance. The coordination of these major approaches is the purpose of the Part Six of the text, as the planning and buying of insurance are reviewed.

[1]Plato, *The Republic,* Book I, 377-B.

It is my feeling, and I believe it also would be that of John Magee if he were still alive today, that each of the approaches to studying insurance and risk has significant value for the general college student, the student who plans a career in insurance *and* the businessman who is pursuing a program of continuing education in his chosen occupation. For this reason the present text should prove adaptable for continued and successful use for a "principles" or introductory risk and insurance course, for some of the more advanced college courses, and for company educational and professional programs such as those of the Insurance Institute of America. Suggested assignment schedules for 30 and 45 class sessions in using this text are offered immediately following this Preface.

A major rewriting and reorganization of the text has been undertaken in this Seventh Edition. Nearly one half of the total pages are completely new or revised material. New sections are included on Introduction to Risk and Insurance, The Structure and Operations of the Insurance Business, Insurance and Government, and Planning and Buying Insurance. More than two thirds (and in four cases, all) of the following chapters are new: Risk and Its Treatment, Insurance and Its Significance, Underwriting and Reinsurance, Insurance Regulation, Social Insurance, Automobile Insurance, Group Life Insurance, Life Insurance Contract Features, and Coordinating Insurance Programs. More than half of ten other chapters are new material, including such important chapters as Insurance Marketing, Insurance for Indirect Losses, Multiple-Line and All-Lines Insurance, Health Insurance, and Group Health Insurance.

This is the first general insurance text to use the new 1958 C.S.O. Table figures in its illustrations and examples of life insurance premium calculations (see Chapter 21). The risk management concept is emphasized in the early chapters, and the current trends in "packaging" of insurance coverages are explored in several others. A Personal Insurance Review and a Case Study for Business Risk Management (based on the risk problems of a modern shopping center) appear in the final chapter.

Major attention has been given to preparing adequate outlines for each chapter. These outlines are given in detail at the beginning of each major part of the book, and are used as the basis throughout each chapter for the subheadings. Careful deletion of some of the former questions "For Review" at the end of each chapter has been done, and new questions have been added. The criteria for choosing questions have included the need for (1) review of important specific concepts, (2) variety in type of questions, (3) provoking organized thought on relationships among various ideas, and (4) instilling curiosity in the student. A summary has been written at the end of each chapter, for the purpose of providing a brief coordinated review of the fundamental points.

Extra material is included in several appendixes. The section on the history of insurance is excellent supplementary information for teachers and advanced students, and the references on this topic are as thoroughly documented as in any available insurance text. Some of the more important insurance contracts and forms are included in the chapters, while others appear in the appendixes. Many teachers will also desire to obtain sample insurance contract kits for their classes from the Insurance Information Institute (110 William Street, New York 38), the Institute of Life Insurance (488 Madison Avenue, New York 22), or the American Mutual Alliance (20 North Wacker Drive, Chicago 6).

No project of this size can result without many persons deserving considerable credit. General thanks, of course, go to my wife, Lee, and children, Tina, Jan, Paul and Carol, who have patiently withstood the trying times which naturally result whenever work has assumed priority over family leisure. This I hereby guiltily acknowledge to have occurred much too frequently during the past two years. To my many former teachers and students I also extend sincere appreciation for their undefinable but important part in shaping my ideas.

Primary and special thanks go to Dr. Edison L. Bowers, who read and commented on every page of the typescript. For those persons who provided help on individual chapters, I also wish to thank: Mr. Maynard W. Whitelaw, Mr. John L. Sybrandt, Mr. W. L. Such, Dr. Davis W. Gregg, Mr. Gene C. Moore, and Mrs. Dorothy T. Layman. For typing assistance, Mrs. Eleanor Sapp met each necessary deadline with excellent work.

With the inborn ability to simplify things, children often analyze their parents in a concise manner. Some years ago my oldest daughter solved the traditional kindergarten query of "What does *your* Daddy do?" by telling a friend: "He's a *book* doctor!" I guess that sums up my role in this text as well as can be done, though I might add that I hope the treatment is successful. I also wish that any teachers or colleagues, or their "patients," will be kind enough to send me their own diagnosis. The responsibility for my diagnosis of the needs of insurance education, of course, in spite of much indebtedness to others, remains my own.

COLUMBUS, OHIO
May, 1964

DAVID L. BICKELHAUPT

SUGGESTED ASSIGNMENT SCHEDULE FOR SEVERAL COURSE LENGTHS

For 30 Class Sessions*	For 45 Class Sessions*	Topic	Chapter
1	1	Risk and Its Treatment	1
2	2	Insurance (What It Is, How It Works)	2
3	3	Insurance (Fields and Significance)	2
4	4	Contract Fundamentals	3
5	5–6	Insurance Marketing	4
6	7–8	Insurance Loss Payment	5
7	9	Underwriting and Reinsurance	6
8	10–11	Insurance Regulation	7
9	12	Social Insurance (Basic and O.A.S.D.I.)	8
10	13–14	Social Insurance (Other Programs)	8
11	15–16	The Fire Insurance Contract	9
12	17	Fire Forms and Additions	10
13	18	Insurance for Indirect Losses	11
14	19–20	Transportation Insurance	12
15	21	Examination	
16	22	The Liability Risk	13
17	23–24	General Liability and Workmen's Compensation	14–15
18	25	Automobile Insurance Laws	16
19	26–27	Automobile Insurance Contracts	16
20	28–29	Crime and Miscellaneous Insurance	17–18
21	30–31	Multiple-Line and All-Lines Insurance	19
22	32–33	Life Insurance Principles and Premiums	20–21
23	34–35	Individual Life Insurance Contracts	22
24	36	Group Life Insurance	23
25	37–38	Life Insurance Contract Features	24
26	39	Annuities	25
27	40–41	Health Insurance	26
28	42	Group Health Insurance	27
29	43–44	Coordinating Insurance Programs	28
30	45	Review Session or Examination	

*The length and number of class sessions are based on the assumption that the normal course will contain either 30 or 45 individual classes of about one hour each, with outside reading assignments in preparation for the classes averaging about two hours each. Some variation of the suggested timing is natural, depending upon the interests of students and teachers, and the desire to use other supplementary materials. Several of the assignments may be easily shortened, if necessary, by omitting a portion of the material at the end of the chapter.

TABLE OF CONTENTS

*See detailed outline for each Part beginning on first page of each Part.

PART V. *Life and Health Insurance* ... 593

PART VI. *Planning and Buying Insurance* ... 845

Appendixes

Index

LIST OF FIGURES

LIST OF TABLES

PART ONE

Introduction to Risk and Insurance

CHAPTER 1 *RISK AND ITS TREATMENT*

I. What Risk Is
- A. Uncertainty and Risk
- B. Economic Risk
- C. Perils, Hazards, and Losses

II. Classifications of Risk
- A. Speculative and Pure Risks
- B. Personal, Property, and Liability Risks
- C. Insignificant Risks
- D. Insurable Risks
- E. Gambling Risks

III. The Treatment of Risk
- A. Avoiding Risk
- B. Ignoring Risk
- C. Retention of Risk (Including "Self-Insurance")
- D. Loss Prevention
- E. Transfer of Risk
- F. Risk Management: Coordinated Risk Treatment

IV. Summary

CHAPTER 2 *INSURANCE AND ITS SIGNIFICANCE*

I. What Insurance Is
- A. Insurance Defined
  1. Economic
  2. Legal
  3. Business
  4. Social
  5. Mathematical
- B. Summary

II. How Insurance Works
- A. The Insurance Equation
- B. Probability and Uncertainty
- C. The Law of Large Numbers
- D. Statistical Data

III. The Fields of Insurance

A. Social and Voluntary Insurance

B. Commercial Insurance

1. Personal Insurance
2. Property Insurance
3. Multiple-Line and All-Lines Insurance

C. Cooperative Insurance

D. Voluntary Government Insurance

E. Summary

IV. A Brief History of Insurance

A. Ancient Insurance Ideas

B. The Middle Ages and the Merchant Era

C. The Eighteenth Century and Insurance in Early America

D. The Expanding 1800's

E. Twentieth Century Growth

V. The Significance of Insurance

A. General Benefits

B. Statistical Evidences

VI. Summary

Chapter 1

RISK AND ITS TREATMENT

THE beginning student often desires in the first few pages of an insurance text a concise explanation of what *insurance* is. Such a start is filled with danger, for insurance is a subject of immense scope.

Almost everyone is familiar today with some aspect of insurance. A tremendous variety of concepts emerges in our everyday use of the word. Thus one person may think of insurance as a legal contract, while to another it means a business organization, a social device, a career, or an important part of the family budget. The many different connotations suggest that any attempt to define insurance should be deferred until a basis for understanding has been established.

WHAT RISK IS

A logical basis for such understanding is the concept of *risk,* which is the foundation for insurance. Without risk, there would be no need for insurance.

But what widespread risks do exist! No one ever reaches the state of absolute certainty. From the moment of birth until life has ceased every individual, no matter who he is or how he lives, constantly faces the possibility of unexpected and unwanted happenings. The essential element of risk is unpredictability, a tendency that actual results may differ from predicted results.[1]

Examples of risk are everywhere. They range from the unavoidable to those assumed by choice. Human existence itself creates such risks as not knowing when death, ill health, injury, or unemployment will occur. An example of risk by choice would be the formation of any form of business enterprise. The risk present in drilling a new oil well is an obvious example, while a more common venture is the investing of money in real estate. Indeed, anyone who owns property automatically assumes the risk of such losses as fire, windstorm, theft, or liability lawsuits. The inability to predict when or

---

[1]Davis T. Ratcliffe, "Risk," *The Journal of Insurance,* Vol. XXX, No. 2 (June, 1963), pp. 269-70.

if these losses may occur are risks the property owner acquires with his ownership.

Uncertainty and Risk

Several warnings are necessary in using the word risk. *Uncertainty* is often used as a synonym, although when so used it usually refers to objective (measurable or quantified) uncertainty.[2] Economists and statisticians use this concept when they measure probability or chance of loss. The probability of heads occurring when tossing coins is referred to as 1 out of 2 or ½. This is not necessarily true for just one toss, or ten, or even more, but it is true objectively, given a sufficient number of tosses to predict the result accurately. Uncertainty about a given probability actually occurring is reduced as the number is increased, as we shall see later in discussing the law of large numbers.

Note that risk is not only chance of loss, for anything that is certain not to happen (0 percent chance of loss) or certain to happen (100 percent chance of loss) does not involve objective risk. Anywhere between the points of certainty, 0 percent and 100 percent probability of loss, involves some unpredictability and thus risk. The greatest uncertainty appears at 50 percent chance of loss.

Subjective uncertainty, which involves a feeling or state of mind as to expected results, differs from the above concept of objective uncertainty. Lack of knowledge as to the real facts, prejudices, unwarranted high hopes or other factors can cause different predictions. Therefore different subjective risks occur, and these often deviate from the underlying objective risk.

Economic Risk

The student must contemplate these differences to understand risk. Further distinction is also necessary for meaningful analysis. For example, are all risks economic ones? One might rush to answer yes, but a second thought would suggest that while most risks have financial consequences, not all necessarily do. Usually one thinks of economic results when he considers risk, but psychological, spiritual, and other risks could be identified as well. Inability to predict the loss of friends or character or moral values are risks as well as the more obvious loss of economic values. Many definitions of risk refer to it as "uncertainty of financial loss," which indicates the major concern about risk centers on economic risk.

---

[2]Alan H. Willett, *The Economic Theory of Risk and Insurance* (Philadelphia, Pa.: University of Pennsylvania Press, 1951), pp. 5-6; and Frank Knight, *Risk, Uncertainty and Profit* (Boston: Houghton Mifflin Company, 1921), pp. 233-34.

Perils, Hazards, and Losses

Terminology becomes important in the serious study of any subject. It is the basis for communication and understanding. Terms that are loosely used in a general or colloquial sense can lead only to misunderstanding in a specialized study area such as insurance.

Perils. In contrast to risk, which is the unpredictability of results or happenings, the word *peril* should be used to identify the unpredictable occurrence. Thus it refers more specifically to the *cause* of risk (rather than just general inability to predict). Examples of perils are commonplace, and include fires, automobile accidents, thefts, earthquakes, windstorms, forgeries, water damage, illness, and hundreds of other undesirable occurrences.

The law has coined the term "acts of God" to describe perils operating without human agency or intervention and not preventable by human foresight or care. Fires caused by lightning are often so considered, but the element of human agency is regarded as having intervened in fires otherwise caused. Storms or blizzards are considered acts of God, as are earthquakes, extraordinary floods, and other forces of nature.

Hazards. The various factors contributing to the peril are termed *hazards*. Ordinarily, there are many separate hazards that attach to any particular object or person. The sum total of the hazards constitute the perils which cause the risk.

A practice of the insurance business divides hazards into two major classifications. The first of these is termed "physical hazards" and includes everything relating to location, structure, occupancy, exposure, and the like. The term "moral hazards" is applied to those perils that have their inception in mental attitudes. Included in this second group are the hazards created by dishonesty, insanity, carelessness, indifference, and other causes psychological in nature.

Physical hazards include such conditions: waste paper piled under a staircase, gasoline stored on the premises, weak construction which may fail in a heavy wind, unsafe brakes on a car, holes in a sidewalk, inadequate inventory checks in a store, improper water drainage systems, and many others. These examples each would increase the chance of a loss occurring in regard to a specific peril such as fire, wind, water, theft, or other accident.

When a particular form of insurance is contemplated on a given property, the insurer must make an appraisal of all the hazards involved. He must, therefore, know something of the local climatic and meteorologic expectations. He must know the inherent hazards of the risk due to material, construction, use of the property, and problems of location such as conditions of neighboring property. Finally, there is the question of facilities for minimizing the loss in the event of the happening of the contingency insured against. So, measuring the hazard involves the problem of rating.

The term "moral" as applied to that group of hazards which grows out of the *mental attitudes* of individuals is in a degree a misnomer. This is true because, while there are mental attitudes that are the outgrowth of carelessness or mental instability, and thus most decidedly contribute to a risk, in no sense do they involve moral turpitude. While the term *psychological* might be more apt, a reason for the term "moral" is found in the fact that particular emphasis is given to the effecting of fraud through the deliberate destruction of insured property. It must be remembered, however, that the term "moral hazard" is in no way limited to a classification of the cases involving moral instability but includes in its scope all factors contributing to risk that are mental in their nature.

Appraisal of moral hazard requires the study of the character of the person under consideration in the light of his reputation. When an individual in one set of circumstances will resort to subterfuge in order to gain his ends, no great pressure will be required to stimulate similar action in a new situation. In looking up the record of an insured, therefore, the insurer is always interested to learn of questionable transactions, even though not directly connected with the business of insurance. Evidence pointing to the fact that his insured ever defrauded any other person, or had a previous bankruptcy record, as well as any record of attempting to secure credit upon false or fraudulent statement, are indications of possible moral hazard in regard to insurance. Investigators also concern themselves with the insured's reputation in trade. They will inquire as to his rating with the banks, as to his standing with competitors in his field, and finally as to the regard in which he is held by those with whom he transacts business. An individual who has a reputation for being sharp in his dealings, who is noted for taking unfair advantage of legal technicalities, or who has repudiated contracts in the face of possible financial loss is regarded as one likely to resort to other unethical methods to serve his ends if a new situation should present itself. The possibility of sabotage is regarded as a moral hazard. In the case of strikes, striking employees have in the course of rioting set fire to the property of employers. In retaliation against strikebreakers, striking employees frequently have destroyed the homes, automobiles, or other property of the strikebreakers. Finally, in the normal hazard category are to be found those abnormal mental cases known as "pyromaniacs," in which the individual acts under an irresistible impulse to set fires.

A distinction is sometimes made between "moral" and "morale" hazards, including as examples of increasing chance of loss such morale conditions as carelessness and indifference. Laziness, disorderliness, and lack of concern for others are termed morale problems rather than dishonest (moral) ones. Leaving car doors unlocked increases automobile thefts, bad smoking habits increase fire losses, and hurried, unthinking action can cause many personal injuries.

Losses. An economic *loss* is the undesirable end result of risk. It is the decrease or disappearance of value in an unexpected, or at least relatively unpredictable, manner. In general terms, not all losses have to be related to risk; some losses are the result of foreseeable actions, as for example the giving of a birthday gift. Other losses may be expected because they are known always to occur, such as depreciation of physical properties which can be expected as well as predicted fairly accurately. Many losses, however, cannot be predicted and become the result of risks. Illustrations include losses of property due to fire or theft or other perils, losses of income due to property destruction or personal perils of death or disability, increased expenses such as medical costs, and loss of assets due to legal liability for losses affecting other persons.

CLASSIFICATIONS OF RISK

Speculative and Pure Risks

Two basic kinds of economic risks are (*a*) speculative risks and (*b*) pure risks.[3]

Speculative risks involve both the chance of loss and the chance of gain, whereas in pure risks there is only the chance of loss or no loss. Such risks are "pure" in the sense that they do not mix both profits and losses. The business of insurance is concerned with the economic problems created by pure risk.

Speculative risk, because it involves an element of both profit and loss, may sometimes be nullified by a process known as "hedging." For example, a manufacturer who buys raw material may suffer a severe loss if the price of the raw material falls before the finished product is offered on the market. If the price of the raw material rises, he will enjoy a speculative profit. Since a manufacturer is in business to make a profit on his manufactured goods, he is interested in relieving himself of the speculative risk. This may be accomplished by "hedging." At the time he buys his raw material he will sell short an equal amount for delivery at about the time his finished product

[3]Some authors prefer to differentiate basic types of risk as "fundamental" (those universal and impersonal) and "particular" (those individual and personal). See C. A. Kulp, *Casualty Insurance* (New York: The Ronald Press Company, 1956), p. 3. Another distinction is sometimes made between "dynamic" and "static" risks, but essentially the meaning is the same as "speculative" and "pure" risks, respectively. See Robert I. Mehr and Bob A. Hedges, *Risk Management in the Business Enterprise* (Homewood, Ill.: Richard D. Irwin, Inc., 1963), pp. 3-9.

is offered on the market. "Selling the material short" means selling goods he does not have by obligating himself to make delivery in the future. Thus if the manufacturer sells raw material on a current market for delivery in the future and the market advances, he will lose money on his short sale but will make up the difference on the goods in process. If the material sold short declines in price, the manufacturer will make a speculative profit on the short sale but a corresponding loss on the manufactured goods. The net result of a perfect hedge is to eliminate speculative risk and make the cost of the raw material reflect the current market price at the time the goods are offered for sale.

A *pure risk,* because it involves only the possibility of loss or no loss, cannot be neutralized by an opposite contract, as in the case of hedging. Take the case of the manufacturer already cited. His plant may be destroyed even though he may have taken every means within his power to prevent such losses. The temporary shutdown of the property because of the happening of some contingency may interrupt profits. Trusted employees may abscond with company resources. Customers may go into bankruptcy and fail to pay accounts. There are innumerable risks of this nature which cannot be handled by hedging and which cannot be eliminated by prevention. It is the burden of such risks that is shifted by insurance.

Personal, Property, and Liability Risks

The risks confronting man are ordinarily divided into three classifications: (*a*) risks involving the person, (*b*) risks involving loss or damage to property, and (*c*) risks involving liability for the injury to the person or property of others.

The first of these classifications of risk is ordinarily termed "personal" and is chiefly concerned with death and the time of its occurrence. It is perfectly apparent that of death there is no uncertainty; but the time of its occurrence is uncertain. And, aside from death, there is the risk of incapacity through accidental injury, illness, or old age.

The second classification of risk is that which arises from the destruction of "property." The possible loss of a cargo or ship at sea is considered a risk to those engaged in maritime operations. Fire, lightning, windstorm, flood, and other forces of nature offer a constant threat of loss to real estate, as well as all kinds of personal property and property involved in any form of transportation. Consequential losses arising indirectly from the direct physical losses also may occur, including loss of profits, rents, or favorable leases.

The third classification of risk is occasioned by the operation of the law of liability and may be termed "third-party risks." Whenever an individual is legally liable for an injury to another, as, for instance, through an accident when the driver of an automobile is negligent and injures a pedestrian, or when a person is injured on someone's property, such a risk is termed a third-party risk. It is so called because when insurance is used to shift the burden of responsibility, the insurance company and insured person have agreed that a "third party" (the injured person) will be paid for injuries for which the insured is legally liable.

Insignificant Risks

It is apparent that innumerable risks attaching to the wide range of human activities are of little consequence. For example, a man may lose his pen or break his eyeglasses. There is a loss, but its severity is not sufficient to cause acute suffering or seriously affect the future course of the injured person's business or standard of living. Such risks may be ignored. The destruction of a factory by fire, the serious interruption of production through engine breakdown, theft by dishonest officials, and other losses involving large sums are, however, matters of concern. The test of insignificance is measured by its importance to the parties involved. What may be unimportant to a rich person or large business firm may be crucial to a poorer person or small enterprise.

Insurable Risks

Because of the element of expense in carrying on the business of insurance, premiums are weighed with a charge to provide for this cost. In the case of risks that involve a threat of no great consequence, the cost of handling the business would make the rate prohibitive. Hence, to make a risk insurable, the danger of loss must be sufficiently great to make the cost element a minor factor in the premium charged.

A second requisite of an insurable risk is the necessity of its being of a nature that permits a reasonable statistical estimate of the chance of loss, and possible variations from the estimate. As a corollary to this requirement, the risk must be one of which there are a large number in existence, though insurers occasionally cover isolated risks concerning which there is no previous experience. Most insurance is written, however, to cover risks where losses may reasonably be expected and where mathematical treatment or judgment based upon experience permits an estimate of losses sufficiently exact to make possible a workable estimate of their probable cost. When experience extends over a number of years and the number of risks is great enough, a premium can be computed that will assure a sum sufficient to pay losses and compensate the carrier; provide stability and permanence in the business; instill confidence in the insured; and, through the promise of stabilized earnings, assure the business of new capital when needed.

While the business of insurance places great emphasis upon statistical data and the use of the mathematical theory of probability, it is not an essential requirement that the probability of the occurrence of the contingency to be covered by insurance be definitely known. In certain of the older forms of insurance, future expectation on the basis of past experience can be computed with a fair degree of accuracy. When new insurance forms are instituted, it becomes necessary to make rates that are dependent upon what is sometimes called "underwriting judgment," and in some instances this is nothing more than an approximation or guess to be adjusted with the accumulation of experience.[4]

Other requirements for an insurable risk also relate to the prime requisite that the risk must be reasonably calculable. The need for large numbers applies not only for total risks accepted by an insurance company, but must also be met within each class of risks. Thus a large number of homogeneous, or similar, risks must be present to make a risk insurable.

The losses should be definite, for otherwise estimates of possible loss are difficult. Many insurance contract provisions aim at the objective of making the insured risks as clear and definite as possible.

Ordinarily, no catastrophe (very large) possibility of loss should be associated with an insurable risk. A few such risks, if accepted with smaller risks, would make accurate predictions of loss impossible.

Insurable risks must also normally be accidental in nature. Insurance is intended to cover fortuitous or unexpected losses. Intentional losses caused by the insured are usually uninsurable because they cannot be reasonably predicted, and payment for them would be against public policy for encouraging such actions as fraud or arson.

The student should note that these requirements for an insurable risk are not absolute. In total each insurable risk must meet most of the requirements, but many insurable risks do not have all of the characteristics mentioned in this section. Insurability is thus best described as a relative matter, in which the insurable quality of the risk is determined by appraisal of all the requirements to-

---

[4]For example, in the field of aviation in many instances underwriters not only lack a true statistical base, but are faced with the necessity of providing insurance that will keep pace with the rapid advances in the field. The advent of jet- and rocket-propelled aircraft created a need for insurance in a field where statistical data were entirely lacking. In a civilian passenger aircraft an amount at risk may be as much as several million dollars. In a field so limited an adequate spread by type of risk is impossible. The company assumes the risk on the basis of its best judgment.

gether. Many common kinds of insurance do not perfectly meet each of the requirements. Consider, for example, the following: Is theft insurance "definite" (i.e., Was the item really stolen, or just lost?)? Are all drivers "similar" in regard to risk of automobile accidents? (Obviously not, though they may be relatively similar within age, type of car, and other classifications.) Is a fire caused by carelessness always "accidental"? Aren't windstorms such as Hurricane Carla, Donna, and others "catastrophic" in nature? Careful analysis in applying each of the requirements for an insurable risk to a particular peril shows that few, if any, are "perfect" insurable risks. Most are only relatively good ones, and some are fine examples of bad ones.[5]

Gambling Risks

The presence of a risk as a condition precedent is the factor that removes insurance from the category of a gambling contract; it is also upon this prior existence of risk that the requisite of insurable interest (discussed later) rests. Modern insurance practice holds any contract lacking this element to be against public policy.

Insurance, then, does not permit the creation of a risk but is, on the contrary, the transfer of a risk already existent. Contrasted to this is a bet; so far as the individuals in the transaction are concerned, no risk had heretofore existed, but one is created. Such a transaction is economically unsound. The buyer of insurance is a buyer of security, and for a specified sum the seller of insurance furnishes that security. The contract is mutually beneficial.

Gambling operations may involve many of the attributes of insurance, such as large numbers, spread of risk, homogeniety of risk, predictability, no catastrophe element, and so on. Probably this is the reason so many uninformed persons think of insurance as gambling, and sometimes even feel that they have "lost the bet" if they fail to have a loss equal to the cost of insurance. The distinction is not in the method of operation, which may appear similar, but in the fact that insurance concerns itself with an existing, economically useful risk. Gambling creates the risk at the time the transaction is made.

THE TREATMENT OF RISK

Following an understanding of what risk is and is not, the next most significant knowledge needed about risk is an answer to the

---

[5]Note that many contract details and company underwriting restrictions deal with this problem, trying to improve the insurability of a peril by such methods as limitations on the amount of coverage, locations, prohibited or restricted types, specific contract definitions, deductibles, reinsurance, and many other ways.

question: "How is risk handled?" or "After it is known what risk is, what can be done about it?"

In classifying the kinds of risk in the previous section some possible answers to these questions have already been suggested. Speculative and pure risk were distinguished so that the emphasis is placed upon pure risks, involving chance of loss or no loss, but not those risks having economic gain as a predominant feature. Hedging was explained as one example of a method for dealing with speculative risk. Personal, property, and liability risks were identified to show that pure risks are of many varieties. Insignificant risks were mentioned as ones which could be ignored. Gambling risks were excluded from consideration because they involve the creation of risk, rather than the treatment of existing economic risk.

A major part of the preceding section introduces the concept of insurable risks. One might think that an insurance text could stop right there and conclude that insurance is *the* answer to the problem of handling risk. No such easy, pat answer is intended, for no risk, in theory or in practice, should be handled with insurance as a perfunctory solution. A proper solution should include full consideration of all the available alternatives to dealing with risk. The methods of treatment include: avoiding risk, ignoring risk, retention of risk (including "self-insurance"), loss prevention, and transfer of risk.

Avoiding Risk

One of the most obvious methods of handling risk is to avoid as many risks as possible. If one does not want to have to try to predict economic losses, he can avoid some losses by various decisions in his everyday life. A family can decide to rent instead of buy a home, thereby avoiding the risk of losing the home value through the peril of fire. A business may lease its automobiles and avoid assuming the risk of losing those values (even though it may be accepting in the lease another risk, that of legal liability for its return in good condition). A person who is worried about poisonous snakebites or heat exhaustion can live in the Arctic, or at least locate in areas with a minimum of risk from such perils. The risk of airplane accidents, drownings, and sports injuries can be avoided largely by keeping away from airplanes, water, and sport events, respectively. For the majority of persons who do like to own property, participate in sports, and live in the temperate zone, however, avoidance of risk is no practical solution to the many risks which are involved in normal activities. True, some unusual risks with high chance of loss can be avoided, but realistically the avoidance of risk is only a major alternative in regard to a restricted number of economic risks. For all the other risks we face, other solutions must be considered.

Ignoring Risk

Another alternative method of handling risk is the simplest way of handling risks which are already in existence. Doing nothing about risk is common, and many of the insignificant risks described earlier are met by such nonaction. If it really is an unimportant risk which will not cause financial hardship to an individual or business firm, then the logical action becomes a negative one. A homeowner may not insure all his property against loss, and feel that the risk of loss of such minor properties as a glove, pen or pencil are risks he is willing to assume without doing anything about it. Similarly, a business may decide not to protect smaller buildings or values they consider irrelevant to their normal business operations.

Ignoring risk can be done consciously and intentionally, as in these examples, or unintentionally through plain lack of knowledge, thought, or foresight. Purposeful ignorance of risk is a meaningful alternative of treating risk, while unknowingly ignoring risk is perhaps better classified as a method of *not* meeting risk rather than dealing with it.

Retention of Risk (Including "Self-Insurance")

Once risk has not been avoided, but exists because it has been assumed, another alternative choice of action (beyond just ignoring it) appears. If it is recognized as an important risk, some action is appropriate whenever possible.

Accompanying risk retention a number of choices may be made. The risk may be retained and many things done to reduce the losses to a minimum, as well as to put into effect plans for meeting the losses that do occur. Some of the efforts belong in the loss prevention category (discussed in the next section), while others involve partial attempts to create reserves or savings funds to meet losses.

Only the most complete and formal plans for retaining risk are properly described as *self-insurance* plans. Although many businesses may call their risk retention plans self-insurance, often they may be only partial methods of keeping risk within the firm. Briefly, to deserve the title of self-insurance, the plan must include certain requisites which apply similarly to requirements for a sound insurance company operation.

Some of these requirements have already been discussed under the heading of insurable risks. To be self-insurable, the same characteristics are necessary. These include the need for large numbers of important, homogeneous, accidental risks, which have the quality of being definite and calculable, and do not involve the chance of a large catastrophe loss. For the most part, large businesses are the only ones who can meet these requirements properly. Self-insurance is not realistic for individual or family risk problems.

Self-insurance also requires attention to other points. The plan must, in effect, do almost everything a normal insurance company would do for the business. It should have management's full support and understanding; it should provide essential loss prevention activities whenever economically feasible; it should normally involve a savings fund (not just a "reserve" on the balance sheet) to meet unanticipated losses; and it should provide important records-keeping and loss analysis data. The size of the funds necessary depends on many factors, including the financial stability of the firm, the maximum probable losses expected, the possible repetition of losses within a certain period, and tax considerations.

The main consideration is care in setting up and administering the self-insurance plan, not beguiling oneself into a feeling of security when the plan is not adequate. This solution to treating risk is not possible for many smaller businesses, but can be used successfully by larger firms when judicious steps are taken to assure that the plan really is one of self-insurance. The most common example of self-insurance is in the field of workmen's compensation (industrial injuries), while some of the largest businesses also use this method for meeting part of their automobile or fire insurance risks.

Loss Prevention

It is natural when a pure risk threatens that every reasonable step be taken to minimize the results of it through the agency of prevention. Thus, we build fire-resistive structures. We install protective devices in boilers to eliminate accidents, and inspections are made to detect latent defects. Installations are available to control lightning. Safety devices guard much industrial machinery today, and inspections by such firms as Underwriter Laboratories inspect most of our electrical appliances. Construction is aimed at the reduction or elimination of tornado, earthquake, and hurricane losses. Steps to prevent losses extend from efforts of the individual to community undertakings. Some of the larger projects, such as those involving flood control, are carried on by the government.

In contrast to prevention, insurance saves nothing. Insurance pays the owner of the property, and the payment is made out of the fund to which all insured members have contributed. The sum total of all property is still lessened by the amount of loss. In an effort to reduce the cost of insurance to a minimum, insurance stimulates use of protective measures; and to the extent that it is successful, it is an agency for the actual preservation of property. On the other hand, insurance perhaps contributes to a certain amount of loss through incendiarism, suicide, or other losses instigated in an effort to defraud insurers.

More often the two methods of prevention and insurance are combined. The owner of capital goods subject to a number of risks may take every known precaution, install every known safety device, and still have losses. Or it may be that in weighing the costs, insurance up to a certain point is the more attractive. In any instance, insurance begins where prevention ceases. The cost of prevention cannot be termed a payment for insurance even though it is a payment for security. The concept of insurance does not include prevention but limits itself to the provision of indemnity where the risk to the capital covered remains in existence. The same psychological drive that gives the idea of insurance its momentum has likewise given rise to the development of preventive measures, the two ideas having a common purpose and progressing along parallel lines.

Loss prevention is not the same thing as risk prevention or reduction. The unpredictability (risk) may still be the same, even though the chance of decreasing value (loss) is reduced, or a reduction of contributing factors (hazards) to the cause of loss (peril) occurs.

Transfer of Risk

Some of the most important risks and losses faced by individuals and businesses cannot be avoided, ignored, retained, or prevented. The sole method left for consideration is the transfer of as much of the unpredictability as possible to someone else.

Risks may be shifted to others not only by insurance but also by several other techniques. Since insurance and its significance is discussed in the next chapter, suffice it to say at this point that insurance is based upon a transfer of risk and it has become a major method of treating many types of pure risk.

Hedging has been shown earlier to be a method of transferring some speculative (loss *or* gain) risks. Pure risks (loss or no loss) can be met through several legal methods. One of the simplest is *incorporation,* in which a business firm is permitted to issue stock shares which define and limit the possible loss for those who invest in the corporation.

Another common method of shifting some pure risk is a *lease* contract. A wide variety of legal responsibilities are transferred from one party to another in this manner. For example, proper maintenance is often stated in a lease to be under the care of the person (lessee) who rents property from an owner.

Bailees, or persons holding property of others temporarily, often accept by *bailment contract* or common law certain risks from the property owners. Liability for damage to goods is shifted from owner to bailee in hundreds of everyday business situations, such as railroads, airline companies, laundERIES, warehouses, parking lots, and repair shops.

Most risk transfer methods are far from complete. The unpredictability in regard to *some* perils in *some* circumstances for a *limited* length of *time* for a *limited amount* may be transferred to others. Still, the major risks of families and business remain with them, unless the final method of risk transfer, *insurance,* is used.

Risk Management: Coordinated Risk Treatment

The five basic methods of treating risk discussed above may be integrated in a process known as *risk management.*[6] Both personal and business risks can be taken care of, or "managed," but most efforts and principles of risk management have centered on business risks. The term is a relatively new and popular one, though its exact meaning and scope are neither fully understood nor accepted.[7] It is not all management of a business. In fact, it does not concern all risk and the term as it has evolved thus far is really "(pure) risk management," it being understood that the process does not deal with speculative risks. Only "pure" risks, involving basically chances only for "loss or no loss" but none for gain or profit, are the intended area of the risk management function.

Risk management is clearly more than just *insurance management,* a concept which would be primarily limited to decisions of when, how much, how and where to insure uncertainties previously described as insurable-type risks. If one is to manage (pure) risks, he must almost always insure some risks and be an "insurance buyer."[8] He must also do much more than this if he deserves the title of *risk manager.*

The risk management function is perhaps best described and understood in terms of the decisions which are a part of it. The process begins with a recognition of the existence of various risks. It moves to an identification or classification of risks such as is found in the earlier part of this chapter. Next a choice must be made as to

[6]Robert I. Mehr and Bob A. Hedges, *Risk Management in the Business Enterprise* (Homewood, Ill.: Richard D. Irwin, Inc., 1963), p. vii.

[7]The origin of the term is not precise. One of the earliest uses of the phrase in a major insurance text appeared in Chapter 35 of the 4th edition of *Insurance,* by Mowbray and Blanchard. Chapter 36 of the 6th edition gives a brief but concise explanation of the history, functions, and principles of risk management.

[8]It is interesting to note that the only trade journal of the professional society of some 1,500 "risk managers," *The National Insurance Buyer,* is published by the American Society of Insurance Management. Such inconsistency of terminology is mute evidence of the newness and difficulties of precise definitions in the rapidly evolving field of risk management. Time and growth of knowledge should alleviate such problems in the coming decades.

what methods should be used to meet each specific risk identified. Some risks may be avoided, others ignored, some retained under planned programs of self-insurance, some prevented (*loss* prevention, basically), and some transferred by such as method as insurance.

The most significant characteristic of risk management is that it is a synthesis of all these methods of dealing with risk. Even the consideration of one peril, such as fire, usually requires that a risk manager for a large firm integrate risk avoidance, retention, prevention or minimization of losses, and transfer. In essence, the process is one of coordinating the available methods of risk treatment.[9] The technique is useful in describing both the insured's treatment of risk, as well as explaining the need for a "comprehensive team effort" by the insurer.[10]

An introductory text in the field of insurance should not lose sight of its major premise, i.e., that for most personal risks and the vast majority of business risks, insurance is the most effective method of meeting important risks. If this were not true, then the subject for study in this text might be called risk management. The predominant method of treating pure risk is insurance, however, and it is here that this book rests its emphasis. Given a familiarity with the process of risk management from which decisions to insure stems, the student needs most to discover and evaluate the wide scope, techniques and benefits of insurance. It is on the insurance method that the following chapters concentrate, though risk management will not be forgotten as a needed concept in the study of insurance.

SUMMARY

Any introduction to insurance requires an understanding of *risk*, which is unpredictability. It is the uncertainty about financial loss which serves as the foundation and reason for existence of the technique of insurance. Because actual losses tend to differ from expected ones, both in an objective as well as a subjective sense, the insurance institution arises as one of the more common methods of meeting economic risk.

The financial losses resulting from risk are caused by many *perils*, such as fire, windstorm, explosion, collision, injury, disease, and

---

[9]Many articles delineate the duties involved in risk and/or insurance management. They describe, fundamentally, the steps outlined here. For further information, one of the best compilations of such references appears in *The Growing Job of Risk Management* (New York: American Management Association, 1962).

[10]Goodwin Clark, Jr., "Risk Management as a Team Effort," *The Annals of the Society of Chartered Property and Casualty Underwriters,* Vol. 16, No. 3 (Fall, 1963), p. 250.

untimely death. *Hazards,* some physical and some moral, are the contributing factors to the perils which cause loss.

Risk is so prevalent in our everyday life that classification of its many types is essential in order to study it properly. The differentiation between *speculative* risk (involving both the opportunity for loss or profit) and *pure* risk (where there is only the chance for loss or no loss) is basic, for insurance concerns itself with pure risks in almost all cases. Risks may also be classified as (1) *personal,* (2) *property,* and (3) *liability* risks. *Insignificant* risks may be separated from others in order to concentrate efforts on more important risks that deserve treatment. *Insurable* risks must meet, at least relatively well, the requirements of (1) importance, (2) reasonable calculability through large numbers of similar risks, (3) definiteness of loss, (4) no excessive catastrophe peril, and (5) accidental nature of the risk. *Gambling* risks create uncertainty of financial loss, while insurable risks transfer an already existing risk and thereby perform the economically useful function of reducing uncertainty about loss.

The treatment of risk may encompass several *alternatives.* Some risks may be *avoided;* others may be *ignored,* either purposefully or through ignorance. *Retention* of risk may be of several types, ranging from taking care of losses out of current income to unfunded reserves to true *self-insurance* plans meeting all the requisites of sound insurance methods. *Loss prevention* is extremely important in treating some risks, but ineffective or impossible in regard to others. *Risk transfer* is often an important choice in handling risk, and insurance as a method of risk transfer becomes of major significance for many situations.

The process of *risk management,* or coordinated risk treatment, becomes a synthesis of all the methods of identifying and dealing with pure risks.

FOR REVIEW

1. Why is an understanding of risk important to the study of insurance?
2. Distinguish between the use of the terms: "risk," "uncertainty," "peril," "hazard," and "loss." Why should they be differentiated?
3. An author has said: "The *risks* which families and businesses face are all pervasive. For the study of insurance it is meaningful to classify *risks* in several *different* ways. By doing so, one can learn for *which* risks the insurance technique is best adapted to provide a *solution* to the important *problems* of risk." How would you explain the reasons why each of these statements is true, with particular reference to how each of the underlined terms is necessary to proper knowledge about insurance?
4. Why is it necessary to distinguish between:
   a) "Pure" and "speculative" risks?
   b) "Preventable" and "insurable" risks?
   c) "Gambling" and other risks?
   d) "Personal," "property," and "liability" risks?

5. Are all risks insurable? Why or why not?
6. Mr. I. M. Secure is considering purchasing a new home, and recognizes that "risks" will be created if he does.
   a) Describe the risks he will have.
   b) What alternatives does he have in treating his risks? Discuss the pros and cons of each method and indicate your recommendations, with reasons.
7. Both physical and moral hazards may be involved in many risks. What is the purpose, and what are the problems, of identifying these types of hazards?
8. Are each of the requisites for an insurable risk met by risks that are insured? Why or why not? Explain each of the requirements briefly, and give an example of a risk which is sometimes insured that does *not* satisfy each requirement very well.
9. Are risks transferred by means other than insurance? Explain, with examples.
10. Discuss the shortcomings of a plan of "self-insurance" for a state, for a municipality, and for a business.
11. In your opinion is "self-insurance" ever advantageous? If so, under what circumstances?
12. What is "risk management," and how does it relate to insurance?

Chapter 2

INSURANCE AND ITS SIGNIFICANCE

WHAT INSURANCE IS

THE concept of *insurance* is complicated by its many possible meanings and definitions. It may be described in a number of ways, each meaningful and correct but emphasizing different aspects of its purpose, method, or results. Most important to the student of insurance is an understanding of the variability of its definitions, rather than a blind acceptance of any one description.

Insurance Defined

A definition of insurance may be developed from several viewpoints: economic, legal, business, social, or mathematical. Regardless of which viewpoint is taken, a full interpretation should include both a statement of its objective as well as the technique by which the purpose is achieved.

Economic. In an economic sense, insurance provides certainty or predictability, aiming at reducing uncertainty in regard to pure risks. It accomplishes this result by a "pooling"[1] or sharing of risk. Usually the process involves a transfer of risk, which in the preceding chapter was the method of treating risk under which insurance was introduced.

Legal. From a legal standpoint, an insurance *contract* or *policy* is used to transfer risk for a *premium* (price) from one party known as the *insured* or *policyholder* to another party known as the *insurer* or *insurance carrier*. The burden of risk is shifted by a legally binding contract from the insured to the insurer. Numerous court decisions have given legal status to insurance, including such early definitions as: "Insurance is a contract by which the one party, in consideration of a price paid to him adequate to the risk, becomes security to the other that he shall not suffer loss, damage, or prejudice by the happening of the perils specified to certain things which may be exposed to them."[2] The insured, by virtue of his contract, ex-

---

[1]C. A. Kulp, *Casualty Insurance* (New York: The Ronald Press Company, 1956), pp. 9-10.

[2]*Lucena* v. *Crawford,* 2 B. & P. N.R. 269 (H.L. 1806).

changes the possibility of an unknown large loss for a comparatively small certain payment. It is not really a guarantee against losses occurring, but a method of assuring that repayment, or *indemnity*, will be received for losses that do occur as the result of risk. Many new problems in defining insurance have occurred. The complexity of such problems as differentiating today from variable annuities, warranty service contracts, employee benefit plans, and hospital and medical benefit plans has been thoroughly emphasized.[3]

Business. As a business institution, insurance has been defined as a plan by which large numbers of people associate themselves and transfer, to the shoulders of all, risks that attach to individuals. Insurance may also be looked upon as an important part of the financial world, where insurance serves as a basis for credit and a mechanism for savings and investments. Insurance as a business is a common way of thinking about what insurance is, for many persons have contact with the thousands of insurance organizations and their more than a million employees. It has become a major part of the free enterprise economy.

Social. An adequate definition giving recognition to both the end of insurance and to the means for effecting it has been admirably stated thus: "We should define insurance, then, as that social device for making accumulations to meet uncertain losses of capital which is carried out through the transfer of the risks of many individuals to one person or to a group of persons. Wherever there is accumulation for uncertain losses, or wherever there is a transfer of risk, there is one element of insurance; only where these are joined with the combination of risks in a group is the insurance complete."[4]

To effect insurance, persons who are exposed to loss from some particular peril agree to contribute to indemnify whichever member of the group shall, because of the peril, suffer loss. It is the more usual practice to contribute to a common fund and, out of this fund, to make payments to those who have suffered loss. The payment to the fund represents the cost to the individual of his losses because of the specified peril. Thus, a person owns a house valued at $10,000 which may be totally destroyed by fire. He may, however, for the payment of a definite sum (the insurance premium),

[3]Herbert S. Denenberg, "The Legal Definition of Insurance—Insurance Principles in Practice," *The Journal of Insurance*, Vol. XXX, No. 3 (September, 1963), pp. 319-43.

[4]A. H. Willett, *The Economic Theory of Risk and Insurance*, Columbia University Studies in History, Economics, and Public Law, Vol. XIV (New York: Columbia University Press, 1901), p. 388. See also reprinted edition, published under the auspices of the S. S. Huebner Foundation for Insurance Education (Philadelphia: University of Pennsylvania Press, 1951), p. 72.

eliminate the financial consequences of a $10,000 loss. He does so by exchanging an uncertain large loss for a certain small cost. The sum total of such individual transactions makes insurance a social method by which unfortunates (those having losses) are compensated by the whole group.

In the strictest interpretation of the term, aside from its customary use in the field of business, contributions to a fund by beneficiaries are not essential. As has been said: "The collective bearing of risks is insurance. It is insurance, whether the individual contributes specific premiums to meet each specific risk, or whether he receives free insurance out of the general resources of the community or of an industry. It is insurance whether the contributions are voluntary or compulsory."[5] It is conceivable that groups rely entirely upon assessments after losses to indemnify the sufferers and in such instances accumulate no funds in advance. In the case of insurance enterprises in which the government functions as the carrier, a fund may be accumulated, or the beneficiaries may depend for their insurance payments upon the taxing power. As a business, insurance evidences its strength on the basis of a demonstrated ability to pay, and hence the established practice of accumulating a fund out of which losses are to be paid.

Mathematical. Mathematically, insurance is the application of certain *actuarial* (insurance mathematics) principles. Laws of probability and statistical techniques are used to achieve predictable results. The details of how this is done are covered in the next section, though here it is important to recognize that the basis for a good description of the method of insurance is mathematics. A sound mathematical definition of insurance is a reasonable way of explaining what insurance is, as it provides predictability through the use of known principles of statistical probability.

Summary

Insurance is thus defined in several ways, and probably no one brief definition does justice to its many important viewpoints. It may be an economic system for reducing uncertainty through pooling of losses; a legal method of transferring risk in a contract of indemnity; a business conducted for profit and providing many jobs in a free enterprise economy; a social device in which the losses of few are paid by many; or an actuarial system of applied mathematics. It is all these and more, depending upon how one views the major purposes, methods, and results of insurance.

---

[5]Sir William Beveridge, *Insurance for All and Everything, the New Way,* Series VII (London, 1924), pp. 6-7.

HOW INSURANCE WORKS

The Insurance Equation

It is sometimes not quite clear to the layman how any organization can assume a large risk for a comparatively small premium and, when called upon, make payment immediately after commitment. For example, many life insurance companies pay money for policies issued and in force for less than a year. Insurance of buildings calls for the payment of thousands of dollars in indemnity in return for the payment of what amounts to a few dollars in premium, and so it goes throughout the other branches of insurance. Insurance companies deal primarily with groups. In the case of life insurance, the insurance company is not concerned with when one is insured or another will die, but it is vitally concerned with how many will die each year out of a large group. Knowing this within reasonable limits, the life insurance company adjusts its premium charges so that it will take in enough money to be able to carry on the business and to pay all claims. In the case of other forms of insurance, the procedure is the same. For example, in the case of fire insurance on buildings, the insurance company is interested not in whether specific buildings will burn, but what will be the ratio of losses to premiums when a large group of buildings is considered. This equality between the receipts in the form of premiums and what is paid out in losses constitutes what may be termed the *insurance equation.*

In addition to securing sufficient funds in the form of premium payments to meet all losses, insurance companies must collect enough money to carry on the business. There are expenses such as rental of buildings, payment of salaries, cost of supplies, taxes, agents' commissions, and the like—all of which form a part of the cost of doing business and must ultimately find a place in the premium paid by the policyholder. Certain of the insurance companies provide special services in engineering, rate making, conducting tests, and inspections designed to save property and, by the same token, to reduce premium charges. The companies that support these engineering and research projects must absorb their cost as part of the cost of carrying on the business.

While the insurance premium must, in the long run, cover the cost of all losses and also the expenses of doing business, if the premium is to be a fixed sum, there must be some source to take care of any deficiency as a result of losses or expenses beyond the normal expectation of the insurer. Surplus is the means by which these unexpected losses or expenses are paid. Capital put up by the stockholder of an insurance company is another source for stock insurers. Such capital in no way belongs to the policyholders of the company but is a guarantee that all losses and expenses will be paid. Stockholders who invest funds in an insurance project do so for a profit, and, accordingly, in the computation of the premium some provision must be made to compensate the owner of the capital invested in the enterprise. An alternative to using stockholders' capital to assure financial solvency is the use of assessments. Smaller mutual companies sometimes use assessments, if loss and expenses have exceeded original estimates.

In addition to the foregoing elements that enter into the making up of the premium, conservative companies make an additional charge to set up a reserve for catastrophes. In the computation of premiums, losses are based upon a normal expectation. Insurance underwriters know, however, that from time to time abnormal situations develop, as, for example, the influenza epidemic of 1918, the various fires that have from time to time destroyed large areas in our important cities, and accidents that have caused the death of a large number of people at one time. Catastrophes of this sort cannot be foreseen, but, because they do happen, preparation must be made for them. Insurance underwriters regard a reserve for catastrophes as of paramount importance, and this factor must be taken into consideration in computing the premium. Small companies operating on a local basis frequently have no such reserve. The company that makes no charge in its premium for a contribution to a catastrophe reserve may be able to cut the costs of insurance to its policyholders and remain solvent; but should it experience a catastrophe of any sort calling for unusual or extraordinary payments, it might be faced with an embarrassing situation.

Summarizing, the factors that enter into the computation of a premium may be listed as follows: (1) the cost of losses; (2) the cost of doing business; (3) the cost of capital; and (4) the cost of a reserve for catastrophes.

These costs vary with the different kinds of insurance contracts written. The loss cost may be as much or more than 90 percent of total premiums (as it is for hospitalization insurance), or about 55 percent (as for automobile insurance). It may be as little as 5 percent in such kinds of insurance as title, steam boiler explosion, or fidelity bonds, in which loss prevention services are more feasible and important than payment of losses. The cost of doing business is affected greatly by the marketing system used and the services rendered to the policyholder by the agents of insurance companies. Capital, assessment, and reserve costs are also variable according to the legal type of company, the state laws, and the decisions arrived at by management in conducting the business of insurance.

The insurance equation, stated in more complete terms than just that premiums and costs must be equal, is a revision of a basic accounting concept that total outgo and income must be equal. For an insurance business, total income (i.e., premiums, interest earnings, and miscellaneous income) must in the long run equal total payments and reserves (i.e., losses, costs of doing business, reserves, and cost of capital or assessments).

Probability and Uncertainty

Another explanation of how insurance works centers on the application of the essential concepts of probability and uncertainty.

While it is the function of insurance to assume the burden of the risks which individuals are unwilling to carry, the insurer is able to reduce the sum total of all the uncertainties involved in the risks that he carries to a reasonable degree of certainty. Therefore, within calculable limits the insurer is able to foresee the normal losses, and estimate the catastrophe losses, that will occur in a given number of instances. He is thus able to compute the premium charge to pay all losses, as well as to cover expenses and profits. For each individual the degree of uncertainty may be extreme and the possibility of loss enormous. For the insurer this element of uncertainty is reduced to a minimum through the utilization of the statistical sciences and the application of the mathematical principles of probability. The insurer is concerned not so much with the fact that there will or will not be losses as with his ability to predict their extent and fix his premium charge accordingly. The ability to do this places the insurer on a footing quite different from the insured.

By means of the application of the theory of probabilities it is possible for the insurer to predict within comparatively narrow limits what the losses will be. Were it not for this ability, insurance would be nothing more than the accumulation of many small chances into one enormous chance. As a matter of fact, it is nothing of the sort. Whereas in each individual case the element of uncertainty is extreme, in the sum of the accumulated cases a reasonably definite loss may be predicted.

The uncertainty element is not entirely eliminated. Some insurance companies are more successful than others. Although every company endeavors by a judicious selection to eliminate specially undesirable risks, every company, nevertheless, is certain that in spite of its best efforts losses will occur. Its entire business structure is predicated upon this conclusion. The possibility of estimating and planning for future losses through the utilization of the theory of probabilities is what gives to the business of insurance its stability and makes possible the dealing in risks on a basis of comparative certainty.

Probability measures the chance of occurrence of a particular event. The theory evolved has, in the field of insurance, proved to be an instrument of incalculable importance. The measure of probability is expressed algebraically by means of a fraction whose numerator is the number of favorable (or unfavorable) possibilities, and whose denominator is the number of all possible cases. Using the following notation, in which n represents the number of ways an event can occur, a of which are to be considered as favorable and b as unfavorable, then the probability of p, a favorable outcome, can be expressed $p=a/n$, and the probability of an unfavorable outcome is written $p_1=b/n$. A simple illustration of the formula is found in the experiment of tossing a coin. There are but two ways in which a coin may fall: either head up, or tail up. The probability that it will fall head up is found by using the number of possible successful chances as the numerator of the fraction and the total number of chances as the denominator; thus we have the probability of tossing a head as ½. The probability that it will fall tail up is the same.

With relation to any given event, the two extremes are certainty and impossibility. Between the two there are varying degrees of probability. It will be recognized, however, that the degree of certainty and the degree of probability do not represent similar concepts. If a thing is certain to happen, then its probability is represented by unity, or 1. If it is impossible that it should happen, there is no probability, or probability is represented by 0. Impossibility, then, is negative certainty. That is, the event is certain not to happen. When the chances for and against the happening of an event are equal, the probability is expressed by ½. At this point the uncertainty is greatest.

An inductive process may be used for measuring risk. The method involves the three stages of observation, hypothesis, and generalization. Observation consists of accumulating sufficient statistical data for the purpose. On the basis of the data, a hypothesis is formed and then verified. When a proposition has been verified by repeated experience, it is regarded as probable. The more extended the experience, the more probable is the hypothesis. When further observation fails to produce further information, the generalization is made. For example, it is held, after a sufficient number of observations, that water freezes at 32° Fahrenheit. In the case of observed data involving risks for which insurance is to be provided, an established trend is assumed to be the result of a natural cause inherent in the subject matter. The generalization made from the observations is used as a basis for measuring risks.

The Law of Large Numbers

In addition to the general use of laws of probability, one principle in particular is of great importance to insurance. This is the *law of large numbers,* which briefly states that actual results tend to equal expected results as the number of happenings increases.

Only occasionally is insurance concerned with the happening of a particular event. It is more often concerned with the number of times an event may be expected to happen over a series of occasions. Certain happenings that appear to be the result of pure chance, when isolated instances are considered, occur with surprising regularity when a large number of instances have been observed. The regularity of the happening increases as the observed instances become more numerous. The impossibility of predicting a happening in a particular case gives place to probability when a successive series of possibilities is considered.

Applying these conclusions to insurance, we find that every year a certain number of dwellings burn, or injuries and deaths occur. The contributing causes are so numerous that it is not always possible to draw definite conclusions from cause to effect. It is to be learned from observation that the operation of all causes effects a certain result. Now, if we isolate a small group of cases, we may find a wide variation between the actual experience of that group and the expectation as determined by the past experience of the entire group. If the number of cases is too small, the variation may be far out of line either in one direction or the other. As the period of observation is lengthened, the variations tend to cancel each other; and as the number of cases is increased, the extent of irregularities is lessened.

Because of the operation of the law of large numbers, often termed the "law of averages," insurers have learned the wisdom of including in their portfolios the largest number of risks possible. For this reason insurers limit the amount they will carry on a single risk and attempt to secure a geographical distribution large enough to minimize the danger of large losses from a single catastrophe. A great number of small risks properly distributed ensures a more regular and more accurately predictable loss ratio than in the case of concentrated and unequal distribution. The greater the number of risks, the more stable and certain will be the business.

In certain instances the question of probability is not readily subjected to statistical treatment. Nevertheless, insurers have been willing to estimate the probability and insure the risk. A case in point arises when an attempt is made to reinsure a ship overdue. Years ago, when travel was slower and when there was no wireless communication, ships due in port were anxiously awaited. When the time for arrival passed with no word from the expected ship, anxiety turned to apprehension. In such instances, notwithstanding the fact that ships were not uncommonly late in making port, insurers, anxious to lighten the load, frequently sought reinsurance on the ship, "lost or not lost." The high rate and the chance of gain appealed to the reinsurer.

Statistical Data

In using the mathematical laws of probability and large numbers, frequent reference has been made to the need for adequate statistical data. Unless accurate statistical information is available, predictions in the form of probabilities will be defective. Therefore, in each of the fields of insurance, carefully compiled statistics are assembled to determine loss ratios and to accumulate experience as a basis for rate making.

The statistical data used in estimating the number of deaths for life insurance purposes, arranged in a table showing how many persons at a given age will probably die during each year, is known as a "mortality table." It is a tabulation of the mortality experience of a large group of people so arranged that arithmetical deductions of mortality for each age are readily available, and it is used as a basis for computing life insurance rates for the different types of policies for the different ages and classes of insured. The mortality experiences of life insurance companies have been accumulated. Important investigations have been carried on with a view to determining the experience in the cases of special classes of insured lives. Studies have been made of risks involving different nationalities, occupations, geographical distribution, and the like. Other studies involve the classification of personal characteristics, such as unusual weights and heights.

In other fields of insurance such as fire, casualty, and marine, data are accumulated and classified. Since property insurance rates are made to apply to different classes, the classifications must first be created and tentative rates established before statistics are available from actual experience. In the field of fire insurance, statistics are developed on details of construction, occupancy, protection, and exposure pertaining to different types of buildings. These data are coordinated with individual surveys by inspectors trained for the purpose. The results of these individual surveys, coupled with surveys of individual cities and towns, together with scientific tests and researches dealing with hazardous materials, taken in consideration with fire loss experience, all enter into the final figure that becomes the insurance rate.

For a number of years casualty rating bureaus predicated their formula for premiums on the average experience for a five-year period. When this was reduced to three years, in the light of rapidly changing conditions, the experience was still found not too satisfactory. To adjust experience to present-day conditions a trend factor was introduced. For example, if the automobile loss experience continued to rise over a period of three years it was not expected that the forthcoming year's experience would be measured by the data immediately available. The trend factor attempts to reflect in a current rate structure rapidly changing factors, such as the changing value of the dollar, changing wage levels and material costs, as well as trends in medical costs and court verdicts, that reflect a higher standard of living. In the field of casualty insurance careful records are retained on accident frequency and the average loss per accident. Loss records are kept in all other fields, too.

Judgment must contribute to the final determination of some insurance rates. It is the constant aim of rate-making authorities to reduce judgment to a minimum, however, and to predicate rates as far as it is possible upon a purely scientific basis which rests on the use of statistical data in applying known laws of probability and large numbers.

THE FIELDS OF INSURANCE

Social and Voluntary Insurance

Insurance as a part of our economic structure is divided into two great parts: (1) *social insurance* and (2) *voluntary insurance.* Figure 1 indicates the relationship of the various facilities available for risk bearing by insurance.

Social insurance is compulsory and is designed to provide a minimum of economic security for those in the lower-income groups; it concerns itself primarily with the unfavorable contingencies that may follow injuries, sickness, old age, unemployment, and the premature death of the family wage earner. The term social insurance could conceivably include all insurance, since all insurances possess widespread social implications and involve large groups. However, the concept here is limited to those insurance plans which are required by government, usually are administered by federal or state governments, and have for their object the provision of a minimum standard of living. The compulsion element is predicated upon the experience that some persons cannot or will not voluntarily purchase insurance, and the obligation of the government derives from the duty to protect the general welfare of its citizens.

Social insurance is designed to provide an answer to dependency problems of society. The amount of protection is not based on a premium measured by a mathematical appraisal of the risk, as in the case of private insurance. It embraces large groups of citizens, and the cost is distributed sometimes among those who participate and sometimes among all citizens. The plan undertakes to furnish for each insured and his family a layer of protection adequate for their basic needs.

Social security legislation provides for programs of insurances and assistances. There are, at present, nine programs embraced by the term social security. They comprise five forms of social insurance and four public assistances. Four of the five *social insurance* plans are now in effect in this country. These are (*a*) federal Old Age, and Survivors' and Disability Insurance, (*b*) state workmen's compensation systems, (*c*) federal-state systems of unemployment

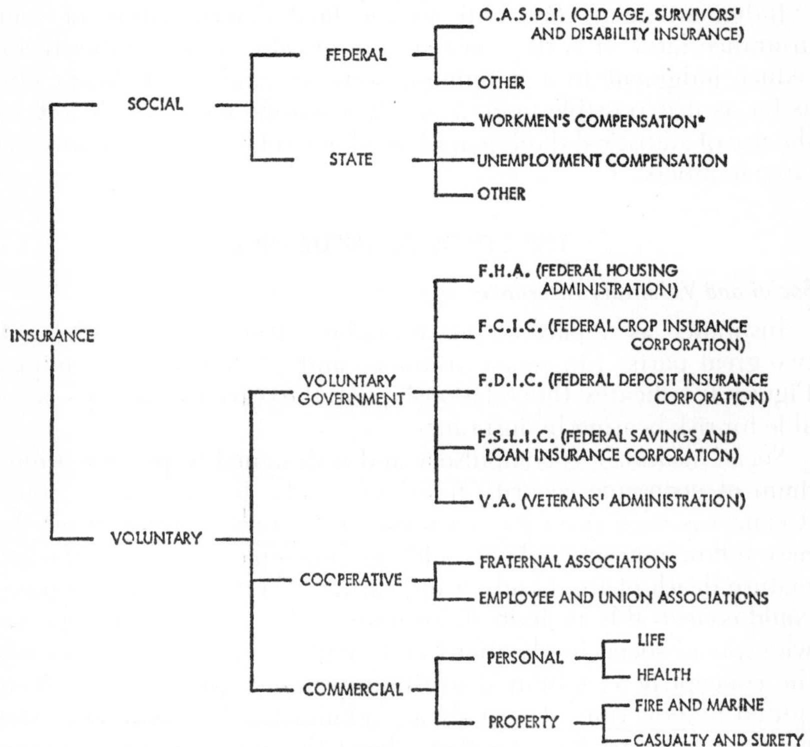

FIGURE 1. The Fields of Insurance

compensation, and (*d*) state-sponsored (in four states) temporary disability insurance, sometimes referred to as "cash sickness" insurance. The fifth, health insurance, has been advocated for such groups as the aged. *Public assistance,* in contrast to social insurance, includes no contributions or payments directly from the individuals or employers. It is financed by general tax revenues, and recipients of social assistance programs must meet certain standards of "need" to become eligible for benefits.[6] There are two categories: (*a*) noninstitutional and (*b*) institutional. The noninstitutional category includes federal-state programs of: (*a*) old-age assistance, (*b*) aid to the blind, and (*c*) aid to dependent children. Institutional care provides facilities of different types for many who are otherwise unable to maintain themselves.

Contributions for social insurance benefits are compulsory for covered groups. Social insurance thus limits the freedom of the individual. With respect to this coverage, he has no choice. In a strict sense, it is not an undemocratic process; rather, it changes the method of reaching a desirable objective. It reverts to earlier group methods that required every individual not only to provide for himself and his family but also to contribute, if able, to the needy in the community. Compulsory insurance has proved more satisfactory than charity.

Social insurance is treated separately in greater detail in a later chapter. The remainder of this section stresses the kinds of voluntary insurance, and especially the commercial branch of insurance which is the basis of the private sector of insurance.

Voluntary insurance represents those forms of insurance which do not have the element of governmental compulsion and which are sought by the insured to meet a recognized need for protection. Voluntary insurance divides itself into three groups: (1) commercial insurance, (2) cooperative insurance, and (3) voluntary government insurance.

Voluntary insurance includes the vast business of insurance carried on by privately owned companies, and a wide range of insurance protection is offered by these organizations. *Commercial* insurance represents that division of the field usually thought of as the "insurance business," including those privately formed companies organized with profit as a normal business objective. In addition to the commercial companies there are certain nonprofit organizations that offer insurance protection to group members, such as those belonging to fraternal lodges or unions. These nonprofit organizations form a class known as *cooperative* insurance. They are not to be confused with commercial mutual companies which are in a sense cooperative but which are operated like other commercial companies, including the payment of salaries or commissions, and form in a true sense a part of the commercial insurance category. Only organizations that plan their operations strictly on a nonprofit basis fall logically into the cooperative group. Finally, the government appears in the voluntary field by making insurance available

[6] J. C. Turnbull, C. Arthur Williams, Jr., and E. F. Cheit, *Economic and Social Security* (2nd ed.; New York: The Ronald Press Company, 1962), pp. 14-15.

where the hazards are so great that private companies cannot well assume the risk, such as the insurance of soldiers' lives in wartime. A few activities closely allied with the function of supervision also are illustrations, for example, the insuring of deposits of certain kinds of banks. These insurance functions have important social implications but are all classed as *voluntary government* insurance because there is no element of compulsion connected therewith and the choice of whether or not insurance will be carried rests with the insured.

Commercial Insurance

Commercial insurance is the most important of the kinds of voluntary insurance, and the most highly developed of all the forms of available insurance protection. A vast number of insurance forms have been developed to meet the needs of insureds for family protection and for the protection of business enterprises. When the term "insurance" is used, it is usually commercial insurance to which reference is made.

Commercial insurance, in contrast to the cooperative plans, receives its motivating force from the profit idea. Agents are located throughout the country. They present their insurance plans to prospects and receive as their compensation a commission on the business they produce. Officers of these companies are paid salaries for their services, and the operations of the companies are in every sense commercial enterprises.

Commercial insurance falls logically into two major classifications: (1) *personal* insurance and (2) *property* insurance. Partly the outgrowth of historical development and partly the result of legal restrictions, commercial insurance in this country is written by companies specializing in particular forms of insurance. Chiefly these are life and health insurance companies, fire and marine companies, and casualty and surety companies. Many companies now extend their activities to include several or all of the categories.

Personal Insurance. The two principal consequences of risk which insurance at the present time covers are: (1) personal[7] insurance, the loss of earning power by persons and businesses, and (2) the loss of property.

The loss of earning power by persons results from their death, injury, illness, old age, or loss of employment. The branches of insurance covering some of these contingencies have not, it seems,

[7]Note that another classification of all kinds of insurance might contrast "personal" versus "business" insurance, depending on the nature of the purchaser (family as opposed to business firm purchases). The above division is based, instead, on the nature of the perils; i.e., whether they are more directly concerned with losses due to loss of (1) earning power of a person or (2) values of a physical property.

acquired names in keeping with their purposes, so that death is a contingency covered by life insurance, and disease is a contingency covered by health insurance. Unemployment insurance indemnifies for the loss of employment. Certain of the perils bearing upon the loss of earning power have been noticed in connection with the coverages of social insurance. In the field of commercial insurance, however, life contingencies form the basis for one of its most important branches.

Life insurance in its simplest form undertakes to protect the insured's family, creditors, or others against pecuniary loss which may be the outgrowth of the death of the insured. The loss occasioned by death, against which life insurance attempts to provide protection, is the cessation of the current earning power of the insured. Applying an economic interpretation to the concept of death, the permanent loss of current earning capacity amounts to an "economic death." From an economic standpoint, death may be (1) actual, (2) living, or (3) retirement. The first classification represents the so-called "casket death." Permanent disability from the economic standpoint is "living death," while living beyond the period of earning capacity represents "retirement death."[8]

Health insurance provides benefits for medical, surgical, or hospital expenses or for time lost because of injury or illness. While health insurance is written by life insurance companies, injury and illness are also viewed as casualties, and casualty and multiple-line insurance companies write a large volume of this type of business. In addition to these carriers, there are a number of companies that limit their business to forms of health coverages, including accident insurance.

Property Insurance. Property,[9] used here as a synonym for *ownership*, is the right to use and dispose of an animal or thing for a legitimate end without the interference of any other person. In the category of property insurance is included every form that has for its purpose the protection of persons against loss arising from the ownership or use of property, as above defined.

There are two general classifications of property insurance. The first undertakes to indemnify the insured in the event of loss growing out of damages to, or destruction of, his own property. The second form undertakes to pay damages for which the insured is legally liable, the consequence of negligent acts that result in injuries to

---

[8]S. S. Huebner, *The Economics of Life Insurance* (New York: Appleton-Century-Crofts, Inc., 1959), p. 11.

[9]Although a sound argument (see *ibid.*, p. 48) can be made for including a person's earning power as one of his most valuable "properties," the distinction here between personal and property insurance seems justified on the basis of more generally accepted use of the term "property."

third parties. The first of these is known as "direct loss insurance," and the second form is known as "liability insurance."

There are a great number and variety of coverages. Traditionally, a more meaningful division of property insurance is the major groupings of fire and marine, casualty and surety insurance. Most states have permitted companies to write *multiple-line* insurance since the early 1950's, and now many companies write all of these major kinds of property insurance.

Fire insurance in its simplest form provides indemnity for direct loss or damage caused by fire. It may be written to cover not only direct loss but consequential (indirect) loss as well, such as loss of profits resulting from a fire which closes a business for several months. The fire field has been extended to include a number of perils closely allied to fire or from which fire may be expected to develop. In this latter group are to be found policies insuring against loss caused by such perils as explosion, smoke, earthquake, windstorm, and riot. Damage to property from these perils frequently results in serious injury to the property insured, with further damage caused by fire following the disaster. It is not always easy to establish a line of demarcation between one cause and the other, and it was a natural consequence that fire insurance should be extended to cover both classes of peril. Thus we have in the fire insurance business policies covering direct and consequential loss, and policies covering the so-called *allied lines.*

Marine insurance covers goods primarily while in the process of transportation. It includes protection against the perils of fire and allied lines, and also many other perils of navigation and transportation such as theft, sinking, collision, and so on. Although often written by fire insurance companies, marine insurance and its contracts are quite unique in their flexible and broad protection. They may insure one's own property while in transit, or one's legal liability for others' property (such as a railroad, airline, or trucking firm has for goods in its care).

The first type of *casualty* insurance written on a commercial basis in this country was accident and health insurance in 1850. This was followed by insurance covering accidents to steam boilers written in 1867. Both were specialized forms, and the cause of the loss in each case focused attention upon some form of accident involving a certain degree of violence. Around this nucleus developed that form of insurance to which the term "casualty" is applied.

Casualty as an insurance term is not easy to define. Accepting casualty to mean accident—that is, a mishap proceeding from an unknown or unexpected cause—casualty insurance might be presumed to mean a contract whereby an insured who suffers loss or damage when an accident or casualty is the cause of the loss is reimbursed for the loss suffered. Since this definition might be made to apply to almost any form of insurance, it hardly serves as a guide for classifying coverages. By a process of elimination, this most recent of the major insurance groups is said to comprise those insurance coverages not to be classified as marine, fire, or life.

This process of elimination does not result in strict accuracy, nor can a logical definition readily be devised. Resort, therefore, is necessary to the statutes for accurate definition; and because of this it follows that the definitions, while alike in principle, may differ in phraseology and minor detail in each state.

The major kinds of casualty insurance today are automobile insurance, workmen's compensation insurance, health insurance, and the various other kinds of liability insurance besides automobile liability (called "general" liability insurance). The miscellaneous categories of casualty insurance are numerous, and most states include the following minor categories (in terms of sales volume) of insurance in the laws which license casualty insurance companies: theft, glass breakage, steam boiler explosion, credit, title, water damage, aircraft, animal life insurance, fidelity and surety bonding.

It will be noted that the foregoing definition specifically mentions title insurance. By the process of elimination already mentioned, title insurance would be included in the casualty group; but because of the nature of the risk, it possesses many of the characteristics of a guarantee. It will also be noted that the section allows casualty companies to write fidelity and surety business. While there are companies that specialize in these forms, it is quite the usual practice to include fidelity and surety lines as part of the casualty classification.[10]

In the strict sense, all corporate bonds in which a surety agrees to answer for the nonperformance of a principal are surety bonds. As a matter of practice, bonds are divided into two major classifications: (1) fidelity bonds and (2) surety bonds. In the case of a fidelity bond, the obligation of the employee is implied rather than contractual, and the bond undertakes to reimburse an employer for loss of money or property growing out of the dishonest acts of the employee. The surety bond, in contrast, obligates the surety to hold himself responsible for the performance of an expressed obligation. In order to establish a claim under a fidelity bond, the employee would have been guilty of a dishonest act. In the case of a surety

---

[10]The classification plan of the National Association of Insurance Commissioners states: " 'Casualty' as used throughout the plan includes suretyship." Prior to the advent of corporate suretyship, a surety bond was defined as the promise of one person to answer for the debt, default, or miscarriage of another. The suretyship contract originated as a credit device and made its appearance in ancient times with the earliest development of business activities. Corporate surety bonds were offered first in England during the early part of the eighteenth century.

bond the coverage is much broader; and while a dishonest act may give rise to a loss, it is equally true that a loss may originate through negligence or lack of ability on the part of the principal. An example of a surety bond is that required for executors of estates.

With the development of corporate suretyship and the intimate association of this business with insurance, suretyship now is generally regarded as a branch of the business of insurance and is included in the casualty classification.

Multiple-Line and All-Lines Insurance. For many years, the business of property insurance was carried on chiefly by companies devoting their efforts to a single "line," or major kind, of insurance. A fire company wrote only fire insurance, and a casualty company only the various kinds of casualty insurance mentioned above. Monoline insurance companies were the normal method of operation in American insurance. The "American" system of separating insurance into compartments of fire and casualty lines was strengthened by state laws which licensed companies for one or the other of these major fields of property insurance, but not both.

Since 1900 the separation of fire and casualty insurance has gradually broken down in what has been called the multiple-line insurance trend. Gradually the restrictions have disappeared and today all states[11] permit a fire or marine insurance company to write all casualty lines, or a casualty company to write all fire and marine kinds of business. Many company groups have written multiple-line insurance since the 1920's, and individual companies often have been licensed for the broad fire-casualty market since legislation permitted them to do so during the last decade. Note that the term has been accepted to denote not just several kinds of insurance, but the combination of at least two kinds of insurance, specifically the traditional fire and casualty lines.

The real multiple-line insurance change has centered in recent years (since the 1950's) on combinations of coverages in a single multiple-line package contract. The Homeowner's Policy is the best example, combining fire, theft, and liability protection in one insurance contract for the family. Many new business contracts for stores, industries, and service businesses have also evolved.

The newest trend in broader insurance organizations and contracts is the *all-lines*[12] which combines *personal* and *property* insurance. To differentiate the term from multiple-line insurance, it is

---

[11]By specific statute, or by insurance department rulings in five states. See David L. Bickelhaupt, *Transition to Multiple-Line Insurance Companies* (Homewood, Ill.: Richard D. Irwin, Inc., 1961), p. 37.

[12]For discussion of the forces behind and impact of all-lines insurance, see Dan M. McGill (ed.) *All-Lines Insurance* (Homewood, Ill.: Richard D. Irwin, Inc., 1960).

best to describe all-lines insurance as all kinds of insurance, including life and health protection.

The term all-lines should not be used in a technical sense, for few, if any, companies or contracts do include every possible kind of insurance. In a general sense, however, the term is useful today to describe the broadening nature of insurance operations which combine a relatively large group of traditional types of insurance including fire, casualty, life, and health lines.

The trend so far has been evident mostly in the formation of many large all-lines company groups. Most major property insurance companies have formed or bought life insurance subsidiaries. Some state laws have prevented life insurance companies from owning property companies, but permissive legislation is to be expected in the years ahead. All-lines insurance contracts are not yet permitted in most states, though life insurance for a homeowner's mortgage has been combined with the Homeowner's Policy in a few new contracts.

Cooperative Insurance

The term "cooperative" is applied to mutual associations usually operating under fraternal, employee, industrial, or trade-union auspices. The associations are organized without regard to the profit motive and represent, in fact, an effort to accomplish the ends of social insurance by private enterprise.[13]

In the United States the cooperative idea is evidenced primarily in the operation of fraternal societies, employee mutual sick benefit associations, and trade-union benefit associations. The associations are ordinarily small and to a large extent local in their operation and management. The tendency to bring together persons having a common racial origin or religious belief has manifested itself in these membership organizations.

Employee mutual sick benefit associations provide cash payments to members when sick and sometimes at the time of death. Membership is limited as a rule to the employees of a particular industrial establishment, although some are organized on an occupational basis. Some of these associations are financed solely by the pay-

---

[13]This has been pointed out in a study sponsored by the Federal Security Agency thus: "With its emphasis on collective effort and common needs, co-operative insurance is the real forerunner of social insurance. Association for the common good and collective responsibility for the risks and dangers common to all members of the group have distinguished co-operative insurance from the beginning. As in social insurance, which is usually restricted to persons whose annual earnings are small, those who are insured by co-operative effort are in the main in low-income groups—laborers, artisans, and small tradespeople" (Elizabeth L. Otey, *Cash Benefits under Voluntary Disability Insurance in the United States,* Federal Security Agency, Bureau of Research and Statistics, Report No. 6 [Washington, D.C., 1940], p. 68).

ments of the members, and in other instances the employer company contributes. Membership is usually voluntary, though in some instances all employees of an organization are required to join. In the case of trade-unions, some unions have provided benefits for their members on a national basis, though the tendency recently has been to permit management of such benefits by local organizations. Certain of the unions have organized insurance departments and provide for the writing of life and accident insurance. In addition to the foregoing, benefits in the form of hospital treatment, homes for the aged and disabled, and special provisions for the treatment of tuberculous members have been provided.

Blue Cross, Blue Shield, and other medical insurance plans are an interesting combination of social and private insurance. They emphasize the nonprofit, cooperative objective, and are administered in most states under special state statutes which remove them somewhat from the commercial category of voluntary insurance. Such plans include representative membership in their boards of directors from medical groups and the public.

To a certain extent the facilities of cooperative insurance run parallel with those offered by the commercial insurance companies. The cooperative organizations, however, are set up to meet requirements of special classes of persons and to provide, for the most part, an insurance program that may be represented as a minimum. There are a great many people who are not eligible for the facilities of the cooperative organizations or are eligible only for a limited participation.

Voluntary Government Insurance

Insurance that falls into this category is principally distingushed from social insurance in that there is no element of compulsion. The various plans offered have wide social significance and are designed to benefit the entire community.

In this category are to be found such plans as the insurance of loans by the Federal Housing Administration, insurance of growing crops by the Federal Crop Insurance Corporation, insurance of many bank deposits by the Federal Deposit Insurance Corporation, insurance of shares by the Federal Savings and Loan Insurance Corporation, insurance against loss by enemy action by the War Insurance Corporation, and government life insurance for servicemen administered by the Veterans' Administration.

Government voluntary insurance, in the usual course, provides protection in fields where private insurance cannot safely enter. This is because of lack of experience in the field or because of the catastrophic perils connected with the insurance. Coverage of such perils on a safe basis is beyond the capacity of private enterprise.

In some instances there is an overlapping of government voluntary insurance and insurance offered by commercial insurance companies.[14]

Summary

The fields of insurance have been described briefly in this section. The major classification emphasizes the difference between social and voluntary insurance. In essence, this is the distinction between compulsory government insurance and private insurance. Voluntary insurance includes the major categories of commercial, cooperative, and voluntary government insurance. Commercial insurance is divided into personal (life and health) and property types of protection, and traditionally in property insurance the major groupings of fire, marine and casualty insurance are important. With recent trends toward broader insurance operations and contracts, the terms multiple-line insurance and all-lines insurance have become significant.

Another useful method of discussing the field of insurance is to classify and analyze the legal types of insurers and their organization in the marketing of voluntary insurance. Chapter 4 will use this approach in studying the fields of insurance.

A BRIEF HISTORY OF INSURANCE

History is important in obtaining a proper perspective for the study of any subject. It is particularly significant in insurance, for the roots of the insurance idea go far back in the pages of history. This section merely serves an an introduction to the wealth of knowledge which history contains about insurance. The student (and his teacher!) is encouraged to delve further into insurance history by referring to Appendix A, "A History of Insurance," where more complete detail is offered on pertinent areas in the development of insurance. By learning more about the past, one can better understand the present and appraise the future of insurance.

Ancient Insurance Ideas

Insurance has a rich and colorful history. It is a part of many ancient civilizations, and almost any economic history contains references to practices which can be identified as the forerunners of modern insurance techniques.

---

[14]An example is to be found in the insurance of registered mail and parcel post by the Post Office Department. Although the insurance is ordinarily supplied as a concomitant of the service of transportation, coverage for mail shipments is also afforded through private insurance carriers. The shipper has the right to elect, if he desires insurance on his shipment, to purchase it either through the Post Office Department or through a private carrier. The government does not exercise a monopoly but offers the insurance as a service.

The evolution of insurance is not so precise that one can point with confidence at a single civilization, or year, or transaction and say: "That was the beginning of insurance." Certainly, however, the origins were present in Biblical times. Some authors even describe insurance arrangements (perhaps not as it is known today, but, nevertheless, with similarities of purpose and method) thousands of years before the Christian calendar began.

The Babylonians and Hindus used contracts known as "bottomry" loans to shift the burden of risk from owners of ships and cargoes to moneylenders who agreed to cancel the loan if the ship or cargo was lost during a voyage. The charge for the bottomry loan, if the venture was successful, was a high one which combined both interest and the cost of risk. Insurance has been called "the handmaiden of commerce," for it was with early commercial activities and the great dangers of travel and trade that such contracts appeared. The Phoenicians, Greeks, and Romans developed agreements that correspond in most essentials to written contracts used two thousand years later in marine ventures to the New World. Moneylenders and traders used these loan-insurance agreements in their vast negotiations throughout the ports of the Old World.

Not only were risks shifted from one party to another in ancient times, but the idea of sharing and pooling risks was also used. Chinese merchants divided their cargoes among several ships for perilous voyages on the rivers of ancient China, for the purpose of not having any one merchant suffer a total loss of cargo because of one disaster. The famed storage of grain during the "Seven Fat Years" in preparation for the "Seven Lean Years" is adequately explained in the Bible to denote a clear recognition of the principle of community and group sharing of risk.

Life insurance, too, can be traced to ancient civilizations such as Rome. Burial funds were common in those days. In Greece religious organizations collected and dispersed funds for burial costs of members. The Egyptians left many evidences in the tombs of the pyramids that burial societies were then in existence. Feudal guilds included such services in their system of dues, although documentation is difficult in the tracing of their use through the Dark Ages.

The Middle Ages and the Merchant Era

Perhaps the real origins of insurance stem from the advances made in commerce during the Middle Ages. Venetian decrees in the fifteenth century regulated marine insurance contracts, and the Hanseatic League used indemnity contracts for trade with all of Europe. The Mediterranean trade with Europe and the Near East rapidly expanded the need for specialized services in the guaranteeing of financial solvency in the face of navigation disasters.

A new financial specialist known as an "underwriter" (who underwrote his name on a contract of insurance as he accepted maritime risks) appeared. In the coffeehouses of England, particularly, the individual insurer grew in significance as England and France forged to the peak of their naval supremacy. Lloyd's of London became the best-known center of marine insurance, and remains today as an important source of worldwide insurance on ships and cargoes.

Fire insurance appeared in the seventeenth century, prompted by a disastrous fire which destroyed 85 percent of London in 1666. The failure of several insurance schemes in this period led to increased desire by the public for stronger insurance plans. One famous plan by Nicholas Barbon, a building contractor who guaranteed to repair houses he built if they later were damaged by fire, was doomed to early failure because of lack of recognition of the substantial risks assumed in the agreement.

The Eighteenth Century and Insurance in Early America

The beginnings of corporate insurance, as opposed to individual insurers whose guarantees were limited to their personal fortunes, appeared in 1720. The "Bubble Period," during which speculators and insurers alike failed in a financial panic of widespread repercussions, brought forth restricted charters from Parliament for two insurance companies, the London Assurance Corporation and the Royal Exchange Assurance Corporation. These companies had a monopoly on corporate insurance, and perhaps the wisdom of the royal charters is evidenced by the fact that these two insurers still are strong companies today.

Colonial America naturally took ideas from England for the first companies in the United States. Much of the early insurance was written by branch offices of English insurers. But new American companies sprang up to meet the needs of a growing America. Benjamin Franklin organized the first incorporated fire insurance company, the Philadelphia Contributionship, in 1752. The Mutual Assurance Company (1784) was known as the "Green Tree" because of its "fire mark," a plaque used on insured houses to identify them for the fire-fighting companies maintained by the insurance company. The oldest joint stock company was formed in 1794 to do a fire and marine business (and for a few years, life insurance, too) under the name of The Insurance Company of North America. In life insurance, other companies were started: the Presbyterian Ministers' Fund in 1759, and the Episcopal Corporation in 1769. The business was small, however, and probably there were fewer than one hundred policyholders until after 1800.

The Expanding 1800's

Economic expansion in the early 1800's found two more life insurance companies ready for business: the Pennsylvania Company for the Insurance on Lives (1809) and the New York Life Insurance and Trust Company (1830). Other companies well-known today were formed before 1850, including the New England Mutual Life Insurance Company (1836) and Mutual Life Insurance Company of New York (1843). By mid-century, twelve more new companies were organized, and the beginnings of scientific actuarial mortality tables appeared. Life insurance quadrupled in the decade following the Civil War.

The fire insurance business prospered, also, while growing pains developed in the form of concentrated city construction, and expanding market problems as the first agency systems were developed. Disastrous city fires tested the strength of the fire insurance companies, and pointed toward crucial needs for improved building codes and fire-fighting equipment. The Chicago Fire in 1871 is famous, as it resulted in a property loss of over $150 million, which was an especially huge loss for that time. Almost $100 million of the losses were insured. Numerous other fire disasters were almost as important, however, as each tried the resources and services of the insurance companies: fires in New York in 1835, New Orleans in 1854, New York in 1862, Portland, Maine in 1866, and Boston in 1872 ($75 million property loss, just one year after the Chicago fire!).

State regulation of insurance began about 1850, as several states established boards or commissions for the supervision of the business. Solvency and tax revenues were the prime objectives of the new laws, through deposit, investment, reserve, and premium tax requirements. The first separate insurance departments began in 1855 (Massachusetts) and 1859 (New York). Men such as Elizur Wright became the stalwart proponents of better insurance regulation, as abuses were corrected and mathematical standards improved in many phases of the insurance business.

Twentieth Century Growth

The development of insurance in the 1900's has paralleled the major economic changes of the times. The expansion of the railroads, the advent of the automobile age, the mass production techniques of modern industry, the wars, the introduction of the airplane, and the changing social conseiousness of an affluent society—all these factors and many more closely affected the rise of insurance as a major business of the twentieth century.[15]

---

[15]Some excellent insurance company biographies are available which clearly show how insurance reacted to the major events of the nineteenth and twentieth centuries. The author has seen nearly a hundred such historical works which tell much about insurance history. Representative of these publications are: Marquis James, *Biography of a Business* (New York: The Bobbs-Merrill Company, Inc., 1942); Hawthorne

Some of the landmarks in fire insurance were the San Francisco fire of 1906 (property loss of $350 million), the New England hurrican of 1938, Texas City ship explosion of 1947 (3,500 killed or injured), the East Coast windstorm of 1950 (over 1.5 million separate insurance claims), the South Amboy explosion of 1950 (400 persons dead or injured), and the increasing number of recent windstorm catastrophes such as Hurricanes Donna and Carla. Transportation risks changed as the railroads encountered competition from the motor truck and airline industries. New chemicals, radioactive materials, and industrial processes have caused continual risk analysis innovations for property insurance.

Major developments in casualty insurance were the rise of workmen's compensation insurance since 1911 to a $2 billion a year business, and the growth of automobile insurance to insure 91 million drivers and 75 million automobiles today at a cost of $8 billion per year. Negligence laws have increased the need for many other forms of liability insurance. Concentrated valuable properties have expanded crime insurance needs, and high medical costs and loss of income have sky-rocketed health insurance to a multibillion dollar part of the casualty insurance field.

Life insurance, too, has undergone significant change since 1900. Many new companies have competed for the growing needs of a prosperous economy, until today over 1,500 life insurance companies are in business. Group insurance through employers for their employees has shown rapid growth in the past fifty years, and today group pensions, life and health insurance play an important part in labor negotiations. New mortality tables have been adopted, reserve tests strengthened, and merchandising methods changed to encompass family plans and complete estate programming. The life insurance companies had a most remarkable record for a financial institution during the Great Depression of the 1930's, with less than 1/10 of 1 percent of policyholder funds lost during that period. Life insurance amounts in force have grown seven-fold since 1930 to over $700 billion today.

THE SIGNIFICANCE OF INSURANCE

Chapter 2 has already presented some examples of the wide scope, nature, and benefits of insurance. This final section serves to review and reappraise the combined effect of insurance in the home, business, and government.

Daniel, *The Hartford of Hartford* (New York: Random House, 1960); Thomas C. Chubb, *And There Were No Losses* (New York: John B. Watkins Company, 1957); and Nicholas B. Wainwright, *A Philadelphia Story* (New York: Frederick Fell, Inc., 1952).

Insurance in the United States today is regarded as a basic part of our society, ranking in importance with agriculture, commerce, banking, manufacturing, transportation, and communication. In its several branches, the business of insurance provides the factor of protection now regarded as essential in our economic and industrial organization.

While there is scarcely anyone who does not at some point or other make contact with the business of insurance, there are few indeed who, without some reflection and investigation, have an adequate idea of the great size and importance of the business. There is no industry which is not dependent upon it and no individual who does not owe to it substantial credit for daily comforts and conveniences.

General Benefits

The benefits of insurance are numerous. A partial listing of the advantages of insurance would include:

1. *Peace of mind.* Almost everyone has a basic desire for some security, or peace of mind. To the extent that insurance provides certainty or predictability, it helps an individual or business by improving efficiency of actions by reducing anxieties. This is a psychological factor that is difficult to measure in terms of specific benefits. It is nonetheless important in our everyday life.

2. *Keeps families and business together.* The existence of insurance often supplies the financial aid which permits a family or business to continue despite serious adversities which have occurred. A death or disability of a husband can bring financial disaster to a family. With family income stopped, the wife or children may have to give up their home and accept undesirable alternatives such as foster homes, living with relatives, or accepting relief payments. A fire or liability suit can cause the failure of a business. Such perils can be met through insurance, which provides money at the time of need in order to keep the family or business intact.

3. *Increases marginal utility of assets.* From an economic standpoint, insurance serves as an intermediary between those who have small need for a minor amount of capital or income (i.e., the cost of insurance) and those who have great needs for immediate use of large sums to meet losses they have suffered. Basically, insurance takes the least useful "last" dollar of low marginal utility from all policyholders, and repays the important "first" dollars[16] of high marginal utility to those unfortunate persons having severe losses.

---

[16]An exception to this statement is the use of deductibles, which may not pay the policyholder until after the loss has exceeded a specified minimum.

4. *Provides a basis for credit.* One finds it impossible to visualize the credit economy of today without insurance. Several kinds of insurance are invaluable as the foundation for credit transactions. Personal and business bank loans of many kinds use life insurance (either face values or cash values) as a guarantee that the loan will be repaid in spite of uncertain contingencies such as death or disability of the borrower. Fire insurance is invariably used by mortgagees who loan money with real or personal property as collateral. The creditor must know that his collateral will not disappear in a fire, windstorm, or other loss, and this security is accomplished through proper amounts of insurance being purchased by the debtor for his home or automobile.

5. *Stimulates saving.* Many kinds of insurance are important for the fact that they encourage thrift. An insurance premium, though small in relation to the possible loss it protects against, is basically a prepayment in advance of potential loss. All the payments are gathered together to form a fund from which those few who do suffer losses are paid. In essence, the plan of insurance encourages all to save in order that unfortunates are repaid for their losses. In addition, life insurance has special advantages in stimulating saving. The long-term contracts, often over a whole lifetime, build substantial cash, emergency, or retirement values. A policyholder treats his regular premium payment as an obligation to his family or beneficiaries, and greater savings result than in any other good-intentioned but irregular savings program.

6. *Provides investment capital.* The savings held as assets by insurance companies are not stagnant. They provide a gigantic source of important capital for our economy. The Institute of Life Insurance reviews the creative force of almost $140 billion of life insurance company assets at midyear 1963, by showing how these funds are used: government, railroad, utility and industrial *bonds,* $66 billion or 47 percent; home *mortgages,* $49 billion or 34 percent; *stocks,* $6 billion or 5 percent; *loans* to policyholders, $7 billion or 5 percent; *real estate* $5 billion or 4 percent; and *cash and miscellaneous,* $7 billion, or 5 percent.

In addition to the large sums invested by life insurance companies, property companies had $33 billion[17] of investments. These companies have heavy investments in bonds, and a much greater investment in stocks than the life companies. If the assets of social insurance programs are added to the $173 billion total assets of insurance companies in 1963, over $250 billion is seen as the investment of

[17]The 1963 *Fire Insurance Index* by *The Spectator* (Philadelphia) totals the assets of 1159 property companies as $32.9 billion on December 31, 1962.

insurance in the United States. The tremendous impact of such assets on families and businesses is apparent, when one considers that the assets of all banks totaled only about this same amount.

7. *Advantages of specialization.* It is common sense that an insurance organization that specializes in risk-bearing can usually perform its services more efficiently than someone else. When a business transfers its risk to an insurer it says in effect: "Here, you take care of those bothersome unpredictable risks of loss, and we'll pay attention to the main purposes of our business." The productive aspect of insurance thus emerges an an incentive to business or individuals, relieving them of fortuitous losses so that more effort, manpower, and capital can be directed toward the work for which they are best suited. For example, a department store is normally better off to shift its pure risks to an insurance company and then concentrate its efforts on greater sales or other merchandising services. The alternative of "self-insurance" or do-it-yourself insurance is better only when a very large store can do a better job of insuring than the insurer. Even in such a rare case, the store must further consider the loss of profits it has in effect lost (the "opportunity costs" in an economic sense) because it is using time and personnel to provide its own insurance program.

8. *Loss prevention.* Insurance benefits society by making considerable effort toward prevention of losses. This result is a subsidiary goal for most kinds of insurance, but undoubtedly more loss prevention work occurs because of insurance than would occur without it. The net effect is advantageous, as lives are saved or property values preserved. Examples are fire prevention campaigns, motor vehicle safety research, health education by life insurance companies, elevator and boiler inspections, and many others.

9. *Special benefits of individual kinds of insurance.* In addition to the above eight examples of general benefits of many kinds of insurance, each particular kind has some special benefits which make it significant to our economy. For example, consider the special purposes and achievements of life insurance. A separate list of benefits of life insurance includes: establishes an immediate and liquid estate, encourages gifts to charity, aids in planning for education costs, reduces mortgage worries of a widow, offers a safe and reasonable investment service, provides retirement income, and so on. For each particular kind of insurance a supplementary list of special benefits might be developed. The student should think about such fields as transportation insurance, theft insurance, bonds, and hospitalization insurance to provide additional examples of these benefits.

10. *Negative considerations.* It would be unfair to consider only the benefits of insurance without mentioning possible negative con-

siderations. The institution of insurance is not maintained without costs to the policyholders. Expenses of operating an insurance company and its agency system must be balanced against the benefits enumerated above. From an economy viewpoint, insurance manpower could be used elsewhere in providing useful products and services. Insurance, like other worthy institutions, occasionally has adverse effects such as the encouragement of fraud to collect dishonest claims, or increases in carelessness when one feels completely insured.

Statistical Evidences

The major contributions of insurance can be summarized concisely in employment, asset, and sales figures which show its size and diversification throughout our economy.

Over a million persons are employed in the voluntary sector of insurance in the United States. This means that about one out of every fifty *employed persons* directly receives his livelihood from insurance. Not all these persons are in insurance sales work, either, for almost two thirds of insurance employment is nonsales work.[18] Many men and women are needed by insurance for such jobs as underwriters, claims personnel, accountants, secretaries, file clerks, statisticians and actuaries, advertising experts, research specialists, investment counselors, and management positions from top executives to personnel managers to field managers of many types. Few people realize that insurance employment exceeds that found in many other major parts of our economy, such as banking or mining or chemical products.

Another measure of significance has already been introduced in referring to the *assets* controlled by insurance organizations, and the *investments* which stem from the use of these assets. Few other institutions, even financial ones, can compare with the several hundred billion dollars of funds put to use by insurers. Virtually every area of our economy receives some capital from investments made by the insurance business. In the race into space aiming toward the United States placing a man on the moon, an estimated $5 billion of life insurance funds have provided capital for research and manufacture of jet aircraft and spacecraft.[19] Another major use of the assets held by insurers (in fact, their major purpose) is the payment of *losses*. In 1962, life companies alone paid over $9 billion to policyholders and beneficiaries, including almost $4 billion of death pay-

---

[18] *Life Insurance Fact Book* (New York: The Institute of Life Insurance, 1963), p. 99.

[19] "The Insurance Industry's Role in the Space Age," *The Spectator* (Philadelphia: Chilton Company), September, 1963, p. 34.

FIELD OF INSURANCE	1962 Premiums[7] (To Nearest Billion Dollars)			
Fire and Marine Insurance	$ 3			
Casualty[1] and Surety Insurance	12			
Total Property Insurance		$15		
Life Insurance	$ 14			
Health[2] Insurance	5			
Total Personal Insurance		19		
Total Commercial Insurance			$34	
Cooperative[3] Insurance			4	
Voluntary Government[4]			1	
Total Voluntary Insurance				$39
Federal[5] Insurance			$ 14	
State[6] Insurance			5	
Total Social Insurance				19
TOTAL INSURANCE PREMIUMS[7]				$58

1. Excludes health insurance of about $1 billion, and includes 1/2 of homeowners and commercial multiple-peril premiums of $1 billion (other 1/2 apportioned as fire insurance).

2. Includes approximately $1 billion of health insurance written by property companies and $1.6 billion of workmen's compensation insurance written by private insurers.

3. Estimated total of such plans as Blue Cross and Blue Shield ($3.7 billion); and fraternal and employee benefit associations. Note that including these amounts in health insurance totals above would increase the health field to $9 billion.

4. Estimated total of F.D.I.C., F.H.A., F.S. & L.I.C., V.A., and F.C.I.C. insurance.

5. Includes $12 billion O.A.S.D.I. taxes; remainder Civil Service, R.R. Retirement and miscellaneous.

6. Includes approximately $2 billion unemployment compensation; $2 billion state and local retirement funds; $.5 billion state workmen's compensation funds; and remainder miscellaneous.

7. Including as "premiums" the compulsory amounts paid under social insurance plans, which are technically better described as taxes.

Sources: Spectator Fire, Casualty, Life and Health Indexes (1963); Life Insurance Fact Book (1963); Source Book of Health Insurance Data (1963); and Budget of the United States Government (1963).

FIGURE 2. Premium Volume of the Fields of Insurance

ments and over $5 billion of living benefits such as annuities and policy dividends.[20]

Premiums, the amounts paid by policyholders to insurers, are a most important measure of the gigantic nature of insurance. Figure 2 reviews the $58 billion total sales volume of insurance, according to the previously discussed major fields of insurance activity in the United States.

The conclusion is clear. By any measure of employment, assets (and their use), or premium volume, the institution of insurance is of major significance in the economic activity of the Unted States. It employs over a million persons, it holds some $250 billion of assets, and annually has an income of over $58 billion. The interests of everyone are closely affected by the giant size and scope of insurance. Insurance is the cornerstone of the private property system and an essential element of our free enterprise economy.

SUMMARY

More important than any one single definition of insurance is the recognition that *insurance* may be defined in a number of different ways. A definition from economic, legal, business, social, mathematical, and other viewpoints can each be meaningful in explaining the purpose and method of the insurance mechanism.

The *insurance equation,* showing that an insurer's expenditures cannot exceed its income without decreasing financial solvency, is one method of indicating how insurance works. Also important in analyzing the insurance method is the study of the application of the principles of *probability,* the *law of large numbers,* and the prime need for adequate *statistical data.*

Classifying the fields of insurance helps organize its many parts into basic divisions. *Social* insurance of a compulsory nature is contrasted with *voluntary,* or private insurance, which includes *cooperative, voluntary government,* and *commercial* approaches to the distribution of insurance. The commercial type, which is generally thought of as "the insurance business," is subdivided into (1) personal and (2) property insurance. *Multiple-line* and *all-lines* insurance are two new terms describing recent trends in the business.

The perspective of history aids one to appreciate the growth and problems of insurance today. From its ancient beginnings to its recent rapid development in the twentieth century, insurance ex-

---

[20]*Life Insurance Fact Book, op. cit.,* p. 37. The amazing explanation of how employment, assets, premiums, investments, and losses are related in the everday business efforts of a single giant life insurance company is interestingly told in Robert Sheehan, "That Mighty Pump, Prudential," *Fortune* (Chicago: Time, Inc.), January, 1964, p. 99.

hibits a vitality and continued responsiveness to the basic needs of our economy and society.

Benefits of insurance, from the general peace of mind it creates to the specific economic stimulation to savings and investment capital it represents, are persuasive evidence of its signficance throughout the world. As a business with billions of dollars of income, hundreds of billions of assets, and millions of employees, it justifies itself as a powerful force in the free enterprise economy.

FOR REVIEW

1. An adequate description of "insurance" requires an explanation of *what it is, its purpose,* and *how it accomplishes its goal.* The essential parts of what may be termed "insurance" all stem from an analysis of these three parts of the description.
   a) Explain how you might describe *what insurance is.*
   b) What is, in relation to risk, the fundamental *purpose* of insurance?
   c) Discuss briefly *how* insurance accomplishes the purpose set forth in (*b*).
2. Define "insurance" and compare the contract with the ancient contract of bottomry.
3. Why is it that there are many ways of defining insurance? What do you consider the best definition, and why?
4. It is said that the risk that an insurance company carries is far less than the sum of the risks insured. For example: "The aggregate danger is less than the sum of the individual dangers. . . ." (William Roscher, *Principles of Political Economy.*) Do you agree or disagree? Give reasons.
5. Insurance has a long and colorful history. To know where insurance in the United States has come from, one needs to answer these questions:
   a) How old are some forms of insurance?
   b) How were loans and insurance related?
   c) Did the guilds have insurance?
   d) How did marine commerce encourage insurance?
   e) How and when did insurance become a specialized business of risk-bearing?
   f) How did the London fire in 1666 effect insurance?
   g) When did insurance *companies* begin?
   h) How did insurance start in America?
6. Describe the method of determining probabilities for the purposes of insurance underwriting when the risk to be insured is of a nature that affords no precedent whatsoever.
7. Explain how predictability is achieved through the use of the insurance method.
8. Describe the use made of statistics in the field of life insurance, and in fire insurance.
9. It is sometimes stated by those interested in the business of insurance that the development of social insurance is in fact a threat to the insurance business. Those who express this opinion evidence a fear that some day all the business of insurance will be handled by the government. As a point of departure for discussion, indicate whether or not in your opinion the government's participation in the field of social insurance constitutes a threat to the private insurance business.

10. How do social and voluntary forms of insurance differ? Identify the basic kinds of each, as to their purposes and methods of operation.
11. What kinds of perils (causes of loss) are included in fire insurance? Marine insurance? Casualty insurance? Personal insurance? Multiple-line insurance? All-lines insurance?
12. How do cooperative types of insurance vary from commercial and voluntary government types? Give examples of each.
13. Why is the term "casualty" insurance misleading? How did it evolve?
14. How does insurance differ from assistance? Why is the distinction important?
15. How has the scope of social insurance changed over the years? Give examples of some of the changes of greatest significance.
16. A newspaper article recently commented on the relationship of premium income to losses in the fire insurance business and concluded, in effect, that if a company received $1,000 in premiums and paid out $600 in losses, it made a profit of $400. Does this seem reasonable? Is the conclusion correct?
17. What are some of the benefits of insurance?
    a) To the individual?
    b) To the business economy?
    c) To society?
18. "Over-insurance leads to fraud, full insurance to carelessness, and even partial insurance to some diminution of watchfulness." This statement is made by Willett in *The Economic Theory of Risk and Insurance.* It sounds like a severe indictment and is unquestionably true. Justify insurance in the light of this statement.
19. Mr. I. M. Sure is a family man who has all of his real and personal property insured against loss. What other kinds of insurance does Mr. Sure need besides property insurance?

PART TWO

The Structure and Operations of the Insurance Business

CHAPTER 4 *INSURANCE MARKETING*—Cont'd

3. Farm Mutuals
4. Factory Mutuals
5. Fraternals

C. Lloyd's

1. Lloyd's of London
2. American Lloyd's

D. Reciprocals

E. State Insurers

F. Self-Insurers

G. Summary

III. MARKETING METHODS

A. Agency versus Direct-Selling Systems

B. Life Insurance Agency Systems

C. Property Insurance Agency Systems

1. Independent Agency System
2. Exclusive Agency System
3. Summary

IV. TYPES OF INSURER REPRESENTATIVES

A. Agents

1. Life
2. Property

B. Solicitors

C. Brokers

D. Service Representatives

V. THE PROFESSIONAL CONCEPT OF INSURANCE MARKETING

VI. THE CONSUMER VIEWPOINT OF INSURANCE PURCHASING

A. Selecting the Insurer

B. Selecting the Agent or Broker

VII. SUMMARY

CHAPTER 5 *INSURANCE LOSS PAYMENT*

I. SIGNIFICANCE

II. PURPOSE

III. INSURANCE CLAIMSMEN: TYPES AND ORGANIZATION

A. Agents as Adjusters

B. Staff Adjusters

C. Independent Adjusters

D. Adjustment Bureaus

E. Public Adjusters

IV. CLAIMS PROCEDURES

A. Fire Insurance Losses

1. Rights and Obligations
2. Special Problems

B. Marine Insurance Losses

C. Liability Insurance Losses

D. Workmen's Compensation Insurance Losses

E. Life Insurance Losses

V. SUMMARY

CHAPTER 6 *UNDERWRITING, REINSURANCE, AND OTHER FUNCTIONS*

I. RELATIONSHIP OF MAJOR INSURANCE FUNCTIONS

II. UNDERWRITING

- A. Purposes
- B. Selection of Risks
  1. The Agent and Company as Underwriters
  2. Sources of Underwriting Information
- C. Rating of Risks
  1. General
  2. Fire Insurance as an Example
     - a. Rating Bureaus
     - b. Rate Analysis
     - c. Classification
     - d. Class Rates
     - e. Specific or Schedule Rates
     - f. What the Insured Can Do to Lower Rates
- D. Special Problems
  1. Deductible Clauses
  2. Minimum Premiums
  3. Annual and Term Policies
  4. Installment Plans

III. REINSURANCE

- A. Reinsurance Agreements
  1. Specific or Facultative
  2. Treaty or Automatic
- B. Reinsurance Contracts
  1. Share-of-Risk Contracts
  2. Excess-of-Loss Contracts
- C. Retrocessions
- D. Summary

IV. OTHER FUNCTIONS OF INSURERS

V. SUMMARY

Chapter 3

INSURANCE CONTRACT FUNDAMENTALS

PRIVATE insurance is usually created by a written contract. For this reason the legal technicalities of contract law are of extreme importance to the field of insurance. The insurance contract is the tangible product of the systems devised to handle risk through a transfer of the burden of unpredictable events which may cause financial loss. It is the means by which risk transfer is accomplished, and this makes insurance fundamentally dependent upon legal principles of contracts.

The importance of contract law to insurance is magnified by the fact that many persons think of the physical piece of paper upon which the insurance *policy* contract is written as the whole of insurance. Since this document is what one sees as he purchases insurance, he may unconsciously assume that this is all there is to it. One tends to forget that there are many other parts of insurance. The risk transfer, the application of the law of large numbers, the freedom from worry, the inspections and loss prevention services, the advisory functions—all these services tend to be forgotten when only the contract of insurance is considered. Even the payment of losses in dollars of currency (a most tangible result) is neglected in such thoughts by insurance purchasers, that is, unless they happen to suffer losses for which reimbursement is paid! Buyers of insurance thus are familiar with the general fact that insurance is legal in nature. Before studying more specifically the principles of insurance law, however, one should review the other basic attributes of insurance.

INSURANCE A FUTURE, CONTINGENT, SERVICE, RISK CONTRACT

Many writers characterize insurance as an "intangible" product, as opposed to goods such as clothing or automobiles that can be seen, felt, and frequently used in everyday life. The description is perhaps valuable as a general introduction to insurance, but it is misleading as a simple answer as to why insurance differs so much from other economic products. The real differences in the insurance product and its marketing as compared with general production and marketing of goods can be summarized: the insurance contract is unique in that it is a *future, contingent, service, risk* contract.

Unlike most physical goods which one purchases, insurance is not normally used immediately. At least the policyholder does not realize that he is using the insurance from the moment the contract goes into effect. Only the unusual person stops to think that he is obtaining a significant benefit immediately, and continually throughout the contract period of protection. The relief of anxieties and freedom from worry as to the financial results of harmful losses is a real insurance benefit. The policyholder often forgets this, however, and contemplates only that the insurance is purchased to obtain a loss payment sometime well into the *future.* A fire, an automobile collision, a death, or a retirement are all future considerations to the insurance purchaser.

More than that, the average policyholder buys insurance with the conviction that such perils will not really cause losses to him. He buys it "just in case," but at the same time thinking that "it will never happen to me." This quality of insurance emphasizes its *contingent* nature. The feeling of contingency is supported by fact, too. It is only the unfortunate minority who actually suffer loss who need the services of loss payment. Families may continue insurance for many years without an automobile loss, or a lifetime without a fire or theft loss to their home. A business may continue through millions of man-hours of work without a disabling injury to any of its employees. The very nature of insurance is based on contingencies that may or may not occur, and normally only occur infrequently.

Preceding comments have suggested the need for considering insurance as a *service* contract rather than a single physical product. It is, in fact, a bundle of services in regard to *risk* or unpredictable financial losses. Naturally, then, insurance becomes a unique product. The policyholder needs help in understanding its varied benefits. That is why in the marketing of insurance the personal contact of an agent is so often necessary. Through him the prospective insurance buyer learns about his needs in regard to risks. He finds out how insurance prevents losses, transfers his risks, pays benefits in case of losses, and renders many auxiliary services in return for the cost of the policy contract.

GENERAL LEGAL REQUIREMENTS

The rights and obligations of the parties to an insurance agreement are determined largely by reference to the general laws which govern contracts. The agreement by which insurance is effected is a contract in which the insurer,[1] in consideration of the payment of a specified sum, agrees to make good the losses suffered through the happening of a designated unfavorable contingency. The insurance contract need not of necessity be in writing, but as a matter of business practice such agreements are ordinarily written. Even social insurances, such as unemployment compensation, are written, though the terms appear in a state law rather than in a private agreement.

A contract has been defined as "an agreement enforceable by law." A more complete definition would include certain essentials which the law requires: (1) the *offer* and its *acceptance,* (2) the *object* of the agreement must be *legal,* (3) the *parties* must be *competent,* and (4) generally a *consideration* is essential. A lack of any of the essential elements is fatal to the enforcement of the agreement.

Insurance contracts, as all contracts, must meet the general requirements for a valid and enforceable contract. Examples of insurance situations in which these four general requirements might be lacking are: (1) a policyholder whose offer to purchase has not yet been accepted by the company; (2) a proposed agreement in which no insurable interest exists (see later section of this chapter); (3) a large life insurance contract taken out solely by a minor; and (4) a life insurance application in which the prospect has not paid the initial premium.

SPECIAL LEGAL CHARACTERISTICS

Personal Nature

The insurance contract is *personal* and follows the person rather than the property concerned. We speak of "insuring property." Yet this is not technically the situation. Insurance actually provides repayment of a loss arising out of some undesired happening. It is impossible to guarantee to a person that he will not lose his possessions, or even to guarantee to replace them with like and kind. It is possible, however, to provide for indemnification to the person who has incurred the loss. Hence, if an individual should pay for a fire insurance contract and subsequently sell the property without arranging with the insurer to transfer the insurance to the new owner,

[1]The terms *assured* and *insured* are used interchangeably, though formerly each had a different meaning. As early as 1826, Charles Babbage in his *Comparative View of the Various Institutions for the Assurance of Lives* stated: "*Assurance* is a contract dependent on the duration of life, which must either happen or fail. *Insurance* is a contract relating to any other uncertain event which may *partly* happen or *partly* fail; thus in adjusting the price for insurance of houses and ships, regard is always had to the chance of salvage arising from partial destruction."

there would be no payment by the insurer in case of fire because there would be no loss on the part of the original insured. The measure of insurance payment is loss to the insured, not loss of specified property.

The reason for the importance of the personal characteristic of insurance is that many insurance contracts are not freely assignable by the policyholder to other parties. Most insurance contracts (life insurance being an exception) represent a personal legal agreement between insurer and insured. To permit a fire or automobile insurance contract to be assignable without the insurer's approval would be unfair to the insurer. Only by knowing and investigating each policyholder they insure can the insurance company correctly appraise the risk they are accepting. A parallel illustration of a personal contract in the entertainment field may help the student realize the value of this aspect of insurance. A personal appearance contract by Jack Benny could not be fulfilled by Jack's manager sending someone else to appear for him.

Conditional Nature

The obligation to perform on the part of one of the parties to an agreement may be conditional upon the action of the second party. A clause in an insurance contract requiring such a performance is usually referred to as a *condition.*

Where a contractual obligation is subject to a condition, the condition may be either (*a*) precedent, (*b*) concurrent, or (*c*) subsequent. In the case of a condition precedent, there is a requirement that something must be done or must have happened before the other party to the contract is obligated to perform. In the case of a condition concurrent, the rights of the party subject to the condition are dependent upon his doing or being prepared to do something simultaneously with the second party to the contract. In the case of a condition subsequent, the rights of the party are determinable upon a specific event. Payment and delivery are said to be concurrent conditions, even though payment actually may be made prior to delivery. The law interprets conditions concurrent to involve a situation where there is a readiness and willingness to perform the mutual obligations. Failure of one relieves the other of obligation. It is a common practice in the insurance business to regard conditions which must exist prior to the formation of a valid insurance contract as conditions precedent. When this is the case, all others are regarded as conditions subsequent.[2] An example of a con-

[2]For a discussion of the semantic problem in conditions precedent and subsequent see Bertram Harnett and John V. Thornton, "The Insurance Condition Subsequent—A Needle in Semantic Haystack," *Insurance Law Journal,* No. 315 (April, 1949), p. 275. Reprinted from the November, 1948, issue of the *Fordham Law Review.*

dition subsequent is the normal requirement in an insurance contract that an insured who suffers a loss must give proper notice and proof to the insurer before the claim is payable.

Strict Compliance Nature

Contracts of Adhesion. The insurance contract, in that it is ordinarily prepared in all its details by the insurance company, and the insured has no part in drawing up its clauses or determining its wording, is said to be a "contract of adhesion." In applying for insurance, the applicant either accepts the policy as prepared by the insurer or he does not purchase the insurance. To be sure, contracts are modified to meet individual needs, but even when so modified, the contract with its amendments is prepared by the insurance company. A contract of adhesion is contrasted to a "bargaining contract" in which both parties contribute to its terms and conditions.

Benefit of Doubt to Insured. Since the insurance company has the advantage in drawing up the agreement and is expected to be able to represent clearly the intent of all the parties, it is now a rule, generally enforced, that where the terms of the policy are ambiguous, obscure, or susceptible of more than one interpretation, the construction most favorable to the insured must prevail.[3] The rule is predicated on the assumption that the insurance company, in drawing up its contract, is under a duty to make its meaning clear. When the company has failed to be clear, the insurer, and not the insured, must suffer.[4] In other words, the "benefit of the doubt" goes to the policyholder.

Insured's Obligation to Read Contract. Where there is no ambiguity, however, the contract is to be enforced in accordance with

---

[3]*Knouse* v. *Equitable Life Insurance Company of Ohio,* 181 Pac. (2d) 310.

[4]The rule of construction followed by the majority of courts that the terms and provisions of an insurance policy in cases of ambiguity are to be construed more strictly against the insurer and more favorably to the insured is not the invariable rule. Since the rule is predicated on the assumption that the company that draws the contract is in a better position to know its meaning than the insured and, hence, interpretation should be in favor of the insured, it follows that this reasoning does not hold when the wording is not that of the insurer but is taken from the statutes (*Funk* v. *Aetna Life Insurance Company,* 96 F.[2d]28; *Coyne* v. *American Policyholders Insurance Company,* 120 Conn. 645; *Haitner* v. *Aetna Casualty & Surety Company,* 189 So. 365; *Brown* v. *Great American Indemnity Company,* 298 Mass. 101). Again cases have been evidenced where the rule has not been applied when the intent may be gathered from the entire contract (*Mick* v. *Royal Exchange Assurance,* 87 N.J.L. 607). On this point a Maryland court has held that "the rule adopted in some jurisdictions, that insurance contracts are to be construed most strongly against the insurer, has been distinctly repudiated by this court, and the sounder view that the intention of the parties as gathered from the whole instrument now prevails" (*Jones* v. *Jones,* 146 Md.1). However, where intent is not clear and an ambiguity exists with respect to an insurance contract prepared by an insurance company, the rule here definitely applies, and the terms and conditions of the contract are construed against the insurer and in favor of the insured.

its terms. Nothing may be added to the contract, nor may its meaning be distorted by interpretations. Consideration must be given to the entire context to determine the nature and extent of coverage. If the contract is clear and understandable, it is to be enforced in accordance with the generally understood meaning of the terms used.

A corollary to the strict compliance rule is that the law holds a person to be bound by the terms of a written contract which he signs or accepts, regardless of whether or not he has taken the trouble to acquaint himself with all its terms and conditions.[5] Too many insurance contracts are complicated and difficult to understand. It is probably safe to state that, regardless of the clarity or obscurity of the terminology, most people do not read their policies. The insured assumes that the policy meets his needs and lets it go at that. It is no defense, however, when the loss occurs, to claim ignorance of the terms of the policy because of failure to read the agreement. Summarizing a line of decisions, the court said in the case of *Grace* v. *Adams:* "It has often been decided that one who accepts a contract and proceeds to avail himself of its provisions is bound by the stipulations and conditions expressed in it whether he reads them or not."[6]

Oral Evidence. In connection with the insurance contract the question of admissibility of *parole,* or oral, evidence frequently arises. The rule of law applying to parole evidence has been expressed in the following terms in a leading case: "It is a fundamental rule, in courts both of law and equity, that parole contemporaneous evidence is inadmissible to contradict or vary the terms of a valid written instrument."[7] The insurance authority Richards states: "In the absence of fraud or mutual mistake the written contract, if there be one, is the best and only admissible evidence of what the contract is as to all matters which it purports to cover."[8]

While the contract in the ordinary course is not subject to modification by parole evidence, the language of the policy is nevertheless not binding in clear cases of mutual mistake of fact or where there is a mistake on one side and fraud inducing it on the other.

---

[5]This is the general rule. However, some observers have noticed a disturbing tendency in recent cases which seem to say that the insured does *not* have to read his policy. Charles Pachner cited a half-dozen cases at the 1963 Denver C.P.C.U. Convention (his address on "Legal Dilemma of a Service-Oriented Profession" to be published in the 1964 C.P.C.U. *Annals*) to show what he believes to be a trend away from the general rule.

[6]100 Mass. 505.

[7]*Northern Assurance Co.* v. *Grand View Building Assn.* 182 U.S.308 (1902).

[8]G. Richards, *Law of Insurance* (4th ed.; New York: Baker, Voorhis & Co., 1932), p. 105.

In instances in which fraud or mutual mistake enters into the transaction, the injured party has relief in equity and may ask that the written contract be reformed to correspond to the real agreement.[9]

Indemnity Nature

Insurance in its essence is a contract of *indemnity,* or replacement. By this is meant that insurance provides compensation or reimbursement for actual damage sustained by the insured. This being the case, the total policy amount (face value) is not the amount payable in the event of a loss but rather represents a maximum limit to the liability of the insurer. An exception to the use of indemnity in insurance is the "valued policy," such as in life insurance, where the full policy amount is paid for a total loss. Under the indemnity rule, in the case of a property valued at $5,000 and insured for $10,000, the insurance company would be liable only to pay $5,000 to the policyholder who suffered a total loss. If, for any reason, the insured receives reimbursement for the loss from any other source, or reimbursement in part, the liability of the insurer is reduced in the same amount.[10]

Property Insurance. The destruction or damage of the *property* described in the contract of insurance is not the contingency upon which the insurer promises to indemnify the insured; it is only when the insured has suffered a loss that the insurer may be called upon to make a payment under the contract.[11] In most cases of property insurance the approximate value of the property can be estimated before the loss, or determined after a loss, within reasonably narrow limits. Some cases provide special problems, however, such as older buildings that are now used for different purposes than when they were built. For example, a large stable or coach house now used for a garage at the rear of a residence would probably never be replaced as it was before being destroyed by fire. Here the functional value of the building is more important than the replacement value. The insurer would usually limit the insurance amount written to its functional value.

Liability Insurance. *Liability* policies paying for damage to other persons or their property are a special example of indemnity. They were formerly written as contracts of indemnity. If the insured was held to be legally liable in any given case, the policy undertook to indemnify him for his loss. In the case of bankruptcy,

[9]*Ibid.,* p. 107.

[10]The United States Supreme Court has set forth the rule by stating that, where there is a contract of indemnity and a loss happens, anything that reduces or diminishes that loss reduces or diminishes the amount which the indemnifier is bound to pay. *Chicago, St. Louis & New Orleans R.R.Co., v. Pullman Southern Car Co.,* 139 U.S. 79.

[11]*Draper* v. *Delaware State Grange Mutual Fire Ins. Co.,* 91 Atl. 206.

if the insured could not settle the claim, the insurance company was not obligated to do so because in such a situation the insured suffered no loss.

Insurance companies later offered liability policies containing the so-called "bankruptcy clause." This provided that, whether or not judgment was enforceable against the insured, the insurance company assumed the obligation to pay a claimant if the insured were legally liable for damages that came within the scope of a contract. The liability policies as now issued are regarded not as contracts of indemnity against loss but as contracts of indemnity against liability.[12]

In setting the limits of insurance for liability policies, care must be taken to write the policy amount high enough to take into consideration the unknown nature of jury verdicts. The policyholder should often purchase higher limits than the minimum, or standard, limits available in buying liability protection.

Life and Health Insurance. *Life* insurance and many *health* insurance contracts are also special illustrations of modifications of the indemnity principle. Here it is the difficulty of determining precise values that prevents the contract from being, strictly speaking, based upon indemnity. One cannot say that the life of a person is worth (or not worth) precisely \$10,000 or \$50,000 or \$300,000. Thus the life insurance contract agrees to pay a certain stated amount, rather than an amount determined after the loss to be a repayment for the loss. There can be no question raised by the insurer paying the loss as to whether or not the loss of life actually resulted in an equivalent economic loss to the insured or his family.

Valued Policies. A special case of the indemnity doctrine concerns the *valued policy* in property insurance. Just as the life insurance contract is valued so that the amount of insurance shall be regarded as the true value of the insured's life, so in property insurance there are properties that, because of their nature, are extremely difficult to appraise accurately. In this category fall works of art, curios, rare and unusual collections, family portraits, and heirlooms. Because of the difficulty of arriving at any satisfactory agreement as to value following a loss, it is deemed advisable in this class of business that the insurer and the insured agree upon a value at the time the policy is issued. From the insurer's standpoint, this

---

[12]The difference between a liability contract and an indemnity contract has been clearly set forth in the language of the courts in the following terms: "There is a well-recognized difference between contracts of indemnity against loss and contracts of indemnity against liability. In the former the insurance company does not become liable until loss has actually been suffered and the amount of the insurance does not became available until the insured has paid the loss, whereas in the latter case the obligation of the insurance company becomes fixed when the liability attaches to the insured" (*Klotzbach* v. *Bull Dog Auto Fire Assn.* 267 S.W. 39 [1924]).

value must be one that unquestionably will make the preservation of the property more attractive to the insured than would be its loss accompanied by the payment of the insurance. Thus an irreplaceable painting by Picasso may be valued and insured at $100,000. If total loss results, the policy amount determines the amount of the insurance claim payment. Even if the painting actually turns out to be worth at the time of loss only $75,000, the full amount of $100,000 is paid.

In writing a contract of this type there is no violation of the indemnity idea. Rather, an agreement is made in advance as to the amount necessary to indemnify the insured in the event of loss or damage to his property. The use of the valued policy in such situations is regarded as sound practice because such articles of unique value may be subject to honest differences of opinion at any particular time.

Valued Policy Laws. From time to time there develops a demand by the public for *valued policy laws* in connection with the insurance of other types of property. The opportunity to use such policies to overinsure have caused insurance authorities to frown upon the general use of this contract. Nevertheless, some state statutes have been enacted that make valued policies mandatory for insurance on homes or other property. When such laws have been enacted the statutes provide that whenever an insured property shall be *totally* destroyed, the amount of insurance in force shall be taken as conclusive evidence of the true value of the property and the loss, regardless of the actual value or loss of the property. Such laws are based upon the reasoning presented by the property owner that it is unjust for him to pay for insurance over a number of years and then, if his property is destroyed, to get less than the face of the policy. The reasoning has its appeal. The fact remains, however, that experience in the insurance business had proved that there is less injustice if the responsibility for fixing a reasonable amount of insurance is placed upon the insured than is the case if the insured is permitted to make a profit through the destruction of his property if he is successful in effecting its overinsurance. This being the case, the valued policy laws as they apply to property in general are believed to invite carelessness and fraud and in many instances to stimulate overinsurance. In a specific case in which the property insured is carefully appraised by both the parties at interest prior to the issuance of the policy and an agreement is reached, the valued policy will not violate the indemnity rule.

Insurable Interest

Closely related to the concept of indemnity is the requirement that all insurance contracts contain an element of *insurable interest.*

An insurable interest is a right or relationship in regard to the subject matter of the insurance contract such that the insured can suffer financial loss from damage, loss, or destruction to it. Without an insurable interest, a contract is a wager or gambling contract. When an insurable interest exists, no profit results, for the insured merely receives repayment for the loss he has suffered. Examples of insurable interest include: a property owner for losses due to fire; a mortgagee for fire and other property perils; a bailee for losses to property in his care; a homeowner or automobile driver for liability losses he may suffer; any person for life insurance on his own life; a wife for life insurance on her husband; a creditor for life insurance on his debtor. A mere expectancy of loss without a legal basis is not an insurable interest. Thus a son cannot insure the property of his father, even though he expects to receive the property through his father's will.

Subrogation Rights

In common law it is held that a person who causes a loss, or who is primarily liable, ought ultimately to be made responsible for the damages sustained. In connection with the law of insurance, it is a matter of equity that the insurer, upon paying the insured the amount of the loss, has a right of action against the person responsible for the loss.

The right of the insurer against such persons does not rest upon any contractual relationship but arises out of the nature of the contract of insurance as one of indemnity. If the insured is indemnified, it would be inequitable for him also to try to collect from the parties responsible for the loss, since such rights as he had now belong to the insurer. Subrogation is also a fair principle in that it holds the wrongdoer responsible for the results of his wrongful actions, instead of permitting him not to pay only because an insurance contract was in force. The overall cost of insurance is also reduced to policyholders in this manner.

The doctrine of *subrogation* gives the insurer whatever rights the insured possessed against responsible third parties. The rights to which the insurer is entitled are those that exist at the time of the loss. From the time of the loss the insured is bound to maintain his position as it then existed and may not release or in any other way alienate without their consent any rights that might prove beneficial to the insurers.

The right of subrogation by the insurer is limited in amount to the loss payment which has been made to the insured. The insurer cannot make a profit by subrogating against the person who caused the loss. In fact, oftentimes subrogation rights are of little value to the insurance company. There may be no doubt that someone else was responsible for the loss, but in order actually to recoup its loss payment the insurer must (1) prove the liability of the wrongdoer and (2) the negligent party must have the financial ability to pay for the loss he caused. In many cases the time, expense, or difficulty of legal proof may prevent the insurer from using its subrogation rights to recover the loss payment.

A common illustration of subrogation is in automobile insurance, where the insurer first pays the insured under his collision insurance for damage to his car. Then the insurer takes over the rights of the policyholder by subrogation and brings suit against the other driver involved in the accident to receive reimbursement.

Effect of Concealment, Representations, and Warranties

Concealment. Since the contract of insurance concerns itself with risk and uncertainty, it has been established as a fundamental doctrine of insurance law that neither party practice *concealment.* Both parties to the agreement must stand on equal footing. This doctrine makes mandatory the affirmative disclosure to the insurer of all *material,* or important, facts which are the exclusive knowledge of the insured. For example, if there is knowledge on the part of the owner that the property insured was at the inception of the agreement in grave danger of destruction, and if this information is not disclosed to the insurer, an unbalanced agreement will result.

The earliest development of the doctrine of concealment was in connection with marine insurance, and in this branch today the doctrine has yielded least to modification. Eminent insurance authorities agree that a concealment of a material fact need not be intentional or fraudulent in order to make the policy voidable, and that it is no defense to plead mistake, forgetfulness, or inadvertence. If the insurer, had he possessed all the facts, would have declined the risk or accepted it upon different terms, then the policy is voidable.

The terms "void" and "voidable" are sometimes used interchangeably, but such use is not correct. A *void* agreement is one that is entirely without legal effect. The law makes certain requirements essential for the validity of a contract, and in the absence of these essentials the contract is void. A contract having an illegal object is void, and neither party can enforce it.

A *voidable* contract is one that may be affirmed or rejected at the option of one of the parties but is binding on the other. In the case of insurance a situation may develop in which the insured has failed to comply with a condition of the contract. The company may elect to fulfill its part of the agreement or may choose to void the contract and revoke the insurance coverage. There are frequent instances in which the insurance company has a technical right to claim a forfeiture, but in the interests of equity and good public relations it decides not to exercise that right.

The strict interpretation of the concealment doctrine persists in marine insurance due to the nature of the business. A ship or cargo may be insured in London, New York, or other insurance or business center; yet the insured property may be located in some far corner of the globe. More often than not, the property is beyond the possibility of inspection by the insurer. Hence, full reliance and dependence must be placed upon the insured for all pertinent facts. If, as a result of ignorance, mistake, forgetfulness, or other cause, the pertinent and material facts are not put into the hands of the insurer, the full responsibility for the failure rests upon the insured and the insurer may save himself from loss through voiding the policy.

In the case of fire insurance, a different situation is presented. The property insured is ordinarily convenient for inspection, and consequently those material facts essential for an appraisal of the risk are within the range of the insurer's observation. The modified doctrine, as generally adopted by the courts with reference to policies of fire insurance, and extended to include other property forms except marine coverages, accepts the view that, when it is not made the subject of express inquiry, the concealment must be intentional to void the policy. The insured needs only to answer fully and in good faith all inquiries made by the insurers. One exception to the rule provides that when there are facts bearing on the risk that are unusual and extraordinary to a degree that they would not ordinarily be anticipated for inquiry or readily discovered by the insurer, the obligation for affirmative disclosure is present, whether or not express inquiry has been made.

Representations. A *representation* is a statement made by the insured to the insurer at the time of or prior to the formation of the contract. Since it is the right of the insurer to have a full knowledge of the subject of insurance, it frequently becomes necessary for him to depend upon statements of the insured, from whom it is most convenient to ascertain the pertinent facts. A *misrepresentation* (false statement) on the part of the insured of any material fact has the same effect as a concealment and affords a basis for a rescission of the contract by the insurer.

The difference between concealment and misrepresentation may readily be seen. The insured is said to conceal if he maintains a silence when obligated to speak; to misrepresent, if he makes a statement which is not true. While concealment must be conscious, willful, or intentional, at least so far as fire insurance is concerned, in order to make the policy voidable, misrepresentation resulting from negligence, mistake, or oversight may make the insurance voidable if concerned with a fact which materially affects the risk.

Warranties. To avoid the necessity of showing in a particular case whether a fact is material or not, the insurer frequently makes it a provision of the policy that all representations shall be deemed warranties. When such a provision is incorporated in the policy, the application for the insurance is made a part of the policy, and the answers to specific questions on the application are deemed *warranties* which, if false, make the policy voidable by the insurer.

The difference between a warranty and a representation is found in the fact that a warranty is a part of the contract itself and must therefore be strictly complied with, while a representation is an incidental statement preceding the contract and not actually a part of it, though it may be an inducement to it. The difference in effect is that in order to make the contract voidable a warranty need only be false, while a representation must be both false and material.

In relation to insurance, warranties are classed as either affirmative or promissory. Those in the first group relate to representations made prior to, or contemporaneous with, the issuance of the policy. The warranties that are included in the second group concern themselves with things agreed to be done or conditions to be maintained during the life of the policy.

It is now held that a statement, in order to constitute a warranty, not only must be intended as such but must be definitely indicated as a warranty either through its incorporation into the policy or its being specifically referred to as such. Where there is any doubt as to whether or not a warranty was intended, the statement is to be regarded as a representation and must be shown to be material in order to defeat the policy.

Many states by legislative act have modified the strict application of the doctrine of warranties. Where the doctrine has been thus modified, the insurance is voidable sometimes only if a loss occurs during a breach or is caused thereby, or sometimes only if the breach materially increases the risk. This, in effect, makes most warranties in insurance contracts today to be considered as representations. It is wise, however, not to tamper with warranties incorporated in insurance policies but to comply with them to the letter, for it is still the tendency of some courts to enforce the original strict rule, declaring the policy voidable when a warranty is breached, regardless of how trivial or immaterial to the loss it may be.

Effect of Fraud

A false representation of a material fact, or the nondisclosure under circumstances that make it tantamount to a misrepresentation, *with the intent and result* that it be acted upon by another party, may constitute *fraud.* Usually a false representation is required. However, a nondisclosure or concealment amounts to a false representation if active steps are taken to prevent discovery of the truth. This is the case if a representation is made that is in part truth but certain facts are suppressed. The same is true if there is a duty to disclose facts and failure to disclose them implies that they do not exist.

To constitute fraud the representation must be of past or existing acts. It follows, therefore, that expressions of opinion, belief, expectation, or intention do not constitute fraudulent statements. The representation must be of material fact and of a character that would lead to reliance upon it by the party to whom it is made. Commendatory expressions of value or false representations made where the parties deal on equal footing and have equal means of knowledge are not held to be fraudulent.

The representation must be made with knowledge on the part of the person making the statement that it is false. Knowledge is imputed if the person making the statement does so in reckless disregard as to whether it is true or false. Finally, in order to constitute fraud the misrepresentation must be relied upon by the party intended to be injured and action by him must result in his injury.

To constitute fraud, then, there must be an active attempt to deceive and the attempt must be successful to the extent that prejudice or injury results to the party relying on the misrepresentation. In such cases the contract becomes voidable at the option of the injured party.

The requirements for proving fraud are difficult to meet. An insurer must prove intent on the part of the insured to defraud. Intent involves premeditation and it is hard to show what a person thought before he acted unless his actions repeatedly or very clearly indicate his intent. If proved, fraud is a serious matter, however, and may subject the insured to criminal as well as civil penalties. Purposeful destruction of property by fire for fraudulent objectives, or *arson,* is an example. A more common but perhaps equally serious example is the intentional exaggeration of any insurance claim for the purpose of receiving overpayment for a loss.

Waiver and Estoppel

One of the most perplexing doctrines in the entire field of insurance concerns the questions of waiver and estoppel. The problem is centered around the modification or contradiction of the terms of an insurance contract by some action of one or both of the parties.

Estoppel prevents one from alleging or denying a fact the contrary of which by his own previous action he has admitted. For example, a company or its agent may issue a policy which is known to them to violate certain contract conditions. If the agent led the insured to believe that his policy was valid and the insurance effective, he would be estopped from denying liability on the contract.

Waiver is defined as the intentional relinquishing of a known right. The knowledge of an agent is presumed to be the knowledge of the principal or, in the case of an insurance contract, the insurer. An agent who issues a policy in which he knows the conditions are being violated is said to waive those conditions.

There are three periods during which there are some differences in the operation of the doctrines and their effects: (1) the period of negotiation, and up to and including the time of the delivery of the contract, (2) the period from the delivery of the contract until the time of the loss, and (3) the period from the occurrence of the loss through the time covering all subsequent negotiations.

It is generally conceded that any knowledge in the possession of the company at the inception of the policy contract will be sufficient grounds for estopping the company in later presenting the facts as a defense of a claim under the policy. If a company with full knowledge of the facts were to issue a policy that was unenforceable, that company would be guilty of fraud. The condition that might otherwise make the policy voidable is presumed to be waived.

The second period concerns itself with the operation of the doctrines during the interval between the delivery of the contract and the happening of the loss. In this period, if knowledge of the violation of a policy condition comes to an agent, he is obligated to cancel the policy. Failing to do so, he waives the violation, and the company is therefore estopped from setting up the violation as a defense in denying liability. If an agent with knowledge of a violation of a policy condition were to collect a premium, he would have waived the violation, and therefore the company would be estopped from using it as a defense.

The final period, beginning with the occurrence of the loss and carrying through the subsequent negotiations, is regarded by company representatives as the most difficult and confusing to handle. For example, it is held that grounds for a waiver of a defense have been established if a company with knowledge of a defense asks an insured to pay a premium or file proofs. A denial of liability under a policy waives the conditions of the policy as to filing proofs and gives the insured an immediate right of action on the policy. In fact, almost any act taken by the representative of a company toward the ascertaining of the amount of the loss and its adjustment may be construed as the waiver of a known violation of a policy condition. Adjusters must act with extreme caution in such instances. To give all parties greater freedom and latitude in their actions, when there is a possibility that liability may be denied because of a policy condition, it is common for the parties at interest to sign a *nonwaiver agreement*. This agreement is for the purpose of relieving the company of waiving any right or acknowledging liability through any act, statement, or deed of its representative in the capacity of adjuster during the preliminary negotiations of investigating and ascertaining the loss.

Agency Law Principles

With the development of modern large-scale enterprises, much business must be entrusted to representatives. In the case of corporations this is particularly true. Since the major part of the insurance business is in the hands of corporate organizations, the part played by the agent is important.

Agency involves a *principal* who authorizes a second party, an *agent,* to create, modify, or terminate contractual relations between himself and a third party. As a general rule, an agency relationship may be created by any legally qualified parties, though contracts which delegate authority to an agent must, like other forms of agreement, have as their purpose a legal object.

The principal usually expressly confers definite and certain authority upon the agent. This is the custom in the business of insurance. A carefully drawn document, the *agency contract* or "commission of authority," designates the parties and outlines the authority of the agent to act for the company.

To create an agency relationship, it is not necessary that the agreement be reduced to writing. As a matter of fact, no particular formalities are essential, and the authorization may be written or oral. To the general rule, however, there are exceptions. One of these is of particular concern in the case of an agent authorized to write surety bonds. Here the agency must be created under seal. The agent is then said to possess the "power of attorney."

Agency by Estoppel. A principal may by his conduct be estopped from denying the existence of the agency. If the principal permits one holding himself out to be an agent to act in such a way that third parties may reasonably believe that an agency relationship exists, and if a third party relies upon the attitude of the principal, the principal will be estopped from denying the existence of an agency. The agency thus created is said to be an *agency by estoppel.*

The application of this principle to insurance may be illustrated thus: Suppose an agent is suspended by the company, and the company neglects to secure the blank policies and other supplies. Should the suspended agent later issue a policy, he will have acted after the termination of his authority and after he had been deprived of his powers as an agent to assume risks or issue policies.

But, since he had the forms and policies in his possession, it would be manifestly unfair to an innocent third party, who in good faith bought and paid for the insurance, to have the company deny liability on the ground that the agent had lacked authority. In such a case, the company will be estopped from setting up lack of authority as a defense, and it will be bound on the policy.

Agency by Ratification. Sometimes a person may hold himself out as having authority whereas, as a matter of fact, he has no authority to act for a given principal. Contracts entered into between one presumed to be an agent and a third party, when the agent is without authority and there is no element of estoppel, cannot bind the supposed principal. If, however, the principal later ratifies the act of the unauthorized agent, the agreement becomes effective and binding upon the principal from the inception of the original agreement. This situation creates an agency by *ratification.*

Ratification may be either expressed or implied from any act, expression, or conduct which would definitely indicate the intent of the principal to adopt the transaction. Ordinarily, an expression of approval, acceptance of a benefit, promise of performance, or partial or complete performance on the part of the principal will constitute a ratification as will the bringing of a suit based upon the agreement in question. An agreement made by an unauthorized agent must be ratified or rejected in its entirety. It is obviously unfair for a principal to accept the benefits of an agreement, ratifying it to that extent, and yet divest himself of burdensome obligations on the ground of lack of an agent's authority.

In the field of insurance this principle is illustrated by the following situation: It often happens that an agency is suspended by the company for one reason or another. If, for example, an agent is slow in remitting balances, the company may terminate the agency and prohibit the writing of further business in its name. If while such a status exists the agent issues a policy in the name of the company that suspended him, the company will be deemed to have ratified the transaction and assumed full liability under the contract if it fails upon receipt of its copy of the policy to demand immediate cancellation. Aside from the element of ratification, in this same case the principle of estoppel may likewise be operative. A company may ratify an unauthorized policy at any time, even after the occurrence of a loss.

Apparent Authority and Limited Authority. In connection with the law of agency the scope of *apparent authority* assumes an extremely important place. There can be no question concerning the responsibility of the principal for those acts of his agent acting in accordance with definite instructions. It sometimes happens, however, that the limits of an agent's authority are not readily ascertainable. In such an instance, assistance may be gained from the principle that invests an agent, in addition to those powers expressly conferred, with such incidental powers as are necessary for effecting the purposes for which the agency was created. Again, the general uses and customs of the community in which the agent is operating tend to expand or limit his authority. Ordinarily, therefore, it is sufficient to bind the principal when dealing with third parties if an agent with expressly conferred powers is acting within the scope of his apparent authority.

A principal may from time to time modify or limit the powers of his agent. As between principal and agent, the agent is bound by these limiting instructions. On the other hand, a third party having knowledge that an agency exists is under no obligation to search out and explore in order to learn the existence of uncommunicated limiting instructions. In the case of limiting instruction, when notice is given third parties, they are, of course, bound by them; but in the absence of such notice, insureds are in no way affected if, in their dealings with the agent, he acts within the scope of his apparent authority.

An example of the operation of this principal may be found in the custom of insurance companies of issuing to their agents lists of risks that the company will not write. For example, the following coverages are included in the list of so-called "prohibited risks" of one fire insurance company: amusement park and fairground properties, farm property, ice houses, roadhouses and roadside stands, sawmills, and bowling alleys. The lists vary with companies, so that some lines accepted by one company will be refused by another. Some companies are liberal in their underwriting while others are extremely conservative. Some companies have, in addition to prohibited risks, lists of properties which may only be insured after specific referral to the company and special inspection. It is possible, therefore, for an agent to write a policy in a company that prohibits the risk, deliver the policy, and accept the premium. In this situation, should a loss occur before the report of the policy reached the company or cancellation had been effected, the company would have a right of action against the agent but would be bound to the third party if the latter had no knowledge that the agent lacked authority to issue the policy.

SUMMARY

The legal nature of insurance is based on the use of written contracts (called "policies"). The insurance policy must meet the general requirements for a valid contract agreement. In addition, insurance policies have special legal characteristics which are important in understanding the relationship of insurance to the law. These characteristics include the nature of insurance as a future, contingent, service, risk contract, as well as the personal, conditional, strict compliance and indemnity characteristics which make the insurance contract a unique product. Special laws apply to insurance in regard to insurable interest, subrogation, concealment, warranties, representations, fraud, waiver, and estoppel. Agency law is particularly significant to insurance because of the common use of agents in the marketing of insurance contracts.

FOR REVIEW

1. Explain the significance of the statement that insurance is "a future, contingent, service, risk contract."
2. Identify three special legal characteristics of insurance, and explain the reason for the importance of each to the policyholder.
3. From the insurer's standpoint, why are the following important in the insurance transaction:
   a) Its strict compliance nature?
   b) Its indemnity nature?
   c) Insurable interest?
   d) Subrogation?
   e) Agency law?
4. Must insurance contracts be in writing? Why or why not?
5. X insures a dwelling against loss by fire. During the policy term the building burns. X is not the owner of the building at the time of the fire. Having accepted the premium, is the insurer liable?
6. The strict compliance rule is justified by the fact that the insurance company has an advantage in drawing up the insurance agreement. In your opinion, are insurance contracts sufficiently complex to concede a real advantage on the part of the insurance company?
7. Distinguish between a "warranty," a "representation," a "concealment," and "fraud."
8. B, an agent, is suspended by the Blank Company. The company representative takes its supplies from B's office. B reissues an expired policy, collecting and retaining the premium. Is there any liability on the part of the company for which the agent purports to act, or must the policyholder suffer the loss?
9. In the foregoing situation, after suspension but before the supplies are taken up, B issues a policy carrying a large premium. He is without authority to do this but reports the policy to the company in due course. The company accepts the premium. Upon what theory is the agent's act validated?
10. X approaches the Blank agency for $10,000 insurance on his dwelling. The agent states the insurance is bound, but before he can enter the facts upon his binder, his mind is diverted and he completely forgets the matter. It is next brought to his attention a few days later by X, who reports a serious fire. What is the position of X, and what is the position of the Blank agency? Which of his companies, if any, are liable?
11. X, an agent, has instructions not to insure certain prohibited properties. Carelessly, an employee of the agent issues a policy on a prohibited risk. Before notice reaches the home office of the company the property burns. Discuss the questions of liability involved.
12. What examples can you give of possible violations of the concept of indemnity in insurance? Indicate *how and why* they deviate from the indemnity approach.

Chapter 4

INSURANCE MARKETING

INSURANCE is based upon the legal contracts of insurance whose fundamentals have been introduced in Chapter 3. Imperative to a full understanding of the rather unique product of insurance is the fact that insurance is more than just a policy contract. It includes many other service benefits prior to, at the time, of, or after the contract itself is written.

The services of insurance may be considered from the viewpoint of the insurer; that is, what services or functions does the insurer provide to the policyholder? In the succeeding chapters of this section are discussed the primary functions of insurers. Once the insurance contract has been designed, these functions include (1) the marketing of insurance, (2) the underwriting and reinsurance function, (3) the insurance loss payment, and (4) miscellaneous services such as loss prevention, records-keeping, statistical analysis, and many other related activities.

It may be helpful for the student to think of insurance in terms of the traditional producer-consumer relationships. The insurer is the producer; the consumer is the purchaser or policyholder of the insurance contract. The missing link between the producer and consumer is the marketing system used in getting the insurance product (the policy *and* its services) from the insurer to the insured.

This chapter differentiates among the various kinds of insurers, their marketing methods, and their representatives. The professional concept of insurance marketing is explained, and the concluding section takes a look backward to see how the insurance consumer views the insurance market.

THE INSURANCE MARKET

A *market*, in a strict sense, is a meeting of people who have as their purpose the transaction of business by means of private purchase and sale. The term has come to mean either the region in which a commodity can be sold or the group of persons who might be expected to purchase. It has come as well to mean the place of purchase. As examples, there are the stock market, the grain market, or for that matter the local market for the purchase of foods.

In insurance terminology, market is used to indicate both the area of distribution and the available source of the different coverages. In the first instance persons in the middle salary brackets might be referred to as a market for retirement annuities. Large industrial organizations are a market for group pension plans. The second and more restricted use of the term applies it to the place or source for the purchase of different forms of coverage. For instance, the market for war-risks marine coverages would probably become restricted with the outbreak of a major war. Again, one might indicate that Lloyd's is a market for certain unusual and special risks.

One further concept of insurance marketing has already been discussed in Chapter 2, where the fields of insurance were classified into various personal and property lines of business. In addition to knowing *what* risks are the subject of insurance, one must know *who* distributes the insurance product and *how* the marketing is accomplished.

The insurance buyer has little difficulty in placing ordinary risks—that is, in finding a market. As a risk tends to involve special features, the limitations of the market evidence themselves. Because a company writes fire insurance or casualty insurance, it does not follow that it will write all fire or casualty lines. Every company selects risks on the basis of underwriting judgment, but more than this there are many classes that one company or another will not write at all. For example, some fire companies will not insure saw mills. Virtually every company has its list of prohibited risks. In the casualty field motorcycle races, aviation meets, rodeos, and carnivals are risks that some companies will not accept.

Local agents may limit their business to either life or property insurance or they may embrace all forms of the business. An all-lines agency represents companies that will afford facilities for all the classes of insurance that its customers require. Frequently, the limitations of the local agent require that he seek outside facilities. In such an instance he is said to "broker" the line, or as much of it as he is unable to handle. The transaction involves a division of commissions.

The insurance buyer for a large organization has direct touch with the insurance market and its limitations. In selecting an agent to handle the business of his concern, he must investigate the facilities of his agent with a view to determining to what extent his firm's needs can be met. The more usual coverages such as fire insurance, automobile liability insurance, and the like are obtainable in every community through a local agency or a company representative. For other coverages, and this is particularly true of some of the more hazardous lines that are not written in volume, the market is more limited. It is true that almost every measurable risk is insurable. It does not follow that every agent has the facilities for placing every insurable risk. Familiarity with the market and ability to place unusual lines are evidences that the agent or broker is well informed and keeping abreast of developments in his field.

TYPES OF INSURERS

The *insurer* that bears, or carries, the risk of insurance is sometimes referred to as a "risk bearer" or "insurance carrier." Insurers are divided broadly into six groups, as follows: (1) *stock* companies, (2) *mutual* companies, (3) *Lloyd's* organizations, (4) *reciprocals* or interinsurers, (5) *state* insurers, and (6) *self-insurers*. Stock companies, Lloyd's, and sometimes state insurers are essentially noncooperative in their operations; the insureds have no ownership in the funds out of which losses are to be paid. The others are mutual in their nature. Certain types of state insurance are included in this latter classification.

Stock Companies

In the United States a corporation organized to write insurance under the laws of a particular state is considered a *domestic* company by that state but is usually termed a *foreign* insurer by all other states. The term *alien* insurer is generally applied to those companies incorporated in some foreign country. *Stock insurance companies* have for their purpose the conduct of one or several of the different classes of the insurance business. Strict laws enacted by the various states govern their operation; and they are obliged to satisfy the designated authorities as to their capital, reserve fund, assets, and investments. The contracts they issue are written for a definitely stated consideration (premium), and so far as the insured is concerned the transaction has no interest for him beyond indemnification in the event he suffers loss. He receives no benefit (dividend) from the earnings of the company and pays no assessment or additional premium if losses exceed income.

Stock companies are organized as profit-making ventures. The capital subscribed by the *stockholders* serves as an extra amount, in addition to premium payments, out of which losses can be paid. Additions made to the surplus serve the same purpose. Stock insurance carriers assume risks with the profit element in view, and the stockholders are entitled to any of the residual profits after losses and expenses have been paid and proper reserves set up.

The facilities of stock companies are often worldwide in their scope and are being continually adjusted to meet changing conditions. In the United States stock companies generally write their business through local agents, allowing them a commission on the business. The agents, in turn, act as insurance advisers to their insureds. Some insurance is purchased through brokers, who represent the policyholder.

The absence of any form of contingent liability by the insured in stock insurance guarantees the policyholder that his first cost is the final cost. Advocates of mutual insurance contend that stock companies tend to overemphasize the importance of this point.

Stock insurance companies thus have as their basic characteristics: (1) they are owned by stockholders who supply capital funds serving as part of the financial security for the firm's operations, (2) they issue contracts for a fixed cost (the contracts are nonassessable), (3) they are often large companies who do business in many kinds of insurance throughout the world, and (4) they operate through agents who are usually paid on a commission basis.

Mutual Companies

A mutual insurance company is a corporation owned, operated, and controlled by its *policyholders*. It is organized under general laws for the purpose of providing insurance for its policyholders at cost. Every policyholder is a member of the company. There are no stockholders. The mutual policyholder-members elect the board of directors. The board elects the executive officers who actually manage the company. The mutual corporation assumes the risks of its policyholder-members. As a consideration for the assumption of this risk, each policyholder-member, except in the case of certain farm mutuals, pay or agree to pay in advance a premium and, where their contracts so provide, a specified assessment where premium contributions are inadequate. When the premiums in a given period are more than adequate to meet losses and expense, part or all of the excess is returned to the policyholder.

There are a number of different kinds of mutual insurers. These include (1) *general-writing* mutuals, (2) *class* mutuals, (3) local *farm* mutuals, (4) *Factory Mutuals,* and (5) *fraternals.* They may differ greatly in some characteristics, but each is incorporated and is owned by the policyholders who often receive dividends if the company operations are successful.

General-Writing Mutuals. This type of mutual company is closest in similarity to the stock companies. Legally, they are different because they are owned by the policyholders, have no stockholders, and usually pay policyholder dividends. However, they are like the stock companies that operate on an advance-premium basis over a wide variety of types of insurance and geographical area.

A few may issue "assessable" policies which provide that the insurance company may assess each policyholder an amount beyond the original premium cost if the losses and expenses of the company require it. A majority of these advance-premium mutuals issue a nonassessable contract, however, in which the maximum cost of the insurance is set when the policy is begun. The general standard for writing nonassessable policies requires a mutual to possess substantial amounts of surplus to provide for the financial solvency of the company in spite of temporary periods of heavier than normal losses or expenses.

In most states the general-writing mutuals must comply with the same reserve, investment, policy form, and regulatory laws as apply to stock companies. Their organization requirements are somewhat different, as a minimum number of policyholders are required to start a company and the board of directors must be set up in the charter and by-laws as subject to the control of policyholders rather than stockholders.

Many of these general-writing mutuals issue dividends to policyholders. If the original premium charge (which may be the same as the published stock company tariff rates) permits, a return is made at the end of the policy period for any excess amount beyond the losses, expenses, reserves, and reasonable increases in the surplus of the company. The actual amount of the return is unknown to the policyholder until after the insurance contract expires, it being dependent upon the experience of the company for that policyholder classification. The net cost (original premium less dividend) to the policyholder is thus somewhat uncertain until the dividend is paid.

Class Mutuals. Certain mutuals confine their operations to selected risks of a definite class and hence are called *class mutuals*. There are companies which insure primarily certain kinds of businesses such as milling and grain operations; others insure lumber and allied lines, hardware risks, drug manufacturers, and numerous other classifications. These organizations have a store of specialized information for their respective fields.

Farm Mutuals. There are said to be over 2,000 *farmers' mutuals*. They insure about three fourths of the insurable farm property. These companies find an important place in every rural community.

Farm mutual contracts are written in two ways, either in a limited or an unlimited liability policy. Most of them are assessment contracts, and many require no advance premiums at all, relying entirely on assessments at the end of the policy period. A member who belongs to a company in which liability in unlimited binds himself to pay his pro-rata share of all losses and legitimate expenses of the company. The unlimited liability for assessment has caused some concern to many who fear that a serious catastrophe might involve them in assessments greater than they could meet. It is said, on the other hand, that because farm risks are so scattered, a farmers' mutual with a reasonable number of risks is comparatively free from the catastrophe hazard, unless perhaps located where prairie or forest fires, or widespread windstorms are a menace. About seven tenths of the farm mutuals operate with the unlimited assessment plan.

It is the usual small size, limited area, and the assessment features which cause farm mutuals to be separated from other types of class mutuals. Some special state laws also apply specifically only to farm mutuals, concerning their limited scope of operations in the property insurance field. They are particularly well known for their activities in insuring farms against the risks of fire, lightning, and windstorm perils. A few farm mutuals are unusual in that they operate over a considerable territory and use advance premiums.

Factory Mutuals. An important group of insurance carriers in the mutual group base their operations on the belief that fire prevention should be the first and basic aim in any effort to secure low-cost insurance. The first company in the group, later to develop into the important Factory Mutual System, was organized in 1835 to insure manufacturing properties and from the beginning gave practical application to the prevention idea.[1]

As the idea grew, a technical staff of trained engineers studied the problem of prevention, and a laboratory for research and testing was maintained. Slow-burning construction was advocated; special hazards were studied with a view to providing safeguards; and when new fire-prevention developments appeared, their adoption was encouraged. It was this group that was largely responsible for the adoption of the automatic sprinkler.

The Factory Mutuals require insureds to deposit with them large premiums, estimated from past experience to be in excess of all loss requirements. At the end of the policy period, deductions are made for expenses and actual losses paid, and the balance is returned to the insured.

The Factory Mutuals limit their commitments to the highest grade of protected properties and insist that their insureds meet their standards before acceptance. More recently the companies have shown a tendency to enlarge the scope of their operations and, instead of limiting them strictly to factories, have written other classes of risk, including hospitals, churches, and schools.

---

[1]The Factory Mutual Fire Insurance System is the outgrowth of the idea of a New England manufacturer who interested other manufacturers in a plan to share losses on their factories on a mutual basis. The originators of the plan undertook a careful study of the causes of fire; and through the inauguration of a program of prevention, members of the group were able to reduce materially the cost of their insurance protection. A mutual company was formed and later other similar companies were organized. As the size of lines increased, insurance was distributed among the different companies of the group. There are now eight companies organized together as the Associated Factory Mutual Insurance Companies, cooperating in engineering and inspection work, adjustment of losses, or other phases of the business with resultant efficiency and economy.

The cost of administration in the Factory Mutual System includes the cost of inspection and engineering services. Because of the cost of inspections, surveys, consultations, conferences pending improvement of the risk, the insurance plan, and other services rendered, companies in the group do not solicit small risks.

Policies of the Factory Mutual System are broad in their scope and especially adapted to the needs of their insureds. Full insurance coverage is usually required. Companies in the Factory Mutual System make their contracts in their home offices. Manufacturers in states other than the home state of the company concerned are considered as having come to that state for insurance. On this basis it has been held that the company does business in its own state, and accordingly there exists no need for formally entering other states. It is the policy of the Factory Mutuals, however, to become licensed in all states where a sufficient volume of business is developed.

The essence of Factory Mutuals is in their characteristics of large deposit premiums, insurance for large manufacturing risks, and emphasis on loss prevention techniques.

Fraternals. Of the basic types of mutual insurers only the general-writing mutuals and *fraternals* are active in the field of personal life and health insurance. A fraternal is a special type of mutual, organized under special state statutes for the providing of certain insurance for their members. The operations of the fraternal are closely related to and controlled by the by-laws of the lodge organization. Only about 2 percent of the life insurance in the United States is written by fraternals.

Lloyd's

In contrast to insurers that operate as corporations are the *Lloyd's insurers* whose basic characteristic is that they are *individual* insurers. Although this type of insurance is only used for a few percent of the total insurance sales in the United States, the concept of insurance written by individuals is important. Historically Lloyd's organizations are significant, too, and in the world market they are very predominant for unusual and difficult risks to insure. Two types of Lloyd's should be distinguished: "Lloyd's of London," which is by far the most important, and the "American Lloyd's" which are small and few in number.

Lloyd's of London. One of the most famous institutions for the insurance of risks is located in London and still bears the name of the coffeehouse[2] in which it originated. In the process of develop-

[2]Some intriguing books, and even movies, have been written about Lloyd's of London. For two books on the subject, see C. E. Golding and D. King-Page, *Lloyd's* (New York: McGraw-Hill Book Co., Inc., 1952), and Ralph Straus, *Lloyd's, The Gentlemen at the Coffeehouse* (New York: Carrick and Evans, Inc., 1938).

ment, Lloyd's has become a great corporation. But as a corporation it neither subscribes to policies of insurance nor directly issues them. Insurance is still written by individual underwriters, who are themselves members of the corporation but who in their undertakings of insurance sign "each for himself and not for another." The insurance carrier, then, is not Lloyd's but the underwriters at Lloyd's.

Membership in the Corporation of Lloyd's has been compared with membership in the New York Stock Exchange. The Exchange sets up standards with which its members must comply. Yet a purchase of a security from a member is a transaction between that member and his customer. So with Lloyd's. It is itself a permanent organization made up of an ever-changing body of members, who are in the first place elected to membership and whose places are filled following death or resignation.

Until recent years the Corporation exercised little actual control over its members, and they operated with great freedom, limited only by the opinion and regard of the other members. Recent developments have resulted in the adoption of numerous regulatory measures, such as, for example, limiting a member's commitments to a ratio to his capital deemed proper by the Corporation. There is now also a reserve fund requirement.

It is required that all current premiums be segregated under a deed of trust as a fund out of which claims may be paid. The great pride taken by the members in the enviable record of the institution is a safeguard, as is the searching and far-reaching annual audit.[3]

There are no insurance companies in Lloyd's or any connected as underwriters in the Lloyd's organization; and there are no devices of any sort designed to limit the liability of any insurer, whose every penny stands squarely behind any risk he may assume. Corporations are not admitted to membership, and each underwriter is liable for underwriting obligations under Lloyd's policies without limit and to the full extent of his assets. If the underwriter whose name appears on a policy is unable to pay a claim, the insured has no claim whatever against either Lloyd's or the other underwriters for more than the share of the loss they themselves specifically assumed. There is, however, a further element of protection in the guarantee fund and in the guarantee policies that members take out insuring one another, as well as in the fact that other members would in all probability make good the losses of a bankrupt member to maintain the prestige of their institution. There is ample

[3]The Assurance Companies Acts of 1909 and 1946 regulate the insurance activities of Lloyd's underwriters. The act requires each underwriter to pay all premiums derived from his insurance activities into a trust fund under a trust deed approved by the British Board of Trade to be held for payment of underwriting liabilities. The law requires an annual audit of underwriting accounts by an auditor approved by the governing committee of Lloyd's.

precedent for this last-mentioned procedure, though there is no legal obligation whatsoever.[4]

The organization is composed of approximately 2,400 "name" underwriters who, severally and each for himself, as members of underwriting syndicates assume insurance risks. There are almost 300 syndicates, with a membership varying from 6 to as many as 100 in each. The syndicate is operated by an agent, who is also frequently its organizer. While each member assumes the risks to which he is committed, business is not carried on by him personally but in his name. The agent is the one who actually does the underwriting and commits his "names" to the risk.

Again, when a policy is desired through Lloyd's, business is transacted not with the underwriters or syndicate agents who underwrite for their "names" but through a broker. With an adequate description of the risk, the broker circulates among the underwriters offering the line. Each underwriter who wishes signs a slip (underwrites his name to it, hence the term underwriter) carried by the broker, indicating the amount for which he will commit his syndicate. When the broker has obtained enough signers so that the amounts they assume will total the required insurance, Lloyd's Policy Signing Office draws up and issues the policy. This document, however, is not signed by the Corporation but by the individuals, who must themselves pay in the event of loss. The Corporation of Lloyd's itself participates in no direct way in the business of insurance. Its functions are purely to supervise transactions and guard the reputation of the institution.[5]

The fame of Lloyd's of London is heightened by the specialty risks of unusual nature which have been insured there. Examples include the on-schedule opening of the 1964 New York World's Fair; Khrushchev's safety on his 1959 visit to the United States, Elizabeth Taylor's illness in the filming of "Cleopatra" (on which a $2 million loss was paid); Marlene Dietrich's legs and Jimmy Durante's nose against accidental injury; missile launchings; and a wide variety of unique risks. Many of these obtain widespread publicity for

---

[4]Since 1939 a trust fund known as "Lloyd's American Trust Fund" has been maintained in the United States for the protection of American policyholders. The American trust fund of each "name" consists of all premiums or other funds payable to it in connection with American business. The United States trust agreement provides that the trustee shall always be a bank or trust company organized under the laws of the United States or of any state and shall be a member of the Federal Reserve System. In 1963 the American Trust Fund totaled some $450 million for Lloyd's policyholders.

[5]The following clause is now made in part of every Lloyd's policy: "No Policy or other Contract dated on or after 1st January, 1924 will be recognized by the Committee of Lloyd's as entitling the holder to the benefit of the Funds and/or Guarantees lodged by the Underwriters of the Policy or Contract as security for their liabilities unless it bears at foot the Seal of Lloyd's Policy Signing Office."

Lloyd's of London, although more important in its everyday work in insurance are the many marine, aviation (twenty syndicates specialize in this area), and excess liability risks involving millions of dollars of potential loss.

London Lloyd's is licensed directly only in two states, Illinois and Kentucky, though Lloyd's brokers and agents operate throughout the United States and the rest of the world.

Lloyd's (American). In the United States there have developed groups of individuals and individual voluntary partnerships which have entered the business of underwriting risks upon a plan based to some degree upon that followed by Lloyd's of London, and from the similarity these organizations have been termed "Lloyd's Groups."

In the American groups, each member ordinarily holds himself liable for a given amount upon any desired number of risks, but as a general rule these are definitely limited by a specified maximum. The strict regulations governing membership, deposits, and audits of the London Lloyd's are not a requisite of the ordinary American group. Each organization depends upon the financial strength of its individual members; and the name Lloyd's carries with it no particular significance as to financial position, integrity, and past reputation so far as the American groups are concerned. While it is true that some of these groups have operated with success for some time in this country, others, lacking the stricter regulation exercised abroad, have operated with indifferent success and, in certain instances, because of inadequate resources or questionable practices, have brought the name under a cloud.

Confusion has sometimes existed in the minds of insureds who have associated the name "Lloyd's" with the original organization in London and, relying upon the strength, reputation, and credit of that organization, have not understood that the American Lloyd's and the London organization have no connection.

Reciprocals

The *reciprocal,* or interinsurance association, is a development of mutual insurance. Each policyholder under this form of insurance contract is insured by all of the others; and he, on the other hand, insures them. Each insured is also an insurer. While the plan is effectively mutual in its operation, it is not in the true sense mutual because the individual subscribers in their capacity as underwriters assume their liability as individuals.

The funds of one subscriber may not be diverted to meet the obligations of another subscriber with respect to a claim. Thus the funds held by a reciprocal are not available in their entirety for the payment of individual claims but represent, rather, the sum total of individual credits held for the account of individual subscribers. These subscribers are required over a period of years to accumulate reserves, representing a multiple ranging from two to five annual premiums, before underwriting earnings, if any, are returned in cash. A separate account is maintained for each subscriber, and out of this is paid only his individual share of each loss. There is no partnership liability on the part of one subscriber to others, and the liability of each subscriber is definitely limited.

Reciprocal insurance is quite distinctly an American development. A group of New York businessmen, believing fire insurance rates on their property to be too high, met to devise a cooperative form of fire insurance that would provide themselves with insurance coverage at cost. The original plan provided for the building up of a fund through the annual payment by each member. This fund was to be increased each year at the same rate until a maximum of five times the annual premium was built up. Finally, if the losses of members at any time exceeded the total reserve, each member of the group was obligated to contribute to the insurance fund an amount not in excess of ten times that premium. Thus, if a member of the group paid a premium each year of $500, his liability for assessment was limited to $5,000.

The policyholders, or subscribers, appoint a manager to whom is entrusted the responsibility of carrying on the business; he derives his authority from a power of attorney and is in turn known as an "attorney-in-fact." A very important element of control over the attorney-in-fact is provided by an advisory committee. In addition to controlling the investment and custody of all funds over the amount required to operate the exchange, this committee has complete control over the manager through its power to replace the attorney-in-fact by a majority vote of its members. Since the members of the advisory committee are the chief officers of large corporations whose assets are largely insured under the protection of the policies of the reciprocal exchange, the committeemen have interests identical with the insureds. Intimate information concerning developments is furnished the committee through monthly reports and regular audits, in addition to frequent meetings. The control exercised by the committee is considered a vital element in the plan.

In a reciprocal that maintains no engineering organization, the compensation of the attorney-in-fact represents the entire cost of carrying on the business. The powers of the attorney-in-fact, as conferred by a power of attorney, signed by all who join the group, are sometimes very broad. Such limitations as are provided are often not made the subject of inquiry by prospective insureds, and it sometimes happens that an insured under a reciprocal contract is unaware of the extent of the rights he has conferred and the obligation he has assumed.[6]

This form of organization, investing almost absolute power in the hands of a single individual, has tempted unscrupulous promoters to utilize reciprocals to their own ends. When the limit of liability is not carefully provided for and understood, a reciprocal in the hands of an unscrupulous attorney might prove to be disastrous to the insureds. Several organizations have failed because of corruption. Since reciprocals are not incorporated, no assets beyond the limited liability of the members are normally available to prevent insolvency.

The major characteristics of reciprocals are the dual nature of each insured as an insurer (with stated limits of liability), the system of individual accounts, and the use of an attorney-in-fact under the control of an advisory committee. Reciprocals are relatively unimportant in the total business of insurance (only a few percent of the total), but in certain areas and for specific lines such as automobile insurance they have become of some significance. Although usually small, a few reciprocal exchanges have grown to substantial size(such as the Farmers Insurance Exchange (Los Angeles), the Inter-Insurance Exchange of the Automobile Club of Southern California, and the United Services Automobile Association (San Antonio, Texas).

State Insurers

Already discussed has been the differentiation between social and voluntary types of insurance. The above types of insurers—stock, mutual, Lloyd's, and reciprocals—comprise the major part of the voluntary (private) sector of insurance.

When a state or nation performs the functions of an insurance carrier, the insurance so provided is generally termed *state insurance*. In this form of insurance enterprise the government manages the project and assumes the liability for payment of claims.

State insurance falls into two general categories. The first embraces those projects of a social nature, such as the Social Security program of the federal government. The second classification includes the writing of insurance risks by the state in competition with privately owned insurance carriers.

---

[6]Until 1914 there were fewer than 15 reciprocal exchanges for the purpose of handling fire insurance, and only 1 for other risks. With the development of the automobile, however, casualty and automobile reciprocal exchanges began to multiply, so that within a decade there were over 100. Those in control of the older and more conservatively operated reciprocals have been concerned with the tendency of enterprising attorneys-in-fact who have failed to incorporate in their plan certain features of safety to be found in the older organizations and believed to be essential to a sound reciprocal exchange.

In competition with private enterprise, perhaps the most progress has been made in this country by state insurers in the field of workmen's compensation. State funds of this type are in their essence mutual insurance carriers operated by the state. Some states have made for themselves a monopoly of the compensation business, while others have entered the field as free and open competitors of privately owned and operated carriers.

The operation of state funds has met with varying degrees of success. In some instances they have functioned to the entire satisfaction of all parties concerned; in others there has been some question as to their efficiency, or, in some cases, the experience has been decidedly unsatisfactory. Indicative of the difficulties involved, it has been pointed out that, when competition is lacking, there is a tendency toward inefficiency; and when competition is permitted, the governmental insurance office is hardly in a position to hold its own in the race because it lacks the business organization and trained staff of the well-established companies. State insurance carriers, moreover, are frequently obliged to assume risks that a privately operated company would scarcely consider. A final difficulty or deterrent factor to state insurance, considered by many to be of great importance, is to be found in the possibility of insurance projects becoming involved in political problems.

Self-Insurers

The plan by which an individual or concern sets up a private fund out of which to pay losses is termed *self-insurance*. Where self-insurance can be successfully carried out, there is no doubt that it furnishes the least expensive of all the possible forms. The fund, as it accumulates, belongs to the insured, and he can invest it as he may deem prudent. He pays no commissions to agents, and other costs of operation are reduced to a minimum. No fees are required by the state. Benefits to be derived from care reflect directly to the owner-insurer.

If the owner of a large plant exposed to loss from a single fire cancels all outstanding insurance and instead deposits the annual insurance premium in a fund to meet losses as they occur, it is sometimes said that he is insuring himself. While such a procedure is ordinarily included in the category of self-insurance, it is *not*, as a matter of fact, insurance at all. There is no hedge, no shifting of the burden or risk. It is merely a chance that no serious loss will occur—at least until the fund has reached a figure sufficient to meet it.[7]

---

[7]From time to time press notices give evidence of the falacious reasoning that prompts a saving of insurance premiums through their deposit into a fund under

(Continued on next page)

On the other hand, the setup of a chain store company with 1,000 retail outlets widely distributed geographically and much alike physically lends itself readily to a self-insurance plan. If an insurance premium is charged to each store, a fund sufficient to meet any loss that might occur at one time will rapidly accumulate. If each individual store of the chain has an extremely rapid stock turnover and low inventory, the loss to a single store will in no case be great. It will not in any instance be sizable enough to cripple or handicap the business seriously.

To institute a plan of self-insurance there must be a wide distribution of risks subject to the same hazards. The number of the greatest corporations in the country, with a wide distribution of property, that insure their property in commercial companies and forego the temptation to build up funds of their own even in the face of years of favorable experience affords evidence that comparatively few organizations have an ideal setup for this plan. Certainly no company or individual with a limited number of risks should attempt to use it.

Summary

The organizations which provide insurance protection and service are numerous and varied in terms of size, objectives, and operations.

In property insurance as of 1963 the stock companies numbered about two thirds (700) of the total of almost 1,150 insurers, and wrote about $11.4 billion of premiums of the total $15.7 billion. Almost 400 mutual companies (or one third of the total insurers) wrote $3.7 billion in premiums. About 60 of the major reciprocals and Lloyd's organizations wrote approximately $.6 billion in premiums.[8] Thus stock companies were predominant, writing about three fourths of the total business, while mutuals wrote about one fourth, and all other insurers wrote less than 4 percent of the total premiums.

In life insurance an entirely different situation exists. At the end of 1962, 89 percent of the life insurers were stock companies, or over 1,300 of almost 1,500 companies. In terms of life insurance

---

the name "self-insurance." States and their political subdivisions are frequent sufferers. Typical is the following credited to *The National Underwriter:* "Knoxville, Tennessee.—In the face of the destruction by fire of Gibbs school building, with loss estimated at $500,000, Knox county school board officials have publicly admitted the failure of a 'self-insurance' plan adopted some years ago. The insurance fund, to which is being added $10,000 annually, now contains only $87,141 against the $500,000 loss." Quoted by *Fire Insurance Facts and Trends,* National Board of Fire Underwriters, Vol. VII, No. 1 (February, 1951), p. 4.

[8] *1963 Fire Insurance Index* (Philadelphia: The Spectator), p. 3. These figures exclude the minor volume of about one-half billion dollars of premiums written by almost two thousand very small local or farm mutuals. These mutuals, often of the assessment type, are numerous; but they are significant only in rural markets rather than on a national basis.

amounts in force, however, the mutual companies predominated, having 60 percent of the total of almost $700 billions of life insurance in force.[9] The typical stock life insurer was smaller and younger in comparison to the larger and older mutual life insurers.

MARKETING METHODS

Agency versus Direct-Selling Systems

Insurance is distributed from the insurers to policyholders in a variety of ways. Most important is an *agency system* of representatives who operate under the authority given them by the insurers to make legal transactions with the consumer of insurance. The complex nature of insurance, and its usual significance to the insured, make such personal contact through an intermediary essential to the sale of most insurance.

Only in the case of carriers who restrict their lines to a local territory do the insureds in the usual course of business come in contact with company officers. In the greater number of cases the contact between insured and carrier is made through an agent who is paid by the company he represents. The discussion of insurer representatives in the next section assumes major importance when the widespread use of agency systems in marketing insurance is realized.

A further exception to the general rule that insurance is sold mainly through agents is in the case of *direct-selling systems* under which the insurer deals directly with the insured through employees of the insurer. In specialized and limited lines of insurance these systems may assume some importance. Many health insurers operate in this manner by using direct-mail advertising. All correspondence is direct from the company to the prospect, and the insurance contract is written and serviced without an agent. Examples also exist in the other fields of insurance. For example, the Factory Mutuals deal directly with insureds in writing fire insurance for large businesses. A few automobile insurers have applied the system successfully in writing automobile insurance. Even in life insurance the growth of group life insurance is evidence of more direct contact with the insured by salaried employees of the insurer instead of depending entirely upon the traditional commissioned agents for insurance marketing.

Life Insurance Agency Systems

A distinction should be observed between the usual agency method of marketing life insurance as opposed to property insurance. In life insurance the insurers normally use agents who repre-

---

[9] *1963 Life Insurance Fact Book* (New York: The Institute of Life Insurance), pp. 17, 97.

sent only one insurer. The agent sells life insurance for one company, and therefore is more directly related to the needs, rules, and policy forms of that insurer. A *general agent* often provides field supervision of the sales in a given territory for the company and is in a position similar to a wholesaler of manufactured products who distributes goods for one major producer. The general agent works under the authority of the company he represents and hires, trains, and directs the activities of his life agents. He is paid a commission for the business his agents write, but the actual acceptance of the life insurance contracts is performed at the home office of the life insurer.

Property Insurance Agency Systems

In property insurance two major agency systems of marketing are used to distribute the fire, automobile, and other casualty insurance contracts: (1) the *independent agency system* and (2) the *exclusive agency system.*[10]

Independent Agency System. Traditionally the predominant method has been an agency system in which the agent in contact with the policyholder is one who represents several or many insurers. This is known as the *independent agency system.* The agent is independent in the sense that he may place his business with any one of a number of insurers (perhaps as few as five or as many as thirty) whom he represents as agent. He sells on a commission or fee basis as an independent contractor for insurers that recognize ownership, use and control of policy and expiration records as belonging to the agent. The agent often has the authority to bind the insurer immediately for many of the kinds of insurance he writes for his policyholders. A branch office or general agency of each insurer may supervise the activities of the agent on the local level.

Exclusive Agency System. The *exclusive agency system* of marketing property insurance has risen in recent decades with the growth of automobile insurance and simplified insurance coverages (nonbusiness) for the individual. Here the agent normally represents only one company, as in the case of the typical life insurance agent. His agency contract limits his representation to one insurer, or a few which are under common management. It reserves to the insurer the ownership, use and control of policy and expiration

---

[10]The primary terms used here have caused much confusion in recent years. In late 1963 the Committee on Property and Liability Insurance Terminology of the American Risk and Insurance Association agreed upon the basic terms used above: (1) direct-selling system, (2) independent agency system, and (3) exclusive agency system to describe marketing systems in insurance. It is noted that one recent book on this subject uses these terms, and the source is recommended for further information on the changes in insurance marketing. See John N. Cosgrove, *Competition in Insurance Marketing* (Cincinnati, Ohio: The National Underwriter Company, 1960).

data. The agent may have binding authority. The larger exclusive agency insurers, such as State Farm Mutual, Allstate, and Nationwide Mutual, have made tremendous increases in their sales of automobile insurance in the last decade and are beginning to show substantial gains in fire, homeowners, and even life and health insurance.

Summary. The advantages and disadvantages of these two marketing systems in property insurance are not easily seen by the policyholder. Certainly the terms are often misleading. Less desirable than the above contrast between independent and exclusive agency systems are the two terms *American Agency System* and *direct-writing system,* which have been extensively used to describe, respectively, these two competing systems of marketing. Obviously, the direct-writing system can be just as "American" as the American Agency System, and the American Agency System just as "direct" as the direct-writing system! Even with the newer suggested terms, one should point out that an independent agent *is* dependent to a certain extent on the insurers he represents, and an exclusive agent may have some measure of independence from his insurer. Also, the exclusive agency system is not automatically better or of higher caliber as it may imply. In fact, its critics call it the "captive" agency system!

The insured must analyze his choice in terms of both cost and service from the agent, regardless of the name of the agency system. The main advantage of the exclusive agents is lower cost, through reduced commissions or decreased expenses due to centralization of some functions such as policy writing, records-keeping, billing, training, advertising and sales methods. The independent agents have substantial advantages in representing more than one insurer, and in their ownership of expirations. Since no one insurer is the best in all lines and all territories, the agent serves an important purpose in serving as an expert in choosing the best companies to write insurance for the individual needs of his clients. He thus has a wider choice and variety of coverages, prices, and services for his policyholders.

It is fair to predict that no one agency system will be destroyed by the other in the current era of changing distribution patterns of insurance. Each system has some merit and each will retain and increase its share of the market in the proportion that it meets the real needs of the insurance consumer.

TYPES OF INSURER REPRESENTATIVES

The insurance buyer is often most concerned, and rightly so, with the representative of the insurer with whom he has direct contact. The legal type of insurer or the marketing system used is often of secondary importance to the insured. The applicant for insurance makes contact with the insurer through one or more of the following: (*a*) agents, (*b*) solicitors, (*c*) brokers, and (*d*) service representatives.

Agents

The agent is a company representative, and the authority under which he operates is delegated through the medium of an agency contract. An agent may be a natural person, a partnership, or a corporation. The significant feature of the agency relationship is that the agent is appointed and authorized by an insurance company to act as its representative with authority to solicit, negotiate, and effect contracts of insurance or annuities in its behalf.

The powers of the agent are governed by the document creating the agency, sometimes termed a "commission of authority." The terms *general agent, local agent, state agent,* and *special agent* among others, are frequently used in the insurance business. The local agent who makes contact with the applicant for insurance may be designated *general agent, regional agent,* or simply *agent.* All of these terms have a specialized significance within the business and may represent the nature of the position of the agent with the company or the commission arrangement. Legally, regardless of company terminology, an agent is either a *general agent* or a *limited agent.* A general agent can bind a risk and thereby make insurance effective immediately and prior to the actual delivery of the policy. If the agent's powers are limited or restricted, he must operate within the scope of the authority delegated to him. It has been noticed that secret limitations do not bind a third party, and the agent may bind as principal if he is acting within the apparent scope of his authority.[11] The authority of agents in the different fields has been so well established that the buyer of insurance will have little difficulty in determining its extent and limitations with respect to any class of insurance. A brief summary follows:

Life. In the strict legal sense, company officers act in the capacity of agents in issuing policies and otherwise conducting the affairs of the corporation. However, as the term "agent" is used in the insurance business, regularly salaried officers of the company are by definition excluded. The life insurance business customarily limits the authority to issue or modify life insurance contracts to company officers. Life insurance agents are limited agents. Generally

[11]It is in accordance with the weight of authority that a local agent of an insurance company who is furnished by it with blank policies to be filled out, countersigned, and issued by him has all the powers of a general agent. This includes among other powers the authority to waive any provisions of the policies which he is authorized to issue (*Liverpool & London and Globe Insurance Company* v. *Delaney,* 190 Miss. 404; 200 So. 440).

speaking, life insurance agents are authorized to solicit, receive, and forward applications for the contracts written by their companies. The agent is not authorized to receive payments or any money due or to become due to the company except the first premium due on the application obtained by him. An exception is the "industrial" life insurance agent, who does collect renewal premiums regularly at the home of the policyholder. He is authorized to collect the first and subsequent premiums and forward them to the company, following the company rules in the matter of receipt. An agent may, under special authorizations, collect funds other than the first premium on his own business; but the authorization will outline the procedure, and the receipt to be delivered will be the regular form used by the company and forwarded to the agent for the purpose. The authority of the life insurance agent in the matter of collections is, therefore, limited.

From time to time the company may assign specific duties in connection with the solicitation of applications. Unless he has special instructions, the agent must carefully limit his activities. Specifically, an agent is not authorized to accept risks of any kind, to bind the company, or to modify a contract in any way. He does not have the right to extend the time for paying of premiums or to waive a forfeiture. He may not bind the company by any statement, promise, or representation.

Property. Agents appointed to represent fire, marine, and casualty companies in effecting property insurance are, as a rule, granted the powers of a general agent. The limitations to their authority are set forth in the commission of authority and agency agreement. Such agents may bind their companies by oral contract as well as waive policy provisions. Among other responsibilities they inspect risks and collect premiums due.

Surety agents as a rule operate under a limited authority. It is the general practice to authorize them to sign bonds in certain classifications within prescribed limits. Few agents have authority to bind or in any way to commit a surety company on a contract bond. Attorneys, architects, and contractors know of the limitations of the authority of local agents to execute bonds. Where there is any question that a particular bond may require special authorization, it is considered excellent practice to insist that there be attached to the bond a duly authenticated copy of the agent's power of attorney.

Solicitors

A *solicitor* is an individual authorized by an insurance agent or broker to solicit contracts of insurance or annuities. He acts only on behalf of one agent or broker. He does not have authority to bind the company with respect to risk but, in connection with his business activities, is authorized to collect premiums. The solicitor transacts business in the name of the agent or broker by whom he is employed, and the employer is responsible for his acts or omissions within the scope of his employment.

Brokers

Like the agent, a *broker* may be a person, partnership, or corporation. The broker acts on behalf of the insured. He is an independent contractor and is remunerated, usually, on a commission basis. His principal function is to assist the applicant for insurance in placing risks. The broker has been termed an anomaly in that he serves the insured, yet is paid by the insurer. The broker is a middleman between the insured and the company agent. In the early days when the broker made his first appearance in the insurance business, it was contended that he rendered no service since he did for the the insured only what the company officers were ready and willing to do. Men of ability and integrity made their livelihood from this occupation, and their value to the insurance company was finally recognized and admitted. By informing themselves of rates, forms, and other technical features of the business, they became increasingly useful to the insured. Since they secured their remuneration in the form of a commission from the company, their service to the insured had the additional attraction of being free. Brokers are now recognized intermediaries between the company and the insured.

There is sometimes some confusion on the part of uninformed insureds dealing with a broker because they do not differentiate between an insurance broker and an agent. The insurance agent is acting under specific and delegated authority from his company and is authorized to bind his company within limits of his delegated authority. The broker, on the other hand, has no such authority and in most jurisdictions is recognized as the agent of the insured. This has been modified in some states by statutes which specifically provide that, for the purposes of collecting premiums and delivering policies, the broker is an agent of the company but, for all other purposes, is agent of the insured.

Because the broker is held to represent the policyholder, the insured is bound by the acts of the broker with respect to the negotiations between insurer and insured. Fraudulent acts of the broker are binding on the insured when perpetrated in his behalf. As in other agency relationships, the insured as principal is charged with the broker's knowledge. Any misrepresentation or breach of warranty perpetrated by the broker makes the insured responsible as if he himself committed the acts. This is partly why the status of the broker sometimes causes confusion, for he is rendering impartial services to the insured but is paid by a commission from the companies with whom he places business. The same rule holds concerning mistakes. A mistake in issuing orders for coverage or accepting a policy that does not meet the requirements of the insured is the responsibility of the insured and not the issuing company. Notice of cancellation may be given to the broker and effectively terminate coverage. The broker may serve as the agent of the insured to substitute one policy for another and otherwise negotiate with the insurance company for protection for the account of the insured.[12]

It is important to understand clearly that the broker on his own authority cannot make insurance effective. He is not a party to an insurance contract as an insurer. He negotiates insurance contracts on behalf of third parties who are insureds but never on behalf of the company from which he derives his remuneration.[13]

For certain lines there is a limited market which requires the use of an *excess line broker* (see several illustrations which follow). This is due to the fact that in some instances the particular classification has a high loss ratio and in others the amount of insurance required is so great that it taxes the facilities of the ordinary markets. Then there are lines fraught with great uncertainty. Particularly in this category is to be found products liability coverage of new and untried products that might with failure bring about catastrophic claims. In this category are to be found cosmetics and medicinal products. It frequently happens that a new risk is carried in whole or in part by the market represented by excess line brokers during an early period of uncertainty. As time passes and the nature of the risk becomes clearer, more and more of it is absorbed by the local market.

There are brokers who specialize in placing excess lines or lines that are otherwise difficult to place. In some instances the brokers are obliged to seek a market such as that afforded by Llyod's of

[12]The difference between an agent and broker has not always been clearly established in the minds of insurance buyers. To further confuse the issue, it may here be pointed out, a given individual may act both as agent and as broker. The simplest illustration is to be found in the case of an agent, who commits his own companies for a part of a line, and acts as broker in placing any excess his own companies are not able to handle, through another agency.

[13]The courts have recognized that the function of an insurance broker, like that of other brokers, is to bring parties together for the purpose of commerce and trade without having any special property rights in the contract which results from his efforts, except for a commission which he earns immediately upon consummation of the transaction. Notwithstanding the fact that the insurance broker is held to represent the applicant for insurance and not the company, it is generally held that the payment of an insurance premium to a broker is payment to the insurance company. On this point Section 121 of the Insurance Law of the State of New York reads: "Any insurer which delivers in this state to any insurance broker a contract of insurance pursuant to the application or request of such broker, acting for an insured other than himself, shall be deemed to have authorized such broker to receive on its behalf payment of any premium which is due on such contract at the time of its issuance or delivery or which becomes due thereon in not more than 90 days thereafter."

London, and in other instances the business is placed for a premium, higher than locally established rates, with companies that have not been licensed to do business in a particular state and are known as "nonadmitted companies."

The type of risk that in the ordinary course is placed by the excess line broker might include liability coverage on motorcycle and automobile racing, fireworks displays, amusement parks, aviation shows, circuses, and the like. Where capacity is a problem, there is usually some feature of the risk that tends to make underwriters limit the amount they will carry for their various companies. In the case of burglary, for instance, a large warehouse containing readily moveable valuable items such as cameras, television sets, and the like with limited burglary alarm and watchman service may call for the assistance of the excess line broker in handling the portion of the risk that the local market is unable to absorb.

The market for excess lines may include companies with a home office in the United States, or they may include foreign markets such as London, Canada, or South America. Domestic nonadmitted companies are those charted in one of the states but not licensed in all states. Foreign companies may or may not be admitted or they may be licensed in one or more states and not in others. The nonadmitted character of much of the market handling excess lines business tends to invite the careful scrutiny of the prospective insured. The excess line broker may not always deal with the insured directly but may be sought out by the insured's broker. Much of the line may be placed in the local market with an accommodation line placed by the broker with nonadmitted companies. It is to be presumed that the originating broker will satisfy himself with respect to the financial positions, adjusting facilities and practices, and general attitude toward claims of the company with which he places excess lines. It will be poor consolation to the insured, however, if he discovers the relationship to be an unsatisfactory one after a loss. It is always desirable that excess lines be placed, so far as it is possible to do so, with companies licensed in the state where the business is placed. If this is impossible, the insured should carefully check the broker's sources of information in order to become satisfied personally with the financial responsibility of the company in question as well as its reputation.[14]

While the major part of life insurance production is handled by company agents, there are a number of *life brokers* who devote all or most of their time to life insurance but place the business they produce with the company that they feel to be in a position to

[14]It is sometimes possible to secure a "service of suit" clause in policies obtained in a foreign market. Such a clause is quite customary in policies obtained in the English market. By virtue of the clause, suit may be served on local representatives of the company and action may be brought against it in courts having local jurisdictions.

handle and service the line adequately. Group insurance has proved a fertile field for brokers. Since underwriting rules of companies differ so widely, the placing of a group risk may involve its submission to several companies. Brokers with a number of company contracts and knowledge of the extent and limitations of the particular field as set up by the company underwriters are admirably situated to handle lines of this sort.

A significant volume of brokerage business arises from life agents who fundamentally represent one life company but place business in another because clients want the particular plan it offers or because they may place it on a more favorable basis in view of the underwriting limits of their own company. While this type of business is classed as brokerage, the agent is to be distinguished from the life broker who is attached to no particular company and originates business and places it where the best market is to be found. Specialists in estate planning, group insurance, pension plans, or other specialized fields where transactions are large and competition keen are fields in which the life broker is more and more making his influence felt.

Service Representatives

Many companies employ specialists on a salary basis to work with and assist agents in writing specialized lines. Such employees are termed *service representatives* and may help an agent to effect insurance in the company employing the representative. General agents employ service representatives to work with and assist agents in soliciting and effecting insurance in one or in all the companies represented by the general agent. Company officers, managers, or general agents of insurance companies employed on a salary basis are not included in the category of service representatives.

The requirements for obtaining a license to act as agent, broker, or solicitor differ in the various jurisdictions. The agent's qualifications and licensing law recommended to the National Association of Insurance Commissioners calls for the state to license agents, solicitors, or brokers but does not make this requirement with respect to service representatives.

Examples of service representatives are common in both the life and property insurance fields. In property insurance, "special agents" are used by many companies to initiate agency contracts, help the agent on special sales problems and generally keep the agent informed of new contracts and services of the insurer. Engineering and appraisal services are often provided by company specialists in conjunction with local agents. Company claims adjusters also work in cooperation with the agents on many of the losses involving large amounts or special problems.

In life insurance the service representatives include advanced underwriting specialists who aid the life agent in estate programming and tax planning. Many salaried training specialists are used by general agents to recruit, supervise, and help the new life agent. Most companies writing group life and health coverages provide salaried company representatives who aid the life insurance agent in writing group contracts.

THE PROFESSIONAL CONCEPT OF INSURANCE MARKETING

The insurance business is placing increasing emphasis upon the value of education and training. Training is predicated upon the premise that no longer is the insurance producer a mere canvasser for business; but rather, on the basis of education and training, he is in a position to diagnose the insurance needs of his clients. With the emphasis upon education and the focusing of insurance protection in such a manner that the needs of the applicant are cared for on the most economical basis possible, the professional idea of personal service was developed.

Emphasis on the professional status of the insurance underwriter has been in some instances a source of misunderstanding. Reference to the professional concept and professional ethics has led some to assume that the use of the term "profession" carries an implied reflection upon the term "business." This is not the case. The professional concept recognizes two types of business negotiation. Where representatives of differing interests meet on opposite sides of a bargaining table, each knows that the other is "trading" to make the best possible deal for the party he represents. There is nothing unethical in this type of transaction. Each party relies upon his own knowledge and ability; he serves the interest he represents. This is understood by all parties to the transaction.

The professional underwriter brings to the service of his client a fund of technical knowledge and a background of experience; he may also call upon his company associates for assistance. These include highly trained specialists. The professional concept makes the underwriter the representative of the client in working out an insurance program that, in the light of the client's resources, will best meet his needs. The underwriter and the client are on the same side of the bargaining table. The underwriter can be successful only to the extent that he satisfies the needs of his clients. This is now a fundamental concept in the training programs of the insurance business.

The insurance business makes available training and educational facilities[15] at all levels. Correspondence courses and special home office training courses are offered. For those who wish to become spe-

[15]See Mildred F. Stone, *The Teacher Who Changed an Industry* and *A Calling and Its College* (Homewood, Ill., Richard D. Irwin, Inc., 1960 and 1963, respectively).

cialized experts at the top of their profession, with evidence in recognition of their qualifications, there are the vigorous educational programs and the examinations of the American College of Life Underwriters and the American Institute for Property and Liability Underwriters, Inc. The creation of the American College of Life Underwriters in 1927 was a notable development in insurance education. With the objective of establishing higher educational standards in life and health insurance, the organization awards to properly qualified persons, by national written examinations, the professional designation C.L.U. (Chartered Life Underwriter).

In 1940 the American Association of University Teachers of Insurance (now the American Risk and Insurance Association) passed a resolution "endorsing in principle the establishment of professional standards for property and casualty insurance." There was thus initiated a movement that resulted in the formation in 1942 of the American Institute for Property and Liability Underwriters, Inc., with the following purposes: (*a*) to establish educational standards and administer them so that properly qualified property and casualty underwriters shall be recognized with a professional designation; (*b*) to encourage and foster the training of students in educational institutions and under competent instructors in qualified groups outside educational institutions for the career of professional property and casualty underwriters; and (*c*) to cooperate with educational institutions in general property and casualty insurance education. As in the case of the American College, a designation is awarded to qualified underwriters who successfully pass a series of five written examinations involving not only insurance knowledge but also related business subjects such as accounting, economics, law, management, and finance. In this instance it is C.P.C.U. (Chartered Property Casualty Underwriter).

About 12,000 persons have now achieved the coveted designation of C.L.U., and over 4,000 have their C.P.C.U. designation. In addition, tens of thousands of others have partial credit or are currently improving their capabilities through the C.L.U.-C.P.C.U. programs. Also important are the Certificate Courses offered by the American College in the area of company and agency management, health insurance, group insurance, pensions and estate planning, and its continuing education program, jointly with the American Society of Chartered Life Underwriters, for practicing C.L.U.'s.

The Insurance Institute of America (I.I.A.), associated closely with the C.P.C.U. program, has a number of study programs for property and liability insurance and insurance adjusting. An intermediate sales training program in life and health insurance is offered by the Life Underwriter Training Council which each year enrolls more than 20,000 persons in its courses.

The professional concept assumes a client's reliance upon a person of particular skills or training. Professional ethics require conduct that will warrant implicit confidence on the part of a client. The insurance underwriter is sometimes compared to the clergyman, the doctor, or the family lawyer. This is particularly the case in the field of life insurance. To the extent that the insurance salesman is an expert bringing specialized knowledge concerning the principles and usage of insurance unselfishly to the service of his clients, whatever the line of insurance, the analogy is good. It is, therefore, proper to emphasize the professional status of the insurance underwriter.

It is proper, as well, at this point to indicate that not all insurance agents or brokers are fully qualified to render a professional service. There are many agents who are needed in the insurance business without the skill and educational requirements necessary to plan satisfactorily the life estate or serve the needs of a complex business establishment. More and more, however, the broadening use of insurance to meet a wide variety of family and business financial needs suggests that the insurance man of the future shall often have to be of professional caliber.

THE CONSUMER VIEWPOINT OF INSURANCE PURCHASING

Selecting the Insurer

It might seem, at first thought, that the selection of the insurance company would be one of the first and most important decisions of the insurance buyer. However, the applicant, to a large degree, leaves the choice of companies to his broker or agent. This is not to say that companies and their reputations are not carefully scrutinized. It is rather to say that companies enjoying the best reputations ordinarily attract high-grade representatives. With state regulatory agencies carefully scrutinizing the financial position of companies, their ability to pay can rarely be expected to become a matter of question. The attitude of companies with respect to claims may differ, however, and the insured is concerned with the company's attitude regarding technicalities and the reputation for satisfactory dealings with insureds at time of loss.

The insured is interested in knowing the scope of the contracts offered by a company and whether or not it is liberal with respect to underwriting. A company that is selective in choosing risks may prove unsatisfactory when a buyer has a more difficult type or risk to be insured. The insured should find out about the facilities and reputation of the claim department. He is also interested in knowing the facilities for rate analysis and loss-prevention recommendations that may favorably influence insurance costs.

The size of a company is not a controlling factor in its selection: financial strength and size are not necessarily equivalents. The trend of a company's growth, over a period of years, is signficant and helpful. The buyer who limits his purchases to well-known and recognized companies and places his business with an agent or broker of outstanding reputation in his profession will probably have accomplished as much as may be expected of anyone in choosing the best possible carrier.

Selecting the Agent or Broker

Insurance premiums contain a charge for the services of the agent or broker. It is the responsibility of the purchaser of insurance to determine whether or not he is getting a full measure for the payment of an insurance premium. If his agent or broker is only an order taker, he is getting something less than full value for his premium payment.

Placing insurance on the basis of personal friendship or social connections is quite as logical as selecting a doctor, lawyer, or architect on the same basis. These may be contributing factors, but the qualifications of the underwriter should be basic in making the determinations.

Some years ago it was the practice—and with some insureds it still is—to distribute insurance with a number of agents. Frequently this distribution was made on a reciprocity basis to create good will, or on a patronage basis to distribute a line among a number of friends. Sounder practice today suggests selecting one agent or broker to handle an entire insurance account. Skilled agents, as well as the insurance buyer, should prefer this practice. They would rather have fewer accounts for which they are fully responsible than a wide participation in risks where they contribute little in the way of service. Sometimes the account may be split so that fire lines are handled by one agent, casualty lines by another, and life insurance and pension business by the life underwriter.

The suggestion has been made that large accounts be offered for competition on an annual basis. Some buyers have attempted the plan with not too satisfactory results. The agent who secures an account in open competition will do the best he can to service the account, but if he does not regard the insured as a permanent client, there is a tendency to let the applicant do his own servicing. Insureds have found the plan detrimental in that in a period of unfavorable losses a company may have no assurance of continued coverage and competing insurers will be reluctant to participate. Thus, the insurance buyer may seriously limit his market. This will not be the case where a company may expect over a period of years to recoup losses incurred in an unfavorable year. From the standpoint of the buyer as well as the underwriter, a permanent relationship on a professional basis seems to work out in the long run to the best advantage of all.

Whether to select an agent or a broker as the intermediary in placing insurance will depend largely upon local conditions. The situation that prevails in a given community will depend largely upon custom and in many instances upon the state law. In some large cities much of the business of insurance producers is in the hands of brokers, and very little contact with applicants for insurance is made directly by agents. In most areas opposite conditions prevail, and business is handled largely through company representatives with agency contracts.

It is to be pointed out that insurance agencies and brokerage firms vary from the individual operator to organizations involving a large personnel and offering a wide degree of specialization. These organizations differ in the services they are able to offer, their methods of doing business, the types and kinds of insurance they handle. It is, therefore, encumbent upon the buyer of insurance to determine, in selecting the agent or broker with whom he intends to deal, whether or not the particular individual, or his concern or organization, has the experience and service facilities to meet his requirements.

A substantial part of the insurance premium represents commission or salary, to the agent. In the event that no service or inadequate service is rendered for this part of the premium, the insured is paying for something he actually does not get. Normally the insurance consumer needs the services of a competent agent who performs the wide variety of services essential to proper insurance protection. These include helping the policyholder understand his needs, analysis of significant risks, explanation of alternative coverages and contracts, arranging for credit or installment payments, frequent reviews of the insurance program to adjust to changing risks, loss prevention or engineering services, appraisals, aid in prompt claims payment, and many other important duties.

The agent who represents one or more companies may technically have his market limited to the facilities of these particular companies. A broker who is in the habit of placing his business with one company or a small group of companies is in very much the same situation. In the case of unusual lines both agents and brokers should be in a position to know where a market for such lines exists. For excess lines, or unusual lines, they are in a position to find a market that might not be known to the ordinary insurance buyer. In such circumstances the experienced agent or broker will place risks offered to him either with his own company if he is an agent, or with his usual contacts, if he is a broker. He will often be able to give his clients the benefit of any competitive situation that may make its appearance in the insurance field.

Some companies will rely for production of business upon full-time salaried salesmen. They deal directly with their insured without using the intermediary of the local agent or broker. Representatives of such companies are thoroughly versed in all the lines which the company has to offer. Such a representative ordinarily does not place insurance outside his own company. Where he meets a situation that requires insurance protection not offered by his own company, he may be able to suggest another carrier. However, the insurance buyer may himself be obliged to make a new contact for the purposes of placing the particular risk.

Whatever the point of contact selected by the applicant for insurance, the reputation and the "know-how" of the company representative is to a large degree responsible for the selection of the insurer. Much of the success of the insurance consumer in having proper insurance is based upon the choice by the insured of his agent or broker. For the businessman, or even for the family spending a substantial portion of income on insurance, it is not a selection to be made in a haphazard manner.

SUMMARY

The marketing of insurance has been presented in Chapter 4 as one of the most important and difficult functions of the insurance business. It is essential in order that insurers obtain the large number of separate risks upon which to base their predictions of future losses and costs. The sale of insurance is difficult because of the unique features of the insurance product—the contingent, future, and sometimes complex legal nature of its services.

The insurance market in the United States is serviced by many types of insurers. Over 4,000 insurers provide the vast number and variety of property, liability, life, and health contracts needed by the American public. In terms of sales, the *stock* companies predominate in the property-liability insurance lines, writing some three fourths of the total business. In life insurance, *mutual* insurers write 60 percent of the business, even though they number only about 10 per cent of the number of insurers. Mutual insurance organizations are found to vary greatly in terms of size and type, from large general-writing insurers, to specialized kinds of class, farm, Factory, and fraternal insurers. *Lloyd's, reciprocals, state,* and *self-insurers* are important examples of the great diversity of objectives, organization, and operations of insurers, even though in volume they account for minor parts of the total insurance business.

The major method of insurance marketing is through the use of *agency* systems as opposed to *direct-selling* systems. Life insurance and property insurance have traditionally used different agency systems to accomplish the distribution of insurance. Substantial changes of recent years in property insurance indicate increasing competition between *independent agency* systems and the *exclusive agency* system. The number of companies an agent represents, and whether or not he has ownership rights to the policy records of his clients, are the distinguishing features of these competing agency systems.

The insurance policyholder has contact with the insurer through agents, brokers, solicitors, and service representatives. He rarely is in a position to select the insurer directly, but often relies upon the judgment and advice of these persons in making his choices among contracts, coverages, and insurers. It is partially the heavy reliance of the consumer upon the agent and other such persons that creates the tremendous need for the growing professional concept in insurance. From the viewpoint of the insurance consumer, it is expected that the higher standards of ethics and education shall markedly influence the purchase of insurance in the future.

FOR REVIEW

1. What is "the insurance market," and why does the insurance buyer need to know about it?
2. Distinguish between a stock and a mutual company, and explain why the differences may be important to the policyholder.
3. What are the advantages and disadvantages of assessment mutuals and general-writing mutuals? Why are each important in the insurance market?
4. What was the underlying motive that prompted the organization of the Factory Mutuals? The class mutuals?
5. Discuss the points of similarity and the differences between London Lloyd's and
   a) The American Lloyd's.
   b) Mutual insurers.
   c) Reciprocals.
6. The text states that the liability of a member of a reciprocal association is several and not joint. Explain the difference between the operation of a reciprocal and a mutual with respect to the distribution of financial resources held by the organization for the payment of losses.
7. In what class of insurance carriers is the major volume of each type of insurance business written?
8. "Mr. . . . pointed out that a survey of 162 . . . . school corporations showed that they paid $920,000 in premiums and had $220,000 in losses for a five-year period. *The Star*, commenting on the survey, says the fire insurance companies have therefore made a 'lush profit' of $700,000 which in the opinion of the reporter, conclusively proves the need for the state to enter the insurance business." This statement appeared in the insurance press in connection with the discussion of a proposal for the establishment of a state fund to insure public property. Figures such as these encourage the uninformed with respect to "self-insurance" projects. Explain the fallacious reasoning that leads to a recommendation for "self-insurance."

9. In what kinds of insurance are state insurance and "self-insurance" most often used? Why?
10. Distinguish between an agent and a broker. May an individual under certain circumstances be both an agent and a broker? May he be both an agent and a broker in dealing with an individual insured with respect to placing one specific line? Give reasons for your answer.
11. X, an insured, operates a retail store and feels that for business purposes he should divide his insurance business so that as many customers as possible will participate. Can you see any dangers in this practice?
12. D, an agent, writes automobile insurance for E company. X applies for automobile insurance. The agent knows that the applicant has a poor record and has been denied insurance elsewhere. Nevertheless, anxious for the business and collateral lines that will come with it, the agent writes the policy and delays sending the report to the home office. The agent feels that, if the policy is in force for a month, the company will then let the matter pass and not request cancellation. However, a serious accident happens in the meantime. What is the position of the parties?
13. Outline briefly the difference in the powers of the typical property-liability insurance agent and the agent for a life insurance company.
14. Under the general rules of principal and agent the principal owns the agent's records and, therefore, the expirations. How is this rule modified under the so-called "independent agency system"? May a company withdrawing from an agency turn these records over to a competing agent? Would your answer be different if the agent was an "exclusive agent?"
15. What does the "professional concept" of insurance marketing include? Does this explanation offer any reasons as to why agency systems are more important in marketing insurance than direct-selling systems?
16. Explain three criteria which a business man should follow in choosing his insurer, and three other factors of importance in selecting an insurance agent or broker.

Chapter 5

INSURANCE LOSS PAYMENT

THE payment of losses is not the only function of insurers, but certainly it is the most obvious of the important purposes for many kinds of insurance. Without claims culminating in loss payments there would be no insurance business. For this reason it is appropriate to discuss the payment of insurance losses at an early point in an insurance text, even before a more detailed understanding of specific contract details is attempted.

In reading this chapter it is suggested that the student not be overconcerned with some illustrations which seem to require specific knowledge about some of the pertinent phrases and language of particular insurance contracts. Such references are necessary to serve as examples of loss payment techniques and problems. They will also serve as an introduction to the later chapters which discuss the analysis of insurance contracts in more detail. It is the purpose of this chapter to provide a broad picture of insurance in action, using specific illustrations from each of the major fields of insurance to show the scope and methods of paying insurance losses. The final section of this chapter on claims procedures, in particular, should be read by the beginning insurance student for general information rather than detail.

SIGNIFICANCE

The basic function of loss payment is commonly referred to as *insurance adjusting*. The term is not very satisfactory, but it has become well fixed in the business of insurance. It is hoped that some better term may be adopted in the future, for the connotation of an "adjustment" is something that always requires a compromise or change before settlement is reached. Since this is not true, a better phrase might be *claims payment,* with the persons who do this work referred to as *claimsmen.* However, since the more common reference today is to adjusting and adjusters, these terms will be used frequently in this chapter. It should be recognized, in spite of this common practice, that insurance adjusting does have the same objective as the perhaps more accurate terms of loss payment or claims payment. A loss, a claim, and an adjustment may logically be three different amounts, though here the phrase adjustment is used to mean whichever of the three amounts the final insurance payment is determined to be.

Loss payments are a daily part of the routine of the insurance business. The repayment for the values which have been lost is often the point at which the policyholder has the strongest possible realization of why he purchased the insurance contract. Up to that time he may have had a feeling that there were a number of vague reasons why he purchased the protection. When he actually receives a loss check which makes it possible for him to rebuild his home or replace his automobile, he has specific and tangible knowledge as to why he needed the insurance. He often may wonder what he possibly would have done if he had not had the proper insurance coverage.

PURPOSE

The insured who has honestly suffered loss or damage need approach the insurance company in no apologetic frame of mind. The claim settlement which he asks for is his by right of purchase. His contact with the adjusters is a routine transaction from the insurance company standpoint. It should be the objective of both to arrive at a fair and equitable measure of the loss. There may, and frequently will be, areas of disagreement. With both parties resolved to reach an equitable adjustment, disagreements usually are readily reconciled.

Insurance adjusters today are indoctrinated with the conviction that it is encumbent upon them to deliver the goods which the agent has sold. The insurance business recognizes that years of insurance programing and planning will come to nothing if the insured is faced with difficulty in effecting an adjustment following a loss. The new adjuster is taught at the outset that it is his function to settle the claim equitably and not, as is sometimes believed, for the least sum to which he can get the insured to agree. This has been carried so far that adjusters are instructed when an insured does not know what is due him under his contract to take steps to explain what amounts should be included in his claim. By the same token, in the interest of equity in the business, adjusters are trained to recognize sharp practices and to resist padded claims or fraudulent demands. Fairness to the uninformed and resistance to wrongful claims is held to be for the benefit both of the insurance business and, in the long run, the insured who must pay rates predicated upon loss experience.

From the point of view of the individual company, claims adjustments afford an attractive area of competition. Where premium rates are fixed, there can be no competition on the basis of price.

The service that the company can offer may include expert planning, elaborate loss-prevention service and the like. If it fails in effecting a prompt and equitable adjustment following loss, however, it will have failed in the most crucial of all competitive areas.

This is not to say that there should be competition among companies that will result in overpayemnt of claims. In the long run this benefits no one. There is no one who recognizes prompt services and sound practices with respect to the settlement of claims more readily than the agent or broker. If he becomes dissatisfied with the adjustment practices of a company, he will direct his business into other channels. Likewise, experienced insurance buyers soon learn the reputation of a company with respect to its claim service. However well pleased a company itself may feel with its procedures, if they are not up to the standards required by the industry, the company will in time find it more and more difficult to sell contracts. As time goes by for such a company, claim adjustments will be less and less of a problem for, with a dwindling business, it follows that there will be a falling off of claims. This is not a healthy situation since claims make the business, and good public relations demand that they be treated accordingly.

The loss adjustment is set in motion when an insured files a notice of loss with his insurer. The adjustment is the means for effecting the ultimate aim of insurance. Of the many thousands of insurance policies written, claims are filed under only comparatively few. It is the purpose of the adjustment to determine the question of liability for a given loss and reach an agreement with respect to the loss or damage where liability is found to exist.

INSURANCE CLAIMSMEN: TYPES AND ORGANIZATION

Since the insurance policy is a contract, the terms and conditions are carefully stated so in the event of a loss the insured has his contract to follow in effecting an adjustment. As a matter of practice, a company representative approaches the insured and, if investigation shows the loss to be legitimate, undertakes to effect a settlement, sparing the insured as much technical detail as possible. All such persons who aid in the loss payment are termed *claimsmen* or in more common language, *adjusters.* Adjusters fall into five categories: (1) agents as adjusters, (2) staff adjusters, (3) independent adjusters, (4) adjustment bureaus, and (5) public adjusters.

Agents as Adjusters

Local agents are usually authorized to settle and sometimes to pay small losses. It is common sense on the part of the insurer to allow the agent, whenever possible, to pay losses to the policyholder. After all, the agent is usually closest to the claimant, knows him, is familiar with the insurance contracts he has for the insured, and normally has the earliest facts on the occurrence of the loss. The agent has, too, a prime interest in seeing that his client receives prompt and fair treatment in the loss payment. The satisfaction of the policyholder is important to the agent, in terms of goodwill and the continued business that he is able to do with the insured and his friends.

In property insurance many agents have the authority of their companies to settle a claim immediately with the policyholder. For smaller and uncomplicated losses this is the most expedient and efficient way to pay claims. For example, the local agent may be given permission by his companies to settle all losses of certain kinds up to a stated dollar amount. For a new agent or a small agent this authority may only extend up to $100. For larger and more seasoned agents the authority may extend to several hundred dollars, and in addition, the agent may be given responsibility for actually issuing checks in the name of his companies. Custody of such a checkbook, of course, must be carefully controlled by the company. For the agent it is a valuable way in which he can render prompt service to his policyholders with a minimum of paperwork to all parties concerned. Some of the kinds of losses where this practice is becoming more and more prevalent are fire, windstorm, and medical payments under home and automobile contracts, and automobile collision and miscellaneous damage (to the insured's car).

In larger losses, or ones which involve more complex adjusting methods such as in liability insurance, it is necessary to provide specialized help to the agent and insured. One or more of the four other types of claimsman will be used in such cases. Again, this is reasonable because it is the duty of the insurer to see that losses are equitably paid to the policyholder. An agent with little legal background should not be permitted to attempt to settle liability claims, nor should one with little experience in adjusting an infrequent business interruption loss be given sole authority to determine the company's liability and amount of loss payment. It must also be remembered that the funds for loss payment are the prime responsibility of the insurance company. In some cases the agent, if given too much authority in the adjusting of losses, may be overzealous in his efforts to please a friend or important policyholder with a wrongful claim payment. Such a situation would be improper for the insurer, for the agent, for the policyholder, and for other policyholders whose rates may be raised in the future by careless or exaggerated claims paid.

In life insurance the agent is often involved directly in the loss payment. The claims procedure for smaller contracts is a simple one —notice to the company and a birth and death certificate are often all that is required before the policy amount can be paid. The life agent usually forwards the death notice and certificates to the insurer and the check is issued by the company for delivery to the policyholder's beneficiary by the agent. Life insurers do not have the problem of determining the extent of loss payment that is common in property insurance losses, for the contract itself states the amount to be paid upon loss. For the larger policies, various installment payment options in place of a lump-sum cash payment may need to be explained by the agent. In such cases, and also in the more frequent problems of health insurance in connection with life insurance contracts, the life agent may need and be required by his company to use special personnel from their claims department.

Staff Adjusters

The contact between local agents of fire, marine, and casualty companies and the home office is maintained through a field man, known as a special agent, state agent, or general agent. Among other functions, the field man has jurisdiction over loss adjustments. Company employees who make adjustments are known as company or *staff adjusters*. In the casualty field, in particular, they may devote their entire time to loss settlements. Casualty claims lend themselves to the services of staff adjusters since, in most instances, only one company is concerned with the claim. In such fields as automobile insurance and the other casualty fields, the volume of claims is such that the companies have found it to their advantage to maintain claim offices staffed by specialists in the various lines they write. These companies, however, frequently utilize the services of company bureaus if the claim develops in a location where it can be better or more economically serviced by such a bureau.

In fire insurance, company field men may handle the loss or it may be turned over to an adjustment bureau. At one time, if a loss occurred with a sizable number of different companies interested, since it was not feasible for representatives for all the companies to participate in negotiations, the loss was referred to a "committee." Limited use is still made of committees. When this plan is followed, the company writing the largest amount of the business is said to have the "top line" and is expected to look after the details of the adjustment. It is usual to form a committee of three or more adjusters and to turn the loss claims against all companies over to the committee, although any field man interested is permitted to sit in on the settlement. It is the usual procedure for all companies to follow the recommendation of the committee. More recently the tendency to use company-owned bureaus has evidenced itself. If only one company is interested in the loss, the field man may handle it himself or in conjunction with the agent of the insured.

The use of staff adjusters depends on the volume and kinds of business written in the territory in which the loss occurs. To support a full-time staff adjuster in a given area the insurer must have enough claims to be adjusted. Some companies use staff adjusters almost exclusively, while others are more apt to use the services of the other types of adjusters available.

Independent Adjusters

Independent adjusters are experts who have made loss adjusting a business. Some have specialized in particular fields, and they are called upon when technical skill of a particular nature is required. Others in the field possess a general knowledge and understanding of adjustment procedure and handle losses when it is impossible or inconvenient for the company representatives to give prompt attention. Some independent adjusters operate as individuals within a limited area. Others have built up sizable organizations and extend their operations over a wide area; and some accept assignments on a national basis.

The independent adjuster works for the insurers who request his services. A typical use would be in automobile insurance where the insurer has only a small volume of business in a given area, or where the policyholder has an accident while traveling there. For the occasional claim which occurs in the territory it would be expensive and inefficient to send a staff adjuster from the home or branch office to settle the claim. Instead, the insurer hires an independent adjuster to do the job. The independent adjuster often builds up a continuing working relationship with particular companies, as well as accepting infrequent adjusting assignments from a larger number of insurers.

Adjustment Bureaus

Adjustment bureaus are becoming more and more important as factors in all fields of claim adjustment except life. These bureaus have numerous branches. Their sole business is claim adjustment, and they are owned through stock distribution by the insurance companies. The bureaus are not organized for profit, and an effort is made to adjust charges to meet expenses. If a profit is earned, it is distributed in due course; but, if there is a deficit, it is met by assessment. Bureau adjusters are highly trained and experienced men who devote their entire time to adjusting losses. Companies look with favor upon the trend toward bureau adjustment, feeling that it tends toward an equitable treatment of all members of a community and eliminates competition among adjusters and agents in the matter of building a reputation for generosity over their competitors by excessive claim payments. Bureau adjusters, being company representatives, are interested in the production end of the business. In the general interest of the business it is their aim to effect a prompt and satisfactory adjustment with a minimum of controversy or litigation; and, on the other hand, they are equipped to cope with fraud or false claims.[1]

Public Adjusters

As the name implies, *public adjusters* represent the public in contrast to the adjusters who represent insurance companies. The public adjuster is retained *by the insured* to represent him in negotiating the loss settlement. He offers his services on the basis of bringing expert insurance knowledge, particularly in estimating damages and effecting loss settlements, to the insured. It is sometimes assumed that a company adjuster is biased and will make borderline decisions to the advantage of the insurance company. As a matter of fact, such situations are the exception, although in a loss there may be a wide area for differences of opinion. It is usually a basic principle of public relations in the insurance business to settle all losses fairly in accordance with the terms of the policy. Many insureds, however, feel inadequate to approach the problem of adjustment without assistance they feel represents their interests. Sometimes they retain an attorney to represent them in negotiations or turn the loss over to a public adjuster.

In some states public adjusters are required to obtain a license from the insurance department of the state. An examination may be required before a license is issued, and the state licensing authority exercises control over the practices of the adjusters to the end that their operations are ethical and follow established business practices. The insured, of course, assumes the responsibility for the selection of a public adjuster.

The actions of such an adjuster can involve something more than working out loss details and effecting a settlement. This is so since the courts have held that a public adjuster acts as agent for the in-

---

[1]The General Adjustment Bureau, operated on a nationwide basis, was formed in the early 1930's as the outgrowth of a merger of a number of adjusting organizations. First known as the Fire Companies Adjustment Bureau, Inc., it later changed its name to the General Adjustment Bureau, Inc. The ogranization has a national headquarters in New York City but in the interests of simplifying administration it has been departmentalized. There are the Eastern, Southeastern, Southwestern, Western, Pacific Coast, and Rocky Mountain Departments with headquarters respectively at New York, Atlanta, Dallas, Chicago, San Francisco, and Denver. Operations are carried on in 48 states, and annually over two million losses are adjusted with less than one in 100,000 going to court. It has over 700 branch offices with approximately 6,200 employees. One separate company-owned organization, the Underwriters Adjustments Company, has headquarters in Chicago and provides adjustment facilities for 13 states in the Midwest.

sured within the scope of his employment. If the public adjuster, in an attempt to get a generous adjustment, perpetrates a fraud, then the policy is voided quite as much as if the fraud were perpetrated by the insured. This is true whether or not the fraud is successful. This is based upon the rule that an attempted fraud of an agent acting in the scope of his employment binds the principal. To permit any other holding regarding the operations of a public adjuster would open wide the door to fraud and permit a circumvention of policy conditions. All that would be necessary to perpetrate a fraud upon the insurance company, with immunity from the consequences for the insured, would be a complete delegation by the insured of the responsibility for the adjustment of a loss to a third party whose acts might be disavowed at the option of the insured. Thus, it has been held that, if the insureds do not themselves personally attempt fraud, but if fraud has been attempted by a public adjuster working in their behalf, the responsibility for the attempted fraud rests with the insured and the policy may be voided.

CLAIMS PROCEDURES

It does not come within the scope of a general insurance text to give consideration to all the aspects of claims adjustment procedures. For the purpose of outlining the pattern to be followed, consideration will be given here to examples of the following claims: (*a*) fire, (*b*) marine, (*c*) liability, (*d*) compensation, and (*e*) life. The examples are selected because of the significant differences of one class from the other.

Fire Insurance Losses

Rights and Obligations. The fire insurance contract imposes certain definite obligations upon the insured immediately upon the occurrence of a loss. Two of these, the requirement of the notice of the loss and the obligation to file a proof of loss, are conditions with which the insured must comply before there is any liability on the part of the company. The insured is obligated to take the first step, and until he does so there is no requirement on the part of the company to effect an adjustment.

The purpose of *notice of loss* to the company is to convey the information that a loss has occurred, so that it may take whatever steps it deems necessary to safeguard its interest. Obviously, any unreasonable delay in notice might hamper investigations or otherwise injure the position of the company. What constitutes immediate notice is subject to interpretation and is dependent upon circumstances surrounding each case. The insured must exercise due diligence and forward the notice without unnecessary delay. If there is no reason to prevent it, notice should be given the day the loss occurs, or at least the day following.[2]

The condition of the policy requiring the insured to render a *proof of loss* is the second obligation placed upon the insured as a condition required before recovery under his policy. This document has to do with the knowledge and belief of the insured as to the time and origin of the fire, title to the property, cash value of each item and the amount of loss thereon, encumbrances, other insurance, and the like. The proof of loss, unless waived, must be furnished within 60 days.[3] The policy requires that the statement be furnished to the company, but if the proof is given to its duly authorized agent, the requirement has been compiled with. Blank forms designed to meet the requirements of the insurance company in the matter of the proof of loss are obtainable, and their use to a considerable degree lessens the possibility of a technical error or deficiency.

The proof of loss is a statement of fact concerning the property, the loss, and the insurance. It has for its purpose the supplying of information as a basis of settlement. Information necessary to indicate compliance or noncompliance with the policy terms and conditions is supplied. If this information is found to be satisfactory, concern is then with values, a point of the utmost importance to all parties to the contract. The insurer is obligated to indemnify the insured to the extent of the *actual cash value* of the property destroyed or damaged, with deductions for depreciation, and with a limit fixed by the cost of repairing or replacing the destroyed or damaged property within a reasonable time with material of like kind and quality. The obligation to pay the loss rests upon the company. The obligation to prove the loss rests upon the insured. The essential element in proving the loss is to be found in the ability to demonstrate the values of the property.

A misconception which may lead an insured into difficulty is found in the idea that after a fire the damaged property should not be touched until examined by the fire insurance adjusters. The insured is under no obligation to leave the property undisturbed; on the contrary, he is definitely required to do everything reasonable

[2]In a New York case, the policy was in a safe in the building that was burned and could not be obtained until about the time notice was given, 53 days after the fire; and notice was held sufficient. In another case, a notice given 14 days after the fire, unaccompanied by any fact or circumstance excusing the delay, was held not to be immediate notice.

[3]It has been held that the 60-day period begins to run from the termination of the fire, not from its beginning, but the requirement that proofs be furnished within 60 days after the fire is not complied with if proofs are deposited in the mail on the sixtieth day and do not reach the company until the sixty-second day. There is no specific requirements as to where the proofs shall be filed.

to *prevent further damage.* An insured who fails to protect his property adequately from further loss after the fire cannot collect for the additional loss thus occasioned.

When the damaged goods have been segregated, the insured is required to make a complete *inventory,* stating the quantity and cost of each article and the amount claimed as a loss. The inventory is used as a basis for determining value and simplifies the problem of determining the loss. If the goods destroyed were purchased by the insured in the open market, there is usually an established market value; and the quotations on the day of the fire, plus freight and handling charges, less discounts, form the basis of the valuation for adjustment purposes. If the insured is not entitled to claim market value, as in the case of a manufacturer, the acquisition cost must serve as a basis, to which is added appreciation to cover any increased cost of manufacture, or from which is subtracted depreciation if costs or values have decreased.

When the satisfactory valuation has been obtained and the element of loss computed, the figures thus obtained will serve as the basis for settlement. The representatives of the company and the insured will verify the figures and undertake to reach an agreement as to the amount of the loss and damage.

In the event an agreement cannot be reached, provision is made in the policy for an *appraisal procedure* which either party may demand. Aside from those cases in which the honest intent of one or the other of the parties may be questioned, there are instances in which an honest difference of opinion results in a disagreement as to the amount of loss or damage. To expedite settlement, in case the insured and the company shall fail to agree, provision is made to submit the loss to appraisers. The method of selecting appraisers is set forth in the policy. Awards signed by two or by three of the appraisers determine the amount of the loss. The finding is conclusive, and from it neither party can appeal, except on the ground of irregularity in the appraisal such as fraud, corrupt practices, mistake, or willful misconduct on the part of the appraisers. The burden of proof rests with the party seeking to set aside the findings of the appraisal, and unless there is clear and strong evidence of partiality, conspiracy, fraud, or palpable error, the presumption is in favor of fairness.

The number of cases in which appraisal proceedings are actually used is infinitesimally small. Most adjusters who have spent a lifetime in loss adjusting have never had a loss go to appraisal procedure. It is a procedure seldom used, but still of potential value to both parties to the contract. Besides appraisal, when an insured has complied with all the conditions and requirements of his policy and still fails to effect a settlement, he may then have recourse to *law suit* in the courts. In order that questions of liability may not accumulate against insurers and be revived at indefinite dates, the policy sets a limit within which suit must be filed. The usual policy provides: "No suit or action on this policy, for the recovery of any claim, shall be sustainable in any court of law or equity unless all the requirements of this policy shall have been complied with, nor unless commenced within twelve months next after the fire."

The fire insurance contract provides for two *options of settlement by the company:* the payment of damages for the loss, or the restoration of the subject matter of the insurance to its former condition.[4]

If a company feels that it may rebuild the damaged property to its own advantage rather than make a payment for damages, it may elect to do so. If the insurer elects to rebuild, he is held to have abandoned the alternative mode of settlement, and the insurance contract is at once converted into a building contract. The amount of damage recoverable for a breach is not thereafter limited to the amount of insurance. When the insurer elects to rebuild, he must complete the operation; and he is liable for damages, including rent, resulting through delay. When separate insurers elect to rebuild, in case of breach, it has been held that the owner may proceed against one of the insurers and collect full damages, leaving this company to seek contribution on its own account from the others.

The option to repair or replace involves the insurance carrier in the business of building construction, and the liabilities incurred make choice of rebuilding most unattractive. It is very uncommon to exercise the option. Companies prefer, when at all possible, to settle all losses by a cash payment.

In the case of merchandise, the insurer may sometimes settle a troublesome loss by agreeing upon the sound value of the damaged goods and then turning the damaged items over to a salvage company to be sold. The amount realized is credited to the insurance companies, who in turn pay the insured a total loss. However, the insured has no right to ask the company to take the property and salvage it. The policy specifically covers the point by stating there can be no abandonment to the company of the property. When, however, the appraisal indicates a loss with a salvage to be realized by the insured less than the insurance company believes it can real-

---

[4]The restoration privileges of the insurer are stated in the following clause: "It shall be optional with this Company to take all, or any part, of the property at the agreed or appraised value, and also to repair, rebuild or replace the property destroyed or damaged with other of like kind and quality within a reasonable time, on giving notice of its intention so to do within thirty days after the receipt of the proof of loss herein required."

ize, it may on its own account exercise the option to take all or part of the goods at the appraised value.[5]

While it has been held that an insured renders his policy void when he sells goods without giving the company the right to exercise the option to take the goods, it has likewise been held that after an appraisal the company must take some steps to indicate its intention to exercise the option before it can claim breach of condition, and that to ask the insured to keep the goods 30 days, while awaiting the company to indicate its intention, is unreasonable.

Special Problems. In the event of a *total loss of merchandise*, a physical inventory is, of course, impossible. The value of the destroyed property must be determined by an entirely different procedure. This is accomplished through recourse to the books and accounts of the insured. If the books are properly kept, inventories accurately taken at stated periods with all items carefully recorded at original cost, and a record kept of additions as made and of the income from sales, it is comparatively simple to compute the value of goods on hand at the time of the fire.

To accomplish this, one must take an inventory as a starting point, add to this purchases made, and deduct sales. Since the record of purchases is made on the basis of cost, and sales income is recorded on the basis of selling price, to arrive at the value of the goods on hand it is essential to reduce the item of income from sales to a figure that will represent the cost of the items sold, and not the selling price. To do this, it is essential that one know the margin of profit. The gross markup will not furnish this figure. It is obtained by finding the cost of merchandise sold during a period of a year and subtracting this figure from the income from sales for a year. This difference will be the profit for the year. Reducing the figure representing profit to a percentage of sales, one may then use this percentage figure to determine the cost of goods sold.

When the margin of profit has been determined, it is a matter of simple addition and subtraction to arrive at the value of the inventory when the fire occurred, and hence the amount of the loss. The method of determining value of inventory follows:

---

[5]While some insureds feel that it is an advantage to have the insurance company pay them a total loss and take the damaged property for salvage, there are others who see a disadvantage in this procedure. The insurance company has a right, of course, to rehabilitate the damaged property to the best advantage possible and place it on the market. The owner of the damaged merchandise may object to having it placed on the market in competition with new goods. This is so particularly of a manufacturer who is offering his product on a competitive market. For this reason many insureds prefer to keep the salvage and dispose of it on the best possible basis, giving consideration to all factors of the market.

STATEMENT OF LOSS

Inventory of stock on hand at beginning of year (cost)			$
Adjustment for depreciation			$
Actual value of stock at beginning of year			$
Subsequent purchases			$
TOTAL goods to be accounted for			$
Sales	$		
Less profit (%)	$		
Cost of goods sold	$	Deduct	$
Value of stock on hand at time of fire			$

The problem of determining value and loss or damage is more difficult for *machinery or buildings*. In the case of machinery and buildings designed for use over a long period of years, the problems of depreciation and obsolescence become factors of major importance. The solution of the difficulties they present are by no means so simple as accounting practice would indicate.

In relation to a fixed asset, *depreciation* has been defined as the inevitable decrease in value resulting from wear, tear, and the lapse of time. When the decrease in value is the outgrowth of an improvement in a manufacturing process or a discontinuance in the demand for the product manufactured, the loss is due to obsolescence. Depreciation and obsolescence do not run parallel, and arbitrary charge-offs on the straight-line basis certainly offers no accurate measure of the value. A property built during a period of low construction costs might actually be growing more valuable each year as building costs advance; yet a straight-line depreciation of some arbitrary percentage, say 5 percent, would furnish a book value of less than cost, whereas the actual value would be greater.

Because of the difficulties involved in fixing a value in the case of fixed capital for the purposes of an insurance adjustment, it is essential that a satisfactory and competent *appraisal* (an expert estimate of valuation—not the loss appraisal procedure mentioned earlier) be available as a point of departure. The insured understands that he must pay substantial sums annually for his insurance protection. He should likewise understand that the cost of an adequate appraisal is a proper charge when the placing of insurance is carried on in an efficient and businesslike manner.

When an adequate appraisal of buildings has been made by competent appraisers and has subsequently been kept up to date the problem of valuation for *total loss* is not a difficult one. When no appraisal has been made, however, some starting point must be found. A set of blueprints covering building plans, with the date of construction, furnishes such a point. The search for data often must proceed further to reliable information concerning dates of subsequent replacements or additions. An inquiry among older residents of the vicinity, a study of newspaper files, building permits, and, when pertinent, the record of property transfers will generally serve to fix the date of construction, which in turn serves to fix the depreciation when the replacement cost has been found.

Two methods are advocated for fixing value in the instance of the total destruction of the property when neither appraisal nor plans are available as a guide. One is the "discount method," based upon computing future earnings on the basis of past experience. Value is found by a process of discounting that portion of the income which remains after deducting land returns. This process is followed because land is a permanent investment, but the buildings have a measurable usefulness. Another method, known as the "square-foot method," is based upon the assumption that if a given building of a known type and construction costs a certain sum, its cost may be reduced to a square-foot basis, and the unit thus obtained may be applied to measure the value of other buildings of like construction. Both methods are faulty to some extent, but each can serve as a check on the other.

When an accurate appraisal is made within a reasonable time or when the date and cost of construction are known, values may be brought up to date with a table of price index trends. The table is computed with reference to a base year, and relative costs for any year may be found. When the present replacement value of the building is found by means of the table, it is then depreciated to compensate for its age.

In the event of *partial loss* to a building, the customary procedure in effecting an adjustment is to obtain from a reliable contractor or builder an estimate of the cost to repair and replace the damaged property. Frequently, a builder representing the insured and another representing the insurer work together in making the estimate of loss. They proceed together, calculating costs, item by item, and agreeing so far as possible whenever a discrepancy occurs in their estimates. When there are points of difference, these can be referred to the interested parties, and usually an agreement can be reached. Failure to agree in the case of partial building losses is frequently due to a misunderstanding on the part of the insured as to his coverage. Frequently claims are made for items not properly to be included in the estimate of damage. Changes in construction requirements due to building ordinances, making replacement cost more than the cost of the damaged parts, will not usually permit a claim for the extra cost. The policy does not undertake to replace old with new. Depreciation is, therefore, to be deducted from the replacement figure, although this need not be at a flat rate. Different parts of the building will be subjected to different depreciation figures, depending upon the state of the repair. For example, if a house had been painted a week before a fire, but its wooden shingles were 20 years old, and both paint and shingles are damaged, obviously no depreciation will be charged in the paint item, but the figure will be heavy in the shingle item. Architect's fees do not represent a proper claim in minor losses. When, however, the damage is such as to necessitate the employment of an architect before necessary repairs can be made, the fee represents part of the cost to repair or replace and may properly be included in the computation of the loss.

Several other special problems[6] of fire insurance losses are discussed in a later chapter on limitations on the insurer's liability. These include the important problems of *contribution and apportionment* where several contracts insure the same property, *coinsurance* requirements to encourage insurance amounts reasonably close to total values of the property, and *nonconcurrence* which involves conflicting provisions in different policies.

Marine Insurance Losses

The adjustment of marine losses involves a considerable degree of technical knowledge and, accordingly, is usually entrusted to experts. The adjuster is presumed not to represent any particular interest but to effect an equitable apportionment of the loss. His adjustment is not binding until made so by agreement but it serves in practice as the basis of settlement.

In order to establish a claim under the policy, it is necessary to present certain information which is obtainable from existing documents. As a source of proof that the loss was caused by one of the perils insured against, reference may be made to the log of the vessel. The same information, when incorporated in a document made by the master under oath, is termed the "master's protest." In the case of a claim on a cargo, the bill of lading is presented to show that the goods on which the loss is claimed were actually aboard the ship in question. The invoice of the goods serves as a basis for arriving at the value of the shipment and of determining whether or not the insurance is adequate. The insurance policy or certificate is necessary in order to determine to whom the loss is payable; and in the case of a hull loss, the certificate of enrollment showing ownership is essential. Having established a loss caused by a peril insured against and having furnished evidence of interest in the subject of the insurance, the claimant is then entitled to payment within 30 days.

---

[6] One of the most complete references to details of property loss adjustments is Prentice B. Reed, *Adjustment of Property Losses* (New York: McGraw-Hill Book Co., Inc., 1953). Another valuable reference is William C. Moore, *A Primer on Adjustments* (5th ed.; Indianapolis, Ind.: The Rough Notes Company, 1964). This book contains a good section on the new "Guiding Principles" effective in late 1963 for many overlapping insurance coverages.

An unusual circumstance prevails in ocean marine insurance if the ship has not been heard from after a reasonable time. It is then *presumed to have been lost* and a claim for an actual total loss may be made. The courts have held that there is no time fixed by law after which a missing vessel should be presumed to be lost. The length of time necessary to elapse must of necesssity depend upon the circumstances in each case, such as the vessel, her speed, the voyage, and her facilities for communication. In England, a notice of missing vessels is posted at Lloyd's, and 10 days thereafter claim may be made upon the insurers for total loss. In this country, 30 days may run after the presumption arises before the payment for loss is due.

When the cargo, or a part thereof, is thrown overboard or a part of the vessel is sacrificed for the purpose of lightening or relieving the vessel in case of necessity or emergency, the property sacrificed is said to have been "jettisoned." By the provisions of the ancient Rhodian law, property jettisoned to save other property must be contributed for by the property saved. This is the law today. The contribution is termed a *general average loss.* There are three essentials, each of which must be present, in order to establish a claim for general average. The sacrifice must be (1) voluntary, (2) necessary, and (3) successful.

It follows, therefore, that if a mast is carried away in a storm, even though the ship rides more easily thereafter, there can be no claim for general average. The act was not voluntary. The reverse is true, however, if the captain orders the mast cut away. Again, if the property for which the sacrifice is made is not saved, obviously the owners derived no benefit from the sacrifice and are accordingly under no obligation to contribute to a general average claim.[7]

The term *salvage* when used in connection with insurance and maritime law has two distinct meanings: the property which is saved or the compensation due to those who voluntarily assist in

---

[7]Because of the great difference in the detailed rules for the adjustment of general average losses in the different parts of the world, reference is frequently made in the policy to the code to be followed. The regulations commonly used are known as the "York-Antwerp Rules." This code was adopted by the Association for the Reform and Codification of the Law of Nations at meetings held at York, England, in 1864, and at Antwerp, Belgium, in 1877, and was revised and amended in 1890 at the Liverpool, England, conference, and was again further amended at Stockholm, Sweden, in 1924 and in 1950 at Amsterdam, Holland. The rules cover specifically such questions as the amount to deduct from the cost of repair of ships of different ages and construction, as well as questions involving the cutting away of wreckage, voluntary stranding, jettison of deck cargo, loss of sale, damage to engines in refloating the ship, expenses of lightening the ship when ashore, damage to the cargo in discharging, temporary repairs, loss of freight, and other disputable points. In addition to a reference to the rules in the policy, it is customary to provide in bills of lading for their use. Where, however, the rules do not apply, the law applying at the port agreed upon is used in effecting the adjustment.

saving a ship or cargo in peril. Salvors have a legal interest in the property saved, and if they and the owners of the property are unable to agree upon an amount for a reward the amount is fixed by an admiralty court. There is no fixed rule as to the amount of salvage. A vessel deserted by her crew without the intention of return is said to be a "derelict." In such case an old rule awarded the salvors one half of the property saved. This rule is now held to be an upper limit for salvage in the case of a derelict, with one third of the value as a lower limit. In cases other than derelict, the amount depends upon danger, risk, time expended, and skill necessary to save the threatened property. The work of salvors reflects to the benefit of the marine underwriters, and the marine policy assumes the liability for salvage obligations.

In the fire insurance policy, it is provided that there can be no abandonment of the damaged property to the insurers. in marine insurance the situation is not the same, and there are total losses that are actual and those that are constructive. When the subject of the insurance is wholly destroyed, irreparably damaged, or taken from the insured without hope of recovery, the loss is total and *actual*. When the loss becomes total only because the subject matter of the insurance is abandoned, or the entire property is not actually destroyed, the loss is termed *constructive*. There is a constructive total loss when the subject of the insurance has some measurable value and is available to the interested parties where it lies. So far as the insured is concerned, the loss is total, although there may be some salvage to the underwriters. An actual total loss does not require that the property be annihilated. It is sufficient that it be so destroyed that it no longer remains the thing it formerly was; or that it be beyond human means of recovery, as when it is sunk; or that it be irretrievably gone, as when it is captured.

Not in every case of partial loss is the insured entitled to abandon and claim a total loss. The rules in England and the United States are not identical. In England, when the cost of recovering the ship or goods would exceed their value when recovered, or when a ship is so damaged by a peril insured against that the cost of repairing would exceed the value of the ship when repaired, abandonment is permitted. In this country, abandonment is held to be justified, with the consequent claim for a total loss, if the cost of repairs or expenditures will be in excess of 50 percent of the value of the property when restored. Occasionally, American insurers issue a policy containing the English provisions.

A *particular average loss* differs from a general average loss in that it remains where it falls without contribution from other interests and it differs from a total loss in that the property insured is not destroyed or lost in its entirety. A part of a shipment may be totally lost, in which case the loss is total of the part and not one of particular average. The rules for ascertaining the amount of a particular average loss differ to a considerable degree with the interest involved. The more common interests which are the subject of insurance are the hull, the cargo, and the freight.

When a vessel's *hull* is so damaged that there is an evident loss, but not of a degree to warrant abandonment to the insurers, the measure of indemnity is predicated upon the cost of repairs less improvements resulting therefrom. Subject to the limit set by the face of the policy, the insured is entitled to the reasonable cost of repairs, less the customary deduction when the repairs are supplied "new for old." The question of deductions to be taken because of new for old is not altogether the simple problem today that it was formerly. In the days of wooden vessels, an arbitrary rule allowed a deduction of one third of the cost of repairs. With the advent of metal vessels, the arbitrary rule of one third was held to be excessive, particularly in the case of new vessels, and, as a consequence, a modified percentage depending upon the age and condition of the vessel and the character of the repairs became usual.

If the vessel is not repaired and the cost, therefore, is not available as a guide in the settlement of the claim, the insured is entitled to such lessening in the value of his property as is attributable to the unrepaired damage. When partial repairs are made, the insured is entitled to their cost, less allowable deductions, plus the depreciation resulting from that part of the damage that remains unrepaired. If the ship is sold in her damaged state, it has been held that the amount recoverable is her value before the casualty, less the amount for which she sold. If a sale of the damaged property is effected, the burden rests upon the insured to show that the full value of the salvage is realized.

When certain items of a *cargo* are totally destroyed, the loss is determined in the case of a valued policy by arriving at a figure determined by the proportion that the part lost bears to the value of the whole. Thus, if 5,000 barrels of potatoes are insured for full value at $10,000, and 1,000 barrels are totally destroyed, the loss is 20 per cent of the insurance. In the same case, if the policy is not written on a valued form, the indemnity is the insurable value of the destroyed or lost property measured by the invoice or cost price, plus freight, insurance, and charges for such items as packing, agents' commissions, and customs. If the goods are delivered at their destination in a damaged state, the difference between the sound and the damaged values at the port of arrival is determined. If the policy is valued, the amount of damage is reduced to a percentage and applied to the valuation as fixed by the policy.

A partial loss of *freight* interest may be the result of a partial loss to either ship or cargo, or both. The measure of indemnity is determined by finding the proportion that the lost freight interest bears to the total freight interest at risk. The percentage thus found is applied to the insurable value, in the case of an unvalued policy, or, if the policy is valued, to the amount stated in the contract. If part of the cargo is lost so that it cannot be delivered to its destination, there is a total loss of part of the freight. If the goods are delivered, though damaged, the freight is collectible, and there is no loss. If, because of a peril insured against, the voyage is discontinued and only a part of the freight is collected, the difference represents a loss.

Liability Insurance Losses

The adjustment of liability claims differs from direct damage contract claims in that the *claimant is not the insured.* The adjuster, in representing the company, is not dealing with a customer of the company as is the case in settling the usual direct damage property loss.

From the outset a liability claim carries with it an element of conflict with respect to the measure of damages. Mental attitudes frequently intensify the degree of conflict. Different individuals have a different approach and attitude to a given situation. The owner of a new Cadillac car may take great pride in its appearance. He might require a scratch on a fender to be removed at considerable expense. To another individual a scratch on the fender is but an incidental injury to be expected as part of the wear and tear of the car. He would neither spend a substantial sum to repair the scratch nor expect an insurance company to do so. On the other hand, there are those who are unreasonable in their demands where insurance is involved. Frequently, for example, where a damaged fender could be repaired, the insured will insist upon a new one. Finally, a difference in the attitude of a claimant from that of a defendant regarding the extent of an injury is natural. This is particularly the case if bodily injury is involved. Persons injured in accidents tend to exaggerate the nature and extent of the injury, while it is natural for the defendant to discount or minimize its importance.

Determining an adequate amount to compensate for a *personal injury* is not a simple process.[8] This statement is supported by the number of verdicts in widely different amounts for seemingly identical injuries. In no other area of loss adjustment are there so many imponderables and uncertainties. Even where all the factors are known and some of them are readily reducible to a monetary

[8] Many legal references would indicate this difficulty, and authors have written many pages on the subject. For example, see Patrick Magarick, *Successful Handling of Casualty Claims* (Englewood Cliffs, N.J.: Prentice-Hall, Inc., 1955).

amount, there will be others where the measure of damages will to a large degree be influenced by the fallibilities and prejudices that are characteristic of human nature.

The difficulties involved become apparent when disinterested witnesses, jurymen, and judges attempt to assign a monetary value to a severe personal injury. It can be argued that a disabling injury is the occasion of a more severe financial loss to a wage earner than to a housewife. Who can measure the loss of the housewife's care of small children? Who will differentiate with respect to the nature and amount of pain suffered? What impact will social position, financial circumstances, and reputation of the claimant have upon the amount of the settlement? Finally, what will be the effect of the ability, resourcefulness, forensic talents, and persuasiveness of the claimant's attorney if the case goes to trial? All of these factors must be weighed by the adjuster in an attempt to reach a settlement that he feels he can conscientiously recommend to his company.

Injuries that involve primarily a loss of time are not too difficult to handle. The value of the time usually is ascertainable. The same is true with respect to medical bills and hospital expenses, if any. The area of uncertainty in such cases involves suffering and inconvenience. Since the claimant tends to be conscious of loss of time and out-of-pocket expenditures, when these are taken care of, particularly if the injury is not severe, no great difficulty may be anticipated in closing the claim. These cases are settled on the basis of a generally accepted formula. This gives consideration to (*a*) wages lost because of the injury, (*b*) wages that may be expected to be lost, (*c*) age of the injured person at the time of accident, (*d*) number of dependents, (*e*) amount of medical care expense, (*f*) nature of the injury, (*g*) extent of pain suffered, and (*h*) social status of the injured person. For a person suffering from a broken limb where recovery may be expected, time lost as represented by income lost together with expenses plus a settlement for suffering is the usual measure of damages.

The situation is quite different with more serious injuries. In the case of fatality some states limit recovery by statute. Where there is a statutory limitation for death, the law may specify "instantaneous death." In such an instance claim may be made for the statutory limit for death with an additional amount, if the injured party is not killed instantaneously, for "conscious suffering." The amount claimed for conscious suffering will, of course, depend upon the magnitude of the injury and the length of time covered by the conscious suffering. Where death is not instantaneous, in addition to the statutory limitations and the award for conscious suffering, damages will include a sum for loss of wages, medical expenses, and the loss to dependents of the support of the deceased. When the injured party lives and suffers permanent injury, the problem of damages becomes increasingly complex. A comparison of verdicts where cases have gone to trial affords only a partial solution. In some low verdict areas the judgments vary substantially from other high verdict areas. The verdicts should be based upon a realistic approach to the conditions surrounding the injured person.

The extent of a claim for *damage to property* is measured by the amount of the loss occasioned the property owner. The measure of loss to any property is the difference in value between the property undamaged and the property in its damaged condition. While the cost of repair may serve as a measure of damage, there is no obligation to restore a property to its original condition if the cost of repair exceeds the value of the property before the accident giving rise to the claim. For example, an old automobile virtually demolished is worth as a claim the value of the car before the accident less its salvage value. It may cost considerably more than this figure to restore the car, but such a cost is not a proper claim for damages.

There is one point in respect to property damage liability claims that must be differentiated from direct loss insurance claims. There is no limitation of consequential loss in any liability damage claim, and loss of use may be a factor in determining the amount of the claim. Under a direct loss physical damage policy the liability of the company to the insured is limited by the policy coverage.

Following an accident that may involve a claim for damages, whether the insured feels himself to be liable or not, *notice* should be given the insurance company as promptly as possible. Companies have printed forms indicating the nature of the data they require. The company will require all pertinent information bearing upon the accident. The insured will be expected to use reasonable discretion and initiative in acquiring and recording this information. Where there is personal injury, an estimate of the extent of the injury is required. Whether or not the insured persons received first aid or medical attention is significant information. If injured parties receive medical attention, the name of the attending physician should be ascertained. If they were hospitalized, the name and location of the hospital should appear in the report. The name and address of all witnesses are required; and, if an automobile is involved, the name and address of the owner as well as the car license number should be taken. If the driver is someone other than the owner, his name, address, and driver's license form essential parts of the report. It is important to note the exact location of the accident together with weather conditions. The condition of the highway should be noted and a detailed sketch made showing the relative positions of the cars just before and after the collision. In complying with the state requirements for reporting accidents, insureds will at the same time make duplicate copies of any written forms or reports and hold them for the insurance adjuster. If one or more members of the police force are present, a notation should be made of their names or badge numbers.

Not everyone realizes the extent to which he surrenders control of adjustment when he relies for protection on a liability policy. Liability policies vest complete control of claims and all litigation arising out of them with the insurance company. The power to settle claims granted by the policy is irrevocable. In very clear language it is provided that the insured shall not admit or voluntarily assume any liability, offer to settle any claim, or incur any expense without the written consent of the company. An exception to this requirement may permit the insured to provide immediate medical and surgical relief that appears to be imperative at the time of the accident. Even in such an instance he must admit no liability. This is so even though he believes himself to be liable. An admission of liability by insured can cause him to have no further protection under the policy.

The logic of the requirement is obvious. The rule is predicated upon the assumption that the policy limits are adequate to pay the claim, and on this basis control of settlement should remain with the party who is to pay the indemnity—that is, the insurance company. In contemplating the situation the courts have pointed out that, if the insurer entrusted the matter of making settlements to its numerous policyholders, it would have a precarious existence indeed. As has been said: "We are all apt to be pretty generous when it comes to spending the money of others . . ."[9] Even when there may be a verdict in excess of the policy limits, control of the adjustment must in the last analysis center with a single determining agency and by virtue of the contract this is the insurance company.

When the report of an accident involving a claim reaches the company and coverage is verified, the insurance company immediately sets in motion the procedure leading to a settlement. Before any determination as to the extent of liability may be reached, company representatives will conduct an *investigation* to determine whether there was, in fact, negligence and whether the negligence was the proximate cause of the damage. The object of the investigation is to secure a complete and full background of the accident to be used as a basis for effecting an adjustment. All pertinent facts are secured promptly from the insured, and then contact is made immediately with claimants. In personal injury cases it is customary

[9]*Wisconsin Zinc Company* v. *Fidelity and Deposit Company of Maryland* 162 Wis., 39; 155 N.W. 1081.

to secure from the claimant his consent to interview his doctors and obtain a report from them.

After the insured and claimants have given their statements, the investigation broadens out to include any records or notices which the police may have and a copy of the police report, if any. All witnesses are interviewed and, where obtainable, written statements are taken. Investigators avoid the use of technical or legal phraseology. Each statement is prefaced by the name of the witness, his address, his relationship to the insured, if any, as well as other identifying data. There should be no uncertainty as to who the witness is and where he may be reached. He will state how he happened to be on the scene of the accident and then follow these preliminary statements with a chronological factual report. Conclusions and opinions are avoided. A factual statement in simple straightforward terms is the essence of a good report. The purpose of investigation is twofold: (*a*) the establishment of a theory of liability and (*b*) the determination of a settlement value of the claim.

The summary report prepared by the adjuster will contain all pertinent information and reach a conclusion as to liability. It will then appraise the nature of the injuries. In the case of property damage a reasonably close approximation may be given. In the case of personal injuries a settlement value is assigned in an amount which, in the adjuster's opinion, would be a proper and advantageous settlement from the point of view of the company. Such an evaluation does not undertake to establish a "bargain" figure for the company but, rather, establishes a reasonable figure that would enable the company to close the case without suit. Any points that will be of benefit to bring the case to a conclusion, such as the attitude of the claimant or his attorney, are mentioned.

While the control of an adjustment rests with the insurance company, the company in settling a loss is by no means permitted to make its own interest the prime motivating factor in arriving at a decision. The company may determine whether or not an offer or compromise of a claim shall be accepted or rejected. In determining the action to be taken concerning an offer of compromise, the insurance company is obligated to give fully as much consideration to the interests of the insured as it does to its own. The insuring agreement obligates the insurance company to defend any suit against the insured with respect to the perils covered alleging injury, sickness, disease, or destruction, even if such suit is groundless, false, or fraudulent. The insurance company may elect to effect a settlement within the policy limits; otherwise it must assume the defense of the insured.

A serious question develops when there is an *offer to settle within the policy limits* and the insurance company feels the amount of the offer to be excessive. The position of the company becomes a precarious one when it refuses an offer of settlement within the policy limits on the ground that the amount is excessive and elects to go to trial. If a judgment is then awarded against the insured in an amount in excess of the policy limits, the insured may argue that the claim should have been adjusted on the basis of the earlier favorable offer. The insured may then claim that the insurance company, having failed to make a favorable adjustment, should pay the full amount of the trial award. The insurance company is fully within its rights in making every effort to settle the claim on the most favorable basis possible. If the conduct of the company is such, where there is a conflict of interests, that the insured suffers (*a*) because of negligence or (*b*) bad faith, then the company may be held liable for the full amount of damages without regard to policy limits. These two rules, one known as the *negligence rule* and the other the *bad faith rule,* are matters of grave concern to insurers since by virtue of their operation a company using what it believes to be all reasonable care and operating within the policy contract may virtually wipe out policy limits. There is protection for the insureds since the insurance company cannot abandon or neglect a defense or deliberately take an action in its own interest at the expense of the insured except at its own peril.

The liability insurance adjuster is forced in many instances to hard decisions. He is faced with many situations where he feels that the amount of the claim is excessive. Where such is the case he is quite justified in refusing to make a settlement. In every such instance, when, after trial, a judgment is in excess of the policy limits, the adjuster knows that he may be faced with a claim for the full amount of the judgment based upon alleged bad faith. However, the insurance company has the right to do everything within its power to protect itself as to the amount it must pay within the limit of its obligation. If the insurance company operates in good faith in its effort to negotiate a settlement and in doing this allows a case to go to trial, the company cannot be held responsible for any difference in judgment that may be rendered over the policy limits.

Following an accident that results in a claim for damages, the responsibility of the insured does not cease when he turns the adjustment over to the insurance company. The *cooperation clause* obligates the insured to render full assistance in the settlement or adjustment of a suit and prohibits the insured from admitting or assuming liability. The clause is held to be a material condition; and if the insured fails to comply with its requirements, he forfeits his right to indemnity under the contract. The breach, to warrant forfeiture, must be substantive and material. Failure to comply to the letter in matters that are slight or inconsequential cannot have the effect of jeopardizing the insurance. The careful insured, however, will not attempt to determine what is consequential but will fully disclose, as accurately as possible, all information which he may have and work with the company adjusters to effect a satisfactory settlement quite as diligently as if there were no insurers.

Violations of the clause may be the outgrowth of (*a*) inconvenience or (*b*) bias in favor of the claimant. The insured may feel it to be inconvenient to attend trial. He may feel that it is the responsibility of the company to make the investigation and he may negligently disregard the obligation to secure the names of witnesses or other pertinent information; or, having information of value, he may negligently withhold it. Any willful obstruction on the part of the insured to the defense of the company violates the cooperation clause. The insured has a duty to give a full and truthful account of all the circumstances leading up to and attending an accident and, if the insurance company requires it, he must attend court and testify to these facts as a witness.

When liability has been established and a value placed on the claim, insurance companies prefer to make a prompt *settlement.* While an adjuster may draw away from a claim that is manifestly unreasonable, it is axiomatic with adjusters that litigation is to be avoided if possible. Nothing is to be gained by bringing to trial a case that can be settled reasonably in any other way, and the nearer a case comes to litigation the more expensive it becomes. This is true because, even though the claimant may get no more as a result of suit than had been offered during negotiations, the legal expenses increase. Most cases, therefore, are settled as a result of negotiations between the claimant and the insurance adjuster. If a settlement cannot be reached, the claimant may then sue the insured. It is the responsibility of the insurance company to provide the necessary defense and, within the limits of the policy, pay any awards in damages that may follow from the court action.

Not all liability claims are settled for their estimated value. There are many instances where there appears to be definite liability but where the amount of the claim seems excessive. If the claim is not too excessive, the company may elect to pay rather than assume the uncertainties of litigation and the additional attendant costs. There are other situations in which liability is doubtful and there is every reason to believe the company could win if the case were litigated. Here again the question of costs presents itself. If the case can be settled for a reasonable sum, regardless of liability, the company may prefer to close the case with such a settlement. Frequently, claims originating from premises accidents are for medical payments. Where the claimant is willing to accept such a settlement it is often to the advantage of the company to make the payment. If the case goes to a jury and negligence is found, the verdict may be much higher than the medical payments claim, and the cost of defense will, in any case, be sizable. Finally, there is the case that on the basis of the investigation would indicate no liability. However, because of the limitations of witnesses, coupled with uncertainties as to a sympathetic jury or a persuasive opposing attorney, as well as the trend of verdicts in the jurisdiction, discretion may be the better part of valor. A reasonable settlement is to be preferred to the risk of an excessive verdict resulting from a trial. In such cases the attorney for the claimant is usually willing to negotiate a settlement since his client's position is uncertain. On the other hand, if the company denies all liability he has little to lose by bringing suit.

From the foregoing it is apparent that a loss may be settled at any one of several stages. The claims adjuster may settle following the investigation. Failure to settle may result in suit. After a suit is filed, the case may be settled before trial, sometimes "on the courthouse steps." If the case goes to trial, settlement will be based upon the verdict except in the unusual situation where an appeal is entered. Every effort should be made to effect a satisfactory adjustment in the earliest possible stage.

Workmen's Compensation Insurance Losses

Claims for injury or disease made by workmen against employers are (*a*) compensation claims or (*b*) liability claims. The employer covered by workmen's compensation and employers' liability insurance contemplates that all claims will be settled as compensation claims. As in the case of liability coverages already noticed, claimants are persons other than the insured. The adjustment of compensation claims follows a somewhat different pattern from the liability claim based on negligence. While the investigation of compensation claims is essential, the investigation concerns itself with coverage and the nature and extent of the injury without the necessity of determining negligence or the degree of negligence. The liability feature of the policy is designed to complete the protection for the employer by providing liability protection when negligence may be a factor and when for some reason the injury or the injured employee is not within protection of the compensation act.

Compensation claims are based upon the provisions of a workmen's compensation act or an occupational disease act. When an employer obtains an insurance policy meeting the requirements of such acts, all liabilities with which he might be charged under the acts are assumed by the insurance company. Benefits are prescribed in the act. Workmen's compensation insurance is, in fact, group accident insurance limited to occupational injuries. Not only do the acts relieve the injured workmen of the necessity of proving negligence but they also deny workmen the right to sue under the common law.

Common law suits may be brought, however, by employees against employers for injury that does not come within the scope of the compensation acts. Such suits, for example, may be brought for the contraction of occupational diseases that are not compensable. To hold the employer liable the employee must be able to show that the contraction or aggravation of the disease was caused by the negligence of the employer. There is no statutory limit to such common law suits. Insurance covers for a specific limit of employer's liability.

Compensation acts are "liability without fault" statutes and establish a uniform payment for the injured employee measured by the nature and extent of the injury. The standard of recovery varies from state to state but is, in every instance, fixed by the legislature. This being the case the amount of the award for any compensable injury is not a problem.[10] In this respect, it is to be pointed out that compensation awards, while designed to relieve the burden for workmen injured on the job, do not attempt to adjust the compensation to the needs and circumstances of each individual. To this end awards for injuries established by compensation statutes afford little or no criteria for comparison with awards where injury results because of negligence and liability is thus established. In establishing arbitrary awards for compensation claims, which are in many instances less than could be anticipated in negligence cases, the legislatures have based the amount of these awards on the assumption that prompt payment without delays, costs, and litigation is better for all parties than fuller compensation subject to such contingencies.[11]

As in all insurance investigations the adjuster first determines the coverage. The first step following a report of an accident is to determine that the injury reported was one "arising out of and in the course of employment." Every accident, or disability possibly attributable to an accident, that involves an employee of an insured covered by compensation insurance is the subject of immediate investigation by the compensation insurance adjuster.

Compensation laws require that an injured employee give notice of an accident or injury within a specified period, usually 30 days. Upon receiving notice of the injury of an employee, the employer

---

[10]In the discussion of compensation claims adjustment, it must be recognized that the laws in the different jurisdictions will introduce differences in the detail of procedure. The overall pattern, however, is much the same in all jurisdictions.

[11]*Ruso* v. *Omaha & Council Bluffs Street Railway*, 98 Neb. 436; 153 N.W. 510.

proceeds immediately to notify the insurance company and the industrial commission.[12] If, after a check of the policy, the adjuster is satisfied that the claim is one within the scope of the policy issued by the company he outlines a plan of operation based upon the facts contained in the accident report. The injured person is interviewed and, if he is in a position to make one, a signed statement is taken. Signed statements are also taken from any available witness to the accident as a part of the routine investigation. A death case may require a postmortem examination in order to determine compensability. If an autopsy is required, steps must be taken to secure the consent of relatives. The death certificate, coroner's reports, newspaper reports, and the like are all sources of information. In the process of investigation the adjuster undertakes to secure reliable witnesses, and where possible these data are fortified by signed statements.

When the adjuster has completed his investigation, he incorporates all pertinent data in a report to the company, including a narrative report of the accident. An appraisal is made as to the effect of the injury on the particular individual. A written report of the attending physician, or any suggestions with respect to treatment, are incorporated in the report. If the accident involves any elements that afford any promise of recovery under subrogation, the facts are fully covered. While it is the expectation of the company to arrive at an agreement for compensation following the first investigation, it is sometimes necessary in borderline cases to make subsequent checks to determine the full extent and nature of the injury for the purposes of determining compensation. When a final appraisal of the injury has been made, a complete breakdown of benefits due by weeks and amounts is determined. The report will cover payments for medical benefits as provided in the compensation act or any expected payments that are anticipated. In this item are included all expenses incidental to examinations and medical treatment.[13]

---

[12]The situation varies from state to state depending upon the law. Some states operate their own "funds"; some have a single administrator instead of a commission. Procedures for filing claims, making appeals, and so on, also vary.

[13]The adjuster is particularly interested in seeing that the injured person receives proper medical care. For a time the amount available for medical care under compensation laws was limited. The earlier laws have been broadened, and at the present time in some jurisdictions there is no limit on the period of time which the employer is obligated to provide medical care. This is now considered good business from the point of view of the injured employee, the employer, and the insurance company. The best medical care will operate to reduce the period for which indemnity payments are required. This tends to reduce the overall cost of the injury. The employee is benefited by being rehabilitated or being permitted to return to work at the earliest possible date. The cost of the claim to the insurance company is reduced. A reduction in costs to the insurance carrier ultimately reflects in a reduction in the cost of the insurance to the employer.

At the conclusion of the investigation, the adjuster undertakes to reach an *agreement* with the employee with respect to compensation under the provisions of the act. When such an agreement is reached, a memorandum concerning the details signed by all parties is filed in the office of the compensation commission. If, upon review, the commission finds the agreement to be in comformity with the provisions of the compensation act, it is approved. If the agreement is found to be not in conformity with the act, the agreement is disapproved. If, on the other hand, the insurance adjuster and the employee fail to reach an agreement in regard to the compensation, appeal for an award must be made to the commission. Where the state authorities have failed to approve the agreement for compensation, or where no agreement has been made, any person interested in the proceedings may file a *petition* for an award of compensation.

Within a time specified in the act following the filing of a petition for an award, a copy of the petition is sent to all other parties named therein. Or notice may be given to the interested parties in a manner to be determined upon by the commission. A time limit is set after notice of filing of the petition for all parties interested in opposition to file an answer. Failure on the part of any party opposing the petition to file an answer within the time specified in the law does not tend to delay the action, and hearing proceeds upon the petition as filed without the answer. The state insurance authorities fix a time for hearing, and notice is given to all parties. Provision is made that the hearing usually be held in the town where the accident occurred.

If it is established from the petition that the compensation agreement has not been reached because there appear to be facts in dispute, provision is made to hear all witnesses that may be presented, or by agreement the claims from both parties to such facts may be presented by affidavits. Where there is no dispute with respect to facts, the parties may file with the commission an agreed statement of facts for a ruling upon the applicable law. From the evidence thus presented at the hearing the commissioner, or other state authority acting in behalf of the commissioner, makes a summary decision regarding the merits of the controversy. The findings of the commissioner both of fact and rulings of law are filed in the office of the commissioner, and a copy of the findings is mailed to all interested parties. The decision reached at such a hearing, in the absence of fraud, upon all questions of fact is final and binding upon all the parties at interest.

Compensation laws set a time limit within which a petition for compensation award is to be filed. If an agreement as to compensation or a petition for an award is not filed within the time limit established in the act, the employee's claim for compensation is barred. While compensation is being paid, under any agreement of award, and any of the parties at interest feel that conditions have so changed that payments should be adjusted either upward or downward or discontinued altogether, the party who wishes the change may ask for a review. Upon review by the compensation commission, the award may be increased, diminished, or discontinued altogether; the action will depend upon the facts as presented at the time of the review.

When the injured employee returns to work or is fully recovered, the employer notifies the insurance company and the supplemental report is filed with the industrial accident commission. In either instance the case is closed and compensation terminated. A supplemental report is also required if incapacity recurs or if the injured employee dies.

Life Insurance Losses

In the ordinary course, the settlement of life claims devolves upon the life insurance agent. Unlike other fields of insurance, for the usual life insurance case there is no specialized claim adjuster whose function it is to ascertain the amount of the claim and make payment to the insured or his beneficiary. In the unusual situation where a claim is questioned, the law department of the company will cooperate with the claims department and local legal assistance may be retained if the circumstances seem to warrant such action.

Since life insurance in its simplest form undertakes to pay a stipulated sum or equivalent annuity upon the death of the insured, most claims are death claims. However, such policies as the endowment contract provide that a stipulated sum or annuity equivalent be paid upon the survival of the insured to a fixed date or age. The choice as to the method of payment may be made by the insured or by the beneficiary if the insured has not made a choice. The life insurance policy does not provide for payment upon death of the insured but rather for payment upon submission of *proof of death* to the company. This notice may be given by a beneficiary, the legal representative of the insured, or any interested party. The insurance company has its own forms for proof of death. These are supplied by the company representative who cooperates with the interested parties in securing their prompt completion. Every effort is made by company representatives to effect the promptest settlement possible in the circumstances.

Life insurance contracts now issued provide that the policy shall be *incontestable* by the company after a certain designated period during the lifetime of the insured, usually two years. The clause gives the company time to investigate any factors bearing on the application, and at the same time results in greater certainty to insured and beneficiary after the two year period. The incontestable clause prohibits the insurance company from raising defenses later that would be hard for the policyholder or his beneficiaries to disprove, such as those based upon misrepresentation, concealment, warranties, or misrepresentations amounting to fraud. Thus it is rare that these so-called "inception factors of defense" are considerations in determining the validity of a life insurance claim. Occasionally, however, under the incontestable clause the company has the right to contest payment if the applicant has by his acts concealed material facts or resorted to fraud to secure the policy. Thus, for example, if an applicant for insurance secures a policy and dies within a year and it can be shown that he was suffering from tuberculosis but sent a substitute to pass the medical examination, there would be no obligation to make payment. In order to void such a contract it would have to be contested within the period of limitation established in the policy. After the period of limitation set forth in the incontestable clause, the policy is payable in accordance with its terms.

In determining the liability of the insurer for a death claim under a life insurance policy, the question of whether or not the insured committed *suicide* may upon occasion become important. The policy provides for a return of premiums paid in the event of self-destruction within a period of a year or in some instances within two years. If suicide is suspected but cannot be proved, there is a presumption against it. This means that the life insurance company, if it undertakes to contest the payment of a policy on the basis of suicide, must establish the fact by a preponderance of evidence. This is accomplished when the evidence is such that no other reasonable inference may be drawn from the circumstances.

In cases where policies provide that, if the insured dies as a result of *accidental death,* double (or sometimes more) the face of the policy is to be paid the beneficiaries, proof must be submitted that the death was accidental. The whole question of accidental death in borderline cases, as it applies to life insurance policies, is surrounded by uncertainty. This arises out of (*a*) court decisions and (*b*) the different wording of the various insurance contracts themselves.[14] Death by accidental means must usually be "independent of all other causes." Policies may provide further that there is no liability if death is due, directly or indirectly, to disease or bodily

[14]In *Landress* v. *Phoenix Mutual Life Insurance Company* (291 U.S. 491), Mr. Justice Cardozo referred to accident insurance law as the "Serbonium bog." The reference from Milton's *Paradise Lost* (Book II, line 592) reads "A gulf profound as that Serbonium bog. Betwixt Domiata and Mount Casius old, Where armies whole have sunk."

or mental infirmities. In such case it might be assumed that there should be no liability if disease or bodily infirmity contributed in any way to the death, and liability results only if accident alone was the cause of the death. A strict interpretation of this clause might work serious injustice since the average normal person is rarely free from all infirmities. With this in mind, it has been stated that a policy of insurance is not accepted with the thought that the coverage is restricted to an Apollo or a Hercules.[15]

It is the responsibility of the company representative when claim is made for double indemnity to determine whether or not there is coverage. Where there is any doubt as to whether disease is a contributing cause in any given death, the final resort for determination is a jury.[16] To establish a case it must be shown that the accident or injury probably caused the insured's death. The causal connection between the accident or injury and the insured's death must be shown to be possible. The company representative will complete for the beneficiaries proofs of claim when death is beyond question accidental. In situations involving doubt a complete report is submitted to the claims department of the home office. Here a decision is made indicating the company's opinion pertaining to liability. If the company denies liability for double indemnity and the beneficiary brings legal action, then attorneys are retained and the case is finally settled on the basis of the court decision.

If the life insurance provides for a lump-sum settlement, it is a simple matter to close the claim. It is equally simple if the policy provides for a distribution under one or a combination of the *settlement options*. If, however, there is no provision made by the insured for a settlement other than a lump-sum payment, and the needs of the beneficiary are such that the use of one or more of the settlement options is indicated, then the settlement of the claim will take on additional complications.[17] This may involve a completely planned settlement, utilizing the policy proceeds for cash, interest, installments, or life income payments. A planned settlement may be an agreement made with (*a*) the policyowner or (*b*) the beneficiary. An agreement with the policyowner may provide for the distribution of endowment or cash surrender benefits to the policyowner himself as retirement income, or for the distribution of benefits payable at the insured's death to designated beneficiaries. An agreement with the beneficiary, following the death of the

---

[15]Justice Cardozo in *Silverstein* v. *Metropolitan Life Insurance Company* (254 N.Y. 81; 171 N.E. 914).

[16]*Bennett* v. *Metropolitan Life Insurance Company,* 14 C.C.H. Life Cases 97; 212 Pac. (2d) 970.

[17]For examples of some of the problems and their solutions, see Burt A. Richardson, *Settlement Procedures in Life and Health Insurance* (Decatur, Ga.: Victor Publications, 1963).

insured, may utilize one or more of the settlement options to provide for differing needs. As a matter of contract, combination options are subject to the consent and approval of the insurance company. Not only are options combined, but the agreement may include the power to change from one option to another, the privilege of increasing or decreasing installment payments, and withdrawal privileges.

SUMMARY

This chapter has reviewed one of the major functions of insurers, the payment of losses. As it is more popularly known, *insurance adjusting* has the purpose of providing prompt and fair settlement of all claims made under the contracts of insurance. The process must be equitable not only to the insured, but also to beneficiaries, other third parties, and the insurance organizations involved. The payment of losses is performed by the insurers or their agents, often with the help of different insurance claimsmen known as *staff* adjusters, *independent* adjusters, *public* adjusters and adjustment *bureaus.* The claims procedures vary considerably among the various fields of insurance. The steps to be taken, the documents used, and the problems encountered are illustrated by reference to the contracts of fire, marine, liability, workmen's compensation, and life insurance.

FOR REVIEW

1. How would you describe the purposes which (*a*) the policyholder and (*b*) the insurer should have in effecting a loss payment under an insurance contract?
2. After a fire in the plant of X, the insured telephones his agent, notifying him of the loss. Does this comply with the requirements of the New York standard policy?
3. X owns a warehouse in which pianos and other musical instruments are stored. A fire occurs on the top floor burning a hole in the roof. He advises his employee following the fire to touch nothing until the adjusters arrive. Is this good advice? Explain your answer.
4. B operates a filling station. One of the attendants lights a match in order to light a cigarette. The lighted match ignites gasoline fumes, and the resulting explosion wrecks the filling station. Is this a fire loss?
5. In adjusting a fire insurance loss it becomes necessary to determine "the actual cash value of the property at the time of loss" in order to determine the extent of the fire insurance company's liability. Reference is frequently made to "sound" value in connection with insurance losses. Is there any difference between the two? Would "assessed value" or the "appraised value" for the settlement of an estate have any bearing upon actual cash value?
6. Who adjusts insurance losses? Why are different types of claimsmen used in the various fields of insurance? Include reference to the major advantages of an insurer using the different types of claimsmen which you have identified.

7. Compare the special problems of loss payment in:
   a) Fire insurance.
   b) Marine insurance.
   c) Liability insurance.
   d) Workmen's compensation.
   e) Life insurance.
8. Under the fire insurance contract, what are the obligations of the insured after a loss has occurred?
9. Are valuation problems in a fire insurance loss different for buildings, merchandise, and other types of property? Explain.
10. To save a ship, a certain part of the cargo was jettisoned. In opening the hold, water destroyed a substantial part of the remaining cargo. May the owner of the damaged goods make a general average claim as a result of the water loss?
11. In marine insurance losses, why are the following terms important in settling losses: constructive total loss? particular average? salvage? freight interests?
12. Why are loss payments under liability insurance contracts fully under the control of the insurer rather than the insured? Does this mean that the policyholder has nothing to do in regard to a liability claim under his policy?
13. If a suit has been tried and the defendant found to be liable for damages within the limits of the policy, what is the position of the liability insurance company if it insists upon an appeal and the higher court renders a verdict in excess of the policy limits?
14. X brought action against Y, an insured, for alleged personal injuries. X offered to settle for a sum that was within the policy limits. The insurance company refused the offer and allowed the case to go to trial. The policy limits were $5,000. The claimant obtained a verdict of $7,500. X was unable to collect the $2,500 in excess of the policy limits from Y, and so she brought action for this amount against the insurance company. She argued that the insurance company owed her the full amount of the verdict because it had refused her offer to settle within the policy limits. Is this situation, in your opinion, one in which the insurance company may be liable for an amount in excess of the policy limits?
15. What is different about liability insurance losses as opposed to property insurance losses? Do these characteristics make loss payments easier or more difficult to make? Explain.
16. Following the Texas City disaster, action was brought against the federal government in which approximately 273 suits were consolidated. Claims of 8,485 persons were involved, and the damages claimed amounted to $360 million. Negligence was alleged. It was this negligence of the federal government, it was claimed, that was the proximate cause of the disaster. It was brought out in the trial that the federal government manufactured ammonium nitrate fertilizer, which was a dangerous explosive and a fire hazard, and, with knowledge of the danger involved, permitted the material to be handled and shipped in the city area without giving warning to the public. What is the significance of this suit from the point of view of the insurance company? What is the significance of the findings by the trial court that each shipment was held to be dangerous to the public and that the government was liable for the damage? What was the effect of reversal on appeal? Where did the insurance companies stand with respect to payment during litigation?

17. B drives a truck for the X company. All drivers for the company are given a set of safety regulations. All drivers are warned not to exceed the legal speed limit while driving on the highways. X is seriously injured while driving at 45 miles an hour in an area where the legal limit is 25 miles an hour. The employer contends that there is no compensation liability for the injury because the injured employee was violating specific instructions of the employer at the time of the accident. What is your opinion?

Chapter 6

UNDERWRITING, REINSURANCE, AND OTHER FUNCTIONS

PART Two of this text has approached the study of insurance on a functional basis. The major activities of insurance organizations have been analyzed on a separate basis, including individual chapters on the designing of the insurance product (or contract fundamentals), the marketing of insurance, and the payment of losses. A final major part of the process of insurance is *underwriting*, the selection and rating of the risks which are insured.

RELATIONSHIP OF MAJOR INSURANCE FUNCTIONS

The functions of an insurer are necessarily closely related to each other. No one activity exists alone, and each has many direct effects on the other. For example, the types of contracts offered by an insurer may determine how they are distributed through an agency system to the policyholders. Agents often are important in helping to redesign insurance contracts to meet specific needs of the insurance market. How loss payments are made is affected considerably by the objectives and scope of the marketing system used.

The interrelationship of the major insurance activities is nowhere more apparent than in the underwriting process. An insurer who has organized a good system of distributing a wide range of insurance contracts, and set up logical procedure for loss adjustments, still cannot operate successfully without proper attention to the selection and pricing of its product. This chapter emphasizes the underwriting techniques of insurers. The *underwriters*[1] of a company are those who have the task of accepting or rejecting (or revising, perhaps) insurance contracts which the marketing system brings to the insurer. Whether or not the underwriting function is

[1]The term is often used in a variety of other ways besides the meaning here. In everyday insurance language it frequently is used to refer to the agent or salesman. Even the professional designations of C.L.U. (Chartered Life Underwriter) and C.P.C.U. (Chartered Property Casualty Underwriters) use the word underwriter in a broad sense to mean one who writes or does business in insurance. Sometimes the underwriters are the actual insurers, as when one refers to the underwriters at Lloyd's of London.

properly carried out, of course, has an important effect on the frequency and size of insurance losses.

A complete summary of insurance underwriting cannot be attempted in one chapter. Some of the specific methods and problems of underwriting must be deferred until later when a greater familiarity with the various insurance contracts has been achieved. Here the student should strive for a basic knowledge of the general functions of selecting and rating risks in insurance. The process of *reinsurance,* or insurance purchased by insurers, is so closely connected with underwriting that it also is discussed in this chapter.

UNDERWRITING

Purposes

Underwriting is a function not found in other businesses. As opposed to marketing or financing and other normal business functions, it is a unique activity of insurance. (The only activity closely related to it is the credit selection process of banks and savings and loan institutions.) One might ask why underwriting is found only in the insurance business, and why it is so important as to be classed as one of the major functions of an insurer.

A general description of the process is simple: underwriting is the selection and rating of risks which are transferred to an insurer. Selection implies that there are some acceptances and some rejections, or risks that will not be accepted for insurance. An understanding as to why risks must be selected by an insurer, and some rejected, will explain both the uniqueness and the importance of insurance underwriting.

Suppose an insurer was willing to write an insurance contract for every individual who asked for protection against loss. Or suppose it automatically accepted every person or business to whom the marketing force of the insurer had sold the idea of completing an application for insurance. Would it be sound business practice for an insurer to operate in this manner? The student may at first answer: "Of course. The company needs large numbers of risks and a diversification or spread among various kinds of risks, geographical locations and so on. Why shouldn't an insurer accept all the separate risks it can get?" After further consideration the student might add: "Naturally, the insurer won't want the *bad* risks, or those which seem to offer a high probability of loss, for it will lose money in writing such poor risks."

A more complete answer might then suggest itself. The insurer does not want bad risks, it is true; but even bad risks could be accepted if the price charged for the contract were high enough to pay for all losses and expenses and still permit the insurer a profit on the business. Here is the crux of the problem—the insurer must only accept policyholders who will in total be *profitable* risks. The purpose of underwriting is thus found to be the acquisition of insureds who, at least in the long run for all those selected by the insurer, will return a profit to stockholders (or policyholders of a mutual-type insurer).

An important corollary to understanding the underwriting function is the fact that most insurance prices are based upon an *average* rate for an entire class or group. Some insureds within each class will be better than average and some worse than average. Which type of policyholders will an insurer who does no selection of risks tend to have? A moment's thought will indicate the extent of the problem: those persons who are better than average are most likely not to want or need the insurance, and conversely, those persons who know they are worse than average will be most likely to desire the insurance contract. This result is natural, for in everyday language the bad risks, at the average rate, are obtaining a bargain.

The tendency for insurance contract applications to include a preponderance of "poorer than average for the class" risks is found throughout the field of insurance. Whenever the applications result from free choice on the part of the individuals who wish to transfer their risks to an insurer, the choice will be against the insurer. This tendency is called *adverse selection,* and every insurance company must be aware of its existence and results. Where adverse selection against the insurer exists, the results can be financial disaster, as the insurance company ends up with poor risks but obtains only an average price for the loss protection it provides. The result is apt to be the opposite of the stated purpose of insurance underwriting —a large, safely diversified, profitable group of risks.

Illustrations of adverse selection, if underwriting selection were not practiced by insurers, will show why an insurer cannot just accept all insurance applications. In life insurance, who would be the most likely persons to apply if no medical examinations were required before the contract were written? Naturally, those persons in poor health are likely to die much sooner than the average person in the population. In fire insurance, who would be sure to apply for a fire insurance policy? Most likely, those persons who have had frequent fire damage, or those who have obvious hazards such as inflammable products, poor fire protection, uncertain heating appliances, careless employees, and the like. In theft insurance, also, the typical application would tend to come from applicants who have had many thefts, or those situations where valuable properties were exposed to temptations created by lack of proper burglary or robbery protection.

The major need for insurance underwriting thus stems from the tendency toward adverse selection which without underwriting would be ruinous to insurers. Even with selection by the insurer of the risks it will accept, some adverse selection always exists whenever a class or group rate is used. Profitable risks can only be achieved by careful selection of risks which reasonably offsets the adverse selection factors involved in insurance applications. The insurers also need to know as much as possible about the policyholders it accepts, for only then can fair classifications and sufficient prices be determined. The process of underwriting is the means by which the insurer evaluates the potential risks it has been asked to accept. A compromise is often necessary between two objectives: (1) to obtain a *large number* of individual risks within each classification so that reasonable predictability of losses is possible, and (2) to obtain *homogeniety* of risks within each classification so that reasonable equity between the better and poorer individual risks is achieved. The care with which an insurer combines these objectives is vital to its underwriting success and thus the success of the whole operations of the insurer.

Selection of Risks

Underwriting involves both the selection of risks and the pricing of the contracts which are to be issued. These two parts of underwriting are closely related. If an adequate price for a class of risks has been established, the insurer must underwrite to secure at least an average group of policyholders. Otherwise, losses paid will exceed the premium income for paying losses. If the pricing for an insurance contract is inadequate, then even normal underwriting methods will fail to produce a profitable group of insureds. The alternative in such a case is to increase prices or practice severe risk selection, only accepting the best risks of each class. Despite the necessary inter-relationship between pricing and selection in the underwriting process, the two parts are separated in this section in order to provide a sufficient number of examples of each.

The Agent and Company as Underwriters. The choice of policyholders for most insurers begins with the underwriting done by the agent. Except for the relatively few applications which are initiated by the insured himself, there is substantial selection of risks performed by the agent in most lines of insurance. Each time an agent prepares a prospect list or, for example, telephones Mr. White instead of Mr. Green to sell insurance, he is providing the first step in underwriting. If an insurer employs high-caliber and well-qualified agents, they often will try to choose their clients from good homes, reasonably high-income groups, good neighborhoods, less dangerous occupational groups, and so on.

Even though the agent does some underwriting for the insurer, most of the underwriting is performed by salaried employees in the home offices and branch offices. This is true for a combination of reasons. The agent, though he should have his companies' interests in mind as he sells insurance, cannot perform all the needed underwriting services. His position is not completely unbiased, either, for he is paid on a commission basis regardless of the quality of the contracts he sells. Sometimes he may not be qualified to make the selection, as for example in life insurance where medical examinations are usually essential. Again, the agent may not have all the necessary information to make proper underwriting choices, as in automobile insurance where only preliminary underwriting information is secured by the agent. The company is in a much better position to check with the state motor vehicle department for the applicant's past accident record, and with credit investigation companies for financial and moral faults. The lack of data by the agent, and his technical inability in specialized fields such as medicine or engineering, place the prime responsibility for underwriting with the insurer. This is logical, for it is the insurer that is accepting the risks, and the insurer that is obligated to pay the losses in the insurance contracts.

The general technique of the insurance company is to provide underwriting rules to be carried out by its agents and company personnel in the underwriting departments. Agents receive both instructions on what risks not to write as well as encouragement in the form of directives and sales contests which specify which types of contracts and what kinds of policyholders are particularly desired. In fire and liability insurance, prohibited lists are common. These lists may specify bars and bowling alleys, for example, as uninsurable.

Other types of applicants are often specified as insurable only after the insurer has detailed information and an opportunity to have a company representative investigate or inspect the property of the applicant. Examples of such a referral situation, where the agent may not have authority to bind the coverage immediately, are steam boiler explosion risks and comprehensive liability risks for businesses.

The binding authority which many agents possess for putting the contract into effect immediately is a good example of the fact that agents do perform important underwriting services for their insurers. Many property insurance contracts go into effect in this manner. The insurer receives the application and the contract which has been put into effect at the same time. It may then request cancellation under the contract terms, but this would be an unusual case after the agent has written the business. The insurer is more likely, even in somewhat doubtful cases, to continue the protection and perhaps ask for additional information prior to renewal of the contract. Underwriting by the insurer, and agent, takes place not only at the time of the original application but also at each expiration and renewal of the insurance contract.

Sources of Underwriting Information. The sources of underwriting information upon which insurers rely include: (1) the applicant, (2) the agent, (3) the insurer's own inspection or claim department, (4) company bureaus and associations, and (5) outside inspection agencies. The applicant for an insurance contract often makes written as well as oral statements. Signed written statements are normal procedure in life and health insurance, and the applications become a part of the contract. Automobile and business risk applicants also frequently prepare written statements as a means of giving the company basic underwriting details. Agents for many kinds of insurance provide their companies with reports, opinions, and recommendations which are valuable aids to the insurer in selecting its policyholders. Many insurers maintain separate inspection departments to provide the company underwriters with physical inspection and engineering reports on the properties of applicants. The insurer's claim department, too, may be a source of important underwriting data for renewal decisions.

Insurers also combine efforts to maintain bureau or association lists of undesirable insurance applicants. The Medical Information Bureau (M.I.B.) for life insurance, and the Index Bureau of the National Bureau of Casualty and Surety Underwriters for automobile insurance, offer a centralized index service of applicants who have been refused insurance, had frequent losses, or had suspicious or fraudulent claims.

Many kinds of insurance use outside agencies to supplement the information gathered from the applicants, agents, and insurer representatives. Physicians supply life insurance companies with medical reports after physical examination of the applicants. Standard financial reference services such as Dun and Bradstreet are used for many insurance applications from businesses. Automobile insurers have in recent years increasingly used credit investigations[2] as routine checks on new applications, especially for younger drivers. These are not just financial investigations for credit purposes, but also are valuable in determining poor habits or moral problems of the prospect from such sources as employers, neighbors, or associates.

Rating of Risks

General. The pricing of insurance contracts is a specialized part of underwriting which requires the services of experts. Basically,

[2]By such organizations as Retail Credit Company, Hooper-Holmes and others. Life insurance companies have used such services for many years as a common procedure.

insurance rates are calculated by *actuaries* who apply sound principles of mathematics to the particular pricing problems of insurance. The manuals, rate charts, and formulas which the actuaries develop for the insurers and company bureaus are used by the agents as they quote the contract price of insurance to the policyholders.

The fundamental part of most insurance rates is the estimate of future losses. The task is complicated in some kinds of insurance by the lack of data in regard to past loss experience. In some types of insurance, such as life insurance, the job of setting correct prices is aided by a wealth of past experience, but hampered by the need for predictions involving many years into the future. The scope of life insurance mortality data is amazing, and its techniques of analyzing and graduating the recorded data are the field of study known as actuarial science. The methods and calculations are sufficient to merit separate study of these procedures in later chapters of this text.

Fire Insurance as an Example. As an example of property insurance rating methods, the field of fire insurance offers a valuable insight into the many different factors which must be considered in setting the price to be charged for insurance. The problems involved are numerous, and it is through cooperation of insurers in rating bureaus that many of the solutions are reached.

Rating Bureaus. The work of fire insurance rating is placed in the hands of specialized rating bureaus. Headquarters for the various organizations are located at strategic points throughout the country. Jurisdiction over a specific territory is assigned each organization, and branch offices sufficient to meet the territory's needs are located in the important congested areas. There are about 40 such organizations handling the problems of fire rating in this country.[3]

[3]Fire insurance rates are regulated by the state. The All-Industry Fire Marine and Inland Marine Rate Regulatory Bill makes provision for (*a*) rating organizations and (*b*) advisory organizations. Every insurer is obliged to file with state authorities all rates, plans, and rules which he proposes to use except inland marine risks which by general custom of the business are not written according to manual rates or rating plans. An insurer may satisfy its obligation to make such filings by becoming a member of or a subscriber to a licensed rating organization which makes such filings, and by authorizing the state insurance authorities to accept such filings on its behalf. A corporation, an unincorporated association, a partnership, or an individual may make application for license as a rating organization. The application specifies the kinds of insurance for which rates are to be provided. Among other things the application must state the qualifications of the applicant to act as a rating organization. If the state insurance authority approves, a license is issued authorizing the applicant subject to law to promulgate rates. Section 6(*d*) of the bill provides: "Any *rating organization* may provide for the examination of policies, daily reports, binders, renewal certificates endorsements or other evidences of insurance, or the cancellation thereof, and may make reasonable rules governing their submission. Such rules shall contain a provision that in the event any insurer does not within sixty days furnish

(Continued on next page)

Some operate only within one state, while others combine several states within their territorial jurisdiction.

It is the function of the rating bureau to apply the schedule in use in the territory to each property that is the subject of insurance. The task is large, and to accomplish it requires a huge staff of inspectors, engineers, and scores of experts highly trained in specialized fields. Rate manuals and tariffs are published, and corrections are furnished from time to time to insurance companies and their representatives. Application for a new rate, or for rerating a building already rated, may be filed with the rating organization either by the owner of the property or by an insurance agency or company interested as an insurer.

Rate Analysis. The premium charged the insured for fire insurance is based upon a rate fixed by the rating authority to whom this responsibility has been delegated. The insured who handles his affairs in a businesslike manner will not be content to be told that the rate on his building is 2 percent per annum when he knows that across the street a property owner pays one half of 1 percent. First, he will want the discrepancy justified, and, second, he will want to know to what extent a downward revision of his own rate is within his control. This information is all obtainable through an analysis of the makeup of the rate.

The effort to eliminate, so far as possible, the element of judgment and substitute therefore a set of scientifically determined working rules has had the effect of making the problem of rate determination for a sizable structure a complicated and technical procedure.[4] The average insurance agent is not equipped to make, nor will he presume to make, a rate analysis. This work is assigned to highly trained experts who have qualified by education and experience for this branch of the business. The agent and the insured, however, may take the makeup of the rate when the work is com-

---

satisfactory evidence to the rating organization of the correction of any error or omission previously called to its attention by the rating organization, it shall be the duty of the rating organization to notify the (commissioner) thereof. All information so submitted for examination shall be confidential." In contrast to a rating organization, Section 10 (*a*) of the bill defines an *advisory organization* as follows: "Every group, association or other organization of insurers, whether located within or outside this state, which assist insurers which make their own filings or rating organizations in rate making, by the collection and furnishing of loss or expense statistics, or by the submission of recommendations, but which does not make filings under this Act, shall be known as an advisory organization." Fire insurance rating organizations check the rates on all policies issued by subscribers or members. The home office copy of the policy is submitted through the rating organization. This serves as a check against errors and precludes discrimination.

[4]No claim can be made to an invincible plan that will provide an accurate rate for every building in relation to all other buildings. What has been accomplished is the establishment of rating systems that, within workable limits, appraise the hazards for individual risks and fix a reasonable rate on the basis of this appraisal.

pleted by the rating authority and, upon inspection, determine where it will be profitable to eliminate hazards for which charges are made and thereby reduce the rate.

Fire insurance rates as promulgated by the bureaus fall into one of two categories: (1) class and (2) specific. Class rates are sometimes known as "tariff rates." The terms "class," and "tariff" are interchangeable, and the term customarily used in the community is frequently the outgrowth of local custom.

Classification. Fire insurance risks are classified for rate-making purposes by (1) perils, (2) occupancy, (3) protection, and (4) structure.

It is apparent that the experience for a given unit of insurance will vary with respect to the nature of the *perils* covered. For purposes of classification by perils, the following groups have been established; (*a*) fire; (*b*) time element and loss of income (business interruption, use and occupancy, errors and omissions, profits and commissions, rents, leasehold, and extra expense); (*c*) extended coverage endorsements; (*d*) windstorm and hail (except growing crops); (*e*) water damage, including sprinkler leakage; (*f*) riot, civil commotion, and explosion; and (*g*) earthquake.

In the residential risks *occupancy* category are dwellings and farms, housing developments, single-ownership apartment buildings, boarding and rooming houses, nurses' and sisters' homes, and fraternity and sorority houses. The mercantile building category includes stores, dwellings, and all types of mercantile buildings together with contents. The nonmanufacturing category includes office and bank risks, and also telephone exchanges, telegraph central stations, and radio and broadcasting facilities. Included in this category are hotels, commercial boarding and lodging houses, clubs, theaters, auditoriums, and other places of amusement. It also includes garages, service and filling stations, educational institutions, libraries, and museums, as well as buildings used for warehousing and storage. The manufacturing category includes buildings and contents such as those used in the manufacture of food and kindred products, clothing and cloth products, textiles, furs and fur goods, paper and pulp, and other manufactured items. To be included in the sprinklered category, the risk must be equipped with an approved automatic sprinkler system with all principal hazards of the property adequately protected.

Classification by *protection* divides risks into (*a*) protected and (*b*) unprotected. A protected risk is one located with 500 feet of a public hydrant connected with a town or city water supply. Moreover, the risk must be within 1½ miles of an available, regularly organized and equipped fire station.

Risks are classified as to *structure* thus: (*a*) fire resistive, as classified by the rating bureau having jurisdiction; (*b*) brick, as classified by the rating bureau having jurisdiction; (*c*) frame, as classified by the rating bureau having jurisdiction; (*d*) wind resistive, in connection with extended cover endorsements and windstorm coverages; and (*e*) earthquake resistive, applicable to earthquake coverages. Generally speaking, to be classified as fire resistive, a building must have all bearing walls of brick, stone, or reinforced concrete. All floors, roofs, nonbearing walls, curtain and panel walls in skeleton construction, and principal partitions must be of brick, concrete, or other incombustible material. The second group, those buildings classified as brick, are required to have walls of brick, stone, concrete, or equivalent masonry construction, though the interior and roof construction may be of wood. Frame additions, which are not in excess of one third of the ground floor area, do not have the effect of removing the building from the brick classification. All risks not classified as either fireproof or brick fall into the third group and are classified as frame. In the case of windstorm and earthquake coverages, if the rating bureau having jurisdiction has not promulgated definitions, fire-resistive construction is regarded as the equivalent of wind-resistive, and fire-resistive construction and dwellings are regarded as least hazardous in the earthquake category.

Class Rates. Class rates apply to all properties that fall within a given category or classification. Classifications are defined according to differentials with respect to major features of (*a*) construction, (*b*) occupancy, and (*c*) class of fire protection. The construction classification concerns itself with whether or not the building is frame or brick and whether or not the roof is combustible or noncombustible. Occupancy is considered in connection with dwelling risks and concerns itself primarily with the number of families. With respect to fire protection, towns and cities in each state are grouped into classes, and all communities falling within a particular class take the same rates.

The outstanding example of class rating is to be found in detached dwelling houses or residential homes. Class rates are promulgated to apply to all dwellings not subject to some special hazard. Class-rated dwellings are subdivided into groups in accordance with construction, with a rate assigned to each class. The rate also varies as to the classification of the city or town and the number of families occupying the property. In addition to class-rated dwellings, some jurisdictions apply class rates to buildings such as churches, apartment buildings, and others where the elements of construction and occupancy are similar enough to permit a ready grouping into rate classes.

Specific or Schedule Rates. When class rates do not apply, the rate is said to be "specific." *Specific rates* are promulgated by the rating bureaus for mercantile, manufacturing properties, and all types of business establishments. Public buildings and schools are likewise so rated. Specific rates are determined by the application to the particular risk of a schedule or formula designed to measure the relative quantity of fire hazard with respect to the particular risk. The system is known as *schedule rating.* Specific rates are published for individual towns and cities, and each building with its contents is individually rated.

Schedule rating is a plan by which hazards with respect to any particular risk are measured. A schedule has been defined as ". . . an empirical standard for the measurement of relative quantity of fire hazard."[5] It undertakes to produce an equitable tariff of fire insurance costs. The schedule rate is a development of the recognition of the differences in hazards with respect to different risks. Schedule rating takes into consideration the various items contributing to the peril of fire. Among these are the construction of the building under consideration and its occupancy with a view to determining which features either enhance or minimize the probability of loss. Credits and charges representing departures from standard conditions as to building construction, occupancy, protection, and exposure are incorporated in the schedules. Thus, a schedule rate is the sum of all charges less the sum of its credits, and the schedule itself constitutes a standard for the measurement of the fire hazard.

Schedule rating has not by any means solved the fire insurance rating problems. A schedule, of itself, is an arbitrary and empirical standard. As among several or many risks using the same schedule, equity and uniformity as among insureds may be obtained. However, where several different schedules are in use, and each produces a different result with respect to a given risk, the question may properly be asked as to whether the schedule in use is producing a rate that meets the objective of the rating laws. It would appear that in a territory where different schedules are in use and each produces a different result not all can be correct.[6] It is also true that even though the schedule in effect produces an equitable

[5]Jay S. Glidden, *Analytic System for the Measurement of Relative Fire Hazard, an Explanation* (Chicago: Jay S. Glidden, 1916), p. 17. Mr. Glidden was the author of this explanation of the Analytic System but it was copyrighted by J. V. Parker. The Analytic System for the Measurement of Fire Hazard, that is, the rating instrument itself, was originally copyrighted by A. F. Dean, then by J. V. Parker, and is now copyrighted by R. D. Hobbs.

[6]One rating organization uses a total of 128 different schedules, according to the report of an examination made by the state insurance department. The report points out that for some classes different schedules are used in different areas under the jurisdiction of the bureau. In the report of the examination it is stated: "A review of the requirements of the schedules showed that in many cases there was duplication; in other cases it was difficult to determine which schedule should be used; and it was also noted that the use of each schedule would produce a different rate."

rate, unless risks are resurveyed periodically to pick up changes and new hazards, inequities result.

Fire protection provided by towns and cities is known as public or municipal protection. Municipal protection is an important consideration in all schedule rating. The National Board of Fire Underwriters has prepared a *Grading Schedule for Cities and Towns* of the United States based upon an analysis of conditions in more than 500 cities.[7] In municipalities under 30,000 population, engineering surveys may be made by the fire insurance rating organization having jurisdiction. In such instances the National Board Rating Schedule is used as a basis in evaluating the protection and hazards in the community. The schedule takes into consideration not only the natural and structural conditions that have a bearing on the hazards but also the status of laws designed to control unsatisfactory conditions. The schedule is based upon a maximum of 5,000 points of deficiency divided in accordance with the relative importance of each factor under consideration. The relative value of the deficiency points is as follows:

Water supply	1,700 points
Fire department	1,500
Fire alarm	550
Police	50
Building laws	200
Fire prevention	300
Structural conditions	700
	5,000 points

On the basis of the application of the foregoing schedule, cities and towns are classified according to the number of deficiency points into Classes 1 through 10. Appendix B on "Fire Insurance Rating Notes" reviews the classification system and explains the care which goes into the grading schedule. Even climatic conditions such as snow, dryness, tornadoes, floods, and earthquakes are evaluated in relation to their effect on fire insurance losses. The ten grades of protection, from the highest Class 1 to the lowest Class 10, are used as the basis of schedule applications to specific rates. They are also used to determine minimum rates on dwelling house property.

It is evident that the control of the basic rate in many communities falls only indirectly within the control of the individual. However, so far as he can throw the weight of his influence, cooperating with other citizens, civic-minded bodies, mercantile associations, and the local city government with a view to securing the approval

[7]National Board of Fire Underwriters, *Standard Schedule for Grading Cities and Towns of the United States with Reference to Their Fire Defenses and Physical Conditions* (New York, 1942).

of conditions that reduce or eliminate fire hazards, he can contribute to a lower community rate.

The two most widely used schedules are known as the *Universal Mercantile Schedule* and the *Analytic System.* The first of these found early acceptance in the East (and later in some southern states), and the second, introduced by A. F. Dean late in the nineteenth century, found wide acceptance in the West. The Analytic System is now widely used throughout the country; it is more generally known as the Dean Schedule, taking its name from the author of the plan. The schedules are basically different in their fundamental analysis of the factors affecting insurance risks, but they are alike in that they establish an arbitrary point from which to build up the rate based upon the various physical hazards of the risk. A schedule of additions and reductions is computed and the difference applied to the arbitrary point of departure.

The *Universal Mercantile Schedule* was designed to rate mercantile risks, and because it was designed to be applicable to all such risks, it was termed the "Universal" schedule. This plan of rating takes as its point of departure a standard building in a standard city. A standard city is described as one having wide level streets, gravity water works, adequate fire and police protection, and building conditions meeting a rigid set of requirements. A standard building, although not fireproof, represents the ideal for ordinary construction.

The schedule makes use of (*a*) a basis rate, and (*b*) a key rate. The basis rate is the rate of the standard building in a standard city noticed above. Charges, known as "deficiency charges," are made for deviations from a standard city. Deductions from the basis rate are made for exceptionally good features of environment. The key rate is intended to measure the average rate of a standard building in the community under consideration. The specific rate that applies to the particular building is found by making adjustments to the key rate. If there are any deficiencies in the structure or any unusually favorable features, the key rate is modified accordingly. For all unfavorable features, additions are made to the key rate, and deductions are made for the favorable features. Thus, by computing charges based upon a schedule of specific hazards, the rate for a standard building in the particular city in question is converted into the rate for the building under examination.

To find a rate for a particular building, using the Universal Mercantile Schedule, the additional charges for the various hazards and credits for protective devices or exceptionally good features are applied to the key rate of the city or town. Schedules are adapted to the particular class of property to be rated. The Universal Mercantile Schedule, while using flat amounts in increasing the key rate with respect to features of construction, allows adjustments for occupancy, protective devices, and management charges to be applied to the key rate on a percentage basis. Provision is also made for deductions from the rate in percentages for exceptionally good features of construction.

It is with the specific makeup of the rate that the insured is concerned. He wishes to know for what he is being charged, how much, and whether it will pay him to correct the hazard and remove the charge. With his agent or broker, he can go over the specific charges for the various hazards and the credits for protective devices or exceptionally good features. In connection with the occupancy of the structure, there are two charges. The first of these is included in computing the building rate, and the other is a differential added to the building rate to determine the rate on the contents themselves. Appendix B, "Fire Insurance Rating Notes," shows a standard mercantile building schedule, which indicates the detailed method of charging for hazards in arriving at a rate.

The *Dean Schedule,* or the Analytic System for the Measurement of the Relative Fire Hazard, is fundamentally different from the Universal Mercantile System. From the insured's point of view the two schedules are similar in that their charges and credits are added to a basis rate.

Perhaps the outstanding difference between the two schedules is to be found in the method of applying charges and credits. With the exception of certain after-charges for untidiness and carelessness which represent flat sums added to the rate, all charges for other hazards deemed to be inherent in the risk are made in terms of a percentage of the basis rate. This practice is based upon certain fundamental assumptions. It is assumed that every risk absorbs a ratio of the hazards to which it is exposed and that, by the same reasoning, it transmits a ratio of absorbed hazards. The risk itself radiates hazard inherent to it. The ratio of radiated, absorbed, and transmitted exposure is modified by the structure of the building, clear space intervening, and fire department protection. Because of these assumptions that hazards are radiated, transmitted, and absorbed as ratios, adjustments are made as percentages rather than flat charges. This is in contrast to the Universal Mercantile System in which flat charges are made for defects in the building as compared with standard, although certain unusual features in the building may permit a final credit in terms of percentages. Because of the wide acceptance of the Analytic System and the underlying philosophy, certain of the important features of the schedule will be noticed.

The Analytic System defines a risk as a building or other structure together with its occupancy or occupancies. There are four features or elements of risk. These are: (*a*) structure, (*b*) occupancy, (*c*) exposure, and (*d*) protection.

Buildings are classified into A, B, or D construction. Buildings of fireproof construction receive the A designation, those of brick and stone construction are class B, and class D includes buildings of frame construction. The schedule does not state in so many words that a standard building is thus and so but simply provides charges or credits for departure from the standards for individual items.

Occupancy is recognized as a prime factor among the causes of fire. A building itself does not cause fire, but its ability to resist fire will prove a contributing or deterring factor after a fire occurs. Even in the case of buildings damaged or destroyed by a fire spreading from another building, the cause of the loss may be traced to occupancy in the exposing risk. The Analytic System carefully classifies and analyzes occupancy features as causes of fire.

Full consideration is given to the exposure factor. That fires originating in one building spread to another has long been recognized by fire insurance underwriters. It has been found that the hazard of exposure as a cause of fire ranks second to that of occupancy.

The classifications established under the Standard Grading Schedule of the National Board of Fire Underwriters, already noticed, are used as a basis for rating public protection. In addition to public protection, the property owner may provide private protection by means of fire hose, fire extinguishers, watchman's service, sprinkler systems, and the like. Credits are incorporated in the rating plan that give recognition to private protection.

One of the outstanding advantages evidenced through the use of the Analytic System is found in its recognition of what has been termed the "principle of relativity." The sum total of all the hazards that contribute to a particular risk are all a proportionate part of the risk. It is the recognition of this important principle that brought about the use of percentages to effect charges and credits rather than the use of flat charges as had been the case with respect to schedules prior to the Analytic System. The same percentages apply with respect to given hazards whenever they are found. Appendix B, "Fire Insurance Rating Notes," gives complete examples of the method in which percentage debits and credits are applied, and how they are proportionally charged as between locations and time periods.

Another principal point of difference between the Analytic System and the Universal Mercantile Schedule lies in the determination of the *basis rate*. Instead of attempting to establish a basis rate for a standard risk in a standard city, the Dean Schedule gives consideration to the degree of fire protection and efficiency of fire-fighting facilities as represented by the classifications established under the Standard Grading Schedule of the National Board of Fire Underwriters.

The basis rate is determined by (*a*) the construction of the building; (*b*) the class of exterior fire protection; and (*c*) in the case of B and D buildings, the height of the building. Basis tables are prepared for each state or rating territory, and the tables used are determined by the underwriting experience in the territory involved. Percentage charges are added to the basis rate to secure the specific rate of the property under consideration. These charges reflect conditions of the building construction and occupancy. Credits are subtracted for protective features and superior structural conditions. The exposure hazard is recognized, and charges are added for any unsafe condition which can readily be corrected by management.

The first fire insurance rates which were quoted on a class minimum-rate basis were, in fact, basis rates. With the advent of schedule rating and the analysis of risks to the end that charges or credits could be made for specific hazards, there always remained with respect to every risk an unanalyzed portion. This portion, sometimes referred to as "the residium of unanalyzed hazard," actually constituted a basis rate, since it was to this rate that other charges were added.

In connection with the Dean Schedule, there is actually no difference between the charge in a schedule termed a "basis rate" and the other charges, except that the basis rate includes only those factors which of themselves are too obscure or unimportant to be separately scheduled. Thus, any factor that can be identified as a hazard has a relative value attached to it. This applies to such features as floor openings, occupancy, height of building, structure, and the like. To the remaining indefinite or unidentifiable factors a lump-sum charge is attached, and this is the basis rate.

The schedule provides for standard basis tables for each of the three classes of construction. The fireproof tables have the lowest rates, the brick table rates are intermediate, and the frame table is the highest. Tables are divided into ten columns, each column representing a class in the Standard Grading Schedule of the National Board of Fire Underwriters.

The master Basis Table assumes that a city in the tenth class will have a rate of $1.00. On the basis of experience the relative rate for a building located in a first-class city is determined. Then, the relative value of the protection among all the other classes is established.

Occupancy as it contributes to the start of fire or its spread is an important feature of the Analytic System. While a number of fires spread from exposure, and this feature is considered by the system, a very large proportion of all fires are due to the hazards of occupancy alone. As a matter of fact, exposure fires are, for the most part, due to hazards of occupancy in the building of origin.

The system recognizes three general classes of occupancy. These are: (*a*) mercantile, (*b*) industrial, and (*c*) miscellaneous. Mercantile occupancies include all risks in which the principal business consists of the sale or storage of merchandise. Both wholesale and retail establishments are included. Industrial risks comprise those in which the principal business consists of the production of materials or the manipulation of materials in the manufacture, packing, or shipping of merchandise. The miscellaneous category consists of occupancies classified as neither mercantile nor industrial.

The Analytic System recognizes that the cause that starts a fire is quite a different factor from the medium that spreads it. The consequences of a fire vary with the nature of the *occupancy*. The factors of hazard found in occupancies are recognized to be: (*a*) causes, (*b*) media, and (*c*) effects. Causes are defined as the things which originate combustion. Media are the substances on which the causes act with reference to their latent energy or combustibility. Effects are defined as the relative susceptibility of media to damage as the direct or indirect results of fire commonly known as "damageability."

The schedule provides an alphabetical occupancy list with charges to be applied based upon the combustibility and damageability of the occupancy. In effecting classification of combustibility consideration is given to: (*a*) the facility with which the substance will ignite or take fire, (*b*) the rapidity of its combustion when started, and (*c*) the intensity of combustion as indicated by quantity. In giving consideration to damageability the effect of fires may be either (*a*) direct or (*b*) resultant. Direct effects are those caused by the actual combustion of the substances themselves or by change in their molecular structure caused by the heat of adjacent combustion. Resultant effects are those that are incidental to fires, caused either by the efforts to suppress combustion or to remove merchandise from burning premises or by the effects of adjacent combustion other than heat. The most usual resultant effects of fire are from smoke, water, dampness, change of temperature, breakage, and the like. In the case of both combustibility and damageability, the charges to be made in the rate are determined by reference to the Alphabetical Occupancy List for the occupancies named therein.

What the Insured Can Do to Lower Rates. The details of schedule rating are many, and the refinements to which the measurement of hazards have been carried make the problem of rating seem to many insureds complicated and involved. The insured, however, is primarily interested in knowing that it is possible, through the elimination of chargeable construction defects or the installation of protective devices, to lessen materially the insurance premium for the protection he requires. Each of the following paragraphs reviews the major parts of the rate makeup, and what can be done by the insured to lower his cost of insurance.

In connection with rate analysis, one of the first points in the rate structure for consideration is charges for features of construction classed as "other than standard." Here frequently the variation from the requirements may be only slight, and by means of some inexpensive modification the risk may be made standard and a substantial saving effected. In the case of skylights, cornices, stairs, heating, lighting, electrical wiring, and the like, slight alterations to correct defects frequently result in savings far in excess of a normal return on the amount invested.

In both the Universal and the Analytic systems of rating charges incorporated in the rates are dependent, among other factors, upon the construction of adjoining buildings, the distance between risks which affect each other, protection, and the hazards of the exposing risk. If a building of superior construction is exposed on any side by a highrated risk, it is frequently possible to eliminate the exposure charge. When a brick wall contains one or more unprotected openings, the rate may be materially lessened by entirely closing the openings when feasible, or by otherwise protecting it. Standard firedoors, standard fire shutters, wire-glass windows set in steel sash and frames—all contribute to the elimination of exposure charges, and their installation frequently proves to be profitable.

The rate of a particular risk is affected as well by the occupancy of the property. It frequently happens that a hazardous occupancy is eliminated and, through neglect or oversight, no application is made for rerating. This is more likely to be the case when the change of occupancy occurs in a risk, not directly under the control of the insured, but which exposes his property. Whenever the insured finds that there have been any changes in occupancy since the promulgation of his rate, in either his own or adjacent property, an investigation to ascertain their effect upon his rate is in order.

At the end of the schedules is a space for a charge for hazards growing out of faults of management. These are not inherent in the risk but are usually the outgrowth of carelessness or indifference. Since such hazards are readily corrected, a charge is made which aims to make their elimination profitable to the insured. Charges are made for such hazards as broken plaster or windows; smokepipes improperly placed near combustible material; improper receptacles for oily waste, ashes, or cloths used for cleaning; the accumulation of rubbish; and other indications of slack housekeeping and carelessness. If, unknown to the insured, aftercharges of this sort have crept into his rate, he will find it inexpensive to correct them. Frequently when a property changes hands the new owner may of his own volition clean up conditions that carry an aftercharge in the fire rate of his building. Unaware that this charge is part of the rate, he may continue to pay for the hazard through failure to notify the rating board of its removal.

Perhaps no single improvement to a property will have a greater effect on a rate reduction than the installation of an automatic sprinkler system. Sprinkler systems found their first extensive use in factories but are now used in almost every type of structure. In buildings where the temperature is below the freezing point of water, a dry system is available. The pipes, instead of being filled with water, contain air under pressure up to the sprinkler head. When a sprinkler head is opened, the compressed air is released, and water then flows through the system and through the opened valve to drench the fire. The cost of sprinkler installation is considerable. There are certain minimum requirements that make the charge seem unreasonably high for risks involving small values. When values are under $50,000, there is little incentive for the installation of a sprinkler system, unless considerations other than rate reductions predominate. When large values are involved, it is usually found that over a term of years the savings on the insurance premium will pay for the sprinkler system. The capital investment having been returned in the form of premium reductions, the saving then continues as a gain for the property owner.

Credits on the rate are allowed for protective features less elaborate and complete than the automatic sprinkler system but nevertheless designed to minimize the risks. Among these are approved fire extinguishers, automatic thermostatic fire alarms, watchman service, fire pails, and standpipe equipment. When the installation of this type of equipment is contemplated, care should be exercised to see that it meets the standard of rating requirements. Considerable money might be spent for equipment that would receive no credit on the rate because of failure to meet the required specifications. A slight rearrangement of present equipment or the addition of new equipment may make the required difference. The same rule applies in connection with present installations. A property owner might install fire extinguishers for his own protection in a haphazard manner which seems to him to be suitable. To secure a rate credit, he may, however, need a few more extinguishers or a better distribution of those already installed. The expense of such readjustments of protective features to comply with requirements for a rate credit is frequently negligible.

When plans are being approved for new construction, their submission to the fire insurance rating organization will frequently bring forth suggestions to increase the safety of the property and lessen the insurance cost. A slight addition to the thickness of a wall; a change in roof specifications; an increase in the thickness of a floor; changes in floor openings, elevators, vents, light shafts—all may become profitable investments by saving on insurance premiums. While much may be done in the way of correction after a building is completed, obviously when the architect can make corrections in the drawings to eliminate chargeable hazards, the planning stage is the point at which to catch and eliminate the defect. Moreover, at this stage, at a very small cost or even at no extra cost, defects can be eliminated that, because of expense, would be beyond consideration in a completed building. Such a change might be the substitution of metal stud and lathing for wood. Obviously, after the building is completed such a change is out of the question. Through submission of the plans and specifications to the rating bureau, a complete rate analysis may be obtained for study before final acceptance and approval of the plans.

In connection with this discussion of fire insurance rates, emphasis has been placed upon the money saving to be effected by the correction of hazards. This is but one benefit, and perhaps the least important of a number. The owner of a building, stock, or business purchases insurance to indemnify himself in the event of loss. In spite of adequate insurance protection—and frequently the insurance is less than adequate—the insured will suffer various consequential losses in the event of fire. He is, therefore, interested in taking steps to minimize, so far as possible, all known hazards with a view to increasing the safety of his property entirely apart from the saving in insurance premium. Preservation of lives may be another basic reason.

Special Problems

Deductible Clauses. A deductible clause in an insurance contract provides that the insurer will pay a loss only when the loss is in excess of a specified amount. The clause made its early appearance in marine contracts because marine underwriters recognized that in the case of goods particularly susceptible to damage there would be innumerable claims where the losses would be insignificant. They felt such losses, particularly if they were almost certain to happen, should be borne by the insured. If the insurance carrier were to be responsible, the necessity was created of adding to the insurance rate a definite sum to cover the damage that was almost sure to happen. There seemed to be little point in adding to a rate the amount of a loss that could reasonably be anticipated. This being the case, the marine underwriters provided in their contracts that they were to be relieved of all partial losses on certain types of goods, and in other classifications the loss to be collectible must exceed a designated percentage of value. The provision was first attached to the policy in the form of a memorandum, and for that reason such clauses to this day are referred to as "memorandum clauses."

The percentage of loss is sometimes called the "franchise." It will be noticed that there is no loss payable unless the loss amounts to the percentage or franchise. If the loss reaches this figure it is paid in full. In marine insurance, on the contrary, another clause known as the "deductible average" provides that a named percentage of the loss is always deducted from the claim, and the amount above this deductible is paid the insured. This is also known as a "straight" deductible.

The deductible principle has found its way into other branches of insurance. For example, in automobile insurance, the owner of an automobile might be perfectly satisfied to have small damages repaired himself. If the insurance company is liable for the repair of minor losses, the cost of handling the claims is entirely out of proportion to the damage sustained. There also is a tendency on the part of the insured to ask for more extensive repairs if insurance is involved than would be required if he, himself, is making the damage good. For this reason, automobile insurance involving loss or damage to the car of the insured is frequently written with a straight deductible clause providing that the company is not liable unless the loss exceeds an amount named in the clause, and then the liability is only for such amount as the loss exceeds the specified deduction.

Small deductibles written in connection with property insurance are sound in theory. They effectively eliminate most of the small "nuisance" claims and in the long run provide for a lower insurance premium. As a matter of fact, it is sometimes stated that the insured is in effect receiving advance payment of the small losses in the form of a reduced premium charge where a deductible is used. Some find it difficult to believe that small losses will have any important adverse effect upon loss ratio. It is pointed out, however, that adjustment and overhead expense in settling nuisance losses is out of all proportion to the amount of the loss. A $25 loss payment often may involve more than $25 in agents' and adjusters' time, completion of necessary forms, records keeping, and so on. The loss records show that the adjustment and payment in full of such claims do indeed unfavorably influence the loss ratio with a resulting increase in premium charges.

It has not proved feasible, in connection with most property insurance, to provide a franchise type of deductible for payment in full if the loss exceeds the amount of the deductible. For example, in the case of a $50 deductible there is a grave temptation to stretch a $40 or $50 loss to the point where it exceeds the deductible, if by so doing the full amount of the claim is to be paid. A new approach, which is in effect a combination of the straight and franchise deductibles, is found in the so-called "variable," "diminishing," or "modified" deductibles. In the case of a $50 loss or less, the full amount of the deductible applies. The amount payable for loss between $50 and $500 is 111 percent of the amount in excess of $50. When the loss is $500 or more, the loss deductible disappears. This is illustrated as follows:

Amount of Loss	*Deductible Amount*	*Loss less Deductible*	*Amount Collectible*	*Franchise Amount*
$ 50......................	$50	0	0	$50.00
100......................	50	$ 50 × 111%	$ 55.50	44.50
400......................	50	350 × 111%	388.50	11.50

If the deductible amount is $100, then 125 percent is used to determine the amount payable for loss between $100 and $500. This works out as follows:

Amount of Loss	*Deductible Amount*	*Loss less Deductible*	*Amount Collectible*	*Franchise Amount*
$100......................	$100	0	0	$100.00
200......................	100	$100 × 125%	$125.00	75.00
400......................	100	300 × 125%	375.00	25.00

The franchise is the net deductible amount or insured's contribution and disappears when the amount of the loss reaches $500. Many of the new Homeowner's contracts now use this type of deductible.

Sizable deductibles have been introduced recently in the field of fire insurance. Forms allowing deductibles at the insured's option ranging from $5,000 up to $250,000 are offered. A schedule of rate credits is applicable according to the percentage of value represented by the deductible amount which the insured selects. Table 6–1 is such a schedule. Reference to the table will indicate, as an example, that a policy written with $100,000 deductible will reduce the insurance premium by 33 percent. The higher the percentage which the deductible bears to the basis of insurance the greater is the credit allowed. Where $100,000 deductible represents 25 percent of the basis of insurance, just over half the premium is saved. These policies are written with the requirement that no other insurance will be provided to apply to the deductible amount.

Experience shows that the frequency of losses varies with the size of the loss. The less the amount of the loss the more frequent the occurrence. If an insured can handle losses up to a given point and eliminate such losses from his insurance coverage the loss experience will be reflected in a much lower rate and accordingly a premium savings. The aim of this deductible has no relationship with nuisance claims, as is the case with $50 and $100 deductibles; its sole purpose is the reduction of insurance costs.

TABLE 6–1

Credits Applicable to Deductible Insurance

	Percentage Relationship of Deductible to Value												
Deductible Amount	*Less than 5*	*5+*	*10+*	*15+*	*20+*	*25+*	*30+*	*35+*	*40+*	*45+*	*50+*	*75+*	*90+*
$ 5,000....	16%	19%	22%	25%	29%	34%	38%	43%	47%	52%	50%	76%	91%
10,000....	19	22	25	29	33	37	41	46	50	55	58	76	91
15,000....	21	24	27	31	35	39	43	48	52	57	59	76	91
20,000....	23	26	29	33	37	41	45	50	54	58	60	77	92
25,000....	25	28	31	35	39	43	47	52	56	59	62	77	92
50,000....	29	32	35	39	43	47	51	55	59	62	64	77	92
75,000....	31	34	37	41	45	49	53	57	61	64	66	78	93
100,000....	33	36	39	43	47	51	55	59	63	66	68	78	93
250,000....	39	42	45	49	52	56	60	64	68	71	72	80	93

Minimum Premiums. There are certain fixed costs that attach to the issuing of an insurance policy. For example, a fire insurance rate may call for 27 cents for each $100 of insurance written for a period of one year. Obviously if one asked for $100 of insurance, the insurance company could not profitably issue a policy for 27 cents. A certain amount of expense is involved in the preparation of the rates and in the purchase of supplies. Likewise, there is the expense of office labor required in preparing the policy. That cost alone often exceeds $5.00 per contract written, according to many office efficiency studies. For this reason it is customary to require a minimum premium, sometimes referred to as a "policy fee."

In some fields of insurance a large part of the expense in connection with the carrying of the risk involves inspections or other such services. If this is the case, if the amount of insurance ordered does not bring the premium up to a specified minimum, the underwriting requirements indicate a charge that must be met regardless of the rate. Finally, there are types of risk that companies accept on a short-term basis only with reluctance. This is because there is a tendency on the part of the applicant for insurance to apply for such coverage for a period of 30 or 60 days only when he senses peculiar circumstances that tend to increase the risk. If such insurance were written at the manual rate in smaller amounts, there would be a tendency to create a situation of adverse selection against the company. Hence, the minimum premium has to be set at an amount sufficiently large to reimburse the company for the risk.

Annual and Term Policies. The time specified in the policy during which the coverage is effective is its *term.* A policy written for one year is called an *annual policy,* while a policy written for a longer period is called a *term policy.* Certain types of risks are accepted on an annual basis only; others are written for a longer term with a reduction in the rate; still others are written for less than one year at an increased short-term rate.

When policies are written on the term basis with a prepaid premium for the entire term, it is the usual rule in property insurance to charge for all years after the first year a premium equal to 85 percent of the annual premium rate. While a policy may be written for any period from one to five years, the usual terms are three and five years. Hence, on the basis of a charge of 85 percent of the annual premium charge for each year subsequent to the first year, the premium for three years figures 2.7 times the annual rate, and for five years the premium is 4.4 times the annual rate if the premium is paid in advance. Since policies are written based upon rates, conversion tables are available to convert the annual premium to a term premium. Appendix C, "Rates for Prepaid Term Insurance," is such a conversion table. Reference to the one-year rate of $1.00 in that table will show the two-year rate to be $1.85, the three-year rate to be $2.70, the four-year rate to be $3.55, and the five-year rate to be $4.40.[8]

Policies may also be written for a period less than a year. Short-term policies are ordinarily written for a special purpose, such as to bring about an expiration date at a particular time or to add to insurance during the period of a temporary inventory increase. Policies written for less than a year are charged for on what is termed the *short-rate basis.* Appendix C, "Short-Rate Cancellation Table for One Year," contains the data for short-rate premium calculations. For example, a 180-day contract would cost 60 percent of the annual rate, or for a 60-day contract, 27 per cent of the annual premium would be earned or charged by the insurer.

Installment Plans. For some insurance, term rates are allowed permitting installment payments. For example, in the casualty field

[8]It is interesting to note that in the early days of fire insurance perpetual policies were offered and a small number of companies continue the practice today. The amount of insurance written under these contracts is comparatively small but for insureds who have held them, they have considerable appeal. Perpetual policies are written under a continuous contract for a single premium. The coverage may be terminated by either the company or the insured and when so terminated the premium deposit is returned to the insured. While the insurance is in force, the investment return on deposits is used to pay claims and operating expenses.

2½ times the annual premium plus 5 percent is the charge for a three-year term policy if paid in installments of 50, 30, and 20 percent for the first, second, and third years, respectively. In the case of prepaid insurance there are many who feel the prepaid premium does not warrant the saving, particularly in the case of large premiums where interest is a factor. To permit taking advantage of term discounts and provide at the same time for equal annual installment payments the deferred premium payment plan (DPP) has been devised. The plan provides for an annual DPP rate which is 35 percent of the three-year prepaid rate whether the policy is written for three or five years. The plan allows for term insurance but permits premiums to be paid in equal annual payments. Conversion tables are provided for converting annual premiums to DPP plan premiums. Appendix C, "Conversion Table–Annual Rate to Deferred Premium Payment Rate," is an example of such a table. Reference to an annual premium of $1.00 will show that on the DPP plan the insurance may be purchased for 94 cents annually.

In some states, the annual installment premium plan has been extended to provide for premium payments on the monthly basis. Insurance companies have long provided financing plans for monthly premium payments that involved signing a loan application and note, with the premium being advanced by a lending institution. The policyholder then paid off the note. The new plan eliminates the loan concept. This plan provides for an extra premium charge and is arranged to require each installment to be paid up one month in advance of any premium due date.[9] This allows the company to issue prior notice of cancellation in the event of nonpayment of any premium installment with the result that the coverage is not impaired during the notice period and continues to the end of the period for which previous payment has been made.

A wide variety of premium payment plans have recently appeared in insurance. With automobile insurance costs rising, and the concept of account selling (all insurance of a policyholder with one insurer) gaining favor, the policyholder is often faced with the need for spreading his insurance premiums over a number of payments. Some insurance companies have set up separate finance plans to permit the insured to do this on a quarterly, semiannual, or monthly basis. Larger agencies have also designed such finance plans to aid their clients.

REINSURANCE

In order to secure a large number of similar risks to permit the prediction of losses with a reasonable degree of certainty, insurance

[9]The extra premium charge is $2.25 for each $100 of annual premium or annual installment, and on the quarterly plan the charge is $1.88 per $100 of premium.

companies have devised the practice of *reinsurance*. Reinsurance is the transfer of insurance business from one insurer to another. Its purpose is to shift risks from an insurer, whose financial safety might be threatened by retaining too large an amount of risk, to other *reinsurers* who will share in the risks of large losses. It also tends to stabilize profits and losses, and permits more rapid growth.

Reinsurers are of two basic types: those that do a reinsurance business only, and those that write mostly insurance but also write some reinsurance. Most reinsurance in the United States is written by the full-time "professional" reinsurers. However, in the past decade an increasing number of insurers have organized reinsurance departments.[10]

If risk is concentrated in large amounts on a few properties, obviously the variation from the average may and probably will be great. For this reason, the insurer seeks to limit its lines and secure the widest possible dispersion of risks. For example, if it can be shown that over a period of time one dwelling house in a thousand will be destroyed each year by fire, then the contribution of $10 by each of a thousand homeowners will make up a fund sufficient to pay the loss for the one $10,000 house. If in the group of houses there is a house valued at $20,000 and the owner of that house pays $20 into the fund, that is, $10 for each $10,000 coverage, the fund at the end of a year will total $10,010. If, however, the $20,000 dwelling should be destroyed, the fund would be inadequate to reimburse the owner for his loss. In order to enable an insurance company to provide the full coverage for such a house at the established rate, the business has devised the practice of reinsurance.

Reinsurance Agreements

There are two principal forms of reinsurance agreements in regard to the method by which the reinsurance goes into effect: (*a*) specific, or facultative, reinsurance, and (*b*) treaty, or automatic, reinsurance.

Specific or Facultative. *Specific* reinsurance, also termed *facultative* reinsurance, is a form which concerns itself with a specific optional transaction. Each contract under specific reinsurance is written on its own merit and is a matter of individual bargaining between the original insurer and the reinsurer. It is termed facultative because the reinsurer is under no obligation, through previous

---

[10]The increase has been from 28 reinsurance departments of American insurers in 1945, to over 70 in 1963, according to Mr. Donald Chadwick, Reinsurance Secretary of the Atlantic Companies, who referred to the trend in his talk at the 1963 C.P.C.U. Annual Meetings in Denver, Colorado on September 24, 1963. He also is the author of "Evaluating a Reinsurance Program" in the June, 1953 *Annuals of the Society of C.P.C.U.*, pp. 57–68.

agreement or reciprocal arrangement, to accept the risk. In other words, he retains the faculty or privilege to accept or reject a line, as offered.

The procedure is simple and was, in fact, the first form of reinsurance of which we have any record. Modern practice has given rise to newer standard procedures. Nevertheless, specific reinsurance is still widely used because some risks will always fall outside the scope of the automatic arrangements discussed next. Because the underwriting requirements are burdensome, few insurance companies doing only a reinsurance business write this form of coverage, and the bulk of such business is exchanged between insurers that do reinsurance as a small part of their total business.

Treaty or Automatic. *Treaty* or *automatic* reinsurance exists when two or more companies enter a contract which undertakes by reinsurance to cover risks that at the time of the agreement may be undetermined. The reinsurer agrees to insure a proportionate part of a designated class of business written by the insurer. Treaty reinsurance embraces future contracts as well as those in existence at the time the agreement is executed. Treaties controlling the major part of the business today obligate the reinsurer, within the limits set in the agreement, to assume the ceded (reinsured) lines. When the reinsurer is obligated to accept a specific part of each risk assumed by the original insurer and the original insurer on its part is obligated to cede a like portion of the risk, the liability of the reinsurer attaches as soon as the original insurer assumes the risk. Automatic[11] protection is thus assured for the original insurer, as the reinsurer has agreed beforehand to accept all risks within the terms of the treaty.

A special type of treaty arrangement is the *reinsurance pool,* which is an exchange of reinsurance among two or more insurers according to an automatic agreement. Each reinsurer receives a certain amount or proportion of the risks or losses of the other reinsurer or reinsurers, and each cedes or gives to all the others a predetermined part of its risks or losses. These pools are valuable for spreading infrequent catastrophic types of risks among insurers of a company group or fleet.

Reinsurance Contracts

The facultative and treaty reinsurance agreements may use either of two basic ideas in distributing the insurance risk between the

[11]Sometimes the insurer retains the option as to what it will reinsure and the treaty is termed an "open treaty" or "facultative treaty." Here the automatic part of the arrangements for reinsurance are limited to the general type of reinsurance contract and its provisions, but the actual risks and amounts to be ceded to the reinsurer are subject to negotiation.

original insurer and the reinsurer. The reinsurer agrees to accept either (1) a *share* of the *amounts of risk* which the insurer writes or (2) an *excess* of the *losses* which exceed certain established limits. A special type of contract which is not regularly used by an insurer is called "portfolio reinsurance." This occurs when the reinsurer takes over all the risks of certain lines of insurance from the original insurer, oftentimes when the insurer is discontinuing such business.

Share-of-Risk Contracts. Reinsurance contracts that share risks may involve two fundamental ways[12] of distributing the business written by the insurer. In one type, known as *quota or pro rata share,* the insurer cedes a fixed proportion of every insurance contract of a given kind. For example, in fire insurance it might be arranged that the insurer keep only one third of each risk and the reinsurer accept two thirds. In such case the reinsurer would receive two thirds of the premium (less commissions paid by the insurer to agents), and pay two thirds of any losses. This form of reinsurance contract enables the original insurer to write much larger amounts of insurance than it otherwise could, and is particularly useful to smaller companies that want to expand rapidly.

Another common type is the *surplus share,* in which the reinsurer does not participate in every risk of the original insurer, but accepts only the part of the risks that go over certain limits. Usually the limit is established in relation to the "line" retained by the original insurer, and the reinsurer may, for example, agree to take three lines above the retention. The reinsurer does not participate unless the insurance exceeds the net retention. Surplus treaties are one of the most common types of reinsurance arrangement, and often a second or third surplus treaty is used, involving several different reinsurers on the same risk for amounts up to five or ten times the amount of risk kept by the original insurer.

Excess-of-Loss Contracts. The second basic type of reinsurance contract, *excess-of-loss,*[13] is designed to afford protection against large *losses* only. This coverage is used when protection is desired either on a single risk, against a single large loss irrespective of the number of risks involved, or against an accumulation of losses in ex-

---

[12]Reference here is primarily to the property-liability reinsurance contracts. In the life insurance field two basic types are also used: the "coinsurance" type and the "yearly renewable term" type. Since life risks involve total losses only rather than total or partial losses, the analogy of reinsurance contracts between the life and property fields is not complete. Basically, however, the "coinsurance" type is closest to the share-of-risk contract, and the "yearly renewable term" is most like an excess-of-loss contract.

[13]Excess-of-loss reinsurance is sometimes confused with "catastrophe covers," which have similar goals of protecting against large losses only, but are written as direct insurance between policyholder and insurer.

cess of a stipulated limit. The coverage may be limited to a certain area, such as a designated city, or may be nationwide in its scope. Again, the coverage may be limited to a definite class, where a company desires to protect underwriting profits by having the reinsurer pay all losses when the loss ratio exceeds an agreed percentage of the earned premiums. This is called "excess-of-loss ratio" reinsurance. Other variations include "excess catastrophe" and "aggregate excess" reinsurance.

Unlike the quota share cover, in the case of loss under excess-of-loss reinsurance there is no obligation on the part of the reinsurer until the gross claim is shown to be in excess of the amount payable by the ceding company. Sometimes, in order to arrange the reinsurance in such a way as to hold the ceding company interested in the gross amount of the loss settlement, the agreement is written so that the ceding company continues to participate in the excess loss up to an agreed percentage.

Excess-of-loss contracts are the type of coverage by which many insurers, especially in casualty insurance, cover the catastrophe risk. American and foreign companies accepting reinsurance write the coverage, and London Lloyd's write many of these increasingly popular reinsurance contracts.

Retrocessions

Reinsurance enjoys no immunity from the operation of the principles governing sound practice for insurers. The reinsurer also must avoid a concentration in conflagration areas or catastrophe situations, and must maintain a wide distribution of its risks. Since the reinsurer may have lines ceded from a number of different sources, it is easily possible that it might find itself with an unwarranted accumulation of risk in a single policyholder, given locality or class. To relieve itself of this unsatisfactory accumulation, the reinsurer would itself have to resort to reinsurance. The act of reinsuring any part of a reinsurance is termed *retrocession.*

In compensation, casualty, and life risks the reinsurer sometimes finds an unusual line offered. The amount in excess of the net retention of the original insurer is often far greater than the reinsurer is willing to carry. In such a case, it may prefer to accept the entire excess, and in turn seek reinsurance through retrocession, retaining only as much of the risk as it deems prudent.

Summary

The entire area of reinsurance and retrocession is an example of the essential need for spread of risk among many risk bearers. Much of the process goes on without the policyholder being aware of its existence, since he is not a party to the reinsuring arrangements.

Yet it is an important part of the security behind many insurance contracts.

Consider a hypothetical illustration of an agent who sells $3 million of fire insurance on a manufacturer's plant. Three insurers may each take $1 million of coverage in separate policies. Perhaps Insurer A has a quota share treaty reinsurance agreement with Reinsurer W, that takes two thirds of this $1 million policy. Insurer B may have a surplus share treaty with Reinsurer X to take five "lines" above a $100,000 retention by Insurer B. This would leave $400,000 to be arranged by Insurer B in a facultative reinsurance agreement with Reinsurer Y in a second surplus agreement. The third $1 million policy may be spread to Reinsurer Z in an excess-of-loss contract, in which Insurer C agrees to take care of all losses up to $200,000 and Reinsurer Z will pay any loss exceeding that amount up to $1 million. Any of the reinsurers, or all of them, may decide their total risk is too great, and through retrocession transfer some of their risk to other reinsurers. The example illustrates how one policyholder's risk may result in several insurance contracts, and many reinsurance and retrocession agreements.

The reinsurance area is noted for several unusual characteristics: its international character, its extreme flexibility and freedom from insurance regulation as to forms and rates, and its high level of business conduct on a basis of good faith between the contracting parties. A substantial reinsurance business is conducted in the United States by reinsurers from other countries, or by branch companies of foreign reinsurers. These companies compete actively with the full-time professional United States reinsurers and with the reinsurance departments of U.S. insurers which have increased so rapidly in recent years. The widespread market for reinsurance is partially responsible for the great flexibility which reinsurers have in designing new and special contracts for the individual needs of insurers. The large and sometimes complex nature of reinsurance arrangements, and the necessarily high caliber of reinsurance personnel for such contracts, makes reinsurance a unique part of the insurance business.

OTHER FUNCTIONS OF INSURERS

Space does not permit the extensive discussion of the many other functions which insurers perform in addition to the contract design, marketing, loss payment and underwriting activities discussed in the past four chapters. It is important to note in summarizing the structure and operations of insurers, however, that other activities than those reviewed are necessary in carrying out the business of insurance.

From the standpoint of insurer organization, in some organizations these auxiliary functions may be performed under the supervision of the marketing (or "production" or "agency") department, the claim department or the underwriting department. In other insurers, separate status is often accorded to these other activities.

Included in this group of functions are those performed by the legal department, the actuarial department, the accounting department, the statistical and research department, the public relations department, the advertising department, the education department, and the investment department. Also, a large number of other internal services may be grouped together under an administrative department that provides secretarial, purchasing, filing, printing, mailing, storage, employment and employee benefit functions.

Only a few of these activities are unique enough to insurers to warrant separate treatment in any insurance text. Nevertheless, how such services are performed in an insurance organization is significant in understanding how they are related to the major insurance functions.

The legal department, for example, often works closely with the claims department of property and liability insurers. It generally is also responsible for meeting general incorporation, licensing, and taxation laws of the many states in which the insurer does business. Oftentimes it helps design insurance contracts in regard to legal interpretations, drafts agency agreements, and provides general legal counsel for the insurer. In life insurance it offers substantial aid to the sales and underwriting departments by reviewing estate tax problems and planning settlement options.

The actuarial department is most closely related to the rating or underwriting department of insurers. Life insurance companies, in particular, need a separate actuarial staff to diagnose mortality trends, determine costs for the various contracts, and provide research for many phases of the insurer's activities. Close cooperation is needed with the accounting and statistical areas, to coordinate expense, loss cost, and other studies.

Separate research departments are not common for most insurers, but increasingly the need for economic and social research is being realized. Some companies now have substantial staffs to analyze economic trends, policyholder opinion surveys, market potentials, investment opportunities, and other factors important to insurer operations.

A public relations department is maintained by some insurers. News releases, claim dissatisfactions, and general service to the community and public are part of its activities. Coordination with the claims, education, and advertising departments may be essential in many of its projects.

Education is another growing area of insurance organizations.

Several hundred directors of such activities for insurers are joined together nationally in a professional effort to improve insurance education through the Insurance Company Education Directors' Society. Many insurers today provide extensive programs of education for management development, training of claimsmen and underwriters and regular separate schools for agents and employees.

Investments form an important part of the income for both life and property insurers today. Finance experts often work as a separate department of an insurer to determine the best investments for the assets of the insurer. They must follow some state regulation which limits the investment media which can be used, especially for required reserves of the insurance contracts. Much individual choice is possible, however, among various government, utility, industrial, and mortgage bond investments. For the voluntary reserves and surplus of the insurer, many forms of stock, real estate, and other investment holdings must be carefully considered.

Many general administrative services are necessary for efficient operation of an insurer. Personnel managers, purchasing experts, clerical and filing help, secretaries, and many other jobs are numerous. The paperwork essential to insurance organizations creates employment for many thousands of persons, and a successful insurer must be well organized in these areas to provide efficient results. Automation offers substantial help today for many problems in these services, but it is unlikely that the current ratio of two nonsales jobs for each sales job in insurance will change rapidly.

SUMMARY

The selection and rating of the risks accepted by an insurer is the function of insurance *underwriting*. It is a process of close relationship to the other major functions of product (or contract) design, marketing and loss payment. The purpose is to obtain a safe distribution of risks which will produce a reasonable profit for the risk bearer.

Many sources of underwriting information are used in order to select those risks to be insured and reject those risks which should not be insured. Both the insurance agent and the insurance company perform some of the underwriting activites in most kinds of insurance. In life insurance, and the more complicated, larger business property-liability exposures, the basic underwriting decisions are more likely to be made by the insurer. Oftentimes, additional parties such as rating bureaus, credit investigation companies, medical examiners, and financial services may be used to help the insurer in reaching its conclusions on underwriting.

If risks are accepted, it is also imperative that adequacy, reasonableness, and equity are achieved in the *rating* (pricing) process.

As an example of how *class,* or average, and *specific,* or individual, rates are set for insured properties, fire insurance rates are analyzed. Special problems which occur in many lines of insurance include the adjustments in the rating methods which allow for deductibles, minimum premiums, term policies, and installment payment plans.

Reinsurance is the transfer of risks from one insurer to an additional party known as a reinsurer. Sharing the risk is often essential in order to obtain stability of results, continued growth in the operations of the insurance company, and, at the same time, in order to meet the needs of policyholders for reliable insurance protection. Reinsurance *agreements* are classified as (1) *specific* or *facultative* and (2) *treaty* or *automatic.* Reinsurance *contracts* are numerous in kind, but may be simply divided into (1) *share-of-risk* and (2) *excess-of-loss* contracts. Many combinations of the basic types are prevalent, and the needs of the reinsurance market often also encourage various *retrocessions* among reinsurers.

The major functions of insurance are supplemented by several auxiliary activities, including the services performed within the insurer organization in such areas as the legal, actuarial, accounting, statistical and research, public relations, advertising, education, and investment departments.

FOR REVIEW

1. How is the function of underwriting related to the other major functions of an insurance company? Cite several examples.
2. Since many insurance rates are class, or average, rates, why doesn't an insurer just accept all applicants for protection in a given class and thereby benefit from the "law of large numbers"?
3. Can the insurer rely upon the agent for performing the selection of proper risks? If so, to what extent? If not, what are the limitations?
4. Discuss the use made by insurance companies of inspection reports. What other sources of underwriting information are commonly used in various kinds of insurance?
5. Discuss the problem of moral hazard arising out of an attitude of indifference engendered by a lack of self-interest. What should be the attitude of the underwriter when indifference on the part of the insured may be a factor?
6. What is a class fire rate, and how is it found? How does a specific fire rate differ, and how is it determined? Give an example of the use of each type of fire rate.
7. You are the risk manager for a large corporation. An expansion program calls for the construction of 20 large warehouses situated in strategic locations throughout the country. Heretofore warehouse construction has been of brick and in many instances sprinkler systems have been installed. The immediate requirement for 20 warehouses is a drain on available capital and the architect has suggested frame construction. This will make a heavy cut in the immediate cash outlay. Purely from a financial point of view, as risk manager, what possibilities will you consider that may lead to the rec-

ommendation that the directors do not abandon the policy of superior construction for the warehouses?

8. The Medical Office Building has just been completed, and application for fire rate filed. It is now discovered that a substantial charge is included in the rate because the building was constructed with wooden interior walls. Wherein did the owners fail concerning this rate? What other features of this risk would heavily influence the insurance rate which the building owners will have to pay?
9. If there were two cities with identical fire departments, explain how it would be possible for one city to have more deficiency points than another. Can the classification of a city for its fire insurance rate be made a community affair and, by focusing public interest on the deficiency factors, perhaps bring about a reduction?
10. It is stated that, in purchasing insurance, consideration should be given to possible losses even though their occurrence is remotely probable. X claims that he cannot afford to insure remotely probable losses. Discuss from a rating standpoint.
11. What is the purpose of a "schedule" fire insurance rate? How do the two principal schedule rating systems, the Universal Mercantile Schedule and the Dean Analytic Schedule, differ?
12. How can an individual business property owner lower his fire insurance costs?
13. There have been those in the insurance industry who have criticized insurance with substantial deductibles as encouraging self-insurance and, hence, detrimental to the insurance business. Do you think insurance with deductibles of $10,000 or upward has a place in the insurance business? Discuss.
14. What are the purposes in the normal use of: deductibles? term policies? installment plans?
15. For the purposes of insurance underwriting, indicate the principal reasons for making use of reinsurance.
16. Distinguish between: *(a)* "facultative" and "treaty" reinsurance; *(b)* "reinsurance" and "retrocession"; and *(c)* "share-of-risk and "excess-of-loss" reinsurance.
17. X operates a department store with an inventory of $250,000. His insurance is divided among a number of companies with expirations scattered throughout the year. B, an agent, in an effort to secure the entire line, offers to combine the coverage and deliver a single policy for $250,000 to the insured. Knowing this to be reinsured, what advantages and disadvantages are to be found in the agent's suggestion?

PART THREE

Insurance and Government

CHAPTER 7 *INSURANCE REGULATION*

- I. Why Insurance Regulation Is Needed
- II. Methods of Insurance Regulation
  - A. Self-Regulation of Insurance
  - B. Government Regulation of Insurance
    - 1. Government Legislation
    - 2. Administrative Action
    - 3. Court Action
- III. Kinds of Insurance Regulation by the States
  - A. Formation and Licensing of Insurers
  - B. Insurer Operations
    - 1. Contracts and Forms
    - 2. Rates
    - 3. Expense Limitations
    - 4. Reserves
    - 5. Asset and Surplus Values
    - 6. Investments
    - 7. Agents' Licensing and Trade Practices
    - 8. Taxation
  - C. Liquidation of Insurers
- IV. Summary

CHAPTER 8 *SOCIAL INSURANCE*

- I. Description and Objectives
  - A. "Social Security"
  - B. Public Assistance and Social Insurance
  - C. Veterans' Benefit Programs
- II. Background
- III. The Social Insurance Programs
- IV. Old Age, Survivors, and Disability Insurance
  - A. Eligibility
    - 1. Covered Employment
    - 2. Insured Status
  - B. Benefits
    - 1. Types of Benefits
    - 2. Size of Benefits
    - 3. Special Earnings and Disability Requirements

- C. Administration
  1. Tax Collection
  2. Individual Accounts
  3. Approval of Benefits
- D. Financing
  1. Tax on Employer and Employee
  2. Need for Understanding
  3. Pay-as-You-Go Assessment Plan, with Contingency Trust Funds
  4. Income Shift among Generations
  5. A Current Recipient "Bargain"
  6. Future Self-Supporting Cost Estimates
  7. Needed Research on Effects

V. UNEMPLOYMENT COMPENSATION
- A. Eligibility
  1. Covered Employment
  2. Individual Requirements
- B. Benefits
  1. Amount
  2. Duration
- C. Administration
  1. Federal Standards
  2. State Administration
- D. Financing

VI. WORKMEN'S COMPENSATION
- A. Eligibility
- B. Benefits
- C. Administration
- D. Financing

VII. TEMPORARY DISABILITY (NONOCCUPATIONAL) INSURANCE LAWS
- A. Eligibility
- B. Benefits
- C. Administration
- D. Financing

VIII. OTHER SOCIAL INSURANCE PROGRAMS
- A. The Railroad Retirement and Unemployment Acts
- B. Government Employee Retirement Systems
- C. Required Liability Insurance
- D. Miscellaneous and Future Programs

IX. SUMMARY

Chapter 7

INSURANCE REGULATION

ALL forms of private business enterprise have some regulation of their activities, either by self-imposed rules and customs or by specific regulations by government. Sometimes the government provides extensive controls for business organizations, including almost every phase of the operations from creation to liquidation. For other businesses there is minimum government regulation, perhaps only for the purposes of providing necessary tax information.

WHY INSURANCE REGULATION IS NEEDED

The insurance business is among the types of private enterprise subject to much government regulation. It is generally classed as a business which is "affected with a public interest." This characteristic is the reason why many forms of government supervision[1] of insurance are deemed necessary. Although competition is an effective regulator for some businesses, in insurance uncontrolled competition would work a hardship upon the buyers of insurance, most of whom do not understand insurance contracts. Much of the insurance written is to protect third parties who have not participated in making the contracts. The value of the contracts depends upon the ability of the insurance companies to fulfill their promises to the public, sometimes many years after the issuance of a policy. Ability to carry out the provisions of contracts depends upon many factors including the efficient operation of the insurance company, the selection of satisfactory risks, the determination of proper premium rates, and the wise investment of adequate reserves. Consequently, the needed integrity and long-range financial stability of insurers place insurance in an area which has traditionally been considered appropriate for government regulation.

---

[1]Some authors prefer the use of the word "supervision" to that of regulation, feeling that regulation has a stronger connotation of active direction. The distinction is not widely accepted, however, so the terms are used interchangeably in the chapter. See Adelbert G. Straub, Jr., "Communication in the Art of Insurance Supervision," a paper presented to the Zone Four Insurance Regulation Institute of the National Association of Insurance Commissioners, Michigan State University, February 11-13, 1958.

The question of how much regulation is necessary is a more difficult problem. Apparently insurance falls into the category of heavily regulated business, but does not belong in the same class as banks and public utilities which are examples of the most complete public regulation requirements. Many banks are subject to federal charters, while insurance companies are not.[2] Public utilities, unlike insurance companies,[3] have close government control of their organization (under "certificates of necessity"), their complete rate schedules, and their maximum profit return in relation to invested capital. The extent of public regulation of insurance is reviewed in succeeding sections of this chapter by descriptions of the major methods and kinds of insurance regulation.

METHODS OF INSURANCE REGULATION

The state government is undoubtedly most important in the regulation of insurance. Before considering this and other phases of government insurance regulation, however, it is logical first to summarize the field of self-regulation of insurance.

Self-Regulation of Insurance

To the extent that a business provides adequate self-regulation for itself, government regulation is often unnecessary, or at least diminished in some degree. In insurance it is not realistic to think that the entire job of regulation can be done by internal, as opposed to external, methods of supervision. C. A. Kulp, whose authoritative chapter on regulation of the casualty insurance business remains as one of the finest analyses of self-regulation, points out that the insurance business does discipline itself more than most persons realize:

> The extent of self-regulation is very considerable. No business has more incentive to cooperative effort or more to lose by failure to cooperate; in general also, insurers are given wider legal leeway in cooperative action than other businesses . . . . The privilege and the responsibility of cooperative action do not preclude public regulation of the group or of the individual members. As a matter of fact, there is a clear tendency in public regulation rather toward both greater group responsibility and closer regulation of individual insurers.[4]

---

[2]Though such charters have been advocated for parts of the business. For example, interstate life insurance company charters on a voluntary basis are suggested in "Are Federal Charters Coming?" *The Spectator*, July, 1961, pp. 34–45.

[3]All insurers are not technically "companies," or corporations, but the use here refers to all private insurers. Social insurance systems such as are discussed in Chapter 8 might be considered much closer to the concept of a public utility, and their regulation and administration are correspondingly more akin to government regulation of public utilities.

[4]C. A. Kulp, *Casualty Insurance* (New York: The Ronald Press Company, 1956), pp. 533–34.

As illustrations of self-regulation in insurance Kulp goes on to review the major functions over which insurers and their trade associations exercise considerable control. He discusses the following areas: (1) rate making and policy drafting, (2) claim administration, (3) hazard prevention, (4) research, and (5) public and legislative relations.[5] The work of such organizations as the National Bureau of Casualty Underwriters (N.B.C.U.), the Mutual Insurance Rating Bureau (M.I.R.B.), the National Council on Compensation Insurance (N.C.C.I.), and the National Association of Independent Insurers (N.A.I.I.) is discussed in relation to their importance to contracts and rates. To this list would have to be added the many state and regional fire insurance rating organizations, and the new Multi-Line Insurance Rating Bureau (M.L.I.R.B.). In claims, the Health Insurance Council (H.I.C.), the International Claim Association (I.C.A.), the Association of Casualty and Surety Companies (A.C.S.C.), the National Auto Theft Bureau (N.A.T.B.), the National Inter-Company Arbitration Agreement (N.I.C.A.A.), and the National Board of Fire Underwirters (N.B.F.U.) provide valuable help in regulating claim practices. Many of these organizations are also active in hazard prevention work, cooperating with other such associations as the National Safety Council (N.S.C.), the Insurance Institute for Highway Safety (I.I.H.S.), the American Society of Safety Engineers (A.S.S.E.), Underwriters' Laboratories (U.L.), and many others. In research activities, the insurance business sponsors such important cooperative efforts as the Institute of Life Insurance (I.L.I.), the Insurance Information Institute (or I.I.I., for property-liability insurance), the Life Insurance Agency Management Association (L.I.A.M.A.), the American Mutual Alliance (A.M.A.), and the research bureaus of the N.A.I.I., N.B.F.U. and A.C.S.C. In public and legislative relations the insurers themselves, as well as many of the above insurance organizations, supply many representatives directly to industry committees who tackle the major problems of insurance. Oftentimes these industry committees work in conjunction with government regulatory bodies to draft legislation, coordinate programs and offer constructive aid to the formulation of action designed to improve both self-regulation and public regulation of insurance.

In evaluating the success of self-regulation in insurance it is important to mention that widespread differences exist between the United States and other countries. Extremely different methods and results may be found in particular lines or classes of insurance, or in one state as opposed to another. Self-regulation is no panacea; it works in some parts of insurance extremely well, while in others

[5] *Ibid.*, pp. 534–42.

it is disappointingly ineffective. Kulp evaluates its performance for casualty insurance as best in rate making and hazard reduction.[6] Other authorities emphasize the difficulties and continual inadequacies of self-regulation in any aspects of insurance which are closely related to competition,[7] such as regulation of production costs, commissions, advertising, and rates.

In some foreign countries, such as England and the Netherlands, self-regulation has worked well. Very little government regulation exists, to the extent that a general comment has been heard: "In England, insurers may do anything, the only requirement being that they publicize what they are doing!" Still, cooperative action of the insurers has succeeded in achieving high standards of financial solvency (backed by interinsurer funds and guarantees) and fair treatment to policyholders.[8] The reasons attributed to the excellent success of self-regulation in England include the philosophy, attitudes, and traditions of English insurers, as well as their smaller number and size.

Other countries, such as Germany and the Scandinavian nations, follow the strictest patterns of governmental regulation of insurance, including approval procedures for most forms, commissions, and rates. The United States seems to fall between these two extremes of very little as opposed to very extensive self-regulation. Self-regulation is relied upon much more in the United States than in Germany, but much less than in England.

Government Regulation of Insurance

Three basic methods of providing insurance regulation are available to government: (1) legislation, (2) administrative action, and (3) court action. Corresponding to the three main branches of the government, each of these methods is significant in the supervision of insurance. Legislation is the foundation of insurance regulations, for it makes the law. The insurance laws of each state are often combined in what is known as an *insurance code*,[9] and these codes are of primary importance. Administrative action is also very important, as many of the specific applications of insurance laws are left in the hands of the insurance *superintendent or commissioner* in each state. Court action is of lesser importance, but of great value

---

[6]*Ibid.*, p. 542. The term hazard reduction as used here means loss prevention.

[7]G. F. Michelbacher, *Multiple-Line Insurance* (New York: McGraw-Hill Book Co., Inc., 1956), Chap. 22 "Development of Governmental Supervision," p. 527.

[8]For an excellent though somewhat out-dated review of English insurance regulation, see A. J. Bohlinger and Thomas C. Morrill, *Insurance Supervision and Practices in England* (New York Insurance Department, 1948).

[9]The insurance code for an individual state may be bound in a volume which today often exceeds several hundred pages.

in regulation because of its ever-present potential effect in providing detailed interpretations of troublesome parts of the law.

Government Legislation. The regulation of the insurance business by the states is now well established. The practice takes its point of departure from a series of court decisions and has been continued in the face of some contention that, because of the number of jurisdictions, insurance might better be regulated by the federal government. The classic case is *Paul* v. *Virginia*, in which the United States Supreme Court decided in 1868 that insurance "is not a transaction of commerce," and thus can be neither interstate commerce, nor subject to federal regulation.[10] Until 1944, a period of 75 years, the Paul decision was upheld by the Supreme Court.

In 1941 complaints were made to the Department of Justice that certain insurance company practices were in violation of the Sherman Antitrust Act. As a result a momentous 4 to 3 decision was handed down in 1944 by the United States Supreme Court before one of its largest audiences in history. This case, *United States* v. *South-Eastern Underwriters Association et al.*,[11] now known to the legal profession and to the insurance business as the *S.E.U.A. case*, held insurance to be commerce. Thus, because of its interstate nature, it would often be subject to federal regulation. As a matter of practice, because of delegation of authority by Congress, the regulation of the business of insurance remains a state function.

The specific delegation to the states of the power to regulate insurance occurred with passage of Public Law 15 in 1945.[12] Congress made the Sherman Act, the Clayton Act, and the Federal Trade Commission Act applicable to the business of insurance after January 1, 1948 "to the extent that such business is not regulated by state law." In other words, jurisdiction for regulating interstate insurance was left with the individual states as it had been for many

---

[10]Today it is difficult to rationalize such a decision, but in 1868 it was understandable as the now-famous decision stated: "Issuing a policy of insurance is not a transaction of commerce. The policies are simply contracts of indemnity against loss by fire entered into between the corporations and the assured for a consideration paid by the latter. These contracts are not articles of commerce in any proper meaning of the word. They are not subjects of trade and barter, offered in the market as something having an existence and value independently of the parties to them. They are not commodities to be shipped or forwarded from one state to another and then put up for sale. They are like other personal contracts between parties which are completed by their signature and the transfer of the consideration. Such contracts are not interstate transactions, though the parties may be domiciled in different states. The policies do not take effect—are not executed contracts—until delivered by the agent in Virginia. They are, then, local transactions, and are governed by the local law. They do not constitute a part of the commerce between the states any more than a contract for the purchase and sale of goods in Virginia by a citizen of New York, whilst in Virginia, would constitute a portion of such commerce." *Paul* v. *Virginia*, 231 U.S. 495.

[11]64 U.S. 1162.

[12]Also known as the McCarran-Ferguson Law, C 20, 79th Congress, 1st session.

years, but the important proviso was added that would permit the federal government to take over insurance regulation whenever the state regulation became inadequate. The specific nature of this rather general requirement has not been fully settled, though the most recent cases indicate that federal jurisdiction will not usurp the states' powers as long as legislative action to provide insurance supervision has been taken.[13] Most states increased heavily their insurance regulation in laws passed between 1944 and 1948, as a result of the S.E.U.A. decision and Public Law 15, and have continued their efforts to retain the power to supervise insurance for the states. Investigations totaling thousands of pages of testimony have been carried out by the Senate Judiciary Anti-Trust and Monopoly Committee.[14] Alleged inadequacies in state insurance laws have been pointed out, but no recent federal legislation has taken over any significant part of state regulation of insurance.

The development of insurance regulation by the states has, in the above manner, had a colorful history. Many of its interesting facets are included in Appendix A, "A History of Insurance." Interesting details on some of its other landmarks, such as the Armstrong Investigation of 1905, the Merritt Committee Investigation of 1911, the Temporary National Economic Committee studies in 1939–41, and the investigations of health insurance practices in 1910 and 1951–58, are contained in numerous other volumes.[15]

In summary, the regulation of insurance by governmental legislation has been found to be almost completely a matter of insurance laws passed by the individual states. Their insurance codes have the distinct disadvantage of lacking uniformity. The critics of state regulation emphasize the possible duplication, complexity, and inefficiency which may be the result of nonuniformity. However, advocates of federal regulation for insurance must provide much stronger arguments than just simplicity and economics, for today the political and social repercussions of any trend away from states' rights are overwhelming.[16] The taxes and fees paid by insurers to the states in the annual amount of over $600 million[17] are stark evi-

---

[13]*F.T.C.* v. *National Casualty Company* (1958) and *F.T.C.* v. *Travelers Health Association* (1959).

[14]Report of the Committee of the Judiciary, Subcommittee on Anti-Trust and Monopoly, Report No. 1834 (86th Cong. 2d sess.) (Washington, D.C.: U.S. Government Printing Office, August, 1960). The report is about 250 pages, but testimony and exhibits total nine volumes of almost 6,000 pages.

[15]Including Appendix I of the classic reference: Edwin W. Patterson, *The Insurance Commissioner in the U.S.* (Cambridge, Mass.: Harvard University Press, 1927); and Chapter 34 of Albert H. Mowbray and Ralph Blanchard, *Insurance* (New York: McGraw-Hill Book Co., Inc., 1961).

[16]Kulp, *op. cit.*, p. 615.

[17]According to the 1962 state insurance department data, compiled as of the end of 1961 by the Insurance Industry Committee of Ohio, Columbus, Ohio.

dence of the stakes involved. Legal precedent to date has firmly established the regulatory responsibility, and its benefits in tax revenue, for the individual states.

Administrative Action. The broad powers which the ***insurance*** *commissioner*[18] of each state possesses are the key to the enforcement of insurance laws by the states. The administrative powers of the commissioners are derived from statutes which create the office. Usually these statutes are not very detailed in defining the authority and responsibility of the commissioner. With the vast number of bills and laws[19] which today concern insurance matters, and the general increased reliance on administrative law, the position of commissioner has become increasingly important in state government. His wide authority extends from licensing of companies and agents to requiring annual reports from the insurers to approval of forms and rates (in some but not all lines of insurance) and investigation of complaints of many kinds.

In most states the insurance commissioner is appointed by the governor and is a member of his cabinet. The logic of this method of choosing the head insurance regulatory official is that the governor is ultimately responsible for the business success of his term of office, and therefore should be able to appoint a person to carry out this responsibility. The prime disadvantage of this method is the short[20] tenure of office for many insurance commissioners, especially in states where the majority political party has frequently changed. In several states where the job of insurance commissioner is an elective office the disadvantageous situation of a short term in authority is also complicated by the vagaries of voter appeal. One wonders if the electorate could choose a person of the necessary high caliber and integrity with any better measure of success than appointments by the governors have produced. The dilemma of obtaining better commissioners and longer terms of office seems unavoidably tied to the political party system of our governmental system. Many observers, while criticizing the perhaps too broad powers of the insurance commissioner and his political method of

---

[18]A large majority of the states use this title, or "commissioner of insurance"; six states use the title "superintendent of insurance"; and four are "director of insurance." *Best's Insurance Reports—Fire and Casualty 1963* (New York: A. M. Best Company), p. vi.

[19]Alice Chellberg, in a speech at the 1963 C.P.C.U. Convention in Denver on September 25, 1963 (to be published in the 1964 C.P.C.U. Annals), notes that the number of bills closely associated with insurance exceeded 10,000 in the state legislatures during 1962!

[20]Consider, for example, the recent experience of Ohio, where four different superintendents of insurance have been in office between 1959–63. N.A.I.C. 1963 President Lee I. Kneckelhan of Washington referred to the estimated average term of office among all appointive commissioners as 2½ years in the *National Underwriter* (Fire and Casualty Edition), October 28, 1963, p. 11.

selection, marvel at the handicaps which are often overcome by generally low-paid but high-caliber insurance commissioners.[21]

The insurance *department* with which most insurance commissioners carry out their duties may vary from a few persons in some of the smaller states to well over 600 employees in such a state as New York. Many departments have existed since the 1800's. The New York Insurance Department has been in operation for over 100 years.[22] Its competent personnel have been responsible for an excellent record of supervision in that state, and for a vast influence upon insurance regulation in many other states that have relied upon New York as a guide for their insurance legislation and administrative action. An example of the means by which capable employees of an insurance department are developed to provide career service in insurance regulation is the seven-volume publication by the New York Insurance Department of their in-service training program.[23]

The major powers of the insurance commissioner have been mentioned as licensing, examination, and investigation. Each insurer in a state, after following the required incorporation procedure if they are a domestic organization, must be *licensed* for the lines of business it plans to write. The commissioner has broad interpretative powers in deciding whether or not an insurer is qualified, financially and otherwise, to operate in his state. After issuance, licenses are usually renewable on an annual basis. Again, the insurance commissioner has considerable power to refuse to issue a renewal license, as well as the power of suspension or revocation. He also conducts examinations through his department which determine the issuance of insurance agents' and brokers' licenses.

The *examination* of insurers, once they have been licensed, is also an important task of the commissioner. Continued solvency of the insurers is the major objective of such detailed examinations which are conducted according to law at intervals of from three to five years. The checking of assets, liabilities, and reserves is part of this procedure, as well as a review of almost all underwriting, investment, and claim practices of the insurer. A zone system is used in cooperation with the National Association of Insurance Commissioners[24] to avoid unnecessary duplicate examination by many

[21]Kulp, *op. cit.*, p. 562.

[22]John Gudmundsen, *In the Public Interest: One Hundred Years of Insurance Supervision in New York State* (Published by the Insurance Industry Committee for the New York Insurance Department Centennial), January, 1960.

[23]Aldebert G. Straub, Jr. (ed.), *Examination of Insurance Companies* (New York Insurance Department, 1953–55). These volumes are an extensive source of reference for many topics of interest to students of insurance regulation.

[24]This is a voluntary association of the top insurance administrator from each state. It has been important since 1871 for not only the Zone examination procedures, but also for its indirect influence on uniformity of insurance laws in the states. Recom-

states. In this way the examination of insurers licensed in many states is standardized and simplified, and the results of the regular zone examination accepted by all states in which the insurer does business. In the intervening years between complete examinations of insurers, every state requires the filing of an *annual statement* with the insurance commissioner. This is a report of current financial condition and changes which have occurred during the year. A standard N.A.I.C. form is used which for most details provides uniformity of the information requested in the statement.

The *investigation* powers of the insurance commissioner in most states extend to a wide variety of powers to determine whether or not insurers or their representatives are meeting the requirements of the statutes. Free access to records and books of the insurers, and hearings on such matters as rate violations or unfair trade practices are examples of his authority. As a result of such procedures, which are often informal, the commissioner may issue administrative rulings or advisory opinions in regard to the business conduct of insurers or their agents. In extreme cases he may declare the insolvency of an insurer in liquidation or rehabilitation proceedings. All such powers have as their major goal the protection of insurance policyholders and claimants. These parties should not treat the functions of an insurance commissioner as a guarantee against any and all possible loss, but the insurance regulatory powers provide important means of preventing or reducing such losses and abuses.

Court Action. The extremely broad authority of insurance commissioners is subject to some measures of review and interpretation by the courts. The *notice* and *hearing* procedures which are conducted by the commissioner in order to arrive at official rulings may be reviewed by the courts to determine if he has carried out his duties in conformity with the statutes. The discretionary power of the commissioner is also subject to *mandamus* (relief against breach or abuse of official power) and *injunction* (to prevent irreparable injury) actions by aggrieved parties.[25] Examples are actions to compel the commissioner to issue a license to an insurer, or to prevent its cancellation. In addition to the courts being used in private actions (or by the attorney general of the state) against an insurance commissioner, the reverse may be true. The commis-

---

mendations and model laws are discussed and studied by its committees, and given publicity in semiannual meetings. The prestige and position of these officials have given some effect to the adoption of their suggestions by the states. However, major criticism in recent years has been aimed at the N.A.I.C. for its inability to bring about greater uniformity in the insurance legislation of the states.

[25]Robert E. Dineen, Clifford R. Procter, and H. Daniel Gardner, "The Economics and Principles of Insurance Supervision" in *Insurance and Government* (New York: McGraw-Hill Book Co., Inc., 1962), p. 24.

sioner may, for example, petition the courts to enforce compliance with laws or rulings.

KINDS OF INSURANCE REGULATION BY THE STATES

The specific state laws which regulate insurance cannot be discussed in detail in this chapter. The insurance codes, as well as the general business laws, of each of the fifty jurisdictions vary too much to attempt a complete treatment of the subject. For specific insurance laws, administrative practices, and court decisions, the lawyer and the student of insurance must refer to the regulatory activities in a particular state. However, a general picture of the kinds of insurance regulation in the states is also necessary. This section of the chapter summarizes the regulation usually found in the more important insurance jurisdictions, such as New York State. The reader must take care to compare his own specific state laws and rulings with the general review as presented here.

Insurance regulation by the states is largely aimed at the insurers that conduct an insurance business within their jurisdiction. Some regulation is also provided for agents, brokers, and other persons who are part of the marketing of insurance contracts and services provided to insurance policyholders. Regulation of insurers falls into the following categories: (1) formation and licensing requirements, (2) supervision of operations, and (3) liquidation procedures. The second category includes a wide variety of regulatory controls, some extensive and some slight, over such activities as contract forms, rates, reserves, assets, and trade practices.

Formation and Licensing of Insurers

Insurance companies are required to meet specific standards of organization, often higher ones than are set for general business organizations. The rationale for such higher standards has been discussed in the first section of the chapter. Basically, the need is for methods which have the objective of ascertaining the solvency, competence, and integrity of the insuring organization. The first step is *incorporation,*[26] an introductory process in which the state recognizes and approves the existence of a new legal identity. Early insurance companies achieved this legal recognition through separate application to the state legislature. Starting in the latter half of the nineteenth century special incorporation statutes were passed in most states and today all but one state uses this method of forma-

[26]Reciprocals, Lloyd's associations, fraternals, and some health insurance associations do not legally become incorporated by this process. They do, however, file similar statements of present status and proposed activities as stated in their charter and by-laws.

tion for insurance companies.[27] The New York Insurance Law,[28] for example, outlines in detail the procedure to be followed under the incorporation statute, including: written proposal to the Superintendent of Insurance, name to be used, territories and kinds of business in which operations are planned, and public notice in newspapers of intention to incorporate.

The next step, *licensing*, is a check on the insurer's financial condition to ascertain that it has the required capital and surplus for the kinds of insurance permitted in the license. The statutory requirements for licensing must be met by *domestic* (insurers domiciled, or having their home office in the state), *foreign* (out-of-state), and *alien* (out-of-the-United States). The requirements sometimes vary among these three types of insurers, but the laws usually specify at least as high standards for foreign and alien insurers as for domestic insurers. Standards also vary by legal type of insurer, with mutual company requirements being somewhat different from those for stock companies. For example, the financial requirements for mutual companies are stated in terms of surplus, rather than capital plus surplus, and additional requirements are set for the minimum number of policyholders with which to start a mutual company.

The financial standards for insurers to obtain a license are tremendously variable in the different states.[29] In some states as little as $25,000 of capital or surplus is required to write a specific kind of insurance such as fire. Each additional kind of insurance for which the company is to be licensed requires an additional amount of capital or surplus. For multiple-line insurance, including all kinds except life insurance, the states also exhibit wide variation: "The strictest state sets its requirement at $3,550,000 . . ., which is over thirty-five times the standard of the two most lenient states which requires only $100,000 . . . ."[30] Twenty-one states require less than $500,000, twenty-two between $500,000 and $1,000,000, and nine jurisdictions set $1 million or more as the minimum standard for a new domestic multiple-line company.

The licensing procedure is not dependent alone on financial requirements. Many states give the Insurance Commissioner leeway to apply considerable judgment in acting, or refusing to act, upon a license application. The objective of licensing is ostensibly to assure a preliminary method of lessening the chance of financial in-

---

[27]Rhode Island, where insurers must petition the General Assembly.

[28]*New York Insurance Law*, Secs. 48–49.

[29]And, in many states, to continue to keep the license, the financial requirements must be maintained.

[30]David L. Bickelhaupt, *Transition to Multiple-Line Insurance Companies* (Homewood, Ill.: Richard D. Irwin, Inc., 1961), p. 65.

solvency of the insurer. On the basis of the same objective, a license may be denied for many other reasons, including bad faith or reputation of the proposed incorporators or management of an insurer. General managerial ability is undoubtedly as important as capital and surplus requirements in achieving sustained financial stability for an insurer.

Insurer Operations

As a protection against insolvency and unfair treatment of policyholders, insurance regulation continues after the formation and licensing of an insurer. The states exercise some control over many phases of the operations of insurers. The basic idea of continual regulation is that most obligations of insurers extend years into the future, and the state should provide supervision to see that the promises in the contract are fulfilled. Variations in the way insurer operations are supervised are strikingly different among the states, and among the various kinds of insurance. Most states do provide some regulation of the following types: contracts and forms, rates, expense limitations, reserves, asset and surplus values, investments, agents' licensing and trade practices, and taxation.

Contracts and Forms. The strictest regulation of contracts is applied in fire insurance, where each of the states stipulates the exact wording for the standard fire insurance contract. All states require a standard fire insurance contract, and almost all states use the New York form.[31] Many differences in the wording of other contracts are found, however, and independent companies and the various rating bureaus may have individualized contracts which vary in some impartant particulars. Life insurance contracts are not standard contracts in the sense that similar form or benefits are required. Most states do, however, provide some uniformity by requiring a number of "standard provisions" in life contracts, pertaining to such items as the grace period, loan and surrender values, and the like. The best examples of little regulation over contracts and forms are found in the marine and health fields. Except for a few required provisions, these contracts are the most nonuniform of insurance contracts and should be carefully studied by policyholders in order to determine what benefits, conditions, and exclusions they contain.

Rates. The price of insurance contracts is also controlled to a varying degree in the different lines of insurance. In some kinds of insurance, such as marine insurance, practically no regulation exists in the states. In other kinds, the supervision of rates is indirect, as in life insurance where the regulation is aimed at minimum reserves

---

[31] See Chapter 9.

which must be maintained (and thus prices which must be charged to be able to pay losses and expenses).

Most other major kinds of insurance are subject to some direct-rate regulation. The statutory standards are set forth in an insurance rating law. Every state[32] now has such a law, and most of them have the same basic objectives as set forth in the National Association of Insurance Commissioners' "All-Industry Bill" which served as a model for many of the laws as they were put into effect between 1946 and 1948.

The early attempts to establish rate making on a sound basis through the establishment of the various regional organizations generated a hostility on the part of the public to insurance cooperation. Opposition was voiced on the ground that cooperative action was monopolistic and contrary to the public interest. At the outgrowth of this opposition various state legislators undertook to prohibit cooperative rate making by the enactment of bills (known as "anti-compact laws"), which prohibited combinations between insurers for the joint fixing of rates. It became apparent, however, that unlimited competition, far from being in the public interest, could also be injurious. An inadequate price for insurance can result much easier than for other products. Insurance costs, and thus prices, must be based upon estimated minimum costs of losses, expenses, and services to be provided for many years ahead. Insurance commissioners realized the importance of safeguarding the solvency of the companies, and it was found that the disastrous consequences of unrestricted competition could be avoided through the organization of rating bureaus. Rates could be predicated upon statistical information accumulated from all available sources and the loss experience of member companies. Laws were then enacted authorizing the association of companies for the purpose of making rates.

Basic standards recognized by rating laws required that: (1) rates shall be reasonable and adequate for the class of risks to which they apply, (2) no rate shall discriminate unfairly between risks involving essentially the same hazards and expense elements or between risks in the application of like charges and credits, (3) consideration shall be given to the past and prospective loss experience, including the fire conflagration hazards, if any, (4) consideration shall be given to all factors reasonably attributable to the class of risks, and (5) consideration shall be given to a reasonable underwriting profit. Rates are considered reasonable when they produce

[32]C. Arthur Williams, Jr., *Price Discrimination in Property and Liability Insurance* (Minneapolis: The University of Minnesota Press, 1959), p. 55. The author notes on page 94 that it was not until 1951 that all states had effective legislation for regulating insurance rates, even though one of the first comprehensive rating laws was enacted in 1909.

sufficient revenue to pay all losses, to pay expenses of doing business, and, in addition, to produce a reasonable profit for the insurance carriers.

Rating laws provide specifically that there is no intent to prohibit or discourage reasonable competition; neither do they prohibit or discourage uniformity in insurance rates, rating systems, rating plans, or practices. The insurance department passes upon the reasonableness of the rules and regulations of rating organizations. A rating bureau may not be organized and withhold its facilities from certain companies or groups of companies. All companies have the statutory right to become bureau subscribers. Any company not eligible as a bureau member may secure the services of the bureau by paying reasonable fees and binding itself to the rules of the organization. It is the intent of the laws to permit concerted rate making but it is not the intent to require it. While a company the rates of which meet with the criteria indicated in the statutes may join with others in making rates in concert, it is not obligated to do so.

When rates have been promulgated, to allow any return of the insurance premium developed by the rate to an insured, except dividends to a class, is regarded as discrimination. A concession in rates is contrary to the law whether made in the form of a direct payment or credit on premium or by means of any subterfuge. The statutes do not prohibit the payment by one broker or agent of a part of his commission or other compensation to other licensed agents or brokers. Statutes generally do not allow the owner of extensive property holdings to become a licensed agent or broker for the purpose of placing his own business.

The proposed rates are not actually made by the states (except in Texas and Massachusetts), but by the rating bureaus or by individual insurers if their size and experience justify separate rates. The bureau method is used in fire insurance, workmen's compensation, surety bonds, automobile insurance (by some but not all insurers) and other lines. Individual company rate making has increased in the past decade and has become an important factor in automobile insurance and the new forms of multiple-line homeowner's and commercial policy contracts.

Approval of the proposed rates is required by the insurance commissioner, even though it may be that "the statutes providing for rate regulation are vague and their objectives are contradictory."[33] Some states require prior approval before the rates can be used; others permit the use of new rates immediately (so-called "no prior

[33]Frederick G. Crane, *Automobile Insurance Rate Regulation* (The Ohio State University: Bureau of Business Research Monograph Number 105, 1962), p. 67.

approval" laws) but the insurance commissioner may disapprove them within a certain time limit. A few states, such as Ohio, require prior approval for some kinds of insurance, such as fire insurance, but no prior approval before use of other kinds such as automobile insurance.

Rate approval is not required for all property and liability insurance. Most states do not apply the All-Industry type of rating laws to special lines such as aviation and health insurance and reinsurance.

Expense Limitations. Other than direct regulation of insurance prices by required rate approval, some state laws supervise the cost of *life* insurance by limiting the expense portion of the premium. The New York law is most influential in this regard; because all companies doing business in that state must conform to its limitations for all insurance contracts it writes anywhere. Maximum commissions and allowances of 55 percent during the first year are set for business written by life insurance companies.

Reserves. It is the practice for the states to require insurers to set up as a liability a reserve considered as adequate to provide a fund to meet policy obligations as they mature. The only insurers excepted are certain types of mutual companies operating on an intrastate basis and usually confining their operations within a small local area. In the case of these local mutuals, the reserve requirement may vary, depending upon the assessment liability provided in the policy.

In the case of life insurance the reserve is an amount which, augmented by premium payments required under outstanding contracts and interest earnings, will enable the life insurance company to meet its policy obligations. More specifically, the reserve is that portion of premiums paid on level premium life insurance policies which is held to meet future policy obligations. These include death benefits, policy loans, surrender values, and the like. It is represented by assets which the company invests but is, in fact, a company liability to be disbursed to meet policy obligations. In life insurance there is no provision for the cancellation of the policy and a return of unearned premium. The life insurance policy does provide, however, upon the surrender of the contract for the return to the insured of certain values termed "nonforfeiture values."

In the field of property insurance the *unearned premium reserve* must at all times be adequate to pay a full proportionate return premium to policyholders in the event of the cancellation of a policy before it expires. The reserve should be adequate to reinsure the business, if necessary. The basic purpose of the reserve is to meet all liabilities under the contract and to pay expenses of claim services incurred with respect to the business. The reserve requirement in both life and property insurance is the establishment of an accounting practice that will make available funds for the proper settlement of claims or payment of losses and, at the same time, account for income received but not yet earned.

A second type of reserves required of property insurers is the *loss reserve*. Since many contracts of this type do not involve immediate payment of all losses that have occurred, reserves must be set up to assure their future payment. For example, a workmen's compensation claim may be made against the insurer today. In many cases the loss payments may be made gradually according to law during a long future period of disability. In automobile liability cases it may be several years after a loss before a court decides who is liable and for how much. In such cases, an estimate of the reserve that will be needed to pay the insurer's obligation is made and carried on its books as a loss reserve. In this way, losses and loss expense for claims that are known but not yet paid are provided for by the insurer under the loss reserve laws of the states.

Assets and Surplus Values. The value of assets appearing in the balance sheets of insurance companies must be correct in order that liabilities, reserves, and residual surplus items have true meaning. Securities held by insurers are valued by a committee of the National Association of Insurance Commissioners. The insurance commissioner of each state does not have to use these values but in practice almost always does in fulfilling his regulatory duties. Stocks are usually valued at end of the year market values, while some bonds (especially those nonamortizable) are given estimated or "Convention" values. The result is a good example of voluntary and state regulation working together for the proper regulation of insurance. For some insurers, such as mutual life companies, both surplus accumulation and distribution are subject to regulation aimed at providing equitable treatment for all policyholders.

Investments. To protect the solvency of insurers, most states have laws governing the types of securities that may be purchased for investment. The strictest regulations apply to life insurance companies, since they hold many billions of dollars of assets for many years for their policyholders.

The investment of assets by property and liability insurers is also supervised, although the laws are more lenient. Uniformity among the state laws is practically nonexistent. Only a few general characteristics of the regulations are discernible. The laws of specific jurisdictions must be consulted for application in any one particular state. General practice aims at requiring the safest types of investments for all assets held as reserves (unearned premium and loss reserves) and other liabilities. Cash, bonds of high grade and specified experience, and perhaps preferred stocks of proven quality may be permitted for those assets. Although many exceptions among the states can be found, the remainder of assets (representing capital and surplus) may be invested in a wider range of securities, including common stocks meeting certain minimum requirements. Limitations on real estate holdings, size of single investments in relation to total assets or surplus, investments in out-of-state companies, and many other restrictions are also found in the state statutes.

Life insurance companies are subject to vigorous supervision of their investment portfolios. Each annual statement filed with the insurance department lists every individual investment with detailed information about its acquisition, costs, values, and earnings. The insurance laws require a high standard of investment for life insurers, of a quality comparable to those required for savings banks. Mortgages and bonds are the prime investments in the portfolio of life insurers, involving a large majority of total assets. Some limited permission is granted in most states for other investments such as stocks, which may be limited, for example, to about 5 percent of assets, or a proportion of surplus. Real estate holdings, especially commercial properties and housing projects, are also limited to a maximum of between 10 and 20 percent in various states. The legality of all holdings of the insurer are checked carefully in periodic audits and meticulous inventories of the securities.

Agents' Licensing and Trade Practices. An important control on insurer operations is maintained through laws in all states which require insurance agents and brokers to be licensed. The insurance departments usually administer these laws, with the objective of permitting only competent and trustworthy representatives to be used by the insurers. The standards vary tremendously, from mere payment of a license fee to a comprehensive written examination following required attendance in insurance courses approved by the department. New York's written examinations, with ninety classroom hours of study also required since 1955, have begun to influence other states to raise their licensing requirements for insurance agents. The examinations are often divided into separate tests for life insurance, health insurance, and multiple-line insurance. In states that license brokers, the examinations for insurance brokers are usually more difficult and extensive than those given to agents.

Special laws, called *countersignature laws,* require that all property insurance contracts written in a state must be signed by an agent who is a resident of that state. Agents must also represent only insurers that are authorized and licensed in the state. An exception is made under some *surplus line laws* which in some states permit a specially licensed agent to represent unauthorized insurers in cases where the risks cannot be fully protected by licensed insurers within the state.

Unfair trade practices in insurance are made illegal in all states under legislation similar to the Federal Trade Commission Act. These laws aim at retaining jurisdiction for the states (under the provisions of Public Law 15) in preventing fraudulent and unethical acts of agents and brokers. They provide fines and, more important, suspension or revocation of licenses as penalties for violations. Examples of such unfair practices in insurance include: (1) *rebating*, the returning of any part of the premium (except in dividends) to the policyholder by insurer or agent as a price-cutting sales inducement, (2) *twisting*, a special form of misrepresentation in which an agent may induce the policyholder to cancel disadvantageously the contract of another insurer to take out a new contract, (3) *misappropriation*, in which the agent unlawfully keeps funds belonging to others, (4) *commingling*, which some states prevent by requiring a separate bank account for the agent's premium funds, and (5) *misleading advertising*, which includes many regulations for full and fair information in advertisements by insurers and agents. The insurance commissioner has broad powers in preventing the above unfair practices and exercises his authority by investigating complaints as well as initiating investigations of any questionable acts of insurers or their representatives.

Taxation. Revenue for the states has become an important reason for insurance regulation. The insurers pay what amounts to a sales tax on premiums received from all their policyholders. This *premium tax* is usually about 2 percent, although some states charge 3 percent of premiums. The tax is paid by insurers; its cost, of course, is included in the price of insurance contracts and thus is paid indirectly by the policyholders. Premium taxes and other miscellaneous license fees are now a sizeable amount in the states, exceeding $600 million in 1961.[33] That the taxes are primarily for revenue purposes rather than to pay for the cost of insurance regulation is obvious from the statistics. Only 4 percent, or $24 million,[34] of the above total tax revenue and fees in 1961 was used for operation of the state insurance departments. Some states used less than 2 percent[35] of the tax revenue for insurance department regulation, while only a few used more than 7 percent.[36] If public regulation of insurance is lacking in any respect, the state legislatures should first look to see if the insurance departments are provided with adequate funds and manpower to carry out the necessary supervision of insurance in a consistent and equitable manner.

---

[33]See footnote 17.

[34]*Ibid.*

[35]*Ibid.* Michigan, Ohio, Missouri, Oklahoma, West Virginia, and Mississippi.

[36]*Ibid.* New York, Texas, Massachusetts, South Carolina, and Puerto Rico.

Liquidation of Insurers

The insurance commissioners of a state not only officiates at the birth and growth of an insurer, but also, if necessary, at its demise. An insurer may be liquidated for a number of reasons, including financial insolvency. Some liquidations may be voluntary in nature, in order to effect a corporate reorganization or merger. Reinsurance of all outstanding liabilities and contracts may be achieved so that no loss results to policyholders. New York State, for example, has maintained a record since 1908 that no life insurance policyholder of a New York licensed insurer has suffered loss through a company failure. In supervising a liquidation, the insurance commissioner acts under the insurance laws as the official in charge of rehabilitation (if the company can be restored to financial stability through reorganization) or liquidation if the company is dissolved. The purpose of both actions is to conserve as much as possible the assets of the insurer and provide fair treatment for the claimants, policyholders, and investors.

SUMMARY

Insurance is a highly regulated form of business because its characteristics include complexity, future promises, and heavy reliance by the buying public on the integrity and financial security of insurers. The individual states provide the basis for insurance regulation, although many kinds of self-regulation by the insurers and their voluntary associations are also important. Government regulation of insurance is more strict in the United States than in some other countries such as England. Each state legislature has enacted many insurance laws (known as an insurance *code*) which are administered by an insurance *commissioner* with broad interpretative powers to carry out his duties through an insurance *department*. Court cases may clarify regulation by interpreting and enforcing insurance legislation and administrative actions.

The power of the states to regulate insurance was challenged in the famous S.E.U.A. case in 1944. The result was that Congress passed Public Law 15 to grant continued jurisdiction over insurance specifically to the states. The federal government may have only residual jurisdiction in regulating insurance where the states do not provide adequate supervision. This potential power has not been used to any great extent as yet, although the trend suggests that increased attempts to use these residual powers might be expected in the future.

The typical state laws regulating insurance include many kinds, from licensing requirements when an insurer is organized to active controls over many facets of its operations. Tremendous variety exists among the states in the extent and detail of these laws supervising insurer operations. Some regulation is present in most states, however, of contracts, rates, expenses, reserves, assets and surplus values, investments, licensing of agents and brokers, and unfair trade practices. Many rules apply separately and differently to the various kinds of insurance, especially in life insurance as compared with property insurance. Insurance departments also collect substantial revenue in the form of state taxes on premiums, and aid in rehabilitating or liquidating insurers when necessary. The wide scope, the extreme variability among the states, and the importance of sound insurance regulation make these concepts essential to a good understanding of insurance.

FOR REVIEW

1. Why would "uncontrolled competition work a hardship upon the buyers of insurance?"
2. Insurance has long been subject to regulation. In your opinion, why is it logically a proper subject for regulation? The business is carried on by privately owned companies, not public utilities, and there is usually no right on the part of the public to demand and receive their services. They compete for business just as do automobile companies, merchants, and other business enterprises. Should not competition be the sole regulatory force?
3. Is "self-regulation" an effective means by which the insurance business can be regulated? Cite several examples.
4. Explain the relationship among the three basic methods by which government regulates insurance, i.e., (1) legislation, (2) administrative action, and (3) court action.
5. Does the federal government, or do the state governments, provide most of the regulation for insurance? Briefly explain the important part which (1) the Paul v. Virginia case, (2) the Southeastern Underwriters (S.E.U.A.) case, and (3) Public Law 15 had to play in the development of insurance regulation to its present situation.
6. It has been stated, regardless of the S.E.U.A. decision, that Congress could probably have exerted control over the business of insurance on the ground, not that insurance was commerce, but that it *affected commerce.* Discuss this point.
7. The Brief for Appellees in the S.E.U.A. case indicates that state experience is now hostile to competiton. To quote from the brief: "Their experience has taught the States that unlimited competition in fire insurance—as distinguished from other businesses—leads to: (1) insolvency of insurers which in turn injures the assured public since they will not only have paid out their money for nothing but, worse, will have relied in ignorance on a worthless indemnification; (2) competition going to greater extremes than in other businesses; (3) increased fire losses due to failure to take proper precautions to minimize hazards; (4) discrimination in favor of the influential assured whose business is sought rather than the average assured; and (5) a greater concentration of wealth and power in the larger, at the expense of the smaller, companies." Discuss briefly each of these points.
8. The insurance commissioner (or superintendent) in each state has powerful regulatory duties. Discuss several of the major functions of this offi-

cial. What are some of the principal problems in connection with proper insurance supervision by the commissioner?

9. Evaluate the need for state regulation of insurance in each of the areas of (*a*) incorporation and licensing, (*b*) operations, and (*c*) liquidation.
10. Briefly discuss the extent of state regulation of insurance as to: (*a*) contracts and forms, (*b*) rates, and (*c*) reserves. Include examples of how the regulation differs for some of the major fields of insurance.
11. Are insurance rates highly regulated? What are the objectives of the states in regulating the price charged for insurance contracts? How do the "All-Industry" rating laws attempt to achieve these purposes, and what are the alternatives to such laws?
12. What types of restrictions are placed upon investments by insurance companies?
13. In addition to income taxes and other taxes which may apply to many business enterprises, are insurers subject to any special form of taxation? If so, explain the kind and extent of such taxation.

Chapter 8

SOCIAL INSURANCE

IN addition to regulation of private insurance, governments are closely related to insurance in many programs of *social insurance*. The quest for economic security through application of the insurance technique is not limited to individuals—it is a desire of society as a whole as well as of private citizens, families, and businesses.

DESCRIPTION AND OBJECTIVES

"Social Security"

In general, the idea of society providing or requiring systems for obtaining economic security is popularly expressed as "social security." Oftentimes, the specific nature of this term is clouded by misconceptions and misunderstandings. To many persons "social security" means a particular program, most frequently that of Old Age, Survivors, and Disability Insurance (O.A.S.D.I.). Other persons often use the term in referring to the broad range of programs by which our federal, state, and local governments help bring economic security to individuals. In this broader sense, "social security" could include almost all government activities, from federal employment offices and minimum wage laws to municipal efforts to bring new industry to a certain city or area.

"Social security" is thus not used with preciseness in our everyday language. However, it ordinarily does involve reference to those *assistance* and *insurance* programs which are required, subsidized, or actually provided by government.

The objective of "social security" is simply restated as security for the members of a society. It is basic economic certainty which is the goal. "We are aiming at a minimum level of well-being for the people of this nation. Because we live in a money economy, that means the minimum of income and services essential to decent human existence."[1]

Although there are few persons who would quarrel with the overall goal as quoted, many observers will differ in defining the

[1]William Haber and Wilbur J. Cohen (eds.), *Social Security: Programs, Problems, and Policies* (Homewood, Ill.: Richard D. Irwin, Inc., 1960), p. 5.

more specific nature of the objective, and particularly in designing the method by which the goal should be accomplished. For example, should the objective be certainty in regard to *all* possible causes of financial adversity? Or should society pick out a few of the major kinds of unpredictable losses—such as old age, unemployment, or industrial injury—which affect a major part of the population? What is a *major* kind of loss and part of the population? How can such widespread social risks be differentiated from the same causes of losses which may be essentially individual[2] in their origin? And what about the *method* of providing a social solution to what have been identified as essentially social problems, i.e., those in which the community as a whole will have to bear the costs if nothing is done to meet the economic losses they bring? (The next section, on public assistance versus social insurance, tackles this question.)

A final example of the difficulty in defining the goals of "social security" is the question of just what constitutes a minimum level of well-being. In our industrialized and urbanized society, the minimum "floor-of-protection" must be translated into a specific income (or certain services) to enable each person to maintain the necessities of life. Obviously the needs include food, shelter, and clothing, and most of the early programs aimed at these essentials. Even if agreement is reached on the quality and quantity of these basic needs, and that is no mean task,[3] how is allowance made in a broad national program for "differentials in living costs and customs from one area of the country to another, variance in wage levels, and population mobility?"[4]

Public Assistance and Social Insurance

The distinction between "assistance" and "insurance" is important. A *public assistance* program is based on the concept of "need." Benefits are available to its recipients only after they have shown (by either lacking sufficient assets or income, or both) that society should help them in meeting basic minimum standards of food, shelter, and clothing. *Social insurance* programs are those systems

---

[2]Such as, for example, injuries that are nonoccupational or unemployment that results from quitting work for personal reasons.

[3]Should the food minimum include steak instead of hamburger, at least once in a while? Should nutrition and calories be the only criteria, or reasonable variety be included in the goal? Is housing only a roof and four walls, or should neighborhood and other factors be considered?

[4]Edwin J. Faulkner, "Social Security and Insurance—Some Relationships in Perspective," *The Journal of Insurance,* Vol. XXX, No. 2 (June, 1963), p. 207. The author also points out that there has been no universal agreement on the minimum level of protection, or whether it should include things such as an automobile, tobacco, or travel.

in which (1) the elements of the insurance technique[5] are present and (2) the plans are required, and often also conceived, financed, or administered, by government with the objective of meeting certain economic security standards for a society.

Examples of programs generally held to be those having the characteristics of public assistance are: (1) the Old Age Assistance (O.A.A.) program and (2) federal-state aid to dependent children, the blind, and permanently and totally disabled persons. Examples of plans usually included as social insurance are: (1) the Federal Old Age, Survivors, and Disability Insurance program (O.A.S.D.I.), (2) the state unemployment compensation systems, (3) the state workmen's compensation plans, (4) the state temporary disability (nonoccupational) insurance plans in four states, and (5) other programs such as the railroad retirement and unemployment systems, and sometimes, federal government civil service and state retirement systems.

Veterans' Benefit Programs

More than 40 different benefits and services[6] are available to veterans of service in the U.S. Armed Forces. Because these benefits are not public assistance programs based on "need," and many of them do not meet the requirements outlined above for social insurance plans, they are mentioned separately here. Such a wide range of benefits are available that it is not appropriate to try to distinguished each benefit under the normal categories of public assistance or social insurance.

The Veterans' Administration administers many of the benefits. Primarily these are available to the veteran himself, but many of them are also paid or available to survivors or members of the veteran's family. A partial list[7] includes: (1) compensation for service-connected disabilities, (2) pensions for non-service-connected disabilities, (3) compensation to survivors of servicemen who died in service or from a service-connected cause, (4) pensions for survivors of veterans who died from a non-service-connected

---

[5]This is where many definitions differ. Some authorities suggest that the only requirement is the combination ("pooling") of separate, independent risks in sufficient number to provide reasonable predictability. Other persons state that is also necessary to have such characteristics as (1) transfer of risk, (2) a legal, contractual obligation, and (3) a fund or other means on which to base future solvency of the plan, and (4) equity of costs in relation to potential benefit payments. See C. Arthur Williams, Jr., "Social Insurance—Proper Terminology?", *The Journal of Insurance*, March, 1963.

[6]A summary of these benefits and services is available from the Superintendent of Documents (Washington, D.C.: U.S. Government Printing Office) in a booklet titled "Veterans' Administration Fact Sheet, IS-1."

[7]*Social Security Handbook* (Washington, D.C.: Social Security Administration, U.S. Department of Health, Education, and Welfare, January, 1963), pp. 285–86.

cause, (5) benefits payable under U.S. Government Life Insurance or National Service Life Insurance, (6) veterans' burial expense payments, and (7) medical services of many kinds through Veterans' Administration hospitals. Supplemental and special payments to those payable under the Social Security Act are made to widows of a veteran who died of a service-connected cause. These bring the monthly payments up to a normal maximum of $128 per month.

Some examples of veterans' benefits administered by other agencies are: (1) retirement pay from the individual branches of the armed services, (2) Social Security (O.A.S.D.I.) wage credits for earnings while in the service, (3) burial space in national cemeteries, (4) farm and home loan benefits through various agencies, and (5) reemployment rights under the U.S. Department of Labor, Civil Service Commission and state employment offices.

In all, the veterans' benefit programs entail a broad and important range of benefits and services for a particular, but large, segment of the population today.

BACKGROUND

Social insurance in the United States is largely a product of the twentieth century, and particularly of the last 30 years. Workmen's compensation insurance appeared in the second decade of the century, but the real impetus toward extensive social insurance systems came in the 1930's with the passage of the Federal Social Security Act of 1935. In addition to providing support for public assistance programs such as Old Age Assistance, the Act was the direct means by which the Old Age Insurance system (now O.A.S.D.I., including survivors and disability benefits) and the state unemployment compensation plans began. Temporary disability (nonoccupational) laws created another major division of social insurance in four states during the 1940's.

The Social Security Act was by far the most outstanding landmark in the development of social insurance. "One of the remarkable things about the Social Security Act is that, born in a depression with millions out of work, its principal features were long-range programs that would have no immediate effect on the problems of the unemployed and the aged."[8] The depression of the 1930's was a factor in this legislation, undoubtedly, but the reasons for the recognition of the needs and the choice of a gigantic social insurance program for the solution were more deep-rooted.

The economy of the United States had rapidly changed from an agricultural and family-oriented society to one in which the vast

---

[8]Merrill G. Murray, "Social Insurance Perspectives: Background Philosophy and Early Program Developments," *The Journal of Insurance*, Vol. XXX, No. 2 (June, 1963), p. 184.

majority of the population lived in urban surroundings and worked in industrial pursuits. The result was to create an increasing interdependence among all wage earners. Instead of depending upon individual and family initiative, ingenuity, and thrift to provide support in hard times, the individual found that he must turn to the government and society as a whole to help him through economic hardships. The Great Depression focused the problem on the plight of the aged segment of the population, and the unemployed group, and from this grew the Social Security Act. The growth of social insurance from this beginning has been made possible by an unparalled economic upswing in the recent decades, bringing a high standard of living in the United States to support the continuing interest in alleviating the problems of industrial injury and disease, old age, unemployment, and disability. The concern is still evident today, with the current federal administration pledged to major efforts in reducing unemployment and a general "war on poverty."

The amendments to the O.A.S.D.I. program have been steady during the past 25 years. Survivorship benefits were added for widows and children up to age eighteen in 1939, even before the first retirement benefits for old age began. Liberalization has proceeded in almost every session of Congress, including 1946, 1950, 1952, 1954, 1956 (when disability benefits were introduced), 1957, 1958, 1960, and 1961. It has "expanded from coverage of a relatively limited group of workers to embrace all but a few gainfully employed Americans."[9]

THE SOCIAL INSURANCE PROGRAMS

In a textbook of this scope, only a limited summary of the major provisions of the basic social insurance programs can be offered. The student desiring additional detail and further information about each of the social insurance systems is referred to comprehensive publications[10] which concentrate on social (as opposed to private) insurance against economic insecurity.

The remainder of this chapter will aim at establishing a familiarity with the four most important types of social insurance today: (1) Old Age, Survivors, and Disability Insurance, (2) unemployment compensation, (3) workmen's compensation, and (4) temporary disability (nonoccupational) insurance. The section on

[9] Faulkner, *op. cit.*, p. 203.

[10] John G. Turnbull, C. Arthur Williams, Jr., and Earl F. Cheit, *Economic and Social Security* (2d ed.; New York: Ronald Press Co., 1962). See also Haber and Cohen, *op. cit.* For an extensive bibliography of references, a 221-page booklet is recommended: *Basic Readings in Social Security* (Washington, D.C.: U.S. Government Printing Office, U.S. Department of Health, Education, and Welfare, Social Security Administration Publication No. 28, 1960).

workmen's compensation will be abbreviated, since Chapter 15, "Employers' Liability and Workmen's Compensation," will discuss many of its aspects. References are also to be found to the O.A.S.-D.I. program in Chapter 28, "Coordinating Insurance Programs." Several miscellaneous types of social insurance are introduced at the end of this chapter, such as the railroad retirement and unemployment programs, government employee retirement plans, and several acts requiring liability insurance.

The general significance of the four primary social insurance programs is seen in the size of the yearly taxes (or, in the smaller part of the programs, insurance premiums) which now support them. As noted in Figure 2 of Chapter 2, the total taxes and premiums are nearly $20 *billion* a year, or nearly one third of the combined private and social insurance fields. More than half of the annual cost of social insurance today goes for the O.A.S.D.I. program, which exceeds $12 billion.

Each of the social insurance plans have basic features with which the student of insurance should be familiar. The programs are analyzed in the following sections of the chapter on the basis of (1) eligibility, (2) benefits, (3) administration, and (4) financing.

OLD AGE, SURVIVORS, AND DISABILITY INSURANCE

The largest and best-known social insurance system in the United States, O.A.S.D.I., is often mistaken as the only part of the 1935 Social Security Act, which actually provided also for nine other separate programs.[11] Title II of the Act created the trust funds and requirements for the O.A.S.D.I. program.

Eligibility

Covered Employment. More than nine out of ten employed persons are now covered by the plan. The only major types of workers not covered by O.A.S.D.I. are (1) some government employees, (2) private physicians, (3) some ministers, (those who have not elected to be covered), (4) some agricultural workers, and (5) some employees of nonprofit organizations (those which have not elected to become part of the system). Many federal government employees are covered under other retirement systems, and many state and local government workers are included in O.A.S.D.I. as a result of federal-state agreements. Thus, very few working persons are not now a part of the program. Both wage earners and self-employed persons are included.

---

[11]*Social Security Handbook, op. cit.*, p. 2. These include one other type of social insurance, unemployment compensation insurance, five public assistance programs, and three child welfare services.

Insured Status. To be entitled to benefits it is necessary that a person be engaged in employment covered by the Act for at least a certain prescribed minimum number of quarters (generally, a calendar quarter of a year in which at least $50 in wages, or $100 in self-employment, is earned). Workers become eligible for benefits by becoming "fully" or "currently" insured. *Fully insured status* is necessary for most benefits. It is usually attained by having 40 quarters, or 10 years, of coverage. However, the requirements may also now be met by having worked a much shorter period, including at least 1 quarter of coverage for each calendar year after 1950 (or after the year in which he attained age twenty-one) prior to his death, disability, or retirement. A minimum of 6 quarters is required. *Currently insured status* gains eligibility for survivorship benefits to a widow with children, and the worker must have been in covered employment during at least 6 of the last 13 quarters.

Benefits

Types of Benefits. There are three basic types of benefits available to those persons who achieve eligibility under the O.A.S.D.I. program. These are: (1) payments for *death,* including a small lump-sum payment and important survivors' income payments to widows with dependent children, (2) income payments for *disability,* if it is permanent and total, and (3) income payments after *retirement* age, to either or both husband and wife (or to a child under eighteen, or any age if disabled). Thus, in essence, O.A.S.D.I. pays in the case of dying too soon (before economic lifetime is completed), being disabled to a point which prevents earning an income, and living too long (beyond normal working lifetime of age sixty-two or sixty-five).

In reference to the insured status of the worker, the following *types* of benefits are paid:[12]

1. If the worker is *currently* insured:
   a. lump-sum death payment
      (1) to widow, widower, or anyone paying burial expenses
   b. survivorship income payments
      (1) to widow with one or more dependent children under age eighteen
      (2) to a dependent, unmarried child prior to age eighteen, or if the child is disabled before then
2. If the worker is *fully* insured:
   a. lump-sum death payment as in 1.*a.*
   b. survivorship income payments, as in 1.*b.*, and *also*
      (1) to widow at age sixty-two or more
      (2) to dependent parents at age sixty-two or more

[12]Adapted from *Social Security Handbook, op. cit.,* p. 24. Payments to a widow will stop if she remarries; payments to a wife or dependent husband will stop if a divorce is granted.

- *c.* retirement income payments
  - (1) to retired worker at age sixty-two or more
  - (2) to dependent wife or retired worker, at her age sixty-two or more
  - (3) to dependent child of retired worker, prior to age eighteen, or if the child is disabled before then
- *d.* disability income payments
  - (1) to disabled worker under age sixty-five, *if* he also meets the special requirement of 20 quarters of coverage out of the 40 calendar quarters ending with the quarter in which disability is found to have started
  - (2) to dependent wife of disabled worker, at her age sixty-two or more
  - (3) to dependent child of disabled worker, prior to age eighteen, or if the child is disabled before then

3. If the worker is both *fully and currently* insured:
   - *a.* survivorship income payments
     - (1) to dependent widower, age sixty-two or more, of a deceased woman worker (as well as all benefits shown in 2.*b.*)
   - *b.* retirement income payments
     - (1) to dependent husband, age sixty-two or more, of retired woman worker (as well as all benefits shown in 2.*c.*)
   - *c.* disability income payments
     - (1) to dependent husband, as in 3.*b.* (as well as benefits in 2.*d.*)

Generally, the major benefit of a worker being "currently" insured is to enable the widow and dependent children to receive substantial *survivorship* income. If the worker is "fully" but not currently insured, the major benefits include (1) survivorship income and (2) *retirement* income and (3) *disability* income (if special 20 of 40 quarters requirement is met, too). "Fully *and* currently" insured status enables such three classes of income payments to be paid to dependent widowers or husbands. The lump-sum death payment (maximum of $255) is payable in the case of either a fully *or* currently insured worker.

Size of Benefits. As to *size* of the benefits payable under the O.A.S.D.I. program, two calculations are important. One is the *primary insurance amount* (P.I.A.),[13] which is the amount of monthly income payable to the insured worker at retirement or for total disability. The benefit rates for all other types of benefits are calculated as percentages of the P.I.A.

The tables of benefits are related to the *average monthly earnings* (A.M.E.), with indicated minimum and maximum amounts payable. A person's A.M.E. is figured (under the 1960 new-start[14] method) by counting all the years of earnings after 1950, or age twenty-one

[13]The mathematical complexities of the necessary calculations are compounded by new formulas which were developed with each of the O.A.S.D.I. amendments. The 1958 amendments replaced the old formulas with tables of benefits, and simplified the process. The old formulas are used, where applicable, if they produce higher benefits than the tables.

[14]The old-start method includes all years after 1936.

if later, then subtracting out the five years of lowest earnings and any years of total disability, and dividing the person's total remaining earnings (up to specified maximum taxable earnings in each year, which have changed from $3,600 in 1951 to $4,200 in 1955 to $4,800 in 1959) by the number of months in those years. Earnings for active duty in the uniformed services of the United States since 1956 may be included, and prior service may earn wage credits of $160 per month.

The benefit formulas and tables are heavily weighted in favor of the low-income worker. As revised in 1958, for example, the primary insurance amount is figured on a basis which takes almost 60 percent of the first $110 of average monthly earnings, and only a little more than 20 percent of the next $290 of average monthly earnings. The minimum monthly primary benefit is $40 and the maximum $127 under the 1961 amendments. Average primary benefit in 1962 was approximately $80 per month.

Percentages of the P.I.A. are applied in the following manner for the various types of O.A.S.D.I. payments:

1. Lump-sum death payments—3 times the P.I.A., up to $255 maximum.
2. Survivorship income payments—82½ percent of the P.I.A. to an elderly widow, dependent widower, or a dependent parent; and 75 percent of the P.I.A. to each dependent child and to the mother of such children. Maximum family benefit is $254 a month.
3. Retirement and disability income payments—100 percent of the P.I.A. to the retired or totally disabled worker; 50 percent of the P.I.A. to the elderly wife, dependent husband, or child of the insured worker.

The following Table 8-1 shows the amount of monthly benefits payable under O.A.S.D.I. provisions, at selected average monthly earnings, for the more common types of benefits. Over 10 million retired beneficiaries (or their dependents) are now receiving O.A.S.D.I. benefits, as well as nearly 3.5 million survivors, and over .5 million disabled persons.

Special Earnings and Disability Requirements. Some special provisions apply for determining retirement status and amounts payable. A retired person, under an annual earnings test,[15] may have deductions made from his O.A.S.D.I. benefits. A person under age seventy-two is not considered fully "retired" if he earns wages or self-employment earnings of over certain amounts. If annual earnings exceed $1,200 in a taxable year, his monthly benefits are reduced on the basis of the excess earnings: $1.00 for each $2.00 of

[15]The test also applies to all other O.A.S.D.I. recipients under age seventy-two, except disabled persons. As an example, suppose your monthly benefit amount is $100. If you earned $1,600 in the year, your O.A.S.D.I. benefits for the year would be reduced to $1,000; if you earned $2,000, the O.A.S.D.I. benefit for the year would be $650.

TABLE 8–1

Examples of O.A.S.D.I. Monthly Benefits at Selected Average Yearly Earnings

Average Yearly Earnings after 1950	*Examples of Monthly O.A.S.D.I. Payments*				
	$800 or Less	*$1,800*	*$3,600*	*$4,200*	*$4,800**
Retirement at 65, or later, or total and permanent disability benefits	$40.00	$ 73.00	$105.00	$116.00	$127.00
Retirement benefits at 62	32.00	58.40	84.00	92.80	101.60
Wife's benefit at 65	20.00	36.50	52.50	58.00	63.50
Wife's benefit at 62	15.00	27.40	39.40	43.50	47.70
Combined husband's retirement benefit at 65 or later, and wife's benefit at 65	60.00	109.50	157.50	174.00	190.50
Combined husband's retirement benefit at 65 or later, and wife's benefit at 62	55.00	100.40	144.40	159.50	174.70
Widow's benefit, 62 or over	40.00	60.30	86.70	95.70	104.80
Widow's benefit under 62, and 1 child under age eighteen	60.00	109.60	157.60	174.00	190.60
Widow's benefit under 62, and 2 children under age eighteen	60.00	120.00	236.40	254.00	254.00
Maximum family payment	60.00	120.00	240.00	254.00	254.00

SOURCE: "Your Social Security" (U.S. Department of Health, Education, and Welfare, Social Security Administration, May, 1963), p. 9.

*Because earnings of $4,800 cannot be credited for any year before 1959, benefits in this column will not generally be payable for a few years to come.

annual earnings between $1,200 and $1,700, and $1.00 for each $1.00 of annual earnings over $1,700.[16] No reduction in benefits is made for any month in which the beneficiary did not have $100 in wages or provide substantial services in self-employment. In applying the earnings test, income is only counted if it results from continuing work after retirement, i.e., it does not include income from investments, other pensions or other sources not requiring active employment. After reaching age seventy-two, the earnings test does not apply, and the person may earn unlimited income without reducing O.A.S.D.I. benefits.

[16]*Social Security Handbook, op. cit.*, pp. 229–33.

The requirements for disability income payments also deserve special note. These are cash benefits,[17] not medical care services, for severe, long-lasting disabilities which prevent a person from engaging in substantial gainful activity in earning a living. Disability income is payable to (1) disabled workers,[18] and their dependents and (2) dependent children age eighteen or over, if the disability occurred before age eighteen. The benefits are for total disability of a long-continued and indefinite duration. A waiting period of six months is applied, during which no benefits are paid. The disability may be a physical or mental impairment, based upon medical evidence.[19] Examples include loss of two or more limbs, vision, hearing, speech, and diseases such as multiple sclerosis and severe cancer. A separate wage tax and trust fund was established in 1956 to provide the disability benefits under O.A.S.D.I. The monthly disability benefits for an insured worker are the same as if he had reached retirement age sixty-five, or the primary insurance amount. Payments stop if the insured person dies, becomes no longer disabled according to the definitions in the law, or reaches retirement.

Administration

The Old Age, Survivors, and Disability Insurance system is administered by the federal government. More than 100 million individual account records are maintained by the Social Security Administration in Baltimore, Maryland. The Commissioner of Social Security supervises ten divisions of management, actuarial services, claims, planning, research, hearings and appeals, accounting, and other functions. Regional and field services are performed through district offices located in 613 major cities.[20] These offices inform the public about their rights and obligations in connection with O.A.S.D.I.

Tax Collection. The taxes for the program are collected by the Internal Revenue Service. Employers deduct the required amounts from the wages of their employees and forward these amounts, plus the employer tax, to the District Director of Internal Revenue. Self-employed persons pay their O.A.S.D.I. taxes directly to the I.R.S. with their income tax statements. All the taxes are credited to the two trust funds, the Federal Old-Age and Survivors Insurance

---

[17]Another type of disability benefit under O.A.S.D.I. is the "disability freeze" provision, which permits a totally disabled worker to eliminate his years of such disability in the calculation of his insured status and average monthly earnings.

[18]Until 1960, no disability payments were made until the disabled person was fifty years old.

[19]*Social Security Handbook, op. cit.*, Chapters 5 and 6, pp. 65–87.

[20]The position of the Social Security Administration in the federal government is explained in *A Basic Guide to Organization and Function of the Department of Health, Education, and Welfare* (Baltimore, Md., 1964), pp. 10–14.

Trust Fund, and the Federal Disability Insurance Trust Fund. These funds are used only for the administration and benefit payments of the O.A.S.D.I. program. They are held until needed by investment in securities of the U.S. government.

Individual Accounts. As soon as a worker first performs work covered by the Social Security Act, he must apply for a card which identifies him by name and number. The assigned account number is used for the worker's entire life, and is the basis for the crediting of his earnings. Reports from the worker and his employer each year are the source of the earnings credits.

The worker may check[21] at any time on the status and record of his earnings under O.A.S.D.I. In fact, he should check regularly to see that his earnings have been reported and recorded properly. Unless this is done at least once every three years, it may be impossible under the law to make corrections, if mistakes have occurred. Valuable rights to earnings credits may be lost if the individual does not do this.

Approval of Benefits. It is also important for each worker and beneficiary to understand that O.A.S.D.I. benefits must be applied for, as they are not paid automatically. When application is made for benefits, at death, disability, or retirement, certain proofs are required to be presented to the district offices. Marriage and birth certificates, proof of support for dependents, and medical proof of disability, are required before the various benefit payments can be made. Since certain time limits apply, it is important that these proofs be rendered promptly. Usually the applications must be completed within two years after eligibility, but back payments may be limited to one year. Thus delay can be costly to the O.A.S.D.I. recipients who neglect or postpone proper application and proofs for benefits.

A system for hearings before one of seven regional representatives, and an appeals council in Washington, are maintained for reconsideration of any decision in regard to eligibility or amount of O.A.S.D.I. benefit claims.

Financing

Tax on Employer and Employee. The O.A.S.D.I. program is paid for by taxes levied under the Social Security Act on the earnings of workers. In the case of wage earners in covered employment, both the *employer and employee* each pay an equal tax on the earnings; self-employed persons pay a tax which is slightly less than one and a half times the tax which a wage earner pays.

---

[21]By writing to the Social Security Administration, Baltimore 35, Maryland. Forms for this purpose are available through local district offices.

Originally the tax began in 1937 at 1 percent on both employer and employee. The schedule of taxes was set up to be increased periodically as the program got underway and the number of O.A.S.D.I. beneficiaries increased. Revisions in the schedule[22] have occurred several times since 1950, and the present tax rates and scheduled increases are:

Year	Employee	Employer	Combined Employer-ee	Self-Employed
1963–65	3⅝%	3⅝%	7¼%	5.4%
1966–67	4⅛	4⅛	8¼	6.2
1968 and after	4⅝	4⅝	9¼	6.9

The tax is applied against only the first $4,800[23] of annual earnings. Thus the maximum current tax, in 1964, is 3⅝ percent each from employer and employee on a maximum earnings amount of $4,800, or $174 a year. The combined employer-ee maximum tax is $348, and in 1968 it will be $444 under the present anticipated tax schedule. Self-employed persons now pay a maximum of just over $259, and in 1968 will pay over $331 a year.

Need for Understanding. Many of the misconceptions about the O.A.S.D.I. program are related to its financing. Even though "by design or otherwise, the social security law is so complex as to discourage effort by most people to understand it,"[24] it seems imperative that more persons *should* try to learn how the program works. With annual costs exceeding $12 billion, or about one half of total personal savings, the person who misunderstands the program (or does not attempt to understand) is certainly not fulfilling an important obligation to his society, family, and himself.

Pay-as-You-Go Assessment Plan, with Contingency Trust Funds. One popular misconception concerns the basic purpose and method of the financing system. O.A.S.D.I. is not based on an actuarially funded plan as are individual life insurance contracts and annuities issued by the private insurance business. The solvency of the plan rests on the right of the federal government to levy taxes and to change benefits or taxes in the future, if necessary. The financing of O.A.S.D.I. is nearly a *pay-as-you-go*[25] plan, as is seen in the fact

[22]The tax on both employer and employee changed from 2 percent in 1956, to 2¼ percent in 1957, to 2½ percent in 1959, to 3 percent in 1960, to 3⅛ percent in 1962, to 3⅝ percent in 1963.

[23]The maximum tax base began in 1937 at $3,000 a year, was increased to $3,600 in 1947, $4,200 in 1955 and $4,800 in 1959.

[24]*Faulkner, op. cit.*, p. 204.

[25]In theory there is perhaps nothing wrong with such a plan, whereby current costs are paid by current contributions, as long as it is recognized as such. A fully funded plan, involving $300 to $500 billion of assets, could have undesirable political and economic effects, too.

that current annual contributions (taxes) just about equal current beneficiary payments. The trust funds, of about $20 billion currently, are merely a partial reserve against the much larger amounts which will be paid under the system in future years. Obligations to current O.A.S.D.I. insureds now exceed 15 times the amount in the trust funds.

The nature of the financing method is thus comparable to an *assessment* system, in which the assessments levied on the future working populations will sharply increase as payments from the system expand. The trust funds are similar to a *contingency fund* rather than a full-reserve from which to pay future benefits. They are designed to smooth out and slow down the increases necessary during a 50-year period or more as the system matures.

Income Shift among Generations. A most important effect of O.A.S.D.I. is the shifting of income from one generation of workers to another. Today's taxes on workers are not, as is popularly believed, being set aside in order to prepay the current contributors their future benefits at death, retirement, or disability. Current taxes are used to pay current recipients, which means generally that the working generation today is paying now for the retired (or disabled or dying) generation. The retirement benefits of a person age thirty today will be paid, not from his own taxes for the next 35 years, but from the taxes levied on his working children in the 1990's and thereafter.

A Current Recipient "Bargain." If a recipient of O.A.S.D.I. retirement payments believes that he has fully "earned" the right to his benefits (by the taxes he paid up to age sixty-two or sixty-five), he should reconsider the extent of his actual contributions. On the average, the current beneficiary of retirement income has paid about 4 percent of the value of his benefits. Even at maximum tax rates since 1937, total taxes would be less than $3,000 each for employer and employee. The value of husband and wife income benefits of $150 per month at age sixty-two, for example, would exceed $20,000. In other words, it would cost many times the taxes paid, in order to purchase a retirement annuity similar to the O.A.S.D.I. benefit.

The "bargain" that recipients of social security payments are now receiving is being paid for by the current working generation. Young entrants to the system today will pay two or more times the benefits that they will, on the average at current benefit schedules, receive.[26] The low-cost bargain look of O.A.S.D.I. benefits will disap-

[26] Ray M. Peterson, "How to Preserve Our Social Security System," Address before the Council on Employee Benefits, New York City, October 27, 1961, p. 8. A wide variation exists between how much the average new entrant to O.A.S.D.I. pays, and how much he will receive in benefits, depending upon his age, wage level, marital and family status. For a single person, it may approach 400 percent or more; for a married person, 200 percent; and for a married person with two children, about 170 percent.

pear as the scheduled tax increases take effect, and as the average insured worker has paid into the program for a longer period before he or his survivors begin to collect benefits.

The sizable benefits in relation to normal contributions are today a function of the fact that the program has not yet reached the mature stage when the number of new beneficiaries each year will be relatively stable. Now, many recipients qualify for benefits with perhaps only a few years of taxes paid. The rapid expansion of the number of O.A.S.D.I. recipients will continue during the next several decades.

Future Self-Supporting Cost Estimates. The financing of the O.A.S.D.I. program is designed to be self-supporting. As long as the system continues indefinitely, future estimates of expenditures and receipts (and changes in the law, if necessary) can be made to assure the solvency of the plan. The long-range estimates are difficult to evaluate. The Advisory Council on Social Security Financing, and actuaries of the Social Security Administration, review and revise these estimates periodically. High-cost estimates and low-cost estimates for the future vary by billions of dollars. For example, O.A.S.D.I. income will exceed outgo for only 12 years after 1965 in one set of high-cost estimates; in low-cost estimates the income will exceed outgo for about 80 years.[27] The differences in the estimates stem from the complexity and relative unpredictability of the assumptions which must be made. Future mortality, birth, marriage, divorce, remarriage, immigration, and disability rates all have to be included in the estimates, as well as basic employment data, interest earnings, and many other factors.

Needed Research on Effects. The effects of O.A.S.D.I. financing have reached a significance which suggests much more economic and sociological research in this area is warranted. The results on income redistribution, labor force participation and productivity, consumption, savings, investment, and economic growth all should be considered as major questions for analysis.[28]

UNEMPLOYMENT COMPENSATION

The impetus for the states to establish unemployment compensation systems was established in the Social Security Act of 1935. A tax-offset device was used, in which most employers were required to pay a 3 percent federal payroll tax *unless* the state created a state unemployment plan which met certain standards. As a result, all states within a few years passed unemployment statutes, permitting

---

[27]Haber and Cohen, *op. cit.*, "Financing Old-Age, Survivors, and Disability Insurance," Chapter 13, p. 158.

[28]See Chapters 3 and 4 of Margaret S. Gordon, *The Economics of Welfare Policies* (New York: Columbia University Press, 1963).

employers a 90 percent credit on the federal tax. This left a .3 percent federal tax to provide general administration for the state systems.

Eligibility

In order to be eligible for unemployment compensation, an employee must have been working under covered employment, and must also meet certain individual requirements.

Covered Employment. Not all workers are covered by the unemployment compensation laws of the states. About three out of five workers are covered, however. The main exceptions are: (1) self-employed persons, (2) employees of firms with fewer than four workers, (3) agricultural workers and domestic servants, (4) employees of nonprofit organizations, state and local governments, (5) maritime and railroad workers. Separate federal legislation covers the last category, and many states have unemployment compensation laws which require (or permit, on an elective basis by the employer) coverage for some of the workers of smaller firms, some domestic servants, nonprofit organization employees, and state and local government workers.[29]

Individual Requirements. In order to collect unemployment compensation benefits, a worker in covered employment must meet several important requirements. He must be unemployed through no fault of his own, which ordinarily disqualifies for benefits any worker who has voluntarily quit his job, been discharged for misconduct, is involved in a labor dispute, or refuses suitable employment. The states vary considerably in these definitions for disqualification, and some permit unemployment benefits to workers unemployed because of an employer lockout or even a strike by the employees.

The unemployed worker must be *willing and able to work.* As proof of this, he must register for work at a public employment office, file a claim for benefits, not be sick or disabled, and be available to take a suitable job if it is offered to him.[30]

A third major requirement for benefits is that the worker must have a prescribed minimum amount of recent work before the unemployment occurred. State laws vary considerably here, also, ranging from those which prescribe minimum earnings standards in a base period to those which require a minimum number of weeks of previous employment.[31] The purpose is to show some substantial

[29]Gordon, *op. cit.,* p. 126. For example, 23 states covered firms with fewer than four workers, and 30 states covered many of their employees.

[30]*Social Security Handbook, op. cit.,* pp. 270–71.

[31]Gordon, *op. cit.,* pp. 126–27. Requirements vary from earnings of $150 in Hawaii to $800 in the state of Washington, and from 14 weeks of employment in Michigan to 20 in New York.

recent attachment to the active labor force, and contributions by the employer to the unemployment system.

Benefits

The laws of each state must be consulted in order to determine the amount and duration of unemployment benefits. Normally, the purpose is to provide a *temporary* replacement of a *part* of the worker's full-time weekly earnings.

Amount. Within stated minimum and maximum limits,[32] the size of the weekly benefits is usually aimed at about onehalf of normal wages. Because of rising wages in recent years, the maximum limits are most important, and over half of the new claimants have been eligible for maximum payments in many states. The maximums vary from $28 to $55 weekly, with the average payment falling in between these two figures. Twelve states provide additional dependents' benefits, which increase the range of the above maximums from $30 to $70.

Duration. The state unemployment compensation systems do not aim at a solution to long-term or permanent technological unemployment problems. Typically, most states provide benefits only for 26 weeks. Supplementary benefits for periods of high unemployment have become available in recent years in some of the states, although the maximum duration of payments has not been extended beyond a 50 percent increase. Usually this means a total maximum duration of 39 weeks.

Special provisions in many of the states provide (1) some proportional payments for partially unemployed persons who may replace some of their wages with odd jobs and (2) a waiting period of one week before unemployment payments can begin.

Administration

The direct administration of unemployment compensation systems is performed by the state governments, with the federal government participating indirectly through the standards it sets for meeting the requirements of the tax-offset law.

Federal Standards. Since all or a portion of the state unemployment administrative expenses (as well as the 90 percent tax-offset) depends on the state conforming to the federal standards, the requirements are usually met. These include provisions[33] that: (1) all state unemployment taxes be deposited in an account with the U.S. Treasury, from which only benefits can be paid, (2) benefits be paid only through public or federally approved employment agencies,

[32] *Ibid.*, p. 271.

[33] *Social Security in the United States* (Washington, D.C.: U.S. Government Printing Office, 1959), p. 26.

(3) full payments be made promptly when due, (4) workers have the right to appeal decisions of the state agencies, (5) permit workers to refuse unsuitable jobs, under prescribed standards, and (6) administrative personnel be employed on a merit basis.

The U.S. Secretary of Labor in the Department of Labor has the responsibility of determining state compliance with the federal requirements.

State Administration. The area of state administration is still quite broad, for it must actually carry out the federal requirements as well as make many of its own decisions in regard to the unemployment compensation program. For example, the state decides the major questions of (1) eligibility (what workers are covered and how they qualify for benefits), (2) benefits (how much and for how long), and (3) financing (how much employers will be charged as a tax on payrolls).

The actual administrative work implementing the unemployment compensation law in each state is performed by the *state employment security agency.* Most of the states use independent departments of the state government, or independent boards or commissions. In some states these agencies are under the state department of labor. Benefit claims are handled in about 1,800 local offices of the employment agencies of the states.[34]

Financing

The basic source of funds for the state unemployment systems is a payroll tax levied on employers.[35] The standard tax rate on employers is 3 percent[36] of the wages up to $3,000 for each worker, of which one tenth goes to the federal government and nine tenths goes to the state government under the tax-offset plan mentioned earlier.

A few states have raised the taxable wage base beyond $3,000, although the most significant variation in employers' cost in the various states is found in the *experience rating* systems used in all but one state.[37] Under these plans the tax rate on employers is changed according to the individual experience of each employer. Alternative higher taxes may apply in many states if the reserve funds fall below specified points. The various experience rating plans differ substantially, but most result in the individual employer paying (according to his past unemployment record) rates which

[34] *Ibid.*, p. 26.

[35] Three states, Alabma, Alaska, and New Jersey, also require a small contribution (less than .5 percent) from employees.

[36] The Federal Unemployment Tax Act raised this to 3.1 percent in 1960, and temporarily to 3.5 percent in 1961 amendments designed for extending the benefits beyond normal maximum durations. Current federal portion of the tax is thus .8 percent.

[37] Alaska.

vary between perhaps 1 percent and the maximum standard percent required.

It is the pronounced social, political, and economic effects of unemployment which have necessitated that it be cared for under a social insurance rather than a private insurance system. In addition to the complexity of defining who really is an "unemployed" person, the sizable funds necessary and the cyclical changes in unemployment are problems of substantial nature. A recent study[38] is indicative of the many economic effects of the state unemployment compensation systems: (1) general economic significance, including countercyclical contributions, (2) benefits adequacy or inadequacy, both personal and society viewpoints, (3) labor-force changes, (4) impact of unemployment taxes, and (5) interstate competition in unemployment compensation.

WORKMEN'S COMPENSATION

In an unusual combination of social and private insurance, workmen's compensation laws in all the states require[39] employers to provide certain benefits for *occupational* injuries, and sometimes, for occupational diseases. Workmen's compensation was the first kind of social insurance to develop widely in the United States, many of the laws being enacted before 1920.

The statutory requirement in most states can be fulfilled by the employer purchasing workmen's compensation insurance from a private insurer. Many states also have established workmen's compensation state funds for insuring employers, and seven states require that the benefits of the law be insured (unless a qualified "self-insurance" plan for larger employers is maintained) only with such state insurance funds.

Further details of workmen's compensation insurance, and the derivation of state workmen's compensation laws from the former system of employers' liability, are presented in Chapter 15. Discussion here will be limited to a brief description of the major features of the programs.

Eligibility

Benefits under workmen's compensation laws are payable to many, but not all, workers. From a very restricted list of hazardous occupations 50 years ago, the laws have been extended to apply to most employers. Although not all jobs are covered, about two thirds

---

[38]Richard A. Lester, *The Economics of Unemployment Compensation* (Princeton, N.J.: Princeton University, Industrial Relations Section, 1962).

[39]Note that about half the states have an "elective" rather than "compulsory" law. However, the loss of common law liability defenses to the employer usually provide strong encouragement in the elective states for the employer to choose workmen's compensation.

of the employees in most states do have coverage under workmen's compensation, with the following typical exceptions: (1) employees of firms with less than a minimum number of workers, the minimum ranging from two to eight, (2) farm workers, (3) domestic servants, (4) casual labor, and (5) employees of charitable or religious organizations.

In order to qualify as a death, injury, or disease covered by workmen's compensation, the employee must show that it arose *out of and in the course of employment*. In other words, it must be a work-connected loss. Many states exclude losses that are the result of an employee's intoxication, gross negligence, or willful misconduct.

Benefits

Workmen's compensation laws provide definite *schedules* of benefits for different injuries or illnesses. Variations among the states are wide, but most statutes require two basic types of benefits: (1) medical care costs and (2) income payments to the worker or his family. One half of the states also have some type of rehabilitation provision in their workmen's compensation laws.[40]

Medical care benefits are quite complete under the laws of most states. Classification of the extent of medical care under the various state laws shows 36 jurisdictions which have no arbitrary limits, or unlimited authority to extend the limits, on duration or amount of medical benefits payable.[41] The remaining jurisdictions have some arbitrary limits on the extent of medical care provided.

Income benefits under workmen's compensation laws are usually based upon the worker's wages at the time of injury or sickness. Weekly payments are made to either the worker or to his survivors. Disabilities may be either partial or total, and either permanent or temporary. Lifetime payments are possible, but many states set a specific maximum duration of payments, such as six to ten years. Both minimum and maximum weekly benefit amounts are also usually set in the laws. To discourage malingering, a maximum benefit amount of about two thirds of the normal weekly wage is established. Some laws provide lump-sum benefits in place of income payments for certain disabilities. A waiting period of from three days to one week is common, before weekly benefits begin.

Administration

State governments are the administrators of the workmen's compensation laws. In most states, this function is carried out through special *state commissions* appointed for this purpose. They work

[40]Earl F. Cheit, *Medical Care under Workmen's Compensation* (Washington, D.C.: U.S. Government Printing Office, U.S. Department of Labor Bulletin 244, 1962), p. 53.

[41]*Ibid.*, pp. 3–9.

closely with the employers and their insurers in performing the necessary administrative duties. Oftentimes, the work of the commissions takes on an advisory and quasi-judicial nature.

The rules and procedures for filing, reviewing, and investigating claims for benefits are set forth in the laws. Decisions are reached, subject to the approval of the commissions, through various methods of direct settlement, formal agreements, or hearings.

Financing

The direct responsibility for financing workmen's compensation benefits is placed upon the employer. Either through the purchase of a private insurance contract, "self-insurance," or insurance in a state fund he must pay for the benefits as provided in the state laws.

The cost of workmen's compensation insurance varies widely from state to state, among the various occupations, and for each individual employer. The liability or restrictiveness of the benefits in the state law is an obvious cost factor. More hazardous occupations may have workmen's compensation costs which exceed 20 percent of payroll, while other occupations with minimum industrial injury and disease perils may have costs of well under 1 percent of payroll. From year to year, the average premium cost approximates 1 to 2 percent of payroll for all occupations combined. Individual employers are given incentive to reduce losses through the many loss prevention techniques by various experience rating plans, which adjust the insurance costs according to the losses and expenses of each particular business firm.

TEMPORARY DISABILITY (NONOCCUPATIONAL) INSURANCE LAWS

In addition to disability income for occupational injuries or sickness, four states have compulsory temporary disability laws which provide income payments for non-work-connected disabilities. These states are New York, New Jersey, California, and Rhode Island.

The need for these laws stems from the fact that most state unemployment compensation systems require that the recipient of unemployment benefits be willing *and able* to work. Only a few states permit payments to disabled, unemployed workers.

Eligibility

The coverage of most workers is similar to that found under the usual unemployment compensation system, and a few categories of employment are excluded.

The individual worker is required to show that he cannot carry out the regular duties of his job, due to illness or injury. Certain disabilities, such as pregnancy or intentional self-inflicted injuries, may be excluded. He must also have had specified minimum earnings for a required time before becoming disabled in order to qualify for temporary disability benefits.

Benefits

The weekly benefit rates[42] have the purpose of replacing one half or more of the wages lost due to disability. Minimum benefits are $10 per week (except for New York, where $20 is the minimum) and maximum benefits vary from $35 per week in New Jersey to $65 in California.

Benefit duration is also limited. Payments are made for a maximum of 26 weeks in three states, and 20 weeks in New York. A waiting period of 1 week (7 consecutive days) applies in all four states.

Administration

Three of the states administer the temporary disability laws under the supervision of the state unemployment compensation board, commission, or department. New York uses the workmen's compensation board to administer the disability payments.

Rhode Island is the only state which requires that the employer must provide the benefits through an exclusive, or monopolistic, state fund. The other three states permit the employer to choose between private insurers providing a group accident and health insurance contract, a state fund, or a "self-insurance" plan. The alternatives to a state fund must meet the requirements of the law as to eligibility of workers for benefits and the amounts and duration of the payments.

Financing

The *employee* is required to pay all or a portion of the costs of the temporary disability benefits in each of the four states. The tax is based on payroll, and varies from 1 percent of the first $3,600 of annual wages in Rhode Island and California, to .5 percent of the same wage base in New Jersey, to .5 percent of their wages (up to a maximum of $.30 per week) in New York.

In two states, *employers* also bear part of the costs. In New Jersey, the employer pays .25 percent of the first $3,600 of wages (modified by experience rating) and in New York the employer pays all additional costs of the program beyond the stated employee contribution.

It is interesting to note that all four of the temporary disability laws appeared between 1942 and 1949. Although many other states

[42] *Social Security in the United States, op. cit.*, pp. 38–39.

have considered legislative bills for such laws, none has been passed in over 15 years. It appears that the private insurance business has expanded its efforts for coverage of the nonoccupational disability income peril, and successfully provided in many states the needed coverage in this area of insurance. Temporary disability thus remains as covered by both social insurance systems, in four states, and as private insurance in the remaining jurisdictions.

OTHER SOCIAL INSURANCE PROGRAMS

Although the four social insurance programs discussed previously in this chapter are the most important and widespread, other social insurance systems have developed some significance. Among these are the railroad retirement and unemployment plans, the government employee retirement plans, several required liability insurance statutes, and some miscellaneous programs.

The Railroad Retirement and Unemployment Acts

The railroads, for several reasons including early strong unionization of employees, established a pension system before the Social Security Act of 1935. Therefore, the railroad industry was excluded from the 1935 Act, although later provisions have correlated the two systems by permitting combined credits for survivors' benefits under either O.A.S.D.I. or the Railroad Retirement Act. A retiring worker can qualify for retirement benefits under both programs if he has been employed long enough under both railroad and other covered employment of O.A.S.D.I.[43]

Railroad workers have one of the most extensive social insurance benefit programs in the United States. Retirement benefits are paid at age sixty-five (or reduced amount at sixty-two) if the worker has 10 years of railroad service, or at age sixty if he has 30 years of service.[44] The amounts are generally higher than O.A.S.D.I. payments, and are calculated on a formula which takes into account both average monthly earnings and years of service. Survivors benefits to widow and children are payable in lump-sum and monthly payments, while the children are under eighteen, and later when the widow reaches age sixty. Disability payments are payable to a worker if he is permanently disabled (1) for *his* regular job, after 20 years of service, or age sixty and 10 years of service and (2) for *all* regular work, after he has had 10 years of service.

Unemployment and sickness benefits are payable under the sep-

---

[43] *Ibid.*, p. 280.

[44] *Ibid.*, p. 281. The formula is 3.35 percent of the first $50 of monthly earnings, 2.51 percent of the next $100, and 1.67 percent of the remainder. This sum is multiplied by the employee's years of service, with a maximum of 30 years credit up to 1967.

arate Railroad Unemployment Insurance Act.[45] A railroad worker who is out of a job may be paid specified benefits of $4.50 to $10.20 a day for up to at least 130 days in a benefit year, or longer if his past service exceeds 10 years. A waiting period of 14 days applies, with benefits payable for all days out of work over 7 (or over 4 for subsequent unemployment in same benefit year).

The federal government administers the railroad social insurance program through a separate Railroad Retirement Board. The systems are financed by current taxes on the first $400 of monthly earnings: (1) 14½ percent shared equally by employer and employee, for the Retirement Act benefits and (2) 4 percent by the employer only, for the Unemployment Act benefits. It is noted that both the benefits and the costs of the railroad programs are higher than O.A.S.D.I. and other state programs of social insurance.

Government Employee Retirement Systems

Federal employees, state employees, and some local government employees have separate social insurance programs which provide retirement, disability, and survivorship benefits.

The federal government employees, excluding members of the armed services, are most often covered under the provisions of the Civil Service Retirement Act.[46] Special programs are used for some groups, such as foreign service officers and members of Congress. Such federal employees as are not included in these plans are generally included under the O.A.S.D.I. program.

The Civil Service Commission administers benefits for several million federal civil service employees, who are eligible for (1) retirement and disability annuities (at least comparable to O.A.S.D.I. benefits, in most cases, and based on earnings and length of service) and (2) survivorship benefits to widows and children of employees. In contrast to O.A.S.D.I., an employee who leaves government service before retirement, after 5 years of service, is entitled to withdraw his contributions, or leave them with the program until an annuity is payable at retirement. The system is financed by a 6.5 percent tax on the base pay of employees, and an equivalent amount from the employing federal employing agency.

The Federal Employees' Group Life Insurance Act in 1954 inaugurated group life insurance coverage for federal employees, who are covered unless they choose not to be included. Employees pay two thirds of the cost. Benefits for survivors and life insurance even beyond retirement age is provided. Over 2.5 million persons were covered for more than $15 billion at the end of 1963. Private insurance companies have underwritten the coverage in this very siz-

---

[45] *Ibid.*, p. 283.
[46] *Ibid.*, pp. 287–88.

able group life insurance contract. In 1960 health insurance benefits also became available to federal employees, with an optional choice among Blue Cross-Blue Shield, a group private insurer plan, and other alternatives. Benefits differ widely. The federal government pays a portion of the costs.

Almost three fourths of state and local government employees are covered by retirement systems which provide old age as well as disability payments. The plans vary widely, and generally, in comparison with the other systems discussed previously, the benefits may be somewhat lower and may require longer periods of service for eligibility. The employee contributions, which most systems require, may be taken by the employee after a minimum number of years of service, if he retires early or leaves government service. Many of the plans do not include survivors' benefits beyond a return of the worker's contributions, although increasing evidence of extension of benefits in this area is found in such plans as those for policemen, firemen, and others. Some state and local government employees are entitled to O.A.S.D.I. benefits, if the political subdivision has entered into a voluntary agreement with the federal government to have them included.

Required Liability Insurance

To achieve social objectives, some kinds of liability insurance are required by government. These requirements guarantee payment from a negligent person to an injured, innocent accident victim. The most widely discussed type of *compulsory liability* insurance is *automobile* liability insurance. It is not discussed as a major type of social insurance, because the coverage is far from universal. Only three states, Massachusetts, New York, and North Carolina, have adopted such legislation. The remaining states prefer to encourage an automobile driver or owner to purchase such insurance through "financial responsibility" laws, which do not make the insurance mandatory at the time of registering a car for a license. The advantages and disadvantages of these alternative solutions to the unpaid automobile accident victim problem are discussed in Chapter 16, "Automobile Insurance."

In addition, some states require liability insurance for selected situations. The owners of public vehicles, such as buses and taxicabs, often must meet state requirements by purchasing automobile liability insurance with specified limits of coverage. Young drivers under twenty-one years of age or less are required to carry automobile liability insurance in some states. The Interstate Commerce Commission requires motor vehicle common carriers to purchase liability insurance with prescribed minimum limits. Milk distributors in some states are required to carry compulsory products liability coverage. Many other examples may be found, even outside the liability insurance field. For example, bonds are often required in state statutes for such situations as public construction contracts, and certain state officials such as treasurers. The federal government requires bonds in several cases, including trustees of union funds and aliens. Court bonds are required by many courts in many legal procedures. All of these are illustrations of government-required insurance contracts, but the limited nature of their application to special situations tends to cause them not to be included in the usual discussion of social insurance.

Miscellaneous and Future Programs

Most other government insurance plans, upon analysis, will be found to lack the compulsory nature which this text has included as a requisite for *social insurance.* Some plans may lack other characteristics which are important in describing social insurance, such as widespread application to meet reasonably universal problems of maintaining economic security in a society.

Chapter 2, in describing the fields of insurance, also identified several insurance systems which were defined as "voluntary government" plans, where the government may provide the insurance but permits the coverage to be purchased on an optional basis. Included in this category, but often-times confused with the types of social insurance reviewed in this chapter, are such programs as those of National Service Life Insurance, the Federal Crop Insurance Corporation, Federal Housing Administration insurance of mortgages, title insurance under Torrens title laws in some states, and life insurance issued by a state fund in one state (Wisconsin). The Federal Deposit Insurance Corporation, which insures bank deposits up to $10,000 per account, and the Federal Savings and Loan Insurance Corporation, which insures such institution shares up to $10,000, also are usually[47] included in this classification of "voluntary government" insurance plans.

A few other plans might be included as social insurance. These plans include those in some states and municipalities which have "self-insurance funds" for insuring government property against fire and other perils. Although some of these plans may qualify as true insurance systems, many lack some of the requirements for sound use of the insurance technique. In connection with workmen's compensation, many states have established a "second injury fund" which encourages the hiring of handicapped workers. The employer is required to pay for a second disabling injury only to the extent

[47]An exception should be made in the case of national and state banks which are required to carry this insurance, and thus fall within our definition of social insurance.

that it separately causes loss of income, and not for the combined results of both the first and second disability. The balance of payments comes from the state's second injury fund.

The future of social insurance is apparently well established. It would be hard to conceive of abandonment of any of the major social insurance programs which have been discussed. The typical trend seems to be in the direction of expansion of existing programs. Each has developed by increasing its coverage, and the application of its requirements to new and wider groups of persons. Benefits have rarely been reduced, but often extended as to kind, amount, and duration. Illustrative of the possible trend is the current consideration of medical care costs as an additional coverage in the O.A.S.D.I. program. The ultimate development in this area, as in all social insurance programs, will be determined by many factors. The desires of the public, as expressed in government legislation following economic, social, and political considerations, will conclude the issues.

SUMMARY

Social insurance, with the objective of *basic economic security* for the individual in a society, is a large and growing field of insurance. Its *compulsory* nature is contrary to the method of private or voluntary insurance. However, in return for the giving up of some individual freedom of choice, social insurance legislation by the government does result in a "floor of protection" for a broad segment of the population, against certain major risks.

The development of social insurance in the United States has occurred almost entirely in the twentieth century, especially during the last 30 years. At least in the provision for three primary perils, those of (1) *old age,* (2) *unemployment,* and (3) *occupational injury and disease,* the decision has been strongly in favor of requiring the employer or employee (or both) to participate in social insurance programs. A fourth peril, income loss due to *temporary nonoccupational disability,* is a newer and much less universal type of social insurance. These plans, and several other less important social insurance plans for special groups or areas, are to be contrasted with *public assistance* programs based upon the concept of government payments to individuals who met certain criteria of "need."

The fundamental characteristics of the four most significant types of social insurance today may be summarized in terms of eligibility provisions, benefits, administration, and financing. For more complete evaluation of these large and varied programs the reader is referred to the material in the chapter and the publications noted in its references.

TABLE 8–2

Summary of Features of Four Major Social Insurance Programs

Type of Program	*Eligibility Provisions*	*Types of Benefits*	*Who Administers?*	*Who and What Finances It?*
O.A.S.D.I.	Covered employment, with certain time and earnings to become insured	Income for retirement, total and permanent disability, and to survivors	Federal government	Earnings tax on employer and employee
Unemployment Compensation	Covered employment, with specified individual qualification requirements	Temporary income to willing and able unemployed workers	State government	Payroll tax (mostly state) on employer
Workmen's Compensation	Covered employment, and injury or disease arising out of and in the course of employment	Medical care costs, work disability income, and rehabilitation	State government	Insurance purchased by employer
Temporary Disability Benefit Laws	Covered employment, with specified time and earnings requirements	Temporary income for nonwork disability from illness or injury	State government	Payroll tax on employee, or employee-employer

Several other social insurance programs are briefly mentioned, including the railroad industry retirement and unemployment programs; federal, state, and local government employee retirement plans; and compulsory forms of liability (especially automobile) insurance in some states. The history of most social insurance programs indicates continued expansion and growth of the systems.

FOR REVIEW

1. How does the objective and method of "social insurance" differ from that of "public assistance"?
2. Give several examples of the types of insurance included in (*a*) "social insurance" and (*b*) "public assistance." How does the Social Security Act of 1935 relate to these two terms?
3. Justify or criticize, from a social standpoint, the need for a federal government old-age insurance program, in view of the fact that federal and state grants already are provided for the needy aged.
4. The statement is sometimes made that the cost of workmen's compensation, as well as of old-age insurance, is not an actual additional cost. In one way or another these costs have always been borne. Discuss.

5. In connection with the Social Security program, one of the major methods for attaining the objective is to be found in federal grants-in-aid. These grants-in-aid go to the state for certain kinds of relief, such as: pensions for the needy aged, and blind; mothers' pensions; maternal and child health services; aid to neglected, crippled, and other handicapped children; and public health protection. To what extent, if any, may these payments be regarded as insurance?
6. If more than nine out of ten workers are now covered by the O.A.S.D.I. program, why shouldn't, or can't, everyone be brought under the compulsory provisions of this law?
7. What is the distinction between "fully" and "currently" insured status under the O.A.S.D.I. program? What difference does it make to the worker or his family?
8. What is the basis for determining the size of the O.A.S.D.I. benefits payable? What other factors are considered, and how do these help carry out the social objectives of the program?
9. Retirement benefits for old age were the original purpose of O.A.I. in 1935. Then, in 1939, survivorship benefits for the worker's dependents were added to make the program O.A.S.I. In 1956, disability benefits were included, so that the present program is titled O.A.S.D.I. What kinds of disability benefits were added, for whom, and what is the extent of these benefits?
10. Discuss the O.A.S.D.I. taxes in terms of their past development and prospective future increases, especially in regard to their economic incidence and impact.
11. Briefly explain two common misconceptions about the O.A.S.D.I. program, pointing out why the misunderstandings probably exist and why they are fallacious.
12. Compare and contrast unemployment compensation and workmen's compensation as to (*a*) eligibility requirements, (*b*) benefits, and (*c*) administration.
13. It is sometimes said that a state can enact an unemployment insurance law best suited to its individual needs. What is the necessity for the federal government setting up minimum federal standards?
14. Who pays for the costs of (*a*) O.A.S.D.I., (*b*) unemployment compensation, (*c*) workmen's compensation, and (*d*) temporary disability (non-occupational) benefits?
15. Should compulsory automobile liability insurance be classed as a type of "social insurance"? Explain why or why not.

PART FOUR

Property and Liability Insurance

CHAPTER 9 *THE BASIC FIRE INSURANCE CONTRACT*

I. THE STANDARD FIRE INSURANCE CONTRACT
   - A. The Need
   - B. Methods
   - C. Development
   - D. Benefits

II. THE INSURING AGREEMENT
   - A. Inception and Termination
   - B. Personal Nature
   - C. Actual Cash Value
     1. Repair or Replacement Costs
     2. Consequential Losses
     3. Insurable Interest
   - D. Perils Insured Against
     1. Fire Defined
     2. Friendly and Unfriendly Fires
     3. Direct Loss
     4. Lightning
     5. Loss by Removal
   - E. Property and Location
   - F. Assignment

III. CONDITIONS AND EXCLUSIONS
   - A. Concealment or Fraud
   - B. Excluded Property
   - C. Excluded Perils
   - D. Suspension
   - E. Added Perils and Provisions
   - F. Cancellation
   - G. Loss Provisions

IV. SUMMARY

CHAPTER 10 *FIRE FORMS, CLAUSES, ENDORSEMENTS, AND ALLIED LINES*

I. FORMS
   - A. Purpose
   - B. Preparation and Use

CHAPTER 10 *FIRE FORMS, CLAUSES, ENDORSEMENTS, AND ALLIED FORMS*—cont'd

- C. Types
  - 1. Specific Coverage
  - 2. Blanket Coverage
  - 3. Floating Coverage
  - 4. Automatic Coverage
  - 5. Schedule Coverage

II. CLAUSES

- A. General Use
- B. Nuclear Clause
- C. Water Exclusion Clause
- D. Liberalization Clause
- E. Standard Mortgage Clause
- F. Coinsurance Clause
  - 1. Purpose
  - 2. Justification
  - 3. Formula and Examples
  - 4. Valuation Problems and Solutions
- G. Other Clauses Limiting Insurer's Liability
  - 1. Prorata Distribution Clause
  - 2. Three-Fourths Value and Three-Fourths Loss Clauses

III. ENDORSEMENTS

- A. Purpose
- B. General Use
- C. The Extended Coverage Endorsement
- D. The Additional Extended Coverage Endorsement
- E. Broad Form and "All-Risks" Endorsements

IV. SPECIAL AND ALLIED FIRE LINES

V. CONCURRENCY

VI. SUMMARY

CHAPTER 11 *INSURANCE FOR INDIRECT LOSSES*

I. NATURE AND CLASSIFICATION

II. TIME ELEMENT LOSSES

- A. Business Interruption Insurance
  - 1. Importance
  - 2. Purpose
  - 3. Distinguished from Profits Insurance
  - 4. Business Interruption Loss
  - 5. Business Interruption Insurance Amount
  - 6. Business Interruption Forms
- B. Contingent Business Interruption Insurance
  - 1. General Forms
  - 2. Off-Premises Power Plant Insurance
  - 3. Selling Agents' Commissions Insurance
- C. Rents and Rental Value Insurance
- D. Extra-Expense Insurance
- E. Tuition Fees Insurance

III. NO TIME ELEMENT LOSSES

- A. Profits Insurance
- B. Leasehold Interest and Excess Rental Value Insurance

CHAPTER 11 *INSURANCE FOR DIRECT LOSSES*—cont'd

CHAPTER 12 *TRANSPORTATION INSURANCE*

CHAPTER 13 *THE LIABILITY RISK*

CHAPTER 16 *AUTOMOBILE INSURANCE*—cont'd

- G. Part III—Physical Damage
  - 1. Comprehensive (Excluding Collision) Coverage
  - 2. Collision Coverage
- H. Part IV—Uninsured Motorists
- I. Policy Conditions
  - 1. Claims Provisions
  - 2. Other Provisions

III. THE COST OF AUTOMOBILE INSURANCE

- A. Increasing Costs
- B. Rate Regulation
  - 1. Price Competition
  - 2. Nonprice Competition
  - 3. State Regulation
- C. Premium Factors
  - 1. Classification of Automobiles and Contracts
  - 2. Private Passenger Automobile Liability Premiums
  - 3. Private Passenger Automobile Physical Damage Premiums
  - 4. Private Passenger Automobile Discounts

IV. SUMMARY

CHAPTER 17 *CRIME INSURANCE AND SURETYSHIP*

I. CRIMES AGAINST PROPERTY

- A. Nature and Definitions
- B. General Divisions of Crime Insurance Coverages

II. ANALYSIS OF CRIME INSURANCE COVERAGES

- A. Basic Parts of Crime Policies
  - 1. Declarations
  - 2. Insuring Agreements
  - 3. Exclusions
  - 4. Conditions
- B. Residence Theft Insurance
- C. Burglary Insurance
  - 1. Mercantile Open Stock Policy
  - 2. Safe Burglary
- D. Robbery Insurance
  - 1. Messenger and Interior Robbery
  - 2. Paymaster Robbery
- E. Forgery Insurance
- F. Liability Insurance for Crime Losses
- G. "Package" Crime Insurance
  - 1. Storekeepers', and Office, Burglary and Robbery Policies
  - 2. Money and Securities Policy (Broad Form)
  - 3. Comprehensive Dishonesty, Disappearance and Destruction Policy

III. SURETYSHIP

- A. Nature and Development
- B. Insurance and Suretyship
- C. General Divisions of Suretyship

IV. ANALYSIS OF FIDELITY AND SURETY BONDS

- A. Basic Features
  - 1. Penalty of the Bond
  - 2. Obligation to Bond
  - 3. Effect of Fraud

CHAPTER 18 *MISCELLANEOUS PROPERTY AND LIABILITY INSURANCE*

CHAPTER 18 *MISCELLANEOUS PROPERTY AND LIABILITY INSURANCE*—cont'd

- E. Contract Provisions
  - 1. Assignment
  - 2. Subrogation
  - 3. Conditions Supporting a Claim
  - 4. Adjustments
  - 5. Measuring Indemnity
  - 6. The Term
- F. Use of a Group Policy

IV. Boiler and Machinery Insurance

- A. Nature
- B. The Basic Contract
- C. Direct Losses
  - 1. Steam Boilers and Vessels
  - 2. Engines
  - 3. Electrical Machinery
  - 4. Turbines
- D. Indirect Losses
  - 1. Consequential Loss
  - 2. Use and Occupancy
  - 3. Outage
  - 4. Power Interruption

V. Glass Insurance

- A. Basic Coverages
  - 1. Broken Glass
  - 2. Frames
  - 3. Temporary Plates
  - 4. Obstructions
- B. Other Contract Features

VI. Summary

CHAPTER 19 *MULTIPLE-LINE AND ALL-LINES INSURANCE*

I. Multiple-Line Insurance Characteristics

- A. Nature
- B. Development
- C. Significance
- D. Purposes

II. Multiple-Line Insurance Contracts

- A. Personal Multiple-Line Contracts
  - 1. Homeowner's Policies
    - a. Who Is Covered
    - b. What Is Covered
    - c. When Coverage Applies
    - d. Where Coverage Applies
    - e. How Coverage Applies
  - 2. Other Personal Multiple-Line Contracts
- B. Business Multiple-Line Insurance Contracts
  - 1. Manufacturer's Output Policy
  - 2. Block Policy Contracts
  - 3. Commercial Property Form
  - 4. Office Contents Form
  - 5. Industrial Property Form
  - 6. Public and Institutional Property Plans
  - 7. Service Businesses Multiple-Line Contracts
  - 8. Farmowner's Policy

CHAPTER 19 *MULTIPLE-LINE AND ALL-LINES INSURANCE—*
cont'd

III. All-Lines Insurance
   A. Nature and Extent
      1. Life Insurers May Become All-Lines Groups
      2. Property-Liability Insurers Are Becoming All-Lines Groups
   B. The Future

IV. Summary

Chapter 9

THE BASIC FIRE INSURANCE CONTRACT

FIRE insurance is one of the most familiar kinds of insurance. Few persons owning property want to be without the protection afforded by a fire insurance contract. Logic suggests that fire insurance be one of the first insurance contracts discussed in a beginning insurance text. It is generally known to its many policyholders, and in addition, is one of the most standardized of all insurance contracts.

THE STANDARD FIRE INSURANCE CONTRACT

The purpose of fire insurance is simple indeed: to indemnify a named insured in the event that certain described properties should be destroyed or damaged by the peril of fire. Seemingly a proposition so simply stated might readily lend itself to a contract simply drawn, and one the terms of which might be easily understood by all the parties concerned.

The Need

Such, however, was not formerly the case. No uniform form of agreement was used by the fire insurance companies in issuing their contracts, and each devised a policy form to meet its own requirements. Ordinarily the policies were prepared in the home offices of the companies, but where agents were entrusted with this responsibility, extreme variability appeared and complicated the situation. In an effort to incorporate conditions to meet different situations, the contracts began to grow extremely cumbersome and unwieldy. The average policy became so long and complicated as to put a satisfactory interpretation of its meaning well beyond the capacity of the average insured. In fact, it became so ponderous and bulky that even those trained in the law found it difficult to interpret.

As the business of fire insurance developed, it became increasingly evident, both to the companies and to the insuring public, that the cumbersome documents frequently used were creating a situation that was fast becoming intolerable. A shorter document, explicit in its provisions, and fair to both insured and insurer was vitally necessary to the continued success of the business. Out of the recognition of this need developed the contract to which we now refer as a "standard policy."

Methods

Two basic methods of creating standard insurance contracts are available in any field of insurance. The first is to have insurers, by custom or agreement, use uniform language in the contracts. Many insurance contracts today are standardized to some degree by this method. Even if some of the details of the contract are different, the basic provisions may become quite similar by this process.

The second method is standardization by legislation. In Chapter 7 it was noted that one kind of insurance regulation was to require certain contracts or parts of contracts to be used by all insurers. In life and health insurance some "standard provisions" are reqiured, although this does not make all such contracts uniform. In property and liability insurance one of the most completely standardized contracts is found in fire insurance. Its slow and gradual development is evidence of the difficulties involved in standardizing a product such as insurance.

Development

An early step toward standardization of the fire insurance contract was undertaken by the New York Board of Fire Underwriters, who recognized the chaotic state of affairs. Long before the state government intervened, they appointed a committee which drew up and presented a policy that seemed to be eminently fair and to meet fully the needs of the time. It was adopted by many of the companies whose business headquarters were located in New York. However, there was no element of compulsion in its adoption. Many companies continued with their own forms as before, and even where the new form was adopted there grew up a tendency to incorporate amendments, thereby destroying such uniformity as at first had been obtained. It became evident to insurance men, as well as to the general business world, that any decided reform, in order to be effective, must come through legislation.

Massachusetts was the first state to adopt a standard policy form. In 1873, the legislature drew up a form, which it enacted into a statute, thereby introducing a new era in fire policy writing. The Massachusetts form, sometimes known as the "New England standard policy," was not well received by the insurance business.[1] It was

[1]Only three states followed it: Maine, New Hampshire, and Minnesota.

stated that the members of the legislature entrusted with drawing up the policy failed to secure the advice and cooperation of the insurance interests, with the result that an unsatisfactory form was developed. The form was not considered suitable for general adoption by the companies, and unless its use was enforced by law they disregarded it.

The outstanding development came in 1887, when the New York State Legislature authorized the drawing up of a new standard form and made it the only legal one for writing fire business within the state. A committee was formed and insurance operators and lawyers were invited to cooperate, the aim being to draw up a policy so good that it would satisfy not only New York but also every other state. Clauses were painstakingly discussed, opinion everywhere was sought, and nothing was incorporated into the policy until it was agreed to be fair to all parties concerned. The New York policy in its final form was favorably received by both businessmen and insurance interests. The form evolved in New York was deemed so satisfactory that in numerous instances it was taken over by other states in its entirety, without alteration. In other cases it was slightly altered, but in its essentials it remains unchanged.

Since the New York policy was adopted in 1887, certain of its provisions have been nullified by court decisions. To eliminate certain inequitable features as well as those rendered null by court decisions, the National Convention of Insurance Commissioners recommended a new standard form in 1914, which was adopted by New York State in an amended form in 1918.

The net result found different states using three standard forms, the 1887 and the 1918 New York forms and the New England form. While all of the policies were very similar and the differences well known to insurance men, it was felt from the point of view of the buyer that the situation would be immeasurably better if a standard form could be drawn that would be acceptable in all jurisdictions. At a meeting of the National Association of Insurance Commissioners held in 1936 it was recommended that a special committee be appointed to study the problem. There was some thought that an entirely new contract should be drawn, but this idea was discarded in favor of modifying the 1918 New York form to meet present-day needs. Tentative drafts were presented in 1937 and 1938.

The final outgrowth of this study was the adoption by act of the New York Legislature of the new standard policy now known as the "1943 New York form." The form became mandatory in New York, July 1, 1943, and was soon adopted by a large majority of the states. When reference is made to the "standard fire policy" throughout this text the "1943 New York form" is indicated. The student, however, should be on guard in any particular instance to check the policy of the state in question to determine whether or not the 1943 New York form is standard in the area or to what extent the form in use varies from that form.

Benefits

The new form is much simpler and considerably shorter than any of the older standard forms. The use of the new standard form since 1943 benefits the policyholder. An insured might carefully study the conditions of one or all of his policies and be satisfied that his needs for insurance coverage were satisfactorily met. Before the adoption of a standard form, a change in policy forms may have occurred, and some obscure change in wording might have materially altered the coverage. Eternal vigilance, therefore, was necessary in order to be sure that the coverage remained as desired. The standard policy eliminates this danger and provides a uniform continuity of coverage from policy to policy.

Another advantage of standardization is the economy of printing uniform contracts. Time and costs are reduced when it is understood that standard contracts are used. Discrepancies in the wording of policies, often considered of trifling importance by the insured, frequently give rise to questions of coverage and consequently to difficulties in adjustment. With a standardized form, such discrepancies are reduced to a minimum, with a consequent simplification of adjusting problems.

Finally, under a uniform policy there tends to grow up a body of insurance law, as reflected in court decisions, that finds ready application to questions as they present themselves. The meanings of the terms used are clarified and fixed; the conditions of the contract and the meaning of terms tend to become well understood by insurers and insureds. The misunderstandings thus eliminated tend to reduce litigation to a minimum.

The benefits of the 1943 New York standard fire contract do not extend to all parts of what an insured finally sees as his policy contract. Parts of the final and complete contract may vary among different companies. For example, the *declarations* (statements by the insured, rates, property description, etc.) part on the first page may vary somewhat in its style and wording. Also, the *forms* and *endorsements* attached to the basic parts of the policy contract may be partially uniform by custom, but also may be quite different in extending or restricting the coverage to certain perils, places, or properties.

Standardization by law pertains to two essential parts of the contract, the *insuring agreement* and the *conditions and exclusions*. Figures 3 and 4 show the verbatim required language of the 1943 New York standard fire contract. The insuring agreement usually appears on the first page of the policy, with the declarations. The conditions (often called stipulations) and exclusions are found usually on the back of the first page of the policy, as in Figure 4. Together, these two parts are the standard contract. The remainder of this chapter discusses in detail the two basic standard parts of the 1943 New York fire contract. The forms, clauses, and endorsements used in connection with the standard contract, and special and allied fire lines of insurance are treated in Chapter 10.

In Consideration of the Provisions and Stipulations herein or added hereto and of

.. Dollars Premium

this Company, for the term of .... } from the .... day of ...., 19.... to the .... day of ...., 19.... { at noon, Standard Time, at location of property involved,

to an amount not exceeding .... Dollars

does insure ....

and legal representatives, to the extent of the actual cash value of the property at the time of loss, but not exceeding the amount which it would cost to repair or replace the property with material of like kind and quality within a reasonable time after such loss, without allowance for any increased cost of repair or reconstruction by reason of any ordinance or law regulating construction or repair, and without compensation for loss resulting from interruption of business or manufacture, nor in any event for more than the interest of the insured, against all DIRECT LOSS BY FIRE, LIGHTNING AND BY REMOVAL FROM PREMISES ENDANGERED BY THE PERILS INSURED AGAINST IN THIS POLICY, EXCEPT AS HEREINAFTER PROVIDED, to the property described hereinafter while located or contained as described in this policy, or pro rata for five days at each proper place to which any of the property shall necessarily be removed for preservation from the perils insured against in this policy, but not elsewhere.

Assignment of this policy shall not be valid except with the written consent of this Company.

This policy is made and accepted subject to the foregoing provisions and stipulations and those hereinafter stated, which are hereby made a part of this policy, together with such other provisions, stipulations and agreements as may be added hereto, as provided in this policy.

FIGURE 3. **Insuring Agreement from First Page of 1943 New York Standard Fire Policy.**

THE INSURING AGREEMENT

The fundamental part of any insurance contract is its *insuring agreement*. This section of the fire insurance contract is not identified as such, but it is readily discerned as the central part of the agreement. In its paragraphs the insurer obligates himself to indemnify the insured for loss or damage to the described property within a stated period by the specific perils of fire and lightning. The short nature of the insuring agreement as shown in Figure 3 should not mislead the student to think that it is unimportant. It is the core of the legal agreement between the parties, and each phrase has much meaning. The significance of each part of the insuring agreement is discussed in the following analysis.

Concealment, fraud. This entire policy shall be void if, whether before or after a loss, the insured has wilfully concealed or misrepresented any material fact or circumstance concerning this insurance or the subject thereof, or the interest of the insured therein, or in case of any fraud or false swearing by the insured relating thereto.

Uninsurable and excepted property. This policy shall not cover accounts, bills, currency, deeds, evidences of debt, money or securities; nor, unless specifically named hereon in writing, bullion or manuscripts.

Perils not included. This Company shall not be liable for loss by fire or other perils insured against in this policy caused, directly or indirectly, by: (a) enemy attack by armed forces, including action taken by military, naval or air forces in resisting an actual or an immediately impending enemy attack; (b) invasion; (c) insurrection; (d) rebellion; (e) revolution; (f) civil war; (g) usurped power; (h) order of any civil authority except acts of destruction at the time of and for the purpose of preventing the spread of fire, provided that such fire did not originate from any of the perils excluded by this policy; (i) neglect of the insured to use all reasonable means to save and preserve the property at and after a loss, or when the property is endangered by fire in neighboring premises; (j) nor shall this Company be liable for loss by theft.

Other Insurance. Other insurance may be prohibited or the amount of insurance may be limited by endorsement attached hereto.

Conditions suspending or restricting insurance. Unless otherwise provided in writing added hereto this Company shall not be liable for loss occurring

(a) while the hazard is increased by any means within the control or knowledge of the insured; or

(b) while a described building, whether intended for occupancy by owner or tenant, is vacant or unoccupied beyond a period of sixty consecutive days; or

(c) as a result of explosion or riot, unless fire ensue, and in that event for loss by fire only.

Other perils or subjects. Any other peril to be insured against or subject of insurance to be covered in this policy shall be by endorsement in writing hereon or added hereto.

Added provisions. The extent of the application of insurance under this policy and of the contribution to be made by this Company in case of loss, and any other provision or agreement not inconsistent with the provisions of this policy, may be provided for in writing added hereto, but no provision may be waived except such as by the terms of this policy is subject to change.

Waiver provisions. No permission affecting this insurance shall exist, or waiver of any provision be valid, unless granted herein or expressed in writing added hereto. No provision, stipulation or forfeiture shall be held to be waived by any requirement or proceeding on the part of this Company relating to appraisal or to any examination provided for herein.

Cancellation of policy. This policy shall be cancelled at any time at the request of the insured, in which case this Company shall, upon demand and surrender of this policy, refund the excess of paid premium above the customary short rates for the expired time. This policy may be cancelled at any time by this Company by giving to the insured a five days' written notice of cancellation with or without tender of the excess of paid premium above the pro rata premium for the expired time, which excess, if not tendered, shall be refunded on demand. Notice of cancellation shall state that said excess premium (if not tendered) will be refunded on demand.

Mortgagee interests and obligations. If loss hereunder is made payable, in whole or in part, to a designated mortgagee not named herein as the insured, such interest in this policy may be cancelled by giving to such mortgagee a ten days' written notice of cancellation.

If the insured fails to render proof of loss such mortgagee, upon notice, shall render proof of loss in the form herein specified within sixty (60) days thereafter and shall be subject to the provisions hereof relating to appraisal and time of payment and of bringing suit. If this Company shall claim that no liability existed as to the mortgagor or owner, it shall, to the extent of payment of loss to the mortgagee, be subrogated to all the mortgagee's rights of recovery, but without impairing mortgagee's right to sue; or it may pay off the mortgage debt and require an assignment thereof and of the mortgage. Other provisions relating to the interests and obligations of such mortgagee may be added hereto by agreement in writing.

Pro rata liability. This Company shall not be liable for a greater proportion of any loss than the amount hereby insured shall bear to the whole insurance covering the property against the peril involved, whether collectible or not.

Requirements in case loss occurs. The insured shall give immediate written notice to this Company of any loss, protect the property from further damage, forthwith separate the damaged and undamaged personal property, put it in the best possible order, furnish a complete inventory of the destroyed, damaged and undamaged property, showing in detail quantities, costs, actual cash value and amount of loss claimed; **and within sixty days after the loss, unless such time is extended in writing by this Company, the insured shall render to this Company a proof of loss,** signed and sworn to by the insured, stating the knowledge and belief of the insured as to the following: the time and origin of the loss, the interest of the insured and of all others in the property, the actual cash value of each item thereof and the amount of loss thereto, all encumbrances thereon, all other contracts of insurance, whether valid or not, covering any of said property, any changes in the title, use, occupation, location, possession or exposures of said property since the issuing of this policy, by whom and for what purpose any building herein described and the several parts thereof were occupied at the time of loss and whether or not it then stood on leased ground, and shall furnish a copy of all the descriptions and schedules in all policies and, if required, verified plans and specifications of any building, fixtures or machinery destroyed or damaged. The insured, as often as may be reasonably required, shall exhibit to any person designated by this Company all that remains of any property herein described, and submit to examinations under oath by any person named by this Company, and subscribe the same; and, as often as may be reasonably required, shall produce for examination all books of account, bills, invoices and other vouchers, or certified copies thereof if originals be lost, at such reasonable time and place as may be designated by this Company or its representative, and shall permit extracts and copies thereof to be made.

Appraisal. In case the insured and this Company shall fail to agree as to the actual cash value or the amount of loss, then, on the written demand of either, each shall select a competent and disinterested appraiser and notify the other of the appraiser selected within twenty days of such demand. The appraisers shall first select a competent and disinterested umpire; and failing for fifteen days to agree upon such umpire, then, on request of the insured or this Company, such umpire shall be selected by a judge of a court of record in the state in which the property covered is located. The appraisers shall then appraise the loss, stating separately actual cash value and loss to each item, and, failing to agree, shall submit their differences, only, to the umpire. An award in writing, so itemized, of any two when filed with this Company shall determine the amount of actual cash value and loss. Each appraiser shall be paid by the party selecting him and the expenses of appraisal and umpire shall be paid by the parties equally.

Company's options. It shall be optional with this Company to take all, or any part, of the property at the agreed or appraised value, and also to repair, rebuild or replace the property destroyed or damaged with other of like kind and quality within a reasonable time, on giving notice of its intention so to do within thirty days after the receipt of the proof of loss herein required.

Abandonment. There can be no abandonment to this Company of any property.

When loss payable. The amount of loss for which this Company may be liable shall be payable sixty days after proof of loss, as herein provided, is received by this Company and ascertainment of the loss is made either by agreement between the insured and this Company expressed in writing or by the filing with this Company of an award as herein provided.

Suit. No suit or action on this policy for the recovery of any claim shall be sustainable in any court of law or equity unless all the requirements of this policy shall have been complied with, and unless commenced within twelve months next after inception of the loss.

Subrogation. This Company may require from the insured an assignment of all right of recovery against any party for loss to the extent that payment therefor is made by this Company.

FIGURE 4. Conditions and Exclusions from Back of First Page of 1943 New York Standard Fire Policy

Inception and Termination

A contract of insurance need not be in writing. Every day there are literally thousands of property insurance contracts made without so much as a scratch of a pen. A policy is ordered by the insured, and the insurance agent agrees that it shall become effective immediately or at a designated time. When insurance coverage of this sort is effected, it is ordinarily for a short period, pending the drawing up and delivery of the formal contract or policy. Insurance in such an instance is said to be "bound." In every insurance agency a record of some sort is provided in which bound risks are entered. No particular form is required, and upon receiving an order for insurance, the agent will enter in his book the name of the insured, the date, and hour the insurance is to become effective, the property to be covered, all pertinent information and conditions to be incorporated in the policy, and the amount of insurance. He will then apportion the insurance among the companies he intends to commit to the risk, with the amount at risk for each company indicated. From the moment the companies are committed, their liability begins, unless a future time is indicated. Where written evidence of the agreement is desired, a form, called a *binder*, is provided for the purpose. Pending delivery of the policy, the binder would ordinarily be given to the insured for a large contract, or for one which is to be in effect for a number of days. Fifteen days is a normal maximum of coverage under a binder.

When a policy is issued following a binder, it is the custom to date the policy back to the inception date indicated in the original binder. This procedure is by no means necessary, and a binder may be carried for a certain time and paid for separately, to be followed by the issuance of the policy at a new and later date. Under the standard policy, the insurance becomes effective on a given day at noon standard time and is written for a term to expire likewise at noon on a specified day.[2]

When the day and time indicated for termination arrive, the coverage automatically ends. One exception exists, as liability under the policy continues for loss after the time of expiration of the policy when the cause originated before that time. It is held that, if a fire causing damage breaks out before the policy expires, the company is liable for all the damage (subject to the maximum policy amount) even though most of the damage was occasioned by a continuance of the fire after the time for the policy to expire.

At the present time, fire policies are usually endorsed with a full reinstatement of loss clause. The clause is not part of the insuring agreement, but is found in added pages of the contract. It provides that any reduction in the amount of the policy because of a

[2]When no particular time has been designated, there has been considerable uncertainty. In the New York standard form this uncertainty has been eliminated by the inclusion of the condition: "The word *noon*, herein stated, means noon of standard time at the place of loss or damage."

loss shall be automatically reinstated to the extent of, and concurrently with, the repair or replacement of the property damaged or destroyed.

Another provision of importance to the determination of the time during which the coverage is in effect is the permission for cancellation of the contract. The methods by which cancellation can be accomplished are set forth starting on line 56 of the conditions, and shall be discussed below.

Personal Nature

The policy contemplates indemnifying the owner of an interest for loss actually sustained through the destruction by fire of the property insured. There is no agreement to pay a stated sum in the ordinary fire policy. The amount which appears on the face of the policy expresses the limit of liability of the company; the amount payable in any situation is to be determined by measuring the actual loss or damage. This amount is payable, however, not to anyone who may own the property damaged or destroyed, but only to the person or persons named in the policy as insureds. Property is not insured, as is sometimes stated, but the person named in the policy is insured if he should suffer loss as the outgrowth of the perils covered. It follows, therefore, that the insurance policy is of value only to the named insured. Other interests in the property covered by the contract have no interest in the policy, or rights under it, unless their rights are specifically incorporated in the agreement. Legal representatives, such as heirs or executors of the named insured are included in the wording of the insuring agreement.

Actual Cash Value

The fire policy undertakes to indemnify the insured "to the extent of the *actual cash value* of the property at the time of loss. . . ." Regardless of the amount written into the policy, the amount collectible is limited to the actual cash value of the property insured.[3] The objective is repayment for the real loss sustained. That amount *may* be "market value" or "book value," but often is not. For many types of property, actual cash value is measured by replacement cost less depreciation.

The insurance contract does not undertake to supply "new for

---

[3]An exception is the valued policy discussed in Chapter 5. Another exception is the so-called "replacement coverage" sometimes written to insure buildings, equipment, machinery, and contents other than household furniture in dwellings for the difference between the actual value at the time of the loss and the cost of repairing, rebuilding, or replacing if the property is totally destroyed. Under the policy terms, replacement coverage is payable only if the property is rebuilt. Many Homeowner's contracts today include this feature if the policyholder has at least 80 percent of his total values insured.

old." Depreciation, as used in connection with fire insurance, includes the element of economic obsolescence. Thus, a property whose value is lessened by age and use, changing business conditions, neighborhood changes, and the like is subject to depreciation when its value is computed for the purpose of loss adjustments.[4] Actual cash value, which represents the actual value of the property destroyed expressed in terms of money, could not be determined without giving consideration to depreciation of the physical property plus obsolescence.[5]

Repair or Replacement Costs. Time and other factors frequently become an element in the question of valuation. The policy provides that its liability shall be limited by the actual cash value at the time of the loss and adds the additional restriction: ". . . but not exceeding the amount which it would cost to repair or replace the property with material of like kind and quality within a reasonable time after such loss, without allowance for any increased cost of repair or reconstruction by reason of any ordinance or law regulating construction or repair." Thus, when the value exceeds the cost of repairing or replacing, the replacement cost becomes a limit on the amount recoverable. For example, in a rapidly growing community suffering from a housing shortage a family moving in might be willing to pay considerably more than replacement cost for immediate occupancy. This cost would not represent insurable value. As a matter of fact, in the long run the difference between cost and replacement would disappear. However, the difference while it exists is not covered by the fire policy.

The clause limiting the loss to the "cost to repair or replace" is not held to afford any remedy to the insured; rather it expresses a privilege granted to the insurer. It places an upper limit upon the loss. This limit is the cost, less depreciation, of replacing the damage with materials such as were destroyed. If because of building laws, or for any other reason, the cost of reconstruction is in excess of the limitation thus expressed, the liability of the company is not thereby increased.

It sometimes happens that insured property, within areas in a mu-

---

[4]By limiting the loss to the cost of replacement, there is sometimes an element of confusion in the case of manufactured goods. It is the intent of the policy to indemnify the owner of the destroyed property but not to include in the figure any element of profit. If the manufacturer can make the goods in his own plant, his manufacturing costs represent the figure of the loss. It sometimes happens that a manufacturer cannot exactly reproduce the destroyed goods. There is on record a case in which particular grades of whiskey were destroyed. The court ruled that because of the element of age, the cost was to be ascertained by the cost of replacement at the date it was destroyed. In this case, because of the special characteristics attaching to the goods, the processing costs could not serve as a limit because the goods could not be reproduced within a reasonable time.

[5]*McCarney* v. *Newark Fire Insurance Co. et al.*, 159 N.E. 902.

nicipality restricted to specific requirements as to construction, fails to meet the requirements of the local building ordinance adopted after the building in question was constructed. Fire policies as now written do not cover the increased cost of repairs when the increase is made necessary as the outgrowth of a building code. For example, rebuilding a frame building in a downtown area may be prohibited. The policy would not pay the increased cost to rebuild the property with fire resistive materials such as brick or steel. Frequently, an ordinance also makes mandatory the demolition of a building when a substantial part of it is destroyed by fire. The New York form thus definitely settles these questions, and does not pay for either demolition costs or other increased costs because of building codes. A special additional endorsement to the contract is necessary to cover such losses.

Consequential Losses. Unless the liability for *consequential,* or *indirect* loss is specifically assumed under the contract, such a loss is not covered. Included in the category of consequential losses are those arising out of business interruption, such as loss of profit on goods destroyed that might otherwise have been profitably sold. Also, a building rendered unfit for use will deprive its owner of income and its occupant of the use value of his business location. Sometimes leases are drawn with a fire clause, permitting cancellation by one or both parties in the event of a serious fire. Such a cancellation may deprive a businessman of a valuable long-term lease. The consequential damage may form an important part of any fire loss; but, unless it is specifically assumed in the contract, it is not covered by the policy. Chapter 11 discusses these indirect losses and the special kinds of insurance developed to meet them.

Insurable Interest. It is the element of insurable interest that takes insurance out of the wagering classification and makes it one of indemnity. Any definition of insurable interest to include within its scope all specific instances must of necessity be broad. Every interest in property, or liability concerning it, when the nature of the interest or liability is such that the insured may suffer loss from the destruction of the property, constitutes an insurable interest which may be insured. Many different persons, in addition to owners of property, have insurable interests.[6]

---

[6]Insurance policies are written to cover: (*a*) loss to buildings, whether the insured has a legal title, equitable title, or beneficial ownership; (*b*) loss of income in the forms of rents; (*c*) the interest of a bailee in the use of a chattel or the bailee's liability for its destruction; (*d*) the interest of a person having a specific lien; (*e*) the interest of a partner in partnership property; (*f*) the interest of a contractor in a building under construction where payment is withheld or the right of payment arises on completion; (*g*) the liability of a carrier to an owner; (*h*) freight payments due a carrier depending upon a delivery of a shipment; (*i*) the interest of a

Continued on next page

A mere expectancy without a legal basis is not insurable. A general creditor, therefore, has no insurable interest in the property of his debtor unless he has by some legal means acquired a specific lien, such as a judgment lien. Neither has a legatee or a devisee an interest in an estate prior to the death of the testor. To constitute insurable interest there must be present the element of financial loss. If the interest in a property is limited to a hope or expectancy, there is no insurable interest.

There may be several insurable interest in the same property. While the insurance contract is one of indemnity, it is possible that the sum of the insurable interests exceeds the total value of the property. This situation is not usual. Although all the various interests noted are insurable, the interest should be definitely stated in the policy contract.

Compliance with the requirements of an insurable interest originally required that the interest in the property exist both at the time the policy was issued and at the time of the loss. The doctrine has now been modified to recognize as valid a policy issued upon property where no insurable interest existed at the time the policy was issued, but which was later acquired and was retained at the time the loss occurred. It is this extension of the doctrine that validates a policy upon a stock of goods that is being increased or changed from time to time.

There is no warranty as to ownership in the New York standard policy of 1943. The insuring clause limits the amount that may be recovered to the "interest of the insured." Hence, if the insured is something less than sole and unconditional owner, he may not collect unless his interest in the property is such that the damage is actual loss to him. It is the intent of the policy to provide indemnity for loss sustained. This was not accomplished in some of the older policies that voided the contract under the so-called "moral hazard" conditions.

Executors, trustees, and heirs have frequently been concerned with the validity of the insurance, covering the property of the deceased, in effect before his death. Formerly, the passing of property by death was considered to have voided the insurance in effect in the name of the deceased. A grave element of danger would exist in such a situation, however, and to make the coverage continuous a

---

leaseholder in the event his lease is terminated by fire; (*j*) undivided part interest in real estate owned outright or for life only; (*k*) fractional or divided interests; (*l*) improvements on leased property made by tenants; (*m*) the reversionary interest of a beneficiary where an estate has been entailed; (*n*) the interest of a mortgagee; (*o*) the interest of a vendor or vendee in possession; (*p*) the interest of a stockholder in corporate property in which the holdings are large enough to represent an insurable interest.

policy remains effective for his legal representatives in the event of the insured's death.

Perils Insured Against

Fire Defined. The standard fire policy provides insurance first of all "against all direct loss by fire." The word *fire* is not defined in the contract, but has been explained in detail as the courts have interpreted its full meaning. Fire is produced by combustion, yet not all combustion is fire. The presence of heat, steam, or even smoke is evidence of fire, but taken by itself will not prove the existence of fire. Heat sufficient to cause charring or scorching, unless accompanied by ignition does not constitute fire. A frequently cited definition laid down by the United States Circuit Court of Appeals serves as a basis for doubtful cases. The case concerned spontaneous combustion in wet wool. Defining "fire," the Court said: "Spontaneous combustion is usually a rapid oxidation. Fire is oxidation which is so rapid as to produce either flame or a glow. Fire is always caused by combustion, but combustion does not always cause fire. The word 'spontaneous' refers to the origin of the combustion. It means the internal development of heat without the action of an external agent. Combustion or spontaneous combustion may be so rapid as to produce fire, but until it does so, combustion cannot be said to be fire."[7] To constitute fire, combustion must proceed at a rate sufficiently fast to produce a flame, a glow, or incandescence. Regardless of the amount of heat, there can be no fire until ignition takes place.

Friendly and Unfriendly Fires. The insurance contract contemplates the provision of indemnity for loss arising from the happening of an unfavorable contingency. The element of accident in the cause is essential. Hence, a fire deliberately kindled and remaining within the limits intended for it is termed a *friendly fire*, and any damage that it may do is not covered by the fire policy. However, when a fire spreads beyond the confines intended for it and beyond the control of its custodian, it ceases then to be a friendly fire, and the damage it causes is a loss under the fire policy.

The flame of a gas jet or the fire in a stove, a fireplace, an oil burner, or a furnace is in each instance regarded as a friendly fire. Damage from such fires, in the form of smoke, soot, or heat, is not a damage covered by the fire policy. Thus, a lamp or oil stove left burning in a room may smoke, send soot throughout the premises, and do hundreds of dollars' worth of damage. The loss is not covered by the fire policy. On the other hand, if the fire escapes from the confines in which it is intended that it remain, the fire becomes

---

[7] *Western Woolen Mills Company* v. *Northern Assurance Co.*, 139 Fed. 637.

unfriendly (hostile), and the fire policy covers whatever damage is thus done. Consequently, if a breeze blows a curtain against the flame in a fireplace, and the curtain burns, the property thus destroyed is covered.

Direct Loss. The insurance contract specifies that a loss to be covered under the policy must be a *direct* loss. This has been construed by the courts to mean that fire must be the immediate or proximate cause of the loss, as distinguished from the remote cause. Loss or damage caused by smoke, heat, water, or other materials used to extinguish the fire, damage caused by the fire fighters, and unavoidable exposure at or following the fire are direct losses covered by the policy.

In a train of circumstances culminating in a result, the *proximate cause* is held to be the efficient cause: that is, the one that sets intervening agencies in motion. Thus, the courts have held that causes that are merely incidental to a superior or controlling agency are not proximate causes, even though they be nearer in time to the result. Hence, a fire may be the direct cause of a loss or damage, even though some intervening agency may form part of the chain of circumstances set in motion by the fire. For example, it was held that a fire in the tower of a building, where it was confined with but slight damage, was the proximate cause of a large machinery loss in a part of the building remote from the fire. The fire in the tower burned electric wires that caused a short circuit. This in turn set in motion a train of circumstances causing a general breakdown of the machinery. The entire loss was held to be by fire. In the case of a steamboat which caught fire and sank following a collision before the goods on board, which had been insured against loss by fire, had burned, it was maintained that the boat might have been saved after the collision but for the intervention of the fire. Because, however, the fire prevented the use of the available means and appliances for saving the boat, fire was the proximate and immediate cause of the loss.

There are numerous examples of cases in which fire has been held to be the direct cause of the damage growing out of the collapse of walls, which formed a part of ruins. When a building was destroyed by fire and part of the ruined walls fell two days later, damaging a neighboring property, the insurance company covering the second property was held liable for a fire loss. In an extreme case in Alabama, the court held the insurance company liable on the fire policy when the damage from the falling wall occurred during a high windstorm four months after the fire.

On the other hand, if a fire engine on the way to a fire accidentally strikes and damages insured property, the fire is not held to be the controlling agency in this case, and the fire insurers are not responsible for the loss. The cause of the accident and the cause of the fire are held to be independent, and damage to the property by the fire truck is attributable to the accident or its cause, and not to the fire.

When an unfriendly fire sets in motion a chain of circumstances that results in the destruction of the insured property, the loss is covered by the fire insurance policy. This rule, however, is subject to some modification. For example, it has been held that, where fire spreads to an insured building and there causes an explosion, the insurer is liable for all the damage. On the other hand, in the case of an explosion caused by a fire, concussion damage to neighboring properties is not covered by their fire policies. As to whether or not the policy covers in a given situation resolves itself into a determination of the intent of the contracting parties. In what is now held to be a leading case on proximate cause, Justice Cardozo, speaking for the court, points out that general definitions of proximate cause give little aid. "Our guide," he says, "is the reasonable expectation and purpose of the ordinary businessman when making an ordinary business contract."[8] Fire must reach the thing insured or come within such proximity to it that the damage is within the compass of reasonable probability. Then, fire is the proximate cause, because then we may suppose that it was within the contemplation of the contract. In those circumstances where there is more than one cause, and these causes are independent of one another, the courts have held that the nearest is the one to be charged with the disaster.

Lightning. The 1943 New York standard policy includes loss by *lightning* as well as by fire in the insuring clause of the policy. Lightning is frequently the cause of serious loss, though there is neither indication of fire nor, for that matter, evidence of presence of heat. The difficulty of determining at what point the lightning damage ended and the fire loss began was eliminated by including both perils specifically in the contract.

Under the provisions of the older standard policies, damage from lightning is not covered unless fire ensues, and in that case the coverage extends only to the damage caused by the fire. In other words, if lightning succeeded in wrecking a building, and the wreckage were then to catch fire, the fire insurance policy would cover the loss of the wreckage but not the lightning damage. Most such older policy forms are endorsed to include the lightning peril.

Loss by Removal. The loss incurred by removing property endangered by fire has been definitely assumed under the terms of the New York standard policy. The insured is obligated to do everything reasonable to save threatened property. When damage is sustained

[8] *Bird v. St. Paul Fire & Marine Insurance Company*, 224 N.Y. 47, 120 N.E. 86.

in the operation of removal, the fire would normally be considered the direct and proximate cause and the insurer, therefore, is liable. To avoid any doubt the contract specifically lists removal as a covered peril.

The removal must be deemed reasonably necessary in order to charge the insurance carrier, and the threatened danger must be of a nature that would prompt a careful and prudent uninsured person to take a like action in his own interest. Losses caused by breakage and exposure when there is no element of gross negligence, as well as cost of removal, are cause for proper claims. Losses by theft, however, are specifically excluded later in the contract (line 24) from the coverage.

The insurance follows the property to whatever point it is removed and continues in effect in the new location. It covers prorata, or proportionally, on the old location and on each new location, for a period of five days after the fire. When the five-day period has elapsed, the insured must make provisions for new or continued coverage in the new locations, or he will be without insurance as to these locations.

Property and Location

The standard fire contract is a *named perils* or *specified perils* contract. This means that it covers only the listed perils described in the sections above (fire, lightning, removal). Any other perils, if they are to be included, must also be specifically listed in added forms or endorsements to the contract. The coverage of *property* is also limited to the listed and described property in the contract. Buildings, machinery, merchandise, household contents, and personal property are all examples of property commonly included in the policy. Both real and personal property may be included in the same contract, but no coverage applies unless the property is named and described.

The contract is also basically a named *location* coverage. It applies only at the location described in the policy and would not protect (except with written permission from the insurer) against loss elsewhere if the property were moved. Some of the forms attached to the basic policy, it will be noted in Chapter 10, do make the coverage applicable automatically to other locations than those specifically named.

Assignment

Assignment is the transfer of the legal right or interest in an insurance contract to another. It is generally held that a right under a contract is assignable without the consent of the other party in the absence of statute or of an express provision in the contract. In connection with fire insurance an assignment under the terms of the contract is valid only with the consent of the insurer. An exception is the case of an assignment of rights to a claim, after a loss has occurred.

It frequently happens that, with the sale of an insured property, it is desired to transfer insurance to the new owner. In such a situation it becomes necessary, in order for the assignment to be effective, to secure the consent of the company. This is accomplished by having the policy endorsed with the company's consent as well as the insured's assignment of interest. Ordinarily, an assignment carries with it only such rights as are possessed by the assignor. In the case of a fire insurance policy the transfer is not, in the strict sense of the word, an assignment, but rather a novation. A novation is a new contract, in this case between the insurer and the assignee. The relationship between the two original parties is terminated, and a new contractual relationship established.

To accomplish the same end, another and more common method is followed. The policy without assignment is delivered to the office of the company or its agent, with the request that the insured under the policy be changed and the coverage transferred from the insured named in the policy to the newly designated insured. This is accomplished by means of an endorsement, drawn by the agent and signed by him, stating that the interest of the named insured has on that date terminated, and that it is understood and agreed that from then on the insurance shall continue in effect for the benefit of the newly designated insured.

CONDITIONS AND EXCLUSIONS

Concealment or Fraud

It is specifically provided on lines 1–6:[9] "This entire policy shall be void if, whether before or after a loss, the insured has wilfully concealed or misrepresented any material fact or circumstance concerning this insurance of the subject thereof, or the interest of the insured therein, or in case of any fraud or false swearing by the insured relating thereto."

Fraud most frequently makes its appearance in connection with the adjustment of claims. Incorrect loss statements are prepared, salvage concealed, books falsified, false testimony given under oath, and false proofs executed and sworn to. It has sometimes been offered as a defense that the false statements made in connection with the claim were for some purpose other than to defraud the insurers, as when a claimant contended that his statements were made to

[9]The following references to lines are to the numbered 165 lines of the back page of the 1943 New York Standard Fire Policy. These "Stipulations and Conditions" are reproduced in Figure 4 of this chapter.

substantiate statements previously made to a credit company. The courts have held, however, that a false statement on oath concerning the subject matter vitiates the policy, whether or not the purpose was to deceive the company.

Excluded Property

Under the New York standard policy certain types of property are excepted from the coverage of a policy while other types are uninsurable in any case. On lines 7–10, the policy reads: "This policy shall not cover accounts, bills, currency, deeds, evidences of debt, money, or securities; nor, unless specifically named hereon in writing, bullion or manuscripts." If bullion or manuscripts are to be included in the coverage, they must be specifically mentioned. With the exception of these articles, personal property in which an insurable interest exists may be covered by the fire policy. The forms added to the contract must also be read carefully for excepted property, such as automobiles which are excluded in the Dwelling Property Form. Some other contracts[10] specifically include coverage on money or other of the above items which are excluded in the standard fire policy.

Excluded Perils

Lines 11–24 name several perils which are excluded from the standard contract, including *war* (in its various forms), some orders for destruction by *civil authorities, neglect* by the insured to prevent further damage, and *theft.*

In order to eliminate catastrophic war risks all fire policies exclude loss caused by any of the following: (1) hostile or warlike action in time of peace or war, including action in hindering, combating, or defending against an actual, impending, or expected attack (*a*) by a government or sovereign power (*de jure* or *de facto*), or by any authority maintaining or using military, naval, or air forces; or (*b*) by military, naval, or air forces; or (*c*) by an agent of any such government, power, authority, or forces, it being understood that any discharge, explosion, or use of any weapon of war employing nuclear fission or fusion shall be conclusively presumed to be such a hostile or warlike action by such a government, power, authority, or forces; (2) insurrection, rebellion, revolution, civil war, usurped power, or action taken by governmental authority in hindering, combating, or defending against such an occurrence. The difficulties of defining a term such as war are obvious in the lengthy description of the excluded actions associated with the term.

---

[10]For example, the Homeowner's contracts often cover up to $100 on money and $500 on securities. Commercial risks can use the Broad Form Money and Securities Policy, Accounts Receivable or Valuable Papers contracts.

The danger of assuming unpredictable risks which are not accidental in nature leads to the exclusion of property destruction by civil authorities. The exclusion does not apply to orders for destruction made to prevent the spread of a fire, such as the dynamiting of a block of houses to stop a conflagration. These losses would be covered, but others, such as the condemnation of a building by health authorities, are excluded.

The insured must be reasonably prudent in doing all he can at and after a loss to prevent as much damage as possible. Examples of unreasonable actions which might deny him coverage are: not attempting to obtain nearby available help in removing endangered property from a building; failing to turn in a fire alarm as soon as possible or; not arranging to have property, such as machinery, dried off after a fire to prevent rust damage.

Suspension

In order to protect the insurer with respect to changes in the risk, the coverage in certain situations is suspended. This policy condition is for the most part concerned with an increase in the hazard. It is important to notice that they do not have the effect of voiding the policy absolutely but rather act to suspend or restrict the insurance coverage.[11] When the conditions that suspend the coverage no longer prevail the insurance reverts to full force and effect.

When the risk is written and the rate fixed, it is assumed that the risk will remain constant during the life of the policy. If there is any change, the insurer should have the opportunity either of canceling the policy or of securing a higher premium.

It might be contended that the one clause suspending the coverage if the hazard was increased would be comprehensive enough to include the others within its scope. In every case what does constitute an increase in the hazard is a matter of fact, and hence in litigated cases is a matter for the jury to decide. The framers of the standard policy thus undertook definitely to incorporate a few special situations which in their opinion increased the risk to a degree that warranted a suspension of the coverage. Vacancy is one such increased hazard.[12]

In event of riot and explosion, the policy is not suspended, but

---

[11]On lines 28–37 it is stated: "Unless otherwise provided by agreement in writing added hereto this company shall not be liable for loss or damage occurring (*a*) while the hazard is increased by any means within the control or knowledge of the insured; or (*b*) while a described building, whether intended for occupancy by owner or tenant, is vacant or unoccupied beyond a period of sixty consecutive days; or (*c*) as a result of explosion or riot, unless fire ensue, and in that event for loss by fire only."

[12]Though many policies include coverage for vacancy or unoccupancy in the wording of an attached form such as the Dwelling Property Form.

loss is restricted to damage by fire only. Until the 1943 New York policy, loss caused directly or indirectly by riot was not covered. This created a serious gap in the fire coverage and also left an important source of doubt in instances where it was not altogether clearly established whether or not the fire could be attributed to a riot.

The basic policy now does not cover sabotage, vandalism, and other like damage that might originate from a riot but does include within its scope losses caused by fire. In the case of both riot and explosion, if there is loss prior to the inception of the fire, the liability of the fire insurance company extends only to the value of the property at the time the fire started. In other words, if a property is partly demolished by explosion or riot and a fire follows, the fire policy is not responsible for the wreckage caused before the fire, but only for the loss caused by the fire to the property in its wrecked condition.

The difficulty of differentiating such losses is today avoided in the many contracts which include explosion and riot perils in commonly used endorsements to the fire policy.

Added Perils and Provisions

Lines 38 through 55 provide for adapting the standard contract to include additional perils, properties, and provisions. Emphasis is placed, however, on the fact that such additions must be made in writing and attached to the basic policy.

It was the aim of the framers of the standard policy to draw up an insurance agreement that would treat fairly both the insured and the company, and one that would be comprehensive enough in its scope to satisfy every situation. Since it was designed for use in connection with all classes of property, and since its use has extended to insuring nearly every known insurable interest, it can readily be seen that it would be impossible to devise a complete contract that would meet all needs. The policy is also designed to cover perils other than fire and refers, in the insuring clause, in addition to fire, lightning, and removal, to "the perils insured against in this policy." To make provision for the inclusion of further perils, lines 38–41 provide: "Any other peril to be insured against or subject of insurance to be covered in this policy shall be by endorsement in writing hereon or added hereto."

Insurers have found, as the outgrowth of experience, that with the extension of the fire coverage to include other perils it is sometimes necessary to clarify further the extent of the coverage. Recognizing that such situations would develop, they have incorporated a further clause permitting endorsements or riders. The policy is arranged with a blank page for the attachment of these additions. In this space is attached, first of all, an addition known as a *form.* It contains a description of the property to be insured and includes, as well, a number of *clauses* pertinent to the particular contract, and the risk to be insured. *Endorsements* may also be added extending the coverage to include such perils as windstorm, explosion, damage from falling aircraft, and many other extensions or restrictions on the policy coverage.

The doctrines of waiver and estoppel have found frequent application in the enforcement of insurance contracts. The standard policy undertakes to require waivers to be in writing to be effective. To this end the antiwaiver clause is incorporated in the standard policy. Familiar with the difficulties and with what seemed to be abuses arising from parole waivers, the makers of this clause intended that a waiver to be effective should be in writing. In this they were not entirely successful. The courts have held that just as other provisions of the policy may be waived, so may the one that requires waivers to be in writing. It is held that this clause, indicating the form and manner of making waivers, may itself be waived by anyone with authority to do so. Thus, in spite of the antiwaiver provision previously cited, parole waivers may still be evoked to contradict or modify the written terms of the policy.

Cancellation

The insured may at any time have the policy canceled, and no advance notice by him is required. He is obligated on demand to surrender the policy and is penalized as to premium. The premium to be returned by the company represents the balance after charging for the expired term on the *short-rate*[13] basis. If the policy has been canceled for a convenience and is being renewed in the same company for the same or a greater amount, it is the custom of the companies to charge the earned premium on the prorata rather than the short-rate basis.

When cancellation is ordered by the company, five days' notice must be given every named insured or interest. In the case of a mortgagee, the policy provides on lines 68–73, that the policy may be canceled by giving to such mortgagee a ten days' written notice of cancellation. It is to be noted, therefore, that, while named insureds are to receive five days' notice, the mortgagee receives ten. When the Company cancels, a *prorata* premium only may be charged for the period which the policy has run, and not short rates, as is the case when the insured cancels.[14]

[13]Chapter 5, page 164, gives an example of the effect of a short rate cancellation, and Appendix C contains a short-rate cancellation table.

[14]To cancel a policy effectively, the company must notify the premium payer, all parties named as insureds, and all parties named as mortgagees. The notice must

(Continued on next page)

The New York standard form makes cancellation effective upon proper notice, without tender of the unearned premium, provided notice is given the insured that he is entitled to a return premium that will be paid him upon request.

Loss Provisions

All the remainder of the wording in the conditions and exclusions pertain to rights and obligations of the parties to the contract. The importance of these sections of the required 165 lines in the standard policy is indicated by the fact that more than one half of the lines are used to enumerate provisions which apply following a loss.

Mortgagee requirements after a loss are discussed on lines 74–85. The mortgagee must file proof of loss if the owner does not, and if the insurer pays the mortgagee, he may take over any rights against the mortgagor. Other mortgage provisions may be added to the policy, and often are so included in the forms attached to the basic part of the contract. (See next chapter for example of the standard mortgage clause in the Dwelling Property Form.) These added mortgage provisions will be separately referred to in the next section of this chapter.

An important limitation on the payment made by the insurer for a loss appears on lines 86–89. The *prorata liability clause* limits the liability of the insurer by stating that "This Company shall not be liable for a greater proportion of any loss than the amount hereby insured shall bear to the whole insurance covering the property against the peril involved, whether collectible or not." Thus, if Company A had $10,000 fire insurance on a building, and Company B had $5,000 on the same building, each insurer would pay a proportionate share of any loss. If the loss were $9,000, Company A would pay two thirds, or $6,000, and Company B would pay one-third, or $3,000, of the loss. The purpose of the prorata liability clause is to prevent double payment of a loss to the insured, which would be a violation of the indemnity principle. Since more than one policy contract is a common occurrence in fire insurance, it is

---

state unconditionally the company's determination to cancel at a specific time. Notice of cancellation does not become effective until actually received. Therefore, the time will not run on the notice until actually in the insured's hands. The time is not computed from the instance of receipt. The first day, that is, the day the notice is received, is excluded in the computation of the time; and beginning with the next midnight, the days are counted, running from midnight to midnight.

When it is not convenient to reach the insured and serve the notice personally, the company sends a notice by registered mail. Elaborate forms have been prepared for the purpose. Some are so printed as to become, when folded, envelopes, thereby avoiding the possibility of the insured's claiming to have received an empty envelope. Sometimes these notices are made in duplicate, and the postmaster is asked to witness the inclusion of the notice in the envelope. Finally, a demand is made for a personal return receipt.

necessary that each insurer specify by the wording that he will pay only his proportionate share of a loss.

The insured is required in lines 90–122 to take certain actions following a loss. The acts are conditions which must be met as specified, or the insured may not be able to collect his claim against the insurer. The insured must: (1) give immediate written notice of the loss, (2) protect the property from further damage, (3) separate the damaged and undamaged property, (4) furnish an inventory of the damaged property, its costs, values, and losses sustained, (5) render a written *proof of loss* within sixty days,[15] including detailed information about the loss (its time, origin, insurable interests, occupancies, insurance contracts in force, and so on), and (6) exhibit to the insurer the property and books of account.

Although seldom used, appraisal proceedings are provided for on lines 123–40. Either insurer or insured may, if they do not agree on the lost amount, ask for an appraisal. Both select a competent and disinterested appraiser, and the two appraisers choose an umpire who settles any differences in the two appraisals of loss. The method sometimes avoids resorting to the courts for determination of a difficult loss settlement.

The following section (lines 141–47) states the right of the insurer to repair, rebuild, or replace the property destroyed or damaged with like kind and quality of materials. This right is rarely exercised, for the insurer much prefers to make a financial payment for loss rather than to go in the repair business. It does act as a maximum ceiling on payment, however, in case an insured refuses to accept reasonable payment for his loss. The insured may not abandon his damaged property to the insurer and claim a total loss (lines 148–49). The loss is payable by the insurer within sixty days after proof of loss is received (lines 150–56), though most are paid well in advance of that required time. The insured, according to lines 157–161, may not sue the insurer until all the policy requirements have been complied with, nor after one year following the loss.

The final section of the New York standard policy definitely incorporates the doctrine of *subrogation* into the policy with this clause: "This Company may require from the insured an assignment of all right of recovery against any party for loss to the extent that payment therefore is made by this Company." Though the right of subrogation exists without being expressly incorporated into a contract, the insurer is thus protected from having this right destroyed by action of the insured. To this end it is essential that an insured

[15]In New York State, by statute, the companies must request the proof of loss from the insured. See New York Insurance Law, Section 172, and Max J. Gwertzman, *A Legal Analysis of the Standard Fire Insurance Policy* (New York: Insurance Advocate, 1963), p. 41–42.

be extremely careful that in making contracts he waive no rights of recovery against another party in event of loss. Such a waiver by an insured might so change the nature of the risk as to void the policy. It is the proper procedure for the insured to have the waiver acknowledged by the fire insurance company and its consent endorsed upon the policies.

Although subrogation cases are much rarer in fire insurance than in automobile or liability insurance, there are some situations in which the insured's right of action against a negligent third party is extremely valuable to the insurer. For example, a neighbor may cause your garage to burn, because he was careless and burned leaves too close to your property. Your fire insurer would pay your loss, but would expect to take over your rights to sue the neighbor for his carelessness. Another example frequently arises when you are having repair work done on your property. Suppose the electrician is negligent and sets fire to your property. Again, your insurer will pay your loss, but will expect to have the opportunity to bring action against the electrician or his employer for recovery of its loss payment.

SUMMARY

The basic fire insurance contract is an important introduction to the study of insurance policies. It is the most standardized of all insurance contracts, since the exact wording is required by state statutes. Most of the statutes base their requirement on the 1943 New York Standard Fire Policy. Only a few states permit any variation of that standard contract wording, and even then the differences are not great. The evolution of the 1943 standard policy through legislation and other methods of standardization is discussed in the beginning of this chapter. Also of significance is an understanding of the benefits derived from such contract uniformity.

The introductory part of the 1943 New York Standard Fire Policy contains the *declarations* in which the insured, the property, the location, the insurance amount, the insurance rate and premium, and the term of the policy contract are identified. Next comes the *insuring agreement,* in which the insurer makes its fundamental promise to indemnify the insured for the actual cash value of his losses. This value does not include consequential or indirect losses, and will not exceed the insurance amount, the insurable interest of the insured, nor the cost of repair or replacement. The insurer's promise is reimbursement for direct losses due to certain named perils, specifically fire, lightning, and removal from the endangered premises. The courts have defined the meaning of what is and is not a "fire," and what constitutes the covered "unfriendly" fires.

A further major part of the standard contract is the section containing 165 lines known as the *conditions and exclusions*. Loss payment under the contract may not be made to the insured in case of concealment, fraud, excluded property or perils, suspension or cancellation. The insured must also meet certain requirements in case a loss does occur, including proper notice, proof of loss, and appraisal proceedings or subrogation when necessary.

Provision is made in the above sections of the standard fire policy for addition of other perils and provisions. The forms, clauses, and endorsements discussed in the next chapter are the means by which this is done.

FOR REVIEW

1. What significance do the following terms have in the field of fire insurance:
   a) Standard policy?
   b) Insurable interest?
   c) Proximate loss?
   d) Actual cash value?
   e) Friendly fire?
   f) Prorata liability clause?
2. Why should, or should not, the fire insurance contract be a standard contract?
3. Is it necessary that an insured have an insurable interest in a property, both at the time the policy is issued and at the time of the loss? Why or why not?
4. Policies are sometimes written to read: "John Doe, as his interest may appear." Is the insurance valid in such an instance if John Doe is not the sole and unconditional owner, or must John Doe's interest be specifically described? Give reasons for your answer.
5. The dwelling house of X is in danger of loss by fire because of sparks falling from a neighboring fire. A representative of the insurance company that covers the dwelling of X is at the scene of the fire. X suggests that wet blankets on the roof might save the building and the agent agrees. Later, when X presents a claim for the value of the blankets, the company denies liability. In your opinion has X a claim?
6. What has the phrase "*direct* loss by *fire*," in the New York Standard Fire Policy, been interpreted to mean? Explain fully.
7. Is the actual cash value to be paid under a fire policly based upon: (*a*) assessed property valuation? (*b*) cost to the policyholder? (*c*) full replacement value? (*d*) an amount proved to be what the insured had offered the property for sale?
8. A policy is delivered to X covering "on building and contents." X contends the description is too vague and wishes the contents item to enumerate in considerable detail the items and classes of items to be covered. What is your opinion as to the best practice?
9. A fire engine on the way to a fire collides with an automobile and demolishes it. The owner of the automobile claims his loss to be directly caused by fire. Are his fire insurers liable? The show window of a store is broken in the accident, too; is this covered by the storeowner's fire insurance?
10. The accumulated soot in a chimney catches fire, and as a result considerable smoke damage follows to the contents of the building. There is no

fire outside the heating plant or chimney. Are the fire insurance companies liable for the loss and damage?

11. C entered into an oral contract to purchase a foundry from its owners. The consideration agreed upon was $25,000. Of this amount, $20,000 was to be secured in the form of a loan from a bank. The deed of conveyance from the owner of the foundry to C, and the deed of trust and note to be executed by C, were prepared and placed in safekeeping with the bank. The papers were to be signed on the morning of May 1, and, on the afternoon of April 30, C purchased fire insurance in the amount of $12,000. During the night of April 30 the foundry buildings and contents were almost completely destroyed. What is the position of C with respect to the insurance?
12. A roast cooking in the oven overheats, becomes badly burned, and smoke permeates the house, damaging both the dwelling and furniture. Is the smoke loss covered under the standard fire policy?
13. Some Kleenex on a mantelpiece accidentally caught fire. A person standing nearby gathered up the flaming tissue with a towel and threw it into a fireplace. Later it was learned that a diamond ring, which had been placed on the mantelpiece, had been accidentally thrown into the fireplace with the burning Kleenex and was destroyed. Is this a fire loss? In another situation some jewelry was thrown into a furnace with rubbish and destroyed. Is there any difference between this situation and the foregoing one that would have a bearing upon determining whether or not the fire insurance company is liable?
14. A fire in a furnace, after getting out of control, seriously damaged the furnace and appurtenant parts. When the fire was discovered it had apparently excaped from the furnace and enveloped the entire furnace pit. Quite definitely the fire was a friendly fire at the outset, but increased in fury until it became a hostile fire. Damages were in excess of $2,000. Is the fire insurance policy liable?
15. X, while under the influence of liquor, negligently throws a lighted match into a pile of shavings and starts a fire that destroys his woodworking plant. Are the fire insurance companies liable for the loss and damage?
16. A church located on the corner of Union and Main streets has three addresses: one that appears in the church records, one that appears in the city directory, and one that appears in the records of the city street department. Which number should be used in writing the policy?
17. B owns a camp in which he uses an oil stove for cooking purposes. While unattended, the flame in the stove creeps unusually high and saturates the building with smoke. Will the fire policies be liable?
18. *a)* X has $5,000 worth of cereals stored in a warehouse. There is no fire in the building, but a fire a block away fills part of the building with smoke. The cereals are damaged by the odor. Is this a fire loss?

    b) A stock of goods stored in a warehouse is extremely susceptible to moisture. Will the fire policies on the stock cover a moisture loss if there is no fire whatsoever in the premises—although the stock absorbs moisture because of the water put on a fire in neighboring premises?

Chapter 10

FIRE FORMS, CLAUSES, ENDORSEMENTS, AND ALLIED LINES

FIRE insurance contracts are fundamentally, but not completely, standardized by the legislative requirements which make the insuring agreement, conditions, and exclusions uniform in the basic part of the policy. The differences appear in the forms, clauses, and endorsements which are attached to and become a part of the fire insurance contract. By these additions the contract is completed, clarified, and extended or restricted to meet the needs of the many different policyholders who purchase fire insurance. Some of these additional parts of the contract are uniform and used with many policies. Rating bureaus and company customs help provide considerable standardization of some forms and endorsements, and most states require approval of these by the insurance commissioner to prevent unfair wording. Many other forms and endorsements are highly individualistic, varying among different insurers or insureds to meet specific purposes. This chapter reviews the more common forms, clauses, and endorsements, as well as a number of separate contracts closely associated with fire insurance.

FORMS

Purpose

The statutory fire contract has been seen to include the insuring agreement, and the conditions and exclusions. A *form* is necessary to complete the contract. The form constitutes a third section of the contract and contains information essential to clarifying the terms of the policy. Particularly the form contains a description of the property to be insured as well as a number of clauses pertinent to the particular contract. The insuring agreement and the stipulations and conditions are general in their application. By means of the form the contract is tailored to the specific risks and to the particular needs of the insured.

Preparation and Use

Standard forms are prepared by rating organizations, each designed for a particular class of risk. The number of specialized forms is myriad. There are forms for dwellings, stores, farms, apartments, and many others. There are forms prepared with blank tops, that is, with no description of the property to be covered but with the clauses and permits used in connection with the class of risk. These are available for standard-type risks where the wording of the descriptive material is specialized in nature.

The wording of the form is not prescribed by statute. Forms are usually printed with spaces left for typing details, such as the name and address of the insured and the amount of insurance. If the form is specially prepared for an individual insured, it may be, and usually is, printed in its entirety. The standard forms noted above are printed and distributed to agents. There is no requirement, however, that the form be printed, and where it satisfies the needs of the insured it may be mimeographed, typed, or even handwritten. Since standard forms are available for the more usual type of risk, it is the general practice to use them. If there is no standard form available to meet the needs of a special situation, the insured may have his own form prepared.

It is quite customary in the case of sizable risks to prepare and print a special form. Where this is done, the approval of the rating authority must be obtained before the form can be used. This approval serves two purposes. The form must afford the insured the protection he contemplates and give him the benefits of the various liberalizing clauses to which his premium entitles him. On the other hand, the form must also be checked to prevent discrimination against other insureds through an extension of the coverage not provided for in the rating structure.

Insureds who have familiarized themselves with the conditions of standard forms and policies are sometimes inclined to confuse the modifications permitted in the form with the terms and conditions of the policy. It is of the utmost importance to recognize that certain coverages and privileges, as well as certain restrictions and conditions, originate in the form attached to the policy, and not in the policy itself. It is essential for an insured, whose plan of insurance requires a number of policies on the same property, to have his policies carefully checked and to see that the forms are identical.

Types

Although there are dozens of various forms used in connection with the fire contract, the form will fall into one of the following five categories: (1) *specific,* (2) *blanket,* (3) *floater,* (4) *automatic,* or (5) *schedule.* A brief description of each type will indicate their particular characteristics.

Specific Coverage. This is the most common form in use. It covers primarily one kind of property in one definite location. When the building and contents are insured with definite amounts covered on each, the policy is specific. An example of this type of form is the first page of the *Dwelling Property Form* in *Figure* 5. Appendix D, "Forms, Clauses, and Endorsements," contains the other pages of the *Dwelling Property Form* and another example (from the business world), the "Manufacturing Form—Buildings and Contents."

The Dwelling Property Form is a good example of the purposes of forms: completion and clarification of the contract. In addition, it provides some important extensions of coverage. The term "dwelling"as used in the declarations is defined to include building and outdoor equipment and fixtures. "Contents" includes all household and family personal property, with a few exceptions such as animals, automobiles, and boats. Without these definitions, there would be many problems in determining what is covered by these items in the standard fire contract.

The extensions of coverage are four: (1) the insured may apply up to 10 percent (of the amount of insurance on the building) for *private structures* such as a detached garage; (2) he may also apply up to 10 percent (of the building insurance amount) for the loss of *rental value* of the dwelling while untenantable due to the perils insured against, with a maximum limit of one twelfth of the 10 percent each month; (3) *off-premises contents* are covered up to 10 percent (of the amount of insurance on the contents) for losses of family personal property while it is away from the premises, including in hotels, college dormitories, summer residences, and so on; and (4) for *improvements, alterations, or additions* by an insured tenant, 10 percent (of the contents insurance amount) may be used. The extension of coverage noted for private structures and rental value apply as an additional amount of insurance; the off-premises and improvements contents coverage are not an additional amount of insurance beyond the amount stated in the declarations of the standard contract.

Blanket Coverage. A blanket policy covers the same kind of property in different locations, or different kinds of property at a single location. Thus, several buildings in different locations may be insured under a blanket policy, as may stocks of goods or merchandise located in a different warehouses or stores, or building and machinery at a single location.

Floating Coverage. A floating policy, termed in the insurance business "a floater," is used to cover goods in different locations when it is difficult or impossible to furnish an accurate description of the location. One form of floater covers certain specific goods wherever they may be, usually within certain prescribed limits as to territory. For example, the equipment of a traveling theatrical

Form D—No. 1

DWELLING PROPERTY FORM (NOT FARM) — Edition January, 1962

(SEASONAL PROPERTY SHALL BE SO DESCRIBED ON FIRST PAGE OF POLICY)

Insurance attaches only to those items specifically described in this policy for which a specific amount is shown, and, unless otherwise provided all conditions of this form and the provisions of the policy to which it is attached shall apply separately to each item covered.

SECTION I

(A) **Unless the occupancy is otherwise described on the first page of** this policy, or by endorsement(s) attached thereto, the term "dwelling" shall mean a building occupied exclusively for dwelling purposes by the number of families stated in this policy, but in no event by more than 4 families.

(B) Any loss hereunder shall not reduce the amount of this policy.

(C) If this policy is cancelled at the request of the Insured, the total premium retained by the Company shall be not less than the minimum set forth in customary short rate table.

SECTION II

(A) **DWELLING COVERAGE:**

When the insurance under this policy covers a dwelling, such insurance shall include additions in contact therewith; also, if the property of the owner of the described dwelling and when not otherwise covered, building equipment, fixtures and outdoor equipment, all pertaining to the service of the described premises and while located thereon, but not lawns, trees, shrubs or plants. Also, materials and supplies located on the described premises or adjacent thereto, intended for use in construction, alteration or repair of structures covered hereunder.

(B) **Dwelling Coverage Extensions:**

(1) The Insured may apply up to 10% of the amount of insurance applicable to the principal dwelling item under this policy as an additional amount of insurance to cover private structures (other than the described dwelling and additions in contact therewith) appertaining to the described premises and located thereon, but not structures used for commercial, manufacturing or farming purposes, nor any structures (except structures used principally for private garage purposes) which are wholly rented or leased to other than a tenant of the principal dwelling covered hereunder.

(2) The Insured may apply up to 10% of the amount of insurance applicable to the principal dwelling item as an additional amount of insurance to cover rental value, as hereinafter defined and limited in Section VII, but not exceeding 1/12 of said 10% for each month the principal dwelling or appurtenant private structures (except those used for commercial, manufacturing or farming purposes) or parts thereof are untenantable as a result of physical damage to the described building(s) or the equipment therein, or the equipment on the described premises, caused by a peril insured against.

SECTION III

(A) **CONTENTS COVERAGE:**

When the insurance under this policy covers contents, such insurance shall cover all household and personal property usual or incidental to the occupancy of the premises as a dwelling (except animals, birds, aircraft; motor vehicles other than motorized equipment used for maintenance of the premises; and boats and their equipment other than rowboats and canoes and their equipment), belonging to the Insured or for which the Insured may be liable or, at the option of the Insured, belonging to a member of the family of the Insured, or to a servant thereof, while contained in the described dwelling or appurtenant private structures (except those used for commercial, manufacturing or farming purposes), or while in the open on the described premises.

(B) If, during the term of this policy, contents covered by this policy is removed to another location within the limits of this State and occupied in whole or in part as the Insured's residence, this policy shall cover such property while at such new location up to the amount applicable to contents and shall cease to cover at the former location, except that during the period of removal this policy shall cover at each location in the proportion that the value of the described property at each location bears to the aggregate value at both locations.

(C) Loss due to change of temperature shall be limited to such loss resulting from physical damage to the described building(s) or to equipment therein or to equipment on the described premises caused by a peril insured against. This Company shall not be liable hereunder for any loss specifically excluded under (a) the Riot provisions of the Extended Coverage Endorsement if effective under this policy; nor, (b) the provisions of the Vandalism and Malicious Mischief Endorsement, if also attached.

(D) Loss shall be adjusted with and made payable to the named Insured unless other payee is specifically named.

(E) **Contents Coverage Extensions:**

(1) The Insured may apply up to 10% of the amount of insurance applicable to the contents item under this policy, not as an additional amount of insurance, to cover property so defined (except rowboats and canoes) belonging to the Insured or members of the Insured's family of the same household, while elsewhere than on the described premises but within the limits of that part of Continental North America included within the United States of America and Canada, and in the State of Hawaii. This extension of coverage shall in no wise inure directly or indirectly to the benefit of any carrier or other bailee.

(2) The Insured (if not the owner of the described premises) may apply up to 10% of the amount of insurance applicable to the contents item under this policy, not as an additional amount of insurance, to cover improvements, alterations or additions to the described dwelling and private structures appertaining thereto except those used for commercial, manufacturing or farming purposes.

SECTION IV

As respects the 10% extensions under the Dwelling Coverage and Contents Coverage items: It is a condition of this policy that in the event the Insured elects to apply the 10% optional provisions, this Company shall not be liable for a greater proportion of any loss than would have been the case if all policies covering the described property had contained identical optional provisions and the same election were made under all policies.

SECTION V

Outbuilding Coverage: When the insurance under this policy covers specifically described appurtenant private structure(s), such insurance shall include, if the property of the owner of the appurtenant private structure(s) and when not otherwise covered, building equipment, fixtures and outdoor equipment all pertaining to the service of the described premises and located thereon, but not lawns, trees, shrubs or plants.

SECTION VI

Trees, Shrubs or Plants Coverage: When the insurance under this policy covers trees, shrubs, or plants, such insurance shall cover only those located on the described premises which are not grown for commercial purposes, and this Company shall not be liable for more than the limit specified on the first page of this policy for any one tree, or any one shrub, or any one plant.

SECTION VII

Rental Value Coverage: When the insurance under this policy covers specifically on Rental Value, such insurance shall cover the rental value (as hereinafter defined) of dwelling and appurtenant private structures (except those used for commercial, manufacturing or farming purposes) or parts thereof described in the dwelling coverage item. Rental Value Defined: The term "rental value" shall mean the fair rental value of the building(s) or parts thereof, as furnished and equipped by the owner whether rented or not. Loss of Rental Value shall be limited to such loss resulting from physical damage to the described building(s) or the equipment therein, or the equipment on the described premises, caused by a peril insured against and shall be computed for the period of time, following loss, which would be required with the exercise of due diligence and dispatch, and not limited by the expiration date of this policy, to restore the property to a tenantable condition, less such charges and expenses as do not continue.

SECTION VIII

When the Extended Coverage Endorsement applies to this policy, this Company shall not be liable for loss caused by wind or hail to metal smokestacks, or, when outside of buildings, cloth awnings, signs, radio or television antennas including their lead-in wiring, masts or towers, unless liability is assumed as a separate item(s) by endorsement to such Extended Coverage Endorsement and additional premium(s) paid therefor.

SECTION IX

Deferred Premium Payment: In consideration of the Insured's election to pay the premium in equal annual payments as indicated on the first page of this policy, the premium for this policy is hereby made so payable, provided that no payment shall be less than the Minimum Premium applicable.

Default in making any payment shall be construed as a request of the Insured to cancel this policy, in which case this Company shall, upon demand and surrender of this policy, or after notice of cancellation in accordance with the policy conditions, comply with the said request.

If this policy is cancelled, either at the request of the Insured or at the election of this Company, this Company shall refund to the Insured only the excess of paid premium over earned premium. In the event the earned premium exceeds the paid premium the Insured shall pay this Company the difference.

FIGURE 5. **First Page of the Dwelling Property Form**

company are located in different hotels, theaters, trains, boats, automobiles, and terminals. A floater would cover this equipment whereever it might be, so long as it remained within the limits prescribed. Such limits might be a single state, the continental limits of the United States, or worldwide.

Automatic Coverage. Automatic coverages are written with "reporting forms." They are used when it is difficult, if not impossible, to provide the insurance company with an accurate statement of values because of changes or fluctuations, even though full insurance coverage is desired. The term "automatic insurance" has been applied to this type of coverage because the amounts are automatically adjusted without action on the part of the insured as the amount of risk increases or decreases. The multiple-location contracts utilized by chain stores fall within this category. So long as the required reports are accurately made within the limits of the policy, the insurance automatically adjusts itself to intervening inventory changes. The automatic builder's risk form has the same effect. A building in the process of construction adds value day by day. Monthly reports are required, but a loss at a point between two reports will be protected by full insurance as the values of that day show.

Schedule Coverage. Schedule forms are a variation of specific coverage and are indicated for certain large risks. All the buildings and their contents belonging to an insured may be grouped on a single form covering for specific amounts, instead of being written as specific insurance on separate policies. While specific amounts of insurance are indicated for each unit of the property, the policies as written cover proportionately every unit represented by the schedule. For full coverage the insured must provide himself with policies aggregating the total set forth in the schedule. An organization with widely scattered property, such as a state, a municipality, a church, or a university, frequently finds this form to be desirable as a means for simplifying the clerical supervision of insurance detail.

CLAUSES

General Use

Following the descriptive matter in the form, there are a number of *clauses* modifying the policy conditions. These clauses differ with the character of the risk, being sometimes permissive, sometimes liberal, yet often restrictive in their nature. Clauses have the effect (*a*) of extending or limiting the coverage provided by the statutory wording of the standard policy and (*b*) modifying the statutory provisions to meet the insured's requirements with respect to the perils covered. Clauses are usually printed in standard forms as separate sections. The first few words of each clause are printed in boldface, and this boldface printing is usually the name by which the clause is known. Appendix D, "Forms, Clauses, and Endorsements," may be referred for exact wording of most of the following clauses, as contained on the second page of the Dwelling Property Form, the Manufacturing Form, and many other forms.

Several of the more important clauses are discussed separately below. The *nuclear clause* and the *water exclusion clause* are significant restrictions on the coverage in many forms. The *liberalization clause* may provide an important extension of coverage to the insured if changes occur in the forms during the policy period. The *standard mortgage clause* is essential whenever the insured property is subject to a mortgage loan. The *coinsurance clause* is used on most business property insurance contracts, and it is imperative that businessmen understand its purposes and limiting effect on loss payments. There are numerous other clauses, and these are included according to the form, the type of coverage, and the particular needs of the insured.

Nuclear Clause

It is not the intent of the fire insurance contract to cover nuclear radiation or radioactive contamination. There is a mandatory *nuclear clause* which must be attached as an endorsement to all fire policies, which provides that the word "fire" does not embrace nuclear or radioactive contamination. The exclusion applies to any such loss whether it be direct or indirect, proximate or remote, or whether it be in the whole or in part caused by, contributed to, or aggravated by fire or any of the other perils insured by the policy. A radioactive contamination, whether controlled or uncontrolled, is not to be construed as either explosion or smoke. Direct loss by fire resulting from nuclear reaction or nuclear radiation or radioactive contamination is covered. The intent of the clause is to exclude radioactive contamination but not to limit coverage with respect to other perils enumerated in the policy.[1]

Insurers provide special facilities for both atomic energy liability and physical damage coverages. These risks are handled by insur-

[1]Indicative of the disastrous consequences of an atomic explosion, the Atomic Energy Commission reported the cost of cleaning up what was termed a "minor atomic mishap." On November 20, 1959, a small amount of solvent exploded at the Oak Ridge Laboratory, scattering about one fiftieth of an ounce of plutonium into the air. All persons within a four-acre area turned in laboratory clothes to be decontaminated. They were checked physically. The plant equipment was shut down and buildings washed with detergents. Roofs were resurfaced, lawns dug up, and the sod removed and buried. The surface of a sizable area of asphalt roads was chiseled and buildings completely repainted. The cost of this minor mishap amounted to approximately $350,000 (*Time*, Feb. 15, 1960, p. 104).

ance pools. The mutual industry has organized a 105-company combination property damage and liability facility known as the Mutual Atomic Energy Reinsurance Pool (MAERP). There are two stock pools, the Nuclear Energy Liability Insurance Association (NELIA) with 140 stock casualty companies and the Nuclear Energy Property Insurance Association (NEPIA) with 189 member stock companies. By means of these pools the insurance industry has available limits up to $60 million per location for liability coverage and up to $65 million per risk for physical damage coverage. Private insurance may be augmented by government funds. The Price-Anderson Act, effective since September 2, 1957, supplements private insurance by authorizing the Atomic Energy Commission to provide a licensee U.S. government indemnity to the extent not available to private insurance interests, up to $500 million per nuclear incident.

Water Exclusion Clause

Since the fire policy commonly is extended to include perils other than fire and lightning, to clarify the situation with respect to water damages the *water exclusion* clause disclaims liability with respect to losses resulting from, contributed to, or aggravated by any of the following: (1) flood, surface water, waves, tidal water or tidal wave, overflow of streams or other bodies of water, or spray from any of the foregoing, all whether driven by wind or not; (2) water which backs up through sewers or drains; (3) water below the surface of the ground including that which exerts pressure on or flows, seeps, or leaks through sidewalks, driveways, foundations, walls, basement or other floors, or through doors, windows, or any other openings in such sidewalks, driveways, foundations, walls, or floors. If fire ensues the company is liable only for the damage caused by the fire. If the policy covers other perils the same rule applies.

In coastal areas, this clause assumes major importance. The hurricanes of recent years in Texas, Florida, New Jersey, and other states along the Eastern Seaboard have brought public criticism for this exclusion. However, the concentrated and catastrophic nature of water damage by flood and hurricane in low-lying areas does not justify its being a part of the fire insurance contract. Separate policies, often through special contracts with Lloyd's of London at very sizable costs, are available. Loss prevention through construction techniques designed to meet such special perils are also a reasonable answer to these problems.

Liberalization Clause

From time to time rating agencies make provision for extending coverage to include features previously not available. Sometimes the liberalizing feature originates in legislative action. To save insurance agencies the necessity of endorsing policies every time a change is made that would reflect to the benefit of the insured, a *liberalization clause* has been prepared. The clause may be a part of the form or it may be attached to the policy at any time as an endosement. When the clause is made a part of a fire insurance policy, it gives the insured the benefit of any advantageous change that develops. Following is an example of such a clause:

> If during the period that insurance is in force under this policy, or within 45 days prior to the inception date thereof, on behalf of this Company there be filed with and approved or accepted by the insurance supervisory authorities, in conformity with law, any forms, endorsements, rules or regulations by which this insurance could be extended or broadened, without additional premium charge, by endorsement or substitution of form, then such extended or broadened insurance shall inure to the benefit of the Insured hereunder as though such endorsement or substitution of form had been made.

The purpose of extending the protection afforded by the clause so that it is retroactive for a period prior to the inception date of the policy grows out of the fact that a policy might be written with obsolete forms or lack a new feature permitted that had not come to the attention of the agent at the time the policy was prepared. By attaching the liberalization clause, all of these benefits automatically accrue to the insured without specific mention of each in the contract or by subsequent endorsement.

Some insurance companies have gone even farther than this. For the protection of their agents, they have given them letters indicating that they will treat all existing policies as if they were endorsed with the liberalization clause. This means that in the event of loss, if any privilege or extension of coverage is permitted under the rules of the rating bureau, the insured will get the benefit of them.

Standard Mortgage Clause

This clause is often found as part of standard forms. It is completed by inserting the name of the mortgagee if the property is encumbered and the interest of the mortgagee is to be insured. The *standard mortgage clause* may also be added to the policy at any time in the form of an endorsement. The clause constitutes a separate and distinct contract between the insurance company and the mortgagee.

There are two forms in common use, the one referred to as the "full contribution mortgage clause" and the other known as the "noncontribution mortgage clause." They are identical except for the contribution clause incorporated in the full contribution mortgage clause, which provides:

In case of any other insurance upon the within described property this company shall not be liable under this policy for a greater proportion of any loss or damage sustained than the sum hereby insured bears to the whole amount of insurance on said property, issued or held by any party or parties having an insurable interest therein, whether as owner, mortgagee, or otherwise.

The effect of the contribution clause is apparent; and, when used, it makes it imperative that all policies covering the property be written concurrently. When the noncontribution clause is used, the mortgagee may proceed under such policies as contain the clause and require to be paid to him the full amount of the loss or damage without reference to other policies on the same property not so endorsed. The contribution form is the one most widely used and appeals to the insurance companies as better protecting their interests. On the other hand, if all policies are identical, using either form, the protection under either is identical and there is no advantage to the insured, whichever the form.

The basic purpose of the mortgage clause is to protect the interests of the mortgagee, or creditor. It vests the mortgagee with legal rights as the contracting party. The clause avoids the necessity for a separate policy by the mortgagee, or an assignment which is far less certain to protect the creditor.

Every device conceivable to protect the interests of the mortgagee has been incorporated into the clause, with the result that the broadest and most complete form of protection has been thereby provided. Provision is made that if the owner defaults in premium payment, the mortgagee shall pay on demand for future protection, if he desires the insurance to remain in effect. Upon refusal of the mortgagee to pay, the policy may be canceled, and the mortgagee is not liable for payment of premium earned previous to the making of the demand.

The most important liberalizing feature of the clause is that which provides that the policy shall not be invalidated by any act or neglect of the mortgagor or owner of the property, or by any foreclosure or other procedure, or notice of sale relating to the property, or change in title of ownership, or increase in hazard. The mortgagee, who is often a bank or other financial institution which could not keep track of possible violations by many mortgagors, obtains certainty of insurance coverage for the property used as collateral for the loan. Such duty as is imposed upon the mortgagee by the clause is concerned only with changes in ownership, occupation, or increase in hazard, when such changes are known by the mortgagee. If the hazard is thus increased, the insurer may make demand upon the mortgagee for the premium, which the mortgagee is obligated to pay; otherwise, by the terms of the agreement, the policy becomes null and void.

Coinsurance Clause

The *coinsurance clause* has for its aim an equitable control of the amount of insurance the insured shall carry. It effects this control by limiting the liability of the insurance company to that proportion of the loss which the insurance amount bears to a given percentage of the value of the property at the time of the loss or damage. A number of clauses, seeking to accomplish the same purpose and having the same general meaning, have been devised, such as the average clause, contribution clause, percentage coinsurance clause, reduced-rate average clause, reduced-rate coinsurance clause, and reduced-rate contribution clause. Because of the common use of a requirement of insurance equal to 80 percent of the value it is common practice to refer to the clause as the "80 percent coinsurance clause."

The coinsurance clause for business properties is often termed the "reduced-rate contribution clause." The following clause is one now used:

> In consideration of the reduced rate and (or) form under which this policy is written, it is expressly stipulated and made a condition of this contract that in the event of loss this Company shall be liable for no greater proportion thereof than the amount hereby insured bears to . . . % of the actual cash value of the property described herein at the time when such loss shall happen, nor for more than the proportion which this policy bears to the total insurance thereon.
>
> In the event that the aggregate claim for any loss is both less than ten thousand dollars ($10,000.00) and less than five per cent (5%) of the total amount of insurance upon the property described herein at the time such loss occurs, no special inventory or appraisement of the undamaged property shall be required.
>
> If this policy be divided into two or more items, the foregoing shall apply to each item separately.

The above coinsurance clause is found in many of the printed forms attached to the standard fire contract, such as in the Manufacturing Form reproduced in Appendix D. The clause may also be added to some contracts as a specific additional endorsement to the contract, if such wording is not already included in the form. The last two paragraphs of the foregoing clause are not, in fact, a necessary part of the coinsurance clause but are invariably made a part in general practice. Their effect in connection with coinsurance will be noticed in due course.

Purpose. The purpose of the coinsurance clause is to provide equity among policyholders by encouraging each to carry a reasonable amount of insurance (usually 80 percent or more) in relation to the full value of their property. The policyholder receives the benefit of a reduced rate as compared with the "flat"[2] rate for fire insurance, in return for a promise to the insurer that he will insure at least up to the stated coinsurance percentage. While the coinsurance clause does not make mandatory the carrying of insurance up to a specified percentage of value, losses are adjusted as if insurance in such an amount were carried. Where there is a deficiency, the insured is said to be carrying that amount of risk himself and is, therefore, a *coinsurer* to the extent of the deficiency. The coinsurance clause is the simplest method devised to effect an equitable adjustment of charges on the assumption that insurance to a predetermined percentage of value will be carried. For complete protection the insured should carry at least the percentage of insurance contemplated in the rate. Otherwise, he himself becomes a coinsurer of his own risk and must contribute to the payment of his own loss.

Justification. To understand the reason for coinsurance, one must consider the function of the insurance *rate,* or cost per $100 of insurance. Insurance undertakes to shift the burden of risk from the individual, through a distribution of the cost of risk, to those of a great many. Since a fire in a property need not destroy it totally, and since fire losses vary in degree—there being a great many small losses as compared with the number of total losses—unless each insured carries an adequate percentage of insurance to value, the burden of risk will not be equitably distributed.

Insurance premiums have been compared to a tax rate. In every community, taxes to defray community expenses are raised by an assessment levied upon property valued by assessors for that purpose. If each individual were to indicate a value upon which he was willing to be taxed, the benefits, if equally distributed, would bear heavily upon some and lightly upon others. So in fire insurance, if one individual pays on a low percentage of his total value and another pays on a high percentage, experience shows that the latter pays proportionately more for the protection he receives. If one insured insures in the amount of 50 percent of his value, another 20 percent, and a third 80 percent, and if each receives his loss paid in full up to the face of his policy, those carrying the smaller amounts of insurance to value pay less than their share of the average premiums. To create an equitable situation, the amount of insurance to value carried by each insured should be uniform. The coinsurance clause requires that the insured carry insurance to a certain stipu-

[2]A "flat" insurance rate, which is the alternative to the coinsurance rate, is not based on any assumed amount of insurance in relation to value of the property. Losses are paid in full, up to the amount of the insurance, regardless of whether the insurance amount is close to full value, or only a small part of it.

lated percentage of value or, failing to do so, bear a percentage of the loss.

A mathematical illustration of the foregoing statement is to be found in the fact that statistics show most fire losses to be small in relation to values of the properties. The Insurance Bulletin Number 6 of the Chamber of Commerce of the United States says: "the purpose of the coinsurance clause is to distribute the fire loss equitably among policyholders . . . . . The fire loss data indicates:"

Ratio of Loss to Value	*Percent of Building Fires*
Between 0 and 20 percent of value	86
Between 20 and 40 percent of value	8
Over 40 percent of value	6
Total	100

These data show that an insured could, if the coinsurance clause were not required, carry a small amount of insurance and yet be paid for almost all of his losses. The conclusion is that he should be encouraged to carry high amounts of insurance in relation to value (1) in fairness to other policyholders, who would otherwise be paying more than their fair share of total premiums, and (2) in order to have insurance in adequate amounts for one of its most important purposes, paying for large losses.

Formula and Examples. The application of the coinsurance clause may be expressed in the following formula based on the wording of the clause.

Let

I.C. = insurance carried (the amount of insurance)
I.R. = insurance required (the coinsurance percentage × the value of the property at the time of loss)
L = the amount of the loss

Then

$$\frac{I.C.}{I.R.} \times L = \text{THE AMOUNT THE INSURER PAYS}$$

Suppose an insured purchased $60,000 of insurance from Company X on a building valued at $100,000. If an 80 percent coinsurance clause were made a part of the contract, and a loss of $40,000 occurred, the amount Company X would be obligated to pay would be:

$$\frac{\$60{,}000}{\$80{,}000} \times \$40{,}000, \text{ or } \frac{3}{4} \times \$40{,}000 = \$30{,}000$$

The insured would be a coinsurer to the extent of $10,000, since he had not insured the property to 80 percent of the value as he promised. If he had insured the property for $80,000 the loss would be paid in full by the company:

$$\frac{\$80{,}000}{\$80{,}000} \times \$40{,}000, \text{ or } 100\% \times \$40{,}000 = \$40{,}000$$

The second case, where the insured carried the $80,000 as required by the coinsurance clause, illustrates the important principle that the insured is *not just paid 80 percent of the loss*[3] when coinsurance is involved, but is paid the full loss amount (up to the amount of the policy) whenever he at least meets the minimum required insurance amount. In the operation of the foregoing formula it is to be remembered that the insurer is never liable for an amount in excess of the policies, and hence, if the insurance was for $80,000 and the loss was $90,000, the insurer would be liable only for the $80,000 policy amount.

It is frequently stated in insurance literature that when the loss is total, the coinsurance clause is inoperative. This statement is not correct. The clause is operative in every loss. However, when the loss is total, the percentage of the loss that limits the amount the insurance is required to pay will exceed the face of the policies. Therefore, because the full amount of the policies is payable in the event of a total loss, the impression follows that the clause is inoperative. Suppose, for example, that the loss was total in our previous case (instead of only $40,000) when the insurance carried was $60,000. Then the insurer would pay according to the coinsurance clause:

$$\frac{\$60{,}000}{\$80{,}000} \times \$100{,}000, \text{ or } \frac{3}{4} \times \$100{,}000 = \$75{,}000$$

But since the indicated loss payment of $75,000 exceeds the policy amount of $60,000, the policy amount becomes the maximum payment, and $60,000 is paid.

A different example might involve several companies insuring the same property. Assume:

Company X has $20,000 of total insurance of $140,000.
Company Y has $40,000 of total insurance of $140,000.
Company Z has $80,000 of total insurance of $140,000.
Value of property is $200,000.
Loss of $120,000 occurs.

[3]This is a common mistake by students who assume this is how the coinsurance clause works. The insured is paid the full amount of the loss (up to the insurance amount) *if* he meets the coinsurance requirement, and is *only* penalized when he does not have the required amount of insurance.

Application of the coinsurance clause, and the prorata liability clause would be:

$$\frac{\$140{,}000}{\$160{,}000} \times \$120{,}000, \text{ or } \frac{7}{8} \times \$120{,}000 = \$105{,}000 \text{ to be paid}$$

$$\text{Co. X would pay } \frac{\$\ 20{,}000}{\$140{,}000}, \text{ or } \frac{1}{7} \times \$105{,}000 = \$15{,}000$$

$$\text{Co. Y would pay } \frac{\$\ 40{,}000}{\$140{,}000}, \text{ or } \frac{2}{7} \times \$105{,}000 = \$30{,}000$$

$$\text{Co. Z would pay } \frac{\$\ 80{,}000}{\$140{,}000}, \text{ or } \frac{4}{7} \times \$105{,}000 = \$60{,}000$$

Total payment $105,000

Valuation Problems and Solutions. Since the amount for which the insurer is liable is dependent upon a percentage of the actual cash value of the insured property at the time of the loss or damage, it is immediately apparent that the question of *valuation* is of the utmost importance. Moreover, so far as values are concerned, the entire burden is placed squarely upon the insured.

In connection with *stocks* of merchandise there is little difficulty. When inventories are carefully taken, and old stock is properly depreciated, the value of an inventory within reasonable limits can be ascertained through the record of purchases and sales. It is important to emphasize, however, that in connection with a business enterprise that has sharp seasonal inventory increases, insurance written with the reduced-rate contribution clause should be adjusted to meet these seasonal advances. Retail stores, as a rule, add considerably to their stock just before the Christmas holiday season. If their insurance is adjusted to meet their average needs throughout the rest of the year, a fire during the period of the high inventory value might result in the insured's unwittingly becoming a coinsurer.

If the merchandise insured is a commodity with a shifting market and large values are involved, the insured must carefully follow quotations affecting his goods and adjust his insurance to cover any market appreciation. It makes no difference that the insurance to value was correct when the policies were issued. The adjustment will be effected upon the basis of values at the time of the loss.

In the case of *machinery and fixtures* there is little occasion for difficulty. Values are reduced each year through charge-offs made for depreciation and obsolescence. However, when the value used for insurance is the book value, care must be exercised that this value represents the actual value. In other words, it sometimes happens that an extremely conservative depreciation program will result in carrying fixtures and machinery below their actual cash value. While the books of account may serve as evidence to indicate value, they are by no means conclusive. An adjustment contemplates actual cash value, not book value.

Real estate affords the most difficult problem in valuation. Because of changing wage scales, material prices, and other market factors, building values are constantly fluctuating. The price trend is slow, and for that reason deceptive. A ten-year-old factory building that cost $100,000 and depreciated each year on the company's books may, as an actual fact, have a depreciated replacement value far in excess of the original cost. Thus, an insurance program based upon the original cost, less depreciation, might be nothing less than disastrous.

A difficult problem is presented when market value and replacement value differ widely. Economic changes in communities sometimes result in properties being offered for sale at a fraction of their replacement cost. Where the market value is very much below the replacement value, the question of coinsurance becomes confusing. If a building would cost $40,000 to rebuild, yet sold for $10,000, how much should be carried to avoid becoming a coinsurer? The answer is, of course, that because of economic obsolescence, depreciation,[4] and changing neighborhood conditions, the building has lost 75 per cent of its replacement cost. Its insurable value is $10,000. A partial loss will have to be replaced upon a basis of new construction. It is, therefore, wise to eliminate the question of values for coinsurance purposes and to write such a risk flat. Careful underwriters are reluctant to incorporate a coinsurance clause into a form covering any building when the depreciation, however caused, exceeds 40 percent.

The difficulty of valuation is somewhat eased by *property exclusions* which exclude certain types or parts of property from the valuation for coinsurance purposes. When the property is of such a type that 80 percent or 90 percent of the value seems considerably more than any probable loss, particularly when a substantial part of the value can be damaged by fire but slightly, exclusions may be

[4]Suggested annual rates of depreciation, in their particular application, are subject to a considerable degree of modification. The care of the particular building and the operation of the forces that cause depreciation must in each case be considered. A type of building whose life is estimated at 50 years might well be considered at the end of 20 years to be 40 percent depreciated. Some economic change in manufacturing process or in consumer demand might make the building and plant almost useless. On the other hand, favorable developments might eliminate entirely the element of economic obsolescence, and the element of depreciation be limited to such deterioration as remained following an extensive program of repairs and improvement. The contrasting situation, of course, is found when repairs are neglected and the building is allowed to deteriorate and decay.

made in the coverage. By the use of endorsements effecting such exclusions, the total value of the property insured may be substantially reduced, thereby reducing the amount of insurance made mandatory by the coinsurance clause to avoid becoming a coinsurer. Policies covering personal property in which there are ownership interests other than that of the insured may be endorsed to exclude the insured's interest. Some of the kinds of property frequently excluded by endorsement include brick, stone, or concrete foundations, cost of excavations and underground piping, and special patterns, models, or dies which may be separately insured.

Risks equipped with approved automatic sprinklers, and complying with inspection requirements and such other standards may use a special form containing provision for a *guaranteed amount of insurance* as an alternative to the 90 percent reduced-rate contribution clause. When such a permit is given, it is usual to require that the guaranteed amount be the full value of the property, and it is further required that a new statement of values be filed every year. Following is a form of the guaranteed-amount clause: "In consideration of the reduced rate and (or) form under which this policy is written, it is expressly stipulated and made a condition of this contract that in the event of loss this Company shall be liable for no greater proportion thereof than the amount hereby insured bears to $............ nor for more than the proportion which this policy bears to the total insurance thereon." The operation of this clause is identical with that of the reduced-rate contribution clause, with the one exception that the amount of insurance to be carried is agreed upon in advance. Fluctuating values, therefore, will not penalize the insured, as is possible with the usual coinsurance clause if the insurance coverage is not adjusted to meet the changes in valuation.

Incorporated into the reduced-rate contribution clause is the so-called *5 percent waiver clause.* It is a clause entirely separate and apart from the coinsurance clause, but practice has so associated the two that one is commonly considered to be a part of the other. The purpose of the waiver clause is to relieve the insured of the necessity of taking a physical inventory of the undamaged property in the event of small losses. The clause in no way suspends the operation of the coinsurance feature of the contract. It merely relieves the insured of the burden of verifying, by an actual inventory at the time of the loss or damage, the figures as shown on his books. This warning is necessary because of the misapprehension, frequently voiced, that small losses are outside the operation of the clause. Such is not the fact, and even though an inventory is not taken, if the figures as submitted show insufficient insurance to value, the insured becomes a coinsurer, regardless of the size of the loss.

The greatest *disadvantage* of the coinsurance clause is the possibility of misunderstanding by the insured. Insurance agents who recognize the value of coinsurance are sometimes reluctant to advise an insured to adopt it. This is due to the fact that insureds who believe they understand the operation of the coinsurance clause frequently put the details out of mind. When the loss occurs and the companies point out that the insured must contribute to the loss, any misunderstanding results in an embarrassing situation. If the clause is to be used, and it is so used because of substantial rate savings to the insured, proper education and explanation to the insured is essential. The insured should understand his responsibility and possible penalty.

While an insured may secure a reduced rate by incorporating the coinsurance clause in the form, it does not always follow that a change from a flat-rate coverage to a coinsurance coverage will result in a premium saving. The requirements of the clause as to the amount of insurance necessary may result in a considerably increased total premium. The rate per thousand will be less, but because of the necessity of adding additional insurance the total charge may be more.

Other Clauses Limiting Insurer's Liability

Several other clauses are used in special situations to provide the insurer and insured with a contract fair to both parties.

Prorata Distribution Clause. The *prorata distribution clause*, sometimes referred to as the "average clause," has the effect of dividing the total coverage under a blanket policy to apply specifically upon each separate location, in the proportion that the value at each location bears to the sum of the values at all the locations. When no coinsurance clause is used under a blanket form, this clause is usually mandatory. The reason can readily be seen. If a person owned ten dwellings in widely separated locations, each valued at $10,000, a blanket policy covering all the dwellings for $10,000 would be full insurance in each location. Barring a catastrophe, the insured would be able to cover $100,000 in property values for the premium on a $10,000 policy.

For this reason, insurers offer the alternative of using the 90 percent coinsurance clause on such policies, or the prorata distribution clause. When the first alternative is the one followed, in the instance of the ten houses just cited, the insured will be obligated to carry $90,000 insurance, unless he elects to become a coinsurer. If he chooses to write a blanket coverage with the prorata distribution clause, whatever amount he carries will cover proportionately on each house. Thus, a $50,000 blanket policy with the clause would cover one half on each house, or $5,000 only.

In connection with contents the clause permits a coverage that is a great convenience. Frequently the insured is the owner of stocks running to huge values that are constantly shifting from one location to another, but whose total value is more or less steady. When the subject of the insurance may, in the course of the insured's operations, be shifted from building to building, or when shipments are being made from time to time and incoming purchases received, it is not a simple matter to keep an accurate account of values in every location or to shift insurance coverages to follow changes in value. A blanket policy with the prorata distribution clause automatically shifts the coverage as the relative values shift. It serves to provide an automatic coverage.

If adequate insurance to value is carried, the clause is far superior to specific insurance in such a situation. With specific insurance, a stock might be depleted in one location and increased in another. If the fire occurred where the inventory was high, particularly if the specific policies were written with coinsurance, the insured would be a heavy loser, even though his other locations were over-insured.

Examples of the operation of the prorata distribution clause, both in cases where insurance is adequate and those where it is insufficient, appear in Appendix D.

Three-Fourths Value and Three-Fourths Loss Clauses. Two additional clauses are used occasionally for properties located in communities which have no public fire protection facilities.

The *three-fourths value clause* limits the amount of the insurer's liability on a given property to three fourths of the cash value of the property at the time of the loss or damage. The clause is used when it is deemed to the insurer's advantage that the insured assume a substantial share of the risk. Frequently, premium concessions are made when the clause is used. Where a fire once started more often than not results in a total loss, it is believed that the clause serves to minimize carelessness. The clause is without effect upon the amount payable under the insurance policy, unless the damage is in excess of three fourths of the value of the property, Thus, small partial losses are paid in full.

A second clause, having much the same object as the three-fourths value clause, is the *three-fourths loss clause*. From the point of view of the insured the provisions of this clause are more stringent than those of the former. Instead of limiting the insurer's liability to three fourths the value of the insured property, it limits the liability to three fourths of any loss. Therefore, under the terms of this clause, whether the loss is large or small, the insured is obliged to bear one quarter of it. The clause places a considerable burden upon the insured and has as a purpose the elimination of carelessness, as well as the action of a deterrent in the event that moral hazard may be involved.

ENDORSEMENTS

Purpose

An *endorsement* is a provision added to the insurance contract whereby the scope of its coverage is clarified, restricted, or enlarged. Certain endorsements, such as those that extend the perils covered, may be as long as the form and may be attached when the policy is issued.

General Use

Many endorsements are merely typewritten additions to the contract, changing or clarifying some part of its coverage. An endorsement may be added to the policy changing its amount or term. Errors may be corrected in the same manner. If a property is sold, the insurance may be continued for the benefit of the new owner by means of an endorsement. Clauses may be added to the policy in the manner of an endorsement when the form does not of itself meet the needs of the insured. Such endorsements are frequently in the nature of permits. For example, a permit may be added to the policy authorizing removal of the insured property and providing for coverage in another location. Endorsements may be used to effect changes in the contract, such as amount, rate, location, and interest insured. The policy provides for permission to add endorsements in that part of the conditions termed "added provisions."[5]

The Extended Coverage Endorsement

Some years ago a packaged endorsement, known when it was first introduced as the "supplemental contract," provided in a single endorsement *extended coverage* protection against the perils of windstorm, explosion, hail, riot, smoke, and several other perils. The term "supplemental contract" has long since been dropped. The present usage recognizes that the endorsement is not, in fact, an additional contract but is rather an extension of the protection of the fire insurance contract to cover other perils without at the same time increasing the face amount of the policy.

One of the most comprehensive extensions of the fire insurance contract, and one of the most common and important endorsements in all fire insurance, is the *Extended Coverage Endorsement No. 4 (ECE No. 4).*[6] The endorsement, when attached to the fire insurance

[5]Standard fire policy, lines 38–48.

[6]Several variations of extended coverage forms are used in various parts of the country. Comments here refer to the No. 4 endorsement, and care should be taken

(Continued on next page)

policy, by means of a single document extends the policy to include the following perils: (*a*) windstorm; (*b*) hail; (*c*) explosion; (*d*) riot, riot attending a strike, and civil commotion; (*e*) aircraft damage; (*f*) vehicle damage; and (*g*) smoke damage.[7] There is no choice on the part of the insured as to which of these seven perils he wishes to include; all are automatically included in the package-type endorsement. A copy of ECE No. 4 appears as part of the Dwelling Property Form in Appendix D "Forms, Clauses and Endorsements."

The extended coverage endorsement, which has been used for over thirty years, does not increase the amount of insurance provided in the policy to which it is attached. The coverage is effected by a clause that substitutes the new perils to be covered for the word "fire" as it appears in the insuring clause of the statutory contract. If a loss is caused by one of the perils named in the extended cover contract, the same substitution is made for the purposes of applying the policy coverage. All the policy provisions are applied with respect to a loss attributable to a peril covered by the extended coverage endorsement exactly as they would be applied to a fire loss.

With respect to windstorm and hail losses, there is a $50 deductible in most jurisdictions. In some jurisdictions full coverage is available for an additional premium, but the $50 deductible is the more usual. The deductible applies to each structure separately and to personal property in the open. In some jurisdictions the deductible applies to both a building and its contents. Outdoor radio and television antennas and aerials, including their lead-in wiring, mast, and towers, are excluded from the windstorm coverage, but can be added for an additional premium.

The Additional Extended Coverage Endorsement

Another widely used endorsement is available to owners or tenants of private dwellings and is known as the *Additional Extended Coverage Endorsement (AECE).* This form was prepared in the late 1950's in response to a demand for a broader protection to meet some dissatisfaction evidenced with the limitations in ECE No. 4. In fact, this form may only be used when ECE No. 4 is a part of the policy.

---

to identify the specific type. Extended coverage contracts are distinguished from consequential loss contracts in that the damage under an extended coverage contract represents a direct loss, but from a hazard other than the hazard covered by the fire insurance contract. Consequential loss contracts, as has already been noticed, cover indirect losses. Consequential losses due to fires are insurable, as is presently to be noticed, and extended cover contracts may likewise be endorsed to include consequential losses occasioned by the hazard covered in the contract.

[7]An endorsement identical to ECE No. 4, except that it provides protection against loss by waves or overflow, is known as the "Coastal Extended Coverage Endorsement."

It is not, actually, an all-risks coverage but does broaden the policy to provide a very comprehensive insurance protection. The AECE varies in the different jurisdictions, but one of the latest available forms provides insurance for ten additional named perils for a nominal additional premium. These are: (*a*) water damage from plumbing and heating system; (*b*) rupture or bursting of steam or hot-water heating systems; (*c*) vandalism and malicious mischief; (*d*) vehicles owned or operated by the insured or by a tenant; (*e*) fall of trees; (*f*) objects falling; (*g*) freezing of plumbing, heating, and the like; (*h*) collapse; (*i*) landslide;[8] and (*j*) glass breakage.

While the endorsement undertakes to provide a more comprehensive cover than that provided by the ECE, it is important to emphasize that it is not an all-risks coverage. As broad as this makes the contract, it does not cover all risks of loss. AECE insures only against the ten additional perils specified.

The endorsement does not in any way restrict the coverage afforded under the fire insurance contract, nor does it in any way limit the extensions provided in ECE No. 4. To avoid maintenance claims and thereby make possible the use of the endorsement at a low premium rate, there is a $50 loss deductible applicable to each peril for each occurrence. The deductible applies separately to both buildings and contents. As in the regular Dwelling Property Form, there is a general exclusion of liability for loss caused directly or indirectly by earthquake, backing-up of sewers or drains, or by floods, inundation, waves, tide or tidal waves, high water,[9] or over-flow of streams or bodies of water.

Basically, the AECE was beneficial in adding several perils which could be significant to some policyholders, and often may have been

---

[8]The purpose of including landslide as a peril was to provide coverage for earth movement losses not directly caused by subsidence in mining areas. Under the original ECE, landslide, as such, was not one of the perils included in the form. The form did, however, insure against the collapse of the property but excluded a collapse caused by subsidence, and there was no definition given of "subsidence." This gave rise to varied opinions as to the exact meaning of the word, and it was discovered that a common legal definition was this: "Subsidence is any movement of the soil from its natural position." With this broad definition, landslide would come within the exclusion pertaining to collapse, and yet the framers of the form had not so intended it. Under the old form it was the practice to attribute to the word "subsidence" a narrower definition and consider it only as a falling or sinking of the earth, thereby giving the broadest coverage possible for collapse. Subsidence losses normally occur in coal-mining sections where properties have been built over abandoned mines. As a result of the varied interpretations of the exclusion in the old form under the collapse coverage, the new form includes the additional peril of landslide, as well as collapse, with the subsidence exclusion still pertaining to each one.

[9]Recent coastal storms have made these much misunderstood exclusions, although it is clear that most of such losses are not covered by ECE No. 4 or AECE, except for wind damage done separately from the damage by water. See Max J. Gwertzman, *A Legal Analysis of the High Water and Wavewash Exclusion* (New York: Insurance Advocate, 1962).

assumed to have been included in ECE coverage. For example, water damage to contents after a windstorm which broke a window or wall are covered in the ECE. Water damage from building systems was added in the AECE. Also, explosions (except those caused by steam) are covered in the ECE, while steam explosions are covered in the AECE. Riot is covered in the ECE, while the AECE adds vandalism and malicious mischief, with which riot might be confused. Damage of vehicles to the property (other than by an insured) is included in the ECE; damage by vehicles by the insured or his tenants, such as fence or garage losses, are covered by the AECE. These examples show the attempt of the AECE coverage to provide the insured with more complete protection, without some of the gaps in coverage which the ECE included.

Broad Form and "All-Risks" Endorsements

The appeal of the addition of the ECE and AECE has prompted the development of special "package" or "comprehensive" forms. Popular forms for dwellings include a number of perils in addition to those insured under the fire policy with extended and additional extended coverage endorsements. These forms are sometimes referred to as "dwelling packages."

There are forms that attach to the fire policy and require no special policy for their use, known by various names such as "Broad Form" and "Special Form" to mention two. The Broad Form Endorsement has gained such popularity in some territories as to often replace the ECE and AECE, since it combines both of these in one form. It is still a named perils coverage, covering only those perils it specifically mentions.

The most inclusive endorsement is on an all-physical loss basis and includes "all risks," automatically covering all risks of physical loss to the property except those specifically excluded in the form.

The use of these endorsements to expand the coverage of the fire policy has been overtaken by the development of special complete contracts which include the basic fire coverage and extended coverage, and in some forms the AECE perils (or, in others, "all-risks" coverage), as well as liability and other casualty insurance. The Homeowner's contracts are typical of these new package policies, and many homes are now insured in this manner. Business properties, too, are now written in package policies including all fire and allied lines, theft, and liability perils. These contracts are discussed separately in Chapter 19, "Multiple-Line and All-Lines Insurance."

SPECIAL AND ALLIED FIRE LINES

As can be seen by the endorsements studied in the previous section, the field of fire insurance does include more than just the peril of fire. Windstorms, explosion, water damage, smoke and many other perils are often included in the contract. A number of other miscellaneous perils are associated with fire insurance, and included in the general term of *special and allied fire lines* of insurance. Some of these perils are written by endorsements on the fire contract; others are written predominantly by the fire insurance companies in separate contracts.

Appendix E, "Special and Allied Fire Lines," can be referred to for details of these many coverages. They are sometimes of importance to particular insureds, but their relatively infrequent use makes it unnecessary to include full discussion of their characteristics in this chapter. One of the most common is *sprinkler leakage insurance,* for damage done by accidental discharge of water from automatic sprinklers in a building. Legal liability for such sprinkler leakage damage is also an important type of coverage for those insureds who are responsible for sprinkler equipment. *Builder's risk insurance* is a special contract available for the changing values and ownership interests during construction. *Crop insurance* is written for specified types of crops for damage by weather, insects, and disease. *Flood insurance* is a difficult and expensive type of protection, but is available in some special marine policies. *Multiple-location contracts* are very important for larger businesses who need the flexible and automatic coverage of reporting forms. Some of the other special and allied lines forms discussed in Appendix E are: water damage liability, tenants' improvements and betterments, deferred payments, supplemental mortgage interest, blanket tornado and windstorm, contract of supply, fire apparatus charges, and standing timber insurance.

CONCURRENCY

Policies designed to cover identical properties should be exactly alike. When there are discrepancies, the insurance is said to be "nonconcurrent," and this may have the effect of complicating the problem of adjustment, or providing inadequate coverage under permits and clauses even though the face of the insurance may be sufficient.

Nonconcurrency most frequently manifests itself in the form of a combination of specific and blanket policies. The owner of several buildings forming part of one establishment may take out specific insurance on certain of the buildings and blanket insurance covering several or all of the buildings. Another form of nonconcurrency is to be found when there are several policies covering on a given risk, but some written with coinsurance and others without the clause. Policies sometimes cover the contents of a building and extend to cover in adjacent yards, while other policies covering on the same risk do not provide the protection in the yards.

There are many examples of nonconcurrent contracts in fire, inland marine, and casualty insurance. Most of the problems are solved by intercompany cooperation under what are known as the *Agreement of Guiding Principles.* It is agreed in advance by almost all major insurers that any disputes in regard to overlapping coverages will be settled according to these rules of priority and apportionment. The new set of *Principles,* effective in November, 1963, specify which contract or groups of contracts is to be primary coverage for stipulated losses, and which is to be excess coverage. For example, coverage on a limited-purpose basis is paid before any other insurance, such as a "blanket" policy, affording a broader scope of coverage; and coverage specific as to location applies before other "floater" type contracts. Thus the participation of several different insurance contracts in a loss is settled in an orderly and consistent manner, and the insured receives his payment without unnecessary delay.

For all practical purposes it is not essential that forms be absolutely identical. Policies are regarded as concurrent if the coverage is identical so far as terms and conditions affecting the liability are concerned. When, however, policies are identical line for line and word for word, the ideal situation is attained. In the instance of many large and important risks, to arrive at this ideal, special forms are printed, and the use of these forms only is permitted in writing policies of the insured.

SUMMARY

The additions to the basic fire insurance contract are plentiful. Many *forms* are used to complete and clarify the contract coverage. Five general types of forms are: specific, blanket, floating, automatic, and schedule. One common specific form used for residential property is the Dwelling Property Form, while the Manufacturing Form is an example of a fire form used for business properties.

Clauses are found in many policy additions, and several are important enough to have special titles. The nuclear clause, water exclusion clause, liberalization clause and standard mortgage clause are found in the forms used with most all fire contracts. Several clauses which limit the liability of the insurer to the policyholder are used in many business insurance contracts. The coinsurance clause is most significant, for it grants to the insured a substantially reduced rate if he promises to purchase a reasonable amount (usually 80 percent) of insurance in relation to the value of the insured property. The penalty is also severe if the policyholder does not meet the coinsurance requirement, for then the loss payment is made in the proportion that the insurance carried bears to the insurance required. The purposes and operation of the coinsurance clause are equitable, but care must be taken to be sure no misunderstandings develop.

Changes in the fire contract also occur through the use of *endorsements,* which can modify such items as the parties, interests, amounts, locations, descriptions, or duration of the policy. Several of the most common and uniform types of endorsements add more perils to the contract coverage. The Extended Coverage Endorsement, the Additional Extended Coverage Endorsement, and the more recent Broad Form Endorsement and "All-Risks" Endorsement all extend the contract to include many perils of loss associated with fire insurance. These include windstorm, smoke, explosion, water damage, vandalism, vehicle damage, and many other perils which can cause considerable property loss.

Special and allied fire lines refer to policies such as sprinkler leakage, flood, crop, timber, and many miscellaneous contracts. The importance of concurrency among all fire contracts and additions of a policyholder is emphasized.

FOR REVIEW

1. Why is it that there are so many different forms and endorsements which may be added to what is supposed to be a *standard* fire contract?
2. Identify and contrast the purposes of the standard mortgage clause, the coinsurance clause, and the prorata distribution clause.
3. The Extended Coverage Endorsement is one of the most widely used of all insurance endorsements. What is extended, and how is it accomplished?
4. Would you, as an insured, prefer to have a "named perils" or an "all-risk" contract? Explain.
5. X owns a building valued at $100,000. A fire causes damage in the amount of $22,500. Adjusters, upon checking the policies, find two policies for $10,000 each, written with a 90 percent coinsurance clause, and five policies for $5,000 each, written flat. For how much is each company liable?
6. The owner of a building of fire-resistive construction contends that it is not economical for him to insure it with an 80 percent coinsurance clause because he is less likely to suffer a total loss than is the case when the building insured is of frame or other inflammable construction. Is the reasoning correct?
7. A manufacturer stores his finished product in three warehouses, so situated that they would probably not all be affected by a single fire. The total liability in any one location is limited to $50,000. The company therefore carries a blanket policy of $50,000, assuming that no loss will occur in excess of that amount. Wherein is the program unsound?
8. The contents of a retail store have a sound value of $40,000. A loss develops in the amount of $35,000 on merchandise and $4,000 on furniture and fixtures. There is in effect insurance in the amount of $25,000, written with a 90 percent coinsurance clause. How much of the loss will the insurance companies pay, and how much of the loss must be carried as uninsured?
9. It is stated, as a general rule, that the insured is penalized in the case of a partial loss if his insurance is insufficient to meet the coinsurance requirements of the policy. Where is the dividing line above which, in the event

of a partial loss, the insured will no longer be penalized to the extent of becoming a coinsurer?

10. B operates a department store and carries insurance equal to 100 percent of his values, with an 80 percent coinsurance clause. Is he permitted to do this? If your advice were asked, what recommendation would you make concerning his coverage?
11. Building costs have increased so much in recent years that, unless property insurance has been brought up to value, present insurance is inadequate. Today it takes about $2.50 to buy as much building today as $1 bought 15 years ago. In other words, it takes $25,000 now to buy as much house as $10,000 did in 1949. B built a new home in 1949 costing $22,000, which he insured for $20,000. The same year he built a new business block that cost $100,000 and insured it for $80,000 with the 80 percent coinsurance clause. Insurance has been renewed each year without increase.
    a) Assume a $10,000 fire loss to the dwelling and the same loss to the business property. Explain how much the insurance would pay in each instance.
    b) How much would the insurance pay if the loss to each property was $40,000?
12. X completes a new building at the cost of $500,000. He sends for his insurance agent and, giving him the figures, asks for full protection. Y recommends $400,000 insurance with the 80 percent coinsurance clause. His competitor, B, contends that he can supply the 80 percent coinsurance coverage and save the insured 10 percent or more of the annual premium. How can this be effected?
13. Mr. I. M. Insecure has the following fire insurance on his business property, which is valued today at $200,000: $120,000 of insurance, with 80 percent coinsurance clause included in the policy contract.
    a) Is his friend, Mr. B. A. Success, correct when he tells him that he is not carrying enough insurance to meet serious losses and the coinsurance requirement? Explain.
    b) What would be paid in case of a $72,000 loss? Show your method.
    c) A $180,000 loss? Show your method.
    d) How would you explain to Mr. Insecure the reasons why he should be encouraged to carry more insurance in relation to his property values, and how the coinsurance clause does this in an equitable manner?
14. Criticize the following statements which have been made about the coinsurance clause as it is used in fire insurance contracts on business properties:
    a) "The application of the coinsurance clause is easy, for the insurance company merely pays 80 percent of the fire loss."
    b) "The purpose of the coinsurance clause is to make more profit for the insurance companies."
    c) "As a policyholder, it is not important to meet the 80 percent coinsurance amount, as you promised in the contract, because in a large loss it does not matter whether or not you met the 80 percent requirement."
    d) "Changing values of such properties as real estate or inventory stocks do not affect the responsibility of the policyholder who insures with the normal coinsurance clause as part of the contract."
15. What is "nonconcurrency," and how are some of its problems solved?

Chapter 11

INSURANCE FOR INDIRECT LOSSES

INSURANCE for direct damage or destruction of property is important, and obvious to most property owners. Fire, wind, water, and many other perils are known and respected by most persons who usually understand the values which may be lost by the immediate damage done to their property by these perils. Much less recognized and understood are the oftentimes equally significant losses which may result from indirect losses.

NATURE AND CLASSIFICATION

In contrast to direct loss coverages, which apply to the physical loss or damage to the subject of the insurance, *indirect loss coverages* extend to provide indemnity for losses that accrue as a consequence of actual damage to the property. For example, if a store is insured against loss or damage by fire, and an accidental fire destroys the building and merchandise, such losses under the terms of a fire policy are direct losses. The fact that the owner of the store will lose profits because of the interruption of his business is an indirect loss which has occurred over and above the actual physical damage to building and merchandise. Also, the fire insurance policy does not cover profits on goods manufactured. Hence, if such goods are destroyed by fire before they are sold, this fact gives rise to a loss of potential profits. The loss of use of a property, or the loss of rental income from a property destroyed by fire, is not included in the direct loss policy. Indirect loss policies do not extend the fire policy as to perils, but provide an extension of insurance against losses associated with the direct loss by fire. The indirect effects of other perils in addition to fire, such as windstorm, explosion, riot, water, and so on, may also be insured.

Indirect loss that is attributable to the intervention of a time element following physical damage to property before the property may be restored for normal use is known as a *time element loss.* The coverages to provide insurance are known as time element coverages. Among the time element losses are: (1) losses due to the *interruption of business* by damage to the insured's property, (2) *contingent* losses due to business interruptions, (3) loss of income from *rents,* or loss of *rental value,* caused by damage to the property, (4) *extra expense* incurred to conduct business or maintain a home on a temporary basis following loss, and (5) loss of *tuition fees* by educational institutions.

In contrast to contracts involving a time element, there are many other indirect losses that have no relationship to time required for restoration of property to normal use. Among these are: (1) loss of *profits* on *manufactured goods,* (2) loss of *leasehold,* or excess rental value interest, due to cancellation of lease following damage of property subject to lease, (3) loss of perishables due to *temperature* change, (4) loss due to damage to *parts of matched sets,* (5) losses growing out of *errors or omissions* in placing insurance, (6) losses that are the difference between actual value and *replacement cost* new (depreciation), (7) loss due to damage to *accounts receivable* records *and* other *valuable papers,* and (8) loss of profits and expenses due to *rain.*

TIME ELEMENT LOSSES

Losses that are dependent upon the time necessary to restore the property to normal operations are among the best known kinds of indirect losses. The amount of the loss is largely determined by the element of time after the loss which is required to repair, rebuild, or restore property to normal use. The losses include lost profits, lost income, lost use of property, contingent losses to other parties, and increased expenses.

BUSINESS INTERRUPTION INSURANCE

Importance. There is no fixed relationship between property damage loss or value and business interruption loss or value. The importance of *business interruption insurance* becomes apparent when it is recognized that a small property loss in a vital section of the plant may cause a total suspension of operations with a resulting loss far in excess of the actual property damage loss. Losses occasioned by interruption to business during the rebuilding period after a property loss are often heavy, and not infrequently of greater consequence than the loss occasioned by the destruction of the physical plant or material. Consider, for example, the disastrous effects possible as the result of destruction of an essential elevator or escalator in a department store. On the other hand, it is conceivable that a very substantial property damage might occur without serious interruption of operations.

The great need for business interruption insurance for mercantile risks is shown by the relationship between gross earnings (sales less cost of goods sold) and average inventory. Illustrations of this comparison include grocery stores with gross earnings of four times the dollar value of average inventory, drugstores with twice as much gross earnings as inventory, and gasoline stations with six times greater gross earnings than average inventory.[1]

Purpose. Business interruption insurance, also known as *prospective earnings insurance* and *use and occupancy insurance,* protects against the loss of prospective earnings because of the interruption of business by fire or other perils. The contract is one of indemnity for the net profits not realized, plus such fixed charges and expenses as necessarily continue during the interruption, but only to the extent that such fixed charges and expenses would have been earned had no interruption due to an insured peril occurred. Business interruption insurance undertakes to keep the business in the position that it could have maintained for itself had there been no interruption.

Distinguished from Profits Insurance. Business interruption insurance is to be distinguished from *profits insurance* in that profits insurance looks to the past, while business interruption indemnity looks to the future. Profits insurance, it will presently be noted, protects the insured against the loss of potential net profits on finished stock in the hands of a manufacturer or on any finished stock held in storage. In the event that this stock is damaged or destroyed, the direct loss insurance will cover only an amount necessary to repair or replace the damaged property. It will not cover potential profits. Hence, profits insurance is necessary for complete indemnity. Time is not a factor in determining the profits insurance loss. In the case of business interruption insurance, on the other hand, time is the essence of the contract. It looks to the future and undertakes to protect the insured agains loss of future earnings as a result of the interruption of the business conducted in, or with, the physical property described in the policy.

The difference between the two forms of insurance is emphasized when it is realized that profits insurance on a mercantile stock will cover only the profit prevented on the stock on hand which is damaged or destroyed. For example, if a mercantile stock turns over ten times each year, it would mean that an interruption of six months in the business would result in a loss of five turnovers of the stock. Business interruption insurance would cover this loss, but profits insurance would cover only the loss of profits on the inventory actually on hand and damaged at the time of the loss.

Business Interruption Loss. A business establishment is operated for its earnings. Every going business at any given time finds itself in one of three situations: it is being operated at a profit, at

[1]John D. Phelan, *Business Interruption Primer* (Indianapolis, Ind.: The Rough Notes Co. Inc., 1960), pp. 72–73. The importance of business interruption insurance is also apparent in the statement that "43% of all businesses suffering a serious fire loss never reopened–despite the fact that most carried insurance on building and contents." (p. 8).

cost, or at a loss. While business interruption insurance aims primarily to indemnify the insured for loss of profits because of an enforced cessation or limitation of operations, it does not follow that an insured has no loss if the business is not making a profit. When a plant is shut down, certain fixed charges must go on if the business is to continue to function. The policy, therefore, not only covers loss of net profits on business prevented from being carried on, but includes also the payment of such continuing fixed charges and expenses as must continue during the business interruption, to the extent that they would have been earned had there been no loss. Finally, the coverage makes allowance for expenses incurred for the purpose of reducing loss, to the extent that they do reduce loss.

It follows then, that, if a business is operating at a profit and a fire causes suspension, the loss includes both the profit item and the fixed-charge item, plus any costs incurred for minimizing the loss. If the business is operating at cost and a fire occurs, the loss is the same, less the profit item. If the business is operating at a loss, it may still be earning part of its fixed charges, and to the extent that these are earned they represent a loss if business is suspended. A year's interruption then, represents the profits that would have been earned had there been no cessation of operations, plus a year's fixed charges and expenses.

Comprehensive worksheets have been prepared for business establishments in order to estimate their potential business interruption loss, and the year's loss of such a concern may be computed as follows:

1. Estimated GROSS BUSINESS INCOME from sales or services for 12 months following .... $________
2. Discounts allowed .... $________
3. Allowances for returns, etc. ..... $________
4. Charge-offs for bad accounts .... $________
5. Net cost of merchandise, or raw stock (whichever applies)* ..... $________
6. Total 2 through 5. Deduct from 1 .... $________
7. ESTIMATED GROSS EARNINGS .... $________
8. Salaries and wages that may be discontinued if operations cease . . $________
9. Water, power, fuel, etc. (discontinuable portion) .... $________
10. Delivery service, light, heat, power, telephone, insurance and tax rebates, and other operating expenses that may be discontinued. $________
11. Total of 8 through 10. Deduct from 7 .... $________
    Balance represents ESTIMATED BUSINESS INTERRUPTION LOSS .... $________

*This includes anything, such as packaging, that goes out the door with the product, is used up and consumed in the manufacture of the product, or any services contracted outside, such as delivery service.

Business interruption *loss* is thus estimated by calculating *gross earnings* and subtracting out *expenses* which would *not continue* after damage to the physical property has occurred. The remainder is an estimate of the future profits and continuing expenses which would be lost as a result of the interruption of business.

For the average small mercantile establishment, business interruption loss can be determined with the knowledge of (*a*) turnover and (*b*) markup.[2] For example, a jewelry store has a low turnover with a high markup and seasonal peaks. On the other hand a meat market has a relatively low markup with a high turnover. In the case of a jewelry store with a stock valued at $40,000 with a 75 percent markup, the gross earnings on one turnover would be $30,000. If the turnover is twice each year then the annual gross earnings would be approximately $60,000, or an average of $200 a day for 300 working days. The business interruption loss for a year would be $60,000, less the discontinuable expenses. On the assumption that these expenses were estimated at $10,000, for example, then the business interruption loss, if the business was stopped completely for one year, would be $50,000.

Business Interruption Insurance Amount. The estimate of the necessary *insurance* amount to cover a $60,000 business interruption *value,* or gross earnings, would involve several other considerations. First, in a serious loss, would the jewelry store be able to get back in business, at least partially (perhaps at a temporary location), sooner than one year after the loss? Any factor such as the type of building construction and the availability of facilities for restablishing the business are important factors for determining the percentage of business interruption value to be covered. Second, would the earnings of the store be subject to substantial fluctuation during the year, as for weddings in June, or Christmas in December? If so, the estimate of lost earnings must be for the peak periods of the year, rather than only considering the per diem average loss. This suggests the coinsurance requirements of the particular contract form to be used in writing the business interruption insurance. The forms often require that insurance shall equal either 50, 60, 70, or 80 percent of the gross earnings determined as the insurable value. These coinsurance requirements give the insured a wide latitude in the event of fluctuating earnings. For the average mercantile business 50 percent of the business interruption value is ordinarily adequate. Losses for minor peak periods are automatically covered so long as adequate insurance to value is carried, but where the business is heavily seasonal larger amounts are indicated.

Thus, for the jewelry store in our example perhaps 70 percent,

[2]Averages for a large number of classes of business have been determined by and are available from Dun and Bradstreet and other such financial services.

or $42,000, of the estimated business interruption value might be chosen as the insurance amount. Such a choice would be made on the assumption that it would rarely take longer than about eight months for the jeweler to get back in business in full. Also, in case of a shorter period of interruption, if it occurred during peak seasonal sales periods, the insured would have coverage for the larger losses which might result from the ill-timed shorter period.

One of the more difficult estimates to make for business interruption is that for *continuing expenses*. In establishing liability for such fixed charges and expenses as must necessarily continue, the insured is faced with the necessity of segregating these charges to determine his potential loss. A study of the usual business establishment will reveal two types of continuing expenses: (1) *full* continuing and (2) *variable* continuing. Thus, such items as salaries of officers and superintendents must be paid during a shutdown. Rent of undestroyed property, branch offices, distributing points, mortgages, and the like must be paid in full. Bond interest; interest on notes and other obligations; taxes; insurance premiums that must be continued, such as liability coverage, business-life contracts, and insurance upon other property—all are fully continuing expenses.

In the category of variable continuing expenses the range is wider. Salaries of key employees, such as foremen and others necessary to keep the organization intact and ready to resume operations, must continue. The remainder of the payroll may be discontinued. Part of the annual depreciation and maintenance charges should be classified as continuing, though the amount that could be figured in a loss would depend upon the property damage loss. Charges for electricity, telephone, and the like are variable during a shutdown with perhaps only the minimum charges for meter service continuing. Noncancellable contracts, such as those for advertising, membership in trade associations, professional retainer fees, and the like are to be included as continuing to the extent that they must be paid because of legal liability to do so or because they are necessary to maintain the business organization as a growing concern.

Fully continuing expenses offer but little difficulty in estimating business interruption loss. To appraise the variable group of continuing expenses properly requires a careful analysis of the entire overhead expense of the business. Some costs are delayed and well hidden, as for example, rising unemployment compensation costs. One special difficulty is that the variable type often is dependent upon the length of the business interruption. If one estimates the shutdown to be brief, for example, almost all payroll is usually a continuing expense. However, as the interruption becomes one week, one month, two months, and so on, some of the ordinary payroll for unskilled workers is avoidable by laying off the least important personnel.

In addition to providing indemnity to the insured for loss of profits and continuing expenses as a result of fire or other peril insured against, the policy agrees to pay *expenses incurred for reducing the loss* under the policy. This element is not computed in arriving at the business interruption insurable value for, as a matter of fact, it adds nothing to the company's risk. The operation of this clause is illustrated by the following example. Assume that a seasonable business suffers a fire just as it is about to fill a number of large orders. The loss of profits and continuing expenses is estimated to be $80,000, and work will probably be totally suspended for 90 days. As the insured does not wish his customers to go to another concern, he rents a neighboring property, sets up machinery, and is operating at full capacity in 45 days. Although the accomplishment of this feat involves working night and day shifts at increased labor costs, as well as other extraordinary expenses, and the total cost amounts to $20,000, the insured considers it worthwhile since he is thereby able to keep his contact with valuable customers. If by the expenditure of $20,000 the insured is able to reduce the loss to $40,000, for example, the insurance company is obligated to pay the $40,000 loss of profits and continuing expenses, plus the expediting expense item of $20,000. This makes the total outlay of the insurance company $60,000 instead of $80,000 had the expediting expense not been incurred.

Business Interruption Forms. At one time there were several business interruption forms, each adapted to special situations. A nationwide study resulted in the adoption of two basic forms, one for mercantile and nonmanufacturing risks and one for manufacturing risks. The forms make no daily or weekly limitation of payment but require coinsurance (sometimes called "contribution") based upon the annual business interruption value of the business. These forms have an advantage over the older per diem[3] and weekly forms in that they automatically adjust to fluctuating earnings. The company is liable for any loss during the period of coverage, whatever the amount, provided the face of the policy is equal to the coinsurance percentage of the business interruption value, or gross earnings.

Since loss is paid without any per diem or weekly limitation, seasonal or daily fluctuations in earnings are automatically taken care of. The forms take into consideration the prospective insurable interest as one lump sum and pay the actual loss sustained as it appears at the time of the business interruption. In the case of a department store, for example, this would mean a high amount of

[3]Per diem valued forms of business interruption insurance are still written. Some tax and loss settlement advantages offset in some cases the disadvantages of a per day limitation. Power plant coverages may still be written on a valued basis, and in this field the term "use and occupancy" still prevails.

indemnity for Saturdays, with lower amounts for the less active days, as well as higher sums for the periods of greatest activity, such as during the Christmas shopping season, and lesser sums for the dull periods between seasons. Likewise, department store operators contend that in order to keep their organizations intact during short periods of suspension, they must continue all or part of their force of employees and, for this reason, may wish to include in the coverage the item of ordinary payroll. This increases the insurable value and with the operation of the coinsurance clause requires additional insurance. On the other hand, a business establishment, such as a manufacturing plant, that hires a large number of that class of employees known as ordinary labor may exclude such payroll from its insurable value or it may insure it for a limited period or for the entire policy period, whichever coverage best meets its needs.[4]

The *gross earnings form* is most widely used today for most businesses. The business interruption loss is estimated as discussed previously, and a choice made as to the coinsurance percentage desired. The rate decreases as a higher coinsurance requirement is used.

The insured's *ordinary payroll* is covered, though if blanket payroll coverage is not desired it may be excluded by endorsement. Ordinary payroll is defined as the entire payroll expense for all employees of the insured except officers, executive, department managers, employees under contract, and any others who under any circumstances would, of necessity, be retained during a period of shutdown. If full coverage is not required, that portion known to be noncontinuing may be excluded from coverage.[5]

Forms have been written in some jurisdictions with an *agreed amount* instead of a percentage of coinsurance, if the insured files annually a statement of income and expenses with the rating bureau. The agreed-amount form has the advantage of eliminating the danger that the insured may become a coinsurer because of a deficiency in insurance, but it has the disadvantage that it requires

[4]Business interruption indemnity used to be written under five distinct forms: per diem, per week, two-item coinsurance, gross earnings, and specified-time coinsurance forms. The two-item coinsurance forms are sometimes referred to as "contribution forms." The per diem, weekly, and monthly forms limited indemnity to an amount for each period specified. The gross earnings forms are now more flexible than the older forms and are adaptable to any form of business. Today the gross earnings form is by far the most predominant form in use.

[5]Mercantile establishments particularly have felt the need for retaining the entire staff during a period of shutdown. The need, however, is not limited to mercantile establishments. Competitive labor conditions, such as developed during wartime, brought into sharp focus the necessity of retaining employees of all categories to be available when the business reopens rather than relying on the recruiting of a new staff built around key employees.

the insured to file data that he sometimes is reluctant to make available.

A relatively new and promising solution to the difficulty of estimating coinsurance needs accurately is the *"no coinsurance" earnings forms* available in most states. These forms are designed for small and medium-sized business, and provide a simple method of determining the amount of insurance. The insured estimates his need for business income for one month after a loss, and the policy is written for four times that amount.[6] Many smaller firms, needing several thousand dollars of coverage per month, find this form increasingly attractive in terms of simplicity. Its disadvantages are that it is not permitted for manufacturers, and may be higher in cost for larger firms than the gross earnings form.

The business interruption forms contain a number of special exclusions, and the nature of these depends upon whether or not the policy is designed for a mercantile or manufacturing risk. Certain of these exclusions that are applicable to both classes of risk appear in all forms. In the category of special exclusions the policy provides that there shall be no liability for (*a*) the destruction of any finished stock, (*b*) any increase of loss which may be occasioned by any ordinance or law regulating construction or repair of buildings, (*c*) suspension, lapse, or cancellation of any lease or license, contract, or order, (*d*) increase of loss due to interference with rebuilding by strikers, and (*e*) consequential or remote loss.

Contingent Business Interruption Insurance

This type of indirect loss policy is available to indemnify the insured in the event of loss due to damage or to the destruction of property not owned or operated by the insured but upon which the insured is dependent in whole or in part for the continued operation of his business.

General Forms. There are two forms of contingent business interruption insurance. These are: (*a*) *contributing properties* coverage and (*b*) *recipient properties* coverage. The first form provides indemnity in the event that the insured suffers a business interruption loss due to the destruction of or damage to other plants furnishing materials, parts, or services to the plant of the insured. The prime example of the need for such insurance was the disastrous fire at Livonia, Michigan, in 1953. A $50 million fire destroyed an essential transmission plant which supplied many General Motors

---

[6]The four times one month's loss of gross earnings is the result of a common limitation in the contract of no more than 25 percent of the insurance being available during the first thirty days after loss. In many western states the requirement is 33⅓ percent, so the insurance amount is commonly set at three times the first month's estimated loss.

automobile manufacturers. The vast business interruption suffered as a consequence by the automobile manufacturers was a contingent business interruption loss to them, resulting from the destruction of the contributing properties.

The second form, recipient properties coverage, insures against loss caused by damage to or destruction of other plants to which the product of the insured plant is sold. Recipient properties coverage is a required form for the manufacturer who as a subcontractor supplies materials or parts to a prime contractor. In the event that the plant of the prime contractor, termed in the policy the "recipient property," is damaged or destroyed so that the prime contractor is no longer able to take the product of the insured, his business interruption losses are covered under his recipient properties coverage. Such insurance is most important when the supplier sells a large proportion of his total goods to a single large buyer, and when the product has limited other market possibilities.

Off-Premises Power Plant Insurance. Another type of contingent business interruption coverage is a specialized contingent form covering the continued flow of utilities. Insurance may be written to cover loss attributable to the interruption of the supply of electricity, heat, gas, or water. The source may be either a public utility or a privately operated source. Since the coverage applies with respect to utilities received from plants *outside* the premises of the insured, the coverage is, in fact, a form of contributing properties business interruption indemnity. Coverage may be provided for the interruption of the supply of any one or of several named utilities, to protect the insured against interruption of power, light, or other utility due to fire damage at the source of supply. It may also be written to cover against tornado, explosion, vehicle damage, and all the other hazards insurable under the fire extended coverage endorsement. Interruption due to damage to transmission lines may be covered, as well as property damage at the generating plant.

Selling Agents' Commissions Insurance. The commission lost where goods already manufactured and sold but not delivered are damaged or destroyed may be insured under the profits form to be discussed in the next section as a type of no time element loss. The loss is identical to the loss of profits to the owner of the goods but is measured by the commission earned through the sale but lost through inability to secure delivery of goods sold.

In contrast to this type of commission is the selling agent who handles large quantities of the output of one or more manufacturing establishments. He does not purchase for his own account but secures his income from placing orders. He may be a commission agent, broker, or factor. A person or concern operating in one of these capacities is not solely concerned with goods manufactured but not delivered. He is concerned with the interruption of a continuous flow of the goods he undertakes to sell and may suffer a severe loss if this flow of goods is interrupted. The loss may be covered under a *selling agents' commission form* of contingent business interruption insurance.

The selling agents' commission form has a particular appeal when a substantial volume or all of the business of the selling agent is derived from the output of a single plant. It also appeals to the agent or salesman who spends the entire year on the road taking orders for a future seasonable delivery. Orders for calendars and advertising novelties, for example, are taken the year around, but deliveries are made about December 1. If a representative working on a commission basis were to have orders in for a year and the plant were destroyed before delivery of the goods, he might, depending upon his contract, suffer a substantial loss. Under a commissions coverage, the goods need not have been completed, since it is sufficient to support a claim if the concern for which the goods were sold is unable to make deliveries because of a peril covered by the policy.

Commissions insurance is written with a coinsurance clause with the usual requirement at least 80 percent of insurance to value. The rate charged is the rate for business interruption insurance at the location where the goods sold by the agent are manufactured.

Rents and Rental Value Insurance

If a property is rendered untenantable by fire, there is, in addition to the direct loss or damage, a loss of rental income if occupied by a tenant, or a loss of use if occupied by the owner. Losses from this source are insurable under a rents or rental value form of business interruption insurance.

Rents insurance indemnifies the owner of a property in the event that his rental *income* is cut off or interrupted by fire or other peril included in the coverage. *Rental value* insurance covers the occupant and indemnifies him for the *loss of use* of the premises. The occupant may be the owner, in which case his indemnity represents the rental he must pay to secure premises similar to those destroyed or damaged. If the occupant is a tenant under a lease drawn so that his payments must continue during the untenantable period, he can be indemnified on the the same basis as if he were the owner.

Rents insurance is a particularly important coverage for estates whose holdings are largely real estate, the beneficiaries of which would be seriously inconvenienced if their income should be interrupted for any lengthy period. Trustees might personally be willing to assume the risk on their own property but are frequently unwilling to take the risk as trustees if the beneficiaries of the trust depend largely upon the income from the real estate in question.

Rental forms in common use are written with coinsurance. The requirements vary from 60 percent to 100 percent. The rate is less as the ratio of insurance to value required by the coinsurance clause increases.

If the form is based upon the rental value for the length of time required to rebuild the property if totally destroyed, the amount of insurance necessary for full coverage is the amount of income received during the estimated period. If the form contains the 100 percent coinsurance clause, the period estimated as the time required to rebuild should be generous; otherwise, when a loss occurs, the insurance may be found to be inadequate.

In seasonal risks, the months of customary occupancy are incorporated into the form, and the policy is written to limit its liability for loss of rental value only during this period. A summer home, with a rental value of $1,500 for the months of June, July, and August, would be insured for $1,500 for one year under a seasonal form. If damaged in September and repairs could reasonably be completed before the following June, there would be no liability under the policy. Damage in May that could not be repaired until September would require the payment of the face of the policy. When a property is untenantable for a month or fraction thereof during the indicated usual period of occupancy, indemnity is paid on a prorata basis.

The period for which a loss may be collected begins with the happening of the fire, or other contingency insured against, and runs for the period required with the exercise of reasonable diligence to restore the property. The loss must originate during the term of the policy, though the liability may continue beyond its termination.

Wherever rent must be paid by a business as a continuing expense, this loss is covered under the regular business interruption gross earnings contract. However, rental value insurance may also indemnify a business tenant for rent payments he is obligated to make under a lease during the period the property he occupies is untenantable. The question presents itself as to whether or not there is duplication in the two coverages. To an extent there is, and sometimes the gross earnings policy is endorsed to provide that if the insured's interest is otherwise insured under a rent or rental value policy, then rental value is to be eliminated from all consideration under the business interruption policy. The purpose of eliminating the rental coverage from the continuing expenses is, of course, a premium savings. The need for rental coverage in addition to business interruption is only in that situation where the insured knows or fears his business is not earning fixed charges. Under the gross earnings policy the insured recovers rent only to the extent that he would have earned fixed charges during the period operations are suspended. Rental value insurance is not dependent upon whether or not the rent is earned but makes payment to the insured during the period he is obligated to pay.

Extra-Expense Insurance

Extra-expense insurance covers, subject to the policy limits, all extra-expense or additional charges incurred by the insured *in order to continue* as nearly as practicable the normal conduct of his business following damage or destruction of buildings or contents by an insured peril. This may cover the cost of doing business at a location other than the usual premises of the insured. It is sometimes confused with business interruption insurance, which covers loss when the business cannot be continued. Extra-expense insurance covers the additional cost of carrying on a business following a loss. The difference in the two forms of insurance should be quite apparent.

The business interruption policy does contain an extraordinary expense item and for many classes of risk the business interruption policy satisfies the needs of the insured. However, extraordinary expenses under the business interruption policy are limited to the extent that loss under the policy is reduced. Extra-expense insurance sets no such limitation, and provides for any extraordinary outlay to keep a business in operation. It provides for the extra expense over and above normal operating costs to provide the means to permit the insured to continue as nearly as practicable normal business operations immediately following damage or destruction to buildings or contents by the perils insured against. The policy does not cover loss of income in any respect.

The amount paid to the insured for his extra expenses is limited by (1) the basic policy insurance amount and (2) a percentage of the total insurance amount which is set as a maximum which may be used each month following the beginning of indemnity. For example, a common requirement is a limitation of 40 percent during the first month, 80 percent during the first two months and 100 percent for the first three months or thereafter.[7] The period of indemnity continues during the period necessary to restore the property to normal use.

Some types of businesses have a special need for protection against extra-expense losses. Such firms as banks, milk distributors,

[7]Coinsurance is not used in connection with extra-expense, although the above monthly limitations serve a similar purpose in encouraging the insured to purchase an adequate amount of insurance.

newspapers, laundries and many others must provide, at all costs, continuous service to their customers. Otherwise, their clients are immediately lost to competitors. These businesses need somehow to continue daily service, and extra-expense insurance is an important means by which this can be accomplished. Extra help, overtime pay, expensive substitute quarters, advertisements of continued services available at temporary locations, air freight costs to replace needed machines, and many other costs are typical of the extra expenses of these firms.

There is a form of extra-expense coverage, known as *additional-living-expense,* available for residents of dwellings and written in connection with rental value insurance. This form bears the same relationship to rental value insurance that extra-expense insurance bears to business interruption insurance. Rental value coverage indemnifies the insured for the rental value of the home during the period it is unfit for occupancy because of a loss caused by a peril covered by the insurance. The additional living-expense form reimburses the insured for excess expenses necessitated by securing temporary living quarters during the period the property is not habitable.[8]

The additional-living-expense contract covers *necessary* living expenses. To establish a claim the expenses must be *incurred.* Thus, an insured may not create excessive charges to provide quarters more luxurious than those which he occupied. There must be a reasonable relationship between the two. Conversely, he may not move in with relatives or occupy less desirable quarters on a temporary basis and collect on the ground that he *could have* obligated the company for the better quarters under the terms of his policy. The insurance company undertakes to indemnify the insured for excess payments which the insured himself has actually made to house his family adequately.

The contract provides payment for the period required to restore and make habitable the damaged property, subject always to the policy limits. If the family establishes itself in permanent quarters other than those vacated because of the loss, the insurance payments terminate.

Insurance is not written with a coinsurance requirement, but the payment in any one month under the contract is limited to 25 percent of the face of the policy. This means that with excess costs of $100 monthly and an interruption of use of the premises of one month, $400 insurance would be required. This same insurance would pay $100 monthly for four months, but not $400 for one

[8]Some cynical soul has coined the term "mother-in-law insurance" for extra-living expense cover, presumably because it obviates the need for going to live with in-laws while repairs to a dwelling are being made.

month even if a necessary incurred expenditure could be shown. It follows, therefore, that insurance should be at least four times the first monthly anticipated claim and should be in an amount sufficient to last for the time the family may be expected to occupy substitute quarters.

It is to be remembered that additional-living-expense insurance does not pay the full cost of substitute quarters but only the excess cost of the new quarters above the usual costs of living in the uninhabitable damaged property. Includable expenses in a typical claim for additional living expenses might be: the *extra* costs of a hotel or motel for several weeks (perhaps followed by further rental of an apartment or house), eating meals out, laundry costs, extra travel expenses and many other items.

Tuition Fees Insurance

Private schools, run for profit, are dependent upon the income derived from tuition fees for their maintenance. A fire that destroys any substantial part of the property of the school might necessitate a temporary suspension of operations, with a consequent obligation to refund tuition collected or to cancel charges already made. Nor is there any assurance, with the work of reconstruction and repair completed, that all the students formerly enrolled will return. Thus, the consequences of the fire from this angle alone may be far reaching enough to disorganize the entire program of the school.

The insurance, as written, indemnifies the insured for loss occasioned by the necessity to return, or the failure to receive, tuition fees as the outgrowth of a fire. If a fire occurs during a summer vacation, the loss is computed on the basis of the attendance for the previous year. The policy pays for the loss of tuition fees sustained after the expiration of the policy if the fire occasioning the loss occurred during the policy term. Recovery is not limited to the time required to restore the damaged property. Protection extends to the day preceding the beginning of the first school year following the date that restoration and repairs have been completed. Thus, if a school building is destroyed or damaged during a school term, resulting transfers may not be determined until the opening of the next school year. The policy further provides that if the reconstruction period runs to a date within 30 days of the opening of the next school year, loss of tuition due to uncertainty of the plans for the reopening is covered. This provision covers a loss where rebuilding is possible during the vacation period but transfers result because of the students' uncertainty regarding the completion date.

Under the tuition fees coverage the insured is required to carry insurance in an amount equal to the normal tuition fees for the fiscal year covered by the policy. If a loss occurs and the insured fails to carry the required amount of insurance, the company is liable only for that proportion of the loss which the insurance bears to the normal tuition fees for the fiscal year in which the loss occurs. This is in effect a 100 percent coinsurance requirement. Some forms permit use of a coinsurance requirement of a lesser amount.

The insured is obligated immediately following the loss to take all reasonable steps to eliminate any expense which does not necessarily continue. He is expected to make use of other available property or take advantage of any other reasonable steps that will reduce the amount of the loss. The cost of this procedure as well as the savings effected are taken into consideration in arriving at the amount of the loss for which the company is liable.

NO TIME ELEMENT LOSSES

Indirect losses in which the time required for restoration of the physical property is not the determining factor in the payment of an insurance loss are of several types. Insurance of these losses is not as important as the time element losses previously discussed. Yet, for the policyholder who is exposed to such losses, the consequences of not considering insurance protection for them can be serious. Generally, the need for insurance of no time element losses arises in specialized situations, but some are of more than merely infrequent occurrence.

Profits Insurance

Profits insurance indemnifies the insured for loss of profits on finished goods. It is written by attaching a special form to the fire, windstorm, explosion, earthquake, or other peril insurance contract. Under the fire or other direct loss contract, the measure of the damage to the insured is the cost to repair or replace. In the case of manufactured goods, this is limited to the manufacturing costs. It may happen, therefore, that if a warehouse is filled with completed goods not yet delivered, their destruction will result in a substantial loss to the insured because his direct damage loss will be settled on the basis of cost to him rather than on the basis of the price for which the goods may be sold.

In the case of seasonable goods, the profits of an entire year may be lost if fire occurs just before it is time to deliver the finished product. Christmas toys, for example, are ordinarily delivered during the month of October, but the manufacturing process takes place during the entire year. If the year's stock of toys of a manufacturing establishment is destroyed late in September, the loss of profits will be serious. Nor is the loss of profits serious only to business establishments that make seaonable deliveries. Any business that has substantial amounts of finished stocks in storage is faced with a probable loss of profits.

The distinction between profits insurance, which covers profit loss on only one turnover of the goods, and business interruption insurance covering perhaps many business turnovers, has already been made earlier in the chapter.

Two forms of profits insurance are written. One limits the liability of the company for loss of profits to the percentage of loss ascertained and adjusted under the property loss or damage policies. This form provides that if the direct loss on stock is determined to be 50 percent, the loss of profits is limited by the same percentage.

A second form, known as the "unlimited form," adjusts the profits item without regard to the percentage of loss on stock. It is quite possible that a partial loss on stock might so damage the merchandise as to eliminate entirely the profit item. Under the unlimited form, there could be a percentage loss under the direct damage contracts with a total loss of profits. The unlimited form is regarded as the most satisfactory protection. From an underwriting point of view, the risk is greater and the premium charge correspondingly higher.

Profits insurance is usually written only for a manufacturer and not for merchandise held for sale by a retail merchant. Loss of profits for a retailer is covered in business interruption insurance. It is expected that the retail merchant can replace at cost much of the damaged stock and resume business in the period during which his building is being restored. The merchant would collect only the profits that were not earned in that period. On the other hand, the manufacturer is in quite a different position. He has on hand merchandise completed and ready for delivery. The finished goods cannot be replaced by the manufacturer for delivery according to the contract at the cost to him. The manufacturer would have realized his profit on this merchandise had there been no loss. Time needed for restoration is not a factor in the loss of the profit. Profits insurance covers this lost profit.

Delayed profits contracts have been issued covering the loss of profits due to unusual delay in the completion of a contract. Ordinarily, this risk would be written only in the face of the most unusual circumstances. In wartime, for example, the construction of ships is feverishly carried on, and a completed ship is often worth substantially more than its replacement cost. Here the time element is of great importance. It follows, in such instances, that if a ship near completion were totally destroyed, its value would be considerably in excess of the cost of building a new ship.

Contingent profits insurance is a special form used by insurance agencies whose commissions are contingent upon the loss experience of the agency. It sometimes happens that the agreement between the agent and the company provides for an agreed commission, plus a contingent commission if the loss experience does not exceed a certain percentage of premiums. As the year's end approaches and the contingent commission is earned, there is ever present the possibility of a serious loss or even a conflagration that might have the effect of wiping out the contingent earnings of the agency. An insurance agency may provide insurance against the loss of these anticipated contingent earnings.

Leasehold Interest and Excess Rental Value Insurance

Leases as they are ordinarily written contain a cancellation clause which provides that either party to the lease may terminate it at his option if a designated percentage of the property is destroyed. It follows, therefore, that if a tenant possesses a long-term lease particularly advantageous to him, the lease will in all probability not be continued if the owner can terminate it. The tenant then loses his valuable interest in the lease.

Leasehold value represents the increased rental value of premises to a lessee in excess of the actual rental paid by him under the terms of his lease. Thus, if 10 years ago a lease were executed on a property calling for $1,000 monthly rental to run for a period of 20 years, it might be quite possible that, owing to a change in business conditions, the same property would today bring $2,000 a month. If this is so, the holder of the lease has a leasehold interest in the property valued at $1,000 a month for the remaining 10 years. Assuming the property is destroyed to an extent that permits the owner of the property to cancel the lease, the holder of the lease has lost the equivalent of $1,000 a month for 120 months. The insurable value is the discounted value of $120,000, or the present value of $1,000 a month for 120 months. Leasehold insurance does not cover in the event of cancellation of the lease for any reason other than the happening of a loss due to one of the perils insured against.

In addition to the situation where a tenant is paying a rental less than the actual rental value measured by the current market for the property, there are other situations that create an insurable interest in a lease. These are; *(a)* the payment of a bonus to secure a location, *(b)* expenditures for betterments and improvements, and *(c)* advanced rent payments. It often happens where good locations are scarce and held under long-term leases that a concern may find it profitable to pay a substantial lump-sum *bonus* to a present tenant to secure his location. This sum, of course, would be lost entirely if the premises were destroyed and his lease canceled. The bonus is amortized over the period of the lease and may be insured under a special form designed for the purpose. The policy is written for a face amount equal to the bonus with the amount of insurance decreasing monthly to reflect the amortization of the bonus.

Tenant's *improvements* are insured for physical loss or damage under a tenants' improvement form. There is no conflict between this form and the leasehold interest form covering an amount invested in betterments. The leasehold interest form covering benefits follows the pattern of the bonus form. It defines leasehold interest as the insured's interest in improvements and betterments to a particular building during the unexpired term of his lease. If the building is destroyed or damaged to the extent that the lease is canceled, then the leasehold improvements and betterments coverage indemnifies the insured. In the case of partial destruction of the premises, with no lease cancellation, the leasehold improvements and betterments coverage pays nothing. Here the insured requires tenants' improvements insurance to pay the cost of repairing physical damage to the property. To obviate double insurance the improvements and betterments leasehold form provides that in the event of the cancellation of the insured's lease by fire, any amount payable to the insured under property damages policies for the direct loss or damage to improvements and betterments is to be deducted from the amount recoverable under the leasehold policy.

In some situations substantial amounts of *advance rent* are payable in advance. Without any interest in the betterments, a property owner may agree to make certain renovations for a prospective tenant and, as an aid to financing them, require the advance payment of rent for a year or more. In other instances the owner, as a convenience to himself, may require rent paid annually in advance with no provisions for refund under any circumstances. The cancellation of such a lease would leave the tenant without the use of the property for the unexpired term of the lease and accordingly he would lose a prorata share of the advance rent. This form of advance rent may be covered, as in the case of the bonus and improvements, with the amount of insurance decreasing over the term of the lease.

In writing a leasehold-interest policy, the fire clause in the lease furnishes the key to the entire underwriting problem. Oftentimes a copy of the lease is attached to the policy. When the clause vaguely states the rights of the parties to terminate the lease in the event of a fire, a leasehold interest under such an agreement is uninsurable. A satisfactory form of fire clause will require that the property be over 50 percent destroyed by fire before the lease may be canceled. Discounts from the rate are sometimes allowed if the fire clause requires a 75 percent or more destruction before the right of cancellation arises. From the point of view of the underwriter, the higher the percentage indicated, the more favorable is the risk. If no specific clause appears in the lease, statutes in the state where the property is located govern in case of fire. When the statue is considered adequate from the insurer's viewpoint, a leasehold-interest policy may be written, incorporating into the form the stipulation that the statute of the state is to be followed in the matter of right to cancel.

Rates for leasehold interest are governed by the building rate. Since a leasehold interest reduces in value from month to month as the term of the lease runs toward expiration, with no value left at expiration, the amount collectible is less each month. For this reason the form itself provides for this continued reduction in the amount payable, decreasing the original face amount of the policy as it approaches expiration. The premium, so that it may be equitable, is based upon an average of the amount the insurer has at risk during the policy term. The average is found by adding the insurable value at the beginning of the policy term to the insurable value at its termination and dividing by two the sum so found. The average thus obtained is multiplied by the rate, and the resulting amount is the premium for the policy term.

The leasehold contract is one of indemnity, and the loss under the policy is payable only if the lease is terminated. As in the case of other fire insurance policies, the contract is one of indemnity. There are a number of forms covering leasehold interest, but they all follow much the same pattern. A widely used form provides, in the case of cancellation of the lease, for the payment of the gross leasehold value for a period of three months. The leasehold value for the balance of the term is discounted on the basis of a discount rate established in the policy.

Leasehold-interest policies may be written on an annual basis or for a term, as may the fire policy covering the direct loss. Upon renewal, or at any time during the policy term, if a change in the leasehold value takes place, the insurance may be adjusted to cover accordingly. A leasehold interest may run to great value, and executors or trustees particularly should recognize their obligation to protect and preserve this value as an asset, just as they would protect an asset represented by ownership of physical property. This value, however, is frequently overlooked.

A converse of the leasehold-interest contract is found in the *excess rental value policy* which undertakes to protect the *owner* of buildings who has an advantageous lease which, if canceled, could not be renewed on equally favorable terms. This is in contrast to the leasehold-interest policy, which provides indemnity if the lessee is obliged to cancel a lease that is worth more than the price he is paying.

The excess rental value policy operates in the following manner. Assume a lease written 10 years ago for a period of 20 years and calling for a monthly payment of $2,500. Assume further that on the present market the most the property would bring is $1,500. Under these circumstances, the property owner has an insurable excess rental value in the lease of $1,000 a month for 10 years. If the property should be destroyed by fire so that the lessee could elect to cancel, it is apparent that this would be the logical procedure for him to follow. In these circumstances, if the owner of the property restored it and offered it for rent, his income would be reduced by $1,000 a month. As in the case of leasehold interest, the insurable value is determined by discounting the monthly payments and finding their present lump-sum value.

Temperature Damage Insurance

If a temperature change follows a fire loss and the fire originated in the insured premises, any loss to stock caused by the change is generally held to be covered by the fire insurance contract. The situation is not so clear if the stock is located in a building that secures its heat or refrigeration from a plant located some distance away. Because of the uncertainty that exists, the policy issued on cold storage warehouses, breweries, packing plants, greenhouses, creameries, and other such risks (where there is a liability for loss or damage by interruption of power or change of temperature), usually exempts the insurer from such indirect liability.

Because of the nature of stocks or merchandise or material in process located in buildings where temperature change may be one of the most serious hazards, policies may be endorsed to provide *temperature damage insurance* for loss caused by failure of heat or refrigeration. The rules covering the attachment of the endorsement are not the same in all jurisdictions. In some instances no premium is charged if the source of heat or refrigeration is located within the insured premises. An additional premium may be charged if the source is located outside the premises.

Matched Set or Parts Insurance

Another source of indirect loss is found where one part of a matched set is damage or destroyed. The risk is one that is especially important to the garment trade. Here it is customary to send different parts of a garment to several locations for a part of the processing. Insurance companies writing policies on garment manufacturers' stock eliminate the possibility of consequential loss claims by endorsing the policy to provide that the insurance will not cover any loss or damage by the insured perils due to the reduction in value of remaining parts of clothing or suits, unless such other part or parts are in the same fire section. If it is desired that the consequential damage risk be assumed by the insurance company, an endorsement is provided which includes indirect damage to clothing whether caused by fire at the insured's location or elsewhere. Jewelers also find a need for *matched set insurance* on such articles as earrings, bracelets and necklaces, where the value of the set may be more than proportionally lost by damage or loss of one part.

Errors and Omissions Insurance

Financial institutions that lend money with real estate as security are always faced with the possibility that, through some neglect on the part of the owner of the property, insurance in force when the loan was made will not be renewed. Painstaking care in checking expirations still leaves a loophole—the outgrowth of an error on the part of the employees to whom this responsibility has been assigned.

The *errors and omissions policy* for lending institutions protects against losses arising out of failure to have in force proper insurance to protect the mortgaged property as a result of error or omissions. The policy protects only the mortgagee and applies only when, through error and omission, specific insurance is invalid, insufficient, or has not been provided. To establish a loss under an errors and omissions policy, the failure of specific insurance must be the outgrowth of some unintentional act of either the mortgagor or the mortgagee, and the damage to the property, the subject of the mortgage, must be of a nature to impair the mortgaged security. Ten percent coinsurance is ordinarily required, but in any case a minimum premium is required. It frequently happens that the minimum premium will purchase more insurance than the minimum of the coinsurance requirements.

Errors and omissions insurance is not strictly property insurance. The property encumbered as security for a mortgage is not covered for the benefit of the owner. It is designed to protect the lending institution from loss due to the destruction of its security if insurance through error has not been placed or renewed. The insurance company after paying a loss is subrogated to the rights of the insured. The debt of the mortgagor remains unchanged; and, if it is collectible, the insurance company must be reimbursed. This has a bearing upon the nature of the forms available.

The most prevalent errors from which losses arise involve the elements of carelessness, delay, or oversight. It may happen that the mortgagor has agreed to deliver his policies to the bank. Before he can do so, a loss occurs. After the loss, it develops that his insurance is insufficient to cover the mortgage debt. The errors and omissions policy indemnifies the mortgagee to the extent of his loss. When property is sold and the deeds are passed but the insurance, through oversight or inadvertence, is not transferred, the errors and omissions coverage would step into the breach to protect the mortgagee. Changes in ownership, incorrect description, errors in entering expirations at the bank, failure to report change of occupancy or increase of hazard when known, errors in ordering or binding coverage, incorrect statement of ownership, oversight in ordering renewal —these and scores of other errors that might invalidate the coverage or jeopardize the protection are covered by the policy.

Another important hazard covered in the policy is concerned with coinsurance. When there is not insurance enough to value, both insured and mortgagee are affected by the operation of the clause. Naturally banks take precautions to see that proper insurance to value is carried. If, however, the insurance is insufficient, the bank is protected by the errors and omissions coverage.

Depreciation Insurance

The fire insurance contract covers the insured for loss or damage to the extent of the actual cash value of the insured property at the time of the loss. Cash value is determined by giving consideration to depreciation. It follows, therefore, that an insured property whose value is lessened by age and use, changing business conditions, neighborhood changes, and the like, may be covered for full value under a fire insurance contract and yet the insurance may be less than the amount necessary to replace the loss or damaged property.

Not all insurers are willing to write insurance in an amount sufficient to insure the full replacement cost of the insured property. They point out that there is an element of moral hazard in providing insurance that will replace in its entirety an old and partly obsolete building in a new condition. There are others who contend that in most instances the element of moral hazard is negligible and that an insured has every right to buy insurance that will place him back in business after a fire without contributing to the replacement cost of his building an amount measured by depreciation.

Depreciation insurance, sometimes called *replacement cost*[9] insurance, pays for full replacement cost new of the insured property, without deduction for depreciation. It provides indemnity for the expenditures the insured is obliged to make over and above the amount of the loss covered by full insurance under the standard fire policy in order to restore the property to its full usefulness as before the loss or damage. Depreciation insurance substitutes a figure representing the cost of replacement new for the term "actual cash value."

Depreciation insurance through replacement cost endorsements or clauses has become increasingly important in the past decade. Homeowner's contracts for residential risks and business multiple-line package policies both often include such protection now. Depreciation insurance is written ordinarily to cover buildings only, but including machinery and equipment incidental to the service of the building. Coinsurance is invariably required. Some underwriters

[9]Formerly the term depreciation insurance used to be applied to separate policies, covering this risk, while "replacement cost" referred to endorsements to the fire policy. Note that in the former case only the difference between replacement cost and actual value is covered.

insist upon 100 percent of value, though in some instances policies are written on an 80 percent basis. The coinsurance percentage applies to the full replacement cost and not to the actual cash value, as would be the case with ordinary fire insurance. In the usual course, liability under the policy accrues on an actual cash value basis until repair or replacement has actually been effected. This means that if the property is not repaired or replaced, the only liability of the company will be on an actual cash value basis. Some companies specify a time limit within which repair or replacement must be completed. It is usual to provide that repairs or replacements shall be completed with due diligence and dispatch, ordinarily within 12 months.

Accounts-Receivable and Valuable Papers Insurance

Accounts-receivable and valuable papers insurance are two separate forms. Contrary to most of the types of indirect loss insurance discussed in this chapter, the coverage is provided both by casualty and inland marine underwriters.[10] When written as an inland marine policy, a form is attached to the basic schedule property floater. The forms are very much alike but are modified to meet the requirements of the property insured. Both provide "all risks" coverage.

The *valuable papers and records* forms provide insurance under two headings: (*a*) specified articles, and (*b*) all others. Specified articles are listed and valued, and the amount per article is the agreed value for the purposes of loss adjustment. All other papers and records, are covered in a blanket amount, not separately valued. The insurance covers only while the papers and records are contained in the premises named in the policy. It is required that the insured papers and records be maintained in a fireproof safe or receptacle named and described in the policy at all times except when they are in actual use. There is an extension of the coverage not exceeding 10 percent of the combined limits of insurance, but in no case in excess of $5,000, while the papers and records insured are being conveyed outside the premises or temporarily within other premises for any purpose other than storage.

Many persons and businesses have a great need for valuable papers insurance. Lawyers, doctors, authors, architects, photographers, banks, insurance companies and agencies, and many others suffer extensive losses when their records are damaged. Indeed,

---

[10]At one time, valuable papers and accounts-receivable policies were written both by casualty companies and inland marine underwriters using their own rates and forms. Effective April 5, 1954, the National Bureau of Casualty Underwriters and the Inland Marine Insurance Bureau announced revised rules and rates applicable to these policies and new forms developed cooperatively by the two rating organizations. Identical coverages now may be obtained from either marine or casualty insurers.

protection for the expenses of replacement (or irreplaceable values) is present to some extent in almost every business.

The *accounts-receivable form* contains the same provisions noted above and may be written (*a*) on a reporting form, or (*b*) for a lump sum on a nonreporting form. For the reporting form monthly reports of values are submitted. For the nonreporting form a statement of the average monthly balance and the largest monthly balance during the latest 12 months is required. No monthly reports are submitted and no audit of the policy is made. The reporting form provides greater flexibility where there is a considerable fluctuation in values. The nonreporting form appeals to smaller insureds who do not wish to be faced with the responsibilities entailed in monthly reports.

The policy covers as follows: (*a*) all sums due the insured from customers, provided the insured is unable to effect collection thereof as the direct result of loss of or damage to records or accounts receivable; (*b*) interest charges on any loan to offset impaired collections pending repayment of such sums made uncollectible by such loss or damage; (*c*) collection expense in excess of normal collection cost and made necessary because of such loss or damage; and (*d*) other expenses, when reasonably incurred by the insured in reestablishing records of accounts receivable following such loss or damage. A department store using many charge accounts for its sales is a good example of need for this policy. Were its records destroyed, many accounts would be uncollected. Even when duplicate records are maintained they are seldom complete and foolproof as an alternative method of treating this risk.

In the case of installment sales contracts or certain other financing operations notes are taken rather than to carry the amount due in an open account. The accounts-receivable policy is not suitable for such operations. Notes fall in the category of securities and are insurable under any of the policy forms that extend to cover securities, such as, for example, the money and securities broad form policy.

The accounts-receivable policy does not cover accounting, bookkeeping, or billing differences or other losses attributable to accounting procedures. The policy also excludes losses "due to alterations, falsifications, manipulations, concealment, discrepancies, or disposal of records of accounts receivable committed to conceal the wrongful giving, taking, obtaining, or withholding of money, securities, or other property, but only to the extent of such wrongful giving, taking, or withholding." Losses due to electronic or magnetic injury, disturbance, or erasure of electronic recordings are not covered unless caused by lightning. Inherent hazards in the equipment are not considered as insurable under the accounts-receivable policy.

Both policies exclude fidelity loss attributable to fraudulent or criminal acts of any insured or any such act committed in collusion with an insured or a partner or officer of the named insured if a corporation or copartnership. The usual war damage and nuclear radiation or radioactive contamination exclusion appear, as well as the exclusion applying to wear, tear, vermin, or inherent vice. The exclusions, in all, are few in comparison with the broad "all risks" coverage of these policies.

Rain Insurance

It would seem to be a far cry from covering direct loss or damage to property by fire to include insurance for loss of profits due to *rainfall.* However, the extension of the fire insurance contract to include loss or damage growing out of unfavorable weather conditions followed a logical sequence. The first step included fire damage associated with windstorm and earthquake losses, which became logical extensions of fire insurance. With the development of windstorm and earthquake business interruption coverages, indemnity was provided for loss growing out of the interruption of the business rather than for property damage. It was, therefore, but a logical further step to provide indemnity for losses due to the interruption of a business activity when weather is the cause of the loss. The result has been to extend the coverage provided by fire insurance companies to rain insurance which pays for loss incurred as result of rain, hail, snow, or sleet. It indemnifies for: (1) loss of funds advanced for expenses and (2) for loss of income on events when unfavorable weather such as rain, hail, snow, or sleet is the cause of the loss.

Unlike other forms of insurance, rain insurance attaches for a very brief period, usually for only a few hours in a single day. The policy provides that, if rainfall occurs within certain specified hours, the indemnity is payable. There are two types of coverage available. One provides for the measurement of the amount of precipitation, and the findings of an established weather station are usually relied upon for these readings. If, however, there is no such station within a reasonable distance of the event for which coverage is provided, a rain gauge is set up at some convenient location, and the reading is under the supervision of some responsible person agreed upon by the parties. The nonmeasurement contract provides that payment shall be made under the policy if rain in any amount shall fall during the specified hours.

Typical situations when rain insurance can be helpful in providing needed protection are graduation exercises, circuses, baseball and other sports events, and many charity benefit performances.

There are six forms of rain insurance coverage. All of them are strict contracts of indemnity. Each undertakes to pay only for loss sustained. If a certain event is insured against loss due to the fall of rain but there is a full attendance and no loss can be demonstrated, the company is under no liability to make payment. This is an extreme situation, for ordinarily any event insured against loss due to rain would suffer some lessening of income because of rain. The measure of damages is the amount of loss that the rain actually caused. This is determined in different ways for different types of events.

Form A—Income Expectancy. This form, known as the "income expectancy form," covers indoor or outdoor events for which there are certain fixed expenses and the income expectancy may be determined on the basis of the experience of a previous year.

Form B—Abandonment. Form B is written for events that will have to be abandoned or postponed in case of rain.

Form C—Experience. This form is used largely to cover annual events, such as fairs, races, meets, and the like. The policy covers the difference between the gross income received and the anticipated incomes set forth under the terms of the policy.

Form D—Valued. This form, unlike the other rain insurance forms, pays the face amount of the policy in the event of the prescribed amount of rainfall designated in the policy.

Form E—Advance Ticket Sales. There are certain types of events that rely for patronage on an advance sale of tickets. Where the tickets are subject to refund in the event of rain, Form E protects the insured against loss from refunds.

Form F—Advertising Sales. This form is sold only to publishers and provides a specialized type of coverage. It undertakes to reimburse the publisher for refunds for any advertising space sold for a special event under an agreement to make a refund in the event of rain.

To place rainfall insurance, an application for the policy must be made at least seven days before the policy attaches. Local agents are not authorized to bind rainfall insurance without authorization from the home office of the company, and the business is not accepted until the premium has been paid in advance. It is an unusual type of insurance in comparison with more common insurance contracts, but nevertheless an indirect loss coverage which both attracts attention and provides a needed security to the policyholder.

SUMMARY

Insurance for indirect losses is much more important than policyholders realize. Although most property owners recognize the seriousness of fire, windstorm, and other related perils which may cause direct damage or loss to their home and businesses, they often fail to discern the far-reaching indirect consequences of such losses.

The indirect results of property losses are of two general types: those whose costs are related to the time element required for restoration, and those where the extent of loss is not directly affected by the time needed to regain normal use of the property. Insurance for *time element losses* includes the basic *business interruption* contract for payment of lost profits and continuing expenses following damage to property due to such perils as fire, wind, and explosion. The gross earnings form reimburses for these losses, which oftentimes can mean disaster to the financial stability of a business firm. Without proper insurance for business interruption losses, many businesses fail because they rely heavily on continued income and profits to maintain their solvency.

Contingent business interruption insurance is also imperative in cases where direct damage to the property of others may cause substantial indirect loss to a business. Such cases, where a business is dependent upon one or a few market outlets, or sources of product or power supply, are more frequent than might be supposed. *Rents and rental value* insurance are also available where one's property losses result in not only repair or rebuilding costs, but in addition mean the loss of rental income or use of property for a length of time after the damage has occurred. Sometimes *extra-expense* insurance is more appropriate, in cases where the prime concern is in maintaining continuance of service to customers instead of insuring the losses that may result from an interruption of business. *Tuition fees* insurance is a specialized need of colleges and schools.

No time element losses are quite varied in the kinds of insurance they require. *Profits* insurance on goods already manufactured is significant for manufacturers who have sizeable inventory accumulations before delivery to the consumer. *Leasehold* insurance is necessary in situations where the tenant may lose his favorable long-term lease contract as a result of a specified extent of direct damage to a building. Other special contracts are available to policyholders who may suffer indirect losses due to *temperature damage* to perishables; more than proportional loss of value because of damage to one part of a *matched set* of clothing or jewelry; and reduction of collateral security values by financial institutions who find that *errors or omissions* have been made in maintaing proper basic insurance on mortgaged properties. *Depreciation* insurance can be purchased on property to cover the additional loss above actual cash value which often occurs when replacement costs exceed current values. The indirect losses associated with "all-risk" losses of *account-receivable* records and *valuable papers* is protected by contracts written by both property and casualty insurers. And finally, *rain* insurance can protect loss of profits and expenses due to unfavorable weather contingencies.

In all, the wide field of indirect loss insurance is important to both policyholders and insurers for its essential need and potential for supplementing basic property insurance contracts.

FOR REVIEW

1. Why is insurance for indirect losses an important form of insurance protection?
2. B occupies loft space as a tenant in a two-story building. The building is destroyed by fire. What is the liability of the business interruption policy in the event (*a*) the owner decides not to rebuild, (*b*) the owner decides to rebuild a four-story structure, and (*c*) the owner will rebuild, but takes several months to determine exactly what course he will follow?
3. D operates a neighborhood grocery store. His earnings have been fairly stable, gaining about 5 percent a year until last year, when the gain was 15 percent. He attributes this to a new subdivision recently started nearby. He is concerned about forecasting gross earnings for the purpose of his business interruption coverage. Advise him.
4. It is, of course, obvious that indirect losses can be serious. It is a natural tendency for owners of property to insure the physical property and neglect intangibles. Discuss the impact of a failure to insure consequential or indirect losses.
5. X claims the coverage he requires in a business interruption policy is "indemnity for loss of net profits plus fixed expenses." The wording of the policy provides that the insured will "recover the reduction in his gross earnings less any expenses which do not necessarily continue. . ." Reconcile the policy statement with the insured's understanding of the coverage.
6. X, the president of B company, in adjusting a business interruption loss, contends that he is covered under a perdiem form for $200 a day, and therefore insists this is the company's liability. As a company adjuster, what would be your answer?
7. B claims that the gross earnings business interruption contract with 50 percent coinsurance should be purchased only where a relatively short period of business interruption appears likely. He states that it will cover a total cessation of business for six months only. Explain the error in this statement.
8. The A.B.C. Company has a business interruption insurance value of $100,000. This includes annual net profits and expenses. The company carries a business interruption policy for $80,000 on the 80 percent coinsurance form. During the month of February, as a result of fire, the store is closed for 20 business days. It is during a period of slack business, and the loss amounts to $200 per day. How is the loss computed?
9. For the purposes of determining business interruption insurable value, distinguish between gross earnings for a mercantile risk and for a manufacturing risk.
10. B contends that since he does not own the building in which his business is located he does not need business interruption coverage. In the event of a fire or other damage he claims he would move to a new location. Advise him.

11. A store carries a "no-coinsurance earnings" insurance policy for $10,000. Assuming a loss of $5,000 monthly for three months, what is the liability of the company? Why may such a policy be better than the gross earnings form?
12. Show the amount of insurance required under a gross earnings BI form with 50 percent coinsurance based on the following data: (*a*) net sales, $310,000; (*b*) merchandise at beginning of year, $40,000; (*c*) merchandise purchased during year, $150,000; (*d*) merchandise at end of year, $20,000. Assume in your calculations an estimated 15 percent increase in business for the year for which your computations are made over the year for which the data are available.
13. Is BI coverage limited to the fire peril, or may it be extended to include other perils?
14. The C.D.E. Manufacturing Company is operating at a loss and therefore sends its BI policy for cancellation on the ground that there will be no interruption of profits in the event the plant is shut down. Is the reasoning correct?
15. Give several examples of the need for *contingent* business interruption insurance.
16. B is the president of a company engaged in the manufacture of an article enjoying a seasonal sale. He recommends to his board of directors that the anticipated profits to be derived from goods stored in a warehouse be covered by insurance. One of the directors objects to the purchase of the policy on the ground that in the case of a partial loss the profits policy pays a profits loss in proportion to the direct damage loss. He feels that all profits are wiped out if goods are partially destroyed. What is your answer to this objection?
17. B is the trustee of an estate whose beneficiaries are dependent for their income primarily from the rent of a small-business block. How may the trustee assure the beneficiaries a continued income even though the buildings be destroyed?
18. Fire insurance policies written to cover merchandise in packing houses, cold-storage warehouses, markets, and other like institutions, unless specifically endorsed to anticipate the risk of damage by temperature change, may leave the insured in an uncertain position in the event that fire disables the refrigerating apparatus. How is this problem met?
19. Describe a unique feature of each of the following "no time element" coverages for indirect losses:
    a) Rain insurance.
    b) Accounts receivable insurance.
    c) Valuable papers insurance.
    d) Errors and omissions insurance.
    e) Depreciation insurance.

Chapter 12

TRANSPORTATION INSURANCE

THE previous three chapters have discussed the basic fire and allied lines insurance contracts, and insurance for indirect losses. Another important part of property insurance is the very broad field of *transportation insurance,* which is concerned with the perils of property in (or incidental to) transit as opposed to property perils at a generally fixed location.

MAJOR DIVISIONS

Transportation insurance, usually known in the insurance business as *marine* insurance, has two major divisions. The first of these, *ocean marine* insurance, is very ancient in its origin and has to do primarily with the insurance of sea perils. The second division, of comparatively recent origin, is *inland marine* insurance.

Inland marine insurance is not limited, as might be expected, to the risks of lake, river, or other inland waterway transportation, but covers the risks of all transportation on or over land, such as railroad, truck, train, and airplane. Waterborne perils may form part of the risks covered by an inland marine policy when such perils form part of the transportation risk. In the process of development, inland marine insurance has been extended to include a wide range of policy forms that embrace every conceivable method of transportation, outside of those risks that fall definitely within the ocean marine category.

OCEAN MARINE INSURANCE

Scope and Development

Insurance historians tell us that the insurance of ocean marine perils preceded almost all other types of insurance. The earliest of the ocean marine policies insured against the total loss of the vessel. An early step in the evolutionary process placed liability upon the insurance carrier for partial losses growing out of sea perils while an insured shipment was aboard ship, even though the ship itself eventually arrived in port. Shippers also began to discover that, even though they covered their goods while waterborne, damage such as total destruction by fire while they were on the docks at one end of the voyage or the other, could be quite as disastrous as a total loss of the vessel at sea. The first extension of ocean marine coverages, then, was to provide insurance on the cargo while on docks or quays. From this, it was but a step to make the coverage effective at the warehouse of the shipper and terminate at the warehouse of destination. This form of cover was provided by the so-called "warehouse-to-warehouse clause." Thus was ocean marine insurance brought ashore.

The ocean marine business is highly specialized in its operation and is carried on primarily by large insurers. Lloyd's of London is one of the famous insurers of marine perils. Insurance is provided for: (*a*) ships or *hulls,* (*b*) goods or *cargoes,* (*c*) earnings such as *freight,* passage money, commissions, or profit, and (*d*) liability (known as *protection and indemnity*) incurred by the owner, or any party interested in or responsible for insurable property by reason of maritime perils.

Ocean marine contracts are now commonly written to protect merchandise while in transit and include the perils of both land and water conveyances between the warehouse at point of origin and the warehouse at point of destination. Forms have been developed for special commodities. For example, flour and mill products shipped to northern Europe and the United Kingdom may be covered against "all hazards and dangers of transportation," from the time of leaving the mills in the interior of America by any conveyance by land or water, until safely delivered at any point of destination. Cotton is insured under ocean marine contracts during processing in compresses, while being shipped by land by either trucks or railroads, and on steamers until delivered abroad at point of destination. Other products, notably wool, are afforded a similar type of contract. It is the intention of the underwriters to assume particularly the perils of the sea but to extend the coverage so that the owner may know that his insurance is continuous from the time the products leave his hands until delivered into the hands of the consignee. This inclusion of land perils in the ocean marine contract focused attention upon the land transportation hazards, where ocean perils were not a factor.[1]

The Basic Contract

The modern ocean marine policies take their point of departure from the Lloyd's contract adopted in 1779. This form appears in the first schedule of the Marine Insurance Act of 1906, in which Great Britain codified its marine insurance law. It is notable that even here the Lloyd's form is not made mandatory. The perils clause in

[1]The development of insurance for land perils resulted in the establishment of that branch of the business to which is applied the term "inland marine."

Lloyd's marine policy form as it is used today follows the original pattern and reads as follows:

> TOUCHING The adventures and Perils which we the Assurers are contented to bear and do take upon us in this Voyage, they are, of the Seas, Men-of-War, Fire, Enemies, Pirates, Rovers, Thieves, Jettisons, Letters of Mart and Countermart, Surprisals, Takings at Sea, Arrests, Restraints and Detainments of all Kings, Princes and People, of what Nation, Condition, or Quality soever, Barratry of the Master and Mariners, and of all other like Perils, Losses and Misfortunes that have or shall come to the Hurt, Detriment or Damage of the said Goods and Merchandises and Shipe, etc., or any Part thereof.

The foregoing perils clause covers three classes of risk: (*a*) fire, (*b*) perils of the sea, and (*c*) war. In the United States, the Lloyd's policy serves as the general frame around which the various contracts offered by the insurance companies have been built. The value of the ancient phraseology, and the reason for its retention, lies in the fact that in the long period of its use meanings have been definitely settled through the process of litigation. The policies have been enlarged and extended, and many of the clauses that first found their way into the Lloyd's contract as endorsements are now included in the printed forms as permanent parts of the contract. Because of the international nature of marine insurance and because of the exigencies of competition, coverages have assumed a considerable degree of uniformity. In the United States the American Institute of Marine Underwriters has developed a number of standard cargo clauses reflecting the generally accepted practice in the American marine market. These clauses have met with considerable approval on the part of underwriters, brokers, and insureds. The fact remains, however, that in the field of marine insurance there are no standard forms made mandatory by law.

The contract is positive in its nature, stating definitely the perils that the insurance covers. In contrast to the situation in fire insurance, in marine insurance the policy is usually written on a *valued form,* and unless full insurance to value is carried, the insured must contribute to any loss an amount proportionate to the deficiency. In the settlement of a loss under a marine policy, the liability of the insurer is similar to that of an insurer under a fire policy with the *100 percent coinsurance* clause. The principle is so thoroughly understood that it is recognized as established in law and need not be inserted in the policy in the form of a coinsurance clause.

War risks still appear in print in the perils clause of the hull policy, but war perils are excluded by virtue of a clause known as the *free-of-capture and seizure clause* printed into the form. The F.C. & S. clause may be canceled out, and when this is done the perils clause is restored to its complete form and covers war perils.

However, in this country when it is the intent to cover war perils it is the usual practice to write a separate war-risks policy with a perils clause indicating in detail the war perils to be covered and the conditions applicable to this particular contract.

That part of the clause which follows the recitation of fire, war risks, and sea perils which reads *"and of all other like perils, etc.,"* might seem to carry with it the implication that the ocean marine policy is an all-risks agreement. This is not the case. It is held that the clause applies only to perils of the same nature as those previously enumerated. All losses which are the outgrowth of perils described in the policy are covered, but here the extent of the "other perils" clause ends.

The Insurable Interests

As in the case of fire insurance, the insured must have a financial interest in the subject of insurance in order to effect an enforceable contract. This interest must be at risk, and the indemnity for which the insurer is liable is measured by the loss sustained. When valued policies are used, they have the effect of making the agreed valuation binding upon both parties to the insurance. It is not necessary that the insured have an interest equal to the whole value of the subject matter, nor is it necessary that the interest exist when the insurance is effected, but it is absolutely essential that it exist at the time of the loss.

Ocean marine policies have been classified into four groups based upon the interest covered as (1) hulls, (2) cargo, (3) freight, and (4) liability. Policies are also classified as either (1) time or voyage policies or (2) valued or unvalued contracts.

A *voyage* policy covers the subject matter for the voyage named in the policy, while a *time* policy provides coverage for a fixed period of time. Most marine insurance policies are *valued;* that is, the parties agree at the time the insurance is placed upon the value of the thing insured, and this value is set forth in the policy. *Unvalued* policies, rarely used in marine insurance, provide that the value of the thing insured be ascertained following a loss.

Hull. Hull policies cover on the various types of vessels for which marine insurance is written. There are a number of subdivisions in which the policy is adapted to a particular type of risk, such as, for example, ocean steamers, sailing vessels, builders' risks, port risk policies, fleet policies, and the like. Policies may cover the liability risk by incorporating in the form a collision or running-down clause.

Hull policies, in the interest of a lower premium, are written providing for either a deductible average or a minimum franchise form. When the *deductible average* form is used, any sum agreeable to the parties may be written into the contract. It may range from a few hundred dollars to hundreds of thousands, depending upon the risk and the amount of loss the insured is willing to carry. Under deductible average, the deduction is made from any loss. Under the *minimum franchise* form no claim is paid unless the loss reaches a certain limit, but if the loss reaches or exceeds the designated limit, it is paid in full. This is the most frequently used form of deductible. Ordinarily 3 percent is used, but sometimes this is as high as 5 percent. If a larger sum is required to indicate the minimum for which a claim may be made, it is common practice to eliminate percentages and instead to incorporate into the policy a lump-sum figure.

The *builders' risk form* covers the perils peculiar to ship construction. The policy attaches from the laying of the keel and, while usually written for a period of a year, may be written for the estimated period of construction until delivery to the owner. It covers against the perils found in the usual hull contract and covers not only the hull itself but tackle, apparel, engines, boilers, machinery, boats, and all furniture and fixtures as well as all material in the yard, buildings, workshops, or on docks and quays used in the work of construction. The policy covers against fire, and risks of launching may be included if required. General average and salvage charges are covered, together with liability risks assumed under the collision and protection and indemnity clauses. Excluded are claims originating from loss of life and personal injury, whatever the cause, including claims under workmen's compensation and employers' liability acts. The policy does not cover losses originating in strikes, riot, civil commotion, earthquake, or war risks. Consequential damage through delay is not covered, nor is damage to boilers, engines, and material while in transport, except in the port where the construction is taking place.

In the early days of American shipping, a vessel was owned jointly by a group of individuals or by a single individual. With the advent of steamships and the development of large companies to operate fleets of vessels, it was found that insuring the *fleet* under a single coverage had certain advantages. The most important of these was the inclusion of the less desirable and older risks in the policy at an average rate. The poorer vessels, if they were offered individually, might be rejected altogether by the underwriters or accepted only at a very high rate. Ships operated as fleets, and ostensibly owned by one company, are frequently, as a matter of law, separately owned. This individual ownership is effected through the agency of the corporate form of business organization. A corporation is formed to hold each ship in the fleet, and another corporation formed to operate it. This legal device has the effect of limiting liability claims in cases of accident to the single vessel involved and places the other vessels of the fleet beyond the reach of claimants. Fleets organized on this basis call for the *single-vessel* coverage.

Where navigation is seasonal, as in the case of the northern lakes, the vessel is of necessity in commission during only a part of the year. Policies are written, nevertheless, for a period of a year, since fire and other perils are matters of concern whether or not the ship is in commission. The insurer is interested in the location and conditions surrounding the ship during the winter months and incorporates the winter-mooring clause in the policy requiring satisfactory conditions. Likewise, if the vessel be laid up in port during the season open for navigation for a specified consecutive number of days, a return premium is allowed. In the case of yachts operating on the Great Lakes or on the coasts within specified northern limits, it is customary to include in the policy the express warranty that they will be laid up and out of commission during the winter.

Cargo. Cargo policies may be written under a *single risk form* providing insurance for a particular ship, or they may be written under *floating or open forms,* which provide coverage for goods of a certain class up to a certain limit, their values to be declared subsequently. Freight coverage may be included in such policies. If the person shipping a cargo seldom has occasion to make shipments, he secures a single risk policy covering the specific shipment for a particular voyage. On the other hand, the insured who has many shipments in the ordinary course covers them under an open-cargo form. This form automatically covers all the shipments in which the insured may have an insurable interest on and after an effective date.

Open-cargo forms are designed to accommodate exporters or importers who are constantly shipping goods throughout the entire year. It often happens in such cases that goods consigned to them have been shipped prior to their actual receipt of notice, and goods on the dock ready for shipment may be placed aboard ship and under way before notice is in the hands of the owner. To provide the automatic attachment of insurance, open-cargo forms are written on either imports or exports. Under the export form, provision is made for the insured to issue certificates of insurance so that he may be able to furnish without delay evidence of the fact that insurance has been effected. The import policy is sufficiently broad to attach coverage even before the insured knows that the cargo is shipped. From the time it becomes effective the policy attaches on all shipments consigned to the insured, or other parties, if an insurable interest exists in the insured. Shipments insured under open policies covering imports are reported to the company as required in the policy.[2] Individual certificates of insurance are not required, since it is the interest of the insured in shipments consigned to him that is covered.[3] Cargo policies are sometimes written before the insurable interest of the insured attaches. It is essential, however, that the insured be interested in the subject matter insured at the time of the loss. A policy may also be written to cover shipments which the insured is under instructions to insure for the account of others.

Freight. Policies issued to cover freight interests are usually designed to cover hull or cargo interests as well. For example, in the case of hull policies the freight interest is usually included, and in the case of cargo policies the freight is included in the valuation. If a ship undertakes a voyage, and the freight to be earned is not payable until the cargo is delivered, the total loss of the ship will also involve the loss of the freight to be earned on the cargo. Hence, in insuring the hull for a voyage, it is a normal procedure to include the income expected from freight for the voyage. In the case of a cargo shipment, the shipping charges will represent part of the value at the port of destination. Hence, in cargo shipments it is customary to add shipping costs, that is, freight, to the value at the port of embarkation. This form of insurance bears a close resemblance to the purposes of business interruption insurance discussed in Chapter 11.

Liability. Damage to an insured ship as a result of collision constitutes one of the perils covered under the marine policy. The policy without special provision does not cover the liability of the shipowner for damage he may do to the craft with which his ship collided. To cover this liability, the *collision* or *running-down clause* is made a part of the hull policy. In case both vessels in a collision are found to be responsible, liability of each vessel is fixed in proportion to the degree in which each vessel is determined to be at fault. The collision clause is limited to provide indemnity only in

[2]Since the import policy covers automatically all shipments made to the insured, it is not at all unusual to have substantial values at risk before either the insured or the insurance company knows of the shipment. The safe arrival of a shipment does not relieve the insured of the obligation to report the shipment and pay a premium thereon. All shipments are covered from the time the interest of the insured attaches, and in turn he is obligated to pay the agreed premium for all covered shipments.

[3]The difference between the requirements of the exporter and the importer with respect to certificates may be noticed. When financial advances are made upon cargoes in transit, those who become parties to the transaction will require evidence that their interest is protected by insurance. Aside from special policies so written as to be assignable, the need is met by a privilege accorded the insured under the open form of issuing insurance certificates upon forms provided for the purpose. The form indicates the right of the named insured, or his order, to the insurance, and therefore, it is to the holder of the document properly endorsed that the underwriters are liable in case of loss.

the case of liability for physical damage to another vessel and its freight and cargo, including loss of use of the damaged vessel. The clause does not assume liability for damage to cargo in the custody of the insured vessel, or damage to persons, or damage to docks, piers, breakwaters, and the like.

A problem early presented itself in providing collision insurance for fleets under a common ownership. It is a basic principle of liability law that an owner cannot recover damages in the case of a collision of two ships owned by himself, since he cannot sue himself as a wrongdoer. Thus there would be no payment under the ordinary collision clause. The situation is covered by the so-called "sister ship clause." This provides that in case of collision between two ships the property of a single shipowner or under the same management, the insured shall have the same rights under the policy as he would were the vessels owned separately.

The exclusions in the collision clause were designed to set limitations upon the extent of the collision liability. The demand, however, presented itself for a more comprehensive coverage, and as a result the collision liability provided in the R.D.C. clause may be augmented by *protection and indemnity insurance.* The coverage is usually provided in a separate policy, though in some instances it is attached to the hull policy by means of an endorsement. It provides a comprehensive liability protection against losses excluded under the hull collision liability.

The collision clause, as originally written, obligated the underwriters to assume only three fourths of the collision liability. Other exclusions, such as liability for loss of life or personal injury and damage to docks, piers, and the like, were excluded and continued to be excluded under the collision clause in the policy. When the R.D.C. clause was written only to cover three fourths of the liability of the vessel owner, efforts were made on the part of owners to share this one-fourth portion of collision liability on a mutual basis. To do this they grouped together in clubs. Vessel owners contributed to the expense of the club and to losses incurred on the basis of tonnage to be protected by the club. While the R.D.C. clause may now be written on a 4/4 basis, the exclusions still in the clause with respect to liability for persons and property leave the vessel owner with a wide area of liability unprotected. With the development of legislation in the nature of the employers' liability, owners became increasingly conscious of the need for insurance protection other than that provided by the R.D.C. clause. When the clubs began to assume liability for personal injury, the basis for P. & I. insurance was laid.[4]

---

[4]The first P. & I. clubs were said to have been organized in England, with others closely following in the Scandinavian countries. During World War I pressure for

The coverage is a highly specialized form of protection. It concerns itself with marine legal liability insurance with respect to vessel operations. The policy "protects" and "indemnifies" the vessel owner with respect to his legal liability as the owner and operator of the insured vessel. The policy covers liability with respect to (*a*) crew members, (*b*) persons other than employees, (*c*) cargo, (*d*) other vessels and fixed objects, and (*e*) miscellaneous claims including liability for customs or other fines or penalties.[5]

Coverage for liability of the insured for personal injury to and death of *crew members* is a source of a large number of claims. This phase of the coverage differs considerably from other liability contracts, since negligence is not necessarily a condition precedent for liability. A seaman who is injured or becomes ill while in the service of a vessel is entitled to wages to the end of the voyage, maintenance, and medical care unless the injury or illness is the result of willful misconduct. If the injury or illness is so severe that the injured seaman must be left in a foreign port the shipowner is obligated to pay cost of transportation to the port where the seaman joined the voyage. If negligence of the vessel is a factor, the seaman may bring suit against his employer.

Liability of the vessel to *persons other than employees* for bodily injury and death is covered. This protection extends to include claims of passengers, stevedores, and any other persons who may be working on the vessel or who may be on board. Claims of persons injured in a collision are also covered.

Any responsibility on the part of the vessel owner for damage to *cargo* carried by it is covered. Cargo damage frequently arises when a ship is not in proper condition to accept it or if it is improperly stowed. There are laws that provide certain immunities with respect to claims for cargo damage, but if damage is attributable to negligence the cargo owner may proceed against the ship and recover his loss. Claims resulting from improper stowage, contamination, unseaworthiness of the vessel, and shortages are all covered.

Damage to *other vessels* for which the insured vessel is liable where actual collision is not a factor is covered. Damage to *fixed objects* such as piers, docks, bridges, and aids to navigation is covered. Damage resulting from collision with a bridge or marine cable

broader liability coverage from the shipowners of the United States resulted in the establishment by American underwriters of P. & I. coverage.

[5]The exclusions in the collision liability clause which the P. & I. policy undertakes to pick up and for which it provides protection appear in the Syndicate hull form in the following terms: "Provided always that this clause shall in no case extend to any sum which the Assured, or the Charterers, or the Surety, may become liable to pay or shall pay for removal of obstructions under statutory powers, for injury to harbors, wharves, piers, stages, structures, or any other objects (excepting other Vessels and property thereon), consequent on such collision, or in respect of the cargo, baggage or engagements of the Insured Vessel, or for loss of life, or personal injury."

may run to very sizable sums. If a negligently operated vessel causes another vessel to run aground or collide with a third vessel, protection and indemnity on the negligent vessel responds for damages.

Liability for *customs*, immigration or other *fines*, or *penalties* for the violation of the law for which the owner, master, or agents of the vessel are liable are covered. If the owner of the vessel suffers a loss due to a deviation for the purpose of landing an injured or sick seaman, the policy covers port charges, insurance, fuel, stores, and provisions consumed as a result of the deviation. Extraordinary expenses incurred as a result of quarantine are covered, as are reasonable expenses in defending claims under the policy.

The protection and indemnity policy contains the same "sister ship clause" found in the running-down clause. Moreover, unlike the usual liability policy, the coverage will pay damages if property belonging to the insured, such as docks and wharves, is damaged. The P. & I. policy is written on a deductible basis with deductibles ranging from $250 to as high as $15,000 or more a claim.

Under the terms of the Longshoremen's and Harbor Workers' Compensation Act,[6] every employer is obliged to secure the payment of compensation either by insurance or by qualifying as a self-insurer for the "disability or death, of an employee resulting from an injury occurring upon the navigable waters of the United States (including any dry dock), if recovery for the liability or death through Workmen's Compensation proceedings may not be validly provided for by state law." This requirement does not extend to include the master or crew of any vessel. Failure to secure payment of compensation carries with it a penalty of fine not more than $1,000 or by imprisonment for not more than a year, or both. The insured's liability for compensation may be endorsed upon the fire and marine policy that has been extended to cover P. & I. risks.

Special Features

Ocean marine contracts are important for several additional clauses and features. A few of these, such as the "implied warranties" and the "Inchmaree clause" are unique. Other features are found in many insurance contracts, but were derived from the ocean marine field. These include the "average" and "memorandum" deductibles, coinsurance, the "sue and labor" clause, and assignment provisions.

Implied Warranties. In dealing with ocean marine insurance it is essential to be familiar with the doctrine of implied warranties. Warranties of this class need not be and seldom are incorporated

[6]Federal Act 808, passed by the Sixty-ninth Congress and approved March 4, 1927.

into the policy for, by law, without any expression on the part of the parties, they are made a part of the agreement. As is the case with all other warranties, strict compliance is necessary, and they form a condition precedent before any obligation exists on the part of the insurer. If the condition be broken at the inception of the risk, there is no contract whatever and the policy is void.

Among the more important of the implied warranties are those that have to do with (*a*) seaworthiness, (*b*) deviation, and (*c*) legality. The insurer has a right to expect that the vessel insured is *seaworthy*. Generally speaking, the ship must be tight; properly equipped to withstand the common dangers to be anticipated; with cargo properly stowed and not in excess of safe carrying capacity; with necessary food, fuel, water, and other stores; with a competent master, officers, and crew; and with a pilot when one is required by law or usage. The *deviation* warranty provides that the vessel insured must not deviate from the proper course of the voyage. It is based upon the reasoning that the insurer is entitled to have sufficient knowledge of the voyage contemplated in order to judge the perils involved. To vary the voyage amounts to a variation of the risk. To comply with the warranty of *legality*, the adventure must be lawful and, so far as it is within the control of the insured, must be carried out in a lawful manner.

Inchmaree Clause. A decision having a lasting influence upon the policy of marine insurance was rendered in the case of the steamer "Inchmaree." A check valve had become closed with salt, with the result that a donkey pump was damaged. Claim was made to the underwriters on the ground that the loss was covered under the "and all other perils, losses, and misfortunes" clause. This was held not to be the case. In appeal it was held that whether due to negligence or accident the loss had not been caused by any of the perils set out in the policy, or other like perils and, therefore, the loss was not covered. To counteract the effect of this decision and to provide indemnity for the insured for damage to the hull or machinery resulting from the negligence of the master or crew, as well as from explosion or latent defects, a machinery clause, more commonly known to insurance underwriters as the "Inchmaree clause," was introduced into hull policies. It is used in hull policies insuring steam vessels or others using machinery.

The purpose of the clause is to place negligence in the list of perils insured against; in other words, to make the insurer liable when negligence is the proximate cause of the loss. To make the situation clear: if, as result of negligence, a member of the crew sets fire to the ship, the policy covers if it insures against the peril of fire. If, however, insufficient fuel is placed aboard a ship and the master is obliged to burn spars and furniture to bring her into port, this is not a fire loss within the terms of the marine policy. Negligence in providing the proper fuel is the proximate cause of the loss, and negligence of this nature is covered under the clause.

Average and Memorandum Clauses. In connection with maritime insurance losses, the term *average* appears frequently. The etymology of the term is not altogether certain, though the contention that it is derived from the French word *avaire* and means "loss" or "damage" is in line with its present-day use. A *general average loss*[7] is one made to fall on all the interests at risk in a given voyage. The term *particular average* is used when the loss is to some part of a risk and is of a nature to carry with it no right of contribution from other interests. The term as used today, though held by some writers to be obviously inaccurate, has by common acceptance come to mean "partial loss."

It was early recognized that, under the broad coverage of the marine contract, insurers would be continually harassed by claims for trifling losses whenever shipments of certain susceptible types of merchandise were covered. As early as 1749, in an effort to solve the problem, a clause was added to the policy in the form of a note or *memorandum clause* designating certain goods upon which the underwriter was relieved of all partial loss. On other goods less susceptible to damage no loss was to be paid unless the damage amounted to a certain percentage of the value. In the early Lloyd's policies the memorandum was attached following the signatures. The clause is now inserted in the body of the contract itself. The list that appears in modern cargo policies has been considerably enlarged. The old terminology continues generally in use, although clauses as used today are by no means uniform.

Under the memorandum clause, which states that a loss must equal a certain percentage of the value before liability exists, the claim is paid in full without deduction once liability is established. The percentage mentioned in the memorandum clause is known as the "average limitation," and it is a "franchise" type of deductible. There is no provision for an average limitation in the event of general average claims. The memorandum clause does not operate if the ship is stranded.

In modern cargo policies, the objective of the memorandum clause is attained by the use of the *free of particular average clauses*. These are closely related to the memorandum clause but differ in that items pertinent to the particular shipment or risk are mentioned rather than a long list designed to forsee every eventuality.

Because the memorandum clause is not sufficiently specific to meet all situations, a F.P.A. clause may be attached to the policy

[7]See examples and further explanation of general average losses in Chapter 5.

definitely effecting more specific limitations. For example, some insurances are issued with the intention that a loss shall be paid only if total. In such an instance, an F.P.A. clause is attached, providing that no partial losses shall be paid.

The following is an example of the clause known as the "free of particular average American conditions" clause (F.P.A.A.C.): "Free of particular average unless caused by the vessel being stranded, sunk, burned, or in collision but including jettison and/or washing overboard irrespective of percentage." The foregoing clause is used particularly when the insurer is willing to issue a policy on a cargo shipped on deck. In the case of underdeck shipments, approved merchandise is ordinarily covered under the following clause: "Free of particular average under 3 percent unless the vessel be stranded, sunk, burned or in collision, each package separately insured." This clause has the effect of relieving the insurer of the burden of paying petty claims, but if the loss to any package equals 3 percent it is paid in full. This second clause follows the "free of particular average English conditions" form (F.P.A.E.C.) and is the one most frequently used. By the terms of the American conditions clause, there is no liability on the part of the insurer for a partial loss unless caused by one of the enumerated accidents. Under the English conditions clause, the underwriters are liable if one of the casualties enumerated happens during the voyage, whether it is or is not actually the cause of the loss.

Coinsurance. In the development of marine insurance, the coverage was expected to equal the full value of the subject of the insurance. When rates were promulgated, it was understood that the amount designated in the policy represented the full value of the risk. Failure to designate full value had no effect upon the insurance in case of total loss, and the full amount of the insurance was paid. In event of partial loss, however, the insurance company was obligated to pay only that portion of the partial loss that the amount of insurance bore to the value of the risk. In other words, it was a 100 percent *coinsurance* clause. To illustrate: If a cargo valued at $50,000 is insured for $25,000 and there is a loss of $10,000, even with $25,000 insurance the full amount of the loss cannot be collected. Since the amount of insurance to value is one half, the amount for which the insurance carrier is liable is likewise one half. It follows, therefore, that in the case of any partial loss, unless full insurance to value is carried, the insured must contribute to any loss an amount proportionate to the deficiency. This principle is thoroughly established in marine insurance and is so universally followed that mention of it in the contract is regarded as unnecessary.

Sue and Labor Clause. A section of the perils clause provides that in case of loss or misfortune the insured or his representatives are both permitted and obligated to take certain designated steps to prevent, limit, or reduce loss. This clause, known as the *sue and labor* clause, not only affords the insured the privilege, without prejudice to his rights, to take such steps as are reasonable to minimize or avert loss but likewise places upon him a definite obligation to do this. The clause is, in fact, an independent contract and operates as a collateral agreement separate and apart from the provision to indemnify for loss or damage from the named perils. Payment made to an insured for expenses incurred under the sue and labor clause are not regarded as a partial loss and, therefore, are not subject to percentage restrictions that may apply to particular average claims. Likewise, it is quite conceivable in the case of a total loss that compensation under the sue and labor clause might sometimes be payable over and above the face of the policy.

To establish a claim under the sue and labor clause the expenditure must have been made to avert a loss for which the underwriters would be liable. The steps taken must be the act of the insured or his agents, and must definitely be in order to save the ship or goods insured from damage by the perils insured against in the policy. It has been held, for instance, that money expended to defend a collision suit when collision was covered by the policy does not come within the scope of the clause. Salvage charges may not be paid by the clause when voluntary salvors act to save the insured property. If the salvors act under contract with the insured, the situation is different, and the charge is a proper one.

Assignment. Marine policies are assignable unless under the terms of the contract assignment is specifically prohibited. The protection under a marine policy extends in the first instance only to those for whose account the policy was issued. An assignment is without effect because of lack of insurable interest unless the subject matter of the insurance is likewise transferred. The assignment may be clouded with doubt when the interests of the assignee are such as to change materially the character of the risk. This, of course, is not the case if the subject matter of the insurance has been destroyed. If, for example, after a loss covered by the policy the policyholder wishes to assign his right of action to another, he may do so.

Marine cargo insurance policies are drawn in such a manner as to permit assignment before a loss and without the consent of the company. The matter is covered in the policy so that assignment may be made without question by writing the insurance "on account of whom it may concern." In the case of hull policies, insurers, foreseeing the importance of moral hazard, have definitely settled the question of assignment by incorporating in the policy a clause making the policy void if assigned without their consent.

Other special features of ocean marine contracts, such as war risks and express warranties, are presented in Appendix F, "Other Special Features of Marine Insurance Contracts."

Rates

Ocean marine insurance has long been written on the basis of judgment rates quoted by underwriters after an appraisal of the entire risk. As in other fields, statistical data are accumulated. However, because the perils covered under a marine policy and the perils of each particular voyage tend to differ in so many respects, it is not easy to determine a rate that may be promulgated and generally applied. Even in the case of ships that are nearly identical in construction and follow similar courses, differences in management, upkeep, and policies of operation could easily have the effect of requiring entirely different rates. Ships sailing over an identical course present different risks in summer from those in winter. In some seasons cyclones may create a hazard, and in other areas there is a seasonal hazard created by icebergs. Entirely aside from the season, there are hazards to navigation that attach to particular voyages, such as, for example, fogs, shoals, inadequate aids to navigation, tides and currents. In some areas inadequate anchorages create special hazards, as do unprotected harbors and dangerous approaches. Vessel construction is also a consideration, not only in the rate charged for the vessel itself, but as well in the rates for cargo transported in the vessel.

After all the physical factors applying to the ship itself and the condition of the voyage have been taken into consideration, weight is given to such factors as the nationality of the vessel, the reputation of the owners, the conditions of the coverage, and the effect of trade customs. In no other branch of the insurance business is judgment so important a factor.

For convenience, marine insurance underwriters promulgate advisory rates for certain types of shipments. It is customary to quote rates for cargo shipments made upon approved ships. These rates cover the shipment against perils of the sea while it is waterborne and cover as well (*a*) rail and local truck risk to or from interior places in the United States, (*b*) rail and local truck risk to or from the ports and interior places rated, and (*c*) customary incidental lighterage risk to or from the ship at the seaport.

In the case of a policy producing a sizable volume of business, the underwriter would probably be willing to quote a rate lower than those suggested in the published manuals. Conversely, a policy on susceptible merchandise, regardless of the volume of premium, might require rates higher than those quoted. Again, the reputation of the shippers, their experience record, and the classification of the ship would operate to modify the suggested rates.

Unlike other forms of insurance written in this country, the ocean marine insurance market tends to be international in its scope. American insurance underwriters in quoting rates and soliciting business must be in a position to meet competition from abroad. This they have always been able to do, to the end that ocean marine insurance forms a large and important branch of the insurance business of the United States.

Vessel construction is an important factor in ocean marine rate making. Data bearing upon the construction and type of a vessel are assembled by *classification societies* and made available to insurance underwriters through periodic publications known as "classification registers." Two of the most widely known of the classification registers are *The Record* published by the American Bureau of Shipping and *Lloyd's Register of British and Foreign Shipping.* From the registers are to be obtained the nationality of the vessel, the number of decks and their condition, the condition of the rigging, pertinent information touching upon the engine and boiler, as well as the equipment of the vessel, together with the port and date of last survey. The classifications regarding seaworthiness are based upon exhaustive data bearing upon construction, period of elapsed service, and other pertinent characteristics.

The rules of classification societies are accepted as standards for the construction of ships and their machinery. Because of the international character of shipping and marine insurance, international agreements have been effected on fundamental principles governing safety regulations. These agreements provide for the mutual acceptance of technical standards, but the details of administration of the standards remain with the various societies.

Pleasure Craft Insurance

The number of ships engaged in commerce is small, compared with the number of motorboats and yachts owned privately and used solely for pleasure purposes. Marine insurance is written on private yachts and motorboats in a special broad form policy designed to meet the insurance needs of the owners of such craft.

For a term of one year, time policies are written covering hull, spars, sails, materials, fittings, boats, furniture, provisions, stores, machinery, and boilers. If new, boats are valued at their purchase price; if secondhand, at cost, plus improvements. The policy is valued, and full insurance to value is required.

The policy covers damage to the insured vessel caused by perils of the sea and other waters described, fire and other perils usually found in the marine policy, including general average and salvage charges. The Inchmaree clause and the collision clause are made a part of the policy. Exclusions include: pilferage; war risks; strikes; riots and civil commotions; loss on account of any illicit trade; damage to sails, spars, or masts sustained while racing; loss of tender while in tow; liability for personal injury and for damage to docks, buoys, and other property not included in the coverage of the collision clause. Partial losses are covered in full if equal to the franchise expressed in the policy, which is usually 1 percent; and, when repairs are necessitated, no deduction is required "new for old."

Certain cruising limits are designated in the policy, and to leave these limits without consent of the insurer constitutes a deviation and voids the policy. Forms usually provide for automatic reinstatement if the insured vessel returns to the cruising limits undamaged. If furniture, tackle, or other property of the vessel is stowed ashore, apart from the vessel itself, the property is covered against fire only, and the amount applying on the property is deducted from the amount covering the yacht and property on board. On the values thus covered ashore, a limit is usually set at 10 percent of the insured value of the vessel.

In order to secure more adequate protection than is afforded by the collision clause, the yacht owner may have his policy endorsed with a protection and indemnity rider, of which two forms are usually written. The one form includes liability for loss of life and personal injury, while the other covers only property damage. The customary coverage is the same as the amount insured on the hull, with a specified limit for each individual claim for personal injury. Larger amounts of insurance than a limit set by the hull value are obtainable, and often advisable for pleasure craft owners.

INLAND MARINE INSURANCE

Inland marine insurance is much more recent in its origins than ocean marine contracts. The impetus appeared in the railroad age and grew rapidly during the automobile and airplane eras to create the need for inland marine insurance coverages.

The Need

With the development of railroads into great systems representing vast investments, for many years shippers tended to look to them for reimbursement in the event of loss or damage to the goods shipped. The situation was by no means ideal. Railroads regarded themselves as primarily in the transportation business and not the business of insurance. While it may be presumed that it was the intention of the management of railroads to settle equitably all claims for which they were legally liable, questions of fact and of law frequently entailed much litigation and delay. The situation as it existed was aggravated by failure of shippers to understand thoroughly the effect of limitations of liability incorporated in the bills of lading.

Because of these conditions, there developed a growing tendency on the part of shippers to seek transportation insurance from insurance companies. This demand was crystallized at the time of World War I when the government took over the transportation systems of the country. The delays and disputes that had developed prior to the war were brought into sharp focus when it became apparent that the government was a factor in any claim for reimbursement. Rather than be faced with delay and litigation as well as being disturbed by the element of uncertainty, private insurance was sought as a solution of the problem of land transportation risks.

About the same time that the railroad situation was giving stimulus to inland marine insurance the automobile was becoming an increasingly important factor in the transportation system. While the shipper had a reasonable degree of assurance of the financial responsibility of railroads, in many instances he had little or no assurance of the ability of the trucking concern to meet promptly a heavy claim for loss or damage. With the introduction of trucking, a second feature made its appearance. Many times the shipper himself owned the trucks; therefore, unless the contents were insured by a separate carrier, the goods were in transit with no provisions whatever for reimbursement in the event of loss.

To a lesser degree, the airplane exerted its influence. Shipments are now made regularly by airplane; but, in the beginning, shippers were apprehensive lest this method of transportation prove particularly hazardous.

Another important factor in the need for inland marine insurance is the fact that the common carrier is *not* always liable for the loss or damage to the goods owned by the shipper. The common law liability of the carrier has been thus expressed: "The law charges this person thus entrusted to carry goods, against all events, but Acts of God, and of the enemies of the King."[8]

The early common law has been modified in but few respects. A carrier now is still not responsible for a loss occasioned by an "act of God," nor is he held responsible for a loss caused by an order of the public authority or one occasioned by a public enemy. Acts or defaults of the shipper are exempted; and the carrier is not responsible for losses growing out of the inherent vice or nature of the goods. In no instance may a common carrier be freed from liability because of its own negligence.

Because of this stringent liability, shippers have been accustomed to look to the carrier for reimbursement for loss or damage. While

[8] *Coggs* v. *Bernard,* 2 Lord Raymond 909; 1 Smith's Leading Cases 369.

the carrier remains responsible, developments in recent years have tended not to curtail the principle of liability but to limit the amount for which the carrier may be held.

When goods in the hands of a common carrier have reached their destination and have been placed in reasonable safety, the status of the carrier changes to that of a warehouseman.[9] The difference in status becomes apparent when it is recognized that insurance against losses by fire, burglary, or other perils which involve no negligence would afford the shipper no protection if his goods were in the hands of a warehouseman. While in the custody of a carrier, however, the common law liability of the carrier would attach. Thus the status of the protection which the shipper may expect from the carrier can automatically change. Failure to provide adequate protection to meet such situations may entail a serious loss to the shipper.

Up to this point, the discussion of the carrier's liability presupposes the ability of the carrier to settle losses for which it is liable. Because of the size and financial strength of railroads, the question of ability has not been an important factor. With the use of motor trucks as carriers, the owners of the trucks have viewed their liability as a very serious risk indeed. It is conceivable that the destruction of a shipment might entail a loss far in excess of the value of the truck upon which it was being transported. This led to a demand for insurance covering the legal liability of the carrier for damage to shipments entrusted to his care.

With the introduction of policies providing for the legal liability of carriers, it was but a step to provide the same protection for other bailees who had temporary custody of goods for owners. Not all persons operating transportation facilities come within the legal classification of common carriers. Some truckmen who do not operate regularly established routes, or who work primarily for one or two customers, accept goods as a bailee; in this instance, they are liable for negligence and are not, as in the case of a common carrier, insurers of the goods.[10]

---

[9]The laws in all jurisdictions are not the same as to precisely when the change becomes affective. Under the Uniform Storage Tariff, the carrier is obligated to send notices of arrival to the consignee and is liable as a carrier or insurer for 48 hours after the first 7:00 A.M. after notice of arrival has been sent to the consignee. In some states no such notice is required. After the expiration of the period set forth limiting responsibility as a carrier, the carrier then becomes a warehouseman and is liable only for losses growing out of negligence.

[10]Under most bills of lading issued today whether by railroads, truckmen, or railway express agencies, the carrier, whether common carrier or bailee, is not liable for loss or damage caused by "acts of God." It follows, therefore, that a shipper who sends merchandise to a consignee is exposed at his own risk to such irresistible disasters as earthquakes, violent storms, lightning, and unprecedented floods. In addition to this, many carriers exempt themselves under what is known as *released* bills of lading which restrict their liability to a certain dollar amount for loss or damage to property in their custody.

Development of Inland Marine Insurance

Inland marine insurance does not refer only to the insurance of transportation risks on inland waterways. It is, in fact, a comparatively new branch of insurance that developed out of the need for inland transportation insurance involving either land risks or waterborne risks, or both.

When the demand first made its appearance, it was natural that appeal for the coverage should first be made to marine underwriters. These companies were thoroughly conversant with the problems of transportation risks and under the terms of their charters were authorized to write the business. However, as the demand for inland marine coverages developed into a veritable boom, fire and casualty companies were attracted to the business. This, too, was logical. The ocean marine policy required substantial modifications in order to meet the needs of inland perils. Some of the old marine clauses were retained, but there were also incorporated in the policy features to be found in both fire and casualty policies. The risks covered involved not only transportation hazards but so many of the fire and casualty hazards that it was not always easy to determine which were the dominant factors.

Because of the flexibility of the transportation policy, much broader coverages were available under inland marine contracts than could be obtained under the old fire or casualty contracts. The inland marine contracts were particularly desirable when there were concentrated values. In the case of furs, jewelry, art treasures, and the like, instead of insuring the risks against burglary, fire, malicious mischief, earthquake, and other innumerable specific perils, a single policy covering "all risks" had a tremendous appeal. When, as was usually the case, the all-risks policy could be obtained for a cost must less than was required for an accumulation of separate policies, the appeal of the marine policy to the buyer of insurance was natural.

Because of the transition of inland marine insurance from the competitive and flexible ocean marine field, this new form carried with it an adaptability not to be found in the older established fire field. While the fire insurance business was enlarging the scope of its activities to include perils other than fire, as compared to the marine business, the pattern was comparatively rigid. There was little flexibility with respect to policies and forms, and business for the most part was written at rates established by the bureaus.

The competitive spirit and flexibility of inland marine rates and coverages attracted business that seemed normally to belong in the casualty and fire fields. This caused fire insurance underwriters to pause and give serious consideration to the fact that substantial blocks of properties were being written at rates less than the established fire rates. This was accomplished by merging storage risks with transportation risks. A storage risk, before or after shipment, was covered under a transportation policy and frequently at rates less than the fire rate for the location. Competition flared between fire insurance companies and the marine underwriters. In some instances, the fire department of an insurance company found that it was losing lines written at established rates that were turning up in its own marine department at rates less than the promulgated bureau rates.

The first efforts to bring order to the confusion that developed were made by the fire insurance companies. As an initial step, they undertook to provide forms that would parallel the coverage offered by the marine underwriters. They then formed an organization known as the Interstate Underwriters Board which promulgated a definition of marine insurance which became effective in 1929.

About this time the state supervisory authorities began to view the situation with concern. In the spring of 1931 the Superintendent of Insurance of the state of New York called a general meeting of all interested parties. A committee representing all insurance interests undertook to work out a definition of marine insurance. On June 2, 1933, the definition was published and approved with slight modification by the National Association of Insurance Commissioners and by resolution was adopted unanimously as the definition of marine underwriting powers. With some modification the definition as adopted became effective in 36 states and was known as the "Nation-Wide Definition and Interpretation of the Insuring Powers of Marine and Transportation Underwriters."

In June, 1953, the definition was considerably broadened and modified and in its new draft adopted by the N.A.I.C. In its present form the title has been shortened to *The Nation-Wide Definition* and it is divided into two parts. The first part provides the conditions under which marine and transportation policies may cover (*a*) imports; (*b*) exports; (*c*) domestic shipments; (*d*) bridges, tunnels, and other instrumentalities of transportation and communication; and (*e*) personal property floater risks. The second part of the definition is known as the "restrictive section." Originally there were eight kinds of risks which were prohibited unless approved under permissive sections. Under the recent revision of the definition the limitations in the restrictive section are reduced to six, and these concern themselves largely with risks where the element of transportation is ordinarily lacking.

Another step to introduce some stability to the inland marine business and put an end to unregulated competition was the formation of the "Inland Marine Underwriters Association" in 1931. The work of the Inland Marine Underwriters Association was making itself felt through the development of uniform rates, forms, and commissions throughout the industry when the impact on the Southeastern Underwriters case made itself felt. There probably would have been no serious need for any modification of the work of that organization but for the requirement that concerted rate making must now be brought within the purview of state regulations.

The Inland Marine Underwriters Association was reorganized and renamed the Inland Marine Insurance Bureau. It qualified under the new rating laws as a rating body. The I.M.I.B. filed rates and forms, and thus the activities formerly carried on by the I.M.I.B. were made subject to the regulations of the various states. Since the time of its organization, I.M.I.B. rates and forms have set the pattern for a substantial area in the field of inland marine insurance.

It may be pointed out here that in the transportation field many of the contracts are still unregulated. Truckmen's cargo liability, department store floaters, and other inland marine transportation policies do not lend themselves well to either a rigid form or promulgated rates.[11] There are standardized forms for bridges and tunnels, but no rates have been filed since the characteristics of each particular risk are determining factors with respect to rates. Pipelines and radio and television towers are all written on tailormade forms designed to fit the requirements of the particular risk and the needs of the insured, and there are no rate filings. In the floater field salesmen's samples, contractors' equipment, floaters, installation risks, and fine-arts and rug dealers' policies are still in the unregulated area.

Classes of Inland Marine Insurance

Basically, to be eligible for an inland marine contract, the risk must involve an element of transportation. Either the property is: actually in transit; held by persons (bailees) who are not its owners; at a fixed location, but is an important instrument of transportation; or is a movable type of goods which is often at different locations. Taking the ocean marine contract as the basis transportation policy, inland marine underwriters have incorporated features of the fire and casualty policies to meet the needs of adequate land transportation insurance.

There are four divisions or classes of inland marine insurance. These are: (1) *property in transit,* (2) *bailee liability,* (3) *fixed transportation property,* and (4) *personal* and *commercial floaters.*

Inland marine policies are written both on an all-risks or a named-perils basis. When a policy is written on an *all-risks basis,* it provides

[11]Parcel-post and registered mail policies are exceptions in the transportation field where form and rate filings have been made.

broad automatic coverage of all risks without naming each peril in the contract. The only risks not included are those specifically excluded in the listed exclusions of the policy. All-risks coverage does not necessarily include all losses, however, for some losses are certainties and do not involve risk. There must be a loss attributable to some unpredictability that could not have been foreseen. Thus losses due to innate tendencies to deterioration or wear and tear are not covered.

Policies written on a *named-perils basis* may provide a coverage limited to a few perils, or one that is virtually but not actually all-risks.[12] The extent of the coverage will depend, of course, upon the number of the perils which are specifically listed as being included in the policy coverage. Another name for such a contract is a "specified perils" policy.

The wide variety of inland marine insurance contracts will be apparent as the classes of coverage are discussed. Appendix G offers a detailed list of the prospects for marine and all risks contracts, indicating for over 70 kinds of individuals and businesses the types of insurable property and form of policies recommended. For example, manufacturers are shown as prospects for the following inland marine contracts: trip transit, motor truck cargo, parcel post; and floater policies for neon signs, exhibitions, installations, installment sales, salesmen's samples, patterns, garment contractors, and many others.

Exclusions vary with the type of contract. All contracts follow a general pattern with the addition of exclusions in certain instances where, because of the nature of the property insured, the additional exclusions are necessary to delineate properly the extent of the coverage. In a named-perils policy it is customary to exclude loss by leakage, breakage, marring, scratching, wet or dampness, and like losses unless the loss or damage is a direct result of a peril covered by the contract. In all-risks contracts losses attributable to wear and tear or gradual deterioration are excluded. All policies exclude losses caused by the risks of war as well as losses attributable to any weapon of war employing atomic fission or radioactive force whether in time of peace or war. There is no liability for loss of goods confiscated by any government or public authority nor will the policy extend to cover risks of contraband or illegal transpor-

[12]For example, it is reported that a policy written on the George Washington Memorial Bridge spanning the Hudson River at New York covered against the perils of fire; explosion; collision; lightning, flood, rising water, floating ice, tornado, hurricane, cyclone, windstorm, waterspout, tidal wave, cloudburst, rainstorm, falling meteor, earthquake, or other acts of God; malicious mischief, banditry, sabotage, anarchy, or other acts of violence; strikes, labor disturbances, riots, or other civil commotion; collapse or failure; and seizure or detention, either on account of any illicit or prohibited trade or war.

tation or trade. Even in an all-risks contract certain losses such as breakage of statuary, glassware, bric-a-brac, porcelains, and similar fragile articles unless caused by specifically named perils are excluded. Losses caused by strikes, riots, or civil commotion may be excluded. Finally, it is customary to exclude loss or damage by any process while the property is actually being worked upon, unless the loss can be traced directly to certain perils named in the contract. Reference in every instance should be made to the particular contract to determine the nature of the exclusion with respect to a particular risk. In some instances because of the nature of the property a list of exclusions is long and often technical in application.

A valuable aid to the student of insurance is the understanding that all insurance contracts must have some exclusions. In analyzing any policy, it is most helpful to keep in mind the *general types of exclusions* which he normally may expect to find. These include losses that are: (1) *uninsurable* or *catastrophic*, (2) *usually separately insured* in other contracts, (3) *excessive or unusual*, thus requiring special information, endorsements, and premium charges, (4) *normally expected*, thus not really risks, and (5) *not accidental* in nature.

Property in Transit. The major class of inland marine insurance is protection for property frequently exposed to loss while it is in transportation from one location to another. Several different contracts are available for these risks, including the basic inland transit floater, trip transit policy, processing floater, department store floater, and special forms which insure only one type of transportation, such as express, motor truck, parcel post, registered mail, first-class mail or armored car and messenger shipments.

The *basic inland transit policy* in the insuring clause states briefly that the policy covers for an amount "not exceeding the limit(s) of liability as stipulated in the form or endorsement(s) attached hereto." This is followed by a space on the face of the policy for the attachment of the proper form or endorsement.

The basic inland transit floater policy lists neither perils nor exclusions. These appear in the form or endorsement attached. The policy is designed so that it may be modified to fit the particular needs of the insured. There are standardized forms to cover goods, wares, and merchandise shipped by common carrier. Policies may be issued to cover a single shipment or, as in the case of the open-cargo form, merchants, manufacturers, or others who ship and receive goods continuously may cover all shipments under an open form. In certain instances, policies are prepared for specialized risks, based on the inland transit floater contract.

The form attached to the basic policy lists the perils covered, as well as the exclusions. If there are any features peculiar to the type of risk that make additional conditions necessary, these are made part of the form and are referred to as "special conditions." The more important clauses in the basic policy follow the pattern already noticed in connection with ocean marine insurance. Among these are clauses covering misrepresentation and fraud, machinery, notice of loss, a sue and labor clause, and an average clause. Territorial limits for the coverage are established.

The basic inland marine transit policy contains certain other clauses that parallel to a considerable degree clauses already noticed in connection with fire insurance contracts. It is provided that adjusted claims shall be paid within 60 days, but no loss shall be paid if the insured has collected for the loss from others. Provision is made for the usual appraisal, court suit, and cancellation procedures when they are necessary.

To meet the needs of insureds who are constantly shipping or receiving goods, policies may be issued to cover all their shipments, either incoming or outgoing or both. There are two forms of policy in use. The coverage they afford is the same; the difference is in the manner of computing the premium. An *annual form* requires a deposit premium calculated at agreed rates and based on an estimated valuation of shipments to be covered during the policy period. At the end of the policy term an audit is made of the total value of all the actual shipments, and an additional premium is charged or a return premium paid to the insured. The *open policy* requires not a deposit premium but a monthly report with premiums due and payable when the report is made.

Transportation policies are issued to cover specified risks or may be written "all-risks." The policies differ depending upon the nature of the conveyance as well as the susceptibility to loss of the property being shipped. Coverage may be provided for an insured who ships exclusively by truck, whether his own or public trucks. The policy may be limited by endorsement to trucks owned by the insured or it may cover only public trucks.

Trip-transit certificates are available for single shipments. The policy is issued to cover such shipments as merchandise, household furniture, livestock, and heavy machinery while in transit by freight, express, motor truck, and inland or coastwise steamers. The same perils may be covered as are covered under the annual and open forms. Unless provided by endorsement, the company is not liable for loss caused by theft, robbery, civil commotion, strikes, riots, war, and like perils.

Contracts are from time to time issued covering on unique, unusual, or extremely rare properties that are, in fact, inland marine contracts; but, because of the peculiar features of the risk, they often intrigue the public interest and are regarded as special forms of insurance. The perils covered by the policy and the exclusions incorporated in the document are planned in each instance to meet the requirments of the owner of the particular shipment. Exhibits, films, paintings, valuable stamp collections, and many strange and unusual risks involving transportation hazards have been covered. It would be difficult to draw a line beyond which marine underwriters are unwilling to go in insuring special transportation risks.[13]

The insurance requirements with respect to certain shipments necessitate the use of other special forms adapted both to the nature of the perils to be covered and to the means for effecting the shipment. Certain of these forms have within limits become reasonably standardized. The more usual of these are:

a) "Express Shipments." When confined to express shipments the transit policy covers all risks of fire, lightning, cyclone, tornado, flood, earthquake, landslide, theft, pilferage, short delivery or non-delivery, transportation, and navigation.

b) "Parcel-Post Policy." One of the most widely used of all inland marine coverages, this form insures the safe arrival of merchandise shipped by parcel post, first-class mail, or registered mail.

c) "Registered Mail Policy." This policy covers shipments by registered mail and by express. It is designed for business institutions having large values at risk in the mails or in express shipments. Such values are usually concentrated in currency shipments or shipments of securities.

d) "First-Class Mail Policy." The first-class mail policy provides a broad coverage for securities and detached coupons with the exception of United States government securities or coupons. It provides the same protection for the items covered that the registered mail policy affords, at the same time allowing the insured to utilize a less expensive means of shipment.

---

[13]Insurance of $100,000 was placed on a copy of the Gutenberg Bible that covered while the book was on display at a luncheon in commemoration of the 500th anniversary of printing. It was reported that a policy was issued by Lloyd's in an amount of £ 10,000 (equivalent to $48,000 at the then current exchange) covering on a 1-cent stamp of an early British Guiana issue. The stamp at the time was part of a collection on its way to London to be sold at auction. The entire collection of which the stamp formed a part was said to have been insured for £ 30,000. When the Dionne quintuplets were being filmed for their first feature-length picture, extreme care was taken of the film because any change in the appearance of one of the children might make the retaking of a scene impossible. As a matter of fact, it is reported that during the making of the picture two of the quintuplets cut teeth. Make-up men pointed out that in each case the new tooth radically altered the shape of the babies' mouths as they sometimes appeared in the photographs. Films, as they were taken, were carefully guarded in a steel-lined vault and were insured against earthquake, fire, theft, hurricane, scratches, or mishaps of any sort that could prevent satisfactory development. Another policy is reported covering four million cryptolaemus bugs for $20,000. The insects were imported to destroy the mealy bug which in turn was destroying citrus fruit in this country.

e) "Armored Car and Messenger Insurance." This policy provides much the same protection as that found in the registered mail policy except that it provides insurance for shipments of money, securities, and other valuables made by armored motorcars and messengers.

f) "Processing Floater." There has developed in many lines of business the custom of sending goods and merchandise from the premises of the owner to various locations for processing. This policy covers property such as yarns, cloth, metals, plastics, leather, rubber, paper, glass, foods, and other similar properties when (*a*) the property is owned by the insured and is being processed by others and (*b*) while such property is in transit. Property owned by the insured on the insured's own premises is not covered nor are stocks of merchandise not undergoing processing operations wherever located. The policy is written on a named-perils basis.

g) "Department Store Floater." A special form of transit policy designed to meet the needs of department stores covers incoming and outgoing shipments of goods and merchandise usual to dry goods stores, department stores, or other retail merchants who ship and receive merchandise. The policy covers all risks of loss or damage to the property insured from any internal cause subject to the usual inland marine exclusions.

Bailee Liability. Insurance to meet the needs of persons who have temporary custody of the goods or property of others has resulted in the inland marine field in the development of *bailee liability coverages.*

The term "bailment" pertains solely to personal property. For a bailment to arise, it is necessary that personal property pass temporarily into the possession of a person or persons other than the owner. A bailee may be a carrier, a laundryman, cleaner, dyer, garagekeeper, or other person having possession of goods whose title is in another.

Bailments have been classed as *(a)* exceptional and *(b)* ordinary. In the first category are public carriers and innkeepers, who are subject to exceptional duties and liabilities. Ordinary bailments include business transactions with the element of hiring such as (*a*) hire of services, (*b*) hire of custody, and (*c*) hire of carriage. Examples of these three types are cleaners and dyers, warehousemen and transportation carriers.

In dealing with bailments the degree of care required of the bailee differs. An innkeeper would be expected to handle money in quite a different manner from the way a trucker would be expected to handle a load of coal. What constitutes ordinary diligence in one set of circumstances would be construed as gross negligence in another. In ordinary business contracts, in the absence of special agreement, a bailee is obligated to take ordinary care of the property as a reasonably careful owner of similar goods would exercise with respect to them.[14]

With respect to bailees there are various statutory liabilities that apply in specific cases. Included in the category are carriers, warehousemen, and public garagekeepers, among others. Bailees are invariably liable for negligence. Negligence is defined as "failure to exercise the care that the circumstances justly demand."[15] The negligent performance of a required duty, or failure to perform the duty, will create a legal liability for damages on the part of the bailee. This is a liability imposed by law and not a liability which is the outgrowth of contract.

The first step in providing insurance to protect the bailee is to cover his legal liability for loss. Under such a policy in order to establish a loss, there must be (1) legal liability on the part of the bailee and (2) loss or damage due to a peril covered by the policy. It is obvious that many losses would involve no legal liability, yet the bailee, because of his relationship with his customers, would wish to make good for loss of property while in his custody. There are now three forms of bailee policies written: *(a)* for the sole benefit of the bailor, *(b)* for the sole benefit of the bailee, and *(c)* for the benefit of both. The legal liability type of coverage affords limited protection. It is more usual today and more satisfactory to provide direct damage insurance which pays for damage to the property in the hands of the bailee whether or not there is any element of legal liability.

Many forms of insurance are written that have a bailee interest.[16] There are three such major inland marine forms: (1) motor-truck carriers, (2) bailees' customers, and (3) furriers' customers.

With the recent increases in volume of shipping by truck, legislatures have provided statutory enactments compelling licensed public truckmen to purchase a prescribed minimum coverage for *truckmen's legal liability* for their shipments. The legal liability of a truckman as a carrier may be written under a blanket form or under a gross receipts form on a named-perils basis. Under the

---

[14]*Levine* v. *Wolff*, 78 N.J.L. 306; 73 Alt., 73; *Mortimer v. Otto,* 206 N.Y. 89; 99 N.E. 189.

[15]It has been noticed that a public carrier is not liable for loss or damage to goods due to an act of God. The negligence rule, however, makes such a carrier liable if through the negligence of the carrier the lost or damaged goods was brought within the operation of the destructive forces of the act of God. (*Schwartz* v. *Adsit,* 91 Ill. App. 576).

[16]For example, fire policies frequently contain clauses in the following or similar terms: ". . . his own or held in trust or on commission or sold but not removed." This clause insures the interest of a bailee even in the absence of a lien interest or a liability interest (Edwin W. Patterson, *Essentials of Insurance Law* [New York: McGraw-Hill Book Co., Inc., 1957], p. 127).

blanket form a list is made of the trucks operated by the insured and a limit of liability set for each truck. The premium is computed by applying the rate to the aggregate liability. Under the gross receipts form the rate is applied to the total receipts of the business. This form is considered to have an advantage in that a percentage of every charge goes for insurance and, when the trucks are idle or empty, no insurance costs accrue.

Customers' goods insurance, or *bailees' customers policies,* are written on a named-perils basis and cover direct damage, without regard to legal liability, to goods in the custody or control of the insured for services such as cleaning, repairing, laundering, or the like. While the policy may be adapted to the needs of any business institution there are three forms that have attained wide acceptance: laundries, dyers and cleaners, and rug and carpet cleaners.

Furriers and department stores accepting furs for storage offer as part of their service *furrier's customers insurance* protection on the stored items. The policy is written on a special inland marine form, and insurance certificates are furnished the dealer to issue to customers. The dealer is named in the policy as the insured, and all furs or garments for which certificates have been issued are covered. The coverage is for all risks and provides not only legal liability coverage up to the valuation on the receipt issued to the owners of the furs but also direct loss or damage without regard to legal liability. If the insured elects to purchase the coverage, the policy may be endorsed with the excess legal liability endorsement which covers the insured for any legal liability for which he may be held in excess of the receipt valuations.

Fixed Transportation Property. Bridges, tunnels, and other instrumentalities of transportation and communication are insurable under inland marine forms, although as a matter of actual fact they are fixed property. They are so insured because they are held to be an essential part of the transportation system.

Marine policies must exclude buildings, their furniture, fixtures, fixed contents, and supplies held in storage. Also, marine policies invariably extend to cover more perils than those included in the usual fire policy which may cover fire, tornado, sprinkler leakage, hail, earthquake, explosion, and riot and civil commotion. In order for a risk to qualify for a marine contract, there must definitely be included some additional marine peril such as collapse, collision, or flood. The bridge policy which is written either to cover *(a)* direct damage or *(b)* use and occupancy will indicate the nature of the perils included.

Bridges are owned not only by various governmental units, such as states and their political subdivisions, but also by carriers such as railroads, and not infrequently by companies who have built the bridges and operate them for profit from the tolls. Enormous sums are invested in a single structure and if the bridge represents the major asset of the company, the purchasers of securities are interested in the steps taken to preserve the value of the assets. Likewise, state, county, and municipal authorities, as well as corporation directors, are impressed with the concentration of value in a single risk.

Bridge insurance covers direct loss or damage to the bridge and its approaches "however caused" with a limited number of exceptions. The policy does not usually cover losses caused by or resulting from strikes, lockouts, labor disturbances, riots, civil commotions, sabotage, vandalism, malicious mischief, or the acts of any person or persons taking part in any such occurrence or disorder. The policy, however, may be extended at an additional premium to include these perils. The usual policy does not cover loss arising from any act of government, from the violation of law, or from war risks. The coverage is terminated in the event of a suspension of use of the insured bridge through the operation of any ordinance or law, through injunction or court procedure, cancellation of license, or like cause. Losses occasioned by failure of the insured to maintain the structure properly are excluded, as are losses caused by neglect of the insured to use reasonable means to save and protect the property at or after any disaster covered by the policy. Use and occupancy losses are not covered under the policy, but the coverage may be written to include loss due to the total or partial suspension of use of the bridge caused by the perils insured against.

It has long been recognized that bridges were susceptible to serious damage, but there has been a tendency to regard the possibility of total loss as remote. Examples of actual losses show that serious losses are possible, and that insured amounts should be substantial.[17]

In both use and occupancy and direct property damage insurance, minor losses are excluded. In the use and occupancy policy a defi-

[17]The collapse of the $6,400,000 Narrows Bridge over Puget Sound, November 7, 1940, four months after its completion demonstrated beyond question the very real possibility of heavy losses. The bridge was insured under an all-risks inland marine form and the cover, it is reported, was divided among 22 companies The property damage cover was $5,200,000 and the loss determined to be $4,000,000. The insurers agreed to pay the Washington State Toll Bridge Authority this amount in cash, the state to retain all salvage and to retain interest in the portions of the bridge still standing, such as piers and anchorages. Indicative of the amounts at risk under a bridge policy, insurance on the Tappan Zee Bridge which spans the Hudson River was covered for $62,400,000 direct damage and $6,000,000 business interruption. The policy covered perils of fire, lightning, floods and rising waters, ice, collision, explosion, and other applicable extended coverage perils. Calling for a premium of over $300,000 for three years, the risk was underwritten 50 percent by 46 American companies and 50 percent by underwirters at Lloyd's. A 1964 loss of sizable proportions involved the collapse of a multimillion dollar bridge in South America after a freighter hit the bridge supports.

nite number of days is indicated, and no liability for loss arises unless the period of suspension exceeds the period indicated, and then only for the period in excess. In the direct damage form, the coverage is subject to an agreed deduction, ordinarily not less than $1,000. Unlike the usual marine form, bridge policies are written with an 80 percent coinsurance clause.

A builder's risk form is available to cover structures under construction. The cover includes, in addition to the structure, materials at the site to be used in construction work during the period of actual construction and until the work is completed, accepted by the owners, or until the policy expires.

Next to bridges and tunnels in terms of insurable values, come piers, wharves, docks, and bulkheads. The perils of fire, earthquake, windstorm, and other perils ordinarily included in the fire contract may not be covered. Flood risks, collision, or collapse are insurable under the marine contract. Marine railways and drydocks, however, are insurable against all risks. Water pipelines are insurable, as are oil pipelines and power transmission lines. Radio towers are covered and here the principal peril is collapse. Airway beacons and floodlights are insurable, as are stop-and-go signals. Dams may be insured and the peril here is collapse or damage from ice or debris.

Floaters. In inland marine insurance, the term *floater* is used in the sense that it provides insurance to follow the insured property wherever it may be located, subject always to territorial limits of the contract. Floater policies may be classified as *(a)* personal and *(b)* business.[18] In the personal floater category are to be found the policies covering such items as jewelry, furs, silverware, and works of art. In the business floater category are to be found policies covering contractor's equipment, farm equipment, theatrical property, salesmen's samples, stock floaters which include processing risks, stocks of fine-art dealers, consignment, installation and installment sales floaters.[19]

The basic contract for all floaters is the *Scheduled Property Floater Policy.* It is a very simple policy that states on its face the usual insuring clause indicating that the policy covers "on property described below or in schedule attached." It then states that the policy "is made and accepted subject to the foregoing provisions and

[18]The Nation-Wide Definition separates personal property floaters into two main divisions: (1) policies covering individuals, and (2) policies covering individuals or generally. In the second classification are included policies covering risks on movable property that may belong to an individual but frequently belongs to, or is used by, a business enterprise. Personal property floaters are written to cover not only the interest of the owner but also the interest of a bailee.

[19]One of the best texts available for further reference on the many floater policies is William H. Rodda, *Inland Marine and Transportation Insurance* (Englewood Cliffs, N.J.: Prentice-Hall, Inc., 1958).

stipulations and those hereinafter stated, which are hereby made a part of this policy, together with such other provisions, stipulations and agreements as may be added hereto . . ." With this basic policy the property to be covered may be listed and forms with additional clauses and stipulations attached. The standard clauses that appear in the basic property floater are in many cases repetitions of clauses that have appeared in policies already noticed.

Personal Floaters. Everyone has personal property sometime or another at other than a permanent location. The baggage of a traveler is a pertinent example, as is clothing at a laundry, an overcoat in a checkroom, or equipment used for sports.

Recent developments in the insurance of household contents that provides coverage for a part of the personal effects away from the permanent abode of the insured have tended to minimize the importance of coverage against named perils where the amount at risk is small. However, a number of personal property floaters are available that provide a broader protection or insurance on articles of higher value.

There are a number of important floater policies covering personal effects that are prefixed by the term "personal." The policies are so different and their names are so similar that it is important at the outset to distinguish the different forms. Those most likely to be confused are: *(a)* the Personal Property Floater Form, *(b)* The Personal Effects Floater, and *(c)* the Personal Articles Floater. Closely akin to the foregoing are the Tourist's baggage Form, the Householder's Protective Floater, and the Householder's Floater.

The "Personal Property Floater" is perhaps the most important policy in this group and provides an all-risks coverage for the personal property of the insured, not only while away from his residence but in the residence as well. The policy provides protection for "personal property owned, used or worn by the person in whose name this policy is issued and members of assured's family of the same household, while in all situations, except as hereinafter provided." The policy thus covers virtually every piece of personal property, with only a few exceptions such as boats, automobiles and business property. Unforeseen and unexpected perils are automatically included in the all-risks protection, and only a few perils are excluded, such as breakage of fragile articles, wax, and wear and tear. The importance of this former classic example of all-risks insurance has been decreased in recent years with the availability of similar broad coverage in the Homeowners' Policies (see Chapter 19).

The "Personal Effects Floater" provides all-risks protection for the insured on personal property away from his residence. It is broader than the Tourist's Baggage Policy in that it does not specifically list the personal effects to be covered.

The "Personal Articles Floater" provides all-risks coverage in a single policy for furs, jewelry, cameras, silverware, and other classes of property formerly insured under separate contract.

The "Tourist's Baggage Floater" is a restricted form of the Personal Effects Floater and covers on a named-perils basis certain named articles such as are usually carried by travelers while the property is outside and away from the permanent residence of the insured. The form is seldom used because of the limited coverage provided.

The "Householder's Protective Floater" is a form similar to the Personal Property Floater but written on a named-perils basis. It is designed to provide coverage for lesser values and at a lesser rate than is provided by the Personal Property Floater.

The "Householder's Floater," sometimes known as the "Dwelling and Contents Floater," like the Householder's Protective Floater is designed to meet the needs of insureds who do not have values suffiicent to require a broader policy and who are satisfied with a a named-perils protection at a lesser rate.

It is the intent at this point to distinguish briefly between forms that might easily lead to confusion. The more comprehensive personal property floater is listed here as an inland marine contract, and properly so. However, since the policy covers property located in the permanent residence of the insured, it is not, in the strictest sense, a marine contract. The uniform definition of marine insurance originally excluded the cover, but in a number of states administrative authorities early made an exception permitting it. The insurance had popular appeal and in time the policy was authorized in every state. The revised definition specifically includes in the category of marine insurance the Personal Property Floater as one of the personal property risks covering individuals. Hence the contract continues to be handled as an inland marine coverage.

Inland marine floaters, depending upon the nature of the risk, utilize one of three forms. These are (*a*) blanket, (*b*) scheduled, and *(c)* blanket and scheduled. There are many classes of personal property that involve in the aggregate substantial values but include no single item or items sufficiently valuable or distinctive to require scheduling. Such properties are insured under the *blanket* form. For example, the "Food Freezer Policy" covers the contents of food freezers against loss by spoilage resulting from the mechanical breakdown or failure of outside power on a named-perils basis. Another example, the "Golfer's Equipment Floater," is an all-risks blanket policy.

Scheduled property floaters are used to cover properties involving a number of items each of substantial value. Assuming correct valuation of the scheduled items, the policy provides full insurance to value for each separate item included in the schedule. Such policies may be written on a very broad all-risks basis with the few exclusions that are typical of all inland marine policies. With respect to certain items, the exclusions may vary. Almost any type of floating property may be covered under the form, although for certain classes, such as musical instruments and objects of art, a special policy is used. To be covered under this policy, the property must be carefully scheduled. It must be described in detail sufficient to indicate clearly the item to be covered, and, when more than one item is covered, each must be separately valued. Some of the more usual classes of property for which the coverage is more or less standardized, will be discussed.

The "Musical Instruments Floater" is designed to provide a comprehensive coverage for musical instruments. The coverage is written on a broad all-risks form or on a limited form insuring against loss or damage caused by fire, lightning, cyclone, tornado, flood, theft, and transportation perils. The coverage was originally designed to cover rare and costly instruments owned either by professional concert artists or by private individuals. The business has now extended to cover all types of instruments, whether owned by amateurs or professionals. Miscellaneous equipment used in connection with the instruments, such as music, cases, racks, and the like, may be insured with the 100 percent coinsurance clause and up to 10 percent of the face of the policy. Otherwise, each item must be scheduled and valued.

The "Cameras, Projection Machines, and Equipment Floater" provides an all-risks coverage on cameras, projection machines, and equipment for both professionals and amateurs.

The "Furs and Jewelry Floater" covers individual fur pieces or fur coats and jewelry which belong to the insured, or to members of his family residing permanently with him, on a worldwide basis. The policy covers against all risks. Each piece of fur insured must be specifically scheduled in the policy and carefully valued. When new, the cost price is acceptable as a valuation; otherwise, an appraisal by a reliable furrier is preferable. It is an underwriting practice not to insure furs for an amount greater than their cost. When both furs and jewelry are both insured under a single policy, an advantage is found because, as aggregate values exceed designated limits, the rate on the excess drops. A further reduction in the premium may be obtained if a $50-deductible clause is made a part of the policy.

The "Outboard Motors and Motorboats Floater" covers both the boat and the motor. The boat is covered against direct loss or damage caused by fire, theft of the entire boat, or loss or damage caused by collision with another vessel. The motor is covered separately whether on board or attached to any boat or while ashore, against transportation perils, theft of the entire motor, fire, collision, and marine perils, including loss overboard. In addition to the usual exclusions, the policy is void if the boat is rented, used to carry passengers for hire, or used in illicit trade or in any official race or speed test.

There are certain types of personal property that lend themselves, for the most part, to a combination *blanket and scheduled* form of coverage. Items that have an unusual value may be scheduled, and other items covered on a blanket basis. The Personal Property Floater, the Householder's Protective Floater, and the Dwelling Contents Floater, already noticed, are all examples of scheduled and blanket personal property forms. Another example is the "Fine-Arts Policy." Under this form, the owner of paintings, tapestries, sculpture, and other articles of rarity, historical value, or artistic merit may secure an all-risks coverage. The policy is used in insuring private or public collections of paintings, etchings, pictures, tapestries, valuable rugs, statuary, marbles, bronzes, antique furniture, antique silver, manuscripts, rare porcelains, glass, books, and other valuable items. Special forms adapted to particular needs are available for museums, art galleries, dealers, or other commercial enterprises. A final example is the "Wedding Presents Floater." In order to protect wedding presents, wherever they may be and until permanently located, the Wedding Presents Floater provides a worldwide coverage against all risks. To comply with the Nation-Wide Marine Definition, the policy must be written to expire not over 90 days after the wedding. As in the case of the Silverware Floater, the policy may be written on a scheduled, blanket, or combination basis.

Business Floaters. Property that is frequently moved about in connection with a business or profession may be insured under a business or commercial floater. Some business floaters are prepared as modifications of the transportation policy, while others are written on a form prepared for the particular risk. Some of the more widely used commercial forms will be described.

The "Physicians' and Surgeons' Equipment Floater" is designed to cover professional instruments and equipment used by the insured in the practice of medicine or dentistry. It is an all-risks policy covering in the territorial United States and Canada. It insures instruments and equipment carried by the insured from place to place, and such instruments not customarily carried are excluded from the protection. Office equipment including furniture and fixtures but excluding radium is covered. If there are any unusually valuable instruments they may be scheduled, though for most physicians or surgeons blanket insurance is adequate.

The "Salesmen's Floater policies" insure samples to be transported from place to place for display to prospective customers. There are many classes of samples as there are types of business. Obviously, a case of shoe samples, with only one shoe of a kind, is less of an attraction to thieves than is a case of jewelry. Some samples are shipped by railroad or other transportation company, while others are transported in the automobile of the salesman. Again, extremely valuable items are carried in cases constantly in the care of the salesman or custodian. Salesmen's Floater policies are written under one of three general forms, though any form may be modified within limits to meet a particular need. The forms are referred to as "limited," "broad," and "all-risks."

The "Radium Floater Policy" protects one of the most peculiar types of property ever made the subject of insurance. It is a rare substance, now widely used by the medical profession, particularly in the treatment of cancer. Infinitesimal amounts have a very high value. In spite of the great care exercised in handling so valuable a substance, losses frequently occur. It is to indemnify the owner of radium in the event of its loss from any cause, war risks and gradual deterioration excepted, that the all-risks radium floater is written. Radium covered by the policy must be individually itemized and so described that the insured item can be identified. Blanket insurance covering miscellaneous items is not written. Full coverage insurance equal to 100 percent of the value must be carried; otherwise, the insured becomes a coinsurer for the deficiency.

"Installation Floaters" are written for a number of concerns whose business requires the complete installation of their product in working, or serviceable, order in the premises of the customer before delivery is completed. For example, houses specializing in store fixtures contract to remodel a given location, which may require anything from a new front to interior decoration. Machinery is often delivered installed, as are organs, carillons, many other items. The business at any time will have goods partially installed in numerous locations and in transit. Such risks may be insured against fire and transportation perils, and perils on the premises to which they have been consigned until installation is complete.

The "Conditional Sales Approval Floaters" may be written covering department stores and other businesses against loss of goods sold on the installment plan, loaned, leased, or sent on approval. The development of merchandising has made it a usual practice to send out to prospective customers on approval or for trial such commodities as rugs, refrigerators, television sets, furniture, washing machines, and the like. Sales frequently involve installment payments. The policy covers goods in transit against fire, collision, cyclone, flood, theft, sprinkler leakage, and breakage when the damage exceeds a specified minimum. It covers in buildings, excluding premises owned, rented, leased, or used for storage or exhibition purposes by the insured.

There are six forms of "agricultural machinery equipment and farm animals floaters." These forms all contain the basic conditions of the schedule property floater. Each is designed for a particular class of risk: (*a*) the Mobile Agricultural Equipment Floater, (*b*) the Equipment Dealers' Floater, (*c*) the Livestock Floater, (*d*) the Mobile Agricultural Equipment and Farm Livestock Floater, (*e*) the Monthly Reporting Livestock Floater, and (*f*) the Horse and Wagon Floater. In addition, the conditions of the Scheduled Property Floater have been modified to insure winter range livestock. Some companies also write livestock mortality insurance on valuable animals, chickens, turkeys and other poultry, and dogs or other pets on a named-perils basis.

The business floaters here noted serve only as examples of the many parts of inland marine insurance. Policies are also written on neon signs, theatrical equipment, rolling stock, livestock and farm machinery, contractor's equipment, patents, scientific instruments, mortician's equipment, and the like. An inland marine floater policy may be adapted to almost any conceivable type of risk involving property that is moving from place to place.

A final example of inland marine insurance adaptation in the business area are the *inland marine block policies.* Originally written for jewelers, and said to have originated with the underwriters at Lloyd's of London, inland marine underwriters provide block form policies for jewelers, furriers, camera or musical instrument dealers, construction equipment and agricultural equipment dealers, to mention but a few. The policies are written on an all-risks basis with the list of exclusions tailored to meet the particular class of business to be covered. The insured's goods are covered without limitation as to time on his own premises. This is in contrast to the usual marine contract. In addition, the block policy provides in a single package coverage for: (*a*) goods on premises of others; (*b*) goods in transit, including salesmen's samples; and (*c*) goods of others in the custody of the insured. With the exception of the Jewelers' Block Policy where forms have been standardized, there are variations in the terms of the other forms just noticed. Because the jewelers' form is the oldest and has become standardized, this will be noted as an example of a block policy.

The "Jewelers' Block Policy" is written to provide comprehensive coverage for retail and wholesale jewelers, manufacturing jewelers, watch dealers, pawnbrokers, silverware dealers, and diamond wholesalers. The policy provides an all-risks cover. The exclusions are not, in fact, serious curtailments of the cover but, rather, list perils that are to be specifically insured or perils not ordinarily insurable in any case, such as inherent vice or insufficient or defective packing. There are five specific limitations in the policy with respect to coverage. The limitations apply as follows: (1) to property at the premises named in the policy; (2) to property shipped by first-class registered mail, railway express, or armored-car sevice; (3) to registered air-mail or express shipments in a given day to one recipient at the same address; (4) to property handled by customer parcel delivery service and parcel transportation services; and (5) to property in custody of insured's personnel away from the premises.

The policy covers stock usual to the business of a jeweler against loss or damage "arising from any cause whatsoever" but subject to the exclusions indicated in the contract. In addition to property of the insured himself, the policy provides protection against loss of property owned by customers of the jeweler but entrusted to him for some purpose such as for repair. To this extent the policy provides a bailee's customers' protection. It also covers the insured's liability for property entrusted to him by dealers who are in the jewelry trade. Thus, if the insured during the holiday season has a consignment of diamonds sent him for a period of ten days and, as a result of a fire, they are lost or destroyed, the insured's liability to the lender is covered.

Policies as written generally cover "in or upon any place or premises whatsoever" in the United States and Canada, and while being carried in transit. Conditions and stipulations found in the policy are lengthy and comprehensive. Particular emphasis is given to a number of warranties that appear. The insured is required to keep an accurate inventory in such a manner that the exact amount of loss can be determined. The insured also warrants that he will maintain during the life of the policy protective devices and watchmen's service described in the proposal.

SUMMARY

This chapter presents a survey of the field of transportation insurance. The tremendous scope of ocean and inland marine insurance is readily apparent. Its basic protection is for movable types of property, those properties actually in transit, or special fixed properties closely associated with transportation. The insurance extends, in some cases, to aspects of liability coverage, as well as the basic kinds of direct and indirect losses discussed in previous chapters.

Ocean marine insurance is significant for its historical language, its broad insuring clause and its many special features which have been adapted for other lines of insurance. Coinsurance, valued policies, warranties, deductibles, and many other insurance contract provisions have been derived from ocean marine insurance.

Inland marine insurance concentrates upon, but is not limited to, land transportation perils. The need for this type of insurance grew rapidly in the twentieth century as railroad, automobile, and air transportation developments made the world a place of increasing mobility. The traditional methods of insurance were challenged with extreme competition as insurers adjusted to the changing requirements of protection.

The Nation-Wide Definition helped identify the scope of inland marine insurance to include (1) property in transit, (2) bailee liability, (3) fixed transportation property, and (4) "floater" contracts. The many types of inland marine contracts within these classifications provide policyholders with a wide selection of broad coverages. Considerable flexibility is possible in most of the policies, even though some have become reasonably uniform in their basic provisions. Personal floaters of many kinds are available for individuals who need insurance on valuable types of movable property. Businessmen have many similar floater contracts to insure their varied properties at all locations, under either schedule or blanket forms of coverage. The floater and "block" policies of inland marine insurance have been, undoubtedly, of great importance in the recent development of multiple-line package contracts during the past decade.

FOR REVIEW

1. Why does a businessman need to know about bailments, and how does insurance relate to these situations? What difference does it make whether the bailee is a gratuitous or a paid bailee?
2. Of what importance to a midwest businessman is knowledge about ocean marine insurance? Is there any reason for an individual homeowner to understand ocean marine insurance, too?
3. Is the ocean marine policy a standard contract? Explain your answer.
4. The owner of a cargo of goods expects to get a better price for them in the market to which they are being shipped. If he ships them in the own vessel and insures them, may he, in the event of total loss, collect the cost of the goods to him at the shipping point or the value of the goods at the point of destination?
5. X ships 1,000 typewriters and 500 calculating machines to a branch in South America. During the voyage, because of heavy weather, about half the packing cases are broken and the contents of each severely damaged. X makes a claim under the marine contract for his loss and he is told that because there has been no accident or fortuitous happening, there is no liability on the part of the marine insurance company. The loss, it is claimed, is due to improper crating. Does this conclusion coincide with your understanding of the law? Explain.
6. Importers frequently purchase goods to be shipped them on a C.I.F. (cost, insurance, and freight) basis. By so doing, the goods which they import are insured for the account of the consignee by the shipper. Is such insurance adequate?
7. Briefly explain the importance of the following principles in ocean marine insurance:
   a) Warranties.
   b) Protection and indemnity insurance.
   c) Deductibles.
   d) Assignment.
   e) Coinsurance.

8. A "yacht" includes in its definition any vessel or motorboat used for pleasure purposes. Yacht and motorboat insurance is written under both a marine form and under a form covering the fire risk only. What additional protection is afforded under the marine form for pleasure craft that the fire policy cannot give?
9. *a)* A steamer with her machinery, including a donkey engine, was insured by her owner. The donkey engine was used to pump water into the main boilers. A valve was inadvertently closed and the engine was damaged. The closing of the valve was not the outgrowth of any action of the sea, yet it caused a substantial loss to the owner. Does the marine insurance policy afford protection?
   b) When the *Ellaine* was built, a defective steel frame was cast and put into the vessel. The defect was concealed by the builders through the use of metal and a steel wash. The defect, when discovered by the owners, was reported to the insurer, and a claim for the defect was filed under the Inchmaree clause covering loss or damage "through any latent defect in machinery or hull." Does the clause cover this loss?
10. Why did the need for inland marine insurance develop, and what factors have contributed to the growth of this field of insurance?
11. Why did most states adopt *The Nation-Wide Definition*, and what were its important effects in the insurance business?
12. Classify the basic parts of inland marine insurance and give an example of each type.
13. What *general* types of exclusions should you expect to find in insurance contracts (even in "all-risks" inland marine policies)? Illustrate each general type of exclusion with a specific exclusion found in some inland marine contract.
14. Recent floods in this country have brought forcibly before property owners the danger of damage to property by flood and rising waters. What form of flood insurance may be obtained?
15. X consigned a shipment of goods to an express company with instructions that they be held at the place of destination until called for by the shipper or his agent. The express company held the goods in its warehouse for four months. While the goods were in the warehouse, an unusually heavy rainstorm occurred. Part of the shipment was on the floor of the warehouse. Because of the seepage of water into the building, the goods on the floor were damaged. The express company made every effort to minimize the damage. The damaged goods were removed to another room, dried, and repacked. Advise the express company of its liability.
16. X, a truckman, carries the truckmen's legal liability coverage in the amount of $5,000. While carrying a shipment of oriental rugs, valued at $15,000, his truck overturns and catches fire. He is able to save part of the shipment, and the actual loss is $4,000. What is the collectible amount of insurance?
17. X, an employee of B's hotel, allowed a trunk being transported from the railroad terminal to become wet, destroying $300 worth of clothing. B denies liability on the ground that the truckman was negligent. Is B liable? If so, is the risk insurable?
18. The insurance manager of a large mercantile corporation recently stated that credit sales are growing so tremendously in volume, and so grave is the danger of congestion in values, that an insurance coverage of the risk is necessary. Many customers may not feel that they should be called upon to pay for something which was not fully theirs at the time the loss occurred. What form of coverage will provide adequate insurance, and what type of concerns need it particularly?

19. In a recently reported fire more than 200 bundles and packages of laundry were destroyed. Assuming that the laundry was entirely free of neglect and that there was no liability on the part of the owner of the laundry to make good the loss to the individual customers, is there, nevertheless, an insurable loss to the laundry because of the damage to the packages?
20. The state of Connecticut owns Gilbert Stuart's life-size portrait of George Washington. This work of art has been appraised at $250,000. Would the fine-arts floater policy cover loss to this picture occasioned by the malicious throwing of acids upon it? Explain.
21. What types of business "floater" contracts might a department store consider in its insurance program? Bailee liability contracts? Transit inland marine contracts?

Chapter 13

THE LIABILITY RISK

INDIVIDUALS and businesses are confronted today with a world which places heavy emphasis on legal requirements and rights. Whether one likes it or not, rarely can he ever make important decisions or changes for his family or business without considering its legal implications. A birth, a death, a marriage, a divorce, a purchase of a home, a new employment, a new car, a sales contract, or the formation of a business enterprise—all these actions have significant legal consequences. The liability risk which accompanies these and many other everyday events of our lifetime is the subject of this chapter.

SCOPE OF THE LIABILITY RISK

Because of the prevalence of claims, almost everyone is aware of the liability risk in operating an automobile. The risk, however, also attends every form of human endeavor. Every business or professional activity is to some degree in danger of suffering loss because of liability claims based on negligence. If a negligent act or omission interferes with the rights of any individual, the party responsible for the negligence is liable for damages to the injured party. Entirely aside from the negligence hazard, there is always the danger of alleged negligence which may be damaging to reputation and which may result in expensive litigation.

Then, there may be the breach of liability assumed under a contract, or of an implied warranty. If a buyer makes known the purposes for which goods are required to a seller and relies on the seller's skill or judgment, there may be an implied warranty that the goods are fit for such a purpose.

To meet the legal consequences of negligence, or breach of implied warranty, or expenses of defense if negligence or breach is alleged, the principle of liability insurance has been extended into all fields of personal, business, and professional activity. Liability for loss and damage may arise in manufacturing and construction operations, in the maintenance of property, in the operation or use of property, in the course of rendering professional services, and while engaging in recreational activities, selling or serving goods, and entertaining guests. In fact, in business, recreation, or entertainment, casualties may and do occur giving rise to huge claims.

MAGNITUDE OF THE LIABILITY RISK

The owner of a property knows the limit of direct loss. This limit is the value of the property. Thus, a building that cost $10,000, if completely destroyed, will result in a loss to the owner of $10,000. An automobile that cost $3,000, if stolen and never recovered, represents a loss of no more than $3,000, plus any expenses incurred in an effort at recovery. In the case of liability claims, the limit is not marked by the value of the property involved and, as a matter of fact, may not be fixed with any reasonable certainty. This characteristic is in contrast to the situation in direct property insurance, where the maximum possible loss can be readily determined as the total property value.

Liability claims, therefore, may far exceed the capital invested in an enterprise. More than this, it requires a substantial sum of money to prove there is no liability when a groundless claim is made. If there is liability and the injury is serious, such as one involving permanent disability or the marring of the appearance of an individual, the verdict can be such, in the absence of adequate insurance, to bring financial ruin to an individual or business. The former limits for which liability policies were written are no longer regarded as adequate. Courts are taking judicial notice of dollar depreciation, and verdicts that would have been considered excessive in the past[1] are no longer regarded as sufficient to compensate an injured person for loss sustained as the result of an injury. The decreased value of the dollar has been recognized by appellate courts in refusing to reduce verdicts which formerly might have been considered excessive. Claims running into enormous sums are constantly being paid. The public is becoming liability-minded, and rare indeed is the accident that is not made the basis of a claim for damages. The annual size of liability payments today in the United States has caused William E. Knepper, a past-president of the International Association of Insurance Counsel, to refer to this multibillion dollar cost as "the injury industry."

Liability verdicts today are not only high and thus potentially

---

[1]For example, in 1902 an award of $4,000 was held to be excessive for the loss of a right leg (*Chicago Railroad Company* v. *Jackson,* 55 Ill. 492; 8 Am. Rep. 661). In 1896 a verdict of $1,100 was held adequate for the loss of a right leg to a seven-year-old girl (*Berry* v. *Lake Erie Company,* 72 F. 488); and in 1911 a verdict of $10,000 was reduced to $5,000 in the case where both legs had been amputated (*St. Louis Railroad Company* v. *Hesterly,* 98 Ark. 240; 135 S.W. 874). The records of old files are filed with settlements that come within the $5,000 limit. More recent decisions indicate these limits to be sadly inadequate.

ruinous to financial condition, but they are also extremely variable and unpredictable for an individual or business. Any random sample of newspapers will reveal such headlines as the following: "Man Is Paid $260,000 for Car Accident," "Court Upholds $625,000 Damage Award in Insect Bite Case," "$325,000 for Girl Drowned in Backyard Swim Pool," "$190,000 to Five-Year-Old Boy for Injuries," "$300,000 for Loss of One Eye," "Hardware Store Sued for $2 Million Shopping Center Fire," "Ask Million for Injuries to Girl, 8," and many others. Ten years ago losses were considered very large if they exceeded $50,000 or $100,000.[2] Today numerous examples of $500,000 to $1 million for *one* person's injuries have appeared. For a single accident involving several or more persons, the claims and verdicts skyrocket to millions of dollars.

Contrary to popular notion, the size or location of the state no longer seems to have a bearing on the maximum verdicts handed down by the jury, as is seen in the highest single person awards of New York ($1,000,000), Illinois ($750,000), Oklahoma ($650,000), Ohio ($625,000), Florida ($550,000), and Delaware ($470,000).[3]

High verdicts are by no means limited to automobile accidents, as the above actual newspaper headlines show. On a single day of November, 1963, two losses of obvious sizable liability consequences appeared in the news: "Indiana Skating Rink Coliseum Explosion Involves 68 Persons Dead, 400 Injured"; and "Georgia Factory Explosion Will Cost $2.5 Million."[4]

While it is true that the majority of liability claims are settled or receive verdicts for far less than the original amounts asked in a court suit, it is poor consolation for the individual or business faced with a claim which may spell financial ruin after several years of uncertainty. The trend is significant, too, for the defendant often may be required to pay an award far beyond his expectation of maximum loss at the time when he placed his insurance.

The large claims for liability are not always against big corporations, either, as many examples show. A California housewife was sued in 1962 for over $800,000 of damages to residential homes, on

---

[2]For a long list of awards ranging from tens of thousands to over $100,000, see Melvin M. Belli, "The Adequate Award," reprinted with some additions from the March, 1951, edition of the *California Law Review* in the *Insurance Law Journal,* No. 343 (August, 1951), p. 577. See also "Verdicts or Awards Exceeding $50,000" in *NACCA Law Journal,* Vol. VIII (November, 1951), p. 229, and in Vol. IX (May, 1952), p. 244. The same author has written two sets of books: *Modern Trials* (six volumes, 1954-60, with supplements), and *Modern Damages* (three volumes, 1959-60, with supplements), published in Indianapolis by Bobbs-Merrill Company.

[3]Bernard J. Daenzer, "Higher Verdicts–Higher Limits," *The Weekly Underwriter,* Vol. 189, No. 20 (November 16, 1963), p. 14.

[4]"The Real Why of Insurance," *The National Underwriter,* November 8, 1963, p. 40.

the basis that she was negligent in starting a backyard fire without a fire permit! The variability of liability claims, even for similar type accidents, is self-evident in the following recent contradictory headlines: "Failure to Yell 'Fore' Costs Golfer $25,150," and "Golfer Must Accept Risk of Being Hit."[5]

Direct loss or damage to property destroys values already acquired, but a liability claim may destroy more by obligating the party held responsible for the loss or injury to make payments for years in the *future*. Cases are on record in which individuals who believed themselves to be judgment proof were obliged to readjust their entire standards of living and make weekly payments out of their incomes until judgments were satisfied. Because of the size of awards now being made in damage cases, a court judgment may reach out to take bank deposits, securities, real estate, and, in addition, a part of one's earnings for years to come.

Bankruptcy has sometimes been suggested as a way out for a person without assets and said to be judgment proof. This is not altogether a simple procedure, and the consequences in the way of injury to business reputation and credit standing amount to a lasting injury. Even this process of avoiding a legal obligation is being brought to an end through legislative enactment. In many states failure to satisfy a judgment up to a given amount will deprive a car owner of his right to drive, and in some jurisdictions he faces a possibility of a jail sentence. Travelers familiar with the laws of their own state do not realize that they are subject to the laws of the place where an accident occurs and are not always prepared with adequate liability insurance limits. In addition to involving a driver in a maze of legal difficulties and technicalities while he is distant from home, the difficulty may have legal reverberations in his home state. Where reciprocal agreements exist the failure on the part of the motorists to pay a judgment in a neighboring state may definitely affect his standing at home. For example, when the failure to satisfy a judgment takes with it the right to drive, bankruptcy to wipe out the monetary obligation would not at the same time restore the right to drive.

During recent years, great loss and annoyance have resulted from *fraudulent* claims for alleged injuries. A number of individuals and gangs have been apprehended, but the menace has grown to such proportions that casualty companies have organized central index bureaus in different sections of the country for the filing and tabulating of casualty claims. This system brings to light duplication of claims for the same alleged injury, and the frequency with which the

---

[5]The first headline is from a Columbus, Ohio newspaper; the second from Atlanta, Georgia.

names of doctors and lawyers appear in connection with doubtful claims "spots" them for observation.[6]

Aside from the professional fakers of claims there are the amateurs to be considered. In this group are to be found persons who measure damages, not by the extent of the injury, but by what they can get. When involved in any accident, however slight, they go to bed immediately and experience all kinds of symptoms. These cases stubbornly refuse to yield to the most expert medical treatment until a satisfactory financial adjustment has been effected. The recovery then is phenomenal. Cases of this type, where the injury is slight or frequently where there is no injury, have cost property owners hundreds of thousands of dollars. Every claimant knows that it is expensive to contest a suit and that the defendant, disliking the attendant publicity, prefers a settlement even when he knows he is being held up. Payment of claims of this type, when there is no liability or when claims are in excess of damage, is termed "buying one's peace." Such settlements are not easily affected by one inexperienced in the adjustment of liability claims. A property owner who relies upon himself to evaluate such claims would do better to buy his peace of mind through liability insurance, and then let the insurer use its professional loss adjustment services to minimize the harmful effects of fraudulent claims.

THE BASIS FOR LEGAL LIABILITY

Liability Imposed by Law and Assumed Liability

In contrast to direct damage insurance, which indemnifies the insured when the loss is the result of injury to his own person or property, liability insurance policies cover instead the liability *imposed by law* for damages to others. Liability imposed by law is to be distinguished from assumed liability. *Assumed liability* arises when a party by contract agrees to be responsible for loss or damage whether or not the liability is one imposed by law.

Liability insurance policies undertake basically to pay, on behalf of the insured, all sums which the insured shall become obligated

[6]Faked claims are made in almost every conceivable situation. Sometimes they are made in such a manner as to prompt a quick adjustment to avoid unfavorable publicity. An example in point is the case of the man who often carried a dead mouse in his pocket. Going into a restaurant, he would order a chicken pie. After eating a part of it, at a favorable opportunity he would slip the mouse under the pastry and leave it there until it was well soaked. Watching until a waiter was at hand, he would open the rest of the pie and "discover" the dead mouse presumably cooked therein. To avoid any possible scene, settlements were promptly made.

Another case run to earth by the insurance companies was that of a man who would swallow a nail or a tack in a restaurant and allege it to have been in the food. X-ray pictures would be presented in due course, and damages claimed and paid. His fraud was finally brought to light by the insurance checkup.

to pay by reason of the liability imposed upon him by law. This has, in insurance terminology, sometimes been shortened to the more convenient but inaccurate term "legal liability." All liability which is assumed or imposed by law is "legal," since the rights of the injured party to damages is enforceable in courts of law. Standard liability forms cover only liability imposed by law. In addition, certain contracts include as a matter of practice limited contractual (or assumed) liability coverage. If additional contractual liability is required, this may be included by specific arrangement in the policy contract.

In the direct damage insurance contract there are two parties to the agreement—the insurer and the insured; the insured receives payment from the insurance company to indemnify him for a loss. In the case of liability insurance, the party who is injured or suffers a loss to his property is not the insured and, hence, is not a party to the contract. Because of this, liability insurance has sometimes been termed *third-party insurance*. The term is entirely in order, but in using it one should remember that the third party is not an insured and usually has no right of action against the insurance company.

Liability Insurance Not Accident Insurance

Liability insurance does not undertake to make good the loss or damage caused by the insured. It is not automatic payment for all accidents which cause damage. Rather, it undertakes to defend the insured when claims are made against him and, *if* he is legally liable for the loss or damage, to settle with the claimant on the best terms possible. The liability insurance policy undertakes to make such payments to injured persons, or to the owners of damaged property, as the insured would himself have been obligated to pay because of the liability imposed by law. If investigation indicates no liability, it does not alter matters if the insured feels in a particularly generous frame of mind and wishes a prompt and generous settlement. The insured in justice cannot contend that he is paying a premium for such a settlement. Briefly stated, if there is no negligence on the part of the insured, and hence no legal liability, there is no obligation on the part of the company to make any payment to a claimant. The company, however, is obligated to defend the insured against groundless claims, to bear the expenses thereof, and to make settlements subject to the limits of the policy in the event of unfavorable verdicts.

In cases in which the question of liability is not clear, the insurer may, and frequently does, make a settlement. By so doing, the company saves the expense of litigation, and the insured is spared the inconvenience attendant upon a trial. The option of making such a settlement rests with the insurance company or its representatives.

Implied Warranties

In connection with sales or a contract to sell, the law imposes certain obligations termed *implied warranties.* It is the law in most jurisdictions that where a buyer, expressly or by implications, makes known to the seller the particular purpose for which goods are required, and it appears that the buyer relies on the skill of the seller or his judgment, there is an implied warranty that the goods are reasonably fit for the purpose for which they were sold. This rule applies whether the seller grew or manufactured the goods or whether they were purchased by him from a supplier. Thus, in any situation where a merchant recommends goods to a customer or selects them for him, there is always a possibility that the seller may be held liable for any injury attributable to the goods so recommended or selected.

It may be noted in passing that aside from breach of implied warranty a tort liability may develop in connection with sales. A seller may be held liable on the ground of negligence if the thing sold is imminently dangerous to life or health and owing to negligent manufacture or construction injury follows. Again, liability may follow if such products are supplied to a user without giving proper notice of their dangerous qualities. The dividing line between liability growing out of a breach of implied warranty and liability attributable to negligence is not always clear. The point to be emphasized is that the seller may be held liable for injuries which the product may cause after it leaves his hands.

Legal Wrongs

A claim based upon liability imposed by law develops as the result of the invasion of the rights of others. A legal right is defined as the power of capacity residing in one person of controlling, with the assent and assistance of the state, the action of others. The invasion of such a right is a legal wrong. The wrong may be (*a*) criminal or (*b*) civil. A *criminal wrong* is an injury involving the public at large and is punishable by the state. The action on the part of the state to effect a conviction is termed a "criminal action." *Civil wrongs* fall into one of two classes: (1) torts and (2) breaches of contract. *Torts* are wrongs independent of contract, such, for example, as assault, fraud, libel, slander, and negligence. A *breach of contract* is the unjustifiable refusal or neglect of a party legally bound to perform the duties imposed by contract. While the state takes action with respect to crimes, civil injuries are remedied by court action instituted by the injured party termed a "civil action." The remedy is, in the usual course, the award of damages. The consequences of a crime are not insurable, but the liability for damages growing out of a civil wrong may be covered.

Negligence

Negligence is a tort. Much of the liability imposed by law stems from accidents attributable to negligence. If negligence can be shown to be the proximate cause of an injury to another, the negligent party is liable to the injured party for damages. Negligence is the failure on the part of an individual to exercise the proper degree of care required by circumstances. It may consist in the failure to do what was required under the circumstances, or it may consist in the doing of something that ought not to have been done. Behavior in any circumstances that fails to measure up to that expected of a careful prudent person in like circumstances constitutes negligence. Faulty judgment may result in liability for negligence, even though the motive behind the act was the best.[7]

If the negligent party acts in the capacity of agent or servant of another, the responsibility may attach to the wrongdoer himself, or the principal or master may be held liable. This point is a matter of tremendous importance because it makes the owner or operator of a property liable personally for the torts of those he employs if the tort is committed while the agent or servant is acting within the apparent scope of his authority or engaged in the business entrusted to his care.

Contributory and Comparative Negligence. Except where statutory enactments have modified the rule, anyone who seeks to hold another liable for negligence and who has himself been negligent has no legal basis for his claim. This is due to the common law rule that anyone who is himself so negligent as to contribute to the injuries or damage complained of cannot recover from another for these injuries. Such a person is said to be *contributorily negligent.*

In cases in which contributory negligence is alleged as a basis for denying liability, the claimant frequently advances the plea that the alleged contributory negligence was, in fact, not a proximate cause of the accident and, therefore, did not contribute to the injury. It is contended that, in spite of the alleged contributory negligence of the claimant, had the defendant exercised reasonable care, he could have avoided the accident. As a result of such contentions there has developed a rule known as the "doctrine of last clear chance," which holds that, although the claimant is negligent, liability nevertheless attaches to the defendant if he had a last clear chance to avoid the accident.[8]

---

[7]Reference to the circumstance indicates that the degree of care necessary to escape the charge of negligence varies. For example, a surgeon setting a fractured limb must exercise an entirely different degree of care from that exacted of a tailor fitting a suit of clothing.

[8]The doctrine is said to derive from what attorneys refer to as the "Hobbled-Ass Case" (*Davies* v. *Mann*, 19 Eng. Rul. Cas. 189), decided in England in 1842. In this

Continued on next page.

The old common law doctrine of contributory negligence, in its strict application, does not always produce entirely equitable results. A very slight degree of negligence on the part of an injured person would bar recovery under the strict application of the common law rule. Some states have enacted statutes that provide that contributory negligence shall not bar recovery for damages. Such statutes introduced the idea of *comparative negligence* and provide that contributory negligence shall not bar recovery, but rather that damages shall be diminished by the jury in proportion to the amount of negligence attributable to the person injured or the owner or person in control of the property damaged.[9]

At first glance the idea of having a person, for example, pay 80 percent of the damages in an accident for which he has been held 80 percent negligent, seems to have substantial merit. In the same example, however, the other party would be required to pay 20 percent of the damages to the person who was primarily responsible for the occurrence of the accident. The critics of the comparative negligence law used in some states point out this drawback. Legal authorities also stress other faults in the law: the extreme difficulty or impossibility of charging a jury to define liability with a precise percentage measuring stick, and the noted tendency to increased litigation.[10] For these reasons the contributory negligence rule as reasonably applied in most states seems preferable to most observers as the general rule of negligence.

Presumed Negligence. In order to establish a case, the claimant in ordinary circumstances must show a failure to exercise reasonable

---

case a donkey was left tied in the street in such a way that it interfered with the passing of carriages. The defendant in the case drove his carriage against the donkey and pleaded that the owner of the donkey was contributorily negligent in leaving it so tied. The court held that contributory negligence was no defense unless the donkey being so tied was the immediate cause of the injury. It was pointed out: "Although the ass may have been wrongfully there, still the defendant was bound to go along the road at such a pace as would be likely to prevent mischief."

[9]For example, see the Mississippi Code of 1942, Section 1454. See also Revised Statute of Nebraska, 1943, Section 21-1151 which provides: "In all actions brought to recover damages for injuries to a person or to his property caused by the negligence of another, the fact that the plaintiff may have been guilty of contributory negligence shall not bar a recovery when the contributory negligence of the plaintiff was slight and the negligence of the defendant was gross in comparison, but the contributory negligence of the plaintiff shall be considered by the jury in the mitigation of damages in proportion to the amount of contributory negligence attributable to the plaintiff; and all questions of negligence and contributory negligence shall be for the jury." A handy refernce to these statutes is *Statutes Affecting Liability Insurance* (11th ed.; New York: Association of Casualty and Surety Companies, December, 1963).

[10]Anyone with serious injuries would almost always file a counter suit in a comparative negligence state. Even if the jury decided he was really 99 percent responsible for the accident, 1 percent of a large amount might be enough incentive for such a suit by the guilty party.

care. The burden of the proof, therefore, is on the claimant. In certain cases, however, *presumed negligence* may be imputed from the facts. The legal doctrine which applies—*res ipsa loquitur*, "the thing speaks for itself"—establishes a prima facie case of negligence. If the injury was caused by an inanimate object within the control of the defendant, when common experience has proved that such objects cause injury only when there is negligence, presumed negligence may apply as an exception to the common law rule that a plaintiff must prove the defendant's fault. The doctrine finds its logic from the circumstances that place in the hands of the party controlling the instrumentality causing the injury material facts and evidence bearing upon the accident that the injured party would have no way of knowing.

The doctrine operates when an accident causes an injury: (*a*) if the instrumentality would not normally cause injury without negligence, (*b*) if inspection and use of the instrumentality is within exclusive control of the party to be held liable, and (*c*) if the party to be held liable has superior knowledge of the cause of the accident and the injured party is unable to prove negligence.[11] There must be no contributing negligence and the accident must be of such nature that injury would not ordinarily occur without negligence.[12] The rule applies only when the circumstances attending an accident are such as to justify the conclusion of negligence. The inference of negligence is to be deduced, not from the happening of the accident itself, but from the attending circumstances; and the inference must be the only one that can reasonably be drawn.[13] If a definite cause for the injury can be established, or if it can be shown that the injury probably resulted from an unavoidable cause or was not the result of a defect in the instrumentality causing the injury, or resulted from an act of a third person or from causes due to other than a human agency, the rule does not apply.[14]

---

[11]*McCloskey* v. *Kopler et al.*, 329 Mo. 527; 46 S.W. (2d) 557.

[12]The doctrine arose in old English cases. In these cases all theories of the cause of an accident, other than that of negligence, are logically excluded by the facts themselves. In 1809 a sailor was injured when a crash broke an axle of the stagecoach in which he was riding. He sued and proved the broken axle as well as his injuries by being thrown from the coach. The court held that the evidence established a prima facie case and inquired, "What other evidence can the plaintiff give?" (*Christian* v. *Griggs*, 170 Eng. Rep. 1088). The great Chief Justice Mansfield speaking for the court stated: "In many cases of this sort, it must be equally impossible for the plaintiff to give the evidence required. But when the breaking down or overturning of a coach is proved, negligence on the part of the owner is implied. He always has the means to rebut this presumption, if it be unfounded, and it is now encumbent on the defendant to make out that the damage in this case arose from what the law considers a mere accident."

[13]*Francy* v. *Rutland Railroad Company*, 119 N.E. 86; 22 N.Y. 482.

[14]*Corpus Juris Secundum*, Carriers, Sec. 764 (e); 10 *American Jurisprudence*, Carriers, Sec. 1625.

Liability and Damages

Requisites for Liability. To do a wrong, the act or omission must be *voluntary*. Thus, if a person in the course of saving himself from great danger injures another without intent, there is held to be no voluntary act and hence no liability. On the other hand, it is no defense if the act which injures a party was done without intent to do an injury or if the motive behind the act was good and praiseworthy.

A second requisite for the fixing of liability is found in the rule that the voluntary act of the wrongdoer must have been the *proximate cause* of the injury. To be held a proximate cause there must have been a continuous succession of events from the causal act to the final event causing the injury. If there was an independent and intervening cause, the continuous succession of events was broken. Neither a natural force nor the involuntary act of another is held to be an intervening cause. Thus, a fire negligently ignited and spread by the winds is one continuous succession of events. If a third party, while watching the fire, were deliberately pushed into the flames and injured, there would not be a continuous sequence, and no liability for the injury would attach to the party responsible for the fire.

Kinds of Damages. With respect to negligence the person guilty is liable for damages in such an amount as will reasonably compensate the injured party for (*a*) personal injuries, (*b*) property damage, and (*c*) any other losses for which the negligence is the proximate cause.

In the case of *personal injuries*, damages may be assessed for (*a*) pain and suffering, (*b*) disability whether temporary or permanent, and (*c*) disfigurement.

Compensation for *property damage* is measured by the difference in value of the property before and after injury. While cost of repair and replacement may serve as a measure of damage, this does not always reflect the actual amount of the damage. If the cost to repair the damaged property is in excess of its value, then the measure of damage would be the value of the property immediately before the accident, less the salvage value immediately following the accident. There is no obligation on the part of the person liable for the damage to replace the property in its original condition.

Other losses may also be a part of damages in a liability claim. An injured person may collect for medical and nursing expenses. Loss of income due to inability to work is often a large amount in liability cases. If a wife is injured, the husband may collect for the value of her services as well as for "consortium," the term which the law applies to the companionship of the wife.[15] A parent may

[15]At common law the right to maintain a suit for loss of consortium was limited to the husband (*Koscialak* v. *Portland Railway, Light & Power Company,* 126 S.E. 307;

collect for the loss of services of an injured child and the expenses attendant upon the injury. In the case of death the heirs or next of kin may collect damages for the loss of the life. Some states fix a statutory limit for an instantaneous death; but, if the party retains or regains consciousness after the injury and ultimately dies, the damage for conscious suffering is added to the damage for the death.

Types of Liability Insurance

The damages resulting from legal liability may be insured in several types of liability insurance. Chapter 14 discusses general liability insurance, Chapter 15 workmen's compensation and employers' liability insurance, and Chapter 16 the significant field of automobile liability insurance.

In writing liability coverage insurers separate the property damage from the bodily injury covers. Hence, the liability insurance field is divided into two major classifications: (1) *bodily injury liability insurance* and (2) *property damage liability insurance.* A large number of liability policy forms are offered by insurance companies providing insurance protection against liability growing out of the class of accidents described in each policy. The most recent development in the liability field is a comprehensive policy, designed to include all the known business exposures of the insured, as well as losses that may grow out of unknown and unforeseeable exposures.

Bodily injury liability policies are ordinarily written setting forth a limit applicable to *each person* and a limit applicable to *each accident.* Thus, an automobile bodily injury liability contract may have limits of $10/20,000. This means that in any one accident not more than $10,000 will be paid by the company for the claim of the given individual and not more than $20,000 as the aggregate of all claims for bodily injuries growing out of a single accident. In the case of property damage liability a limit of liability is set applicable to any one accident. Standard limits are usually set at $5,000. The exceptions to this practice are found where an aggregate limit for the policy term is established. Thus, in the case of malpractice liability coverages, a standard limit of $5,000 per claim with a $15,000 aggregate for the policy term is the practice. Finally, policies are written with a limit for each person, another limit for each accident, with an aggregate limit for the policy term. Thus, a products liability contract has standard limits of $5/10/25,000.

---

189 N.C. 120). Until recently the view was rarely questioned. This view found its way into the opinions in most jurisdictions. However, a change in direction in thought on the matter grew out of a suit filed by a wife who was injured in the District of Columbia in 1947 and received compensation under the District of Columbia Workmen's Compensation Act. The Federal District Court dismissed the action; but on appeal the Court of Appeals, in a decision by Justice Bennett Champ Clark, declared that it recognized that a husband is entitled to recover for the loss of his wife's consortium, said the reverse also was true, and authorized the wife to file suit.

Insureds have frequently been instrumental in causing injuries to persons under circumstances in which negligence could not be imputed. In the circumstances, the liability insurance company is obligated to make no payment to the injured party. The situation frequently has become a source of annoyance and embarrassment. This was particularly the case in connection with the ownership of an automobile where the owner felt himself to be morally obligated to make payments to injured passengers. Sometimes misunderstanding developed with respect to the liability of the company. Not infrequently such situations became the occasion of temptation to collusion. The injured passenger, claiming negligence on the part of the insured, has frequently attempted to collect for injuries sustained. Where there is actually no negligence the insured sometimes finds himself in an unhappy position. In order to provide for the payment of medical expenses for injury without liability, that is, where no negligence is involved, liability policies are endorsed to provide medical payments coverage. The protection is not technically liability insurance, but is often an important part of the liability insurance contract.

Liability insurance may also be divided, as in the property insurance field, into direct and indirect types. One type is written to cover the primary or *direct* liability of the insured, and a second type of contract is written on *contingent* liability. Contingent liability insurance covers the insured in cases in which the liability might reasonably be expected to attach to another party directly liable for the accident, but when the insured might still be held indirectly liable. Such a situation might arise in the relationship of contractor and subcontractor. A subcontractor might be liable for an accident, but the injured party, having no knowledge of the relationship, would in such case proceed against the general contractor.

SPECIFIC KINDS OF LIABILITY SITUATIONS

Many kinds of special liability situations exist. The following discussion of some of these important aspects of liability is not complete, but merely illustrative of the wide scope and variety of the liability risk. Many other examples will be found in the important chapters on employers' liability and automobile insurance which follow.

Real Property Ownership

A dangerous or defective condition maintained on a property is termed in law a "nuisance." The owner of a property is responsible for injuries attributable to a nuisance if it can be shown that the dangerous condition was created by him or by his agent or by a former holder of title. In the latter instance the nuisance is presumed to have been adopted if the owner makes no effort to correct it. The same is true of a nuisance known to the owner and created by a stranger. A tenant is responsible for a nuisance created by himself or his agent or one created by the landlord, if the tenant adopts and makes use of it and does not effect a correction.

In the case of property owners, the prudence and diligence required differ with respect to the position occupied by the person entering upon the property. The law divides such persons into three classes: (1) trespassers, (2) licensees, and (3) invitees. One who goes without any right upon the lands of another is a *trespasser.* One who enters upon another's lands with permission expressed or implied is a *licensee.* One who is expressly invited to enter and comes in the interest of the occupier of the property as well as his own is an *invitee.* Milkmen, postmen, and many salesmen fall into this class.

It is held that trespassers take the risk of defects in the premises, whether they be hidden or open, but that trespassers cannot be intentionally injured by a trap or otherwise very dangerous situation. The licensee likewise takes the premises as he finds them, but with this difference: he has the right to expect the occupier of the premises to warn him of any hidden dangers. The invitee, on the other hand, may hold the occupier of the premises liable for any loss or damage caused by a defect which, though unknown to the occupier, is of such a nature that a reasonable and prudent man would have discovered it by exercising reasonable diligence.

Snow and ice on public sidewalks may be the occasion of a liability claim, although not all jurisdictions have the same laws. The general rule holds that the owner of a property is not responsible for injury or damage caused by snow or ice that falls and forms naturally on sidewalks. A duty to correct the situation may arise if the owner of the property through invitation, implied or direct, makes a use of the sidewalks for his own purposes, such as for the convenience of customers or tenants. Municipal codes may require snow or ice removal within specified time periods after its accumulation. If some act of the tenant results in collections of snow or ice in a form other than that which collects naturally and thereby creates a dangerous situation, liability for injury may follow. Ice formed by the natural flow of water over a sidewalk is usually held not to create liability. An overflow from a defective gutter or a drain left in defective condition through neglect will create liability.

When private property is open to the public, the public by implication is invited to use all the facilities generally made available. The owner or tenant is obligated to exercise reasonable care to maintain the property so that it is reasonably safe. He is expected to use reasonable foresight to anticipate any injury that might occur. A landlord is generally held liable, in the case of rented or leased premises, for injuries which occur due to defects on the parts of a property under his control that are used by the public and by tenants in common.

The proprietor of a business or the owner of a property is expected to maintain his property in accordance with standards of construction regarded as generally acceptable for public use. If the design is such that it creates a dangerous condition, the owner or tenant may be held liable for injuries. With respect to stairways, entrances, ramps, and the like, the design should be standard and there should be no dangerous conditions such as an unusual slippery condition, or absence of standard lighting and handrails. When a person has knowledge of the conditions of construction or the existence of any danger and deliberately exposes himself to it, he is presumed to have assumed the risk of injury.

Attractive Nuisance Hazards

There is a line of decisions known as "Turntable Cases." A decision of the Supreme Court of Minnesota, in 1875, held that a boy injured by a railroad turntable was not in a position of a trespasser.[16] It was held that the turntable so strongly attracted young boys that they were induced to play upon it, and, this fact being known to the railroad, it was bound to use ordinary care to protect them from harm.

The original theory held that any person who maintained a nuisance visible from the highway that, because of its nature, attracted and allured children was liable for injury to children playing with or near it. This has since been modified by the decisions so that now the object in question need not be of itself a nuisance, or need it be actually visible from the highway. To constitute an attractive nuisance, it is sufficient if it is attractive to children and dangerous to them. The doctrine of attractive nuisance holds the owner or tenant of a property obligated to exercise reasonable care in the protection of children in cases where they might through attraction be injured.

Objects that might become attractive nuisances are contractors' equipment, such as concrete mixers, cranes, and the like. Ladders on light poles, artificial pools, tramolines, mill property, machinery of any description, power lawn mowers, unlocked automobiles, unguarded hoists, elevators, and scores of other properties may all give rise to liability claims on the attractive nuisance theory.

Liability for Servants and Agents

Aside from the responsibility that attaches to the individual wrongdoer when he acts in the capacity of agent or servant of an-

---

[16] *Keep* v. *Milwaukee and St. Paul Railway Company,* 21 Minn. Rep. 207.

other, the responsibility may also attach to the principal or master. This is predicated upon the legal doctrine *respondeat superior* which holds a master responsible for acts committed by his servants in pursuit of his business. Thus, the principal or master becomes liable to third parties for damage caused by the negligence of an agent or servant, so long as the agent or servant is acting within the scope of his authority or engaged in the business entrusted to his care. The severity of the rule is recognized when it is found to apply, fixing liability upon the master or principal, if the wrongful act committed in the course of employment is contrary to express instructions. For example, if a bank messenger is forbidden by his employer to use his car during business hours and, contrary to orders and in the course of his employment, uses the car and accidentally kills a man, the bank may be held liable for the tort (or wrong) of its servant.[17] It is definitely settled that the principal cannot escape responsibility by showing that the agent acted contrary to his orders; nor can he avoid liability by showing that his agent was doing work other than that which he was instructed to do.[18]

Trustee Liability

There is a legal principle which holds trustees personally liable for injury to third parties based upon some breach of duty. The law reasons that the assets of a trust may not be diverted to the payment of judgments that might otherwise be obtained since to allow such diversion would defeat the purposes of the creator of the trust and might even destroy the trust. Contrary, therefore, to the situation that exists in the case of master and servant, trustees are held personally responsible for damages growing out of injuries caused by their negligence in handling trust property.

The erroneous opinion is sometimes expressed that the "trust fund doctrine" that makes the trust fund immune from claims from dam-

[17]The United States Supreme Court has held: "A master is liable to third persons injured by negligent acts done by his servants in the course of their employment although the master did not authorize or know of the servant's act or neglect, or even if he disapproved or forbade it." *Singer Manufacturing Co.* v. *Rahn,* 132 U.S. 158.

[18]When the injured party seeks to hold the master or principal for the wrongful act of a servant or agent, there are three points to be determined. First, it must be shown that a tort was in fact committed. Second, it must be shown that the wrongdoer was actually a servant or agent. Finally, it must be shown that he was acting within the apparent scope of his authority and in the furtherance of his master's or principal's business when the wrong was committed. For instance, it has been held that, if an employee steps aside from his business, however brief the time, and during this interval wrongs another, there is no responsibility on the part of the employer. The possession of the employer's car or other vehicle is not sufficient to hold the employer liable for the employee's tort, but the employer is not freed from liability if the employee combines his own business with that of his employer. The test of liability is said to be found in the affirmative answer to the question: "Was the servant engaged in the apparent furtherance of his employer's business?"

ages as a result of the negligent acts of trustees relieves the trustee as well. This is not the case. Even though a trustee is not permitted to charge the trust with the consequences of his negligence, a trustee may be required personally to settle for third-party injuries.

Parents' Liability for Children's Acts

A child acting in such circumstances as to constitute himself the agent of his parents is subject to the law of agency and thereby may commit a tort for which his parents are liable. In the relationship between parent and minor child, the law goes one step further. Parents have been held negligent, and therefore liable, when children have been given possession of dangerous instrumentalities. An example would be giving a child a gun or knife with which harm is done to others.

While parents are frequently involved in litigation as the outgrowth of acts of children committed without any apparent malicious intent, the parent is not legally liable for all the acts of his minor children, and the child may himself be liable for his own wrongful acts. It is, therefore, entirely possible that a child be legally liable for, but unable to meet, damages in a situation in which the parent cannot be held liable. There is a difference between the liability of a parent for acts of his minor children and the liability of the children themselves for their own acts. In liability policies in which the contract itself does not extend to cover the liability of children, if the insured wishes the coverage as well as protection for his own liability for their acts, he should have the policy endorsed accordingly.

When a car has been negligently operated by a minor child, parents have been held liable under a legal theory that has come to be known as the "doctrine of the family automobile." The reasoning behind the conclusion that the parent is liable does not in every case follow the same line. Sometimes the conclusion is based upon the doctrine of agency, and sometimes upon the ground of dangerous instrumentality. Again it may be based upon the theory that the car was furnished for the family and that any liability arising from its intended use should attach to its owner.

Liability for Acts of Animals

The keeping of a mischievous animal with knowledge of its propensities to injure or damage is a basis for absolute liability. In this group are to be found pets and other domestic animals. The element of knowledge, to which the law applies the term *scienter*, is essential in the case of animals ordinarily held to be harmless. Scienter means knowledge of the viciousness of the animal or other harmful propensity. Some states have abrogated the rule of scienter by statute with respect to dogs, and in such states the owner is liable for injury notwithstanding a lack of knowledge of vicious propensities. To fix liability upon the owner of a domestic animal, the beast need be neither vicious[19] nor ordinarily classed as dangerous.[20] Wild animals, such as are to be found in a menagerie, are kept at the owner's peril; and the liability is absolute, regardless of diligence or absence of fault.

Products Liability

In virtually every state, on the basis of either the enactment or specific legislation or judicial interpretation, retailers, wholesalers, and manufacturers may be held liable for injury arising out of the use or consumption of merchandise away from the premises of the vendor. The liability for injury frequently arises with respect to food products. There is an equally great hazard with respect to the sale of nonedible merchandise.

Almost every manufacturer or distributor has some products liability exposure. In some cases, the risk is exceptionally high, as for example in the case of the small manufacturer of an essential part for airplanes. An improperly constructed electronic system, or even a simple nut or bolt, could be held responsible for the loss of a $6 million jet aircraft.

Other cases may be less spectacular, but illustrate the widespread nature of products liability risk into areas well beyond the common examples of bad food products. A Rhode Island case in 1960 involved a suit against a fire alarm company for $25,000 when the fire whistle stuck while a home burned! Some of the more famous recent products liability cases have been against drug and chemical firms, such as the Salk polio vaccine multimillion dollar personal injury losses, and a Texas case of over $11 million damages which resulted when a wrong chemical was negligently put into cattle feed.

The broadening of products liability risks is apparent in cases involving everything from automobiles to salmon to hair lotion. Soaps, deodorants, and cigarettes have been claimed to cause injuries and sickness ranging from allergies to fatal diseases such as cancer.[21]

---

[19]In a case decided in the Supreme Court of Vermont, an old man called at a farm house to buy potato seed. A young mastiff ran to meet the visitor and, jumping up, put his paws on the old man's shoulders. The visitor fell and broke his leg. Suit for damages was brought and defended on the ground that the dog was only playful and that the owner could not be liable unless the dog was vicious and he (the owner) had knowledge of the fact. The Court held that it was sufficient to fix liability if the owner knew that the dog was rough at play and might reasonably commit the injury complained of.

[20]In 1962 a California woman asked $25,000 damages from a neighbor for being kicked by a "giant" and "vicious" rabbit in her backyard.

[21]"Products On Trial: Courts Widen Seller's Liability for Damages," *The Wall Street Journal*, August 31, 1960, p. 1.

Liability of Charitable Institutions

There has been a tendency to hold that charitable institutions, including churches, hospitals, orphanages, and other like institutions having a religious or charitable objective, are immune from liability for injuries caused by negligence. While based upon an abundance of legal citations, the theory that charitable organizations are fully immune from the responsibility for the negligence of employees or agents is far from safe.

There is an old doctrine that takes its point of departure from early English law that holds that the rule *respondeat superior* does not apply in the case of injuries occasioned by the negligence of the agents or servants of a charitable organization. The doctrine has been perpetuated by the decisions in a number of states.[22] It is in reliance upon these decisions that the immunity theory is advanced.

The situation is not as simple as this. First of all, the question arises as to whether the institutions actually wish to avoid a moral responsibility. Many institutions, even in the face of the doctrine of immunity, carry liability insurance on the ground that there is a moral obligation to reimburse persons injured through the negligence of their employees. Such policies contain an endorsement that stipulates that the company will not take advantage of the immunity defense without the written consent of the insured.

Entirely aside from the element of moral obligation, however, there is a wide diversity of opinion with respect to the doctrine of immunity and more and more courts are tending to hold charitable institutions responsible for negligence. The decisions range from full immunity to general responsibility.[23]

More important, in jurisdictions where the immunity doctrine has in the past prevailed, changing conditions with respect to the operations, income, property, and ability to meet damage claims has gradually set in a trend from immunity to liability.[24] More recent

[22]In *Fire Insurance Patrol* v. *Boyd* (120 Pa. 624; 15A, 553), the court stated: "This doctrine (that a public charity is bound to apply its funds in furtherence of the charity and not otherwise) is hoary with antiguity and prevails alike in this country and in England as early as the reign of Edward V, and it was announced in the year book of that period."

[23]*McDonald* v. *Massachusetts Gen. Hosp.*, 120 Mass. 432 (1876), the first American decision to adopt the immunity doctrine, relied on an English case without realizing that the English decision had been overruled 10 years earlier. Massachusetts thus established a precedent based on an overruled case followed for years by many other American courts. The early decision in this country has long since ceased to serve as a binding precedent in most jurisdictions. Some judges argue that since the rule has been followed for so many years it is the responsibility of the legislature to change it. These represent the minority.

[24]Charities are now held to be in a much different position than when the liability question was first before the courts. Then they were largely small institutions—many connected with churches—and of limited means. As has been stated: "Today they have become, in many instances, big business, handling large funds, managing and

decisions are tending to reject completely the immunity doctrine; and in some instances the more recent decisions are holding the concept as unsound from the beginning.[25] The current rules in the different jurisdictions fall into three groups: (1) some states extend immunity to all the negligent acts of all a charity's employees, (2) some have a rule of partial or qualified immunity, and (3) some have repudiated the immunity doctrine in its entirety and apply to charities the tort rules that are applied to individuals and corporations. In the circumstances, therefore, because of the erosion that is taking place with respect to the doctrine, it is extremely unwise for any charitable institution to assume on the basis of the old decisions that it is immune from liability for the negligence of its agents or employees.

Government Liability

Stemming from the feudal concept that held to a belief in the divine right of kings, the doctrine of sovereign immunity was borrowed in this country from England. In effect, this doctrine said that "the King can do no wrong," and thus could not be liable to anyone. Federal and state governments and political subdivisions of the state such as counties and towns adopted this immunity from liability for the torts of its officers and agents. Incorporated municipalities for a time did not enjoy this immunity. Over the years the immunity was extended to municipalities but in an effort to curtail it and extend liability the courts developed a distinction between governmental and proprietary activities. The concept still maintains that the sovereign cannot be sued without its consent, and in performing governmental functions the municipality is held to share the sovereign immunity. The difficulty with respect to liability develops in the determination of precisely what constitutes a governmental function.

---

owning large properties and set up by large trusts or foundations. It is idle to argue that donations from them will dry up if the charity is held to respond for its torts the same as other institutions or that the donors are giving the funds or setting up large foundations for charitable purposes with the expectation that the charities they benefit will not be responsible like other institutions for negligent injury. Such charities enjoy endowments and resources beyond anything thought of when the matter of immunity was first being considered." *Foster* v. *Roman Catholic Dioceses of Vermont,* 17 C.C.H., Negligence Cases 858. See also *Administrator* v. *Hospital of St. Vincent de Paul,* 107 S.E. 785.

[25]In *Wendt v. Servite Fathers* (76 N.E. [2d] 342), insurance was carried and the decisions was based upon the fact that in purchasing insurance a fund separate and apart from the trust fund of the eleemosynary institution was established to be used as compensation to any person or persons injured by the insured. The decision briefs a case for the abolition of the immunity rule, but the decision itself hold that, where a charitable institution carries liability insurance, there is liability to the extent of the insurance protection. This has given rise to a new doctrine that a charitable institution waives immunity by carrying liability insurance.

Injury to an individual caused by a municipal officer engaged in a proprietary (profit-making) function is held not to be within the immunity that goes with governmental functions. The question is not at all settled, but with the development of new activities on the part of municipalities, there is a tendency on the part of the courts to regard many of them as outside of governmental functions. Among the activities regarded as proprietary are: the operation and maintenance of utilities such as water works, sewer systems, electric plants, airports, and the like. There is a difference of opinion with respect to street cleaning, garbage collection, and swimming pools, to mention but a few. The line of demarcation between governmental functions and proprietary functions is extremely nebulous, but the distinction is having the effect of extending the liability of states and cities to the end that the area of the operation of the immunity rule is narrowing. In the case of proprietary functions it is the tendency to hold the municipality to the same degree of liability as attaches to private enterprise.

There has also been a tendency to curtail the scope of immunity to governmental functions through legislation. For example, in specific instances states frequently allowed individuals to bring suit as the result of special legislation. In other instances states have set up administrative boards to investigate claims and, following the ordinary rules of liability, recommend legislative action. Other states have passed laws curtailing governmental immunity or eliminating it entirely.[26] The Federal Tort Claims Act makes the federal government liable for injuries to individuals in the same manner and to the same extent as a private individual. As a result of the decisions and legislative enactment, governmental immunity differentiates with the different jurisdictions and where there is a differentiation between governmental functions and proprietary functions there is no clear-cut line of separation.[27] It appears therefore, that there are areas of certainty and more important areas of doubt. The tendency to hold more governmental units responsible for liability is clear, but the differences among various states and other units are still extremely varied.

The question also presents itself as to the personal liability of individuals whose negligence gave rise to the loss or damage. Some courts have held that public policy should in any case prevent a diversion of public funds from public uses to settle private dam-

[26]For example, New York law provides: "The State hereby waives its immunity from liability and action and hereby assumes liability and consents to have the same determined in accordance with the rules of law as applied to actions in the Supreme Court against individuals or corporations, provided the claimant complies with the limitations of this Article." 113 N.Y. Laws 1929, ch. 467.

[27]James Fleming, Jr., "Inroads on Old Torts Concepts," *NACCA Law Journal*, Vol. XIV, p. 226.

ages.[28] Such a holding does not preclude suit against a municipal officer, trustee, or employee individually.[29]

Generally speaking, the liability of public officers for private suit for negligence depends upon their positions and the nature of the act giving rise to the suit. Judges are held to have absolute immunity. In the case of officers holding lower positions, distinctions have been drawn as to the nature of the wrong. For example, there is held to be no liability with respect to the exercise of a purely judicial or discretionary function. In the case of ministerial functions responsibility may attach. Thus, in the case of a discretionary function, a municipal officer may not be held liable if he does not act, but, once he undertakes to act, his status becomes ministerial and there will be responsibility for damages.

Professional Negligence

The treatment of a patient by a medical practitioner (such as a surgeon, physician, or dentist) in a manner contrary to accepted rules or with lack of skill, with injurious results constitutes malpractice. Liability for damages may arise out of error or mistake made in rendering or failing to render professional services or made by any person for whose acts or omissions the practitioner is legally responsible. Liability for personal injury in such instances is known as *professional* or *malpractice* liability.

The doctrines are not limited to the medical fields, and they extend into other professional fields.[30] Accountants, architects, advertisers, attorneys, members of collection agencies, directors of corporations, insurance brokers or agents, public notaries, real estate agents, stock brokers, surveyors, civil engineers, and title abstracters all may be held accountable for their professional errors or mis-

---

[28]*Devers* v. *Scranton,* 308 Pa. 13; 161 Atl. 540; *Taylor* v. *Westerfield,* 233 Ky. 619; 26 S.W. (2d) 557.

[29]Personal liability of members of a school board with respect to school-bus accidents is unsettled. Because of this uncertainty, automobile liability policies are written to cover municipalities, boards, or districts and, without extra charge, may be endorsed to cover the legal liability of individual board members, bus owners when hired busses are used, and their drivers.

While it is accepted that a municipality cannot be sued for damages resulting from accidents caused by fire apparatus, the Supreme Court of Vermont has held that the fireman driving the apparatus does not enjoy the same exemption and must answer for damages when he is at fault. In other cases in which the state could not be held, state officials have been held individually liable.

[30]Numerous articles in recent years stress in further detail the major importance and problems of professional liability. See, for example, in *The Spectator:* "Lawyer Finds Need for Legal Protection" (December, 1959, p. 43), "Crisis in Malpractice Plans" (April, 1960, p. 34), "Trust Officers Need Protection" (July, 1960, p. 48), "Mistakes Happen, So Even Architects Need Liability Plan" (January, 1961, p. 54). Also, looseleaf services such as *Policy, Form and Manual Analysis* of The Rough Notes Company, Indianapolis, Indiana, contain thorough reviews of these malpractice liability needs.

takes. Failure to meet a standard of skill and care generally accepted for any of these professions or occupations, or performing operations in a negligent manner with resulting injury to the client, may obligate the responsible party to defend himself against claims for damages. In contrast to malpractice liability where personal injury gives rise to the damages, liability is the outgrowth of monetary loss.

In the case of the professional man, defense is an important factor. While in other damage cases a settlement to avoid suit where liability is not clear or even is denied may be the most inexpensive and expedient way to handle a claim, the professional man cannot afford to jeopardize his reputation in this manner. He therefore often needs the right to refuse to allow payment for an alleged injury. Not only is he open to claims for damage based upon failure to exercise the standard of care required in the circumstances, but he may become involved in suits for damage occasioned by the acts of professional or technical assistants. Claims are sometimes based upon alleged moral turpitude. Malpractice claims have also been threatened with the aim of eliminating or reducing a fee.

Nonownership Liability

It is in connection with the ownership and operation of automobiles that some of the most perplexing questions of liability are presented. In the absence of specific statutes providing the contrary, it is the rule that, when a car owner lends his automobile (in good mechanical condition) to another who uses the car for his own purposes, the car owner is not usually called upon to pay for damages arising out of the operation of the car. On the other hand, if the operator of the car doing the damage occupies the position of servant or employee of the car owner, the owner of the automobile is held liable.

Thus, a car owner is responsible for the conduct of a chauffeur while on the business of, or engaged in furthering the interests of, his employer. The liability is predicated upon the doctrine *respondeat superior* and applies with respect not only to chauffeurs and other servants driving cars owned by their employers but as well to salesmen, agents, clerks, or other employees who in the course of their employment use *their own cars* in transacting business for their employers. The most difficult problems arise in this last-named situation when an employer is held liable when the car is not owned, leased, or hired by him. For instance, the employee of a laundry or grocery store delivers a package on his way from work riding in his own car; a bank employee or director goes out to inspect property using his own automobile; a collector or subscription solicitor for a newspaper, an employee of a contractor going from one job to another, a salesman, reporter, collector, or scores of others acting in their employers' interest and driving their own automobiles may involve their employers in huge accident claims. The danger is particularly acute in that the employee may have very little resources, while the employer is a logical target at which to aim heavy damage suits.

Other Special Situations

There are many special situations. The operator of a drugstore may incur liability claims, the outgrowth of compounding prescriptions which, in fact, is a form of malpractice liability. He may also incur products liability from dispensing food, soft drinks, medicines packaged under his label, or for the improper maintenance of his store premises. Any person who sells packaged foods may be subject to a liability claim based upon alleged injury from their use.

Owners and occupants of buildings may find themselves responsible for the acts of independent contractors. Property damage liability and personal injury may flow from an explosion. Injury may result from the operation of elevators. The liability for owners of automobiles for accidents is well known. The same liability may develop from accidents caused by motorboats and sailboats. Restaurant owners are liable not only for the maintenance of the premises but, as in the case of drugstores, for the wholesomeness of the food that is served. Private schools and colleges may be held responsible for injuries on their properties. Particularly, this is the case with reference to restaurants, gymnasiums, swimming pools, grandstands, crowded auditoriums, and the like. In some instances the school itself may be liable for accident or injury, and in others liability may attach directly to a teacher[31] or trustee. Injury to others may grow out of participation in sports. Hotels, airports, gasoline dealers, and the owners of parking lots—all have particular problems. In fact, a person may incur liability simply walking along the street, as in the case of a man who is smoking and is jostled into another person, burning that person with a lit cigar. Such a burn, if it were to mar the face of a woman, could result in a very substantial claim, indeed.

There are situations where the relationship between individuals in a transaction is uncertain. In a given situation, if an individual is an employee, one set of rules applies; if he is an independent contractor quite another set applies. In many business relationships there is a considerable area of doubt. If the status is misjudged, a

---

[31]Fortunately, for teachers and colleges the liability is not without some limit. In a 1959 case, the New Jersey supreme court ruled against a Columbia University student who had sued for $8,065 damages, claiming that the college had "failed to teach him wisdom." The judge sagely observed that "wisdom cannot be taught, if in fact it can be defined"!

party to such a transaction may find himself unexpectedly faced with a serious liability claim. Beverage manufacturers, bottlers, refiners, distributors, storekeepers, owners of teams, trucks, and bicycles—all are responsible for any injury that may be caused by their negligence. In every instance the party concerned must exercise such care as a reasonably prudent person would use in the circumstances; and failure to do this, whether deliberate or unintentional, creates a liability for injury and damages if a person or property is injured as a result.

SUMMARY

The *liability* risk pervades every important family or business decision today. Almost everyone recognizes to some extent the potential loss which can result from legal responsibility placed upon a negligent person for the injury done to other persons, or the damage done to property of others. Few persons, however, recognize the full scope and significance of legal liability in our society.

Liability may either be (1) imposed by *law* (2) assumed specifically in a *contract* or (3) implied in a *warranty*. Most liability insurance concerns the first type, although many such insurance policies may also include liability under contract or warranty obligations. Liability insurance is not accident insurance, for payment is made only when a legal wrong has been shown to have caused injury to another.

The types of negligence upon which liability are based vary according to the state laws. Most jurisdictions apply the doctrine of *contributory* negligence, while others use one of *comparative* negligence. Types of liability coverages include *automobile* liability, *employers'* liability, *and* general (or "all others") liability insurance.

Many specific kinds of special circumstances exist which create, as well as vary, the concepts of liability. *Ownership* of property is a common illustration of a situation which causes potential liability to the public for any injuries or damages. *Attractive nuisance* hazards are a particular burden to property owners, causing a high degree of responsibility to children for their injuries. Other important liability obligations are those involving (1) *agents,* (2) *trustees,* (3) *parents,* (4) owners of *animals,* (5) manufacturers and distributors of *products,* (6) *charitable* organizations, (7) *governmental* units, and (8) *professional* persons. *Employers* may even be held liable in cases of *non*ownership, for example, when automobiles of their employees are used for the benefit of the business organization.

The range of liability is so wide as to cause a major problem in determining the best methods of meeting its uncertainties. The penalty of inadequate preparation for treating the perils of liability are severe, as it may encompass the entire financial resources of a family or business.

FOR REVIEW

1. What is the relationship between the doctrine of "negligence" and liability insurance?
2. Why is liability insurance sometimes considered more important than property insurance? Cite several examples, including at least one illustration of the possible effect of an "attractive nuisance" on your property.
3. Distinguish among the basic types of "legal liability" and explain why the differences are important to insurance buyers.
4. What are the basic kinds of liability insurance, and how do these differ from accident insurance?
5. The "comparative," "contributory," and "presumed" negligence rules may each bring about important results to a person who is injured. Give an example of each of these rules, showing its results to the claimant.
6. An unusual and violent storm damaged the roof of a building in which B occupied space as a tenant. Water entered and damaged the tenant's goods. The tenant in turn sued the owner. A judgment for the tenant was reversed upon appeal. Why?
7. A customer eating in a restaurant alleges that he has been ill because of having been served spoiled sardines. An examination of the food shows that the sardines were not spoiled and that the claim is obviously a fake. Suit is filed. Is the insurance company covering the risk obliged to defend a suit in a fake claim?
8. X operates a place of amusement and contends that he has resources to meet any liability claim. He states that most claims are minor in their nature and that, even in the case of a death, which he conceives virtually impossible in connection with his business activities, he would have ample resources to meet it. Even in the case of a wealthy organization, does this sound like good judgment?
9. X is the father of a two-year-old son who was killed by an automobile as he ran from the sidewalk into the path of an oncoming car. A nine-year-old sister had been placed in charge of the boy by his mother. She was playing in a swing on a nearby porch when she saw her brother run toward the road. The sister made an effort to stop the child, but before she could reach him the accident happened that caused his death. The father, who brought action against the car owner, was not present at the time of the accident, yet the car owner was held not to be liable, on the ground of contributory negligence on the part of the father. Does this seem reasonable?

   Suppose the child had not been injured but had caused the car owner to swerve and crash into another car. Would the parents have liability in such a case?
10. X is is an employee of the federal government and drives a postal truck. Since the federal government may not be sued, the claim is made that the driver of the truck, while acting in the capacity of a servant of the federal government, may likewise not be sued. Is this contention correct?
11. *a*) X is a teacher in a Sunday school and suffered an injury to one of his legs when a piano fell while being moved. In your opinion is the liability of the church so remote as to free it from the possibility of damages in the event that suit is filed?

    b) X was injured by a fall on a church property. She brought action on the ground that her injury was caused by the "corporate negligence of the church." She recognizes that the church, as a charitable organization, may take advantage of the charitable immunity defense, but contends that at the time of the injury she was an invitee and not a beneficiary of the church as a charitable organization. Do you think she has a case?

12. You are a member of the governing board of a large hospital. The hospital is maintained by a religious organization as a nonprofit and charitable institution. The hospital has never carried liability insurance, on the ground that a charitable hospital is immune from liability for negligence. A friend has just told you of a death in another hospital, caused by the administration of the wrong type of blood to a patient during an operation. A hospital technician had labeled the blood of the deceased Type 2 when, in fact, it was Type 4. Suit for $25,000 was brought against the hospital for wrongful death. What do you think of the position of the hospital? Would the case influence you with respect to liability insurance for the institution with which you are connected?
13. R.M., a student 15 years of age, had an eye injured as a result of the explosion of a pressure guage in the school laboratory. Do you feel that there is any legal liability on the part of the town board of education?
14. W.H. purchased a used car from the G Motors Company. After driving it a few blocks, at a speed of about 25 mph, he applied his brakes. The brakes locked and the car skidded on the sidewalk and injured B. An examination of the car showed that grease on a brake drum (from a leaking grease cell) had apparently existed for a month or longer. B, the injured party, claims the dealer should be responsible for his injuries and bring suit. Do you think he has a case?
15. X, a trustee of a large estate, is sued by B, who is injured on one of the properties owned by the estate. In your opinion is X liable or is the estate liable?
16. The agent of a large life insurance company, on the way to attend a convention, meets with an automobile accident and a passenger riding with him is seriously injured. The life insurance company has no interest in the automobile and no knowledge of the passenger. In your opinion, if the agent was negligent in the operation of the car could the insurance company be held liable?
17. X occupies a seat in a box in a ball park. He is struck by a foul ball. Has he a case against the management because of his injuries?
18. B, a bank messenger, purchases for his own use a secondhand automobile. His employers discover the ownership of the car and forbid him to use his automobile at any time upon the bank's business upon the pain of dismissal. B is delayed at the bank one afternoon and, in order to carry a package of bonds to the post office before the registry window closes, uses his own automobile, but without the knowledge of his employers. On the way to the post office he strikes and kills a child. Suit is filed against the bank and the bank denies liability on the ground that it had expressly forbidden the employee to use his automobile in the course of business. In your opinion, may the bank escape liability?

Chapter 14

GENERAL LIABILITY INSURANCE

THE liability risk discussed in Chapter 13 is insured by several categories of liability insurance. For treatment in this text, the basic kinds are divided into three chapters. Chapters 15 and 16, respectively, analyze the important areas of (1) employers' liability (and workmen's compensation) insurance and (2) automobile insurance, including automobile liability coverages.

THE SCOPE OF GENERAL LIABILITY INSURANCE

The third major category of liability insurance is a miscellaneous group which includes all other forms of liability protection. The purpose of this chapter is to introduce the several distinct coverages which constitute the area of *general liability insurance.*

By the use of basic conditions applicable to all general liability policies and special provisions applicable to the particular contracts, coverages are available for a large variety of liability risks. Underwriting rules and classifications and rates for the several general liability lines are to be found in a publication known to insurance people as the "Liability Manual." When reference is made to the Liability Manual, the insurance underwriter has in mind a group of at least ten separate manuals.

The scope of general liability insurance may, to some degree, be determined from the titles of these manuals. The first six manuals deal with *business liability* risks, and the remaining four are concerned with *professional liability* risks. The ten manuals are: (1) Owners', Landlords', and Tenants' Liability Manual, (2) Manufacturers' and Contractors' Liability Manual, (3) Contractual Liability Manual, (4) Product Liability Manual, (5) Elevator Liability Manual, (6) Owners' or Contractors' Protective Liability Manual, (7) Physicians', Surgeons', and Dentists' Professional Liability Manual, (8) Hospital Professional Liability Manual, (9) Druggists' Liability Manual, and (10) Miscellaneous Medical Professional Liability Manual.

In addition to the foregoing separate manuals there is a supplement which treats comprehensive business liability coverages, such as the Comprehensive General Liability Policy. The *Personal lia-*

bility coverages are included in other manuals of instructions for writing individual liability protection for residences, sports, and comprehensive personal liability.

COMMON CONTRACT FEATURES OF THE BASIC PARTS

Liability policies, like most insurance contracts, are divided into four main parts: (1) declarations, (2) insuring agreements, (3) conditions, and (4) exclusions. The *declarations* identify the insured and provide other underwriting data. The *insuring agreements* outline the coverages in broad terms. The *conditions* enumerate the duties of both the company and the insured through a definition of terms and the setting forth of the obligations assumed by both parties. The *exclusions* set up limitations by taking away certain coverages that the insuring agreements would otherwise provide.

Declarations

Policies may be written on a general provisions form, or on a schedule form. The general provisions form is a basic contract containing the provisions that apply to all general liability policies. The special provisions applicable to one or more of the several forms of liability insurance available are attached in the form of an endorsement or rider. By this means, insurance to meet the needs of an applicant may be provided in one or several of the available classifications in a single contract. For example, owners', landlords', and tenants' bodily injury and property damage and elevator bodily injury and property damage, constituting four distinct coverages, may all be included in a single sheet. Insurance is afforded only for such coverages as are indicated, or scheduled, by specific limits of liability entered in the declarations for each of the coverages desired.

The *declarations* are made a part of the contract either by means of the insuring agreement or as one of the conditions of the policy. When named in the insuring agreement, the company agrees, in consideration of the payment of the premium and of the statements contained in the declaration, to pay, on behalf of the insured, all sums which the insured shall become obligated to pay by reason of the liability imposed upon him by law for damages arising out of the perils covered by the policy. A condition covering declarations provides that the named insured, by accepting the policy, agrees that the statements in the declaration are his agreements and representations; that the policy is issued in reliance upon the truth of such representations; and that the policy embodies all agreements entered between the named insured and the company or any of its agents relating to the insurance.

Wherever the word "insured" is used in the contract without

qualification, it includes any director, executive officer, stockholder, or partner of the insured, if the named insured is a corporation or partnership. The coverage to directors, executive officers, stockholders, or partners applies only while they are acting within the scope of their duties as such, and does not apply in connection with their general affairs. Coverage is specifically limited to acts performed in connection with the furthering of the interests of the business of the insured in his particular capacity.

The statements made by the insured in the declarations thus include the basic information which identifies the insured, his business, its location, the duration of the policy contract and other pertinent information about the contract. Especially important is the schedule of types of liability, each of which may be included in the contract *if* there is a limit of liability and premium charge indicated in the declaration.

Insuring Agreements

The company agrees in the *insuring agreements* to pay on behalf of the insured all sums which the insured shall become legally obligated to pay as damages because of the perils insured against. Usually, two specific types of liability are separately named in the insuring agreements: *bodily injury* liability and *property damage* liability. The first covers damage to other persons, the second covers damage to the property of others. In the case of bodily injury liability, the coverage extends to include liability for loss of services for which the insured may be legally liable. Property damage liability specifically covers liability for loss of use of the damaged property.

Liability policies may be written to assume liability imposed by law *caused by an occurrence* instead of *caused by an accident,* as is the usual practice. In recent years there has been a growing demand, particularly in connection with owners', landlords', and tenants', contractual, and products liability coverages for policies written on an occurrence basis. An additional charge is often made when a policy is written on an occurrence basis.

By way of distinguishing between the two insuring clauses, an accident is defined as "a sudden and unforeseeable event." An occurrence may be any event. Anything that happens is an occurrence. An accident must happen at a definite time. Thus, gradual damage cannot be construed as an accident. A policy, therefore, written on an occurrence basis is broader than the policy covering damage caused by accident in that it provides for gradual damage. Following is a definition of occurrence used to put a bodily injury contract on an occurrence basis: "Occurrence means an event, or continuance or repeated exposure to conditions, which unexpectedly causes injury during the policy period. All such exposure to substantially the same general conditions existing at or emanating from each premises location shall be deemed one occurrence."

A policy written on an occurrence basis would cover injury caused by a lotion sold as a cosmetic. Damage from the use of a lotion is rarely instantaneous, though its use over a continued period might cause damage. Fumes escaping from a manufacturing plant might kill crops. Airplanes flying over a fur farm have frightened the animals and prevented breeding. Paint on homes has been damaged by repeated exposure to dust and chemicals from trucks going to a construction site. There have been other claims because of the lessening in value of property caused by a manufacturing process. There have been sickness and disease claims, the outgrowth of unsanitary conditions where no accident has been involved.

Unquestionably, a policy written on an "occurrence" basis is broader than a policy written on a "caused by accident" basis, even with the limiting language that appears in the definition here noticed. The insured must determine whether or not, for his risk, the broader form is essential or even desirable. The broader form is not always available where coverage on an accidental basis may be easily obtained.[1]

One exception to the accidental nature of the liability coverage is that assault and battery committed by an employee of the insured is covered by the policy. Assault and battery is regarded as a very real peril, and claims originating from an assault by an employee on a member of the public are frequent. The policy does not cover assault and battery if committed by or at the direction of the named insured.

A final important part of the insuring agreements is that all general liability policies provide that the company will provide investigation, defense, and settlement of all claims made under the policy. These costs may be considerable, and are paid in addition to the policy limits stated in the contract. The insurer is obligated by the

---

[1]Insurers willing to write bodily injury liability on an occurrence basis frequently will not write property damage liability. This grows out of the apprehension that claims for damage would materialize where buildings and their contents suffered gradual deterioration from recurring conditions such as smoke from industrial plants. Again, there are situations such as those where waste is channelled into streams. Claims for damages develop that cannot be traced to a sudden and unexpected event. Insurance carriers are not prepared to cover this class of risk for policyholders, except by specific endorsement and increase in premium after careful consideration of the catastrophic possibilities of the by-products liability peril to property.

The need for "personal" injury instead of "bodily" injury coverage is apparent in several recent cases of libel, slander and nonphysical injuries. A Michigan truckdriver received a $150,000 award in 1964 for psychotic results of an accident in which no physical injury was involved. The case caused *Time* (February 16, 1964, p. 75) to define "emotional trauma" as "a state of mind precipitated by an accident, stimulated by an attorney, perpetrated by avarice, and cured by a verdict"!

wording to defend claims, even if they are fraudulent or falsely made against the policyholder.

Conditions

Certain *conditions* are found in all general liability policies and are applied to all coverages. Notably there are those that are concerned with (*a*) notice of accident, (*b*) notice of claim or suit, (*c*) assistance and cooperation of the insured, (*d*) action against the company, (*e*) other insurance, (*f*) subrogation, (*g*) policy changes, (*h*) cancellation, and (*i*) statutory conflict.

The policy provides that upon the occurrence of an *accident,* written *notice* shall be given by or on behalf of the insured to the company or any of its authorized representatives "as soon as practicable." The notice is required to contain particulars sufficient to identify the insured and also reasonably obtainable information respecting the time, place, and circumstances of the accident. Names and addresses of the insured and of available witnesses should also be included.

If a *claim* is made *or* a *suit* is brought against the insured, the insured is required to forward to the company immediately every demand, *notice,* summons, or other process received by him or by his representatives. The word "immediately" takes on considerable significance. Any undue delay in notifying the company with respect to any legal action brought against the insured may seriously jeopardize his position with respect to the insurance.

The insured may not wash his hands of the claim once he has turned it over to the insurance company. He is obligated to render every reasonable *assistance and cooperation* in connection with the settlement of a claim and to participate in hearings and trials if required to do so. The insured may not, except at his own cost, make voluntary settlements or payments or assume any obligations or incur any expense other than for immediate medical and surgical relief that appears imperative at the time of the accident. The settlement and adjustment of the claim is fully within the control of the insurance company.

No action shall lie *against* the *company unless,* as a condition precedent thereto, the insured shall have fully complied with all of the terms of the policy, nor until the amount of the insured's obligation to pay shall have been finally determined either by judgment against the insured after actual trial or by written agreement of the insured, the claimant, and the company. This precludes an injured party suing the company directly prior to an adjustment, and it precludes any legal action by an insured against the company until he has complied with all the policy conditions. After a settlement is made, any person or organization or legal representative thereof who has secured such judgment or written agreement may, thereafter, take action to recover under the policy to the extent of the insurance. If an action is brought against the insured and another person or organization, the policy specifically precludes any right of such person or organization to join the company as a codefendant in any action against the insured to determine the insured's liability.

The final section of this condition provides that bankruptcy or insolvency of the insured or of the insured's estate shall not relieve the company of any of its obligations thereunder. This clause now appears in all liability contracts. A strict contract of indemnity would relieve the liability company of any payment if the insured were bankrupt and unable to pay. The laws now require liability companies to pay where liability is determined, even if the insured would not have been able to pay in the absence of insurance.

The policy covers as contributing insurance if there is *other insurance* covering the loss. The policy contributes proportionally on the basis of limits of liability. Under the general liability policy the company is not liable for a greater proportion of any loss than the applicable limit of liability stated in the declaration bears to the total applicable limit of liability of all valid and collectible insurance against such loss. Assume, for example, the policy has an applicable limit of liability of $10,000. Assume two other policies have like limits. That means that there are three policies with an applicable limit of $10,000, or a total of $30,000, covering on the loss. Assume the loss is finally adjusted for $6,000. Each company then would contribute one third, or $2,000, to the payment of the loss.

Another condition gives the right of *subrogation* to the insurance company and places certain obligations on the insured to maintain and transfer such rights to the insurer. With respect to any payment under the policy, the company is subrogated to all the insured's rights of recovery. The insured is required to execute all papers required and to do everything that may be necessary to secure to the company such rights. Any action that the insured takes in the way of executing releases might defeat the right of the company with respect to such claims against wrongdoers. It might also jeopardize the insurance protection of the named insured and provide a basis for voiding the coverage.

It is provided that *policy changes* may be effected only by written endorsement. This condition both permits such changes, as well as making sure that the insured knows that they should be in writing and attached to the contract.

The usual *cancellation clause* provides that the insured may cancel the policy at any time on a short-rate basis. If the company elects to cancel, it must pay a return premium on a prorata basis and give five days' notice of cancellation.

It is usual to provide that if any of the terms of the policy are in *conflict with statutes* of the state in which the policy is issued, it is automatically amended to conform to such statutes.

Exclusions

As for all insurance contracts, liability policies must include some basic *exclusions* for perils or property that the contract cannot cover or for which the contract does not expect to provide protection. General liability policies invariably exclude liability for injury imposed by workmen's compensation laws. This peril is covered by workmen's compensation insurance. There is also an exclusion extending to bodily injury, sickness, disease, or death of any employee while engaged in the employment of the insured. Such claims as do not fall within the purview of workmen's compensation are covered by employers' liability insurance. Liability assumed by the insured under any contract or agreement is excluded, except that some contracts provide a limited contractual liability coverage. Contractual liability may be covered with respect to any liability contract by endorsement. Elevator liability is excluded unless coverage is particularly provided in the declarations.

There is no liability with respect to the ownership, maintenance, or use of power-driven vehicles, draft or saddle animals, watercraft, or aircraft. Nor is there any liability for injury to or destruction of property owned, occupied, or used by, rented to, or in the care, custody, or control of the insured. Damage to buildings or their contents from causes originating within the premises, such as water damage that may be covered by water damage or sprinkler leakage insurance, is excluded. Injury to or destruction of premises alienated by the insured out of which the accident arises are excluded. The exclusions vary with the coverage, but the foregoing appear in one form or another in all general liability policies.

The purposes of such exclusions are to exclude uninsurable risks, risks that are normally covered in other separate contracts, or to exclude risks that it would be inequitable to include for all policyholders. Perils and property in the last group may often be added to the contract by specific endorsement and an additional premium.

SPECIFIC CONTRACTS OF GENERAL LIABILITY INSURANCE

The field of general liability insurance may be divided into three distinct types of contracts, those providing protection, against (1) *business* liability perils, (2) *personal* or individual liability perils, and (3) *professional* or malpractice liability perils. Since *medical payments* coverage is technically not insurance against liability, but is often included in liability contracts, a separate section at the end of this chapter is devoted to this important type of insurance.

Business Liability Insurance

The most common types of business liability policies are the Owners', Landlords', and Tenants' Policy (O.L.T.), the Manufacturers' and Contractors' Policy (M. and C.), and the Comprehensive General Liability Policy (C.G.L.). The first two named are schedule contracts, in which the basic premises and public liability perils are included and, usually on an optional basis, additional specific liability perils may be included as indicated in the schedule part of the declarations. Thus many of the kinds of liability that will be discussed may be included in the O.L.T. and M. and C. policies, such as contractual, products, elevator, protective, and trustee liability. The C.G.L. Policy is an "all-risks" type of liability insurance, which means it automatically includes all kinds of liability perils (without specific scheduling or naming of each) except those specifically excluded. For this reason the C.G.L. Policy is discussed after the separate kinds of liability are introduced.

Owners', Landlords', and Tenants' Public Liability The O.L.T. Policy covers loss or expense, or both, resulting from claims upon the insured for damages on account of bodily injuries, death, or property damage alleged to have been accidentally suffered by any person or persons not employed by the insured. The accident must be alleged to have been caused by reason of the ownership, maintenance, ordinary alterations and repair, or use of the premises occupied by the insured. There is no restriction with respect to the use of the premises. Thus, if for any reason the insured enlarges his activities or changes the nature of his business, the coverage is not affected. With respect to newly acquired premises or elevators, automatic coverage is provided, although the company must be notified within a stated number of days if the coverage is to be continued.

The perils under this form of coverage are twofold as to location. Types of businesses in which the principal exposure is within the place of business fall into one category, while in a second type of business the outside peril constitutes a substantial part of the exposure. The *on-the-premises* peril not only includes claims from tripping, falling on stairs or slippery floors, and the like, but extends to sidewalks and passages adjacent. Examples of claims also include: blood poisoning as a result of scratching a wrist while fitting a glove, collapse of a chair in which a customer was seated, injury to an eye caused by demonstration of a perfume atomizer, and many others. The outside or *off-premises* peril is important where appliances are sold and demonstrated on the premises of the prospect. Electric refrigerators, radios, television sets, cleaners, and other household devices are demonstrated and installed in the customer's home. Accidents during demonstration or installation may involve the employer of the salesman in a heavy claim for damages.

Two basic types of liability are included in the O.L.T. Policy, and separate limits of liability apply to each: (1) *bodily injury* liability and (2) *property damage* liability. Under the *bodily injury* protection the company agrees to pay on behalf of the insured all sums which he becomes legally obligated to pay because of bodily injury, sickness, or disease including death suffered by members of the public. To be covered, the injury must be the outgrowth of an accident while the policy is in force arising out of ownership, maintenance, or use of the premises described in the declarations. Protection is provided for operations carried on at and from the premises of the insured. Coverage, therefore, extends to accidents off the premises if caused by employees of the insured engaged in the same type of operation as conducted at the premises. Automatic coverage on newly acquired locations or undertakings is provided if the company is notified within 15 days after acquisition of the new risk. This feature does not apply if the insured is covered by other valid and collectible insurance.

Protection is afforded under *property damage* liability for injury to or destruction of property of others, including loss of use. It provides property damage coverage under the same conditions that bodily injury protection is afforded. Excluded are losses to buildings or contents caused by discharge, leakage, or overflow from plumbing, heating, refrigerating, or air-conditioning systems, or from automatic sprinkler systems. Rain or snow losses caused by defective roofs, open window skylights, or the like on premises of the insured are excluded. There is no coverage because of injury to property owned or controlled by the insured caused by alteration or repair.

The standard limits for the Owners', Landlords', and Tenants' Liability Policy is $5,000 per person and $10,000 per accident with a limit of $1,000 per accident for property damage liability. Many types of business require much higher limits. This is particularly the case where there is any possibility of a catastrophe loss. Limits may be increased above the standard amounts for an additional premium. The rate for such increased amounts of coverage decreases per thousand dollars of protection as the policy limits are raised. For example, limits as just mentioned may be increased from 5/10/1 to 10/20/5 for about a 10 percent increase in premium, or about 20 percent for 25/50/10 limits. Many business firms should carry limits of 50/100/25, or more, on their liability policies.

The policy may be used in connection with the operation or ownership of any type of real estate, as well as many types of business establishments. Apartment houses, for example, are a source of claim from falling plaster and similar accidents. Signs, pipes, dark stairways or stairways with insufficient guards, torn carpets or coverings, defective railings, and the like are sources of other accidents from which claims may develop. All classes of property, not even excepting churches, have been the sources of very substantial claims.

Manufacturers' and Contractors' Liability. The M. and C. Policy provides protection for the manufacturer similar in nature to that afforded under the owners', landlords', and tenants' coverage but adapted to meet the needs of the manufacturer. Coverage applies to all premises and all operations of the insured including owners', landlords', and tenants' exposures, unless they are definitely excluded. The policy automatically extends protection to newly acquired premises without any requirement of notification on the part of the insured with respect to such acquisitions. Premium, of course, is required for any exposures acquired during the policy term.

Insurance is provided against the two primary perils: bodily injury liability and property damage liability. Separate limits are written for each hazard, and it is optional whether the insured carries property damage coverage. The policy establishes a limit for each accident and an aggregate limit establishing the total liability of the company during the policy period.[2]

Bodily injury liability covers the public liability of the insured for any accident arising out of operation of the insured's business. The clause is extended to cover the legal liability for such accidents occurring on or about the premises described in the policy and includes accidents caused by the insured's employees in his business. It also covers losses caused by such employee while engaged in the insured's business away from the premises. Property damage coverage provides protection of the same nature with respect to injury to or destruction of property, including loss of use of such property, for which the insured is held legally liable.

Employees are not regarded as members of the public while engaged in the performance of their duties, but it is possible for an employee to be injured on the premises under such circumstances as to be classed as a member of the public. Applicants for employment, visitors to the plant, salesmen, collectors, deliverymen, employees of contractors, children, and trespassers—all form a part of the public.

Liability for accidents for which another form of insurance is designed is excluded. Such accidents are those caused by automobiles or elevators. New construction work or the demolition of buildings is excluded. Accidents caused by the employee of a contractor or subcontractor are not covered, and there is no protection for liability for accidents caused by employees under age or by contract convict labor.

When written to cover the liability of a contractor, the protection

---

[2]In the case of contracting operations the aggregate limit applies to a project.

applies at specified locations, or a blanket policy may be written to cover all locations. Included in the policy is liability for loss when the accident is caused by the use of hoists, elevators, teams, or automobiles on the premises. Contractors engaged in road paving and street construction are protected in the setting up, taking down, and operation of the machinery and equipment used in their work while they are at the place and while they are being taken to and from the place of work. This includes such equipment as steam shovels, concrete mixers, road rollers and graders, tractors, and other similar equipment.

Contractual Liability. In cases of liability assumed by contract, specific insurance is necessary if adequate protection is to be provided. The coverage may be provided by endorsing other public liability policies such as the owners', landlords', and tenants' form, or it may be included as an insuring clause in any scheduled liability policy. The comprehensive liability policy automatically covers certain assumed liability, such as railroad "sidetrack" agreements (see below), and other assumed liability agreements may be included by endorsement. Separate contractual liability policies may be issued, but it is considered preferable to write contractual liability in connection with the public liability coverage carried.[3]

Under the terms of the contract, the company agrees with the insured to provide liability insurance for personal injuries or property damage that the insured has agreed to assume. The policy covers only liability assumed by the insured under a written contract, and the agreement under which liability is assumed is identified in the policy usually by reference, but in some instances a copy of the indemnity provisions of the contract is attached to the policy. The party with whom the indemnity agreement is made is referred to in the contract as the "indemnitee." Any liability that the indemnitee may incur as a result of the operations of the insured, and which is covered in the agreement between the indemnitee and the insured, is included within the scope of the policy protection. The policy covers only the liability assumed by the insured to the indemnitee indicated in the agreement.

This policy finds frequent use in providing protection for contractors who are required to assume the responsibility for all liability of a municipality before a permit is issued for the contractor to use city streets to store material, to bridge sidewalks, or otherwise to use public facilities in connection with his operations. Also, it is the

---

[3]When a contractual liability endorsement is attached to another liability policy, no additional insurance is provided, but the insurance protection afforded by the policy is extended over a broader risk. With a separate policy, additional insurance for the contractual risk is provided, and losses paid by the contractual policy will not limit the insurance available for losses under other policies.

custom of railroads to insert a clause in "sidetrack agreements" with property owners, requiring that the parties for whose convenience the siding or spur track is built shall assume all responsibility for injuries to persons or loss to property arising out of the use, existence, or maintenance of the siding. If the policyholder insuring his liability under an owners', landlords', and tenants' contract is not aware of the exclusion of contractual liability and does not take steps to provide the coverage under an endorsement or under a contractual liability policy, he may find his insurance cover sadly inadequate.

Products Liability. Claims for damages caused by or alleged to be caused by the consumption, use, or handling of goods away from the premises of the insured are specifically excluded from the coverage of the general liability policies issued to merchants and manufacturers. To meet the needs of insureds in various lines of business, the products liability coverage has been developed. Liability protection is provided under this form against loss caused by any article manufactured, handled, or distributed by the insured. While bodily injury liability is the more usual form of protection carried, property damage liability is written if the insured requires this coverage. The protection is available as a separate policy or may be made a part of another contract, such as any of the personal liability or the scheduled liability policies.

The products liability coverage pays claims for damage caused by mistakes, imperfect ingredients, or foreign substances, as well as improper handling, labeling, packing, or delivering. The policy does not cover products consumed on the premises of the insured or any liability for injury to employees. Goods manufactured, sold, or distributed in violation of law are never covered. It is the intent to provide liability protection for defects, errors, or mistakes made in connection with the manufacture or preparation of products offered for sale. The protection extends to include losses attributable to defective materials. It is not necessary that the product actually be sold since injury attributable to samples or souvenirs is covered.

The policy covers only for amounts for which the insured shall become legally obligated to pay as damages if the accident causing the loss occurs: (*a*) away from the insured's premises and (*b*) after the insured has relinquished possession of the product to others. The policy is written with three limits: (*a*) a limit per person, (*b*) a limit per accident, and (*c*) an aggregate limit. The limit per person injured in a given accident applies to each person. The per-accident limit fixes a total liability for claims from one common cause, such as from one prepared or acquired lot of goods. The aggregate limit is the total liability for all damages under the policy. Basic limits are $5,000 for each person, $10,000 for each accident, with an aggregate limit of $25,000. Higher limits may be purchased, and often should be, for adequate protection.

The manufacturer's policy may be endorsed to protect the retailer against claims resulting from the manufacturer's negligence. Retailers sometimes require this protection in connection with a sales agreement. Protection limited to the manufacturer's negligence is limited in its nature. Full liability for vendors of a manufacturer or distributor may also be written.

Purchase-order agreements are sometimes written with a "hold-harmless" clause under the terms of which the manufacturer agrees to hold the retailer harmless for liabiilty claims attributable to the handling of his product. The hold-harmless agreement is an assumed liability and excluded under the products liability policy. The policy may be extended by agreement to cover this form of assumed liability.

The contractors' and manufacturers' liability policy excludes coverage on accidents that occur after an operation has been completed. Contractors have been held liable on the grounds of defective work after a job has been completed and turned over to the owners. A products liability policy may be written to provide liability protection for contractors with respect to completed operations.

Elevator Liability. The elevator liability contract provides protection to the insured for his legal liability to the public growing out of accidents contributed to by the ownership, care, maintenance, or operation of the insured elevator. The coverage extends to claims originating in accidents to persons while entering or leaving the elevator or caused by elevator wells or equipment.

The elevator liability protection may be written to cover (*a*) bodily injury liability, (*b*) property damage liability, and (*c*) collision coverage. The first two of these coverages are liability forms. The third is a form of physical damage coverage and provides insurance against loss through accidental damage to the insured elevator.

The greatest source of elevator claims is found in elevators of the passenger-carrying type, such as those used by hotels, apartment buildings, office buildings, stores, and other properties where elevators are installed to carry members of the public. It is also true that in factories, warehouses, garages, and other properties where elevators are installed only for freight, accidents often occur which involve members of the public. It may be noted that bodily injury to any employee of the insured engaged in the course of his employment is not covered, and the insurance does not apply to structural alterations or new construction or demolition operations.[4]

---

[4]Injury to employees is covered by employers' liability or workmen's compensation insurance. Protection during structural alterations or demolition operations may be provided by the owners' protective liability policy.

Elevator liability protection may be made a part of the owners', landlords', and tenants' form, or the manufacturers' and contractors' form. The elevator liability, however, is not so covered unless the elevators are described in the application for the policy and specifically written into the contract. If no O.L.T. or M. and C. Policy is carried, the elevators may be separately insured under an Elevator Liability Policy.

Accidental damage to the insured elevator itself is provided by an endorsement. This is known as the "elevator collision endorsement" and is made part of the liability policy. This is not itself a liability coverage, although it is written only in connection with property damage insurance. It covers loss or damage to the insured elevator resulting from collision of the elevator or objects carried in the elevator with other objects. The coverage indemnifies the insured for loss or damage to other property owned, leased, occupied, or used by the insured if the loss is occasioned as the result of a collision of the insured elevator.

Protective or Contingent Liability. Several types of protective or contingent liability insurance may be important to certain policyholders. The Owners' and Contractors' Protective Liability Policy is designed to provide owners of property a protection for the contingent liability that may develop as the result of an accident caused by the negligence of a contractor.[5] Contractors purchase the coverage to provide themselves the same protection for claims that develop as the result of alleged negligence of subcontractors. The policy is primarily a "defense" policy. However, there are numerous recorded cases in which judgments have been awarded against an owner or against a contractor when it would appear that the primary liability should attach elsewhere. Hence, the policy is used by contractors carrying on a big project in which substantial parts of the operation are sublet to other contractors. Members of the public frequently recognize only the general contractor and file their suit for damages against him; or, if they do recognize the subcontractor, they file a joint suit. The purpose of the protective liability policy is to provide defense for the general contractor in the event that he is drawn into litigation of this character. If judgment is rendered against the insured, the policy indemnifies him, subject to the policy limits, to the extent of the judgment plus expenses incurred in investigation and defense.

The protective policy, while primarily purchased for its investigation and defense provisions, provides direct liability protection in

[5]In contrast to the owners', landlords', and tenants' form and the manufacturers' and contractors' liability coverage, each of which provides premises hazards protection as well as protection for business operations performed by the insured, the protective contract furnishes protection for claims made against the insured growing out of accidents in the operations of independent contractors. The coverages do not overlap.

those situations where the law holds the owner or principal contractor liable in spite of the negligence of an independent contractor. These situations develop in connection with (*a*) unlawful work, (*b*) responsibility that cannot be delegated, and (*c*) inherently dangerous work. The violation of a municipal ordinance bringing about an accident would fall in the first category. The principal contractor cannot delegate to others duty to the public, such as maintenance of a sidewalk in safe condition. Where an extremely hazardous operation, such as, for example, blasting, is a part of an operation, the principal contractor may not escape responsibility for injury to the public on the ground that the dangerous work was let to a subcontractor.

Another form of contingent liability is insured in the Principal's Protective Liability Policy. This form provides insurance protection in an area where the liability is uncertain. There are business establishments which carry on their operations in such a manner as to leave the status of their operators in question. While from the point of view of the business they may be regarded as independent contractors, in some instance it is quite possible for determining liability that their status be construed as that of an employee. Whatever determination is made will require liability protection for the owner of the business establishment. If the status of the worker is that of independent contractor, the business, nevertheless, may be responsible to the public for his negligent acts performed in the course of his operations in behalf of the business.

For business establishments that distribute their products under arrangements whereby the products are purchased by a canvasser and resold to the public, the principal's protective policy covers the insured whether the canvasser is determined to be an employee or an independent contractor. It accomplishes this by stating in the contract that the persons concerned are to be regarded as independent contractors or employees of independent contractors. The policy provides protection under two insuring clauses: (*a*) liability to independent contractors and (*b*) liability for independent contractors. Thus, if the insured is held liable for injury or damages to a person described in the policy as an independent contractor, the insurance covers. On the other hand, if the insured is held liable for injuries to members of the public because of an accident arising out of the activities of his business operations carried on by a described independent contractor or his employee, protection is also afforded.

The policy is tailored to meet borderline situations such as confront newspaper publishers in their distribution arrangements, as well as bakeries, ice-cream manufacturers, milk distributors, and others who operate on a basis that is ostensibly that of an independent contractor.

Trustee's Blanket Liability. The protection afforded by this policy is the same as that coverage provided by the standard Owners', Landlords', and Tenants' Policy, with the addition of coverage for an insured who is interested as neither a beneficial owner or tenant. The trustee's blanket policy is useful not only to individuals acting in the capacity of trustees but particularly so to banks and trust companies. The policy is written to cover all properties held in trust at the time the policy is effected, and a special endorsement provides the same coverage on newly acquired properties and automatically excludes properties no longer held by the trust.

Rates are based upon the manual rates for each property covered. There is no charge for including the trustee as an additional interest, and the charge for each beneficial ownership is indicated so that each estate may be charged with its proper portion of the cost.

Comprehensive General Liability. Casualty insurance companies now often write a Comprehensive General Liability Policy designed to include in a single contract insurance protection against all the liability perils to which an insured may be subject. Prior to the introduction of this policy it was necessary for the insured, in building up his liability protection, to select in schedule policies the single perils he felt met his needs. The danger of this procedure is to be found in the possibility of gaps in the coverage of the policies or of an unforeseen exposure for which no coverage has been provided. Also, claims sometimes develop as the result of exposures that do not come within the scope of any of the named-perils policies. With a comprehensive policy covering all public liability, the insured has the most complete liability protection that can be purchased.

The comprehensive policy is so broad that it covers all third-party liability because of bodily injury, sickness or disease, and injury to or destruction of property. While policies may be written so that the insurance is limited to liability for bodily injury and damage to property *caused by accident,* the bodily injury coverage may be extended by endorsement to remove the cause-by-accident limitation. This is necessary where professional liability is a factor. Professional liability claims originate from circumstances that frequently may not be included in the category of an accident.

The policy provides full automatic coverage for all included exposures: that is, if a claim arises because of the acquisition of some property creating a liability peril subsequent to the writing of the policy, the coverage automatically attaches.

The policy is written to include the perils ordinarily insured by the following separate policies or endorsements: (*a*) owners', landlords', and tenants'; (*b*) manufacturers' and contractors'; (*c*) elevator; (*d*) contractual; (*e*) products; and (*f*) protective. The so-called "unknown perils," when the insured may be subject to some peril about which he knows nothing or a peril which usually would not be covered by any named-perils policy, is also covered.

With respect to contractual liability, the policy covers: (*a*) warranty of goods or products; (*b*) liability assumed under written lease, easement, or side-track agreements; (*c*) written agreements required by municipal ordinances; and (*d*) written escalator or elevator maintenance contracts. Other types of assumed liability are excluded. Forms not automatically covered may be included by endorsement.[6]

Exclusions under the policy have been reduced to a minimum. While not all contracts are identical, the following exclusions are found in one form or another: (*a*) assumed liability except as noted above; (*b*) employees of the named insured; (*c*) automobiles away from premises; (*d*) watercraft away from premises; (*e*) aircraft on or away from premises; (*f*) property in the care, custody, and control of the insured; and (*g*) water damage liability including sprinkler leakage. Not all policies include the water damage exclusion; but when water damage liability is not to be covered, the policy is endorsed accordingly. On the other hand, if the exclusion is found in the policy, water damage protection may be included by endorsement.

Premiums for the comprehensive liability form are computed by determining manual rates for all known exposures when the policy is written, and to the premium thus determined a charge is added to provide for the unknown peril.

It is expected that the automobile perils away from the premises will be covered by a separate automobile liability policy. However, comprehensive automobile cover may be included in the same contract that provides the comprehensive general liability. Where necessary, other liability exclusions may be covered by endorsement. It is the intent to make the policy available as a combination of all the known liability policy forms that, in the ordinary course, would apply to the risk plus an overall coverage designed to make the protection complete.[7]

Professional or Malpractice Liability Insurance

Professional or malpractice insurance was first written to indemnify professional practitioners for loss or expense resulting from claim on account of bodily injuries because of any malpractice,

[6]It is apparent that in spite of the term "comprehensive" that applies to the general liability policy, there are limitations to the contractual liability coverage provided. The general liability policy may be endorsed, for an additional premium, to provide complete automatic contractual liability coverage. This point is important since the insured ordinarily assumes that the comprehensive liability policy covers all liability known and unknown. This is true regarding liability imposed by law, but true only with respect to liability assumed under a contract if complete automatic contractual liability is endorsed on the policy.

[7]It is to be noted that workmen's compensation and employers' liability protection are not included in the basic policy or by endorsement. The peril regarding employees is covered only under the workmen's compensation policy.

error, or mistake committed, or alleged to have been committed, by the insured in the practice of his profession. Professional practitioners in every field find themselves defendants in heavy damage suits. Recently, professional liability insurance has been extended into fields to cover losses where monetary damages are a consequence of the professional services of the insured attributable to negligence and involving no bodily injury.

The original malpractice policies were written to cover physicians, surgeons, hospitals, and the like. Policies are now written to cover morticians, accountants, attorneys, surveyors, and many others. Not all the separate forms are discussed here. Although the medical forms are presented here because of their many unusual liability features, the growing importance of professional liability insurance for many nonmedical professional groups should not be forgotten.

Physicians', Surgeons', and Dentists' Liability. This form provides coverage for liability arising out of malpractice, error, or mistake made in rendering or failing to render professional services in the practice of the insured's profession. It covers acts or omissions committed by the insured or by any person for whom the insured is legally responsible.

The insuring clause providing indemnity to the insured for damages on account of malpractice or mistake is very broad. Any claim whatever arising from injuries either real or alleged comes within the scope of the policy. The insured is covered whether the act occasioning the claim is his own or the act of any assistant acting under the insured's instructions. An assistant need not necessarily be in the insured's presence to be deemed to be acting under the instructions of the insured. A specialist called in to cooperate in the care of a patient or to perform an operation is not an assistant. The policy covers such claims as loss of services of husband, wife, or other member of the family; errors in prescribing or dispensing drugs or medicines; and claims arising through the performance of autopsies. It also defends counterclaims in suits brought for the collection of fees.

Physicians and other professional practitioners have frequently been victimized by claims based upon alleged moral turpitude while engaged in professional practice. Such claims are covered by this contract, as are claims based upon undue familiarity, anesthesia, hallucination, assault, slander, libel, and malicious persecution. The policy covers claims for personal injury, for property damage, for care and loss of services, and losses of an intangible nature. The policy is a very broad professional coverage but is not broad enough to cover the personal liability of the insured for claims that cannot be traced to the professional practice of the insured.

The physicians', surgeons', and dentists' liability policies as usually written exclude liability for any partner of the insured unless the liability is specifically assumed. X-ray therapeutic work is specifically excluded under all policies, although protection is obtainable through endorsement with the payment of an additional premium. X-ray used for diagnosis and the taking of pictures does not fall in the therapeutic exclusion. The policy excludes claims in cases in which it shall have been legally established that the damage was caused by the insured, or any assistant of the insured, while under the influence of intoxicants or narcotics or while engaged in or in consequence of the performance of a criminal act. Finally, the policy excludes claims arising by reason of the liability of the insured as proprietor in whole or in part of any hospital, sanitarium, dispensary, clinic, or other business enterprise.

A feature peculiar to this policy is the requirement that the insurer secure the consent of the insured before compromising any claim. When the insured feels his professional reputation is at stake, he may require the company to resist the case to the court of last resort, even though the claimant offers to compromise on a basis satisfactory to the company. The company obligates itself to defend the insured's reputation at the risk of huge judgements and to pay, subject to the policy limits, such award as may be made against the claimant plus the full costs of the defense.

Policies are written on an occurrence basis with a limit per claim and an aggregate limit of liability for the policy period. The per-claim limit is in contrast to the per-person limit to be found in certain of the other liability policies, and the aggregate limit has no reference to a single accident. Basic limits are $5,000 per claim with a $15,000 aggregate. The premium is based on a flat charge for the insured plus other additional flat charges to cover professional assistance, if any. Obviously, most insureds should purchase much higher limits than the basic ones. In addition to the policy written for an individual, policies are written to cover groups and partnerships.

Druggists' Liability. This is a malpractice coverage which also extends to provide product liability insurance protection.

The contract provides insurance against loss and expense arising or resulting directly from claims upon the insured for damages on account of bodily injury or death as the result of actual or alleged error on the part of the insured or his employees in preparing, compounding, dispensing, selling, or delivering any of the drugs, medicines, or merchandise customarily kept for sale in drugstores. Coverage is also provided for claims arising out of the consumption or use of beverages, food, or other products, including merchandise of every character. This extends to losses caused by errors in labeling or delivering. Hence, a claim originating because two correctly compounded prescriptions were accidentally exchanged in delivery is covered. Likewise, errors in reading or interpreting the physician's prescriptions and carelessness on the part of a clerk referring to a wrong number in a refill are covered.

The policy does not cover (*a*) bodily injury or death suffered by an employee of the insured in the course of his employment, (*b*) claims arising directly or indirectly from the willful violation of a penal statute, ordinance, or regulation committed by or with the knowledge or consent of an insured or of a store manager employed by the named insured, (*c*) liability assumed by contract, and (*d*) damage to insured's own property or that in his care, custody, or control. The exclusions for the most part are those to be found in all liability contracts and have to do with claims that are ordinarily covered by workmen's compensation insurance together with the usual exclusions covering assumed liability and property of the insured or that in his care, custody, or control.

The exclusion with respect to claims attributable to illegality assumes some significance in connection with this coverage. For example, the illegal employment of clerks, sales of prohibited drugs or drugs contrary to statutory regulation, or the compounding of a prescription by a person other than one legally qualified, unless by an assistant in his presence and under his direction, will in each instance void the coverage so far as these acts give rise to claims. Violation of the Medical Practice Act by prescribing treatment or violation of the Harrison Narcotic Act or of statutes or ordinances governing the sale of alcoholic liquors has the same effect. However, if the insured or his manager does not intentionally violate the law, the policy protects him from the illegal actions of his employees who may knowingly commit an illegal act.

Coverage is on an occurrence basis. The injury to be covered must happen during the policy period, though claims attributable to the use of goods or products sold prior to the inception date of the policy, at the premises covered by the policy, are covered.

Hospital Liability. As in the case of the druggists' policy, this form is a combination of malpractice and product liability. It is designed for use by hospitals, clinics, dispensaries or infirmaries, convalescent or nursing homes, homes for the aged, mental-psychopathic institutions, sanitariums, and health institutions other than osteopathic institutions.

Coverage is provided for liability arising out of malpractice, error, or mistake made in rendering or failing to render medical, surgical, dental, or nursing treatment, including the furnishing of food or beverages in connection therewith. Product liability insurance is included, both on and off the premises, for drugs or medical, dental, or surgical supplies or appliances furnished or dispensed by the insured. Insurance is afforded for liability arising out of the performance of autopsies or other handling of deceased human bodies. Coverage includes bodily injury and property damage liability, but it is not limited to these. For example, a claim based on mental anguish would be covered. As in the case of the physicians' and surgeons' form, coverage is on an occurrence basis. The source of the claim must have occurred during the policy period, but there is no time limit on the appearance or discovery of the injury.

The exclusions are concerned with the following: (*a*) liability arising out of the performance of a criminal act; (*b*) liability on account of injuries to employees; (*c*) liability of an insured, if an individual, for his personal acts or omissions of a professional nature; (*d*) liability assumed under any contract or agreement; and (*e*) liability arising out of motor vehicles, watercraft, or aircraft.

Miscellaneous Medical Liability. This coverage is provided by endorsing one of the other professional liability policies. The policy to be used depends upon the professional classification of the applicant for insurance. The physicians', surgeons', and dentists' form is used to cover chiropodists, chiropractors, nurses, optometrists, physiotherapists, and veterinarians, whether self-employed or employed by others. When employed by others, the form may be used to cover pharmacists, opticians, dental hygienists, and laboratory, X-ray, or physiotherapy technicians.

The hospital form is used for blood banks and medical or X-ray laboratories. Proprietor opticians are covered by endorsement of the druggists' form.

The basic limits of liability are $5,000 for each claim with an aggregate of $15,000 for a policy year. Increased limits are available.

Personal Liability Insurance

In the same way that liability insurance is needed by many businesses, protection is also important for numerous personal or individual situations. The ownership of residential property, participation in sports activities, the keeping of pets or animals, and many normal everyday activities all involve a responsibility upon individuals not to cause injury or damage to other persons or their property.

Three basic policies are discussed in this section for: (1) residence liability, (2) sports liability, and (3) comprehensive personal liability. The last category includes a special contract for farmers which is a combination of personal and business liability insurance.

Residence Liability. The liability peril of the private dwelling is covered under a special form to cover either an owner or a lessee.

A low flat rate covers the bodily injury legal liability exposure. If desired, the policy may be extended to provide property damage coverage. One of the special perils covered in the residence policy is the liability for bodily injury sustained by a member of the public by reason of the insured's ownership of dogs. The policy also covers injuries caused by saddle animals and teams owned and used only by the insured.

A special feature of the Residence Liability Policy permits the extension of the policy by endorsement to include protection from loss when the claim is made by a servant or other employee injured in the course of employment. Public liability policies as a rule exclude the coverage of employees, since workmen's compensation or employers' liability forms are available, and this risk is expected to be covered by specific insurance. Since in most states the workmen's compensation laws do not apply to farm laborers or domestic servants,[8] the insured may neglect his exposure to loss from this source. He may insure his liability to such employees by extending his residence liability policy.

The residence liability policy was at one time the most common form of personal liability insurance. The use of the Comprehensive Personal Liability Policy (and the Homeowner's Policy which includes the same coverage) has made this form much less popular.

Sports Liability. A policy covering the golfer's liability for claims on account of bodily injury or death suffered or alleged to have been suffered by a member of the public by reason of the insured's participation in any game of golf was one of the first of the liability policies in the sports liability group. The policy was known as "golfers' liability insurance." Then provision was made to extend the policy if the insured participated in other forms of sport, such as tennis, baseball, basketball, football, hunting, and fishing.

The policy was soon replaced by a broad sports liability form which extends to cover the insured for liability for bodily injury the result of any athletic sport or game. It likewise protects the insured while using saddle animals not owned by the insured and while using for other than commercial purposes bicycles, canoes, or rowboats, as well as power boats or sailboats not owned or chartered by the insured.

With the advent of the Comprehensive Personal Liability Policy, individual sports liability forms for nonprofessional individuals are seldom written. The comprehensive form includes sports protection. The separate form is maintained here because of the common recognition of the importance of sports liability perils, and its place in the development of the broader comprehensive policies. Sports

[8]Some states require workmen's compensation insurance if there are more than a certain number of domestic employees, such as two or four.

liability policies are also still issued to professionals, since the comprehensive personal liability excludes business or occupational pursuits.

Comprehensive Personal Liability. There are two forms designed to provide comprehensive liability protection for individuals. These are: (*a*) the Comprehensive Personal Liability Policy and (*b*) the Farmers' Personal Comprehensive Liability Policy. Both contracts are designed to provide comprehensive liability protection for a named insured and the members of his household. However, there are certain perils in the farm risk not found in the usual household, and the farmers' comprehensive form is adapted to them.

Both of these forms incorporate in a single document the risks that were at one time separately insured under such forms as the sports liability contract, residential liability, dog liability, and a number of others.

In the liability insuring clause, the comprehensive personal liability policies, unlike most liability policies, cover under a single limit the liability of the insured for damage on account of bodily injury to members of the public and to employees and for damage to the property of others caused by an occurrence. The minimum single limit is $10,000, but, as in the case of other liability coverages, policies for larger limits are frequently written. The single limit represents the maximum liability of the company regardless of the number of persons injured or the extent of property damage attributable to a single occurrence. The contract excludes assumed liability, except liability assumed under a written contract relating to the premises. The intent of this wording of the insuring clause taken together with the exclusion is to provide protection to an insured who has assumed certain liabilities in a "hold-harmless" clause under a lease.[9]

Under both forms, two full-time residence employees are covered without charge if they are not entitled to benefits under any workmen's compensation law. In the event that there are more than two residence employees, it is required that the employees covered be declared and employers' liability insurance protection be included in the contract.

Legal liability coverage for damage to nonowned premises and furnishings caused by (*a*) fire, (*b*) explosion, or (*c*) smoke loss caused by the faulty operation of a heating or cooking unit may be provided by endorsement. This protection appeals to tenants, particularly those who rent valuable seasonable properties. It protects them

[9]The comprehensive policy provides protection for many types of losses that happen rarely but, when they do happen, may involve the parties in serious litigation and frequently heavy damages. For example, children playing with firearms sometimes shoot and kill one of their group. Injuries caused by children riding bicycles; throwing rocks; engaging in sports, coasting, Halloween pranks, and the like; and damage to parked cars—all may originate a claim.

from damage suits growing out of injury to or destruction of home or home furnishings which have been rented to them if the loss is caused by one of the perils noted.

The fact that personal liability claims are relatively infrequent tends to make the rate for the comprehensive personal liability form moderate. The protection, however, is a valuable one when a claim does, in fact, materialize. The modest premium of perhaps $10 to $20 a year prompts the purchase of this insurance, which provides protection against a very real possibility of heavy damages. Many persons consider it as essential to the insurance protection of a home as fire insurance.

Under the *Comprehensive Personal Liability Policy* there are two basic coverages: (*a*) liability including bodily injury and property damage and (*b*) medical payments.

The liability protection covers an insured against claims from bodily injury to members of the public or to employees and from damage to the property of others. The liability is, therefore, a combination of public liability and employers' liability insurance within the limits of a single insuring clause.[10] The medical payments protection provides reasonable medical expense in connection with injuries to employees and to members of the public injured on or off the premises of the insured. It applies, regardless of legal liability, if the injuries are attributable to the activities of the insured, his family, an employee while engaged in the employment of the insured, or an animal owned by or in the care of the insured. The basic limit is $250 per person. Injuries to family members of the household are not covered. The C.P.L. is liability insurance, and not accident coverage for everyone.

Premises protection applies to accidents that happen on the premises of the insured, such as his permanent residence, whether a dwelling owned by him or an apartment that is rented; a summer cottage, whether owned or rented; and even a cemetery lot. The policy extends to provide protection for injuries attributable: (*a*) to pets or the use of saddle horses, bicycles, and small boats; (*b*) to sports, such as golfing, hunting, or fishing; and (*c*) to any type of accident away from home for which the insured or any member of his household is held responsible. The contract covers liability of the insured and the members of his family and household for loss or damage that is the outgrowth of personal activities, except in an automobile accident or business or professional acts.

---

[10]The employers' liability coverage provides protection for the insured but no benefit to the injured employee unless the insured is legally liable for the injury under the common law. Liability under workmen's compensation law is excluded; and, where such law applies, the risk should be covered by workmen's compensation insurance.

Business pursuits of the insured are not covered in the basic policy, but the policy may be extended to include them if the insured is employed on a salary. Incidental business pursuits on the premises, such as a doctor's office, art or music studio, and the like, may be covered by such an endorsement. Medical payments coverage in connection with the business pursuits endorsement is optional.

The *Farmers' Personal Comprehensive Liability Policy* is written with three insuring clauses: (*a*) liability, (*b*) medical payments, and (*c*) animal collision.

The liability coverage affords bodily injury and property damage liability insurance protection similar to that afforded under the comprehensive personal liability form, including important product liability as well. The medical payments coverage follows the same pattern.

The animal-collision cover is optional and provides a limited form of livestock mortality insurance for the insured. The policy pays the insured for loss by death of cattle, horses, sheep, hogs, and the like if death is caused by collision between the animal and a motor vehicle not owned or operated by the insured or by any of his employees. The animal collision applies only to animals (except dogs) killed in a public highway while not being transported.

Contractual liability with respect to liability assumed under written contracts with relation to the premises or with respect to warranties of goods and products is covered. Otherwise, as in the Comprehensive Personal Liability Policy, assumed liability is excluded.

Medical Payments Coverage

Medical payments insurance provides necessary medical, surgical, ambulance, hospital, professional nursing, and funeral expenses, *regardless of negligence or liability* on the part of the insured, for a person injured or killed in an accident covered by the liability policy. The importance of the coverage is that it avoids delay and difficulty in providing legal liability in the case of many smaller injuries.

This form of insurance may be written with premises, elevators, and operations liability coverages, but it may not be written with products liability. It is an optional coverage with the Owners', Landlords', and Tenants' Policy, the Manufacturers' and Contractors' Policy, and the Comprehensive General Liability Policy. It is automatically included in the C.P.L. policies.

Medical payments coverage written with general liability contracts provides, in addition to a per-person limit of coverage, a second limit per accident. The limit thus established is independent of bodily injury liability limits. There is no coverage for injury to the named insured, any partner of the insured, or any employee while engaged in his employment. With respect to tenants there is no coverage for injury to a tenant or other person residing regularly on the premises covered by the liability policy; and there is no coverage for an employee of the tenant or resident while engaged in his employment. Thus it is *not* accident insurance for a whole family or business situation.

Not only is medical payments coverage not available for products liability, but there is an exclusion in the basic coverage with respect to products and completed operations. Thus, if a restaurant were to carry on O.L.T. (owners', landlords', and tenants') policy and a customer suffered from poisoning, there would be no medical payments coverage. On the other hand, if the same customer fell and was injured, the medical payments coverage would apply.

Some business establishments have a first-aid station with a nurse and often a physician together with other first-aid assistance as part of their regular organizations. Where this is the case a discount is allowed from the medical payments premium. At the same time the policy excludes liability for payment for services rendered by the named insured or any of his employees.

The value of medical payments coverage for a business is in the goodwill it can create on the part of customers. Without delay, or the customer having to prove that the business is legally liable for the injury, the coverage can pay for X-rays and treatment of common injuries such as minor sprains, cuts, bruises, or simple fractures.

SUMMARY

The field of general liability insurance, which includes all forms of liability coverage except automobile liability and employers' liability (and workmen's compensation), has an important place in the insurance market today. From the standpoint of potential loss to the insured, it is essential protection of assets against the financial disaster which a large liability claim might bring to an individual, a business, or a profession.

The basic parts of all general liability contracts are the declarations, insuring agreements, conditions, and exclusions. The common features are noted, especially those provisions which are pertinent to liability contracts: the distinction between "caused by accident" and "occurrence" coverage; separation of "bodily injury" and "property damage" liability in most policies; requirements for immediate notice to and cooperation with the insurer; importance of subrogation; and the usual exclusions to be expected in liability policies.

Specific contracts are discussed in some detail, pointing out the three distinct types of (1) business liability insurance, (2) professional or malpractice liability insurance, and (3) personal liability insurance.

Business liability coverages mentioned are the common schedule liability policies: the Owners', Landlords', and Tenants' Policy and the Manufacturers' and Contractors' Policy. Contractual, products, elevator, protective or contingent, and trustee liability are separately analyzed. The popular Comprehensive General Liability Policy is introduced as a broad, "all-risks" kind of liability insurance which provides good automatic protection for many changing business liability situations.

The special nature and extensive coverage of *professional or malpractice* insurance is recognized in presenting several of the basic forms for study: the physicians', surgeons', and dentists'; the druggists'; the hospital; and miscellaneous medical malpractice contracts.

Personal liability insurance is noted as just as essential as the many business and professional liability coverages. Residence and sports liability are shown to be the forerunners of the broader personal liability contracts used today. The Comprehensive Personal Liability Policy, and a special form of it for farmers, has increased significance now as a single-limit coverage for residence and off-premises liability protection for sports, animals, and a wide variety of personal acts of the whole family. Many policyholders now have this protection in the various Homeowner's policies.

Medical payments coverage is explained as a valuable supplement to the liability policies. It is customarily included in the personal liability forms, but often is optional in the business liability forms. The rationale for its use with liability insurance is based on its convenience and payment to the injured person without delay, and the resulting goodwill it brings to the insured.

FOR REVIEW

1. Give several examples of the reasons why liability insurance coverage on an "occurrence" basis is generally considered broader than coverage for an "accident."
2. The Owners', Landlords', and Tenants' Policy covers both premises and off-the-premises liability. It may also include protection for elevator, protective, contractual, and products liability if the policy provides for this coverage. Explain the need for each of these types of liability insurance by a property owner.
3. X is the owner of a building which he has leased in its entirety to a second party. He feels, therefore, that he has no need for a public liability policy since, under the terms of the lease, the tenant has assumed all liability in the event that anyone is injured on the premises. Is the owner thereby relieved of all risks?
4. B is the owner of a store property which he listed for rent with X, a realty agent. The agent, on a given afternoon, showed P through the

property. P followed the agent from a lighted room into a dark room. As he passed into the darkened room, he fell into an open trap door, sustaining serious injuries to leg, back, and spine. P brought suit and in the course of the trial was asked why he did not see the opening in the floor and if his vision was obscured by the darkness. P, the plaintiff, replied: "When somebody is with you, you don't look down to watch if there is a hole there." Do you think the circumstances are such as to hold the owner or agent, or both, liable for P's injuries?

5. X is the president of a bank and is considering the application of the Y company for a large loan. X discovers that Y leases a mechanical apparatus and in the agreement undertakes to hold the lessor "harmless" from all losses caused by the operations of the leased machines. How can the borrower satisfy the bank with reference to this hazard?
6. X was a guest at the Blank Hotel. In the state in which the hotel is located, the innkeeper is liable by statute for goods of his guests "placed under his care." Upon arrival X turned his car over to a hotel employee, who drove it to the garage of the hotel and parked it. When X was ready to depart he called for his car and it was not to be found. X sued the hotel. The hotel in turn denied liability on the ground that it took no possession, custody, or control of the car, and made no charge for parking it, and that X was contributarily negligent for having left his keys in the automobile. The hotel company claimed that the innkeeper's law does not apply to an automobile or its contents. Do you believe X has a case against the Blank Hotel company?
7. It was contended that X, a general contractor undertaking to repair a bridge, failed to provide either a barricade or lights, and as a result an automobile accident occurred which seriously injured the driver. Suit was filed against X and damages in an amount of $20,000 were awarded. How could the contractor have protected himself with insurance? Would your answer change if subcontractors were hired by X?
8. X is covered by a Comprehensive General Liability Policy. As a result of an error, he caused the arrest of B. B brought action against him for false arrest and alleged mental anguish. Does the policy cover?
9. B, the insured, operated a dog kennel and was covered by a Comprehensive General Liability Policy. His neighbor, M, brought suit for an injunction to restrain B from operating the kennel on the grounds that it depreciated the value of M's property and that his health had been impaired. M did not ask for money damages. B's insurance company refused to defend the suit, so B retained his own counsel and successfully fought his case in the court. He then brought action against his insurer to recover expenses. Should the company have conducted the defense?
10. A druggist carries an Owners', Landlords', and Tenants' Liability Policy. A claim is made for illness caused by eating food served in the store and claimed to have been spoiled. Another claim is filed on the ground that illness was caused by consuming fruit juice purchased at the store and used to make punch at the home of claimant. A third claim is filed based upon an alleged error in the compounding of a prescription. Which of these claims is/are covered under the policy? Explain why or why not.
11. B, a customer of a restaurant, alleged that he became seriously ill as a result of eating spinach in which pieces of glass were later found. He brought suit against the restaurant, and a verdict of $500 was rewarded. Is this risk insurable? Do other businesses (besides restaurants) have such liability? Explain.

12. X threatens a doctor that unless he pays $1,000 he will bring suit against him alleging malpractice. It is an attempt to extort money by threat of injuring the doctor' reputation in the community. Does the Doctor's Malpractice Liability Policy cover against such a claim?
13. Professional liability policies, ordinarily known as "malpractice liability," were written to cover bodily injury growing out of error or mistake committed, or alleged to have been committed, by a professional practitioner in the practice of his profession. It can readily be understood that there is a grave risk in the case of physicians, hospitals, druggists, and other like practitioners. Discuss the extension of professional liability to include other professional groups, such as lawyers.
14. An employee of an electric company, calling at the residence of X to read an electric meter, steps on a golf ball left on the back porch, falls, and break his leg. Is the liability of the owner of the ball covered under the Comprehensive Personal Liability Policy?
15. Mrs. B, a maid working in the house of X, was engaged in cleaning clothing with gasoline supplied her for the purpose by her employer. The gasoline fumes vaporized and resulted in an explosion which caused the death of Mrs. B. Mrs. B's husband brought suit for damage against the employer. Has he grounds for a claim? How can X protect himself against such claims?
16. Mr. Homeowner invited guests for dinner at his home. The following events occur which made him realize the magnitude of the liability risk property owners face:
    a) Mr. A fell as he came up the front steps because a weak railing came loose. He spent several weeks in the hospital and was unable to work for three months.
    b) Mrs. B ran down the front steps as she was leaving and sprained her ankle.
    c) A six-year-old child of Mr. and Mrs. C turned on the buzzsaw in Mr. Homeowner's workshop and was seriously injured.
    d) Mrs. D suffered food poisoning that evening.

    Identify the *liability principle* which each of these occurrences illustrates, and indicate the reason why the Comprehensive Personal Liability Policy of Mr. Homeowner would or would not cover the losses.

Chapter 15

EMPLOYERS' LIABILITY AND WORKMEN'S COMPENSATION

WHY and how employers' liability has been supplanted in the United States by the workmen's compensation laws is evident in a brief review of the relationship between employer and employee in our changing industrial society. The development has been one progressing from common law liability which defined an employer's responsibility to his employees for work injuries, to employers' liability statutes, and finally to the workmen's compensation laws of the twentieth century.

EMPLOYERS' LIABILITY

Common Law Liability of Employers

At common law an employer is liable to employees for damages due to injury when the negligence of the employer is the cause of the injury. However, the burden of proof in the case of accidental injuries rests squarely upon the employee to show that there was negligence on the part of his employer, and that this negligence was the cause of the injury.

The employer has three strong defenses against injury claims by his employees. Under the *contributory negligence rule,* the employee must also show that he did not himself contribute to the negligence. It has been further held that when an employee has knowledge of the ordinary risks involved, he is paid for assuming those risks and, therefore, cannot recover for injuries caused thereby. The doctrine has been extended to apply in cases in which the employee continues to work without complaint after the discovery of failure on the part of his employer to afford proper protection. The employer's defense against such claims is referred to as the *assumption-of-risk rule*. Finally, the common law relieved the employer of responsibility when the cause of the injury was the willful wrongdoing or negligence of a fellow servant. This defense is known as the *fellow-servant rule*.

Modifications of the Common Law

The difficulty of an injured employee's establishing a case of liability can readily be understood. Through statutory enactment and a tendency on the part of the courts to interpret the rules favorably to employees, the position of the worker has been somewhat bettered. The class of fellow servants has been narrowed to include only those who work with the injured person, not the foreman or manager. A statute in 1856 abolished this defense in the case of employees of railroads. Other laws followed but were to a degree nullified by employers who required workmen to sign contracts releasing them from liability.

With the changes brought about by industrial development and the widespread substitution of machinery for hand labor, it became increasingly apparent that the problem of loss due to industrial accidents was still far from a satisfactory solution. In an effort to correct the situation, a number of states adopted *employers' liability acts* by which the position of the employee was immeasurably improved. The employers' liability legislation was the outgrowth of a recognition of the need for liberalizing existing law in favor of the employee. The English laws of 1875 and 1880 mark a turning point in liability legislation. Under the law of 1880 the employer was held responsible for defective machinery when it was the cause of an accident, as well as for the negligence of foremen and others in authority. The old rules of liability were otherwise broadened. This law is important as serving as a model for the laws subsequently adopted in the United States.

Employers' liability acts were fought every inch of the way in the courts, and certain of the earlier acts were declared unconstitutional on one ground or another. Defects in the earlier laws were corrected. The Federal Employers' Liability Act of 1906 was held unconstitutional, but upon its reenactment in a new form it was upheld by the United States Supreme Court. This law abrogated the fellow-servant rule and modified the operation of the rules of contributory negligence and assumption of risk. Finally, the law provided that contracts or other devices intended to exempt the employer from liability created by the act shall be void.

Negligence on the part of the employee was still a factor, and many accidents occurred where negligence could not be shown. Great expense and delay were occasioned by both employer and employee in litigation, and the award of a jury in any case was often unpredictable. The disadvantageous position of the employee was still severe, for the immediate result of his filing a suit or making a claim against the employer was twofold: he lost his job, and he incurred expenses which usually he could ill afford.

WORKMEN'S COMPENSATION LAWS

Employers' liability acts in all jurisdictions in the United States have now been superseded by *workmen's compensation laws.* Even though the liability acts were designed to improve the position of the employee, and, in fact, did accomplish this, they were, nevertheless, far from satisfactory.

The theory behind workmen's compensation legislation completely disregards the old idea of liability based upon negligence. Rather, the theory is based upon the idea that neither the employer nor the employee is to be burdened with the cost of industrial accidents. This cost is to be charged directly to the employer, *regardless of liability,* and then passed on to the consumer as a part of the cost of production.

Compensation laws make the employer responsible for indemnity to the injured employee without regard to the matter of fault or negligence. The amount of indemnity to apply in particular cases is predetermined by the law. It is sufficient to provide relief for the injured workman, although it does not equal the compensation received while employed. The laws undertake to make indemnities correspond to injuries; and if the injuries are fatal, benefits are provided for the employee's dependents. Both medical expenses and income benefits are included.

Constitutionality

Just as employers resisted the trend toward liberalization under the employers' liability acts, so they questioned the constitutionality of the first attempts toward the establishment of the compensation principle. The New York Legislature was the first to enact a compensation law. The law was passed in 1910 and was modeled upon the English law of 1897. A test was immediately made of the constitutionality of the act. The court held that the statute that sought to impose a liability upon an employer "who has omitted no legal duty and has committed no wrong" was unconstitutional in New York. Proponents of the act then set about to amend the state constitution. The amendment was adopted in 1913, and a new compensation law enacted in 1914.

In the period between 1910 and 1914 a new plan was evolved to overcome the constitutional difficulties, giving the employer a choice as to whether or not he would be governed by the workmen's compensation act. The employer and the employee might, if they wished, retain their rights at common law, or they might elect to accept the compensation law. The courts had already passed upon the right of the legislature to abrogate the common law defenses. As an incentive to employers to avail themselves of the compensation act, the elective laws provided that if an employer fails to accept the compensation law, he loses the defenses of contributory negligence, negligence of a fellow employee, and assumption of risk by an employee. With the loss of the common law defenses and the uncertainty as to jury awards, plus litigation costs, the compensation alternative offers an attractive haven. It follows that, although as a matter of theory employers are entirely free to elect to be bound by the act or not, the choice is, as a matter of fact, so one-sided that employers find it desirable to assent.

As a result of court decisions and legislative enactments, there are today two types of compensation laws in force. In one instance compensation is compulsory, and in the other instance it is elective. The New York law as finally passed and held constitutional is compulsory. The vast majority of states have adopted the elective plan, under which form of law the matter of assent to the act is voluntary. In some states employees may exercise an option. Where a choice is afforded employees, they are usually presumed to have assented unless they specifically indicate the contrary.

Scope and Benefits of the Laws

In the beginning, workmen's compensation laws were enacted to protect employees engaged in certain industries regarded as hazardous, such as coal mining, blasting operations, and explosive manufacturing. The tendency in compensation legislation has been to enlarge the application of the laws, and exemptions of classes of employees decreased rapidly in the different jurisdictions. No state at present brings all occupations within the operation of the law, but most are covered regardless of the extent of danger in the work. Agricultural, domestic, and casual labor is ordinarily exempted; and it is usual to exempt employees when an establishment engages fewer than a designated number of workers.

Compensation is provided for all injuries arising out of and occurring in the course of employment. No benefits under compensation acts are allowed for the injury or death of an employee when it is proved that such was occasioned by the willful intention of the employee to bring about the injury or death, or that the injury or death resulted from the intoxication of the employee while on duty. An exception to the regulation covering intoxication is sometimes made if the employer knew that the employee was intoxicated, or that he was in the habit of being intoxicated while on duty.

While the benefits differ in different states, there are points of similarity in all the acts. *Definite schedules of benefits* are provided for different types of injury. While in certain cases, lump-sum settlements may be made, it is usual to provide for the payment of benefits on a weekly basis. The lump-sum benefits, when used, are in lieu of weekly benefits. For example, perhaps $9,000 might be paid for the loss of a leg, or $10,000 for an arm, or $5,500 for an eye. The states vary greatly in terms of the size of the lump-sum settlement.

To discourage malingering, the more common weekly benefit is set at a fraction of the injured employee's weekly wage. This ranges from 50 to 90 percent of the average weekly wage, subject to a sum set as a maximum and another set as a minimum. Thus, a state might allow 66⅔ percent of the injured employee's weekly wage, but would in no case allow a sum in excess of $50 or below a minimum of $10. When the law provides a minimum, it does not mean that an injured employee whose average wage is less than the minimum will receive the minimum amount as compensation. It operates rather to prevent the application of the percentage of the weekly wage allowed, to reduce a wage below the designated minimum. A maximum total payment is usually set as a multiple of the weekly benefit. Variations among the states are great, but normally the duration would not exceed six to ten years of payments, or a total of perhaps $10,000 to $25,000.

In order to eliminate the excessive expense of handling small losses and to prevent malingering when the injury is of no serious consequence, most laws provide a period of from a few days to one week during which no compensation is paid. This interval is called a "waiting period," and it acts as a kind of deductible. Some laws provide that in cases of serious injury involving a protracted period of payments, indemnity shall be payable from the date of the injury, regardless of the waiting period.

An important feature of compensation legislation is the fixing with as much detail as possible the exact benefit due in each specific type of injury. Substantial variations appear in the provisions of the acts of the various states, but the following injuries or disabilities are usually specifically provided for: (*a*) fatal injury, (*b*) temporary total disability, (*c*) permanent total disability, (*d*) temporary partial disability, and (*e*) permanent partial disability. Some laws provide benefits in the case of such disfigurements as might be a handicap in securing employment.

Thus, the basic benefits are for the peril of *industrial injury,* and include *medical expenses* (often with maximum limits, although many states provide unlimited amounts) and *income* within the limits explained above. An increasing number of states also now provide *rehabilitation* benefits.

Most states also include some protection for the worker against the peril of *occupational disease*. Occupational diseases are defined as diseases peculiar to the occupation in which the employee is engaged and due to causes in excess of the ordinary hazards of employment. In recent years, suits claiming compensation for such diseases as those developing from exposure to chemical fumes and dust, skin abrasions, frostbite, and even prolonged industrial noise, have come increasingly to the attention of employers.

Liability for occupational disease is based upon the common law doctrine requiring the employer to use all reasonable precautions to safeguard the employee from injury and to warn him of the existence of any particular danger. By statute in one form or another occupational diseases have been covered in many jurisdictions—in some by the workmen's compensation laws, and others by separate occupational diseases acts. Some laws provide compensation for every injury, including diseases, resulting from the employment. Such a law is regarded with disfavor by employers and insurers. The all-inclusive provision, it is felt, tends to create doubts in the minds of all parties concerned and causes needless and wasteful litigation. A solution of the difficulty is offered by the schedule method used in a number of states. In these states a schedule of well-recognized occupational diseases is drawn up, to which other diseases may be added when industrial changes lead to new diseases traceable to an occupational risk. The trend in the last few years, however, has been from schedule to full cover of occupational diseases.

Not all diseases contracted in the course of an occupation may be attributed to the work or its nature. In the case of an occupational disease there must be a cause-and-effect relationship between the occupation and the disease as well as a frequency and regularity of the occurrence of the disease in the particular occupation.[1] To clarify the difference between an accidental injury and an occupation disease certain of the states passed amendments to their workmen's compensation acts.[2] In other instances the act was so clearly drawn as to evidence legislative intent to exclude occupational diseases without reference to the term in the act.

The problem both to the insurers and to employers created by the inclusion of occupational diseases within the scope of workmen's compensation is a serious one. Insurers and insureds alike have raised two questions: first, since occupational diseases in general are progressive and recurring, at what point of time does liability for compensation begin; and, second, which employer, in the event there are more than one, is liable? The trend of court decisions indicates the answers. When inability to work or earn because of certain express conditions occurs, the case is compensable. In other words, compensation starts from the time of actual disability. It has been

[1]An occupational disease has been well defined as "An occupation or industry disease is one which arises from causes incident to the profession or labor of the party's occupation or calling. It has its origin in the inherent nature or mode of work of the profession or industry, and is the usual result or concomitant" (*Victory Sparker & Spec. Co.* v. *Franks*, 147 Md. 368; 128 A. 635).

[2]For example, Connecticut amended its Workmen's Compensation Act to define a personal injury to include only an "accidental injury which may be definitely located as to the time when and the place where the accident occurred, and occupational disease as herein defined." The definition of an occupational disease was given as "a disease peculiar to the occupation in which the employee was engaged and due to causes in excess of the ordinary hazards of employment as such."

held that employees are insured "in their then condition," and if their employment causes a disease to continue until they are incapacitated, the insurer at the time of the incapacity is liable.

The seriousness of the situation becomes evident when it is realized than an employee may be suffering over a long period from an occupational disease that is progressive in its nature. Many times, subsequent to the onset of the disease, he may have changed his employment, yet the employer for whom he is working at the time his disease reaches a stage resulting in incapacity must bear the entire brunt of the compensation.[3] The tendency of many large employers to require preemployment physical examinations may discourage the hiring of partially incapacitated workers.

Administration of the Laws

While in some five[4] jurisdictions the administration of compensation law is left with the courts, the more usual method is to leave it with a special *state commission* (or administrator) appointed for the purpose. When the courts have jurisdiction, cases are heard by a judge or a referee appointed by the judge.

In the interests of simplification and to expedite the settlement of disputed points, legislatures have preferred the appointment of a commission. These commissions have been invested with varying powers, including general supervision over the administration of the compensation act, with power to make rules and regulations for the purpose of carrying out its provisions. Power is granted to prescribe forms and to arrange the procedure in such a manner as to effect a speedy and inexpensive disposition of proceedings. The state compensation administration is quasi-judicial, but much more supervisory and administrative. Its primary objective "is the substitution of a quick, informal administrative process for that of the courts."[5]

---

[3]An exception exists in those states with "second injury funds" (see later section of this chapter). Insurance underwriters are always apprehensive of the effect upon health of new materials and processes. The death of a woman late in 1951, a cancer victim, recalls one of the most famous occupational disease cases in compensation insurance history. The disease was diagnosed as cancer in 1950 and was attributable to radon gas latent in the woman's system for the past 33 years. This was the forty-first death in a group that contracted a fatal illness in 1918 as the result of radium poisoning. Workers swallowed particles of radium when they wet with their lips the tips of brushes used in painting numerals on watch and clock dials. The 1951 death was the fourth of this kind among the 41 reported; 37 died within five or six years after symptoms of the poisoning first made its appearance. The lethal nature of the process was, of course, unknown until the catastrophic effect had made its appearance.

[4]C. A. Kulp, *Casualty Insurance* (New York: The Ronald Press Company, 1956), p. 122.

[5]*Ibid.*, p. 123.

Varying in degree with different states, commissions are given authority to appoint investigators to report on circumstances surrounding an industrial accident when they deem such an action necessary. When the facts are in dispute, the commission hears the evidence, and decisions are made. Some states use a "direct settlement" method, others a "formal claim petition" method, and others a "hearing" method. Most states, however, use a "formal agreement" method in which employer and employee agree on the benefit amounts, subject to approval by the state authority.[6] In the absence of fraud, the decision of the commission upon all questions of fact is final.

Financing of the Benefits under the Laws

It is the employer who has the direct responsibility for paying benefits to qualified workers in accordance with the workmen's compensation laws. Indirectly, the consumer may be paying these costs if the product is one of relatively inelastic demand (where price increases do not decrease sales).

To guarantee that the benefits will be paid to the worker, the employer is required in all states to have some form of insurance. In many states he is given a choice among private insurers or state funds, and self-insurance. The next section of this chapter explains these alternatives available to the employer.

Regardless of the insurance method chosen, the costs of workmen's compensation benefits are substantial. Nationally, the cost of workmen's compensation is over $2 billion a year. The costs vary considerably by state, type of occupation and individual business firm. The general level of benefits is determined by the state laws which set forth the medical and income percentage, duration, minimum and maximum payments. Different classifications have extremely different costs, as the rates may vary from a few cents per $100 of payroll for such classes as office workers to over $30 per $100 for hazardous occupations such as sawmill operators or steeplejacks.

Workmen's compensation is obviously a major cost factor for many businesses. Many industrial injuries may be prevented (or at least reduced in frequency or severity), and the individual employer often directly benefits from decreased losses through the individual rating plans discussed later in this chapter. Still, the overall cost of workmen's compensation to business and industry is important, as its costs normally vary from year to year from 1 to 2 percent of payroll.

---

[6] *Ibid.*, pp. 123–26.

WORKMEN'S COMPENSATION INSURERS

Employers are usually offered options as to how they shall guarantee the payment of injury claims.

Insurance may be provided either through a *state fund* or by *private insurers* (stock, mutual, or reciprocal) authorized by the particular state to transact the business of workmen's compensation. Situations in the various states differ as to exact requirements. On one end of the scale there are state funds with a monoply[7] of the compensation business; a second group has state funds in competition[8] with private insurers; a third group of more than thirty states entrusts the business of compensation insurance to private insurers. As an alternative in each of the three groups, in almost all states the employer who can provide satisfactory proof of financial ability may carry his own risk; that is, he may *self-insure.*

From time to time the question of whether or not a state shall establish or abolish a state fund becomes a political question. Advocates of the state fund contend that, since workmen's compensation insurance is virtually compulsory, it should be the duty of the state to provide a means for effecting the insurance. It is further argued that with respect to a compulsory coverage it is inappropriate that it be a source of profit to private insurance. It also is argued that, since the cost of workmen's compensation insurance is a cost of production, to allow a profit reflects an unnecessary charge to the consumer.

In answer to this, those who favor private insurance raise the question as to whether a state fund does, in fact, provide protection at the lowest possible cost. In the absence of competition, inefficiency in management may evidence itself with a resulting higher cost differential than that established by the profit accruing to insurance companies. Proponents of private enterprise point out that competition affords a superior service to policyholders. They point out that insurance companies are able to provide insurance on an interstate basis and in connection with the statutory requirements of workmen's compensation coverage provide, as well, employers' liability protection, medical expense coverage, and other forms of protection not available through a state fund established by statute. It is further pointed out that under private insurance the cost is definitely established. While the cost may be definitely established under a state fund, an unseen cost may develop if the taxpayer is

---

[7]The "monopolistic state fund" means that private insurers may not write any workmen's compensation insurance for risks in these states. The states are: Ohio, West Virginia, Nevada, North Dakota, Wyoming, Washington, and Oregon. The first two named permit self-insurance as an alternative.

[8]The "competitive state funds" are used in many large industrial states, including New York, Pennsylvania, Michigan, and California.

called upon to subsidize the fund to maintain its solvency. Finally, it is pointed out that in a system of private enterprise any activity that may be carried on to advantage by private business establishments should not be relegated to the government.

The pros and cons of private insurers versus state funds are difficult to remove from political considerations. All of the seven monopolistic funds have been in existence for many years and those states are very reluctant to give up or change a system that has been in operation so long a time. One recent investigation of the Oregon state fund, in comparing it with private insurers in Massachusetts, concludes that the private insurers provide superior marketing and administrative services and higher benefits at a somewhat increased cost.[9]

The question of whether or not to self-insure the risk of workmen's compensation is another important decision for most of the larger employers. The general arguments in favor of self-insurance are the alleged lower administrative costs, increased managerial benefits of direct contact between employer and employee, and safety of the plan.[10] One of the best[11] analyses of self-insurance plans confirmed these advantages a number of years ago. However, the choice is not a simple one, for it involves careful consideration of many factors. The *particular* employer in a particular occupational group in a particular state or states at the present time must be evaluated. Critics of self-insurance point out the increased administrative burden on a self-insured employer, the loss of a third-party guarantor of benefits, the lack of a third-party to intervene as an impartial body between employer-ee and the decrease in valuable loss prevention and loss analysis services[12] by the insurer.

Federal government encroachment into the workmen's compensation field has been a recent topic of serious interest. The total and permanent disability benefits available under the federal Old Age, Survivors' and Disability Insurance program since 1956 have been broadened to overlap the state workmen's compensation benefits. It is pointed out that a disabled employee in 40 states may be eligible for the benefits of both programs to an extent in which his tax-free income *after* disability exceeds his normal net earnings.[13]

---

[9]Mark R. Greene, "Marketing Efficiency and Workmen's Compensation—A Case Study," *The Journal of Insurance,* Vol. 24, No. 4 (December, 1962), pp. 467–502.

[10]C. A. Kulp, *op. cit.,* pp. 432–33.

[11]Howard M. Teaf, Jr., *Self Insurance of Workmen's Compensation Insurance in Pennsylvania* (Harrisburg, Pa.: Special Bulletin Number 40, Department of Labor and Industry, Commonwealth of Pennsylvania, 1934).

[12]J. M. Sweitzer, "Monopolies Lag in Workmen's Compensation," *The Spectator,* May, 1962, pp. 37–40.

[13]See "Which Way in '62?" in *The Journal of American Insurance,* January, 1962, p. 1; and A. W. Brown, "The Folly in 'Federal,'" February, 1963, p. 5.

THE STANDARD WORKMEN'S COMPENSATION AND EMPLOYERS' LIABILITY POLICY

There is no standard workmen's compensation policy in the sense that a standard form is required by statutory enactment. Because of the diversity of the compensation laws as enacted in the various states, it was at first feared that a large number of different forms would be necessary to meet all requirements. This, the insurance carriers believed, would create confusion, and in an effort to solve the difficulty the company executives undertook to develop a standard form sufficiently broad to meet the requirements of insureds and at the same time meet the legal demands in each jurisdiction. Insurance executives, after many conferences with representatives of the various industrial accident commissions, developed the form that came to be known as the "Standard Workmen's Compensation and Employers' Liability Policy." That the policy served well is evidenced by the fact that only one major revision has occurred since its introduction more than 50 years ago. It simplified and clarified the older form by adapting it to changes in coverage and rating concepts adopted since the enactment of the first workmen's compensation law.[14] The revision undertook to reduce to a minimum the number of endorsements that developments in the field made necessary with respect to the original policy. With the new revision the majority of policies may be issued to the average risk without endorsements. There are a few situations, due to statutory requirements, manual rules, or underwriting practices, where endorsements will still be required.

The standard provisions for workmen's compensation and employers' liability policies follow the pattern of liability policies, with four main divisions: (1) declarations, (2) insuring agreements, (3) exclusions, and (4) conditions. Efforts have been made to follow the language of comparable provisions in liability policies. This rule makes for consistency and contributes to the understanding of both forms of insurance.

Declaration

The declarations consist of six items and cover such pertinent information as the name of the insured, policy period, states where operations are carried on, and liability limits for employers' liability.

---

[14]National Council on Compensation Insurance, *Workmen's Compensation and Employers' Liability Insurance Policy and Endorsement Forms* (Memorandum Accompanying Releases of the Standard Provisions for Workmen's Compensation and Employers' Liability Policies, October 1, 1954), p. 1. See also Willard J. Gentile, *The Workmen's Compensation and Employers' Liability Policy* (rev. ed.; New York: Roberts Publishing Company, 1963), p. 7. The new form is approved for use in 42 states and the District of Columbia, but does not apply in Arizona or the 7 states which have monopolistic state funds.

Premium information and certain other data that may be required by the company appear here. Basically the declarations provide the underwriting data relied upon by the company for the issuance of the policy.

The page of the policy devoted to the declarations is divided into six items. Certain information common to all insurance coverages is found here, as well as some items peculiar to this contract.

Item 1 calls for the name of the insured, the address, and the form of business organization; that is, whether the business is carried on as an individual proprietorship, partnership, corporation, or other form. Then are listed all usual workplaces of the insured at or from which operations covered by the policy are located. The requirement of listing "usual workplaces" calls for the listing only of permanent locations and does not require that every place where work may be carried on appear in the declarations.

Item 2 states the policy period. The policy runs from 12:01 A.M. Standard Time at the address of the insured. This reference to the address of the insured as stated in Item 1 of the declarations is very important. In the case of a risk that extends to a number of states and includes more than one time zone the time of an accident at the place of occurrence would not coincide with the time used to determine the inception and termination of the policy period.

Item 3 is perhaps one of the most important of all declarations. It states that Coverage A of the policy applies to the workmen's compensation law and any occupational disease law of the state or states listed. The entries on this item indicate the extent of coverage. By listing a state in Item 3 the policy extends to provide insurance for the entire liability of the insured under compensation and occupational disease laws of that state. The policy covers all operations of the insured in the state or states listed which are not specificially excluded or otherwise insured. In the case of a concern operating on a nationwide basis, Item 3 may list the states to be covered by inserting "All states except. . . ." The excepted states are then listed. When this practice is followed, states with monopolistic state funds, states in which the company is not qualified to write compensation insurance, and states where the insured has not complied with the formal requirements necessary to bring himself and his employees within the provisions of the workmen's compensation law must be listed as exceptions.

Item 4 classifies the operations of the insured. The estimated total annual remuneration of all employees is given as a premium basis. The rates per $100 of remuneration are listed together with the minimum premium for the policy and the total estimated annual premium. The deposit premium is given. If premium adjustments are to be made on a semiannual, quarterly, or monthly basis, this is indicated. Policies may be written without reference to an interim premium adjustment in the declarations by an endorsement known as the Periodical Audit Endorsement.

Item 5 supplies a single limit to apply to the employer's liability feature of the coverage. Sometimes provision is made for a different limit of liability for certain operations, and in some states there are special requirements touching upon this matter. In such instances the limit of liability is clarified by endorsement. This limit applies only to employers' liability coverage and not to workmen's compensation. Compensation benefits are all fixed by the law.

Item 6 may not appear in all policies, since it is optional with the company. It is designed to provide notice to the company of locations not intended to be covered by the policy. Actually to exclude a location not intended to be covered and not otherwise insured would require a policy endorsement. Some states require that the entire compensation obligation of an employer be insured in a single policy. Except where such a requirement exists, locations not intended to be covered, whether they are otherwise insured or not, may be excluded by endorsement. Listing excepted locations in Item 6 is for the information of the company only, and whether or not Item 6 appears in the policy, locations otherwise covered by the policy may only be excluded by specific endorsement.

Insuring Agreements

There are four sections to the insuring agreements. They are designated by Roman numerals and are sometimes known as Agreements I, II, II, and IV. Insuring Agreement I concerns itself with coverages known as Coverage A and Coverage B. Coverage A provides coverage for the insured's liability under the workmen's compensation law of the state or states indicated in the declarations, and Coverage B provides an employer's liability coverage with respect to injuries arising out of and in the course of employment. Insuring Agreement II covers the matter of defense, settlement, and supplementary payments. Insuring Agreement III provides for definitions. Insuring Agreement IV is concerned with the application of the policy by limiting liability to disease or injury that originates within the policy term.

The Standard Workmen's Compensation and Employers' Liability Policy basically affords the insured a twofold coverage. It undertakes, first of all, to assume the insured's liability under the workmen's compensation law of the state or states in which the coverage is effective by reading the law into the contract. In addition, the policy provides public liability coverage with respect to injuries arising out of the course of employment. The coverages are provided by *Insuring Agreement I* and appear in two parts, as follows:

I.

Coverage A—Workmen's Compensation

To pay promptly when due all compensation and other benefits required of the insured by the workmen's compensation law.

Coverage B—Employers' Liability

To pay on behalf of the insured all sums which the insured shall become legally obligated to pay as damages because of bodily injury by accident or disease, including death at any time resulting therefrom, sustained in the United States of America, its territories or possessions, or Canada by any employee of the insured arising out of and in the course of his employment by the insured either in operations in a state designated in Item 3 of the declaration or in operations necessary or incidental thereto.

Coverage A takes notice of the definition of "workmen's compensation law." This is defined in Insuring Agreement III and applies with respect to the state or states indicated in the declarations. By inserting a name of a state or states in the declaration the policy extends to cover the liability of the insured under the workmen's compensation law of that state. If a state has a separate occupational disease law, Coverage A of the policy covers the liability of the insured under that law. In a state where there are separate laws for occupational disease and workmen's compensation, it is possible to use the policy to provide coverage only under one of such laws. When this is the intent, the law, under which no coverage is to be afforded, is specifically excluded from the policy by endorsement.

Coverage B provides protection for the employer (even though he may be operating under the compensation law) who may find himself faced with a common law or employers' liability claim. It is quite possible that such a claim might be filed, particularly in those states providing employees with the option of coming within the operation of the compensation act. It is not altogether clear in some states whether or not the workmen's compensation acts have the effect of repealing employers' liability laws and terminating common law liability, although this is generally regarded to be the case in most jurisdictions. In addition to liability coverage for injury, a broad common law disease coverage is afforded. It is to be noticed that the word "disease" appears in Coverage B and not "occupational disease." Thus, coverage is afforded with respect to a liability claim attributable to any disease to which the employment may be alleged as a contributing cause.

Coverage B has the effect of completing the compensation protection and affords the insured the satisfaction of knowing that liability claims for injuries not covered by the compensation laws, even though groundless, will be defended by his insurance company. Coverage B affords protection only with respect to injuries "arising out of and in the course of employment." This means that a claim for coverage must be traceable to the operations of the insured in a state specified in the declarations. Other claims would be covered by one of the standard liability policies. To avoid duplication in coverage there is usually an exclusion in liability policies with respect to employers' liability. The exclusion in the liability policy specifically refers to injuries "arising out of and in the course of employment."

Since compensation benefits are fixed by law, there is no limitation with respect to them in the policy. A policy limit for Coverage B is established in the declarations. A widely used limitation is $25,000, although for many business institutions this limit is not considered adequate. The insured may elect higher limits, but Coverage B is always written with a definite limitation established in the declarations.

Insuring Agreement II is similar in effect to like clauses in liability insurance coverages. The clause obligates the company to undertake the defense of the insured and places the matter of negotiation and settlement with the company alone. There is the usual requirement to pay bond premiums and expenses incurred by the company in effecting a settlement. Likewise, the company is obligated to reimburse the insured for reasonable expenses incurred at the company's request.

Amounts paid for bonds, investigations, and other expenses incurred in connection with a claim are all in excess of the limit of liability with respect to liability coverages and in addition to the amounts required to be paid under a compensation law. In other words, the company always pays the full amount of the benefits provided by the compensation law, regardless of the amount of expense incurred in effecting a claim settlement. If the action is brought under Coverage B, the insured has the benefit of the full amount of the limit of liability for the adjustment of claims. Expenses incurred in effecting the adjustment are in excess of that limit liability.

Insuring Agreement III concerns definitions. These definitions are closely coordinated with the coverages provided under Insuring Agreement I, which uses such broad terms as "the workmen's compensation," "states," and "bodily injury by accident or disease." Insuring Agreement III clarifies the meaning of these terms with respect to coverage.

Definition (*a*) ties the term "workmen's compensation laws" as found in Coverage A to the state or states indicated in Item 3 of the declaration. If the state has a separate occupational disease law by virtue of Insuring Agreement III, Coverage A provides occupational disease coverage. Under the circumstances, in a state having separate laws for compensation and occupational disease, if it is the intent of the insured to provide coverage for accidental injuries only and not for occupational disease, the coverage not to be provided must be specifically excluded from the policy by endorsement. The definition of "workmen's compensation law" does not include the U.S. Longshoremen's and Harbor Workers' Compensation Act. It follows, therefore, that no insurance is automatically afforded for the insured's obligation to employees subject to this Act even if the operations are carried on in the state designated in Item 3 of the declaration.[15] Finally, the definition states that it "does not include those provisions of any such law which provide nonoccupational disability benefits."[16]

Definition (b) makes the word "state" mean any state or territory in the United States and the District of Columbia. This precludes limiting the term to its more restricted use. Risks in a territory or the District of Columbia may be covered on the same basis as a state if listed in the declarations.

Definition (c) clarifies the meaning of "bodily injury by accident" and "bodily injury by disease" in such a way that there cannot possibly be any overlapping. This prevents accumulation of limits. Hence, it would be impossible, under the definition, for an injured employee to claim an accidental injury and then, if a disease followed as a result of the injury, to hold the company liable for an occupational disease disability. Under the terms of the definition any given injury may be one or the other, but it cannot be both.

Definition (d) is usual to liability policies and provides that with respect to coverage (b) assault and battery shall be deemed an accident unless committed by or at the direction of the insured.[17]

Insuring Agreement IV limits coverage by the policy to injury by accident or by disease that occurs during the policy period and

---

[15]Because of the wide difference in longshoremen's risks they are not automatically included in the definition. The company is thus afforded an opportunity to underwrite maritime risks apart from other lines. If they are to be insured, such risks are included in the policy by endorement.

[16]By virtue of an extension of the New York Compensation Law nonoccupational disability benefits are brought within the purview of that law. Whether other states follow or not, the clause is incorporated in the policy to exclude coverage for nonoccupational disabilities.

[17]An assault to be compensable, as in the case of all other accidents, must be one "arising out of and in the course of employment." The Court of Appeals in affirming an award to the claimant in *Heiz* v. *Ruppert*, 218 N.Y. 148, touched upon the necessity that the assault arise out of the claimant's employment in the following terms: "Altercations and blows may, however, arise from the act of a fellow-servant while both are engaged in the employer's work and in relation to the employment. The employer may be badly or carelessly served by two men engaged in his work, and yet it may be inferred, when one injured the other in a quarrel over the manner of working together in a common employment, that the accident arose out of the employment and was not entirely outside of its scope, if it was connected with the employer's work and in a sense in his interest." If the assault is not compensable and suit is brought against the insured for the purpose of Coverage B, the assault is held to be an accident and the company will provide defense.

clarifies liability with respect to an occupational disease that has been developing over a considerable period of time. The first part of the agreement states that the policy applies only to an injury occurring during the policy period. The second part makes the insurer liable for an occupational disease that has developed over a long period of time. In the case of silicosis, for example, an employee may be exposed over a period of years, during which the workmen's lungs are gradually becoming affected. Finally, he becomes disabled. The company which is covering at the time of the last injurious exposure of the employee is liable for the benefits provided in the law. In other words, if A has been working in granite quarries all his life and is now found to be disabled, even though several companies provided coverage over the years, the insurance company covering when the last injurious exposure developed assumes the liability.[18]

Exclusions

There are six exclusions. They are designed primarily to clarify coverage and to prevent overlapping. Other workmen's compensation insurance is excluded in order to avoid duplicate coverage. Domestic or farm employment is excluded unless it is covered by the compensation law. Under Coverage B, the employers' liability coverage does not apply to assumed liability in a contract, employees hired in violation of law with knowledge of the insured, suits filed after 36 months after the end of the policy, or obligations under unemployment or disability benefits laws of the states.

Conditions

The conditions follow closely those in policies making use of the national standard provisions program for liability policies.

Compensation premiums are computed as a percentage of the payroll of the insured. The premium that an employer must pay for his workmen's compensation coverage depends on (*a*) the type of business he operates, (*b*) the number of employees in his establishment, and (*c*) the total amount of remuneration that he pays them. This information is found in the declarations. *Condition 1* of the policy deals with the manner of premium computation. It is a rather long condition of five paragraphs. The first of these incorporates by reference "the manuals in use by the company." By virtue of this clause the preparation of the policy is enormously simplified. If an employer should carry on operations not mentioned in the declara-

[18] This is not the case in all states. For example, California and Connecticut, in occupational disease cases, require contributions from successive insurance carriers of the same employee. In these states the policy is endorsed amending Insuring Agreement IV so that this policy condition complies with the state law.

tions, it is clear that the premium will be computed for those operations by the use of manual rates. The insured, moreover, agrees that any change in classifications, rates, or rating plans or any changes in benefits provided by the workmen's compensation law all become a part of the policy and the effective data made known to the insured by the issuance of an endorsement by the company.

The second paragraph of Condition 1 then goes on to describe what is meant by "remuneration." Unless otherwise provided by endorsement, the policy provides specifically that the remuneration of all employees engaged in operations covered by the policy, whether executive officers or not, shall be included in the payroll submitted for determining the compensation premium.

The second section of the paragraph includes all other persons performing work "which may render the company liable under this policy for injury to or death of such person." This means, for example, that if an employer sublets work to a subcontractor, he must include the payroll of that subcontractor in his compensation premium unless that subcontractor already carries compensation insurance. This exception is set forth in the latter part of the paragraph. In other words, the paragraph provides that the insurance company shall be entitled to a premium based on every dollar of remuneration paid to employees who will have a right to make a claim against the company under a covered compensation law.

Workmen's compensation premiums, since they are based on the actual payroll for the period covered, cannot be computed until the end of the policy term. The policy is written with an estimated payroll. At the end of the policy term an audit is made; and if the estimated premium is in excess of the actual premium developed by the audit, the difference is returned to the insured. On the other hand, if the estimated premium is less than the premium developed by the audit, the insured is billed for the difference.

If the risk is a particularly large one, arrangements may be made to determine the premium due on a periodic basis shorter than a year. The third paragraph of the condition covers this situation. This means, briefly, that if a deposit premium is paid at the beginning of the policy term the deposit is retained in its entirety until the end of the policy term and an adjustment is made at that time. For example, if an estimated premium of $2,000 is paid at the beginning of a policy term and an audit at the end of six months indicates a premium of $1,500 for that period, the insured is billed for the full amount of the $1,500. No credit is allowed for the $2,000 deposit premium. If a $1,500 premium is developed for the second six months, then the $2,000 deposit is credited to that premium and a balance of $500 returned to the insured. On the other hand, if during the second six-month period the audit develops a premium of $2,500, then the $2,000 would be credited to that premium and the insured billed for the additional $500.

The next paragraph of Condition 1 places an obligation on the insured to maintain all the necessary records for the purpose of computing the premium. The company may elect to ask the insured to forward those records at such times as the company may direct for the purpose of computation of premium. However, as a matter of actual practice in risks, other than the smaller ones, it is the practice of the company to send an auditor to the office of the insured and there check payrolls and records. The right of the insurance company to records of the insured is limited to "the information necessary for premium computation." The insurance company therefore has no right of access to any other records or files.

The final clause of Condition 1 deals with the method of premium computation already noticed. The clause precludes any misunderstanding with respect to the premium indicated in the declaration. It clearly states that the premium is an estimated one. It again incorporates the rules, rates, and rating plan to be found in the manuals of the insuring company as part of the contract. There is a saving clause at the end of the paragraph which provides that the premium due the company shall be dependent neither on the validity of the compensation law nor on its constitutionality. In other words, if the company assumes the risk, even though all or part of the law may be declared invalid, the right of the company to retain the premium is not thereby jeopardized.[19]

Most of the remaining thirteen conditions in the Standard Workmen's Compensation and Employers' Liability Policy are ones which have been already noticed in connection with previous insurance contracts. Several of the clauses specify rights of the *insurer* to: (1) inspection and audit of the insured's books, (2) written notice of injuries, claims, or lawsuits, as soon as practicable, (3) assistance and cooperation of the insured in hearings, trials, obtaining witnesses and the like, (4) proportional contribution from other insurance payable for covered losses, (5) subrogation for payments made under the contract, and (6) assignment of the contract only when the insurer consents to it in an endorsement.

Rights of the *insured or his employees* are also explained in several of the conditions. The insured who has complied with the policy terms has the right of action against the insurer if the employers'

[19]There is an optional condition that may be inserted in the policy following Condition 1 covering the matter of policies written for a period longer than one year. It makes all the provisions of the policy apply separately to each consecutive 12-month period. If the first or last period is less than 12 months, the shorter period is treated on the same basis that a short-term policy would be treated had it been wirtten separately. Premiums for each 12-month period are computed as provided in Condition 1 already noticed.

liability benefits are not paid as provided. Changes in the policy may be made by endorsement, and all terms in conflict with the compensation law are made to conform to it. The insured may cancel the contract at any time, and he also has the right to ten days' notice in case the insurer cancels.

One of the unusual conditions (Number 8) introduces a feature hitherto not found in liability coverages. The policy, in addition to protecting the named insured, states that the provisions of the insuring clause relating to workmen's compensation or employers' liability are the *direct obligation* of the insuring company *to any injured employee* or, in the event of his death, to his dependents. Since the contract is made primarily for the benefit of employees and their dependents, they have a direct right of action against the company and are in effect insureds under the policy as much as if specifically named.

For the further protection of the employee, the policy provides that the obligations of the insuring company to him shall not be affected by the failure of the employer in any way to comply with the policy requirements. Further, a default by the employer in the payment of the premium after an accident will not jeopardize the position of the employee. Failure to give the company the notice required by the policy does not react to the disadvantage of the employee; nor does the death, insolvency, bankruptcy, legal incapacity, or inability of the employer. The placing of the employer's business in the hands of an executor, receiver, trustee, assignee, or other person does not in any way affect the responsibility of the company to the injured employee. A notice to the employer of an injury is presumed to be notice to the company, so far as any obligation rests upon the injured party, and the knowledge of the employer is held to be the knowledge of the insurer. The insuring company shall be bound by all the findings or orders rendered against the employer.

SPECIAL RATING PLANS

In addition to the classifications and rates referred to in the declarations, which provide the basis for workmen's compensation premium costs, the insured may have several opportunities to benefit from individual risk rating plans. These features include experience rating plans, premium discount plans, retrospective rating plans, second injury funds, and deductible plans.

Experience Rating Plan

Experience rating bases its findings upon the past experience *of the particular risk* under consideration. The experience of the particular risk is compiled in much the same manner that data are collected for arriving at the manual classifications. If the injury history shows a cost below normal for the class, a credit in the rate is allowed, while an unfavorable experience results in a debit. This credit is applied to the manual rate to find the new or adjusted rate. When the risk is very large, the experience is the sole basis for composing the rate without reference to the manual. Such risks are said to be self-rated. To qualify for experience rating, the risk must produce a designated minimum premium figured at manual rates. In a large number of states, the minimum premium required is $1,000. There are variations, according to some states, from $400 to $800. For the purpose of determining experience, the plan requires a period of not less than one year and not over five years, although the rule is not the same in all states.

The term "standard premium" is used to designate that premium determined by applying manual rates to the employer's payroll modified by experience rating. In those instances where the annual standard premium exceeds $1,000 the insured has available to him four plans from which to choose that will further modify the premium charge. These include (*a*) the premium discount plan and (*b*) three retrospective rating plans.

The Premium Discount Plan

Workmen's compensation rating plans recognize that certain factors that enter into the premium charge do not increase proportionately as the premium increases. The principal factors considered are: (*a*) losses, (*b*) claim expense, (*c*) engineering and accident prevention, (*d*) administration and payroll audit expenses, (*e*) acquisition costs, and (*f*) taxes. Under the premium discount plan a definite portion of the first $1,000 of premium is allocated for company expenses and acquisition costs. As the size of the risk increases certain company expenses and acquisition costs are graded down. It is the purpose of the plan, as the premium increases, to give credit for those expenses that do not increase proportionately. Premium in excess of $1,000 is grouped in brackets and a discount applied. The discount is greater in the higher brackets. The net effect of this plan is to provide a reduction from the standard premium as the premium increases in amount. The theory upon which these premiums are computed is sometimes referred to as the "principle of graded expense."

The premium discount plan, in contrast to the retrospective plans, does not provide for a modification of the premium as a result of current loss experiences. It does, however, take into consideration past experience since the discount is applied to the standard premium, which, in turn, is modified by experience rating. The discounts applied for are for the purpose of reflecting a lower ratio of expenses and acquisition cost to premiums in the higher brackets. The net effect is to provide a lower premium than would be the case if the standard rates applied uniformly to the entire payroll.

Retrospective Rating Plans

Retrospective rating plans differ from the premium discount plans. Modification for *current loss* experience is the distinguishing feature of the retrospective plans. These plans are not separate and apart from experience rating but are, in effect, supplementary. While experience rating looks definitely to the past to determine the rate for the future, retrospective rating permits the insured to influence his premium by his current performance. Instead of assuming that the future will equal the past, retrospective rating gives consideration in its final charge to the actual experience during the policy term. Measured from the inception date of the policy it is an arrangement whereby at a future date a premium will be computed based upon the losses which actually occurred during the policy period.

It is apparent that at the inception date of the policy the actual anticipated experience can only be estimated. Under the retrospective plan, if the experience is particularly good, a credit reflects to the insured in his premium charge. If the experience is unsatisfactory, the cost to the insured is reflected in an increased premium. For the protection of the insured, upper limits to the cost are established; and for the protection of the insurance company, lower limits are established. The term "cost plus" has sometimes been applied to this rating plan.

The retrospective plan provides for the determination of a basic premium, which is a percentage of the standard premium, developed by applying the regular manual, schedule, or experience rates to the payroll of the insured. This basic premium provides for the agent's commission, home office expenses, audit, and safety inspection expenses, and, since the company guarantees the cost will not exceed an upper limit, there is a small charge for insurance. This insurance charge or loading, as it is termed, provides actually for losses that develop in excess of the maximum premium. There is no charge in the basic premium for claims expense or premium tax. These are computed when the losses are determined. Loss expense is added to the amount of actual losses when the final premium is determined. The losses plus loss expense produces an amount known as the "converted loss figure." The converted loss figure plus the basic premium is increased by the amount of tax required in the particular state. This practice limits loss expense and taxes to actual disbursements on the particular risk and precludes any overcharge that might lurk in an estimate.

In actual operation the plan provides for three premiums: (1)

minimum retrospective premium, (2) maximum retrospective premium, and (3) retrospective premium. The plan provides that the insured shall pay, in any case, the premium known as the minimum retrospective premium. On the other hand, he is protected in that he never may be called upon to pay more than the maximum retrospective premium. The premium he will actually pay will probably fall somewhere between the two; this is known as the "retrospective premium." It is determined by adding to the basic premium the losses incurred, modified to provide for taxes and claim adjustment expenses. Under the plan, the premium charged may be the minimum retrospective premium, and this is considerably less than the manual rate. It may be more than the minimum retrospective premium, depending upon the experience of the risk, but the possibility of excessive losses is cut off by the provision that the premium may never exceed the maximum retrospective premium.

The retrospective rating plan gives the insured the same credit for decreasing administration and acquisition expenses as does the premium discount plan. In addition, however, the retrospective rating plan reflects current losses in the current premium charge. This is, in fact, a protected profit-sharing plan. With a good experience, the insured shares the profits. With an unfavorable experience, he shares the losses. The amount of loss in any year is subject to a definite limit. From the standpoint of the insured, this is particularly attractive because he gets immediate credit for such care as he may exercise in reducing his loss experience. From the point of view of the insurance company, it is equally attractive because anything that will stimulate activity on the part of the insured to cut his losses will in the long run reflect to the benefit of the insurance carrier.

There are five forms of retrospective rating: Plans A, B, C, and J, which apply to workmen's compensation only, and D, which may also apply to liability, automobile, burglary, and glass insurance. These plans are alike in principle but vary in detail, principally with reference to the fixing of the maximum and minimum premiums. In addition, several states have adopted retrospective plans of their own. All of the plans, however, are alike in that they aim to have the current premium predicated upon the loss experience of the current year.

Second-Injury Funds

With the advent of experience rating, and more particularly with the advent of retrospective rating, the attention of the insured has been focused on all factors that may contribute to his loss experience and hence his workmen's compensation cost. Great emphasis has been placed upon accident prevention service, and it has been natural to carry the attention of the insured from accident prevention to physical factors. This has directed attention to incapacitated employees and more particularly to employees so incapacitated that a second injury would result in total disability.

The term *second injury* in compensation parlance refers to an injury that, taken in connection with a previous injury, will result in an incapacity greater than would have been the case had there been no previous injury. For example, persons who have lost an eye, or a hand, or are otherwise partially incapacitated, could become totally incapacitated as a result of another injury that in itself would not have resulted in total incapacity Unless the statutes provide specifically to the contrary, the cost of disability arising out of the second injury reflects upon the employer in whose employ the second injury is sustained. The end result of this situation is to place an undue burden upon the employer who retains in his employ the person who is already seriously injured.

To counteract this situation, a number of states, by statute, have limited the liability of the employer in such instances to payment for the disability resulting only from the second injury. The statutes in such circumstances provide that such injured workmen, after having received all of their regular compensation benefits from their employers, will be entitled to additional weekly benefits during the continuance of incapacity out of the second-injury fund administered by the state. It is usual to provide that the fund be financed by contributions from insurers writing compensation insurance. Payments for the second-injury disabilities are made out of this fund. If the injury is total, special compensation is provided. It is also provided that, if the injured workman is able to secure employment, but not at the level at which he was previously employed, he may receive compensation based upon the difference between his present weekly earnings and the weekly earnings before the second injury occurred.

Deductible Plans

In the interests of lower premium charges, insureds have sometimes preferred to assume losses up to an agreed point. Coverages of this kind have been written under two forms. The first insures against loss in excess of a designated amount arising from the single accident. Such a coverage is termed *excess insurance*. The second form is the same in principle but applies the policy limitation to each claim, instead of to a single accident. This form is called *deductible average insurance*.

These coverages are considered unsatisfactory from the insurance carriers' standpoint and for that reason are rarely written. Insurance companies prefer that risks with a low loss ratio reduce insurance costs through experience and retrospective rating. There is a grave danger that important hazards will be overlooked by an insured who knows that his losses above a predetermined amount are covered by insurance. When every loss has a bearing on the insured's costs, care is taken to eliminate all hazards. This lessens the possibility of catastrophes, as well as of occasional accidents.

OTHER POLICY BENEFITS

One of the most important benefits of workmen's compensation insurance is the impetus to loss prevention efforts which it provides to both insurer and insured. The individual risk rating plans have been shown to be of direct benefit to employers who lower their insurance costs by good loss experience.

Loss prevention in industrial injuries and disease has also been achieved by considerable activities of the insurers. They undertake to inspect the workplaces covered and to suggest to the insured such changes or improvements as may operate to reduce the number and severity of accidents. A high accident frequency may be attributable to poor management and indifference. Management sometimes overlooks hazards attributable to poor housekeeping such as obstruction in passageways and aisles, slippery floors, lack of adequate handrails or guards, and the like. Improvements in housekeeping may be effected at modest cost. Safety meetings for the education of management and employees require some time and effort. If management is sincerely interested in reducing costs by improving its loss ratio and will cooperate with the inspection and engineering service of the company, improvement can frequently be effected.

Insureds realize that industrial injuries are a direct source of monetary loss. Work is interrupted; superintendents and others lose time from productive effort; machinery is broken and goods spoiled because of the mental upset of witnesses to the accident. These and other factors tend to make the "hidden costs" of industrial accidents a serious drain, even though the employer's obligation to the injured man is covered by insurance. These indirect costs, including such items as loss of time by other employees, cost of replacement or rehiring, decreased productivity and morale, are estimated at four times the direct costs of workmen's compensation insurance.[20]

Inspection service is becoming an increasingly important factor in the placing of compensation insurance. An unfavorable loss experience coupled with poor or indifferent management would place a business in the category of an undesirable risk from the insurance company standpoint. On the other hand, hazardous occupations are

[20] H. W. Heinrich, *Industrial Accident Prevention* (New York: McGraw-Hill Book Co., Inc., 1950), pp. 50–61. This book is a classic pioneering effort in the field of loss prevention.

insurable if management evidences an interest in loss-prevention activities. Some companies have organized highly specialized engineering and research services for the purpose of investigating and studying extra-hazardous working conditions and of devising, if possible, safer methods and conditions. In new manufacturing processes, where there is no previous industrial experience, the expert knowledge of experienced research engineers proves of great assistance in discovering safe methods. If a favorable experience is reflected in the premium, the direct saving is often substantial.[21]

SUMMARY

Employers' liability and workmen's compensation insurance is an unusual combination of social and voluntary insurance. The risk is now largely a social one, since by virtue of the *workmen's compensation laws* in each of the states the employer is required to provide certain benefits for industrial injuries and some occupational diseases. These laws have replaced, in most cases, the earlier negligence system in which the employee had to prove that the employer was responsible for the injury or sickness of the worker. Instead, the workmen's compensation system places liability on the employer *regardless of fault* on the part of employer or employee.

Workmen's compensation insurance is still, however, an important part of the voluntary sector of insurance because three fourths of the coverage is written by private insurers, as opposed to state funds set up for this purpose. Administration of the laws is technically the work of state workmen's compensation commissions, but in many cases the insurers are most important in carrying out the payment of benefits to the employees. The security of the benefits according to the law is assured by the insurance method, through *private insurers* (in most states) and *state funds* (competitive, or monopolistic), or optional systems of *self-insurance* by the employer.

The benefits of the workmen's compensation laws are threefold: *medical expenses,* weekly *income* payments during incapacity (or lump-sum settlements for certain losses of limb or eyesight), and *rehabilitation.* The variety of the benefits among the states as to amount and duration of benefits is very great. The eligibility for benefits also differ in each state, but generally speaking the vast majority of workers, except those in domestic or agricultural occupations, is covered.

The Standard Workmen's Compensation and Employers' Liability

---

[21]Accident-prevention services provided by casualty insurers include, among others, the following: (1) engineering consultation service, (2) periodic inspection service, (3) employee and supervisor training programs, (4) distribution of informative material, (5) claims services, (6) employee safety meetings, and (7) advisory committees to work with supervising officials.

Policy is used to create excellent uniformity of coverage by insurers. The *declarations* provide essential underwriting and premium calculation information. The *insuring agreements* include one for (1) "all compensation and other benefits required of the insured by the workmen's compensation law" and (2) others which provide, within a specified limit, employers' liability protection and defense for claims which may fall outside the compensation statutes. The *exclusions* are few, involving mostly assumed liability and violations of law by the employer. The *conditions* contain details of how the premium is to be calculated and adjusted for changing payrolls, and specify the other rights of the insured and insurer in connection with the policy. The policy benefits are made a direct obligation of the insurer to injured employees.

Special rating plans are commonly used to make the cost of the workmen's compensation policy vary directly with the individual employer for whom it is issued. *Experience rating* for past loss experience, *premium discounts* for decreasing administrative expenses of larger insureds, *restrospective rating* for *current* loss experience, *second injury funds* and *deductible plans* are all used to give the employer more direct incentive to use every available means of loss prevention and reduction of industrial injuries and disease.

FOR REVIEW

1. Indicate several differences that distinguish claims made under the workmen's compensation policy from other casualty claims.
2. State workmen's compensation laws are either (*a*) compulsory or (*b*) elective. Explain. They also are either (*a*) monopolistic or (*b*) competitive in nature. What does this mean?
3. Why have workmen's compenation laws been adopted in all of the states? Shouldn't injured employees be able to show negligence on the part of the employer before the employer should be held liable?
4. What kinds of benefits are provided by the workmen's compensation laws? How are the amounts determined?
5. The workmen's compensation policy provides (*a*) liability coverage and (*b*) compensation coverage. What is the extent of the protection afforded under each?
6. B conducts a trucking business in his own name. If he should decide to incorporate would it be necessary to secure a new compensation coverage, assuming the risk and the management remain exactly as before?
7. Give an example of the following types of disability: (*a*) temporary, (*b*) permanent partial, (*c*) permanent total, and (*d*) occupational disease.
8. X operates a trucking business and his experience has been most unfavorable. His workmen's compensation insurance carrier cancels the coverage. In an effort to get new insurance the proprietor of the business makes several deliberate misstatements. Shortly afterward, because of negligence in the maintenance of a steam shovel, one man is killed and two other dangerously injured. Upon learning the fact, the insurance company denies liability on the ground that the policy was obtained through deliberate

misrepresentation of material facts. To whom may the injured employees and the legal representative of the deceased employee appeal for damages?

9. From time to time there is considerable agitation for the replacement of all privately written compensation insurance by monopolistic state funds. The claim is made that insurance will be offered at cost and will thereby reflect lower premium charges. There are a few monopolistic funds, while some states offer state funds as an alternative to private insurance. Why, in your opinion, has not the state monopoly idea been more widely adopted?
10. Mrs. X is a salad maker in a restaurant and contracts an annoying skin affection caused by handling certain types of vegetables as a part of her work. Would you call this an occupational disease? Would this be covered under the workmen's compensation laws?
11. Are occupational diseases covered by the standard compensation policy without special endorsement?
12. It has been stated that insurance companies make it difficult for physically handicapped employees to secure employment because of penalties in the compensation rate. Insurance companies deny this and point out that they do not in any way penalize the physically handicapped. Employers answer that although no specific penalty is indicated, injuries reflect in their experience rating and, as a result, they cannot afford to hire the physically handicapped. If you were an employer operating a large industrial plant, would you feel safe in employing persons injured in industrial accidents or disabled veterans? Predicate your answer purely on the financial implications.
13. X, an employer, is told that the workmen's compensation policy affords a coverage as broad as the act. He conducts a business at B Street. A new business outlet is shortly opened in another part of the city, and the employer expects to report the payroll at this location at the time it is audited. Is he protected at the new location?
14. A.B. filed suit against his employer for $60,000. He claimed that he had contracted silicosis because the paint plant in which he worked was not properly equipped with health-protecting devices. He was awarded $10,000. The award was followed by a flood of suits from other employees. How would the position of the employer be better if the disease were covered by the compensation act?
15. What characteristics make the workmen's compensation policy (*a*) simpler than other insurance contracts and (*b*) sometimes more difficult to write than other insurance contracts?
16. What special rating plans are used in workmen's compensation insurance? Briefly explain their primary purposes.

Chapter 16

AUTOMOBILE INSURANCE

THE "automobile economy" of the United States today is an amazing world of mobility, responsibility, and danger. It has provided many opportunities and advantages for work and recreation, yet at the same time it has created substantial risk and insurance problems. Could anyone really have imagined a generation or so ago that 80 million motor vehicles would be traveling today over our highways? Or could they have foreseen the awesome effects of this era in terms of death, injuries, and monetary costs?

The annual toll has now reached alarming proportions: over 40,000 persons killed, over 1.5 million persons injured and at least $8 billion of lost wages, property damage, and medical and insurance costs. It is easy to lose the proper perspective of such figures, but a simple comparison shows that more than twice the number of American deaths have been due to automobile accidents during the twentieth century than were due to all the wars since the Declaration of Independence.[1]

THE NEED AND REQUIREMENTS FOR AUTOMOBILE INSURANCE

With such obvious needs for insurance protection, it is little wonder that the automobile insurance field has grown to a gigantic size, exceeding $7 billion in annual premiums. Three basic questions are emphasized in the review of automobile insurance in this chapter: (1) By whom, and how, is automobile insurance needed and required? (2) What provisions of the usual automobile insurance contracts provide the necessary coverage? (3) What are the costs, and to whom?

Viewpoints on the Need for Automobile Insurance

More than many other kinds of voluntary insurance, automobile insurance must be looked at not only as an individual solution to an individual problem of risk, but also must be considered in its social or public aspects. The uncertainty of financial disaster due to an automobile accident is so widespread a risk today that any reasona-

[1]Calvin H. Brainard, *Automobile Insurance* (Homewood, Ill.: Richard D. Irwin, Inc., 1961), p. 7.

ble method of treatment for the risk becomes partially individual and partially social in its methods and objectives.

The individual who owns or uses an automobile (or other motor vehicle) has some of the familiar risks which all property owners face. He may lose part or all of the value of his automobile through a variety of perils, such as fire, theft, or collision. In addition, he has an enormous risk in not knowing if his automobile will cause damage to the property of other persons, or injury to other persons, for which he may be held liable. He and his family may also suffer personal losses due to medical care expense and lost income as a result of an automobile accident. In summary, the individual risks require protection from three important fields of insurance: (1) property, (2) liability, and (3) accident.

Another viewpoint from which automobile insurance should be considered is that of the victim. If he is an *innocent* victim, certain legal rights accrue to him against the parties responsible for his property damage or personal injury loss. To obtain payment, he must usually prove the other party liable. Time and costs may be involved in carrying out the legal right, and even then the negligent party may not be able to pay for the results of his irresponsibility. The result is that some innocent victims of automobile accidents remain uncompensated.

Perhaps no such sympathy and concern need be wasted on the other group of automobile accident victims, i.e., those who were responsible through their own negligence for their losses. However, from society's viewpoint the effects may be similar regardless of who[2] was the cause of the accident. The victims and their families may become burdens of the government, through various public welfare programs.

The need for considering all of the three viewpoints in reaching a conclusion about how to treat the automobile risk suggests that some governmental action encouraging or requiring insurance is necessary. Each of the following solutions shows that this is true, although the method and extent of the requirements differ greatly in the various types of laws designed to cope with the problem.

Current Solutions

The federal government and a number of states have enacted legislation making adequate automobile coverage a condition which must be met before a license is issued to operate in certain fields of

[2]And indeed, some accidents may be the result of negligence of society itself. For example, consider the possibility of some accidents which may be caused largely by improper highway engineering, construction, and safety directions. A fair appraisal of the automobile accident risk leaves most losses in the realm of individual responsibility, however.

business. Common carriers such as truckmen, taxicabs, or bus operators fall in this category. The Interstate Commerce Act provides that all interstate common carriers furnish evidence of liability insurance to the Interstate Commerce Commission. In addition to the state laws that apply only to common carriers, there are in some jurisdictions motor carrier acts requiring a certificate of insurance on file with the state authority in the case of private transit carriers. A few states also require insurance before issuing an automobile registration or license to certain groups of persons, such as minors under the age of twenty-one or eighteen.

The most important types of automobile insurance legislation, however, apply to all or nearly all automobile owners or drivers. These include the two basic types, automobile (1) *financial responsibility laws* and (2) *compulsory insurance legislation.* Several other laws will be discussed later which are designed either to permit everyone to purchase insurance protection, such as "assigned risk" plans, or to meet the financial needs of accident victims, such as "unsatisfied judgment funds" and "uninsured motorist coverage."

Financial Responsibility Laws. In connection with the operation of an automobile, 47 states encourage the purchase of insurance by means of financial responsibility legislation. These laws are designed to make it impossible for the reckless and financially irresponsible motorist to secure a license to drive a car unless there is a guarantee that he is able to pay and will pay, within the limits established by the statutes, damages for which he becomes liable.

The earliest financial responsibility laws differed in detail from state to state but were alike in principle. Instead of requiring a motorist to purchase insurance before his car is licensed, the laws operate on the principle that once a motorist has demonstrated himself to be a careless driver *by becoming involved in an accident* for which he is found liable, he must prove his financial responsibility or lose his license to drive.[3]

To strengthen the financial responsibility legislation by eliminating the possibility of the first victim remaining unpaid under the

---

[3]This type of plan was generally held to fall somewhat short of the objective of the sponsors of financial responsibility legislation. One of the earliest such laws was passed in Connecticut in 1925. Motorists irresponsible financially continued to operate cars on the road without insurance. The impact of the possible loss of license to drive was lessened since many who met with injuries in automobile accidents were unwilling to incur the cost of a suit if it appeared at the outset that the judgment would be uncollectible. In such circumstances, the person responsible for the accident suffered no penalty.

Even in the cases where the license was revoked the party responsible for the accident could, under this type of law, have his license restored by furnishing proof of financial responsibility for future accidents. This usually meant the purchase of an insurance policy to cover future accidents. There was no relief for the injured party whose accident made mandatory the financial provisions for future accidents.

so-called "one bite laws," a new type of law was enacted. Under this type of law the motorist must immediately establish his ability to answer for damages if involved in an accident.[4] If the motorist is not insured, he is required to furnish security that in the judgment of the state authorities will satisfy any judgment that may be recovered against him. In contrast to the earlier laws, which required the motorist to establish his ability to answer for damage only after a judgment had been awarded and then only with respect to future claims, the newer type of law requires motorist involved in an accident to provide security immediately to cover any possible judgments that may be expected to result from the accident that has already occurred.

The statutes require at least minimum bodily injury limits of $5,000 per person and $10,000 per accident, and property damage limits of $1,000. Most states require higher limits, such as 10/20/5, and a few require even higher limits.[5] There is no waiting until the motorist is convicted of a traffic violation or a judgment awarded for damages. The motorist must be prepared immediately to respond to damages upon the happening of an accident.

The law applies to the accident that has occurred as well as to accidents that may happen in the future. Laws of this type are known as "security-type laws" and are in contrast to the earlier laws in which only future accidents were considered. This type of law provides a powerful incentive to insure since motorists understand that, following an accident, failure to satisfy the state authorities with respect to financial responsibility will result in the immediate suspension of license and registration. Financial responsibility must be evidenced at the time of any accident involving personal injuries, although many states do not apply the law to small property damage accidents under $50 or $100.

Because of the legal requirements of the financial responsibility laws, the technicalities involved and the uncertainties concerning the operation of the different state laws, motorists have turned to insurance to help fulfill their legal liabilities. The percentage of insured drivers has increased from less than 50 percent 20 years ago to over 80 percent in many states today. Some of the states with

---

[4]This type of law first appeared in New Hampshire in 1937. In many states the present legislation is based upon a model safety responsibility law, Article IV of the Uniform Vehicle Code. The requirements of the law are often applied not only after an accident, but also in other specified cases where the motorist has a certain number or type of serious motor vehicle violations, such as reckless driving or speeding.

[5]These laws differ substantially in the different jurisdictions. For a comprehensive summary of these differences and an outline of the important features of the different security-type laws, see *Analysis of Automobile Financial Responsibility and Related Laws,* Complied by the law department of the Association of Casualty and Surety Companies, New York, 1963.

particularly effective financial responsibility law enforcement have increased the percentage to above 90 and 95 percent insured.

Compulsory Liability Insurance Legislation. In contrast to the financial responsibility laws enacted in the majority of the states that have legislated in the field, Massachusetts in 1927 went one step further and made the demonstration of financial responsibility a condition precedent to obtaining registration. All owners of automobiles are required to produce an insurance policy[6] *before license and plates will be issued.* In essence, this is mandatory financial responsibility required in order to own and use a car. It was not until 30 years later (1957) that a second state, New York, adopted such a law. North Carolina became the third state to do so, in 1958.

Since the enactment of the law in Massachusetts, there have been two opposing schools of thought concerning the subject. Advocates of compulsory insurance point out the danger of a serious accident when an uninsured and financially irresponsible driver is liable for damages and unable to pay. In such a case, the financial responsibility law, they contend, offers no assistance for past accidents. As a guarantee of protection to the public against financial loss, compulsory insurance is held by its advocates to be superior to the usual financial responsibility law.

Opponents of the law object to the compulsion forced upon every car owner, whether he is a good or a bad driver. They contend that it tends to accelerate recklessness, thereby causing more accidents instead of lessening them. Insurance companies have little opportunity to select their risks, and the loss experience is disheartening. Claim suits tend to increase abnormally, the courts are congested, and rates are perhaps higher as a result of unfavorable experience.[7] There is also a belief that property damage claims are fraudulently converted into bodily injury claims since only the bodily injury coverage is required by one of the laws (Massachusetts).

Another criticism is leveled at the tendency of the compulsory laws to provide less protection, as many persons expect the required minimums to meet their full needs. Policy coverage also tends to be restricted by political considerations, as promised lower rates are secured by limiting the policy coverage. In Massachusetts, for example, the basic policy does not cover, unless it is endorsed to do

---

[6]The laws also permit, as an alternative, the filing of cash, bond, or collateral in amounts equivalent to the required insurance contract limits of liability. Practically speaking, the insurance policy is the only method ever used.

[7]Claims do increase, as much as 25 percent or more, for example, in the first few years following compulsory law in New York and North Carolina. New York and Massachusetts also have the two highest basic coverage rates in the country. However, these facts may not be proof that the laws are bad, for it may also be an indication that they have succeeded in their objective of paying automobile accident victims for their losses.

so, (1) accidents occurring on private property, (2) accidents occurring out-of-state, or (3) guests in the car. A final objection raised is the possible threat to private enterprise which may result from the compulsory law, with a state insurance fund perhaps usurping a field of insurance which now accounts for 40 percent or more of the business of property-liability insurers.

The lack of competent and unbiased data[8] leaves many of the arguments for and against compulsory automobile liability insurance unsolved. It is an emotionally charged problem, yet one of extreme importance to both society and the private insurance business. The idea and objectives are reasonable in many respects, but often misunderstood as automatically bringing a full solution to the problems.[9]

Neither the compulsory laws nor the financial responsibility laws do much to increase the prevention of accidents, which is perhaps the fundamental and most-needed goal. Better enforcement of existing motor vehicle and safety laws is essential, and tackles the problem at its root. The increasing and unnecessary losses on the highways should not be condoned under any of the current or proposed solutions to the automobile accident victim problem.

The future will undoubtedly bring further action by the states in attempting to achieve better solutions. The compulsory law, having been adopted in only three states, is apparently not a popular choice. It has been defeated in many bills introduced regularly in the past three decades in many states. The current trend seems to be in the direction of strengthening the financial responsibility laws through the adoption of one or more of the following other types of laws or programs, in conjunction with existing statutes.

Other Laws and Programs. Three further plans are directed toward solving portions of the automobile accident victim problem. The assigned risk plans aim at making insurance available to almost all persons desiring coverage; and the unsatisfied judgment funds and uninsured motorist coverages have been developed to assure payment of losses to innocent victims.

Assigned Risk Plans. Every state has felt the necessity of making insurance available to all who are entitled to it. Since private insurers have the right to select risks, it sometimes develops that an

---

[8]Two earlier qualified studies are now out-dated for evaluation of the current situation. See *Report by the Committee to Study Compensation for Automobile Accidents* (Columbia University: Council for Research in the Social Sciences, 1932) and *The Problem of the Uninsured Motorist: A Report by Deputy Superintendent George H. Kline and Special Assistant Carl O. Pearson to Superintendent of Insurance Alfred J. Bohlinger* (State of New York Insurance Department, 1951).

[9]For example, contrary to popular belief, full protection of the unpaid automobile accident victim does not necessarily result. Accidents caused by hit-and-run drivers, drivers of stolen cars, drivers of illegally registered cars and out-of-state cars, and victims who themselves are negligent, are not covered.

applicant may have difficulty in securing adequate insurance. To preclude a state fund or other insurance provided by the state, provision has been made under the *assigned risk plan* for an equitable distribution of individually rejected risks.

The plans are not the same in all states, but they follow a similar pattern. Generally, if an insured has been refused insurance by one or more private insurers, he may apply to the manager of the assigned risks plan. If, upon investigation, the applicant is found to be eligible for insurance, the manager of the plan assigns the risk to a company writing the type of insurance required. Assigned risks are rotated among the different companies in proportion to the business that each insurer writes in the state. All insurance companies are obligated[10] to accept risks as assigned unless absence of good faith can be shown. An applicant who can be shown to be engaged in illegal operations such as gambling, dealing in narcotics, or other illegal enterprise, or one who has been a habitual violator of the law need not be accepted as an assigned risk. Insureds covered as assigned risks include not only those persons with poor accident records,[11] but also high-rated classifications such as the under-twenty-five age group in some territories.

The policyholders who purchase their insurance protection through the assigned risk plans usually pay a higher rate than other insureds. A surcharge of 10 to as high as 200 percent is applied, depending on the policyholder's accident record, motor vehicle violations, and other factors. The latest figures available show that the higher charges do not usually offset the poorer loss experience for these undesirable classifications of automobile insureds.[12]

[10] A decision of the United States Supreme Court held in 1951 that a company writing automobile liability insurance must assume its share of assigned risks. The constitutionality of the California law requiring companies to accept assigned risks was questioned, and the answer given that the police power of the state "extends to all the great public needs." In taking steps to make available means for the compensation of innocent victims of highway accidents, the Court held that California did not go beyond permissible limits. *California State Automobile Association Inter-Insurance Bureau, Appellant,* v. *John R. Maloney, Insurance Commissioner,* 340 U.S. 105; 71 Sup. Ct. 601; 95 Law Ed. 788.

[11] Only extreme cases or many law violations or accidents result in being refused insurance coverage in the assigned risk plans. In what must be a classic case, consider the problem of a thirty-nine-year old driver who had 50 accidents in a nine-year period, including 28 in the most recent three years. Surprisingly, in only 2 accidents was he found at fault and in none were there any serious injuries! *The Columbus Dispatch* (Ohio), February 19, 1964, p. 37A.

[12] *The Mutual Memorandum* (Chicago, Ill.: American Mutual Alliance, Vol. 45, No. 3, January 22, 1964). Combined data for all states except Massachusetts for the period 1938-61 show loss ratios (premiums earned to losses incurred) of 1.18 for bodily injury liability and .90 for property damage liability. In 1961 the ratios were 1.06 and .88, respectively. Individual states showed bodily injury loss ratios in 1961 as high as 1.83 (South Dakota), 1.49 (Minnesota), 1.44 (Arkansas), and 1.13 (New York). These figures do not include the expenses of the assigned risk contracts.

Unsatisfied Judgment Funds. Three states have adopted legislation[13] which provides the innocent victim of an automobile accident with a source of payment for losses caused by a financially irresponsible motorist. A separate *unsatisfied judgment fund* is established, with the purpose of paying bodily injury, and in some states property damage,[14] losses (1) if the victim proves, by obtaining a judgment against him, that another party was negligent in causing the accident and (2) if the victim shows that he cannot recover the judgment, i.e., it remains unsatisfied.

Certain minimum limits apply as a deductible, and maximum amounts of coverage also are specified.[15] The negligent motorist is not relieved of liability for the damages or injuries he has caused; his driving privileges are revoked until the U.J.F. has been reimbursed for the amount paid to the innocent victim.

The basic financing of these funds is by a levy usually assessed against the uninsured motorists of the state. However, North Dakota and Maryland also charge insured motorists a $1.00 fee at the time of registration, and New Jersey and Maryland charge the insurance companies writing automobile business in the state ½ of 1 percent of their net direct-written premiums.[16] The fees charged to the uninsured motorists have risen sharply in recent years, from $3 to $15 a year in New Jersey, and from $8 to $70 in Maryland. This fee is for the right *not* to purchase automobile liability insurance, and does not provide any liability protection for the uninsured motorist.

An evaluation of the merits for and the disadvantages of unsatisfied judgment funds is no easy task. The article by Dr. Hashmi includes reference to the following benefits: (1) providing some recourse to innocent victims, (2) keeping more irresponsible motorists off the road, (3) a small reimbursement of the funds, of about 5 percent, by the uninsured motorists, and (4) a broadening scope of coverage. He points out the similarity to compulsory insurance and criticizes the (1) financial inequity of the costs being paid by insured motorists, (2) the deficits which have resulted in the funds from inadequate levies, and (3) the complicated, expensive and cumbersome procedures used by the funds. He does not predict much further growth, but suggests the future may bring adjustments

---

[13]North Dakota (in 1947), New Jersey (in 1952), and Maryland (in 1957). The basic idea for these systems came from funds established earlier in several provinces of Canada.

[14]Sajjad A. Hashmi, "Unsatisfied Judgment Funds," *The Journal of Risk and Insurance,* Vol. XXXI, No. 1 (March, 1964), p. 93. New Jersey and Maryland include property damage over $100 in amount.

[15]*Ibid.,* pp. 93–94. The minimums are $100 in New Jersey (for property damage only) and Maryland, and $300 in North Dakota. The maximums are $10,000 per person, $20,000 per accident, and $5,000 property damage.

[16]*Ibid.,* pp. 94–95.

which bring about a combination of U.J.F. and the uninsured motorists plans which are discussed next.[17]

Uninsured Motorists Coverage. Another method of providing compensation for victims of automobile accidents caused by financially irresponsible motorists is the *uninsured motorists endorsement.* This coverage became available in the early 1950's and has received increasing attention as a solution to the problem. For a small cost (usually about $5.00 a year, or less) the insured motorist may extend his own automobile insurance contract to include protection for his family against the possibility of losses caused by persons who cannot pay for their legal liability. Hit-and-run cases are also covered, where the victim cannot usually collect his damages because he has no one to ask for payment.

The standard form of this coverage is treated in further detail in the later discussion of the Family Automobile Policy. Different contracts may have somewhat different wording, so the insured should read the endorsement to determine the extent of protection.

The state laws are also important, as some 14 states now require an uninsured motorists endorsement to be included in automobile insurance contracts. The provisions vary considerably.[18] In many other states the coverage is available on an optional basis. New York, in 1959, established a plan which gives all residents of the state U.M. coverage for automobile accidents within the state. For coverage outside the state, an optional coverage is available. The costs for the mandatory coverage are paid by assessments against the insurers, although indirectly this means the costs are met by insured motorists.

Uninsured motorist coverage accomplishes the objective of payment to innocent victims without a separate system such as the U.J.F. It is usually not necessary that the victim secure a judgment against the wrongdoer; only that he had no liability insurance. Delays and administrative costs are reduced by having the insurer make the settlement with the injured party or his representative subject to an arbitration process when necessary.

Additional Alternative Solutions. Two other solutions to the problem of the unpaid automobile accident victim should be briefly mentioned. A system of *automobile compensation,* similar to benefits paid under the present workmen's compensation laws in the states, has been advocated. Such a plan is based on the assumption that our present system of legal liability is unworkable for deter-

[17]*Ibid.,* pp. 96–110.

[18]For example, all provide bodily injury coverage, but the limits may vary from 5/10 to higher amounts. Property damage coverage is provided in a few states, such as South Carolina and Virginia (with a $200 deductible). Financing varies from most states where the insured motorists pay the entire cost, to the above two states where the uninsured motorists are charged a fee which establishes a U.M. fund.

mining and providing for losses resulting from automobile accidents.

In Canada, the province of Saskatchewan[19] has applied this doctrine to pay injured parties regardless of fault, on the theory that automobile accidents are a social rather than an individual cost and responsibility. Although the possible benefits of such a plan are recognized, in terms of less delay, less difficulty in measuring damages (since the scale of benefits is set by the law), and a reduction in some inequities of the liability system, there are many serious drawbacks. The difficulty of setting benefit levels, the inappropriateness of comparing the very different workmen's compensation risk with the automobile risk, and the great possibility of fraud are noted.

If concerted efforts are made to preserve and correct the deficiencies of the automobile liability system of the United States, it seems unlikely that such a completely different solution to the present problems will occur. However, the possibility should not automatically be discounted. At least one United States insurance company[20] has already established an experimental program in which, for a small additional premium, the automobile policyholder may purchase an alternative compensation benefit for all persons involved in the accident.

A final observation on the need for automobile insurance protection is made. *If* everyone were completely insured through his own *accident insurance* for all medical costs and loss of income which might result from automobile accidents, there would be no need for automobile liability insurance nor any problem of unpaid victims. As a solution to the fact that some persons would not voluntarily insure, however, due to ignorance, financial inability or personal conviction and optimism, this is a solution of theory rather than practicability.

THE FAMILY AUTOMOBILE POLICY

Basic Policy Forms

Automobile insurance is not a field in which all contracts are alike. Several different contracts are used for different types of risks. Most commercial motor vehicles are insured under a contract known as the *Standard Automobile Policy,* while most personal vehicles are insured today in a policy which became available in 1956 called the *Family Automobile Policy.* Another contract, the *Special Automo-*

---

[19]See *Saskatchewan's Automobile Accident Insurance Act Explained* (rev. ed.; Regina, Saskatchewan: Government Insurance Office, 1963).

[20]Nationwide Mutual Insurance Company. Note that this is a limited benefit, with specified limits such as a $5,000 death benefit, $2,000 medical expenses, and $5.00 a day for one-half year for loss of income. The injured person still has the option to sue, so the plan really combines some features of liability, compensation, and medical payments coverage.

bile Policy was introduced in 1959 for the personal automobile risk, and under a variety of names[21] it has attracted a portion of the market.

There are some similarities among the most common automobile contracts, and some provisions have been standardized by voluntary action of insurers who use forms developed by various rating bureaus.[22] However, in general the automobile insurance market is one with a product which is relatively unstandardized. About 700 insurance companies sell automobile insurance, and in addition to price competition the field is known for nonprice competition in the form of contract variations. Some contract differences are significant to the insurance buyer, others may be better described as sales "frills" and attention-getting features. It is a wise automobile owner (and also a most unusual one, unfortunately) who reads his automobile insurance contract to determine what he has purchased.

The Family Automobile Policy (F.A.P.) has been chosen for analysis in this text as the most universally used automobile insurance contract. This form was designed for the family automobile insurance market and is shorter and simpler than the Standard Automobile Policy which was drafted for insuring all kinds of automobiles, trucks, busses, taxis and other motor vehicles. The Standard Automobile Policy includes many conditions, definitions, and provisions that do not apply to family cars.[23] By omitting such irrelevant terms the F.A.P. policy provides, in the clearest language pos-

[21]Different companies may call a contract which has most of the features of the Special Automobile Policy by such other names as the "Economy Auto Policy," the "Special Package Auto Policy," and other titles. The basic features are usually: (1) a *single liability limit* of $25,000, or more, coupled automatically with smaller limits of coverage for medical payments, uninsured motorists, and accidental death, (2) some *restrictions* in coverage, such as (*a*) medical payments coverage is on an excess basis above other applicable insurance and (*b*) no liability payments to a relative of the insured if he is a resident of the same household, and (3) *lower premium* cost, due to factors such as reduced commissions, direct billing to the policyholder from the insurer on a three or six-months basis, and the differences in coverage already noted.

[22]The main ones are the National Bureau of Casualty Underwriters, the Mutual Insurance Rating Bureau and, (for physical damage rates) the National Automobile Underwriters Association.

[23]In the F.A.P. public or livery conveyance exclusion no longer applies to the named insured or spouse with respect to injury resulting from his occupancy of a nonowned automobile, other than as the operator thereof. This provides protection for a claim that might originate from the direction of a taxi by the insured. The contractual liability exclusion has been deleted so that the policy will cover the named insured when he has signed a hold-harmless agreement in connection with the use of a rented driverless car. The trailer exclusion has been deleted, subject to the business use exclusion, with a view to providing a more comprehensive coverage. Because "occurrence" replaces "caused by accident" in the liability coverages, a "caused intentionally" exclusion has been added so that any occurrence resulting in a claim through the deliberate act of the insured is eliminated. This is the same exclusion that is found in the comprehensive personal liability policy. There is no workmen's compensation exclusion since this exposure has only a limited application to the family use of an automobile.

sible, protection for families with respect to the normal use of automobiles by members of such families.

Basic Insurance Coverages

There are two major divisions of the automobile insurance business. The first provides the *casualty* (mostly *liability*) coverages and the second, the *physical damage* coverages. The casualty coverages are: (*a*) bodily injury liability, (*b*) property damage liability, (*c*) medical payments coverage, and (*d*) uninsured motorists coverage. In the physical damage category are to be found those forms of automobile insurance that protect the insured from loss or damage to the car itself, and are (*a*) fire, (*b*) theft, (*c*) collision, and (*d*) a number of miscellaneous coverages, such as windstorm, hail, earthquake, explosion, water damage, flood, riot and civil commotion, and vandalism and malicious mischief. All the perils mentioned in (*d*) are often combined with fire and theft coverage in what is called "comprehensive physical damage" coverage.

Because automobile physical damage insurance is so intimately associated with the automobile liability business, the discussion of the two classes of business in one chapter is logical. In fact it is now the accepted practice to provide both liability and physical damage coverages in a single contract, though separate contracts may be obtained if desired. That is why the F.A.P. policy is often titled the *Family Combination* Automobile Policy.

Basic Parts of the Contract

Like all insurance contracts, the Family Automobile Policy contains four fundamental types of provisions. These are: (1) the declarations, (2) the insuring agreements, (3) exclusions, and (4) conditions. The actual physical arrangement of the F.A.P. is varied somewhat from these groupings. It is almost to be expected that the F.A.P. is relatively longer than some other insurance contracts. The variety of the coverages just noted, and the importance of many of these different types of protection, cause the need for explanation in legal terms of the extent of coverage provided under the contract.

The F.A.P. is usually divided into about five pages, beginning with a *declarations* page as shown in Figure 6. The insuring agreements and exclusions are combined in the next three pages of the policy, which contain four separate parts as identified in Figures 7, 8, and 9 on the following pages. The parts include: (1) *liability*, (2) *expenses for medical services*, (3) *physical damage*, and (4) *protection against uninsured motorists*. The final page of the policy is shown in Figure 10, containing a list of *conditions*. Some of these conditions apply to only a part of the coverages and others apply to all of the parts of the contract.

Declarations

The declarations page as shown in Figure 6 includes most of the basic information about the insurer, the insured, the policy period (usually one year, beginning at 12:01 A.M.), the premiums, and the limits of liability for each of the coverages. Toward the bottom of the page are found several items which give the insurance company

FAMILY COMBINATION AUTOMOBILE POLICY

No.

RENEWAL OF NUMBER

SPACE FOR COMPANY NAME, INSIGNIA, AND LOCATION

DECLARATIONS

Item 1. Named Insured and Address: (No., Street, Town or City, County, State)

SPACE FOR AGENT'S NAME AND MAILING ADDRESS

Item 2. Policy Period: (Mo. Day Yr.) (Months)
From to
12:01 A.M., standard time at the address of the named insured as stated herein.

Occupation of the named insured is IF MARRIED WOMAN, GIVE HUSBAND'S OCCUPATION OR BUSINESS (ENTER BELOW)

Item 3. The insurance afforded is only with respect to such of the following coverages as are indicated by specific premium charge or charges. The limit of the company's liability against each such coverage shall be as stated herein, subject to all the terms of this policy having reference thereto.

CAR 1 PREMIUMS	CAR 2	LIMITS OF LIABILITY		COVERAGES
$	$	thousand dollars each person thousand dollars each occurrence	A	Bodily Injury Liability
$	$	thousand dollars each occurrence	B	Property Damage Liability
$	$	dollars each person	C	Medical Payments
$	$	$ Actual Cash Value* $ 100	D	(1) Comprehensive (excluding Collision) (2) Personal Effects
$	$	Actual Cash Value less $ deductible	E	Collision
$	$	$	F	Fire, Lightning and Transportation
$	$	$	G	Theft
$	$	$	H	Combined Additional Coverage
$	$	$ 25 per disablement	I	Towing and Labor Costs
$	$	thousand dollars each person thousand dollars each accident	J	Uninsured Motorists
$		Form numbers of endorsements attached to policy at issue		
$	$	Total Car 1 - Car 2		
$	Total Premium			

* STRIKE OUT "ACTUAL CASH VALUE" AND INSERT AMOUNT IF POLICY IS WRITTEN ON STATED AMOUNT BASIS.

Item 4. Description of owned automobile or trailer

	Year of Model	Trade Name	Body Type; Model	Identification Number (I) Serial Number (S) Motor Number (M)	F.O.B. List Price or Delivered Price at Factory	Purchased Month, Year	New or Used	Class & Rating Symbol	Sub-Class (if any)
Car 1									
Car 2									

Item 5. Loss Payee: Any loss under Part III is payable as interest may appear to the named insured and (NAME AND ADDRESS—ENTER BELOW)

Item 6. The owned automobile will be principally garaged in the town or city designated in Item 1 above, unless otherwise stated herein: (ENTER BELOW)

Item 7. During the past three years no insurer has canceled insurance, issued to the named insured, similar to that afforded hereunder, unless otherwise stated herein:

Countersigned: By____________________
Authorized Representative

FIGURE 6. Page 1 of the Family Automobile Policy (The Declarations)

important data upon which the classification and premium for the insurance contract are based. These items include the description of the automobile[24] and its use, whether or not a mortgage or loan is in existence on the car, the location where it will be principally garaged, and whether or not within the past three years any insurer has canceled automobile insurance for the insured.

It is noted that the "Coverages" listed in the right-hand column of the declarations are identified as A through J. The contract is a "schedule" type of policy, as the policyholder may choose the coverages he desires to include by scheduling the limits of liability for each coverage and paying the appropriate premium charge. Only Coverage A and B (bodily injury and property damage liability) are required; the remaining coverages are optional. The usual contract will include most of the coverages: Coverage C (medical payments), Coverage D (comprehensive), Coverage E (collision), and perhaps Coverage J (uninsured motorists). Coverages F-H (fire, lightning, transportation, theft, and combined additional coverage) are not necessary if Coverage D (comprehensive) is included, since all those perils are included in the comprehensive coverage. Coverage I (towing and labor costs) is a minor coverage which may not be selected by many policyholders.

The declarations page also refers by number to any endorsements which are attached to the later pages of the contract. On the bottom lines the contract is confirmed as a legal contract by signatures of authorized representatives of the insurer.

Part I—Liability

Bodily Injury and Property Damage. The basic promise of the insurer in the liability portion of the automobile policy is to pay for injuries or damages for which the insureds become legally liable. Liability decisions aim at making those persons responsible for a loss to pay for it. Coverages A and B promise to pay "on behalf of" the insured for liabiilty losses arising out of the ownership or use (see Figure 7) of automobiles covered in the contract. Both injury to other persons, including death, and damage to the property of other persons are included. Gratuitous payments are not a part of liability coverage; a legal responsibility must exist before the insurance company will pay the injured party under this provision of the contract.

Defense and Supplementary Payments. With respect to insurance afforded by the policy for bodily injury liability and property damage liability, the obligations of the company extend to other important related promises. The first of these has to do with the

[24]Or automobiles. Space is provided for two cars, since many families insure more than one car in the same policy, with a reduction in cost of about 20 percent.

obligation to defend and is sometimes known as the "defense clause." The second type of additional agreement is divided into four sections. These "supplementary payments," including the de-

RESERVED FOR YOUR COMPANY'S NAME

Agrees with the insured, named in the declarations made a part hereof, in consideration of the payment of the premium and in reliance upon the statements in the declarations and subject to all of the terms of this policy:

PART I — LIABILITY

Coverage A—Bodily Injury Liability; Coverage B—Property Damage Liability: To pay on behalf of the insured all sums which the insured shall become legally obligated to pay as damages because of:

A. bodily injury, sickness or disease, including death resulting therefrom, hereinafter called "bodily injury," sustained by any person;

B. injury to or destruction of property, including loss of use thereof, hereinafter called "property damage";

arising out of the ownership, maintenance or use of the owned automobile or any non-owned automobile, and the company shall defend any suit alleging such bodily injury or property damage and seeking damages which are payable under the terms of this policy, even if any of the allegations of the suit are groundless, false or fraudulent; but the company may make such investigation and settlement of any claim or suit as it deems expedient.

Supplementary Payments: To pay, in addition to the applicable limits of liability:

(a) all expenses incurred by the company, all costs taxed against the insured in any such suit and all interest on the entire amount of any judgment therein which accrues after entry of the judgment and before the company has paid or tendered or deposited in court that part of the judgment which does not exceed the limit of the company's liability thereon;

(b) premiums on appeal bonds required in any such suit, premiums on bonds to release attachments for an amount not in excess of the applicable limit of liability of this policy, and the cost of bail bonds required of the insured because of accident or traffic law violation arising out of the use of an automobile insured hereunder, not to exceed $100 per bail bond, but without any obligation to apply for or furnish any such bonds;

(c) expenses incurred by the insured for such immediate medical and surgical relief to others as shall be imperative at the time of an accident involving an automobile insured hereunder and not due to war;

(d) all reasonable expenses, other than loss of earnings, incurred by the insured at the company's request.

Persons Insured: The following are insureds under Part I:

(a) with respect to the owned automobile,
  (1) the named insured and any resident of the same household,
  (2) any other person using such automobile with the permission of the named insured, provided his actual operation or (if he is not operating) his other actual use thereof is within the scope of such permission, and
  (3) any other person or organization but only with respect to his or its liability because of acts or omissions of an insured under (a) (1) or (2) above;

(b) with respect to a non-owned automobile,
  (1) the named insured,
  (2) any relative, but only with respect to a private passenger automobile or trailer, provided his actual operation or (if he is not operating) the other actual use thereof is with the permission, or reasonably believed to be with the permission, of the owner and is within the scope of such permission, and
  (3) any other person or organization not owning or hiring the automobile, but only with respect to his or its liability because of acts or omissions of an insured under (b) (1) or (2) above.

The insurance afforded under Part I applies separately to each insured against whom claim is made or suit is brought, but the inclusion herein of more than one insured shall not operate to increase the limits of the company's liability.

Definitions: Under Part I:

"named insured" means the individual named in Item 1 of the declarations and also includes his spouse, if a resident of the same household;

"insured" means a person or organization described under "Persons Insured";

"relative" means a relative of the named insured who is a resident of the same household;

"owned automobile" means

(a) a private passenger, farm or utility automobile described in this policy for which a specific premium charge indicates that coverage is afforded,

(b) a trailer owned by the named insured,

(c) a private passenger, farm or utility automobile ownership of which is acquired by the named insured during the policy period, provided
  (1) it replaces an owned automobile as defined in (a) above, or
  (2) the company insures all private passenger, farm and utility automobiles owned by the named insured on the date of such acquisition and the named insured notifies the company during the policy period or within 30 days after the date of such acquisition of his election to make this and no other policy issued by the company applicable to such automobile, or

(d) a temporary substitute automobile;

"temporary substitute automobile" means any automobile or trailer, not owned by the named insured, while temporarily used with the permission of the owner as a substitute for the owned automobile or trailer when withdrawn from normal use because of its breakdown, repair, servicing, loss or destruction;

"non-owned automobile" means an automobile or trailer not owned by or furnished for the regular use of either the named insured or any relative, other than a temporary substitute automobile;

"private passenger automobile" means a four wheel private passenger, station wagon or jeep type automobile;

"farm automobile" means an automobile of the truck type with a load capacity of fifteen hundred pounds or less not used for business or commercial purposes other than farming;

"utility automobile" means an automobile, other than a farm automobile, with a load capacity of fifteen hundred pounds or less of the pick-up body, sedan delivery or panel truck type not used for business or commercial purposes;

"trailer" means a trailer designed for use with a private passenger automobile, if not being used for business or commercial purposes with other than a private passenger, farm or utility automobile, or a farm wagon or farm implement while used with a farm automobile;

"automobile business" means the business or occupation of selling, repairing, servicing, storing or parking automobiles;

"use" of an automobile includes the loading and unloading thereof;

"war" means war, whether or not declared, civil war, insurrection, rebellion or revolution, or any act or condition incident to any of the foregoing.

Exclusions: This policy does not apply under Part I:

(a) to any automobile while used as a public or livery conveyance, but this exclusion does not apply to the named insured with respect to bodily injury or property damage which results from the named insured's occupancy of a non-owned automobile other than as the operator thereof;

(b) to bodily injury or property damage caused intentionally by or at the direction of the insured;

(c) to bodily injury or property damage with respect to which an insured under this policy is also an insured under a nuclear energy liability policy issued by Nuclear Energy Liability Insurance Association, Mutual Atomic Energy Liability Underwriters or Nuclear Insurance Association of Canada, or would be an insured under any such policy but for its termination upon exhaustion of its limit of liability;

(d) to bodily injury or property damage arising out of the operation of farm machinery;

(e) to bodily injury to any employee of the insured arising out of and in the course of (1) domestic employment by the insured, if benefits therefor are in whole or in part either payable or required to be provided under any workmen's compensation law, or (2) other employment by the insured;

(f) to bodily injury to any fellow employee of the insured injured in the course of his employment if such injury arises out of the use of an automobile in the business of his employer, but this exclusion does not apply to the named insured with respect to injury sustained by any such fellow employee;

(g) to an owned automobile while used by any person while such person is employed or otherwise engaged in the automobile business, but this exclusion does not apply to the named insured, a resident of the same household as the named insured, a partnership in which the named insured or such resident is a partner, or any partner, agent or employee of the named insured, such resident or partnership;

(h) to a non-owned automobile while maintained or used by any person while such person is employed or otherwise engaged in
  (1) the automobile business of the insured or of any other person or organization,
  (2) any other business or occupation of the insured, but this exclusion (h) (2) does not apply to a private passenger automobile operated or occupied by the named insured or by his private chauffeur or domestic servant or a trailer used therewith or with an owned automobile;

(i) to injury to or destruction of (1) property owned or transported by the insured or (2) property rented to or in charge of the insured other than a residence or private garage;

(j) to the ownership, maintenance, operation, use, loading or unloading of an automobile ownership of which is acquired by the named insured during the policy period or any temporary substitute automobile therefor, if the named insured has purchased other automobile liability insurance applicable to such automobile for which a specific premium charge has been made.

Financial Responsibility Laws: When this policy is certified as proof of financial responsibility for the future under the provisions of any motor vehicle financial responsibility law, such insurance as is afforded by this policy for bodily injury liability or for property damage liability shall comply with the provisions of such law to the extent of the coverage and limits of liability required by such law, but in no event in excess of the limits of liability stated in this policy. The insured agrees to reimburse the company for any payment made by the company which it would not have been obligated to make under the terms of this policy except for the agreement contained in this paragraph.

Limits of Liability: The limit of bodily injury liability stated in the declarations as applicable to "each person" is the limit of the company's liability for all damages, including damages for care and loss of services, arising out of bodily injury sustained by one person as the result of any one occurrence; the limit of such liability stated in the declarations as applicable to "each occurrence" is, subject to the above provision respecting each person, the total limit of the company's liability for all such damages arising out of bodily injury sustained by two or more persons as the result of any one occurrence.

The limit of property damage liability stated in the declarations as applicable to "each occurrence" is the total limit of the company's liability for all damages arising out of injury to or destruction of all property of one or more persons or organizations, including the loss of use thereof, as the result of any one occurrence.

Other Insurance: If the insured has other insurance against a loss covered by Part I of this policy the company shall not be liable under this policy for a greater proportion of such loss than the applicable limit of liability stated in the declarations bears to the total applicable limit of liability of all valid and collectible insurance against such loss; provided, however, the insurance with respect to a temporary substitute automobile or non-owned automobile shall be excess insurance over any other valid and collectible insurance.

FIGURE 7. Page 2 of the Family Automobile Policy (Liability Insuring Agreements)

fense clause, indicate obligations that the company assumes to pay *in addition to the policy liability limits.*

Defense Clause. Under the terms of the defense clause, in addition to the obligations assumed by the company to defend the insured, there is also reserved to the company the right to make investigations and effect a settlement under terms deemed expedient to the company. This affords the company an important right but carries with it a corresponding obligation. It places the control of settlement in the hands of the company and takes it entirely out of the hands of the insured. The company, however, is thereby obligated to use every reasonable means to effect a settlement within the policy limits. The company is obligated to defend fraudulent or groundless suits.

Cost of Investigating and Defense. The cost of investigating a claim, the negotiations for settlement, and the cost of defense are all paid by the company. This is true, even in the case of a false or fraudulent claim or in the case of a claim excessive in amount. Defense costs frequently run to sizable amounts. In the case of an appeal, interest on the amount of the judgment not in excess of policy limits is covered.

Bond Premiums. If the insured is arrested because of an accident or violation of a traffic law, arising out of the use of an automobile, and bail is required for his release, or if as a result of an automobile accident a claimant secures a writ of attachment on any property of the insured including the automobile, the cost of the bail bond or the release of attachment bond not to exceed $100 is paid by the company. In the case of an appeal from a judgment to a higher court, a bond is required, and the premium for the bond is paid. This feature is more important than the actual cost of the bond. While the company is not obligated to apply for or furnish bonds, it usually does this, thereby relieving the applicant of any obligation to deposit cash or bonds as collateral to the surety.

First-Aid Expense. In the case of an automobile accident involving personal injury, an insured may feel obligated to secure first-aid medical or surgical treatment without exploring the matter of liability, or even regardless of liability. Where treatment of injured is imperative, the cost is covered.

Other Reimbursable Expenses. If it becomes necessary as part of the adjusting procedure to ask the insured to incur some expense, the policy provides for reimbursement. This clause clarifies any doubt where it might be construed under the cooperation clause that the insured should bear some or all such expenses. Loss of earnings on the part of the insured due to the interruption of his personal affairs is not covered. Actually, it is the intent of this clause to reimburse the insured for actual cash outlay made at the request of the insurance company.

The coverages provided under the supplementary agreements, with the exception of amounts paid or obligations incurred in the settlement of claims and suits, are in addition to applicable policy limits. Assume, for example, a claim of an individual amounts to $12,000 with a policy limit of $10,000. If the company spends time and money in investigation, provides appeal bonds, and otherwise runs up expenses to $2,000 for the purposes of effecting a $10,000 settlement out of court, the insured is fully protected. The $10,000 claim is paid, and the company bears all settlement costs in addition. Moreover, if at the time of the accident the insured provided first aid, this is not used to reduce the company liability but is assumed by the company in excess of the liability limit of the policy.

Persons and Automobiles Insured. The insured named in the declarations and the insurance company are the contracting parties under the automobile liability insurance contract. Over a number of years the contract has been broadened to include within the scope of its protection the family of the insured and others driving the owned automobile *with the permission* of the named insured. The term "named insured" means the policyholder and his spouse,[25] if the spouse is a resident of the same household. "Insured" may include not only the named insured but also any person while using the owned automobile and any person or organization legally responsible for its use. An example would be an employee driving his car on an errand for his employer. The clause affording these extensions of coverage is sometimes referred to as the *omnibus clause.* The insurance with respect to any person or organization other than the named insured does not apply to certain persons or organizations such as those operating automobile sales agencies, repair shops, or the like.

It frequently develops that the owner of an insured car has occasion to drive a car other than his own. It may be that he is on a trip with a friend and they alternate in driving. He may borrow a friend's car. He may be asked in some emergency to render a service and be offered the use of a car owned by another. The situations are innumerable in which an individual may find himself driving a car other than his own. While the insurance on the other car protects its owner or any person driving the car with the permission of the owner, it is not always known whether the borrowed car is insured or not, and even if insured the limits may be inadequate.

The individual named as the insured (the husband or wife) *or*

[25]Note that children or other relatives are not permitted to extend the permission to use the car. A son who permits a girlfriend to drive (or a daughter who permits a boyfriend to drive) provides no coverage to the driver.

other relatives have *drive-other-car coverage* for the occasional use, with permission of the owner, of private passenger automobiles other than the insured car. Coverage for the use of *nonowned* automobiles extends to a person or organization legally responsible for the use of a borrowed car by the insured, provided that person or organization is not the owner. This means, for example, that if a volunteer worker on a drive is sent on an errand in a borrowed car and he meets with an accident, his own insurance would cover not only himself but any liability that might attach to the organization or person in whose interests the errand was performed.

The extension of coverage does not apply to a car furnished for the regular use of the insured. It is the intent to make impossible the purchase of insurance on one automobile and then have it extended to protect other cars owned by the insured or members of his household. Any car, either owned or rented, under the constant control of the insured and which he may use as often as he wishes, would not be covered, even though he elects to use it only occasionally.[26]

The policy does not cover any automobile used in a business or occupation of the named insured except a private passenger, farm, or utility (load capacity under 1,500 pounds) automobile operated by him or under his direction. This means, of course, that coverage does not extend to trucks, buses, or other commercially operated vehicles.

The policy provides that with respect to bodily injury and property damage liability coverages the term "insured" is used severally and not collectively. The inclusion of more than one insured does not operate to increase the company's liability. Sometimes, where there has been more than one insured, each has claimed that as to himself he is covered for the full policy limits. This has never been the intent of the policy.

The protection provided in the automobile insurance contract includes not only coverage with respect to the automobile described in the declarations together with equipment, but also includes (*a*) a temporary substitute automobile, (*b*) a newly acquired automobile, and (*c*) trailers.

If an insured is using a car temporarily while his own is out of commission, he is covered. An example of such a situation is to be found in the case where an automobile dealer loans the insured an automobile for use while the insured car is in a garage for repairs.

[26]A broad form drive-other-car coverage is available at an additional premium charge, and this coverage is needed when the insured frequently drives hired cars or when the insured uses a car furnished for his regular use. Nonownership liability insurance is also very important for many businesses, where if an employee drives his own car on company business, the employer needs such coverage when an accident results.

If the insured car is withdrawn from normal use the insurance attaches to a substitute automobile. This is true even if the insured car is destroyed.

This coverage, as well as the protection for driving a nonowned automobile, is *excess* insurance which applies only over and above any other valid and collectible insurance. The insurance policy of the car owner applies as primary coverage.

A newly acquired automobile which replaces an owned automobile insured by the policy is covered for bodily injury, property damage, and medical payments during the remainder of the policy term without notice to the company. A newly acquired automobile that does not replace an insured car is automatically covered but notice is required by the company within 30 days of delivery date. If the insurer does not insure all the private passenger automobiles of the insured, then there is no automatic coverage. There is no additional premium if one car replaces another. Where the number of cars is increased, an additional premium is required.

The definition of the automobile automatically extends bodily injury and property damage liability coverages to all trailers designed for use with a private passenger automobile without description and without charge. Home trailers are so covered, but physical damage insurance for such trailers is not included. Trailers used for business purposes with a car other than a private passenger automobile are not covered automatically by the policy.

Exclusions. Ten specific exclusions from the coverage of Part I—Liability are enumerated. For example, the policy does not apply while the automobile is used as a public livery conveyance unless such use is specifically declared in the policy. Also, the policy now states that "bodily injury or property damage caused intentionally," such as assault or battery, is not covered by the policy. Assault may be defined in general terms as any willful or unlawful attempt or offer with force or violence to do a corporeal hurt to another. Battery may be defined as any willful and unlawful use of force or violence upon the person of another. Under the terms of the policy, any injury or damage committed by an insured or at his direction is specifically excluded as an action.[27] Otherwise, the policy covers. A case in point would be a situation where a chauffeur, following a minor accident, became involved in an altercation with another party concerning responsibility for the accident and in a fit of anger struck him.[28]

---

[27] *Columbia Casualty Company* v. *Able et al.*, 30 CCH Automobile Cases 693.

[28] Those who in the past have held that an intentionally inflicted injury cannot be regarded as an accident rely on the definition of an accident as an "untoward and unforeseen occurrence in the operation of an automobile which results in the injury to the person or property of another." *Ohio Casualty Insurance Company* v. *Marr*, 98 F.

A rather important exclusion excludes damage to property owned or transported by the insured, and property rented to or in charge of the insured, except a residence or a private garage. It is the intent of the policy to pay for losses for which the insured is legally liable. If the insured damages his own property, quite obviously he is not subject to suit for damages, for he cannot sue himself. Property damage liability would cover the damage by an insured Mr. Lynch, for example, to the garage doors of a garage he rents, but would not cover damage to a business building which he leases. Likewise, damage to his own garage would be excluded.

Other exclusions which have not yet been mentioned include automobile liability (1) of insureds covered under special nuclear energy liability contracts, (2) arising out of operation of farm machinery, and (3) involving injuries to employees in the domestic employment of the insured if they are covered by the workmen's compensation law, or fellow employees of insureds other than the named insured.

Financial Responsibility. The purpose of this clause is to uphold the intent of any financial responsibility law. The courts have held that financial responsibility statutes have been passed to secure the solvency of operators of automobiles upon the highways and to guarantee their ability to discharge judgments arising out of accidents in which they might be involved.[29] The clause, in effect, makes the liability of the insurance company to the injured party absolute, whenever an injury within the purview of a financial responsiblity act occurs.

For example, if the insurance company had a valid defense against the insured because of a material misrepresentation, the policy with respect to the injured claimant under the financial responsibility law cannot be voided. The insured is obligated to reimburse the company for payments that it makes that otherwise it would not have been obligated to make. The company may proceed against the insured and collect the amount of the payment. The clause, therefore,

---

(2d) 973. On the basis of this definition it was contended that an automobile liability policy would not cover any intentionally inflicted injuries. With the passing of time, decisions tended to include as accidents (*a*) injuries caused by intentional acts of employees not at the direction of the insured, (*b*) injuries inflicted by a third party on a public conveyance, and (*c*) where the injury was attributable to reckless conduct in contrast to willful or intentional conduct. Since, on the basis of these decisions, there was reason to believe assault claims would in some instances, at least, be covered by the policy, it was deemed advisable to clarify the situation once and for all. This was accomplished by inserting in the policy the clause just noticed, which brings an assault within the definition of accident unless it is committed at the direction of or by the insured.

[29]*Hartford Accident and Indemnity Company* v. *Wolburst et al.,* 28 CCH Automobile Cases 1013.

does not provide for any coverage (for the insured) not already written into the contract, nor does it operate to extend policy limits.

Policy Limits. The limits of liability are stated in the declarations, with three specific limitations in dollar amounts applied to Coverages A and B. Standard limits in Coverage A usually provide up to $10,000 for bodily injuries to, or death of, any one *person;* and subject to the same limit for each person, $20,000 for bodily injury or death involving more than one person in a single *occurrence.* Coverage B provides a standard property damage liability limit of $5,000 for each occurrence.

An occurrence involving one injury of $12,000 and a second injury to another person of $4,000, would bring the total claims to $16,000. However, the liability under the $12,000 claim is limited to $10,000. The $4,000 claim is payable in full. The company's liability for claims amounting to $16,000 is $14,000, that is, $10,000 plus $4,000. The other $2,000 the insured must pay himself.

Because judgments growing out of automobile claims frequently run to high figures, the standard limits are often inadequate. To meet the requirements of the individual insured, rates are provided for higher limits in both the personal injury and property damage coverages. Illustrations of the need for high liability limits are found in Chapter 13, "The Liability Risk." Three further examples are frightening and almost unbelievable. Automobile crashes involving a few cars are bad enough, but can you imagine these three multiple-car accidents?: (1) a 1963 California crash on the Santa Ana Freeway in a fog which resulted from one stopped car fixing a flat tire, with a toll of 1 dead, 24 injured, 20 demolished cars and at least 200 cars involved, (2) a 1964 East River Drive crash in New York City during a slight snowstorm which caused a skidding car to end up in a 34-car pileup, and (3) a 1964 London expressway crash in a fog which caused nearly 100 cars to crash successively into each other, with 5 persons killed and over 100 injured![30]

Because of the trend to high judgments where bodily injuries are involved, there are many who feel that $50,000 is the minimum adequate lower limit, and many policies are written with upper limits from $100,000 to $300,000 and in some instances even higher. Property damage claims also frequently run to substantial amounts, so careful consideration should be given to increasing these limits beyond the standard amount, too.[31]

[30]*Time,* January 4, 1963 and March 20, 1964, p. 63; and *Newsweek,* February 3, 1964, p. 34 respectively.

[31]For example, consider the value of several new automobiles today, where the insured may be held liable for the damage to or destruction of two or more such vehicles. Also, buses or trucks (including valuable cargos, perhaps) may be involved. Damage to other property than vehicles is a potential source of very large losses. One driver was held liable for over $50,000 for fire damage resulting from an auto

Since in the majority of cases claims can be satisfied out of the amount set by the standard limits, and only the occasional or disastrous claim will run into large amounts, the insurance company can and does write the excess limits at an additional premium very much less than that charged for the standard limits. For example, the increase to 25/50 limits is less than 20 percent more (and to 100/300 limits is only about 40 percent more) than the usual 10/20 bodily injury limits. Property damage premiums are increased only about 20 percent when the limits are raised five times, from the usual $5,000 to the more adequate $25,000.

The increasing number of judgments of large amounts are not the only reason for carrying high liability limits, either. Even though the actual payment to the injured claimant may eventually be relatively small, the insured who has a $50,000 limit, and a $75,000 suit against him, may spend several years with a $25,000 uninsured worry before the settlement or court trial is completed.

Other Insurance. The final clause in Part I—Liability explains what happens when more than one automobile insurance policy applies in a given loss situation. If the insured has more than one policy in effect for the owned car (such a case would be very unusual, probably resulting only from a mistake or misunderstanding), each policy will contribute to the loss on a proportional, or prorata, basis according to its limits of liability.

Much more common is the case in which the driver is not the owner of the automobile. In such situations, "the insurance with respect to a temporary substitute or nonowned automobile shall be *excess* insurance over any other valid and collectible insurance." This means that the owner's insurance policy pays the loss up to the full limits of its liability, and only then does the driver's insurance policy pay (within its maximum liability) for the remaining amount of the unpaid loss.

Suppose Mr. DeMaria borrows Mr. White's car, and is held responsible for an accident. Mr. White's insurance contract will provide the primary coverage for any liability claim, and Mr. DeMaria's insurance contract, under its "drive-other-car coverage," will provide coverage only on an excess basis for the accident. The car owner's liability insurance pays first; the driver's liability insurance pays only if needed. The method is one of the many reasons why it is important for a car owner to be careful to whom he loans an automobile, for the owner's insurer will pay first for resulting damages or injuries.

---

accident which resulted in damages to a new bridge. Skidding into a gasoline pump or a water hydrant has caused damages exceeding $100,000. Damage to a store front caused a $27,000 claim recently. Many other examples are to be found in a wide variety of circumstances where the auto accident causes a chain reaction of events.

Part II—Medical Payments

For a small additional premium[32] the policyholder may include Coverage C in the Family Automobile Policy to cover the cost of medical services for himself, his family, and anyone else in his car. This is really automobile accident insurance for medical care costs, and the protection applies without regard to whose fault the accident was.

The advantage of having automobile medical payments coverage in addition to liability insurance is that it pays promptly, without having to wait for determination of liability. It also avoids many embarrassing or difficult liability claims or lawsuits by friends injured in your car, and provides coverage for you and members of your family who are usually unable to sustain a liability claim against you. Under the "guest laws," in some 27 states,[33] the persons in your car often must prove "gross negligence" by the owner or driver, too, which makes it unlikely that the liability portion of the contract will apply in many cases for the occupants of your car. Medical payments coverage avoids these problems of establishing legal liability, and in addition pays for many injuries which may be considered moral rather than legal responsibilities.

Coverage is quite broad, for all reasonable medical expenses (including surgical, dental, ambulance, hospital, nursing) are paid, as well as funeral expenses, up to the policy limit. Injuries occurring "in, upon, entering into or alighting from" the automobile are covered. The high cost of medical services today makes the need for such protection obvious.

The persons covered are described in two separate clauses. Division 1 supplies very broad coverage for the named insured and household relatives if they are injured in either automobiles owned by the insured, in nonowned automobiles, or even when struck by an automobile as a pedestrian. Division 2 provides other passengers coverage in the owned car of the insured (driven by named insured, relatives, or anyone else using it with his permission under the "omnibus clause"); and also passengers in nonowned private cars being operated by the insured, his family, or servants.

The exclusions aim at eliminating duplicate coverage or types of protection usually available under business rather than individual insurance contracts. Excluded are: (1) injuries in owned vehicles used as public or livery conveyances, or homes, (2) injuires

---

[32]From about $5 to $20 per year, depending on the basic charge in the policy for bodily injury liability, and the limits of coverage chosen. The standard limit is $500 per person but, for example, if that limit costs $6, the limit may be raised to $2,000 for $10 and to the maximum $5,000 limit for $13.

[33]See *Statutes Affecting Liability Insurance* (11th ed. New York: Association of Casualty and Surety Companies December, 1963).

to the family, while in or being struck by a farm type tractor while not on public roads, or other rail or crawler-tread vehicles, (3) injuries to persons other than the family, while in nonowned automobiles used as public vehicles, in the automobile business or in any other business, except when a private passenger automobile is used by the named insured, (4) injuries by any person employed in the automobile business if covered by the workmen's compensation law, and (5) injuries due to war.

An "other insurance" provision is similar to the clause in Part I of the contract, with coverage in nonowned or temporary automobiles being excess coverage over the medical payments insurance of the other car owner.

Figure 8 contains the entire wording of both Part II—Expense for Medical Services, and Part III—Physical Damage, as found in the Family Automobile Policy.

Part III—Physical Damage

Physical damage coverage for *your own automobile,* or others that you or your family drive, is provided in the F.A.P. under several separate coverages, D through H, if the declarations page indicates a premium charge and policy limit for the protection. This coverage should not be confused with property damage liability, which is the damage to the property of other persons for which you are held liable.

The policyholder may choose the limited coverage of Coverage F (fire, lightning, and transportation), Coverage G (theft) and/or Coverage H (combined additional coverage), if he desires. However, most automobiles are insured under Coverage D (comprehensive) and Coverage E (collision). Coverage I (towing and labor costs) is also included by some policyholders for emergency road service up to $25 per disablement.

The importance of physical damage insurance is related to the value of the automobile, and the need and ability of the owner to replace or repair the vehicle if it is damaged. Since most newer automobiles today are large items of value in relation to the assets of a family, most owners do need this insurance protection. However, as the value of an older car decreases, a time may be reached when physical damage insurance is not necessary to cover a possible maximum loss of a few hundred dollars. It is unwise to go without this coverage, however, if the value of the automobile is such that your income or assets could not readily replace the car as required for your work or family.

Sometimes the car owner has little choice as to whether or not he purchases physical damage insurance. Most installment contracts for the purchase of automobiles require that sufficient physical

PART II — EXPENSES FOR MEDICAL SERVICES

Coverage C—Medical Payments: To pay all reasonable expenses incurred within one year from the date of accident for necessary medical, surgical, X-ray and dental services, including prosthetic devices, and necessary ambulance, hospital, professional nursing and funeral services:

Division 1. To or for the named insured and each relative who sustains bodily injury, sickness or disease, including death resulting therefrom, hereinafter called "bodily injury", caused by accident,

(a) while occupying the owned automobile,
(b) while occupying a non-owned automobile, but only if such person has, or reasonably believes he has, the permission of the owner to use the automobile and the use is within the scope of such permission, or
(c) through being struck by an automobile or by a trailer of any type;

Division 2. To or for any other person who sustains bodily injury, caused by accident, while occupying
(a) the owned automobile, while being used by the named insured, by any resident of the same household or by any other person with the permission of the named insured; or
(b) a non-owned automobile, if the bodily injury results from
  (1) its operation or occupancy by the named insured or its operation on his behalf by his private chauffeur or domestic servant, or
  (2) its operation or occupancy by a relative, provided it is a private passenger automobile or trailer,

but only if such operator or occupant has, or reasonably believes he has, the permission of the owner to use the automobile and the use is within the scope of such permission.

Definitions: The definitions under Part I apply to Part II, and under Part II:
"occupying" means in or upon or entering into or alighting from.

Exclusions: This policy does not apply under Part II to bodily injury:
(a) sustained while occupying (1) an owned automobile while used as a public or livery conveyance, or (2) any vehicle while located for use as a residence or premises;
(b) sustained by the named insured or a relative while occupying or through being struck by (1) a farm type tractor or other equipment designed for use principally off public roads, while not upon public roads, or (2) a vehicle operated on rails or crawler-treads;
(c) sustained by any person other than the named insured or a relative,
  (1) while such person is occupying a non-owned automobile while used as a public or livery conveyance, or
  (2) resulting from the maintenance or use of a non-owned automobile by such person while employed or otherwise engaged in the automobile business, or
  (3) resulting from the maintenance or use of a non-owned automobile by such person while employed or otherwise engaged in any other business or occupation, unless the bodily injury results from the operation or occupancy of a private passenger automobile by the named insured or by his private chauffeur or domestic servant, or of a trailer used therewith or with an owned automobile;
(d) sustained by any person who is employed in the automobile business, if the accident arises out of the operation thereof and if benefits therefor are in whole or in part either payable or required to be provided under any workmen's compensation law;
(e) due to war.

Limit of Liability: The limit of liability for medical payments stated in the declarations as applicable to "each person" is the limit of the company's liability for all expenses incurred by or on behalf of each person who sustains bodily injury as the result of any one accident.

Other Insurance: If there is other automobile medical payments insurance against a loss covered by Part II of this policy the company shall not be liable under this policy for a greater proportion of such loss than the applicable limit of liability stated in the declarations bears to the total applicable limit of liability of all valid and collectible automobile medical payments insurance; provided, however, the insurance with respect to a temporary substitute automobile or non-owned automobile shall be excess insurance over any other valid and collectible automobile medical payments insurance.

PART III — PHYSICAL DAMAGE

Coverage D (1)—Comprehensive (excluding Collision); (2)—Personal Effects:
(1) To pay for loss caused other than by collision to the owned automobile or to a non-owned automobile. For the purpose of this coverage, breakage of glass and loss caused by missiles, falling objects, fire, theft or larceny, explosion, earthquake, windstorm, hail, water, flood, malicious mischief or vandalism, riot or civil commotion, or colliding with a bird or animal, shall not be deemed to be loss caused by collision.
(2) To pay for loss caused by fire or lightning to robes, wearing apparel and other personal effects which are the property of the named insured or a relative, while such effects are in or upon the owned automobile.

Coverage E—Collision: To pay for loss caused by collision to the owned automobile or to a non-owned automobile but only for the amount of each such loss in excess of the deductible amount stated in the declarations as applicable hereto. The deductible amount shall not apply to loss caused by a collision with another automobile insured by the company.

Coverage F—Fire, Lightning and Transportation: To pay for loss to the owned automobile or a non-owned automobile, caused (a) by fire or lightning, (b) by smoke or smudge due to a sudden, unusual and faulty operation of any fixed heating equipment serving the premises in which the automobile is located, or (c) by the stranding, sinking, burning, collision or derailment of any conveyance in or upon which the automobile is being transported.

Coverage G—Theft: To pay for loss to the owned automobile or to a non-owned automobile caused by theft or larceny.

Coverage H—Combined Additional Coverage: To pay for loss to the owned automobile or a non-owned automobile caused by windstorm, hail, earthquake, explosion, riot or civil commotion, or the forced landing or falling of any aircraft or its parts or equipment, flood or rising waters, malicious mischief or vandalism, external discharge or leakage of water except loss resulting from rain, snow or sleet whether or not wind-driven; provided, with respect to each automobile $25 shall be deducted from each loss caused by malicious mischief or vandalism.

Coverage I—Towing and Labor Costs: To pay for towing and labor costs necessitated by the disablement of the owned automobile or of any non-owned automobile, provided the labor is performed at the place of disablement.

Supplementary Payments: In addition to the applicable limit of liability:
(a) to reimburse the insured for transportation expenses incurred during the period commencing 48 hours after a theft covered by this policy of the entire automobile has been reported to the company and the police, and terminating when the automobile is returned to use or the company pays for the loss; provided that the company shall not be obligated to pay aggregate expenses in excess of $10 per day or totaling more than $300.
(b) to pay general average and salvage charges for which the insured becomes legally liable, as to the automobile being transported.

Definitions: The definitions of "named insured", "relative", "temporary substitute automobile", "private passenger automobile", "farm automobile", "utility automobile", "automobile business", "war", and "owned automobile" in Part I apply to Part III, but "owned automobile" does not include, under Part III, (1) a trailer owned by the named insured on the effective date of this policy and not described herein, or (2) a trailer ownership of which is acquired during the policy period unless the company insures all private passenger, farm and utility automobiles and trailers owned by the named insured on the date of such acquisition and the named insured notifies the company during the policy period or within 30 days after the date of such acquisition of his election to make this and no other policy issued by the company applicable to such trailer.

"insured" means
(a) with respect to an owned automobile,
  (1) the named insured, and
  (2) any person or organization (other than a person or organization employed or otherwise engaged in the automobile business or as a carrier or other bailee for hire) maintaining, using or having custody of said automobile with the permission of the named insured and within the scope of such permission;
(b) with respect to a non-owned automobile, the named insured and any relative while using such automobile, provided his actual operation or (if he is not operating) the other actual use thereof is with the permission, or reasonably believed to be with the permission, of the owner and is within the scope of such permission;

"non-owned automobile" means a private passenger automobile or trailer not owned by or furnished for the regular use of either the named insured or any relative, other than a temporary substitute automobile, while said automobile or trailer is in the possession or custody of the insured or is being operated by him;

"loss" means direct and accidental loss of or damage to (a) the automobile, including its equipment, or (b) other insured property;

"collision" means collision of an automobile covered by this policy with another object or with a vehicle to which it is attached or by upset of such automobile;

"trailer" means a trailer designed for use with a private passenger automobile, if not being used for business or commercial purposes with other than a private passenger, farm or utility automobile, and if not a home, office, store, display or passenger trailer.

Exclusions: This policy does not apply under Part III:
(a) to any automobile while used as a public or livery conveyance;
(b) to loss due to war;
(c) to loss to a non-owned automobile arising out of its use by the insured while he is employed or otherwise engaged in the automobile business;
(d) to loss to a private passenger, farm or utility automobile or trailer owned by the named insured and not described in this policy or to any temporary substitute automobile therefor, if the insured has other valid and collectible insurance against such loss;
(e) to damage which is due and confined to wear and tear, freezing, mechanical or electrical breakdown or failure, unless such damage results from a theft covered by this policy;
(f) to tires, unless damaged by fire, malicious mischief or vandalism, or stolen or unless the loss be coincident with and from the same cause as other loss covered by this policy;
(g) to loss due to radioactive contamination;
(h) under coverage E, to breakage of glass if insurance with respect to such breakage is otherwise afforded.

Limit of Liability: The limit of the company's liability for loss shall not exceed the actual cash value of the property, or if the loss is of a part thereof the actual cash value of such part, at time of loss, nor what it would then cost to repair or replace the property or such part thereof with other of like kind and quality, nor, with respect to an owned automobile described in this policy, the applicable limit of liability stated in the declarations; provided, however, the limit of the company's liability (a) for loss to personal effects arising out of any one occurrence is $100, and (b) for loss to any trailer not owned by the named insured is $500.

Other Insurance: If the insured has other insurance against a loss covered by Part III of this policy, the company shall not be liable under this policy for a greater proportion of such loss than the applicable limit of liability of this policy bears to the total applicable limit of liability of all valid and collectible insurance against such loss; provided, however, the insurance with respect to a temporary substitute automobile or non-owned automobile shall be excess insurance over any other valid and collectible insurance.

FIGURE 8. Page 3 of the Family Automobile Policy (Medical Payments and Physical Damage Insuring Agreements)

damage insurance be purchased to protect the value of the car used as collateral. Two warnings are important in these cases: (1) the insurance which the bank or other creditor suggests or requires is usually limited to coverage on the car itself, and should not be misunderstood as including the very important liability or other automobile coverages, and (2) if the insurance cost is included in the finance plan, be sure to ask what coverages are included and know the cost involved.

Comprehensive (Excluding Collision) Coverage. The comprehensive automobile coverage is, with the exception of collision losses, virtually an all-risks physical damage coverage. It is now widely written instead of the limited coverages that formerly were used for fire, theft, and other named perils. Protection is afforded for any direct and accidental loss of, or damage to, the automobile covered and its normal equipment.

Although the broad wording of the contract "to pay for loss caused other than by collision to the owned automobile or a non-owned automobile" (used by an insured) would automatically include losses on an "everything but" basis, the clause does give specific examples of the types of perils which are not considered to be collision losses, and are therefore covered. Among these perils are the following: fire, theft, windstorm, earthquake, strike, flood, vandalism, malicious mischief, riot or civil commotion, falling objects, breakage of glass (except intentional breakage), explosion, hail, and lightning.

There are many strange and unexpected losses included in this coverage. Mention may be made of cases involving damage to a fender kicked by a horse, damage to the finish of an automobile caused by arsenic tree spray or paint, damage by Fourth of July firecrackers, battery acid, Halloween vandals, and the like. Damage by animals, such as running into a dog, deer, cow, or other animal, is now specifically stated in the policy to be included under the comprehensive coverage. The damage to be covered must be accidental. To break a window to get into a car with keys locked inside is not an accidental damage. Breakage of glass due to a collision is included as a comprehensive physical damage loss.

There is an extra clause which provides the insured and his relatives with limited coverage for robes, wearing apparel, and other personal effects while in or upon the automobile. Such losses are covered only if caused by fire or lightning, and a $100 maximum limit applies.

Another "supplementary payment" is provided in a clause which grants reimbursement for actual transportation expenses incurred following a theft of the automobile. This is a type of "loss of use" coverage, and is limited to $10 per day up to a maximum of $300 or the value of the car, begining 48 hours after the theft has been reported to the police and the insurer, and ending when it has been returned to use. The amount paid is in addition to the loss payable for the damages caused by the theft.

An unusual marine coverage is also payable, as an additional amount, for "general average and salvage charges for which the insured becomes legally liable." Such a loss might occur while the automobile is being transported on a ferry boat, and the car owner becomes liable for a proportional share of a voluntary sacrifice of the ship or its cargo to prevent a sinking.

Most of the other provisions of this section are applied to both comprehensive and collision coverages. Many are similar to the definitions, clauses, and exclusions already discussed in Part I of the Family Automobile Policy. The coverage applies to the owned automobile while it is being used by either the named insured or anyone else using it with his permission. Nonowned automobiles (or drive-other-car coverage) are covered while used with the owner's permission by the insured or by his relatives, as long as the cars are of the private passenger type and not owned by or furnished for regular use to them. Newly acquired automobiles are covered, and additional new cars if the insured has all his automobiles insured with the company and notifies the insurer within 30 days after acquisition.

Home, office, store, display, or passenger trailers are not included. Other exclusions are: (1) damage due to wear and tear, freezing, mechanical or electrical breakdown or failure (except caused by theft), (2) damages to tires,[34] unless damaged by fire, vandalism, malicious mischief or theft, or coincident with other losses covered by the policy, and (3) loss caused by radioactive contamination.

The insurer's limit of liability is usually for indemnity based upon "actual cash value" of the automobile,[35] although some contracts, especially for business vehicles, use a stated value form. The actual cash value wording protects the policyholder for losses on the basis of value as of the time of the loss, not exceeding the cost of repair or replacement. A special limit of $500 applies to a nonowned trailer used by the insured. Other valid and collectible physical damage insurance of the insured on the automobile applies on a prorata basis, except on nonowned automobiles where it applies as excess insurance.

Collision Coverage. *Collision* insurance reimburses the insured for damage to the automobile sustained by reason of a collision with another car or with any other object, movable or fixed. The policy in Coverage E now also specifically includes loss to the automobile caused by upset, by defining a collision to include an upset.

As in medical payments insurance, even if the insured did not

[34]Note that ordinary flat tire losses are not included. To be covered by physical damage, the loss must be due to a collision or other identifiable covered peril.

[35]The principle is the same as that as used in the fire insurance policy. No dollar amount for payment, except the maximum limit, is stated in the contract. Replacement cost, less reasonable depreciation, is the basis.

carry collision insurance, he *might* be able to recover damages from another person who caused the accident. However, since (1) the insured or the driver of his automobile may be responsible for the loss, either with or without another car involved in the accident *and* (2) if another party is responsible for the damage, the insured must prove him negligent *and* (3) there may be delay and uncertainty in collecting from a negligent person (who may not have sufficient assets or insurance to pay the damages), the automobile owner is wise to consider purchasing collision insurance himself. Then, regardless of whose fault the loss is, he will be paid for the damages.

Collision losses are one of the most common situations in which *subrogation* may apply. If the policyholder collects the damages from his insurer, then the insurer may take over his rights to sue the responsible party and recover the payment made to the insured. Whether or not the insurance company will actually do so depends on many factors, including the accident facts, who was liable, the size of the loss and whether or not proof is readily available against another person who is likely to be able to pay for the damage he has caused.

Collision insurance also is a common illustration of the use of the *deductible*. Most automobile collision contracts require the use of a deductible, either of $50 or $100. Some contracts use higher deductible amounts, and variations of the straight deductible form are sometimes used. Occasionally, full coverage without a deductible is available, but the high cost of this farm usually makes the cost prohibitive. It is the basic purpose of a deductible to avoid the high cost and administrative expense of frequent small collision losses.

The normal collision deductible provides that there shall be no liability on the part of the insurer unless the loss exceeds a named amount. Then the amount of the loss payment is only so much of the loss as exceeds the deductible amount. For example, under a $50 deductible form, if the loss is $40, there is no payment by the insurer. In case of a $200 loss, the insurance company pays the policyholder $150.

Deductibles of $100 or more are being used with increasing frequency today. The reduction in cost to the insured usually justifies his decision to accept a larger portion of collision losses himself. The decrease in premium cost often may be $30 or more (depending on the basic cost and classification) for the $100 deductible as compared with the $50 deductible.

Ordinarily, the insured should not expect to receive the deductible amount from the insurer if the insurer is successful in subrogation proceedings against another negligent party. The cost of the legal proceedings must be considered, although company practices in these situations vary. The insurer does not profit in subrogation cases, and often only recovers a part of the payment it has made to the insured.

The collision coverage applies under the same definition and exclusions already discussed above in relation to comprehensive physical damage. A most important result of these provisions is the fact that the collision insurance applies not only to the named insured's operation of the automobile, but also while other persons are operating the car with his (or his spouse's) permission. The named insured and his relatives also are provided, on an excess basis, with collision coverage for nonowned or temporary substitute automobiles which they use.

Part IV—Uninsured Motorists

The recognition of need for insurance to pay the insured, his family, and their passengers for bodily injury caused by a negligent but uninsured motorist has led to the inclusion of Coverage J—Protection against Uninsured Motorists in the Family Automobile Policy. This insurance is optional, applying if the insured selects the coverage[36] and pays a small additional premium for it. Until recent years, it was included in the contract only by a special "uninsured motorists endorsement."

The form may vary somewhat in some of the states which now make this a mandatory coverage in the automobile insurance policy. The usual wording is that found in Figure 9, as it appears on page 4 of the F.A.P.

Coverage is issued for limits of liability corresponding to those specified in the financial responsibility law of the individual state. By definition, an uninsured automobile is one which is not covered by a bodily injury liability policy or bond at the time of an accident. The definition is extended to include a "hit-and-run" automobile when the owner or operator of the car cannot be determined. It also includes other cars, such as stolen or improperly registered automobiles, for which no insurance applies.

Insurance applies whether or not the injury caused by the uninsured motorist results from occupancy of an automobile. A family is, therefore, protected with insurance against accidents caused by uninsured motorists which occur when any member of the family household occupies an automobile, operates a bicycle, or is a pedestrian. In addition to covering members of the family, the insurance also includes protection for guests of the family injured while riding

[36]The reasons for this coverage, and its relationship to the problem of the innocent unpaid automobile accident victim, have been discussed in a previous section of this chapter.

PART IV—PROTECTION AGAINST UNINSURED MOTORISTS

Coverage J—Uninsured Motorists (Damages for Bodily Injury): To pay all sums which the insured or his legal representative shall be legally entitled to recover as damages from the owner or operator of an uninsured automobile because of bodily injury, sickness or disease, including death resulting therefrom, hereinafter called "bodily injury," sustained by the insured, caused by accident and arising out of the ownership, maintenance or use of such uninsured automobile; provided, for the purposes of this coverage, determination as to whether the insured or such representative is legally entitled to recover such damages, and if so the amount thereof, shall be made by agreement between the insured or such representative and the company or, if they fail to agree, by arbitration.

No judgment against any person or organization alleged to be legally responsible for the bodily injury shall be conclusive, as between the insured and the company, of the issues of liability of such person or organization or of the amount of damages to which the insured is legally entitled unless such judgment is entered pursuant to an action prosecuted by the insured with the written consent of the company.

Definitions: The definitions under Part I, except the definition of "insured," apply to Part IV, and under Part IV:

"insured" means:

(a) the named insured and any relative;
(b) any other person while occupying an insured automobile; and
(c) any person, with respect to damages he is entitled to recover because of bodily injury to which this Part applies sustained by an insured under (a) or (b) above.

The insurance afforded under Part IV applies separately to each insured, but the inclusion herein of more than one insured shall not operate to increase the limits of the company's liability.

"insured automobile" means:

(a) an automobile described in the policy for which a specific premium charge indicates that coverage is afforded,
(b) a private passenger, farm or utility automobile, ownership of which is acquired by the named insured during the policy period, provided
   (1) it replaces an insured automobile as defined in (a) above, or
   (2) the company insures under this Coverage all private passenger, farm and utility automobiles owned by the named insured on the date of such acquisition and the named insured notifies the company during the policy period or within 30 days after the date of such acquisition of his election to make the Liability and Uninsured Motorist Coverages under this and no other policy issued by the company applicable to such automobile,
(c) a temporary substitute automobile for an insured automobile as defined in (a) or (b) above, and
(d) a non-owned automobile while being operated by the named insured; and the term "insured automobile" includes a trailer while being used with an automobile described in (a), (b), (c) or (d) above, but shall not include:
   (1) any automobile or trailer owned by a resident of the same household as the named insured,
   (2) any automobile while used as a public or livery conveyance, or
   (3) any automobile while being used without the permission of the owner.

"uninsured automobile" includes a trailer of any type and means:

(a) an automobile or trailer with respect to the ownership, maintenance or use of which there is, in at least the amounts specified by the financial responsibility law of the state in which the insured automobile is principally garaged, no bodily injury liability bond or insurance policy applicable at the time of the accident with respect to any person or organization legally responsible for the use of such automobile, or with respect to which there is a bodily injury liability bond or insurance policy applicable at the time of the accident but the company writing the same denies coverage thereunder or
(b) a hit-and-run automobile;

but the term "uninsured automobile" shall not include:
   (1) an insured automobile or an automobile furnished for the regular use of the named insured or a relative,
   (2) an automobile or trailer owned or operated by a self-insurer within the meaning of any motor vehicle financial responsibility law, motor carrier law or any similiar law,
   (3) an automobile or trailer owned by the United States of America, Canada, a state, a political subdivision of any such government or an agency of any of the foregoing,
   (4) a land motor vehicle or trailer if operated on rails or crawler-treads or while located for use as a residence or premises and not as a vehicle, or
   (5) a farm type tractor or equipment designed for use principally off public roads, except while actually upon public roads.

"hit-and-run automobile" means an automobile which causes bodily injury to an insured arising out of physical contact of such automobile with the insured or with an automobile which the insured is occupying at the time of the accident, provided: (a) there cannot be ascertained the identity of either the operator or the owner of such "hit-and-run automobile"; (b) the insured or someone on his behalf shall have reported the accident within 24 hours to a police, peace or judicial officer or to the Commissioner of Motor Vehicles, and shall have filed with the company within 30 days thereafter a statement under oath that the insured or his legal representative has a cause or causes of action arising out of such accident for damages against a person or persons whose identity is unascertainable, and setting forth the facts in support thereof; and (c) at the company's request, the insured or his legal representative makes available for inspection the automobile which the insured was occupying at the time of the accident.

"occupying" means in or upon or entering into or alighting from.

"state" includes the District of Columbia, a territory or possession of the United States, and a province of Canada.

Exclusions: This policy does not apply under Part IV:

(a) to bodily injury to an insured while occupying an automobile (other than an insured automobile) owned by the named insured or a relative, or through being struck by such an automobile;
(b) to bodily injury to an insured with respect to which such insured, his legal representative or any person entitled to payment under this coverage shall, without written consent of the company, make any settlement with any person or organization who may be legally liable therefor;
(c) so as to inure directly or indirectly to the benefit of any workmen's compensation or disability benefits carrier or any person or organization qualifying as a self-insurer under any workmen's compensation or disability benefits law or any similar law.

Limits of Liability:

(a) The limit of liability for uninsured motorists coverage stated in the declarations as applicable to "each person" is the limit of the company's liability for all damages, including damages for care or loss of services, because of bodily injury sustained by one person as the result of any one accident and, subject to the above provision respecting each person, the limit of liability stated in the declarations as applicable to "each accident" is the total limit of the company's liability for all damages, including damages for care or loss of services, because of bodily injury sustained by two or more persons as the result of any one accident.
(b) Any amount payable under the terms of this Part because of bodily injury sustained in an accident by a person who is an insured under this Part shall be reduced by
   (1) all sums paid on account of such bodily injury by or on behalf of (i) the owner or operator of the uninsured automobile and (ii) any other person or organization jointly or severally liable together with such owner or operator for such bodily injury including all sums paid under Coverage A, and
   (2) the amount paid and the present value of all amounts payable on account of such bodily injury under any workmen's compensation law, disability benefits law or any similar law.
(c) Any payment made under this Part to or for any insured shall be applied in reduction of the amount of damages which he may be entitled to recover from any person insured under Coverage A.
(d) The company shall not be obligated to pay under this Coverage that part of the damages which the insured may be entitled to recover from the owner or operator of an uninsured automobile which represents expenses for medical services paid or payable under Part II.

Other Insurance: With respect to bodily injury to an insured while occupying an automobile not owned by the named insured, the insurance under Part IV shall apply only as excess insurance over any other similar insurance available to such insured and applicable to such automobile as primary insurance, and this insurance shall then apply only in the amount by which the limit of liability for this coverage exceeds the applicable limit of liability of such other insurance.

Except as provided in the foregoing paragraph, if the insured has other similar insurance available to him and applicable to the accident, the damages shall be deemed not to exceed the higher of the applicable limits of liability of this insurance and such other insurance, and the company shall not be liable for a greater proportion of any loss to which this Coverage applies than the limit of liability hereunder bears to the sum of the applicable limits of liability of this insurance and such other insurance.

Arbitration: If any person making claim hereunder and the company do not agree that such person is legally entitled to recover damages from the owner or operator of an uninsured automobile because of bodily injury to the insured, or do not agree as to the amount of payment which may be owing under this Part, then, upon written demand of either, the matter or matters upon which such person and the company do not agree shall be settled by arbitration in accordance with the rules of the American Arbitration Association, and judgment upon the award rendered by the arbitrators may be entered in any court having jurisdiction thereof. Such person and the company each agree to consider itself bound and to be bound by any award made by the arbitrators pursuant to this Part.

Trust Agreement: In the event of payment to any person under this Part:

(a) the company shall be entitled to the extent of such payment to the proceeds of any settlement or judgment that may result from the exercise of any rights of recovery of such person against any person or organization legally responsible for the bodily injury because of which such payment is made;
(b) such person shall hold in trust for the benefit of the company all rights of recovery which he shall have against such other person or organization because of the damages which are the subject of claim made under this Part;
(c) such person shall do whatever is proper to secure and shall do nothing after loss to prejudice such rights;
(d) if requested in writing by the company, such person shall take, through any representative designated by the company, such action as may be necessary or appropriate to recover such payment as damages from such other person or organization, such action to be taken in the name of such person; in the event of a recovery, the company shall be reimbursed out of such recovery for expenses, costs and attorneys' fees incurred by it in connection therewith;
(e) such person shall execute and deliver to the company such instruments and papers as may be appropriate to secure the rights and obligations of such person and the company established by this provision.

FIGURE 9. Page 4 of the Family Automobile Policy (Uninsured Motorists Insuring Agreement)

in the family car or in any other automobile while operated by the named insured or spouse.

The insurance business approached this coverage with some reluctance since the adjustment of a loss involves two interests that are essentially diverse. The company is obligated to pay only if the uninsured is liable. In the case of a disputed claim the company finds itself in the unhappy position of working against its own interests if it presses the interest of the insured to the limit in an effort to establish liability on the part of the uninsured motorist. The contract undertakes to meet the situation by working out an adjustment through an agreement between the insured or his representative and the company. If they fail to agree that the insured is legally entitled to recover damages against the uninsured motorist or fail to agree as to the amount thereof, the matter is settled by arbitration under the rules of the American Arbitration Association.

The protection is to provide for the insured the amount he would have collected from an uninsured driver who is unable to pay because he is without resources. It has been stated that the man who carries liability insurance takes care of the "other fellow." In the case of uninsured motorists coverage, the insurance is comparable to the collision insurance an insured takes out on his own car. Here, instead, it is bodily injury protection for himself—as long as the "other fellow" is negligent and uninsured.

A few exclusions apply. An insured may not collect (1) to the extent that he is entitled to workmen's compensation benefits, (2) to the extent that he is paid by the uninsured motorist, and (3) beyond the stated limits of the coverage, even if other uninsured motorists coverage may apply when an insured is using a nonowned automobile.

Policy Conditions

The final page of the Family Automobile Policy contains 18 conditions which affect the rights and responsibilities of the parties to the contract and its beneficiaries. Some of these conditions apply to all four of the parts of the contract already discussed. Others apply only to certain parts of the contract, as indicated in the wording shown in Figure 10. The more important of these conditions are mentioned in the following paragraphs, if they have not already been treated in the previous sections.

Claims Provisions. Many of the conditions are promises by the policyholder which must be fulfilled before he should expect the insurer to make payments under the contract. Several conditions are restrictions on the liability of the insurer.

Only automobile losses in the *United States and Canada* are covered. Residents of the southern border states, and travelers who visit Mexico, should note that separate protection must be purchased if they wish to be covered while driving in Mexico. Since Canada's required liability limits in some provinces exceed the financial responsibility laws of some states, care should be taken to check the insurance contract and laws before driving in Canada.

The policyholder promises to pay any *premium* adjustment necessary due to an acquisition of replacement or additional automobiles.

CONDITIONS

Conditions 1, 2, 3, 6, 14, 15, 16 and 18 apply to all Parts. Conditions 4 and 5, 7 through 13, and 17 apply only to the Parts noted thereunder.

1. Policy Period, Territory: This policy applies only to accidents, occurrences and loss during the policy period while the automobile is within the United States of America, its territories or possessions, or Canada, or is being transported between ports thereof.

2. Premium: If the named insured disposes of, acquires ownership of, or replaces a private passenger, farm or utility automobile or, with respect to Part III, a trailer, any premium adjustment necessary shall be made as of the date of such change in accordance with the manuals in use by the company. The named insured shall, upon request, furnish reasonable proof of the number of such automobiles or trailers and a description thereof.

3. Notice: In the event of an accident, occurrence or loss, written notice containing particulars sufficient to identify the insured and also reasonably obtainable information with respect to the time, place and circumstances thereof, and the names and addresses of the injured and of available witnesses, shall be given by or for the insured to the company or any of its authorized agents as soon as practicable. In the event of theft the insured shall also promptly notify the police. If claim is made or suit is brought against the insured, he shall immediately forward to the company every demand, notice, summons or other process received by him or his representative.

If, before the company makes payment of loss under Part IV, the insured or his legal representative shall institute any legal action for bodily injury against any person or organization legally responsible for the use of an automobile involved in the accident, a copy of the summons and complaint or other process served in connection with such legal action shall be forwarded immediately to the company by the insured or his legal representative.

4. Two or More Automobiles—Parts I, II and III: When two or more automobiles are insured hereunder, the terms of this policy shall apply separately to each, but an automobile and a trailer attached thereto shall be held to be one automobile as respects limits of liability under Part I of this policy, and separate automobiles under Part III of this policy, including any deductible provisions applicable thereto.

5. Assistance and Cooperation of the Insured—Parts I and III: The insured shall cooperate with the company and, upon the company's request, assist in making settlements, in the conduct of suits and in enforcing any right of contribution or indemnity against any person or organization who may be liable to the insured because of bodily injury, property damage or loss with respect to which insurance is afforded under this policy; and the insured shall attend hearings and trials and assist in securing and giving evidence and obtaining the attendance of witnesses. The insured shall not, except at his own cost, voluntarily make any payment, assume any obligation or incur any expense other than for such immediate medical and surgical relief to others as shall be imperative at the time of accident.

Part IV: After notice of claim under Part IV, the company may require the insured to take such action as may be necessary or appropriate to preserve his right to recover damages from any person or organization alleged to be legally responsible for the bodily injury; and in any action against the company, the company may require the insured to join such person or organization as a party defendant.

6. Action Against Company—Part I: No action shall lie against the company unless, as a condition precedent thereto, the insured shall have fully complied with all the terms of this policy, nor until the amount of the insured's obligation to pay shall have been finally determined either by judgment against the insured after actual trial or by written agreement of the insured, the claimant and the company.

Any person or organization or the legal representative thereof who has secured such judgment or written agreement shall thereafter be entitled to recover under this policy to the extent of the insurance afforded by this policy. No person or organization shall have any right under this policy to join the company as a party to any action against the insured to determine the insured's liability, nor shall the company be impleaded by the insured or his legal representative. Bankruptcy or insolvency of the insured or of the insured's estate shall not relieve the company of any of its obligations hereunder.

Parts II, III and IV: No action shall lie against the company unless, as a condition precedent thereto, there shall have been full compliance with all the terms of this policy nor, under Part III, until thirty days after proof of loss is filed and the amount of loss is determined as provided in this policy.

7. Medical Reports; Proof and Payment of Claim—Part II: As soon as practicable the injured person or someone on his behalf shall give to the company written proof of claim, under oath if required, and shall, after each request from the company, execute authorization to enable the company to obtain medical reports and copies of records. The injured person shall submit to physical examination by physicians selected by the company when and as often as the company may reasonably require.

The company may pay the injured person or any person or organization rendering the services and such payment shall reduce the amount payable hereunder for such injury. Payment hereunder shall not constitute an admission of liability of any person or, except hereunder, of the company.

8. Insured's Duties in Event of Loss—Part III: In the event of loss the insured shall:

(a) protect the automobile, whether or not the loss is covered by this policy, and any further loss due to the insured's failure to protect shall not be recoverable under this policy; reasonable expenses incurred in affording such protection shall be deemed incurred at the company's request;

(b) file with the company, within 91 days after loss, his sworn proof of loss in such form and including such information as the company may reasonably require and shall, upon the company's request, exhibit the damaged property and submit to examination under oath.

9. Proof of Claim; Medical Reports—Part IV: As soon as practicable, the insured or other person making claim shall give to the company written proof of claim, under oath if required, including full particulars of the nature and extent of the injuries, treatment, and other details entering into the determination of the amount payable. The insured and every other person making claim shall submit to examinations under oath by any person named by the company and subscribe the same, as often as may reasonably be required. Proof of claim shall be made upon forms furnished by the company unless the company shall have failed to furnish such forms within 15 days after receiving notice of claim.

The injured person shall submit to physical examinations by physicians selected by the company when and as often as the company may reasonably require and he, or in the event of his incapacity his legal representative, or in the event of his death his legal representative or the person or persons entitled to sue therefor, shall upon each request from the company execute authorization to enable the company to obtain medical reports and copies of records.

10. Appraisal—Part III: If the insured and the company fail to agree as to the amount of loss, either may, within 60 days after proof of loss is filed, demand an appraisal of the loss. In such event the insured and the company shall each select a competent appraiser, and the appraisers shall select a competent and disinterested umpire. The appraisers shall state separately the actual cash value and the amount of loss and failing to agree shall submit their differences to the umpire. An award in writing of any two shall determine the amount of loss. The insured and the company shall each pay his chosen appraiser and shall bear equally the other expenses of the appraisal and umpire.

The company shall not be held to have waived any of its rights by any act relating to appraisal.

11. Payment of Loss—Part III: The company may pay for the loss in money; or may repair or replace the damaged or stolen property; or may, at any time before the loss is paid or the property is so replaced, at its expense return any stolen property to the named insured, or at its option to the address shown in the declarations, with payment for any resultant damage thereto; or may take all or such part of the property at the agreed or appraised value but there shall be no abandonment to the company. The company may settle any claim for loss either with the insured or the owner of the property.

Part IV: Any amount due is payable (a) to the insured, or (b) if the insured be a minor to his parent or guardian, or (c) if the insured be deceased to his surviving spouse, otherwise (d) to a person authorized by law to receive such payment or to a person legally entitled to recover the damages which the payment represents; provided, the company may at its option pay any amount due in accordance with division (d) hereof.

12. No Benefit to Bailee—Part III: The insurance afforded by this policy shall not inure directly or indirectly to the benefit of any carrier or other bailee for hire liable for loss to the automobile.

13. Subrogation—Parts I and III: In the event of any payment under this policy, the company shall be subrogated to all the insured's rights of recovery therefor against any person or organization and the insured shall execute and deliver instruments and papers and do whatever else is necessary to secure such rights. The insured shall do nothing after loss to prejudice such rights.

14. Changes: Notice to any agent or knowledge possessed by any agent or by any other person shall not effect a waiver or a change in any part of this policy or estop the company from asserting any right under the terms of this policy; nor shall the terms of this policy be waived or changed, except by endorsement issued to form a part of this policy.

15. Assignment: Assignment of interest under this policy shall not bind the company until its consent is endorsed hereon; if, however, the insured named in Item 1 of the declarations, or his spouse if a resident of the same household, shall die, this policy shall cover (1) the survivor as named insured, (2) his legal representative as named insured but only while acting within the scope of his duties as such, (3) any person having proper temporary custody of an owned automobile, as an insured, until the appointment and qualification of such legal representative, and (4) under division 1 of Part II any person who was a relative at the time of such death.

16. Cancelation: This policy may be canceled by the insured named in Item 1 of the declarations by surrender thereof to the company or any of its authorized agents or by mailing to the company written notice stating when thereafter the cancelation shall be effective. This policy may be canceled by the company by mailing to the insured named in Item 1 of the declarations at the address shown in this policy written notice stating when not less than ten days thereafter such cancelation shall be effective. The mailing of notice as aforesaid shall be sufficient proof of notice. The time of the surrender or the effective date and hour of cancelation stated in the notice shall become the end of the policy period. Delivery of such written notice either by such insured or by the company shall be equivalent to mailing.

If such insured cancels, earned premium shall be computed in accordance with the customary short rate table and procedure. If the company cancels, earned premium shall be computed pro rata. Premium adjustment may be made either at the time cancelation is effected or as soon as practicable after cancelation becomes effective, but payment or tender of unearned premium is not a condition of cancelation.

17. Cancelation by Company Limited—Part I: After this policy has been in effect for sixty days or, if the policy is a renewal, effective immediately, the company shall not exercise its right to cancel the insurance afforded under Part I unless:

1. the named insured fails to discharge when due any of his obligations in connection with the payment of premium for this policy or any installment thereof whether payable directly or under any premium finance plan; or
2. the insurance was obtained through fraudulent misrepresentation; or
3. the insured violates any of the terms and conditions of the policy; or
4. the named insured or any other operator, either resident in the same household, or who customarily operates an automobile insured under the policy,
   (a) has had his driver's license suspended or revoked during the policy period, or
   (b) is or becomes subject to epilepsy or heart attacks, and such individual cannot produce a certificate from a physician testifying to his unqualified ability to operate a motor vehicle, or
   (c) is or has been convicted of or forfeits bail, during the 36 months immediately preceding the effective date of the policy or during the policy period, for:
      (1) any felony, or
      (2) criminal negligence resulting in death, homicide or assault, arising out of the operation of a motor vehicle, or
      (3) operating a motor vehicle while in an intoxicated condition or while under the influence of drugs, or
      (4) leaving the scene of an accident without stopping to report, or
      (5) theft of a motor vehicle, or
      (6) making false statements in an application for a driver's license, or
      (7) a third violation, committed within a period of 18 months, of (i) any ordinance or regulation limiting the speed of motor vehicles or (ii) any of the provisions in the motor vehicle laws of any state, the violation of which constitutes a misdemeanor, whether or not the violations were repetitions of the same offense or were different offenses.

18. Declarations: By acceptance of this policy, the insured named in Item 1 of the declarations agrees that the statements in the declarations are his agreements and representations, that this policy is issued in reliance upon the truth of such representations and that this policy embodies all agreements existing between himself and the company or any of its agents relating to this insurance.

FIGURE 10. Page 5 of the Family Automobile Policy (The Conditions)

When *two or more automobiles* are insured under the contract, the liability and medical payments limits apply as if there were only one automobile insured. Under the physical damage coverage, each car is covered for its actual cash value. An attached trailer does not serve to increase the limits of the policy.

When an accident occurs the policy requires *written notice.* This is given by or on behalf of the insured to the company or any of its authorized agents *as soon as practicable.* The notice must contain particulars sufficient to identify the insured, as well as reasonably obtainable information respecting the time, place, and circumstances of an accident, together with the name and addresses of the owner or driver of the car involved in the collision and all available witnesses. If a claim is made or a suit is brought against the insured, he is obligated to forward to the company immediately every demand, notice, summons, or other process received by him or his representative.

In the event of an accident that may involve a claim for damages, whether the insured feels himself to be liable or not, notice should be given the insurance company as promptly as possible. Companies, as a rule, have printed forms indicating the nature of the data they require. This, of course, varies to some degree with the nature of the coverage. The insured will be expected to use reasonable discretion and initiative in acquiring and recording this information.

In every instance where there is personal injury, an estimate of the extent of the injury is required. Whether or not the injured persons received first aid or medical attention is significant information. If injured parties receive medical attention, the name of the attending physician should be ascertained. If they were hospitalized, the name and location of the hospital should appear in the report. The names and addresses of all witnesses are required, and the name and address of the car owner, as well as the license number, should be taken. If the driver is someone other than the owner, his name, address, and driver's license form an essential part of the report. It is important to note the exact location of the accident, together with weather conditions. The condition of the highway should be noted and a detailed sketch be made showing the relative positions of the cars just before and after the collision.

In complying with the state requirements for reporting accidents, insureds should make a duplicate copy of any written forms or reports and forward a copy to the insurer. If members of the police force were present at the accident scene, a notation should be made of their names or badge numbers. It is important to note that the insured must make no admission as to liability and make no effort at the scene of the accident to negotiate a settlement of the claim. The insurance company by virtue of the contract has exclusive control over the adjustment of the claim, and the insured may make no attempt to effect a settlement without the consent of the insurance company. By doing so he runs the risk of placing himself outside of the protection of the policy.

With respect to the liability and collision coverages, the insured is not divested of all responsibility once he has turned the adjustment over to the insurance company. In fact, by virtue of the *assistance and cooperation clause* the insured has assumed serious obligations. The clause, in effect, obligates the insured to render full assistance in the settlement or adjustment of a suit and prohibits the insured from admitting or assuming liability.

The clause is held to be a material condition, and if the insured fails to comply with its requirements he forfeits his right to indemnity under the contract.[37] The breach, to warrant forfeiture, must be substantial and material.[38] Failure to comply to the letter in matters that are slight or inconsequential will not jeopardize the insurance. The careful insured, however, will not attempt to determine what is inconsequential but will fully disclose, as accurately as possible, all information which he may have and work with the company adjusters to effect a satisfactory settlement quite as diligently as if there were no insurance.

Breach of the condition may be the outgrowth of inconvenience or bias in favor of the claimant. The insured may feel it to be inconvenient to attend trial, or may feel that it is the responsibility of the company to make the investigation. He may negligently disregard the obligation to secure the names of witnesses or other pertinent information, or having information of value, may negligently withhold it. Where claims are made by relatives or friends, the insured frequently feels in sympathy with their needs and may be tempted to withhold information or color his testimony to favor the claimant. To admit liability untruthfully or to give false information intentionally to build up the case of the claimant constitutes a breach of the cooperation clause.[39] Any willful and avowed obstruction on the part of the insured to the defense of the company, of course, violates the clause. The insured has a duty to give a full and truthful account of all the circumstances leading up to and attending an accident and if the insurance company requires it, he

[37] *Royal Indemnity Company* v. *Morris*, 37 F. (2d) 90,281 U.S. 784.

[38] *George* v. *Employer's Liability Assurance Corporation, Ltd. et al.*, 291 Ala. 307, 122 So. 175.

[39] *Guerin* v. *Indemnity Company of North America*, 107 Conn. 649; *Bassi* v. *Bassi*, 165 Minn. 100; *Finkel* v. *Western Automobile Insurance Company*, 24 Mo. 285.

must attend court and testify to these facts as a witness.[40] Under the terms of the policy he has no alternative.

Most states have adopted statutes which require in substance that liability policies shall contain a provision that the *bankruptcy or insolvency of the insured shall not release the insurer* from the payment of damages or injuries. A policy provision is included to the effect that an *injured party* may maintain an *action directly against the insurer* if, *after judgment,* the execution against the insured is returned unsatisfied. Some statutes provide the right of action for the injured party in case the judgment remains unsatisfied for the specified period.[41] In some instances the right to sue the insurer is conditioned both upon the bankruptcy or insolvency of the insured and upon the existence of a final judgment which establishes his liability.[42] By virtue of this policy condition it is provided that any person who has secured either judgment or written agreement of the insured's liability may recover under the policy to the extent of the insurance afforded. This provision allows the injured judgment creditor to sue the insurance company without the necessity of demonstrating the insured's insolvency through an unsatisfied execution.

To indicate in a legal action that the insured is covered by insurance may result in a mistrial or the judgment for the plaintiff may be reversed. The rule is based upon the assumption that if the jury knows that an insurance company is to pay the damages and not the individual defendant, there will be a temptation to be generous with the company's money and in borderline cases sympathy rather than the facts at issue may be the determining factor.[43] It follows, therefore, that reference to "insurance" directly or by inference may

---

[40] *Francis,* v. *London Guarantee & Accident Company, Ltd.,* 100 Vt. 425, 138 Atl. 780.

[41] The courts have held that the statute governing such contracts of insurance is, in fact, read into the contract even in the absence of the clause required by the statute or, in fact, if the policy contains language contrary to that required by the statute. In *Bosse* v. *Wolverine Insurance Company,* 184 Alt. 359, the rule is stated thus: "Though the contract itself may not expressly embody the provisions of the statute, nevertheless the statute fixes the rights of those claiming under the policy. *Tuck* v. *Hartford Fire Insurance Co.,* N.H. 326, 331. Indeed, the provisions of the statute may be regarded as practically incorporated into the contract."

[42] Some states allow direct action if a public carrier is concerned. Wisconsin and Louisiana permit direct action by any insured. It is the general rule, however, that direct action may only follow if a judgment is unsatisfied.

[43] The logic behind the rule has thus been expressed: "He must have appreciated the effect it would have made upon a jury trying a case between two citizens, when it was made known that a corporation, and not the defendant, would have to discharge the judgment for damages. He must have known that the wavering balances would go down against the 'soul-less corporation.' No amount of admonition to the jury could remove the effects of the testimony, because it could not remove the knowledge that the suit was not one between citizens, but between citizen and a corporation." *Carter* v. *Walker,* 165 S.W. 483.

jeopardize the case of the plaintiff. The rule is not universally accepted in the light of the wide distribution of insurance and the practice of the use of same defense counsel that regularly represent insurance companies.[44] Where, however, the rule is in force, insurance company attorneys conducting a defense will be on the alert to turn it to their advantage wherever the opportunity presents itself. This is entirely proper in a legal action, and it is, therefore, the responsibility of the plaintiff so to conduct himself with respect to the rule that he will not be responsible for a mistrial or a reversal on appeal of any judgment in his favor.

In liability and collision claims, but not with respect to medical payments, the company is *subrogated* to all rights of recovery which the insured may have. The insured is obligated to execute and deliver instruments and papers and do whatever else is necessary to secure the subrogation rights of the company. It is important that the insured do nothing whatever after a loss to prejudice the subrogation rights of the company. In gathering information required for the loss notice the insured should make no statement that would in any way prejudice the position of the company either by relieving another of liability or assuming responsibility himself. The insured may feel himself to be to blame for an accident but he may be mistaken. He should therefore gather his facts, and such admissions, if any are to be made, should be made after due deliberation and consultation with his insurer.

Some special conditions outline the duties of the insured under physical damage losses. These include: (1) *protection* of the insured automobile *from further loss,* (2) a sworn *proof of loss* within 91 days, (3) rights to *appraisal,* (4) *no abandonment,* and (5) *no benefit to bailee.* These obligations are essentially the same as noticed in connection with other property insurance coverages.

Due to the nature of an automobile, the obligation to *protect the damaged property* is significant. Negligence on the part of the insured to exercise reasonable care in preserving the damaged property and protecting it from further loss may result in loss or damage

---

[44]For example: "and, in addition, we would say that the custom of carrying casualty insurance is now so universal and so generally recognized that a mere individual reference to the fact that defendant was thus protected should not constitute error in absence of a showing of injury." *Russell* v. *Bailey,* 290 S.W. 1108. Again in *Howard* v. *Marshall Motor Company,* 106 Kans. 775, 190 Pac. 11, the court states: "I am unable to see why the courts, in respect to the defendant's indemnity, should ever be called upon to 'walk softly like the gods, whose feet are shod with wool,' or why impenetrable obscuration should envelop so simple and so common a situation. Why should not the jury know who the real party at interest is, the same as they may know who is putting up the security for costs or who is paying the expenses of a witness? To invest the fact of the defendant's insurance with the sanctimonious camouflage of a manufactured reverence is, to my mind, the superlative quintessence of judicial ineptitude."

not collectible under his contract. The policy undertakes to reimburse the insured for all reasonable expense incurred in protecting and preserving any salvage, and the insured is obligated to take all reasonable steps to this end. In the case of theft losses, immediate notice should be communicated to the public authorities. However, if he offers any reward for the return of his property, without the specific authorization of the insurer, such a disbursement is not collectible under the policy. The insured is also obligated to make the damaged property available for inspection by company representatives, submit to examination under oath, and make available records and invoices that may have a bearing on the loss.

The appraisal condition is patterned after a similar one in the fire insurance contract. Any request for an appraisal by either the insurer or the insured must be made within 60 days after receipt of proof of loss by the company. It is also a part of the condition that participation in an appraisal by the company in no way is a waiver of any rights. Thus, a company having a defense under the policy may participate in an appraisal without waiving that defense. This makes it unnecessary to take an agreement that no defense is waived as is sometimes the practice where such a clause does not appear in the policy.

The company is never liable beyond the actual value of the insured automobile. When an automobile has become damaged, an insured may feel that it cannot be replaced in a manner to satisfy him or restored to a condition reasonably approximating that before the loss. In such a case, he feels it not at all unreasonable to ask from the insurance carrier the full value of the car, leaving the salvage to the company. Under the policy, the insured has *no* such right of *abandonment,* nor has the company any obligation to settle on such a basis. The company does, however, have the right to take any part or all of the salvage at the appraised value. The measure of the insured's loss represents the difference between the value before the loss and the value of the salvage. It does not matter that salvage is beyond repair, nor is it necessary that the amount of loss be sufficient to repair the damage.[45]

The *no benefit to bailee clause* is found in one form or another in all transportation contracts. The policy expressly excludes liability for loss or damage to the insured automobile when in the possession of a carrier or bailee, if the proceeds of the insurance are to inure directly or indirectly to the benefit of such carrier or bailee. The insured is expected, as in the case of all marine contracts, to pro-

[45]In the case of a used car, the cost of repairing after a loss is often several times the value of the car before the loss. For example, a car valued at $200 before a fire and valued at $80 for junk after the fire represents a loss of $120, and the cost of replacing the car in its original condition has no bearing on the amount of the loss. On new cars, the amount of the damage and the cost of repair are often the same.

ceed against the carrier or bailee. In the process of adjustment the company may advance to the insured, by way of a loan, money equivalent to his loss or damage. The money is to be repaid to the insurance company to the extent of the net amount collected by, or for, the account of the insured from the carrier or bailee after deducting the cost and expense of collection. This condition prevents railroads or steamship lines, otherwise liable, from taking advantage of an insured's insurance which covers a loss of the automobile during shipment.

A few special conditions apply only to the medical payments and uninsured motorists coverages. These provisions require the insured to execute authorization for obtaining *medical reports,* and to submit to *physical examinations* by physicians when and as often as reasonably requested.

Other Provisions. An *assignment* of the policy will not bind the company until the company consents. Because of the nature of automobile coverages, the insurance company wishes to underwrite its insureds carefully. The clause contains provisions as to the application of insurance in the event of the named insured's death. The policy shall then cover the named insured's spouse, his legal representatives in performing their duties, and anyone in temporary custody of the automobile. Medical payments coverage applies to such a person while the owned automobile is used by a relative up to the time of the appointment and qualification of the insured's legal representative.

Cancellation provisions provide for the insurer to give the policyholder 10 days' notice in writing, with a proportional return of unearned premium to the end of the policy period. If the insured cancels, return of premium is calculated on the customary short-rate basis. The Family Automobile Policy and many other automobile insurance contracts have recently limited the right of the company to cancel the liability portion of the coverage. After the initial contract for the insured has been in effect for 60 days, the insurer may not cancel the protection unless the insured: (1) fails to pay the premium due, (2) obtains the coverage through fraudulent misrepresentation, (3) violates terms or conditions of the policy, or (4) or anyone who customarily operates the insured automobile, has had his driver's license suspended or revoked, becomes subject to epilepsy or heart attacks, or has been convicted or forfeited bail in the past 36 months for a felony, criminal negligence in operating a motor vehicle, driving in an intoxicated condition or under the influence of drugs, leaving the scene of an accident without stopping to report, motor vehicle theft, making false statements for a driver's license, or a third violation within 18 months for speeding or other serious motor vehicle violations.

The final condition in the policy *incorporates the declarations* into the agreement. It is stated that the policy embraces all agreements existing between the insured and the company or any of its agents relating to the insurance. Thus it is important that all material information called for appear in the declarations, as the contract is issued by the insurer in reliance upon their truth.

THE COST OF AUTOMOBILE INSURANCE

With the substantial cost of automobile insurance today it is important for any policyholder or student of insurance to know as much as possible about automobile insurance prices. He should at least be familiar with the reasons why its costs are high, how automobile insurance rates are regulated, and what factors determine the costs for the many different classifications of insured.

Increasing Costs

It is a shock to many policyholders to realize that they often pay more for automobile insurance than they do for gas, oil, and maintenance for their car.[46] Automobile insurance costs have increased rapidly, yet in the past decade automobile insurers have lost about $1 billion in writing the protection they provide for policyholders.[47]

The reasons are many. Rate increases have tended to lag behind the rising costs, due to greater competition in the booming automobile ownership market, changing marketing methods (see Chapter 4), reluctance of state authorities to approve higher rates, the difficulty of predicting losses and expenses in a rapidly expanding field, and many other factors.

The fundamental factors are traceable to the loss portion of the premium dollar paid for automobile insurance. In fact, the expense portion of premiums has actually decreased as a percentage of the total, despite the exposure of regular insurance company operating expenses to the tendency toward the higher cost of doing business today as compared with several years ago.

Thus, in analyzing the losses paid by automobile insurers, the reasons for much greater insurance costs are spotlighted. What, for example, would cause bodily injury liability payments, and medical payments, to increase? The factors emerge: (1) more cars, more drivers, more mileage driven, more accidents, (2) sharply rising

[46]A greater shock comes to those automobile owners, especially young persons under twenty-five years of age, who find that their annual cost for insurance may exceed the total value of their older-model car!

[47]Losses and expenses have exceeded premiums received by all automobile insurers by this amount. Investment income, fortunately, has enabled the insurers to stay in business without destroying the financial strength of most companies. Some insurers have succeeded in making a profit; many others have suffered rather consistent underwriting losses.

hospital and medical cost for treating injuries, (3) more loss of income, based on rising wages, when injuries do occur, and (4) a sharp upward trend in the size and number of claims made, settlements paid, and verdicts granted by juries in personal injury cases. The answer is not simple, of course, for many other factors are important and interrelated with one another in the problem.

What about property damage liability, and collision, insurance costs? Here other factors are pertinent: (1) higher property values, for cars as well as property which automobiles damage, and (2) higher repair costs, especially for automobile repairs based on increased labor and materials costs.

It may be true that some of the increased payments under automobile insurance contracts are due to fraud or exaggerated claims, but it can also be readily seen that there are many basic factors responsible for all kinds of automobile insurance to increase during the recent years of economic expansion.

Rate Regulation

The price charged for automobile insurance contracts does vary, not just for different contracts, but also for essentially identical policies. Most studies[48] indicate that the differences in cost to policyholders may even be "substantial" (1) in some areas, (2) in some classifications, (3) among the competing marketing systems, and (4) for certain periods of time.[49] This conclusion is contrary to the fact that many consumer research surveys have consistently found that the majority of persons believe that all insurers charge about the same price.

Price Competition. How can these opposing findings be explained? The reasons are based upon lack of information and understanding by the buying public. As to why the seeming contradiction should exist, two factors loom as most significant. First, the many pricing mechanisms for automobile insurance are not simple. They include many variations in both regulation and practice. Regulatory provisions differ greatly among the 50 states, as to the objectives and wording of the laws and as to the extent to which the laws are applied. Also, the differences appear in sharp focus when one analyzes the numerous automobile insurance markets and the actual practices of the competing insurers. Second, the insurance consumer is, after all, no more sophisticated in his approach to buy-

[48]See Frederick G. Crane, *Automobile Insurance Rate Regulation* (Columbus, Ohio: Bureau of Business Research, The Ohio State University. Published in cooperation with the Griffith Foundation for Insurance Education, Monograph Number 105, 1962), pp. 41–50.

[49]Allen F. Jung, "Rate Variations among Suppliers of Automobile Insurance," *The Journal of Insurance*, Vol. XXX, No. 4 (December, 1963), p. 573. This study was limited to the State of Illinois.

ing insurance than in buying most other goods and services. Decisions are not always carefully calculated, and are made with tremendous differences in education, ability, initiative, and interest. Indeed, like most other products, insurance is probably purchased as often based upon emotional factors and partial information as it is the result of rational decision-making with all the factors at hand.

Nonprice Competition. Another point is most significant. Why shouldn't prices for automobile insurance vary considerably? Contracts do differ in their terms, and even in identical contracts the product is largely a bundle of services, not limited merely to indemnification for loss. It also includes many hard-to-measure benefits. Just as important to most buyers of insurance as the specific price (although cost certainly is a dominant factor in many decisions, and perhaps too many) are such needs as (1) the opportunity to learn about their requirements, and how insurance can provide the best solutions, (2) the advice and counsel of the insurer and agent in making the decision as to proper coverage, (3) the promptness, efficiency, and fairness of the loss payments, and (4) the careful protection of the insured's right to own and drive an automobile by meeting the various motor vehicle regulations of the states. Nonprice competition is very important to the automobile insurance buyer.

State Regulation. The background for the main issue is therefore formulated with the introduction of the above observations. The problem is essentially one of the extent to which there should be price competition as opposed to price cooperation in automobile insurance, or, put another way, the proper extent of public control of price competition[50] in this field.

A brief summary of the current methods of control is warranted. Three legislative methods may be identified: (1) a restrictive approach, (2) a permissive approach, and (3) the "All-Industry" approach.[51] The first method is used extensively in only a few states. Massachusetts and Texas, for example, follow this approach, and a state agency makes the actual rates which must be charged for all or the major part of automobile coverages.

The permissive approach is used in several states, based upon the idea that competition is the best regulator of insurance prices. California and a small number of Western states follow this practice, with laws which provide minimum regulation as long as general objectives of rate adequacy, unexcessiveness, and fair discrimination are met.

Most of the states, as a result of the McCarran Act (Public Law

[50]Crane, *op. cit.*, pp. 101 and 145–53.

[51]*Ibid.*, pp. 68–73.

15, 1945), adopted within a few years laws modeled after bills approved by the National Association of Insurance Commissioners. These are known as the "All-Industry laws," and apply to many forms of property-liability insurance in addition to automobile insurance. They permit insurers to choose among several alternatives: (1) filing their own rates, (2) adopting the rates filed by a rating organization, or (3) using deviated rates based upon their own experience. The rates must be filed with the state insurance department and the insurance commissioner or superintendent may disapprove them within certain time limits if they do not meet certain standards according to definitions in the laws. The laws are basically a compromise between the restrictive and permissive approaches: they permit competition through independent, bureau, and deviated rates, and they provide for regulated cooperation through the rating bureau approach to rate-making. More precise standards for the authorities to follow in evaluating the compliance with the objectives of rate regulation are used, although the diversity of the rules and their application among the states is considerable. Competition is encouraged but somewhat controlled. The result in most states is that the automobile insurance consumer finds, if he looks for it, a reasonable degree of price competition.

Premium Factors

Classification of Automobiles and Contracts. For the purposes of insurance, automobiles are classed as: (1) passenger, (2) commercial, (3) public, (4) dealers', and (5) miscellaneous. These classifications are based to some degree upon the type of car and to a greater degree upon the use of the car. The class designations are for the obvious purpose of differentiating among the various major types of automobile risks. The miscellaneous category includes a number of automobiles designed for special purposes such as fire and police department vehicles, ambulances, hearses, armored cars, auto homes, motorcycles, motor scooters, tractors (not of truck type), and trailers or semitrailers. Automotive equipment not insurable under the automobile policy includes lawn mowers, power shovels, and trench diggers. Risks of this type are normally insured under inland marine contracts.

Commercial vehicles are classified in accordance with the size of the vehicle and the business use classification of the insured. In addition to factors of weight and use, some territories give consideration to a mileage-radius factor. Commercial trucks involving long-distance operations have evidenced that these operations are definitely more hazardous than those confined to a local territory. A surcharge is placed, with some exceptions, on all risks which are customarily operated more than 50 miles from the place where they are garaged. Garage, service station, and other automobile dealers are treated separately from other commercial insureds under special contracts designed for their particular needs.

For rating purposes public automobiles are classified as: (*a*) private livery, (*b*) public livery, (*c*) taxi cabs, and (*d*) buses. The distinction between a private and public livery lies in the use of the car. A private livery automobile is a public automobile of any type with a seating capacity not in excess of eight passengers excluding the driver. To qualify as a private livery automobile, the car must be rented from a garage or the residence of the named insured, with one of his employees in attendance as chauffeur. Such cars are used for social functions or tours and the like. A public livery automobile may operate from a public place, and is hired with a chauffeur by the hour, day, trip, or mile. Because public automobile rates are high and because there is no risk when the car is not in operation, a system or rating has been devised on an earnings basis per $100 of gross receipts or on a mileage basis.

When there are five or more commercial or public cars under a single ownership, a "fleet" policy is issued, based upon discounts and the estimated average future exposure. The advance premium charged is adjusted at the end of the policy term by determining the actual number and use of the vehicles during the policy term.

As noted in the early part of this chapter, the Standard Automobile Policy is the normal contract for insuring most of the types of business-use motor vehicles mentioned above. Variations in the basic contract are frequent, in order to meet the specific needs of the policyholder.

Private Passenger Automobile Liability Premiums. The various Coverages A-J in the Family Automobile Policy each have individual factors which are most important in determining the price charged by the insurer. Approximate charges have been indicated for the medical payments and uninsured motorists coverages as they were discussed. The major portion of the price of automobile insurance applies to the liability and physical damage coverages, which are discussed further here.

Bodily injury and property damage *liability* insurance premiums are dependent first upon a *territorial* designation, according to the state and territory in which the automobile is principally garaged. Some states have as many as 50 separate rating territories, while others have only a few. The differentiation is based both upon the usual rural-urban differences in exposure to loss, as well as the particular loss experiences for several years in the territory. Claims statistics in changing the rates are determined by accidents charged to the location where the car is principally garaged. Thus an accident by a person from a large city is not charged to a small city where the accident may have occurred.

For rating purposes, private passenger cars are divided into classes. Territorial premiums are set for each class on the basis of *ownership* of the car, and *use* and *age* of the driver. The following are the classes now[52] commonly used by many companies[53] for private passenger automobiles:

CLASS 1A	Not used for business, not driven to or from work, no male operator under twenty-five.*
CLASS 1B	Not used for business but driven to or from work less than 10 miles one way. No male operator under twenty-five.
CLASS 1C	Not used for business but driven to or from work 10 or more miles one way. No male operator under twenty-five.
CLASS 2A	One or more male operators under twenty-five and each such operator is either married or not an owner or principal operator.
CLASS 2C	Unmarried male owner or principal operator is under twenty-five.
CLASS 3	Used for business; no male operator under twenty-five.

*Male operator under twenty-five includes an individual who is a resident in the same household. It includes anyone absent while attending school, but not one in active military service unless he customarily operates the automobile.

The Class 1A premium is the lowest, Class 1B is slightly higher, and Class 1C, for driving to or from work 10 miles or more one way, the most expensive of the Class 1 (for no male operators under twenty-five) group. Men under the age of twenty-five (Class 2) pay a much higher premium, based upon the greater accident frequency and severity for this group. Class 2C premiums, for unmarried under twenty-five males, are as much as three times as high as those in basic Class 1A. Class 3, for cars used for business (such as salesmen) has a premium somewhat higher than that for Class 1C.

Farm automobiles and trucks, with a load capacity of 1,500 pounds or less, have special 1AF, 2AF, and 2CF class premiums which are about 10 percent below the corresponding classifications.

The dollar figures for the premiums in each territory vary too much to make a precise illustration valuable. The range of premiums

---

[52]Several other classification systems have been used in the past. During World War II a system correlated car mileage estimates (based on gasoline ration cards) with the premium charge. Statistical studies thereafter showed that the use and age classes measured the differences in expected losses more accurately.

As of May, 1964, a revised classification system was announced, effective January 1, 1965. Most widely affected will be women drivers and young drivers. New classes will be established for unmarried girls under twenty-one, single women thirty–sixty-four, unmarried males twenty-five–twenty-nine, and married or unmarried males under twenty-five (by individual year of age).

[53]Individual insurers can, and do, use other or more classifications. Two recent plans of note are those which establish special classes for younger drivers (1) on the basis of average school grades and (2) on scores in specially designed psychological tests given by the insurance company.

is significant, however. Bodily injury liability premiums for basic rating limits of 5/10 (the actual policy limits are normally 10/20 or more) vary from about $20 for Class 1A in some sections of the country to over $130 in other territories. Class 2C premiums may be over $250. Property damage liability premiums vary less, and may range from about $20 to $30 for Class 1A in most territories. Insureds in the assigned risk plans of the various states may have substantial increases in their premiums as a result of poor loss or motor vehicle violation records.

Private Passenger Automobile Physical Damage Premiums. Automobile *physical damage* insurance premiums are also heavily dependent on the *territory* in which the motor vehicle is operated. The next elements for consideration are the *year* and *make* of the car and its *age*. There are four age groups applicable to the comprehensive physical damage and collision coverages.[54] As the car becomes older, the premium decreases. The make of the car determines a "symbol" class by letter groupings A-Z, and indicates the approximate value of the automobile. In anticipating collision and physical damage losses, it is recognized that a Cadillac owner should pay more than an owner of a lower-priced car, since damage and repair costs will differ substantially.

Collision insurance also uses premiums which vary by use of the car. Commercial cars have two classes, and for the private passenger cars the classes are the same as for liability insurance, except that all Class 1 premiums are the same (no difference is made depending on whether the automobile is driven to work). A final factor of importance is the use of deductibles in collision coverage. As noted earlier, full-coverage collision insurance is extremely high, if it is available. Most policyholders prefer to carry part of the losses themselves, and the $50 and $100 deductible forms are most often used. The insurance buyer should check on the difference between $50 and $100 deductible coverage, for often a saving of $30 or more is possible through the use of the $100 deductible.

Private Passenger Automobile Discounts. Several types of *discounts* in the cost of automobile insurance have become quite important in recent years. One is a *driver training* credit for Class 2 (under age twenty-five) operators. Usually this is about a 10 percent reduction for liability, medical payments, and collision coverage. The drivers must have passed an accredited course of class-

[54]Age groups provided in the manual are as follows: (1) automobiles purchased new not more than 6 months prior to the date insurance attaches; (2) automobiles purchased new more than 6 months but not more than 18 months prior to the date insurance attaches; (3) automobiles purchased new more than 18 months but not more than 30 months prior to the date insurance attaches; (4) automobiles purchased new more than 30 months prior to the date insurance attaches.

room and practice instruction. Another credit of about 20 percent (10 percent on collision) is allowed on Class 1 and 3 automobiles when *two or more automobiles* are insured in the same contract. Insurance premiums for any automobile may be reduced by *temporary layup or suspension of use* of the car for over 30 days. A proportional credit is granted when the coverage is reinstated. Most insurers also have recently introduced a *compact car* discount of about 10 percent, applicable to certain types of the smaller modern automobiles (not classed as sports car), which have been shown in research studies to cause fewer and less serious accidents.

A further major step in discounts is found in the *safe driver insurance* plans based upon the premise that drivers who operate automobiles in a lawful manner and free from accidents are entitled to recognition in terms of reduced automobile insurance costs. Rating plans based upon the nonoccurrence of accidents or convictions, popularly called "merit rating," allow discounts for good drivers of 10 percent or more from premiums developed by the classification system. It may be logically argued that these differences are large and frequently enough applied so that they have become new classes of risks rather than mere discounts.

The plans that operate in the various states undertake to provide individually tailored coverage designed according to the driving record and needs of the individual family. The plans establish automobile insurance premiums that will reflect driver experience. There has been a growing feeling that there is an element of inequity in burdening good drivers that never have had an accident or a moving traffic violation with loss experiences attributable to the few careless drivers. The safe driver plan rewards those with good driver experience with lower rates. Drivers with a record (within the previous three years, usually) of accidents and traffic convictions pay more.

Some plans establish a point system under which drivers that have no points receive the lowest allowable premium. Premiums are advanced for other drivers based upon the number of points they have accumulated. An experience period is established and points are assigned for such convictions as, for example: (*a*) driving while intoxicated, (*b*) failure to stop and report when involved in an accident, or (*c*) driving without a license. A lesser number of points is assigned for a conviction for reckless driving or other conviction for a moving traffic violation.

SUMMARY

Few other fields of insurance today have the interest of the public as does automobile insurance. The need for such insurance is almost universally respected, yet the growth of its coverage has brought to the property-liability insurance business an era of marketing innovations, severe competition, and financial losses unparalleled in modern times.

Automobile insurance should be considered from the viewpoint of the insured and insurer, the accident victim (as an individual), and society as a whole. With the advent of the public measures aimed at solving the problem of the *unpaid innocent automobile accident victim,* the automobile insurance policy has become more than just a private contract. Most states encourage the purchase of automobile liability insurance through *financial responsibility laws* which require insurance for those persons who have had accidents or severe motor vehicle violations. Three states require *compulsory automobile liability insurance* before any automobile can be registered and issued license plates. Several other laws, including the *assigned risk plans, unsatisfied judgment funds,* and *uninsured motorists coverage,* have evolved with the objective of assuring payment of losses to innocent injured persons. The problem is so serious that many alternative programs have been instituted and many others considered.

The Family Automobile Policy is analyzed as the major contract which provides the individual with the automobile insurance he needs. The basic liability and physical damage coverages are evaluated as they appear in the declarations, insuring agreements, exclusions, and conditions of the policy. It is surprising to find that a wide variety of liability, medical payments, collision, comprehensive physical damage, and uninsured motorists coverages may all be included in one broad contract. The protection may extend to the whole family, several automobiles, coverage while driving other cars or while the insured car is being driven by other persons with proper permission, and a large number of "supplementary agreements" which provide legal defense and other important benefits. The relatively few exclusions and the conditions which impose a number of necessary duties on the policyholder are discussed in sufficient detail to show the exact nature of the coverage which is provided.

The over $8 billion annual cost of automobile accidents is shocking in terms of its tragic toll in lives, injuries, and suffering. Analysis of some of the reasons for the rapid increase in the price of automobile insurance indicates that many underlying features of our economy are related to the growth of insurance costs. Regulation of automobile insurance rates is summarized as to its purposes and methods. The automobile insurance premium is shown as the result of many factors, including substantial territorial differences in costs. Widespread variations in price result from the use of specific classifications and discounts developed to measure the extent of risk for different uses of the car, ages of the drivers, and kinds of automobiles.

The key to the family automobile(s?) today is truly the sign of one of the highest standards of living any nation has ever enjoyed. Yet, with the key goes a frightening responsibility for the control of the costs, both physical and financial, which are associated with it.

FOR REVIEW

1. The unpaid innocent automobile accident victim has created an increasing problem for our society. Every state has adopted some legislation to assure that persons are financially able to pay for injury or damage resulting from legal responsibility arising out of the ownership or use of automobiles.
   a) Explain the basic characteristics of the type of law used by almost all states.
   b) Three states have adopted another type of law. How does it differ from the law discussed in *a*)?
2. In reference to question 1, identify any other *statutory* approaches to the solution of this problem. Indicate, with reasons, your estimate of the merit of these solutions.
3. Aside from the answers given in questions 1 and 2, what other alternatives should be considered? Evaluate them as an answer to the problem.
4. Discuss (*a*) the merits and (*b*) the faults of the following solutions to the "unpaid innocent automobile accident victim problem":
   a) Compulsory automobile liability legislation.
   b) Financial responsibility laws.
   c) Unsatisfied judgment funds.
   d) Uninsured motorists coverage.
5. Perhaps part of the solution to the "unpaid innocent automobile accident victim problem" lies in the voluntary efforts of individuals to provide an answer. Each of the coverages in the basic Family Automobile Policy could help alleviate the problem. For *each* coverage in the policy, explain how this might be so.
6. Mr. Riskee has just purchased a Family Automobile Policy with 50/100/10/2 limits for the basic coverages of bodily injury liability, property damage liability, and medical payments.
   a) What kinds of property damage would such a contract cover? Give several examples.
   b) Does the medical payments coverage pay for losses even if Mr. Riskee is not liable for them? Explain. *Whose* injuries does it pay for?
   c) What additional coverages would you suggest for Mr. Riskee to have on his *own* car? Explain each briefly.
   d) Would you recommend that the uninsured motorists coverage be included in this policy? Why, or why not?
7. What are the "supplementary agreements" in the Family Automobile Policy, and why may they be important to the policyholder?
8. Does your Family Automobile Policy cover your wife and children while they are driving the car of a friend? Explain.
9. Mary, a teenage daughter of X, drives with him to the country club. A friend of the family asks Mary to drive his car home. While driving this car Mary becomes involved in an accident that results in a huge liability

claim for personal injury. The friend's insurance is inadequate to cover the claim. Will the insurance on her family car help?

10. Y borrows an automobile from X. X sends his driver with instructions to take orders from Y. In the event of an accident what, if any, is the responsibility of Y?
11. A lends his automobile to B and rides with B to the railroad station. They are in a hurry to catch a train and B negligently attempts to pass another car on a hill with the result that there is a collision and both passengers in the car are seriously injured. Can A, the owner of the car and the named insured, sue B? If so, will A's policy protect B?
12. B carries collision insurance on his car with a $50 deductible. A friend, with $250 deductible collision, loans him a car to go for some friends. On the way he becomes involved in a collision resulting in $250 damages to the other car. He feels morally obligated to settle the damage and is concerned to find that no part of it will be carried by the insurance on the car he borrowed because of the deductible. Tell him how much his loss will actually be, and why.
13. Following an accident you are arrested and convicted of speeding in violation of traffic laws. You are told by a friend that since the accident was the outgrowth of a law violation, your policy will not provide liability protection. Discuss.
14. A young man riding in an automobile attempted to show the young lady driver his skill in blowing bubble gum. He blew a huge balloon and turning to the driver to demonstrate its size attempted further to inflate it. The balloon burst in the face of the driver. The car left its traffic lane and crashed into an oncoming car. Would the automobile liability insurance of the young lady cover if the accident were attributable to his negligence?
15. Mary, the daughter of X, is injured while riding in the car of a friend to a Girl Scout meeting. Does the father's medical payments coverage on the family automobile afford any relief in this situation?
16. The Family Automobile Policy affords much broader coverage than some of the other policies, such as the Standard Automobile Policy and Special Automobile Policy. Indicate as many as possible of these broader coverages.
17. M, the insured, became involved in an automobile accident and claimed he telephoned a report to the agent on the following day. The agent claims no knowledge of the phone call and no further report or information was offered by the insured. Three weeks after the accident suit was filed by the injured party against the insured, and the insurance company denied liability on the grounds that the insured did not give notice "as soon as practicable." What do you think of the position of the insured?
18. X carries automobile comprehensive physical damage coverage. Explain why you think the following losses would, or would not, be covered:
    a) Because of a delay in putting antifreeze into his automobile radiator, there is a freeze-up with serious damage.
    b) Would it be the same if there were damage resulting from the freezing of parts due to lack of lubrication?
    c) Vandals rip the car radio antenna off and dump a can of red paint over the car.
    d) While driving west late one afternoon, X is temporarily blinded by the sun. As a result, X's car collides with another at an intersection. X claims the loss is not a collision but is due to temporary blindness. He claims that the comprehensive policy will pay the claim.

e) The car is stolen and the thieves collide with an oncoming car in an attempt to escape from the police.

f) X carries both comprehensive physical damage and $50 deductible collision coverage. The car skids and strikes a light pole by the side of the road, damaging the windshield to the extent of $100.

19. Mr. I. M. Hazard, while driving friend C's car, made an illegal left turn. He swung too wide and drove over the curb into a clothing store. The car careened on to strike a pedestrian and Mr. B. His car finally stopped as he hit a bus, causing damage to the bus and its occupants. Mr. Hazard had no insurance. C has a Family Automobile Policy with the following coverages and limits: A, $50,000/$100,000; B, $10,000; C, $2,000; D, A.C.V.; and E, A.C.V. with a $100 deductible.

    a) Under these circumstances, does C's policy cover Mr. Hazard as an insured? Explain.

    b) Indicate, with brief reasons, the kind and extent of coverage, if any, which would apply for the following losses:

1) Mr. C's car	$ 2,000
2) Clothing store	15,000
3) Bus	5,000
4) Mr. Hazard	1,000
5) Mr. B	10,000
6) Pedestrian	55,000
7) Two bus passengers	15,000 (each)
8) Court and legal costs	20,000

20. *Who* is protected by the Family Automobile Policy, and *what* automobiles?
21. Suppose a friend asks your advice for proper protection he should have for his new automobile. What explanations would you offer him for the most important coverages, and what approximate limits would you suggest he include in the Family Automobile Policy?
22. Are automobile insurance costs similar for all insureds and for similar protection from all insurers? Should they be? Explain your answers.
23. What factors have caused the rising costs of automobile insurance?

Chapter 17

CRIME INSURANCE AND SURETYSHIP

THE broad field of crime insurance includes any wrongful taking of someone else's property. Suretyship is not technically included in crime insurance, but an important part of suretyship is the fidelity bond business for employee dishonesty. Suretyship also pertains to losses occasioned by acts of neglect as well as crimes, as in judicial and contract bonds.

CRIMES AGAINST PROPERTY

Nature and Definitions

Crimes involving offenses against property, such as robbery, burglary, and larceny, are not always defined identically in the statutes of different jurisdictions. To eliminate any element of uncertainty, policies covering theft losses provide a definition of the peril to be covered. Briefly, *robbery* consists of the carrying away of the personal property of another from his person or in his presence by violence or putting him in fear. *Burglary* is the breaking and entering of the property of another with the intent to commit a felony. This is generally broadened to include theft losses occasioned by person or persons making felonious entry by actual force or violence. *Theft* is the stealing or taking of another's goods. The legal term for theft as used in insurance policies is *larceny*, and in the insurance contract both terms are used interchangeably. Larceny is the taking and carrying away of the personal goods of another with a felonious attempt to steal. Larceny losses would include thefts by sneak thieves, servants, tradesmen, mechanics, or others having access to the premises of the insured. Such losses, of course, would not fall within the category of burglaries and would not be covered by a policy insuring the burglary risk only.[1]

General Divisions of Crime Insurance Coverages

There are two divisions of the insurance business that are concerned with insurance protection against theft losses. These are: (*a*)

[1]It is at once apparent that from the point of view of theft "burglary" and "robbery" coverages are limited in their scope. To be fully covered for "theft" losses those attributable to larceny must be included in the contract. Limited contracts are acceptable if the limitations are thoroughly understood.

nonemployee, or burglary-theft dishonesty insurance, and (*b*) employee, or fidelity dishonesty insurance. The burglary-theft dishonesty coverages, usually known in the business as "burglary insurance," provide insurance against pecuniary losses resulting from the dishonesty of persons who are not employed by the insureds. Dishonesty coverage for employees is known as the "fidelity bond business" and provides protection for the insured resulting from the dishonesty of persons employed by him. The insurance business sometimes uses the term "insider" dishonesty insurance to describe the fidelity bond business, and "outsider" dishonesty insurance is applied to the burglary and theft coverages. The two branches, however, are quite commonly known in insurance terminology as (*a*) burglary and theft insurance, and (*b*) fidelity bonds. Fidelity coverages will receive consideration with the later discussion of the corporate surety bond business.

Burglary and theft coverages have been sometimes grouped into six categories: (1) theft (2) burglary, (3) robbery, (4) forgery, (5) liability for crime losses, and (6) "package" crime insurance. Among the more commonly written forms are: (*a*) Broad Form Personal Theft Policy, (*b*) Mercantile-Open Stock Burglary Policy, (*c*) Mercantile Robbery and Safe Burglary Policy, (*d*) Messenger Robbery Policy, (*e*) Money and Securities (Broad Form) Policy, (*f*) Storekeepers' or Office Burglary and Robbery Policy, and (*g*) Comprehensive Dishonesty, Destruction and Disappearance Policy.

ANALYSIS OF CRIME INSURANCE COVERAGES

Policies in the burglary-theft category follow in general the pattern already noticed with respect to liability policies. There are four sections: (1) declarations, (2) insuring agreements, (3) exclusions, and (4) conditions. Most policies have four pages. The printed policy is included in the first three pages and the fourth, which is virtually blank, is reserved for endorsements.

Basic Parts of Crime Policies

Declarations. The first page of the policy contains for the most part the declarations. At the top of the page, however, following the name of the company is a reference to "the assured named in the declarations forming a part hereof" instead of the actual name of the insured. The declarations then follow and consist of all the essential statements and specifications required for the particular risk. They contain the name and address of the insured and, where pertinent, his business. The policy period is given with a statement of the coverage together with limits of insurance. The premium to be charged will appear, and the premises to which the policy applies will be indicated. The declarations may call for the total amount of insurance to be carried.

The declarations will state whether or not a burglar alarm system is maintained, pertinent information with respect to the premises, whether or not a private watchman will be on duty, or any other warranty with respect to special protective features that reflect in a reduction in premium. Finally, there is a statement with respect to a history of previous losses during the past five years. A statement is also required with respect to any cancellation of theft insurance issued to the insured or whether any such insurance has been declined by any insurer.

Insuring Agreements. The insuring agreements are preceded by a short paragraph in which the company agrees with the insured named in the declarations to indemnify him for certain losses. The insurer does so in consideration of the payment of the premium and in reliance upon the statements in the declarations and subject to the limits of liability, exclusions, conditions, and other terms of the policy. The insuring agreements then describe the perils against which the insurance is written and the property covered.

The insuring agreement may consist of one or more parts, and insurance may be granted under one or more or all of them. While the insuring agreement establishes in a broad way the nature of the perils to be covered, the extent of the protection can be determined only in connection with the exclusions, definitions, and conditions contained in the contract.

Exclusions. The exclusions in theft coverages are designed primarily to establish limits to the coverage. By so doing the insured is saved from paying twice for the same coverage. For example, theft of an aircraft or automobile is excluded, since such vehicles are ordinarily specifically insured. Other exclusions deal with features that apply to the particular type of coverage. Most contracts, but not all, exclude losses attributable to war, insurrection, and the like.

Conditions. The conditions for the most part follow the pattern already noticed with respect to other insurance contracts. They provide for notice and proof of loss, subrogation, assignment, cancellations, other insurance, action against the company, changes, special statutes, declarations and a clause covering payment, replacement, and recovery. These clauses are to be found in one form or another in all theft policies. The notice of cancellation when the company elects to cancel, which in most instances is ten days, is longer in some forms.

The conditions peculiar to an individual policy concern themselves primarily with (*a*) definitions, and (*b*) ownership of the property covered. It has already been noticed that there is a difference in statutory definitions of various forms of theft. To avoid confusion and misunderstanding, the extent of the coverage as respects a given form of theft is clarified by definition in the conditions. Other terms such as custodian, guard, messenger, and premises are carefully defined. Loss is defined to include damage, and business to include trade, profession, or occupation. Other specific definitions appear where the coverage requires it. Following the definitions is a condition with respect to ownership of the property insured. Burglary policies usually undertake to provide coverage for both the property of the insured and property for which he may be held liable.

Residence Theft Insurance

Two theft forms for residences are: (*a*) Broad Form Personal Theft Policy and (*b*) Personal Theft Policy. The first of these furnishes a very broad coverage. There is no restriction as to the nature of the theft. It may be attributable to burglars, servants, occasional employees, or for that matter anyone except relatives permanently residing with the insured. In contrast, the second form provides theft protection to homeowners who either do not require the broad protection afforded under the broad form or cannot afford it. There are numerous exclusions, including mysterious disappearance losses.

The *Broad Form Personal Theft Policy* is the more common, it provides two major types of coverage: (1) theft from premises or a depository, and (2) theft away from the premises.[2] The coverage is very broad in that the word "theft" includes larceny, burglary, and robbery. The peril of *mysterious disappearance* is also named, and it applies to any insured property, except a precious or semiprecious stone from its setting in any watch or piece of jewelry.[3] This means that theft of every character is covered, and it also means that if any piece of insured property is missing, with the exceptions noticed,

[2]The earliest attempts to insure householders against theft losses provided insurance only against loss by burglary. Policies are now written furnishing a broad coverage and include in addition to burglary the perils of robbery, theft, and larceny. The form covering the burglary peril only is still written; and a policy covering burglary, theft, and larceny without the robbery coverage is obtainable. Since so many residence losses are due to sneak thieves and others who enter the premises without the use of force, the broad coverage is preferable because there is less likelihood of misunderstanding. For those willing to risk larceny losses, the restricted form is available at a lower rate.

[3]Including the peril of "mysterious disappearance" affords an extremely liberal coverage. Some companies have eliminated the mysterious disappearance feature as a "claim breeder." The clause, it is contended, is broader than necessary to be useful, and the claims that are presented are costly. Frequently there is grave doubt as to whether or not the claims are actually the outgrowth of theft losses. The companies do not contemplate covering losses caused by carelessness. Loss of a precious or semiprecious stone from its setting in a watch or piece of jewelry is not regarded as a mysterious disappearance or theft, and the loss is not covered by the policy.

and there is no explanation for its disappearance, then the loss is covered by the policy.

Coverage includes the property of the insured, members of his family, relatives, guests, residence employees, and other permanent members of the household. On-premises coverage applies automatically when the named insured moves to new premises. Off-premises coverage is worldwide and extends to provide coverage on property unattended in automobiles and property in charge of a carrier for hire. The policy also covers damage caused by burglars, robbers, and thieves to the insured property or to the premises occupied by the insured, or loss or damage caused by vandalism or malicious mischief.

Property for the purposes of insurance is divided into the following three classes; (*a*) jewelry, sterling silver, and furs; (*b*) other property not specifically insured; and (*c*) specified articles described and insured for specific amounts. Specified limits of insurance are applied to the first two categories, and specified amounts are applied to each article in the third category. If certain particularly valuable items of jewelry, silver, or furs are specifically insured, a specific amount may still be applied under the first group of unscheduled items in the category. Property not specifically insured in the second category includes such personal property as household furniture, clothing, rugs, plated ware, musical instruments, cameras, money, and securities. It is the practice, therefore, to place separate amounts of insurance upon jewelry, watches, gems, and the like and another amount upon household goods and personal property generally. Any particularly valuable items are specifically insured.

It is not necessary, however, to separate jewelry, furs, and silver. When this is done the coverage is said to be divided. An alternative to divided coverage is one of two forms of combined coverage referred to usually as "blanket coverages." From the foregoing it is apparent that the insured may elect one or several combinations of coverage.

Burglary Insurance

Mercantile Open Stock Policy. In its more usual form this policy provides (*a*) burglary insurance, and (*b*) property damage insurance attributable to burglary. The burglary risk is defined in the policy, and, by means of an endorsement in connection with certain carefully underwritten risks, the policy may be extended to cover the undefined risks of theft, larceny, and robbery.

Unlike insurance coverages for money and securities that are written on all risks or broad forms, all-risks policies are never written to cover mercantile open stock, and the policy does not apply to money and securities. The policy is a specified-risk contract covering (*a*) burglary, (*b*) property damage, (*c*) robbery of a watchman, and (*d*) in some instances, theft.

The contract undertakes to indemnify the insured for loss of the insured property caused by *burglary* while the premises are not open for business. The policy covers all merchandise in the insured premises as well as furniture, fixtures, and equipment, but not money and securties. To be within the protection afforded by the policy, the property must be on the premises of the insured as defined in the contract. Show windows or showcases not opening directly into the interior of the premises, as well as public entrances, halls, and stairways, are not within the coverage of the policy. This risk, however, may be specifically insured. The term "premises" is defined to mean only the interior of that part of the building described in the application as occupied by the insured in conducting his business.

Under the terms of the policy there is no coverage for loss or damage to furs or articles made entirely or principally of fur caused by burglary of such merchandise from within any show window outside the building line after glass has been broken from the outside. The risk is insurable; but if this class of merchandise is to be covered in outside show windows, the coverage must be supplied by means of a separate endorsement attached to the policy, for which an additional premium is charged. The policy further provides a limit of $50 for loss or damage to any one article of jewelry. This limit may be increased upon the payment of an additional premium. Property held as a pledge or as collateral for a loan is insured to the extent of the amount advanced, plus accrued interest at the legal rate to the time of the loss, but it is in any case subject to the limit set for jewelry. Under its terms the policy excludes liability if the insured, an associate, or an employee is connected with the burglary either as a principal or as an accessory.

As is usually the case in burglary insurance, *property damage* by a burglary or an attempted burglary is covered. Under this policy this includes not only merchandise but furniture, fixtures, and equipment in the premises. Damages to the premises is covered if the insured is the owner or is liable for the damage.

Theft coverage is provided only by endorsement to the *Mercantile Open Stock Burglary Policy*. Insurers are unwilling to insure merchandise in a retail establishment against the shoplifter type of loss or losses attributable to pilfering by employees of the insured because the terms "theft" and "larceny" are undefined. Theft risks are underwritten as a rule only for those types of manufacturing, wholesale or public warehouse establishments that handle bulk merchandise, such as textiles and fabrics in bales or bolts. Particularly the endorsement is not available to any establishment where there are inevitable stock shortages due to breakage, shrinkage, spoilage, and the like. The theft coverage is almost never issued to a retail establishment. However, it is possible to extend the burglary policy to cover loss occasioned by someone hiding in the premises and making a forcible exit. It will be recalled that "burglary" is defined to mean a theft loss occasioned by a person or persons making felonious entry by actual force or violence. This is "breaking in." Breaking out does not constitute burglary and theft losses attributable to someone's hiding in the premises are not covered unless the policy is extended accordingly. Mysterious disappearance losses are never covered, and wherever a theft is suspected as a result of any shortage of insured merchandise brought to light by an inventory, there is no coverage unless it can reasonably be shown that the shortage was occasioned by theft, larceny, or robbery. The theft coverage provided by the endorsement excludes liability of a loss by theft committed by an employee or servant of the insured. Because of the restrictions and limitations which surround the theft endorsement, it provides only a limited extension to the basic Mercantile Open Stock (M.O.S.) Burglary Policy.

It may be noted in passing with respect to all the coverages that they apply only while the premises of the insured are closed to business. This being the case, the contract is sometimes said to be a "nighttime, Saturdays, Sundays" policy. The exclusions are few. They provide that there is no coverage for (*a*) loss in excess of actual cash value or cost to repair or replace, (*b*) losses contributed to by a change in the condition of the risk or occurring while a protective system for which a premium reduction is allowed is not maintained, (*c*) loss of furs in a show window from the outside, (*d*) loss attributable to dishonesty of employees, and (*e*) loss or damage that cannot be ascertained from the records of the insured. The exclusion relating to change of conditions, as well as the one relating to furs in a show window, may be deleted by endorsement where conditions warrant. The exclusion with respect to dishonesty eliminates duplication with fidelity coverages.

The mercantile open stock burglary form introduces a feature peculiar to this type of policy. The policy contains an average clause sometimes known as the *coinsurance clause*. The rating manual provides for a classification of risks according to the type of business carried on and establishes a limit known as the *coinsurance limit* for each classification. In addition to the coinsurance limit for the classification there is established a coinsurance requirement expressed as a percentage of the value of the stock, and based upon location. The country is divided into fifteen territories, and requirements vary from 80 percent to 40 percent. New York City and Los Angeles are included in the highest percentage group.

The coinsurance limit expressed for a class of business is in a dollar amount. It represents a maximum probable loss for the type of goods in the class. For example, the coinsurance limit might be set at $10,000 for heavy goods such as pianos, but $20,000 for smaller, more stealable goods such as clothing. To determine the amount of insurance to be carried for a given risk and therefore to avoid a coinsurance penalty, it is necessary to know (*a*) value of stock, (*b*) coinsurance limit, and (*c*) coinsurance percentage determined by rating territory.

To avoid penalty the insured must carry an amount of insurance which equals or exceeds the smaller of either the coinsurance limit or the amount determined by applying the coinsurance percentage to the value of merchandise at the time of loss. The operation of the coinsurance clause under the foregoing condition may be illustrated by the following example:

Value of inventory of a television store	$60,000
Coinsurance percentage for specified territory, 60 percent	36,000
Coinsurance limit for specified territory	30,000

To comply with the coinsurance clause, the insured must carry 60 percent of the value of the inventory; but since the coinsurance limit is less than 60 percent of the value of the inventory, the coinsurance requirement is fully satisfied if $30,000 of insurance is carried. The average clause adversely affects the position of the insured in a loss settlement only when the amount of insurance covering the merchandise is less than both the coinsurance limit and the amount determined by the application of the coinsurance percentage. Specific insurance not subject to a coinsurance clause may be written as an alternative, with no specific limit on single articles.

Safe Burglary. The insurance agreement of this policy provides indemnity to the insured for loss of the insured property from within the vault or safe by safe burglary. The term "safe burglary" is defined to mean the felonious abstraction of insured property from the covered safe when all doors of the safe are duly closed and locked by all combination locks and time locks that are a part of the safe. There is a supplemental agreement which obligates the insurance company to pay for damage to the safe or chest covered by the policy or to any property contained therein caused by the commission or attempted commission of burglary as defined in the policy. The property damage coverage also extends to include furniture, furnishings, fixtures, equipment, or other property of the insured. Property insured includes (*a*) money, (*b*) securities, and (*c*) other property. The coverage is not limited to strictly mercantile risks but may be issued to any person or organization owning a safe or vault.

Under this form, money is defined as "currency, coins, bank notes, bullion and travelers' checks, registered checks, and money orders held for sale to the public." Securities, as defined in the policy, include all negotiable or nonnegotiable instruments, such as checks, drafts, bonds, and stock certificates or contracts representing either money or other property. Included in the category are revenue and other stamps in current use. In addition to covering money and securities in the safe, the policy covers other property of any kind kept by the insured in the safe. Personal property, such as jewelry owned by the insured or employees, is covered provided always that there is a sufficiently adequate record to permit a determination of the amount of the loss or damage.

In order to establish a loss under a mercantile safe policy, it must be shown that a *burglary* was actually effected or attempted. Entry to the safe or vault must have been effected by the use of tools, explosives, electricity, gas, or other chemicals upon the exterior of the safe, at a time when it was properly closed and locked by at least one combination or time lock. Evidence of the force used must appear on the exterior of the safe. An adequate set of books must be maintained from which the value of the lost or damaged items can be determined.

Under the safe-burglary policy, the company is not liable for loss or damage to manuscripts, records, or accounts. Losses occurring while combination or time lock, burglary alarm, vault, or private watchman service warranted in policy declarations is not maintained are excluded, as are losses effected by opening the door of the safe, vault, or chest by manipulation of the lock. Losses attributed to manipulation of locks are regarded as theft losses but not in the burglary category. If the manipulation is performed by an employee of the insured, the protection is available through a fidelity bond coverage. Kidnapping coverage is not available in connection with safe-burglary insurance. If an employee of the insured is forced to return to the premises under threat of violence and opens a safe or vault, the loss is not regarded as a burglary loss. If the insured feels that this peril should be covered, he may obtain protection through providing inside robbery insurance with the kidnapping coverage included.

The contract extends to cover *property damage* caused by burglary of insured's safe or any attempt at a burglary. Property damage coverage extends to the insured's safe or vault together with the insured's property within. It also covers property damage to furniture, equipment, and merchandise on the premises, but not in the safe or vault if the loss is attributable to a burglary. If the insured is liable for damages to the premises, this coverage also comes within the scope of the contract. The property damage loss to furniture, fixtures, or merchandise is not covered, however, unless the insured's safe has been entered by force or an attempt at such entry actually has been made.

Rates for safe insurance are quoted per $1,000 of insurance carried and depend upon the following features: (1) type of safe, (2) territory, (3) class of business, and (4) property covered. Safes are classified into seven groups of fire resistive and burglar resistive safes. Discounts are allowed for features that tend to minimize the risk, such as a private watchman, safes equipped with an approved relocking system, premises protected with an approved burglar alarm system, and safes or vaults equipped with certified tear-gas systems. Discounts are allowed when there is more than one safe in a single location. If part of the insurance covers "securities only," "merchandise only," or "securities and merchandise only," a discount of 25 percent is allowed for that part of the insurance that so covers. If the insurance covers loss to securities only, a 50 percent discount from the manual rate is allowed.

Robbery Insurance

Messenger and Interior Robbery. Stores, offices, and other places of business are not immune from robbery during business hours; and messengers carrying money and valuables are held up and robbed on the city streets. Messenger and robbery insurance are two separate forms of coverage available to the insured in a single contract. The coverages are: (*a*) interior holdup insurance, which covers office and store robbery risks; and (*b*) outside holdup insurance, which covers the risk of messenger robbery. Either coverage is available separately.

The interior holdup policy covers loss or damage to the insured property through robbery or attempted robbery and loss or damage to furniture, fixtures, and other property. The coverage is effective on a 24-hour basis and furnishes protection only within the insured's premises. Loss or damage to merchandise stolen from a show window by a person who has broken the glass from the outside, or by his accomplice, is covered while the premises are regularly open for business.

Kidnapping is sometimes resorted to by robbers to hold the owner of a property or his employee, later forcing the person detained to open the premises or supply information, keys, or other means of admission. Kidnapping usually occurs off the premises.

The outside holdup feature of the contract covers the insured for robbery losses if the robbery or attempted robbery takes place outside the premises of the insured. This feature of the contract covers not only messenger robbery but, as well, damage to money, securities, merchandise, or the container in the possession of the messenger resulting from robbery or attempted robbery. The protection applies outside the insured's premises and provides 24-hour protection.

Interior robbery, if written without messenger coverage, does not cover outside the building. In certain types of risk this coverage is desirable when the messenger policy is unnecessary. In cases in which custodians meet customers outside the building, as at filling stations and other roadside places of business, upon the payment of an additional premium the coverage may be extended to include the ground immediately surrounding the store, office, or structure used by the insured in serving his customers.

There is a type of risk in which it is the usual practice for the manager or owner to take home the cash that accumulates after banking hours and up to closing time. This is usually the custom if safe means for leaving the cash on the premises of the business are lacking. Burglary (and robbery and theft, if desired) coverage in the home of the custodian may be endorsed to the messenger or interior robbery policy.

Factors affecting the premium on messenger robbery are the territory, the number of guards accompanying the custodian, the nature of the property covered, and any other protective measures approved as tending to reduce the hazard.[4]

Paymaster Robbery. Many businesses pay their employees in cash and transfer large sums of money from point to point. The policy to cover this is similar to the messenger robbery policy but contains features to fit the particular needs of payroll risks. Coverage is divided into two parts: (*a*) protection outside of premises and (*b*) protection inside of premises.

The policy provides day and night protection for the insured from loss by robbery from a custodian outside the insured's premises of money or checks held solely for payroll purposes. It covers as well an amount not exceeding 10 percent of the amount of the insurance, for money and securities not intended solely for payroll purposes. As in the case of messenger robbery, the bag, satchel, safe, chest, or other container in which money is being transported is covered against loss or damage attributable to robbery or attempted robbery.

Differing from the messenger robbery form, the *Paymaster Rob-*

[4]The premium for interior robbery, as in other robbery coverages, is dependent upon the territory in which the risk is located, the number of persons on duty within the insured's premises, the kind of business, the protective measures, and the kind of property. Credits on the rate under the messenger robbery form are allowed when certain designated precautions are taken. These are: (1) the use of a private conveyance; (2) the use of a locked messenger safe or chest, or satchel or wallet, lined with steel or wire mesh and attached by chain or wire strap to the custodian or vehicle conveying the funds; and (3) the use of a route limited to the interior of the building containing the premises of the insured. There is also a rate credit when the coverage is limited to securities only.

bery Policy covers inside the insured's premises for loss or damage of money or checks intended for payroll purposes. It extends also to cover damage to the premises, furniture, fixtures, or other property within the control of a custodian provided the custodian at the time is engaged in his regular duties in handling payroll funds. Employees of the insured are protected, while on the premises of the employer, against loss of money or checks which is the outgrowth of a robbery or attempt thereat of the custodian. Payroll funds taken by a safe burglary do not come within the protection of the policy. Losses to payroll funds are covered if attributable to the kidnapping of a custodian.

Paymaster robbery broad form is available by endorsement under the Money and Securities Broad Form Policy (see later section). It may cover at the home of the paymaster, or provide a broad all-risks coverage. When so endorsed the policy covers, in addition to robbery, the destruction, disappearance, and wrongful abstraction of payroll funds. The endorsement may be written to cover inside the residence of the insured or provide both inside and outside coverage. War risks are excluded from the protection. The surrendering of the money or securities in any exchange or purchase is not covered under the broad form, nor are fraudulent or dishonest acts of the insured or officers or employees of the insured.

Forgery Insurance

The *Depositor's Forgery Policy* sometimes referred to as a "forgery bond," is issued to individuals, firms, or corporations. It is not issued to banks and building and loan associations. The policy is divided into two sections: (*a*) covering outgoing items and (*b*) covering incoming items. It is the intent of the policy to protect the insured against forgery losses on commercial paper issued or presumed to have been issued by the insured or an authorized agent and to provide forgery protection on incoming paper received by the insured. The insured may elect to cover his own paper only; but if he wishes to insure incoming items, he must provide a combined coverage insuring both outgoing and incoming items. Incoming items are not insured separately.

The *outgoing form* most commonly used serves the requirements of the insured when the hazard from incoming items is not regarded as great. Therefore, checks, drafts, or other instruments accepted by the insured that may be the occasion of loss because of alteration or forgery are not insured under this form. On the other hand, the banks in which the insured maintains his accounts enjoy the same protection as the insured with respect to forged instruments of the insured. This protection to the bank has the effect of eliminating the question of liability between the bank and the insured.

The insurance covers whether the forged signature purports to be that of the insured in the capacity of the drawer of a draft, check, or bill of exchange; the maker of a note; or the acceptor of a draft, bill of exchange, or trade acceptance. The coverage affords protecton against forgery of the endorsement of any payee or other person upon a check or draft drawn by the insured upon his bank.

Retail establishments that in the ordinary course of business take large numbers of checks find the danger of losses from forgery a very real one. Business establishments where the incoming hazard is regarded as important find adequate insurance protection through coverage for *both incoming and outgoing* items. The insurance provided for incoming items covers losses caused by the insured taking forged or altered instruments in the course of business operations in exchange for merchandise or services. Checks cashed by the insured as an accommodation are not within the scope of the coverage. Cash may be given as change when a check is paid whose face value is in excess of the price charged for the article or service without affecting the coverage. The coverage does not extend to indemnify the insured for losses when the check is drawn on an account with insufficient funds, or when the check is returned marked "no account." Such losses are not regarded as due to forgery or alteration and are to be guarded against by the ordinary precautions of those in charge of credits.

With respect to incoming items the insured is required to assume 25 percent of every loss. This is due to a provision in the policy limiting the amount of the insurance carrier's liability for any one instrument to 75 percent of the insured's pecuniary interest in the instrument. This is to be determined by the amount paid for property sold and delivered, or for services rendered, fixed at the time of the transaction, to which may be added any sums delivered against the instrument in question in excess of the amount paid for goods or services. The policy does not cover losses which are the outgrowth of receiving that class of instruments known as a "traveler's check."

A *Family Forgery Policy* is available to cover the named insured, his spouse, and children residing permanently in his household against forgery losses. Contrary to the depositor's form, it applies only to personal financial transations. Business and professional activities are not covered.

There are three forms of protection: (*a*) outgoing items, (*b*) incoming items, and (*c*) counterfeit money. The protection afforded under outgoing items is similar to that already noticed with respect to the Depositor's Forgery Policy. Incoming items receive considerably broader coverage than that provided by the depositor's policy in that protection is afforded not only for loss attributable to the acceptance of forged or altered checks but for loss resulting from forged or altered incoming coupons, drafts, money orders, real estate mortgages, stock certificates, or other negotiable instrument ordinarily traded in the securities market. If the insured gives value or extends credit on the strength of a forged or counterfeit instrument, or one that has been altered or stolen, or one that has been acquired under a lost or stolen transfer, assignment, guarantee, or endorsement, the policy covers the loss. Under the section covering counterfeit money, the insured is protected up to $100 aggregate if he accepts counterfeit United States paper currency in good faith. Liability is limited to $50 for counterfeit currency accepted in any one transaction.

A *Forged-Securities Policy* is provided for banks, brokerage houses, corporations, or other business organizations whose business is concerned largely with issuing securities or with investing or dealing in them. The coverage offered under the Forged-Securities Policy is very broad. Two forms are in general use: (*a*) Standard Form No. 3, and (*b*) Standard Form No. 4. Form 3 is designed for an insured who handles his own securities or retains the custody of securities belonging to others. Form 4 is issued primarily to dealers who issue, sell, and transfer securities.[5] The protection the policy affords may be adjusted to meet the particular needs of the individual insured.

Liability Insurance for Crime Losses

Policies covering the *liability* of the insured imposed by law upon custodians are written as burglary forms. They are included in the burglary category presumably because burglary and robbery are among the principal sources of loss. Two widely used forms are: (*a*) innkeepers' liability, and (*b*) warehousemen's liability.

The *Innkeepers' Liability* form protects the innkeeper in the event he is held liable for the injury to, destruction of, or loss of property of guests. The policy provides no protection directly for the guests. The liability of an innkeeper is considerably greater than that of a bailee. At common law, an innkeeper was at one time absolutely liable as an insurer of the property of his guests when it comes within the care and charge of the innkeeper. Originally, innkeepers were held liable for all losses whether by reason of burglary, theft, fire, or negligence, unless the loss was occasioned by negligence or misconduct of the guest or by an act of God or the public enemy.[6] The common law liability has been modified by statute in all jurisdictions in this country, but the liability resting upon the innkeeper is still severe. The status of the hotel man may in one in-

---

[5]As in the case of bankers' forgery insurance, the protection for security dealers is available as part of the protection provided by bankers' or brokers' blanket bonds.

[6]*Wilkins* v. *Earle*, 42 N.Y. 172.

stance be that of an innkeeper, in another that of a landlord, and in a third that of a bailee or warehouseman. To provide protection against the various liabilities that may arise, the hotel and innkeeper's policy provides insurance against all such liabilities.

Contractual liability is excluded with the exception that written agreements made with a guest before a loss do not fall within this exclusion. Coverage does not apply if the insured has released any third party from its legal liability. Losses caused by spilling or upsetting food or loss of or damage to automobiles or property in automobiles, as well as property in the insured's custody for laundering or cleaning, or merchandise for exhibition, sale, or delivery by guests, are not covered. These liability losses with respect to food, automobiles, and other property in the custody of the insured may be covered by endorsement upon payment of an additional premium.

The *Warehousemen's Liability* form covers warehousemen, packers, and other like bailees for their liability for loss of property in their custody. Burglary and robbery losses from any cause, subject to limited exclusions, are covered. The policy is usually written with a deductible which may be as little as $50 or as much as $10,000 or more. The deductible applies to each occurrence giving rise to one or more claims and not to each claim. Thus, in the case of robbery with loss to several owners of merchandise, the deductible would apply once to the aggregate of all claims. The exclusions include war risks, money, securities, and perishable goods. In some states, because of legal requirements, fire and sprinkler leakage losses are not covered, and these risks are in such circumstances insured separately. There are also the usual liability exclusions with respect to contractual liability.

"Package" Crime Insurance

A very important category today are the "packaged" policies that have been prepared to include one or several of the separate forms of burglary, robbery, or theft protection. These policies result in broader and more economical crime insurance. Some of the most widely used of these contracts are (*a*) the Storekeepers', and Office, Burglary and Robbery Policies, (*b*) the Money and Securities (Broad Form) Policy, and (*c*) the Comprehensive Dishonesty, Disappearance, and Destruction Policy.

Storekeepers', and Office, Burglary and Robbery Policies. The basic form is designed to meet the needs of the small *storekeeper and merchant* and provides at reasonable cost a blanket burglary and robbery coverage. Until this form was made available, the small merchant found it difficult to secure adequate burglary and robbery insurance protection, due to the fact that rules as to protective devices, coinsurance requirements, and minimum premiums were drawn with the larger concerns in mind. The seven basic coverages, provided in the amount of $250 each, are given in the footnote below.[7]

A policy similar to the storekeepers' policy is written to provide a burglary and robbery coverage for *offices*. It protects the insured against loss of money, securities, and other property but excludes merchandise. The class of risk for which the office form is designed includes accountants, architects, attorneys, auditors, insurance offices, brokers, contractors, dentists, doctors, and the like. Specifically excluded are bankers, auctioneers, garagekeepers, ticket-office clerks, theater owners, loan groups, and similar risks. Businesses in which merchandise and other property are held for sale or manufacture, cleaning, repairing, pressing, or storing may not be covered under this form.

The company is not liable for burglary and robbery losses if the loss or damage occurs during a fire in the building. In the case of jewelry, gems (precious or semiprecious), watches, and the like, the company's liability is limited to $50.

---

[7]The storekeepers' form in a single policy covers the insured against loss of money, securities, and merchandise, together with damage to property. The policy covers not only the property of the insured but also property held by him as bailee, in trust or on commission, or as collateral, or in any other capacity where he is liable to the owner for loss or damage. The coverage is provided under seven headings, with $250 insurance applying to each as follows:

1. *Office and store robbery* covers loss of any securities and merchandise by robbery from a custodian within the premises. Only one custodian is required, and the coverage is for a period of 24 hours.
2. *Messenger robbery* covers loss by robbery from a custodian outside the premises anywhere within the United States or Canada.
3. *Kidnapping* coverage protects the insured against loss in case a custodian while outside the premises and under threat of violence shall be compelled to provide means of egress to the premises. The loss must be occasioned by theft within the premises before the premises have been opened for the next business day.
4. *Safe-burglary* coverage provides protection against loss of any money, securities, and merchandise from within a safe or vault in the premises. This coverage is effective when all doors of the safe or vault are locked. To support a claim, entry to the safe must have been made by force or violence, of which there must be evidence in the form of visible marks.
5. Felonious abstraction coverage provides indemnity for loss of money and securities from a *night depository* of a bank or from the residence of a custodian. The theft must be committed by a person making felonious entry by force, of which there is visible evidence.
6. Mercantile *open stock burglary* coverage provides indemnity for loss of merchandise, furniture, fixtures, and equipment. A limit of $50 is placed upon the liability of the company as the aggregate for any loss of jewelry, watches, precious and semiprecious stones, and as in other burglary coverages the theft must have been made by a person or persons making a felonious entry by force and violence, of which there must be visible evidence.
7. *Property damage* is covered where the loss is occasioned by a burglary or robbery actually committed or attempted. Building, furniture, fixtures, and equipment are covered under this section, provided the insured is the owner of the property or responsible for the damage.

When coverage to the extent of $250 is not sufficient, more than one policy in both the storekeepers' and the office burglary and robbery forms may be bought to cover a single risk. The amount applying to each division under a single policy may not be varied. There is no reduction in the coverage in the event of the payment of a loss, but the full amount of $250 applying to each of the coverages remains in force during the policy term.

Similar policies to those for stores and offices are available to service stations and other risks.[8] The specialized forms for banks and churches are discussed in detail in Appendix H, "Special Crime Insurance and Bonds."

Money and Securities Policy (Broad Form). Available to many businesses, this policy has two optional insuring clauses: (*a*) inside protection and (*b*) outside protection. It covers money and securities against all risks of physical damage or destruction including fire. Loss of money and securities from within the premises (or any bank or similar place of safe deposit) covered by the policy extends to disappearance or wrongful destruction losses. The premises section covers, as well, loss of or damage to property caused by burglary or robbery or attempts thereat.

The outside coverage affords the same protection to money, securities, and property injured or destroyed by robbery or attempted robbery while money or securities are in the custody of a messenger or an armored motor vehicle company. The policy does not provide fidelity coverage or open stock burglary coverage. The policy may be written to cover either the premises section or the outside coverage separately, or it may cover both. In the case of a business such as a filling station where money in the course of operations is handled just outside the building, inside coverage may be extended to cover the premises and the entire lot upon which business is transacted.

The policy may be written to cover securities only. This form has a particular appeal to institutions and individuals who own large values in securities. Individuals in the capacity of trustees or treasurers of endowed institutions, investment trusts, holding companies, and brokers frequently have in their possession securities having a

[8]The *Combination Service-Station Policy* is designed to furnish a broad liability and theft protection for service stations. Unlike the storekeepers' policy, which is planned to meet the requirements of most retail establishments, this form is tailored to a particular type of business. The policy does not include fidelity protection because, in the ordinary course, employees of a business of this type would be bonded and the owner of the business would probably not wish to limit the fidelity coverage to an amount that would be included in a package policy. However, if the applicant for the coverage desires fidelity protection, it may be included. Other optional coverages such as products liability and protection for claims growing out of defective workmanship are available.

face value running into large sums of money. Even with the protection afforded by the safe-deposit box, the possibility of loss growing out of mysterious disappearances, entry to the box by misrepresentation or fraud, as well as burglary or robbery constitute a real peril. In addition, fire, theft, tornado, riot, explosion, or other like perils might be the agency for the destruction of the box and its contents.

The Money and Securities Policy (Broad Form) has a particular appeal since, with the exception of certain bonds written for financial institutions, most all policies covering on property insurance specifically exclude losses growing out of destruction of money and securities.

Comprehensive Dishonesty, Disappearance, and Destruction Policy. This contract, familiarly known as the *3-D Policy,*[9] was designed to provide the broadest possible crime coverage for business firms. Since it combines fidelity and burglary coverages, it is a convenient method of insuring all crime perils. It combines in a single document coverages that may be purchased separately and at one time were available only as separate policies. It now makes possible the offering in a single contract of full fidelity coverage as well as complete burglary-theft insurance.

The basic form contains five separate insuring clauses: (*a*) dishonesty insurance (in one of the forms of fidelity bonds discussed in the next section), (*b*) all-risks coverages within the premises, (*c*) all-risks coverages outside the premises, (*d*) all-risks coverages on securities and safe-deposit boxes, and (*e*) forgery insurance on outgoing risks. In addition to the coverages ordinarily obtainable under the forgery, robbery, and burglary policies, this contract provides indemnity for losses of money and securities sustained as a result of "disappearance, destruction, or wrongful abstraction of such property."

The following coverages may be added to the policy by endorsement: (1) forgery coverage on incoming checks; (2) mercantile open stock burglary; (3) mercantile open stock theft; (4) mercantile open stock burglary with a limited amount of theft coverage; (5) broad form payroll inside and outside the premises; (6) broad form payroll inside the premises only; (7) warehouse receipts forgery; (8) securities of lessees of safe deposit boxes; (9) burglary coverage on office equipment; and (10) theft coverage on office equipment.

Because of the breadth of the coverages provided by the 3-D

---

[9]The student is referred to other sources for information about the 3-D Policy's salability, and some policy details not included here. See Harold F. Gee, *Comprehensive 3-D Primer* (Indianapolis: The Rough Notes Company). Republished about every four years.

Policy, and the insuring clauses that may be included in the contract, protection may be extended to virtually every conceivable type of dishonesty loss. The insured is not required to carry protection under all of the insuring clauses but may elect to adjust the protection under the policy to his own immediate requirements. The policy does not have a uniform penalty applying to each of the insuring clauses; an optional amount may be elected to apply to each of the various clauses, subject always to the underwriting rules of the company.

The broad protection of the 3-D Policy, and its advantages of convenience, have made it one of the most popular methods for businesses to insure their crime and fidelity bond perils. Another similar policy to the 3-D Policy is the *Blanket Crime Policy,* which uses a single insurance amount for all the insuring agreements.

SURETYSHIP

Nature and Development

The contract of suretyship is a credit device that made its appearance with earliest development of business obligations. Under the terms of a surety agreement, or *bond,* one party becomes answerable to a third party for the acts or neglect of a second party. The party holding himself responsible is the *surety,* and the one for whose debt or obligation the surety is responsible is the *principal debtor,* or more commonly referred to as the *principal* or *obligor.* The person protected by the agreement is called the *obligee.*

Before the writing of surety bonds became an established business, persons acting in a fiduciary capacity or occupying positions of trust requiring sureties were obliged to appeal to relatives or friends. While it was not unusual for the *personal* surety to require compensation for participating in the agreement, more often than not the surety signed his name to a bond without remuneration and purely as a favor. This practice was the source of many difficulties, not to say loss and hard feeling.

Corporate surety bonds were offered first in England around 1720, when a company offered to insure masters against loss through the dishonesty of their servants. This project is sometimes said to mark the first effort in the field of corporate suretyship. It made no lasting mark in the field of insurance, however, and it was not until 1840 that the corporate fidelity business became established with the organization of an English company to write the business. The first American company was organized in 1853, following enactment by the New York Legislature of a law authorizing the formation of corporations to insure the honesty of employees.

Corporate suretyship was slow in developing. There was considerable resistance to the substitution of the impersonal corporation for the locally known personal surety. However, there was the growing reluctance on the part of individuals to assume gratuitously obligations in which they had no immediate interest. Corporate sureties were more and more accepted, and, as the idea became better known, individuals became increasingly reluctant to assume obligations without remuneration that corporations were ready and willing to assume for a consideration.

A second feature that tended to stimulate the development of corporate suretyship was the permanence and stability of the surety corporations. They are subject to the regulations provided by the statutes; they have a lasting and permanent organization. It is their chief function to meet losses when they come. In the case of the individual surety, if the bond runs for any considerable period of time, the financial status of the individual may prevent him from meeting his obligations. It is also easy to investigate the standing of a corporate surety. It is not so easy to know the status of an individual or to be assured that financial reverses may not change that status without the knowledge of the other parties to the bond. Because the parties in whose interest a bond is written can exercise no supervisory control over individual sureties and have no way of assuring themselves of continuing solvency, individual sureties are unable to supply a bond with the same safety and stability as can a surety company. For this reason, those requiring bonds tend to insist upon satisfactory corporate sureties.

Insurance and Suretyship

With the advent of the corporate surety company, the courts have given a different interpretation from that given to the bonds upon which individuals gratuitously appeared as sureties. The corporate bond is issued by the surety for a compensation fixed by itself, and based on a contract drawn by itself, in which numerous clauses are incorporated setting forth or limiting its liability. As a result of these differences, the courts have held that in the case of a bond issued by a surety company, the rule of *strictissimi juris* favoring the surety does not apply. Thus, the bond of a surety company is regarded as a contract of insurance instead of suretyship, and the obligee occupies the position of the insured. Following the rule of insurance law, the contract is interpreted in his favor wherever ambiguity or uncertainty exists.

Surety bonds are also handled by agents writing other lines of insurance, and the contract is in general appearance similar to the contract of insurance. In other ways it is markedly different.

Strictly speaking, the surety contract is not a contract of insurance. Individuals may act as sureties, and in such instances the agreement has little in common with the contract of insurance. The form of the agreement, however, differs from the insurance contract in that there exists a *right of indemnity* between the surety and the principal debtor. In the event that the surety is called upon by the obligee to make good a loss under the bond, the surety in turn may proceed against the principal, who is primarily liable on the agreement. This is in contrast to the insurance contract, which obligates the insurance company to pay losses in accordance with the policy terms without recourse to any other party to the contract. The surety is liable to the obligee for a loss, but between the surety and the obligee, there is always the party primarily liable, that is, the principal. The principal is a party to the contract and liable thereunder. The liability of the principal is to be contrasted with the liability of third parties against whom an insurer may proceed under its rights of subrogation. In the case of subrogation, the third party is not a party to the contract.

Insurance anticipates that there will be losses, the outgrowth of the happening of the contingency covered by the policy. In the surety contract, on the other hand, the undertaking of the surety is secondary. The agreement is drawn in such a form that the surety is not liable until after the failure of the principal to perform a specified obligation. Failure may be occasioned by dishonesty, incompetence, or lack of resources. The surety underwriter, therefore, after giving due weight to the nature of the obligation covered by the bond, is interested particularly in knowing the qualifications of the principal to fulfill his undertaking. Surety bonds are usually written on the assumption that there will be *no losses.* They are written to strengthen the credit or provide a guarantee for the principal; and, only if the principal fails or defaults is the surety liable.

As a matter of actual practice, corporate suretyship is, in fact, regarded as a part of the insurance business. Much the same methods are followed in carrying on the business, and the same agency system is used by both bonding companies and insurance companies writing direct loss and casualty risks. Statutory enactments in a number of jurisdictions refer to the corporate guarantee and surety contracts as contracts of insurance and both are regulated by state insurance departments.[10]

---

[10]It is not difficult to reconcile the surety contract with an insurance definition that states the contract of insurance is one that shifts the burden of risk. The end should be distinguished from the means. The means employed with respect to property insurance (pooling of risks, contributions to a common fund, certainty of loss, and the like), if compared with the practices involved in underwriting most bond classifications, will evidence a difference between suretyship and insurance practices.

It may be conceded that a literal interpretation of the form of the agreement may take the surety contract out of the definition of insurance. In a broad sense, however, the surety contract is in fact the purchase of certainty on the part of the parties requiring a bond; and because of the association of the surety business with the business of insurance and because of the attitude of the courts in the interpertation of surety contracts, for all practical purposes the surety business may well be, and generally is, included as a part of the business of insurance.

General Divisions of Suretyship

Bonding companies arbitarily divide bonds into two classes: (*a*) *fidelity bonds* and (*b*) *surety bonds.* In the strict sense, all corporate bonds in which a surety agrees to answer for the nonperformance of a principal are surety bonds. The difference between a fidelity and a surety bond lies in the nature of the obligation. In the case of a fidelity bond, the obligation is implied rather than contractual, and the bond undertakes to reimburse an obligee (the employer) for loss of money or property growing out of dishonest acts of the principal (the employee). The surety bond, on the other hand, obligates the surety to hold himself responsible for the performance of an expressed obligation of the principal. To prove a loss under a fidelity bond, the principal must have been guilty of a dishonest act. In the case of surety bonds, the coverage is considerably broader. While a dishonest act may give rise to a loss, it is likewise true that negligence and lack of ability on the part of the principal may create a liability on the part of the surety.

The business of corporate suretyship has developed into three broad divisions. These are: (1) fidelity bonds, (2) judicial bonds, and (3) contract bonds. For purposes of rating, these bonds are separated in the manual into six classes as follows: (1) fidelity, (2) judicial, (3) contract, (4) depository and miscellaneous, (5) license and permit, and (6) federal. A brief summary of each class follows.

As noted in the chapter on theft coverages, under *fidelity bonds* the surety company undertakes to reimburse employers for dishonesty losses of employees. The employer may be an individual, a firm, a corporation, or the public.

Judicial bonds, sometimes referred to as "court bonds," are those required in court proceedings. There are two categories of judicial or court bonds. The *fiduciary* obligations are those filed in behalf of an executor, guardian, or trustee. In the second category are those involving a *financial guarantee,* which are the type filed with the court for bail or when a case is appealed.

Contract bonds guarantee to the person owning a property when he enters into a contract for construction that the work will be completed in accordance with the terms of the agreement. The contract bond guarantees the performance of contracts and the credit of the persons who obligate themselves to build or perform some specific service. If the contractor fails to complete his obligation in accordance with the terms of the contract, the surety company either completes the work or indemnifies the obligee for his loss.

Depository and miscellaneous bonds include bonds that guarantee bank deposits and a number of other miscellaneous forms such as those filed in connection with the duplication of a life insurance policy or lost securities.

License and permit bonds, in connection with licenses or permits issued by states or their subdivisions, are required to provide indemnity to the public authority or third parties in the event of violation of the terms of the license or permit.

Federal bonds are required by the federal government in connection with the granting of a permit, bonds required in connection with federal immigration laws, and all bonds required in connection with export and import duties.

ANALYSIS OF FIDELITY AND SURETY BONDS

Basic Features

There are certain features which are common to many fidelity and surety bonds. These characteristics will be discussed briefly before some of the more usual types of bonds are analyzed in reference to the details of their specific provisions.

Penalty of the Bond. When a designated sum is written into the bond as a limit of the liability of the surety, the sum so written is the *penalty,* and the bond is a *fixed penalty bond.* The penalty corresponds to the face of an insurance policy.

Bonds are written in which no amount of penalty is fixed. Such a bond guarantees that the surety will pay whatever damages arise from the nonperformance of the obligation assumed by the principal. Such bonds are known as *open covenant bonds.*

Obligation to Bond. It is important for those who hold positions of trust to understand that losses to property in their care occasioned by their negligence carries with it a personal liability. It has been held by the courts that failure to provide fidelity coverage upon an officer of a bank by the directors is negligence, and the directors may be held liable for dishonesty losses. The effect of such a rule is to place the responsibility of adequate fidelity bonding of bank employees squarely upon the directors, and failure on their part to take the necessary steps may result in their being obliged personally to make good losses that occur. Statutory requirements may be regarded as minimum requirements. What constitutes adequate bonding coverage must be decided by the circumstances surrounding each particular case.

Effect of Fraud. If a surety has been induced by fraud of the principal to become a party to the bond, this fraud will not constitute a defense against an innocent obligee who has acted relying upon the bond.

As to the obligation of the obligee to inform the surety of facts having a bearing on the risk, there has been some uncertainty. It was originally held that the contract was *uberrimae fidei* and, as in the case of marine insurance, the insurer was entitled without inquiry to all information affecting the risk known by any party to the agreement. The opinion now prevails, however, that a surety, entering into a contract, will have taken steps to secure such information as is required.

When inquiry is made by the surety and disclosures by the obligee are incomplete, insufficient, misleading, or false, the contract is jeopardized. If questions are put to an employer in the form of an application and the answers are not true, the surety may be released from his obligation if the misrepresentation is material. If the answers in the application are declared to be warranties, incorrect information, whether the result of carelessness or the intent to mislead, may void the obligation of the surety through the operation of the doctrine of warranties.

Waiver and Estoppel. As in the case of other contracts of insurance, the doctrines of waiver and estoppel apply in connection with surety bonds. When a surety company delivers a bond, knowing a cause for holding it invalid, the delivery amounts to declaring the contract to be valid, and the defense is waived. The same is true if a premium is accepted with knowledge by the surety of an existing defense.

Again, if a company proceeds to adjust a loss, knowing that strict compliance with the contract conditions as to notice or proofs of loss is lacking, it will be held to have waived such compliance. If a company has held incomplete or insufficient proofs until the time for filing satisfactory and acceptable proofs has elapsed, it will be estopped from denying liability on the ground that the proofs retained were insufficient.

Statute of Frauds. Unlike other contracts of insurance, which are usually in writing but which need not necessarily be, surety contracts fall within the statute of frauds. At common law, contracts of guarantee or suretyship were valid without written evidence. However, the fourth section of the English statute of frauds, which is substantially followed by the statutes of most of our states, requires that an agreement to answer for the debt, default, or miscarriages of any other person shall be *in writing* or that there shall be some written evidence to support the agreement. This being the case, liability under fidelity and surety bonds is legally enforceable only if supported by written evidence of the agreement.

Assignment. Contracts of guarantee and suretyship are, as a general rule, assignable. This rule holds even before a breach unless, by its terms, assignment of the contract is limited or restricted. Fidelity bonds are not assignable before a loss without the consent of the surety because, by the very nature of the agreement, a definite principal is contemplated by the company, and another, therefore, may not be substituted.

Subrogation. In contracts of suretyship, upon the payment by the surety of a debt of the principal, the surety is subrogated to all the rights of the creditor against the principal whose debt has been paid. This includes all securities, funds, liens, priorities, or equities held by the creditor as security. When the surety fulfills an obligation of the principal, it is subrogated to the rights of the principal in the engagement.

In the case of cosureties, that is, when more than one surety is liable equally on the same obligation, if one of the sureties pays the obligation in full, he has a right of contribution from the others.

Acts Discharging Surety. When a surety is liable for the honesty of an employee, the principal, upon the discovery of any dishonesty in connection with the duties for which he is bonded, is obligated to dismiss the dishonest employee at once or to continue him in his position only after having secured the consent of the surety. Failure to follow this procedure will release the surety from any liability for loss occasioned by further dishonest acts of the employee. In the case of suretyship for the officers or agents of corporations, where a conspiracy between such officers or agents might have the effect of discharging all sureties and therefore defeat the purpose of the bond, the rules do not apply. Acts of immorality outside the guaranteed employment need not be disclosed.

Unless provided in the bond, no particular degree of supervision over the bonded employee is required. It is usual, however, in the case of corporate fidelity bonds to require periodic examinations or audits of the principal's accounts. The requirement may be incorporated in the body of the bond or as a part of the application. In either instance, the provisions are in the nature of warranties, and failure to comply fully therewith affords grounds for relieving the surety.

If the bond secures a contract, a material alteration in the contract by the obligee without the surety's consent has the effect of releasing the surety. Contractors' bonds, as a rule, contain a clause permitting changes, alterations, or additions without the consent of the surety. Even with this clause, if a change is such that the work becomes essentially different from that originally contemplated, there is ample precedent to indicate that the nonconsenting surety may be released.

Cosureties. Bonds issued in very large amounts are sometimes signed by more than one surety. Each company obligated on such a bond is known as a *cosurety.* Under the terms of the bond, a limit may be set on the liability of each surety. When the individual limits of liability for the cosureties are set, it becomes necessary to do this through an agreement entered into between the sureties, known as a "side agreement."

Reinsurance. The laws of the various jurisdictions in this country fix a limit to the liability to be assumed by a surety company on a single risk. When attractive business is offered but the limit of liability is in excess of that which the company may legally assume, or is willing to assume, it may write the bond and reinsure the excess liability with other surety companies, just as insurance companies reinsure their excess lines.

Indemnitors. An indemnity agreement is used when a bond is required by an applicant whose financial position or background of experience is such that he is just short of meeting the company's standards. The *indemnitors* are individuals who assume much the same responsibility in connection with the writing of a surety bond as that assumed by an accommodation endorser of commercial paper. In the event of a default by the principal, the indemnitors assume the obligation. The surety, if called upon, may in turn seek reimbursement from the indemnitors.

It is frequently asked upon what grounds a surety company can justify asking for indemnitors if it is in the business of surety underwriting and is paid a premium for assuming the risk. The answer is the same as that which justifies a bank in the business of lending money requiring endorsers before lending upon a unsecured note. The credit of the applicant is otherwise insufficient.

Considerable misunderstanding sometimes arises when indemnitors are called upon to fulfill the obligations assumed under the indemnity agreement. Optimism on the part of the applicant for the bond and an impatience to place the business on the part of the company agent sometimes result in an incomplete understanding of his position by the indemnitor. The tendency to regard the agreement as a "mere matter of form" frequently leads indemnitors into unforeseen and unconsidered difficulties.

Surety companies are insistent that, if a bond is written with indemnitors, it is the duty of the agent to see that the agreement is carefully read by all parties thereto and that the obligation to pay is clearly understood.

Capacity. To be bound on a contract of surety, the party to be bound must have the capacity to enter into the engagement. Since the same rules apply as in other forms of contract, the agreement of an infant is voidable, as is that of an insane person, a drunkard, or any other not in a position to give his consent freely.

In the case of corporate suretyship, the capacity of the corporation to enter the agreement would rarely be a matter for question, though in the event of the incapacity of the principal the question of the liability of the surety is sometimes raised. It is settled that, if the principal is an infant, insane, or otherwise incapacitated, this defect does not affect the liability of the surety; and this is true even when the surety becomes a party to the agreement without knowledge of the incapacity of the principal, unless induced through fraudulent concealment or mirepresentation. If the contract of the principal is void because of positive illegality, the agreement binding the surety is likewise void and without effect.

Fidelity Bonds

General Classes. A fidelity bond pays an employer for loss growing out of a dishonest act of his employee. Fidelity bonds are classified as to extent of protection against (1) larceny and embezzlement and (2) dishonesty. For the purposes of underwriting, bonds are classified as: (1) bonds required by private employers to cover loss through dishonesty of employees and (2) bonds required of public officers for the faithful performance of their duties. These classifications are differentiated in the subheadings immediately below.

As to form, bonds are written as follows: (1) individual bonds, (2) schedule bonds, and (3) blanket bonds. Schedule bonds are written as (*a*) name schedule, (*b*) position schedule, or (*c*) discovery on either name or position schedule. Blanket bonds are subdivided into (*a*) commercial blanket, primary or excess, and (*b*) blanket position. Since these classes represent some of the most important fidelity coverages, each will be discussed briefly in following separate sections.

In addition to the foregoing, a large number of blanket bonds are written for financial institutions in which the fidelity coverage forms only a portion of the protection afforded. The specialized nature of these bonds makes them less frequently used by general business, so their discussion is reserved for more complete analysis in Appendix H, "Special Crime Insurance and Bonds."

Larceny and Embezzlement, and Dishonesty Forms. The larceny and embezzlement form is a restricted cover and limits indemnity of the surety to an amount indicated in the bond for losses growing out of larceny and embezzlement committed by the employee named in connection with his duties in a specified position. Because larceny and embezzlement are crimes, some companies have contended that conviction in the courts is a condition precedent to recovery.

In contrast to the more limited form, the dishonesty bond binds the surety to pay the employer for pecuniary loss sustained either of money or of property, including property for which the employer is responsible. The perils include fraud, dishonesty, forgery, theft, embezzlement, wrongful abstraction, misappropriation, or any form of dishonesty committed by the bonded employee while the employee holds any position at any location.

Public Official Bonds. The law requires that certain public officials be bonded, but losses frequently occur attributable to the acts of minor employees not covered by the statute. It is now possible to provide a blanket bond for public employees that extends protection against all dishonesty or against all losses resulting from failure to perform the duties of the position as required by law.

There are four forms of blanket bond written for public officials. These are (*a*) public employees' honesty blanket bond, (*b*) public employees' honesty blanket position bond, (*c*) public employees' faithful performance blanket bond, and (*d*) public employees' faithful performance blanket position bond.

Coverage under the faithful performance form provides protection against loss from failure of employees to perform faithfully the duties of the office as required by law or to keep accurate accounts of all properties and monies in their control. In contrast, coverage under the honesty forms is limited to loss from dishonest or fraudulent acts committed by employees.

The bond covers all officers and subordinates (except treasurers or tax collectors) who are not required by law to furnish an individual bond to qualify for office. All such employees of a municipal subdivision may be covered on a single bond; or a separate bond may be executed for the different divisions or departments of any state, county, city, town village, or other political subdivision.

Individual Bonds. The simplest type of bonds for private employers are individual bonds, which are written to guarantee against loss growing out of dishonest acts of a named individual. An application is required of the principal, and on the basis of this application an investigation is made by the surety company. If the risk is acceptable, the surety company signs the bond, and this in turn is delivered to the employer.[11] In the beginning, fidelity bonds were

[11]Ordinarily, the principal as well as the surety signs all bonds. In the case of individual bonds, it is customary still to require the principal to sign. In the case of a

(Continued on next page)

all individual; and, if several persons were to be bonded in the employ of a given concern, a separate bond was written for each. The bonds ran for a period of one year, with the result that considerable confusion was experienced in keeping all employees covered and bonds renewed as they expired. To overcome this difficulty, the schedule bond was devised.

Name Schedule Bonds. The name schedule bond was the first of the schedule forms to be developed. It was a simple step to list the names of all the employees to be covered and provide surety protection in a single document. The name schedule bond, as in the case of the individual bond, guarantees the employer against dishonesty loses and extends the protection to all the employees listed in the schedule attached. The insuring clause indicates the acts of dishonesty to be covered and limits the coverage to the amount indicated in the schedule as applying to the particular employee concerned.

The name of each bonded employee is listed in the schedule, and the limit for which he is bonded is set after his name. This permits compactness in the contract itself and, at the same time, flexibility in the amount of coverages. For example, the treasurer of a concern may be bonded on a name schedule bond for $25,000, while outside salesmen may be provided with satisfactory coverage in the amount of $1,000. As new employees are added to the staff, their names may be included in the coverage by endorsement; and, if an employee severs his connection with the organization, coverage for him may be removed from the schedule upon notice to the surety company. The bond will at all times indicate the names of the employees bonded and the amount for which each is covered.

As is the custom in writing schedule bonds, the persons named in the schedule are not required to sign the bond. Each employee is required to sign an application in which he agrees to indemnify the surety against any loss caused by him once his name is included in the schedule.

Position Schedule Bonds. The principal difference between the name schedule bond and the position schedule bond is to be found in the method of preparing the schedule. In the name schedule bond, as has already been noticed, defaults of persons designated by name are covered. Under the position form, instead of naming the persons to be covered, the list of positions appears in the schedule, and persons holding those positions are covered by the bond.

This bond appeals particularly to business concerns having a

---

fidelity bond, this is not essential; in the case of schedule bonds, the practice has been abandoned. Signature of the principal in the case of a fidelity bond is not necessary because the principal is liable for any dishonest act without regard to the bond itself.

considerable turnover in personnel. In the schedule, every position to be covered is listed; and, if two or more persons occupy the same position, the number in that position must be listed. For example, it would be logical that a schedule show the position of treasurer, but it might show twenty positions of outside salemen. If two or more persons concurrently occupy a position, each must be bonded for the same amount. If the number of employees concurrently occupying a position is not correctly stated in the schedule, the employer is obliged to contribute to the loss only to the extent that the bond does not cover every employee.

Under the position schedule bond, an automatic coverage is provided which protects the employer in the event that additional positions are added to the same designation as positions already included in the schedule. The automatic coverage continues for a period of 60 days. Within that time the employer is expected to file a written request that the new position be included in the schedule, and failure to do so will result in termination of the automatic coverage. New positions of a class not already designated in the schedule may also be automatically added, but in this case it is usual to set a limit for the liability of the company. Such a limit is placed by a number of the important surety companies at $5,000. As before, the automatic coverage continues for 60 days and is terminated at the end of that period unless written request for continuation is filed by the employer and the coverage is accepted by the surety.

Discovery Bonds and the Contract Term. Schedule bonds as they are usually written provide coverage only if loss is sustained while the coverage is in force or discovered within a certain designated period after cancellation. Thus, if a bond was terminated on December 31 of a given year and liability was cut off after 12 months, a loss discovered after the expiration of the cutoff period would be outside the coverage. The *discovery bond,* on the other hand, covers losses regardless of when they may have been sustained, provided they are discovered while the bond is in force. Thus, if a fraud were perpetrated covering a long period of time, it would make little difference under the discovery bond exactly when the loss did occur, provided the loss is discovered while the bond is in force.

If the coverage of an individual employee is terminated under a discovery bond, the surety remains liable for any losses caused by that employee prior to cancellation, provided always that the loss is discovered while the bond is in force. If coverage under the bond is canceled as to a given employee and he is retained in service and a substitute is not placed for him in the schedule, the bond provides that the surety shall not be liable for losses discovered after cancellation. If a bond is terminated as to all employees by the employer, the surety is not liable for any losses discovered after cancellation. If the bond is terminated by the surety company, the employer has 60 days within which to discover losses.

Both individual and schedule fidelity bonds may be written either on a *term basis* or on a *continuous basis.* If written for a term, the period is usually a year and the bond expires at the end of the term, as does an ordinary insurance policy. The continuous bond remains in force until canceled. Bonds written for a term are continued through the agency of a continuation certificate which provides that, in consideration of the payment of the stipulated premium, coverage continues effective for a period indicated in the certificate. The value of the continuation certificate is to be found in the fact that it eliminates the need for drawing new bonds each year, with the attendant necessity on the part of the employer of carefully checking the new coverage to see that it meets his needs. No certificate is required in connection with the continuous form; and, if premiums are paid when due, the bond remains in force until one party or other to the agreement takes steps to effect termination.

Fidelity bonds of all types may be canceled at any time by the employer or bonding company. If the company wishes to cancel, notice is required; and conditions governing the notice are incorporated in the bond. Term bonds, of course, terminate automatically; but continuous bonds remain in effect and cover indefinitely unless canceled. As they apply to an individual employee, they terminate in accordance with the terms of the bond on his death, designation, or discharge.

There are two types of *restoration clauses,* and it is important to recognize the difference between them. Under one form, the bond is automatically reinstated to its full amount after a loss. However, the amount reinstated is effective only for future losses.

The most comprehensive restoration form is known as the "retroactive restoration clause" and is available for primary commercial blanket bonds and is also part of the coverage under certain of the bankers' blanket bonds. The retroactive restoration clause has the effect of automatically restoring the full face of the bond as to prior losses following the discovery of a dishonest or fraudulent act.

Under the simple restoration form, a bond covering $25,000 would automatically be reinstated as of the date of a loss to the full amount. A loss of $20,000 discovered on the first of the month would be covered in full. A loss that occurred in the previous month and discovered later would have only $5,000 coverage to apply. A loss that occurred in point of time subsequent to reinstatement would have the full amount of the bond to apply. Under the retroactive restoration cover, the situation is different. For example, if during any year a loss is discovered, the bond is reinstated in full. If a loss antedating the first loss is discovered later, that loss also is covered in full.

Commercial Blanket Bonds. It was found in connection with individual and schedule bonds that they involved considerable detail and care where there were frequent changes in personnel. In addition, losses frequently developed that were traceable to unbonded or inadequately bonded personnel. *Commercial blanket bonds* or *blanket fidelity bonds,* a term by which they are sometimes known, cover all employees. As noticed, there are two forms: (*a*) *primary commercial blanket bonds* and (*b*) *blanket position bonds.*

The primary commercial blanket bond is written in a lump-sum amount. The aggregate lump sum applies collectively to all employees. The blanket position bond, on the contrary, follows the pattern of the primary commercial bond in that it covers all the employees of the insured; but it differs with respect to the application of the penalty of the bond. While the primary commercial bond applies the aggregate collectively to all employees, the blanket position bond applies the penalty to each employee. In the case of the blanket position bond, the company is theoretically liable for the penalty of the bond multiplied by the number of employees. The difference operates to limit the liability of the company to the penalty of the bond where several employees are in collusion under the primary commercial blanket bond. However, under the blanket position bond, the full penalty of the bond applies with respect to each employee.

The definition of employees covered by the primary commercial blanket bond and the blanket position bond is identical. Both bonds cover all natural persons (except directors of the insured, if a corporation, who are not also officers of the corporation) who are in the regular service of the insured. They must be compensated by salary, wages, or commission and must be under the direction of the insured in the performance of their duties. The bond does not cover factors, brokers, commission merchants, consignees, or other like representatives or agents. Territorial coverage includes all of the United States and Canada; and, if desired, coverage may be extended to include approved employees in foreign countries. Executive officers of a corporation owning a majority of stock may be excluded from the coverage. Others excluded are canvassers, chauffeurs, collectors, demonstrators, drivers, driver's helpers, and outside salesmen of companies in certain designated lines of business. These employees are known as "Class A special employees." The effect of including employees in this category in the blanket bond is to build up the rate unduly high. For this reason, special Class A employees are usually excluded from the blanket bond and covered for a limited amount under a schedule bond. This plan results in a substantial saving in premium.

The primary commercial blanket bond provides that the payment of a loss shall not reduce the amount payable for any other loss whether sustained before or after the shortage under consideration. In other words, there is no reduction in liability for a loss, though the limit with respect to any one employee is the penalty of the bond. This provision is unnecessary in the blanket position bond since the full penalty of the bond applies to each employee and a loss payable with respect to one employee in no way affects the coverage on the others. Regarding the discovery period, there is a difference. The primary commercial blanket bond allows 12 months, whereas the blanket position bond allows 24 months. In both instances, the period commences to run only if the bond is canceled in its entirety. Both forms provide group coverage in that fraudulent or dishonesty losses are paid if attributable to one or more employees even though the guilty party may not be designated.

Judicial Bonds

All bonds filed in judicial proceedings are included within the category of judicial bonds. Judicial bonds are sometimes referred to as "court bonds," but this term is more commonly used to designate a particular class of judicial bonds.

The field is divided into two groups. *Fiduciary bonds* constitute the first group and include those bonds which guarantee the faithful performance of a trust administered under the supervision and jurisdiction of a court. The second group includes all those bonds required of litigants in a court action. This is the group to which the term *court bond* is usually applied.

The coverage afforded by each subdivision is quite different. Fiduciary bonds provide a guarantee that the principal will discharge his trust honestly and in accordance with the law. The coverage is broader than one strictly against dishonesty since it covers also losses occasioned by negligence or lack of ability. Court bonds differ in that they are given in connection with litigation and the obligation is the payment of money. Honesty, integrity, high standing, or ability have no effect in determining the obligation if the litigation is in the end decided against the principal. Since bonds of this class involve the payment of money, they are sometimes termed "monetary obligations." Examples include injunction, appeal, and bail bonds.

Fiduciary bonds are of two classes: (*a*) probate bonds and (*b*) fiduciary bonds other than probate. Probate bonds are those required by the various probate courts of those entrusted with the administration of estates of decedents or the management of the estates of incompetents or minors. The classification of fiduciaries other than probate embraces all those bonds required of fiduciaries appointed by courts other than probate, such as, for example, receivers, assignees, or trustees in bankruptcy.

Court bonds may be divided into numerous subclasses. One division distinguishes between bonds required in proceedings at law and those required in equity. Bonds filed in proceedings at law may be further classified as bonds to be filed in: (*a*) civil actions or (*b*) criminal actions.

More detailed information on many of the judiciary bonds are contained in Appendix H, "Special Crime Insurance and Bonds."

Contract Bonds

The four main classes of contract bonds are as follows: (1) construction, (2) supply, (3) maintenance, and (4) miscellaneous.

Under the first heading are to be found bonds such as those guaranteeing construction where the work contracted for on completion becomes attached to, or forms part of, the real property. Many contractors involved in public construction are required to furnish a contract bond, and as a matter of good business practice many other private construction projects use such bonds. Supply contract bonds guarantee a supply of material contracted for at an agreed price. A newspaper publisher might require such a bond in connection with a term contract for its supply of newsprint.

Maintenance bonds are given in connection with contracts undertaking to maintain all or part of the work in good condition for a term after completion. An example is to be found in the agreement frequently inserted in construction contracts stipulating, for example, that a roof will be maintained in good condition during a period of years. The purpose of such a bond is, in effect, to provide a guarantee against defective materials or workmanship, though sometimes the obligation extends to include efficient and successful operation for a term of years.

The miscellaneous group includes a wide variety of bonds not classified under one of the other headings, such as a compensation bond of a self-insurer under a workmen's compensation act, and the bond of a lessee guaranteeing to make certain improvements to the property leased or guaranteeing the payment of the rent during the term of the lease.

Although contract bonds are not infrequent in the business world, they do cover situations which are not as common as the need for fidelity bonds. Therefore, specific analysis of the above classes of contracts is not attempted here. The reader is referred to Appendix H, "Special Crime Insurace and Bonds," for further information about each of the specific contract bonds. The final section of Appendix H also contains more details about the surety bonds other than the fidelity, judicial, and contract bonds, including depository, license and permit, and federal bonds.

SUMMARY

While the statistics may show a decline in the crime insurance departments of some insurers, it is wrong to assume that the need for such protection has diminished. In fact, the rising crime rates testify to the *increased* needs. The fiction of the decline in crime insurance premiums is merely an accounting change, as many of the crime policies discussed in Chapter 17 are now contained in the Homeowner's Policy and other multiple-line coverages for businesses discussed in Chapter 19. The trend toward "packaging" of crime coverages with other property and liability protection will probably continue in the future.

However, the unique features of *crime insurance,* and *suretyship,* are such that separate treatment seems well justified. Very little, if any, of the information in this chapter is rendered obsolete by the newer multiple-line contracts. The principles and language in the contracts, their underwriting and marketing and claims problems—all require careful study as in the past.

Crimes against property include *burglary, robbery, theft,* and *forgery.* Insurance for each of these perils may be written in separate policies, and aside from the residence theft contracts most of the policies are designed for business risks. Some businesses also have a legal liability for property in their possession, which may be subject to crime losses. Many policyholders combine several of these perils in broad crime contracts such as the Storekeepers', and Office, Burglary and Robbery Policies, the Money and Securities Policy (Broad Form), and the Comprehensive Dishonesty, Disappearance and Destruction Policy.

Suretyship differs somewhat from insurance, in the strict sense, but is generally accepted as part of the insurance business. Its principal differences are the presence of an *obligor* (*principal*) and *obligee* in the surety bond; its common assumption of few, if any, losses; and the primary liability of the principal before the surety is called upon to pay a loss.

Fidelity bonds are insurance against the dishonesty of employees. Many types are written, including individual, name schedule, position schedule, discovery and commercial blanket bonds. The primary commercial blanket and the blanket position bonds are used to provide the broadest possible fidelity coverage for the employer.

Other types of *surety* bonds are *judicial* and *contract* bonds. The wide variety of these contracts, designed for specific businesses and situations, is so extensive that a number of them are treated in detail in Appendix H, "Special Crime Insurance and Bonds."

FOR REVIEW

1. Classify the basic parts of the field of crime insurance. Why is such classification important to understand?
2. Identify several of the "package" crime insurance contracts and explain their advantages to the insured.
3. A storeowner usually should not consider only the special contract (the Storekeepers' Burglary and Robbery Policy) for his crime insurance needs. What are its disadvantages, and what other contracts should he perhaps have?
4. A fiction writer describes a masked man entering a store and at gunpoint taking the cash on hand. As a side comment he remarks that the burglary policy had not been renewed. The inference is that had it been renewed the storekeeper would have been reimbursed for his loss. This is not a correct inference. Why?
5. In an effort to open a safe in a dwelling, a burglar's explosion severely damages a fine oil painting. The burglar fails in his attempt to open the safe and takes nothing. Is the property damage loss covered under the burglary policy? Would a quantity of paper money which was destroyed beyond salvage be covered?
6. To what extent are forgery losses a matter of risk to (*a*) the individual or business institution writing the check, and (*b*) the bank called upon to make payment?
7. What is the purpose of the fidelity bond? How does it differ from judicial and contract bonds?
8. B was elected to the board of directors of the First National Bank. Shortly afterward a new cashier was hired and ordered to furnish a bond in the amount of $25,000. The directors neglected to check up on this matter, and the bond was never filed. In the course of several years a huge shortage developed and B was asked to contribute with the other directors in restoring the amount of the loss on the ground that the directors were negligent. B refused on the ground that this was the responsibility of the president of the bank. In your opinion will he be forced to contribute?
9. What are the similarities and the differences between "insurance" and "suretyship"?
10. What is the function of an indemnitor in the field of corporate suretyship?
11. B has always placed his insurance with the X agency. He has been in the habit of calling this agency from time to time as he requires insurance coverage, instructing the agent to bind the needed coverage, and deliver the policy when convenient. Under what disadvantage does B operate in undertaking to have a bond coverage so bound?
12. B has never carried a bond on any of his employees but recently, startled by reports of losses, has determined to provide coverage on a position-schedule basis. Outline how a "discovery bond" would be of advantage to this employer.
13. X is the treasurer of a corporation and is bonded in the sum of $25,000. A loss occurs amounting to $100,000. A former bookkeeper, now deceased, is involved—as are probably other members of the bookkeeping staff. The treasurer is suspected of collusion, but the officers are unable definitely to identify each employee's actual responsibility for the shortage. What is the position of the corporation where each employee concerned is specifically bonded? What suggestion would you make concerning the type of bond which this business should have?
14. X is the treasurer of a savings bank and is bonded for $25,000. Defalcations totaling $75,000, extending over a period of eight years, are discov-

ered. In no one year would the loss exceed the penalty of the bond. The directors of the bank contend that the surety company is liable for the amount embezzled on the ground that each annual premium payment made the bond for each year a separate contract of indemnity, and that the surety company is, therefore, liable under its terms to make good the embezzlement for each separate year. In your opinion, how strong is the case of the bank and how much may it collect?

15. Probate bonds are required when a person is appointed by the court to safeguard the estate of an incompetent. Indicate cases in which a court will make such an appointment. What other types of judicial bonds are there?
16. If a bond covers a public official for the "faithful performance of his duty," what coverage does the bond provide in addition to dishonesty?
17. The representative of the Consolidated Insurance Agency has advised the officers of a bank supplying money to build an apartment building that they should insist upon both a contract bond and a completion bond. The borrower states that because the contractor is supplying a contract bond, this is all that is necessary, since the contract bond obliges the contractor to complete the work in accordance with the terms and specifications. What is your opinion as to the need of a completion bond?
18. The Blank Surety Company supplies B, a contractor engaged in street paving, with a maintenance bond conditioned that B will maintain a certain street in good condition for a period of five years after its completion. Owing to an unforeseen defect in the subsoil, a section of the road caves in. There is nothing wrong with the workmanship or the materials put into the job. Is the contractor obligated to replace the paving? If he fails to do so, is the surety liable?
19. Contrast the protection afforded by the blanket position bond and the primary commercial blanket bond.
20. Either of the blanket bonds mentioned in Question 19 may be included in the "3-D Policy." What other coverages does this popular contract contain?

Chapter 18

MISCELLANEOUS PROPERTY AND LIABILITY INSURANCE

WITH the exception of Chapter 19, "Multiple-line and All-lines Insurance," the present chapter concludes the discussion of property and liability insurance in Part Four of this text. Prior chapters have treated fire, indirect loss, transportation, liability, workmen's compensation, automobile and crime insurance. In Chapter 18 are the remaining types of miscellaneous property and liability insurance, including *aircraft, credit, title, boiler and machinery,* and *glass* insurance. Each of these types of insurance has some unusual features which are not found in other insurance contracts.

There are several other kinds of property and liability insurance which, because of their limited use in special situations, are treated in Appendix I, "Supplementary Information on Miscellaneous Property and Liability Insurance." The reader is referred there for additional explanation of aircraft insurance coverage details, and brief explanations of such unusual types of insurance as (1) *patent protection,* (2) *livestock* insurance, (3) *career coverages,* (4) *libel liability,* and (5) *contingency coverages.*

AIRCRAFT INSURANCE

Development

Aircraft insurance received little attention until after World War I. There were no special forms to cover aviation risks, and the few policies that were issued made use of the ordinary fire or automobile forms. By 1920, a number of companies had definitely entered the field, but the early experience was far from successful. Underwriting at the outset was characterized by a considerable element of trial and error. The volume of business was small; values in single risks were great. Experience upon which to predicate rates was lacking. Early insurers charged high premiums, imposed heavy deductibles, and used some complicated policy conditions.

By 1963 the civilian aircraft industry was well established as a major factor in the transportation system of the United States. In 1962 over 50,000 active aircraft were in service, including 2,000 owned by 55 U.S. certified air carriers who carried over 58 million passengers and a billion ton-miles of mail and freight for an operating revenue of $3 billion.[1]

Insurers

For a considerable period, insurance companies organized into underwriting syndicates to handle the growing aircraft business. Such syndicates still account for a substantial part of the business, especially the protection for the large airline transportation and aircraft manufacturing companies. Within recent years insurers are insuring on an individual basis many planes and helicopters that are privately owned or are owned by industrial concerns using aircraft in connection with their operations.

With the passage of federal regulatory legislation, the business of aviation attained stability. The control of aviation activities exercised by the federal government through the Civil Aeronautics Authority, the Civil Air Board, and the Federal Aviation Agency has made mandatory safety measures that might otherwise be disregarded. Control is exercised with respect to the certification of pilots, and regulations cover aircraft flights in the United States. Adequate insurance facilities now exist in this country for handling aviation risks of every description. Policies follow a somewhat standardized pattern (though not by regulation) and competition is a strong factor with respect to rates and liberality of coverage.

Basic Nature

At first glance the aircraft coverages seem to parallel the automobile coverages. Basically, the coverages are the same. They are divided into two classifications: direct loss and liability coverages. However, the perils in aircraft insurance differ in so many ways from those in automobile insurance that coverages have been developed and modified which vary widely from the automobile policies in many important features. Excluded from discussion here are the aviation accident insurance contracts issued to passengers, which are a type of health insurance treated in Chapter 26.

As compared with the automobile risk, aircraft insurance involves much larger sums. A modern jet airliner equipped to carry as many as 200 people costs $8 million or more. In connection with aviation, direct loss insurance, depreciation, and obsolescence are factors of tremendous importance. Losses are in many instances much greater than and different from those attached to the automobile. One of the most important of the factors influencing losses is the physical condition, training, and experience of the pilot. While it is true that inexperienced drivers of automobiles are responsible

[1] *1963 Britannica Book of the Year* (Chicago: Encylopaedia Britannica, Inc., 1963), p. 186.

for many accidents, the incompetence of a pilot is disastrous. The adage has developed: "Good pilots die in bed."

The liability peril stems from the same source as that of automobile liability and is based upon the accepted common law rules of negligence. However, the decisions tend to hold the operators of aircraft absolutely liable without the common law defense of contributory negligence; in addition to this, the trend of legislation is in the direction of absolute liability.

Because of the large amounts involved and the peculiar nature of the risk, the underwriting problems are usually handled by agents or managers who are specialists in aviation coverages. In total, the aircraft insurance business has become an unusual blend of features —combining aspects of automobile, fire, liability, and inland marine insurance in a specialized insurance area which also has close dependence on reinsurance techniques.

Classification of Aircraft

Planes are classified in accordance with the use to which they are put, as (*a*) private business, and pleasure and (*b*) commercial. The first classification applies to individuals or corporations not engaged in commercial aviation who own or use aircraft for pleasure or business. This classification extends to the transporting of guests without charge, executives, and salesmen, and includes other uses in connection with business or pleasure.

The commercial classification includes aircraft operated by a flying school, sales agencies, taxi, or similar operations of a fixed base operator. Since the rates for a coverage are less if the policy excludes student instruction or the renting of aircraft to others, the commercial classification is sometimes subdivided into (*a*) commercial and (*b*) limited commercial. The term "commercial" is defined as the use of the aircraft for hire or reward including student instruction and rental of the insured plane to persons other than the owner. The "limited commercial" classification provides for the use of the aircraft for commercial aviation purposes including student instruction and rental to others but differs from the broader commercial classification in that it excludes passenger carrying for hire. Dealers or distributors fall into a special-risks group as do a number of risks involving unusual conditions, such as, for example, flying boats, multiengine aircraft, manufacturing risks, scheduled airline operations, and flying clubs.

Types of Contracts

The basic policy forms include: (1) *hull policies* which cover the risks of loss or damage to the insured aircraft itself; (2) *aircraft liability coverages* which are written to cover public and passenger liability and property damage liability; (3) *admitted aircraft liability coverage* which provides for voluntary settlements to injured passengers; and (4) *medical payments coverage* which provides medical expenses regardless of liability. These contracts, and a *comprehensive light plane policy* which combines many of these coverages, are each discussed separately in the following sections.

In addition, special forms are written for (*a*) *hangar keeper's liability* which covers the bailee's liability with respect to aircraft stored for safekeeping or repair; (*b*) *airport and air meet liability* which provide protection similar to the owners', landlords', and tenants' forms generally written for property owners; (*c*) *products liability* which covers manufacturers, sales or repair organizations, and the like against liability claims attributable to defective products or work; (*d*) *aircraft workmen's compensation and employers' liability;* (*e*) *aviation personal accident* insurance; and (*f*) *cargo liability* covering legal liability for loss or damage to cargo or baggage. Cargo liability is to be distinguished from cargo insurance. Cargo insurance, strictly speaking, is not classed as an aviation line but is written by fire companies in their inland marine departments. These special forms (*a*) through (*f*), are treated in Appendix I, "Supplementary Information on Miscellaneous Property and Liability Insurance."

In aviation insurance, distinction is made between ground coverages and flying coverages. Hangar fire, windstorm, and theft perils come within the scope of ground coverages. Accidental damage or "crash insurance," public and passenger liability and property damage form the more important flying coverages. The ground coverages provide indemnity only if the loss occurs while the aircraft is on the ground and not in motion. The flying coverages include damage to the machine arising out of flight and liability coverages. For the purposes of insurance, an aircraft is deemed as not in flight under all circumstances, except during the period of time commencing with the actual takeoff run and continuing thereafter until it has safely completed its landing run. The distinction is an important one, frequently developing borderline cases giving rise to doubt as to the exact status of the coverage. If under flight coverages the insured is covered under a participating or deductible form and under the ground coverages the insured has full protection, the amount of liability of the company will differ depending upon whether the accident happened just prior to actual takeoff, immediately after landing, or during flight.

Only aircraft licensed by the United States Department of Commerce are regarded by insurers as risks eligible for insurance. Since the skill and experience of the pilot are said to constitute 90 percent of the company's risk in underwriting aviation insurance, particular emphasis is centered upon the qualifications and character of the pilots who will fly the insured planes.

Hull Insurance. The hull policy provides insurance against direct loss or damage from the perils defined on the schedule of coverages attached to the policy. Policies are written either on a named-perils or an all-risks basis. When written on a named-perils basis, the policy may be arranged to include any or all of the following coverages: (1) fire, (2) crash insurance, (3) stationary land damage, (4) windstorm, (5) amphibious mooring, and (6) theft. These perils are similar to coverages under other property insurance contracts, and "crash insurance" is merely a different name for the same type of protection afforded by automobile collision coverage. When written on an all-risks basis, the policy provides complete hull coverage both on the ground and in the air and includes such perils as crash damage, tornado, cyclone, windstorm, earthquake, flood, hail, sleet, snow, collapse of the hangar or building in which the plane is stored, denting, marring, or scratching while in the care or custody of a hangar keeper, and every other conceivable risk which may damage the plane.

The exceptions are few. They are wear and tear, deterioration, or conversion (taking without authority) by a person in possession of the aircraft, or loss due to mechanical breakage or structural failure. While the policy does not cover loss due to mechanical breakage or structural failure, damage by collision or fire which results from such breakage or failure is covered. The all-risks form may, however, be written covering all risks with the exception of specifically excluded perils. For example, a policy can be written "all risks excluding crash" or "all risks excluding crash but including fire in air except following crash." Various other exclusions may be incorporated in the all-risks policy depending upon the requirements of the insured.

Aviation hull covers run to very large sums. Even the lower-priced privately owned planes run to values considerably in excess of automobiles, but in the case of the larger risks the difference is wide and policies involving hundreds of thousands of dollars on a single plane are not at all unusual.

There are two classes of hull cover. These are protection of the insured plane (*a*) in flight and (*b*) not in flight. The insured aircraft is defined in the policy to include not only the plane itself but also all equipment that is built into the plane and forms a part thereof. Included as part of the aircraft are engines, propellers, operating and navigation instruments, and radio equipment attached to or usually carried on the aircraft. Detached parts not replaced by other similar parts and tools which are standard for the make and type of aircraft are covered.

The policy provides that the insurer will pay the insured value of the plane in the event of total loss subject to whatever deductions are provided in the schedule of coverage. The rates for hull insurance are based on the assumption that the aircraft is insured for 100 percent of value. No coinsurance clause actually appears in the contract, but the practice of requiring insurance 100 percent to value is in line with that followed generally in inland marine business. In all hull policies, total losses are subject to depreciation at prorata of 20 percent per year for new aircraft and 15 percent for used aircraft. New aircraft are held to be planes less than three months old at the time the insurance attaches.

There are certain combinations of perils that have become generally accepted forms of hull insurance. These are: (*a*) Coverage on the ground and in flight. This coverage pays for any loss or damage to the insured aircraft including disappearance if the aircraft is unreported for 60 days after takeoff. (*b*) Coverage except while in flight. This coverage pays for any loss of or damage to the insured aircraft except loss while in flight. (*c*) Coverage except while in flight and taxiing. This form provides comprehensive protection while the aircraft is stationary. (*d*) Fire, explosion, lightning, and transportation. This protection extends to cover the insured plane while in flight and while taxiing if the damage is attributable to one of the named perils. (*e*) Named-perils ground coverage. This policy usually includes fire, transportation, theft, windstorm, and taxiing accidents. (*f*) Named perils, ground and air. This provides for any loss of or damage to the insured aircraft whether in flight or not in flight. The perils may be the same as those written for named-perils ground coverage. (*g*) Fire under all circumstances except following crash. This is a form of fire insurance ordinarily written upon planes in hangars to cover a catastrophe fire hazard.

With the exception of the comprehensive light plane form mentioned later, which *may* be written on an all-risks basis, the hull policies heretofore noted are named-perils forms. This is true even though, as noted, the term "comprehensive" is sometimes applied where the combined coverages embrace virtually all of the usual perils.

Within recent years, particularly with the emphasis given to all-risks forms in inland marine and the automobile comprehensive form, the demand for identical protection has evidenced itself in the aviation field. The more usual all-risks hull coverages include: (*a*) all risks while not in flight, (*b*) all risks while not in flight but including fire while in the air but excluding fire following a crash, and (*c*) all-risks ground coverage extended to include all risks while in flight. This last form is the most comprehensive obtainable and covers every peril to which the plane may be subject by providing complete ground coverage together with collision and crash damage cover.

Deductibles apply upon much the same basis as in the case of named-perils coverages. In the case of light planes, 5 percent of the insured value applies but not less than $100 or more than $300 if the aircraft is not ordinarily housed in a hangar. If the plane is maintained in a hangar, the deductible is $25. There is no deduction with respect to losses caused by theft, transportation perils, lightning, explosion, or fire. Where ground and in-flight risks are both covered, the ordinary deductibles applicable to both classes of peril apply separately.

Public Liability and Property Damage. These coverages, with the exceptions to be noted, afford essentially the same insurance protection as similar coverages in automobile insurance. Although the automobile liability policy generally covers the passenger hazard, the aviation liability policy does not; and it makes no difference in the latter case whether the passenger is carried for a consideration or is a guest.[2]

In contrast to the automobile policy which provides for protection against loss attributable to liability imposed by law for accidental injury, some aviation policies provide coverage without a special endorsement on an occurrence basis. As aviation liabilities are written there is some question as to the exact line of demarcation between an "accident" and an "occurrence." The substitution of the term "occurrence" for "accident" is intended as a broadening of the coverage. Actually the term "occurrence" which literally means an event is limited by definition in the policy. By definition the word "occurrence" whenever used in the policy means either an accident or a "continuous or repeated exposure to conditions, which results in injury during the policy period, provided the injury is accidentally caused." The definition then goes on to state that all damages arising out of exposure to substantially the same general conditions shall be deemed to arise out of one occurrence. The requirement that the injury be accidentally caused is designed to exclude claims resulting from the willful intent of the insured. The use of the term "occurrence" provides coverage for gradual damage. If, for example, an insured knew that some action of his would result in bodily injury and he committed the act in any case, the policy would not cover since the injury would not be accidentally caused. On the other hand, if an occupant of a plane was forced to bail out and landed without injury but contracted pneu-

---

[2]As in the case of automobile insurance, the purchaser of an aviation policy selects the coverages he will carry. In bodily injury liability, Coverage A excludes passengers, while Coverage B covers only passengers.

monia due to exposure, such a sickness or disease claim would be attributable to the occurrence.

The liability policy does not cover: (1) liability imposed upon or assumed by the insured under any workmen's compensation act or plan; (2) liability for injuries sustained by employees or pupils of the insured while carried upon, or operating, or caring for the insured aircraft, or while engaged in the usual course of trade, business, or profession of the insured.

In the case of property damage the coverage excludes: (1) property belonging to, or in the custody of, the insured; (2) property belonging to, or in the control of, the insured's employees or pupils; (3) property which is rented or leased and for which the insured is legally responsible; (4) property carried in or upon the insured aircraft.

When aviation liability policies were first offered, they contained no omnibus clause. As a result, the insurance extended to cover only the person specifically named in the contract. There is now an additional insured clause similar to that found in the automobile liability policy. This is effected by a definition of the term "insured," extending coverage under the policy to others legally responsible for the operation of the aircraft. The exceptions include injuries to an employee by another employee. These injuries would ordinarily be covered by workmen's compensation. Sales service and repair organizations and the like are excluded unless they are the named insured. The effect of the clause is to provide protection to friends or members of the family while they are flying the plane of the insured.

The policy now provides a fly-other-aircraft provision which protects the insured while flying a borrowed plane. This provision is limited to policies issued to insureds who are owners of planes in the private passenger category. The policy also excludes any liability in consequence of operation of the insured aircraft in connection with course racing, or operation for or in connection with other than uses specified in the policy. Intentional low flying is not covered while the insured attempts to perform or permits acrobatics. The policy does not cover crop dusting, spraying, seeding, hunting, bird or fowl herding, or dropping objects from the aircraft. If a special permit or waiver is required from the Federal Aviation Agency for a particular type of operation, the policy does not cover unless specifically endorsed to include the particular operation. The liability policies contain the same exclusions as to unlawful use, geographical limits, and Federal Aviation Agency certificate as are found in the hull policy. In addition, the policy excludes workmen's compensation.

Standard limits for bodily injury liability are \$5/10,000; for passenger liability, the standard limit is $5,000 per seat; and $5,000 is standard limit for property damage. Medical payments coverage is written only in connection with passenger liability, and the standard limit is $500.

Because of the values involved and the possibility of catastrophic accidents, limits higher than standard are the rule. Rate manuals quote liability limits for bodily injury, other than passenger liability, up as high as $100/300,000 and passenger liability up to $100,000 per seat. Property damage rates are quoted with a $100,000 limit. Needs of an insured are often such that requests are made for limits beyond those provided for in a company's rating schedule. Companies are willing to consider such higher limits and have developed a formula for computing the premium charge.

Passenger liability coverage is written with a standard limit of $5,000 per passenger seat. Hence, the lower standard limit of passenger liability coverage is $5,000, and the upper limit is the lower limit multiplied by the number of passenger seats. In determining the limits of insurance the pilot's seat is not counted. Hence, in a four-passenger plane, one seat would be allocated to the pilot and the limit per passenger would be multiplied by three. Higher limits, as in other liability coverages, are available. In the case of transport lines in particular, the higher limits are invariably recommended. However, it has become increasingly the practice to carry high limits in connection with privately owned planes as well. Unlike the automobile policy that pays for far more injuries for temporary disability than for death, injuries to airplane passengers are much more likely to be fatal.

The terrific damage that a crashing airplane can do to both the human body and property emphasizes the need of high limits. Even an accident that is short of being a catastrophe can run the damage claims to huge sums. In the case of property damage the need for high limits, sometimes overlooked, is likewise essential. Taxiing accidents are frequent; and, because of the fragile construction of aircraft, a comparatively slight collision has resulted in damage amounting to many thousands of dollars.

Individuals learning to fly may protect their individual legal liability for death or injury to members of the public, passengers excluded, under a special form written at a comparatively low rate.

Admitted Liability Coverage. A form of liability coverage, closely akin in principle to the medical payments in the automobile field, provides that in the event of bodily injury to a passenger, excluding passengers carried for hire, the company will offer a settlement on a definitely determined basis regardless of whether the insured is legally liable. The policy provides that in consideration of the payment of these benefits, there shall be obtained a release from the claimant relieving the insured from any further liability as result of the accident. In the event that a passenger meets with death, the same benefits are payable to his dependents or estate. If the injured passenger refuses to release the insured from further liability, the policy will pay, up to the amount of the benefits indicated, any legal claims for damages that may be established. It is not necessary, however, to establish legal liability if the claimant signs the required release.

The admitted liability policy is usually issued in connection with an additional passenger third-party liability policy written for substantially greater amounts. This second policy is written as excess over the first policy, and therefore the premium rates are correspondingly low. This policy has proved attractive in that it permits the owner of a plane to offer passengers an insurance service covering injuries without forcing the injured party to prove negligence on the part of the plane owner for the purpose of establishing legal liability.

Medical Payments. The similarity of medical payments to admitted liability coverage is found in the fact that payment is offered the injured passenger without the necessity of establishing liability. Under the admitted liability coverage, however, policy limits are high enough to satisfy a liability claim in the ordinary course and a release is required from the injured party.

Medical payments cover not only passengers but the pilot as well. The payment is made without regard to liability, and no release with respect to further claims is required. Limits for each passenger and pilot ordinarily begins at $500 but may be increased to $2,000 or more depending upon the underwriting practices of the company.

Payments are made for bodily injury to a passenger or pilot if the accident is caused while in or upon entering or alighting from the insured aircraft. The policy may be written to provide the insured the same protection with respect to the use of substitute aircraft. As in the case of the automobile medical payments, payment is made for reasonable expense of necessary medical, surgical, ambulance, hospital, and professional nursing services. Reasonable funeral expenses are paid in event of death.

Comprehensive Light Plane Policy. A special hull policy has been provided for light planes—that is, planes weighing under 2,000 pounds fully loaded—to cover comprehensive risks, including crash. The perils are specifically named, but the policy covers a wide range of additional risks, such as earthquake, flood, denting, marring, and the like that are not usually included in the policies written covering specified perils. The term "comprehensive" derives from the wide number of perils included in a single form.

Unlike the automobile comprehensive, it is not an all-risks cover. Moreover, the insured bears a portion of the loss in the form of participation and in return, therefore, secures a considerably lower rate than otherwise would be the case. A $50 deductible applies to all ground coverages except fire, theft, and transportation. This deductible may be eliminated for the payment of an additional premium. The policy, as ordinarily written, provides insurance against all the named perils with the deductibles and participation as shown in Table 18-1.

TABLE 18–1

Perils	*Deductible*	*Insured's Participation*
Fire (excluding fire following crash)	Nil	Nil
Windstorm	$50.00	Nil
Land damage	$50.00	Nil
Theft	Nil	Nil
Crash (including fire following crash)	Nil	20% to 33⅓% of amount of loss

In case of crash losses, the participation to be borne by the insured depends upon the usage of the plane and the experience of the pilot. Instead of writing the policy on a comprehensive form with named perils as indicated, the light plane policy may be written on an all-risks basis for an additional premium.

Aviation Rates

Aviation insurance, in contrast to other property fields, provides no rating schedule showing rates applicable to different classes of aviation risk. In the aviation field there is an open market. Rates, therefore, are not standard and are to a large degree based upon judgment. Some states require that insurance companies file "rate spreads." Such a filing indicates a minimum and a maximum rate but leaves the actual rate for a specific risk to the judgment of the underwriter.

Some companies furnish rate sheets that provide an average rate for an average risk of a particular class. These rates are not firm, and the final rate quotation is made only after the underwriter has been given an opportunity to appraise the particular risk. Competition influences rates. Factors that enter into the consideration of the underwriter in determining the final rate include the physical condition, age, weight, flying characteristics, and depreciated value of the plane. The business of the insured is a factor, as well as his standing in the community. If the plane is used in connection with a business operation, the period in which the insured has carried on his business is a factor for consideration. The underwriter will also wish to know to what extent the business has operated profitably. The experience of the pilots, the age and physical type of equipment, and the experience of the insured are all factors. The operator with good equipment, good reputation, and a good loss experience secures the most favorable rate consideration.

Rates are ordinarily quoted on an annual basis. There are risks that do not lend themselves to annual quotations predicated upon the number of planes owned. Dealers or business organizations that have an active turnover in the number of aircraft owned may secure a policy providing for periodic reporting of risks with rates, as before, determined on a judgment basis but with premiums computed from the reports of the number and nature of the planes at risk. In some instances crash insurance may be written based on the number of hours the insured plane is flown. Most of the coverages for scheduled airlines are written on a reporting basis, although this is not the universal practice. Some airlines carry their own hull catastrophe coverage but, when the crash hazard is insured by an underwriter, it is usually on an hourly or mileage basis. The rate, as before, is based upon all that apply of the previously listed characteristics of the risk; and it is finally determined in a competitive market by the judgment of the underwriter.

The constant coverages for fleets, such as fire, windstorm, and theft, are not written on a reporting form but are covered for a definite period of time, as in the case of policies covering single planes.

Deductibles and Participations

When insurance companies first undertook to write aviation risks, they imposed heavy deductibles upon the insured. These deductibles were designed to eliminate small losses and, at the same time, place part of the burden of loss on the insured. With a heavy deductible there never could be an actual total loss. Whatever merit the deductibles may have possessed, they placed serious limitations upon the adequacy of the insurance protection. Whatever deterrent they may have exerted toward the elimination of moral hazard losses, there were many who felt that in the hazardous field of aviation the deductibles were too great to provide the protection required. A small plane valued at $10,000 and insured with a 10 percent deductible would involve the company in no liability until a loss exceeded the amount of the deductible. In other words, in the case of a $1,200 loss, the company would be liable for only $200. There were many who felt they could not assume such losses. This was particularly the case with new and growing business establishments. A few losses that could be entirely justified as free of any moral-hazard taint could, nevertheless, result in seriously crippling the business undertaking.

To provide participation of the insured in all losses and, at the same time, limit small claims, the "participation form" of policy, as noted previously for light planes, was offered. The participation form, instead of reducing the loss by a flat amount as is required where the policy is written with a deductible, requires the insured to bear a percentage of each claim regardless of its size. Thus, in the example cited, with a 25 percent participation and a $1,200 claim, the company would pay $900 and the insured would bear $300, the amount represented by his participation.

As the amount of the claim increases, the amount of the participation of the insured may be in excess of the usual deductible. In the circumstances, the insured must determine whether it is more important for him to eliminate all partial losses up to a certain amount and collect all in excess of that, or to bear a percentage of all losses, which increases in dollar amount as the amount of the loss increases. With a $10,000 plane and a 10 percent deductible, the insured would collect, in the case of a total loss, $9,000. The same plane insured with a 25 percent participation would mean that the amount of the claim in the event of a total loss would be limited to $7,500. The use of deductibles and participation forms has the effect of modifying the rate in favor of the insured. The higher the deductible or the rate of the participation, the lower will be the premium charged the insured.

CREDIT INSURANCE

Nature and Development

Credit insurance[3] is a contract under which an insurer, in consideration of a stipulated premium, undertakes to indemnify the insured against loss occasioned by the insolvency of debtors. Most of the insureds purchasing this kind of insurance are wholesalers.

The contract follows the form of an insurance policy; but, because of its nature, the question was raised in the early days as to whether it was in fact a contract of insurance or of surety. While recognizing the similarities between suretyship and credit insurance, the courts have held that credit insurance agreements are in fact contracts of insurance and should be treated as such.

The outstanding distinguishing feature between a strict guarantee and insurance in the credit contract is to be found in the fact that the credit risk is not based upon the individual standing of the

[3]The distinction between *commercial* credit insurance discussed here, and *consumer* credit insurance such as credit life and health insurance, is important. The term "credit insurance" has always been understood to mean the commercial type. For further details of many of the topics in this section, see Clyde W. Phelps, *Commercial Credit Insurance as a Management Tool* (Baltimore: Commercial Credit Company, 1961), 111 pages.

primary debtor but rather upon the credit experience of a large group of debtors belonging to a certain class. A second distinguishing feature is that in the case of a guarantor the agreement is made for the accommodation of the debtor, usually as a basis for securing credit. In credit insurance, the policy is secured by the creditor without any cooperation on the part of the debtor and may be obtained without his knowledge or consent.

Insurance historians date the origin of the idea of credit insurance from an undertaking proposed in 1837 for the organization of a $10 million corporation "to guarantee notes and contracts and collect debts." The idea was not readily adopted,[4] and even during recent years the use of credit insurance has been limited.

Notwithstanding developments to date, credit insurance is still in an experimental stage. It is by no means a major[5] branch of the insurance business, though the demand for the coverage is increasing and appearing in fields where coverage has hitherto been unavailable. The area of *foreign* credit insurance has taken on increased significance as companies have expanded their marketing operations on an international scope in recent years.

Underwriting the Risk

It is not the function of credit insurance to replace credit investigations with a contract of indemnity. Rather, the insurance undertakes to furnish indemnity for unforeseen losses where credit investigations are made, and a reasonable scrutiny of accounts to reduce losses to a minimum is the practice.

Insurance companies place upon the liability they will assume a limitation based upon the *credit rating* of the customers of their insureds. Credit ratings are usually determined by references to the services of established mercantile agencies, such as Dun & Bradstreet, Inc.[6]

In the application for credit insurance a statement is made of the mercantile agency whose ratings are to be used. Under the section

[4]Other early insurers followed much later. The United States Credit System of New Jersey was incorporated in 1889 and was the first organization of the kind to operate over a period of years. This company was unable to weather the depression of 1893 and went into receivership in 1898. The American Indemnity Company appeared in the field in 1891, and other pioneer writers of the line include the Ocean Accident and Guarantee Corporation, Ltd., entering the field in 1895, and the London Guarantee and Accident Company, Ltd., entering in 1905.

[5]Net written premiums in 1962 were only $11.3 million, in comparison to the $16.5 billion fire and casualty business total. See *Best's Aggregates and Averages (1963)* (New York, A. M. Best, Inc.), p. 144.

[6]Dun & Bradstreet, Inc., is the agency widely used as a basis for underwriting, although the ratings of other agencies operating in a specialized field have been accepted. Among these are the Shoe and Leather Agency, Lyon Furniture Mercantile Agency, Lumbermen's Credit Association, National Lumber Manufacturers' Credit Corporation, Jewelers' Board of Trade, and Iron and Steel Board of Trade.

of conditions and stipulations, the policy provides that the governing rating of the debtor is to be understood to be the mercantile agency named in the application, and the name of the agency is inserted in the policy. The latest published rating book of this agency is used to determine the debtor's governing rating for coverage on shipments, and no loss is covered by the policy unless the debtor shall have had, at the date of shipment, a governing rating for which coverage is specified in the "table of ratings and coverage" inserted in the policy. The gross amount covered on the total indebtedness of a debtor is limited, first, by the amount owed by the debtor to the insured at the date of insolvency and, second, by the amounts set opposite the governing rating of the debtor in the aforementioned table.

Credit ratings are classified for underwriting purposes as "preferred" or "inferior." Policies written on preferred risks represent desirable business from the point of view of the insurance company. It is nevertheless true that most policies cover both types of risk. These are known as "combination policies," and set definite limitations on the inferior classifications.

Since control of the extension of credit rests in the insured, underwriters have felt that credit extensions will be more carefully scrutinized by the insured if he is forced under the terms of the policy to bear a part of the loss. Accordingly, policies are written with a *coinsurance* stipulation that the insured bear an agreed percentage of each loss.

The coinsurance features of the contracts vary. Percentages of 10 and 20 are usual. The higher percentages are used when the risk is greater, or in the case of an inferior rating coverage with high limits.

The term coinsurance as used in connection with credit insurance is sometimes confused with its application in the fire business. There is no clause, however, in the credit policy that provides full recovery in the event that insurance to value is carried. In each case the insured is required to carry the indicated percentage of the loss. The condition is comparable to deductible coverage in marine insurance, using a percentage of loss as the amount of the deductible.

The Peril Covered

Credit insurance covers the peril of loss by the insured arising out of the insolvency of customers to whom credit has been extended. The question of the insurability of the risk has been settled by the courts, and it is now held that the peril of loss by the insolvency of customers is as real and definite as is the peril of loss by fire, lightning, or tornado.

The need for the coverage becomes evident when it is realized that credit losses reach a huge figure every year. Estimates place the total at over $1 billion for a single year. The credit insurance contract issued in this country by domestic insurance companies has been available, as a rule, in the past only to manufacturers and wholesalers; but it is now available and used by service organizations such as advertising agencies. Within the past few years, a considerable volume of this latter business has been written. The terms and conditions of the policies issued vary widely. The more usual coverage provides that an insured will himself assume such credit losses as are normal to his particular business. The policy undertakes to indemnify for any *abnormal or excess loss* resulting from the insolvency of debtors to whom credit has been extended in the regular course of business.

There is a tendency to associate credit losses and insolvency with business incompetence. This line of thought assumes that the careful credit analysis of a credit executive will preclude the necessity for credit insurance. While it is true that many credit losses follow business incompetence, it is equally true that a large proportion of credit losses are the outgrowth of physical disaster. There are few individuals who have physical risks scattered throughout the country who would not provide a floater policy to cover them. Automobile dealers and those selling other items such as refrigerators, radios, pianos, and the like invariably provide insurance protection to cover them against losses growing out of perils such as fire, tornado, earthquake, and flood. The same insureds frequently do not see that perils such as fire, tornado, earthquake, and flood can make accounts receivable as valueless as physical property actually destroyed. The accounts of a businessman doing business over a widespread area may be threatened by perils which are of little or no concern in his own area. Experience has shown that every catastrophe carries with it a trail of credit losses that extend their consequences to the far corners of the country. Only the credit men of active firms trading in areas where there have been disasters caused by cyclones, floods, fires, or other catastrophes have any real knowledge of just how far-reaching are their effects in the credit field. This is true because many of the victims of disaster are frequently wiped out so completely that no effort whatever is made to collect their accounts, and there are few records of bankruptcy of this sort. While accounts receivable are beyond reach of physical damage because they represent claims, their asset value is actually subject to every physical hazard that threatens the assets of the creditor.

Types of Contract

In times past a number of forms of credit insurance policies have been issued, varying in some degree or other, and designed to fit varying needs or situations. Because only a few companies[7] now write credit insurance, the available policies are those which the writing companies have to offer. The major difference in the contracts offered is that one type of contract, known as the "general coverage policy," is designed to cover insurable accounts of the insured against credit losses in excess of normal. In contrast to this, "extraordinary coverage" is available providing insurance against credit losses on one or a few accounts. This policy is ordinarily used when a large percentage of the business of the firm is carried on with a limited number of customers or when the outstanding accounts of one or a few customers represent a very substantial proportion of the working capital of the insured.

Policy Provisions

Policy Term. Credit insurance policies are usually written for a term of one year. Two forms are written with reference to the covering of losses that occur after the end of the policy term. Term policies cover losses through insolvencies on sales made during the term, while continuing policies cover losses though insolvencies occurring during the term. It is assumed that continuing policies will be renewed from year to year. Under a term policy, a loss for which the insurer is liable may occur after the end of the specified period for which the policy was written. Credit insurance policies are terminated if the insured becomes insolvent during the policy term or if issued to a partnership and the partnership is dissolved.

Insolvency. Since the insolvency of debtors is the peril covered by a credit policy, it is essential to have a clear understanding of the meaning of the term as used in the contract. In the absence of words limiting the meaning of *insolvency* to a definition set forth in the policy, a debtor need not necessarily be adjudicated a bankrupt to be insolvent. Failure to meet obligations in the usual course of business is sufficient to hold the insurer liable for loss.

In order to eliminate the necessity of depending upon a liberal construction of the policy, most contracts now set forth at some length the conditions which will warrant a claim on the ground of insolvency. Not all contracts agree on what constitutes insolvency. The following description indicates the breadth of the term as it applies to loss adjustments under a widely used form: The insolvency of the debtor shall be deemed to have occurred when: (1) a debtor shall have absconded; (2) a sole debtor shall

[7]Phelps, *op. cit.*, p. 12. Only two companies in 1961 wrote most of the commercial credit insurance: The American Credit Indemnity Company of New York (a subsidiary of Commercial Credit Company), and The London Guarantee and Accident Company, Limited. 1963 *Best's Aggregates and Averages* also lists Old Republic Insurance Company as writing a very small amount ($280,000) of credit insurance. Some 41 other companies are indicated as writing less than $250,000 each.

have died; (3) a sole debtor shall have been adjudged insane; (4) a receiver shall have been appointed for a debtor; (5) a debtor shall have transferred or sold his stock in trade in bulk; (6) a writ of attachment or execution shall have been levied on a debtor's stock in trade and said stock sold thereunder, or the writ returned unsatisfied; (7) a debtor shall have made a general offer of compromise to his creditors for less than his indebtedness; (8) possession shall have been taken under a chattel mortgage given by a debtor on his stock in trade; (9) a debtor's business shall have been assigned to or taken over by a committee, appointed by a majority in number and amount of his creditors; (10) there shall have been a recording of or taking possession under an assignment or a deed of trust made by a debtor for the benefit of his creditors; (11) a voluntary or involuntary proceeding shall have been instituted to adjudge a debtor bankrupt; or (12) a proceeding for the relief of a debtor shall have been instituted in a court of bankruptcy. It is clear that the coverage is not restricted to the legal definition of insolvency. In addition to actual insolvency, the definition extends to provide protection in situations where collection might prove difficult because of impairment of assets.[8]

Primary or Normal Loss. In every business, year in and year out, bad accounts are the occasion of some loss. This loss is to be expected and is absorbed as a charge-off each year. The amount of such losses can be calculated for any business within reasonably close limits and is usually expressed in a percentage of gross sales. This primary loss is recurring and is sometimes referred to by accountants as the *normal loss.* For the purpose of credit insurance it is termed in the policy the *primary loss.*

It is not the function of insurance to provide indemnity for the happening of certainties. Consequently, the element of primary loss is not insurable. Every credit policy indicates a primary loss for the business insured, determined by previous experience and expressed in terms of a percentage of gross sales. There is no liability during a policy term by the insuring company until the insured has absorbed the amount set up as the primary loss.

Method of Adjustment. The policy sets forth the period within which the insured must file a claim in order to be within the coverage. A usual period is 20 days after acquiring knowledge of the debtor's insolvency and before the expiration of the policy. If information of a debtor's insolvency is received by the insured too late to notify the company during the term of the policy, such notification of claim may be filed with the company within, but not later than, 20 days after its termination.

[8]The definition of insolvency in different policies may vary somewhat in wording, but each follows the same general principle.

In filing a claim, the whole account against the debtor is placed with the insurance company for attention and collection. The company provides a form for giving notice, and this notice constitutes authority for the company to place the account for collection with any attorney it may select. The company undertakes to effect an adjustment within a period not to exceed 60 days after receipt by the company of the final statement of claim setting forth the amount ascertained to be due under the policy.

To ascertain the net loss in any adjustment, the gross loss covered is determined and from this amount the following deductions are made: (1) all amounts collected from the debtor or obtained from any other source; (2) the invoiced price of goods returned, reclaimed, or replevined, when such goods are in the undisputed possession of the indemnified; (3) any discount to which the debtor would be entitled at the time of adjustment; (4) any amount mutually agreed upon as thereafter obtainable; and (5) any legally sustainable setoff that the debtor may have against the indemnified.

After the foregoing deductions from the gross loss covered have been made, the remainder is regarded as the net loss. There is then deducted from such net loss 10 percent, or whatever other percentage is named in the policy, for coinsurance. The balance represents the sum payable to the insured. In the case of disputed claims, the company does not undertake to make any adjustment under the policy until the disputed claim shall have been finally determined to be a valid and legally sustainable indebtedness against the debtor or his estate. When such determination has been effected, the claim is adjusted and the amount due the policyholder is then payable.

The policyholder is obligated to assign to the company the claim allowed in adjustment, together with a securities and guaranties relating thereto, and is required to warrant the legal validity of the indebtedness for the amount of the claim. On any claim assigned to the company in the course of an adjustment, the company agrees to remit to the indemnified after deduction of collection charges and expenses: (1) the net amount realized on any claim in which the company has no interest, (2) the net amount realized on any claim in excess of the gross amount covered, or (3) that portion of the net amount realized on any claim, equal to the percentage of coinsurance thereon borne by the policyholder.

The Collection Clause. Most credit insurance policies are now written with a provision affording the insured the right to file past-due accounts with the company for collection. Policies so written permit the policyholder, during the policy term, to file for collection any insured account after it shall become due and payable but before it shall have become more than 90 days past due under the original terms of sale. When a past-due account is filed with the company, it is treated, for the purposes of effecting the adjustment, as if the debtor were insolvent. The company undertakes to effect a collection, and provision is made in the policy to deduct charges on collections following a schedule set forth in the policy. After the collection charges and expenses are deducted, remittance is made to the insured.

Cancellation. Under general coverage policies there is no cancellation privilege. Under extraordinary coverage issued on individual debtors, the company is allowed the privilege of canceling coverage as to future shipments to any debtor. To effect such cancellation, the company is required to give written notice to the policyholder, in which event the coverage granted on the debtor under the provisions of the contract terminates. The termination of coverage applies only to shipments made to the debtor after receipt by the policyholder of the notice of cancellation.

If there is coverage outside the individual debtor contract that would ordinarily be available to the debtor in question, this coverage ceases to attach so long as the debtor owes an amount in excess of the limit of coverage that would ordinarily have been available under the general cover. When the amount owed by the debtor is less than the limit of coverage available after the cancellation of the extraordinary coverage, insurance attaches as to shipments made after cancellation. However, the gross amount covered on shipments made both prior and subsequent to the date of cancellation may not exceed the limit of coverage available after cancellation. Provision is made for the policyholder to effect cancellation of extraordinary coverage upon giving notice to the company. If no claim for loss had theretofore been filed, an unearned premium is calculated on a prorata basis.

TITLE INSURANCE

The Peril Insured

The peril covered by a title insurance contract is loss growing out of undiscovered defect in the title to a property insured.[9] The policy guarantees the title search to a purchaser, mortgagee, or other interested party, covering the insured against loss arising out of *undiscovered defects in existence* at the time the policy was issued.

In contrast to other forms of insurance, title insurance looks backward for the source of a claim, rather than forward. The usual insurance contract covers loss growing out of the happening of some unfavorable contingency subsequent to the issuance of the policy.

[9]An alternative to title insurance appears in some dozen or more states that have passed Torrens Acts. Under the Torrens system, the property owner applies to a court which, after suitable hearing of any claims by other parties, declares and registers absolute title in the name of the owner.

Title defects which may arise following the issuance of a title policy are not within the scope of the coverage. To support a claim, the defect must have been in existence and undiscovered when the policy was issued.

The Need for Title Insurance

The law divides property into two classes—real and personal. The term "real property" refers to land and rights issuing out of land. Title to real property may be acquired in a number of ways, the more common being transfer with the consent of the owner, by will, and by descent regulated by statute. To secure title to the rightful owner, the law sets up certain formalities governing transfers. These formalities are technical and must be complied with in detail; otherwise, the transfer may be defective.

A transaction involving the sale of real estate usually involves substantial sums of money. The purchaser is interested in knowing that the seller has good title to the property being conveyed and that it is free and clear of all liens or other encumbrances. To satisfy himself of the title of the conveyor, he must have a search made at the record office covering all grants, conveyances, wills, liens, encumbrances, taxes, or other matters that might have the effect of clouding the title. A record of all matters affecting the title is made, and the document is called an "abstract."

The abstract in turn is referred to a lawyer skilled in this type of work. After carefully examining the abstract, the lawyer will give an opinion as to the title. The lawyer who undertakes to pass upon an abstract submitted to him has no means of knowing that the document has been correctly made. Neither can he tell that all parties whose conveyances are recorded had full capacity to contract. An examiner may overlook in the record some defect that may be vital, and many defects in title are of a nature that are not apparent from the record. It follows that the most careful scrutiny of the records by a competent attorney will not in every case bring to light existing causes which may prove a title to be defective.

The Title Insurance Company

Title insurance companies are large corporations[10] with resources ample to carry the risks assumed. Unlike other insurance carriers, most of them tend to confine the scope of their activities to a limited territory. This is made necessary by the very nature of the business.

Since the abstract of title is the basis of the contract, title companies have built up elaborate sets of records which are based upon

[10]Statistics concerning title insurance are relatively difficult to obtain. A new source of information was published in 1963: *Title Insurance Companies* (Stamford, Conn.: Philo Smith and Co., Inc.).

the real estate records of the territory in which their operations are conducted. These records are constantly maintained up-to-date and are sometimes referred to as an "abstract plan." This plan eliminates the necessity of making a complete search of title every time a transfer is made; and as time passes the company will find, as the result of extension of its activities, more and more properties upon which policies have been issued. The writing of a new policy upon a property formerly insured involves only a reference to the records covering changes since the issuance of the last previous policy.

In urban communities where values are high and the real estate turnover rapid, title companies render an important service. In communities where values are low and transfer infrequent, the volume of business is often hardly adequate to support a title insurance company. In such communities the purchaser of real estate or mortgagee must be content with an opinion as to title from an examiner without the guarantee of an insurance contract.

The Basic Policy

Title insurance contracts are not at all uniform, and the policies issued in one community may be markedly different in detail from those issued in another. The forms issued to owners and mortgagees providing indemnity for loss or damage by reason of defects in the title or the unmarketability of the title are usually alike in certain essentials.

The insuring clause provides indemnity to the insured, his heirs, and devisees subject to an indicated limit: (1) by reason of any defect of the title of the insured to the estate or interest described in an attached schedule; (2) by reason of the unmarketability of the title of the insured described in the schedule; or (3) because of liens or encumbrances at the date of the policy, except the defects, estates, objections, liens, or encumbrances specifically scheduled as excepted, or excepted by the conditions of the policy.

The schedule describing the subject matter of the insurance sets forth: (1) the estate or interest of the insured; (2) a description of the property, the title to which is insured; (3) the deed or other instrument by which the title or interest is vested in the insured.

A second schedule sets forth discovered defects that are, therefore, not within the scope of the protection. In this schedule are listed all defects or objections to title, liens, charges, or encumbrances that have been discovered as a result of the title search.

Contract Provisions

A final section of the policy contains the conditions and limitations of the contract between the company and the insured. The policy covers such subjects as assignment, subrogation, conditions supporting a claim, and the conditions governing loss adjustment.

Assignment. Assignment of a title policy is not permitted in the usual course unless the policy is held by the owner of a mortgage or other encumbrances, in which case the contract may be transferred to an assignee of the insured. It may also be transferred to the purchaser at a sale under foreclosure where the property sold is bought by, or for, the insured. The company may by special agreement permit assignment in other cases.

Insurance companies view with concern the assignment of policies issued to the owner of an equity because, if the owner sells his property after holding it for a considerable period and at the same time undertakes to assign a title policy, the holder of the policy may be misled into believing that the policy protects him from the date of the transfer. It is apparent, of course, that no insurance company will undertake to cover title defects that may develop after the policy is issued without first having an opportunity to examine the record and determine whether or not it is willing to assume the risk. To obtain adequate and full protection, the only safe method in the case of the transfer of equity is to secure a new policy or have the current policy brought up to date. However, some policies may be assigned with the consent of the company endorsed thereon. Under such conditions, the company is enabled to point out to the new policyholder the nature of the assignment and the necessity for carrying forward the effective date of the insurance.[11]

Policies written for a mortgagee frequently provide that the coverage will follow to a new interest when the nature of the mortgage interest has been changed by foreclosure or other transaction. Thus, a mortgagee insured under the title policy that changes its status to a holder of title under foreclosure, trustee sale, or other legal process for satisfaction of the indebtedness secured by the mortgage continues to be covered under the policy. The provisions in the policy that a new interest in such circumstances will be covered is not in effect an assignment, but rather the continuation of coverage for essentially the same interest even though its legal character has been changed.

Subrogation. Whenever a claim is settled by the company, the policy provides that the company shall be entitled to all rights and

[11]If assignment is permitted with the consent of the company, the following or a similar clause appears in the contract: "No transfer of this policy shall be made, except that a policy held by the owner of a mortgage or other encumbrance may be transferred to the purchaser at a foreclosure sale where the property sold is bought in by or for the insured, and except also in such other cases as this company may, by special written agreement, permit; but no transfer of this policy shall be valid unless the approval of this company is endorsed hereon by its proper officer. Such approval may in any case be refused at the option of this company, and all interests in this policy (saving for damages accrued) shall cease by its transfer without such approval, so endorsed. The liability of this company to any collateral holder of a policy shall in no case exceed the amount of the pecuniary interest of such collateral holder in the premises described in the policy."

remedies which the insured would have had in respect to the claim. The insured is obligated to transfer these rights to the company and permit it to use the name of the insured in any necessary action in connection with recovery or defense. When payment does not cover in full the loss of the insured, the company's subrogation rights are limited to the proportion that the amount paid by the company bears to the entire loss.

Conditions Supporting a Claim. The policy undertakes to defend the insured against suit, promising to defend in all actions or proceedings founded on a claim of title or encumbrance prior to the policy date. The policy then sets forth, in some detail, conditions under which loss may arise, which are, in fact, a description of situations covered by the contract occasioned by actions of ejectment, dispossession, or eviction founded upon a claim of title, lien, or encumbrance.

Adjustments. When liability has been definitely fixed, the loss is payable within 30 days. The company is given the right to demand a valuation of the insured estate or interest. The policy provides that such a valuation be made by three arbitrators chosen thus: one by the company, one by the insured, and an umpire chosen by both. The valuation may be fixed by the agreement of any two.

No right of action accrues until 30 days after a notice of the action of the arbitrators shall have been served upon the company, and the insured shall have tendered a conveyance of the insured estate or interest to a purchaser to be named by the company at such valuation less encumbrances.

A right of appeal from any adverse determination is reserved to the company. Such an appeal is not allowed to operate as a delay in the payment of the loss if the insured provides the company satisfactory security for the repayment of the amount of such loss in the event that determination is ultimately in favor of the company.

Measuring Indemnity. In order to recover under a title contract, the insured must show that a loss has actually been sustained. When the insured is without title, the measure of damages under a title insurance contract would be, in the absence of any unusual circumstance, the purchase price. When title actually passes but a lien is subsequently discovered, the measure of damage is the cost of discharging the lien. When the defect is in the form of an encroachment, the measure of damage is the difference between the value of the property unencumbered and the value with the encumbrance.

The Term. The title insurance policy is personal and does not follow the property. It is usually perpetual, though sometimes the coverage is limited to 25 years. When the property insured is transferred, the insurance terminates, and, if the new owner desires coverage, a new policy is issued. Premiums are paid in a single payment at the time the policies are written, and no further payments are required during the term. Policies have been written containing a provision for a reduction in premium when reissued within five years from the date of the original insurance. This is not the usual practice, however.

Use of a Group Policy

A group title insurance policy is used for the convenience of large users of title policies. Life insurance companies and mortgage companies, for example, are issued a master policy with certificates indicating each risk to be covered. The convenience of such a form is recognized. It has a particular appeal to the mortgagee because he knows precisely the type of coverage he is securing on every risk; and there is no obligation on the part of the legal staff to scrutinize and examine a number of different forms, or even a number of different policies written on the same form, in which changes or modifications might be included in the course of their preparation.

The group form involves no difference in the underwriting procedure. It is simply the use of the master policy form with certificates that has found such general acceptance in other fields of insurance. The group form simply establishes that a uniform set of policy conditions applies to all the risks covered under the policy, and the individual certificates serve as evidence of insurance in the case of each particular risk.

BOILER AND MACHINERY INSURANCE

Nature

Insurance policies issued upon boilers, turbines, electrical machinery, and other similar objects provide coverage for two classes of losses: (1) direct loss and (2) indirect loss. A single policy may cover boilers, machinery, or both. Another name for boiler and machinery insurance is power plant insurance. Total premiums for 1962 were about $70 million.[12]

Direct loss provides indemnity in the following cases: (*a*) damage to insured's property whether to the insured object or to other property; (*b*) damage to the property of others for which the insured may be liable; (*c*) liability for loss of life and injury to employees when the coverage is not prevented by the compensation laws of the jurisdiction; (*d*) liability for loss of life and injury to persons who are members of the public—that is, not employees.

Indirect loss is covered as follows: (*a*) business interruption under a use and occupancy form; (*b*) indemnity for indirect losses caused by an accident when there is no business interruption under the

[12] *Best's Aggregates and Averages* (1963), *op. cit.*, pp. 144 and 212.

outage form; (*c*) consequential loss to perishable materials when caused by accident to the boiler or other object insured.

The Basic Contract

For a number of years a copyrighted standard boiler and machinery policy found wide acceptance. This policy has been replaced by standard provisions to the end that the policies of different companies need not be identical word for word even though the policies incorporate the standard provisions. The basic policy is used for all power plant insurance including, as well as direct damage coverages, the use and occupancy and the consequential loss forms.[13]

The basic policy is completed by attaching a number of schedules. Each schedule defines the "object" to be insured and defines "accident" with respect to that object. The policy states the insured to be covered against loss to an object caused by an accident as defined in the schedules.

The standard provisions allow for seven forms of coverage in the *insuring agreements*, though virtually all companies writing boiler and machinery insurance include only the first five of the following coverages in their printed general policy forms:

1. The *property damage* section provides insurance for damage to property of the insured. Damage to the insured object is covered as well as damage to other property owned by the insured.

2. The *expediting charges* section reimburses the insured for reasonable costs incurred in effecting the speediest possible replacement of the damaged property. These charges include expenses incurred in effecting temporary repairs or extra expense for overtime work or for rushing transportation of material by an agency more expensive than would ordinarily be used. The amount payable under the policy is limited to the amount for which the company would otherwise be liable as direct damage loss on the property, but with a limit for expediting charges usually of $1,000.

3. The *property damage liability* section defends the insured against claims and makes payment for liability for damage to the property of others caused by an insured accident.

4. The *bodily injury liability* section is optional but, if included, covers the insured against bodily injury to persons injured by an insured accident. The usual defense and settlement provisions are included as well as reimbursement for first-aid relief given at the time of the accident. Liability under any workmen's compensation law

[13]There is a special residence form and a form known as the "off-premises explosion form." The special form for small residences covers only explosion of boilers and water heaters and furnace gas explosion. The off-premises explosion form covers the insured against steam boiler explosion losses if the boiler is not owned or operated by him. The boiler may be located in another building or another part of the same building that the insured occupies.

is not covered, but there is no other exclusion with respect to liability to employees.

5. The *legal expenses* section covers the cost of defending liability claims as well as the usual defense costs of interest on unpaid judgments, premiums on attachment and appeal bonds, witness and attorney fees, and other defense costs. These costs do not reduce the amounts available for claim payments.

6. The *riot and malicious damage* section pays for an accident described in a schedule caused by strike, riot, civil commotion, or malicious mischief.

7. The *automatic coverage* section provides protection for newly acquired objects similar to those described in the schedules. It may be added by endorsement for a small additional premium. The clause requires written notice to the company within 90 days after the newly acquired object is put in operation. The coverage for the new object dates from the time of its operation, and the premium is computed accordingly. Coverage already in effect for similar objects applies with respect to the newly acquired object.

Boiler and machinery insurance is primarily a material damage coverage. Bodily injury liability is provided where there is no public liability or workmen's compensation coverage or where the coverage is deemed inadequate to cover damages in the event of a boiler accident. Bodily injury liability provided by the boiler and machinery policy is considered as excess and noncontributing insurance when there is other like insurance. It is effective and applicable only to that portion of the insured's loss that is in excess of valid and collectible indemnity required to be paid under a contract of other similar insurance.

The policy defines the term "one accident." By virtue of this definition the term is made to include all resultant or concomitant accidents, regardless of the number of objects involved as long as they are the outgrowth of a single general occurrence. The policy establishes a single limit per accident that applies to every such general occurrence during the policy term and applies whether or not more than one insured object is involved. If two or more objects are involved, the highest limit applying to any one of the objects governs. For example, if one accident involves both engine breakdown and boiler explosion, and the limit per accident for each object is $50,000, the insured would not have $100,000 protection but $50,000. Any general occurrence which involves one or several insured objects is considered one accident.

Direct Losses

Steam Boilers and Vessels. Coverage for steam boilers is written on the basic boiler and machinery contract and provides indemnity for loss or damage caused directly by the explosion, collapse, or rupture of the insured boilers or vessels.[14] An identifying schedule listing the objects[15] covered, the pressure approved by the company for each, the kind of boiler, the identifying numbers, and other essential data is made a part of the policy.

The boiler policy does not cover explosions in the fire box or tubes of the boiler unless the contract is endorsed to cover furnace explosion. Frequently, gases accumulate from unconsumed coal, and when the power is uneven or combustion is distributed by a windstorm or by other cause, serious fire box or smoke pipe explosions occur. Such explosions often cause serious damage to the insured object as well as to other property of the insured. Personal injury accidents frequently develop in connection with furnace explosions. Furnace explosion coverage is provided by an endorsement to the boiler contract. The endorsement covers up to the limits of the policy: (*a*) damage to the property of the insured, (*b*) the legal liability of the insured for damage to the property of others, and (*c*) the legal liability of the insured for bodily injury caused by furnace explosion.[16]

The boiler coverage excludes liability for loss or damage to property of the insured resulting from an explosion caused by the burning of the structure containing the boiler, or for loss or damage to the insured's property by fire resulting from any cause whatever.

---

[14]The boiler policy is not confined in its use to the insuring of steam boilers but may be used to provide insurance for numerous other vessels in industrial plants which are liable to explosions from internal pressure. Among the vessels upon which insurance is commonly written, and for which rates are provided, are air tanks, hot-water tanks, kettles, kiers, mangle rolls, matrix tables, purifiers, radiators, receivers, refrigerating systems, rolls on paper machines, rotary bleachers, separators, steam drums, steam pipelines, separately fired superheaters, and water heaters.

[15]In connection with boiler insurance it is customary to apply the term "object" when reference is made to the vessel covered. The word "object" is then to be interpreted in accordance with the manual definitions for the specific types. Thus, a boiler is an object, but reference to the manual indicates that with respect to a boiler the term "object" includes the boiler as described and its water columns, steam and water gauges, safety valves, water walls, water screens and water grates, any superheater wholly or partly within the setting of the boiler, any steam economizer not possible of operation with any other boiler, interconnecting pipes and fittings, feed pipe, steam pipe, return pipe, and blowoff pipe to and including the nearest valve in each such pipe. The term also includes that part of any apparatus under pressure of steam or water which is within the furnace of the boiler, even though not directly in the boiler circulation.

[16]The protection furnished under the explosion endorsement and that provided by an explosion policy or an extended cover endorsement to a fire policy providing explosion coverage is sometimes confused. The explosion contract and the extended cover contract cover material damage to the property of the insured described in the policy form. The furnace explosion endorsement attached to the boiler policy covers not only the property of the insured but the insured's legal liability for injury to the property of others as well as bodily injury to others. On the other hand, the explosion contract is broader than the furnace-explosion endorsement in that the explosion losses that it covers extend to furnace explosion from any cause with the exception of steam explosions covered under the boiler and machinery contract.

The liability coverage, however, will protect the insured in the event that he is legally liable for damage to property of others as a result of an explosion caused by fire or as a result of a fire caused by an accident covered by the policy. It follows, therefore, that a boiler policy may cover a loss for which the insured is liable without having any liability for loss to the property of the insured. Fire damage to the property of the insured is covered by the fire policy insuring the property. The policy also excludes liability for loss or damage from the explosion[17] of a boiler while any safety valve limiting the pressure in it is, with the insured's knowledge and consent, removed, rendered inoperative, or set to blow off at a pressure in excess of that approved for it by the company as stated in the policy schedule. Finally, the policy excludes loss from stoppage of the plant or from any other indirect result of an explosion. Indirect loss may be covered under special forms.

Boiler piping is an optional coverage in connection with steam boiler insurance. Unless the policy provides this protection, for which a premium is charged, the insured may find himself faced with a serious explosion loss without any insurance protection. This is so because the same high pressure which may cause a boiler explosion is transmitted to the pipelines. High-pressure pipes frequently pass through parts of a plant where substantial numbers of persons are working and where members of the public may be admitted. In addition, large values in the way of inventories may be exposed to steam or water losses, and injuries to delicate machines could run loss figures into very large amounts. Hence, the failure of steampiping because of an explosion may result in serious damage to merchandise, raw materials, products in process of being manufactured, valuable machinery, and equipment and—of greatest importance—may be the cause of serious personal injury. A high-pressure boiler covered without including steampiping is a boiler only half insured.

Engines. Coverage may be written to insure engines that derive their power from steam, oil, or gas. Pumps, compressors, and refrigerating machines are objects insurable under the form. The policy covers damage caused by sudden and accidental breaking, deforming, burning out, or rupturing of the insured machine or any of its

[17]The boiler policy defines an explosion or rupture as a sudden substantial tearing asunder of the boiler, caused solely by steam pressure, or by the internal pressure of air, gas, or liquid if the boiler is described in the schedule as containing it. "Collapse" is defined as a sudden crushing or forcing inward of the furnace or the flues of the boiler resulting in a rupture thereof caused solely by pressure of its contents. Boiler insurance may be written to provide limited or broad coverage. Limited coverage provides insurance against explosion caused by internal pressure. Broad coverage includes losses caused by accidental burning, bulging, cracking, or collapse of the boiler. Damage caused by dry firing, low-water conditions, and the like are covered under the broad form. Limited coverage is primarily a catastrophe form. Cracking of sections in the case of cast-iron sectional boilers is covered under the broad form.

parts. The damage must manifest itself at the time of the accident by immediately preventing continued operation of the object insured or by immediately impairing its functions.[18]

Flywheels may be separately insured. Flywheel insurance may be written on many other types of revolving machinery, such as pulleys, shaft wheels, gear wheels, fans, blowers, centrifugal dryers, separators, and other rotating objects. The definition of "accident" in engine policies is drawn broad enough to include every form of breakdown. When the engine is insured, all wheels mounted on it are covered. The same types of protection are provided under the engine policy as are afforded under the boiler policy.

Electrical Machinery. Insurance, following the coverage afforded by the engine breakdown policy, is provided under the electrical machinery form to provide protection against losses from breakdown. The term "breakdown" is defined as "the sudden, substantial, and accidental breaking or burning of the machine, or any part thereof, while in use or installed and connected ready for use, which immediately stops the functions of the machine, and which necessitates repair or replacement before its functions can be restored."

Motors, generators, and exciters are insurable as are power and distribution transformers. Miscellaneous electrical apparatus that may be covered includes such objects as switchboards, oil switches or circuit breakers, and units of electrical control and starting for motors.

Turbines. The protection afforded under the turbine[19] policy is essentially the same as that provided in the other power plant policies. Direct and consequential loss to property may be covered, as well as liability for personal injury. Four kinds of coverage are written, each furnishing a different degree of protection:

---

[18]The principal hazard in the operation of a steam engine is the flywheel. It frequently happens that a wheel breaks while in operation. Sometimes a rapidly moving wheel disintegrates with such force that the break is referred to as a "flywheel explosion." The damage caused by such a break is often terrific. The breaking of such a wheel can entirely wreck plant, machinery, or neighboring property, and cause injury and loss of life.

Engine losses, however, are not limited to flywheels. Cylinders explode, hurling fragments with terrific force. Moving parts become crystallized from "fatigue" and give way. Improper lubrication, loosened parts not promptly discovered, or other causes may result in some part of the engine giving way. Because of the force involved, a comparatively slight break of a part may start a chain of events that will end in complete destruction of the plant.

[19]A turbine is a rotary engine which converts the energy of supplied water or steam into mechanical or electrical energy. A delicately balanced rotor enclosed in a heavy outer casing turns upon the impact of the steam or water. The centrifugal force so generated is capable of terrific destruction both to the machine itself and to surrounding property and life. Large units, such as are used for generating power by public utility companies, not infrequently cost millions of dollars. Parts are so heavy that to move them to effect repairs frequently involves large expenditures.

1. *Breakdown insurance* is the most complete form of insurance obtainable on a turbine since it covers all the major hazards, including all types of explosions, the burning out, short-circuiting, or breakdown of electrical equipment, as well as accidents to the rotor, such as the stripping of the blades or other breakdown.
2. *Explosion insurance* is designed to protect the insured from catastrophe losses. Accidents involving the breaking or rupturing of the shaft or rotor and explosions due to steam pressure are covered. An explosion is defined as the "sudden and substantial tearing asunder as a result of the pressure of steam of those parts of the turbine subject to steam pressure; or the sudden and substantial bursting or disruption of the rotor, while revolving, into two or more parts." Losses caused by breaking, cracking, stripping, or loosening of gears or couplings or of movable or stationary blades are not covered. Likewise, the policy does not cover losses caused by short-circuiting, burning, breaking, or loosening of electrical conductors.
3. *Limited breakdown* provides the broad breakdown coverage with the exception that electrical burn-outs on the generator rotor are excluded from coverage.
4. *Combined coverage* provides a combination of turbine explosion and generator breakdown. The steam end of the equipment is provided with explosion coverage only, while full breakdown insurance is provided for the generator and exciter.

Indirect Losses

There are four forms of boiler and machinery insurance covering indirect damage. These are (*a*) consequential loss, (*b*) use and occupancy, (*c*) outage, and (*d*) power interruption. The first three of these forms cover indirect loss caused by accident covered under the policy on the premises of the insured. Power interruption covers the insured for loss of power from a source off the premises.

Consequential Loss. This form is designed to protect the insured against spoilage due to interruption of heat, burn-out of motors, interruption of power, or failure of refrigeration caused by an accident to the insured object. In certain types of risk the consequential loss may far exceed the direct damage caused by an accident.[20] Losses of this character, which are consequences of an accident to the object insured but not directly caused by it, are not covered under the property damage policy contract unless an additional premium is

[20] A small motor furnishing power to a pasteurizer in a dairy might burn out with but a small loss to the motor. However, even a few minutes' shutdown at a certain point in the process of pasteurizing a batch of cream might result in a loss of many hundreds of dollars. A boiler out of commission in a greenhouse, or the refrigerating system in a cold-storage plant, may run a consequential loss to thousands of dollars while the direct damage loss is negligible.

paid and the consequential loss endorsement is attached to the policy. Risks where there is a danger of spoilage to perishable goods caused by an accident to boiler or machinery require consequential damage protection.[21]

Use and Occupancy. Use and occupancy insurance is written as a separate policy covering any of the objects insured under power plant forms or may be added to the direct damage policies by endorsement. In principle the coverage is the same as other business interruption forms having as its purpose the payment of continuing fixed charges and indemnification for loss of profits due to shutdown as a result of accident.

The significance of use and occupancy insurance of power plants should be considered. The violence that attends explosions sometimes leads to an undue emphasis upon direct damage and liability coverages with the neglect of the potential losses that may flow from business interruption. The heart of an industrial plant is its power equipment. Apartments, hotels, public utilities, theaters, and other business establishments are all dependent for income upon the operation of their heating and power plants. While a boiler explosion can cause direct damage losses running to many thousands of dollars, the loss may be multiplied many times if business interruption is not included in the protection.

Outage. This coverage provides for the payment of an agreed amount for the period an insured object is out of use. Interruption of business is not a factor. It differs from use and occupancy which provides indemnity only for loss caused by the interruption of business. There are cases in which an accident to a boiler, power machine, or other object insured would not actually cause an interruption of business, but the accident would nevertheless cause increased operating expenses during the period the insured object is out of commission.

Outage insurance provides for the payment of an hourly indemnity for each working hour that the insured object has been incapacitated because of an accident of the kind insured against for direct damage. The insurance is written by attaching an outage endorsement to the direct damage policy and specifies the amount to be paid for each hour of total outage, as well as the company's limit per accident for each object so covered. The coverage is particularly adapted to schools, apartment buildings, office buildings, drawbridges, public-utility plants, conveyors, looms, cranes, dredges,

---

[21] Contact of refrigerants with food products may result in spoilage. Such contamination damage is sometimes held to be a consequential loss. This may grow out of the fact that refrigeration losses due to power interruption caused by fires are consequential losses. With respect to power plant insurance, contamination damage is a direct loss and not a consequential loss.

shovels, and the like. An accident to the insured object may bring about no cessation or interruption of business, yet it may cause substantial increased costs to handling the business while the insured object is inoperative.

Power Interruption. An accident in a power plant causing loss to a user of the power through the interruption of the service is not covered by the electrical machinery policy. Insurance providing indemnity against loss arising from the total or partial deprivation of usable service furnished by a public utility, when such deprivation is caused by an accidental occurrence to the physical equipment of a public-service system, is provided by the power interruption form. The policy may be written to cover the service of electricity, steam, water, gas, or refrigeration. Two forms of coverage are available: (*a*) hourly indemnity for loss of use and (*b*) property loss due to spoilage. Indemnity for loss of use is paid for the period power is interrupted without regard to the establishment of an actual loss. Indemnity for spoilage is paid on the basis of the actual loss sustained. Business interruption is not a factor to the establishment of a claim under either form.

GLASS INSURANCE

The uses of glass for light, display, and ornamentation have reached such an extent that the investment in the glass used in a structure or in connection with the operation of a business represents the outlay of large sums. The growing use of large plates tends to concentrate substantial values; and glass is peculiarly subject to breakage. The glass insurance field, though small in relation to the whole property and liability insurance business of $16.5 billion, did account for $42 million of premiums in 1962.[22]

Glass set in show windows is particularly susceptible to breakage. Crowds, riots, strikes, runaway automobiles, rocks hurled by passing cars, accidental or deliberate breakage by intoxicated or insane people, window dressing, falling awnings, and the like are some of the factors that contribute to the risk. Other perils to which this and other glass are subject include breakage caused by burglars, defective settings, explosions, sudden temperature changes, hail, snow, ice, windstorms, sudden jar of building, settling of building, and falling articles.

Basic Coverages

The *Comprehensive Glass Policy* provides a coverage that is an all-risks contract, with very few exceptions. It undertakes to pay the insured for all damages to glass, lettering, and ornamentation

[22]*Best's Aggregates and Averages (1963), op. cit.*, pp. 143 and 211.

insured by the policy due to breakage of the glass or by chemicals. The policy also provides coverage for losses that may be incident to glass damage. The coverages as provided are: (*a*) broken glass, (*b*) damage by acids or chemicals, (*c*) damage to frames and bars, (*d*) installation of temporary plates, and (*e*) removal of obstructions. There are only three exclusions: (*a*) fire, (*b*) war including invasion, civil war, insurrection, rebellion, or revolution, and (*c*) nuclear energy.

Broken Glass. The policy provides that the company will replace broken glass, described in the schedule, and any lettering or ornamentation insured under the policy. The replacement service, in a rapid and efficient manner, is one of the prime benefits of glass insurance for many policyholders. Glass broken by windstorm, expansion cracks, flying substances, settling of a building, earthquake, or other accident is covered by the policy. Protection is afforded for deliberate breaks such as those prompted by malice, vandalism, or racketeers. As an alternative to replacing the glass the company may pay for the replacement in cash. When a replacement of a broken plate is made, the policy automatically covers the new plate and no additional premium is required.

Frames. The cost, not to exceed $75, of repairing or replacing window sashes immediately in casings and contiguous to the insured glass is covered if the repairing or replacing is made necessary by damage to or breakage of the insured glass. Cost is limited to replacement with sashes of like material.

Temporary Plates. Coverage is provided for the cost of boarding up or installing temporary plates in openings in which any broken insured glass or glass damage by chemicals is located. Here, again, the limitation is $75, and it is the requirement of the policy that the boarding up or the temporary installation is made necessary by unavoidable delay in replacing any broken glass insured under the policy.

Obstructions. If it becomes necessary to remove or replace fixtures or any other obstruction, in order to replace the broken or damaged glass, the cost of such removal is covered by the policy. The limitation here again is $75. The policy does not cover the cost of the removal of show window displays.

Other Contract Features

The $75 limit in any of the insuring agreements may be increased for the payment of an additional premium in a situation where it appears that $75 will not cover the cost. Unless otherwise described in the schedule, each plate insured is covered as plain plate, flat glass set in frames, and adjustment is made accordingly. Liability of the company is limited to the actual cost of the glass, including its replacement, at the time of the breakage. If lettering or ornamentation is insured, the company is liable for the cost of replacement at the time of the breakage. In no case, however, does the liability of the company exceed the amount of insurance stated in the schedule.

Glass insurance is not limited to the protection of plate glass. The Comprehensive Glass Policy may cover ordinary window glass or many special types of glass. Policies may be written to cover structural glass, such as glass bricks, and blocks, Flexglass, Carara, Opalite, Vitrolite, and other like building glass. Since the Comprehensive Glass Policy covers only breakage and chemical damage, a broader form is sometimes preferred. Stained glass set in leaded sections, such as the glass used in church and memorial windows, may be covered under an all-risks contract. This form excludes only wear and tear, deterioration, and war risks. Marring, scarring, scratches, theft, breakage, or injury caused by fire would be covered under the all-risks contract; scratching, defacement, and disfigurement are not covered under the glass comprehensive policy unless caused by breakage or chemical damage.

Halftone screens and lenses, as well as rotogravure screens, may be insured against all risks. Neon and glass signs are insurable under a Comprehensive Glass Policy, and the coverage may be extended to all risks by endorsement. Such signs are written on either a deductible or full-cover basis. The deductible varies from $10 to $100 for each insured object with a corresponding reduction in premium as the deductible increases.

The policy does not make the filing of a formal proof of loss within a stipulated period of time a condition precedent to recovery, but the company may require the insured to file such a proof under oath on forms provided for the purpose. In the event of loss, immediate written notice must be given either to the company at its home office or to its authorized agent. The policyholder is further required to make all reasonable efforts to preserve the glass and prevent further loss or damage.[22]

SUMMARY

Aircraft insurance is one of the important miscellaneous kinds of property and liability insurance. It is a specialized field, combining many of the characteristics of marine, automobile, and liability insurance. The basic contracts include a hull policy, on the air-

---

[22]Immediate notice affords the company an opportunity for investigation as soon after the accident as possible. Such an investigation is carried on with a view to fixing responsibility for the loss and collecting damages if possible. The requirement obligating the insured to prevent further loss after a break is designed to preserve as much of the glass in the form of salvage as is possible. Sometimes a short crack may be stopped by a glazier, leaving a big salvage in the pane. If left without attention, the crack might run across the pane and cause considerably greater damage.

craft itself, public and property damage liability, admitted liability and medical payments. The large amounts of protection needed in aircraft insurance contracts has led to the use of many deductible and participation arrangements, as well as companies (and their representatives) that specialize in this highly competitive and rapidly growing field of insurance.

Credit insurance protects policyholders, most of whom are wholesalers, against the abnormal credit losses caused by insolvency of their customers. Its unusual features include reliance upon credit ratings by other financial institutions, coinsurance participation in all losses by the policyholder, and strict cancellation provisions.

Title insurance covers the insured for losses arising out of undiscovered past defects of title to real property. It is extremely important in some areas of the United States, but very unusual in other parts of the country. Perpetual contracts with a single premium at the beginning of the policy are written for property owners and mortgagees.

Boiler and machinery insurance is a combination of property and liability insurance. Direct losses to the following kinds of objects, and liability for damages or personal injury resulting from their use, are written: steam boilers, engines, electrical machinery, and turbines. Indirect losses which may be written in connection with the basic contract are consequential loss, use and occupancy, outage and power interruption.

Glass insurance is used by policyholders with large exposures of plate glass and other special kinds of glass. It uses an all-risks contract with very few exceptions, and provides valuable replacement service to the insured.

FOR REVIEW

1. Contrast the use of "deductibles," "participations," and "coinsurance" in aircraft insurance.
2. What forms of aircraft insurance are written to protect the aircraft owner (*a*) against damage to his own aircraft? (*b*) From liability for damages and injuries to other persons or their property?
3. The X Air Lines is the owner of a plane that crashed into a dwelling and killed the inhabitants. The officers of the airlines contend that there was no negligence, that the accident was unavoidable, and that every reasonable and possible precaution to avoid accident had been taken. In the absence of negligence, they contend there is no liability on their part for damages. Assuming that it can be shown that there was no negligence, does it follow that the X Air Lines is free from liability?
4. Is there a standard aircraft insurance contract?
5. X carries a public liability policy on each of his automobiles and on a privately owned and operated airplane. What important differences are found in the aviation policy with respect to claims for personal injury that are not found in the automobile policy?

6. In the month of February, 1937, an airliner flying from Washington to Cleveland ran into bumpy air near Harpers Ferry, Virginia. On one bump the ship dropped approximately 300 feet. Two of the passengers were thrown from their seats, striking the roof so violently that they had to be taken from the plane and sent to a hospital. Suits were filed, and damages in the amount of $200,000 were demanded from the airline. It was contended by claimants that the pilot should have warned passengers to fasten their safety belts. The airline based its defense upon the contention that, since bumps often come wtihout warning, the accident was unavoidable. What is you opinion as to the liability of the airline?
7. It is stated that the owners of Chicago's Merchandise Mart paid $2,500,000 to Chicago & North Western Railroads in order to straddle the railroad yards with its building. The right of the owner of real estate to control of air above his property has from ancient times been regarded as a principle of property ownership. X wishes to prevent aircraft from flying over his property. May he do this? May he claim damages if objects are dropped?
8. The B company owns an airplane valued at $10,000, insured under a crash form with a 10 percent deductible clause. The plane is damaged in the amount of $3,000. The insured contends the company's liability to be $2,700, but the adjuster contends it to be $2,000. Who is right? Explain.
9. Aviation insurers contend that they should have a wide flexibility in quoting rates and that their rates should be exempt from departmental rate approval required of most other forms of insurance under state regulatory procedure. In your opinion have aviation underwriters a case?
10. Explain (*a*) the loss-prevention facilities and (*b*) the service of collection furnished by credit insurance.
11. Explain the meaning of credit ratings used as a basis for determining coverage under a Credit Insurance Policy.
12. Fire, flood, windstorm, drought, crop failure, or other local catastrophes may unfavorably affect the ability of a debtor to meet his obligations. Will credit insurance prevent loss from these sources?
13. What is meant by the statement that "credit insurance is *excess insurance*"?
14. Credit insurance is said to be (*a*) "a guarantee of working capital," and (*b*) "an endorsement of the customer's promise to pay." Explain each of these statements.
15. How does the doctrine of insurable interest apply in the case of title insurance? Give several examples.
16. B purchases a piece of property and is told by his attorney that he need have no concern with title difficulties because a Title Insurance Policy has been secured. May the insured be satisfied that the Title Insurance Policy affords him full protection against all claims growing out of a defective title?
17. For what, and to what extent, is the insurer liable under a Title Insurance Policy?
18. In comparison with many other insurance contracts, what unusual features does a title insurance contract have? Explain three such features briefly.
19. Failure of the brine cooler in the refrigerating system at a southwestern poultry and egg plant endangers over 300 employees. One was killed, eight were injured, and the property loss was in excess of $100,000. Under what kinds of insurance are these losses insurable?
20. It is sometimes said that the inspection feature afforded with a Boiler and Machinery (Power Plant) Policy is of greater value than the insurance feature. Explain.

21. Compare the protection afforded by furnace explosion insurance and that afforded by the Extended Coverage Endorsement of the fire insurance contract.
22. What is the peril insured against by power interruption insurance? Does it cover power interruption attributable to equipment owned or operated by the insured? Explain.
23. What insuring agreements are important in providing coverage under the usual Boiler and Machinery Insurance Policy?
24. What is meant by the statement that "the bodily injury liability coverage of the boiler and machinery contract is excess insurance"?
25. When should a business firm purchase glass insurance? When should it not purchase such insurance?
26. The Comprehensive Glass Policy is an "all-risks" contract. Explain why the following losses would or would not be covered:
    a) Fire in adjoining premises causes the glass to crack.
    b) Scratching of the surface of the glass with some hard object, such as a diamond ring.
    c) Several plates of glass broken during a strike at the insured's property.
    d) Chemicals thrown on the glass ruin the surface of the glass.
27. There are several $75 limits in the Glass Insurance Policy that provide for damage in addition to breakage or other damage to the glass. Explain these limits.
28. What options does the insurance company insuring glass have with respect to loss adjustment, contrary to the practice in most other forms of property damage insurance? Which option is customarily elected, and why?

Chapter 19

MULTIPLE-LINE AND ALL-LINES INSURANCE

ONE of the most dynamic developments in insurance during the past decade has been a trend toward combination of insurance coverages that have been treated for many years as separate and distinct parts of the insurance business. In this final chapter of Part Four, two examples of this trend are discussed.

The first example, *multiple-line insurance,* which combines many of the kinds of property and liability insurance analyzed in Chapters 9–18, is an accomplished fact in numerous companies and contracts today. Chapter 19 includes a concise but reasonably complete description of its nature, significance, purposes, development, and contracts. Since multiple-line insurance is a merging of types of insurance already separately presented in Part Four of this text, unnecessary duplication of the coverage details is avoided.

All-lines insurance, the second example, is a much newer and less complete part of the general trend. Because it involves the combination of *life and health* insurance (discussed in Part Five) with *property* and *liability* protection, only a brief section at the end of this chapter concerns its beginning evidence and potential future development.

MULTIPLE-LINE INSURANCE CHARACTERISTICS

Nature

Multiple-line insurance is the combination of the traditional "lines," or basic types of coverages, known as *fire* and *casualty* insurance.[1] The most common illustration of multiple-line insurance

[1]One might be tempted here to replace the term "fire and casualty" with "property and liability." Historically, under the legal definition by which the states have separated the fields of insurance, the term "fire and casualty" is necessary in describing the origin of multiple-line insurance. However, in theory, *property* insurance is properly contrasted with *liability* insurance as the two fundamental parts of multiple-line (nonlife) insurance. This is the more accepted use of the term today. Property insurance may also generically describe all perils affecting property assets, including fire, theft, and liability losses. *Casualty* insurance creates such difficulties of logical definition as almost to defy its use, but the term has long-standing legal and business acceptance as including the fields of liability, theft, workmen's compensation, automobile, health, surety, title, and a wide variety of miscellaneous coverages. (See earlier discussion in Chapter 2.)

combines fire perils with liability (and/or theft) protection. Individually these basic perils would be mono-line in character; in combination they become multiple-line insurance.

It is necessary in discussing multiple-line insurance to recognize that the term includes many parts. For example, one might refer to, or study separately, such facets as multiple-line insurance *contracts* or multiple-line insurance *companies.* Examples of the difficulties which may result from improper definitions are numerous. A multiple-line insurance company, doing business in both fire and casualty insurance fields, sometimes does not issue multiple-line insurance contracts in which these perils are merged in a single contract.

Other subdivisions of the topic of multiple-line insurance include multiple-line insurance company *groups,* portions of the company organization known as multiple-line insurance *departments,* multiple-line insurance *agents,* and so on. A multiple-line insurance company group involves fire and casualty companies combined by common ownership, management, or reinsurance arrangement. It may have a substantially different history, legal organization, and operations than a multiple-line insurance company which involves only a single company or corporate identity writing both fire and casualty lines of insurance.

For example, many company groups or "fleets" are operated, even today, as closely affiliated enterprises, with the same company officers for several of the individual companies within the group. Other company groups are loosely related, and the separate insurers may have complete autonomy within their activities, and substantially different personnel and practices. However, a multiple-line company by definition must be a single insurer.

Furthermore, basic functions of insurance company activities may be separately defined and discussed under such terms as multiple-line *sales,* multiple-line *underwriting,* multiple-line *rating,* and multiple-line *claims adjustment.*

It is difficult to review in one chapter the entire field of insurance from a multiple-line viewpoint. It becomes necessary to emphasize only portions of what collectively is known as the multiple-line insurance trend. Trends can be seen only in the study of the past. The value of identifying trends lies in the changes that are indicated for the future. In essence, the need is for observing the past in order to learn what the present suggests about the future.

Development

The multiple-line trend has not been a rapid nor a consistent change. Viewed in the perspective of history, the trend appears as a long series of changes, including complete reversal of the trend at some points. The major impetus since the 1930's to multiple-line insurance, however, has been a relatively fast and continuous movement.

Foreign experience of insurance companies with broad charters suggested that early American insurance companies might have adopted similar multiple-line operations. However, mono-line insurance companies were accepted almost from the beginning of American insurance. For whatever reasons of limited capital or special interest in restricted areas of insurance, almost all American insurance companies through the nineteenth century did business within restricted lines of fire, marine, or other specialized areas.

Voluntary acceptance of what became known as the "American system" of mono-line insurance was encouraged and required by insurance department regulations and laws of the states throughout the century. One of the basic reasons for the compartmentization of insurance became, then, restrictive legislation. The states apparently concluded that it was easier and better to regulate insurance by licensing and limiting insurers to do business only in specific categories of insurance.

The first real adoption of the multiple-line principle began in the early 1900's with legislation in some states which permitted fire and marine companies to combine, and then later allowed fire companies to have casualty subsidiaries and casualty companies to own fire companies. The success of the company group or "fleet" operations and the need for broader insurance coverages for automobiles, airplanes, and other valuable movable properties pointed toward an immediate and rapid movement toward multiple-line operations. The trend slowed, however, with the various inland marine agreements in the 1930's which restricted the expanding powers of marine insurance companies. These agreements encouraged many companies to continue mono-line practices in specified types of insurance.

The modern multiple-line trend began with a resurgence of the company groups that wrote both fire and casualty protection in separate but closely related companies. The advantages of broader insurance powers were recognized in the Diemand Committee Report to the National Association of Insurance Commissioners in 1944. In the next five years the states began to permit limited or partial multiple-line operations by passing "partial multiple-line laws." One company could then write both property and liability protection for specified items such as automobiles, aircraft, specified types of personal property, reinsurance, and insurance outside the United States.

Thereafter followed "full multiple-line laws" which gave a single insurance company the legal power to write all forms of fire and casualty insurance. In effect, this legislation broke the legal barriers which had existed between fire and casualty insurance for a century or more. As long as the insurance company met the capital and surplus requirements for the various lines, it could be licensed to write all types of insurance protection except life insurance. A number of years were necessary before all states permitted full multiple-line insurance. The major landmark in this development was the passage by New York State in 1949 of such full multiple-line insurance legislation. By 1955 all states permitted, by specific legislation or departmental rulings, full multiple-line insurance operations in the United States.

The capital and surplus requirements for formation of a multiple-line insurance company vary among the states from $100,000 to over $3,500,000. It is not to be implied that all fire and casualty insurance companies today operate on a multiple-line basis. Insurance organizations doing business only within a single major line of insurance still exist. Most of the larger fire and casualty insurance companies today, however, operate as multiple-line organizations. Practically none of the major insurance companies today restricts its writings to one line.

The legal changes which occurred to create multiple-line companies were of two types. Almost all of the multiple-line insurers began as single-line insurance companies, and broadened their licensing powers and insurance activities to include other lines of protection. Charter amendments permitting the broadened activities, and mergers of fire and casualty insurance companies, were the two major techniques of change to multiple-line insurance companies. Since 1949 these changes have been the most obvious legal indication of the widespread progress of the multiple-insurance trend.

Significance

Multiple-line insurance extends the concept of product diversification to insurance. Just as manufacturers have discovered that it is often better to produce several related products instead of to rely only on one, so insurers now sell protection against both fire and casualty perils. The technique is

> . . . hailed enthusiastically as the technique by which insurance can achieve modern economies and efficiency. It is also berated, just as vehemently, as the cause of many of today's major insurance problems, from changes in policy forms and rating to such dilemmas as how to obtain adequate capital, maintain uniform statistics, train new personnel and revise company organizations.[2]

The increasing scope of the literature pertaining to multiple-line insurance is also evidence of its major significance during the past

[2] David L. Bickelhaupt, *Transition to Multiple-Line Insurance Companies* (Homewood, Ill.: Richard D. Irwin, Inc., 1961), p. 3.

decade. Revision of ideas, operations, articles, textbooks, and insurance courses all attest to the widespread effects of multiple-line insurance.

One of the clearest indications of the place and growth of multiple-line insurance is its sales figures. Proper comparison is difficult until after 1955, the lack of consistent definitions making precise data almost unobtainable. The following table shows the growth of multiple-peril contracts since 1955.

TABLE 19–1

MULTIPLE-PERIL CONTRACTS, 1955–62
(In Millions of Dollars of Premiums Written)

Year	*Homeowner's Contracts*	*Commercial Multiple-Peril Contracts*	*Total Multiple-Peril Contracts*
1955	68.1	*	68.1*
1956	178.9	17.7	196.6
1957	240.7	28.5	269.2
1958	344.7	29.4	374.1
1959	522.6	37.9	560.5
1960	763.7	55.6	819.3
1961	883.9	81.7	965.6
1962	1,039.1	157.8	1,196.9

*Commercial multiple-peril figures not available for 1955.

SOURCE: *Best's Aggregates and Averages* (New York: Alfred M. Best, Inc., 1963), pp. 141 and 209. Included are 771 stock and mutual insurers writing homeowner's contracts and 572 writing commercial multiple-peril contracts.

Thus, Table 19–1 shows the amazing growth record of homeowner's and commercial multiple-peril contracts. In seven years the annual sales have increased from less than $100 million to $1.2 *billion,* or more than a twelve-fold increase! Commercial multiple-line policies, which had a later start, almost tripled between 1960 and 1962. About 7 percent of all nonlife insurance sales were multiple-line contracts by 1963.

Multiple-line insurance company *groups* have grown steadily since the 1940's. Over 150 stock and mutual company groups, including more than 430 separate insurers, were in business at the end of 1962.[3] These groups wrote two thirds of the total fire and casualty insurance premiums of $16.5 billion.

Insurers classified as multiple-line insurance *companies* (single corporate identities writing both fire and casualty insurance) wrote $7.4 billion,[4] or nearly one half, of the above total 1962 premiums.

[3]*Best's Aggregates and Averages* (New York: Alfred M. Best, Inc., 1963), pp. 1–15.

[4]*Ibid.,* pp. 42 and 148. Stock and mutual companies so classified numbered 172.

Purposes

The amazing growth of multiple-line insurance is explained by its purposes or objectives. The motives for the changes are the advantages which are anticipated. If the goals are successfully achieved, they are the advantages of the multiple-line technique. Detailed purposes may vary considerably according to the viewpoint of the party involved, but a study of the fundamental objectives is valuable in understanding why multiple-line insurance has appeared.

From the viewpoint of the *policyholders*, the advantages of multiple-line contracts are conveniently summarized as improvements in (1) coverage, (2) cost, and (3) convenience. In effect, the results are better protection and service at lower costs, and a reduced number of contracts, companies, agents, and premiums for the insured. Cost economies are naturally uppermost in the minds of most policyholders, and these may be substantial. Oftentimes, the combination of coverages in a single multiple-line contract may bring savings exceeding 10 percent (and it may be as much as 30 or 40 percent), as compared with the cost of protection in several separate property and liability contracts. The prime advantage of better coverage and service under a multiple-line contract should not be forgotten, however. Fewer gaps in the protection, such as leaving out theft insurance when the insured chooses among several individual policies covering separate perils, usually results. Also, overlapping coverages or overinsurance which may occur under separate policies are avoided through less confusion in regard to which policy covers which peril.

In many ways the objectives of *companies* entering into multiple-line operations are also those of the policyholder, although further goals may be reasons for interest by the companies. Fundamental to all of the company motives is the general impact which multiple-line operations should have in diversifying the company's business. The "spread of loss principle" which is basic to all insurance is observed in the effects which the acceptance of many kinds of perils have on a company's operations. For example, the averaging of fire losses with liability losses over a period of time should result in greater stability of operating results, and thus financial strength, for a company. A bad year of fire losses may be offset by some profits from theft, liability, or other kinds of insurance.

In addition to stability of earnings and profits, the multiple-line company may have increased profits, power, and prestige as objectives. If multiple-line contracts increase total sales and lower costs through having fewer and larger-size average contracts, then a multiple-line company may obtain greater influence, industry position, and prestige as an insurer. The benefits to policyholders in the above paragraph also redound to the success of the insurer, for satisfied insureds are of great importance in continuing growth of insurance companies.

Possible disadvantages that may accompany the purposes of multiple-line insurance should be mentioned. The policyholder usually does not have quite the freedom of choice which he formerly had in separate contracts. Certain minimum coverages must be included in most multiple-line contracts, and the insured may not delete them. Thus he may be paying for a few types of protection he does not wish to have. The same idea applies to the insurer—he may be accepting a good fire insurance policyholder at the expense of including some questionable burglary or liability business. Another basic problem is the general difficulty of readjusting to change, including the effort, time and costs which change requires. Another example is the uncertainty that arises from new contract wording, the precise meaning of which often takes a number of years of legal interpretation to determine. A final problem is the unwarranted assumption that these broader multiple-line provide automatic and complete coverage for *all* losses. They do not, and cannot, and a false sense of security may be created from undue reliance upon them to accomplish the impossible.

MULTIPLE-LINE INSURANCE CONTRACTS

Multiple-line insurance contracts of many kinds in existence today are obvious examples of the recent rapid progress of the multiple-line trend. The multiple-line insurance contracts of tomorrow undoubtedly will illustrate continuing changes which stress the fact that the multiple-line trend is far from complete. The summary here of multiple-line insurance contracts can only include some of the major multiple-line coverages. For accuracy in detail and timeliness the reader must supplement the concluding portions of this chapter with reference to the bureau and company forms, manuals, and rules applicable under the laws of his own state.[5]

It is important to understand that a number of concurrent and related trends exist. Terminology once again becomes significant in clarifying discussion in this section on multiple-line insurance contracts. Caution must be exercised in using terms which may be

[5]For up-to-date specific information on multiple-line contracts, the reader should consult such loose-leaf, continuing reference services as the *Fire, Casualty and Surety Bulletins* (Cincinnati, Ohio: The National Underwriter Company), the *General Insurance Guide* (Greenlawn, L.I., New York: Werbel Publishing Company), or the *Policy, Form and Manual Analysis Service* (Indianapolis: The Rough Notes Company, Inc.).

confused with the expression "multiple-line." For example, one might discuss *multiple-peril*[6] insurance contracts, but multiple-peril contracts are not necessarily *multiple-line* insurance policies. The two perils combined may be all within one insurance line, such as fire. The Extended Coverage Endorsement is multiple-peril but not multiple-line in nature because it includes only fire and allied lines of insurance. Similarly, the Storekeepers' Burglary and Robbery Policy combines several perils in one contract, but since all are casualty coverages it is not a multiple-line policy. A multiple-line insurance contract is always multiple-peril, but a multiple-peril contract is not multiple-line unless it combines perils from both fire and casualty fields.

Package policies are also easily confused with multiple-line insurance contracts. The technique of including a number of separate perils in one broad package contract is an important, but distinctive, part of the development of multiple-line insurance policies. In package contracts the policyholder must accept substantially all of the perils combined in the package; multiple-line contracts merely involve combining fire and casualty perils, which may be done either by "packaging" (all or none choice by the insured) or "scheduling" (permitting choices as to the coverages included). Most modern package policy contracts are also multiple-line in nature, but the differentiation is necessary in the proper use of these terms.

Similarly, the terms *all-risk* and *comprehensive* may also cause confusion if not properly used. Both of these terms include the attribute of broader coverage in insurance policy contracts, but the precise meaning of each may be widely dissimilar.

Many contracts are called "comprehensive" when they include only a few perils; other such contracts may include many perils. The term is not standardized in the insurance business, and generally refers only to the fact that it is a combination form of comparatively liberal coverage. Examples include the Comprehensive Personal Liability Policy, Comprehensive Automobile Physical Damage Policy and Comprehensive Crime Policy.

"All-risk" contracts are distinguished by the type of insuring agreement used. If the policy lists each peril that it covers, it is a "named perils" or "specified perils" contract. If the contract says it covers, for example, "all risks of physical loss except enumerated exclusions," then it is an all-risks type of contract. Note that "all risks" should not be taken literally, for invariably a few exclusions are specifically identified. Examples of all-risk contracts are the

---

[6]Note that the preceding statistics on multiple-line growth are technically referred to as multiple-peril. The inconsistency is necessary because of the lack of other data available at the present time.

Personal Property Floater, the Dwelling Building Special Form, and the Glass Insurance[7] Policy.

For further discussion, the multiple-line insurance contracts are separated into two basic groups, those essentially personal (individual, family, or nonbusiness) and those designed primarily for business situations.

Personal Multiple-Line Insurance Contracts

The most popular and the best known of multiple-line insurance contracts today are the Homeowner's policies. Of all the changes in insurance policy contracts during the past decade, the use of these forms has been one of the most significant and widely accepted of multiple-line techniques. Some earlier examples of personal multiple-line insurance contracts are briefly mentioned at the end of this section.

Homeowner's Policies. Proper analysis of the Homeowner's policies, as for any insurance contract, stresses the fundamental parts of the policy forms rather than the detail. For complete interpretation of policy contracts coverage it is necessary to refer to the individual insurance contract as a legal document. Much more can be gained by the reader in the following paragraphs by viewing the purposes and component parts of the contract. Such emphasis on the fundamental principles of the policy contract will result in a greater understanding of the essential contract parts. The basic parts do not change substantially, even with frequent policy revisions.

In summary, the proper understanding of Homeowner's policies involve an emphasis on *who* is covered, *what* is covered, *when* and *where* the protection applies, and *how* this protection is provided at a certain price. The old but effective outline of who, what, when, where, and how provides a convenient framework for analyzing Homeowner's policies.

Who Is Covered. As to *who* is covered by the Homeowner's policies, the primary purpose of these contracts is to provide multiple-line coverage to owners who occupy their private residences.[8] A rather important addition to the eligibility rules permits tenants to obtain the same combination of fire, theft, and liability perils in what is known as a Tenant's or Contents' Homeowner's Policy Form.

---

[7]The title of the glass policy is the *Comprehensive* Glass Insurance Policy, which is an example of how the terms discussed above are used in the insurance business without making the distinctions explained.

[8]The purpose of coverage is protection for essentially private and personal residential coverage, although the rules permit insuring under these Homeowner's policies risk situations which include two-family houses, as many as two roomers or boarders, and a variety of incidental business pursuits at the residence such as offices or studios.

Homeowner's policies are insurance for the personal property and personal liability of the whole family.

What Is Covered. The *what* of Homeowner's policies is determined by reference to the property and perils included in the coverage. Since the Homeowner's policies are basically combinations of the Standard Fire Policy (and allied perils forms), the Residence Burglary and Theft Policy, and the Comprehensive Personal Liability Policy, a detailed description of these coverages or reproduction of the forms are not necessary. The present Homeowner's policies used in most states are the third edition of these forms since the early 1950's. Although not every state has adopted the 1959 Homeowner's Program, most states are using this edition of the forms.[9]

A summary table may help to explain the Homeowner's Policy forms. Table 19–2 indicates in general the major property, perils, and amounts of coverage which the five basic Homeowner's forms provide. The most significant result of all these forms is to combine the fire and allied perils, theft, and liability insurance for owners who occupy their homes, or tenants who use Form 4 to achieve this same combination of coverages.

The coverage as to the property and perils also may be illustrated by an example showing the insurance provided by the most commonly used policy, Form 2 (Broad Form):

Property and Perils Coverage	*Amounts of Coverage*
Section I	
a) Home	$20,000
b) Garages or appurtenant private structures	2,000
c) Contents, or personal property	
1. At home	8,000
2. Away from home	1,000
d) Additional living expense	4,000
Section II	
e) Comprehensive personal liability	25,000
f) Medical payments	500
g) Damage to property of others	250

Such protection under a Form 2 Homeowner's Policy would cost about $60 a year on a $20,000 frame dwelling in a Class 1–6 rating territory in the Midwest. Less protection in separate fire, theft, and liability policies would cost as much as $20 more a year. At the present Homeowner's rates, the owner is insuring over $30,000 of his family assets, plus liability, for less than one fifth of 1 percent a year of the values protected. In comparison with Form 2, the above basic amounts of coverage would cost approximately $10

[9]If the reader lives in a state which still uses the policies known as Homeowner's Policies A, B, and C, he should recognize the close similarity of these forms with the newer forms 1, 2, and 5.

TABLE 19–2
Homeowner's Policies, Summary of Coverage

<table>
<tr><th rowspan="2"></th><th colspan="4">Policy Section I
(Property Coverage)</th><th>Policy Section II
(Liability Coverage)</th></tr>
<tr><th>Coverage
"A"</th><th>Coverage
"B"</th><th>Coverage
"C"</th><th>Coverage
"D"</th><th>Coverages
"E," "F," and "G"</th></tr>
<tr><td></td><td>Home.</td><td>Garage or appurtenant private structures.</td><td>Contents or personal property.</td><td>Additional living expenses.</td><td>Comprehensive family liability, medical payments, and damage to property of others.</td></tr>
<tr><td>Amounts</td><td>This amount is chosen as the basic contract coverage.

Minimum $8,000, or $15,000 for Form 5.</td><td>10% of home amount.</td><td>40% of home, or 50% under Form 5 (10% of contents amount applies away from home, with $1,000 minimum).

Minimum for Form 4, $4,000.</td><td>20% of home, or 10% under Form 1.</td><td>Basic amounts are: $10,000, $250 and $250.

($25,000, $500, and $250 under Form 5, and in many states under Form 2.)</td></tr>
<tr><td>Form:
Standard (No. 1)</td><td colspan="4">Fire and lightning.
Extended coverage perils (wind, explosion, smoke, and so on).
Theft, vandalism.</td><td rowspan="5">ALL FIVE FORMS INCLUDE THE ABOVE THREE PERILS OF (1) LIABILITY, (2) MEDICAL PAYMENTS, AND (3) DAMAGE TO PROPERTY OF OTHERS (IRRESPECTIVE OF LIABILITY).</td></tr>
<tr><td>Broad (No. 2)</td><td colspan="4">All Standard Form perils as above, plus miscellaneous perils such as falling objects, collapse, water damage, rupture of heating systems, and freezing (essentially these are the Broad Form fire endorsement perils).</td></tr>
<tr><td>Buildings Special (No. 3)</td><td colspan="4">Building only covered—not contents. "All risks of physical loss" except those specifically excluded (such as flood, earthquake, landslide, war, backing-up of sewers). This form is not used alone, and only can be used in conjunction with Form 4.</td></tr>
<tr><td>Contents Broad (No. 4)</td><td colspan="4">Contents only covered—not buildings.
Covers same named perils as Broad Form 2.
Can be used alone for tenants.</td></tr>
<tr><td>Comprehensive (No. 5)</td><td colspan="4">Covers same "all-risk" perils as Special Form 3, but includes both home and contents.</td></tr>
</table>

less per year under Form 1 (Standard), and $60 more per year under Form 5 (Comprehensive).

The forms have undergone considerable change in recent years. The first step to standardization was in 1957 when the Multi-Peril Insurance Conference[10] was formed by combining the Multiple Peril Insurance Organization (MPIRO) and the Inter-bureau Insurance Advisory Group (IIAG). Two major contract revisions in 1959 occurred, establishing the use of Forms 1, 2, 3, 4, and 5. However, a few states[11] still use the older forms, Homeowner's A (similar to Form 1), Homeowner's B (similar to Form 2), and Homeowner's C (similar to Form 5). A 1961 revision now used in many states makes additional changes in coverage, particularly in increasing the basic liability limits of Form 2 to $25,000 and the medical payments limit to $500.

When Coverage Applies. As to *when* coverage under the Homeowner's policies applies, the minimum duration of coverage is three years. Five-year policies can also be written, and either three- or five-year contracts can be paid for on an annual installment basis. The coverage begins at noon standard time at the location of the home. The insurance agent often has the power to bind coverage immediately for the insured while the policy is being prepared.

Where Coverage Applies. Where the coverage under the Homeowner's policies applies is summarized by noting that the protection is basically at a fixed location—the home of the insured. However, coverages away from the home are also significant. For example, within the limits specified, personal property or contents away from the home are covered on a worldwide basis. The family liability and medical payments to other persons also apply both at home and away from the premises.

How Coverage Applies. How the Homeowner's policies provide the coverage discussed in the preceding paragraphs can be explained in several ways. The policies are *multiple-line* in character, combining fire, theft, and liability protection in one contract. The policies are also *package* contracts, in the sense that they must include certain coverages. The insured is given some leeway in choosing the amounts of coverage on the home, personal property, liability, and medical payments. This characteristic of the insured having to accept basic perils, and to a certain extent the amounts of insurance which are fixed by percentage formulas, makes the Homeowner's policies essentially package rather than schedule-type contracts. Coverages B through F may be increased by endorsement,

[10]In 1963 this organization separated its rating functions, which were transferred to a new bureau, the Multi-line Insurance Rating Bureau. A separate organization, the Fire Insurance Research and Actuarial Association was formed at the same time.

[11]Including New York.

but the only exception to the prescribed minimums is that personal property at home may be decreased to 30 percent of the home amount. The *all-risk* technique is also used in connection with Homeowner's policies in Forms 3 and 5, which covers "all risks of physical loss" to the insured property except for specified exclusions.

Pricing, another part of how the Homeowner's policies work, is accomplished by a so-called *indivisible premium.* This is one which has a combined charge for all basic perils included in the contract. Premiums charts are used to show the cost of the various forms, based upon varying amounts of coverage for the home and the related amounts on the garages, contents, and additional living expense perils. By this process no separate charge is made for each of the individual perils included in the contract. This is contrary to the traditional system in fire insurance in which the premium is calculated by adding together separate charges for fire, windstorm, and miscellaneous perils. The Homeowner's rate is a package premium for the minimum amounts of coverage in the package contract. Additional charges are calculated for the increases in insurance amounts permitted above the mandatory minimums.

Current practice indicates that Broad Form (No. 2) is the most popular Homeowner's Policy Form. Perhaps one fifth of the policyholders use the limited protection of the Standard Form (No. 1, or A), while less than half use Form 2 (or B). However, many agents are finding that "all-risks" coverage is desired by their policyholders. The Comprehensive Form (No. 5)[12] has not been widely used, but an alternative, using Special Form (No. 3) together with Contents Broad Form (No. 4), is being purchased by an increasing number of policyholders. This combination provides "all-risk" coverage on the buildings and Broad Form Named-Perils coverage on the contents. The result is very adequate coverage, only excluding a few known perils such as spillage of liquids or animal damage to contents. It is almost as complete coverage as Form 5.

Deductibles are used in connection with each form. Deductible Clause I applies only to wind or hail losses over \$50 (in Form 5 this amount is \$100). A new feature applies the deductible on a franchise basis, which creates a disappearing deductible. If the loss is over \$500, no deductible applies. For losses between \$50 and \$500, 111 percent of the loss amount above the deductible is paid. Deductible Clause II applies to theft and all miscellaneous perils except fire and lightning. Both of these deductible clauses may be

[12]In effect, Form 5 provides "all-risks" coverage by combining the Standard Fire Insurance Policy (with Dwelling Special Form attached), the Comprehensive Liability Policy and the Personal Property Floater Policy. The higher cost relative to other forms and a mandatory deductible has discouraged its use. Less than one of ten Homeowner's policies are written on Form 5.

eliminated, except in Form 5, for additional cost. In Form 5 the deductible may be changed from $100 to $50, but cannot be eliminated.

One other important feature of the Homeowner's policies is that *replacement cost* coverage is provided on home and garages. Thus depreciation will not be subtracted in calculating the claim payable and the policyholder will receive full replacement cost on these items. The loss must be less than $1,000 and less than 5 percent of the insurance amount, or the property must be insured for more than 80 percent of the replacement cost if the loss exceeds $1,000.

Additional living expenses are included when an insured peril causes the premises to be untenantable. Limits are 20 percent of the building insurance amount under each form, except Form 1 which has a limit of 10 percent.

One final feature is the provision for an endorsement to the Homeowner's policies of insurance for specifically named personal property. Very broad "all-risk" protection can be provided at low cost by scheduling valuable properties such as jewelry, cameras, furs, antiques, artistic objects, and collections. Endorsements may also add protection for earthquake damage and theft from unlocked automobiles.

A few exclusions apply to specific articles as to the amount of coverage. An attempt is made to provide reasonable coverage for valuable or hard-to-value articles such as money ($100 limit), accounts, securities, and boats ($500), manuscripts ($1,000 limit), and jewelry and furs ($1,000 per article, or $250 in Form 5). An additional limitation applies to trees, shrubs, plants, and lawns. These items are not covered for windstorm but are covered for fire and other allied perils up to $250 per item or 5 percent of the home insurance amount for any one loss.

Other Personal Multiple-Line Contracts. A number of other insurance contracts may be classified as multiple-line coverages. Each of these contracts combines fire and casualty insurance perils; in fact their development and use preceded by many years the Homeowner's policies which today are the most popular multiple-line contracts. The Personal Property Floater, the Personal Articles Floater, the Outboard Motorboat Policy and the Valuable Papers Policy are all examples of such contracts. These four policies are better known as inland marine insurance contracts, because they were developed prior to the real impetus and legal sanction for multiple-line contracts. Since each of these contracts has been discussed in previous chapters it is unnecessary here to repeat the details of basic insuring agreements, exclusions, and conditions of the policies.

These forerunners of full multiple-line legislation in the states were a significant part of the mutiple-line trend. Fire, allied, and theft perils were combined in the all-risk, worldwide protection of the Personal Property Floater in the early 1930's. The Personal Articles Floater appeared then, also, designed for articles of high value which were scheduled in a specific list of items such as jewelry, furs, collections, and historical and artistic objects. The Valuable Papers Policy, which also may be used by businesses, provides coverage for hard-to-value properties such as blueprints, plans, and manuscripts. The Outboard Motorboat Policy reveals a strong heritage from the ocean marine field of insurance, and combines fire, theft, and even limited liability protection in one policy.

Business Multiple-Line Insurance Contracts

Five contracts stand out in the development of multiple-line protection for business before 1960. Since then at least six new contracts have appeared, suggesting an increasing impetus to change in the field of commercial multiple-line policies. The fundamental characteristics of each of these contracts will be discussed, but the rapid changes in this volatile area preclude lasting value for any extensive description of all their provisions.[13]

The five policies that are well established by bureau approval and use, even though revisions have been made in the original contracts, include: the Manufacturer's Output Policy, the block contracts, the Commercial Property Form, the Office Contents Form, and the Industrial Property Form.

The six newest contracts include the Public and Institutional Property Policy, the Motel Owner's Policy, the Mercantile Policy, the Apartment Building Owner's Policy, the Office Building Owner's Policy, and the Farmowner's Contract. These contracts are commonly available from many insurance companies. Individual insurers have recently also designed special contracts for funeral directors, homes and ranches, drycleaners, and a wide variety of special categories, although these are not treated in this text.

The Manufacturer's Output Policy. One of the early experiments in multiple-line insurance for businesses was the Manufacturer's Output Policy. It was designed by one insurance company, although today the Multi-Line Insurance Rating Bureau has jurisdiction over this contract. Its basic characteristics are that it covers all personal property of the manufacturer on an all-risk basis while the property is away from the premises of the insured. It was originally a spe-

---

[13]A brief review of current changes in this area is found in the following articles appearing in Winter, 1963 issue of *The Annals of the Society of Property and Casualty Underwriters* (Vol. 16, No. 4): William H. Rodda, "Commercial Multiple Peril Forms and Coverages" (p. 343); L. H. Longely-Cook, "Commercial Multiple Peril Rating Philosophy" (p. 355); and Harry F. Perlet, "Commercial Multiple Peril Rules" (p. 361).

cialized policy for the automobile industry only, but since its inception it has been made available to several hundred classes of manufacturers.

Unlike most insurance contracts the coverage is continuous, remaining in effect until canceled. A minimum premium of $5,000 restricts the contract to large risks. The policy also uses a reporting form in order to adjust the premiums to the property values actually in existence during the year. The rate is an indivisible one calculated specifically for each risk. The property coverage includes improvements and betterments to buildings not owned by the insured, and personal property of others while in the care of the insured. Automobiles are covered at any location, although the basic policy intends to cover primarily personal property away from the premises. Limitations of liability include specified amounts for losses at any one location and losses on conveyances and property at fairs or conventions. Some of the more important exclusions for this all-risk contract include: war perils, infidelity losses by employees, mysterious disappearances, inherent vice, temperature changes, and earthquake or flood damage (except for automobiles and other specified properties).

Block Policy Contracts. Forty years ago, jewelers' block insurance became one of the earliest examples of business multiple-line coverage. It was an inland marine policy, covering on an all-risk basis the entire merchandise and contents of the jeweler's store. Several other similar policies have been regarded primarily as inland marine insurance, even though they also are part of the multiple-line trend. These contracts include the Furriers' Block Policy and a variety of dealer's floaters (equipment, appliances, cameras, instruments, and so on). Fire and theft coverages are provided in all these contracts both on and off the premises, therefore they are characterized as contracts providing very broad protection on a multiple-line basis.

Commercial Property Form. The Commercial Property Form, attached to the fire insurance contract, creates a multiple-line insurance contract for merchants. Retail and wholesale stores may thus obtain all-risk coverage on a basis similar to the inland marine block policies. The perils include all fire and allied perils, theft, and all other perils of physical damage to property. They do not include liability insurance. The property included is the stock, furniture and fixtures, and improvements and betterments of the insured. One endorsement creates a nonreporting contract and provides for a stated limit of liability at each declared location. A second endorsement makes the contract a reporting form by requiring monthly valuation of contents.

Limits are provided for each declared location and a separate limit applies for "any other location." Excluded perils are flood damage at fixed locations, war risk, atomic or radioactive contamination, mechanical breakdown, wear-and-tear, employee fraud, and a number of other miscellaneous perils. Some specific types of property are excluded, as in the Standard Fire Policy and in similar inland marine forms. The policies usually are written subject to a $50 deductible which applies to each loss except fire, lightning, or other specified perils. A bureau form introduced in late 1960 has increased the eligible merchants who may purchase these commercial property forms. The manual, rules, and rating system have changed to permit use of this policy by firms with incidental manufacturing exposure (less than 25 percent of gross sales).

Package multiple-line coverages for business risks have been a rapidly changing part of insurance. Forms that have been adopted in some states have not been approved in others. One of the most promising contracts appeared in 1963, as part of the Special Multiple-Peril Program which now also includes special forms for motels, apartments, offices, and institutions. It is called the Mercantile Program. Its important features include: (1) eligibility of all firms, with a few exceptions, that are engaged to the extent of 75 percent in the buying and selling of merchandise, including retail and wholesale establishments, (2) a comprehensive liability coverage, including products and medical payments if desired, is provided, (3) a new premium and dispersion credit plan applies to the fire coverages, granting credits for number of locations included and the total size of premium, (4) many optional coverages are available, such as glass, business interruption, rents, employee dishonesty, money and securities, and boiler and machinery insurance, (5) in all, it is a package policy for merchants, with many flexible features which permit the insured to include all property and liability coverages except workmen's compensation.

As a hypothetical[14] example, take a retail clothing store in a Midwest city. The lower costs and broader coverage of a Special Multi-Peril Policy under the S.M.P. Mercantile Program might be illustrated by the table on page 584.

In the example, for less cost, the Mercantile Policy adds business interruption, burglary and theft, vandalism and malicious mischief protection, and increases liability coverage to more adequate limits. Other examples might, of course, add similar or greater increases in coverage which would cause the total cost to exceed the original cost of individual policies.

---

[14]Costs are illustrative and not meant to be exact. They would vary in actual practice by substantial amounts according to many factors such as sprinkler systems, store area, territory and protective features. Insurance rates also differ between bureau and nonbureau members.

Individual Policies	Amounts of Coverage	3-Year Cost of Individual Policies	3-Year Cost of Mercantile Package
1. Standard Fire Policy, with Extended Coverage Endorsement	$50,000 on building	$300	$210
2. Standard Fire Policy, with Extended Coverage Endorsement	$70,000 on contents	450	320
3. Public Liability	5/10/5 limits	100	100 (with single limit of $50,000)
4. Business Interruption	$60,000 gross earnings	None Carried	90
5. Burglary and Theft	$10,000 merchandise	None Carried	100
6. Vandalism and Malicious Mischief	Added to fire policies	None Carried	20
Total 3-year cost		$850	$840

Office Contents Form. Very similar to the block policy contracts and the Commercial Property Form is the Office Contents Form. Its features include all-risk coverage for most offices (except medical and dental offices), including equipment, furniture, supplies, other contents of the office, and improvements and betterments if the office is leased. The protection is multiple-line in nature, since it includes theft perils as well as fire and miscellaneous damages. Other parts of the policy are quite similar to the Commercial Property Form, including a rating system which has as its foundation the fire and extended coverage rates plus an extra charge for the additional perils included in the policy.

Industrial Property Form. In 1956 the Industrial Property Form became available for manufacturing businesses. It was designed to provide coverage similar to that of the output policies for automobile and other manufacturers, and was made available to many more industrial classifications, and smaller insureds. It also resembles the Commercial Property Form and the Office Contents Form in not being a policy by itself, but becoming a multiple-line contract when attached to the Standard Fire Insurance Policy. The types of property included are one of its distinguishing features, for it includes business property of the insured, personal property of others held by the insured and for which he may be liable, machinery and equipment, and even buildings (which may be covered if desired). It is intended for fairly sizable businesses, with a requirement that at least two locations must be insured and minimum amounts of coverage must apply at the secondary location. Minimum premiums are

$2,500 (for a named-perils contract) and $5,000 a year (for the all-risk coverage). Reporting or nonreporting forms, and one- or three-year policies are available. The policy is multiple-line in nature because at least some fire and theft perils are mandatory.

Public and Institutional Property Plans. An outstanding new insurance program for schools, churches, hospitals, and government units was inaugurated in 1960. Five parts of the form may be used by the eligible institutions to provide blanket coverage for all real and personal property against the basic fire insurance perils, extended coverage, vandalism, malicious mischief, and sprinkler leakage losses. It is an unusual policy in several respects: (1) credits of 25 percent or more are given if the insured complies with initial inspection requirements, quarterly self-inspections, and an annual statement of values, (2) valuations are controlled by a mandatory agreed amount of valuation and a mandatory 90 percent amount of insurance, (3) a $100 deductible per item applies, as well as a maximum deductible per loss of $1,000 for all perils except fire and lightning and, (4) a minimum premium of $1,000 (lowered to $500 in 1961). The result is a form which emphasizes broad coverage, loss prevention and lower cost, making it a highly competitive and salable new multiple-line insurance contract.

An adaptation of these plans is now available under the Special Multi-Peril Program in some dozen or more states. All-risks coverage on property, and *liability* protection, are provided by this new Institutional Program.

Service Businesses Multiple-Line Contracts. Several of the newest multiple-line business contracts involve protection for businesses which are primarily providing services rather than goods. The output and industrial property policies provided multiple-line coverage for manufacturers; the Commercial Property Form permitted businesses that buy and sell goods to have multiple-line policies; but service industries had to wait until the 1960's for contracts designed specifically for their multiple-line problems. The first of these to become available was a contract for *motel* owners. A number of states have approved this new multiple-line contract, as well as specialized programs for *office* building owners and *apartment* building owners. Together with the previously mentioned *mercantile* and *institutional* package policies, these contracts have become available under what is called the Special Multi-Peril (S.M.P.) Program of the Inter-Regional Insurance Conference.

The outstanding characteristics of these new policies is the provision of property *and liability* coverages in one policy. These policies almost may be characterized as a combination of the package and schedule approaches to insurance. The basic package includes some fire and liability insurance, but considerable leeway is given the insured in selecting at his option other coverages such as theft, business interuption, glass, and other miscellaneous perils. The policies also are essentially named perils in the basic contracts; however, all-risk endorsements are available if the policyholder desires. The result is a policy which may be tailored to the needs of the individual insured. The newest and broadest language for liability coverage is also used in most of these forms, including coverage on an occurence basis and personal injury liability losses such as false arrest and invasion of privacy. A disappearing deductible of the franchise type for losses over $500 is usually a part of the contract. It is to be expected that the approach of these policies to multiple-line insurance will be furthered by the introduction of more such forms for other service-type businesses.

Farmowner's Policy. A final example of multiple-line insurance contracts is a combination of both personal and business multiple-line insurance. Approval of the Farmowner's Policy in many states occurred in or after 1961, and rapid growth in the sales of this policy is indicated. The coverage is quite similar to the Homeowner's forms. Fire, theft, and liability protection is provided on the dwelling, and the policy includes fire insurance and related protection for farm buildings and personal property ($10,000 minimums). The liability insurance is the equivalent of the Farmer's Comprehensive Personal Liability Policy now in use.

Once again, a multiple-line insurance contract has been adapted to the needs of the policyholder. One cannot conclude this section on multiple-line insurance without being impressed by the significant scope and nature of the changes which have occurred. The future undoubtedly will bring continued change to this progressive area of insurance, particularly in the newer and highly competitive field of multiple-line insurance contracts for businesses.

ALL-LINES INSURANCE

Nature and Extent

All-lines insurance is a separate trend, but one almost as apparent and significant as the multiple-line trend today. The all-lines approach combines *fire, casualty, life, and health* insurance. Although this combination may only be accomplished within a single contract or single company[15] in a few examples and a few states, fire and casualty companies have created an all-lines trend in the past several years by purchasing or forming separate life insurance com-

[15]Emphasis is on the phrase "within a single contract or company." In contrast to the multiple-line trend, which started with (1) multiple-line *groups* and (2) extended to multiple-line *companies*, and (3) then to rapid growth of multiple-line *contracts* in the last decade, the all-lines trend is still largely centered on the first phase, i.e., all-lines insurance company groups.

panies. At least 150 insurance companies now have such all-lines affiliations. The result has been many all-lines insurance company *groups,* although all-lines *contracts* and all-lines *companies* are still rare except in limited cases.

Life Insurers May Become All-Lines Groups. Life insurance companies may also logically be expected to expand their operations by starting or purchasing fire and casualty companies in the future. In past years they have been held back by legal barriers preventing a life insurer from owning substantial stock in other insurance companies. Recently, however, such prohibitions have begun to be removed.[16] A gradual development in life insurers entering all-lines operations is probable for a number of reasons: (1) licensing laws in most states still prevent the same insurer from doing business in both life and property fields,[17] so the permitted company group technique of all-lines operations (which is sometimes more unwieldy) will have to be used, (2) about two thirds of life insurance is written by mutual companies, and they are limited in expansion by the amount of their surplus, (3) profits in property-liability insurance in recent years have been small and uncertain, especially in relation to the more stable life insurance field, and (4) the changes necessitated by all-lines operations are considerable, involving such widespread effects within an insurer as to have major impact on management, product development, losses and expenses, underwriting, marketing, education and training, regulation and investments.[18]

Many observers still feel that, despite the problems of life insurers in entering all-lines, the movement will continue to increase. Reasons for the growth are competition, economy, and the growing recognition of the mass market concept.[19]

---

[16]In June, 1961, New York State's highest court reversed a former decision and stated that out-of-state life insurers may purchase fire and casualty companies. Although other legal barriers exist (such as antitrust and monopoly acts) it seems that this decision will hasten the all-lines trend in the decade of the 1960's. See *The National Underwriter* (Life Edition), June 10, June 30, and July 8, 1961, p. 1. The suit concerned the purchase of Aetna Insurance Company by the Connecticut General Life Insurance Company.

[17]Only thirteen states have permitted the "inclusion of life, fire, and casualty writing powers in single insurers." These include Alabama, Alaska, Connecticut, Delaware, Georgia, Maine, Mississippi, North Dakota, Oregon, Rhode Island, South Carolina, Tennessee, and Wisconsin. Since New York is not one of them, any insurer doing business in New York cannot, under the application of the Appleton Rule to out-of-state insurers, use such broad powers. See Hugh D. Harbison, "Legal Environment for All Lines Insurance" in *All Lines Insurance* (Homewood, Ill.: Richard D. Irwin, Inc., 1960) chap. 2, p. 23.

[18]See chapters on each of these impacts of all-lines insurance in Chapters 4–11 of *All Lines Insurance* (Homewood, Ill.: Richard D. Irwin, Inc., 1960). This lecture series of the S. S. Huebner Foundation for Insurance Education was edited by Dan M. McGill.

[19]Thomas C. Morrill, *ibid.*, Chapter 1.

Property-Liability Insurers Are Becoming All-Lines Groups. The predominant action in the formation of all-lines groups has been taken by property-liability insurance companies. Either by purchasing a life insurer, or by forming a new life affiliate, the multiple-line companies have in recent years often become all-lines groups. The growth has been startling, and studies have shown an increase from 51 active all-lines groups at the beginning of 1958 to 91 such groups in 1961, and 150 in 1963, writing over $12 billion in annual premiums.[20] Many more groups have been formed during 1963–64.

Some of the reasons why this trend has emerged in recent years have been concisely reviewed: (1) basically, it caters to the buyer's convenience by affording him one-stop shopping, (2) volatile loss ratios in property and liability insurance have caused these insurers to look to life insurance as a stabilizer for their operations, (3) the property-liability insurers have a ready-made sales force for selling life insurance, and (4) many property and liability insurance agents deal with business firms, which makes a natural entry into the group life insurance business of the employer.[21]

The Future

All-lines insurance has a long way to go before it earns its title. Perhaps in the future there will be contracts that are broad enough really to deserve being called all-lines contracts. At the present time there are only a few all-lines types of policies written by a small number of companies in a few states. An example is life and disability insurance for a home mortgage which is written along with a Homeowner's property and liability protection.

Undoubtedly, increased competition in all-lines selling will be an important part of tomorrow's insurance market. The advantages of survey selling[22] and other such features as automatic monthly check payment plans are obvious to many policyholders. Many agents or agencies have been operating as all-lines sales forces for years. The rapid entry of property and liability insurers into all-lines operations by creating all-lines groups will probably result in many

---

[20]T.J.V. Cullen, "All-Lines Trend Grows in '62," *The Spectator* (Philadelphia: Chilton Co.), April, 1964, pp. 23 and 55–64. See also earlier studies reported in the April, 1962 issue, Kap Soo Bang and William Alrich, "Background for 'All-Lines'," p. 58; in the October, 1958 issue, "All-Lines Groups Write Fifth of U.S. Premiums," p. 38; in the November, 1960 issue, "All-Lines Protection: The Future for Underwriting," p. 38; and in the June, 1961 issue, "What Does All Lines Mean?" p. 64.

[21]Benjamin N. Woodson, "All-Lines Underwriting: New Fashion or New Era?" *C.L.U. Journal,* Winter, 1957, Vol. XII, No. 1, pp. 73–75. See also: "All-Lines Underwriting: Five Years Later," *C.L.U. Journal,* Summer, 1962, Vol. XVI, No. 3, pp. 239–41, which reaches the interesting conclusion that the greatest change of the 1950's has been the "applicability of life insurance methods to the underwriting and sale of personal-line property and casualty coverages" (p. 242).

[22]Edwin L. Overman, "All Lines Survey Selling," *The Spectator* (Philadelphia: Chilton Company), October, 1961, p. 44.

life insurers also becoming all-lines organizations. Considering the advantages which accrue to them by doing so, and the need for protecting their markets, life insurers have sound reasons for evaluating the prospects of all-lines insurance. There is evidence that they are, in such programs as the 1963 meeting of the Life Insurance Agency Managers Association, which had "Operation All Lines—1963" as its theme.

The insurance product of tomorrow may be a direct outgrowth of the trend to multiple-line and all-lines insurance. It may well be a market dominated by "package" contracts of property, liability, life, and health insurance written by "package" all-lines insurance companies.

SUMMARY

The traditional insurance company was for many years an organization which specialized by kind or "line" of insurance. In recent decades an impetus to product diversification has occurred in insurance. Two distinct but related trends have appeared: (1) *multiple-line* insurance, a combination of fire and casualty coverages and (2) *all-lines* insurance, the merging of life and health insurance with fire and casualty protection.

The new terminology must be carefully used, for the delineation of the different changes is complicated. Multiple-line insurance company *groups* developed rapidly during the 1920's and 1930's. Multiple-line *companies* appeared mostly after the late 1940's when enabling legislation permitting such organizations was passed in many states. Multiple-line insurance *contracts* have gained tremendous popularity since 1955, with a twelve-fold increase in seven years to become a $1.2-billion-a-year business.

The purposes of multiple-line insurance are summarized in its advantages of better coverage at lower cost with more convenient contract forms. It may also bring greater stability of operations for insurers.

One of the most popular of multiple-line insurance contracts is the Homeowner's Policy. In one package contract it combines the basic personal insurance needs of the family home—protection against fire and allied perils, liability, and theft. The broad nature of the coverages is explained in terms of who, what, when, where, and how the insurance applies.

Business multiple-line insurance contracts have become a volatile field for sales in recent years. From special contracts designed as "output" and "block" policies for only a few specialized industries and businesses, the number and variety of forms has multiplied rapidly. Now, package-type contracts are available for most commercial, office, industrial, institutional and service-oriented businesses. Most, but not all of these contracts combine liability coverages with the basic fire and theft insurance in order to provide the insured with a broad policy to meet his normal insurance requirements. The Farmowner's Policy is an example of a multiple-line contract which includes both personal and business risks in one policy.

All-lines insurance is a newer development. The best illustration of increasing interest in bringing all life, health, fire, and casualty coverages together is the trend of the last decade (especially the last several years) toward all-lines insurance company groups. Thus far the change has mostly involved property-liability insurers becoming all-lines groups by purchasing or starting life and health insurance companies. For many reasons, including some legal restrictions, life insurers have not yet moved strongly toward all-lines operations. The future, however, is expected by many persons to show continued movement in the direction of all-lines insurance.

FOR REVIEW

1. If multiple-line insurance contracts provide greater coverage than comparable separate policies, how can the multiple-line contract have a lower premium?
2. What is multiple-line insurance, and how does it compare with all-lines insurance?
3. What separate parts can you identify in the multiple-line trend? Why are they significant?
4. Has the multiple-line trend been recent? Rapid? Continuous? Explain the evidence you present.
5. One of the purposes advocated for multiple-line contracts is their lower costs. What permits these lower costs, and is this the only significant result of these contracts?
6. Are all insurance companies now multiple-line companies? Why or why not?
7. Is the multiple-line trend completed? What examples can you mention of mono-line activities in insurance companies or organizations? Do you think they will continue in this manner? Explain fully, indicating how the economic benefits of specialization are involved in your answer.
8. What is the difference between multiple-line insurance and "package" policies? All-lines insurance? Multiple-peril contracts? All-risk policies?
9. What are the goals of multiple-line insurance for the policyholders? For the companies?
10. How have multiple-line insurance companies been formed? What legal problems exist? What other problems do multiple-line operations bring to a company?
11. Mr. Riskee has just been married and purchased a new suburban home. Why would you recommend a Homeowner's Policy to him? What form would you suggest, and why?
12. What personal multiple-line insurance contracts were used before Homeowner's Policies? Why are they considered multiple-line in nature?
13. Give a brief illustration of at least four kinds of liability insurance protection which are included in the comprehensive personal liability section

of the Homeowner's Policy, indicating for each whether or not tenants as well as property owners might incur such losses.

14. What older forms of business multiple-line policies existed before 1960? Where did they come from, and how could they be developed before the "full" multiple-line laws of the late 1940's and early 1950's?
15. What new features does the Public and Institutional Property Plan offer policyholders?
16. Why do you think the personal multiple-line contracts were developed on a large scale before the business contracts using the same technique?
17. For which multiple-line contracts or forms might the following be eligible:
    a) A shoe merchant?
    b) A camera dealer?
    c) A lawyer?
    d) A metal-parts manufacturer?
    e) A building owner?
    f) A university?
18. What implications might the multiple-line trend have for the "independent" and the "exclusive" agency systems of insurance marketing?
19. Some of the Homeowner's Policies use the "named perils" approach in providing protection, while some use the "all-risks" approach. (*a*) Differentiate these two approaches, indicating the basic perils included in one Homeowner's form which uses each approach. (*b*) State your recommendations, with reasons, for the Homeowner's form and limits of coverage to be used by a family owning a $30,000 home.
20. Explain several factors which may (*a*) hasten, and (*b*) several factors which may slow down the all-lines insurance trend. What part of the development of all-lines insurance is most evident now?

PART FIVE

Life and Health Insurance

CHAPTER 20 *PRINCIPLES UNDERLYING LIFE INSURANCE*

I. NATURE OF LIFE INSURANCE
- A. Definition
- B. Compared to Other Insurance Contracts
  1. Not a Contract of Indemnity
  2. A Unique Risk
  3. Insurable Interest Required

II. FUNDAMENTAL LIFE INSURANCE CONCEPTS
- A. The Life Insurance Equation
- B. Actuarial Basis of Basic Contracts
- C. Development from Assessment Plans
- D. The Level Premium Plan for Permanent Protection
  1. Reserves
  2. Combining Protection and Investment
  3. Cash Values
- E. The Investment Function of Life Insurance
- F. Legal Doctrines
  1. Right to Trace Misappropriation
  2. Effects of Divorce
  3. Murder by Beneficiary
  4. Common Disaster
  5. Presumption of Death
  6. Presumption against Suicide
  7. Death by Legal Execution
  8. Rights of Creditors to Life Insurance Values

III. SUMMARY

CHAPTER 21 *ESTIMATING THE LIFE RISK*

I. THE MORTALITY TABLE
- A. What It Is
- B. Where It Comes from
- C. Basic Construction
- D. Actuaries and the Purposes of Mortality Tables

II. KINDS OF MORTALITY TABLES
- A. Different Tables for Different Needs
- B. Development of the 1958 CSO Table

III. LIFE INSURANCE PREMIUM CALCULATIONS
- A. Advancing Premiums as Age Increases
- B. The Interest Factor

II. Insuring Agreement and Face of Policy

III. Application

IV. Standard Provisions
- A. The Contract and Payment of Premiums
- B. The Beneficiary
  - 1. Designation of Beneficiary
  - 2. Change of Beneficiary
- C. Ownership of Policy and Changes
- D. Assignment
- E. Dividends
  - 1. Participating and Nonparticipating Policies
  - 2. Dividend Options
- F. Policy Form Changes
- G. Lapse and Reinstatement
- H. Misstatement of Age
- I. Suicide
- J. Indebtedness and Settlement
- K. Incontestability

V. Cash, Loan, and Nonforfeiture Benefits
- A. Cash Values
- B. Policy Loans
- C. Automatic Premium Loan Option
- D. Extended Term Insurance
- E. Reduced Paid-up Insurance
- F. The Delay Clause

VI. Optional Methods of Settlement
- A. Fixed Installment Payments
- B. Payments for Fixed Period
- C. Life Income Payments
- D. Interest Payments

VII. Disability and Accidental Death Benefit Extensions of Coverage
- A. Waiver-of-Premium Benefit
- B. Total Disability Income Benefits
- C. Double Indemnity Benefits

VIII. Summary

CHAPTER 25 *ANNUITIES*

I. Introduction
- A. Definition
- B. Purposes and Uses
- C. Cost Factors

II. Types of Individual Annuities
- A. By Plan of Distribution
  - 1. Straight or Pure Life Annuity
  - 2. Guaranteed Refund Life Annuities
  - 3. A Variation and Comparisons
- B. By Parties in the Contract
  - 1. Single Life Annuity
  - 2. Joint Life and Survivorship Annuity

- C. By Time When Distribution Commences
  1. Immediate Annuity
  2. Deferred Annuities
- D. By Method of Purchase
  1. Single Payment Annuity
  2. Installment Payment Annuity
- E. Special Annuity and Life Insurance Combinations
- F. Variable Annuities

III. CONTRACT CONDITIONS OF INDIVIDUAL ANNUITIES

- A. General Provisions
- B. No Medical Examination
- C. Not Apportionable
- D. Participation

IV. GROUP ANNUITIES

- A. Nature and Purposes
- B. Eligibility
- C. Retirement Dates
  1. Normal Retirement Date
  2. Optional Retirement Date
- D. Types of Annuities Used
- E. Benefits
  1. Basic Plans
  2. Past Service Credits
  3. Variable Annuity Plans
  4. Death Benefits
  5. Vesting Clause
  6. Change or Discontinuance
- F. Financing Sources
- G. Funding Methods
  1. Pay-as-You-Go Plan
  2. Trust Fund Plan
  3. Individual Policy Plan
  4. Group Permanent Plan
  5. Group Annuities
  6. Combination of Methods

V. SUMMARY

CHAPTER 26 *INDIVIDUAL HEALTH INSURANCE*

I. CLASSIFICATION AND PURPOSE

- A. Definitions
- B. Purpose
- C. Classes
  1. Method of Underwriting
  2. Health Perils
  3. Health Insuring Organizations
  4. Health Insurance Policies
  5. Health Losses and Protection
     - a. Hospital, Surgical, and Regular Medical Expense Protection
     - b. Major Medical Expense Protection
     - c. Loss of Income Protection
- D. Relationship to Life Insurance

- D. Group Medical Expense Insurance
  1. Doctors' Visits (Total Disability Form)
  2. Doctors' Visits (Without Total Disability Form)
  3. Doctors' Visits (In-Hospital Form)
- E. Group Polio and Dread Disease Expense Insurance

IV. GROUP MAJOR MEDICAL EXPENSE INSURANCE
- A. Development
- B. Basic Features
  1. High Maximum Benefits
  2. Deductibles
  3. Coinsurance
- C. Primary Types
  1. Integrated Plans
  2. Basic Plans

V. GROUP ACCIDENT AND SICKNESS INSURANCE
- A. Definition of Disability
  1. Occupational Benefits
- B. Benefit Levels and Duration
- C. Group Accidental Death and Dismemberment Insurance

VI. SPECIAL PROBLEMS
- A Medical Care for the Aged
- B. Dental-Mental-Nursing Care Benefits

VII. SUMMARY

Chapter 20

PRINCIPLES UNDERLYING LIFE INSURANCE

CONSIDER the following riddle. What field of insurance has grown, in one generation between the beginning of 1943 and 1963:[1] (1) from $128 billion to $676 billion of "insurance in force," or total contract values?; (2) from under $4 billion to over $13 billion of "premiums," or annual sales?; (3) from 147 million to 323 million contracts?; and (4) from $35 billion to over $133 billion of assets? The answer: *life insurance.* The reasons for such growth: see the next five chapters, beginning with this chapter on the basic principles and concepts upon which the field of life insurance is based.

NATURE OF LIFE INSURANCE

Life insurance undertakes to protect the insured's family, creditors, or others against financial loss growing out of the death of the insured. The contract embodies an agreement in which the insurer undertakes to pay a stipulated sum upon the death of the insured, or at some designated time, to a designated beneficiary.

Definition

Legal status was given long ago to the definition which indicates the life insurance agreement to be: "A contract by which the insurer, for a certain sum of money or premium proportioned to the age, health, profession, and other circumstances of the person whose life is insured engages that, if such person shall die within the period limited in the policy, the insurer will pay the sum specified in the policy, according to the terms thereof, to the person in whose favor such policy is granted."[2]

Policies provide methods for payment of the proceeds in installments or in some manner other than a lump sum; the choice is made by the insured, or by the beneficiary, if the insured has not

[1] *Life Insurance Fact Book* (New York: Institute of Life Insurance, 1963), pp. (1) 13, (2) 52, (3) 17, and (4) 67.

[2] *Ritter* v. *Mutual Life Insurance Company*, 169 U.S. 139 [1898].

made a choice. The choices are termed "optional modes of settlement," or "settlement options."

In addition to the life policy, which has as its purpose affording protection in the event of a premature death, the life insurance business has developed a second type of contract, termed "the annuity," which furnishes income protection during a period of old age when productive powers have diminished or disappeared.

Compared to Other Insurance Contracts

The essential difference between life insurance and other forms of insurance designed solely to assume the burden of an uncertain peril is that life insurance has, in addition to the function of protecting against uncertainty, the function of accumulation. A considerable part of the premiums paid for life insurance represents a contribution on the part of the insureds to a fund for investment to be administered by the insurer. The establishment of an estate and its management and investment in the interest of the insured are features peculiar to the business of life insurance.

Not a Contract of Indemnity. While the idea of indemnity is emphasized in writing life insurance, strictly speaking one cannot say that the contract is one of indemnity. In buying life insurance an insured undertakes to compensate his estate, dependents, or others to whom he is obligated for the loss occasioned in the event of his untimely death. However, when settlement is made, the beneficiaries under the policy are under no obligation to demonstrate, as a condition precedent to collecting the insurance, a direct pecuniary loss as a result of the decease of the insured. Because of the investment element of the policy, a principal sum accrues for the benefit of the insured, his estate, or beneficiary otherwise designated. It is quite possible, and frequently it is the case, that at the time the policy becomes payable because of the death of the insured, his value as a producer has long since ceased. As a matter of fact, he may have long been a dependent and a charge upon relatives. These circumstances have no bearing whatever upon the right of the designated beneficiary to participate fully in the policy in accordance with its terms.[3]

[3]Life insurance in the early days was widely used as a vehicle for gambling. This was not peculiar to life insurance alone, but life insurance loaned itself admirably to the purpose. Policies were taken out on the lives of important men in public life, leaders in military campaigns, and political prisoners. Frequently the interest on the part of the policyholders in the gain they would derive from the death of the person upon whom the insurance was written was decidedly prejudicial to the best interests of the state. Early opposition to life insurance was not limited, however, to the insurance of the lives of important personages as a gambling feature. There were many

(Continued on next page)

The life insurance contract, therefore, provides for the payment of a definite sum regardless of whether the death of the insured is the occasion of a pecuniary loss to the beneficiary. In fact, quite the contrary may be the case without providing reasons for denying liability on the policy or settling a claim for an amount less than the policy face. In its essence the contract of life insurance is an undertaking to pay a certain sum of money on the death of the insured person, without regard to monetary loss. "This species of insurance," it has been held, "in no way resembles a contract of indemnity."[4]

A Unique Risk. The life insurance policy is a contract of insurance in part only. In other insurance contracts the insurer, for an agreed consideration or premium, undertakes to indemnify the insured against loss or damage caused by the perils indicated in the policy. In all forms of insurance except life insurance, the happening of the unfavorable contingency which gives rise to the loss is uncertain. In life insurance the contingency insured against is death. Death is universal and certain. The uncertainty is the time of its coming. Because the happening of the contingency insured against is certain, life policies, unless written only for a term, provide for certain payment. The uncertain element is the time when such payment must be made.

Although the basic use of life insurance is the protection of life values, life insurance contracts are so carefully drawn that they have found additional uses. Particularly they are used for holding and accumulating assets, and they may also be used as a means for transferring ownership. Finally, because of certain conditions in the contract, it is an admirable instrument for use in connection with the establishment of a trust. All these uses lend value to the services of the business. There is no conflict between the secondary uses and the primary function of life insurance. In many instances the secondary uses supplement and merge with the primary use.

Insurable Interest Required. Although the life insurance contract is not one of indemnity, this fact does not preclude the requirement basic to all insurance of an insurable interest. On the other hand the doctrine of insurable interest in the field of life insurance is considerably broader than in other forms of insurance. In most

---

who felt that the insurance on the life of a person was a thing to be abhorred, and in some instances, it was absolutely prohibited by law.

A turning point in the development of life insurance was reached in 1774, with the enactment of the famous statute 14 Geo. III, c. 48, *An Act for Regulating Insurance upon Lives, and for Prohibiting all such Ins. except in cases where the Persons Insuring shall have an Interest in the Life or Death of the Person Insured.* This statute recognizes that it is possible to have an insurable interest in the life of another to such an extent that the beneficiary under the policy would not find the death of the insured to be preferable to his life.

[4] *Daly* v. *India & London Life. Assur. Co.*, 15 C.B. 365.

states this is governed by statute, and no uniform rule can be set forth. It is generally conceded, however, that so far as a person's *own life* is concerned he is not required to, nor can he, set a monetary value upon it. To this end the courts have held that any person has an insurable interest in his own life for any amount. He may, therefore, buy insurance that is valid and enforceable in any amount which a company is willing to write and upon which he is willing and able to pay premiums.[5]

It has sometimes been held that, to establish insurable interest in close relationships, there must be pecuniary interest in the continuance of the life of the insured. In the case of *husband and wife*, pecuniary interest is conclusively presumed. Actual pecuniary loss growing out of the death of an insured will support an insurable interest as well as an expectation or presumption of pecuniary advantage in the case of certain near relationships. To summarize, not all relationships will sustain an insurable interest, but close relationship will sustain such an interest without the actual immediate establishment of pecuniary advantage in the continued life of the insured. This is particularly the case where there is a close relationship and the policy has been obtained in good faith and not for the purpose of speculation, and where the circumstances are such as to justify the inference that natural affection would operate to protect the life of the insured. Such a relationship gives rise to the presumption of an expected benefit from the continued life of the insured or is sufficient to justify a belief that loss or disadvantage would naturally and probably follow for the beneficiary if the insured dies.

It follows, therefore, that in the field of life insurance, in addition to the interest every individual has in his own life, there are two kinds of loss that will support an insurable interest: (*a*) a loss measurable in terms of money and (*b*) a loss involving a detriment not measurable in terms of money. The first may be covered by a contract predicated upon indemnity. The second may involve, in whole or in part, a feature of indemnity or no indemnity; but the contract has insurable interest and is enforceable because it covers a situation the continuance of which "will justify a reasonable expectation of advantage or benefit."[6]

---

[5]In the broadest possible terms, an insurable interest exists when the insured will suffer a disadvantage if the contingency insured against happens and will enjoy a benefit if the contingency fails to happen. A contract of insurance is "unequivocally unenforceable" without the prerequisite of insurable interest (B. Harnett and J. V. Thornton, "Insurable Interest in Property," *Columbia Law Review*, December, 1948; reprinted in *Insurance Law Journal*, June, 1949, p. 420). The requirement is not one that the insurer may waive. Insurable interest is essential to the life insurance contract, as to all other insurance contracts, if the policy is to be enforceable.

[6]*Warnock* v. *Davis*, above. See also *Geisler, Admx.* v. *Mutual Benefit Health and Accident Association et als.*, 12 CCH Life Cases 866 and 44 C.J.S. 903, 905, Sec. 303a.

A *creditor* may have an insurable interest in the life of a debtor to the extent of the debt, and a creditor of a copartnership likewise has an insurable interest in the life of each copartner. In the case of creditors there is no fast rule as to how much insurance may be taken. The status of the creditor as beneficiary differs if the policy is one taken out by a debtor and is used as collateral for the loan, or if the policy is issued on the life of the debtor and purchased directly from the insurance company by the creditor. In the former case, it is generally held that the amount of the insurance need have no relationship to the amount of the debt. The debtor may take out a policy for any amount he wishes in excess of the debt and deliver it to the creditor as collateral security. When policies are so written, it is held that the right of the creditor to the benefits under the policy is limited to the amount of the indebtedness. If, however, the creditor takes the policy out on his own volition and pays the premium himself without charging it to the account of the debtor, the debtor has no interest in the policy. In any case, the debtor must consent to the issuance of the policy, or he may, in fact, apply personally for the policy in the interest of the creditor. In the first case, therefore, when the policies are collateral to the loan, there can be no question of disproportion between the amount of insurance and the amount of the debt. In the second case, the amount of insurance which a creditor may properly carry on the life of the debtor must not be largely in excess of the amount of the debt. Such a policy has been held to be contrary to public policy.

Aside from the interests of creditors in the lives of debtors and those of dependents in relatives from whom they may expect support or assistance, there are other relationships from which a pecuniary interest arises sufficient to establish an insurance interest under a life contract.

A substantial amount of life insurance is written insuring the life of a *partner* in a business venture for the benefit of the surviving partner or partners. Sometimes the proceeds of such a policy are payable to the firm, and in other instances the proceeds provide a fund with which the surviving partners acquire for themselves from the estate of the deceased partner his interest in the firm.

A corporation may insure the life of a *key man,* such as an important officer or other member of the organization. In the case of a small corporation, where the stock is closely held, the lives of stockholders may be insured, the proceeds to be used to buy the stock of a deceased stockholder, and the stock distributed among the survivors in accordance with a prearranged plan and agreement. Obviously a large corporation with widely distributed stock would hardly have an insurable interest in the lives of any of the stockholders, nor would the stockholders have an insurable interest in each other's lives.

In the case of employees, the question of insurable interest is dependent upon the value of the employee to the business. Obviously, one who could be easily replaced would hardly be one in whom the employer could reasonably claim an insurable interest. A chemist, however, working over a long period of years on research problems, might reasonably be insured. This would be particularly the case if his experiments had not yet materialized but there were reasonable expectation of substantial benefits soon to be forthcoming. It is reasonable to assume that a business might have an interest in other employees occupying key positions, such as the president, executive officers, and department heads. In the event of doubt, however, when insurance seems desirable, valid insurance may be written when the employee himself applies for and secures the policy and designates the employer as beneficiary.

FUNDAMENTAL LIFE INSURANCE CONCEPTS

The Life Insurance Equation

There is no mystery about the life insurance business. The principle upon which it is based is simple. The members of a group large enough to come within the operation of the law of large numbers make payments into a common fund which must be large enough to pay the agreed benefits.

Life insurance, considered in the light of the individual contract, has been to many an incomprehensible transaction. It is known that nothing is as certain as death and likewise that nothing is as uncertain as when it will occur. The company that is willing to agree to pay, in consideration of the payment of a comparatively small premium, thousands of dollars or even millions, whether death occurs immediately after the insurance becomes effective, within a week, a month, a year, or many years, seems to be assuming a risk beyond the understanding of all but a few initiated to the techniques of actuarial science.

The key is to be found in the fact that life insurance deals not with individuals but with groups. No life insurance underwriter can possibly have the vaguest intimation of the length of life of the most promising candidate. An insured may meet with an accident and be killed five minutes after insurance becomes effective. Such happenings come within the calculations of the life underwriter, so long as the transaction is in no way tainted with fraud, because, for every insured in the group who will meet early death, there will be another insured who will live to old age. There will be deaths at all ages, but on the basis of observations death rates for the various age groups may be established.

In its simplest form, here is the method of computing a life insurance premium, assuming 10,000 individuals aged fifty-eight wish to insure their lives for a period of one year for $1,000. Reference to a standard mortality table indicates that the death rate per 1,000 is 17. The life insurance company, therefore, will count on 170 deaths during the year, or payments equal to $170,000. Since there are 10,000 in the group to pay the losses at the beginning, if a premium of $17 is collected from each of these and the death experience is exactly that of the expectation, the insurance company will have $170,000 with which to pay claims, and the account will balance to a cent. In the interest of simplicity, the costs of doing business are at this point not considered.[7]

Since, however, there is no assurance that the death rate will exactly follow the expectation in the given year, insurance companies collect somewhat more than they need to pay the expected claims. In addition to this, they add to the premium enough to pay the operating expenses of the company. Finally, funds are invested and the investment income is used to reduce the cost of insurance. If the company is able to operate at an expense less than it calculated, if the excess collected to provide for emergencies in death claims is not needed, or if the death claims do not equal the tabular expectations, the savings are accumulated and at the end of the business year may be apportioned back to the premium payer as a dividend. Thus, in the long run, the equation balances. Premiums collected and interest earned equal the total of death claims, expenses, and dividends paid.

To summarize, the insurance premium is predicated upon the following assumptions: (*a*) *mortality*, (*b*) *loading* for expenses and contingencies, and (*c*) *interest* to be earned on reserve. The company expects mortality experience to be less than the assumed tabular experience. The loading for expenses is predicated upon experience, and effort is made to keep costs under the amount assumed in the rate calculations. The interest rate is conservative. All these margins provide safety factors. Portions of these margins not needed for safety are distributed to the policyholders periodically by participating companies. The return is, in fact, a policyholder's share of a realized surplus. The term "dividend," while somewhat of a misnomer for the return, has found acceptance in the business. For nonparticipating companies, margins are less and the safety factor is provided by the capital.

Actuarial Basis of Basic Contracts

The multiplicity of existing contracts might give rise to the assumption that a different set of mathematical assumptions is involved for each form. True, each form calls for a premium predi-

[7]The mortality table used for this calculation is the Commissioners' 1958 Standard Ordinary Mortality Table, generally referred to as the "1958 CSO Table." This table is noticed at greater length in Chapter 21.

cated upon the nature of the protection. Computing these premiums is complex and difficult actuarial work. The special contracts are simple in theory. The standard forms of term, whole life, endowment, and annuities are the bases of all calculations.

When the insurance is for the whole life of the insured, the insurance company undertakes to pay a definite sum whenever death may occur. Because of this, the type of insurance is known as *whole life insurance.* The principle upon which it is based is essentially the same as that already described. For example, a large group agrees to pay into a common fund, and out of this fund $1,000 is paid to the beneficiary of each member of the group upon the occasion of his death. Which members of the group will die within a comparatively short time and which will live to very old age, no one knows at the outset. The insurance underwriter does, however, have a very close approximation of how many in the group will die each year until there are no survivors. Knowing this, he knows how many will be paying premiums each year. Computing the annual premium payments and decreasing them by the amount of interest he expects to earn, he is able to compute how much must be received in premiums to have on hand funds to pay the death benefits to each member of the group when death occurs.

The *limited payment policy* is a whole life form but is distinguished from the ordinary life policy, which provides for premium payments for as long as the insured shall live, in that premium payments are made only for a definite number of years. The more usual premium payment periods are 10, 20, or 30 years. So far as premiums are concerned, the contract differs from the ordinary life policy only to the extent that those who survive the premium payment period indicated in the policy are relieved from cash payments for the remainder of their lives. The policy does not mature until death. It is necessary, therefore, that the insurance company accumulate enough money during the premium payment period to pay, when this fund is augmented by interest, the face of all the policies as they mature. On the basis of mortality experience, the insurance company knows, within workable limits, how many premiums it can expect during the premium payment period, and how many policies will mature each year from the inception of the contracts until there are no longer any survivors. Computations are so made that the funds will exactly pay the benefits, and when all benefits are paid nothing will be left.

The *endowment policy* differs from the whole life policy in that the face of the policy is paid if the insured is living at the end of the term indicated in the contract. If the insured dies during this term, the face of the policy is paid, as in the case of the whole life policy, to the designated beneficiary. Thus, with a 20-year endowment contract for $1,000, if the insured lives to the end of the term, he will receive $1,000, but if he dies before the end of the term, $1,000 will be paid to whomever he designates as beneficiary. The insurance company knows, on the basis of its mortality calculations, how many will live to the end of the period. It knows how many survivors will live to pay premiums each year and how many claims will have to be paid during the endowment period. It collects premiums enough to pay all these benefits. Naturally, accumulations must be made as the years go by to pay those policies that mature as endowments.

The *term policy* promises to pay the face of the policy if the insured dies during the stated policy period, such as 5, 10, or 20 years, or perhaps before a certain age such as sixty-five. The whole life, limited payment life, endowment, and term policies each carry a different premium charge. The term policy is the lowest, and there are increasingly higher rates for other forms until the short-term endowment is reached, which calls for the highest premium. This is not a different charge for the same thing; the insured, when he buys his policy, selects the group of which he wishes to become a member. In every case the premium is computed upon the basis of the coverage afforded in the contract. The premium receipts, in every instance, are divided among the members of the group in accordance with the plan determined upon when the group is made up—that is, when the policy is issued.

The *annuity* provides for a periodic payment for a period of years or for life. The annuity idea is the opposite of life insurance in that the annuity is concerned not with accumulation but with liquidation. Each member of the group contributes a lump sum that will provide annuity payments for all the members for life or for the term agreed upon.

The actuary is able to combine term insurance with whole life, whole life with an annuity, and innumerable other forms to work out in a single contract protection that underwriters have determined is needed. Since the special contracts are the actuarial sum of the combined basic contracts, presumably the end might be obtained without the special combination. It is evidence of the competitive nature of the insurance business that the combinations or special policies are made available in such numbers, for convenience and simplicity to the insured.

Development from Assessment Plans

Life insurance in its simplest form provides for permanent insurance written on a year-to-year basis. Based upon the morality experience, a group of insureds of a given age may each be charged a premium sufficient to provide a sum adequate to meet death claims for a year. The next year, since the survivors are older and the mortality experience will show a higher death rate, the premium will be higher than that of the preceding year. The procedure may be continued until all the survivors have died.

The early life insurance societies and associations followed the practice of collecting from each member each year an amount sufficient to create a fund adequate to pay the death claims for the year. Payments to beneficiaries of members who died were made from current income. As the average age of members increased, it was necessary, of course, that assessments increase.

The assessment plan of life insurance makes no provisions for a reserve out of which to pay death claims; rather, the plan is based upon the payment of all benefits out of current premiums. Sums in excess of current needs are sometimes collected to cover variations in anticipated claims and in estimated costs of doing business. Proponents of this plan failed to recognize that in any group there would, as the years went by, be a natural increase in claims unless sufficient new members could be obtained to maintain the relative and average age of the group.

Early assessment companies collected, as a rule, equal annual assessments from each member, regardless of age. It was soon realized that benefits at lowest cost were obtainable when the majority of members were young. Young people, in a society with many older members, began to drop out when the assessments became frequent; and if they wished to continue their insurance, they sought to join organizations made up largely of younger members. The greater the average age of the group, the more frequent were the assessments and the more difficult it became to secure new members. As the younger members dropped out of the older organizations, the inevitable result was an abnormally high rate of assessment, and not infrequently a collapse of the organization. The attendant loss to those old members who had all their lives contributed to the benefits of others was disheartening and often tragic.

Efforts to overcome the inequities growing out of age differentials resulted in plans whereby the assessments were graded according to age on joining the group. Another plan proposed that benefits be reduced as the member advanced in age. A third plan provided that assessments be increased with the increasing age of the member, while another provided for increased assessments at definite intervals. None of these plans has met with success.

The increasing premium charge based upon the age of the insured, provided the premiums are derived from sound data in the beginning, might work out satisfactorily. Actually, the plan is not successful because it provides insurance for a comparatively low premium charge during the period when the member has facilities for paying the maximum premium and builds up to an extremely heavy burden at that time when earning capacity is diminishing sharply or has actually ceased. This feature alone has been the cause of much hardship and disappointment.

Gradually it became evident that it was inequitable to make equal assessments for all ages. Changes, as they were made, were by no means the outgrowth of scientific statistical information. The organizations frequently undertook to use mortality experience but did not always draw sound conclusions about levying their assessments.

The assessment method of writing insurance has proved unworkable. Its serious defect lies in the requirement of (*a*) low premiums in the younger productive years and (*b*) high premiums in the older years of lessening productive capacity. The plan in operation tends (*a*) to defeat the purpose of life insurance and (*b*) to affect mortality experience adversely. The first disadvantage arises because, as premium charges increase, many of those insured feel they no longer can afford to carry the insurance. If the insurance is dropped because of the increased premium rate at a time when the insured has real need of it, the plan has defeated its purpose. The second disadvantage is the outgrowth of the reactions of human nature. It has been found that policyholders drop their insurance because rates are high—only when they feel themselves to be in reasonably good health. The insured suffering from some disease that may shorten his life usually struggles to keep his insurance in force regardless of increased cost. This throws the mortality experiences out of line with the tabular expectation. As the well members drop out and the ill remain, the mortality figures will soar, to the end that the premiums predicated on normal experience will not produce funds adequate to meet the claims.

For both these reasons, assessment insurance is no longer a favored form of permanent insurance protection and business assessment associations no longer occupy an important place in the field of life insurance. Nearly a half century ago a distinguished actuary wrote a fitting epithaph for assessment insurance: "The subject of assessment life insurance represents the pathological side, if I may express it, of life insurance."[8]

The Level Premium Plan for Permanent Protection

One-year renewable term insurance policies are available with premiums calculated on the basis of the amount necessary to insure a person at his attained age for one year. The policies are not com-

---

[8]Miles M. Dawson, "Assessment Life Insurance," *Annals of the American Academy of Political and Social Science,* Vol. XXVI (1905), p. 120.

monly used, however, except in group life insurance, and are designed to fit special situations requiring life insurance on a temporary basis. In the younger age groups, premiums appear particularly attractive; but as permanent insurance handled on a year-by-year basis, the contracts manifest the same defects as assessment plans. For lifetime protection, the yearly renewable term insurance is not recommended.

The defects of the one-year renewable premium plan were regarded as so serious as almost to jeopardize the life insurance plan. To correct these defects, a plan that would not increase the premium with the age of the insured was devised and has become familiar to life insurance policyholders.

The system provides for payment by the insured, at regular intervals, of a premium that is constant throughout the premium-paying life of the contract. This obviates the necessity, and disposes of the disadvantages, of an increasing premium each year. The plan is one of averaging or leveling, and hence the term *level premium.* Based on careful calculations, premiums substantially in excess of the cost of protection are collected in the earlier years of the policy. The excess is invested and the accumulated sum reduces the amount at risk each year. (See Chapter 21 for further discussion and diagrams of the level premium plan.)

Reserves. The law establishes a minimum amount that the company must have available to guarantee future obligations with respect to all policies. This amount is known as the *reserve.* It is sometimes called "reserves required to meet future claims" and sometimes, because the minimum amount is fixed by law, is termed "legally required reserves," or, more briefly, "legal reserve." As the insured grows older, the reserve reduces the risk for the insurance company to the end that a constantly increasing premium is not required to meet the increased mortality rate. See Figure 11. Under the level premium plan the amount of insurance carried by the company, sometimes termed the *net amount at risk,* is the face of the policy less the policyholder's excess payments increased by interest earned from investments. Level premium plans, therefore, are a combination of protection and investment.

Combining Protection and Investment. Life insurance policies are classified as (*a*) temporary or "term" and (*b*) permanent or "whole life." Temporary life insurance provides protection only for the number of years designated in the contract. It is more like the ordinary insurance contract covering property. If the policyholder outlives the term indicated in the policy, the coverage is terminated and no payment is made either to him or to his beneficiary.

Permanent life insurance combines with the element of pure insurance a saving or accumulation feature. Basically the contract is composed of two elements: (*a*) reserve and (*b*) pure life insurance. The reserve represents savings invested for the account of the group. Different forms of permanent insurance are designed to meet specific needs. The element of savings varies, and the premium payment is adjusted to the type of coverage. The amount of the investment account increases each year as premium payments are made. Since pure life insurance, that is the net amount at risk, is on a decreasing basis, if the insured lives long enough the investment element would ultimately equal the face of the policy.

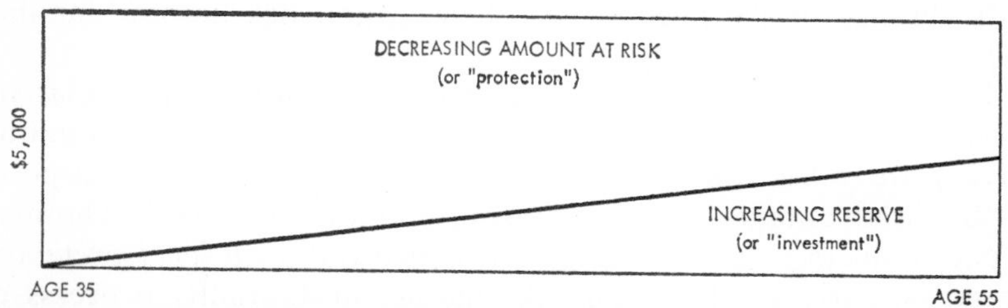

Figure 11. Diagram Showing Decreasing Amount at Risk, First 20 Years of Ordinary Life Policy Issued at Age Thirty-five.

Cash Values. While the reserve is a group matter, parallel with it is a *cash value* allocated to each individual policy. The cash value, which also builds up from year to year, may be withdrawn by the policyholder. The policyholder may also elect to borrow against the cash value.

Borrowing is quite different from withdrawal and sometimes occasions misunderstanding. A loan requires interest, and the question is frequently put: "Why should a policyholder pay interest on his own money?" The question points up a difference between reserve and cash value. The reserve is a group asset and must continually be increased at the rate of interest contemplated in rate calculations if the company is to meet future policy obligations. It makes no difference whether the reserve is invested in bonds or loaned to policyholders. It must continue to earn interest.

On the other hand, if the cash value is withdrawn and the insurance terminated, that part of the reserve designed to meet the maturity of that policy is freed. To withdraw the cash value, then, means the termination of insurance. To borrow the cash value with repayment of principal and interest retains the insurance in force.

The Investment Functions of Life Insurance

Interest is one of the assumptions upon which the calculations of life insurance premiums are based. Hence, the investment of reserve takes on importance. The continued accumulation of life insurance funds is inherent in the level premium system. The investment of these funds in a manner that will earn the necessary interest and assure payment of the principal on maturity is one of the major functions of the insurance business.

Life insurance undertakes to replace income to the dependents of a policyholder or others in the event of his death, and to replace income to the policyholder and his dependents in old age. To the extent that life insurance is purchased for protection, it is a contract of insurance. Emphasis upon the need for income with security, and the trend toward high taxation on current income from other capital assets has brought life insurance to the forefront as an investment outlet. It provides a maximum income with security because life insurance may be planned to distribute both principal and income. To the extent that life insurance is purchased as a source of income, it becomes an investment.

Attempted interpretations of the investment feature of life insurance have sometimes cast unfavorable reflections upon sound investment securities. This is unfortunate since the very foundation of life insurance rests upon sound securities. To state that life insurance is a unique type of investment need not reflect unfavorably upon other types of securities. It is sufficient that it is a particular type of investment carefully worked out to meet a particular need. It can be demonstrated that certain forms of life insurance carried to maturity will afford a yield comparable to that of high-grade securities. Forms of life insurance having an element of investment give policyholders the benefit of the highest type of investment skill and management. The insured has an ownership in a cross section of the accumulated reserve of the life insurance company writing the contract. This represents diversification and a maximum of security.

The usefulness of life insurance as an investment is dependent entirely upon the financial position, resources, and investment needs of the investor. Its unique features are to be found in the fact that investments in life insurance may be arranged so that there will be freedom from seizure from the insured's creditors. It is the only form of investment that may be liquidated on installment plans that involve life contingencies, and the investment objective is protected against failure of completion because of death.

Advantages possessed by life insurance that are characteristic of other high-grade investments include: a safe principal and income, reasonable yield, and ready marketability without sacrifice in value. Life insurance is free from fluctuations and is always available as high-grade collateral for a loan. It may be purchased in face amounts that are convenient and, when used as an investment, frees the owner from the responsibility for the selection of individual investments. Installment purchases are available to fit the convenience of the buyer, and the investment is further protected by the supervision to which the life insurance business is subject.

No other institution can equal the service of life insurance for providing protection against losses growing out of life risks. If capital is limited and income is the primary need, no other investment source meets the situation as does life insurance. The life insurance guarantee may provide not only that the income will be regular and sure but that the period of income cannot be outlived by the recipient. For the inexperienced investor, life insurance eliminates reinvestment problems and risks. In the light of current high taxes and safe interest yields, it is for many virtually the only source of spendable income for old age or for the support of dependents.

Legal Doctrines

There are several legal doctrines applied in the field of life insurance which are fundamental to an understanding of how life insurance works.

Right to Trace Misappropriation. The question presents itself as to the rights of the parties to these values where the insured misappropriates funds to pay premiums. When a defrauded person is able to trace his funds to the payment of life insurance premiums, his rights to the benefits of the policy precede those of both the insured and the beneficiary. This is so because it has been held contrary to public policy to allow the life insurance policy to serve as a vehicle for fraud. The rightful owner of monies used for the payment of life insurance premiums may follow the funds upon the theory which allows a beneficiary to follow trust funds and to appropriate to himself the property into which such funds have been changed.

A difficulty sometimes arises as to what proportion of the misappropriated funds was used to pay insurance premiums. If the premiums were paid entirely from the funds of the party defrauded, he is entitled to the entire proceeds of the policy; otherwise, the defrauded party may secure from the proceeds of the policy only so much as is necessary to reimburse himself.

Effects of Divorce. Where there is no statute covering the situation, a divorce does not deprive the beneficiary of rights under a life insurance policy. In some jurisdictions the statutes make provision for terminating the interest of a beneficiary following a divorce from the person whose life is insured.[9] If there is no such provision

---

[9]In a number of states, divorce terminates the interest of a wife-beneficiary even though the interest prior to the divorce was vested and the insured husband has not reserved the right to designate a new beneficiary. In some instances, laws governing the disposition of property have served to terminate the wife's interest; in one state, it is terminated upon cessation of insurable interest. Other statutes provide that the

in the statutes, when the beneficiary is made irrevocable under the terms of the contract, the beneficiary designated may retain his beneficial interest in the insurance following a divorce.

Murder by Beneficiary. It is well settled that the beneficiary of a life insurance policy cannot recover on the policy if he has feloniously caused the death of the insured. This rule is based upon the principle that one may not profit by his own criminal act.

If the beneficiary is the cause of the death because of an accident, or because he is mentally incompetent and irresponsible and, therefore, not guilty of a criminal act, his rights under the policy remain unaffected.

It was at one time argued that, if an insured was murdered by a beneficiary, the act served to discharge the entire liability of the company. The general rule today holds to the contrary and requires that the proceeds of the insurance be paid to the personal representatives of the insured.[10]

Common Disaster. In the event of a disaster in which both the insured and the beneficiary lose their lives, there is no presumption as to the survivor. So far as the rights of the estate of each are concerned, much may depend upon establishing which of the two outlived the other.

The courts have held that the burden of proof rests upon the representatives of the beneficiary. For example, if a husband insures his life, naming his wife as beneficiary, and both are lost in a disaster under such circumstances as to raise a doubt as to which survived, if the benefits of the insurance are to descend to the wife's estate, it must be shown that she actually survived her husband.

In some states statutory action has been taken with a view to eliminating the necessity of litigation. While not all statutes are the same, the simplest form of legislative enactment provides that, when the insured and the beneficiary have died, and there is not sufficient evidence that they have died at different times, the proceeds of the policy shall be distributed as if the insured had survived the bene-

---

insured shall have the power to designate a beneficiary to succeed a divorced wife, In the absence of governing statute, it is the general rule that a divorce will not terminate the irrevocable interest of a wife-beneficiary.

[10]The courts have reasoned that premiums have been paid to, and retained by, the company and that the money which the company has contracted to pay should, therefore, not be withheld entirely. If there is no beneficiary free from the taint of the crime, the proceeds are payable to the estate of the insured, on the ground that public policy is here not a question.

An exception to the foregoing rule is found in the case in which the insurance policy is procured as a part of an attempt to defraud the insurance carrier. In this case, the beneficiary himself procures insurance with the intent to murder the insured. In such circumstances, the company is relieved of any obligation to pay, not because the death was caused by murder, but because the issuance of the policy was tainted with fraud and, therefore, carried no liability from the beginning.

ficiary.[11] In the absence of such legislation there is no presumption of survivorship in the case of persons who perished in a common disaster with no proof tending to show the order of death. The question of actual survivorship is regarded as unascertainable, and descent and distribution take the same course as if the deaths had been simultaneous.[12]

Presumption of Death. The question arises as to the rights of a beneficiary under a life insurance policy if the insured disappears and is assumed to be dead but actual proof of death cannot be presented. Here the rules with respect to presumptions apply. Unexplained absence for seven years, with no communication with those who might be expected to hear if such person were alive, raises the presumption of the death of the absent party. "The presumption of the duration of life with respect to persons of whom no account can be given ends at the expiration of seven years from the time when they were last known to be living."[13] In order to establish the presumption, it has been held that the absence must be from the last place of residence "which was known to his family or his relatives who would be likely to know whether he was living, and from whom a party in search of the truth would be likely to make inquiries."[14]

The presumption of death is prima facie, that is, it is rebuttable; evidence may always be introduced to show that the person presumed to be dead was seen alive or that a reasonable explanation can be advanced for the absence. In cases involving life insurance, therefore, if the actual time of death is of importance, the beneficiary or any other party who asserts a right based upon the death of the insured must prove by a preponderance of evidence the time that such death took place. There is no help from the law as to the time that the death occurred. The time of death, in absence of evidence, will be set at the end of the seven-year period.

If evidence can be introduced showing good and sufficient reason for a person leaving his place of abode and disappearing for seven years, the presumption does not operate, and a jury must decide on the basis of the evidence submitted. In other words, if sufficient reason can be given to explain the absence to the satisfaction of a jury, the absence is no longer unexplained and the presumption

[11]For example, see the Uniform Simultaneous Death Act. This act has been enacted in 47 states and the District of Columbia. It has not been adopted in Georgia, Louisiana, nor Ohio. However, Georgia and Louisiana have Insurance Law provisions which stipulate that, in the case of simultaneous death, the proceeds will be distributed as if the insured survived the beneficiary—unless the policy provides otherwise. Thus, although in form three states have not adopted the Uniform Law, as a practical matter the principle contained in this law has been enacted in all jurisdictions except Ohio.

[12]*Young Women's Christian Home* v. *French,* 187 U.S. 401.

[13]*George* v. *Jesson,* 6 East. 80, 85 (1805).

[14]*McCartee* v. *Camel,* 1 Barb., chap. 455.

no longer obtains.[15] There may be situations in which an absentee, for reasons of his own, refuses to communicate with family or friends, and yet the presumption of death is not raised. To raise the presumption, the absence must be unexplained.

Presumption against Suicide. Life insurance policies do not pay their full face in the event that the insured meets death as the result of suicide within a limited period, usually two years, from the date of issue of the policy. Hence, it frequently happens that the question of whether or not the insured committed suicide must be settled in order to determine the extent of liability under the policy.

If the question of suicide becomes material and the company writing a life insurance policy denies liability on this ground, the burden of proof rests upon the company to show that there was in fact a suicide. "The love of life is ordinarily a sufficient inducement for its preservation, and, in the absence of proof that death resulted from other than natural causes, suicide will not be presumed."[16] When the evidence permits reasonable doubt as between a conclusion that death was caused by suicide or was the result of an accidental or natural cause, the presumption operates against a finding of suicide. "The law indulges in a presumption that a person will not take his own life, and where the facts and circumstances are as consistent with death from negligence, by accident, or homicide, as by suicide, the presumption is against suicide."[17] Suicide is established when the evidence indicates that death was self-inflicted and permits no other reasonable inference.

Death by Legal Execution. Early policies were issued which excluded liability on the part of the insurer for death of the insured at the hand of the law. The situation is now generally changed. Statutes frequently enumerate the risks a life insurance company may exclude from coverage under the terms of its policy; and, where death at the hands of the law is not a permitted exclusion, the policy would cover such a death.[18] It is now generally held, particularly where the policy contains an incontestable clause, that, in the absence of any express provision touching upon death by legal execution, the policy will cover this death as it does any other.[19]

Rights of Creditors to Life Insurance Values. Since life insurance represents the accumulation of a fund for investment, the rights of creditors to the value of the insurance in the case of the insolvency of the insured are frequently perplexing. It has been established that there is no fraud of creditors on the part of an insolvent

---

[15] *Shaw* v. *Prudential Insurance Co. of America,* 290 Pac. Rep. 694 (1930).
[16] *Union Casualty and Surety Co.* v. *Goddard,* 76 S.W. 832.
[17] *White v. Prudential Insurance Company,* 120 App. Div. 260.
[18] *Prudential Insurance Company* v. *Goldstein,* 43 F. Supp. 767.
[19] *Weeks* v. *New York Life Insurance Company,* 122 S.E. 586; 35 A.L.R. 1482.

debtor when reasonable insurance premiums are paid upon policies and the beneficiaries designated are such dependents as wife or children.[20]

With respect to proceeds, early in the history of life insurance in this country statutes were enacted exempting them from the claims of creditors. With the passage of time, the tendency to liberalize exemptions[21] has manifested itself. It is the law in most states that a third-party beneficiary under a policy effected by any person on his own life is entitled to the proceeds of the insurance against the creditors and representatives of the person whose life is insured.[22]

State statutes that undertake to provide security for a third-party beneficiary for the proceeds of life insurance as against the creditors of the insured differ in the various jurisdictions. In some instances, the exemption applies to specified classes of beneficiaries, such as wife, children, relatives, dependents, or creditors of the beneficiaries. In others, it extends to any third-party beneficiary, assignee, or payee. Exemption privileges apply whether or not the right is reserved in the policy to change the beneficiary. Neither is the right affected if the policy is made payable to the insured if the beneficiary predeceases him.

State exemption statutes fall into one of several broad classifications: (*a*) statutes exempting close relatives, (*b*) statutes exempting all insurance from creditor claims if effected in favor of a person other than the insured, (*c*) statutes exempting a limited amount of protection, (*d*) unlimited exemption, and (*e*) special statutes. Each is discussed briefly in the following paragraphs.

---

[20]In the case of bankruptcy, under the terms of the Bankruptcy Act, the bankrupt is permitted to retain his insurance and keep it in force but is required to turn over an amount equal to the cash value to the trustee in bankruptcy. In this situation it is not necessary that the policies specifically state that they have a cash value, but if as a matter of fact such a value exists, it may be reached. The United States Supreme Court has ruled that, if the state statutes exempt a policy, it is exempt in bankruptcy proceedings. In a few states statutes have been enacted specifically excepting policies with revocable beneficiary if the beneficiary is the wife, child, or dependent relative of the insured. If the bankrupt is a third-party beneficiary, even though he has a vested interest in the policy, it cannot be reached by creditors. Finally, if the bankrupt's policy is written designating irrevocably a third party as beneficiary, the irrevocable interest of the third party cannot be reached by the creditors of the insured.

[21]For complete analysis of the types, extent, and reasons for the protection of life insurance against creditors, as discussed in this section, see Stuart Schwarzschild, *Rights of Creditors in Life Insurance Policies* (Homewood, Ill.: Richard D. Irwin, Inc., published for the S.S. Huebner Foundation for Insurance Education, 1963).

[22]This feature of life insurance has sometimes been said to create an unjust discrimination against creditors. The exemption is justified upon the theory that an individual has definite obligations to wife, children, and dependents, as well as to creditors, and that there is as much justification in placing dependents in a prior position through insurance as there is in putting creditors in a preferred position through a mortgage. The protecton of the interests of a beneficiary by statutory enactment is based upon the premise of an obligation to beneficiaries that may rightfully precede that of personal creditors.

In some states the proceeds of life insurance are protected up to a given amount if payable to certain designated beneficiaries, ordinarily *close relatives,* such as widow, husband, or minor child. In certain states, general exemption statutes protect the proceeds of life insurance from all creditors, including creditors of the beneficiary, without specific mention of insurance. The protection under the general exemption statutes is very broad; but the amount, ordinarily, is sharply limited.

The most widely used exemption statute provides that the *beneficiary or his assignee, other than the insured or the person effecting the insurance,* shall be entitled to the "proceeds and avails" of the policy without any limitation (based on the amount of premium or the face amount of the policy) against the creditors and representatives of the insured. The law provides no protection against creditors of a beneficiary. Neither is the person who effects the insurance protected as an insured or as a beneficiary.[23]

Statutes, in attempting to *limit the amount of insurance* to be exempt from claims of creditors, have made two approaches: (*a*) exempting a limited amount of insurance and (*b*) exempting insurance purchased with a limited amount of annual premium. In a number of states, statutes provide a broad exemption for life insurance benefits if annual premiums do not exceed a given sum—in some instances $500 and in others $250. The terms of the statutes differ; the common characteristic is a limitation of exemptions, based upon annual premium payments.

In a very few states the laws *provide unlimited exemption* of life insurance proceeds of every character from all liability for debt. These statutes protect against creditors of the insured and of the beneficiary. Beneficiary protection may depend upon relationship to the insured.

A number of *special statutes* may apply. They include: (*a*) group insurance, (*b*) fraternal insurance, (*c*) recipients of relief, (*d*) annuitants, and (*e*) recipients of disability income. A number of states provide broad protection against creditors in the case of insurance proceeds of both fraternal benefit societies and insured groups. Protection against creditors of beneficiaries is a characteristic of these statutes.[24]

---

[23]Laws of this type make an exception in protecting the proceeds of insurance against claims of creditors by providing that the amount of any premium paid to defraud creditors shall, with interest, inure to the benefit of the defrauded creditors from the proceeds of the policy.

[24]Under the statutes governing relief, recipients of relief may be obligated to assign life insurance to the relief authority, or the welfare authority may have a preferred claim to insurance proceeds payable to the insured's estate, to the extent of the assistance rendered. Frequently, minimum amounts of life insurance are exempted

(Continued on next page)

SUMMARY

The field of life insurance in one generation has shown more than a threefold increase in assets, sales, dollar value of contracts in force and most other statistical indices. It deserves separate study because of its $13 billion of annual premiums (of the total private insurance business of $33 billion) and because of its many unique insurance features.

Some of the *unusual features* of life insurance are (1) its combination of protection and accumulation, (2) its use of the valued policy concept in place of indemnity as a measure of loss, (3) the certainty of the peril insured against (death) occurring, but the uncertainty as to its time of happening, and (4) the many types of insurable interests which exist by a person on his own life by close relatives, by creditors, by partners and by corporations on the lives of their key employees.

Certain *basic concepts* apply throughout the business of life insurance. The *life insurance equation* states that, in the long run, premiums received and interest earned by a life insurer will equal the total of death claims, expenses, and dividends paid. The *actuarial basis* of each of the basic contracts—term, whole life, endowment, and annuity—can be calculated by considering the effects of (1) mortality, (2) interest, and (3) expenses.

The *assessment plan*, charging at the end of each year the costs that have been incurred, is one of the easiest and simplest methods of determining life insurance costs. Unfortunately, the plan as used in the development of life insurance had many inequities and several false assumptions which made its use unworkable. The *level premium plan* is the soundest method of providing permanent protection in a life insurance contract. It combines protection (or decreasing "net amount at risk") and investment (in the form of an increasing "legal reserve"). Investments thus become very important in life insurance cost and solvency. Many features of life insurance make it an ideal investment medium, as it combines reasonable return, ready marketability, convenience, safety of principal, liquidation by using life contingencies, *and* protection against not being able to fulfill investment objectives due to premature death.

---

from such claims. There are various exemption statutes protecting annuitants. In some instances, the law provides exemption from the purchaser's creditors up to a stipulated monthly sum; in other instances, if the annuity is purchased for another, protection is afforded without specified limitation; in still other instances, protection is extended to creditors both of the purchaser and of the annuitant. In the case of disability income, the laws are by no means uniform, but a number of states have made the matter the subject of special statutes. Sometimes the exemption is limited as to amount, although an exception may be made for debts incurred for necessaries. Where the general statute covering insurance is adequate, the need for special legislation dealing with disability payments is obviated.

Certain legal doctrines are also fundamental in many forms of life insurance. Some of these include: the right to trace misappropriated funds; the effects of divorce, murder by a beneficiary, death by legal execution, and common disaster to both insured and beneficiary; the legal presumption of death after disappearance for seven years; the presumption against suicide; and the substantial protection of life insurance proceeds against the claims of creditors.

FOR REVIEW

1. Develop, in your own words, a definition of life insurance. How does this definition compare with your general definition of insurance?
2. Legally and technically, life insurance is not a contract of indemnity. Why not? Is there a relationship between life insurance and the *idea* of indemnity? Explain your answer.
3. In what ways does life insurance differ from other types of insurance? Why are these differences important (*a*) to the insurer? and (*b*) to the insured?
4. Many situations give rise to an insurable interest in life insurance. Give an example of at least four different insurable interests.
5. The cost of life insurance is based upon three fundamental estimates which must be made by an insurance company. What are they, and how accurately can they be predicted? Indicate any special problems which the insurer may have in predicting these costs.
6. Have economic trends been helpful or harmful in the prediction of the cost factors you have discussed in the answer to Question 5? Justify your answer with full explanation.
7. How is the actuarial basis for the basic life insurance contracts (*a*) similar and (*b*) different?
8. What are the fallacies in the assessment plan when it is applied to life insurance? Can they be overcome by (*a*) modifications of the assessment method of pricing life insurance? or (*b*) by a different premium-paying plan?
9. Permanent forms of life insurance combine protection and investment. How can you tell how much of each is involved in a particular policy at a particular time?
10. How would you explain the advantages of life insurance as an investment to a newly married couple who is considering the purchase of a life insurance contract?
11. X and Y are in no way related. They came to this country as immigrants at the age of 16 and, because of their common interest, a friendship developed that lasted through life. X married, and Y remained single. Y wishes to insure his life, naming X's children as beneficiaries, but is told he cannot do this since, as a matter of fact, no blood relationship exists. Do you agree or disagree? Why?
12. B insures his life, naming his wife as beneficiary. Five years later B is charged with emzezzlement and found guilty. The firm from whom the money was stolen claims the proceeds of the policy. What is the position of the wife?
13. X murders his wife. He is the beneficiary of a life insurance policy covering her life and his mother is an alternative beneficiary. Since a murderer cannot receive the proceeds of a life insurance policy payable because of the murder, and because he was sentenced to prison for life, his mother

claims the insurance. The mother's claim is based on a statute which declares life convicts "officially dead." The deceased wife's administrator also claims the proceeds. Is the alternative beneficiary entitled to the benefits, or should they go to the administrator of the deceased wife?

14. B carries life insurance in the amount of $15,000, naming his wife as beneficiary. On a certain day the wife shoots and kills her husband and immediately thereafter takes her own life. The heirs of the wife claim the proceeds of the policy, as do the heirs of the insured. What is the determining factor covering the payment of this insurance?
15. A is the husband of B. A carries $50,000 insurance for the benefit of B. A's only other living relative is a brother. B's only heir is a nephew. Both A and B perished in an aviation disaster. The brother of A and the nephew of B claim the insurance. To whom will the insurance be paid? Could the problem have been avoided by any special provisions in the insurance policy?
16. A disappears without any explanation; will his wife receive payment as beneficiary under his life insurance policy? Suppose A was a crewman on the submarine *Thresher* which disappeared in the Atlantic last year. Would your answer be the same? Why or why not?
17. What significant advantages does life insurance have to the insured from the standpoint of creditors to the insurance contract values?

Chapter 21

ESTIMATING THE LIFE RISK

LIFE insurance companies must estimate the price of their insurance contracts in a safe and equitable manner. The goal requires analysis of mortality costs, interest earnings, and other expense factors.

Because of a wealth of statistical information available and of favorable trends during the twentieth century, the pricing of life insurance contracts is sometimes considered one of the easiest and most accurate of all insurance rating tasks. However, accomplishing perfect safety of principal and fairness among all policyholders is not as simple as the preceding common compliment to the life insurance business might indicate.

The long-range nature of the necessary predictions for life insurance pricing is one of the complicating factors. Oftentimes the life insurance contract spans forty years or more. Very few businesses attempt to guarantee a fixed price for their product for such a long time into the future as life insurance does. Even most other insurance policies are based upon predictions of costs for only a limited period of one or a few years. First, let us look at the problem of life insurers as they estimate the number of deaths which will cause payments under the various contracts of life insurance.

THE MORTALITY TABLE

What It Is

Since the obligation of the life insurance company to pay benefits depends upon a life contingency, actuaries must know the expected life span of an insured group. The *mortality table* is the instrument by which the probability of living or dying is measured. This is a table showing the probable death rate at each age, frequently in a form showing how many persons, starting with a given number at a given age, will probably die during each succeeding year.

Where It Comes from

Life insurance actuaries have been able to construct tables showing the mortality experience of large groups of people. Applying the principles of the theory of probability and the law of large numbers, they have found that they can readily anticipate the number of deaths and the time of their occurrence in any large group. It is known that the accuracy of predictions is greater, the greater the number of cases under observation. This being the case, in calculating the ratio of deaths, the group, to be reliable, must be sufficiently large to come within the operation of the law of large numbers and permit variations from the average to cancel each other. Insurance actuaries have learned that it is not absolutely necessary to have all the cases in a group started at a given time. If the group cannot be made up of a sufficiently large number of cases at one time, it is found that much the same results are obtained if a small number of lives are insured, and the size of the group is built up by accumulating like cases over a long period of time. In other words, as the groups are increased over time, the actual results tend to equal the expected results.

The number of deaths to be expected in a large group of a given age can be predicted with such a degree of certainty as to provide a basis for a safe calculation of life insurance premiums. The uncertainty in the case of the individual is reduced to a certainty as the individual is absorbed by the group.

The number of living at the youngest age is called the "radix" of the table. The radix is an arbitrary figure. The completed table is an orderly schedule of the number of persons who die at each age and the number who survive out of a given number under observation. The information in a table does not come to actuaries in the form shown. To secure data on 100,000 lives from birth 100 years ago and trace that data until each person died would be impossible, since such data are not available. The mortality table, which appears to give a life history of such a group, is the outgrowth of mathematical computations with the formal arrangement of derived data.

Basic Construction

A completed mortality table seems to suggest that, in its construction, the actuary started with the number of lives indicated in the radix and then followed the history of that group from year to year until there were no survivors. Actually, the actuary determines the mortality rates for all the ages to be included in his table, and from these he builds up a table based upon such radix as he selects. It is a scientific assembly of data in a convenient form in order to show the probabilities of death and survival.

In assembling the data, a large group at each age is selected for observation, commencing with the age at which the table is to begin. A record is made each year of the number who die in each group under observation. By knowing the number of persons constituting a group of a given age and the number of persons dying during the year, the probability that a person of a given age will live one year can be approximated. Applying the probability that a person of that age will live one year to the number living at any given age, the expected number living at the beginning of the next succeeding year may be determined. The process is repeated for each age until a year is reached in which the number dying equals the number living at the beginning of that year.[1] The data are then arranged in the familiar tabular form.

Since the radix of the table is arbitrary, the numbers in the columns headed "Number Living" and "Number Dying" are significant only as they serve as a basis for determining the proportion between the number living and the number dying. The column headed "Death Rate per 1,000" is the basic feature of the table, and from it the other columns are derived.

The arrangement of a table is standard. There are five basic columns. The first of these is headed "Age." The second is the l_x (Number living) column and represents the number living at the age indicated in the age column. The third is the d_x column (Number Dying) and represents the number of these in the l_x column who die before becoming a year older. The fourth is the q_x column (Death Rate per 1,000) and is a figure derived from the first two columns. These columns are usually arranged under the headings appearing in the Commissioners 1958 Standard Ordinary Mortality Table, which appears below in Table 21–1. The final column "Expectancy, Years," often is included to show the expected number of years of life at each age.

---

[1]Expressed in mathematical notations, after the arbitrary selection of the number to represent the radix, the values of p_x are determined; and from these values, the values of l_x may be computed successively for each successive higher age by the use of the relation $l_x p_x = l_{x+1}$. The value of q_x is obtained by dividing θ_x by E_x.

The following notations are used to express the probability of living or dying, utilizing the data in the mortality table:

p_x = the probability that a person aged x will live 1 year,
q_x = the probability that x will die during the year from age x to age $x + 1$,
l_x = number of persons living at age x,
d_x = number of persons dying from age x to age $x + 1$,
${}_np_x$ = the probability that a person aged x will live n years.

Therefore,

$$d_x = l_x - l_{x+1},$$
$$p_x = (l_{x+1}/l_x),$$
$$q_x = (d_x/l_x),$$
$${}_np_x = (l_{x+n}/l_x).$$

In constructing a mortality table based upon the records of insured lives, the notations θ and E are used and the value of q_x for each age is determined by dividing θ_x by E_x, where

θ_x represents the deaths for the year between the ages x and $x + 1$, and
E_x represents the number exposed to risk of death for the year between the ages x and $x + 1$ in the data being used as a basis for the calculations.

TABLE 21–1

1958 CSO (Commissioners Standard Ordinary) Mortality Table

Age	*Number Living*	*Number Dying*	*Death Rate Per 1,000*	*Expectancy, Years*	*Age*	*Number Living*	*Number Dying*	*Death Rate Per 1,000*	*Expectancy, Years*
0	10,000,000	70,800	7.08	68.30	50	8,762,306	72,902	8.32	23.63
1	9,929,200	17,475	1.76	67.78	51	8,689,404	79,160	9.11	22.82
2	9,911,725	15.066	1.52	66.90	52	8,610,244	85,758	9.96	22.03
3	9,896,659	14,449	1.46	66.00	53	8,524,486	92,832	10.89	21.25
4	9,882,210	13,835	1.40	65.10	54	8,431,654	100,337	11.90	20.47
5	9,868,375	13,322	1.35	64.19	55	8,331,317	108,307	13.00	19.71
6	9,855,053	12,812	1.30	63.27	56	8,223,010	116,849	14.21	18.97
7	9,842,241	12,401	1.26	62.35	57	8,106,161	125,970	15.54	18.23
8	9,829,840	12,091	1.23	61.43	58	7,980,191	135,663	17.00	17.51
9	9,817,749	11,879	1.21	60.51	59	7,844,528	145,830	18.59	16.81
10	9,805,870	11,865	1.21	59.58	60	7,698,698	156,592	20.34	16.12
11	9,794,005	12,047	1.23	58.65	61	7,542,106	167,736	22.24	15.44
12	9,781,958	12,325	1.26	57.72	62	7,374,370	179,271	24.31	14.78
13	9,769,633	12,896	1.32	56.80	63	7,195,099	191,174	26.57	14.14
14	9,756,737	13.562	1.39	55.87	64	7,003,925	203,394	29.04	13.51
15	9,743,175	14,225	1.46	54.95	65	6,800,531	215,917	31.75	12.90
16	9,728,950	14,983	1.54	54.03	66	6,584,614	228,749	34.74	12.31
17	9,713,967	15,737	1.62	53.11	67	6,355,865	241,777	38.04	11.73
18	9,698,230	16,390	1.69	52.19	68	6,114,088	254,835	41.68	11.17
19	9,681,840	16,846	1.74	51.28	69	5,859,253	267,241	45.61	10.64
20	9,664,994	17,300	1.79	50.37	70	5,592,012	278,426	49.79	10.12
21	9,647,694	17,655	1.83	49.46	71	5,313,586	287,731	54.15	9.63
22	9,630,039	17,912	1.86	48.55	72	5,025,855	294,766	58.65	9.15
23	9,612,127	18,167	1.89	47.64	73	4,731,089	299,289	63.26	8.69
24	9,593,960	18,324	1.91	46.73	74	4,431,800	301,894	68.12	8.24
25	9,575,636	18,481	1.93	45.82	75	4,129,906	303,011	73.73	7.81
26	9,557,155	18,732	1.96	44.90	76	3,826,895	303,014	79.18	7.39
27	9,538,423	18,981	1.99	43.99	77	3,523,881	301,997	85.70	6.98
28	9,519,442	19,324	2.03	43.08	78	3,221,884	299,829	93.06	6.59
29	9,500,118	19,760	2.08	42.16	79	2,922,055	295,683	101.19	6.21
30	9,480,358	20,193	2.13	41.25	80	2,626,372	288,848	109.98	5.85
31	9,460,165	20,718	2.19	40.34	81	2,337,524	278,983	119.35	5.51
32	9,439,447	21,239	2.25	39.43	82	2,058,541	265,902	129.17	5.19
33	9,418,208	21,850	2.32	38.51	83	1,792,639	249,858	139.38	4.89
34	9,396,358	22,551	2.40	37.60	84	1,542,781	231,433	150.01	4.60
35	9,373,807	23,528	2.51	36.69	85	1,311,348	211,311	161.14	4.32
36	9,350,279	24,685	2.64	35.78	86	1,100,037	190,108	172.82	4.06
37	9,325,594	26,112	2.80	34.88	87	909,929	168,455	185.13	3.80
38	9,299,482	27,991	3.01	33.97	88	741,474	146,997	198.25	3.55
39	9,271,491	30,132	3.25	33.07	89	594,477	126,303	212.46	3.31
40	9,241,359	32,622	3.53	32.18	90	468,174	106,809	228.14	3.06
41	9,208,737	35,362	3.84	31.29	91	361,365	88,813	245.77	2.82
42	9,173,375	38,253	4.17	30.41	92	272,552	72,480	265.93	2.58
43	9,135,122	41,382	4.53	29.54	93	200,072	57,881	289.30	2.33
44	9,093,740	44,741	4.92	28.67	94	142,191	45,026	316.66	2.07
45	9,048,999	48,412	5.35	27.81	95	97,165	34,128	351.24	1.80
46	9,000,587	52,473	5.83	26.95	96	63,037	25,250	400.56	1.51
47	8,948,114	56,910	6.36	26.11	97	37,787	18,456	488.42	1.18
48	8,891,204	61,794	6.95	25.27	98	19,331	12,916	688.15	.83
49	8,829,410	67,104	7.60	24.45	99	6,415	6,415	1,000.00	.50

Actuaries and the Purposes of Mortality Tables

Any table to be used by a life company is the responsibility of the actuary. Statutory enactments limit this responsibility, prescribing the table to be used for certain purposes. The actuary needs the mortality table (*a*) to calculate premium rates, (*b*) to calculate nonforfeiture benefits on lapse or surrender, (*c*) to value contract liabilities, (*d*) to calculate gains and losses from insurance operations, and (*e*) to calculate dividends on participating contracts. The table serves also as a standard for the measurement of the mortality experience in any particular field or group.

A department known as the actuarial department is headed by the company actuary.[2] He may be and frequently is a company officer. The actuarial staff varies with the size of the organization, its needs, and the nature of the business. There may be an associate actuary or several such associates who may head various company divisions. In the actuarial department itself, there often are a number of assistant actuaries, mathematicians, actuarial assistants, and department managers. The work of the actuarial department is closely allied with that of the medical department, and for this reason the work of the medical director in company organization plans may be cleared through the office of the actuary.

KINDS OF MORTALITY TABLES

Different Tables for Different Needs

The mortality table is a basic instrument that serves as a point of departure for actuarial computations. A difference in tables does not mean that one is accurate and the other incorrect. Different tables are computed for different needs.

The rate important to life insurance premium calculations is the mortality rate of insured lives rather than of a mixture of insured and uninsured lives. It is important, as well, that the group of insured lives from which the mortality rate is to be determined be representative of the group to be insured. For example, the field of industrial life insurance bases its contracts on the 1941 Standard Industrial Table, while annuities use an entirely different mortality table.

It might, at first thought, seem reasonable to use the same mortality ratios, based upon insured lives, to construct tables for both life insurance and annuities. Since, however, annuities provide for periodic payments from a given date throughout the lifetime of

---

[2]The title "actuary" is one which may or may not indicate within a company that the person has achieved the professional designation as a Fellow of the Society of Actuaries (F.S.A.). Although many persons may perform actuarial functions, only those who have completed the rigorous examinations of the Society are entitled to use the designation F.S.A. following their names.

the annuitant, the longer the annuitant lives the greater will be the outlay for the insurance company. On the other hand, in the case of life insurance the longer the insured lives the greater will be the income in the form of premium payments for the life insurance company. Hence, while a decreasing trend in mortality rates is a factor of safety for life insurance computations, it tends to make the table unsafe for annuity computations without proper adjustments. However, adjustments for mortality trend alone are not adequate for the determination of accurate ratios. The experience of annuitants has characteristics peculiar to itself.

Annuity computations are essential in determining the value of optional settlements. Mortality data of insured lives prove inadequate for two reasons: (*a*) adverse selection of lives and (*b*) financial adverse selection. First, the beneficiary in poor health, if he has a choice, will elect some form of settlement other than a life income. When impaired risks, through self-selection, are eliminated from the averages, the life expectancy of the remainder will be considerably longer than the average of the entire group.

As to financial adverse selection, it has been found that, when investment yields are high, beneficiaries tend to elect a form that places policy yields within their own control. An upward trend in the investment return prompts withdrawal of policy proceeds, if possible, under the agreement. The tendency to leave funds with the company in a period of low yield places an investment burden upon the company at a time when it may be difficult to secure the required yield. Withdrawal of funds as interest rates increase may necessitate the sale of securities and thus disrupt a long-term investment program. Financial adverse selection definitely adds to costs in the administration of life income optional settlements.

Annuity tables have been constructed based upon the experience of annuitants. Until recently the 1937 Standard Annuity Mortality Table found wide acceptance. In 1952, a new table called the Annuity Table for 1949 was published by the Society of Actuaries based upon more up-to-date data than the 1937 table. For group employee annuitants, the Group Annuity Table for 1951 is often used. These latter tables for the first time take into account increasing longevity and will be noticed in connection with the discussion of annuities.

Ordinarily only persons in good health purchase annuities, and since annuitants as a group live longer than a comparable group of insured lives at the same age it becomes clear that a table adequate for the calculation of life insurance premiums will not serve for the calculation of annuities. As indicated, each mortality table must be based upon the experience of a group similar to that for which the table is to be used in making calculations.

Development of the 1958 CSO Table

The life insurance business is highly competitive and from year to year mortality improvement has been reflected in lower premium costs to the individual buyer. This comes about in mutual companies through increased dividends and in the case of stock companies as a result of competitive rates. Both classes of companies predicate their rates on actual experience. State insurance departments recommend the table to be used in calculating reserves and cash surrender values. The table recommended becomes mandatory with legislative approval.

The American Experience Table appeared in 1867 and was adopted in New York and a number of other states as a standard. This table underestimates the death rate on the basis of present-day experience and, therefore, forms an extremely conservative basis for reserve and nonforfeiture calculations. At the suggestion of the National Convention of Insurance Commissioners an investigation was completed by the Actuarial Society of America and the American Institute of Actuaries and the findings were published in 1918. The data confirmed the experience of the individual companies with reference to the American Experience Table. A new mortality table prepared by a special committee working with the insurance commissioners was presented to the National Association of Insurance Commissioners in 1941, and is known as the Commissioners 1941 Standard Ordinary Mortality Table (1941 CSO Table). The table is based upon the statistics of life insurance company mortality experience during the ten years 1931–40 inclusive. When the table was adopted it was regarded as a milestone in insurance legislation. Actually, in less than a decade the table became in many respects obsolete. No one could have foreseen the improved mortality experience that in effect made the use of the table unrealistic.

The record of mortality improvement sparked an interest in the development of a new table that would more accurately reflect actual experience. A subcommittee of the National Association of Insurance Commissioners and a special committee of the Society of Actuaries undertook to study the problem and prepare a new table or tables. When the National Association of Insurance Commissioners met in 1956, the report of its life insurance committee recommended the adoption of a new table.

As a result, a new table called the Commissioners 1958 Standard Ordinary Table (1958 CSO Table), based upon the mortality experience of 15 large companies for the years 1950-54 and checked for trend to mid-year 1958, was adopted. The model legislation accompanying the new table provides for the permissive use of lower mortality rates for women than for men. The use of the new table permits reserve and cash surrender value factors to be calculated on a later basis than that permitted under the 1941 table. The 1958 table has been adopted for use by most companies in most states, although the older table remains of importance for the many policies issued under the provisions of the 1941 table. For this reason the 1941 CSO Table appears in Appendix J, while the 1958 CSO Table is used in the text examples. By 1966 the 1958 table is expected to be mandatory, rather than permissive as it is now, in most states for new policies.

LIFE INSURANCE PREMIUM CALCULATIONS

The pricing of life insurance is an example of applied mathematics. The mortality tables, interest tables, and basic formulas are used to calculate the charge to be made for the life insurance contract.

Advancing Premiums as Age Increases

The problem of computing the cost of insuring a group at any age for a period of a year is a matter of simple arithmetic. For example, reference to the 1958 mortality table shows that of 9,373,807 individuals living at the age of thirty-five, 23,528 will die within a year. To insure all the members of the group at age thirty-five for $1,000 for one year will require a fund sufficient to pay $1,000 for each member dying during the year—$23,528,000 ($1,000 × 23,528). The premium each insured must pay to contribute his part to all the claims is $2.51 ($23,528,000 ÷ 9,373,807).

To insure the survivors for another year, the charge must be higher, since there are fewer members of the group (9,350,279) to pay the premiums and the number of deaths (24,685) will have increased the mortality rate. The 1958 CSO Table reflects a decreasing mortality rate for age zero through nine years and an increasing rate after age ten. Each year that the insurance is continued after the age of ten, more money is needed to pay the death claims and fewer survivors remain to pay.

Thus, insurance premiums, following the mortality costs for each year, advance each year. As the advanced ages are reached, the cost becomes prohibitive. For example, at the age of eighty-five, of 1,311,348 survivors there will be 211,311 deaths. Hence, to pay the claims will require $211,311,000 ($1,000 × 211,311). Thus to insure a person at the age of eighty-five will cost $161.14 ($211,311,000 ÷ 1,311,348).

While the pure premium charge is comparatively small when the insured is young, this charge increases sharply during the latter part of the life of the surviving members of a group.

The Interest Factor

All life insurance policies provide for the payment of the first premium before the insurance becomes effective. Since premium payments begin at the inception of the contract and benefits are payable at some future date, the element of interest must be introduced into the calculations to establish an equality between sums now due and sums to be due in the future.

Life insurance calculations are performed upon the basis of compound interest, that is, interest upon interest. The annual rate is expressed in simple interest. At the end of the first interest term, the amount of interest is added to the principal, and the interest rate is applied to the sum to find the interest due at the end of the succeeding term. Interest may be compounded annually or oftener.

For example, if $1,000 is invested at 2 1/2 percent for one year, there will be due at the end of the year $1,025. At compound interest, for the purposes of the computation, the amount due at the end of the first year is treated as a new principal. The interest for the second year is therefore $25.63, which added to $1,025, equals $1,050.63, the amount due at the end of the second year. The term *interest earned* is applied to the difference between an accumulated amount at interest less the principal invested. Carrying the process for a third year, the amount due is $1,076.89. The *principal,* or amount invested, is $1,000. The interest earned at the end of the three years is $76.89. Table 21-2 is a section from a compound-interest table and is used to indicate the sum that a principal amount, at compound interest, will produce in a given number of years at the selected interest rates of 2 percent and 2 1/2 percent.

The process of finding the *present value* of an amount due in the future is called *discounting.* The system is the opposite of the compound-interest calculations. If, for example, A has $10,000 due him ten years hence, the debt is obviously worth something less than $10,000, because of the element of interest. We have just seen that $1,000 at 2 1/2 percent compound interest has a value of $1,076.89 at the end of three years. Applying the principle of compound discount, $1,076.89 at the end of three years has a present value of $1,000. As in compound interest, mathematicians have calculated compound discount tables which show the present value of $1.00 at the end of any number of years. Table 21-3 shows the present value of a sum payable years hence.

Since life insurance benefits are sums payable at a future time, the premiums are due and payable at an earlier date than the due date of the benefits; and in establishing the equivalence of benefits and premiums, the discount calculations are basic. The premium is adjusted to the benefit, and not the reverse. One buys, as a rule, a pol-

TABLE 21–2*

AMOUNT OF 1 AT COMPOUND INTEREST

$(1 + i)^n$

n	2%	2½%	n
1	1.0200 0000	1.0250 0000	1
2	1.0404 0000	1.0506 2500	2
3	1.0612 0800	1.0768 9063	3
4	1.0824 3216	1.1038 1289	4
5	1.1040 8080	1.1314 0821	5
6	1.1261 6242	1.1596 9342	6
7	1.1486 8567	1.1886 8575	7
8	1.1716 5938	1.2184 0290	8
9	1.1950 9257	1.2488 6297	9
10	1.2189 9442	1.2800 8454	10
11	1.2433 7431	1.3120 8666	11
12	1.2682 4179	1.3448 8882	12
13	1.2936 0663	1.3785 1104	13
14	1.3194 7876	1.4129 7382	14
15	1.3458 6834	1.4482 9817	15
16	1.3727 8571	1.4845 0562	16
17	1.4002 4142	1.5216 1826	17
18	1.4282 4625	1.5596 5872	18
19	1.4568 1117	1.5986 5019	19
20	1.4859 4740	1.6386 1644	20
21	1.5156 6634	1.6795 8185	21
22	1.5459 7967	1.7215 7140	22
23	1.5768 9926	1.7646 1068	23
24	1.6084 3725	1.8087 2595	24
25	1.6406 0599	1.8539 4410	25
26	1.6734 1811	1.9002 9270	26
27	1.7068 8648	1.9478 0002	27
28	1.7410 2421	1.9964 9502	28
29	1.7758 4469	2.0464 0739	29
30	1.8113 6158	2.0975 6758	30
31	1.8475 8882	2.1500 0677	31
32	1.8845 4059	2.2037 5694	32
33	1.9222 3140	2.2588 5086	33
34	1.9606 7603	2.3153 2213	34
35	1.9998 8955	2.3732 0519	35
36	2.0398 8734	2.4325 3532	36
37	2.0806 8509	2.4933 4870	37
38	2.1222 9879	2.5556 8242	38
39	2.1647 4477	2.6195 7448	39
40	2.2080 3966	2.6850 6384	40
41	2.2522 0046	2.7521 9043	41
42	2.2972 4447	2.8209 9520	42
43	2.3431 8936	2.8915 2008	43
44	2.3900 5314	2.9638 0808	44
45	2.4378 5421	3.0379 0328	45
46	2.4866 1129	3.1138 5086	46
47	2.5363 4351	3.1916 9713	47
48	2.5870 7039	3.2714 8956	48
49	2.6388 1179	3.3532 7680	49
50	2.6915 8803	3.4371 0872	50

*For selected interest rates.

TABLE 21–3*

PRESENT VALUE OF 1 AT COMPOUND INTEREST

$v^n = (1 + i)^{-n}$

n	2%	2½%	n
1	0.9803 9216	0.9756 0976	1
2	0.9611 6878	0.9518 1440	2
3	0.9423 2233	0.9285 9941	3
4	0.9238 4543	0.9059 5064	4
5	0.9057 3081	0.8838 5429	5
6	0.8879 7138	0.8622 9687	6
7	0.8705 6018	0.8412 6524	7
8	0.8534 9037	0.8207 4657	8
9	0.8367 5527	0.8007 2836	9
10	0.8203 4830	0.7811 9840	10
11	0.8042 6304	0.7621 4478	11
12	0.7884 9318	0.7435 5589	12
13	0.7730 3253	0.7254 2038	13
14	0.7578 7502	0.7077 2720	14
15	0.7430 1473	0.6904 6556	15
16	0.7284 4581	0.6736 2493	16
17	0.7141 6256	0.6571 9506	17
18	0.7001 5937	0.6411 6591	18
19	0.6864 3076	0.6255 2772	19
20	0.6729 7133	0.6102 7094	20
21	0.6597 7582	0.5953 8629	21
22	0.6468 3904	0.5808 6467	22
23	0.6341 5592	0.5666 9724	23
24	0.6217 2149	0.5528 7535	24
25	0.6095 3087	0.5393 9059	25
26	0.5975 7928	0.5262 3472	26
27	0.5858 6204	0.5133 9973	27
28	0.5743 7455	0.5008 7778	28
29	0.5631 1231	0.4886 6125	29
30	0.5520 7089	0.4767 4269	30
31	0.5412 4597	0.4651 1481	31
32	0.5306 3330	0.4537 7055	32
33	0.5202 2873	0.4427 0298	33
34	0.5100 2817	0.4319 0534	34
35	0.5000 2761	0.4213 7107	35
36	0.4902 2315	0.4110 9372	36
37	0.4806 1093	0.4010 6705	37
38	0.4711 8719	0.3912 8492	38
39	0.4619 4822	0.3817 4139	39
40	0.4528 9042	0.3724 3062	40
41	0.4440 1021	0.3633 4695	41
42	0.4353 0413	0.3544 8483	42
43	0.4267 6875	0.3458 3886	43
44	0.4184 0074	0.3374 0376	44
45	0.4101 9680	0.3291 7440	45
46	0.4021 5373	0.3211 4576	46
47	0.3942 6836	0.3133 1294	47
48	0.3865 3761	0.3056 7116	48
49	0.3789 5844	0.2982 1576	49
50	0.3715 2788	0.2909 4221	50

icy for a given number of dollars, say $10,000, rather than purchases as much insurance as a given premium will buy. It becomes necessary, then, to know the present value of the benefits to establish the equivalence of premiums.

In computing the net premiums up to this point, only the actual mortality cost has been considered. The factor of interest is introduced, and an accurate figure secured, by reducing the amount of the death claims to their value at the beginning of the policy year. Hence, at the age of thirty-five the actual cost of insuring all the members of the group for one year will be $2.44 ($23,528,000 × .975610 ÷ 9,373,807). This is the net premium for a $1,000 policy written for a term of one year at the age of thirty-five.

To recapitulate:

ONE-YEAR TERM, AGE THIRTY-FIVE NET PREMIUM

No Interest

Number Living	*Number Dying*	*Amount of Policy*
9,373,807	23,528	$1,000

$$\frac{\$23,528,000}{9,373,808} = \$2.51$$

With Interest

$$\$23,528,000 \times 0.97560976 = \$22,954,146.43$$

$$\frac{\$22,954,146.43}{9,373,807} = \$2.44$$

The Net Single Premium

The "net natural premium" represents the amount that each insured must pay into the insurance fund at the beginning of a year so that the beneficiary of each insured who dies during that year may receive the amount of the insurance. This premium has sometimes been defined as "the cost to each individual of the death claims of the group."

The net natural premium, therefore, is computed by applying an interest credit to the natural premium computed from the mortality table. Thus, as already noted, the natural premium on the age of thirty-five is $2.51. Applying credit for an interest earning on the basis of 2½ percent, the net natural premium becomes $2.44.

It is possible to compute a lump sum that will pay in advance and in full the annual premiums on any type of insurance policy. This is accomplished by finding the sum which, if paid when the policy is issued and augmented by interest earnings during the term, will pay the benefit as it comes due. This sum is known as the *net single premium* (N.S.P.).

For a Five-Year Term Policy. The computation may be simply illustrated for the five-year term policy. Assume entrants at the age of thirty-five, each insured for $1,000. The mortality table indicates that during the first year there will be 23,528 deaths, and, accordingly, during that year there will be $23,528,000 paid as death claims. To compute, for example, a five-year term premium, the five-year term. Since, as before, the rate computation is based upon process is repeated for each of the succeeding years throughout the the assumption that the death benefits are paid at the end of the year in which the deaths occur, one group of payments will be due at the end of one year, another at the end of two years, and so on through the five years. To arrive at the basic equation expressing equality between the premiums and the benefits, it is necessary to reduce the benefits to the present value at the beginning of the policy term. The payments due at the end of the first year, therefore, are discounted for one year; those at the end of the second year for two years; and so on throughout the term. The sum of the discounted benefits is then found and divided by the total number of entrants at the beginning of the term, and the result is the net single premium for the term.

To summarize, multiply the number of death claims at the end of each year by the amount of insurance to secure the amount of claim payments for that date. To reduce this amount to the present value at the beginning of the policy term, apply the appropriate discount factor from Table 21–3. The sum of the discounted payments must equal the premium, and this must be paid by all the entrants at the beginning of the policy term. The sum of the discounted benefits divided by the number of entrants equals the net single premium. This is illustrated for the five-year term policy at thirty-five years for $1,000 as follows:

1st year	23,528 claims	=	$23,528,000	due end of year
2d "	24,685 "	=	24,685,000	" " " "
3d "	26,112 "	=	26,112,000	" " " "
4th "	27,991 "	=	27,991,000	" " " "
5th "	30,132 "	=	30,132,000	" " " "

Applying the discount factor,

$23,528,000	×	0.975610	=	$ 22,954,152.08
24,685,000	×	0.951814	=	23,495,528.59
26,112,000	×	0.928599	=	24,247,577.09
27,991,000	×	0.905951	=	25,358,474.44
30,132,000	×	0.883854	=	26,632,288.73
				$122,688,020.93

$122,688,020.93 ÷ 9,373,807 = $13.09

The sum of $122,688,020.93 represents the present value of all estimated death claims during the five-year term. To find the net single premium for each insured, this sum is divided by 9,373,807 (the number of entrants) and the premium thereby determined is $13.09. Thus, if at the beginning of the term each entrant pays $13.09, the insurance company will have sufficient funds to pay to the beneficiary of each insured who dies during the term, assuming 2½ percent interest to be earned, the $1,000 for which he is insured.

For a Whole Life Policy. The net single premium of a whole life policy is computed exactly as for the term policy except that, instead of finding the mortality costs for a definite number of years, the computation runs through the entire mortality table from the year of entrance. For example, for entrants at the age of thirty-five, the mortality cost for each year is found and reduced to its present value at the beginning of the policy term by the application of the appropriate discount factor. The sum of the discounted benefits is found and divided by the number of entrants. The result is the net single premium for a whole life policy at the age of thirty-five. This works out as follows:

Year	*Age*	*Number Living*	*Deaths Each Year*	*Death Claims Payable*	*Discount Factor*	*Present Value of Future Death Claims*
1	35	9,373,807	23,528	$23,528,000 ×	0.975610 =	$ 22,954,152.08
2	36	9,350,279	24,685	24,685,000 ×	0.951814 =	23,495,528.59
3	37	9,325,594	26,112	26,112,000 ×	0.928599 =	24,247,577.09
	[This process is continued throughout the table. In the interest of brevity, only the first three and last calculations are shown.]					
65	99	6,415	6,415	$ 6,415,000 ×	0.200886 =	1,288,683.69
						$3,938,192,458.72

$3,938,192,458.72 ÷ 9,373,807 = $420.13

The present value of the total payments of 9,373,807 entrants at the age of thirty-five from the above calculations is $3,938,192,458.72. This sum divided by the number of entrants gives the amount of $420.13 which is the net single premium for a whole life policy for $1,000 at the age of thirty-five.[3]

Most insureds are reluctant to pay a lump sum for insurance coverage knowing that the premium is necessarily earned by the company in the event of a claim. In the case of an early death, the cost of the insurance would be very high under the single premium plan as compared with the annual premium basis. There is also the practical fact that most persons are not able to pay for life insurance on a single premium basis.

---

[3]The term policy and whole life forms here noted illustrate the method of computing the net single premium. The method is the same for other policy forms. The computations are based upon the interest assumption, mortality assumptions, and benefits provided.

The Net Level Premium

The net single premium represents a full cash-in-advance payment for a life insurance contract. The usual requirement of the insured is a partial payment plan. He wishes to pay for his insurance on an annual basis, or at less than annual intervals, but requires a plan without the shortcomings and defects of the yearly renewable term plan. To provide an installment premium plan mathematically equivalent to the net single premium, a method has been worked out whereby a premium may be charged that remains the same from year to year throughout the premium-paying period. This is known as the *net level premium plan* (N.L.P.).

Utilizing the Annuity Principle. The net single premium takes into consideration the expected mortality experience in determining the amount of benefits to be paid each year. When the present value of the benefits is divided by the number of entrants, no further consideration of mortality expectation is required. Each entrant at an age pays the same premium. This is true whether he dies in 20 days or 20 years; the time of death does not affect the amount of premium he pays.

Under the level premium plan, the time of death definitely determines the aggregate amount of premium paid by each insured. The annual premium is identical for each member of the group; but even though the member dies during the first policy year after the payment of a comparatively small first annual premium, his beneficiary will still receive the face of the policy with no obligation for further premium payments. The insured who pays premiums for many years receives identical treatment. This further spread of the premium risk is part of the insurance feature of the level premium plan.

Since the level premium plan calls for the annual payment of premiums during the premium payment period by living policyholders, it is necessary to examine the anticipated mortality experience to determine (*a*) the number of premiums that may be expected and (*b*) the year in which it may be expected that each premium will be paid.

Annuity plans are based on the payment of installment benefit amounts to all the members of the group that survive from year to year in return for a large annuity premium deposit made previously. The lump sum or cost of the annuity is the equivalent of all of the annual payments discounted and divided by the number of entrants. The problem of converting a net single premium to a net level annual premium is the reverse of determining the cost of an annuity. For the annuity, the payments are known and the cost is found by discounting the payments. To determine the level premium from the known single premium, the net single premium is converted to the equivalent annuity due.

Ordinarily, an annuity contract calls for the first annuity payment to be made at the end of one year and annually thereafter. If the annuity is payable at the first of each year, beginning with the first year, it is called an *annuity due*. In the case of an annuity due, all the entrants receive an annuity payment the first year, but each year thereafter a payment is made only to the survivors. Since every insured in a group pays a premium when the policy is issued, it is the annuity due that is comparable to the annual premiums paid on a level premium basis for a life insurance contract. To convert a net single premium to a net level premium, it becomes necessary to find the annuity due that is its mathematical equivalent.

Converting the N.S.P. to a N.L.P. A net single premium is converted to the equivalent of an annuity due through the use of simple proportion. If an annuity due of $1.00 yearly may be purchased for $20, then to purchase the same annuity due in the amount of $5.00 will take $100. The amount is determined by dividing the cost of the annuity due of $1.00 into the amount available. Therefore, to convert a net single premium into a net level premium, which amounts to the same thing as converting it to an annuity due, the amount of the net single premium is divided by the value of an annuity due of $1.00 for the premium-paying term of the policy.

The Whole Life Annuity Due. To determine the value of an annuity, the mortality table is used to determine the number of entrants at the required age. Contrary to life insurance, annuity payments are concerned with the number of survivors. For a life annuity due for $1.00 a year at age thirty-five, since there are 9,373,807 entrants there will be due immediately $9,373,807. At the end of the second year, since there are 9,350,279 survivors there will be due $9,350,279; but to reduce this amount to its present value the one-year discount factor must be applied. This process is continued, applying the appropriate discount factor throughout the annuity term. The sum of all annuity payments discounted is found and divided by the number of entrants, and the result is the net cost of the annuity due in question. A temporary annuity due of $1.00 a year for five years at age thirty-five is illustrated as follows:

Age		*Number Living*	*Present Value of $1.00 @ 2½%*	*Present Value of Annual Payments*
35	$1.00 due now	9,373,807	$1.00	$ 9,373,807.00
36	1.00 due 1 year from now	9,350,279	0.975610	9,122,225.70
37	1.00 due 2 years from now	9,325,594	0.951814	8,876,230.93
38	1.00 due 3 years from now	9,299,482	0.928599	8,635,489.69
39	1.00 due 4 years from now	9,271,491	0.905951	8,399,516.54
				$44,407,269.86

The present value of all annuity payments is $44,407,269.86. This sum divided by the number of entrants gives $4.74. This is derived as follows: The amount \$44,407,269.86 divided by 9,373,807 equals \$4.74, the individual share of the present value of all annuity payments. This represents the net cost for an annuity payment of \$1.00 a year beginning immediately at the age of thirty-five and continuing for five years.

The five-year term is here used as a simple explanation of the principle. To determine the premium of an annuity due to continue for the whole life, the same procedure is followed to the end of the mortality table. Thus:

Age		*Number Living*	*Present Value of \$1.00 @ 2½%*	*Present Value of Annual Payments*
35	\$1.00 due now	9,373,807	\$1.00	\$ 9,373,807.00
36	1.00 due 1 year from now	9,350,279	0.975610	9,122,225.70
37	1.00 due 2 years from now	9,325,594	0.951814	8,876,230.93
[As for the whole life policy, this procedure is carried out until there are no survivors. As before, only the first three and the last calculations are given.]				
99	1.00 due 64 years from now	6,415	0.205908	1,320.90
				\$222,860,196.46

Individual share equals \$222,860,196.46 ÷ 9,373,807 = \$23.775 = \$23.78

Summary of the N.L.P. Computation. To consolidate what has thus far been stated, it is seen that the computation of a net level premium involves four steps: (*a*) Find the present value of the benefits. (*b*) Divide by the number of entrants in the group to determine the net single premium. (*c*) Find the present value of an annuity due of \$1.00 for the term premium payments are to be paid. (*d*) Divide the net single premium by the present value of the annuity due.

Let:

B = discounted benefits
E = entrants in a given group
A = present value of annuity due of \$1.00 for premium-paying period
N.S.P. = net single premium
N.L.P. = net level premium

We then have:

$$B \div E = \text{N.S.P.}$$
$$\text{N.S.P.} \div A = \text{N.L.P.}$$

We have just computed the value of an annuity due of \$1.00 a year for a five-year term at age thirty-five to be \$4.74. We have also computed the net single premium for a five-year term policy of \$1,000 at age thirty-five to be \$13.09. The problem now is to determine from these two figures the five-year net level annual premium.

If \$1.00 a year for five years has a present value at the age of thirty-five of \$4.74, then it follows that the payment for five years that is equivalent to \$13.09 is \$13.09 divided by \$4.74 or \$2.76. This figure represents the net annual level premium of a five-year term policy at age thirty-five. The solution is a matter of simple proportion:

$$\$4.74:\$13.09 = \$1.00:\$x$$

The product of the means equals the product of the extremes. Hence, we have:

$$\$4.74x = \$13.09$$
$$x = \$\ 2.76$$

Life Insurance Reserves

When a premium for insurance is paid upon a natural basis, the charge is computed to meet the death claims from year to year, plus the cost of carrying on the business. As has already been pointed out, the natural premium increases from year to year.

Up to this point in the computation of premiums, one side of the equation has consisted of benefits to be received, and the other side of premiums to be paid. The aggregate of all premiums, increased by the assumed rate of interest, must produce a fund sufficient to pay all the benefits as policies mature.

Origin. The level premium plan introduced the element of overpayment. During the early policy years, a net premium considerably larger than necessary to meet the mortality costs for these years is collected. As much of that premium as represents excess over calculated costs for each year is reserved for use in the later policy years, when the net level premium payments are insufficient for meeting mortality costs. The reserve, then, does not represent a profit to the insurance company but is held as a trust to meet the claims of policyholders.

A comparison of the natural with the level premium illustrates graphically the need for a reserve under the level premium plan. Figure 12 illustrates the trend of a natural premium. The vertical lines represent the premium charge of each succeeding year. Figure 13 indicates the level premium payments for the same age.

Superimposing one curve upon the other but eliminating for simplicity the vertical lines representing annual premiums, one sees at once the extent to which excess payments are made during the earlier years (Figure 14). The deficiency during the latter years is likewise shown. The area *ABC* represents the excess premiums paid during the earlier years. The area *CDE* represents the excess of the current natural premium during the later years over the amount actually collected from the current level premium. The sum accumulated from the payments represented by *ABC*, plus the interest derived from their investment, represents the reserve accumulated to carry the policy until paid. In computing the adequacy of a re-

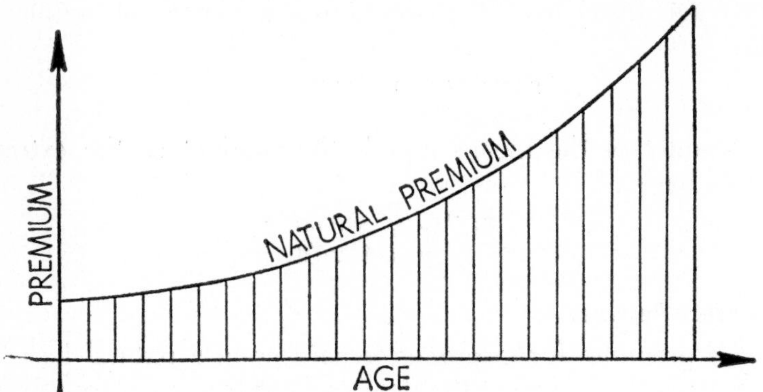

FIGURE 12. Natural Premium Trend

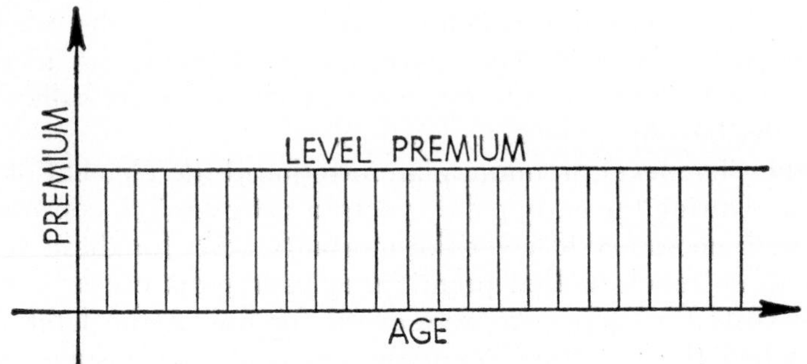

FIGURE 13. Level Premium Trend

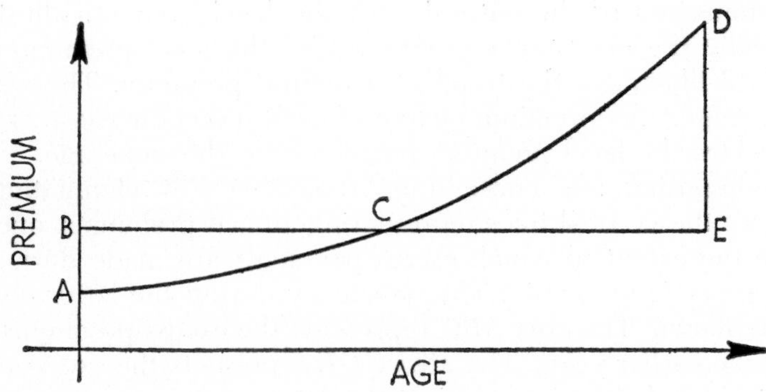

FIGURE 14. Level Premium Reserve Requirement

serve, the company considers all the policyholders of a group. If an individual carries a policy a few years and dies, he pays more than the natural premiums (mortality costs) for his insurance, but this excess is not a profit to the company since his payment to the reserve is necessary for the solvency of the group.

Definition. The *reserve* in life insurance is broadly defined as the difference between the present value of the sum insured and the present value of future premiums. Very simply, the reserve is an amount which, augmented by premium payments required under outstanding contracts, will enable the life insurance company to meet its policy obligations. It is built up out of past premium payments and interest to meet certain requirements determined mathematically. More specifically, the reserve is that portion of premiums paid on level premium life insurance policies which is held to meet future policy obligations. These include death benefits, policy loans, surrender values, and the like. It is represented by assets which the company invests but is, in fact, a company liability to be disbursed to meet the obligations of the policy contract.

During the policy term, for the purpose of computing the reserve the basic equation used for the computation of premiums is as follows: the present value of future premiums plus the reserve equals the present value of future benefits.[4] Transposing the equation, the reserve equals the present value of future benefits minus the present value of future premiums.

With reference to each single policy, the reserve grows as the years pass. The difference between the reserve and the face of the policy at any given time represents an amount termed the "net amount at risk." As time runs, therefore, the net amount at risk decreases until it ultimately vanishes, unless death intervenes to mature a claim.

The statement, frequently made, that the reserve accumulated against a life insurance policy should be paid to the beneficiary along with the face of the policy, is either the outgrowth of a misunderstanding of a basically simple principle of insurance, or is a malicious misstatement deliberately designed to confuse. As a matter of fact, the reserve is not assigned to each particular policy.

The Reserve Account. The fundamental purpose of the reserve is to have available assets to meet the obligations the company assumes for the payment of claims in years to come. The premium calculations contemplate that the reserves will earn interest for the

[4]The technicalities of the various methods used to determine the legal reserves required by the states are explained in Chapters 11 and 13 of Dan M. McGill, *Life Insurance* (Homewood, Ill.: Richard D. Irwin, Inc., 1959). This text is also recommended for the student desiring further explanation of the arithmetic of life insurance, its contracts and its legal aspects.

benefit of policyholders and beneficiaries and they are accordingly invested in securities such as bonds, mortgages, and real estate. The financial statement of an insurance company will show an amount under the heading "Admitted Assets." This represents investments and other credits approved by the state insurance department. The reserve, plus other liabilities and required capital or surplus, must not exceed the admitted assets if the company is to be permitted to continue business.

The ability of the company to meet all claims as they mature depends upon the adequacy of the reserve account. The reserve should never be regarded as an extra amount to meet contingencies or as a profit above mortality experience, for, on the basis of the calculated experience, the mortality costs will ultimately absorb the entire reserve. Only to the extent that actual experience is more favorable than the calculations will there be any excess over claims from the reserve account.

Contingency Reserves. The mortality tables used as a basis for policy valuation in determining minimum legal reserves make no provision for contingencies other than reasonable margins against adverse mortality fluctuations. They do not provide for investment losses, changing expense ratios, or unfavorable mortality experience due to wars or epidemics. A satisfactory method for providing for contingencies is the accumulation of special contingency reserves. The account so accumulated is a known amount over and above policy liabilities on the basis of the valuation formula, in contrast to the reserve, and is called the "surplus." If the surplus is earmarked to be held available for unforeseen emergencies and contingencies, it is often called the *contingency reserve.*

The Gross Premium

The discussion of premium computation has, for simplicity, omitted operating costs. The expense of carrying on the business is estimated on the basis of past experience; this amount is added to the net premium and is known as the *loading*. The *net premium plus* the *loading* is the *gross premium.*

Nature and Purposes. The loading added to the net premium for known expenses and unknown contingencies is not uniform among companies. In mutual companies the loading is frequently heavier than in stock companies. The additional premium strengthens the position of mutual companies, and inequity is avoided through a return of any excess beyond needs for growth, in the form of dividends to the policyholders.

The element of loading provides, first, for operating expenses and, second, for contingencies unforseen in the calculations. The expense element includes such items as the cost of getting business and the cost of collecting premiums. Principal among these items are commissions on new business, subsequent commission payments for a term, and the state tax levied on premiums. Other expense items include the cost of settling claims and, finally, such general business expenses as salaries, rentals, the cost of keeping records, and the like.

Calculations. The loading is an amount per $1,000 of insurance and varies with the kind of policy and age at issue. To arrive at an equitable distribution of the loading requires complex actuarial calculations. These calculations involve the classification of expenses and a determination of the proportion of particular expense items to be charged to each class of policyholder.

Experience shows that expenses may be grouped into one of three broad categories: (*a*) those that vary with the size of the premium, (*b*) those that vary with the amount of the policy, and (*c*) those independent of both. Commissions that represent a proportion of the premium, or premium taxes levied on the amount of the premium, will vary as the amount of premiums vary. For example, the amount of tax and the amount of commission on an endowment policy for $1,000 will be higher than on a whole life policy issued at the same age. On the other hand, the medical examination or cost of writing the policy will be the same in each case. Finally, home office expenses, including salaries, research, accounting, and the like, represent fixed costs that have no direct bearing upon either premium or policy amount but are to be distributed among all the policyholders. Overhead expenses may be assessed against a policy as an amount representing the sum of a number of dollars per policy plus a number of dollars per $1,000 of insurance.

When all the factors are taken into consideration, a loading system determined to be equitable is worked out. This may be a percentage of the premium varying as the amount of the premium for the form of policy increases. The loading may be a combination of a percentage of the net premium for the particular type of policy plus a percentage of the net ordinary life premium at the age of issue. A final method is to increase the net premium by the sum of a fixed amount for each policy plus a fixed amount for each dollar of insurance.[5]

---

[5]A formula for determining the loading due to expense is derived by determining (*a*) variable expenses and (*b*) fixed expenses. Variable expenses may be apportioned by assuming that they are directly proportioned to the number of policies. Fixed expenses are items of overhead that do not fluctuate with volume of new business. For illustration, assume an acquisition expense (exclusive of first-year commission) of $10 per policy plus $10 per $1,000 insurance. In a policy of $2,500 the acquisition cost would be $10 plus ($10 x 2.5), or $35, which divided by 2.5, gives a loading of $14 per $1,000 of insurance.

UNDERWRITING OF LIFE INSURANCE

Medical Examinations

Life insurance companies in computing premiums use exclusively tables based upon insured lives. Since life insurance premiums are computed on the basis of an expected mortality of such a group, the solvency of the company requires that the group of insureds be so selected that the actual experience will occasion no greater payment than anticipated when rates were made.

One method of avoiding insuring applicants who know themselves to be suffering from a physical impairment that might shorten their lives is the medical examination. The purpose of the medical examination is not to find a perfect group for insurance. It undertakes, however, to eliminate from the group those suffering from ailments that tend to increase the mortality beyond that which the mortality table anticipates. Second, it has as a function the detection of such fraud as that of an applicant who, aware of a very serious ailment, makes application for insurance.

Medical examinations when required are made by a physician appointed by the company. Exception to the practice of requiring a medical examination may be made when group policies are issued, though even in such cases an examination may be required of individuals who delay in joining a group. There are certain other exceptions such as industrial policies sold ordinarily for small amounts and payable on a weekly payment plan. In other instances, policies are written making use of the so-called "nonmedical plan," which contemplates placing an increased burden on sources other than the medical examiner for required underwriting information. The medical examination, however, for much of the insurance that is written supplies information for determining whether or not the applicant is acceptable for insurance or upon what basis he is acceptable.

In life insurance computations, it is assumed that the effects of medical selection disappear after five years. A mortality table based upon the subsequent history of lives that have been insured for a period of five or more years is termed an "ultimate table." It has sometimes been contended that the use of such a table affords a mortality rate without regard to medical selection and, therefore, that insurance companies could safely write life insurance without a medical examination.

To refute this contention, actuaries point out that if everyone in a community or country were insured, a medical examination would be unnecessary. A sufficient number of insureds would be included in the group, and the mortality table would reflect the mortality rate with accuracy. Since, however, insurance is purely a matter of volition on the part of the individual, without medical examination there would be a tendency for the unhealthy to seek insurance, while others might neglect or postpone it. The result would be a group of risks unfavorably balanced with defectives and a mortality rate in excess of that anticipated by the table. Where such a situation exists, there is said to be a condition of "adverse selection."

Medical examination or selection without such an examination is not concerned with identifying risks without physical impairment. Medical examination as part of the process of selection undertakes to separate the insurable from the uninsurable and to classify those impaired risks that are insurable into homogeneous groups to which premiums adequate to the risk may be assigned.

Substandard or Impaired Risks

An impaired or substandard risk is one in whom the hazard may be presumed to be increased because of the existence of unfavorable physical condition, family history, habits, or occupation. Through the development of the "extra-risk" type of policy the benefits of life insurance have been extended to many persons who were formerly ineligible because of their classification as impaired risks. The companies approached the problem by means of actuarial studies and were thus enabled to determine an extra premium to be charged to compensate for the extra risk. The result has been the reduction of declined applications for life insurance, to a point in 1962 where they amounted to only 3 percent of total applications.[6]

Impaired risks fall into two groups. In the first group, the insured is charged an extra premium to compensate for the hazards of his occupation. About one in five extra risk policies are of this type. These additional charges for occupational hazards are in some instances moderate and in others, as compared with the usual premium for the age, very severe. The mortality range for occupational hazards varies from an additional charge of one third to three times normal mortality.

The second group of substandard risks includes those with physical impairments. Those of most frequent occurrence include heart disease (30 percent of all extra risk policies); weight problems (20 percent); and other physical impairments (24 percent).[7]

Nonmedical Life Insurance

With a view to reducing acquisition expense, eliminating delay, and to overcoming the sales resistance that sometimes presents itself in the form of an objection to a medical examination, the plan of writing life insurance without such an examination was instituted.

---

[6] *Life Insurance Fact Book* (New York: Institute of Life Insurance, 1963), p. 93.
[7] *Ibid.*, p. 93.

In Canada, where nonmedical life insurance made its first appearance, many life insurance applications were received in rural districts where the services of a physician were not always readily obtainable. This is said to have been one of the major factors leading the Canadian companies to adopt the idea. This same factor—the lack of doctors available for medical examinations—was an important contributing factor to the further extension of nonmedical life insurance business during and after the period of World War II.

For the nonmedical application the agent must secure much of the information otherwise obtained by the medical examiner. He does not undertake anything in the nature of an actual physical examination but secures direct from the applicants specific replies to carefully drafted questions concerning the personal and family history and physical condition. The agent is asked also to determine, as far as possible, that the applicant is in sound health, able to work regularly, and not suffering from any impairment or ailment that requires cessation or interruption of employment. The information obtained by the agent is carefully verified through an independent inspection report, which checks particularly such matters as intemperance or immoral habits. Infrequently the information obtained by this inspection may indicate the possibility of an impairment; in such circumstances a medical examination is required. However, the majority of nonmedical applications are disposed of without an examination.[8]

The objective of nonmedical life insurance is the same as that of contracts written following a medical examination, i.e., to secure an average mortality for the group instead of an abnormally high mortality rate caused by adverse selection. The elimination of the medical examination cost permits a slightly higher mortality experience for the nonmedical life insurance contracts.

In nonmedical coverages, the company limits the amount of insurance and the age range. Many companies make no differentiation between men and women. Some companies set a special-limit coverage for single self-supporting women; others provide the same limits for them as for men, but a different limit for married women. The limit for married women is contingent upon the amount of insurance

[8]There are six principal sources of information upon which life insurance underwriters rely in the selection and classification of risks. These are (*a*) agents, (*b*) statements of the applicant, (*c*) medical examination, (*d*) inspection reports, (*e*) the American Service Bureau, and (*f*) the Medical Information Bureau. The first three are self-explanatory. Inspection reports are obtained from established mercantile credit companies, although some companies make confidential checks through a department set up for the purpose. The American Service Bureau, Inc., makes inspections for member companies. The Medical Information Bureau is a subcommittee of the Association of Life Insurance Medical Directors and serves as a clearinghouse for intimate data on the habits, health, and physical conditions of applicants for life insurance.

carried by the husband. The trend is definitely toward liberalization of limits. Some companies have extended the nonmedical procedure to all applications, at age forty and under, for amounts of $25,000 or less. For ages up to fifty, the limits may be reduced to a maximum of $5,000 or $10,000. More and more companies are writing individual plans, including term insurance and special contracts, with the exception of preferred risk policies available only to above-average risks, on a nonmedical basis. The practices seem to vary greatly by company, but increasing use of nonmedical life insurance is readily apparent.

War Clauses

Life insurance mortality tables cover the experience over a normal period and do not reflect death rates to be expected from major military operations. Hence, to accept insurance on lives of persons in active military service without limiting the liability for war-caused deaths might affect the solvency of the company, or, in any case, affect adversely the position of other insureds as to dividends. Life insurance companies, recognizing this, have invariably attached the so-called "war clause" to policies issued during wartime. Some companies did not make the use of the clause universal but limited it to those of an age liable to military service. Some companies were willing to assume the war hazards on the payment of an additional premium; but, because of the size of the premium, very little of such business was written.

There have been in use two general types of clause: (*a*) the status clause and (*b*) the result clause. The first excludes liability for all deaths occurring while in military service during wartime. The second excludes death resulting from war. There has been considerable objection to the first clause, since it is possible that an insured may die from a normal cause in no way associated with wartime service, in which case the death would, except for the clause, be covered by the policy. This type of clause, however, is the simplest to interpret. The "result clause" is fairer in theory but difficult to administer because of the difficulty of determining whether deaths from disease, exposure, or the like are directly attributable to wartime activities or might have happened in the normal course. Because of its fairness, however, the second type of clause has been the most widely used.[9]

[9]The Life Committee of the National Association of Insurance Commissioners appointed a subcommittee in 1942, to study war clauses and make recommendations to the states for a uniform practice. Aside from requirements officially established, the majority of large insurance companies voluntarily adjusted their practices to the recommendations. With the termination of hostilities in 1945, the subject of war

(Continued on next page)

War clauses cannot be attached to policies already in existence without one. Not all companies follow the same rule with respect to new business. It is generally the practice, however, to use a clause when issuing a policy to members of the armed services. Other companies use such a clause on policies issued to potential draftees. In some instances the clause is limited to those who are classified 1A, and in other instances the companies establish an age bracket and attach the clause to all policies issued to applicants in the age brackets so established. War clauses are not attached to policies issued to civilian defense workers as such, although a clause would be attached by many companies if the worker were in an age group subject to draft or acceptable for military service on a volunteer basis.

For the most part, war clauses adopted are of the "result clause" type. The clause so used excludes coverage on the insured while in the armed forces if death results from war, an act of war or a state of war, while the insured is serving outside the United States or Canada. This clause in no way affects claims for death from normal causes, either disease or accident.[10] The use of the clause does recognize, however, that (*a*) war deaths represent an extra hazard that must be reflected in the premium charge and (*b*) a premium designed to provide full war coverage would be prohibitive. The protection provided by the government for war-caused deaths of servicemen relieves life insurance companies of some of the necessity to provide for the war risk.

SUMMARY

The pricing of life insurance contracts is an *actuarial* function which involves the application of basic mathematical techniques. Estimates of life contingencies come from *mortality tables* which

---

clauses became less urgent. The N.A.I.C. continued their stuides, however, and in 1947 pointed out that relatively little information concerning war mortality was then available. With the outbreak of hostilities in Korea, war clauses again came to immediate consideration. A special subcommittee met to consider the subject. It was pointed out that the experience of the last war was not necessarily a criterion for results in future wars and that companies, within reasonable and justifiable limits, should be permitted to guard against possible future adverse experiences. The time for attaching war clauses to new policies was left to the judgment of management. The committee recommended that the "result clause" be approved by state insurance departments if submitted. Uniformity was recommended to avoid unfair competitive selling.

[10]Following both World Wars I and II, the use of war clauses was abandoned following the termination of hostilities. Our participation in the Korean conflict reestablished the need for such clauses. It is a matter of interest to note that after World War II some companies paid claims on policies on the lives of servicemen where, because of the war clause, they were not legally bound to do so. They did this as a humanitarian gesture after it was determined that such an action would not adversely affect financial stability.

have been constructed in order to predict the probable death rate of policyholders at each age. The long-run nature of the usual life insurance contract with a guaranteed fixed price necessitates careful statistical methods of a scientific nature in estimating the future costs of life insurance.

Different mortality tables are used for various insureds. Individual ordinary policies use the 1941, or more commonly today, the 1958 Commissioners Standard Ordinary (CSO) Mortality Table. Industrial contracts use the 1941 Standard Industrial Table, and annuities may be based upon the 1937 Standard Annuity Table, the Annuity Table for 1949 or the Group Annuity Table for 1951.

Premium calculations for life insurance must consider the *advancing costs* of mortality as age increases, the very important *compound interest* factor, and the process of *discounting* sums to be received in the future to their equivalent present value.

The *net single premium* for a life insurance contract is not a difficult mathematical concept, as illustrated for the five-year term and whole life policies in this chapter. Conversion of the N.S.P. to a *net level premium* (N.L.P.) utilizes the annuity principle to calculate the amount necessary to pay for the policy on a regular installment basis rather than all at once with a single payment at the beginning of the contract. The *reserve* account has its origin in the net level premium system, as excess amounts are collected early in the policy term in order to offset the heavy mortality costs at older ages.

The *gross premium,* which is the amount actually paid by the life insurance policyholder, is calculated by adding a *loading* for known operating costs and unknown contingencies. The basic objectives of safety and equity are considered in these computations.

The pricing of life insurance is part of the larger function of *underwriting,* or selecting the policyholders to be insured. In order to avoid adverse selection and secure at least an average healthy group of insureds, most insurers use *medical examinations* to evaluate life insurance applications. Many *substandard or impaired* risks may also be accepted at increased rates for health defects or occupational hazards. *Nonmedical* life insurance has become increasingly important, written within specified maximum limits at the younger ages prior to age fifty. *War clauses* of various types are sometimes included in life insurance contracts in order to avoid the abnormal catastrophic losses which might occur during wartime.

FOR REVIEW

1. Over a period of years there has been a persistent increase in the death rate from cancer. Heart disease has likewise been showing a consistent increase for many years. What is the effect of these increases upon the reliability of mortality tables?

2. Explain how a mortality table for calculating the cost of life insurance is constructed. Why are different mortality tables used—rather than just one standard table for all calculations?
3. At the time the Commissioners Standard Ordinary (CSO) 1958 Mortality Table was adopted to replace the 1941 CSO Table, this latter table overestimated mortality rates. Did this have the effect of overcharging policyholders for their life insurance protection?
4. Companies writing annuities distinguish between male and female applicants. Indicate why annuity rates could not equitably be based on an average mortality experience of both males and females.
5. Why is it not possible to use the same mortality table to compute a life insurance premium and the purchase price of an annuity? Even though different tables are used for life contracts and annuities, why is it necessary to utilize an annuity table for certain calculations in connection with the life contract?
6. Explain the method of net level premium computation for a term policy for $1,000 for one year.
7. How does the computation of a whole life premium differ from the computation of a term premium for a single year?
8. Using the Commissioners Standard Ordinary 1958 Table with an interest rate of 2½ percent, show the method of calculating the net annual level premium for $1,000 endowment insurance policy maturing at age 65, issued to an insured at the age of 35. In the interest of simplicity, since only the method is required, use four places in the discount table and do not make multiplications, divisions, or additions. Indicate results by letters such as "A," "B," and "C." Show method of computing the first three and the last three years in a series.
9. What is the relationship between annuities and the calculation of the net level premium (N.L.P.)? Why is the N.L.P. computation necessary when the insurer could just charge the insured the net single premium (N.S.P.) without the additional calculation?
10. From where do life insurance reserves come? How would you describe the purpose of the reserve? To what is it equal?
11. The *Dash* Life Insurance Company is a mutual organization, and the *Blank* Life Insurance Company is a stock company. Both use the Commissioners Standard Ordinary 1958 Mortality Table and compute their premiums on a 2½ per cent basis. Which company would you expect to have the largest reserve on a whole life policy in force for 15 years?
12. X has a 10-payment life and a 20-payment life policy in the Great Life Insurance Company. At the end of 20 years which will have the greater reserve?
13. Many life insurance companies engage in an extensive program of life conservation through health education and information. What bearing can the success of such a practice have upon life insurance?
14. What are the sources of surplus to a life insurance company from which it may return a dividend to its policyholders? Should all the surplus be returned to the policyholders?
15. There are two classes of hazards that tend to result in the classification of an applicant for insurance as impaired. Name the classes, together with examples of each.
16. In determining the rate for an impaired life risk, many companies have a practice of giving numerical values to a large number of factors that have a bearing on the risk. The mortality of an average person is considered 100 per cent, and to this basic rate are added charges for unfavorable

factors and credits for favorable factors. It is stated that there are certain forms of impairment which, taken together, have a more serious effect than the arithmetical sum of their individual rating. Discuss and give an example.

17. A news item under the caption *A Substandard Risk?* commented upon a person who was rejected for standard life insurance 45 years ago because of a "bad heart," but who today is enjoying life at 99 years of age and is still taking walks to "stay young." Did the life insurance company make a mistake? Explain your answer.
18. Are medical examinations always required before life insurance is issued? If your answer is *yes,* explain why they are necessary. If your answer is *no,* explain why they are not needed.

Chapter 22

INDIVIDUAL LIFE INSURANCE CONTRACTS

THE life insurance business has developed several methods of distributing life insurance contracts. The purpose of utilizing more than one system of marketing life insurance is to reach the largest possible number of insureds. To accomplish this goal no one technique has proved best in selling the idea of life insurance. Traditionally the efforts have centered on three methods, which are called the major classes of life insurance.

MAJOR CLASSES OF LIFE INSURANCE

The three major classes have been known for many years as (1) *ordinary* life insurance, (2) *industrial* life insurance, and (3) *group* life insurance. The first two categories involve a separate policy contract for each purchaser, and are therefore discussed in this chapter on *individual* life insurance contracts. The third major class, group life insurance, concentrates its sales efforts by combining many individuals in one *group* contract for employers or creditors. The group technique for providing life insurance protection is studied in Chapter 23.

A brief comparison would show the approximate amounts of ordinary life insurance in force to be over 50 percent, group life insurance (including credit life) over 40 percent, and industrial life insurance about 6 percent of total life insurance in force in 1963.

The life insurance business has to a large degree emphasized the sale of *ordinary life* insurance. It is the oldest of the three classes. The protection is issued on the basis of individual applications and may be adapted to almost every insurance need. It is usually written in units of $1,000 and the average policy is for over $6,000. Premiums are computed on an annual basis but may be paid monthly, quarterly, semiannually, or annually. Premiums are due and collectible at the home office or branch office of the company.

In contrast to ordinary life insurance, *industrial life* insurance is written in small face amounts, usually less than $1,000 or $2,000. Premiums are normally payable weekly or monthly and collected by company representatives at the home of the policyholder. There are certain other differences that will be noted as this class is discussed in the final section of the chapter.

Group life insurance is the most recent class development. It differs from ordinary life insurance in that the unit of selection is the group rather than the individual. No medical examination is usually required. Consideration of insurance contracts involving groups will be given special consideration in the next chapter.

BASIC TYPES OF LIFE INSURANCE CONTRACTS

There are a great many different life insurance policies offered to meet the varying needs of individuals. All are either whole life, term, or endowment policies or a combination of one or more of these. Such combinations may include the annuity principle since annuities are a part of the life insurance business. This being the case there are four contracts basic to the life insurance business: (1) *whole life* insurance, (2) *term* insurance, (3) *endowment* insurance, and (4) *annuities.*

Whole life insurance includes those forms where the face amount is paid on the death of the insured whenever death occurs. This is a permanent form of insurance and covers the insured for life. *Term* insurance pays on the death of the insured only if the insured dies during the term covered. If he outlives the period, there is no obligation on the part of the company with respect to benefits of any kind. *Endowments* provide insurance coverage during a stated period, and annual premiums are required to be paid during such a period or until the earlier death of the insured. The face of the policy is payable at the end of the endowment period to the insured or to his beneficiary if he dies during the period. The *annuity* contracts provide for periodic payments to be made from a stated or contingent date for a fixed period or as long as the annuitant or annuitants live. A life annuity is one payable for the lifetime of the annuitant.

These four basic contracts form the foundation of the many life insurance coverages offered in the market. No matter how complex a coverage may seem or how many benefits or options are available, the policy effects its objectives by incorporating in a single contract the features of one or more of the basic contracts. Since annuities are separately treated in Chapter 25, the other three basic types are discussed here.

Approximate annual cost[1] comparison of $10,000 of whole life, term life, and endowment insurance at age twenty-five would be:

---

[1]Costs are necessarily approximate for such general comparison. Participating policies would be slightly higher, with net costs reduced by annual dividends. Nonparticipating policies would be somewhat lower. Extra policy features such as waiver of premium, accidental death benefits, and so on would increase these estimates. See Jerome B. Cohen, "Decade of Decision" (New York: Institute of Life Insurance, 1961), p. 17.

Whole Life	
"Straight or Ordinary Life"	$161.00
"20 Payment Limited Life"	283.00
Term Life	
"5-Year Term"	61.00
"10-Year Term"	73.00
Endowment	
"20-Year"	472.00

In forms of insurance other than life, the contingency insured against may or may not happen. The policies are issued for a term and may run to expiration with no claim made. Some life policies are so written; usually they are not. As life insurance contracts are usually written, if kept in force, the benefits provided must ultimately be paid.

Life insurance policies thus are classified as (*a*) permanent and (*b*) temporary. When the benefits will be payable to someone at some future date, insurance is classified as permanent. Temporary life insurance provides protection for only the number of years designated in the contract. It is more like the usual insurance contract covering property. If the policyholder outlives the term indicated in the policy, the coverage is terminated and no payment is made either to him or to his beneficiary. Whole life insurance forms the basis of most permanent insurance programs, while term insurance provides temporary protection.

Whole Life Insurance Policies

Whole life insurance may be written (*a*) on a straight life basis, (*b*) on a limited payment basis, or (*c*) on a single premium basis. The whole life contract known as the straight life policy when written as ordinary insurance is also known as the *ordinary life policy.*[2] This has been termed the "bread-and butter" policy of the industry. It provides for periodic payment of premiums as long as the insured lives. Benefits are payable at the death of the insured, though a policyholder may stop paying premiums whenever he elects to do so and take the equity he has accumulated in the form of cash or a reduced paid-up policy.

---

[2]The ordinary life policy is the straight life contract with premiums payable throughout life. Efforts have been made to limit the use of the term "ordinary life insurance" to the straight life policy of the ordinary group and use the term "ordinary insurance" to apply to all of the contracts in the ordinary group. As a matter of actual practice this line of demarcation is not well maintained and the term "ordinary life" may mean either ordinary insurance or the straight life policy of the ordinary class. Straight life insurance is an equally important form in the industrial life insurance category. For two recent articles discussing these problems, see *The Journal of the American Society of Chartered Life Underwriters:* Davis W. Gregg, "A Terminology Problem: Is Life Insurance Really 'Ordinary'?" Summer, 1963, p. 197; and Robert M. Crowe, "Life Insurance Is Not Really Ordinary (or Industrial Either)," Winter, 1964, p. 85.

A whole life form known as the *limited payment policy* provides for premium payments for a designated term or until the prior death of the insured. At the end of the premium payment term, the insurance is then paid up for the life of the insured. Under the *single premium life policy,* the premium is paid at the outset of the policy term in a lump sum.

On the assumption that the payment of a single premium is a limited payment policy with payments limited to a period of a year, it may be stated that whole life forms may be reduced to two classes: (1) straight life and (2) limited payment life. When two or more lives are covered in one policy, the term "joint life" is applied to the contract.

In all these forms, the policy matures only on the death of the person whose life is the subject of the insurance; termination of the policy prior to death through nonforfeiture or surrender values precludes, of course, a death settlement. The primary objective of the whole life form is the payment of its face to the beneficiary at the death of the policyholder. In contrast, term insurance pays on the death of the insured if the insured dies during the term covered.

The Ordinary Life Insurance Policy. The ordinary life contract is the most widely sold life insurance policy. For those whose means are so limited that the insurance they can carry is small, the ordinary life policy with the face value payable in a lump sum is the best. The principal purpose of the insurance is to cover burial expenses and cost of the last illness. This represents the absolute minimum of insurance protection. For those with even limited means to provide some protection for dependents, the ordinary life policy best serves the purpose. As the income status improves, higher premium forms may be considered.

The ordinary life policy is used not only for protection but as a means for savings. The policy values are available to the policyholder when he has outlived the need for insurance protection. Even on contracts calling for continuous premium payments to death, the insured may stop payments at any time. The nonforfeiture values enable the policyowner to make one of several adjustments at any time. On retirement the policyowner may elect to discontinue premium payments on permanent insurance and take cash or keep a substantial amount of insurance in force; or, if he prefers, he may use the cash value to augment his retirement income by electing an annuity settlement instead of cash.

The flexibility of the whole life form accounts for its appeal. Basic in the whole consideration, the insurance is permanent. Future uninsurability, the attainment of advanced age, or other contingency cannot terminate the protection. There is no necessity for conversion or redrawing the plan. While certain features permit advantageous changes, the insured does not have to do anything, beyond paying his premium, to keep his insurance in force for life.

The ordinary life policy affords the lowest-cost permanent protection plan available. The policy is issued on a level payment premium basis, and the premiums continue throughout the lifetime of the insured. If the policyholder meets all the premium payments and the policy is not allowed to lapse, he need furnish no further evidence of insurability to be assured of protection throughout his life. For the applicant in moderate circumstances, the ordinary life policy is the contract that will bring the maximum permanent insurance protection for that part of his income which he is able to budget for life insurance purposes.

Many object to the requirement of the ordinary life policy that premiums be paid until death. It is pointed out that in the declining years of a life productive capacity diminishes. To this end it is considered desirable that premiums charges cease after reaching old age. To meet this need, a limited payment life policy is offered.

Limited Payment Policies. The limited payment whole life contract provides for the payment of the face of the policy upon the death of the insured. It differs from the ordinary life policy in that premium payments are charged for a limited number of years only. After the stipulated number of premiums have been paid, the more usual number being for 10, 20, or 30, the policy then becomes a fully paid-up policy. Some are paid up at a specified age, such as age sixty-five or later.

Frequently, policyholders confuse the limited payment life policy with an endowment form and, after making the stipulated payments, expect to receive from the company the face of the policy. The face of the policy is not paid until the death of the insured, although the cash and loan values are higher than under an ordinary life form, the difference depending upon the number of payments called for in the contract. Obviously, the fewer the payments, the faster will the reserve accumulate during the premium payment period. Therefore, a greater reserve will be found under a limited payment life than under an ordinary life form. In either case, the face of the policy is payable only upon the death of the insured.

Under the limited payment form, a policyholder who dies during the early policy years will have paid more for his protection than if he carried an ordinary life policy. On the other hand, the policyholder may find sufficient compensation for the extra outlay in the knowledge that, when he reaches an age when income from personal services will be curtailed, the burden of paying life insurance premiums will also be eliminated.

Comparisons. In arranging the life insurance program, the question of the relative merits of the ordinary life and the limited payment life policies is inevitable. There is no arbitrary advantage of one over the other. As a general rule, when funds available for insurance premiums are scarcely adequate to meet actual needs, the ordinary life form will prove preferable, since more insurance may be obtained for the amount available for premiums. It hardly seems necessary if present needs are being met with difficulty to provide for a future situation that may never develop. Moreover, if the economic status of the insured improves, he may rearrange his insurance and transfer his ordinary life policies to a limited payment plan. As a matter of fact, it is not unusual for applicants for life insurance to buy ordinary life insurance with the definite intention of changing to a limited payment plan at a future time. Added to this, in the case of participating policies, an insured may elect to utilize his dividends by applying them on premium payments to convert the policy into a paid-up form.

If cost is not a determining factor in the arrangement of the life insurance program, the applicant may have fixed insurance charges so arranged that there will be no further payments when he reaches the age at which he expects to retire. If, for example, he is setting up for himself a retirement program, he will probably wish to eliminate as a charge against that income, further life insurance premium payments. In order to keep his permanent life insurance in force throughout his life, he will be able to accomplish this through the agency of the limited payment life policy.

If some change of situation causes the insured to use the nonforfeiture (cancellation) provisions of the policy, the excess of premium over the ordinary life form paid for the limited payment policy reflects to the benefit of the insured. Under limited payment policies, the nonforfeiture values are greater than under the ordinary life policy. Thus, if an insured, during a period when premium payments are no particular burden, elects to make his premium payments in the shortest term consistent with his circumstances, he will accumulate a substantial reserve against an emergency. If he is obliged to discontinue premium payments, his increased reserve will carry the policy fully paid for a longer period than otherwise would have been the case. The shorter the period for premium payments, the greater are the nonforfeiture values.

The single premium policy is the extreme of the limited payment contract. The premium under this contract is paid in a single sum. Because these premiums represent substantial amounts of money, most insureds are unwilling to take the risk of the large single payment. The policies do meet a need, however, in that they provide wealthy persons an opportunity to provide for some future purpose in such a manner that it need not again be brought to their attention.

It may happen that the applicant for insurance foresees the need for a definite sum immediately available at the time of death. There are taxes to be met, the expenses of a last illness, and other immediate needs for funds. Death may occur at a time when estate assets would have to be liquidated at a severe loss. If the applicant does not wish to be concerned with the annual payment of an insurance premium, the single premium form serves his needs.

Modifications. To offset the advantages of the ordinary life policy, that is, its moderate cost, level premium, and the savings element, there are certain shortcomings. There is a tendency for those influenced primarily by cost to be attracted from the ordinary life policy to the term policy, thus unduly delaying the inauguration of a permanent program. To supply an immediate permanent policy with an initial premium less than the ordinary life premium, a *modified life policy* is offered by many companies. The initial cost, for a three- or five-year period is less than the ordinary life policy; thereafter it is slightly higher. Such policies are particularly attractive to young professional persons as they start their careers, or while they are in graduate school prior to beginning fairly high income jobs.

Term Insurance Policies

The earliest form of life insurance contract of which we have a record provided insurance for a term. With the development of incorporated insurers in 1720, life policies were commonly written but, as before, for a term.[3]

Nature. Term insurance is precisely what the name would imply, insurance for a term, or temporary period. This may be contrasted to whole life insurance, which is permanent insurance and covers as long as the insured lives. If term insurance is written for a year, it provides protection equal to the face of the policy for one year, no longer. If it is written for five years, the insurance covers for five years. If it is written for life expectancy, the policy covers for the period of the insured's expectancy of life as shown by the mortality

---

[3]One of the earliest policy forms of which we have a copy was written by the London Assurance in 1720. This policy provides insurance for one Thomas Baldwin on the life of Nicholas Browne for a term of 12 months. The policy reads: "The said Governor and Company, therefore, for and in Consideration of Five Guineas per Cent to them paid, do assure, assume, and promise that he the said Nicholas Browne shall by the Permission of Almighty God, live and continue in this Natural Life, for and during the said term and Space of Twelve Month to commence aforesaid. Or in Default therefor, that is to say, in case he the said Nicholas Browne shall in or during the said Time, and before the full End and Expiration thereof, happen to dye or decease out of this World by any Ways or Means whatsoever, That then the abovesaid Governor and Company will well and truly satisfy, content, and pay unto the said Thomas Baldwin his Executors, Administrators, or Assigns, the Sum or Sums of Money by him Assured. . . ."

table. At the end of the term, whether for one year, five years, or any other period, long or short, coverage terminates, and the policy has no value whatever. It is comparable to a fire insurance policy or other property insurance coverage which is written for a term. If the contingency insured against happens, the policy pays in accordance with its terms. If the contingency fails to happen, the premium paid is fully earned, and the company at the end of the term is under no obligation to the insured.

Uses. When protection for a limited period is the element sought in the purchase of the policy, then the term insurance contract meets the requirements of the lowest possible immediate cash outlay. Because the proportion of loading to premium is highest, this form of insurance is not the least expensive. The low premium charge on term insurance reflects the limited coverage afforded by the policy. Particularly, it reflects the fact that the higher percentage of deaths occurring in the higher age brackets are not covered by the temporary protection of term insurance.

In the light of the low cash outlay required for immediate protection, particularly in the younger age groups, term insurance is recommended for two major uses: (*a*) to provide temporary insurance where the need is created by a special situation and (*b*) to option a permanent program.

Term insurance finds its principal use in providing protection during a period of unusual financial strain. An individual may permit himself to assume heavy obligations as part of a business venture. He is satisfied that, given his health, he will succeed in working his affairs to a satisfactory and profitable conclusion. An untimely death and forced liquidation might seriously cripple his estate. To forestall such a situation, the prudent businessman, whose insurance program is otherwise satisfactory, will frequently buy a term policy to cover the amount of the unusual liabilities for the length of time he estimates will be required for their liquidation. The rate being low, protection is furnished at a minimum cost during the period of uncertainty. When the venture has reached a profitable stage and heavy obligations are cleared, the insurance may be discontinued.

Term insurance is likewise used to provide a fund for the liquidation of some particular debt. Frequently a term policy is carried in connection with a mortgage encumbrance upon the home. Plans for the payment of the mortgage debt may be interrupted by death. In order that dependents may find themselves possessed of a home without encumbrances in the event of the untimely death of the wage earner, a term policy is carried to provide the necessary funds for liquidation.

Term insurance finds an important use in supplying adequate insurance facilities at a low cost during a period when a large amount of insurance is most needed, but when funds for meeting the cost are not available. A young man with dependents who was recently graduated from college wishes the maximum insurance that his money will buy. He, therefore, buys term insurance with the privilege of converting it to another form at a later date. In this instance, his term policy is, in effect an option upon a permanent insurance program, which the insured feels at a later date he can adequately handle. In the meantime he has provided his dependents with a maximum of protection.[4]

Misuses. Much has been said recently about term insurance and its relative merits as compared with a whole life plan written on a level premium basis. Advocates of term insurance as a permanent program either make the statement boldly or at least make it by implication, that level premium insurance represents a higher charge for the same coverage than is obtained by buying yearly renewable term insurance.

Advocates of term insurance suggest as the most economical form of insurance the purchase of a one-year renewable term contract. The cost of this insurance in comparison with that of a level premium plan is low in the younger age brackets but, as the years go on, becomes increasingly higher, until in the later years of life it is, for all practical purposes, prohibitive. Insurance written on this basis follows the natural premium. Under this form the premium income each year pays the current death claims. Thus, in the younger age groups the death rate is low and the premium charges are correspondingly low. In the older age groups the death rate becomes progressively higher and higher, and the effect is felt in a premium that increases from year to year.

The attraction, because of the apparently low premium in the early years, is entirely forgotten in the later years of life, and the abnormally high premium becomes magnified into an almost insurmountable obstacle. This is so because in the earlier years the insured, owing to his ability to earn, is in a better position to pay his premiums, and the premiums are low because the probability of death during these years is slight. As he reaches the age when his ability to earn has a downward trend, premium charges are shooting up along a curve that ultimately becomes perpendicular.

---

[4]An incidental use of term insurance is to provide protection for an insured who wishes to be insured at once, but who, for some particular reason, wishes his policy to be dated and his premiums to come due at a future date. Assume, for example, that an applicant for insurance has a large sum due from investments on January 1 and July 1. During the month of September he decides upon an insurance program which he wishes to become effective at once. He wishes, however, to pay his premiums semiannually on January 1 and July 1. This can be effected by dating his policy January 1 and providing term insurance from the time of the application to the effective date of the permanent policy.

This has always caused policyholders to become bitterly resentful of the increasing premium payments. No matter how painstaking the explanation of the natural premium trend, policyholders have tended to discount the high premiums of later years as too remote to be of importance when attracted in their younger years by the comparatively low premium charges. There is a tendency to wholesale abandonment of the insurance plan when premiums reach a level where the insured cannot or will not pay them.

This, of itself, would have no adverse effect upon the actuarial soundness of the plan but for one other factor. Sick persons do not usually cancel life insurance, regardless of the burden of the premium. Only those who feel themselvs to be in exceptionally good health do this. This results in adverse selection. This means that as the group grows older the insurance company has a group of risks with an abnormally large number of unhealthy persons, while those in sound health continue to abandon their insurance. The ultimate result has inevitably been a total of claims far beyond the average mortality expectation and far beyond the ability of the company to pay on the basis of its premium income.

The unfortunate effects of the use of term insurance for a whole life plan are: first, it does not really insure for the period of a whole life, for the majority of the policyholders are forced to terminate their coverage; and, second, from the standpoint of the companies, the effect of unfavorable selection has made renewable term insurance as a whole life plan impossible on the basis of mortality table expectations.

We sometimes hear it stated, on the other hand, that term insurance is an inferior type of coverage. It is stated that the buyer of insurance gets exactly what he pays for. If he buys a cheap coverage, using "cheap" in the sense of inferior, he cannot expect to get the better product that a higher premium will buy. The reasoning is not sound. The facts of the matter are that the term contract is as safe, as adequate, and in every sense as satisfactory for the purposes for which it is devised as any one of the many types of contracts offered by life insurance companies.

It is just as wrong to say that everyone should automatically "buy term and invest the difference." For policyholders such a system rests on several fallacies, primarily: (1) term insurance cannot always be purchased, for poor health or older age makes it either difficult or impossible to buy and (2) the "difference" (between permanent and temporary protection cost) cannot always bring greater returns at comparable safety, for this depends on size, diversification, costs, mandatory nature, timing, types, and many other features of the alternative investment program.

No life insurance company has the slightest objection to the use of the term policy, or would any underwriter, if he possessed even an elementary knowledge of life insurance theory, show any opposition to the term policy in those situations where its use is indicated. It is not the term policy to which opposition is expressed, but to its misuse.

In spite of everything that may be said, the most important point to consider is the fact that term insurance was not designed to be permanent insurance. For temporary protection to cover an emergency, the policy is admirable. To augment a permanent life insurance plan during a period when the need for coverage is greatest, term insurance is indicated, and a number of combination policies have been worked out by life insurance companies making judicious and generous use of the principle.

Types and Conversion Privileges. Life insurance companies have extended certain privileges in connection with the writing of term insurance with a view to encouraging the insureds under this form to convert their coverage to a more permanent form. The one-year term policy may ordinarily be renewed for a given number of years without medical examination. The policy may likewise be converted into a permanent type policy within a given number of years without medical examination. The particular disadvantage of all term insurance is to be found in the possibility of allowing the policy to run to a point where another medical examination is required and, upon application for further insurance, the applicant is rejected or rated as an impaired risk.

When issued for a term of five years, for example, the policy may often include the privilege (at any time during the term) of converting the insurance without medical examination to a permanent form. Unlike the yearly renewal form, a level premium is charged instead of a premium increasing annually following the natural rate. This type of term insurance finds particular favor with those who intend to make the coverage a part of a permanent program but require low-cost protection for their immediate needs. Through the purchase of this policy, protection is afforded with the assurance that any impairment in health during the policy term will not have an adverse effect upon converting the coverage to a permanent form. In effect, the conversion feature insures the permanency of the insurance.

Term insurance finds a primary use in providing a means whereby an applicant may secure an option on the amount of permanent insurance he deems necessary for his needs before he reaches a position to pay for it. There are, however, a number of other situations for which term insurance is admirably adapted, and numerous special policies have been devised to fit these needs.

Term insurance is used in special situations to supplement permanent insurance in planning the life estate. Policies are available on a

5-, 10-, 15-, and 20-year basis with liberal convertible privileges. Term insurance may also be written on an annual renewable basis to the age of sixty-five or on a level premium covering to the age of sixty-five. In the first instance, the annual premium charges increase each year, following the natural premium trend, and have the disadvantage of becoming extremely high in the advanced ages. In the case of the level premium, the cost is higher than the natural premiums in the first years, but it remains constant.

When an insured carrying a term policy with the privilege of converting wishes to exercise his right, he has two options. The new policy may carry the date of the conversion, in which case the premium is charged on the basis of the then attained age of the insured; or the policy may be dated back to the original date of the term policy. If the insured exercises the second option, he will pay subsequent premiums on the basis of the younger age. He must, however, make up the difference between the term premium and the premium charge for the new policy, plus interest, from the date of the issue of the term policy until the date of conversion.

Endowment Insurance Policies

The ordinary life policy provides for the payment of the amount of the insurance to a designated beneficiary upon the death of the insured. The *pure* endowment reverses the process and pays the amount of the insurance only in the event that the insured lives a specified term. The amount of the insurance is paid to the insured himself if he is living at the end of the period; otherwise, the company pays nothing.

There are few uses for a pure endowment. Pure endowments are sometimes written for children. When it is desired to set up a plan to provide for a child's education, dower, or other specific purpose, this form provides a low-cost means. Under the form, nothing is paid if the child dies before the end of the period, though upon the payment of a slightly higher premium the company will return premiums paid.

Most endowment policies offered by insurance companies incorporate the features of a term life insurance policy. When so written, if the insured dies during the term, the amount of the insurance is payable to a designated beneficiary. If he is living at the end of the period, he himself receives the amount.

Normal Types. The usual endowment policy is thus a combination of pure endowment and term insurance. For example, in the case of a ten-year endowment policy, if the insured lives to the end of the term, the face of the policy is paid under the pure endowment feature. On the other hand, if the insured dies during the endowment term, the term feature of the contract pays the face of the policy and the pure endowment feature pays nothing. By combining the two features in a single plan, the insured guarantees the accumulation of a fund over a given period if he lives, and also guarantees the payment of a fund to his beneficiaries if he dies.

Endowment insurance is written under a number of different forms, each designed to meet particular needs. The terms for which they are written may vary from 5 to 40 years, or they may be written to mature at a designated age, such as sixty or sixty-five years. Again, there are limited payment endowments. For example, an endowment payable at death or at the end of 40 years may be written so that premium payments stop at the end of 20 years.

Uses. The investment feature of endowment insurance makes the premium charge substantially higher than for ordinary life insurance. Obviously, the shorter the term, the higher the premium. A man carrying a ten-year endowment for $20,000 who dies during the term, say at the end of the ninth year, leaves no more insurance to his beneficiary that if he had taken out an ordinary life policy for the same amount. His annual insurance premium, however, is substantially more. (See examples of comparative costs in the early part of this chapter.) To express it differently, for the same premium that the insured pays for an endowment policy he could secure a much greater protection under an ordinary life form. Because of this, it is important to recognize the uses of endowment insurance and to buy it when saving for a particular purpose is to be coupled with insurance.

The first use of an endowment policy is to provide for the old age of the insured himself. There are many who, because of their nature or habits, find saving money irksome and difficult. On the other hand, these people may find it easy to meet obligations. An insurance premium is regarded as an obligation and is paid regularly at fixed periods. Thus, an insured may institute a savings–life insurance program and accumulate a fund that might otherwise prove impossible. The reminder of the insurance company is all that is necessary to keep payments regular.

Endowment insurance is used to accumulate a fund for a particular purpose. Notable in this class are policies designed to provide funds for the education of children. Again, an insured may be desirous of making a substantial gift to a college, church, hospital, or some charity. Through the agency of an endowment policy he may accumulate the sum gradually over a period of years and, at the same time, be assured that the sum will be forthcoming without drain on his estate in the event of an untimely death.

Misuses. Of all the policies offered by the life insurance companies, perhaps none has caused greater misunderstanding than the endowment contract. Much of the criticism that is leveled at endowment insurance is based upon the high premium charge. It is pointed out that if an insured buys a 20-year endowment policy, lives for 19 years and then dies, his beneficiary gets no more than would have been paid if term insurance for the period has been carried. The conclusion suggested by this type of argument would lead the thoughtless insurance prospect to believe that the endowment policy carries a premium entirely out of line with the risk assumed. This is not the case.

It is perfectly true that, if the endowment policy is purchased purely for insurance, there may be a misuse of the contract and the insured may be paying more for his protection than is necessary. Like other insurance contracts, the endowment policy has a very real use. In the situations for which it is designed there is no other contract that will serve as well. To attempt to use it in other situations may result in a poor distribution of that portion of the income set aside for insurance.

An endowment sold purely for the purpose of protection carries with it a much higher cost than less expensive policies, the major function of which is protection. The situation is particularly serious if the resources of the insured for insurance premiums are limited and the need for protection is great. Finally, an endowment insurance policy, if purchased for protection, may defeat its purpose if the insured purchases the policy when young and the term is such that the contract matures when the policyholder has a maximum need for protection with little or no immediate need for a large sum of money. There is always the danger that the policyholder will lose the amount of the insurance money in some unwise business venture or through speculation. At the same time, he will have reached an age when insurance protection is high, and it may be that, because he is no longer insurable, insurance protection is out of the question at any price.

This being the case, insurance underwriters point out the advantage of long-term endowments as compared with those offered by short-term endowments. Particularly attractive are endowments maturing at the ages of sixty or sixty-five. Such policies provide insurance protection for dependents until the insured himself is reaching an age when he will probably retire. The matured endowment may then, through the use of the settlement options of the policy, be used to provide an income for the policyholder himself. As in all forms of insurance, short-term endowments and long-term endowments render their maximum service when adapted to the purposes for which they have been designed.

Other Types. *Life income endowment* insurance provides for the insured the same protection that income policies afford the beneficiary. A certain monthly income is provided, the income to begin at an age selected by the insured when the policy is written. The age which the insured may select as the point at which he wishes the income to begin varies from fifty to seventy. The premium charge varies with the age of the applicant and with the age at which the policy matures.

Policies of this class guarantee a certain income for a definite number of months. Thus, a policy with a principal amount might guarantee to pay at the age of sixty-five the sum of $10 a month for each $1,000 of insurance for a period of 100 months, and for as many months thereafter as the insured shall live. Under the terms of such a contract, if the insured dies after the age of sixty-five but before payment has been made for 100 months, payments will be continued to a beneficiary until the full 100 payments have been made. If the insured dies before the installment payments become due, the face amount of the policy is payable to the beneficiary in a lump sum.

This policy may be written on a limited payment plan if desired. Under such a plan, premiums are paid an agreed number of years from the date of issue of the policy. No further payments are due thereafter, but the income feature does not become operative until the age indicated in the policy. A man at the age of twenty-five might purchase a life income endowment policy payable at the age of sixty-five on a 20-payment basis. After forty-five he would make no more payments, but income would not begin until he reached the age of sixty-five.

Under a *deferred endowment policy* the insured pays the premium for a term, and the amount of insurance is paid to a designated beneficiary when the policy matures. If the insured dies during the term, premiums cease, but the insurance is not paid to the beneficiary until the end of the endowment period.

Policies of this type are frequently sold to provide funds to meet the educational needs of a child. The policy is issued on the life of a parent. The proceeds of the policy are payable to the child when he has attained a designated age. Policies are written to mature at the age, usually eighteen, when the child will need funds for college.

Some parents prefer to have payments made on an installment basis. When this is desired, it can be arranged to have a designated sum paid once a year for four years, or it can be made payable semiannually, quarterly, or monthly for the designated period. The policy is used to prevent the placing of a large sum at one time in inexperienced hands. It may also be used to provide an annual gift over a number of years to a charity, or a gift to some person at a particular season, such as Christmas time, or at a date having particular significance to the donor.

Special Riders and Policy Combinations

Guaranteed Purchase Option. The guaranteed purchase option is a rider or endorsement that can be attached to the ordinary life and endowment contracts. Under the option the policyholder is guaranteed the right, without medical examination, to make periodic additions to his life insurance at standard rates at the time he exercises the option.

For many people this rider proves more satisfactory to option permanent insurance than convertible term insurance. Its cost is low and the additional amounts of permanent insurance are added gradually over a number of years. For example, an insured taking a $10,000 ordinary life policy at age twenty-five may be given five separate options (an added total of $50,000) to purchase an additional $10,000 amount at ages twenty-eight, thirty-one, thirty-four, thirty-seven, and forty.

For many persons the time ultimately comes when they become partially or totally uninsurable. Total or partial uninsurability may result from a deterioration of physical condition or it may be the outgrowth of the applicant's occupation or military status. In the case of partial uninsurability the applicant may obtain some insurance as an impaired risk but for a cost higher than the standard rates for an unimpaired person. In the case of total uninsurability the impact of the inability to provide further life insurance is serious.

The guaranteed purchase option protects against the possibility of being forced to pay more than standard rates and guarantees the availablity of insurance regardless of impairment. The feature has increased rapidly in its popularity during the last five years.

The Double Protection Policy. Another form of permanent insurance that incorporates the term idea is known as the double protection policy. This policy provides for the payment at death of the sum insured and for doubling the amount of insurance payable if death occurs within a period specified when the policy is taken out. Usual periods are 10, 15, or 20 years.

The policy does not carry cash values as high as those afforded under an ordinary life policy, because of the provision for double benefits. The policy is designed for those who require a maximum amount of immediate protection combined with a permanent insurance coverage. The double protection is to supply extra insurance when the need of providing for dependents is the heaviest.

Policies are written in units of $2,000 each and run in the full amount for 20 years or, if the policy is taken out late in life, to the age of sixty or sixty-five. At the end of the period of double protection, each $2,000 unit is reduced to $1,000, and this amount remains in full force to the end of life for the person covered by the policy.

Plans are written in two forms: (*a*) level and (*b*) higher premium reflecting double protection. Premiums may be leveled throughout the lifetime of the insured or, when the double protection feature expires, may be substantially reduced.

One form of double protection policy combines ordinary life insurance with an equal amount of term insurance to age sixty-five. At age sixty-five the amount of insurance is reduced to the amount of ordinary insurance, and the premium is reduced accordingly. During the period the term insurance is in force, a conversion privilege is included. Almost any combination of amounts and term of indemnity may be worked out to fit any family pattern.

Decreasing and Progressive Face Value Policies. Accomplishing much the same result, forms are written covering the insured for a designated amount. When the insured reaches a certain age, the face amount of the policy is reduced. The reduction continues at specified intervals until a second agreed amount is reached, which then constitutes the amount of insurance payable at death. This policy contains no income feature but provides protection in a greater amount for the insured during the years when there is presumably the greatest need of protection.

Progressive ordinary life policies are written so that the amount of insurance will increase each year at a definite rate for a designated term. After the policy has reached a maximum coverage, there are no further increases and the insurance thereafter remains the same. For example, a policy might provide, for each $1,000 insurance, an annual increase of $20 for 20 years. After premiums have been paid for 20 years, there is no further increase and the insurance remains at $1,400. Similar forms are available under the limited payment life and endowment plans.

Return Premium Policy. This contract not only provides for payment of the face of the policy upon its maturity but for the return of all or a certain part of the premiums. It combines one of the ordinary life forms with a provision for an increasing benefit from year to year amounting to the accumulation of premiums that the contract agrees is to be repaid. An extra premium is quoted on a level premium basis. Thus, the insured pays a slight additional amount from year to year in return for the agreement that upon his death not only will the face of the policy be paid but also the premiums thereon or such proportion of them as the policy calls for.

Face Amount plus Cash Value Policies. Policies have been issued that pay, in addition to the face amount, the cash surrender value at the time of death. An understanding of the level premium plan indicates such a plan to be impossible unless additional premium is paid for any payment beyond the face of the policy. The policies that pay the face amount plus a cash value are a combination of two forms of whole life policies. The first provides for the payment of the face amount; in addition, premiums are collected that guarantee an increasing payment, equivalent at any time, to the amount of the reserve. Here again the insured gets precisely what he pays for; that is, any payment in excess of the face amount requires an excess premium payment.

The policy was designed to meet the claim that the cash value is forfeited by an insured at the time of death. The contention that the face amount of the policy plus the reserve should be paid to the beneficiary was heard more frequently in the past than it is today. A growing understanding of the level premium plan has established the impossibility of paying both the face of the policy and the reserve, without additional premium.

Life Income Policies. The life income policy differs from the other forms of ordinary life insurance in that it provides for the payment of a stipulated income to the beneficiary at regular intervals commencing with the death of the insured. The policy may be, and usually is, written with a number of payments certain. In such an instance, if the beneficiary dies before the agreed number of payments have been made, a contingent beneficiary may be named or the remainder paid to the estate of the insured. If the beneficiary survives the period certain, payments will be continued as long as he shall live.

Since this contract provides an annuity for the beneficiary, the beneficiary cannot be changed, so far as the life income feature is concerned, although the guaranteed benefits (payments certain) may be changed on the same terms as govern the change of beneficiary under any life policy.

Life income policies that provide for a number of payments certain are, in fact, whole life policies for the present value of the number of payments guaranteed plus a deferred annuity on the life of the beneficiary. The policies may be written on an ordinary life, limited payment life, or endowment form. The amount of the payments usually is guaranteed for a definite term—as, for example, 20 years—but must continue for the entire life of the beneficiary. Under the endowment form, two lives may be covered. Thus, a husband and wife may take out a policy providing an income to begin at the end of the endowment period. The income under such a policy continues throughout the life of the survivor. If one of the insureds dies during the endowment period, arrangements may be made for the income to commence immediately for the other and continue for life. If the beneficiary does not live to receive the number of payments guaranteed, then the remaining payments are continued in favor of another beneficiary.

Because these policies are purchased ordinarily for the annuity feature, further discussion is reserved until the consideration of annuities.

Principal and Income Policy. This policy provides an income for the life of one beneficiary upon the death of the insured and the payment of the principal amount to a second beneficiary. The income payable to the first beneficiary is determined by a guaranteed rate upon the principal amount. Thus, a principal and income policy for $40,000 with a 3 percent income would pay the first beneficiary $100 a month for life. Upon the death of the recipient of the income, a second beneficiary, or if desired the insured's estate, would receive the $40,000 without deduction. If the first beneficiary dies before the insured, the amount of the insurance is paid directly to the second beneficiary upon the death of the insured.

An income provision of this type may be written with either an ordinary or a limited payment life. A slight addition to the regular premium is made to carry the income feature. When the beneficiary who is to receive the income predeceases the insured, the premium charge from that point on is reduced to the regular premium for the type of policy carried.

This policy finds favor when an insured desires to care for one particular beneficiary for life and then to have his estate distributed. A man with four children might provide a life income for his wife and upon her death a distribution of the insurance to his children. By so doing he accomplishes the same end sought frequently through the agency of a trust. The advantage of the plan over a trust lies in the fact that the principal is guaranteed against loss from unwise investments and a definite income insured.

Joint Life Policies. A policy written to cover one or more lives and payable upon the death of any one of the lives covered is referred to as a joint life policy. The endowment plan may be used; but term insurance is not adaptable to the plan, since separate policies may be carried under the term contract with a premium but slightly in excess of that for a joint term policy. If a term contract were available, it would have no appeal because the narrow differential could not offset the advantage of continued insurance for the survivor after the death of the first of the parties to the transaction.

The terms of the joint life contract follow closely the single life contract. The clause allowing change to other forms of policy differs in that it provides a privilege of change to policies on separate lives. This privilege of change provides (*a*) for conversion to single life policies on the same plan as the joint policies; (*b*) division of the amount so written as not to exceed the face amount of the joint policy; and (*c*) dating of the new policies as of the original date of issue of the joint policy.

The premium charge for two separate policies is less than for a joint life policy for the total of the separate policies. This is so because in the separate policies only the amount written on the individual concerned becomes payable on the occasion of the first death. Likewise, the cash surrender values are usually lower on the joint life policy in proportion to the premium paid. This is so because the insurance company is carrying the risk for the full amount of the policy on all the lives insured and not the full amount on each individual life as is the case with individual policies.

SPECIAL LIFE INSURANCE MARKETS

Many life insurance contracts are designed mostly in order to appeal to certain markets. Although sometimes they are combinations of the whole life, term, and endowment contracts, they often may offer each of the basic policies with special features which make them more attractive to specific kinds of policyholders. Examples of the contracts aimed at special markets are the family plans, juvenile plans, larger policy plans, and the split-dollar employer-ee plans.

Family Insurance Plans

There are three family plans: (*a*) the family income policy, (*b*) the family maintenance policy, and (*c*) the family policy. These plans are a combination of ordinary life and term insurance. The first two are alike in principle but differ with respect to the term feature of the contract. There are a number of varieties of the third plan which undertake to provide in a single policy at a level premium insurance for all the family.

Family Income Form. This is a combination of ordinary life and decreasing term insurance in a single contract. The contract provides that, if the insured dies within an agreed period from the date of the policy, an income will be paid the beneficiary for the balance of the term, and then he will be paid the face amount of the policy. It is thus a combination of decreasing term insurance (for the income benefit) and ordinary life insurance (for the face value). A policy, for example, may be written to provide the income feature if the insured dies within 10, 15, or 20 years from the date of the policy. A $20,000 20-year family income policy, if the insured died 5 years after the contract was taken out, would pay the family $200 per month for 15 years, and then pay $20,000 in a lump sum. If the insured outlives the period indicated, the beneficiary secures the face amount of the insurance immediately upon the insured's death.

This policy finds popular use in protecting a wife and children. A young man with wife and small children, realizing that the proceeds of his insurance might soon be exhausted in caring for and educating his children, provides his wife with an income during the period that the children are dependent. The term of the income is so arranged that, when the children become self-supporting, the income terminates and the face amount of the policy is paid to the wife.

Family Maintenance Form. This policy has much in common with the family income contract. It differs in that the term during which income payments are to be made is a fixed period which commences with the death of the insured. Policies may provide the income feature for a selected period, usually 10, 15, or 20 years from the death of the insured. Regardless of the date of death, if the insured dies within the selected period, income will be paid for the number of years specified. The face amount of the contract, unless otherwise provided, is then payable at the end of the period selected for income payments.

The family maintenance agreement usually provides that the insured may, from time to time, reduce the income period. For example, at the time of issue the insured might have felt the need for an income for a period of 20 years. Some change in circumstances surrounding his family and dependents may make it safe to reduce the income period to 15 years. This reduces his premium; and his children, now older, will still receive protection until they reach the age contemplated in the original agreement. It is usual to provide for reduction of the income period every 5 years. Thus, the policyholder may relieve himself of some part of the premium payment every 5 years and, at the same time, provide a monthly income until the children are fully grown.

Like the family income policy, the family maintenance policy is a combination of ordinary life insurance and term insurance. Since the income feature continues for a period certain, the term insurance is not decreasing but is for a fixed amount. Since the face of the policy is not payable until the end of the income period, as in the family income form, the interest on the face amount of the basic policy enters into the premium calculations. Term insurance is provided for an amount equal to the monthly payments less the monthly interest which would be earned on the basic policy amount.

Family Policy. This is a package form providing life insurance coverage for the entire family. It covers the father, mother, and all living children. It is a condition of the policy that it will cover automatically children yet to be born at no additional cost.

Coverage on the father is usually ordinary life insurance. Protection on the mother and children is for a lesser amount than for the coverage on the father, and is usually term life insurance. Such a package might provide $5,000 ordinary life on the father with term coverage of $1,000 on the mother and each of the children. Coverage on the father may be increased in units of $2,500, with insurance on other members of the family increasing proportionally.

Insurance attaches to newborn children when they become 15 days old and the insurance extends to cover stepchildren and adopted children. Under this plan if the father dies the family receives the insurance on his life and premiums on their insurance cease. When the children reach a designated age, usually twenty-one, their insurance terminates but they have the privilege of buying up to five times the amount of permanent insurance at their attained ages without medical examination. The wife's insurance is often term insurance to the husband's age sixty-five, but some forms insure the wife with permanent ordinary life insurance.

The family policy has proved very popular since its introduction about 1956. Today about one out of eight new policies, representing nearly one fifth of the annual volume of ordinary life insurance purchases, are of the family policy type.[5] It is a convenient and salable contract. Some authorities would point out that sometimes the premium cost which goes toward purchasing the insurance on the life of the wife and children would be better used in purchasing larger protection on the "breadwinner" (the husband) of the family if he is inadequately insured.

Juvenile Insurance Plans

Fraternal and industrial organizations were among the first to provide facilities for the insurance of children. This form of protection was so definitely in demand that the life insurance business entered the field on a wide scale. The insurance of children from the ages of one day upward is now an important branch of the insurance business. On the basis of experience, there seems to be no special hazard involved in insuring juveniles under age twenty-one, and it offers an opportunity for American families to start a thrift program for their children at an early age.

Juvenile insurance is not, in the strict sense, a separate type of policy. It is rather a form modified to meet the needs of young children. The forms most usually written are: (*a*) 20-payment endowment at age sixty-five, (*b*) 20-payment endowment at eighty-five, (*c*) 20-year endowment, and (*d*) educational endowment at age eighteen. Ordinary life policies may, of course, be written; but the premium differential at the early ages between them and the limited payment or endowments is so small that the higher-priced policies have a considerable appeal.

Juvenile policies may now be written, subject to some differing laws of the states, to pay the full face amount of the policy on the

[5] *Life Insurance Fact Book* (New York: Institute of Life Insurance, 1963), p. 22.

death of the insured child. This is contrary to the former practice and laws which scaled cash benefits to the child's age. Notwithstanding the fact that it is now possible in many jurisdictions to secure coverage for the face amount of the policies from the age one, underwriting practice frequently provides a graded coverage from the rated age zero.

A typical form provides a payment of $250 per $1,000 of insurance for the first policy year with full coverage thereafter. Companies may require that the child be at least one month old. No medical examination is required for nominal amounts of insurance. Companies are now willing to write very substantial amounts on juvenile lives, however, and many of these contracts require regular medical examinations before the policies are written.

A feature peculiar to juvenile insurance may provide for the continuance of the insurance in the event of the death of the adult who applies for the policy and who assumes the responsibility for the payment of the premiums. The clause covering this provision, sometimes referred to as the "payer clause," provides for a waiver of premiums in the event of the death or the total and permanent disability of the adult applicant. If a payer benefit is desired, the full medical examination covering the applicant is usually required. If the agent is eligible to submit nonmedical applications in the ordinary course of his business, he may submit a nonmedical application for a payer benefit. In such instances, it is usual to require that the applicant be regularly employed and not over a designated age, and to set a limit on the amount of coverage.

A popular form of juvenile insurance has come to be known as "jumping juvenile" and derives its name from the fact that the face amount of the policy jumps to five times its original value at no added premium or medical examination when the insured child becomes twenty-one years of age. The policy is made available in units of $1,000 and can be purchased on the lives of children from birth up to age fourteen. The more usual forms of permanent life insurance are available, and underwriting practices of companies place a limit on the amount of initial protection. A common limit is $10,000. The advantage of this insurance is that it assures the insurability of a child at the age of twenty-one. It also provides him with low-cost insurance since the premium paid per $1,000 at the age of issue remains constant throughout the life of the policy and does not increase when the child attains the age of twenty-one. Finally, the policy builds up reserves rapidly, providing attractive cash or loan values. Instead of buying an educational policy some parents purchase this form of coverage with the thought that the loan values will be available for education if needed; otherwise the coverage will serve as a start to a permanent life insurance estate for the young person.

Larger Policy Plans

A comparatively recent development, the outgrowth of competition, is that group of policies known as "specials." A distinguishing feature of the specials is that they are for larger than normal amounts, and are issued at lower rates of premium than the similar basic type of contract.

These specials follow generally one of three patterns and are known as (*a*) *minimum amount* policies, (*b*) *preferred risk* policies, and (*c*) *graded* policies with premiums based on size. At the outset special policies were limited to whole life policies, and with a number of companies this is the form still offered. However, in the process of development special policies are now available in virtually every basic insurance plan except term insurance.

Minimum Amount Policies. As the name indicates, this form requires a policy written in an amount equal to or in excess of a minimum established by the company. This could be $5,000, $10,000, $25,000 or any other such large minimum amount. A part of the premium reduction may flow from a lower commission rate paid the agent; the balance is derived from a distribution of certain of the expense items that are fixed on a policy basis. Certain costs that are often the same regardless of policy size include the cost of medical examination, factual data reports, costs of bookkeeping, costs of premium notices, and the like. The cost of such fixed expenses are lower for each $1,000 of insurance as the size of the policy increases.

Preferred Risk Policies. Policies in this category justify a lower premium charge on the basis of rigid selection. Certain classes may be selected, such for example as business and professional men, where the mortality experience is expected to be better than average. Usually, the contracts are also larger in size than the normal contract. A policy designed as an "executive policy," for example, would invariably be for amounts in excess of $5,000 or $10,000.

While there may be some justification for a differentiation based upon flat expense items for the larger policies, it is argued that cutting out of an ordinarily standard group the preferred risks must ultimately result in higher costs for those who are left. In the ordinary course in a group of insureds eligible for insurance at standard rate, there will be some whose experience will reflect better than the average. There are others whose experience will be just the opposite. If the better than average experience is written as a special class at lower than standard rate, it must follow in the long run that the experience of the remainder of the group will inevitably reflect this loss.

Graded Policies, with Premiums Based on Size. This plan of pricing is a logical sequence of the minimum amount policy plan. The same arguments are advanced that certain fixed costs do not vary with policy size. This plan usually provides for size groups, and as the amount of insurance moves from one group to another, the larger the amount of insurance reflected in the particular group, the less is the cost for each $1,000 of insurance.

At one time special policies were limited to standard lives. This is no longer the case, and in many instances they may be written on impaired risks. They may carry with them reduced rates for disability benefits, and this is true with respect to disability for certain of the extra rate classes. A further premium reduction is allowed on many policies issued on female lives.[6]

Split-Dollar Employer-ee Plans

The split-dollar plan involves an agreement between an employer and an employee under which the employer purchases life insurance on the life of the employee. He agrees to contribute to the premium payments to the extent of the increase in the cash value each year or the net premium, whichever is the lesser. The first-year premium, since there is no reserve or dividend credit, is paid in its entirety by the insured employee.

The plan finds its acceptance in providing life insurance for young executives. Any form of life insurance contract may be utilized. The plan is made effective by attaching the split-dollar endorsement to the life insurance contract of which it becomes a part. This endorsement reads: "In the event of the maturity of this policy by the death of the insured, anything herein to the contrary notwithstanding, there shall be paid from the policy proceeds to the X Corporation, its successors or assigns, an amount equal to the cash value of this policy immediately prior to the insured's death and the rights of any beneficiary designated by the insured shall be limited to the excess of the policy proceeds over such cash value."

By use of the plan the employer provides the junior executive with a substantial amount of financial security at a reasonable price. The person whose life is insured pays each year the amount of the premium reduced by any dividends declared and by the amount the cash value of the policy is increased. In other words, dividends are credited on the premium and the employer pays each year an amount equivalent to the increase in cash value. The payment made

[6]Some participating companies attain the object of coordinating net cost with size of policy through dividend adjustment rather than by a decrease in gross premiums. Graded dividends according to the size of the policy are distributed. Dividends are distributed to simplify computations on the basis of size groups, and the policy size group is determined by the face amount of the individual policy. To reflect the better mortality experience of female lives in the case of policies over a given minimum, an additional dividend is sometimes provided over and above that paid on male lives. When a graded dividend program is inaugurated, it does not apply retrospectively since policies in force were sold under a plan that called for a share in the dividend distribution, irrespective of size.

by the employer, however, is more of an investment than an expense, since the cash value of the policy is returned to him when benefits are paid or the policy for any reason surrendered. The plan provides low, net cost life insurance to an employee. The employer provides an incentive benefit which will tend to encourage the continued employment of a valued employee simply by advancing funds that will, in due course, be returned without interest.

The split-dollar plan, from the point of view of the employer consists of allocating a portion of his cash to insurance policy cash values. These values at all times and under all circumstances revert to the employer, though sometimes employers elect to use these values at the time the insured employee retires to augment his retirement income. There is no obligation, however, to do this.

INDUSTRIAL LIFE INSURANCE

A parliamentary committee investigating the insurance needs of the working classes in England about 1854 found that the necessity of paying premiums annually, or even in such shorter periods as were then allowed, made insurance for the poorer people virtually an impossibility.

Nature and Development

To meet the requirements of the industrial classes, insurance companies were asked to provide scientifically sound insurance, with premium payments adjusted to the needs of workers. This was eventually worked out by making the ordinary insurance coverages available and so arranging premiums that they were covered by a small weekly payment. To facilitate matters further, the premiums were collected through the agency of a personal representative who called at the home of the insured each week for the purpose. Insurance so written is termed *industrial life insurance*.

Industrial life insurance has, historically, been of such tremendous importance that it justifies itself as a major class of life insurance. It has introduced the uses of life insurance, and the habit of thrift, to many millions of policyholders. Although industrial life insurance in force has leveled off in recent years at about $40 billion, and now represents about 6 percent of life insurance outstanding as opposed to 18 percent just after World War II,[7] it remains the sole vital source of protection for many families.

Comparison with Other Major Classes

The mortality rate in the industrial life insurance class has been high because of hazardous occupations, unsanitary surroundings, insufficient food, inadequate medical attention, and other factors. The method of collecting the premium and the expense of handling small sums add materially to the cost. The operation of these factors causes the rate for industrial life insurance to be higher than for ordinary life insurance. The mortality cost differential is less than is sometimes assumed.[8] Over the years, improving mortality in the industrial group has materially narrowed the difference in cost. Except for the cost of marketing life insurance in small amounts on the installment plan, the difference in cost would be largely eliminated. However, for many insured the collection service is just as real a benefit as the insurance itself.

A distinguishing feature of industrial life insurance at the outset was the practice of adjusting the amount of insurance protection to a premium unit instead of fixing a premium for the amount of insurance as in the case of ordinary insurance. Policies were issued for 5, 10, and 25 cents, and upward weekly, and the amount of insurance that such a premium would buy depended upon the age of entry. This provided insurance in odd amounts. However, the practice of determining the amount of insurance in round numbers and adjusting the premium to the insurance is becoming more common. Recently there has been an increasing demand for policies in an even $500 of insurance with weekly premiums in odd amounts.[9]

Industrial life policies have been continually adjusted to new developments in the field, and there are now few differences between the provisions in an industrial policy and those in most ordinary policies. The industrial life policy contains many of the nonforfeiture provisions of the larger ordinary policies; and most industrial life policies contain double indemnity provisions without extra premium and, in many cases, provide additional benefits for loss of eyesight or limbs.

The only significant difference between the standard provisions of the industrial and the ordinary life policy is the absence of a provision for policy loans in the industrial life contract. The amounts available for loans under the usual industrial contracts would be of

[7] *Op cit., Life Insurance Fact Book,* p. 28.

[8] McGill refers to one large company that found only a 15 percent (20 years ago it was 40 percent) differential as compared with ordinary policyholders. See Dan M. McGill, *Life Insurance* (Homewood, Ill.: Richard D. Irwin, Inc., 1959), p. 714.

[9] In the early 1940's the Executive Committee of the National Association of Insurance Commissioners delegated to its Committee on Life Insurance the task of preparing a study of industrial insurance. This committee found that, while numerous states had taken effective steps toward controlling industrial life insurance, the legislation was by no means uniform. A Uniform Industrial Standard Provision Bill, prepared by the committee and approved by the Commissioners, has been recommended as a model for the states. The bill would make mandatory the use of certain standard provisions but would allow the substitution of others if more favorable to the policyholders. Many industrial policies sold by the leaders in the field contain provisions considerably more liberal than those suggested by the Insurance Commissioners' subcommittee.

little practical value to the policyowner; and the expense of handling small loans would not be covered by the interest charge.[10]

Industrial life insurance is in the strict sense not a form of insurance protection differing from that offered by ordinary life insurance but rather is a plan adapted to a particular market. The fundamental purposes of industrial and ordinary life insurance do not differ. The first several hundred dollars of any life insurance is usually provided for last expenses and burial. Industrial life insurance provides for these immediate needs and permits a life insurance program adapted to the needs of a low-income family. It provides insurance protection for many who could or would carry no insurance were it not for the extra convenience of the premium collection.

SUMMARY

Life insurance is divided into three major classes: (1) *ordinary,* (2) *industrial,* and (3) *group*. The first two classes are sold as individual contracts on the basis of individual applications from each insured person. The group technique of marketing life insurance to employers and creditors is discussed in the next chapter.

All life insurance contracts are of four basic types, either *whole life, term, endowment,* or *annuity*. Although many more contracts are available which seem to be different, each may be analyzed to find that it is a combination of one or more of the basic contracts. Annuities are separately treated in Chapter 25.

Whole life insurance is the fundamental life insurance contract for permanent protection throughout a lifetime. It pays the face value of the contract at the time of the insured's death. Premium payments may be for all of life, as in the "straight life" or "ordinary life" insurance policy, or they may be restricted to a stated period such as 10, 20, or 30 years, as in the "limited payment life" policy.

Term life insurance provides temporary protection only, for a stated number of years or until a definite age has been reached. It is therefore the type of contract with the lowest premium cost, but it must be noted that it provides protection largely during the younger

[10]The recommended standards of the subcommittee of the Life Insurance Committee of the National Association of Insurance Commissioners provide: (*a*) a grace period of four weeks on weekly premium polices; (*b*) that the policy shall contain the entire contract and that, in absence of fraud, statements of the insured are termed "representations" and not "warranties"; (*c*) incontestability after two years; (*d*) the adjustment of age if misstated; (*e*) dividends on participating policies; (*f*) a stipulated form of paid-up insurance in event of default after three years and provision for cash surrender value after five years; (*g*) reinstatement within two years of default; (*h*) a table of nonforfeiture values available within the first twenty years; (*i*) payment of claims upon receipt of proof of death; (*j*) a descriptive title on the first page; (*k*) limitation of the authority of the agent; and (*l*) a space for the name of the beneficiary. A period of sixty days is allowed for the selection of the nonforfeiture option desired by the insured in the event of default after five years.

ages when the death rate is lowest. When used properly it is an important part of many life insurance programs. It is easily misused, however, as in cases where it is assumed to be the same as a permanent contract. Rising cost as age increases, and limitations on the length of time for which insurability, renewability, or convertibility is guaranteed, make it useful only where the need for protection is temporary. Examples are the young family with limited income and the need for mortgage insurance protection.

Endowment insurance is really a combination of "pure endowment," which pays only if the insured lives to a specified age, and term insurance, which pays if the insured dies before reaching the maturity date of the contract. It has the highest premium cost of the three basic contracts, and emphasizes the savings feature of life insurance. At the same time it provides protection in case a premature or early death prevents the insured from reaching his savings goal. Some of its uses include saving for retirement needs and accumulating funds for special education or charity objectives.

Many policy combinations and riders are available, including *guaranteed purchase options* which protect a policyholder's insurability, and *double protection, return premium, life income, principal and income,* and *joint life* policies.

Contracts designed for special markets today include several popular forms of life insurance. These include the *family* plans, *juvenile* plans, *larger policy* plans, and *split-dollar employer-ee* life insurance plans. The "family policy," combining life insurance on husband, wife, and children, is among the sales leaders of life insurance contracts today, as are the many special contracts at reduced costs for preferred risks and contracts over a minimum size.

Industrial life insurance is individual insurance with the following unique features: small policy amounts usually under $2,000, collection of the premium at the home of the insured on a weekly or monthly basis, and no policy loans. Historically it was of great importance to the growth of life insurance, and even though ordinary and group life insurance today are much greater in volume, industrial life insurance continues to serve an essential purpose in providing basic death benefits for immediate expenses to a large segment of those families with lower incomes.

FOR REVIEW

1. The whole life policy is said to be the most important of all life insurance contracts. Explain *why* this statement may be considered accurate. What qualifications might you attach to this statement?
2. Term, whole life, and endowment life insurance are sometimes misused. Give an example of (*a*) a proper use and (*b*) an improper use of each of the basic types of life insurance contracts.
3. Evaluate the concept of "buy term and invest the difference," indicating

exactly what "difference" is referred to in this idea, and what the primary strengths and fallacies of the technique are for the average life insurance policyholder.

4. Since the 20- or 30-payment life policy costs more than the whole life policy, how can an insurance salesman be justified in offering any but the whole life policy to a prospect?
5. If B purchased a 20-year endowment, a 20-payment life, a whole life, or a term policy, he would pay a different premium for each contract. Nevertheless, if he dies while any of the contracts are in force, each contract pays the amount of insurance provided for. It has been contended, therefore, that life insurance companies charge different prices for the same thing. Show why this is not true.
6. B was recently graduated from college and has entered upon a law practice. He has a wife and child and is at the present time earning approximately $7,000 annually. He is able to save, above his living expenses, $500 annually. He contemplates buying a home but has been advised that he should spend the major part of the amount he is able to save upon life insurance. How would you react to this situation?
7. Endowment insurance is said to be a combination of two forms of insurance coverage. Can you explain what is meant by this statement?
8. It is sometimes stated that the ordinary life policy is in fact an endowment policy. What is meant by this statement?
9. X has inherited from his father $40,000 which he has been able to keep invested to yield 5 percent. In addition to this he earns $12,000 from his professional services. In view of the size of his estate he feels that he has no need for life insurance, contending that his income from personal services is devoted primarily to his own needs and that the income from his investments is entirely adequate to meet the needs of his family in the event of his death. What is your opinion?
10. D is a young man, aged 24, earning an exceptionally good salary. He is unmarried and has no dependents. All the members of his immediate family being in comfortable financial circumstances, D contends that he has no need for life insurance and that he can well afford to lose all the money he earns over and above his immediate requirements for living, which are modest. It is his intention, accordingly to speculate for a period of at least ten years. Is this program a wise one?
11. X is 39 years old, married, and has two children, aged 9 and 12. He feels that, if he were assured of living until his children were grown up and educated, his life insurance needs would be liimted to a sum of $25,000 to provide for his wife. On the other hand, should he die before his children are educated, he feels the need for an additional sum to meet his contingency. He learns of a contract that provides for the payment of the face value upon death; but if death occurs at any time within ten years from date of issue, double the face value will be paid. He makes inquiry of several companies, each of which state that it has no such policy. How could any insurance company duplicate the coverage X wishes to secure?
12. B has purchased a house valued at $20,000 and is paying for it under the monthly payment plan. The monthly payment covers principal, interest, taxes, and property insurance. Assume B to be 25 years of age and his loan to be for $12,000. What additional step might B reasonably take to strengthen his position?
13. Sometimes an employee, under the split-dollar plan, may not have adequate funds to pay even the first premium in full. Can you suggest a way to overcome this obstacle?

14. What are the basic distinctions which differentiate industrial insurance from the other forms of life insurance? How would you appraise the future of industrial life insurance?
15. What are the purposes of the following:
    a) The guaranteed purchase option?
    b) Life income policies?
    c) Joint life policies?
16. Differentiate among the three primary life insurance contracts designed for families. Explain at least one advantage and one disadvantage for each type.
17. Life insurance agents usually find less sales resistance to juvenile life insurance than any to other contract form. Is there a danger in this natural tendency to care more about one's children than about oneself?
18. How are large-amount life insurance policies issued, and what are the advantages to the policyholder?

Chapter 23

GROUP LIFE INSURANCE

IN contrast to the individual contracts issued as ordinary and industrial life insurance is the plan for providing coverage on the lives of a group of persons under one contract. Such plans are called *group life insurance.*

NATURE AND DEVELOPMENT

Almost 40 percent of total life insurance in force in the United States, involving over $240 billion and 100 million insureds, was group life insurance protection near the beginning of 1964.[1] Approximately each six years since 1941 the amount of group life insurance has doubled, and in the decade of the 1950's alone it quadrupled.[2] It has maintained a record of remarkable growth to become one of the giants of the insurance business.

The reasons for its growth are many, but predominant among the factors have been the industrialization of the population, the desire of both employers and organized labor to develop employee benefit programs, and the tax advantages which are included in group life insurance.

As the group life contract was originally written, the members of the group were employees of a single employer.[3] The group concept

[1]"The Tally of Life Insurance Statistics" (New York: Division of Statistics and Research, Institute of Life Insurance, November, 1963). The figures include credit life insurance, which accounts for about 6 percent. Credit life insurance is discussed at the end of this chapter, following treatment of the group life insurance written for employers.

[2]*Life Insurance Fact Book* (New York: Institute of Life Insurance, 1963), pp. 27 and 31.

[3]Attention of the business world was first attracted to group insurance when the Equitable Life Assurance Society of the United States issued a policy effective July 1, 1912, covering the employees of Montgomery Ward & Company who had been in the services of the company a year or more. For the first few years thereafter, life insurance companies were slow to follow the example thus set. However, within a few years the plan had caught the attention of employers everywhere, and life insurance companies entered into the active development of the business. Large and important insurance companies are intensively cultivating the field, and it is unquestionable that the plan affords a socially desirable addition to the business of life insurance.

has been expanded and policies may now be issued to cover other groups for creditors, unions, and trusts. Underwriting rules differ with the companies but the underlying concept for all groups is the same. The form, in a broad sense, is based upon the same fundamentals as any life insurance; but it is unique in the selection of risks and the method of distribution. It differs from other life insurance in that selection based on the group is substituted for individual selection. Mass distribution and mass administration supersede contact with individual insureds. Hence, group insurance may be termed "low-cost, wholesale protection." It has been defined as plan for insuring groups of persons without individual selection of their lives.[4]

By insuring a group under one policy the life insurance business invited the attention of management to an idea that has been far-reaching in its implications. By considering groups of individuals, it has been possible to eliminate medical examinations and most other selection factors. While there may be impaired lives in a group, adverse selection through an undue proportion of impaired lives is reduced to a minimum by the legal and underwriting regulations. The real essence of group insurance is the substitution of group selection for individual selection.

Under the plan, a master contract is issued to the employer, creditor, union, or other person representing the group to be covered. Each person covered in the group receives a *certificate* detailing the protection afforded, such as the amount of insurance, the name of the beneficiary, and the privilege of converting to a standard form of whole life insurance (without evidence of insurability) upon termination of employment. Premiums are paid by the employer or other party who is the policyholder. In some instances a portion of the cost may be paid by the persons insured, or it may be paid entirely by the policyholder. Group insurance has found a receptive market in our economy.

Group life insurance is not to be regarded as a substitute for a program of standard life insurance. It does, however, furnish the bare requirements for all the employees of a business establishment, in the simplest and most economical form. The formula under which most plans are written provides insurance equivalent to about one year's earnings, and the average amount per certificate is nearly $4,500. This gives the deceased worker what has sometimes been called "one year's notice of the demise of the pay check."[5] While not

[4]Davis W. Gregg, *Group Life Insurance* (3d ed.; Homewood, Ill.: Richard D. Irwin, Inc., 1962), pp. 3–4. This work gives a comprehensive analysis of group life insurance principles and practices. An excellent bibliography appears on ages 341–60.

[5]R. Wilfred Kelsey and Arthur C. Daniels, *Handbook of Life Insurance* (New York: Institute of Life Insurance, 1946), p. 20. The quoted remark does not appear in the more recent editions of this booklet, which had its ninth printing of the second edition in 1960 (87 pp.).

in any sense adequate, it does give the family of the deceased a small fund to meet current expenses and bills while an adjustment is in process. For some employees who are otherwise uninsurable under individual contracts, it provides minimum protection and thus achieves an objective desirable from a social viewpoint.

The general term *group insurance* could include several other kinds of insurance than group life insurance. The common principle of group selection has been used extensively for group annuities and pensions (discussed in Chapter 25), and in the many group health insurance coverages (discussed in Chapter 27). To a very minor extent the concept has been tried in the property-liability insurance field, providing automobile insurance for employees on an experimental basis, for example, in a few states which permit such a contract. The present chapter concentrates on group life insurance, including credit[6] life insurance.

UNIQUE FEATURES OF SELECTION AND DISTRIBUTION

The distinguishing features of group life insurance include (1) restrictive legislation which defines and limits its scope and (2) the impact which group selection has on the insurers and insureds who are a part of the plans.

Legal Limitations

In 1917, the National Convention of Insurance Commissioners adopted the following definition of group life insurance:

> Group life insurance is that form of life insurance covering not fewer than fifty employees, with or without medical examination, written under a policy issued to the employer, the premium on which is to be paid by the employer or by the employer and employees jointly, and insuring only all of his employees or all of any class or classes thereof, determined by conditions pertaining to the employment, for amounts of insurance based upon some plan which will preclude individual selection, for the benefit of persons other than the employer, provided, however, that when the premium is to be paid by the employer and employee jointly and the benefits of the policy are offered to all eligible employees, not less than seventy-five per cent of such employees may be so insured.

The definition was recommended to the several states and was adopted by a number of them and by large insurance companies as a basis for writing this class of business. Over the years, the legislatures have enlarged the meaning of the terms "employer" and "group." Not all insurance companies, however, have been willing to enlarge their underwriting facilities to meet this legislative trend.[7]

---

[6]Not all credit lift insurance is issued under group contracts, but it is included in this chapter since more than four fifths of it is written as group coverage.

[7]Careful underwriters view with concern the tendency to extend unduly the group definition. For example, early in 1956 a bill was introduced in the Massachu-

(Continued on next page)

Definition of Size and Type of Group. To encourage uniformity among the states, and to control expansion of the group idea that some thought was getting out of hand, the National Association of Insurance Commissioners in 1946 adopted a model group life insurance law and proposed it for enactment in the several states. The minimum size of the group was reduced from 50 to 25 members for employer or labor union groups and a $20,000 limit was placed on the amount of group life coverage for an individual life. In 1956 another model bill was suggested by the N.A.I.C., lowering the minimum size group to 10, and increasing the maximum individual amount to $40,000, provided that any insurance between $20,000 and $40,000 does not exceed 150 percent of annual compensation. Almost 30 states have adopted these 20/40 limits, although many other states (including New York) have no statutory limit.

Classified by the nature of the group the Model Bill provides for: (*a*) *employer* group life insurance, (*b*) *creditor* group life insurance, (*c*) *labor union* group life insurance, and (*d*) *trustee* group life insurance. In the first category, the contracting parties are an employer and an insurance company. Employees are insured for the benefit of beneficiaries designated by the employee, but not for the benefit of the employer. Creditor group life insurance covers the lives of debtors to the extent of their indebtedness to the creditor, and the creditor is the beneficiary. (See last section of this chapter.) Labor union group life insurance follows the pattern of employer group life insurance except that the members of a union rather than the employees of an individual firm constitute the group. Trustee group life insurance enables two or more employers or two or more labor unions to provide insurance under a single contract through a trustee who acts for the employers or the labor unions.[8] The last two types are not discussed separately here, for their plans are iden-

setts Legislature, presumably having a charitable import, that would allow the members of any nonprofit association in Massachusetts to be covered by a group life insurance policy. The plan called for premium payments to be made from the treasury of the association with the association in turn named as beneficiary. Commenting editorially upon the proposal, *The Standard* had the following to say: "It is hard to imagine a more unsound scheme, or one that does greater violence to the theories of group underwriting. Nevertheless, it has appealing possibilities, such as the prospect that food poisoning of the congregation at a church supper might furnish the funds for a new building." Vol. 158, No. 4 (January 27, 1956), p. 3.

[8]The Insurance Commissioners in revising their definition have definitely set forth the thesis that the essential benefits which flow from group life insurance "should be extended wherever practicable to the largest number of employees consistent with sound underwriting principles." *Report of the Life Insurance Committee of the National Association of Insurance Commissioners, December 14, 1948.* They felt that consideration should be given to federal labor legislation, as well as to the decisions of the courts and the National Labor Relations Board, under which agencies various phases of group insurance, including group life insurance, have been determined proper subjects for collective bargaining between employers and labor unions. Thus, the Commissioner's Model Bill gives legal recognition to labor union and trustee group life insurance.

tical in almost all respects with the normal employer group life insurance contract.

Standard Provisions. The insurance laws of each jurisdiction customarily provide that no group insurance policy shall be issued unless and until a copy of the contract has been filed with the insurance commissioner and formally approved by him. Certain mandatory provisions are, in the ordinary forms of life insurance, referred to as "standard provisions." The National Association of Insurance Commissioners, in 1946, in connection with the revised definition, adopted standard provisions to apply to group life insurance. Wherever the recommended law is enacted, the provisions are required as minimum protection. More liberal provisions may be substituted for the standard provisions if the insurance commissioner having jurisdiction approves.

Any group policy that is on other than the term plan is required to contain a nonforfeiture provision or provisions which in the opinion of the insurance commissioner are equitable to the insured persons and to the policyholder. It is specifically stated, however, that the group life insurance policies shall not be required to contain the same nonforfeiture provisions as individual policies.

The standard group life provisions provide for: (1) a grace period; (2) incontestability; (3) the application being made part of the policy; (4) conditions under which evidence of individual insurability may be required; (5) equitable adjustment of premium or benefits in case of misstatement of age; (6) designation of beneficiary; (7) the issuance of individual certificates; (8) conversion of insurance on termination of employment; (9) conversion on termination of group policy as to any insured or class of insured persons; and (10) the contingency of death during the period within which the insured would have been entitled to an individual policy and before such individual policy shall have become effective.

Selection of Insureds

In making provisions for a minimum of 25 employees to constitute a group, it was the intent of those who drew the Model Bill to require that the number be kept sufficiently large to assure the functioning of the law of averages. In those states where groups smaller than 25 are permitted or where no minimum number is specified, the underlying theory is not changed but the responsibility for determining an acceptable group is shifted from the legislature or the state regulatory authority to the company underwriters. Groups, for the purpose of writing group life insurance, range from a minimum established by law to a maximum dictated by the circumstances.[9]

[9]At the one extreme, a few states define a group as any number in excess of two. At the other extreme, very large group contracts have been written. The Travelers

(Continued on next page)

Group Selection. In passing from the insurance of medically selected lives to the insurance of groups without medical examination, it would be unwise to allow any practice that would permit personal selection against the insurance company. To avoid the element of unfavorable selection, all members of the group must be included, or at least a sufficient number to constitute a fairly representative risk.

As a matter of practice, the group need not include all classes of employees. Groups within an organization may be arbitrarily established. A policy may be issued covering the clerical force and officials of a business; it may insure only employees with a number of years' service; or it may cover the workers in a given department. A few individuals from one department and others from another, even if the total numbers 25, are not eligible unless the insurance is offered to all. If only one division of the employees is offered insurance, a few employees of another group may not be included. On the other hand, any arbitrary grouping is permissible so long as the possibility of individual selection is eliminated.

When the premium is paid entirely by the employers, the group is said to be *noncontributory* and the insurance extends to 100 percent of the members of the group. The group is *contributory* when the premium is to be paid by the employer and employee jointly, and to warrant the insurance such group must include a minimum of 75 percent of the employees in the class.

No Medical Examination Usually. A characteristic of group life insurance is the element of group selection. This being the case, there is no medical examination of individuals insured in the ordinary case. Here is to be found a sometimes overlooked advantage of group life insurance. Since the certificates are issued without medical examination, some persons can obtain protection under the group plan when they could not obtain life insurance at standard rates, or possibly not at all.

Because of the size of the groups it is assumed that the element of individual selection is removed, or at least reduced to an inconsequential minimum. This justifies the elimination of a medical examination. The fact that each of the insureds under a group policy is in regular attendance at his work raises a presumption of a health

---

Insurance Company provides coverage for 575,000 railroad employees and their families in a contract for over $2 billion. This contract is said to be "the largest single private group policy in America" covering members of eleven nonoperating unions employed by approximately 300 railroads. This group is exceeded by the group insurance plan for federal government employees which in 1963 covered nearly 2.5 million persons for a total of $15 billion of life insurance. While the federal government's program is underwritten by private insurers, the Travelers' program calling for an annual premium in excess of $130 million a year is said to be the largest "private" program.

condition warranting insurance. Also, many of the larger employers now require at least some preliminary physical examination before hiring new employees. If an occasional poor risk is included, the law of averages tends to offset such a risk with the exceptionally favorable cases.[10]

There are, however, some instances where evidence of insurability may be required of individuals in group plans. These have to do with situations where adverse selection against the company might be expected to evidence itself. The Commissioners' Model Bill requires that the master policy set forth the conditions, if any, under which the insurer reserves the right to require a person eligible for insurance to furnish evidence of individual insurability satisfactory to the insurer as a condition to part or all of his coverage. The usual conditions are listed as follows: (*a*) If an employee does not take insurance within a definite period (usually 31 days) after he becomes eligible, he may be required to evidence insurability. (*b*) A person who has been dropped for nonpayment of contributions may be required to submit evidence of insurability if he again elects to become an insured member of the group. (*c*) Members of the group who have converted insurance to an individual policy under the conversion privilege may not reenter the group, if the individual policy remains in force, without supplying evidence of insurability. These requirements protect the insurer against individual selection, and at the same time prevent the insurer from selecting against the group by eliminating any impaired risks in the group concerning which it may develop evidence. Impaired risks are insured with the group if insurance is accepted when the group becomes eligible.

THE EMPLOYER GROUP LIFE INSURANCE CONTRACT

This section and the two immediately following discuss employer group life insurance in regard to (1) the employer's contract, (2) the provisions of the employees' certificate, and (3) financing.

Types of Contracts

Group life insurance provides for protection on (*a*) a *term* basis and (*b*) on *permanent* plans. The first group life insurance contracts were written on the renewable term plan, and this practice has been

[10]Group life insurance is to be distinguished from other forms of life insurance that dispense with a medical examination. For example, industrial insurance and, in some circumstances, ordinary life policies are issued to individuals without the requirement of medical examination. In these instances, however, each person submits an application which includes some statements as to present and past health. The insurance company accepts or declines the risk on the basis of the application. Here we have individual selection without the requirement of a medical examination. Group insurance differs in that the group as a unit is accepted or rejected regardless of whether or not it develops that there are some individuals in the group who are uninsurable as individuals.

generally followed through the years. A comparatively recent demand has created a market for group life policies with permanent values such as those offered by individual level premium policies. The level premium insurance may be on a whole life, limited payment, or endowment basis. Some contracts are written combining group term and paid-up life insurance. A number of companies that offer group life insurance on a level premium basis distinguish it by the term "group permanent insurance."

Many of the group life contracts also include some of the group health insurance coverages analyzed in Chapter 27, such as group accident and sickness, accidental death or dismemberment, hospital and surgical or medical expense.

Group Term. It is surprising to some persons to learn that almost all[11] of employer group life insurance is written on a yearly renewable term insurance basis. Knowing the disadvantages which this type of contract has when used as an individual policy (see Chapter 22), the student may wonder how it has served so well for the vast majority of group plans. The answer lies in the participation of the employer, who always contributes to the cost. Thus the increasing cost problem is not fatal to the plan, should the average age of the group increase or mortality experience of the plan grow worse. Group term also offers many advantages in terms of simplicity, flexibility, administration, and full tax benefits to the employer and his employees.

Group term insurance is temporary rather than permanent protection for the employee. The policy could end any year at renewal date, if the employer does not continue it. It also stops when the worker leaves his job for any reason, such as retirement, disability, or resignation, unless the policy is converted to a permanent form of coverage (see section which follows, explaining the provisions for conversion in the employee's certificate).

Group Permanent. With the growing appeal of group term life insurance, those protected by the coverage began to inquire into the possibilities of securing the benefits of the permanent plans[12] under group polices. Particularly, they desired: (*a*) values available to employees on termination of employment, in addition to the right of conversion and (*b*) a plan for paid-up insurance before retirement and while the employee is engaged in active employment. If an employee retires or severs his connection at an advanced age, the conversion privilege may be of little value if he is unable to keep insurance in force on the basis of attained age premiums. Such ac-

[11]Over 97 percent was written on this basis at the beginning of 1964. See "The Tally of Life Insurance Statistics," *op. cit.*, p. 1.

[12]*Ibid.* Although growing, the proportion of total group life insurance on permanent plans was still only about 1 percent in 1964.

cumulated values under a whole life premium would considerably lighten the burden of conversion.

Under many plans, all or part of the group term insurance may be continued in force for the employee after he retires.[13] However, both employers and employees have seen the wisdom of having insurance coverage definitely established, beyond interference by any contingency, by providing for fully paid-up insurance prior to retirement. To attain the objective, several plans have come into use. If the objective is primarily a permanent form of insurance with the accumulation of nonforfeiture values, the whole life policy may be used. If it is the intent to have the coverage paid up at retirement, a whole life form is used with limited payments.

An example of permanent protection without premium payments after retirement, assuming a retirement age of sixty-five, would be a whole life policy paid up at sixty-five. Sometimes the plan extends whole life insurance only to employees who have established themselves sufficiently long in the business as to be regarded as permanent. Such a plan would provide renewable term insurance for a number of years—five years, for example—to be replaced in the sixth year with whole life paid-up insurance at sixty-five. If the employee is too old to permit a limited payment form, then whole life insurance may be substituted.[14]

An alternative form of group permanent insurance is a combination of group term and paid-up life insurance. Under the plan the employee's contributions are applied each year to the purchase of single premium paid-up life insurance at the premium rate for his then attained age. As these amounts of group paid-up insurance build up, the amounts of group term insurance paid for by the employer decrease in such a way that the sum always equals the total death benefit called for by the plan of insurance.

---

[13]*Life Insurance Fact Book, op. cit.*, p. 26. Of the larger plans (over 5,000 employees), nearly three quarters now continue coverage after retirement, compared with one-half ten years ago. Most plans continue the insurance for a reduced amount of protection.

[14]The group insurance contract on a level premium plan, when used in the employer-employee situation, generally contains provisions covering: (1) when and how the employee is eligible for coverage, (2) the benefit formula, (3) restrictions such as suicide clause, (4) optional methods of settlement, (5) underwriting and other conditions under which benefits become effective and terminate, (6) computation and method of payment of premiums, (7) employee contributions, (8) values and privileges on termination of employment, (9) values and privileges in event the contract is terminated, (10) what constitutes the contract, (11) waiver and modification of the contract, (12) amendment, (13) reports and determination of facts, (14) issuance of certificates, (15) dividends, (16) designation of beneficiaries, (17) assignment, (18) incontestability, (19) errors in age, (20) the basis of reserves, (21) tables for all ages and durations showing level premium rate, termination values, etc. See Dennis N. Warters, "Group Insurance on Level Premium Plans," *Transactions of the Actuarial Society of America,* Vol. XLVIII, Part One, No. 117 (May, 1947), p. 97.

Upon retirement or withdrawal from the plan, the employee is entitled to take with him an individual paid-up life insurance policy for the total of his accumulations to date or its cash equivalent in cases where the amount is small. The usual conversion rights apply to any amounts of group term insurance that are discontinued.

The combination of group paid-up whole life and decreasing term insurance is the least costly method of securing at least some permanent life insurance protection for the employee. However, it should be remembered that most of the coverage is term, or temporary coverage.

Policy and Certificate Limits of Insurance

Most life insurance companies fix the *minimum* amount for any one life at $500. A minimum of $25,000 is usually established for the total amount of insurance for a group. Some companies may vary the minimum requirements. In a few instances, a minimum of $1,000 for each life is required; and in some, the minimum total may depend upon whether group casualty lines are carried in the same company that carries the group life insurance. The average group life insurance certificate is for about one year's earnings, or about $4,500.

The *maximum* amount available to an individual employee generally depends upon the statutory limits mentioned previously and the total amount of insurance in force for the entire group. A schedule of maximum amounts as adopted by one of the leading life insurance companies for underwriting purposes appears as Table 23–1. This table represents substantially the standard limits of the

TABLE 23–1

Schedule of Maximum Amounts of Group Life Insurance on Individual Lives

Total Insurance on All Eligible Employees	*Maximum Individual Amount*
Under $100,000	$ 4,000
$ 100,000– 250,000	8,000
250,000– 600,000	12,000
600,000– 1,000,000	16,000
1,000,000– 2,000,000	20,000
2,000,000– 5,000,000	28,000
5,000,000–10,000,000	33,000
10,000,000–20,000,000	38,000
20,000,000–30,000,000	45,000
30,000,000–40,000,000	55,000
40,000,000–50,000,000	65,000
50,000,000–60,000,000	75,000
60,000,000–70,000,000	85,000
70,000,000–80,000,000	95,000
80,000,000 or more	Refer to Home Office

larger life insurance companies. These companies have continuation tables indicating additional limits on very large cases, subject to special review by the home office.

Company practices vary considerably from the indicated limits in Table 23-1. The maximums may be varied, in addition to the total insurance in force on all employees, by such other factors as (1) annual earnings of the employee, (2) number of persons in the plan, (3) special classes for lower income groups, and many others.

Some companies that are competing keenly for business have offered to write very liberal amounts on relatively small cases. The pressures for large limits have developed for a number of reasons, including the following: (*a*) new companies in the field offer to write new coverages or high individual amounts as a competitive factor, (*b*) high-paid employees with small organizations are demanding as much group life insurance as is similarly paid employees of large corporations, and (*c*) increasing pressure of taxes has focused attention upon group life insurance. With respect to the tax situation, large amounts of group life insurance paid for by an employer in a high tax bracket and payable to the employee's family without income taxes, has resulted in a powerful appeal for this type of insurance in substantial individual amounts. Tax legislation changes pending in 1964 seek to limit the tax-free amount of group life insurance on each individual to about $50,000. Above this amount the employee would be required to pay income taxes on the cost contributed to the plan by the employers.

The purpose of requiring minimum limits and setting the maximum insurance per person is to attain a reasonably uniform distribution of insurance within the group. A maximum limitation precludes a concentration of risks in a few lives. A uniform distribution among a group tends to distribute expense so that the expense rate for each $1,000 of insurance is maintained within predetermined limits. The concentration of large amounts of insurance on a few lives tends to increase the average premium for a group and exposes the group to an unfavorable loss experience.

Probationary Period

In order not to build up an undue expense for the insurance of employees classed as "floaters," the group contract may provide that the insurance is not to become effective for new employees until after they have been in continuous service for a designated period. The length of the period will depend upon the experience of the organization buying the insurance. The limit should be set so that all employees come within the scope of the protection as soon as it seems reasonably certain that they have become settled in their positions. The probationary period usually varies between one month and twelve. An eligibility period of 31 days is normal after the probationary period, and during this time the employee may apply for inclusion in the group life plan without undergoing a medical examination. After the eligibility period the employee may still join the plan, but often is required to submit evidence of insurability in order to do so.

Inception and Termination of Coverage

When group insurance is desired, a form is prepared supplying sufficient information to provide a tentative rate. If the result of the preliminary survey is satisfactory to the employer, an application for the insurance is filed. Upon the company's approval of the plan of insurance selected by the employer, and upon the payment of the first premium or an agreed portion thereof, the insurance becomes effective.

It is not required that the master policy actually be issued or delivered before the company assumes the risk. If, however, the policy is to be issued on a contributory form with the employee sharing the cost, the insurance does not become effective until the required minimum number of employees have authorized the deduction from their remuneration as their share of the premium.

Since the policy is usually written on a yearly term basis, the master policy expires, unless renewed, at the end of the policy year. A severance of employment terminates the employee's insurance under the group policy subject to the conversion privilege. Only under the group permanent plans does the worker have assurance that his group life insurance protection (or some part of it) is for all of his lifetime.

In the case of absence from the service of the employer, if the absence of the employee is temporary, occasioned by physical disability or leave of absence, and if the premium is paid by the employer, the insurance may be kept in force.

EMPLOYEE CERTIFICATE PROVISIONS

The employer group life master contract is supplemented by an individual certificate which is given to each insured employee.

Individual Certificate

After a plan has been made for determining the amount for which an employee may be insured under a group policy so as to preclude individual selection, a schedule of classes or divisions may be set up affording preferences to certain members of the group.

If all the members of the group are insured for a uniform sum, the condition against individual selection is most simply satisfied. It frequently happens, however, that such a plan does not satisfy the requirements of the employer. It may be that he wishes to give preference to older employees and executives, or it may be that the amount of insurance he is willing to pay for on one class of employees is, in his opinion, entirely inadequate for another. To meet his needs in such cases, a schedule of insurance amounts may be set up in the contract providing a different amount of coverage for the different classes.

Automatic determination of individual coverage is effected in one of several ways. The more usual of these are: (*a*) a flat amount for all employees, (*b*) an amount based on position, (*c*) an amount based on length of service, and (*d*) an amount based on earnings.

By far the simplest determination is a flat amount of insurance for each employee. This plan has several shortcomings, not the least of which is a failure to recognize the needs of the employee, his ability to pay, his worth to the business, and his period of service.

The most widely used base for determining the amount of insurance is employee earnings. Payroll brackets are established, and all who fall within a given bracket automatically receive a predetermined amount of insurance; or the amount is set at a figure such as one or two times annual salary. This plan recognizes not only ability to pay but, also, within limits, the worth of the employee to the business. It fails to recognize fully the employee's need for protection, however.[15]

Scheduling the amount of insurance on the basis of length of service rewards employees for long service but has several shortcomings. It fails to consider differing income levels and provides lower coverage in the younger age groups, where frequently the needs are greatest. The amount of insurance may increase faster than wages, so that insurance premiums on a contributory plan may become a burden as the employee grows older.

Group insurance allocated on a position basis separates personnel into classes, such as officers, foremen, clerical employees, salesmen, and the like. The amount of insurance is the same for all employees of one class but differs among the classes. This plan recognizes, within limits, both worth and length of service but introduces some administrative difficulties in establishing categories and assigning borderline cases.

Basically, all plans should consider as fully as possible the employee's (*a*) needs and (*b*) ability to pay. It may be, and frequently is, necessary to use more than one plan to accomplish these objectives.

---

[15]Gregg, *op. cit.*, pp. 51–52. Dr. Gregg suggests that earnings do not adequately measure "need" and that some consideration should be given to the number of employee's dependents in scheduling group life insurance. The point is unquestionably well taken.

Beneficiary Provisions

A beneficiary (other than the employer) must be designated. Each employee may designate his own beneficiary. Policies may provide for the payment of the benefits to certain persons other than executors or administrators of the employee if the beneficiary dies before the employee or if no beneficiary has been named. For example, the policy may contain a *facility of payment* provision permitting the company to pay the insurance to the wife or husband, if living; or in equal parts to the surviving children. If neither husband, wife, nor children survive, proceeds may be paid to either the father or the mother or to both equally. If there are no surviving relatives in the foregoing classes, the benefits are payable to the insured's executors or administrators. In some states, payment to relatives is optional with the company; in others, the right of relatives to receive if no beneficiary is named is governed by statute.[16]

The policy indicates the steps required to change the beneficiary. Ordinarily, all that is required is the filing of a written notice on a form provided by the insurance company. In most instances this notice is filed with the employer. Every effort has been made in drawing the policy and writing the law governing beneficiaries to make the objective of the insurance within easy and simple reach. The insurance is designed for family relief. The provisions of the policy are designed to accomplish just this, even though the insured may neglect changing the beneficiary when new circumstances would ordinarily make it necessary. The authorization of payment for expenses of funeral or illness is of enormous value. Credit can frequently be based upon a policy with such a clause where otherwise it might be obtained with difficulty.

Since the employee may change the beneficiary from time to time, the beneficiary has no vested interest in the insurance, and cancellation terminates any contingent interest he may have had.

A beneficiary under a group policy has the right to sue the insurance company; but since there is no contractual relationship in the matter of the insurance between employer and employee, there is no right of action against the employer. In the case of noncontributory insurance gratuitously effected by the employer on the life of his employees, he assumes no obligation whatever to keep the policy in force and may at his option discontinue the insurance without notice either to the insured employee or to the beneficiary. Because of the insurer's more immediate knowledge of terms and conditions of the policy, a statutory requirement for reasonable notice to the employee of the termination of his insurance often is made a part of group life insurance. In the absence of such a statute, in-

[16]For example, see governing statutes of Alabama, Colorado, Massachusetts, New Hampshire, and Wyoming.

surance may lapse without notice to the employee holding a certification of insurance.[17]

Conversion Privilege

Each employee insured under a group policy is usually given the right to continue the insurance as an individual, *without medical examination,* in the event that for any reason his engagement with the employer placing the insurance is terminated. The employee has the right to convert his insurance under the group plan to any of the policies issued by the company, term insurance excepted, for a face amount equal to that of his group certificate. This right of conversion extends for 31 days after the termination of employment.[18]

When the conversion privilege is exercised, the premium charged for the new policy is based upon current rates for the policy required, computed according to the attained age and occupation of the employee at the time of conversion. The right of conversion under older group policies was entirely contingent upon the continuation of the master policy, and failure to renew the group policy terminated any rights of individual certificate holders. Policies now extend the protection of the certificate holder to the extent of providing that, if the group policy for any reason is terminated, an employee who has been insured for five years may convert to an individual policy, without medical examination, in an amount not greater than the amount of his group insurance, but in any instance not greater than $2,000.[19]

Until recently the right of conversion within 31 days of the termination of employment did not carry with it a continuation of insurance without action on the part of the employee. Under the older policies, when employment was terminated, the liability of the insurer to the employee ended. If the employee wished to continue his insurance, he himself was obligated to take the initiative by making application for conversion within 31 days. Failure to make such

---

[17] In the state of New York the statute does, in fact, require specific notification of conversion privileges to certificate holders under employer group plans if the policy is issued for delivery within the state. (Sec. 204, subsec. 3.) The law requires that an employee certificate holder be notified for his conversion privileges within 15 days after he becomes eligible for conversion. Failure to notify within the statutory 15-day period has the effect of extending the conversion privilege. The employee has 15 days after notice within which to act, but in no instance is the privilege extended beyond 90 days.

[18] While the Commissioners' Model Bill as originally drawn provided for the issuance of an individual policy if application was made within 45 days of termination of employment, most states, in enacting the Model Bill legislation, have set this period at 31 days.

[19] See previous footnote. Here, as in the termination of employment with the termination of the master plan, legislation providing for individual policies for certificate holders under the group plan allows 31 days in which application may be made, rather than the 45 days in the Commissioners' original Model Bill.

an application resulted in a lapse in the insurance as of the termination of employment. To eliminate this period of no coverage, policies now provide that the employee shall be actually covered during 31 days following termination of employment. Application for conversion may then be filed after termination of employment, and the new insurance becomes effective at the end of the 31-day period.

Knowing that the purpose of the conversion privilege is to protect the employee (especially the worker who is uninsurable under individual contracts) in his right to maintain life insurance protection, it is incongruous to find that very little[20] group life insurance is actually converted. The reasons may include: (1) ignorance of the important value of the conversion right to uninsurable or substandard applicants, (2) many employees obtain new group life insurance from their new employer, and (3) the higher premium cost, in relation to group term coverage, which the insured must pay for a converted whole life individual contract at his attained age.[21] Still, for many it is a valuable right which should not be overlooked, as evidenced by the extra assessments levied against the employer for converted policies. Adverse selection is quite high, as the most unhealthy persons are most likely to convert their contracts.

FINANCING EMPLOYER GROUP LIFE INSURANCE

Premiums

Premiums on the group life policy, whether under a contributory or a noncontributory form, are paid to the insurance company by the employer. When the employees are to share in the cost of the insurance in the *contributory* plan, their contribution is collected in accordance with the terms of an agreement entered into when the policy is written. The usual procedure is to deduct the premium contribution of the employees from the payroll. Under the *noncontributory* plan, the employee pays nothing and the entire cost is assumed by the employer. Employers may make premium payments to the insurance company annually, semiannually, quarterly, or monthly.

The basic rate for group insurance depends upon the industry in which the employees are engaged. The survey made, following the filing of an application for insurance, gives attention to the occupation of the various employees, sanitary and health conditions, fire protection, condition of the property, and many other employment hazards. When the basic rate is determined, the premium is found for the particular group making the application. This is based upon

[20] Gregg, *op cit.*, p. 72. Less than 2 percent of eligible insurance is actually converted after leaving employment.

[21] *Ibid.*, pp. 72–73.

the amount of insurance carried by each employee and his corresponding age.

The initial premium under a group policy is found by computing a premium on every individual employee and then determining the total. Experience has shown that because of the retirement of a certain number of older employees each year with a replacement in the younger brackets, the age of the group changes little from year to year, and hence the premium is practically stationary for the normal large employee group.

In industries in which the occupation is classed as extrahazardous, or in which a substantial percentage of the employees are classed as of a low industrial grade, or which are located in an unhealthy area, extra loading is added to the premium for the additional hazard.

In the beginning, the noncontributory plan was the general practice. Employees were presented with group insurance as a gift or additional compensation and were not expected to contribute in any way to its payment. The noncontributory form is considerably simpler in operation than the contributory form, in that all employees of a group are automatically covered and the necessity is eliminated for convincing a sufficient number of benefits of the plan to meet the statutory and the underwriting requirements. Also, the problem of apportioning costs among the classes of employees is avoided, and good will is engendered by an outright gift. Advocates of the contributory plan contend that group insurance in the form of an outright gift is less appreciated than that to which the employee must contribute, and also that employees not sufficiently interested to pay part of the costs are not sufficiently interested to appreciate insurance given to them. An advantage of the contributory plan is that it may be used to provide higher benefits than otherwise could be included in a noncontributory plan. Employee contributions in most contributory plans are limited, by state laws as well as by practice, to 60 cents (or less) per month per $1,000 of insurance.

Regardless of the type of plan, the employer is held responsible for the payment of the insurance premium. Under the terms of the contract, the insurance company may collect premiums due from the employer without regard to whether he has been reimbursed by the employees. The group life policy is written so that the insurance company deals only with the employer, so far as premiums are concerned.

Net Costs

The mortality experience under group life insurance plans has generally been favorable. Insurance actuaries have attributed the favorable mortality experience to the fact that numerous employees drop out of the group with advancing years and also to the fact that the entire group must be working when the insurance is effected. Furthermore, an element of favorable selection is found in the care exercised by the insuring company in studying the nature of the hazards involved in the industry when the risk is rated.

In the case of group insurance, there is presumed to be an absence of moral hazard for, because of the very nature of the selection, fraud and speculation are reduced to a minimum. Again, there is an element operating in favor of the company in the fact that in the ordinary course of events the physically unfit and the weaker lives are eliminated, and those who remain are physically fit to carry on their work.

As a result of the operation of the plan, there are certain specific savings not available under the usual insurance plan. Since no medical examination is required, there is a saving of this charge at the outset. Commissions paid on this class of business are substantially lower than those for other classes, thereby reducing the acquisition cost of the business. Finally, the expense in issuing and handling a group life policy is less than the cost of handling a large number of individual policies. Hence, the premium for group life insurance is substantially lower than that for individual policies for most persons.

Studies in various industries have been made as to the actual cost of insurance to the employing company and to the employee. Dividends and rate adjustments based on the actual experience of the group are an important factor in net cost of the plan. It has been estimated that in an average industry the insurance cost will approximate $10 per thousand, or about 1 percent of the total amount of insurance in force. When the employee himself contributes even a small amount weekly, after dividends have been credited, the burden of a group plan upon the employer is relatively light. It has, however, been increasing in recent years as more benefits have been provided, and as many of the plans do not involve the employees in the costs.

GROUP CREDITOR LIFE INSURANCE

The definition of group life insurance in the statutes provides for issuing a policy to a creditor to insure the lives of debtors. It covers that group of debtors who borrow on an installment basis without collateral security. The creditor is named as beneficiary.

Reasons for Use

The policy appeals to lending institutions in that they are assured of repayment of the loan even though the borrower does not live to complete the transaction. Regardless of the ability of the borrower, there is a real danger of not collecting the loan if he dies. In any event, the lending institution is relieved of the difficulty of pressing an unsecured claim against an estate of limited means. From a second point of view, the coverage serves to increase business. The borrower is assured that, if he does not live to pay, he will not leave an obligation for his family to meet.

The growth of this form of insurance is attributable to its appeal both to the borrower and to the lender. From the standpoint of the lending institution there is a guarantee of the payment of any unpaid balance of an insured account at once if the debtor dies before all payments have been made. While it is true that in many instances the problem of collecting might not be serious, if the debt is to cover some luxury item and the family of the deceased is in straitened circumstances, it will be a relief to the lending institution not to be in a position where it will be expected to undertake collection. From the customer point of view there is often a willingness to create a debt if the customer knows that he will be able to pay it, but a reluctance to enter into a situation that might burden his family in the event of his decease. Finally, if the lending institution requires a cosigner or a comaker on the note, such guarantors often more willingly assume the obligation where there is life insurance to guarantee payment in the event of the death of the debtor.

Types of Loans and Insurance Provided

Policies are written to cover debtors making installment loans of the following types: (*a*) unsecured personal loans, and (*b*) indebtedness secured by (1) conditional sales contracts and (2) lease sales contracts. While used at first to secure only limited types of smaller loans on farm equipment, trailers and other items, group credit life insurance soon became very popular for many automobile loans, and then general personal loans. While the tendency to cover mortgage loan on homes is to use individual term policies, the group plan has sometimes been extended to include this class of debtors. The bulk of the loans covered by group credit life insurance, however, continues to be personal loans. An indebtedness fully secured by collateral or an indebtedness created for the purchaser of securities is not covered. Only individual debtors are insured. Comakers and endorsers or officers of a corporation debtor are not covered.

The limitation for each loan set forth in the laws of most states for group credit life insurance is $5,000 or $10,000; but the amount of insurance in each instance is limited to the unpaid balance of the debt, subject to the stated maximum. Ordinarily, like employer group life insurance, no medical examination is required.

Group creditors' life insurance is usually written on a reducing term basis to the end that the amount of life insurance is the amount necessary to pay off the debt entirely. The laws of many states permit this type of group life insurance to cover only in those situations where the debt is required to be repaid in installments and is sold to (*a*) banks, (*d*) credit unions, (*c*) dealers, (*d*) department stores, and (*e*) finance companies. The contract may be written to cover all the debtors of the insured or may be limited to certain types of indebtedness.

Costs

The creditor is responsible for the payment of premiums. The premium is relatively small, since the amount of insurance in force with respect to any one debt decreases as repayments are made. Lending institutions differ in their methods of allocating costs of this coverage. Three of the more usual methods are: (*a*) charging the customer, (*b*) absorbing the cost by increasing the discount rate or service charges, which is the most common method, or (*c*) absorbing the cost as an operating expense. In some instances state laws will influence the choice of method and, in any instance, the method of transacting business by the creditor will have a determining influence.

Provisions

Individual certificates are not issued unless required by law. Individual insurance on the life of any particular debtor terminates (*a*) if the policy terminates, (*b*) if the indebtedness is discharged, or (*c*) if the indebtedness is transferred to another creditor. The insurance terminates, as well, when the loan has become overdue a specified period of time. The policy indicates the overdue period, usually from one to six months, and it is usual to provide that the insurance may be continued with respect to overdue accounts if the creditor continues premium payments for all debtors in a similar default class. If, during any policy year, the number of insured debtors falls below the group underwriting requirements of the company (100 is usual), it may decline to insure new debtors.

The policy covering debtor groups has no conversion provision; consequently, standard provisions dealing with conversions, with beneficiary, and with the requirement of individual certificates do not apply.

Growth and Problems

Credit life insurance is a phenomenon of the credit economy in which we now live. It has eased the task of borrowing by reducing the risk of loss to lending institutions that would suffer by the death of debtors.

Although credit life insurance is still only 6 percent of all life insurance in force, it has been growing faster than any other type, having doubled between 1949–51, and again between 1951–54, 1954–57, and 1957–62.[22] Most of it is issued through group policies, although some results from individual credit policies. Over 40 million certificates under 47,000 master policies were in force in 1963, with an average individual coverage of $800.[23] For a business only starting in the late 1920's, credit life has come a long way.

Such rapid growth has been accompanied, as might be expected, by some problems. One of the most difficult has been a tendency toward such great competition in rates that the states have feared abuses leading to harmful effects on the insureds. States such as New York and New Jersey have set recommended scales for the rates charged under group credit life insurance, with the lowest prices permitted for the largest groups. Other states, such as California, have not legislated the rates to be charged. They have exercised close scrutiny, however, over the business through the insurance commissioner by watching the relationship of premiums to losses in order to see that fair and safe prices result for the borrowers.

Other misuses of credit life have occurred, such as excessive amounts being written and the difficulty of debtors learning the actual cost of the protection. A model bill of the N.A.I.C. has helped curb the possible abuses in more than 20 states which have adopted the bill through recent legislation. With such progress, the future of credit life insurance should remain bright in the credit economy of the United States.

OTHER PLANS TO MARKET LIFE INSURANCE TO GROUPS

Although not technically group insurance, since individual contracts are used, several types of distribution through groups have been developed in life insurance. These methods include franchise (or wholesale) insurance and salary deduction plans.

Franchise or Wholesale Insurance

Groups not sufficiently large to meet the requirement for the group policy (usually groups of fewer than 25) are sold *franchise* or *wholesale* insurance. The National Association of Insurance Commissioners has recommended the size of the groups eligible for the coverage as 5 or more employees of 1 employer, or 10 or more members of a trade, labor, or professional association. There have been some modifications of the recommendations in the state laws during the past decade. Only a few states require 10 or more lives to be insured, over 30 states permit 4 or more lives to be covered, while 16 still establish the limit at 5.

Franchise insurance is a plan for the mass selling of individual policies. Contrary to the group insurance plan, the contracting par-

[22] *Life Insurance Fact Book, op. cit.,* p. 30.
[23] *Ibid.*

ties are the employee and the insurance company. An application for insurance is required from each employee to be insured, and the insurance company issues a policy to each individual included in the plan. While some plans use a master policy issued to an employer, with accompanying certificates delivered to each insured employee as in group life insurance, the more customary procedure calls for individual applications and individual policies. The employer does, however, file an application containing an agreement covering the payment of premiums. The premium may be paid in full by the employee whose life is insured or by the employer and the employee on a cooperative basis.

There is no medical examination except for applicants of age sixty or over unless, for some reason, there is doubt as to the insurability of the applicant or an examination is required by law. Some companies require a medical examination if the insurance exceeds a certain sum. Evidence of the physical condition of the applicant is obtained from the questions answered in the application. Considerable importance is attached to underwriting of individual risks. Table 23-2 shows an example of the medical requirement. The company always reserves the right to require a medical examination at any time, or any other information necessary to arrive at a decision on the application. The company has the right to deny an application for any reason that seems pertinent to its underwriters. Thus, in small groups adverse selection is avoided. Companies do not intend to be unduly selective; wholesale insurance is designed to provide for small groups essentially the same service that other plans give larger groups.

TABLE 23-2

Requirements for Medical Examination for Wholesale Insurance Based on Age and Amount of Insurance

Age Nearest Birthday	*Amount of Insurance up to and Including*	*Medical Requirements*
Up to and including 40	$5,000	No medical examination
Up to and including 59	$3,000	No medical examination
41–59, inclusive	$3,000–$5,000	Short medical examination
60 and over	Any amount	Full medical examination

A minimum and maximum amount of insurance to be issued to each employee is established, and a maximum amount for any class. Amounts of insurance are not automatically changed, as in some other forms of group insurance; and each change requires a new application. If the application is approved, a new policy is issued for the difference between the outstanding amount and the new amount to which the employee is entitled.

Wholesale insurance affords a small business the advantages of group insurance. Many new employees may enter the group without medical examination, and employees leaving the group have the same conversion privileges as in the group policy. The important differences between the group and the wholesale form are the individual applications and the individual policies.

Salary Deduction Life Insurance

Salary deduction life insurance, also referred to as "payroll deduction," "salary budget," "salary savings," and "salary allotment insurance," is a plan for the sale of the regular forms of life insurance by personal solicitation of individual employees providing for monthly premium payments by the employer, who deducts the amounts agreed upon from the salary of the employees. It has some points in common with wholesale insurance and affords both employers and employees many of the same advantages.

The salary deduction plan is designed to assist employees in the higher salary brackets in building up an adequate insurance program by making premium payments convenient and automatic. If the number of applicants meets the general requirements for wholesale insurance—that is, generally, if the group exceeds 10 in number and 75 percent of the group is insured—no medical examination is normally required. A medical statement is always required, and the risk is accepted or rejected on the basis of the information obtained from the application and other sources.

Executive department heads, foremen, and skilled employees are the classes solicited for this type of insurance. The plan has not worked out particularly well for unskilled employees; for them, the group or wholesale plan seems more desirable.

The salary deduction plan allows each participant to select the type and amount of policy he wishes to carry. Premiums may be, and usually are, paid entirely by the employee, although the plan sometimes calls for a contribution from the employer. Rather than being a different life insurance product, salary deduction life insurance is primarily a convenient method in which the employer encourages the employees to purchase regular individual contracts of protection.

SUMMARY

The amazing growth of group life insurance, especially during the past two decades, has made this class of life insurance one of the major factors in the marketing of life insurance. By combining many lives into one group, two objectives are achieved when a master contract is issued to an employer, creditor, union, or trustee: (1) *administration expenses* are substantially reduced and (2) *mor-*

tality costs are kept within manageable limits by the spread of risk among many persons.

Group selection of insureds, rather than individual selection on the basis of medical examinations, is a primary characteristic. Adverse selection by unhealthy persons is avoided by *controls* which are built into the process of group underwriting, such as (1) minimum numbers in the group (set by state laws, usually 10 or 25), (2) maximum amounts of insurance on an individual (often $40,000, but with numerous exceptions), (3) medical examinations required for new entrants to the group, if they do not apply within a stated period, such as 31 days, after eligibility, and (4) special charges for unusual occupational groups. The controls exercised over group selection are often legal requirements, but also include many practical applications of the insurance technique as a part of underwriting rules of the insurer.

The employer group life insurance contract usually provides for *renewable term* insurance, which partially explains the lower cost of this protection in relation to many individual life insurance contracts. Employer participation in the cost of all group life contracts makes term insurance feasible, though it must be remembered that the employee is receiving only temporary life insurance coverage. Permanent protection is available only through (1) the *conversion* privilege, which is an important right to the employee whose employment is terminated and (2) *group permanent* plans, which provide at least some lifetime coverage by using ordinary life, limited payment life, endowment, or combination paid-up and decreasing term insurance.

The *employee certificate* states his amount of life insurance (often related to one or more years' earnings), the beneficiary provisions, and his right to convert to permanent insurance. The premiums for his coverage are paid to the insurer by the employer, often on a *noncontributory* plan as far as the employee is concerned. If the employee shares the cost with the employer, it is called a *contributory* plan. Tax considerations, morale, the interest of unions in such important employee fringe benefits, and other factors determine which method of financing the costs of group life insurance is used.

Group creditor life insurance has had phenomenal growth in our credit economy. Many types of personal loans by banks, savings associations, and finance companies now include credit life insurance on the life of the debtor as part of their regular loan agreements. Rapid development of these plans has brought problems of definition, limitations, and costs.

Franchise (or *wholesale*) life insurance and salary deduction plans are two examples of adaptation of group marketing methods to the sale of individual contracts of life insurance.

FOR REVIEW

1. What factors help to prevent adverse selection against the insurer in the group life insurance contract? Explain each briefly.
2. What characteristics make group insurance different from other insurance plans? Identify and explain the importance of at least three such characteristics.
3. Several different types of minimums and maximums are used in connection with group life insurance. Evaluate the need for such limits.
4. Group life insurance must necessarily be designed to meet basic and average needs of the whole group. How is this accomplished? Explain how three features of the usual group life contract help in achieving the needs of the group.
5. How can term insurance be the normal type of insurance used in group life policies when the increasing cost, during the older ages, makes term insurance (especially the yearly renewable type) unsuitable for many individual life insurance policyholders?
6. Describe at least three factors which have made group life insurance one of the most rapidly progressing classes of life insurance during the last 15 years.
7. Solve this riddle: What kind of life insurance *(a)* has doubled in volume almost every four years since the late 1940's? *(b)* has over 40 million insureds, although it still accounts for only about 6 per cent of all life insurance in force? *(c)* is the only type of group life insurance where the master contract policyholder is permitted to be the beneficiary? *(d)* has the maximum price for the coverage rigidly controlled in many of the states? *(e)* has achieved all its growth despite the fact that most states restrict insurance amount per insured to under $5,000 or $10,000?
8. What type of life insurance is used to provide benefits under most group life contracts? Why is this type used in preference to other available alternatives? Explain fully.
9. In spite of a generous group life insurance program, the executives of the X Company express disappointment in the labor turnover they are experiencing. It was expected that the group insurance would be an important factor in reducing this. In your opinion were the executives justified in their expectations?
10. It is stated that the benefits of group insurance are threefold: *(a)* to the employer, *(b)* to the employee, and *(c)* to the community. Accepting the benefits to employer and employee as self-evident, discuss the possible benefits of group insurance to the community.
11. A plan was submitted to a lending institution under which a life insurance company was to insure the lives of depositors who would elect to make deposits in accordance with the bank's "Insured Life Savings Account." Under the plan there would be a contract between the bank and the depositor directing the bank to issue a "Certificate of Insured Life Savings Account" and to include the depositor in the group life insurance policy. It was contended that such a plan was not within the power of the bank. Do you think such a plan feasible? Does the bank have a right to incur expense in connection with such a plan? Is there any violation of the principal of insurable interest?
12. B, the manager of X Corporation, contends that premiums paid for group insurance should be allowed as corporation expense deductible from taxable income. He makes inquiry of the Collector of Internal Revenue as to whether life insurance premiums are deductible from taxable income

and is told that they are not. Advise B as to the extent that he has received *(a)* correct and *(b)* incorrect information.

13. Some group life insurance underwriters recommend that employees age 65 or more have their group life insurance benefits limited to one half the amount of insurance available to those under 65. Does this seem fair? Is the recommendation based upon a logical approach? Explain your answers.
14. Some group policies contain the stipulation that an employee, in order to secure the benefit of the group insurance policy, must have been in the employ of the concern for a stipulated period of time. Six months is a term frequently indicated. What is the value of such a stipulation?
15. Is the incontestable clause made a part of the group policy? If so, in light of the fact that the policy is issued to employers on the life of employees for a beneficiary other than the employer, discuss its effect.
16. Distinguish briefly the points wherein wholesale life insurance and salary deduction plans differ from group life insurance.
17. To what extent do group life insurance plans *(a)* have standard provisions, *(b)* finance costs through employee contributions, and *(c)* have conversion rights (to permanent life insurance) that are actually used?

Chapter 24

LIFE INSURANCE CONTRACT FEATURES

A HOUSEWIFE spending $50 per month on staple groceries at a favorite market devotes countless hours every year to the process of shopping. Much time is used in reading labels and asking questions in order to determine quality, cost, and potential uses for the products purchased. Yet what happens when the same family purchases a life insurance contract? Probably a part of only one or two evenings are set aside to permit a life insurance agent to visit their home. He tries desperately, with a limited time, to understand their needs and explain how life insurance can provide a solution to the basic family problems of savings and protection. Frequently the wife is not included in the conversations, and if she is, often it is for the final decision only—made on the basis of "Well, if you think it's best, George, then we'd better have it."

A logical purchasing system for a major item in the family budget? Hardly, but then the typical method could be rationalized in terms of the many other hasty and uninformed decisions by the consumer. But wait, shouldn't at least the most important uses of family income be approached with at least some knowledge of the fundamental parts of what is being purchased? Not many persons buy an automobile without knowing at least its size, style, kind of engine, and color. Yet they often spend (or worse yet, don't!) an equal amount[1] of income on life insurance without really knowing what the basic features of the contract are.

Chapter 24 introduces[2] the more important provisions of a life insurance contract. Every potential and actual policyholder should know about the features discussed here, for these rights and benefits are what the contract provides in return for its cost.

---

[1]In approximate figures, a $3,000 automobile purchased once every five years costs an average of $600 a year, or $50 a month. At about age twenty-three, $40,000 of ordinary life insurance would cost a similar amount.

[2]For further information, the student is referred to two excellent references: Janice E. Greider and William T. Beadles, *Law and the Life Insurance Contract,* and Dan M. McGill, *Legal Aspects of Life Insurance* (both published at Homewood, Ill.: Richard D. Irwin, Inc., 1960 and 1959, respectively).

The analysis centers on the provisions found in the usual whole life, or permanent, life insurance contract. Certain of the features may not be found in policies issued as industrial or group life insurance; for example, under such policies limited or no cash and loan values may be present, or the settlement options may be limited to fewer choices.

GENERAL FORM OF THE POLICY

Basically, the life insurance policy is a promise by the insurer to pay a stated amount of money to the policyholder (or his beneficiary). The conditions under which the benefits are paid are significant, and may include death, some types of disability, and in the case of endowments, a certain maturity date set in the contract.

In connection with the fundamental benefits, many important options and privileges are granted to the policyholder. These features combine to make the life insurance contract one of the most flexible agreements ever designed. The owner of the contract, or sometimes his beneficiary, has the right to: (1) stop or change premium payments, (2) change the recipient of the benefits, (3) assign the contract rights, (4) change use of the dividends, (5) change to a different policy, (6) reinstate coverage, (7) take cash or loan values, (8) cancel the policy and receive accumulated benefits in a variety of ways, and (9) use the policy proceeds by receiving lump-sum or installment payments.

The parts of the life insurance contract discussed in this chapter include its: (1) *declarations* (which are found on the "policy face," and in the "application") and *insuring agreement,* (2) *standard provisions,* (3) *cash, loan and nonforfeiture benefits,* (4) *optional methods of settlement, and* (5) *disability benefit extensions of coverage.*

INSURING AGREEMENT AND FACE OF POLICY

On the first page of the policy appears the name of the life insurance company, the name of the insured, the amount of the policy (termed the "face amount") and the names of the beneficiary or beneficiaries. In the insuring agreement the company agrees to insure the life of the person named as insured and to pay to the beneficiary the face amount of the policy upon the notice and proof of death of the insured while the policy is in force.

The type of policy purchased, the policy number, the age of the insured at the time the policy is issued, and the date of issue appear on its face. The face of an endowment policy will indicate that the policy proceeds are payable to the insured if he is living a given number of years from the date the policy is issued. Requirements for premium payments are stated, primarily the date premiums are due and whether they are payable annually, semiannually, quarterly, or monthly. In limited payment policies or endowments, the number of years payments are to be made will be indicated. Any special features of the contract are mentioned, and a statement is made that provisions on subsequent pages form part of the contract. The New York insurance law requires a summary description of the contract at the bottom of the face and on the outside of the folded policy. The signatures of the officers authorized to issue the policy appear at the bottom of the first page.

APPLICATION

As a basis for accepting or rejecting an applicant for insurance, the companies writing life insurance require certain information. This is contained in an *application,* which becomes a part of the contract. Insurers wish to know, for example, the name, residence, age, and occupation of the applicant as well as the plan of insurance applied for, when premiums are to be paid, the beneficiary and contingent beneficiary, and other insurance in force. In addition, they wish to know the family record as to longevity and to have evidence of the physical fitness of the applicant. All this appears in the application. Legally the application constitutes an offer for the purchase of insurance which the company may accept or reject.

If a medical examination is required, there are two parts to the application. The first is a questionnaire completed by the applicant. The second part of the application consists of a report of the physical examination of the applicant made by the examining physician. The first part of the application is signed by the applicant; the second part, by the examining physician. Comments may be added to or required on one or both parts by the agent negotiating the transaction.

The representations by the applicant, in the part of the application which he signs and to the examining physician, should be accurate and carefully considered. Not to relax the requirement for care and accuracy, but rather to make for peace of mind, it is usually provided in the application that, except for fraud, the information supplied need only be substantially true and not literally so.[3] The clause can, under no circumstance, excuse the deliberate withholding of pertinent factual material or an incorrect answer to a

[3]Life insurance policies were formerly written with a clause making the statements in the application to have the force of warranties. The law in most jurisdictions now requires, in the absence of fraud, that statements in the application be considered representations, which must be "material" (or important), and not warranties. Representations made in good faith and without intent to defraud do not have the effect, if not technically correct, of affording the company grounds for canceling the policy or refusing to pay a claim. A deliberate misstatement made with the intent to defraud, or in any way involving bad faith, is a basis for voiding the policy.

question on the ground that the application will still be substantially correct. The person who has no records and cannot recall all pertinent facts—for example, concerning a past physical condition—meets the requirements if his answer is conscientious and reveals all the information at his command.

Statutes controlling life insurance require that the insured be furnished with the entire contract. Policies now make the application a part of the contract and a photostatic copy is attached. When so written, the policy ordinarily provides that no statement shall void the policy, or be used in defense of a claim under it, unless it is contained in the written application and a copy of the application is endorsed or attached to the policy when issued.[4]

STANDARD PROVISIONS

There is no standard policy form required by statute for life insurance contracts, but instead all policies of life insurance newly issued must include the *standard provisions* (sometimes called "general provisions" in the policy) prescribed by the statutes of the jurisdiction. New forms of policies are issued only when approved by the state insurance department. It was early felt that a standard form of policy resulted in too much uniformity of available coverages and, hence, limited the scope of protection the companies wished to make available. To provide more leeway with respect to coverages and, at the same time, adequately safeguard the interests of the policyholders, laws were enacted making certain standard provisions mandatory.[5]

Indicative of the nature of the standard provisions now universally required is the following summary of the ordinary life provisions of the New York law: (1) that there shall be a grace period of either 30 days or one month; (2) that the policy shall be incontest-

[4]But for an exception to the rule, where a false statement appears in the application attached to the policy, consider: "When an insured, in making application for a contract of insurance reveals to the agent of the insurance company the correct answers to questions contained in the application, and the agent, who, acting within the scope of his authority or in the course of his employment, fills out the application blank, and, unknown to the insured and in the absence of circumstances which should arouse his suspicion, inserts in the application incorrect answers to the questions contained therein, the knowledge of the agent is imputed to the insurance company. If such company thereafter enters into a contract of insurance upon the application and collects premiums on such contract, it is estopped from asserting as a defense to a claim arising under the policy that the answers contained in the written application were incorrect. The result is the same regardless of the presence of restrictive provisions in the application limiting the authority of the agent." *National Aid Life Association* v. *Clinton,* 176 Okl. 372, 55 P (2d) 781. See also *Atlas Life Insurance Company* v. *Chastin,* 12 CCH Life Cases 5.

[5]Through the activities of committees of National Association of Insurance Commissioners, as well as the work of such groups as the Committee on Insurance Law of the American Bar Association, most of the important laws governing the business of life insurance are to be found in the statutes of all jurisdictions.

able after it has been in force during the lifetime of the insured for two years from the date of issue; (3) that the policy shall constitute the entire contract between the parties; (4) that, if the age of the insured has been misstated, the amount payable under the policy shall be such as the premium would have purchased at the correct age; (5) that participation must be on an annual dividend basis; (6) that options shall be specified to which the insured is entitled in the event of default of premium after the payment of three annual premiums; (7) that loan values shall be stated; (8) that there shall be a table showing, in figures, loan values and the options available under the policy in default of premium payments each year during at least the first 20 years of the policy; (9) that, in case of a policy payable in installments or as an annuity, a table shall show the amount of installments or annuity payments; and (10) that reinstatement shall be covered.

The law does not prescribe specific wording for the provisions, but wording must be approved by the state superintendent of insurance. Since the standard provisions establish minimum requirements only and a company may file policies with more liberal provisions, the legislation permits considerably more liberality in life insurance contracts than under a standard policy requirement. Other states have enacted legislation similar to the requirements of New York. Because a large majority of all the life insurance companies write insurance beyond the borders of their own states and must, therefore, comply with the standard provision requirements of the state in which they issue their policies, a considerable degree of uniformity has developed in the contracts offered by the important legal reserve companies. The trend of life insurance legislation has been in the direction of greater liberality in the terms of the contract in favor of the insured, at the same time so providing for the regulation of the business that it be conducted on a scientific and safe basis.

The Contract and Payment of Premiums

Taken together, (1) the face of the policy with the insuring clause, (2) the application, and (3) the subsequent pages containing options, privileges, extensions, or limitations, constitute the complete contract of life insurance.

Since premium payments are of vital importance to the validity of life insurance, the policy carefully states how and when premium payments are payable. Policies require the payment of the first premium in advance, while the applicant is in good health. Premiums after the first are likewise payable in advance. Ordinary insurance premiums are computed on an annual basis, though they may be paid semiannually, quarterly, or monthly. Many policies will, for comparative purposes, include in the contract the premium amount if it is paid on these various bases.

The first premium paid satisfies the requirement for a consideration essential to the validity of the contract. The payment of the first premium makes the insurance effective. There is no obligation to pay subsequent premiums, but the payment of such premiums is a condition precedent to the continuance of the insurance. In other words, the premium requirement is not a promise and, therefore, is not binding on the insured. Premiums when due, however, must be paid before there is an obligation on the insurance company to fulfill its part of the contract.

Premiums are required to be paid either at the home office of the company or to an agent authorized to receive payment. The ostensible scope of an ordinary agent's authority will extend to the collection of the first premium but of no other. The first premium payment may be made to an agent delivering the policy, regardless of policy stipulations regarding the receipt, but the authority of the delivering agent to collect extends no further. (Industrial insurance is an obvious exception.)

Obviously, since failure to pay the premium will seriously affect the position of the insured, it is essential to know what constitutes payment and to whom payment should be made. When payment to an agent is authorized, it is usual to require that payments shall be so made only in exchange for the company's official premium receipt, signed by certain designated officers of the company, and countersigned by the person receiving the premium.

It is the rule among life insurance companies to allow a *grace period* following the due date of a premium during which the insurance remains in force. It is the intent to allow a month. To avoid any uncertainty, the grace period is now usually expressed in days, and 31 days are most often allowed. If the insurance policy becomes payable by the death of the insured during the period of grace, any unpaid premium or premiums necessary to complete premium payments for the policy year in which such death occurs, including the overdue premium, are deducted from the amount payable. If the premium is not paid before the end of the grace period, the policy becomes void, and all premiums previously paid are forfeited to the company subject to the nonforfeiture (see later section of this chapter) provisions of the policy.

In emergency, the insured may request of the company an extension of the time within which to pay his premium without allowing the policy to lapse. To keep the insurance in effect beyond the grace period, a written application is filed with the company in advance, and the insured is notified if the company agrees to the extension, together with the terms of extension. Such a procedure is very unusual.

The Beneficiary

The *beneficiary* is the person or interest designated in the contract to receive the proceeds. Oftentimes this is simply done by naming the beneficiary on the face of the policy. If the designation is a complicated one, or if a change is made after the policy is first written, a beneficiary clause may be used, attached in the form of a rider or endorsement to the contract. There are many variations in the preparation of the beneficiary clause. The final form depends upon the objective of the insured. While the life insurance underwriter will cooperate and advise, in the end the arrangement of beneficiary designations is the responsibility of the applicant. A beneficiary may be (*a*) primary or (*b*) contingent. A *primary* beneficiary is the beneficiary first entitled to the benefits of the policy following the death of the insured. A *contingent* beneficiary is entitled to the benefits only after the death of a primary beneficiary. If there are several beneficiaries, the first is the "primary" beneficiary and the others are identified successively as "secondary" or "tertiary."

Designation of Beneficiary. In designating a beneficiary, the owner of life insurance makes a disposition of life values. For many persons this is the only property right they have. Through life insurance life values may be made available to dependents. The beneficiary designation is, in effect, a will making disposition of life values. The disposition of such values deserves as careful consideration as is given to the disposition of physical property by will.

The beneficiary may be designated as (*a*) the insured or his estate, (*b*) a specifically named person or persons, (*c*) a class or classes of persons, (*d*) business organizations, and (*e*) a trustee. Because each has its advantages, the form to be used is important. A careless or thoughtless selection may result in something less than the best practice, and an incorrect choice may defeat the objective of the insurance.

If a policy is made payable to the executors, administrators, or assignees of an insured, the proceeds of the policy are subject to the claims of creditors upon the death of the insured. If no beneficiary is sufficiently designated, the policy becomes payable to the estate of the insured. If the estate is designated as beneficiary, the distribution of the insurance may be made by the insured's will or if there is no will, in accordance with the inheritance laws of the state.

To avoid administrative costs and leave insurance proceeds to the members of a family, the term "family" or "heirs" is sometimes used to designate the beneficiary. This is a *class* designation. The term "family" is susceptible to broad interpretation. It is held to include persons residing with the insured, even though they may not be relatives. It may also include children, stepchildren, or others, even though they have left the household of the insured. When there is ambiguity, intent will govern, if it can be ascertained. Intent may be difficult to establish. Therefore, it is wise to identify the beneficiary as specifically as possible.

If a policy designates the "legal heirs" as beneficiaries, distribution of the proceeds follows the statutes of the jurisdiction governing descent. "Heirs" and similar terms may be interpreted by the courts so broadly as to include persons not originally intended by the insured. On the other hand, the term may not be sufficiently inclusive to carry out his intent. When there is confusion in the interpretation, terms are interpreted in the popular sense rather than by technical definition. This procedure will fulfill the meaning and intent of the insured, and parol evidence is admissible to throw light upon this intent. When the policy is made payable to "heirs" or "family," they receive the proceeds of insurance as beneficiaries, and not by descent as heirs. The proceeds are, therefore, subject to all the protections and advantages that accrue to named beneficiaries.

When a wife is designated a beneficiary without indicating the name, in the case of the death of the first wife, a second wife succeeds as beneficiary. In order to obviate any possible question, it is customary, not only to designate the relationship as wife but also to state the name. In the case of an insurance made in good faith designating a wife as beneficiary, the insurance company in making payment is under no obligation to investigate the validity of the marriage.

When "children" are designated as beneficiaries, the term does not include grandchildren. When it is apparently the intent of the insured, the term "child" will extend to include an adopted child. An insurance policy made payable to wife and children includes all children, whether by the wife designated as beneficiary or by a former wife. It is intended that only the children by the wife designated as beneficiary shall participate, the term "our children" or "children born of this marriage" should be used.[6]

It is entirely in order to designate as beneficiary a business organization such as a partnership, association, or corporation. Life insurance policies are frequently written for the benefit of a business. The settlement options may be limited in such cases, for obviously a life income provision is impossible for a corporate beneficiary. A

[6]It is in order, from the standpoint of law, to designate the members of a group or a class as the beneficiaries of a life insurance policy. Policies may cover such classes as heirs, children, grandchildren, brothers, and sisters or other groups of relatives. Most companies limit the use of class designations and permit only a few types. The limitation is designed to protect the insured and the company. Carlessly worded clauses create a strong possibility that certain individuals may unintentionally be excluded or unintentionally included. A class designation is often used where young children are being named as contingent beneficiaries. In order for unborn children to share in the proceeds, the phrase "to living children," or "children who survive the insured," is used.

trustee may be designated as a beneficiary. Such a designation is made when discretionary power is to be a factor in the distribution of the insurance proceeds.

Change of Beneficiary. With reference to the beneficiary, life insurance policies are written under two forms. Under the first, the beneficiary is named without right of change on the part of the insured, and the insurance designation in such cases is said to be *irrevocable.* A second method of designating the beneficiary retains for the insured the right of change as he sees fit. Here the beneficiary is said to be *revocable,* and most contracts use this form.

The rights of the beneficiary under a life insurance contract vary in accordance with whether the policy is written under an irrevocable or a revocable form. If the right to change the beneficiary is not reserved to the insured, the beneficiary's interest is "vested" from the time the policy becomes effective. If the right to change the designation of beneficiary is reserved, the interest of the beneficiary is limited to an expectancy during the lifetime of the insured and he has no right to the proceeds until the death of the insured. Any rights that a beneficiary may have, whether named irrevocably or not, are dependent upon the conditions of the policy.[7]

When a policy is written with the beneficiary irrevocable, the usefulness of the policy to the insured himself is substantially curtailed. He cannot assign or pledge the policy, nor can he receive any of the other benefits, such as the loan or cash surrender value, without the consent of the beneficiary. The situation is not the same when the insured reserves the right of revocation. There are certain advantages and certain disadvantages in each of the forms. Because of this it is essential to recognize the usefulness of each in particular circumstances and, in procuring life insurance, to make the policy in this respect fit the particular needs of the insured.

If it is desired that the proceeds of the insurance be given to the beneficiary in the form of a gift, especially to avoid taxation in the insured's estate, the irrevocable designation is the proper one. A husband may wish to create an estate for the benefit of his wife and children and so secure it that, in the event of future unforeseen financial difficulties, the accumulated value of the policy will be

---

[7]An irrevocable beneficiary takes a vested interest; but, if the beneficiary is named reserving the right to the insured to change, the beneficiary has only an expectancy. This represents the general rule but is an oversimplification of the situation. A beneficiary may have a vested interest, even though named with the right of change reserved to the insured, if the beneficiary acquires an equitable interest. Such an interest may follow from (*a*) a contract or (*b*) a gift. Equitable interest, for example, may arise between partners who agree to maintain policies each for the benefit of the other (*Smith* v. *Schoelkopf*, 68 S.W. [2d] 346). Completed gifts of policies have been upheld in the courts against beneficiaries named after the time of the gift (*McEwen* v. *New York Life Insurance Company,* 183 Pac. 373; 42 Cal. App. 133).

beyond the control of creditors. Such is the case when the beneficiary is irrevocable. On the other hand, if the insured wishes himself to make use of the policy for the purpose of giving security for a loan, or feels that the time may come when he may wish to surrender or transfer it and wishes to be under no obligation to secure the consent of a beneficiary, the proper form for him to use is that in which the right of revocation is reserved.[8]

Policies as written now usually provide that the interest of the predeceased beneficiary, unless otherwise stipulated, shall thereupon vest in the insured. In this situation, even though the beneficiary originally is designed as irrevocable, the insured may proceed to assign his policy as he wishes.[9]

Most policies provide a simple procedure to effect a change. It is usually stipulated that the beneficiary may be changed as often as desired by filing a written request for endorsement accompanied by the policy at the home office of the company. Policies now provide that upon endorsement on the policy the change becomes effective as of the date of the request. The dating back of the time of the change of beneficiary, whether or not the insured is living at the time of the endorsement, is without prejudice to the company on account of any payment made before the written request for the change reached the home office of the company.

If the insured wants to change an irrevocable beneficiary, the written consent of the beneficiary is required to make a change. Otherwise consent of the beneficiary is not necessary, nor is it required that he be given notice of the change.

Ownership of Policy and Changes

Some policies indicate a life owner. Policies naming a life owner offer the applicant the option of retaining control of the policy or of placing this control with another. A clause is used providing that

[8]The trend is away from naming an irrevocable beneficiary, for such designations cause serious misunderstandings. The advantages of such a designation are limited, and frequently the insured does not realize that he is placing his policy values beyond his own sole control. If it is the definite intent that the beneficiary have a vested interest in the policy, he may be designated as a joint life owner. Such a designation clearly establishes an interest in all policy values and makes it clear to the insured that he is sharing them with another.

[9]The courts have not been in agreement as to the successor in the event that an irrevocable beneficiary dies before the insured. It may be the intent of the insured, in the event that the designated beneficiary predeceases him, that the beneficiary's interest in the policy terminate. Unless provision is made to this effect, the insured may find himself faced with unexpected legal entanglements in the event that the interest of the beneficiary passes to his (the beneficiary's) estate. As stated, policies as written today usually make provision for this contingency by providing that, if a beneficiary predecease the insured, the interest of such beneficiary, unless otherwise stipulated, shall thereupon vest in the insured. This follows the requirement of the New York law.

during the lifetime of the insured the right to receive all cash values, loans, and other benefits accruing under the policy and the right to exercise all options and privileges or to agree with the company on changes or amendments to the policy shall vest alone in the life owner.

Policies written on a form designating a life owner usually provide that, if the designated beneficiary dies before the insured, the interest of such beneficiary shall vest in the life owner. This condition is subject to modification, however, and a provision may be made for the vesting of the beneficiary's interests otherwise, if desired.

Ownership may usually be changed by following a procedure stated in the policy, and it is pointed out that such a change is not the same as an assignment of the policy.

Assignment

A life policy may be freely assigned, and the consent of the company is not required. It is usually provided, under the terms of the policy, that no assignment shall be effective until the company has been notified in writing. The courts have not construed such a clause as prohibiting an assignment. Its effect is to relieve the company of any responsibility arising out of the assignment before the receipt of written notice. It is not required that the assignee have an insurable interest in the life of the insured, though it is essential that the policy be so written at its inception that it is not invalidated for want of insurable interest or other element affecting its validity.

The United States Supreme Court has held that a valid life insurance policy is assignable like any chose in action. The court specifically states that to deny the right to assign a life insurance policy except to a person having an insurable interest is to diminish appreciably the value of the contract. When, however, it is apparent that the policy was procured designating a beneficiary with an insurable interest but transferred to an assignee without an insurable interest, with the intent to provide a wager contract, the courts have held this to be as objectionable as to issue a contract that is in the first instance a wagering contract.

An assignment is to be distinguished from a change in the designated beneficiary. The power to change the beneficiary is a contractual power to appoint.[10] The right of assignment grows out of the nature of life insurance as property.[11] Depending upon the purpose for which it is made, an assignment may take one of two forms: (*a*) conditional or (*b*) absolute. The *conditional* assignment, sometimes

---

[10]*Mutual Benefit Life Insurance Company* v. *Swett,* 222 Fed. 200.

[11]*City National Bank* v. *Lewis,* 74 Okla. 1; 76 Pac. 237.

known as a "collateral assignment," is used in connection with loans or other forms of indebtedness when equities in the policy are used to provide security. Such assignments may be in a definite form fixed in an amount sufficient to liquidate the indebtedness. They may also cover the extent of the creditor's interest. In this instance, the assignment by its terms follows the amount of the debt as it increases or decreases. Evidence that the debt has been extinguished will cancel the conditional assignment. Such an assignment should be canceled immediately, as a matter of record, once the debt it secured has been paid.

An *absolute* assignment conveys to the assignee all right, title, and interest that the insured or policyowner may hold. All incidents of ownership are transferred so that the assignee is placed in the position of the original assignor and has the right to exercise all the powers and privileges formerly held by him. An absolute assignment is in effect an outright sale of all the rights which the assignor has in the contract. His original position can be reestablished only by another absolute assignment conveying his original interest back to him.

Briefly, a conditional or a collateral assignment is designed to make available to a creditor rights under a policy only so long as the debt is outstanding. An absolute assignment is designed to make a final disposition of those rights to the assignee.

Lending institutions at one time were in the habit of asking for an absolute assignment when intended as collateral security. Absolute assignments couched in broad terms tended to defeat their purpose, because an assignment could always be shown to be conditional if such was the intent, regardless of the form used. An assignee under an absolute form that is in fact conditional is frequently unable to exercise specific rights on the ground that the insurance company cannot safely recognize him as sole owner.

As a result of cooperation between banking and life insurance interests, a uniform form has been devised that is free from the defects of the absolute form frequently required by lending institutions and the old collateral forms of life insurance companies frequently too limited to satisfy the needs of the lending institutions. The form, sometimes known as the "ABA Form," is widely used and is as equitable as could be devised; its general use has introduced a needed degree of uniformity.[12]

[12]The form is now available to lending institutions and bears the certification: "Form Approved by Bank Management Commission, American Bankers Association." The form is divided into 11 sections, lettered from A through K. It is a comprehensive document designed exactly to fit the needs of a collateral assignment of life insurance. It adequately protects the lender and sets forth in detail the rights that pass to him by virtue of the assignment. Rights reserved and excluded from the assignment are also detailed. The document adapts itself to the needs of the lending institution and provides protection for the assigner.

If the assignment clause requires the consent of the company, failure to obtain that consent does not invalidate the policy. In such a case the company is within its rights to disregard an attempted assignment and pay the proceeds of the insurance to the original beneficiary. If it does so, it cannot than be obligated to pay the proceeds a second time to an assignee. After the death of the insured, the interests of the beneficiary can be assigned without the consent of the company and without regard to the conditions in the assignment clause of the policy.

The policy condition as to assignment is for the protection of the company but is not binding upon it.[13] The company has every right to waive the policy requirement and recognize any assignment that comes to its attention whether or not it meets strictly with the policy condition. As a matter of actual practice, life insurance companies would make every effort to carry out the intention of the policyowner. They would, therefore, give consideration to any assignment regardless of how the information concerning it came to their attention.

Dividends

The importance of dividends available to many life insurance policyholders is obvious in the fact that about three fourths of life insurance is written by mutual insurance companies. Dividends often reduce the original purchase price of life insurance contracts by as much as 20 percent or more over the life of the policy. The original cost is usually higher, but the use of dividends provides the *chance* of lowering "net cost" if the company does well.

Participating and Nonparticipating Policies. Not only mutual companies issue policyholder dividends, but many stock companies also give their insureds a choice between purchasing participating or nonparticipating contracts. The policies are alike in their essentials. The difference lies in the fact that excess earnings of a participating contract are returned to the insured, whereas earnings of a nonparticipating contract are retained by the company as profit for distribution to the stockholders. Some companies issuing nonparticipating policies supply, as nearly as possible, the features of the participating policy by providing, for a small additional premium charge, an annual increase to the face value of the policy. After the first year, accumulative additions may be drawn in cash.

If the company is a mutual company, or a stock company writing

---

[13]A generally accepted form of assignment clause reads: "The Company shall not be charged with notice of any assignment of any interest in this contract until the original assignment or a certified copy thereof has been filed with the Company at its Home Office. The Company assumes no responsibility as to the validity or effect of any assignment. All assignments shall be subject to any indebtedness to the Company on account of or secured by this Policy."

participating policies, provision will appear in the policy for the distribution of dividends. The dividend represents a return of a part of the premium collected after mortality losses, interest earnings, and expenses have been determined. Dividends are distributed annually and are payable after the policy has been in force for a given period, usually one or two years. Sometimes the payment of the first dividend is contingent upon payment of the premium due to keep the policy in force.

Dividend Options. Policies provide several options with reference to the disposition of dividends. The options are not the same in all policies but follow a general pattern. They may provide for (*a*) cash, (*b*) reduction of current premium, (*c*) paid-up additional whole life insurance, increasing the face of the policy, or (*d*) accumulated deposits with the company, at a guaranteed rate of interest, usually 2½ percent. Some policies also provide for conversion of the basic policy to a paid-up basis, when the policyholder requests, if the accumulated dividends and the policy reserve are sufficient to do so. The accumulation of normal dividends currently issued by most companies will permit many policies to become paid-up after about 25 to 30 years. A similar option to mature the policy as an endowment often applies, whenever the accumulations and reserve are adequate to accomplish the change.

The policyholder may withdraw dividend accumulations at any time, or take the cash value of any paid-up dividend additions his policy has purchased. Many companies permit a change from one option to another, although a change to the option of paid-up additions may require a medical examination to determine insurability.

Policy Form Changes

Prior to an indicated age, usually fifty-five years, the insured may exchange his policy without medical examination for any higher premium-paying policy issued by the company. Exchanges to forms carrying a lower premium are allowed and frequently made, although the contract itself affords the policyholder no contractual right to insist upon a change to a lower premium form.

To make an exchange, the insured is required to surrender the policy he holds for rewriting and to pay the difference between the premiums on the new policy and the policy being surrendered, together with interest thereon. Premiums would be as required for the original age of the insured. A change of this character betters the position of the company in that the reserve on the policy is increased and the amount at risk accordingly lessened. Thus, no medical examination or other evidence of insurability is required.

If a change is made from a higher to a lower premium form, not only are future premium payments lessened but frequently the company is required to make a cash payment representing the reduction in the cash value and thereby increasing the actual amount at risk. Before approving such a change the company will require the insured to furnish satisfactory evidence of insurability.

An increase in the amount of risk under an existing policy from an underwriting standpoint involves hazards identical to increasing the amount of insurance. If an insured holding a $10,000 policy with a $5,000 reserve asks the company to exchange it for a $10,000 policy calling for a lower premium payment and requiring at the date a reserve of only $3,000, he requests the company under the new policy to increase its risk by $2,000. The company, in these circumstances would most assuredly not be justified in effecting the change without evidence of insurability even though the face of the new policy showed no increase. The evidence required is usually the same as for new insurance. It may be a full medical examination, a certificate of health or short-form medical examination, or the change may be granted on the same nonmedical basis as new business, requiring only a current statement by the insured.

Companies are usually willing to issue a policy on a lower premium plan if an increased amount of insurance is taken so that the company receives the same amount of premium. Also, if the insured is having difficulty in meeting premium payments and interest, when the insured has borrowed on his policy, companies are frequently willing to exchange a higher-priced policy for one lower-priced, reducing the premium on the outstanding insurance and reducing or canceling the loan out of the difference in cash values. Of all of these changes, the only ones provided for in the contract are those involving an increase in premium.

Lapse and Reinstatement

Insurance companies are ordinarily willing to revive a lapsed policy and usually stipulate in the contract the conditions under which reinstatement will be made. A typical reinstatement clause in policies today provide that, unless the policy has been surrendered for cash, it may be reinstated anytime within five years after default. Payment of premium and of all overdue premiums, with interest, is required. The insured must also submit evidence of his insurability satisfactory to the company at the time request of reinstatement is made.

The requirement as a condition precedent to reinstatement that evidence shall be submitted to the company of the insured's "then insurability" has been the occasion of some confusion. The older clauses require evidence of "good health," and the change of terminology to "insurability" indicates a requirement somewhat broader than evidence of good health.[14] Thus, today, before agreeing to a reinstatement, the company is interested in knowing not only that no physical ailments tending to shorten life have manifested themselves but also to what extent habits, habitat, occupation, and the like still coincide with the company's standards for insurability. In other words, evidence of insurability includes information about all of the factors bearing upon the risk, and a company is fully justified in declining to reinstate a policy on the ground that it considers the risk uninsurable even though the applicant for reinstatement is unquestionably able to pass a rigorous physical examination.

The clause provides that the evidence of insurability shall be "satisfactory to the company." This seems to place an arbitrary power in the hands of the company and to enable it without reason to refuse to reinstate a policy. Generally speaking, the courts have felt that, if a risk is insurable, the life insurance company will be as anxious to reinstate the policy as it would be to secure a new risk. In the case of an insurable risk, there is no opposition of interests between the life insurance company and the applicant; and it is felt, therefore, that when a company declines to reinstate a policy it has satisfactory reasons.

Misstatement of Age

Since the annual premium on a policy written with a level premium is based upon the attained age at the inception of the policy, applicants have sometimes deliberately misstated their age. In other instances, the misstatement has been the outgrowth of a mistake.

Life policies contain a special clause covering the subject that is equitable to both the insured and the company. The clause provides that if the age of the insured has been misstated, the amount payable under the policy shall be such as the premium paid would have purchased at the correct age. This is determined by the application of simple proportion. If an applicant states his age to be such that the premium for $1,000 insurance at that age is $20 and at the time of his death it proves the correct premium should have been $25, the amount of proceeds payable is determined as follows:

$$\begin{aligned} \$25:\$20 &= \$1{,}000:x \\ \text{Hence, } \$25x &= \$20{,}000 \\ x &= \$800 \end{aligned}$$

[14]The difference has been pointed out thus: "The distinction between 'good health' and 'insurability' might be illustrated in the case of a criminal condemned to death. On the eve of his execution he might be found to be in perfect physical condition, but it could not be reasonably contended that his situation did not affect his insurability" (*Kallman* v. *Equitable Life Assurance Society,* 248 App. Div. 146; 288 N.Y.S. 1032; 272 N.Y. 648; 5 N.E. [2d] 375).

Since age misrepresentation is covered by a special clause, it cannot fall within the scope of the incontestable clause. Age discrepancies are most frequently discovered when proofs of death are being filed. Regardless of the time of discovery, the amount due under the policy is adjusted to coincide with the amount the premium would have purchased had the age been correctly stated. Beneficiaries are sometimes disappointed in receiving less than the face amount of a policy through the operation of this rule and misunderstanding sometimes develops.

Life insurance companies ordinarily do not verify the age of applicants unless the stated age is manifestly incorrect. At the time the policy matures in a claim, the age is checked. If the applicant is uncertain concerning his age or if he knows that verification of his age may be difficult, arrangements may be made with the insurance company when the policy is issued to accept the age given in the application. The company is said to "admit" the age and by so doing agrees not to raise the question at the time of settlement.[15] If any difficulties in proving age are anticipated, it is logical for the insured to do this, for after his death the beneficiary may have considerable difficulty in locating the necessary proof.

Suicide

Suicide is considered one of the hazards covered by the life insurance policy. In some of the older policies, clauses were inserted allowing suicide claims only when the suicide was the result of insanity. It became increasingly apparent that the dividing line between a sane and an insane suicide was extremely difficult to establish. Also, from a social point of view, the dependents of a suicide, sane or insane, are in as great need of the proceeds of life insurance as if the insured had died as the result of an accident or illness.

---

[15]Applicants may arrange with a life insurance company to "admit" the age at the time the policy is issued, or an insured may take steps to do this any time during his lifetime. Such evidence as is available must be submitted to substantiate the age stated in the policy. Sometimes buildings containing public records, baptismal records, or the like are destroyed by fire or the records are otherwise lost. An insured who wishes to forestall the possibility of any question with reference to his age should take the steps indicated to effect an admission of age on the part of the company. The following sources are regarded as satisfactory evidence of birth and are listed in the order of preference: (*a*) a certificate of birth from vital statistics records, made at or about the time of birth; (*b*) a certificate of baptism from church or parish records, made at an early age; (*c*) a legally certified copy of the entire page of the family Bible on which the date of birth appears, together with a statement as to when and by whom the entry was made; (*d*) a school record; (*e*) a confirmation record; (*f*) a certificate of marriage; (*g*) a naturalization record; (*h*) a passport at least five years old; (*i*) an army or navy discharge paper; and (*j*) a life insurance record under a policy issued at least five years previously. This list does not exhaust the possible sources. If none of the foregoing is available, such evidence as is at hand should be submitted to the company with a view to obtaining instructions as to what further evidence is required in order to gain consideration of the application.

Suicide today does not have any effect upon the life insurance proceeds except that, to forestall premeditated suicides for the purpose of defrauding life insurance companies, the policy provides that it shall be in effect for a designated period of time before the full policy benefits become effective. The purpose is thus twofold: (1) to provide payment, regardless of suicide, after the stated period and (2) to limit the payments for suicide within the stated period. A typical clause is expressed thus: "In the event of suicide of the insured, while sane or insane, within two years from the Date of Issue of this policy, the insurance under this policy will be a sum equal to the premiums paid to the Company."

Indebtedness and Settlement

These provisions simply state that any indebtedness to the company will be deducted when the insurer makes a settlement with the insured. *Settlement* includes payments (1) when a policy has become payable due to the death of the insured, (2) when an endowment has reached its maturity date, or (3) when a policy has been surrendered for cash value. The policy is given to the company in exchange for the settlement.

Incontestability

After the death of the insured, which may occur many years after the policy was issued, it would not always be easy for a beneficiary to justify statements made by the insured when the policy was issued. For this reason, a denial of liability by the company on the grounds of fraud could complicate and delay settlements, and possibly deprive a beneficiary of his insurance.

To put an end to the possibility of involving the beneficiary in expensive litigation in effecting life insurance settlements, all life insurance contracts now issued provide that the policy shall be incontestable after a certain designated period. The incontestable clause is a statutory requirement. Two years is the period frequently used, though some policies are incontestable after one year.

It has been contended by some that, if it can be shown that the policy was procured by fraud, it may be voided at any time by the company. Courts have held, however, that *if* a stated period has been reserved in the policy within which the contract may be contested, fraud must be discovered within that time. A policy procured through fraud is not void but is voidable at the option of company. Under the usual incontestable clause the insurer is held to have abandoned voluntarily, after one or two years, its option to contest the contract.

Some policies which have been made incontestable from the *date of issue* have actually turned out less desirable from the insured's standpoint. Here, the courts have held that fraud can *always* be used as a defense, and the policy never becomes incontestable with respect to fraud.[16] Many of the contracts issued by the Veterans Administration to servicemen are of this type.

To become incontestable, as policies are now written, the period must elapse during the lifetime of the insured. If the insured dies during this period, the policy never becomes incontestable. The clause protects the insured because he knows that technical defenses may not be advanced at the time of his death as a ground for denying payment. If the company has a defense, it must present it within a reasonable time, presumably when the insured is living and can answer it.[17]

Some policies exclude the double indemnity benefits (see later section of this chapter) from the incontestable clause. Thus the insurer may still contest the extra benefits for accidental death, even after the stated one or two year period.

CASH, LOAN, AND NONFORFEITURE BENEFITS

Some of the most important provisions in a life insurance contract are the rights the policyholder has in case he defaults in paying the premiums. In order that the insured does not lose the values accrued in his contract, the statutory standard provisions require that *nonforfeiture benefits* be provided for in the policy. Thus the policyholder does *not* forfeit all his benefits, but may exercise certain options at the time he surrenders his contract to the insurer: (1) *cash values,* (2) *extended term insurance,* and (3) *paid-up insurance.* Also, *loan values* are available, even without surrendering the policy.

Cash Values

The amount of cash available to a policyowner on the surrender of the policy is called its *cash value.* Because of the distribution of life insurance premiums toward the payment of business expenses, claims, and reserves, an insured cannot receive back the full amount of the premiums he has paid in. During the years his insurance has been in force he has received the protection provided in his policy contract. He has been a member of a functioning organization, and from his premium payments there has been deducted each year the sum representing the cost of insurance to make good the claims of

---

[16]McGill, *Legal Aspects of Life Insurance, op. cit.,* p. 115.

[17]Some companies have modified the clause by setting up one period for incontestability if the insured lives throughout the period and a second limitation if the insured dies within the period. Such a clause reads: "This policy shall be incontestable after one year from its date of issue unless the insured dies in such year, in which event it shall be incontestable after two years from its date of issue." It provides a one-year period of incontestability but allows at least a full year for investigation if the insured dies within that year.

insureds whose policies matured. He has also contributed his share to the cost of operating the company. The equitable right of the insured to a cash surrender value is measured by the amount obtained by crediting premium payments and debiting expenditures for costs and losses.

Some cash values are usually available after the first year of a permanent type life insurance contract. In the early years of the policy, they are small, but as the policy becomes older the cash values increase more rapidly. For example, a policy might provide for these cash values for each $1,000 of insurance: after 10 years, $139; after 20 years, $290; after 35 years, $540. A table of the cash values at the end of various years is included in the contract, in order that the insured will know the values at any point when he might wish to discontinue the policy.

The cash value forms the basis for the determination of all the nonforfeiture values. Each is the mathematical equivalent of the other. The policy will indicate the provision that will automatically become effective if a premium becomes overdue and the insured fails to make a choice within a stated period, varying from 30 to 90 days. In some states the law specifies the option to be automatic in the absence of a choice on the part of the policyowner. To provide the insured maximum protection, policies are generally written so that, if the insured fails to indicate a choice of options, extended term insurance for the face amount of the policy becomes effective automatically, at the end of the grace period, upon failure to meet a premium payment.

Policy Loans

Under insurance contracts with cash values, the insured may borrow from the company at a specified rate of interest. The table of cash values also shows the loan value, and from it the insured may learn the amount which he may from year to year borrow.

Policies do not have a loan value until a sufficient period of time has elapsed to permit the building up of an appreciable policy value. Most contracts have a loan value after premiums for three full years have been paid, although many policies have some cash and loan values after one year. The interest rate is provided in the policy. A rate of 5 percent is usual today, although 6 percent will be found in some of the older policies. The interest charge is added to the premium payments after the loan has been made.

Failure to repay the loan or pay interest does not void the policy unless the total indebtedness, including accrued interest, equals or exceeds the cash value of the policy. In other words, the loan does not have to be repaid by the insured, but will be deducted from the policy proceeds when they are paid to the beneficiary. When the loan and accrued interest are more than the cash value of the policy, the statutes of some jurisdictions require, and most policies provide, that notice shall be mailed to the insured and any assignee of record at the home office of the company at their last known address and that 31 days after notice shall have been mailed the policy becomes void.

Automatic Premium Loan Option

With this provision the insured may arrange for premiums in default to be treated as a loan. The policy remains in force for its full amount until the total loans, plus interest against the policy, equal the cash surrender value. Not all policies contain this feature, but it is generally available on request without any additional charge in the premium.

This feature is generally a desirable one for the insured to choose at the time when he makes application for the insurance. It prevents unintentional or unavoidable lapsing of the contract should he neglect to pay his premiums on schedule. It applies after the stated grace period for premium payments.

Extended Term Insurance

The *extended term* insurance option provides continued life insurance protection, after premium payments have been stopped, for the full *face amount of the policy* less any existing indebtedness. It will provide protection for such a time as the net cash value of the policy will purchase (with a single premium payment) term insurance at the attained age of the insured. As an example, the extended term benefits might show in the table the following number of years for which protection would be provided without further premiums being paid: after 5 years, over 12 years; after 10 years, over 20 years; after 20 years, over 22 years.

If the policy is an endowment form, the cash value may be sufficient to carry the policy to its original maturity date and leave a balance payable to the insured in the form of a reduced endowment. Usually, extended term insurance goes into effect automatically upon lapse if no other option is selected. The mortality table to be used and the rate of interest for the computations are stated in the policy for this option and the one following.

Reduced Paid-up Insurance

If the insured elects to have his insurance continue in force for life or to the end of an endowment period, he may use his net cash value to that end. If the policy is a whole life policy, a *reduced amount* of insurance is continued and paid to the designated beneficiary upon the death of the insured. If the policy is an endowment form, protection in the reduced amount is continued to the maturity date of the original policy. At maturity the insured receives the reduced amount in cash.

The distinction between the extended term insurance option and the reduced paid-up insurance option should be clear. In the first case the face value of the contract is continued in force, but the protection is temporary. In the second case, the protection is permanent, but the amount is for a reduced face value policy.

Illustrations of the paid-up insurance which would result under this option for each $1,000 of life insurance are: after 5 years, $120; after 10 years, $282; after 15 years, $413; after 20 years, $520; and after 35 years, $769.

The Delay Clause

Life insurance policies written today usually provide that the insuring company may defer the payment of surrender or loan values for a definite period. The period set forth in the contract may be a number of months, as, for example, six months. The company may take advantage of the clause when called upon for a policy loan, except that it will not defer payment if the loan is requested to pay policy premiums. The clause affords the life insurance company protection against a "run" and is virtually identical to the protection afforded mutual savings banks by state legislation. Neither type of institution, except in the face of a drastic run, would ever need the delay privilege.

OPTIONAL METHODS OF SETTLEMENT

If a policy written in the amount of $1,000 or over provides for a lump-sum settlement, it has become an established practice in the life insurance business to insert options giving the insured the right to have the insurance made payable in installments.[18] In case the insured during his lifetime does not elect to have the proceeds of the insurance paid under one of the optional plans instead of as a lump sum, the beneficiary himself upon written notice to the company may take advantage of the options offered. The different modes provided in the policy for settlement other than by the payment of a lump sum are termed "optional methods" or "optional modes" of settlement.

Four basic plans have developed from which are derived the clauses of the life insurance policy providing optional modes of settlement.[19] The specific wording in the contracts, and the company

[18]Many policies, because of the expense factor, restrict the right of the insured to ask for any installments which may be less than $10 a payment.

[19]The newer policies make available as many as seven options: (1) installments for a fixed period; (2) initial payment followed by monthly installments for a fixed pe-

practices, do vary, however. The basic plans include: (1) specified amount installments, (2) specified period installments, (3) life income payments, and (4) interest payments. Examples of the use of these benefits are included in Chapter 28 where life insurance programming and estate planning are discussed.

Fixed Installment Payments

Under this plan, periodic installments are paid to the beneficiary in *amounts specified* in the election so long as the proceeds, together with the interest thereon at the agreed rate, shall suffice, with a final payment of any balance if the remaining amount is less than one such installment. In brief, under this option the policy benefits are distributed periodically to the beneficiary in a fixed amount until principal and interest are exhausted. The guaranteed minimum interest rate is usually 2 percent or more, and additional amounts may be paid by many companies if interest earnings justify a higher rate.

Payments for Fixed Periods

Under this option, a specified sum is paid to the beneficiary for a *specified number of years*. Payment is made in periodic installments for the number of years elected. Installments are increased by participation in excess interest earned by the company over the guaranteed rate. Payments are in such an amount that the proceeds of the insurance, together with interest, are entirely distributed over a stated period. This becomes a useful option in planning life insurance programs (see Chapter 28), when the time for which an income is desired is definitely established.

Life Income Payments

Under this option, instead of paying the beneficiary a fixed amount so long as the money lasts, the beneficiary receives amounts as large as the face amount of the insurance will warrant in installments for his *entire lifetime*. The objective of the option is the distribution of income for the entire lifetime of the beneficiary. It provides protection against his outliving his financial resources. The op-

---

riod; (3) installments for a fixed period and for life thereafter; (4) installments for a fixed amount; (5) proceeds left in trust; (6) joint life annuity; and (7) cash refund annuity. The companies offering these options on their newer policies ordinarily permit the same choices under all older policies. The right to utilize settlement options may be the outgrowth of either (*a*) a contract provision or (*b*) company practice. A number of companies that do not cover the matter in their contract will add the option upon request. It is important, in making a request for a change in an old policy, to remember that, because of the basis of computation and the guaranteed interest rate, many of the older policies provide settlement options more liberal than are obtainable today.

tion is made available in the following forms: (1) the life annuity, (2) the refund annuity, (3) life income with period certain, and (4) joint and survival life income.

The life annuity pays installments only while the beneficiary lives and no return of principal is guaranteed. A refund annuity provides for the payment of installments so long as the beneficiary lives and if he dies before the sum of the installments he has received equals the principal sum of the insurance, the difference will be paid in a lump sum to another beneficiary or the installments continued until the sum of all installments equals the principal amount. A life income with a period certain pays the beneficiary annuity installments so long as he lives but if he dies before the number of certain payments have been received, the installments will be continued to another beneficiary for the balance of the certain period or the value of the remaining payments may be paid in a lump sum. In the joint and survivorship life income option, installments are payable not only over the life of one person but may be continued over the remaining lifetime of a second person. This option appeals to married couples with the idea that payments will continue during the lifetimes of both.

Annuity payments may be made annually, semiannually, quarterly, or monthly. If an annuity option is selected it is not required that the entire proceeds of the insurance be used for the purpose, nor need the beneficiary be limited to the use of a single option. Annuity plans may be combined with other optional methods of settlement to the end that a tailor-made settlement plan can be worked out to fit the immediate requirements of any beneficiary.

The optional methods of settlement are available whether the proceeds are payable as a death claim, or upon maturity as an endowment, or upon surrender of the policy for its cash value. The trend in recent years has been in the direction of making increasing use of settlement options. They assume an important place in determining the type of insurance to be purchased when the insurance program is being set up. The life insurance program is frequently correlated with social security benefits.

The life income option is one of the most important benefits of a life insurance contract, for no other investment can assure an income for a period which will exactly equal an uncertain lifetime. Any other investment asset must either use its income only, or use up some principal as well; and then one cannot know if the principal will be used up before life ends.

Valuable rights to life income may exist in many older life insurance contracts, for these benefits may have been calculated on the older mortality tables, which assume higher death rates than actually exist today.

Interest Payments

Under this plan, the proceeds of the insurance are left with the company. A guaranteed rate of *interest* is paid to the beneficiaries plus any excess interest the company may declare. The interest is payable periodically during the lifetime of the payee.

The person entitled to the proceeds of the insurance may, therefore, leave the money on deposit with the life insurance company, at interest, until he needs it. If he dies, then the face value or other proceeds of the policy (accumulated dividends, for example, less any loans outstanding) become payable to the designated beneficiary of the payee. Oftentimes this option is named as automatic as of the date of death of the insured, pending later choice of another settlement option.

DISABILITY AND ACCIDENTAL DEATH BENEFIT EXTENSIONS OF COVERAGE

Three major types of health insurance benefits are included in many life insurance contracts. The most common are a (1) *waiver-of-premium* benefit for total and permanent disability and (2) *double indemnity* for accidental death. The third type, *disability income,* is less frequently included. It is, however, a very important and much-needed coverage, and recent years have brought added attention to this optional feature of many life insurance policies.

Waiver-of-Premium Benefit

Under the terms of the waiver-of-premium benefit, if the insured becomes totally and permanently disabled by bodily injuries or disease, the payment of subsequent premiums is waived by the company.[20] Virtually all companies today write the waiver-of-premium coverage with many policies.

Permanent disability is presumed after the insured has continuously been totally disabled for a period of at least six months. Later

[20]The waiver-of-premium benefit provides, if proof is received at the home office of the company while no premium is in default "(1) that the insured is totally disabled as a result of disease or of bodily injury which was not self-inflicted, so as to be incapable of engaging in any occupation for remuneration or profit, (2) that such total disability did not arise from disease commencing or bodily injury occurring before the insurance under this policy took effect, and known to the insured, but not disclosed in the application for the insurance under this policy, (3) that such total disability has continued without interruption for a period of at least six months (total disability of such duration being presumed to be permanent during its continuance), and (4) that such total disability commenced before the anniversary of the date of the policy on which the age of the insured at nearest birthday is sixty years," the company during the period of total disability will waive payment of each premium due during the period of total disability. If any premium falls due and is paid during the period of total disability, it shall be refunded. However, no premium shall be refunded if the due date occurred more than a year before the receipt by the company of written notice of the claim.

recovery may be evidence that the disability did not continue as a permanent handicap.

Total disability under such a clause requires that the insured be so disabled as to be prevented from "performing any work or conducting any business for compensation or profit." The courts have given reasonable and not strict interpretation to this phrase. The irrecoverable loss of the entire sight of both eyes or the total and permanent loss of use of both hands, of both feet, or of one hand and one foot are automatically considered to be total disability. Many other disabilities may be shown to be total in their effect.

Total and permanent disability must commence before the anniversary date of the policy nearest the *sixtieth* birthday. This requirement is necessary because nearly everyone would become disabled and eligible for these benefits at some point in old age, were this age limit not specified.

Premiums waived on account of this clause are not deducted from settlements made under the policy. The benefits and values, such as the sum insured, the loan and cash surrender values, and, in the case of participating policies, the dividends—all remain the same as if the premiums had actually been paid in cash. Under the waiver-of-premium provision, the company in effect pays premiums due from the insured during the period of total disability. Indirectly the benefit represents a payment to the disabled insured.

It is an important benefit to add to most life insurance contracts, for it enables the protection to be maintained at a time when it is perhaps most needed. A lengthy disability often reduces one's income substantially, to a point where life insurance premiums could not otherwise be paid. The cost is relatively small, usually under $1 per $1,000 when added to the policy before age forty.

Total Disability Income Benefits

Some policies provide for monthly indemnity payable in case of total disability. The types of disability coverage vary widely. There has been a tendency, at times, to restrict the scope of disability coverage under life insurance policies, and some companies do not write this form of coverage.[21]

---

[21] Annuity benefits for disability were introduced in the life insurance field in 1916. The early policies provided an annual income of $100 for each $1,000 of insurance, paid during total disability in addition to premium waiver without impairing the face amount of the policy. The benefit was soon changed to $10 monthly. Various changes in the contract were offered from time to time, and one company provided policies increasing the income 50 percent after five years of disability and doubling it after ten years.

In the early years, disability benefits were offered by only a few companies; but by 1925, of 50 of the principal companies in the United States, only one did not offer disability benefits. The period following 1925 was one of keen competition and disability business expanded rapidly. Policy provisions were liberalized, and the dis-

Under the more recent policies, insurance companies providing a monthly income benefit for total and permanent disability pay to the insured an amount equal to $5 or $10 for each $1,000 of insurance carried upon receipt of proof that the insured is totally and presumably permanently disabled *before the age of fifty-five.*[22]

Evidence is required that the insured has become totally disabled "by bodily injury or disease so that he is and will be thereby wholly prevented from performing any work following any occupation or engaging in any business for remuneration or profit, and that such disability has already continued uninterruptedly for a period of at least six months." Total disability of six months' duration shall be presumed to be permanent only for the purposes of determining liability under the policy. The coverage is not effective unless the total disability can be shown to have begun before premium default or before the last day of grace. The policy does not cover if the disability arises from bodily injury or disease occurring before the insurance under the policy took effect, and known to the policyholder and not disclosed in the application for insurance.

Income benefits are not written in connection with term insurance policies, nor do they apply in the case of paid-up insurance provided under the nonforfeiture values of the contract. When the insured has reached the age of fifty-five and the income disability provision of the policy no longer applies, future premiums on the policy are reduced by the amount of the premium charge for the disability benefits.

Disability income is not written by all companies, and the companies which write the coverage on an individual policy basis have established underwriting rules that tend to restrict its availability to carefully selected male applicants. On a more restricted basis, policies currently are issued to unmarried women who are employed. Disability income is usually not available for disability that develops after the insured has reached the age of fifty-five or sixty. In some instances, it is not written if the applicant is over forty-five or fifty years of age. Policies now written with the $10 per month clause may provide for the termination of the disability payments at the age of sixty-five with the payment of the face of the policy.

---

ability business of many of the leading companies brought claims far in excess of estimated revenue. The period of depression that followed World War I brought with it economic pressure and want. As a consequence, dishonest claimants found in the disability clause of life insurance a source of income. This phase of the life insurance business found itself facing grave difficulty and fast passed into disrepute. Generally speaking, benefits were sharply curtailed, and premiums for such coverage as granted were advanced.

[22]Since the poor experience with disability income benefits in the 1930's, a trend toward increasing liberality of benefits, particularly in the last decade, has been apparent. Many companies now use the $10 per $1,000 face value benefit, and pay for disability prior to age sixty instead of fifty-five.

Life insurance disability protection may be used to augment other forms of health coverage. It is expensive in relation to the other health benefits in life contracts. As an example, disability income (including the waiver-of-premium benefit) may cost about $5 per $1,000 at age thirty, but cost increases as age advances to over $13 per $1,000 at age fifty. Life insurance underwriters carefully watch disability income limits in relation to income earned by the applicant. Aside from this, companies usually establish an arbitrary upper limit of disability income for any one insured. For example, the limits might be set at $500 per month, not exceeding 50 percent of earned income.

Double Indemnity Benefits

A popular feature of life insurance is the provision for payment of double indemnity[23] in the event that death is caused by accident prior to age *sixty-five.*[24] On the basis of the needs of the beneficiary, it is hard to justify a greater payment if the insured dies as the result of an automobile collision than if he dies of pneumonia. The fact remains, however, that this feature appeals to those who feel the need for high limit accident protection. Some companies now offer triple benefits for specified common carrier accidental deaths, and a few will pay up to 5 times the face value of the life insurance contract.

The double indemnity benefit particularly appeals to individuals who feel their insurance program to be inadequate. The appeal is as great to the person in robust health as to the individual with an ailment that may tend to shorten his life. The premium is comparatively small, often under $1 per $1,000 on whole life policies begun before age forty. Thus, the insured carrying a $10,000 policy may for a relatively small additional premium, get $10,000 extra protection in the event of accidental death. Although double indemnity is payable only in a small proportion of all deaths, life underwriters point out that under the age of forty accidents are one of the largest

[23]The clause in a common policy, for example, provides that if death occurs before default in payment of premium and before the anniversary date of the policy following the insured's sixty-fifth birthday and if such death "results directly and independently of all other causes from bodily injuries effected solely through external, violent, and accidental means and occurs within ninety days from the date of such accident, and if such injuries are evidenced by a visible contusion or wound on the exterior of the body (except in case of drowning and internal injuries revealed by an autopsy), and if such death does not result from suicide while sane or insane, from military or naval service in time of war, from an aeronautic flight or submarine descent, from the taking of poison or the inhaling of gas whether voluntary or otherwise, nor directly or indirectly from disease in any form," the double indemnity is payable.

[24]Many variations in the wording, exceptions, and limits of this clause are used by different companies. In recent years some insurers have used age seventy as the limit for accidental death benefits.

causes of death. Because people are becoming more and more accident-conscious, the double indemnity feature of life insurance has made a wide appeal.

This coverage affords a double insurance protection on a limited basis but *not* double *life* insurance protection.[25] To avoid any possible misunderstanding of the nature and extent of the protection, some companies issue the double indemnity coverage as a separate policy.

The accidental death benefit terminates if premiums due thereon are not paid or if the life policy with which it is written is terminated. The double indemnity feature is not included in the paid-up or extended insurance provision of the life insurance policy in the event of premium default. The coverage may be discontinued upon written request of the insured, and the extra premium charge discontinued.

Double indemnity for accidental death, like waiver-of-premium coverage, is widely written, but on a more limited basis than the life insurance contract itself. Health and occupational hazards are determining factors in both disability and double indemnity coverages. For example, persons in certain occupations are in every sense acceptable for life insurance at standard rates, but the accidental death rate is considerably higher than normal. In this group are to be found farmers, carpenters, machinists, and others in like occupations. Then there are persons suffering from a medical impairment who may be accepted for life insurance at standard, or possibly substandard, rates but whose defect may make an accident more likely or claims more troublesome. For example, a blow or fall that in the normal course would not cause death might, in the case of certain medical impairments, be the occasion of death and give rise to a claim for double indemnity.

Double indemnity is usually declined in cases of organic heart disease or abnormal blood pressure. If there is a loss of vision in one eye or an amputation that does not seriously handicap the applicant, then double indemnity may be written at an advance in premium. Insurance companies tend to reject risks when the hazard is unusual, as in aviation or violent sports. Foreign travel is not now regarded as an increased hazard, but a number of companies prefer not to write risks if the travel is such as to make investigation of the claim difficult or expensive. Finally, companies prefer not to accept

[25]When considering the double indemnity benefits for accidental death as a part of a life insurance program, one should remember that (1) cause of death usually has nothing to do with the needs of dependents and (2) the double indemnity provision sometimes gives a false sense of security. A person may feel that he has, for example $20,000 face value of life insurance in force; whereas (except in the case of death caused by accident) he has only $10,000. There is no objection to including the coverage so long as its extent and nature are understood.

for double indemnity or income disability coverage young people who have not yet entered upon a definite occupation or whose habits have not been sufficiently formed to permit a reasonably accurate appraisal of the moral hazard involved. For this reason, some companies are reluctant to provide double indemnity for persons under twenty, although some companies make it available on the basis of careful selection. After the age of fifty-five, or in some cases sixty, the coverage is not usually available on new policies.

More recently, life insurance companies have scrutinized policies issued with the double indemnity provision with a view to eliminating overinsurance. When the amounts of insurance seem sufficiently large to meet all ordinary personal requirements, life underwriters may restrict the amount of double indemnity. In the case of business life insurance, if the policy is written for a definite purpose and the proceeds of the insurance are ample for the purpose, double indemnity does not find a place in the plan and is not written.

SUMMARY

As a contract which involves one of the major portions of the typical family insurance budget, the life insurance policy merits careful scrutiny by the insured. The contract provisions permit great *flexibility* in adjusting the contract to meet the changing needs of the policyholder. He should be aware of these features, which provide many important advantages throughout the duration of the contract.

The declarations by the insured are contained in the *application,* which also commonly includes the results of a medical examination and becomes a part of the policy. The *face* of the policy states in the insuring agreement the basic benefits which the company is obligated to pay.

The life insurance contract is not uniform among companies. It does, however, contain a dozen or more fundamental "standard provisions," required by the laws of most states. These provide a similarity of the significant features, as a minimum protection to policyholders, although many variations and more-than-the-minimum provisions are found in many contracts.

Some of the standard provisions include the rights of the insured to (1) pay, and change the method of paying, *premiums,* (2) name and change the *beneficiary,* (3) *own* the policy values, (4) *assign* the policy benefits, (5) receive *dividends* as cash, premium credits, accumulations, or paid-up additions, (6) change the policy *form,* (7) *reinstate* coverage after lapsation, (8) receive proportional values even in the case of *misstatement of age,* (9) have benefits payable even for death by *suicide,* and (10) have the policy become *incontestable* after one or two years.

Cash, loan, and *nonforfeiture* values are included in permanent contracts of life insurance. These are set forth in tables of benefits showing the values receivable by the policyholder from year to year. The optional benefits include policy *loans* (including an automatic premium loan in case premiums are not paid), and if the policy is surrendered, (1) *cash,* (2) *extended term* insurance for the full face value for a specified period, and (3) reduced amounts of *paid-up life insurance.*

The *settlement options* provide important choices to the insured or his beneficiary. In addition to lump-sum payment of the policy amount, valuable methods are available to pay the benefits in (1) *fixed installments,* (2) installments for a *fixed period,* (3) *life income* as long as the beneficiary lives, and (4) *interest payments.*

Health insurance, other than for the costs of medical care, is often combined with the life insurance contract in three commonly available extensions of coverage: (1) disability *waiver-of-premiums,* (2) *disability income* for total and permanent disability, and (3) *double indemnity* benefits for accidental death.

FOR REVIEW

1. What reason can you give for the lack of a standard life insurance policy? In what sense is there such a contract today?
2. Briefly identify the following options found in most life insurance contracts: *(a)* Dividend options, *(b)* Nonforfeiture options, and *(c)* Settlement options.
3. Describe a specific instance in which each of the usual settlement options would be appropriate. Do the same for the normal nonforfeiture options.
4. To what extent are the rights of a beneficiary of a life insurance contract affected by an assignment of the contract to a bank?
5. Explain why each of the three types of disability or accident insurance coverages which may be added to many life insurance contracts are valuable to the life insurance buyer. Are they permanent protection? Which type is most common? Which, in your opinion, is most important? Which is most neglected?
6. B insures his life for $10,000, designating his wife as irrevocable beneficiary. He has been allowing the dividends to purchase additional insurance. This year, because of financial reserves, he wishes to utilize the dividends to reduce premium payments. He is advised by a friend that the beneficiary has a vested interest in all the values of the policy and, accordingly, must consent to his decision to apply dividends against the premium. What is your opinion?
7. Y insures his life for the benefit of his wife and children. Upon his death, will only the children living at the time the policy was issued participate? Or will the benefits extend to include children born after the policy was written?
   Children by a former marriage of Y claim they have a right to participate. Is their claim supportable?
8. X insures his life for the benefit of B and later borrows on his policy from the insurance company. X dies, and B contends that he is entitled to the

full face of the policy and that the insurance company should collect the loan from the estate of X. Is B correct?

9. What is the suicide clause? In your opinion, should the usual period of two years be lengthened or shortened?
10. X secures a life insurance policy which excludes the risk of suicide for two years but states the policy to be incontestable after one year. X commits suicide after 18 months, and the company denies liability. The beneficiary files a claim on the ground that the policy is incontestable. Are the clauses contradictory?
11. X is the beneficiary of Y. His policy is written for a face of $10,000 with a double indemnity feature for accidental death. He is found dead under circumstances that might be termed either suicide or accidental death, due to the inhalation of gas. Is it a matter of concern to the beneficiary, from the standpoint of insurance payments, to establish that the death was not suicide?
12. B has a brother, C, who is suffering from tuberculosis. B presents himself at the office of X Insurance Company and applies for a policy, giving his name as C. The policy is issued, and three years later C dies. The incontestable period in the policy is two years. C's children are named as beneficiaries and are entirely innocent of the circumstances surrounding the issuance of the policy, and, in fact, knew nothing of its existence until after C's death. The insurance company, learning of the long-standing case of tuberculosis, refuses to pay, but the attorneys for C's estate contend the policy is incontestable. What is your opinion?
13. A is 28 years old. In applying for a whole life policy he gives his age as 24. He advises a friend that it is absurd to give one's correct age in applying for life insurance because, by giving a younger age, a lesser premium is obtained. The friend seeks advice concerning such an action and is told that a deliberate misstatement of age, with the intent to mislead, constitutes fraud and voids the policy from the beginning. Is this correct? Explain why or why not.
14. In the field of life insurance, reference is frequently made to the term "nonforfeiture values." What is meant by this term? Give several examples of how important they may be to the policyholder.
15. D wishes to provide his wife an income of $100 monthly for life in the event of his death. Since the bulk of his estate will be life insurance, he does not wish the proceeds of his insurance to be exhausted by the payments to his wife. How much insurance is necessary to provide the income for the wife and not deplete the amount of insurance to be paid to the children? How is this accomplished?
16. Few contracts (if any) are more flexible than the typical life insurance contract. Explain at least seven features of the life insurance contract which makes it adaptable to future changes in the needs or abilities of the policyholder.

Chapter 25

ANNUITIES

INTRODUCTION

ALTHOUGH based upon many concepts similar to the individual and group life insurance contracts discussed in Chapters 22-24, insurance annuities are treated in a separate chapter because of some underlying differences. One of the basic distinctions is that annuities generally emphasize *liquidation* of assets rather than *creation* of an estate.

Definition

An *annuity* may be defined as a periodic payment. It may commence at a stated or contingent date and may be continued, to a designated person, for a fixed period or for the life or lives of the person or persons entitled to receive payment.[1] The person entitled to receive payment of an annuity from an insurer is the *annuitant.*

In this brief description, several preliminary observations are implicit. An annuity may be paid as an annual payment, but often it involves a more frequent periodic payment, such as each month. It may start at a fixed date in the future, or it may begin on an unknown future date depending upon an event such as a "life contingency." If payments are not to be made until after the death of some person or persons, it is a *reversionary* annuity.

Once payments have begun, they may be continued for a limited number of years in a *term* annuity. In a more usual form, the duration of the payments is conditional upon the continued life of the annuitant. This is known as a *whole life* annuity. A combination of

[1]An annuity, according to Lord Coke, is "a yearly payment of a certain sum of money for life or years." The term "annuity" carried with it the connotation of an annual payment. This is its original meaning. Annuities antedate by many centuries the contract of life insurance. In ancient Rome in the year 40 B.C., legislation gave rise to the necessity of valuing annuities, and the outgrowth of the law was the development by the Roman jurists of the first-known life annuity values graduated with reference to age. Loans in the Middle Ages and later were repaid in the form of annuities, and governments used life annuities as a means of raising money. The early mortality tables had for their use the determining of the values of life annuities. Life insurance as an offshoot of the annuity has far outgrown its parent in importance. Nevertheless, the business of writing annuities is handled by life insurance companies and is an important branch of the present-day life insurance business.

limits, for a stated number of years *if* living, makes it a *temporary life* annuity.

If the annuity is contingent on the continuation of the life of one person only, it is known as a *single life* annuity. If payable during the lives of a number of persons living at the same time, it is a *joint life* annuity; but if payable to the survivor of several lives, then it is a *survivorship* annuity.

In this chapter annuities are divided into two basic types for discussion: *individual* and *group*. Major sections treat the types of individual annuities, their contract conditions and the annuity as used today in many large group pension plans.

Purposes and Uses

Annuities, in their basic use to liquidate assets, occupy an important place in estate planning and in insurance programming. The settlement options of life contracts (see Chapter 24) are examples of one of the most important uses of annuities. The various forms of annuities written by life insurance companies constitute an important sector of the business through which an essential service is rendered to insureds. For those whose needs are emphasized by retirement requirements rather than the protection of dependents, the annuity is to be chosen instead of life insurance contracts. It is said to be the most certain, convenient, and complete protection against old age and dependency that an individual can arrange through his own voluntary action. It substitutes for speculative outlets a sound and secure means in securing one's own old age or that of another. The security of a sound life insurance company, fortified by legally prescribed supervision, relieves the annuitant of the uncertainties of management and investment.

A second important function of the annuity is to apportion the capital of the annuitant so that it will last him throughout his life. Assuming a substantial fortune coupled with investment skill, some persons prefer to handle their own investments and are able to secure an adequate income for living without drawing upon principal. However, for many persons it becomes necessary upon retirement to use a part, at least, of their capital. The annuity provides an admirable means by which this capital distribution can be spread over a lifetime.

In the case of the individual in modest circumstances but with some capital accumulation, the matter of capital distribution assumes grave importance. It can readily be seen that a man (or man and wife) 65 years old with $50,000 has somewhat of a problem to secure to himself the maximum benefits of the fund during his lifetime. Invested at 4 per cent, his income will amount to $2,000. If he apportions a certain amount of his principal to be spent each year, he may reach a point where income and principal will be depleted and find himself dependent and in need. Even if this point is never reached, the knowledge of constantly decreasing resources, coupled with the knowledge that death must come before a certain time or else need will follow, is psychologically bad.

Where the bare income from capital is insufficient to meet its owner's needs, the investment of the capital in a life annuity will yield, particularly at advanced ages, a sum substantially in excess of the interest yield, and in addition, regardless of how long the annuitant lives, the income is paid for life. The purchase price of a single premium life annuity for a male, age sixty-five is about $1,250 for $100 annually. On this basis an annuitant may obtain an income of slightly over $4,000 a year for life for the payment of $50,000. The annuitant, thus, is freed from financial worry, and the confidence of an assured income for life leads to a serene and favorable mental attitude. It is contended that freedom from financial worry tends to prolong the life of the annuitant and has given rise to the insurance adage, "Annuitants never die."

Cost Factors

According to a technical definition an annuity provides for a yearly payment of a certain sum in money. There is no necessity for the payment of a consideration. Annuities frequently were, and still may be, presented in the form of a gift to the annuitant. When the obligation to pay the annuity is the outgrowth of a contract, a consideration is required. The consideration is the purchase price. In its simplest form it is payable in a lump sum but installment purchase on a semiannual, quarterly, or monthly basis may be arranged. As a branch of the life insurance business, numerous forms of the annuity contract have been developed. These have been designed as the outgrowth of experience to meet the needs of different life situations.

The amount charged for annuity benefits is not ordinarily called the *premium* but rather the *purchase price*. Of a given group of annuitants, some of the contract holders will die in a short time and others will live for a long time, but the number dying each year will follow closely the predictions of the mortality table. The cost of an annuity is based upon the mortality rates of annuitants, just as life insurance is based upon the mortality rates of insureds.

To determine the cost of an annuity by a mortality table based upon insured lives would dangerously underestimate the risk. Individuals who know they have serious health impairments rarely, if ever, purchase annuities. In life insurance groups there will be many impaired lives at retirement age. If annuity costs were based upon the experience of insurance lives and annuities were sold to a group self-selected on the basis of good health, annuity payments would far exceed tabular expectations. Because of this, special mortality tables are prepared reflecting actual experience with annuitants.

In computing the life insurance premium, it has been noted that in the case of the natural premium the amount of the premium increases with age. This has the effect of making the annual amount of a level premium rise with the attained age at the time the policy is written. Stated differently, the younger the insured when the policy is written, the lower the annual premium.

In the case of an annuity the reverse is true. The younger the annuitant, the greater must be the consideration for the annuity to pay a designated sum for life. Obviously $10,000 will purchase a greater income for life for a man of seventy than it will for a man of twenty. Annuities have made a particular appeal to elderly people without dependents[2] who are concerned with providing a maximum income for life on the basis of available resources.

The annuity mortality experience differs substantially from that of insured lives. In a group covered by life insurance in early life there will be a number of impaired risks as retirement age approaches. Some will be on the point of death. Annuitants make their choice usually at the time of retirement. It follows, therefore, that only those who feel to be in sound health would willingly make a substantial payment for a life income. Certainly, the critically ill group to be found among insured lives would not make such a payment.

Annuitants, therefore, constitute a selected group. A mortality table that would accurately reflect death rates for life insurance would seriously overestimate the number of deaths for a group of annuitants. Thus, if annuities were sold on the basis of the table conservative for life insurance, the result would be disastrous, because the annuity is the exact reverse of life insurance. If the mortality for life insurance overestimates the number of deaths, a savings is made that is reflected in dividends. In annuities, overestimation of the number of deaths would reflect adversely upon the financial position of the company. If longevity is greater than that contemplated in the table, premium charges will accordingly be inadequate.

To guard against this contingency, insurance companies base their annuity premiums and reverses upon mortality tables representing the same type of risk as the annuity purchaser. With respect to annuitants another factor must be considered. Provision must be made for the future improvement in mortality which from the

---

[2]If dependents, or other beneficiaries, are desired to have some of the benefits of an annuity, various refund or guaranteed benefits often are included in many annuities.

standpoint of a company selling annuities is an unfavorable development. Annuity tables are now available that assume reduced mortality and increased longevity. These tables now make it possible for insurance companies, pension consultants, and others to calculate the value of annuities, pensions, and settlement options which take increasing longevity directly into account.[3]

TYPES OF INDIVIDUAL ANNUITIES

There are several approaches to the classification of annuities. The method to be used will depend upon the purpose of the classification. Basically, all annuities may be classified (*a*) as to plan of distribution of proceeds, (*b*) as to parties in the contract, (*c*) as to time distribution commences, and (*d*) as to method of purchase. Under the foregoing categories, each annuity is assignable into one of two sub-classes: (*a*) either *straight* life or *guaranteed refund*, (*b*) either *single* or *joint* life, (*c*) either *immediate* or *deferred*, and (*d*) either *single premium* or *installment premium*. Every annuity possesses a characteristic of each of the above classes. Several *special* annuity and life insurance combinations also exist, and a new type of *variable* annuity is noted.

By Plan of Distribution

The *straight or pure life* annuity provides an income to the annuitant for life. Upon the death of the annuitant the liability of the insurance company terminates and there are no payments or benefits due either to a beneficiary or to the estate of the annuitant. In contrast to the straight life annuity, other plans provide payments either for a guaranteed period or for cash refund. In either instance the annuitant receives an income for life. The annuity providing for a certain number of installments, or for a refund, makes provision for a beneficiary if the annuitant dies before receiving benefits up to a designated amount. If payments are to continue for a definite number of years regardless of the happening of any contingency, the annuity is known as an *annuity certain*. If an annuity written by life insurance companies provides for payments to a beneficiary following the death of the annuitant until the payments to the annuitant and beneficiary combined are equal at least to the purchase price of the annuity, the contract is called an *installment refund life* annuity. If the balance is payable upon the death of the

---

[3]One of the four new annuity tables, called the "Annuity Table for 1949" (or A-1949 Table), reflects largely current mortality under immediate nonrefund annuities. The other three tables—the "A-1949 Table Projected 10 Years," the "A-1949 Table Projected 30 Years," and the "Progressive Annuity Table"—are based on the assumption that mortality will continue to decline in the future as it has in the past.

annuitant in a single sum to a beneficiary, the agreement is known as a *cash refund* annuity.

Straight or Pure Life Annuity. This agreement, sometimes called the "ordinary life annuity," provides for the inauguration of payments to the annuitant which shall continue throughout the life of the annuitant but terminate with his death, regardless of how soon that death shall occur. Payments are made to the annuitant annually, semiannually, quarterly, or monthly. Under this type of contract there is no guarantee of a definite number of payments, no cash value, and no provision for refund of any sort upon the death of the annuitant.

The advantage of the form is that under it, annuitants are able to receive the largest possible payments and continue to receive these payments for life. The straight life annuity appeals particularly to persons of advancing age without dependents and of limited means who wish to secure for their remaining days the maximum benefit from their accumulations. The contract is also used by more wealthy persons for the purchase of retirement income as a safety reserve against severe business or investment losses.

Guaranteed Refund Life Annuities. These contracts are much the same in their provisions as the straight life annuity. The payment of a single cash premium secures for the annuitant an annuity for the entire period of his life, payable annually, semiannually, quarterly, or monthly, as the annuitant may elect. The point of difference lies in the guaranteed features, which assure the annuitant (or his beneficiaries) a part or all of the cost of the annuity.

In the *installment refund life annuity,* if the annuitant dies before the aggregate of payments equals the purchase price, payments will continue to a designated beneficiary until an amount equal to the full sum of the single payment has been returned. Under the terms of this agreement the annuitant, or his designated beneficiary, is certain to receive in payments an amount equal to the purchase price without interest. The annuitant, on the other hand, may live long enough to withdraw from the company payments that will aggregate a sum substantially in excess of the purchase price. The annual payments under this form are somewhat less than is the case under the straight life annuity. A modification of this form, permitting an increase in the amount of the payments to the annuitant, limits the refund guarantee to 50 percent of the purchase price of the annuity. This contract is known as a "50 percent refund life annuity."

Another form, a life annuity with *number of payments guaranteed,* is similar to the installment refund life annuity. It provides for regular payments to the annuitant at the agreed interval. The payments continue during the life of the annuitant but, in any case, for a definite number of years. It is thus called an *annuity certain*. This contract pays the annuitant so long as he may live, but the amount to be paid to a designated beneficiary is contingent not upon the purchase price of the annuity but rather on the number of years the annuity has already run. For example, if payment is guaranteed for 20 years and the annuitant dies at the end of five years, payment will be made for a period of 15 years more to a designated beneficiary. If the annuitant, however, outlives the number of years guaranteed, payments will be made to him during his entire life, but nothing is paid to the beneficiary upon his death.

It sometimes happens that a purchaser of an annuity wishes to make provision for final expenses such as, for example, unusual medical expenses and funeral costs. If he places his entire assets in a life annuity without a refund provision, or even if a refund provision is used, he may leave little with which to pay immediate funeral expenses. To cover this contingency, special contracts have been devised which provide an annuity for life, with the additional provision of a lump-sum *cash refund* guaranteed to a designated beneficiary.

A Variation and Comparisons. Under a restricted form of life annuity, the *temporary life* annuity payment is made to the annuitant for a stipulated term of years, but payments are terminated upon the death of the annuitant. Contracts are written with or without refund provisions. The important feature of this contract lies in the fact that, if the annuitant outlives the term of years stipulated in the agreement during which payments are to be made, the entire premium paid is earned by the company, and no further payments will be made. This contract is used when it is desired to provide an income for a limited time. For example, an annuity might be purchased for a young man entering college, providing a monthly payment for him for a period of four years. Such a contract could be written so that, if the young man died before the end of the term, the balance of the purchase price would revert to designated beneficiaries.

The basic value of an annuity is the guarantee to the annuitant that the income provided will not be interrupted by the depletion of capital. There are those, however, who are unwilling to risk a large single outlay representing the purchase price of an annuity and face the possibility of receiving annuity payments for only a short period with no refund. The prospective annuitant is faced with a choice of selecting a contract providing no guaranteed refund, or a contract providing less income and a refund. The greater the refund provision, the less the income.

The reluctance to risk securing a return in annuity payments that is less than the cost of the annuity may operate to the disadvantage of the annuitant. Knowing that the straight life annuity provides the maximum lifetime income for each dollar paid for an annuity, the annuitant must decide (*a*) whether he needs to leave funds for dependents or (*b*) whether his lifetime needs require his entire capital. If the annuitant has no need to provide for dependents, his income will be augmented if he elects an annuity without a refund.

By Parties in the Contract

Annuities are usually written on the life of one person. They can, however, be written on several lives. Both these kinds of contracts are considered individual annuities, because there is just one contract even when more than one life is included as the contingency for payments. Group annuities, written for many employees of a common employer, could be identified as another major division of annuities, as to the number of parties in the contract. However, these annuities are given separate treatment in the final major section of this chapter.

Single Life Annuity. The typical annuity is based only on the life of one person. The payments under the annuity are conditioned on the continued life of the individual identified as the annuitant.

Joint Life and Survivorship Annuity. Sometimes the need of an income involves more than one person. This is usually found when a man and wife without dependents wish to make provision for the old age of both. The contract provides an annuity for the duration of more than one life. A contract widely used guarantees an income for two persons during the lifetime of both and, upon the death of one, continues without reduction until the death of the survivor. Some policies, after the first death, reduce the annuity payments to the survivor to two-thirds. The contract may also be written involving more than two persons; and, when so written, the income is payable without reduction until the death of the last survivor of the group.

Under this type of agreement it is not usual to provide cash surrender or loan value. Likewise, no value or balance is available upon the death of the last annuitant for payment to a beneficiary. Occasionally policies of this type are written with a certain number of payments guaranteed. Under such a policy, the annuitants, or the survivor of the annuitants, receives the agreed income for life, but, if the number of payments made is less than the certain number agreed upon, the balance is paid to a designated beneficiary.

By Time When Distribution Commences

Annuities, classified as to when the first payment is made to the annuitant, are either immediate or deferred.

Immediate Annuity. Although the title is sometimes confusing, an *immediate* annuity provides its first payment at the end of the initial payment period after purchase. If payments are to be annual, the first annuity payment would be due the annuitant one year after the contract began. If payments are monthly, the first payment would fall one month after purchase.

Deferred Annuities. Under most annuity contracts, income to the annuitant does not commence until after a certain number of years or until the happening of some event. A deferred annuity may be written to provide an income at a certain age, or it may be written to provide an income to a beneficiary upon the death of the insured. A deferred annuity may be purchased by the payment of a lump sum, as is essential in the case of immediate annuities, but under most contracts the purchase price is payable in installments during the deferred period. As in other contracts written by life insurance companies, the purchase price may be paid on an annual, semiannual, or quarterly basis.

The *deferred life* annuity guarantees an annuity for life, to commence at some definite and agreed-upon future date. Under this form, a person who wishes an income at the age, say, of sixty-five may make provision for it by regular payments when he is a young man. Deferred life annuities provide a grace period. There is no refund provision upon the death of the annuitant, and no certain number of payments is guaranteed. Usually such contracts are without cash or loan values during the deferred period, and there is no obligation on the part of the insurer to make payment in case the annuitant dies before the first payment becomes due. In case of failure on the part of the annuitant to meet his periodic payments after a stipulated period, a nonforfeiture provision of the policy provides a paid-up annuity for the annuitant, based upon the amount actually paid in.

In its important features the *deferred refund* annuity is the same as the deferred life annuity, with the additional stipulation that the aggregate of the amount payable by the company to the annuitant shall equal the aggregate of the payments made for the annuity. Payments may be made annually, semiannually, quarterly, or monthly or may be paid on a single payment basis. Some policies of this type make provision for a cash surrender value. For example, one company provides that if the contract is surrendered after six years and during the lifetime of the annuitant, the company will pay in cash the full sum of the premiums paid. If the payments have been made for less than six years, a slight reduction is made from the total of the purchase price.

The *retirement* annuity is a deferred annuity used by an individual to provide an income for his own retirement by making convenient payments during the productive period of his life. The outstanding characteristic of the retirement annuity is the provision which allows the annuitant to select a date for the commencement of payments, other than that written in the policy. For example, a young man at thirty may purchase a contract providing an income of $200 a month when he reaches the age of sixty-five. If, however, because of poor health or for any other reason he wishes to retire at an earlier age, he may, subject to limits provided in the policy, elect to have his payments being at an earlier age. In such a case, upon request to the company, an earlier maturity date will be substituted for that written in the contract. The amount of the income will be adjusted to such an income as the purchase price would yield for the new date selected.

Retirement income contracts are written with provisions for optional settlements. The first option provides a life annuity, and under this plan the annuitant receives the greatest amount of the income, and it is paid to him for life. Nothing is refunded to a beneficiary upon the death of the annuitant. The second option provides an income for the life of the annuitant, plus a return. This return, added to the payments already made the annuitant, will equal the full amount paid to purchase the annuity. The final option provides a life income, with payments guaranteed for a number of years certain. Under this form the amount paid to the beneficiary is dependent upon the number of years certain that the contract guarantees.

This contract usually provides for a cash surrender value provided the contract is surrendered before the payments to the annuitant commence. Some contracts provide for loans during this same period. An automatic paid-up annuity becomes effective upon default in the payment of premiums.

The *endowment* annuity, also known as the "retirement endowment," provides for a payment to the named beneficiary if the insured dies prior to the maturity date. If he lives to the maturity date, he may elect either a monthly income for life or a lump-sum settlement.

The contract is, in fact, a deferred annuity similar to the retirement annuity coupled with decreasing term insurance running to maturity. The amount of the term insurance each year is the difference between the face amount of the policy and the cash value. Because of the annuity feature, the cash value increases rapidly; and in policies calling for substantial retirement income with a comparatively small face amount, the cash value may exceed the face amount. If the cash value exceeds the face amount and death occurs, then the greater of the two is payable to the beneficiary. If the insured survives to the maturity date and elects to take the cash instead of monthly payments, the cash surrender value may be greater than the face value. The surrender value or face amount is payable, whichever is the greater.

By Method of Purchase

Single Payment Annuity. Originally, it was contemplated that the annuitant would pay a lump sum in return for a regular income for life or for a term. Life insurance companies continue to sell annuities on this basis, and the contract is known as a *single payment* annuity. No further payments by the purchaser are necessary after the first is paid.

Installment Payment Annuity. However, the single payment is not always convenient, nor will the single payment annuity always meet the needs of the applicant. Life insurance companies, therefore, often sell annuities as an *installment payment* annuity. Arrangements may be made to pay the annual payment semiannually, quarterly, or monthly.

Obviously, only deferred annuities may be purchased on the installment basis. Immediate annuities, it follows from the definition, must be single payment annuities, and they require the deposit of a substantial sum at once. A deferred annuity may be a single payment annuity or an annual payment annuity. Annual payment annuities are always deferred annuities.

Special Annuity and Life Insurance Combinations

For persons who have obligations that are likely to last only a definite period, term insurance admirably meets the need. Such individuals sometimes purchase an endowment insurance policy, feeling that this not only meets the need for protection of dependents but serves to accumulate for the needs of the insured's old age. Sometimes, far more satisfactory results may be obtained by the purchase of a term insurance policy to supply the protection for dependents. An entirely separate contract in the form of a life annuity may be written on the retirement income basis. This provides for a retirement annuity for the insured's own needs and enables him to adjust the insurance program to provide protection for his dependents on the basis of their needs. Under this plan of *term insurance coupled with an annuity,* there does not have to be any correlation or relationship between the old-age needs of the insured and protection for dependents. This provides essentially the same protection as the life policy with retirement income except that the retirement feature and the insurance feature are carried in separate contracts. This permits the independent modification of one or the other to meet changing conditions.

Not to be confused with the joint life and survivorship annuity, the *survivorship or reversionary annuity* is, in fact, a life insurance contract combined in one contract with an annuity agreement. Insurance is placed upon the life of one person, and upon his death the proceeds are used to provide an annuity for a designated beneficiary. Since the payments to the annuitant commence with the death of the other party to the agreement, who is known as a "nominator" or an "insured," a medical examination of the nominator is necessary.

Premium payments under this contract usually continue during the lifetime of a nominator and are payable at the same intervals allowed on other insurance contracts. A modification of this form may be written whereby the premiums will be paid for a definite number of years on the same basis as a 10- or 20-payment life.

If the annuitant dies before the nominator, all premiums paid in belong to the company and there is no refund. The contract has no cash or loan value, though after the premium has been paid for a specified number of years, under the nonforfeiture provision a paid-up annuity based upon the amount of premium actually paid in becomes effective. There are many variations of survivorship annuities designed to fit the needs of particular situations. Contracts of this type are designed ordinarily to provide a life income for some dependent. They may be written, however, so that the nominator himself will benefit from the income after he reaches a certain age, with the annuity to continue to a designated beneficiary upon his death.

The survivorship annuity has many of the characteristics of life insurance. For example, the contract may be written carrying the usual double indemnity benefit, which doubles the amount of the annuity if the death of the nominator is caused by an accident. The contract may also provide for such disability benefits as the company is willing to write, although, since the policy is made for the benefit of an annuitant, the disability benefit is usually confined to a waiver of purchase price payments in the case of the permanent disability of the nominator.

Since the age of the named beneficiary enters into the consideration at the time the contract is issued, there is no provision for a change of beneficiary. If such a change were permitted and a request made to name a beneficiary younger than the first-named beneficiary, the mortality situation would be entirely changed.

Variable Annuities

An annuity was defined as a periodic payment for a fixed period or for life. While annuities sold by life insurance companies are usually for a fixed number of dollars, actually there is nothing[4] in the term annuity that requires that the payment be fixed.

[4]Nothing in theory, at least. In practice, however, the term is thought by many persons to convey the impression of a *fixed* payment. This idea bothers many life in-

One of the principal criticisms of annuities has been that fixed amount payments do not adjust themselves to inflation. To meet this situation, in part at least, a strong movement has been started in the life insurance business to write what has been termed *variable annuities.*

The variable annuity contemplates that part of the funds of the life insurance company set aside to meet annuity payments shall be invested in equities instead of bonds and mortgages. It is not contemplated that the variable annuity be offered as a substitute for the fixed dollar amount annuity, but rather that a certain part of the funds be invested in equities so that the fixed dollar payments will be supplemented by any increased income that the equity investments will produce. The variable part of the annuity would be similar to the use of a diversified mutual investment fund.

Variable annuities are to be written as deferred annuities. This means that payments on the annuity would take place over an extended period as would be the case with annuity payments. Hence, investment in common stocks over such a period would tend to minimize losses that might otherwise occur if all the equities were purchased or sold at any one time.

The idea of the variable annuity is, of course, to make it possible for the purchaser of the annuity to obtain the benefit of a diversified equity investment as a basis for higher retirement income, without losing the benefit of the annuity principle that guarantees income for life with the distribution of principal to enhance periodic payments. The idea is of fairly recent[5] appearance in the insurance field and there is a sharp division of opinion as to the feasibility of such contracts in the life insurance field.

The fact that one major company, and several smaller ones licensed only in the District of Columbia, have successfully marketed the variable annuity is evidence that the concept is workable. There

---

surance companies that feel strongly that to promise a *variable* payment would undermine an important basis of the life insurance business. If this is the true understanding of the layman about an annuity, then a perplexing situation arises when one calls a payment (understood to be fixed in amount) a "variable" (fixed?) "annuity."

[5]One of the pioneers in the field of variable annuities is the College Retirement Equities Fund, a subsidiary of the Teachers Insurance and Annuity Association of America. The CREF was established by a special act of the New York State Legislature in March, 1952, and commenced operation in July of the same year. The variable annuities provided by CREF are a part only of a retirement system for teachers. An individual participant in a retirement plan purchases over a period of years a retirement annuity. He may elect that one quarter, one third, or one half of his premiums be applied to purchase of a variable annuity in CREF and the remainder is used to purchase an annuity in TIAA. See William C. Greenough and Francis P. King, *Retirement and Insurance Plans in American Colleges* (New York: Columbia University Press, 1959). Also, see William C. Greenough, *A New Approach to Retirement Income* (New York: T.I.A.A., 1951); and "Variable Annuities", Chapter 29 in Davis W. Gregg (ed.), *Life and Health Insurance Handbook* (Homewood, Ill.: Richard D. Irwin, Inc., 1959).

are no insurmountable legal blocks to a life insurance company writing variable annuities. The problems connected with it are not simple, however.

Trouble arises in two areas today in connection with variable annuities. One is that many life insurance companies do not wish to offer such contracts in connection with life insurance. They say, in effect, that any future *reduced* annuity payment will be difficult, if not impossible, for the insured to understand. If continued inflation does result, they offer the solution of *additional* life insurance purchases as the method by which to hedge against the decreased purchasing power of the dollar.

A second problem faces those life insurance companies that want to write variable annuities. Although they can legally do so, a dilemma of legal jurisdiction arises. To date, at least, the decision has been rendered that the life insurer must establish a separate company[6] registered under the Investment Company Act of 1940. An exception has been made in the case of *group* variable annuities sold under the provisions of the Keogh Act for self-employed persons. Here the plan is exempt from the S.E.C. jurisdiction, and regulation is provided by the life insurance laws of the states.

Undoubtedly the movement toward variable annuities will continue to be one of the most closely watched developments in the field of life insurance during this decade. The opportunities variable annuities may offer, and the difficulties of legal, marketing, and other adjustments which may be required, are strong evidence of the significance of this idea.

CONTRACT CONDITIONS OF INDIVIDUAL ANNUITIES

Conditions of the annuity agreements vary with companies and with types of annuity. There are certain clauses, however, that either are required by the standard provisions or have been almost universally adopted by the companies. The insuring clause sets forth the undertaking of the insurer and outlines the types and conditions of payment.

General Provisions

All companies reserve the right to require evidence that the annuitant is living before any annuity payment is made to him. They make every effort to save the annuitant from annoyance and usually accept the personal endorsement of the annuitant on the company's check or draft as satisfactory evidence.

[6] The Securities and Exchange Commission ruled in 1963 that Prudential Insurance Company would have to do this to sell variable annuities to individuals. The decision was upheld in January, 1964 by a federal court of appeals, although appeal to the Supreme Court may result.

If, because of misstatement of age, an excess amount has been paid the annuitant, it is charged against current or subsequent payments. The laws covering this subject in the various jurisdictions usually allow the company to charge interest not in excess of 6 percent upon such overpayments. The annuity payments are then adjusted to provide that the amount payable will be that which the annuitant's payment would have purchased had the correct age been given.

It is customary to issue annuity contracts providing for incontestability after one year from issue. In some states the matter is covered by law, and the period named is sometimes two years. If the annuity is written with disability benefits, these may be excluded from the operation of the incontestable clause. Like life insurance, there is usually no restriction after the contract is issued as to traveling, residence, occupation, or military service. The policy and application constitute the entire contract, and power to modify it is limited to certain designated executive officers of the insurer.

The reserve basis is stipulated by indicating the annuity table used together with the interest assumption. The contract may be assigned, but the company assumes no obligations unless the assignment is filed at the home office. In the case of annual payments, a grace period of 31 days is allowed, and reinstatement is permitted within a designated period after default. Reinstatement requires the payment of all purchase price payments in arrears with interest. Nonforfeiture values are usually limited to a paid-up annuity for such an amount as the accumulated payments will buy as set forth in the contract.

No Medical Examination

No medical examination is required for the purchase of the usual annuity. In the case of life insurance, the medical examination serves to forestall unfavorable selection through the insurance of an undue proportion of impaired risk. Since, in the case of an annuity, impairment can in no way adversely affect the interests of the insurance company, a medical examination can serve no purpose. From the standpoint of a life insurance company, the risk lies in the annuitant's living an unusually long life. Consequently, contrary to the situation in the life insurance contract, a physical impairment that tends to shorten life is no barrier to the purchase of an annuity.

An impairment that might make the individual ineligible for life insurance does not necessarily shorten his life. What it does mean is that, of a large group of individuals having such an impairment, the average of their lives will not measure up to normal. Consequently, for these individuals, the purchase of an annuity that will afford them an income after a certain date and a refund for beneficiaries offers an insurance solution not otherwise obtainable. Many persons who are ineligible for life insurance may purchase annuities.

When disability benefits are made a part of the policy, the contract ceases to become a straight annuity agreement and a medical examination is required. Medical examination is also required in the case of a survivorship annuity or any of the special annuity and life insurance combinations.

Not Apportionable

At common law an annuity is held not to be apportionable. This means that an annuitant must be alive at the time a payment is due to receive the payment and no prorata part of a payment is due his estate for the period that elapses between the payment last made and the time of death. This means, in the case of payments made annually, if an annuitant dies a day or a month before a payment is due, no further payments may be made either at the time of death or at the date the next payment would have been due had the annuitant lived. All obligations to the annuitant or his estate are satisfied by the payment of the last installment due prior to the death of the annuitant. The rule has been incorporated into annuity contracts issued by life insurance companies, and they provide that the last payment due prior to the death of the annuitant fulfills the agreement.

Because of this rule, annuities that call for payments other than on an annual basis call for a slightly higher purchase price than if the annuity payments are on the annual basis. This is so because in the long run, if payments are made more frequently than annually, there will be fractional payments made in the last year of the life of the annuitant. Likewise, there will be a few cases where the annuitant will die during the first year following the purchase of the annuity and, if the payments are on an annual basis, nothing will be due his estate.

Participation

Both participating and nonparticipating life insurance companies write annuity contracts, but until recently individual annuity contracts were written on a nonparticipating basis. Annuities were designed to provide the annuitant with the largest possible income. Recent developments, however, notably the lengthening of the average life of annuitants, have made necessary an upward revision of annuity rates. Partly to offset this change, the principle of the participating annuity has been introduced. The idea is to guarantee payments based upon more conservative interest and mortality rates, with a view to returning to annuitants any extra savings over the calculations in the form of a dividend.

Those who oppose the idea of participating annuities contend that the equitable distribution of surplus is not so simple in annuity contracts as in life insurance. This is particularly so with reference to a conservative estimate of the mortality rate. In the case of life insurance, if the mortality table reflects a more severe death rate than is shown by experience, the savings therefrom may be distributed each year to policyholders as a dividend. Annuities, on the other hand, are written for a single payment purchase price; or, in any case, purchase price payments cease after annuity payments commence. It is contended that, if annuity payments are computed upon a conservative mortality table, the payment of dividends to survivors discriminates against those who died early. The idea of a participating annuity is still in its infancy; and from the point of view of selecting a contract, the problem of dividends is as yet not of major importance.

Retirement income plans written by participating companies usually provide for the payment of dividends during the purchase price payment period. Dividends are apportioned after the same plan as used in dividing the surplus under the life insurance contract. Likewise, the contract provides that the holder of the annuity contract may elect to receive his dividends in cash, use them to apply on payments due, or deposit them with the company at interest to be withdrawn on demand.

GROUP ANNUITIES

The annuity principle has had an important application in retirement income plans inaugurated by private business firms. "Annuities set up under pension plans, primarily group annuities, constitute the major portion of all annuities outstanding with U.S. life insurance companies."[7] Some pension plans are fifty years old, but the great impetus for growth followed 1945.[8] The original purposes of pension plans were to improve morale and decrease turnover of labor, by offering faithful employees the prospect of security for old age. Other factors, such as tax inducements, pressure from organized labor, and increasing social and political pressures, become influential forces in the rapid growth of pensions plans.[9]

---

[7]*Life Insurance Fact Book* (New York: Institute of Life Insurance, 1963), p. 35. Of the total 6.3 million annuities with $3 billion annual income, 4.7 million with $2.2 billion income were group annuities.

[8]*Private and Public Pension Plans in the United States* (New York: Institute of Life Insurance, 1963), p. 3. The growth has been from coverage for about 2.8 million persons in 1930 to 6.7 million in 1945 to 25.6 million in 1963.

[9]For a concise explanation of the underlying forces and factors, see Dan M. McGill, *Fundamentals of Private Pensions* (2d ed.; Homewood, Ill.: Richard D. Irwin, Inc., for the Pension Research Council, 1964), Chap. 1.

Nature and Purposes

Group annuities are an important type of insurance contract used in order to guarantee the retirement benefits of employer-employee private pension plans. The pension field also includes many government types of pension programs. Private pension plans are not all insured; in fact, only about one third[10] of the total private pension plan assets are protected by insurance. As a matter of theory there is no reason why any business institution might not set up its own pension plan and administer the fund itself. As a matter of actual practice, many difficulties have been encountered. Privately administered pension plans have in many instances been wrecked by unsound management. Considerable dissatisfaction has resulted because of the uncertainty of employees concerning the status of their pensions.

It was a natural consequence for many businesses to turn the entire problem over to life insurance companies. These companies had the equipment for investment as well as the statistical information to determine payments adequate to meet future problems, and when employers lack either adequate actuarial or investment facilities, it is regarded as good business to turn the administration of such a highly technical project as a pension fund over to an organization trained and equipped to handle this type of business.

With the phenomenal growth of pension plans in the United States in the past decade, uninsured pension plans have again become an important factor in the field. In many instances they have become so large and so important as to be able to command actuarial and management facilities that are in all respects adequate. However, employees have no guarantee of their pension outside the fund unless the plan is underwritten by a life insurance company. There is sufficient leeway allowed the employer to prompt the suggestion that such funds should be subject to some review.[11]

The real purpose of a group annuity as used in a private pension plan is the third-party guarantee it provides for both employer and employee that the benefits will be paid. The administrative and investment services are important auxiliary purposes. The appeal of the insured pension plan is particularly strong for the small and

---

[10] *Private and Public Pension Plans in the United States, op. cit.,* pp. 3 and 13. Of the total of 25.6 million persons covered at the beginning of 1963, 5.8 million persons were included in almost 41,000 insured plans. Of the total assets of $60.6 billion held by private pension funds, $21.6 billion were insured.

[11] It was not until just recently that pension funds became subject to review under the Welfare and Pension Plans Disclosure Act, which became effective in 1959 (with amendments in 1962). For summaries of benefits and financing of the pension plans filing information under the Act, see *Welfare and Pension Plan Statistics: Characteristics of 161,750 Plans Filed as of July 1, 1963* (U.S. Department of Labor: Labor-Management Services Administration, 1963).

medium-size companies, and for many business institutions it affords the only sound basis for the establishment of a pension plan.

When a retirement income plan is put into effect, a master contract is issued to the employer by the insurance company. As in other group contracts, it is usual to give to insured employees a membership *certificate* that outlines the benefits in detail. Circulars and booklets are frequently distributed to employee describing the benefits of the plan. These are for convenience only and refer always to the master group annuity contract for full details.

Eligibility

The employer is primarily interested in providing for employees who reach the retirement age in his employ. He is, therefore, not particularly interested in including temporary or floating labor. This being the case, nearly all private pension plans provide a *waiting period* for eligibility. Other plans require not only the waiting period but a minimum salary or an attained age. For example, a plan might require that employees earning less than $4,000 annually will be eligible for participation in the plan upon the attainment of a salary of at least $4,000 annually or upon the attainment of the age of forty, whichever of these two occurs earlier; but in any case, after the completion of one year of continuous service.

The salary and attained age requirement eliminates those in the category where there is a large labor turnover. Presumably, in this group it would not be usual to add new employees at the age of forty; but if an employee has remained in the service of the company long enough to reach that age, even though he remains in one of the lower-paid categories, it is felt that he is entitled to participate in the retirement plan of the company. The waiting period must be adjusted to fit the individual business. Some employers have little difficulty with labor turnover, and their retirement plan can be made effective immediately with all employees eligible. In some cases, the waiting period has been extended considerably beyond one year.

Some employers feel that all employers should, from the outset, be given a sense of security and permanent relationship. If they become valuable to the business, they will be less likely to change as their equity in the plan becomes established. On the other hand, there are certain groups of employees which exhibit a high turnover; for example, only a small percentage of the younger female employees remain in employment until retirement. The elimination of high turnover groups from the coverage simplifies administration and reduces costs. In the interests of further simplifying administrative detail, the dates upon which eligible employees may enter the plan are set six months apart. Employees' records are checked every year, and salary changes are studied to locate increases or decreases large enough to require a change in the salary classification.

Retirement Dates

Two basic types of retirement dates are included in most group annuities, the normal retirement date and the optional retirement dates.

Normal Retirement Date. "Normal retirement date" means the first day of the month nearest to the attainment of the established retirement age. Since annuity payments commence with retirement, the normal retirement date becomes the normal annuity date. If retirement age is sixty-five, the normal retirement date under such a plan will be the first day of the month nearest the attainment of age sixty-five.

Employees are ordinarily expected to retire and begin receiving annuity payments at the normal retirement date. Factors that affect the selection of the normal retirement age are: (*a*) the age at which social security benefits are available, (*b*) the age at which superannuation occurs in relation to the employee's occupation, and (*c*) the relative cost of providing retirement at different ages. A majority of plans follow the social security program and provide normal retirement for males at sixty-five and females at sixty-two. There are certain occupations, however, where active work to these ages is not possible. In some industries, such as commercial aviation, employees retire at different ages. Airline pilots ordinarily retire at sixty, while other personnel do not retire until sixty-five. The pension plan must recognize situations such as this. Yet to provide a maximum annuity from the available funds, the normal retirement age should remain as near sixty-five as possible.

Frequently at the time the plan is adopted, there are many employees at or near the retirement age. The cost of placing all of these employees upon an annuity at once or within a few years could be prohibitive. Mass retirements, immediately following the adoption of a plan, could also have a disorganizing effect upon the staff. For these reasons, steps are ordinarily taken to spread out the retirement of the older employees. Assuming a normal retirement date of sixty-five years, the retirement of employees who are in the older age groups when the plan is put into effect may be postponed to some age between sixty-five and seventy. Seventy years is usually the limit. For all other employees, and for new employees joining the plan after the effective date, the normal retirement age determines the normal annuity date.

Optional Retirement Date. Pension plans ordinarily also provide for (*a*) an *early* annuity date or (*b*) a *postponed* annuity date.

It may sometimes be advisable, or desirable, for an employee to retire before the normal annuity date. Some plans allow the employee to retire on the first day of any month within the ten-year period preceding the normal annuity date. Virtually all plans make some provision for early retirement. An employee who retires early receives a reduced income. This is so because the period for the accrual of benefits is shortened and the period for which the employee may expect to receive an annuity is lengthened. The amount of the benefit is actuarially determined on the basis of payments and life expectation. Many plans require the employer's approval for early retirement, but some do not.

Arrangements may also be made for annuity payments to commence at a date later than the normal annuity date. In this case, the date on which annuity payments begin is known as a "postponed annuity date." Some plans provide that, when an employee's retirement is postponed, no further annuity credits are purchased. In such a plan, the rate of annuity payments, beginning on the postponed annuity date, usually remain the same as the rate that would have been payable on the normal annuity date.

Making no further payments with the accrual of no further benefits is presumed to encourage retirement at the normal annuity date. Plans, however, are not uniform. Some provide that the annuity will begin at normal retirement age regardless of whether or not the employee retires, which is more equitable where the employee remains at work to accommodate the employer. An employee who leaves the services of his employer before the normal retirement age would not be permitted to elect a postponed annuity date. In all cases, a postponed annuity date requires the consent both of the employee and employer.

Types of Annuities Used

When a plan is established, an employer has to choose a particular form of annuity, which is thereafter known as the "normal form of annuity." This may be (*a*) a *refund* annuity or (*b*) a *life* annuity.

In addition to the normal form of annuity most insurance companies writing group annuity contracts provide optional retirement benefits. The employee may arrange to receive the annuity on a joint and last-survivor basis. Thus, a man can assure himself that he will receive an income so long as he lives and that, if he dies before his wife, she will receive an income so long as she lives. Optional retirement benefits offer the employee an opportunity to convert his full retirement annuity to a reduced amount which will be continued in whole or in part after his death to a named dependent throughout his or her lifetime. The amount of the reduced retirement annuity depends upon the age and sex of the person who is to benefit and upon the percentage of the full retirement annuity the employee elects to be continued for this dependent. The annuitant may elect a larger income during the period that there are two depending upon it and leave a smaller proportion, such as one half, to be paid to his dependent following his death.

The consent of the company, and sometimes the consent of the employer, may be required for the election of an optional plan. If either a refund annuity or a life annuity is named as the normal form, it is usual to offer a contingent annuity as one of the options. The plan has a wide appeal, since old-age income for the wife or other dependents is frequently a greater concern to the family provider than retirement income for himself alone. The contingent annuity option provides for annuity payments in a reduced amount to the employee with a guarantee that payments in a similar or smaller amount, as elected by the employee, will be continued for the remaining lifetime of the person named by the employee as his contingent annuitant. If the option becomes effective in connection with the refund annuity, and the employee or his contingent annuitant, or both, die before making payments equal to the employee's contribution, a death benefit is paid to a designated beneficiary in an amount equal to the unpaid annuity payments.

To preclude selection against the company, it is usually required that the contingent annuity option take effect at the normal annuity date, if elected at least five years prior to that date, or within three months of the effective date of the plan. Otherwise, evidence of good health is required. This rule makes it impossible for an employee, under a plan having a life annuity as the normal form, to elect a contingent annuity if he finds himself in failing health or fatally ill. With the consent of the company, election may be made at any time; and the company may require evidence of good health. The option, once elected, may not be changed or modified without the consent of the company.

Where the normal form is a refund annuity a life annuity option may be elected at retirement providing for maximum annuity payments during the lifetime of the employee after retirement. Where the normal form is a life annuity, a refund annuity option may be elected. The option must be elected within three months after the effective date of the plan or at least one year before the normal annuity date; otherwise the company requires evidence of good health.

Benefits

The benefits under group annuities are determined by: (1) the basic kind of plan, (2) the treatment of past service credits, and such other important conditions as (3) the inclusion of variable annuity provisions, (4) death benefits, (5) vesting clauses, and (6) change or discontinuance provisions.

Basic Plans. There are two basic benefit plans: (*a*) the *fixed benefit plan* and (b) the *money purchase plan.* Under the fixed benefit plan, the benefit is determined in advance; and variables, such as age and sex, determine the cost. The situation is reversed under the money purchase plan; here the cost is fixed and the variables determine the benefit.

The fixed benefit plan receives the widest acceptance and is regarded as equitable in its application. Under the plan benefits are based upon a formula.[12] The plan usually takes into consideration past and future service, but future service plans only are sometimes adopted.

Under the money purchase plan, both employee and employer contribute a fixed percentage of the employee's earnings. Usually their contributions are equal. The joint contributions are applied to purchase whatever annuity credits they will buy for the individual employee, at the time of purchase and at the rates then in effect. Annuity credits for past service may also be allowed under this plan, and are paid in full by the employer.

Under a fixed benefit plan based on earnings, retirement income is more readily estimated than under a money purchase plan; however, under either plan an assumption must be made regarding future earnings. The important point with respect to fixed benefits is to be found in the fact that under this plan it is only necessary to estimate future earnings; to estimate retirement income accurately under a money purchase plan, one would have only to predict future earning rates and the employee's age at which the earning rates will be effective. The fixed benefit plan appeals to employees because under it they can more readily determine in advance the amount of their retirement income. With a predetermined amount of retirement income, the employee may make further adjustments for old age. He can augment the pension by himself purchasing additional insurance or annuities. He can make his personal plans with a degree of confidence that would otherwise not be possible.

Under the money purchase arrangement, there is no way for the

[12]The benefit formula must give consideration to the tax status of the plan. A test of the discriminatory nature of a plan involves the benefit formula. Certain forms of apparent discrimination are permitted, including (*a*) limitation of a plan to clerical employees, (*b*) limitation to salaried employees, and (*c*) exclusion of employees eligible for benefits under a federal or state law. A benefit formula is not considered discriminatory if benefits are integrated with social security benefits. Higher-paid employees should not receive benefits proportionately greater than do the lower-paid employees. This has been accomplished by two basic methods: (*a*) deducting all or a portion of the social security benefits from the income under the private plan or (*b*) reducing the benefit percentage on the first $4,800 of annual earnings by an amount that approximates the benefit percentage under social security. An example of such a benefit formula would provide three quarters of 1 percent of the first $400 monthly income ($4,800 annually) and 1½ percent of the excess monthly earnings over $350 for each year of service. Some plans ignore social security and make the benefit a constant percentage of all earnings for each year of service.

employee to determine definitely what he may expect as a retirement income. The contribution of employer and employee is the same regardless of age or sex and depends upon earnings. Therefore, an elderly man earning a specified amount will receive a much smaller annuity credit for any given contribution than a young man earning the same amount. The plan fails the older employees, who have the urgent retirement problem. For younger employees, the employer contributions of a salary percentage under a money purchase plan are larger than under a fixed benefit plan.

Past Service Credits. It is apparent that many employees with long service will receive little in the way of a retirement annuity if their only benefits are those that accrue for services from the time of the inauguration of a plan. Therefore, most retirement plans provide annuity credit not only for service rendered following the inauguration of the plan but also for past service. This enables employees nearing retirement age to build up an annuity comparable with the annuity ultimately to be received by the younger employees.

Past service credits will depend largely upon the relative ages of the group. In some instances, a maximum period of past service is set, as well as a maximum salary for the computation of past service annuities. For example, a plan may provide that the maximum period of past service to be recognized will be the most recently completed 25 years, and the maximum salary to be considered will be $10,000. Past service benefits are often computed as a percentage of all earnings prior to the effective date of the plan or for a number of years prior to the date set as a limit for past service.

Usually, no attempt is made to average the salary over the period of employment. The age of the employee and the salary at the inauguration of the plan are used for computing benefits, and any compensation for variations during the years is arrived at by the percentages arranged in the schedule of past service benefits. This, however, is not a universal practice. Average earnings or actual earnings for a certain prior period may be used. If current earnings are used, past service benefits are fixed at about three quarters of the future service benefits. This takes into consideration the fact that earnings over prior years have probably increased and that current earnings are probably the highest. Sometimes, limiting the maximum amount of retirement income to be credited to any one person automatically limits the past service credit.

Future service benefits are based upon the actual salary earned from year to year. A percentage of the yearly salary of the employee is deducted, and this combined with a contribution from the employer is used to purchase yearly annuity units.

One of the most perplexing problems in instituting an industrial retirement plan involves the handling of *accrued liability*. Credits for past service must be funded. Employees nearing the retirement age will remain with the employer only a short period before reaching retirement status; and during this time, from some source, the employer must build up capital sums sufficient to meet retirement needs. He may set up a special reserve for the accrued liability. In the past, efforts were made to fund the accrued liability by a single payment to the trustee or to the life insurance company. This was not the usual practice, and for a very practical reason. The accrued liability is usually so large that, for most organizations, a single payment plan is out of the question. Quite as important today, is the fact that, ordinarily, only 10 percent of the accrued liability for past services is deductible for income tax purposes in a single year. For these reasons, installment funding is the common method for handling liability accrued on account of past services.

There are several satisfactory plans of amortization, and the plan to be adopted depends upon the immediate needs of the older employees and the financial position of the employer. A plan widely used divides the aggregate of the premiums of all past service annuities into a number of annual or monthly installments. Since all annuities are purchased on an individual basis, the installments for funding a group liability must be sufficient so that the full amount for the purchase of the annuity will be in the hands of the insurance company before the retirement of any annuitant. Therefore, an employer having a large number of employees near retirement age must fix a very much shorter period of amortization under this plan than if he had only an occasional employee nearing retirement. Under no circumstances will the insurance company guarantee income for past service unless it has been fully funded by the employer. For this reason, annuity installments as they are paid are applied to fund the benefits of employees currently reaching retirement age. Any part of the current installment that remains after the needs for annuities for the coming year have been supplied is set ahead to apply on the needs for the succeeding year. Balances are continually set forward to apply on requirements for the following years. The disadvantage of this plan of allocating the amortized payments is that, if the plan is discontinued, past service payments made up to the point of discontinuance will be credited to those having already retired or are to retire very soon. Those who have not reached retirement status will, in all probability, be deprived of any part of the payments already made by the employer on this account.

A plan somewhat more difficult of administration, but held to be more equitable, apportions the payments made as amortization installments so that they will be distributed to the account of annuitants for several years in advance. One plan provides that, after the current year's needs have been fully met, any excess is applied by allocating one half to the needs of the succeeding year and distributing the other half by applying fractions to meet the requirements of succeeding years on a predetermined basis until the entire surplus has been apportioned. This method distributes the past service fund over a large group of employees. The plan is attractive to the employer because, if an employee dies just prior to retirement, his past service benefits will not have been paid in full and will represent a saving for the employer.

If the employer feels able, he may divorce the past service benefit entirely from the future service feature and purchase a past service annuity for each employee when he reaches retirement status. This is not, however, a usual procedure.

Variable Annuity Plans. In the field of pension planning where both employer and employee are conscious of changing living costs, it is to be expected that the variable annuity will be given full attention. Regardless of the variable annuity concept, employers from time to time have voluntarily adjusted their pension plans so as to bring the benefits to acceptable levels. The variable annuity undertakes, within limits at least, to accomplish these periodical revisions automatically by means of the investment portfolio.

In the group field there are two approaches: (*a*) variables reflecting *stock market trends* and (*b*) variables reflecting changes in the *cost-of-living index*. The first of these follows the pattern already noticed in the discussion of individual variable annuities. The second breaks away entirely from market movements in determining pension amounts.

Variables that reflect stock market trends are sometimes known as "equity unit plans." A part of the money available for employees' pensions is invested in equities. The cash value of these equities is used to provide retirement benefits. As the market value of the equity portfolio rises or falls, the income of the retired employee follows. As previously noticed, the basic underlying thought of this type of investment is found in the conviction that with the continued growth of the country, share values will continue to increase in value and thereby offset simultaneous increases in living costs.

The weakness in the plan is to be found in the fact that often erratic stock market fluctuations show no correlation between stock values and the cost of living. To eliminate downward revision of pensions with a declining stock market without an accompanying lowering of living costs, the variable annuity geared to the cost of living was devised. Benefits are related directly to the cost of living. A part of the employer's allocation to purchase retirement income is invested in equities. It is the intent to take full advantage of capital appreciation as a long-trend proposition. Share values are not allocated to individuals, but the pension fund is used as a source to provide adjustments linked to the cost-of-living index.

Pensioners receiving retirement income based upon a variable annuity are freed to a degree at least from cost-of-living worries that may haunt others retired upon a conventional plan. Those covered by a cost-of-living plan[13] are in an even better position than those covered by equity unit plans.

Death Benefits. If an employee dies before retirement and he has contributed to a pension plan, a sum equal to his contribution is paid to his beneficiary. The plan may be more generous, and contributions may be returned with interest. The accumulations under any annuity plan are substantial, and the death benefit represents a sizable amount to augment the life insurance of the annuitant.

If the death of the annuitant occurs shortly after retirement, the heirs may react unfavorably when they learn that there are no annuity benefits payable to survivors. For this reason, insurers recommend a refund annuity as the normal form. If death occurs before the retired employee has received payments totaling his contributions, the balance will be paid to his beneficiary. The sum so paid is not, strictly speaking, a death benefit but represents annuity payments provided for in the actuarial calculations. If the employee elects the life annuity, it can be pointed out to survivors that the employee's affirmative choice increased his annuity but by virtue of that choice precluded any payment to a beneficiary.

Vesting Clause. If the plan contains a vesting clause, employees withdrawing from the plan prior to retirement will be entitled to the full benefits of annuities purchased during the period of actual service. If the plan contains no vesting clause, the employee is entitled only to a cash refund of his own contributions with or without interest. Under the older plans, annuities were not vested. To vest the interest of the employee in an anuity deprived the employer of any refund of his contributions toward annuities of those who left his service prior to retirement. Most employers felt obligations only to those employees who reached retirement age in their own service. A pension plan without a vesting clause appealed to some employers since in the case of many employees who might other-

---

[13]It is interesting to note the increasing popularity of these cost-of-living adjustments in pension plans. In 1963 a major impetus was given to the idea by legislation passed which provides cost-of-living changes for the pensions paid to federal employees and to retired members of the armed forces. The possible inflationary effect of such changes is one of the disadvantages of broader use of this idea.

wise be dissatisfied with employment or remuneration tended to stay on the job because they did not wish to disturb accumulated annuities.

The best insurance thought today recommends a vesting clause. Through it, the employee secures full title to whatever annuity is purchased for him by both his *and his employer's* contributions. Leaving the plan before retirement does not affect annuities already accumulated. The clause has proved valuable to employers because, by it, employees may be encouraged to carry a greater part of the cost than under a plan containing no vestment clause. On the other hand, employers no longer consider payments made for withdrawing employees as losses, but as additional salary paid during years of actual service.

Change or Discontinuance. Few industrial companies would be willing to enter upon a pension plan that would bind them irrevocably to its continuation. Yet, plans are designed to be permanent. Employers usually point out their intention to continue the retirement plan indefinitely but reserve the right to change or discontinue it at any time. It is usual to protect the employee by providing that discontinuance will not adversely affect the total retirement income already purchased, including the part contributed by the employer.

Contracts ordinarily provide no cash return for the employer after a plan has terminated other than dividends which may fall due. With provision for vesting, the group annuity contract becomes paid up for the amount of contributions made to date. The annuity is then vested in each covered employee. Since the insurance company obligates itself only for the amount of annuity for which payment is received, if the past service benefit has not been fully purchased when the plan terminates, the paid-up annuity will not reflect these benefits. If an employee terminates employment and withdraws his contributions, the benefit of employer contributions is lost to him and applied to other unfunded past service.

Financing Sources

As in other group contracts written by life insurance companies, in order to provide the retirement annuities, the employer may pay the entire cost in a *noncontributory* plan, or employees may pay part of the cost in a *contributory* plan.

The premise that human care is a production cost has led to the inference that the employer should bear the entire responsibility for providing pensions. Some who feel that the pension burden justly is a production cost reason that the payment should, in part, derive from the employee, who in turn allocates it from his wage. This is not considered a departure from the production-cost premise but makes the employee a partner in the transaction. Others hold that since the employer pays the entire amount in any case, crediting part of the cost to the employee as a wage and then deducting it is merely a bookeeping transaction.

The advocates of a *noncontributory* plan contend that a pension, in the strict sense, represents a reward for service and is a form of deferred compensation, which should be a company obligation. And it is also argued that since the employer's contributions need not be regarded as income by the employee, they do not affect his tax position. The full amount of the contribution is used to purchase annuity credits. Employee contributions are made from income after taxes, and net income is thereby reduced by the amount of the contributions. Conversely, since the employer contributions are deductible, the actual reduction of net profits is less than the actual amount of the contribution.

Those who favor a *contributory* form contend that wages are sufficiently high to warrant employee contributions. Such contributions, added to an upper limit of employer contributions, substantially increase the amount of the annuity. The employee scarcely notices the contribution; yet the benefit is marked. The contributory plan follows the pattern set by social security legislation. It invites employee interest, removes pensions from the category of paternalism, and gives the employee a sense of independence in that he is providing for his own retirement through a positive action. Finally, employee participation creates a price consciousness. The employee who asks for increased benefits will be more conscious of their cost if it reflects back as a wage deduction rather than in a reduction of business profits. This is true even if the entire transaction is a matter of bookkeeping.

The controlling argument for a contributory plan is that it usually provides more liberal retirement. The noncontributory plan, on the other hand, provides coverage for younger employees who might not participate in a contributory plan. In addition, the noncontributory plan gives the employer more freedom in determining the nature of the plan, its benefits, and the method of operation.

In the period of high corporate earnings during the 1940's, corporate income taxes were in the higher brackets and tax deduction was an important factor in the strong trend toward the noncontributory plan. In the early 1950's a trend set in toward contributory plans. However, the trend was reversed in favor of the noncontributory plan by the impact of the federal income tax law, which provides that in a qualified plan the contributions of the employer are currently deductible without imposing a tax burden on the employee. Unions have generally preferred noninsured plans for the reason that such plans afford them a greater opportunity for administration and control. Most noninsured plans appear to be on a noncontributory basis.

Funding Methods

A final major characteristic[14] of pension plans is the method by which benefits are financed. Methods of funding retirement plans include: (*a*) a pay-as-you-go plan, (*b*) a trust fund plan, (*c*) an individual policy plan, (*d*) a group permanent plan, and (*e*) a group annuity plan. The first two methods are uninsured; the others are insured plans. The group annuity plan may be under (1) a deferred annuity contract or (2) a deposit administration contract.

Pay-as-You-Go Plan. A pay-as-you-go plan is characterized by the fact that no pension fund is established and payments are made to employees out of current income. The plan may be formal or informal.

An informal pay-as-you-go plan could be quite unsatisfactory. Since there is no predetermined plan, there is always the pressure to reduce retirement payments if the employer is in an adverse financial position. Also, a meager pension may be allocated to an employee with limited savings; or an employee with adequate savings or annuities to supplement the pension he expects to get may find himself retired with little or no company-financed income. A formal pay-as-you-go plan is only slightly better. While there is to be no discrimination as to payments, there is, however, no assurance that the plan will be in effect at the time of retirement or that it will remain in effect throughout the lifetime of the employee. Continuation of the plan is at the employer's discretion.

The inherent weakness of the pay-as-you-go plan is the possibility that the employer may be willing but not able to continue payments. Depression may sorely try the resources of the company, or competitive conditions may prevent the company from showing substantial earnings. When curtailment of expense is necessary, some trimming of pensions may result.

There are, unquestionably, employers operating pension plans on a pay-as-you-go basis that are as sincere as those who have more securely funded plans. In some instances, employers set up reserves for lean years. Yet, because the reserve is within the control of the employer, it may become frozen in the business and little more than a bookeeping account. Even with liquid reserves, retirement costs may become a burden impossible to carry.

---

[14]A thorough analysis of the contract provisions and cost factors is available in Chapters 4–6 and 10–11 of Kenneth Black, Jr., *Group Annuities* (Philadelphia, Pa.: University of Pennsylvania Press, 1955).

A pay-as-you-go plan offers the least assurance to the employee of retirement security and, by the same token, affords the employer a minimum of benefits and satisfaction for funds expended. The trend is definitely away from pay-as-you-go plans and toward adequate funding. Life insurance may be utilized to effect such changes.

Trust Fund Plan. A trust fund may be established for the advance financing of a pension plan. Definite rules govern the fund. Funds are paid to the trustee, who invests and administers them. For the fund to be sound, payments must be based on mortality, severance, and disability experience. Actuarial advice is essential, and a consulting actuary is usually retained to make the original estimates and periodic examinations of the fund. On the basis of the examinations, the amounts required for the fund are adjusted. Contributions to the fund are usually made periodically; but there is no fixed contractual obligation, as in the case of insurance, to make payments at a stated time.

Trust fund plans are usually called "self-administered plans" because the employer retains responsibility, directly or indirectly, for their operation. The investment of the fund is governed by the trust agreement. Investment decisions are usually made by a committee composed of company executives or of representatives of both the employee group and management. As an alternative, investment decisions may be left to (*a*) a trustee alone, (*b*) the pension committee and trustee jointly, or (*c*) the trustee with veto power in the pension committee.

The trust agreement outlines the administration of the plan. Payments may be made directly to retired employees from the trust fund, or the trustee may be authorized to purchase annuities for them. A pension plan is held to be "wholly trusteed" if the trust funds represent the only resources available to pay benefits to beneficiaries as they become due.

The appeal of the "wholly trusteed" plan lies in the hope that the investment experience of the particular employer will be more favorable than the averages used by insurance companies. If investments are limited to United States government bonds and securities legal for trust funds or securities legal for life insurance companies, the margin in favor of the trust tends to disappear. The agreement, however, may include preferred and common stocks. A trust plan is flexible, and the benefits may be revised from time to time as needs of employees change or, more significantly, as changing conditions dictate.

Individual Policy Plan. Under this plan a trustee is named, usually a bank or trust company, and the details of the plan are set forth in the trust agreement. Contributions to the plan may be made to the trustee or paid directly to the insurance company. The trustee arranges for an individual policy for each eligible employee but retains control of it by means of an assignment. A retirement annuity contract may be utilized; but if the employer wishes to provide a more sizable death benefit, he may purchase the so-called "blended plan." This is becoming an increasingly important type of individual policy plan. Under this arrangement, life insurance is provided through the use of whole life or life-to-age-eighty-five policies. Retirement income in excess of that provided by the cash values of the life insurance is funded either by a deposit administration contract or a self-administered fund. The life insurance policies generally contain a guarantee that they can be converted to a full $10 of monthly retirement income for each $1,000 of face amount of insurance.

The individual policy pension trust plan is most useful in providing pensions for groups too small to be eligible under a group plan. The annuities are based upon earnings of the employee when he enters the plan. As his earnings increase, the trustee purchases additional contracts so that the annuity will reflect the benefits set forth in the plan. The normal form of individual annuity purchased under this plan provides payments for ten years certain and life thereafter. Many insurance companies which write individual policy plans offer a "guaranteed issue" plan. The meaning of guaranteed issue apparently varies from company to company, but the concept generally means that each covered employee is issued life insurance, in connection with the pension plan, up to a specified amount such as $10,000, regardless of his condition of health. Life insurance for which an employee qualifies in excess of the specified amount is subject to medical evidence of insurability.

Individual policy plans usually permit the employee to withdraw his contributions if he leaves the company before retirement. Two methods have met with particular favor for handling employees' contributions upon withdrawal before retirement.

The first provides for the return of all contributions paid by the employee, with interest. Some plans do not pay the interest, and they do not have wide appeal. The "with interest" plan conforms with the habit of thought that interest should accumulate with all savings projects. Anticipating withdrawals, the employer foresees dissatisfaction if only the actual funds contributed are returned with no interest. Yet, it is sometimes hard to explain to employees who do not withdraw that they, too, are being credited with interest and are receiving full benefits from their contributions.

The second method permits an employee, upon terminating service prior to retirement, to leave his contributions with the insurance company and retain any paid-up annuity purchased by his own contributions. If the plan provides for vesting, the withdrawing employee will have his paid-up annuity increased, if he has fulfilled the vesting requirements, to the extent of the employer's contribution.

Group Permanent Plan. Group permanent life insurance, aside from providing permanent life insurance protection, has come to be used in connection with retirement plans. When so used, it may follow one of two patterns; (*a*) retirement income insurance or (*b*) life insurance that can be converted to retirement income.

The group permanent plans provide the same protection as comparable individual policies written on a permanent basis. The group plan differs in that being a group contract the life insurance protection is available, up to certain limits, without a physical examination. Companies writing group permanent life insurance require a minimum number of lives to be covered with a minimum amount of insurance on each life.

Group permanent retirement income insurance, plan (*a*), provides for life insurance during the period of active employment with a monthly retirement income at retirement age. This plan leaves no choice to the employee and thus precludes selection against the company. If the employee terminates his employment before retirement age, a portion of the insurance determined by the policy values is continued as paid-up life insurance for the employee.

The second plan, (*b*), is essentially a group life contract but provides that values at termination of employment may be used to purchase retirement income benefits instead of paid-up insurance at retirement. The plan may be written so that conversion to retirement benefits is automatic at the retirement age designated in the agreement. Under such a plan, all of the values represented by the permanent group life insurance are utilized to provide retirement income.

The second plan may be written to provide that the individual employee may elect to use his group insurance values either for retirement income or paid-up insurance. If the choice can be made at retirement, the plan makes it possible for those in poor health to elect paid-up insurance and those in good health to choose an annuity. To prevent adverse selection, the plan usually provides that unless election is made at least five years prior to retirement, the retirement option is available only to employees who can present medical evidence of insurability.

If the group policy provides adequate life insurance during the period of active employment but policy values that will provide inadequate retirement income, supplemental amounts of retirement income benefits may be purchased. Such benefits may be provided by purchasing a single premium annuity at the time of retirement or a supplementary annuity independent of the life insurance protection. A third choice, frequently used in connection with profit-sharing undertakings, provides for deposit, from time to time, with a trustee of amounts to purchase supplemental retirement income in accordance with a predetermined formula covered by contract. This last choice provides for a guaranteed minimum and for periodic increases as profits allocated to the purpose allow.

Group Annuities. The most important type of insured pension plan is the group annuity. By contractual agreement with a life insurance company, the benefits of the pension plan are guaranteed to the employee. In 1960 "over 100 U.S. life insurance companies were actively writing insured pension plans of this type."[15] About one half of the total persons covered by insured pension plans are covered by *deferred* group annuity contracts and somewhat under one half by *deposit administration* group annuity plans.[16]

The *deferred group annuity* contract is perhaps the most generally accepted plan for funding pensions with annuities. The yearly contribution of the employer consists of (*a*) future service contributions and (*b*) past service contributions. Under a contributory plan, future service contributions of employer and employee are combined and applied as received to purchase deferred annuity credits for each employee. Past service contributions are made by the employer only at the end of each plan year, and are purchased and credited to employees in the order of nearness to normal retirement date.[17]

The employer, under this plan, can take no credit for anticipated terminations due to employee turnover. The employer future service contributions each year, with employee contributions, if any, must be sufficient to purchase all future service benefits that accrue in the year. If an employee terminates his services before his benefits vest, the employer will receive a credit as a result of the cancellation of the annuity credits purchased for the terminating employee.[18]

If an employee retires before the normal retirement date, all future service credits will have been purchased. Since past service benefits are purchased in order of nearness to normal retirement date, the employee might well apply for retirement before his past

---

[15]*Private and Public Pension Plans in the United States, op. cit.*, p. 8.

[16]*Ibid.*, p. 9.

[17]Insurance companies normally will accept no more in any one year than 10 per cent of the one-sum cost to purchase all past service annuity credits on the effective date of the plan, to conform with the limitations of past service deductions for tax purposes.

[18]In order for an employer to receive a credit arising from the cancellation of future service benefits, purchased for terminating employees, the employee must be in good health at termination. This is so because there are no credits to the employer for deaths that occur before retirement. Employer contributions are computed by the life insurance company, taking mortality into consideration.

service annuity has been purchased. Any funds for past service contributions not already allocated may be used to purchase this annuity. Otherwise, a special payment will be required of the employer if the retiring employee is to receive the full benefit as promised by the plan.

If the plan is terminated, the insurance company administers all benefits previously purchased. All future benefits are fully funded as of any date. Termination of the plan can have no adverse effect upon benefits accrued from the date of the contract. Future service benefits are fully guaranteed as they accrue. Past service benefits are guaranteed as purchases and are made from past service contributions. These guarantees appeal to employees.

The *deposit administration group annuity* plan uses an unallocated fund of contributions from the employer to purchase each retiring employee an annuity as he retires. Certain types of business have a very large labor turnover, and most of the workers withdraw before retirement age. This is the case when the labor is arduous and can be performed only by young and vigorous employees. On the other hand, there will always be superintendents, foremen, and administrative employees who may remain until they can no longer engage in a gainful occupation. To institute a plan that will not call for the payment into the fund of sums to provide annuities for employees who will inevitably withdraw, the deposit administration group annuity plan has been devised.

Under this plan, the employer makes monthly deposits into a premium fund carried by the life insurance company. The life insurance company accumulates the funds at a guaranteed interest rate and holds them in an undivided employer fund. Employee contributions, if any, accumulate in individual employee accounts. As an employee is retired, the accumulation in his account is used to purchase a part of his retirement income in accordance with annuity rates guaranteed in the contract. The balance of the employee's retirement income is purchased by a transfer from the employer fund. The merger of contributions is made when the employee retires. He receives no benefits from employer contributions into the general fund until this time. At retirement a single premium retirement annuity is provided for the retiring employee for whatever amount is due him under the plan.

The insurance company makes no guarantee to the employee that the full amount of the annuity outlined in the original plan will be forthcoming. This is necessary because if, for any reason the employer fails to provide sufficient funds to meet the needs for the single payment annuities as they become due, the insurance company can pay only such annuity as the funds it has actually received will permit. On the other hand, the plan saves the employer the necessity of advancing payments for members of the group who almost surely will leave before retirement. He also builds up the fund during periods of favorable business and may make smaller contributions during periods of business recession. No withdrawals are ever permitted by the insurance company; and from time to time, the company's actuaries study the group experience to determine whether or not contributions are sufficient to keep the plan on an actuarially sound basis.

Combination of Methods. It is entirely feasible to use more than one method of providing annuity coverages. A usual combination is a group annuity contract and individual annuity contracts. A group annuity contract may be used to provide benefits based on salary up to a given amount, such as $5,000 or $10,000, for all employees. Benefits for employees earning more than the established limit could be provided through individual annuity contracts. The individual contracts, to provide annuities in excess of that financed through the group contract, would be used, ordinarily, when only a very few employees are in the higher brackets.

SUMMARY

Annuities, even though they emphasize liquidation of assets instead of creation of an estate, are an important part of the life insurance business. Many life insurers sell *annuities,* which are promises to pay periodic sums of money to persons known as *annuitants.* Annuities are written either as *individual* contracts or on a group basis as *group* annuities.

The systematic method by which assets are liquidated under an annuity is unique in its use of *life* annuities, under which the annuitant's income continues as long as he lives. The advantage of never outliving one's income, and the benefits of investment diversification and guaranteed income return, make annuities a reasonable choice for careful consideration by many older persons. *Settlement options* under life insurance contracts are often an advantageous method of receiving annuity payments, especially under the life income option.

Classification of annuities helps to explain many of their basic features. The *straight or pure* life annuity is contrasted with the *guaranteed refund* type, in which a minimum amount of dollars (or number of payments) are assured to the annuitant's beneficiary in case of early death of the annuitant. Most annuities do include some kind of refund provisions.

Annuities may also be classified as *single life* or *joint life; immediate* or *deferred* (if income starts sometime after the first annuity period); and *single payment* or *installment* payment. Many individual annuities combine the features mentioned in a guaranteed refund, single life, deferred installment annuity.

Many *special* types of annuity and life insurance combinations have been developed to provide protection for premature death with the annuity guarantees. *Variable* annuities are another type which has begun to receive increasing attention. The legal and practical dilemma of variable annuities is not based on whether or not some hedge against inflation is advisable for financial security, but whether or not (and how) life insurance companies should provide this different kind of contract.

Annuities do not require medical examinations. They are necessarily based upon different mortality tables from those used for life insurance contracts. The 1937 Standard Annuity Table and the Annuity Table for 1949, with some adjustments for trend factors, are in common use.

Group annuities are a major portion of all annuity contracts. The annuity principle has been adopted for use in the rapidly expanding field of pensions, in order to provide a guarantee to employers and employees that retirement income benefits will be paid. Over 25 million persons are now covered by private pension plans that hold over $60 billion of assets. About one third of these assets are protected by *insured* pension plans, as opposed to the alternative pay-as-you-go or trusteed plans. As the most common type of insured plan, group annuity pensions have several characteristics which are significant to analyze, such as their eligibility provisions, retirement dates, treatment of past service credits, the basic benefit formulas, the vesting clause, and sources of financing.

FOR REVIEW

1. What classifications of annuities are important to an understanding of the various uses to which annuities may be put?
2. A fairly common type of individual annuity is a *deferred, installment payment, refund, single life* annuity. Explain the italicized terms and note why the use of these features in an annuity might be expected.
3. Since annuities and life insurance are dependent on life contingencies, why is the medical examination required in the case of life insurance but dispensed with in the ordinary course of writing annuities? What types of annuities require a medical examination and why?
4. The 1958 CSO Table of Mortality is regarded as conservative for use in computing life insurance premiums. The use of this table for the purpose of computing the cost of an annuity would, therefore, be disastrous. Why?
5. X claims that a sound bond is a better type of investment than an annuity since, in addition to income, the principal remains intact. Is this statement correct? Explain why or why not.
6. There is a widespread idea that it requires a large sum of money to purchase an annuity, and that single payment annuities are purchased only by the wealthy. Explain that the contrary is, in fact, the case.
7. Distinguish between the "last survivor annuity" and the "survivorship annuity," including explanation of the type of situation for which each is designed.

8. There are some annuity contracts that do more than effect a distribution of assets in that they have some features of life insurance. Explain the protective features, ordinarily attributed to life insurance, to be found in some annuity contracts.
9. B is 25 years of age. He purchases a retirement income annuity, selecting the age of 60 for the first payment. Because of unfortunate financial reverses, accompanied by broken health, B finds himself at the age of 50 destitute and jobless, with little prospect of being able again to earn a satisfactory living. Must he wait ten years before enjoying the benefits of his annuity, and must he continue his payments on the purchase price during that period?
10. Some life insurance companies are spending large sums of money in advertising retirement income policies. In commenting upon such an advertisement, B, aged 27, states that he believes in life insurance to protect dependents but that he can provide adequately for his own old age. What do you think?
11. "Our advocacy of variable annuities stems from the dilemma of many persons now retired on individual or group pension plans," a leading insurance executive is reported having stated before a legislative hearing of the New Jersey Senate Business Affairs Committee. He went on to say: "Annuity incomes that seemed adequate when purchased years ago today often fail to meet the buyer's needs, primarily because of the impact of inflation on the purchasing power of the dollar." How does the variable annuity undertake to remedy this situation?
12. Some insurance companies strongly favor the variable annuity while others just as strongly oppose the idea. From the standpoint of the business of insurance, indicate such reasons as you can why the variable annuity should not be written by a life insurance company.
13. The trustees of X University have been trying to work out a retirement plan for the members of the faculty. A committee is appointed, and one of its members suggest looking into the possibilities of a group annuity. In your opinion is it wiser to pay the insurance company a premium, with its loading for expense, or to have the committee undertake to set up a fund to be administered by the college?
14. What problems are most apparent today in the development of variable annuities by life insurance companies? Are the obstacles problems of theory, practice, or legal restrictions?
15. Is a variable annuity necessarily the best answer for most individuals who are preparing their future financial plans to meet the effects of inflation? Explain why you believe it to be—or why you believe it not to be—a good and necessary hedge against continued inflation.
16. How are different retirement dates used in pension plans? What are the purposes of having various retirement dates?
17. Explain briefly the basic methods by which benefits are *(a)* determined and *(b)* funded under pension plans.
18. What advantages and disadvantages do group annuities have for pension plans, as opposed to alternatives such as *(a)* trusteed plans and *(b)* individual policy plans?

Chapter 26

INDIVIDUAL HEALTH INSURANCE

IF one were asked to name the major type of voluntary insurance which is a faster growing type of protection, covering more persons, through more insurers, in more contract forms than *life* insurance, the only answer would be *health* insurance. The vast scope of this field of insurance is evident in its over 1,800 insuring organizations that cover more than three out of every four Americans in thousands of different policy contracts.[1] Premiums increased by almost 70 percent between 1957 and 1962, and the total of $9.3 billion was more than three times the amount received by health insurers in 1952.[2]

CLASSIFICATION AND PURPOSE

Definitions

The term *health insurance* applies to those forms of insurance that provide protection against the expenses and income losses arising from illness or injury. Originally a casualty insurance line, but now also often written by life insurance companies, the earliest health protection offered was known as "accident insurance." Later, when sickness coverages were added, it was natural to extend the name of the coverage to "accident and sickness insurance" or "accident and health insurance." The term "disability insurance" has also been used. The older names have by no means been entirely replaced as a part of insurance terminology. However, taken as a part of a personal insurance program with life insurance covering life contingencies, health insurance appears to be a logical term to apply to health contingencies.

Purpose

Health insurance has for its purpose the payment of benefits for loss of income and expenses arising from illness and injury. Not only

[1]*Source Book of Health Insurance Data* (New York: Health Insurance Institute, 1963), pp. 5–6.

[2]*Ibid.*, pp. 36–37.

is the loss of time from productive enterprise the source of loss to the insured but the cost of the care and necessary medical attention adds to the amount of the loss. Health insurance provides protection: (*a*) against the loss of time or earning power and (*b*) the added expense of medical care.

Since a very substantial proportion of the families in the United States are dependent for maintenance on the income derived from their personal efforts, it follows that for these people time is the most valuable asset. There are few indeed, however well situated they may be, who do not rely heavily upon time as an asset. Health insurance undertakes to protect this asset as it is reflected in earning power and in so doing protects the independence and welfare of the family depending upon it. For the family it has been compared to business interruption insurance as applied to business operations. This is true to the extent that it provides income when potential earnings are lost through physical disability.

For those who are dependent upon personal earnings, it follows that incapacity from illness or injury not only interrupts the income produced but also may draw heavily upon family savings for medical, nursing, or surgical care. This being the case, health insurance has a function over and above the indemnification for loss of time or earning capacity. By providing a continued income and resources for expenses atttendant upon incapacity, health insurance serves to preserve family accumulations. Therefore, not only does it provide the means to pay for current expenses but it also makes unnecessary the liquidation of family accumulations such as selling the family car or home or mortgaging them to pay heavy medical or surgical expenses. In this respect health insurance provides property protection.

Classes

Method of Underwriting. Health insurance is written in one of two ways: (*a*) policies covering the individual insured and in certain instances his family and (*b*) policies covering groups of persons. The basic distinction between *individual* and *group* forms of health insurance serves as the division between Chapters 26 and 27 in this text. The method follows the general pattern of Chapter 22, "Individual Life Insurance Contracts," and Chapter 23, "Group Life Insurance."

Health Perils. In regard to the causes of losses, or perils, health insurance may be divided into (*a*) *accident* insurance, for sudden and unexpected injuries and (*b*) *sickness* insurance, for illnesses or diseases. This division was the basis for the traditional description of the fields of insurance, as noted in the definitions given. The terms have been supplanted[3] to some extent by the newer term "health" insurance, describing in one word both of the major perils.

Another way of dividing the perils of good health is to describe the source of the injury or illness as being *(a) occupational* or *(b) nonoccupational.* The distinction is useful in several forms of insurance, especially in social insurance plans by government. Here the classification centers on describing the dangers of poor health as one resulting from the work situation (covered under workmen's compensation insurance in many cases) and all other situations. The outside-of-work causes would usually be provided for by the individual's own voluntary insurance, but in four states they might be compensated under "nonoccupational" or "temporary" disability laws (see Chapter 8).

Health Insuring Organizations. The policyholder has a wide choice among types of voluntary insuring organizations. Of the total of more than 1,800, almost 900 insurance companies, 150 Blue Cross or Blue Shield plans and nearly 800 independent plans are available.[4] The independent plans include those sponsored by communities, labor unions, employers, colleges, and private health clinics. Residents of every state can choose from more than 100 insuring organizations in selecting their health insurance, and in over 30 states the choice can be made among more than 200 organizations.[5]

It is not to decrease the recognition of the important place of the many other types of insuring organizations that this chapter analyzes only the policy forms of the insurance companies. The sheer scope of the complete discussion which would be required in order to discuss all the Blue Cross, Blue Shield,[6] and independent plans necessitates the limitation of the chapter to insurance contracts issued by licensed health insurance companies.[7]

Health Insurance Policies. Individual or family health insurance policies include: (1) commercial policies, (2) industrial policies,

---

[3]The recommendation of the Committee on Health Insurance Terminology follows this pattern, although one can find many evidences that the older terms linger on, and they shall probably do so for many years in the future.

[4]*Source Book of Health Insurance Data, op. cit.,* p. 54.

[5]*Ibid.*, p. 56.

[6]See Robert D. Eilers, *Regulation of Blue Cross and Blue Shield Plans* (Homewood, Ill., Richard D. Irwin, Inc., published for the S. S. Huebner Foundation for Insurance Education, 1963).

[7]Those students desiring further information about health insurance are referred to: O. D. Dickerson, *Health Insurance* (Homewood, Ill.: Richard D. Irwin, Inc., 1963); Edwin J. Faulkner, *Health Insurance* (New York: McGraw-Hill Book Co., Inc., 1960); Davis W. Gregg (ed.), *Life and Health Insurance Handbook* (Homewood, Ill.: Richard D. Irwin, Inc., 1959); and J. F. Follman, Jr., *Medical Care and Health Insurance* (Homewood, Ill.: Richard D. Irwin, Inc., 1963).

(3) mail-order policies, and (4) special purpose policies. The *commercial* policies are written on selected risks with large indemnity limits and provide much of the income protection coverage that is written. Premiums are usually payable annually, semiannually, quarterly, or monthly. *Industrial* policies follow the pattern of industrial life insurance, being designed for persons in the lower-income groups and written with smaller indemnity limits than the commercial policies. Premiums usually are collected weekly at the home. *Mail-order* insurance is characterized by the practice of merchandising by mail solicitation and advertising without the use of agents or brokers. Many of the direct-mail contracts are quite limited in their coverage. *Special purpose* policies include contracts covering special risks such as auto racing, other sports events, travel risks, volunteer firemen, and students. Many policies in this category are "custom tailored."

The commercial policies deserve primary attention in this text. Industrial forms are quite similar to commercial policies, but more restricted in amount and variety of coverage. Mail-order types are quite common, though the tremendous number of these forms, and their great variability, prevents their discussion here. Since they are often very limited in the scope of their protection, it is wiser to concentrate our attention on the more important basic coverages.

The special purpose policies should be mentioned more fully here, however. Many special policies are written to cover travel. Some cover only one form of travel such as travel by airplane, and others cover all travel accidents. The airplane peril is insured frequently by the familiar vending machines located in many airports. Much broader travel accident policies on an annual basis are available through many insurance agents. Several major oil companies introduced an innovation in 1964 by making such travel accident insurance available for purchase through their credit cards and monthly billing.

The so-called "dread disease" policy covers medical expenses in connection with one or a number of specific diseases. Separate policies cover poliomyelitis or cancer. Policies covering a group of diseases may include poliomyelitis, cancer, leukemia, diphtheria, scarlet fever, smallpox, rabies, tularemia, encephalitis, and spinal meningitis, to mention some of the diseases that involve large amounts for medical expenses but occur infrequently.[8]

[8]Dread disease policies and many of these special purpose contracts are sometimes referred to as "limited policies." A limited policy, following a definition suggested by the National Association of Insurance Commissioners, is one "that contains unusual exclusions, limitations, reductions, or contains such a restrictive nature that the payments or benefits under such policies are limited in frequency or in amount." Limited policies may provide either small disability benefits or benefits restricted in duration, or they may provide broad coverage limited to a specified hazard.

Policies are also written to cover injuries sustained while participating in sports, while on vacation, or on duty as a volunteer fireman. In this category also are policies insuring flagpole sitters, divers, steeplejacks, drivers of racing cars, airplane test pilots, and the like. Policies are also written providing insurance for students. Limited policies are offered to many newspaper subscribers, with the coverage usually restricted to small maximum amounts for accidental injuries only.

Indicative of the extent to which special contracts are available, policies are sometimes written paying indemnities for the nonappearance of celebrities because of accident or illness. Policies are also written to indemnify a producer if, due to the temporary or long-term disability of a celebrity because of accident or illness, the theatrical production must be abandoned or a movie production postponed with loss to the producer. These policies are not to be confused with policies written primarily with publicity in mind.[9]

Health Losses and Protection. A final method of classifying the various parts of health insurance is by reference to the kind of loss caused by the interruption of good health.

Health insurance losses fall into one of two major categories: insurance against (1) the cost of *medical care* and (2) *loss of income.* In the process of evolution three important types of insurance protection have emerged. These are (*a*) *hospital, surgical,* and *regular medical* expense protection, (*b*) *major medical* expense protection, and (*c*) *income* protection. The first two of these types help pay the cost of health care. The third type helps replace earnings lost as the result of illness or injury. Income protection policies of necessity are written on an individual basis. Policies covering the cost of med-

---

[9]Such insurance is sometimes termed "cast insurance." Policies are written on a life and health basis and cover either the star of a performance or several stars of a production. Many large claims have been paid. For example, in the filming of *Spartacus* when Jean Simmons had an appendectomy, insurance in the amount of $632,197 was paid. The policy was said to have been written in the Firemen's Fund in the amount of $4.10 million for a premium slightly in excess of $70,000. The illnesses of Elizabeth Taylor in the filming of *Giant* and *Cat On a Hot Tin Roof* resulted in claims amounting to approximately $75,000. Another claim involving Miss Taylor amounting to just over $45,000 developed during the filming of *Raintree County.* When Marlon Brando developed an infection after being injured by a spilled pot of tea, an insurance loss of just over $34,000 occurred. For a report of other like claims see *Time,* December 10, 1960, page 60. Probably the record is the payment of $1,219,172.00 when Tyrone Power, the star of *Solomon and Sheba,* died of a heart attack during the production. The policy secured by United Artists and Theme Pictures covered for $3 million. (John Wesley Noble, "Big Gamble on the Stars," *The Saturday Evening Post,* June 18, 1960, p. 26.)

For examples of policies issued primarily for publicity, large policies have been written on Eddie Cantor's eyes, Jimmy Durante's nose, and Marlene Dietrich's legs. Policies of this sort, however valuable the feature insured, are unquestionably of publicity value.

ical care are written on an individual, a family, or a husband and wife basis.

Hospital, Surgical, and Regular Medical Expense Protection. Hospital expense[10] insurance has two objectives: (*a*) to help pay for costs of room and board and (*b*) to help pay charges for extra hospital services. The policy limits the amount to be paid each day of hospital confinement and there is a limit with respect to the number of days that coverage applies. Other specified miscellaneous benefits are included such as operating room fees and payment for X-ray pictures, laboratory tests, drugs, anesthetics, and the like. Broader contracts include benefits for nearly all types of extra hospital services including maternity benefits. Contracts for individuals are written, but many policies include the whole family in one contract.

The costs of specified operations are covered under the *surgical* expense form. The protection includes surgery in a hospital and may include surgical procedures performed in the office or home. Policies generally list the operations for which benefits are provided together with a maximum amount payable for each. The schedule of operations generally includes all but the most unusual, and it is the practice of many companies to provide for an equitable payment toward the cost of surgical procedures not specifically listed in the contracts. Not all policies covering hospitalization expenses include surgical benefits, but many do. It is often an optional benefit available to the policyholder if he desires it included in the contract.

The *regular medical expense protection* form is designed to help pay for the services of a physician for nonsurgical care in a hospital, at home, or at the physician's office. It is usually written in conjunction with the basic hospital and surgical benefits, and often is an optional coverage. Some policies are written to insure only against the cost of doctor visits to a hospital. This tends to keep the cost of the insurance down and at the same time provides protection when the illness or injury is serious enough to require hospitalization. However, limited home or office care may be included at the option of the insured. If home or office protection is included, liability of the company may start only after several services have been rendered. Blanket medical insurance provides a wide range of services

---

[10]The demand in recent years for hospital expense insurance has resulted in a tremendous growth in the coverage together with many changes in policy forms. The $5.00-per-day allocation for hospital room with specified sums allocated for other expenses sold a few years ago is considered obsolete today. Room benefits run as high as $30 or more daily, and most policies now provide for the payment of miscellaneous hospital expenses on an unallocated basis. The old policies that limited payment for room charge to 30 days for any one accident or sickness may now be replaced with policies that provide for payment from 70 to 100 days or even for a full year. Some contracts offer maternity coverage, while others do not. Usually, maternity benefits are limited to a certain maximum amount.

including care by both specialists and general physicians in the home, office, clinic, and hospital. It may provide preventive as well as curative services, home nursing, X-ray treatment, laboratory and other diagnostic tests, and ambulance service among other benefits. The plans vary but the comprehensive coverages provide a broad protection.

Major Medical Expense Protection. Major medical expense insurance is designed to provide catastrophe coverage against medical care costs. Instead of providing so-called "first dollar" coverage, major medical insurance aims at paying only quite large medical losses. The usual hospital and surgical contracts provide means for the average person to level some of his medical expenses. There are, however, illnesses and injuries that for the average family take on the characteristics of a catastrophe. The serious operation, such illnesses as polio, cancer, multiple sclerosis, and the like, and injuries resulting in total and permanent disability may involve a family in expenses running to thousands of dollars. It is to meet health losses of this type that the major medical form has grown rapidly in popularity in the past decade.[11]

There are three identifying characteristics of major medical insurance: (*a*) the *deductible*, (*b*) *coinsurance*, and (*c*) *high maximum* benefits.

The *deductible* feature obligates the insured person to pay the initial part of his expenses. This is agreed upon in the policy and is called the deductible amount. Under individual and family major medical policies the common range of deductible is between $200 and $750, and sometimes goes as high as $1,000. The purpose is to avoid frequent small loss payments (usually covered by hospital insurance), and consequently keep the cost of the insurance low.

When expenses exceed the deductible amount the policy benefits begin. Under a *coinsurance* feature, the company is then obligated to pay its share of the predetermined expenses. For example, if the insurance company is obligated to pay 75 percent of all hospital, doctor, and other medical bills in excess of the deductible sum, the remaining percentage, or 25 percent, is paid by the policyholder. Another common coinsurance sharing of the losses is 80 percent paid by the insurer, and 20 percent by the insured. The purpose of the coinsurance feature is to prevent overuse of medical facilities and treatment.

[11]Even as compared with other fast-growing health insurance fields, major medical policy growth has been phenomenal between 1953 and 1963: (1) major medical plans, from 2 to 38 million persons protected, (2) hospital expense plans, from 91 million to 141 million, (3) surgical expense plans, from 72 to 131 million, and (4) regular medical expense plans, from 36 to 98 million persons. *The Extent of Voluntary Health Insurance Coverage* (New York, Health Insurance Council, August, 1963), pp. 10, 21.

Finally, benefits are payable up to a *high maximum* specified amount. This amount may be $5,000, $10,000, $15,000, or other sizable amounts. The maximum benefit may be written to apply to each illness or injury or the benefit may limit the aggregate expenses for several injuries.

The deductible and the coinsurance features operate together as follows: with a policy carrying a $300 deductible, in the event of a medical expense of $2,300 the insured pays the first $300 of expenses. With a 20 percent coinsurance feature, the company pays 80 percent of the balance ($2,000). In this instance the liability of the company would be $1,600 and the cost to the patient would be $700.

Many variations of the deductible and coinsurance features are used. In order that the deductible and coinsurance amounts should not operate too severely against the insured, in some instances the policy may provide that the deductible operate on a family basis and not on the basis of each individual illness. For example, in the case of a common accident where three or more members of a family are involved, the policy may provide for a common deductible. Some companies also apply this in the same contagious disease. The example is cited of four members of a family being injured in an automobile accident with a policy written on a $300-deductible basis. If the deductible applies to each injury, this would amount to $1,200. Presuming the family had established an amount of $300 as the sum that it reasonably could carry, the payment of $1,200 would constitute an unduly heavy load. It is conceivable in such circumstances that with medical bills amounting to $1,200 there would be no liability on the part of the insurance carrier. With the deductible applying on a family basis, the situation would be quite different. In addition to the common accident and contagious disease situation, there are a few monthly medical budget expense plans that allow a common family deductible. Ordinarily, however, each member of the family is responsible for his own deductible and his own coinsurance per injury or illness per year.[12]

A form known as comprehensive major medical provides for the payment of 100 percent of all expenses in excess of the deductible up to a given amount and the coinsurance feature applies to all in-

---

[12]Though some companies in the individual and family field of major medical insurance write a *calendar* deductible, the much more common form is the per injury or per illness deductible. The calendar deductible provides that after the deductible has been satisfied once during the policy year, subsequent illnesses of members of the family are covered in full subject to the coinsurance feature, though a small deductible such as $25 applicable to each claim may be imposed for the purpose of eliminating nuisance claims and reducing the cost of administration. In the case of the per illness or per injury deductible, the cutoff is a maximum benefit limit or a period usually of two or three years.

surance in excess. For example, after expenses exceed the deductible a policy may be written to pay 100 percent of the next $500 and 80 percent of the remaining expenses incurred within a designated period after the date of the accident or first treatment for sickness. There are other forms that pay hospital bills without the application of a deductible up to a daily limit established in the policy.[13] The coinsurance and deductible feature applies only to costs over and above room and board. Policies with sizable deductible amounts are designed for those persons with adequate resources to cover ordinary costs of hospital and medical expenses that do not reach catastrophic proportions.

Loss of Income Protection. Income loss is often the most important result of injury or illness, in many cases exceeding the cost of medical care. Loss of income protection becomes an essential part of any good health insurance program. This form, sometimes known as "disability income" protection, is designed to help replace loss of income, or earning power, to the head of a family disabled because of illness or injury.

Income benefits are usually expressed as a weekly or monthly sum, though there are a few policies that specify a daily rate. The definition of "disability" used in the contract is extremely important, as this determines the extent of benefits payable under the contract. The differences between "total" and "partial" disability, and other features, are discussed later in this chapter.

Contracts offered by the various insurers vary greatly. Because there are so many different forms of coverage represented by the different policies of one company and by the differences among companies, there tends to be much competition with respect to selling. One class of competition tends to broaden the coverage. In such cases, emphasis is placed upon the protection afforded rather than upon the premium charged. If emphasis is placed upon a particularly low premium, the coverage under the contract may be expected to be limited. In this field, as in others, it is unreasonable to expect to get more than that for which payment is made. It is incumbent upon the policyholder to give careful attention to the details of the contract because, in a field where there are such a number and variety of benefits available, with emphasis only or primarily upon the benefits, failure to understand the limitations of the policy may lead to disappointment. An insurance company views with concern the possibility of disappointment but cannot be ex-

---

[13]There is a major hospital insurance plan that pays all *hospital* expenses within a given period after an accident or hospital confinement for sickness in excess of a deductible amount up to the full policy limit. A coinsurance factor may be made to the cost of professional nursing care.

pected to redraw a contract to fit the expectations of a disappointed policyholder when he suffers a disability not covered by the contract.[14]

Relationship to Life Insurance

More life insurance companies were writing health insurance at the beginning of 1963 than casualty companies or companies that specialized in health insurance only.[15] Also, even though health insurance is a major (over $1 billion in premiums a year) kind of insurance written by casualty companies, the life insurance companies write more than four fifths of the total health insurance in the United States.[16]

For a considerable period there was some reluctance on the part of life insurance carriers to write health insurance coverages. Limited protection in the form of an income benefit for total and permanent disability and a waiver-of-premium benefit during a period of total disability represented the first attempts on the part of life insurance companies to recognize the insurance of health impairments as a part of the life insurance business. However, in the course of analyzing the personal insurance needs of a family it became readily apparent to life underwriters that loss of time and income attributable to injury or illness could disrupt the family finances. Further examination brought to light the fact that interruption of income was only one factor in disrupting the budget. A life's savings might well be wiped out in a comparatively short period of illness involving surgery, nursing care, hospitalization, and other expensive medical care. Health insurance appeared to be the answer.

---

[14] In view of this situation, the Health Insurance Council serves (*a*) as a medium for development of better understanding of mutual responsibilities in the problems of health insurance, (*b*) as a central source of information regarding health insurance coverages, and (*c*) to provide technical and practical counsel on matters pertaining to health insurance. The council is composed of eight insurance associations that account for more than 90 percent of the health insurance issued by the insurance business. These member associations are: American Life Convention, American Mutual Insurance Alliance, Association of Casualty and Surety Companies, Association of Life Insurance Medical Directors, Health Insurance Association of America, International Claims Association, Life Insurance Association of America, and Life Insurance Conference.

[15] *Source Book of Health Insurance Data, op. cit.,* p. 55. Of the total number of nearly 900 insurance companies actively writing health insurance, almost 600 were life insurers, 250 were casualty insurers and about 50 were monoline (health insurers only). Blue Cross, Blue Shield and independent insuring plans are excluded in this reference. The number of life insurers writing health insurance increased over 100 per cent during the past ten years, while the number of casualty companies writing health insurance increased only 20 percent between 1953 and 1963.

[16] *Health Insurance Index* (Philadlphia, Pa.: Chilton Co., 1963), p. 3. Insurance companies (not included Blue Cross-Blue Shield or independent plans) wrote $5.6 billion of health premiums in 1962, of which $4.5 billion was written by life insurance companies.

Thus life insurers today almost always offer health insurance as an endorsement or "rider" to the life insurance contract, as in total disability[17] waiver-of-premium and disability income benefits, and in extra payments for accidental death. Also, many life insurers write, under regular forms of health insurance, benefits for (*a*) hospital, surgical and medical expense, (*b*) major medical expense, and (*c*) loss of income due to disability.

The close relationship to life insurance, health insurance, and social security benefits suggests that many of the features of these plans should be analyzed together. A complete estate planning program for the family necessitates a coordination of these voluntary and government insurance fields to provide the policyholder with an integrated arrangement for meeting the personal insurance risks. Chapter 28 discusses this need further.

A BASIC POLICY FEATURE—RENEWABILITY

Except for the benefit provisions, in which health insurance contracts differ so widely, probably no feature is more important than the renewability of the policy. Health insurance was originally a casualty line. The early policies followed the casualty practice of covering for a one-year term, and the policies could be renewed only by the consent of the company. Many policies are sold today on a yearly basis with a right to cancel at any time during the policy term, or at least at each policy renewal date.[18]

Influenced by the example of life insurance, a demand arose for a permanent form of health insurance. Policies were developed giving the insured the right to keep his policy in force by the timely payment of premiums just as in the case of life insurance. These policies were said to be "noncancellable" and "guaranteed renew-

---

[17]See Chapter 24, and, for additional information, Kenneth W. Herrick, *Total Disability Provisions in Life Insurance Contracts* (Homewood, Ill.: Richard D. Irwin, Inc., published for the S. S. Huebner Foundation for Insurance Education, 1956).

[18]The main difference in health policies issued by casualty companies and those issued by life insurance companies is the approach to renewals. Life insurance companies normally issue non-cancellable and guaranteed renewable policies. Coverage is usually very similar, although it is possible that casualty companies will write higher limits than life insurance companies because of the difference in the approach. In some instances casualty companies appear to be more liberal in age limits than life insurance companies for the same reason. As for the higher limits of the cancellable policies, this applies more to the area of loss-of-income insurance than to hospital and surgical insurance. Again, as for age limits, while there is available to the older age classes more cancellable or optional renewal coverage, certain of the largest life insurance companies are now issuing a guaranteed renewable lifetime basic hospital-surgical coverage. The age limit for new applicants is seventy-five years. There is also available a fully paid up at sixty-five lifetime hospital-surgical coverage with the age limit for new applicants fifty-five years and a policy with surgical benefits guaranteed renewable for lifetime with age limit for new applicants sixty years. The last mentioned policies are variable-premium-by-class policies.

able." Policies written today fall into one of three broad patterns: (*a*) policies renewable at option of insuring company, (*b*) noncancellable forms with guaranteed premium, and (*c*) noncancellable forms with right to increase premium.

Renewable at Option of Insurer

In this category are to be found three classifications of policies that afford the insurer the right to refuse to renew on any premium-paying date. There are policies that are: (*a*) cancellable at any time, (*b*) not cancellable but renewable at the option of the insuring company, and (*c*) not cancellable but with the insurer's right to refuse to renew restricted.

Policies that are cancellable at any time follow the casualty pattern and afford the insurer not only the right to refuse to renew whenever any renewal premium is due but also the right to cancel the policy at any time on five days' written notice to the insured. When a policy is canceled on any date other than a renewal date, the insured is entitled to a return of the unearned premium computed on a prorata basis. Policies that reserve the right of cancellation to the insurer must also afford the same privilege to the insured.

Policies that are noncancellable but renewable at the option of the insuring company differ from policies that are cancellable at any time in that they may not be canceled during the policy term. The trend in this area today as regards cancellable or optional renewable policies is nonrenewal rather than cancellation. In fact, some cancellable or optional renewable policies are including a provision in the contract of nonrefusal of renewal solely for deterioration of health. In the instance of policies of this category where the insurer may, upon notice to the insured, refuse to renew the policy and discontinue protection, the term "noncancellable" is sometimes erroneously applied. Care should be exercised with this use of the term. A noncancellable contract in the true sense is one that is renewable for a term, or to a given age, at the option of the insured and without any right of the insurer to terminate coverage.

Finally, there are policies which are noncancellable except for certain restricted rights reserved to the insurer to refuse renewal. In policies of this category it is usual to specify in the contract the reason for which renewal may be refused accompanied by an agreement not to refuse renewal for any other reason.

Where the company reserves the right to renew, that is, to discontinue coverage at the end of each yearly period, the company is not only able to give a broader coverage for lower premiums but it also can experiment with new forms of coverage with greater freedom. With optional renewal there is always a way to retire from a line if experience proves the underwriting to be unsound. It is estimated that more than 85 percent of the health insurance policies issued to individuals are so written. However, the guaranteed renewable forms are growing in favor.[19]

Noncancellable with Guaranteed Premium

For permanent coverage a policy must be not only noncancellable but also must be guaranteed renewable for a given period at an agreed-upon premium plan. In such a situation no injury or illness will bring about a termination of coverage within the period fixed at the time the insurance is written. The National Association of Insurance Commissioners has given thought to the minimum requirements for a permanent program.[20]

A noncancellable health policy is defined as a policy which may be renewed at the option of the insured to a given age. This age may be sixty or sixty-five, although policies are written with a limiting age of fifty. The premium rate is guaranteed for the life of the policy. In other words, if premiums are paid when due, the insurance company cannot refuse to renew the policy.

The term "noncancellable" provides for the renewal of the policy, but indicates a specified period within which the insured has the right of renewal. If issued before or at age forty-four, the policy must be continued to age fifty. A noncancellable policy issued after the age of forty-four must be renewable for at least five years and provide maximum benefits for a period of ten years or to the age of sixty-five. A "guaranteed renewable" policy must meet these same requirements, but the premiums may be changed by classes. A promising development offered by some companies guarantees renewal for life with premiums paid up at age sixty-five. The objective is to enable the insured to provide during his earning period for disabilities that may develop after retirement.

The premium rates for policies in this category are considerably higher (two, three or more times) than for policies where the company has the option to refuse renewal. This is so because experience

[19]Advocates of cancellable policies contend that they offer sound protection at the lowest possible cost. They point out that it is easier to insure a doubtful health risk on a cancellable basis. For all practical purposes it is contended that cancellable policies form permanent protection since they usually remain in force from year to year. A 1956 study by the National Association of Insurance Commissioners has shown that only 3/10 of 1 percent of cancellable policies are either canceled or not renewed. This works out to a record of 99.9 percent of the holders of cancellable policies having permanent insurance. The record is impressive, but for the individual whose physical condition has deteriorated the loss of his insurance could be serious. *Cancellable Accident and Health Insurance—a Study and Recommendations,* Industry Study Made at the Request of the National Association of Insurance Commissioners.

[20]Report to the National Association of Insurance Commissioners' Subcommittee on Definition of Non-Cancellable Insurance and Guaranteed Renewable Insurance, December, 1959.

shows that disability increases with age. With a premium remaining the same for the life of the contract, it is apparent that it will be higher in the early years than is necessary to meet claims and lower in the the later years. This being the case the company is required to set up a reserve exactly the same as is required for level premium life insurance.

Noncancellable with Right to Increase Premiums

Policies providing hospital and medical expense benefits involve not only the contingency of sickness but also the uncertainty of the increasing cost of medical care. For this reason policies which may be renewed at the sole option of the insured may contain the provision that the insured may have the right to increase premiums at renewal. In this respect it is important to note that the company cannot increase the premium on the individual insured but must change it by class. While policies providing an increase in premium by class at renewal were originally issued in connection with hospital and surgical benefits, there are now also some income policies on this basis. This form has been found useful in providing so-called "senior citizen" coverage. Hospital-surgical coverage guaranteed renewable with the right to increase premiums by class is available to new applicants to age seventy-five or higher in the area of basic coverage. Other liberal forms are available, and the fact that premiums may not be increased on the policy of the individual insured but only on an entire class affords the insured a wide area of security as respects coverage and stability of premium.

The N.A.I.C. recommendations reflect what is considered good practice today. It can be seen, therefore, that the term "noncancellable" used in connection with a health policy has a limited meaning. Policies may be sold with a shorter noncancellable period than provided in the above recommendations. Such policies should show clearly on their faces the period during which the policyholder has the right to continue the policy. Policies written for a term shorter than that outlined in the above recommendations are not now considered noncancellable in the sense understood by the industry. A noncancellable contract in the true sense is one that is renewable for a term or to a given age, as indicated in the quoted recommendations, at the option of the insured and without any right of the insurer to terminate coverage.

OTHER PROVISIONS IN A TYPICAL HEALTH POLICY

Although a "typical" health contract is as hard to find as the hypothetical "average" man of the U.S. Census Bureau statistics, this section endeavors to describe some of the more important provisions of such a policy. No one specific contract is used as a model; health contracts vary too much among companies and kinds of policies. The best advice to be given to the health insurance policyholder is to read *his* contract, for only then can he tell exactly what his rights and obligations are—and he probably will need the help and advice of a good life, health, or casualty insurance agent to do that.

Many of the provisions discussed in this section are those of the usual (which the student should now recognize as having many variations in the health insurance field) health insurance contract for medical expenses and loss of income. For most individuals or families it is a contract purchased in addition to (1) a hospital-surgical policy and (2) a major medical expense policy. If so, then the medical expenses can be eliminated in the schedule of benefits which applies, and the loss of income becomes the predominant feature of the contract. Oftentimes, the contract may still be titled as an "accident and health" or "accident and sickness" policy. Normally, the provisions discussed here are those found in the cancellable type of contract issued by casualty insurers, i.e., the kind which may be renewed at the option of the insurance company. The provisions, except for the renewability feature, may be quite similar in most of their details to the noncancellable and guaranteed-renewable contracts issued by most life insurers and some casualty insurers.

The general form and content of the insurance policy may be divided into three principal divisions: (*a*) the *policy face and application,* (*b*) the *benefit provisions,* and (*c*) the *standard provisions.*

Policy Face and Application

Briefly, the policy face contains the essential elements of an insuring agreement between the insurer and insured. A summary of the coverage and benefits, a statement of the renewability features, and a reference to the application are usually found here.

The application is required by the company as a basis for the contract. The company relies upon the statements made therein for much of its underwriting information. All states require that the application be attached to the policy form; and both together constitute the contract.

The printed policy face contains the corporate name of the insurer, and it should express the times when the insurance takes effect and terminates. The entire consideration for which the policy is issued should appear in the contract. If reference is made to any standard time by which to determine the term of the policy, the reference should be made to the standard time at the place where the insured resides.

The Application. There is no standard form of application for a health insurance contract, although the applications of most companies follow a general pattern. They undertake to supply the underwriter information that will: (*a*) identify the applicant, (*b*) give adequate information to determine the occupational exposure, (*c*) list health insurance benefits from all other sources and indicate whether insurance will exceed earnings, and (*d*) show past and present physical condition. Finally, the application concludes with an executing agreement. Under its terms the applicant agrees that (*a*) the insurance is applied for, subject to the conditions and provisions of the policy; (*b*) that the policy will not be effective until the initial premium has been paid in cash; and (*c*) that no claim for indemnity will be presented or allowed except in accordance with the policy terms. The insured indicates his understanding that false answers in the application may be used to bar recovery in the event that the answer is material to the acceptance of the risk or the hazard assumed by the company.

When the written application is regarded as part of the consideration for the issuance of the policy, as is usually the case, a copy of the application should be made a part of the policy by attachment or endorsement. The application should be composed of straightforward questions requiring factual answers to be supplied by the applicant. The questions should be so phrased as to be direct interrogatories that permit answers in the form of direct statements of known facts. An application that requires representations based upon indefinite or ambiguous terms or that are in any way inconsistent with the standard provisions of the policy is to be avoided. There should be nothing in the application that would directly or by implication construe the answers made by the applicant as warranties.

Accident Insuring Clause. While the insuring clause providing benefits for accidental injuries follows to some extent the same general pattern, differences in wording that may seem inconsequential to the layman may have the effect of limiting the scope of the coverage. A clause may provide benefits for "bodily injury sustained through accidental means" or the clause may read "accidental bodily injuries." These two clauses point up the difference between a policy that by virtue of its terms covers injury attributable to "accidental means" and one that covers only unintended injuries that are accidental. The importance of the difference evidences itself when it is realized that nearly half of all injuries are the consequence of an intended act and not attributable to an accident.

The "accidental bodily injuries" coverage is the broader and preferable form even in the light of liberal interpretation of the "accidental means" insuring clause. Due to the significance of the different coverages, some consideration of the interpretation of the term "accident" in an insuring clause may be helpful.

A popular or generally understood definition of the term "accident" may not be adequate for the purpose of determining whether or not loss falls within the protection of a policy. In its wording the policy covering "loss attributable to accidental means independent of any other cause" is considerably less broad than a policy containing an insuring clause that reads "against loss resulting from accidental bodily injury."

The term "accidental means" requires special notice. Formerly accidental means was distinguished from an accidental result; and while both could have been covered in some contracts, this was not always the case. There can be no question that the intent of the policy covering loss effected through accidental means is to cover losses that are the results of accidents and nothing else. It must be pointed out, therefore, that unforeseen results of an action that is intended and carried out in accordance with the intent of the person performing the act is not within the scope of the coverage. To constitute an accident, there must have been some event both unexpected and beyond the control of the injured party.

This difference is illustrated by the following example. A man piling wood strains his back and, as a result, is unable to work for two weeks. In piling the wood he did exactly as he intended to do, though the injury to his back was a consequence. There was no accident; therefore, such an injury would not fall within the protection afforded by the insuring clause covering losses attributable to accidental means. If, while piling the wood, the man had slipped and injured himself or dropped a piece of wood with a resulting injury, he would not have done as he intended. There would have been an accident, and the loss, therefore, would have been the outgrowth of an injury effected through accidental means.[21]

There are policies in which the insuring clause reads "through external, violent, and accidental means." Obviously, this clause is considerably more restricted than the one quoted. The words "external and violent" have been eliminated from most of the policies now written. It is well to recognize, however, that their use tends to narrow the coverage considerably.

In contrast to an injury caused by accidental means, there is the situation in which an injury flows from the voluntary act of the injured person when the act is carried out in the ordinary and usual way. The consequence or injury is said to be accidental, but there is no accidental means. Courts have tended to hold the result to be

[21]The United States Supreme Court in 1889 defined "accidental means" in the following terms when it stated ". . . if a result is such as follows from ordinary means, voluntarily employed, in a not unusual or unexpected way, it cannot be called a result effected by accidental means." The Court further stated: ". . . if, in the act which precedes the injury, something unforeseen, unexpected, unusual occurs which produces the injury, then the injury has resulted through accidental means" (*United States Mutual Accident Association* v. *Barry*, 131 U.S. 100).

caused by accidental means if there is any slip or mishap in connection with the performance of the act that caused the disability. The broadest accident policies cover against "accidental bodily injuries" and omit any reference to accidental means. The coverage with the elimination of the accidental-means limitation is broader, and the premium is adjusted accordingly.

It is the intent of the accident insurer to cover disabilities attributable directly to accidents or, in some instances, disabilities that are the accidental consequences of a deliberate act. The policy does not undertake to cover losses attributable to disease or losses to which disease contributed. The phrase "independently of all other causes" that appears in the insuring clauses of many accident policies is very broad and if literally interpreted might nullify the intent of the contract. For this reason court interpretations have tended to favor the insured as against the company. As a consequence, it is now the rule that, if a disease follows an accident as a natural or inevitable consequence, the accident is regarded as the cause of the injury or death. The situation is not changed if the insured is afflicted with the disease before the accident, provided the accident produces results otherwise unlikely. The courts have definitely held that an injury that might naturally produce death in a person in a poor state of health is the cause of his death if he dies by reason of it, even if he would not have died had his previous health been different.[22]

Finally, there is the situation in which there is little evidence of the cause of a death except that it involved violence. For example, when an insured dies as the result of injuries received at the hands of another, the legal doctrine of presumptions operates to hold that the injuries were accidental rather than intentionally inflicted.[23]

---

[22]In the strictest sense, if a disease or infirmity contributes to the disability, the accident policy would not be liable. Defining disease it has been stated: "The words 'disease' and 'bodily infirmity' are construed to be practically synonymous and to refer only to some ailment or disorder of an established or settled character to which the insured is subject, an ailment or disorder which materially impairs, weakens, or undermines the condition of the insured and is so considerable or significant that it would be characterized as disease or infirmity in the common speech of men. These words do not include a mere frail general condition so that the powers of resistance are easily overcome, a tendency to disease, a temporary weakness nor a normal physical change that inevitably accompanies advancing years" (*Bergeron* v. *Prudential Insurance Company of America,* 14 CCH Life Cases 592; 75 Atl. 709). Justice Cardozo, in the now often quoted case of *Silverstein* v. *Metropolitan Life Insurance Company* (254 N.Y. 81; 171 N.E. 914), stated: "A policy of insurance is not accepted with the thought that its coverage is to be restricted to an Apollo or a Hercules."

[23]*Sheppard* v. *The Midland Mutual Life Insurance Company,* 13 CCH Life Cases 1001; 152 Ohio 6; 87 N.E. (2d) 156. In this case the court stated: "One of the well-recognized presumptions of the law is that, where it is shown that death resulted from bodily injury caused by violent and external means without a showing as to how the injury was in fact sustained, there is a presumption that death did not result from suicide, self-infliction of injury, criminal assault of another, or voluntary employ-

The Benefit Provisions

The benefit provisions indicate the amount and nature of benefits for which the company is liable for stated disabilities. Benefits payable under a health insurance policy are payable directly to the named insured except that, in the case of benefits payable in the event of the death of the insured, payment is made to a beneficiary designated in the contract. Since it is through the benefits that the policy undertakes to attain the objective in whole or in part of protecting incomes and reimbursing insureds for expenses incident to disabilities, some of the various available benefits will be individually noticed. The more important of these to be found in disability policies under the classification of benefits are: (*a*) *death* benefits, (*b*) *dismemberment*, (*c*) *total disability*, (*d*) *partial disability*, (*e*) *elective indemnities*, (*f*) *double indemnities*, (*g*) *medical expense benefits*, (*h*) *identification*, and (*i*) *waiver-of-premium* benefit. Since the first benefit, for death, is similar to accidental death benefits already discussed in Chapter 24, no further mention of these will be made here.

Dismemberment or Loss of Sight Benefits. Many health insurance policies that provide benefits for loss of time contain a provision for the payment of lump sums for loss of sight or limbs instead of the weekly or monthly income benefits, but only if the disability is caused by an accident. It is customary to express the lump sums so provided in a multiple of the weekly or monthly benefit. Column 1 in Table 26–1 gives an example.

If no weekly indemnity is provided, it is customary to indicate the indemnity for dismemberment and loss of sight in terms of the principal sum (or death benefit) as shown in Column 2 of Table 26–1.

TABLE 26–1

Dismemberment and Loss of Sight Benefits

	Column 1	*Column 2*
For Loss of:	*Sum Equal to Indemnity for:*	*Sum Equal to:*
Both hands, both feet, or sight of both eyes	200 weeks	Principal sum
Hand and foot	200 weeks	Principal sum
Hand or foot and eye	200 weeks	Principal sum
Hand or foot	100 weeks	½ principal sum
Sight of one eye	65 weeks	⅓ principal sum
Thumb and index finger	50 weeks	¼ principal sum

ment of the means causing death. . . . And even though it is shown that the injuries causing death were received at the hands of another, the presumption is that such injuries were accidentally rather than intentionally inflicted. . . . The reason generally assigned for the recognition of this presumption in the law is that it is man's natural instinct to avoid injury and preserve life; that it is highly improbable that he will intentionally take his own life or inflict injury upon himself, and that ordinarily a third person will not intentionally and criminally inflict injury upon another."

Blindness and dismemberment benefits are often given prominence in the policy and may mistakenly be regarded as an added and attractive feature. As a matter of fact if the policy gives the company the right to substitute a lump-sum payment for continued income payments it may be less broad than a policy providing income payments only. It is preferable that accidental disabilities should receive the same treatment accorded sickness disabilities. A person becoming disabled with a chronic disease would receive a continued income whereas if the policy gives the company the right to make a lump-sum settlement the accident protection may be less broad than the sickness protection. If the disability period is reasonably long, then a health policy that pays income rather than lump sums for blindness and dismemberment, both for sickness as well as accident, provides better coverage than the policy with a special lump-sum benefit.

In connection with these disabilities, when loss of sight is covered, to establish a claim under the policy, the loss of sight is required to be entire and irrecoverable. Some policies require, in order to establish a loss for dismemberment, that the member be completely severed at or above the wrist or ankle joint. Not all contracts are the same. As some policies are written it does not follow that in order to recover the entire member must actually be severed from the body. If as a result of an accident the member becomes practically useless, even though there has been no amputation, the member is lost within the meaning of the policy, and the insurer becomes liable.

Total Disability Benefits. It has been noticed that there is a wide range in the coverages afforded by the various health policies in the market. The definition of "total disability" under one policy may differ entirely from that under a second. For example, one contract may require house confinement as a condition precedent to total disability, while another may define the condition as "inability on the part of the insured to perform any of the duties of his occupation." A third policy may define total disability as the "inability to perform the duties of any occupation whatsoever." Over the years judicial decisions have interpreted the more limited definitions to the end that a broader protection was afforded than a literal application of the definition would seem to permit.

In the past there have been some unreasonable interpretations of the definition "any gainful occupation," and it was these interpretations that led some companies to broaden their coverages to make the insured liable in the event he was unable "to engage in his regular occupation." While this process of evolution was taking place within the business, the courts tended to interpret the "any gainful occupation" clause to mean something more than selling lead pencils on the street corner. If the insured was unable to engage in an occupation for which he was reasonably fitted by education and experience and which would yield him a reasonable livelihood, then the policy was held to cover. As a result of these court decisions the "his occupation" and the "any gainful occupation" definitions are interpreted to mean essentially the same thing. In other words, the "any gainful occupation" is not literally interpreted and does not deny benefits where real disability evidences itself. Some insurance companies still hesitate, however, to include the "his occupation" definition since they fear that they may become liable for claims where there is actually no real economic disability.

Largely as a result of these court decisions, company practices have been modified and coverage is now generally provided if the disability prevents the insured from engaging in any gainful occupation "for which he is reasonably fitted." The common statement of total disability appearing in modern health policies states: "(1) A period in which the insured is unable to perform any and every duty pertaining to his own occupation at the time of the accident; (2) After which period (commonly one year or two years) complete inability to engage in any and every gainful occupation for which reasonably fitted." Monthly disability income may be payable immediately upon incapacity or there may be an elimination period prior to the payment of benefits.[24]

Because of these differences, it is customary to further classify sickness policies as (*a*) house confinement or (*b*) nonhouse confinement; and again policies are classified as (*a*) requiring an elimination period or (*b*) without an elimination period.

Policies are written limiting benefits to that period of disability that requires the insured to remain indoors. Some policies provide full benefits for house confinement with a reduction of indemnity together with a limitation of the period of coverage for nonconfining disability. The clause reads in effect "confinement within doors." Such coverage is terminated when the insured is able to go out on his porch, take walks, and the like even though he has not recovered sufficiently to return to his occupation.[25]

---

[24]The elimination period is a deductible, and is that period at the beginning of a disability for which no benefits are paid. It may provide that weekly or monthly benefits are not payable for the first stated number of days, weeks, or months of disability under total and partial disability provisions of a policy.

[25]A chain of circumstances has tended to obliterate a previously established sharp line of division between confining and nonconfining disability. With the doctor shortage during World War II many patients that in the ordinary course would not leave home had no alternative but to visit the office of their doctors for examination and treatment. Insurance companies did not take advantage of this situation to terminate house confinement coverage. Once this precedent was established it became difficult to revert to the old and original interpretation. Added to the situation created by the

(Continued on next page)

Policies that make no requirement for house confinement provide better coverage. Insurance planners point out that the need of money for living expenses is quite as great during a period of convalescence as it is during a period of severe illness. The type of protection that best suits the needs of an insured depending upon earned income is one that pays benefits all through the period in which he is unable to work and not during a limited period of disability.

Quite definitely where house confinement is required the coverage is in many respects limited.[26] There may be long periods of recuperation where house confinement would be unnecessary but nevertheless the insured would be unable to return to his work. In cases of heart disease, influenza, pneumonia, and the like the period of recuperation may be long and outdoor exercise may be essential to recovery. Even where benefits are payable on a reduced basis this does not satisfy the purpose of the insurance if the insured cannot return to his employment. Rather than rely upon a liberal interpretation or accept a policy with limited payments at the end of the period of "confinement within doors" there will be no problem with a policy where house confinement is not required.

Partial Disability Benefits. Certain policies providing a weekly or monthly benefit may make payments of income at a reduced rate if disability is determined to be partial. Accident policies ordinarily recognize partial disabilities. When so recognized it is usual to provide that the disability manifest itself within a specified time following the accident or it must follow immediately a period of total disability. The shorter the period within which the disability must manifest itself the less favorable the coverage. Some policies are written with no time limit as to how soon disability must begin. A policy that requires disability to be continuous and total from the time of the accident is too limited since frequently real disabilities evidence themselves some time after the accident. For partial disabilities a percentage of the weekly or monthly benefit is provided. Fifty percent of the benefit is usual, though sometimes it is less.

---

doctor shortage, court decisions have tended to liberalize the literal meaning originally attached to the term "house confinement." There is some uncertainty now as to exactly what does constitute "house confinement." The interpretation placed by the company on the term, therefore, is of great significance. It should be noticed that the trend is in the direction of liberalization of coverage interpretation and the tendency is more and more away from a strict house-confining requirement. Many policies do exist, however, with house confinement coverage followed by nonhouse confinement protection.

[26]Some policies are also written with the provision that payment of benefits are to begin with or are related to the first visit of a physician or the date of the first medical attendance. If such a stipulation appears in the policy, it should be incorporated in the benefit clause to which it applies.

Many companies do not recognize partial disability attributable to sickness. It can readily be seen that the dividing line between no disability and partial disability is difficult to locate. However, some companies do make provision for partial disability. It covers only partial disability immediately following a period of total disability. The test of partial disability rests upon the inability of the insured to perform a part of his work. Some policies provide that if the insured is disabled and prevented by sickness from performing at least one half the work essential to his duties, he is entitled during such period of partial disability to one half the weekly or monthly benefit payable for total disability. The policy usually sets a limit to the period for which the insured is entitled to partial disability. This may be a number of weeks, months, or years, or until sixty-five years of age. When provision is made for partial disability following total disability a limit may apply for the total and partial disability combined.

From the standpoint of protection insurance underwriters point out that for employed individuals partial disability provides inadequate protection. Employees usually do not return to their work except on a full-time basis. For such persons partial disability is inadequate. It is pointed out, however, that self-employed persons may work on a part-time basis and for them partial disability supplements reduced earnings while so working.

Elective Indemnity Benefits. In some instances the insured may be offered an elective indemnity in the form of a lump sum, instead of weekly payments during the payment of disability. Such a clause is designed to make an immediate lump-sum settlement more to the advantage of the insured than would be the weekly payments during the period of disability. Table 26–2 gives a schedule taken

Table 26–2

Accident Policy Schedule

For Loss by Removal:	
Of one or more entire toes	$400
Of one or more fingers (at least one entire phalanx)	300
For Complete Dislocation of Joints:	
Hip	600
Knee (patella excepted)	300
Bone or bones of foot (other than toes)	300
Ankle	300
Wrist	250
Elbow	200
Shoulder	150
One or more fingers or toes	50
For Complete Fracture of Bones:	
Skull (both tables)	$650
Thigh (shaft)	600
Arm, between elbow and shoulder (shaft)	600
Pelvis	500
Shoulder blade	400
Leg (shaft)	400
Knee cap	400
Collarbone	300
Forearm, between wrist and elbow (shaft)	300
Foot (other than toes)	250
Hand (other than fingers)	250
Lower jaw (alveolar process excepted)	150
One or more ribs, fingers, or toes	100

from an accident policy, indicating the nature of the options offered under this clause.

Double Indemnity Benefits. Accident policies frequently provide for double indemnity in the event that the injuries are sustained under specified circumstances. Among those circumstances frequently mentioned are: (*a*) while the insured is a passenger in or upon a public conveyance provided by a common carrier for passenger service (including the platform, steps, or running board of such conveyance); (*b*) while he is a passenger in an elevator car, provided for passenger service only, other than elevator cars in mines; or (*c*) while he is in a building whose outer walls collapse, or in a building that burns, if he is therein at the time of the collapse or commencement of the fire. Double indemnity is also granted if injuries are received: (*a*) by the explosion of a steam boiler, (*b*) by a hurricane or tornado, or (*c*) by a stroke of lightning.

As in the case of the double indemnity feature in the life insurance contract, this benefit is devoid of logic. Dependents of a deceased insured have the same needs whether the accident that causes death is lightning, providing double indemnity, or a fall down a flight of stairs where only the principal sum is paid. Or to cite another example, today busses and taxis are construed as common carriers. An accidental death in a taxi calls for double indemnity, but an accidental death in one's own car provides only single in-indemnity.

Some of these benefits take on the characteristic of "window dressing." The chance of securing the additional benefit is often extremely remote, yet it is frequently held out to the insured as an attractive feature to encourage him to buy the particular contract.

Medical Expense Benefits. When provision is made in the policy for hospital expenses it may provide coverage in one of three ways: (1) by percentage increase in the total disability income benefit, commonly 50 percent, (2) a per diem allowance for daily hospital room and board usually with extra allowances for miscellaneous purposes for a maximum number of days, and (3) a blanket expense indemnity for treatment.

When surgical benefits are found in the policy, an additional indemnity is provided in case the insured contracts a disease covered by the policy, by reason of which an operation is necessitated within a designated number of days from the commencement of the period of total disability. The period is usually 90 days. A schedule of amounts is ordinarily provided in the policy, and the amount indicated is payable in addition to other indemnities. Table 26–3 gives a partial list indicating the nature of a schedule of indemnities for operations. The surgical expense provision when contained in or ridered to a modern health policy provides coverage either by a schedule of allowance for the various procedures or again by a maximum blanket indemnity for all treatment. The coverage is in effect while the policy is in force and usually for 90 days thereafter.

Table 26–3

Schedule of Indemnities for Operations

Operation	Indemnity
Abdomen—Cutting into abdominal cavity for diagnosis or treatment of organs therein	$200
Amputation of:	
Thigh	150
Arm, leg, or entire foot	100
Forearm or entire hand	50
Thumb, finger, or fingers (at least one entire phalanx)	20
Toe or toes (at least one entire toe)	20
Chest—Cutting into thoracic cavity for diagnosis or treatment of organs therein	100
Ear, Nose, or Throat:	
Any cutting operation	20
Excision—Removal of:	
Shoulder or hip joint	200
Knee joint	150
Elbow, wrist, or ankle joint	100
Coccyx	20
Eye—Removal of	$100
Any cutting operation on the eyeball	20
Goiter—Cutting operation for radical cure, arterial ligation excepted	150
Hydrocele—Incision and treatment of sac	50
Incision for drainage	10
Inflammation of Joint—	
Incision into joint	50
Mastoiditis—Cutting operation for removal of diseased bone	100
Paracentesis—Tapping of:	
Abdomen	50
Bladder	30
Chest	30
Eardrum	20
Hydrocele	20
Joints	20

Where specified benefits are provided for dismemberment or surgical operations and the policy limits its liability to one such loss as a result of the same accident, hospitalization, or illness, the policy is not regarded as acceptable unless it contains a provision entitling the insured to receive the largest amounts so specified. Where alternative benefits are allowed, the policy should provide a time for making such election at least as long as the time allowed for the giving of notice of injury or sickness. The practice of the business is that the election must be in the best interest of the insured; therefore, when the disability in benefit amount goes beyond the elected sum the insured can return to the disability benefits.

Identification Benefit. This coverage makes provision for bringing notice of the accident to the attention of the relatives or friends of the insured if because of injuries the insured himself is unable to do so. Under a form widely used the company obligates itself upon the receipt of a telegram or other message indicating the nature of the accident to transmit the information immediately to the relatives or friends of the insured. The company further undertakes, subject to a limit of $100, to defray the expenses necessary to put the insured in the care of relatives or friends. The operation of this condition is dependent entirely upon the physical inability of the insured. It does not undertake to pay expenses of communication and transportation except when the insured is so seriously incapacitated that he cannot attend to these matters himself. Companies incorporating this provision in the policy usually follow the practice of providing an identification card or token suitable to be carried on the person of the insured.

Waiver-of-Premium Benefit. Policies are written containing a clause which waives the requirement of premium payments after disability has run for a given period. Such a clause might provide for a waiver of premium after 90 consecutive days of total disability during the indemnity paying period. This means that if total disability lasts more than 90 days and premiums are paid up to that time the policy cannot thereafter lapse during the total disability period. This provision is valuable because during a period of disability the needs of the insured may call for all his resources and he is not required to divert any of them to premium payments. More important, the policy will not be allowed to lapse during the period of illness by inadvertence through failure to attend to the matter of premium payment. In the case of a noncancellable policy that lapsed through failure to meet the premium payment because of illness, an insured upon recovery might find himself without insurance and so impaired physically as to make new insurance difficult or impossible to obtain.

The Standard Provisions

There is no standard health policy; competition has brought scores of contracts to the market. The nearest approach to a standard policy is to be found in the requirements laid down in the *standard provisions* acts adopted by the various states.[27] While there are some deviations in the laws as enacted, in almost every state they are substantially in accord with the Uniform Individual Accident and Sickness Policy Provisions Law approved by the National Association of Insurance Commissioners. Sometimes these clauses are called "general provisions" in the policy contract. In such case they may include some optional provisions in addition to the twelve "standard provisions" adopted by most states.

The standard provisions are concerned with operating conditions and are to be distingushed from the benefit provisions of the policy. Policies must be approved by the insurance department of the state of issue and exceptions in the policy must be given the same prominence as the benefits. It was at one time a requirement that the policy agree with the statutory provision both as to language and number. With the adoption of the Uniform Individual Accident and Sickness Policy Provisions Law, there has been a rec-

[27] Uniform Individual Accident and Sickness Policy Provisions Law, National Association of Insurance Commissioners, 1950.

ognition of the modern-day development of the health insurance business. The law is designed to provide sound future developments by permitting variations in policy provisions where statutory requirements are not appropriate to the coverage provided by a particular policy. While under the law each policy must contain the required provisions or approved corresponding provisions of different wording, there is sufficient flexibility to permit the company to experiment with more liberal policies and claim procedures.

Under the terms of the uniform law, designated provisions must be incorporated in every individual health policy issued. Certain of these provisions are mandatory and are termed in the act "required provisions," while others are permissible and are termed "other provisions." Their purpose is to effect a reasonable degree of uniformity in policies and to phrase important conditions in such a way as to make them understandable. They serve to eliminate the confusion and misunderstanding that attended settlements of claims when it was possible to write obscure limitations and exclusions into the contract. As noticed, there is no requirement with respect to a literal wording of the provisions.[28] This ordinarily provides no

[28]There are twelve required provisions. These are briefly summarized as follows: (1) The policy shall show the entire contract, and changes can be made only after approval by an executive officer of the company and endorsed on the contract. Agents have no right to make changes. (2) A time limit is set upon certain defenses. After three years, misstatement, except fraudulent misstatements, may not be used to void the policy or deny a claim. (3) A grace period, ten days for monthly premiums, seven days for weekly premiums, and thirty-one days in all other instances, is required. The insurer may insert cancellation privileges or the right to refuse renewal. (4) This provision covers reinstatement. Provision is made for automatic reinstatement by acceptance of premium after grace period, but the insurer may require an application for reinstatement and issue a conditional receipt for premium tendered. Insurance becomes effective on the forty-fifth day following date of conditional receipt unless the insured is notified in writing of disapproval of application. (5) Requirement that notice of claim be given within twenty days after occurrence or commencement of loss or as soon thereafter as reasonably possible. Notice given on behalf of beneficiary or insured is deemed notice to insurer. Provision is required for notice at intervals for disabilities that run for a period of at least two years. (6) It is required that a claim form shall be supplied the insured within fifteen days, and if not so supplied the claimant is deemed to have complied with all requirements of the policy as to proof of loss if he submits within the time fixed in the policy written proof covering the character and extent of the loss. (7) Proofs of loss are required. Failure to furnish proof within the time required will not invalidate or reduce a claim if it is not reasonably possible to give proof within the time if proof is actually filed as soon as reasonably possible. Except in the absence of legal capacity, a proof must be filed in any event within a year. (8) Indemnities payable, except periodic payments, are due immediately upon receipt or written proof of loss. The policy must state the terms under which periodic payments are to be paid. (9) This section designates the terms covering payment of claims for loss of life of the insured. (10) This provision gives the insurer the right and opportunity to make examinations and autopsy. (11) This section limits legal actions and provides that no action at law or in equity shall be brought prior to the expiration of sixty days after proof of loss has been furnished. In no case may action be brought after a period of three years. (12) This section covers the right to change

(Continued on next page)

problem since where substituted wording is utilized, it is usually the intent of the company to provide a more liberal treatment than the minimum established by the law.

The more important standard provisions concern rights of the policyholder to: (1) policy changes, (2) incontestability (after two or three years, usually), (3) grace period for premium payments, (4) reinstatment, and (5) change of beneficiary. The insurer is given the following rights in the standard provisions: (1) written notice of loss (usually within 20 days), (2) proofs of loss, and (3) right to examine the insured, and to autopsy.

An example of an optional provision sometimes included in the "general provisions" (along with the 12 "standard provisions") is the *prorating clause.* This clause is justified by insurance underwriters as a protection for the company against premium loss attributable to a carelessly completed application or one in which the applicant deliberately fails to make clear all of the hazards of his occupation. The clause states in effect that if the insured is injured or contracts sickness after having changed his occupation to one classified by the company as more hazardous than that stated in the policy, the company will pay only such portion of the indemnities provided in the policy as a premium paid would have purchased at the higher rate. There is a further limitation in that the company will keep the indemnities within the limits fixed by the company for the more hazardous occupation. This means that when a change of occupation or new duties added to an old job makes the new work "more hazardous," then the indemnity collected in case of disability will be less than that called for in the policy and presumably less than the insured expected to receive.

While there are arguments both for and against including the clause, a policy containing it is somewhat less liberal. A policy that contains a clause explicitly stating that there will be no reduction in any indemnity by reason of change in occupation of the insured establishes once and for all that there can be no reduction in the amount of the indemnity attributable to a change in occupation.

ADMINISTRATIVE AND UNDERWRITING PROBLEMS

For the insurance underwriter, the disability risk involves administrative difficulties that have in the past proved all but insur-

---

beneficiary. The insured has a right to make a change unless he has designated his beneficiary irrevocably. The "other provisions" section of the law deals with the rights of the company in the event of change of occupation or misstatement of age or if other accident and sickness insurance is carried. It describes the right of the company to deduct unpaid due premiums from claims, and treats cancellation conditions and stipulations concerning illegal occupations and the use of intoxicants and narcotics.

mountable. Malingering and fradulent claims have tended to swell the cost of benefits far beyond the expectations upon which premiums were predicated. Overinsurance has aroused the temptation to extend periods of disability that without insurance would unquestionably be temporary. In prosperous years, these administrative difficulties have been fewer than in periods of unemployment. It is an established presumption that depression, with its attendant unemployment, breeds unwarranted claims.

Perhaps the most perplexing problem is determining whether or not the claimed permanent and total disability actually exists. Certain types of disability, involving injuries that are readily apparent, cause little difficulty. There are many cases, however, where moral hazard may be a factor; even more disturbing are the cases of impaired health where the insured honestly feels himself to be totally disabled within the purview of the contract but where the underwriter does not agree.

Careful selection and the strict elimination of overinsurance have been suggested as solutions to underwriting and administrative difficulties. These two measures, together with a realistic attitude toward claim adjustment, will unquestionably help but have proved difficult in application.

Applying the Indemnity Concept

In many insurance contracts it is the usual and accepted procedure to limit the payment to an amount that will indemnify the insured for his loss. In property insurance, the face amount of the policy limits the liability of the company; but if upon the destruction of the property by a peril covered in the contract, it can be shown that the actual loss to the insured was less than the face of the policy, the liability of the company is limited to the actual loss.

Generally speaking, there is no way of fixing a definite indemnity for the loss of life. For health insurance benefits the situation is not quite the same. It is the intent of health insurance to make good to the insured: (1) the cost of medical care and (2) the loss of earnings directly attributable to the disability. It follows, therefore, that it is feasible to measure medical care costs, and to estimate reasonably the amount of income lost by the insured.

Life insurance underwriters undertake to limit disability income coverage on an indemnity basis. Because neither the number of insurance contracts that an insured may obtain nor the amount payable, other than the limit provided in the policy, is limited, control of overinsurance is primarily the underwriter's job. In terms of adequate insurance coverage, there is nothing to be said for overinsurance. In the light of its dangers, there is much to be said against it. Since the contract itself is not usually limited to indemnity (i.e., the insured does not have to prove he did lose a specified amount of income, and even an unemployed disabled person is entitled to collect under disability income contracts), the proper underwriting limits assume major importance in preventing overinsurance.

Overinsurance

Overinsurance creates a continuing moral hazard in the health insurance field. There is overinsurance when the aggregate benefits exceed the loss which the insured suffers. The difficulties attached to disability claim administration could be largely eliminated if benefits could be so limited that employment would be more attractive than unemployment with disability income.

The solution of the problem of overinsurance is not as simple as would appear at first glance. To be sure, human nature being what it is, there are situations where the temptation to prolong a disability is strong if it proves profitable to the insured to do this. Two opposing forces tend to defeat the reduction in benefits as a deterrent to unjustifiable claims. Too drastic a reduction defeats the purpose of insurance. A moderate reduction designed to provide an indemnity for inability to work and at the same time an incentive to return to work affords the ingenious fraudulent claimant opportunities for adjustment that vitiate the incentive.

In an attempt to provide adequate insurance and at the same time protect the insurer against overinsurance, the so-called "limit of issue" clause and the "limit of participation" clause have been devised for use in the contracts providing disability income benefits. The first establishes the maximum amount of benefit of indemnity which the insurer will provide for one person. The second establishes the maximum amount of benefit or indemnity in force in all companies of which the policy in question represents a part.

There is a provision in the Uniform Law covering the matter of insurance with others. This allows the company to reduce benefit payments if additional unreported insurance is found to be in force at the time the claim is presented. If the additional insurance has been reported prior to a claim, the company itself must take action either by adjusting the amount of coverage on a renewal date or taking steps to effect cancellation.

It is at once apparent that cancellation or reduction in the amount of protection cannot be effected in the case of a noncancellable and guaranteed renewable policy. Under the caption "Relation of Earnings to Insurance" the Uniform Law permits the inclusion of a clause known as the "average earnings" clause. It is optional, however, and many contracts may not contain it. The amount of benefit payable at any time is reduced if the insurance in force in all companies exceeds the earned income of the claimant (or specified percentage thereof, such as 80 percent) at the time of the commencement of disability, or his average monthly earnings for the two-year period preceding disability, whichever is the greater. The reduction is proportionate, and benefits are an amount determined by the relationship of the monthly earnings of the insured to the total amount of monthly benefits. The total monthly amount of benefits payable under all coverages upon the insured may not be reduced below the sum of $200 or the monthly benefits specified in all coverages, whichever is the lesser. The clause does not operate to reduce benefits other than those payable for loss of itme.

To avoid the duplication of medical expense benefits the policy may contain a provision for prorating benefits in the event of duplicate coverage not reported to the insurer. This clause, because it introduces problems and questions that are difficult to work out equitably and to the satisfaction of claimants, is passing into disuse. Duplication of expense benefits is now more often avoided as a matter of underwriting practice. If an application is made for a policy calling for expense benefits and inquiry elicits that there is a policy in existence providing similar benefits, the second policy will not be issued.

The crux of the entire underwriting problem is to provide benefits adequate to the needs of the insured and at the same time make a return to employment attractive. The unfortunate experience of health underwriters brings to light the fact that where disability income approximate earned income, the insured is frequently willing to readjust his living to the lesser income.

A disturbing problem is that of establishing benefits as a percentage of net, instead of gross, income. Not only are certain deductions made from a worker's pay, such as social security taxes, group insurance premiums, contributions to a pension plan, but there are other expenses incidental to employment, such as transportation to and from work, union dues, working clothes or uniforms, and lunch money. Added to these are withholding taxes, since disability income is usually free of income tax. A disability income may be substantially less in dollars than the total payroll income and yet serve the recipient as well as, if not better than, his take-home pay.

The problem becomes particularly acute in the lowest-income brackets. If income from the disability benefit is substantially reduced, it will be so low for the legitimate claimant as to defeat its purpose. This group must be included if the health insurance business fulfills its objective of making disability benefits available to other than strictly selected classes.

Exclusions and Limitations on Benefits

Some policies contain exceptions, reductions, or riders of a nature that limit benefits either in frequency or in amount.

Exceptions. An *exception* in a health policy is a provision whereby coverage for a specified hazard is entirely eliminated. It is a statement of a risk not assumed. For example, a statement in the policy that the insurance does not cover hernia would constitute an exception. Some policies provide that losses caused by hernia, sunstroke, freezing, or injuries where there are no visible marks, contusions, or wounds are to be considered only under the sickness provision of the policy.

Other policies except coverage while the insured is in military or naval service. A different form of exception dealing with the same subject matter limits liability only for loss resulting from military or naval service. Liability for certain types of diseases such as heart disease or pulmonary disease may be included as an exception. It is pertinent to note at this point that an exception which excludes liability for "chronic" or "organic" disease from a sickness policy is considered too broad and is not generally approved. Exceptions with respect to diseases should be stated in such a manner that there can be no confusion or misunderstanding as to the extent of the exception. A provision in the policy that the occurrence of a loss covered by the policy affects its cancellation as to losses from injury thereafter occurring is regarded as an exception. Some policies specifically limit coverage to the United States and Canada but in some instances may include Europe. If an insured is undertaking a particular trip for business or pleasure and insurance is required, it is customary for the insuring company to require a statement covering the important features of the proposed trip.

Because of the protection afforded by the workmen's compensation and occupational disease statutes to most people actively employed, some companies issue policies excluding occupational injuries and disease. These policies are known as "nonoccupational." The purpose of the contract is to provide health coverage and effect a savings in premium by eliminating what would be in part, at least, a duplication of coverages if occupational disabilities were covered both by the health policy and workmen's compensation coverage. The nonoccupational coverage has an appeal on premium basis only. This is so because compensation benefits do not always meet the family requirements for disability protection, and this may well be supplemented by a health policy without the occupational limitation.

It is customary for sickness and accident policies to provide that benefits will be payable for disabilities occurring after the policy becomes effective. In other words, it is the intent to exclude from coverage disabilities that have their origin prior to commencement of coverage under the policy.[29] Since it is not always easy to deter-

[29]In group underwriting, preexisting conditions are not a factor of eligibility. Only in connection with individual and family health insurance are they a matter of underwriting concern.

mine the exact time of onset of sickness, it is usual to provide in the policy that no sickness benefits will be paid for sickness contracted and commencing for a given period following the policy date. This period is known as a *probationary period* and may be 15, 30, or some other number of days. The term "waiting period" or "qualification period" is sometimes used.

The probationary period is particularly designed to safeguard the insurance company against applicants who fail fully to disclose knowledge of an existing disease or impairment. Insurance underwriters are particularly anxious to avoid speculative health insurance purchases by applicants who are either not feeling well or know of some incipient disability. The type of risk the underwriter expects to insure is the sound risk who anticipates no disability and shows no evidence of disability, but who may be disabled and thus require the proceeds of the insurance to maintain his family and protect his accumulations.

Not to be confused with the probationary period is the so-called *deductible period.* The probationary period is distinguished from the deductible period in that the former runs from the inception of the policy while the latter runs from the inception of the disability. The deductible period is used to eliminate from coverage periods of disability during which the insured will be on sick leave from his employment and receive full compensation. Or, perhaps it is used in recognition that a short disability of a week or so could be taken care of from savings of the insured.

The coverage is provided by attaching a deductible period rider to the policy. The advantage to the policyholder is that very substantial rate reductions are allowed. The disability benefits may be set to commence when the pay for sick leave terminates. The deductible period may be regarded also as a reduction in benefits, as well as an exception for the shorter disability periods.

Reductions. A *reduction* is a provision which takes away some portion, but not all, of the coverage of the policy under certain specific conditions. In the case of a reduction, payment is made upon the occurrence of a loss, but the payment is limited to some amount or period less than would otherwise be payable had the reduction not been incorporated in the policy. For example, the statement that liability for hernia is limited to one month, where the policy provides indemnity for longer than a month for other conditions, is a reduction.

Under the modern health policy reduction by reason of age is common. Policies sometime provide for payment of only a percentage of the full benefits after the insured reaches a certain designated age. A policy is not regarded as generally acceptable if it does not provide a reasonable period of full coverage prior to the age at which the reduced benefits become effective. Reduction of benefits for specified sicknesses or injuries (except in the case of partial disability under income policies) is not found except in "substandard" policies designed for the insurance of impaired risks. It must be pointed out, however, that individual company underwriting practices may reduce benefits, rider them out, or otherwise qualify them for a preexisting condition for coverage under normal policies. For example, there can be extra waiting periods on specified conditions such as tonsils, adenoids, maternity, and the like.

Riders. Normal health is usually a condition of coverage for a standard risk. However, policies are being issued today to people with impaired health, the specific condition being ridered out or otherwise qualified under the coverage.[30] A recent development provides for full coverage with an increased premium. The amount of the increase depends upon the nature of the impairment. Where an unrestricted policy cannot be issued the impairment *rider* provides protection against all disability hazards excluding only the causes of disability which exist at the time the policy is issued. Policies issued with an impairment rider ordinarily call for no extra premium, but there are situations where both an extra premium and the rider are required to get the insurance.

The rider is an important factor in providing disability insurance. Without its use many applications would otherwise be rejected. By means of a policy with a rider, complete and adequate protection is furnished with the sole exception of disabilities or incipient disabilities that have already manifested themselves. When a rider has been attached to a policy (for example, following an operation), the rider may be removed, after a period to be determined by the company underwriters, if no ill effects have evidenced themselves from the condition covered by the rider. It is not the intent of the insurance underwriter to require a rider limiting coverage when, from an underwriting standpoint, there is no longer a need for such limitation.

Within recent years the insurance of impaired risks in the field of health insurance has made important strides. Such insurance is now available for many types of cardiac conditions, cancer, diabetes, epilepsy, and the like. Several of the leading companies in this field

[30] A "rider" is an endorsement attached to a disability policy which has for its objective a change in the terms of the policy or an alteration in the coverage. It provides, in effect, that after a certain date the policy will not cover or extend to any disability resulting from a designated disease or condition. Some of the diseases and conditions for which riders are ordinarily attached to a policy so that it may be issued to an impaired applicant at standard rates include: asthma, hay fever, anemia, loss of hand or arm, neuritis, peptic ulcers, rheumatism, varicose veins, impaired eyesight, as well as a number of other weaknesses due to previous injury. In determining whether or not a rider is to be required for weaknesses that have developed as a result of previous injury, the underwriter gives consideration to the time elapsed since a disability attributable to the injury has manifested itself.

provide hospital-surgical substandard coverage through the seventy-ninth year. Some companies not listed as substandard wirters issue policies to substandard applicants.

Sometimes, instead of issuing a policy with a rider, the underwriter finds it necessary to ask the applicant for a *postponement* of his application for a period of time to determine what his condition will be following recovery from a disease or other impairment. There are situations which develop following an operation in which it is impossible to determine whether or not the person upon whom the operation was performed will be a proper subject for health insurance. Such a situation does not lend itself to a rider; but if the person concerned shows continued recovery over a period of six months or a year, then he may be accepted for insurance with or without a rider as the case may appear to the underwriter. There are also situations in which an individual has been involved in a number of minor accidents. The repeated injures may be purely fortuitous or they may be the outgrowth of some inherent tendency on the part of the applicant. By virtue of this delay the underwriter may determine whether or not the applicant is acceptable for insurance. In all such situations the underwriter advises the applicant to delay with a view to reapplying at a later date.

Factors Affecting Premiums

Benefits. One of the factors[31] having an important bearing upon the cost of health insurance is the amount and nature of benefits. Some policies are limited in their scope and provide benefits for certain kinds of injuries such as those occurring in an automobile or a common carrier. At the other end of the scale there are policies covering both injury and sickness with benefits so broad that provision is made for almost every conceivable disability. Obviously the cost must of necessity vary with the nature and extent of benefits.

Among the factors that have a bearing upon the cost of benefits are: (*a*) frequency of occurrence (*b*) cost of benefit, and (*c*) duration. It is at once apparent that for determining the incidence of accidental death benefits on costs only the rate of death by accident is required. In the case of surgical benefits both the claim frequency and the amount of the average claim have a bearing. Disability income benefits involve the frequency of disability and the average duration. The premium represents an aggregate based upon the

[31]The factors discussed here refer to those which are a part of insurance company plans. The distinctions in rating procedures for these "experience-rated" policies, and "community-rated" plans such as Blue Cross–Blue Shield, are treated in detail in Duncan M. MacIntyre, *Voluntary Health Insurance and Rate–Making* (Ithaca, N.Y.: Cornell University Press, 1962).

benefits provided. It may vary from as little as $1.00 a year for a limited accident policy such as issued to newspaper subscribers or airplane travelers, to as much as several hundred dollars a year for a broad medical expense and loss of income contract for almost all injuries and diseases.

In addition to the amount and nature of benefits, there are five other factors that enter into the computation of the premium of a health policy: (1) occupation, (2) sex, (3) age, (4) persistency experience, and (5) mortality.

Occupation. Health insurance manuals have an elaborate system of classification of occupations. On determining the occupation of an applicant who is otherwise insurable, reference is made to the manual, which will give the premium charge for the benefits required. In computing these premiums it is the custom to compute basic rates that reflect the average experience of all occupational classes. A reduction from this average is allowed for the less hazardous occupations, and increased premiums are charged where the loss experience is expected to be above the average. Obviously it would be a colossal and probably useless task to quote a premium for every occupation. Actually occupations are grouped into classes which are given alphabetical designation. To evaluate occuptional hazards and assign each to a class is still a task of no little magnitude.[32] The premium charge for a policy advances sharply from the lower-rated classes to the higher, and some of the more liberal policies are not issued at all to those employed in the more hazardous occupations. As a matter of policy, most companies refuse to accept either male or female risks engaged in any work or business involving a direct occupational disease hazard. The same is true if the applicant for insurance is employed under conditions held to be either unsanitary or unhealthy. These risks are classed as prohibited for occupational reasons.[33]

---

[32]The Bureau of Accident and Health Underwriters uses the following alphabetical designations for classes: A, B, C, D*, and D. The Health and Accident Underwriters Conference (now the Health Insurance Association of America) has four manual groupings designated: AAA, AA, A, and B. Both organizations are constantly evaluating occupations and adjusting rates to reflect experience.

[33]Included in the group are workers whose occupation requires the use of such substances as arsenic, mercury, wood alcohol, lead, pottery, acids, poisonous gases, or chemicals. Other typical groups include those engaged in deep-sea diving, tunneling below rivers, acrobats, wild animal trainers, furriers, tanners, and those engaged in dusty trades, such as woodworkers or granite workers. A few occupational groups are in the prohibited category not because of the likelihood of being disabled but rather because of the difficulty of underwriting the moral hazard. These risks include actors, artists, musicians, and others who are self-employed but who have no regular working hours or schedule. Such risks are insurable but are carefully underwritten. In some instances, only accident policies will be written for this latter group, covering death and dismemberment only. A final category for which monthly indemnity is refused is the retired worker who will suffer no loss from inability to work. Such an applicant may secure protection against loss of life or limb from accident, or medical, surgical, and hospital benefits.

Sex. The cost for health insurance benefits for women is considerably higher than for men, and when male and female risks are accepted for insurance, different rating tables are provided for each group or premiums are quoted as a multiple of those quoted for men. Disability income benefits for employed women run from one and one half times to twice the cost for men. Hospital, surgical, and medical expense benefits, exclusive of maternity benefits, usually exceed in cost similar benefits for males by at least 25 percent.

Much of the increased cost of benefits for women is due to the fact that claims are not only more frequent but last for a longer period. This results not only in longer disability income payments but adidtional costs for hospital, surgical, and medical care. There are in addition costs attributable to maternity benefits. In the interest of keeping premium costs down, some policies exclude benefits on account of pregnancy, miscarriage, or childbirth. Because there is a tendency to extend the period of disability while unemployed, some policies exclude benefits if the insured is not gainfully employed away from her residence. All of these factors tend to increase disability costs, with the exception of accidental death and dismemberment benefits, for women over comparable charges for men.

Age. The factor of age, while important, does not have the impact in health insurance that might be expected. Particularly, age is not the same premium consideration under cancellable or optional renewable policies in the fifty-year-and-under class as is found in life insurance. Premiums do not usually vary with each age. However, age very definitely is a factor of increase under noncancellable policies and guaranteed renewable policies; there premium charges range upward year by year by age of issue. All premuims are raised for the senior years, this being justified by the morbidity (sickness) experience tables.

In the case of cancellable or optional renewable policies between the ages of eighteen and fifty for sickness insurance, the factor of age is less important and many companies charge an identical premium for all but the more hazardous occupations. For accident insurance the rates are usually the same for a given manual classification between the ages of eighteen and seventy. An exception is to be found in accident policies providing a principal sum. Where this is the case, a slight increase in premium for each $1,000 of principal sum is charged at the age of sixty. Some companies increase health insurance premiums at the ages fifty and fifty-five. This has caused some dissatisfaction. To counteract it many companies level the cost over the entire policy period and charge the same premium without regard to age as long as the policy remains in force. Under the level premium plan provision is made in the premium charge during the early years of coverage for a reserve that would be available in lieu of a premium increase that would ordinarily be effected at fifty years or thereabouts.

Persistency Experience. Persistency is a very important factor in the calculation of level premiums for health insurance. Lapse rates for accident and sickness insurance are usually higher than for life insurance, but as in the case of life insurance they tend to decrease with duration. Since claim rates tend to increase with advancing years, lapses before the period of high-claim frequency will reflect favorably on premium levels. However, because expenses are higher during the first and early years, lapses during this period may tend to increase the rate level.[34]

Mortality. Rates of mortality of insured lives become a factor in determining premium costs. They are combined with lapses to compute the total assumed decrement. Rates of mortality as applied to disabled lives are combined with recovery rates for use in determining the cost of disability income benefits. Mortality is a negligible factor except for disabilities that cover a comparatively long period. This is so because in shorter periods disability income payments will ordinarily be terminated by recovery rather than by death.

Special Health Insurance Contracts

Several health insurance contracts have been designed for special situations which fall outside of the normal underwriting practices of most insurers. Some insurers issue health insurance coverages under professional overhead, professional accident, and homeowners' disability plans.

Professional Overhead Policies. Indicative of the specialization to be found in disability coverages there is a commercial disability policy that covers professional office overhead expenses incurred during disabilities. There is usually a waiting period before there is liability for payment on the part of the company. This means, for example, that a policy may provide that disability last more than 30 days before benefits are payable.

This is a form of loss-of-time protection with benefit payments monthly. The insured is indemnified in an amount equal to actual business expenses for rent, taxes, public utility services, wages of employees who are not members of the insured's profession, to-

[34]The lapse rate or persistency factor is a matter of concern to the insurance company and a source of waste to the insured. From the standpoint of the company there is the expense of writing and delivering the policy. Medical and inspection fees may run as high as $15, and there is, of course, the overhead of preparing and mailing the policy. Conservation of existing business is held by many to be more important than the securing of new business, and wherever there are lapses every effort is made to secure a reinstatement, and if this is impossible, to secure as complete information as possible concerning the reasons for the lapse.

gether with other customary expenses normally incurred in the operation of the insured's office.

The policy is offered to sole proprietors and partners. It is of interest particularly to architects, consulting engineers, dentists, doctors, lawyers, optometrists, and public accountants, to mention but a few. It must be remembered that this policy does not provide complete disability protection for the insured. It covers only business operating expenses incurred while the insured is disabled. It does not reimburse the insured for salary, fees, drawing accounts, or any other such remuneration. Neither does it cover income from pharmaceutical products. To cover earned income another policy is required.

Professional Accident Policies. Special plans have been made available providing sizable benefits for those whose professional activities would be seriously impaired as the result of an accidental injury. Members of certain professions could suffer a much more serious loss than those engaged in mercantile or other business operations through the loss of the use of fingers or a hand. Policies are written for members of the dental and medical professions as well as laboratory employees providing coverage from $5,000 upward for accidental injuries. Following is an example of such protection afforded by a policy written with a $100,000 limit: accidental death, total disability, or loss of a single leg, arm, or both eyes, $100,000; loss of use of either one hand, foot, or eye, $50,000; loss of use of two or more fingers of one hand, $25,000.

Coverage is provided on a 24-hour basis. It is usual to exclude losses due to (*a*) military service, (*b*) suicide, (*c*) disease, and (*d*) aeronautics other than while riding as a passenger in a licensed aircraft. It is the intent of the policy to provide sizable benefits for any accidental impairment that will seriously interfere with the professional income of the insured.

Homeowner's Disability Policies. It has for a long time been the accepted practice to write term life insurance on a decreasing basis in connection with the mortgage on the dwelling of the insured. The policy is planned so that if the insured dies before the mortgage is paid off, insurance will be available to liquidate the loan in full.

One of the most recent developments in the health field is a policy designed to make available to the insured funds to pay obligations in connection with the purchase of his home that he otherwise would have paid out of income but for a disability. The policy is designed solely for the purpose of making mortgage payments in case the insured is disabled due either to injury or to illness. The insured may receive benefits from other health policies for the purpose of maintaining his family.

The policy provides an inexpensive assurance that with the onset of a temporary disability involving considerable expense, the mortgage payments will be met. The policy is sold only to applicants who are purchasing homes under mortgages. Benefits are payable for a limited period, usually for not over two years.

When the house is purchased, arrangements may be made to include payment of the health policy premiums with the monthly payment on the house. In addition to the payment of principal and interest, a budgeted home purchase plan would include a prorata share of taxes and insurance. If the disability insurance feature is included, the first annual premium is paid when the mortgage transaction is closed. The monthly accumulations during each succeeding year assure a fund sufficient to pay the premium on the disability policy when it becomes due. The contract is a limited policy, covering only in amounts represented by the mortgage installments. Occupational factors are not considered. Since the policy pays only for a limited period, premiums are modest.

The policy is not designed to replace broader disability coverages. It does supplement the broader coverages, but the applicant who feels he cannot afford full disability protection will at least assure himself that his home payments will be protected and that he will not be faced with foreclosure because of a delinquency, in the event of a serious disabling injury or illness.

Several insurance companies now offer both term life and term health insurance in connection with the Homeowner's Policy. This innovation is one of the first examples of a truly "all-lines" insurance contract (see Chapter 19), combining fire, casualty, life, and health insurance together in a single combination policy. The coverages are usually included without a medical examination, based upon statements about prior and present health condition made by the applicant.

SUMMARY

The amazing but oftentimes perplexing variety of health insurance contracts is evidence of both the increased competition and recognition of the need for health insurance protection. As a multibillion dollar-a-year business, health insurance ranks today among the most important and fastest growing types of insurance.

Health insurance is written in either (1) *individual* or family plans (discussed in this chapter), or (2) *group* plans (treated in Chapter 27). The basic health perils of *injury* and *illness* are provided for in contracts of *accident* and *sickness* insurance. Some of the perils are occupational, while many are nonoccupational in nature.

Contracts of health insurance have the purpose of repaying the policyholder for losses involving (1) the cost of *medical care,* or

(2) the loss of *income* due to disability. Protection is offered in many contracts, ranging from very limited policies for specified travel accidents to very broad policies covering almost all kinds of injuries and illnesses.

Three basic contracts should be considered by most individuals and families: (1) a *hospital-surgical-medical* insurance (available in Blue Cross–Blue Shield, insurance company and other independent medical care plans), (2) *major medical* expense insurance, for larger losses of several hundred dollars or more, and (3) accident and health *loss of income* insurance. The third category is most neglected, although life insurance contracts sometimes provide some income protection, and usually include waiver for premiums, for total and permanent disability.

Life insurers are also important in writing much group health insurance, as well as individual long-term noncancellable and guaranteed renewable disability income insurance. This form of protection, and major medical insurance, have made the most rapid advances in health insurance contracts of the past decade.

Besides *renewability* of the contract, many other policy features should be carefully appraised. The definition of "accident" and the many different *benefit* provisions are essential parts of the health contract. *Standard provisions* do not make health policies uniform, but twelve such clauses required by most states do provide the policyholder and insurer with some basic rights and obligations.

The underwriting problems of overinsurance and moral hazard are partially solved by insurers through the use of certain *exceptions, reductions* in the benefits, and *riders* excluding some preexisting poor health conditions. Careful selection is essential for sound health insurance, and the factors affecting premiums must be closely scrutinized, such as occupation, sex, and age.

Among the many special health insurance policies are those designed for professionals, providing loss of income benefits to pay overhead expenses, and extra dismemberment payments. One of the newest innovations is an all-lines insurance contract, the Homeowner's Policy with disability insurance, which combines fire, casualty, life, and health insurance in a package policy.

FOR REVIEW

1. How would you outline the various classes of health insurance? Compare the different ways in which the whole field can be classified.
2. Health insurance contracts are noted for the extreme variability in the scope of the benefits they provide the policyholder. Briefly describe several examples of contracts which you consider as illustrating *(a)* the narrowest and *(b)* the broadest types of contracts.
3. Compare and contrast the hospitalization contract with the major medical

insurance contract as to *(a)* purposes of the contract and *(b)* significant clauses and scope of coverage.

4. What are the characteristic features of major medical insurance? Describe at least three carefully.
5. It has been stated that when major medical expense insurance is first suggested to a prospective insured, he usually objects to the deductible feature and the limit of 75 percent (or 80 percent) on the bills which the company is obligated to pay. Point out why these two features are an advantage to the insured.
6. Health policies for loss of income are written with waiting periods of one (or several) weeks or months. What reasons can there be for buying a policy with a waiting period as long as three or six months, or longer?
7. Which in your opinion is the more important health insurance protection: *(a)* weekly indemnity for loss of time or *(b)* medical, hospital, and surgical benefits? Explain your answer.
8. Health insurance contracts are written to provide substantial benefits if the insured is disabled by poliomyelitis, or the policy may include the so-called "dread disease" covers. What are the advantages and disadvantages of this form of policy?
9. Entirely aside from the moral hazard element, some underwriters contend that a noncancellable health insurance contract is both unsound and illogical if it provides for a life indemnity. Why? Is such a contract needed by most insureds?
10. How is life insurance related to the field of health insurance? What specific types of health insurance coverages are most closely related to life insurance?
11. What are the most important provisions you would look for in analyzing a health insurance contract? Explain briefly at least five such provisions.
12. Is "noncancellable" health insurance really noncancellable? Explain your answer, and indicate why this feature is important to the health insurance policyholder.
13. Which kind of a health insurance contract would you rather have (assuming cost is not a factor in your decision): *(a)* a "guaranteed renewable," *(b)* a "noncancellable" or *(c)* a "noncancellable and guaranteed renewable to age 75" contract? Explain your choice.
14. Are health insurance policies standardized? If so, discuss how; if not, discuss why they are not.
15. Distinguish between the coverage afforded by the insuring clause of an accident policy which provides coverage against injury through "accidental means" and the insuring clause which reads "accidental injuries." Why is this distinction important?
16. B, a diabetic, suffers a leg laceration, the leg becomes gangrenous, and amputation becomes necessary. In another case, C's laceration becomes infected, with resulting severe disability. Do the two situations raise any question of difference with respect to liability?
17. *a)* A, who was 60 years old, died as the result of a heart ailment. There was a red bruise on the side of his leg, and the claim was made that the leg injury was the cause of his death. Have the claimants, under an accident policy, a case?

    b) B, standing at the edge of a dock, fainted, fell into the water, and was drowned. Was death caused by illness or by an accident?

    c) C, in an effort to commit suicide, cut his wrist. Suddenly, changing his mind, he bandages it. The injury is not serious, but two weeks later an infection develops, and it becomes necessary to amputate the arm. What is the position of the accident insurer in this case?

18. B is unloading a truck and as he lifts a heavy package his foot slips on a piece of oily waste and he injures his back. In discussing the case with the insurance adjuster, B denies having slipped, thinking this will be evidence of carelessness. What is the effect of this denial?
19. B's policy provided $10,000 indemnity if he was disabled so as to be prevented from engaging in *any* work or *any* business for compensation. B became deaf and, because of the nature of his business, was obliged to close it out. It was contended that there were other occupations open to a deaf man and that the company, therefore, was not liable. In your opinion is the company liable?
20. X has a heart impairment and is told that it is useless to apply for health policy. To what extent, if any, are persons with heart impairments eligible for health insurance?
21. Explain the difference between an "exemption," a "reduction," and a "rider." Discuss the impact of each on the cost of a health policy.
22. B, an insured under an individual health policy that pays $300 monthly disability income benefits, becomes totally disabled. His monthly income at the time of his accident is $400. He also has a group policy carried by his employer that will pay him $200 monthly. If the individual policy has a clause concerned with the relation of earnings to insurance, what will be its impact on the group policy?
23. Is overinsurance in the field of health insurance a serious problem? Explain how it can occur, its relationship to the concept of indemnity, and what the insurer can do to prevent it.
24. Choose five important factors which affect the cost of health insurance contracts, and briefly show how the prices charged by insurers may vary according to each factor.

Chapter 27

GROUP HEALTH INSURANCE

THE group insurance field includes not only group life insurance and group annuities which have been discussed earlier,[1] but also group health insurance.

NATURE AND IMPORTANCE

As in the other group plans, master contracts are issued to employers, unions, associations, or trustees for the benefit of individuals and their families. The basic characteristics are summarized as: (1) three parties, i.e., (*a*) the insurer, (*b*) the employer (or other "policyholder"), and (*c*) the individual members of the group; (2) insurance based on group rather than individual selection or underwriting; (3) adverse selection reduced by minimum size group requirements, and restrictions on the freedom to choose the insurance, its types and benefits; and (4) simplicity and economy of administration, achieved by employer cooperation and employer contributions to the cost of the plans.[2]

By 1963 the health insurance written by insurance companies was nearly $6 billion, which represented 2.4 percent of disposable personal income.[3] Of the total, group health premiums accounted for over $3.5 billion or 60 percent of total health insurance written by insurance companies.[4] Group health insurance increased by three and one-half times in the decade 1953–63. The largest dollar increases have occurred in group hospital and surgical plans, as the result of growth of employee groups having these health coverages. Factors in the rapid growth have included collective bargaining and union requests for more fringe benefits, favorable tax treatment (premiums are deductible to employer, not taxed as income to employee), and the skyrocketing costs of medical care.

Health insurance for groups follows the pattern generally estab-

---

[1]See Chapters 23 and 25

[2]Jesse F. Pickrell, *Group Health Insurance* (rev. ed.; Homewood, Ill.: Richard D. Irwin, Inc., 1961), pp. 2–5.

[3]*Source Book of Health Insurance Data* (New York: Health Insurance Institute, 1963), p. 37.

[4]*Ibid.*, pp. 37–39. These totals exclude some $3.7 billion by Blue Cross–Blue Shield and other hospital-medical plans in 1962.

lished for life insurance. There are three contract forms: (*a*) group, (*b*) franchise, and (*c*) blanket. Most persons are covered on a group basis. As in the case of life insurance, certificates of insurance are provided for the individuals. Franchise insurance is sold to groups that are too small to qualify for group insurance coverage. Individual policies are issued instead of a master policy and certificates. Blanket insurance covers groups without identifying individually the persons insured. Examples are student groups, and members of a volunteer fire department.

Group health insurance may and often does cover dependents. In many instances an individual is covered by both group and an individual policy. If the group policy does not provide all the coverage required it may be supplemented by an individual policy. For many, however, the group policy may provide the only form of health protection.

Because of the greater opportunities for industrial employment urban residents are more frequently covered under group health insurance policies than are rural residents. Wherever there is a heavy concentration of industry a large amount of group coverage is to be found.

FUNDAMENTAL CHARACTERISTICS OF GROUP HEALTH INSURANCE

Following generally the pattern of individual health insurance plans, the principal kinds of group health insurance may be noted as: (1) *medical expense* reimbursement insurance and (2) *income reimbursement* insurance.[5] The first type provides benefits for all forms of medical care costs; the second pays for temporary or longer term loss of income due to disability, and accidental death and dismemberment benefits.

General Types of Group Health Insurance Contracts

For discussion in this chapter, the above coverages are divided into three classifications of contracts, two covering medical expenses, and one covering loss of income: (1) *group hospital-surgical-medical* insurance, (2) *group major medical expense* insurance, and (3) *group accident and sickness* insurance. Note that the last-named type, although it could conceivably include all health losses including both increased expenses and decreased income, refers in the group insurance business primarily to the income loss repayment for disability, accidental death, or dismemberment.

Eligibility Provisions

Insurance companies have their own underwriting requirements with reference to the size of the group. In some instances no mini-

[5]Pickrell, *op. cit.*, p. 13.

mum member participation is required by the insurer, but there must be compliance with the statutes of the state in which the employer is located. Where there is no minimum number of insureds, it is sometimes required that the total number must be sufficient to meet the minimum annual premium such, for example, as $100.

The first Model Group Accident and Health Insurance Bill[6] suggested the minimum size of the group to include at least twenty-five certificate holders. Subsequent revisions of the model bill reduced the number to ten, and the latest bill, in 1957, mentions no minimum size. The setting of minimums for the size of the group would thus be left up to the underwriting practices of the insurers. Some states do have group health laws or rulings which define group health insurance; 16 states prescribe minimum percentage participation requirements (usually 75 percent); and 28 states set a minimum size group: 4 require two, 7 require five, 16 require ten, and 1 requires fifteen in the group.[7]

All employees may constitute a group, or the employer may select a particular "eligibility group" based on: (*a*) length of time the employee has been with the company, (*b*) a certain salary range, (*c*) occupation, or (*d*) a combination of these bases. In addition to policies purchased by employers to provide insurance for employees, policies also are issued to such groups as members of labor unions or professional associations. A number of policies have been issued to associations or to trusteeships where the insurance is the outgrowth of collective bargaining with a union and the insurance is for the benefit of all the members of the union in an industry or an area.

Group health coverages, for medical expenses, may in many instances be extended to cover the dependents of the insured employee. Dependents' coverage may include hospital, surgical, some forms of medical, X-ray and laboratory, poliomyelitis treatment, and major medical expenses. Qualified dependents of a male employee are his wife and unmarried children less than nineteen years of age. Qualified dependents of a female employee are her unmarried children less than nineteen years of age. Stepchildren, adopted children, and foster children are included in the dependent category if they are actually dependent upon the employee for support and maintainence. If both the husband and wife are covered as employees, the wife is not considered a dependent of her husband. In other words, an employee may not be covered both as an employee and as a dependent.

As in the case of group life insurance, there is an area between the

[6]Recommended to the states by the National Association of Insurance Commissioners in 1940.

[7]Pickrell, *op. cit.*, p. 7.

individual policy and the standard group policy. Franchise or multiple acceptance underwriting in the health field follows very much the same pattern as that established in group life insurance. Each member of the group files an application containing essentially the same data as required for an individual contract. An individual policy is issued to each covered employee containing the statutory provisions applicable to individual policies rather than to group policies. Since, however, underwriting standards contemplate the whole group, these are considerably more lenient than are policies issued on a purely individual basis. Franchise health insurance ordinarily provides nonoccupational protection. Thus, taken in connection with workmen's compensation coverage, 24-hour health insurance is provided. Organizations not covered by workmen's compensation insurance, may be covered for round-the-clock protection.

Costs

Many forms of group health insurance, probably about 60 percent, are written on a "contributing" basis, with the individuals paying a share of the costs. In an employer group this means both the employees and the employer (policyholder) pay part of the cost of the plan. Other plans may be "noncontributory" with the policyholder paying the entire cost. The individual plan participants pay the whole cost of their protection in a few cases, but this is not usual.[8]

The premium charges for group health plans are based on the type, size and duration of benefits, and such other factors as sex, age, geographical variations and environmental factors pertaining to the insured groups.[9] The initial year charges are normally adjusted thereafter on the basis of the actual experience of the group, except for very small groups.

GROUP HOSPITAL-SURGICAL-MEDICAL EXPENSE INSURANCE

The group health plans which provide protection for medical care expenses do so on the basis of two different philosophies. Some plans cover essentially all the specified kinds of expenses "from the first dollar on," and are called *"first dollar"* coverages. Certain maximums are usually set, in terms of number of days of medical care, or in terms of particular maximum dollar limits. These may be set high enough to cover the costs of most normal losses, but often do not

---

[8] *Welfare and Pension Plan Statistics: Characteristics of 161,750 Plans Filed as of July 1, 1963* (U.S. Department of Labor, 1963), p. 14. This shows that of over 128,000 plans having group plans, less than 10 percent involved contributions only from the plan participants.

[9] Charles A. Siegfried, "Medical Expense Insurance-Group and Individual," in Davis W. Gregg (ed.), *Life and Health Insurance Handbook* (Homewood, Ill.: Richard D. Irwin, Inc., 1959), Chapter 44, p. 557.

aim at providing protection for the very large losses. These are the types of contracts discussed in this section, as subdivided into group *hospital, X-ray and laboratory, surgical, other medical* expenses, and *poliomyelitis* expense policies.

An annual survey[10] of new group health insurance plans show: (1) almost 99 percent of the group hospital plans also include surgical benefits, (2) more than 75 percent include in-hospital medical expenses, and (3) about 45 percent include diagnostic X-ray and laboratory expense benefits.

The second philosophy in covering medical expenses under group plans assumes that it is not of prime importance to the insured what kinds of medical care costs are involved. Instead, the plans aim at providing very high ($5,000 to $15,000, for example) maximum limits for *all* medical care expenses. These contracts are called *major medical* (or *catastrophe medical*) policies. Oftentimes, a deductible of several hundred dollars applies, and the insured is paid his expenses above the deductible on a "coinsurance" or share basis with the insurer. These contracts are treated in the next section of this chapter.

Group Hospital Expense Insurance

This coverage is designed to provide benefits to an employee (or other members of the group plan) who because of injury or sickness is confined to a hospital. The coverage is ordinarily written on a reimbursement[11] basis; that is, benefits are payable to the employee for charges actually made. It is usually written as a nonoccupational coverage, to avoid duplication of workmen's compensation benefits. However, there are plans which pay a flat benefit for room and board for each day of hospital confinement, paid without regard to the amount paid by the patient to the hospital. Since the reimbursement plan is the more widely used, this will be noticed here.

The benefits are classified as (1) other than maternity and (2) maternity. The other than maternity benefits are subdivided into (*a*) room-and-board benefits and (*b*) other benefits. Hospital expense benefits often are extended to cover dependents of the certificate holders under the group plan.

Benefits Other Than Maternity. For room-and-board benefits the policy provides a daily limit. This limit is usually not in excess of the

[10] *Group Health Insurance Policies Issued in 1962* (New York: Health Insurance Institute, 1963).

[11] By insurance companies, that is. The Blue Cross plans differ in that they promise to provide certain services, such as semiprivate room accommodations, rather than reimbursement for the hospital charges for such services. The group hospital plans began with service benefits provided to teachers of Baylor University, Texas in 1929. From this beginning, many hospital and insurance company contracts evolved.

charge made for semiprivate accommodations in the area in which the insured employee resides. Generally, the range is between $5 and $30 per day; normally it is between $15 and $20 per day. The employee is reimbursed for the amount of the charges actually made by the hospital. There is a flat sum established as a policy limit, and room-and-board benefits are payable until the limits for any one period of confinement have been reached. The maximum limits may vary from 30 to 150 days and the most common limits are 31 and 70 days.

Other benefits in the other-than-maternity category provide for the payment of hospital charges other than those made for room and board. The patient is reimbursed on the basis of charges actually made by the hospital for medical care and treatment. Professional services other than an anesthetist and professional ambulance service are not covered. The limit placed in the policy for these hospital charges is usually a multiple of the daily limit for other hospital charges. This may be a multiple of 10, 15, or 20 times and sometimes the limit may be much higher. Where limits are high, the plan may require the insured employee to bear a part of the cost after it exceeds a specified maximum. For example, a plan might allow for hospital charges other than room-and-board benefits to be 20 times the room-and-board charge and then agree to pay 75 percent of any excess up to a predetermined limit.

Maternity Benefits. Room and board and other benefits are provided on much the same basis as noticed for other-than-maternity benefits. A limit is established for room and board and other hospital charges that is a multiple of the daily limit specified in the plan; the multiple most generally used is 10 or 15 times. Employees and their dependents are eligible. The normal practice is to make employees insured on the policy date or within 31 days thereafter immediately eligible for maternity benefits. Otherwise the employee is eligible for benefits only if pregnancy begins while insured. In the case of dependent wives it is usual to provide benefits for pregnancies which have their inception while the employee is insured. This is not an invariable rule, however, and for the payment of an additional premium, immediate maternity benefits may be provided on the same basis they are made available for employees.

The policy may be written with a rider carrying with it the privilege of conversion to an individual policy under certain circumstances. It provides in effect that an insured employee may, without submitting evidence of insurability, convert to an individual policy in the event the group hospital expense coverage ends due to termination of eligibility or employment.

Maternity benefits are generally not available under the individual policy. However, these benefits remain in effect for nine months after the termination of group insurance plans unless the insured employee has voluntarily withdrawn from the plan. To secure maternity benefits after termination of insurance, the pregnancy must have begun prior to termination. The benefits that are provided are identical with those that would have been payable if the insurance had remained in force.

Group X-Ray and Laboratory Expense Insurance

Group X-ray and laboratory expense insurance is designed to provide benefits for diagnostic X-ray examinations and laboratory tests or analyses which are not covered by the group hospital expense policy. Since occupational disabilities are covered by many workmen's compensation laws, this form is written on a nonoccupational basis. The employee only may be covered or, as in the case of other group forms, the protection may be extended to include dependents of the employee.

The plan establishes a maximum amount as a limit for all payments during any 12 consecutive months. Benefits are payable for charges actually made to the employee for X-ray examinations or other laboratory tests or analyses rendered necessary because of accidental bodily injury or sickness. Payments are made only for diagnosis and not for treatment.

Usual maximum amounts set as a limit for payments during any 12 consecutive months range from $25 to $75. Benefits are not payable for any tests, examination, or analyses which: (*a*) are made in connection with pregnancy or resulting childbirth, abortion, or miscarriage; (*b*) are made for "check-up purposes" not incident and necessary to diagnosis of sickness or accidental bodily injury; (*c*) are paid for under any other provision of the policy; (*d*) are made during a period of hospital confinement for emergency care following an accidental bodily injury or for a surgical operation; or (*e*) are made during a period of hospital confinement for which room-and-board charges are made by the hospital.

Some plans modify the maximum amount of benefits by establishing a maximum amount in connection with all injuries suffered as a result of any one accident rather than having the limit apply to a 12-month period in connection with all disabilities.

Group Surgical Expense Insurance

As in the case of group hospital expense insurance, this is a nonoccupational form of protection and provides benefits to an employee covered by the policy in the event that a surgical operation becomes necessary. Benefits are payable whether or not the operation is performed in a hospital, and, as in the case of hospital expense insurance payment, is made on a reimbursement basis. The company is liable only for the fees actually charged by the surgeon. This liability is limited by a schedule of maximum surgical benefits that appears in the policy. For serious operations the maximum is about $200, but some schedules go to $500 or more. (See Table 26-3.)

The schedule of maximum benefits is designed to set a limit on the liability of the company for virtually all operations. Companies ordinarily agree to reimburse for any cutting operations which do not appear in the schedule, and adjust the payment to coincide with a comparable operation listed in the schedule. Insurance companies realize that surgical expenses differ in different areas and for this reason provide that the schedule of benefits may be increased. This is done by means of a multiple. Thus, maximum benefits could be made one and a half or two times the schedule that appears in the policy.

Obstetrical benefits may be provided, but policies are written either with or without them. When such benefits are provided, they may extend to both employees and dependents. Benefits are scheduled in maximum fixed amounts for the usual obstetrical services. Eligibility for obstetrical benefits is identical with that noted in connection with hospital expense coverage. Employees insured on the policy date, or within 31 days thereafter, become immediately eligible for benefits. In the case of dependent wives benefits are ordinarily payable only for pregnancies which have their inception while the insurance is in force.

With respect to benefits for which the company is liable after the termination of insurance, as in the case of hospital expense coverage, obstetrical benefits are covered for nine months. The obstetrical extension after the termination of insurance is not available if the employee voluntarily withdraws from the plan. In the case of other disabilities, if the employee or dependent is totally disabled continuously after the termination of the insurance and as a result of this disability is obliged to undergo an operation within three months, the policy covers.

Group Medical Expense Insurance

This form undertakes to reimburse a covered employee for doctors' calls. In some instances it may be extended to include dependents. There are a number of forms, of which the following are typical: (1) coverage for employees only, total disability required; (2) coverage for employees and dependents, total disability not required; and (3) coverage for employees and dependents, payable only if confined to hospital.

Doctors' Visits (Total Disability Form). This is a limited form which reimburses insured employees for expenses incurred in doctors' calls. The employee is covered on a nonoccupational basis, and there are no pregnancy benefits. The company is liable for benefits only while the insured employee is totally disabled. Dependents are not covered since ability to work is a criterion for determining total disability and complications might intervene in determining total disability for an unemployed dependent.

The policy provides a limit for each call, such as $5.00 for office calls and $7.00 for home calls, and a total policy limit is established for all calls. The limit for each call is set at somewhat less than the actual fee is expected to be. This makes the insured employee to some extent a coinsurer. It is intended by this means to prevent malingering and avoid careless abandon in calling for the services of a doctor. The policy covers whether the doctor's calls are made in the home, at the hospital, or at the doctor's office. There is a waiting period during which the employee must be totally disabled and unable to work before benefits begin.

The form is designed to supplement hospital expense insurance or other health insurance. Benefits may be paid on a "day" or a "call" basis. When coverage is on a "day" basis, there is no limit to the number of calls each day for which the company is responsible. In the case of coverage on a "call" basis the company is liable to reimburse the insured employee for only one call each day. When written with disability income insurance, the same waiting period is used. Benefits usually begin with the first day of total disability due to accident, with a waiting period of four or more days in case of sickness. In the case of benefits written on a call basis, the waiting period in the policy indicates the number of calls to be made by the doctor after the insured employee has become totally disabled before benefits begin. As in the case of "day" coverage, the policy may provide benefits beginning with the first call for disability due to an accident but with a waiting period of three or more calls for disability due to sickness. To satisfy the requirements of the waiting period the insured employee may not count more than one call each day. In other words, with a three-call waiting period, benefits cannot commence until after three days regardless of the number of calls made by the doctor.

Provision is made for a limited number of calls after the employee has returned to work. The calls covered are for the same condition which caused the individual to be absent from work. There is no payment for calls made at the time of a surgical operation or in connection with any injury or sickness requiring such an operation.

Doctors' Visits (Without Total Disability Form). A second form providing essentially the same benefits is available to provide coverage for doctor's calls where disability need not necessarily be total. This plan allows coverage to be extended to dependents. No maternity benefits are paid. Under this form a lower level of benefits, and consequent premium saving, is sometimes provided for dependents. It is sometimes felt that the illness of a dependent will not be as severe a financial shock as is the case when the wage earner is incapacitated. In addition to the exclusions with respect to surgical operations and calls connected with a pregnancy, this form excludes calls for medical examination or check-ups where such calls are not directly connected with an injury or sickness. Likewise, there is no liability for calls for eye examination or the fitting of glasses, or for X-ray examinations or laboratory tests.

Doctors' Visits (In-Hospital Form). Another form covers both the employee and dependents but benefits are paid if the insured or his dependents are confined in a legally constituted hospital because of bodily injury or sickness. The plan provides reimbursement for expenses incurred by visits of a physician to a covered employee or dependent while confined in the hospital as a patient admitted on the recommendation of a legally qualified physician. There is no coverage for visits to the home of the insured or the physician's office. Other than limiting the benefits to doctor's calls made at a hospital, the coverage is, in principle, similar to other medical expense plans. Particularly there is no coverage for visits of a surgeon following a surgical operation.

Group Polio and Dread Disease Expense Insurance

This form of group health insurance provides for the payment of specified charges for care and treatment of poliomyelitis or other specified diseases contracted and first treated while insured. The coverage is not written separately but is provided by means of a rider attached to other group policies. Ordinarily it is written with one of the forms of hospital and surgical expense insurance and may be written to provide benefits with a maximum amount of from $1,000 to $10,000. Coverage is provided not only for employees but for dependents as well. Where major medical expense insurance is a part of any group insurance program, the rider is unnecessary since the same benefits are provided under major medical expense.

Polio was the most common disease covered when these plans first appeared. Then, some plans also began to include the larger medical benefits for other "dread diseases," such as leukemia, meningitis, smallpox, typhoid, tetanus, and encephalitis. When so written, the group policy is similar to a major medical contract in a very limited form, since the benefits are only payable for a few particular diseases. However, the other important characteristics of major medical plans, deductibles and coinsurance, are usually lacking. This makes these plans a combination of both "first dollar" coverage and the "catastrophe" type protection discussed in the next section.

The coverage appeals particularly to the employer. The cost is comparatively low and may be borne entirely by the employer. If an employee or dependent is stricken with polio, it is a matter of great satisfaction to the employer to be in a position through his insurance program to see that the victim is cared for generously.

GROUP MAJOR MEDICAL EXPENSE INSURANCE

Development

The fast-growing nature of group major medical expense insurance is derived from (1) the rapid expansion in the use of the group insuring technique for many forms of life and health insurance and (2) the increased recognition of the essential need for protection against the burden of large medical expenses as a result of serious injury or illness. Since both group insurance and major medical expense insurance are primarily innovations of the past two decades, group major medical insurance is truly a modern type of health insurance.

The salient features of major medical insurance have already been noted in Chapter 26. In the field of group insurance the appeal for this coverage has been tremendous. Employers and employees alike have come to realize that the financial protection afforded by the usual hospital and surgical coverages is far from adequate if the illness is serious and prolonged.

Since its introduction in the early 1940's, group major medical insurance has become a highly competitive portion of the health field. The policies offered are not identical with all companies. In fact, one expert concludes that "it is. . . virtually impossible to classify . . . major medical contracts as to specific 'types' because of the many forms such plans may take."[12]

Basic Features

The different methods by which group major medical plans express their basic features may be used to differentiate some of the plans. Special attention is given to provisions which were not discussed earlier in regard to the individual major medical policies.

High Maximum Benefits. The most significant purpose of group major medical insurance is to extend medical care benefits to include payments for catastrophe-type injuries or illnesses. Contrary to most group hospital-surgical-medical plans, which are limited as to type and amount of medical expense, the goal is to provide protection for the larger losses. This is accomplished by using deductibles of several hundred dollars, while at the same time setting the maximum limits payable at high amounts such as $5,000, $7,500, $10,000, $15,000 or more.

---

[12]Pickrell, *op. cit.*, p. 44.

Maximum limits are usually set for each individual either as a lifetime maximum or as a calendar or benefit year maximum. Group policies contain a cutoff provision to forestall abuses when an illness has reached a stage where virtually no care is required and expenses are small. A popular approach to the cutoff idea is through the so-called "benefit year." This plan calls for the satisfaction of a deductible every 12 month benefit year. Thus, if a claim runs over 12 months and the expenses are low, the deductible relieves the company of payment. Another approach is to limit payments for any one disability for a period of two or three years but with one deductible for the period. A third method terminates benefits if the charges during a 60-day or 90-day period fall below a level established in the policy.

When the maximum amount has been paid on behalf of any one person, coverage with respect to that person automatically terminates. The maximum amount may, however, be reinstated upon submission by the individual of evidence of insurability. Since payments on behalf of an individual tend to reduce the amount of effective insurance, it may be desirable to reinstate coverage to the full maximum amount. Hence, it is usual to provide that after benefits have been paid for a given amount, of $1,000 for example, the insured individual may submit evidence of insurability and upon its approval the policy will be reinstated to the full maximum amount.

Benefits are paid for "a bodily disorder, mental infirmity, or bodily injury." It is normal to include coverage for preexisting conditions which cause disabilities during the term of the policy. On a group basis the insurer is able to cover preexisting conditions because unusual adverse selection is prevented. Individuals cannot select against the insurer, since the entire group is included in most of the plans.

All types of medical expenses are included in the coverage, with a few exceptions. The more important types for which protection is provided are: (1) hospital room and board, (2) doctors' services for medical care, treatment, and surgery, (3) professional nursing services by a registered nurse, (4) prescription drugs and medicines, (5) anaesthesia, oxygen, and X-ray examination and treatment, (6) blood, plasma, and surgical dressings, (7) rental of wheel chair, hospital bed, crutches, or other therapeutic equipment, and (8) artificial limbs or eyes. The eligible charges are usually only limited by the maximum amount, and by a general provision which requires that the services, treatments, and supplies be reasonably necessary for the care of the insured.

There are a few excluded charges, in order to prevent duplicate or unnecessary coverage: (1) compensable charges which are paid for under workmen's compensation or state nonoccupational disability laws, (2) confinement in a government-owned hospital (where the insured would not be obligated to pay in the absence of insurance), (3) war injuries, (4) eye, ear, and general health examinations, (5) normal pregnancy expenses, (6) dental treatment or cosmetic surgery, unless necessitated by an accidental bodily injury, and (7) self-inflicted injuries.

Deductibles. Different companies approach the deductible in different ways. There are the (*a*) each illness plan, (*b*) each individual plan, and (*c*) the family budget plan.

With the each illness type of plan the deductible applies to each separate disability. From the point of view of the insured, a weakness in the plan is found in the possibility that he might suffer from two or more disabilities at the same time and be obliged to satisfy the requirements of a deductible with respect to each. Under the each individual plan the deductible is collected but once from a given individual with respect to all eligible expenses incurred within a specified time limit. All expenditures incurred within a definite period time, usually a year, are subject to but one deductible regardless of how many different disabilities are involved. The family budget deductible applies one deductible for all covered members of a particular family with respect to all eligible expenses incurred within a given benefit year. This last plan is predicated on the assumption that one family head will pay all the bills and accordingly the best protection is afforded by the family budget deductible. While this may be so, in order to keep the costs within reasonable bounds a higher deductible was found to be necessary. This higher deductible tended to defeat the objective of the family budget deductible. The each individual plan now seems to be the most popular.

The deductible is designed to eliminate from coverage small claims. Payment of these small medical expenses imposes no burden upon the average family. If every claim large and small is a charge against the insurance, the cost of the coverage would be substantially increased without providing benefits of any importance.

The deductible varies greatly among the different group major medical contracts. It may be as low as $50, or as much as $1,000. Most plans use a deductible of about $200–$500.

Coinsurance. After the deductible amount has been reached, a "coinsurance" factor is applied to all eligible charges. Under this provision the insured pays a stipulated percentage of all the charges (over the deductible amount), such as 20 percent. The insurer pays the remaining percentage, such as 80 percent. The 80–20 plan is most common in the newer contracts, although the 75–25 plan is used in many contracts, and some other variations are in use. The purpose is quite obvious: to prevent overuse of the medical services provided for in the contract. By requiring the insured to participate in a portion of the costs, excessive use is curbed.

Primary Types

Group major medical insurance plans fall generally into one of two primary types: (*a*) integrated major medical plans and (*b*) basic medical plans.

Integrated medical plans, sometimes termed "supplemental," are written where there is already some group protection for hospital, surgical, or medical benefits. *Basic* major medical plans, sometimes termed "comprehensive," are written on groups which have no hospital, surgical, or medical benefits in force on a group basis or may be written to replace all other group health coverages (for medical expenses) already in force.

Integrated Plans. This plan is designed to coordinate major medical insurance with such other group health coverages as are written concurrently. It is the intent that there will be no possibility of double coverage.

At the same time, the deductible feature is retained. There are a number of ways of accomplishing this. A plan in wide use is known as the *corridor deductible*. The plan excludes from eligible expenses covered by the major medical expense insurance all payments under the hospital-surgical-medical plan. Then there is established a deductible, known as the "corridor" of uncovered expenses. A usual figure is $100 or $200. In the case of an illness calling for an outlay of $3,400, for example, with the hospital-surgical-medical plan covering up to $300, and a $100 "corridor" deductible with a 25 percent coinsurance feature, the company would pay $2,250. The basic policy would pay $300. Since the employee must pay the full amount of expenses over the basic coverage up to $100, there is deducted $400 from the total expense before major medical becomes a consideration. This leaves $3,000 for major medical protection, and since there is a coinsurance feature of 25 percent, the liability of the insurer is $2,250 and the insured $750. The total out-of-pocket expense to the individual employee is $850, representing $750 coinsurance and the $100 corridor deductible.

Basic Plans. There are two forms of basic plans described as: (*a*) standard and (*b*) special. The standard plan is identical to the integrated plan just noticed except that there is no underlying group hospital-surgical-medical plan. The special plan differs from the basic plan in that 100 percent coverage is provided for each separate hospital confinement. A number of variations may be introduced in both the standard and special plans. The most frequent of these are (*a*) a pregnancy benefit rider and (*b*) zero deductibles.

The pregnancy benefit rider provides benefits for doctors' and hospital charges incurred in connection with pregnancy. A zero-deductible provision may be applied to the eligible hospital charges or to the eligible surgical charges or to both. Hospital charges are for the most part fixed in advance, and the zero-deductible provision is written without hesitation. It is regarded as desirable, however, that the insured individual have a financial interest in the cost of his surgery, and a zero deductible applicable to surgical charges is less frequently found.

As early as 1954 insurance companies were being asked to quote rates on "comprehensive" plans. A policy was written in that year insuring approximately 500,000 employees and dependents of the General Electric Company. The success of the comprehensive plan unquestionably received impetus from this sale.

The appeal of the comprehensive major medical policy at the time of its inception was its simplicity. By combining into a single coverage the various basic benefits, the problem of coordinating the many coverages was eliminated. There are no internal schedules or limits of benefits that are ordinarily found in hospital and surgical expense plans. The concept of coinsurance and the deductible is maintained. Although the amounts and benefits vary, the basic pattern of the plan is simple. Indicative of the coverage afforded, a typical plan provides an initial deductible varying from $25 to $50 for all claims on a calendar year basis. As a concession to expedite admission to hospitals, full coverage for hospital charges is allowed. All other covered expenses are reimbursed on an 80–20 percent or a 75–25 percent coinsurance basis. There is a lifetime maximum for all claims which may be varied to meet the needs of a particular group. If the lifetime maximum is exhausted by any individual insured, provision is made for reinstatement with the presentation of satisfactory evidence of insurability.

There has been some tendency to veer away from the initial simplicity of the policy pattern because the market for major medical expense insurance and for comprehensive major medical expense coverage is competitive and complex. It is not surprising, therefore, that within a very short time a large number of different types of plans appeared in the market. Prospects did not take kindly to the deductible approach, especially insofar as hospital charges were concerned. It was only after the ideas of catastrophe insurance and a form of "first-dollar" coverage in package form were developed that comprehensive major medical expense insurance became of age.

Recently there has been pressure for a modification of the concept of coinsurance and a further extension of first-dollar coverages. Creating first-dollar coverage for hospital charges has raised the question as to whether or not the concept should be extended into other areas. This has been particularly suggested with respect to the reimbursement for charges made by surgeons. Insurers, however, point out how the extent to which first-dollar coverage is allowed and how the reduction of the insured's coinsurance percentage increases the overall cost of the coverage.

GROUP ACCIDENT AND SICKNESS INSURANCE

In addition to covering medical expenses, group health plans often provide disability *loss of income.* These forms are known as "accident and sickness" insurance, although care should be taken to recognize them as income rather than medical expense reimbursement plans.

Definition of Disability

They are designed primarily as supplemental coverage to workmen's compensation insurance. Under the form the company agrees to pay the designated benefits "if the employee shall become wholly and continuously disabled as a result of nonoccupational accidental bodily injuries or nonoccupational sickness, and thereby be prevented from performing any and every duty pertaining to his employment." While different companies vary in the wording of their policies the quotation from the insuring clause indicates the nature of the protection the company undertakes to provide.

Policies provide for a waiting period, though it is usual in case of disability due to injury to have benefits begin with the first day of disability. In the case of sickness, in order to reduce administrative expense attributable to claims originating from minor illnesses, a waiting period is the standard practice. Three days is about as short a period as is acceptable from an underwriting point of view. A period of seven days is more acceptable and perhaps the most common type of waiting period provision for sickness.[13] Substantial reduction in the premium results from the use of such a waiting period.

Disability income benefits are payable in the ordinary course only when the employee is under the care of a physician. There is usually no provision for partial disability. The test of disability set forth in the policy concerns itself with whether or not the covered employee can perform the duties of his occupation. The determination of disability in the last analysis is in the hands of the attending physician. His certificate sets forth the nature and severity of the disability. There is no limitation with respect to the number of periods of disability in a given year. However, the policy provides that if successive periods of disability are not definitely separated by a period

[13] J. Henry Smith, "Disability Income-Group Coverages," *Life and Health Insurance Handbook, op. cit.,* Chapter 47, p. 599.

of full-time active work or unless it can be shown that there is a different cause for each disability, the two periods will be regarded as one for the purpose of determining maximum benefits. A period of active full-time employment of two weeks between successive periods of disability is a usual requirement in order that the two periods be regarded as attributable to separate disabilities.

The coverage may be written with or without maternity benefits. When such benefits are provided, there is a limitation with respect to payments for any one pregnancy. Six weeks has been found to be an acceptable limitation. For employees insured on the policy date, or in some instances within a limited number of days thereafter, there is no limitation with respect to eligibility. Maternity benefits become effective immediately. In the case of other employees, maternity benefits are payable only if the pregnancy begins while the employee is insured.

Occupational Benefits. Group accident and sickness is usually written on a nonoccupational basis. The coverage is similar to plans required by four states under "temporary disability laws" (see Chapter 8). It is the expectation that occupational injuries will be taken care of by workmen's compensation insurance. In some states, however, the Workmen's Compensation Act does not provide benefits equal to those afforded for nonoccupational disabilities under the group accident and sickness plan. Where this is the case, occupational disability benefits may be included as a supplement to the plan. In such an instance, the plan is written so that the combined compensation and supplemental benefits for occupation disabilities will not exceed the benefit schedule for nonoccupational disabilities. Moreover, payments for occupational disabilities are limited by the policy, and the amount so established cannot be increased if for any reason the employee is not awarded compensation benefits.

Benefit Levels and Duration

Efforts are made to establish benefits at a level sufficiently high to relieve the disabled worker and his family of financial distress due to disability. Benefit levels are generally set at some amount less than the full amount of take-home pay to discourage malingering.

There are a number of plans for determining the benefit amount. Some that have come to general acceptance are: (*a*) the flat plan, (*b*) the earnings plan, and (*c*) the position plan. Under the flat plan, the weekly benefit is the same for all employees. Under the earnings plan, benefits are graded on the basis of earnings and are designed to replace a substantial part of the employee's earnings interrupted by his disability. The position plan calls for the allocation of a flat amount of benefit to a person occupying a particular position such as company officer, foreman, or salesman. Benefits are rarely set up as a salary percentage because of administration costs, but the flat amounts are rounded off so that while providing a reasonable replacement of income they will not exceed 60 percent or in some cases 70 percent of the earnings of the employee. The policy then establishes a maximum duration for the payment of benefits in any one period of disability. A widely used plan is sometimes referred to as the "1-8-26" plan. This provides first-day coverage for nonoccupational accidents, 8-day coverage for sickness (that is, a waiting period of one week), and 26 weeks as the maximum duration for benefit payments. The limit of 26 weeks may be varied. In some instances coverage is for 13 weeks only, and in many other instances it is for 52 weeks. The trend today is toward lengthening the duration of disability income payments. Long term disability, for periods of two, five, or more years, are becoming increasingly popular.

When a plan is put into effect and there is a large number of employees in the higher age bracket, the purchaser of the policy may be faced with the alternative of accepting a shorter maximum period of payment for the older employees or paying a higher premium. Sometimes the policy is written by limiting benefits for employees over sixty years of age. Retired employees may not be retained in the coverage since the purpose of the policy is to replace interrupted income from earnings, and disability would not interrupt retirement income of retired employees.

Group Accidental Death and Dismemberment Insurance

Another form of group health insurance aimed at replacing lost income is group accidental death and dismemberment insurance. This form provides for payment in the event of loss through external, violent, and accidental means of life, sight, or limb. The coverage may be written on either a 24-hour basis or nonoccupational basis.

The form of insurance is not usually written alone but is written in conjunction with other forms of group insurance such as group life, group hospital expense, group major medical expense, or the basic group accident and sickness insurance for disability income discussed above.

As an underwriting practice, life insurance companies establish maximum and minimum amounts of insurance. Coverage for $1,000 is a customary minimum, though where a group life policy is in force with minimums less than this amount, it is usual to have the minimums in both coverages the same. Upper limits are established by company underwriting practices and may be some figure such as $10,000 or $20,000, or more depending upon the nature of the group plan. It is customary, however, to provide the same amounts of insurance for group accidental death and dismemberment insurance as for group life insurance up to the allowable accidental death and dismemberment maximum amount.

By policy definition it is customary to provide that loss of hands and feet means loss by severance at or above the wrist or ankle. Loss of sight means total and irrevocable loss of sight. If an employee is injured to the extent that he suffers more than one of the losses insured against as a result of accidental means and arising out of the same accident, this does not have the effect of increasing the amount of insurance. The total payable for losses arising out of the same accident is limited by the face amount of the insurance. Typical amounts payable are as follows:

For Loss of:	*Amount Payable*
Life	Amount of insurance
One hand	One half the amount of insurance
One foot	One half the amount of insurance
Sight of one eye	One half the amount of insurance
More than one of the above through one accident	Amount of insurance

The company is liable for payment under this form only when loss covered by the policy occurs within 90 days after the injuries are sustained. There is no liability for suicide whether or not the covered employee is sane or insane. Losses caused directly or indirectly by a state of war, any active war, an insurrection, or participation in a riot are not covered. There is no liability for disease of bodily or mental infirmity; medical or surgical treatment thereof; food poisoning or bacterial infection, except only septic infection of and through a visible wound accidentally sustained. There is often no liability for injury which is the outgrowth of riding in an aircraft, except as a paying passenger or as a passenger on a regular scheduled flight of commercial aircraft.

SPECIAL PROBLEMS

Brief mention of several recent developments in group health insurance is made here in order to suggest the scope of the special problems which this field encompasses.

Medical Care for the Aged

A major area of concern is the problem of medical care insurance for the aged. The over-sixty-five group naturally tends to have increasing need for medical care. Unfortunately, their health costs tend to go up sharply at a time in life when income is usually decreasing, with retirement impending or having been reached.

In the past decade strong pressure from proposed government health insurance plans have been focused on the private health insurance business. Several methods of increasing the available and actual protection for the older segment of our society have been evident. Insuring organizations have increased coverage significantly, from 26 percent of the over-sixty-five population in 1953 to 60 percent in 1963. "More than 200 insurance companies are actively issuing health insurance to the aged population . . and four out of five workers covered under group health insurance policies . . . have the right to retain their coverage when they retire."[14]

Alternatives to private health insurance have been advocated, and are being tried. Matching federal grants to states that set up health plans to pay medical bills of the needy aged have begun under the Kerr-Mills Act. Numerous proposals have been made for tying medical care costs into the Social Security program, which would provide a compulsory federal government solution to the problem. A compromise among state-federal-private programs has appeared in the past several years, and is making headway on the problem. These are the interinsurer group hospital, surgical, and major medical plans offered beginning in 1961 on a cooperative basis to the over-sixty-five group in a number of states. The multicompany approach has been adopted in plans known as Connecticut 65, Massachusetts 65, New York 65, Texas 65, and Western 65. Special legislation in other states has opened the door to widespread use of this technique, and the plans have begun to grow rapidly.

The competition in this problem area has been intensified. As one observer notes: "Insuring organizations in the medical care field have thrived upon competition, to the ultimate benefit of insureds in most instances. . . the real question . . . is whether private organizations are capable of sharing with public measures the momentous burden and challenge of financing medical care for citizens."[15]

Dental-Mental-Nursing Care Benefits

The special problems of extending, especially under group plans, medical care insurance to provide benefits for the costs of dental care, nervous and mental disorders, and nursing home care are other areas where the future health insurance plans will meet significant challenges. Partial coverage for mental care costs is available under most new group major medical policies.[16] Some plans include dental and nursing home benefits, but further progress in these areas is needed.

---

[14]James R. Williams, "Health Insurance Continues Healthy Pace," *The Weekly Underwriter,* January 11, 1964, p. 42.

[15]Robert D. Eilers, "Inter-Insurer Arrangements to Provide Over-65 Medical Care Coverage," *The Journal of Insurance,* Vol. XXX, No. 4, (December, 1963), p. 483.

[16]James R. Williams, *op. cit.,* p. 42. Ninety-nine percent had some such protection, and 94 percent had full plan benefits while confined in a hospital.

SUMMARY

The group method of insuring against death and old age has been extended to the perils of injury and illness in the important and fast-growing field of *group health insurance.* Some 60 percent of all health insurance is now written by this technique, largely through employer groups as part of the "fringe benefits" available to workers and their dependents.

Both *medical expense* reimbursement and *income* reimbursement are commonly available to many persons in these group health plans. Eligibility requirements often now permit such policies to be written on small groups of 10 persons or less. The costs are borne, usually, by either employers and employees, or by employers alone.

Medical care costs are covered on a "first-dollar" basis in group *hospital* expense insurance. Oftentimes the contracts include benefits for *surgical* expenses, medical expenses for *doctors* and *diagnostic* X-ray and laboratory expenses. Sometimes special benefits are provided for polio or other "dread diseases."

Group *major medical* expense insurance for severe, catastrophic injuries and illnesses is a most important type of health protection. Very rapid growth of these plans on a group basis has focused attention on the essential nature of insurance for large medical care losses. With high maximum benefits including a broad range of medical costs, substantial deductibles and coinsurance features, the group major medical plans are of two primary types: (1) *integrated* plans supplementing other group hospital-surgical-medical plans and (2) *basic* plans for comprehensive benefits that may have no deductibles for some medical charges.

Group *accident and sickness* insurance aims at the loss of income resulting from disability due to nonoccupational injury or illness. It is thus a complement to workmen's compensation insurance, which continues a portion of an employee's income following a disability resulting from work. The benefit level and duration (normally about one-half year to a full year) are features of prime concern. Income reimbursement for *accidental death and dismemberment* is another form of group health insurance often added to the group insurance contracts.

The special problems of medical care for the over-sixty-five age group, and extension of benefits to include dental, mental, and nursing care costs, are mentioned as examples of major areas in which group health insurance of the future must adjust to meet modern needs.

FOR REVIEW

1. What major types of health insurance losses may be covered in typical group health insurance contracts? What other basic perils besides accidents and sickness may be provided for by the group insurance technique?

2. Two opposing philosophies in group health insurance are the ideas of *(a)* covering all losses on a "first dollar" basis and *(b)* covering only the larger losses on a "catastrophe" or "major medical" basis. With which philosophy do you agree most? Is there any way that the two ideas can be used rationally together?
3. Why can't a policyholder usually be paid for all his medical expenses and loss of income due to health losses? Does this question have particular relevance to group health insurance? Explain why or why not.
4. How does the company avoid adverse selection under a group health insurance plan where underwriting is on a group and not an individual basis?
5. Why are there so many different forms of group health insurance? Why isn't there a group health policy that covers all kinds of health insurance losses?
6. Group health policies for loss of income may be written with a waiting period applying both to disability due to accident and to sickness. However, contracts are frequently written providing no waiting period for disability due to accident, but providing one when the disability is due to sickness. From an underwriting point of view, explain the logic of this latter situation.
7. It is stated that today many hospitals are actually participating in the sponsorship or group budgeting for hospital care. The plans, as a rule, provide for service rather than for benefits payable in cash. To the extent that health insurance companies are able to offer hospital care insurance, how does the method of settlement differ from that of the plans offered by hospitals?
8. X contends that group health coverages are paying for too many types of expenditures in limited amounts. There is a tendency to include coverage for even small predictable claims. Discuss this from the point of view of sound insurance. Do you think the trend will be reversed?
9. A group major medical expense plan sometimes is integrated with a group Blue Cross-Blue Shield plan. What special problems can you see in such a combination of health insurance coverages?
10. One of the principal attractions of major medical expense insurance is said to be the "blanket" nature of the protection it affords. What is meant by the "blanket" protection? How does it compare with other types of group insurance for medical expense?
11. If the deductible in group major medical insurance serves as a safeguard to keep claims down through the elimination of the small claims, why would it not be feasible to write a policy to provide full coverage after the deductible has been satisfied by increasing the deductible and eliminating the coinsurance feature?
12. Group major medical has been one of the fastest growing of all health insurance plans. Identify three of its primary features, and explain why the growth of this kind of insurance has been so rapid in the past decade.
13. X was severely injured in an automobile accident and was hospitalized for three months. Hospital room and board charges were $1,650; other hospital charges, $927; private registered nurses, $3,670; surgery, $2,500. Upon his return home X had a practical nurse for four weeks at $50 per week and then he paid his sister $20 a week for six weeks. Of this $9,067, how much would a major medical expense policy pay if the deductible is $100, the policy limit is $10,000, and the coinsurance factor is 80 percent?
14. Coverage is provided under a "comprehensive" or "basic" major medical insurance policy without an underlying hospital-surgical plan. The de-

ductible amount is $50 with a 20-80 percent coinsurance requirement and a $10,000 maximum. With a total of $6,000 eligible charges, what is the liability of the insurance company?

15. It is the general custom, when group major medical expense insurance is written on a group basis with an underlying hospital-surgical-medical plan, to integrate the two so that there will be no possibility of double coverage and, at the same time, to retain the deductible feature. A widely used plan adopts what is called the "corridor" deductible. Explain the operation of the corridor deductible and distinguish it from the deductible where there is no underlying medical insurance coverage.
16. An employee, to be eligible for disability benefits, must be "wholly and continuously disabled" and "prevented from performing any and every duty of his occupation." Is this coverage broad or limited?
17. Why is much of the group health insurance for income losses primarily a nonoccupational cover? Should it always be of this type?
18. Medical care for the elderly has recently been a matter of considerable study. Older employees *before* retirement can be covered under a group health policy by absorbing the higher age costs in the average group term premium. This is not feasible if the coverage is to be continued for retired employees. How may retired employees be covered? To the extent that your answer does not provide a complete solution, are plans other than private insurance advisable?
19. The treasurer of X Company is advised that if he limits the amount of health coverage for his employees in the older age group, the group premium will be lessened. Is there any justification for the practice? Explain your reasoning.
20. B's teeth have reached a state that makes further filling inadvisable. She is advised to have them extracted and plates made. The bill runs to a considerable sum and B inquires whether or not the charges can be used towards satisfying the deductible in her major medical expense coverage. What would you advise?

PART SIX

Planning and Buying Insurance

CHAPTER 28 *COORDINATING INSURANCE PROGRAMS*

I. SPECIALIZED NEEDS AND THE NEED FOR SPECIALISTS
 A. Specialized Needs
 B. The Need for Specialists

II. THE CHOICE OF METHODS AND MARKETS
 A. Methods of Treating Risk
 B. The Markets for Obtaining Insurance
  1. Criteria for Insurer Selection
  2. Criteria for Agent or Broker Selection

III. PERSONAL INSURANCE PLANNING
 A. Personal Life Estate Programing
  1. The Needs
  2. The Method
  3. Integration with Social Security Benefits
 B. Health Insurance Programing
 C. Home and Automobile Insurance Planning
 D. A Review of Personal Insurance Needs and Costs

IV. BUSINESS INSURANCE PLANNING
 A. Business Life Insurance
  1. "Buy-and-Sell Agreements"
  2. Key Man Life Insurance
 B. The Business Risk and Insurance Survey
  1. Nature
  2. The Need
  3. The Method
  4. Protection during Negotiations
 C. A Case Study for Business Risk Management

V. SUMMARY

Chapter 28

COORDINATING INSURANCE PROGRAMS

THE process of designing and coordinating an insurance program is a part of the broader technique of *risk* management. As discussed in Chapter 1, risk management is summarized as coordinated risk treatment. Implied in this method are several other steps prior to risk treatment, or choice and application of the methods for handling risk. These steps are the identification of risk and its appraisal or evaluation.

Insurance plans or programs should also be coordinated, both with each other and with the other methods for treating risk. For example, the social security benefits should be considered in connection with group and individual life insurance programs. Also, the use of insurance often should be seen as a supplementary action to loss prevention or purposeful risk retention. The title of this chapter is thus used in a broader sense than merely fitting insurance contracts together in a "program," for aspects of providing a program for risk as well as for insurance are included.

SPECIALIZED NEEDS AND THE NEED FOR SPECIALISTS

Planning and buying insurance is basically a problem of decision making for either a personal or a business situation. Each situation is unique in the sense that none is exactly the same, even though some common characteristics may be identified.

Specialized Needs

Every person within a group presents an individual risk problem with conditions peculiar to himself. The same is true with respect to business institutions. While the insurance requirements for a particular class of business may follow a typical pattern, it is nevertheless true that no ready-made plan can safely be assumed to meet any particular need.

For this reason, whether for a person (or family) or for a business establishment, in every case in the selection of insurance coverage it is essential to have an accurate and careful survey of the risks involved. The task then resolves itself into identification, classification, and appraisal, with a view to selecting those risks for insurance that involve the possibility of disastrous losses. Insurable risks must be carefully compared, for it is possible to spend large sums in buying comparatively unimportant forms of insurance coverage while inviting the most serious consequences through a failure to provide essentially needed coverages. Not only are haphazard programs usually more expensive than necessary, but they are also frequently incomplete or inadequate.

The Need for Specialists

It is becoming more and more a recognized fact that the arranging of an insurance program to fit individual needs is work for a trained technical expert. No longer can the insurance agent be a mere solicitor or order-taker. The business or professional man who allows friendship or social contact to be the dominant factor governing the selection of his insurance adviser may find himself without the protection he needs or paying an exorbitant amount for excessive or duplicating coverages. Because of the complex nature of various risks, insurance forms, coverages, and rates, it is essential that the insurance adviser be selected with the same care and discrimination used in choosing other professional assistance.

As the insurance business has developed, for the purposes of planning, the coverages may be divided into (*a*) life and health and (*b*) all other forms, including property and liability. Life and health insurance is highly specialized, and for the most part representatives of life and health insurance companies devote themselves exclusively to these lines. Within the field are specialists who devote themselves to a particular line such as, for example, group insurance or pension plans. In the multiple-line (property and liability) agency, life insurance today is often included to make it an "all-lines" agency. Frequently, the members of the staff who handle the life business ordinarily limit their activities to this field. Also, in the property field there are those who specialize, and, as a rule, in the large multiple-line agency certain persons become the recognized experts in such lines as fire, liability, workmen's compensation, or fidelity and surety coverages.

Most individuals with the help of a professional insurance agent or worker are able to plan their personal and property coverages on a satisfactory basis. The same is true for many business organizations. The owner of the business or one of its administrative officers, with the help of professional insurance persons, can work out a satisfactory insurance program.

Ultimately, however, a growing business reaches a size where the business needs professional representation within its own organization in effecting its insurance program. This is true for two reasons. First of all, the professional agent or broker, no matter how familiar he may be with insurance coverages, cannot be expected to have a sufficiently accurate knowledge of all the ramifications of a huge business organization—such as, for example, American Telephone and Telegraph, U.S. Steel, or General Motors. The knowledge is just too vast to expect that a person outside the organization could determine the insurance needs and the exact extent of these needs on a continual basis. The second reason stems from the first. In the case of an individual or a small business there can be some lost motion in having another person besides the insurance agent or worker making valuations, checking rates and premium charges, and placing insurance coverages. In a small business it might be possible to follow the rule, "When in doubt, insure." This practice might prove to be less expensive and provide as much protection as would result from an expensive program of insurance administration within the firm.

With a large organization, this is not the same. A very small rate differential may mean a difference of thousands of dollars in premium. The expense of surveys to determine necessary improvements to secure even a minor adjustment in rate will pay where the premium volume is large. With reference to coverages, the large concern may quite safely eliminate certain risks from the insurance program and carry others on a deductible or catastrophe basis. While the professional agent or broker can cooperate with the insurance buyer in solving such problems—in fact he is quite essential—it is nevertheless true that the final responsibility for the program rests with the concern itself. It is because of this that the trained "insurance administrator," or "risk manager" in a broader concept, is coming to occupy an important position in the field of business administration.[1] In some cases he heads his own insurance (or risk control)

[1]The number of trained corporate insurance administrators and full-time risk managers is growing fast, although the number in relation to other business administrators is comparatively small. "Insurance buyers," as they are sometimes narrowly termed, have organized for the purpose of recommending more adequate policy forms, coverages for all insurable risks, the elimination of inequities in rates, and the recognition of all factors entering into risk rating. The National Insurance Buyers Association was organized in 1950. This organization absorbed the Risk Research Institute which in turn started in 1932 as the Insurance Buyers of New York. Feeling that this name did not properly represent the activities of its members and the objectives of the organization, the name was changed in 1955 to the American Society of Insurance Management. The present organization undertakes to promote a closer relationship among insurance buyers, to furnish members with insurance statistics and information, to cooperate with insurance underwriters and regulatory bodies in matters affecting the interest of buyers, and to encourage the development of educational facilities in the field of risk management. Present membership is about 1800 persons, and a substantial portion (estimated as high as one fourth) of the total commercial field of insurance, is placed by these persons.

department within the business firm. In medium-sized organizations he may have other financial duties or titles in addition to his risk management functions.

THE CHOICE OF METHODS AND MARKETS

It is an axiom in risk management that insurance is justified economically only in those instances when it covers a level of risk which the insured himself cannot bear without undue hardship. For convenience, to secure the services of the insurer or for other reasons, insureds sometimes insure risks that they are able to carry themselves. Fundamentally, however, it is the risks that could bring disaster or serious financial dislocations that it is imperative to insure.

Methods of Treating Risk

In determining what risks to insure, the risk manager inevitably is first faced with a decision as to whether or not other methods than insurance should be used in taking care of the risks. Consideration should be given to the methods discussed in Chapter 1: (1) avoiding risks, (2) ignoring risks, (3) retention of risk (including self-insurance), (4) loss prevention, and (5) other methods of risk transfer. If these methods are insufficient to meet the risks which have been identified and evaluated, as often they are, then insurance looms as a common and proper solution to the problem of treating risk.

A brief review of risk treatment methods is in order. Some risks may be *avoided,* as for example, in regard to ownership of real or personal property. Instead of owning a building or an automobile, and thereby having such property values subject to the perils, for example, of fire, wind, or theft, the decision may be made to rent a similar building or lease a like automobile.

Many risks are *ignored,* intentionally, because of the small possible loss (in relation to the resources of a person or business) which they involve. Unintentionally, some risks are neglected due to lack of information as to the existence or extent of perils which may cause loss.

Purposeful *retention* of risk includes several categories of meeting risk. Some of the planned efforts include *loss prevention* work (often discussed as a separate method, or as one used in combination with other methods), *reserves,* maintenance and savings *funds.* Each may be valuable for taking care of the smaller, more regular types of risks. Examples of loss prevention include good building construction, adequate fire-fighting and protective equipment, burglar alarms, safety contests, the use of safes for valuable properties, duplicate records and many other techniques. Cost is one of the major limitations, as well as the fact that very few situations exist where the loss is completely preventable. Reserves have the major disadvantage of providing only a bookkeeping limitation on the use of assets; they do not guarantee that cash will be available for meeting losses. The use of maintenance, depreciation, or savings funds for meeting small, frequent, and normal losses may be appropriate, but often are only partial solutions to the problems involved in most risks.

There are a number of types of insurable risks that may, as a matter of policy, be retained without setting up a funded reserve. The nature and extent of such risk retention will depend upon the size of the business, its financial ability to absorb losses, the loss frequently applying to the risk, and the question of whether or not there are any particular advantages to be derived from commercial insurance. Glass, for example, may be the subject for insurance with one concern because of the high value of the plates involved; and with another firm glass may be regarded as a routine maintenance item. Large motor generators may be insured, but coverage may be eliminated on small motors. Some concerns may feel that continuity of operation is more important than the savings of insurance premiums and buy electrical machinery coverage for the inspection service alone. The same may be true with respect to boilers. A concern that easily might handle the cost of repair of a boiler loss could well determine to buy the insurance to forestall business interruption through the inspection service. Sometimes a corporation will go without insurance on all values at a single location up to a given amount. For example, a state might buy insurance on all state buildings where the value exceeds $10,000, and on contents where the value exceeds $5,000. If two buildings are so located as to be subject to a single fire, the risk would be insured. The list of retained risks can be extended indefinitely. The significant point with respect to insurance is that they be recognized and that the retention be a deliberate one.

Self-insurance is feasible where there is a sufficient risk spread with a limited exposure at any one location. Funded reserves are established to pay losses. Regular payments are made to the fund and losses charged to it. It is essential in this respect to distinguish between self-insurance and no insurance. There can be self-insurance only if the number of risks is sufficiently spread and the amount of risk in each location is such that a severe loss will not adversely affect the company or the funds set up for the insurance claims. Over a period of years a premium that ordinarily would be paid for insurance should be sufficient to pay all claims. If there is any great concentration of values in a single location, even though there is an insurance fund equal to the amount of the greatest loss exposure, to go without insurance cannot be termed self-insurance—rather it is no insurance.

By going without insurance, in the case of concentrated value, even with an adequate fund available to pay all losses, the owner of the property is simply placing his fund at risk. With a building valued at $1 million, and $1 million on deposit to meet any fire loss, to go without insurance simply means inviting the loss of $1 million in cash instead of the loss of the building. That is about the only consolation that the special fund affords. If there is no special fund and there is a large concentration of values, the situation is much worse. The owner of the property may have a favorable loss experience over a period of years and during that time he may have accumulated a substantial fund out of premiums to pay losses, but in such a situation he cannot be said to be a self-insurer. He is simply going without insurance and saving the insurance premium. A serious loss might spell financial disaster.[2]

The Markets for Obtaining Insurance

Once the alternatives to insurance have been considered, it may be decided that a substantial part of the risks faced by the business or person are best taken care of by insurance. If this decision is reached, then it remains to choose the place in the open market from which to purchase the proper insurance contracts and services. The choice is limited to those risks and perils which are *insurable*, as discussed in Chapter 1.

The insurance market, as a whole, has been explained and classified in Chapter 4, "Insurance Marketing." The student should review there the types of commercial insurers (stock, mutual, reciprocal, and Lloyd's organizations), the marketing methods (direct selling and agency systems), and types of insurer representatives (agents, solicitors, brokers, and service representatives). The professional concept of insurance marketing is also important to understand.

The consumer viewpoint in purchasing insurance was also summarized in Chapter 4, both in the choice he makes among the many

---

[2] An example of the failure of what was purported to be a self-insurance fund is to be found in the state office building presumably covered under the Michigan state fire fund. It was destroyed in 1951 with an estimated loss of $4½ million; and the balance in the fund at the time was approximately $1½ million. In spite of favorable experience in the past, this partictular loss is indicative of the unexpected source from which a fire may arise. In this instance a 19-year-old highway department employee confessed that he had set the fire to escape the draft for military service. He explained that he had ignited papers in the microfilm division anticipating a minor loss. He hoped for a probationary sentence that would exclude him from army service. It is interesting to note that the state library located in the destroyed building was insured in private companies for a total of $2 million. This was for a premium slightly in excess of $3,000. It would take a great many years of saving insurance premiums to accumulate the amount of such a state loss. To attempt to do so is inviting further loss. Many other examples of the failure of pseudo "self-insurance" plans by business or governmental units have been observed.

insurers offering insurance contracts and in the selection of an insurance agent or broker.

Criteria for Insurer Selection. A review of the criteria which may be helpful in selecting an insurer is appropriate here. The personal or business purchaser of insurance *may* select the insurer; often he does not, for most insurance is sold through the use of agents. In *life and health* insurance, however, it is most common to have the agent represent only one insurance company, so the selection process is a combination one. As the purchaser chooses his agent, he automatically chooses the insurer which the agent represents. Of course the reverse may also be true in those cases where the consumer selects his insurance company (perhaps on the basis of the insurer's advertising or general reputation), and then looks for an agent who represents that insurer. The "exclusive" (one-company representation) agency system, in property and liability insurance, is similar in its effects on the market selection process by the insurance buyer.

Thus, although the purchaser is not always involved in choosing the insurer, he may need to know how to evaluate insurance companies. The need to do this is also particularly important for the large business firm, with perhaps thousands or millions of dollars of coverage written by a few insurers, and in any of the (relatively) infrequent cases where the purchaser does business directly with the insurer without the services of an agent.

Here are some of the criteria to be considered in choosing an insurer:

1.) *Financial strength.* Although surplus, or capital and surplus, is required by all states, requirements vary considerably. The present net worth of the insurer is a starting point in the financial analysis of an insurer, but many other factors may need to be considered. The type of business written, the trends observed over a number of years, the underwriting and investment activities analyzed separately, the adequacy of reserves and the ratios of policyholders' surplus to liabilities (and to net premiums written) are all significant considerations. Basic to all these factors is the general quality of the management, which over a period of time ultimately determines the financial strength of the company.

2.) *Service.* The ability of the insurer to provide proper protection for the insured is essential. Does the insurer specialize in a few lines of insurance contracts, or does it sell all coverages which the purchaser may need and want? Is the insurer experienced in offering all the contracts it will write? Will the insurer tailor-make contracts to meet individual needs of the insurance buyer? Does it have capacity and adequate reinsurance for the largest risks the buyer may require? Is it licensed in all states in which the buyer needs coverage? Can the insurer provide, in addition to indemnification for losses, the necessary engineering and loss prevention services which the purchaser needs? What is the general attitude and reputation of the insurer for prompt and fair settlement of all resaonable claims?

3.) *Cost.* Although often thought to be the most important criterion, cost should usually be considered and compared after the above two criteria are analyzed. Costs do vary, and a too low cost can be just as bad as a too high cost. Lower costs are an obvious direct benefit to the purchaser of insurance, but *too* low costs can result in an unduly strict attitude toward claims payment, inadequate reserves or other financial weakness, or perhaps undesirable decreases in the number or quality of agents and representatives who provide services to the insurance buyer. Initial costs are only part of the necessary analysis, for final costs over a longer period of protection must be considered, including possible rate changes, dividends, assessments, or premium adjustments under audit or retrospective rating plans.

Criteria for Agent or Broker Selection. Since most insurance is written through the agency system, the choice of a competent and reliable insurance agent is often the most important decision for the purchaser of insurance. If an "exclusive" agent who represents one insurer only is chosen, this selection also determines the insurance company with which business is conducted. If an "independent" agent is chosen, the insurance buyer often leaves the selection of the insurer up to the agent, or at least relies heavily on his recommendations of the insurance company with which to write his particular contracts.

The choice is not necessarily limited to one agent, and some purchasers may use several different agents for different lines of insurance. For example, one agent may be used for property and liability contracts, and another for life and health coverages. It is usually not wise to have too many agents, however, for the more that one agent knows about your total insurance account, the better he may be able to analyze the risk and recommend protection for your total needs.

Brokers, who represent the policyholder rather than the insured, may also be valuable in rendering service to the insurance purchaser. With widespread contacts and knowledge of many fields of insurance, many brokers offer significant advice and counsel to their clients. The larger insurance brokerage firms are especially well-equipped to handle the problems of insurance for a buyer with individual and specialized requirements. Sometimes "excess" or "surplus line" brokers are needed to place unusually large or severe types of risks.

Here are some of the criteria that might be used to evaluate insurance agents and brokers:

1.) *Knowledge and ability.* The agent or broker must do a twofold job of education: inform himself about your risk and insurance needs, and help you learn, understand, and appreciate the value of the services he is rendering to you as an insurance buyer. He must bring with him the background and experience necessary to identify, analyze, and treat risk properly. He must learn and teach, ask and answer. Many insureds need the ability of a truly professional insurance person; one who can detect and solve complex problems of varying markets, coverage, forms, and rates.

2.) *Willingness.* The agent or broker must not only be able to do a good job for the purchaser of insurance, but he must also be willing to take the time and make the effort to see that his services (or those of his agency staff and companies) are performed in the most adequate way possible. He must undertake the programing and survey of the buyer's risks and insurance. He should offer to recommend additional legal, accounting, or consulting services when needed. Loss prevention suggestions, and help with filing claims for losses, are important parts of the service he should willingly provide the insurance buyer.

3.) *Integrity and character.* Even the willing and able agent or broker lacks an important requirement if he is unable to command the confidence and trust of the insured. An insurance purchaser who cannot believe and act on his agent's or broker's recommendations is not receiving full value from his insurance dollar. Since insurance advice is purchased in order to obtain certainty, the agent or broker must be able to give his clients both psychological and actual security. Since confidential information from the purchaser is often required in order to perform good insurance counseling services, the agent or broker must respect the buyer's trust with as complete honesty as would a doctor, lawyer, or accountant.

4.) *Representation.* A good agent does not represent poor companies. He must represent or have contacts with one or many insurers that can provide the required protection and services for the insured. All the necessary coverages, including even special or unusual ones, must be available through him in a prompt and efficient manner at a reasonable cost. The insurers he represents should be capable of writing many different kinds of insurance, with a progressive attitude toward newer coverages and forms designed to meet the particular needs of individual buyers.

PERSONAL INSURANCE PLANNING

The first two sections of this chapter have discussed (1) the persons or businesses purchasing insurance for specialized needs and

(2) the choice which the persons or businesses have in selecting the various insurance markets and alternatives for treating risk.

The buying phase is often preceded or combined with the planning of insurance purchases. Good planning is an essential step for good insurance buying, and in the broader sense, risk management, for both personal and business situations. In life and health insurance, the technique of good planning is called *programing;* in all other lines of insurance the process is usually referred to as an *insurance survey.*

Life insurance planning may serve (*a*) the individual and his family or (*b*) a business establishment. The first category is "personal life insurance" and the second is "business life insurance." Life insurance protects business organizations or associates against losses occasioned by the death of members of the firm or key employees. This is a term applied to a specialized use for regular life insurance facilities—it is not a special form of policy developed for business purposes. Business life insurance will be discussed later in this chapter as a part of business insurance planning.

Personal Life Estate Programing

Life insurance programing[3] for the individual or family consists of a study of the need for capital resources and income. The study includes: (*a*) the person's present financial position and future obligations and (*b*) the life insurance facilities available to supply capital to meet his needs. Life insurance is arranged to meet the needs so far as possible and at the least possible cost.

When life insurance programing made its appearance, many felt that it was primarily for persons of substantial means. For those who inherit or acquire great wealth, the problems of taxation, as well as the liquidation of assets for distribution, indicate life insurance as a means for conserving values. However, experience has shown that the individual of modest means, and more particularly the wage earner with dependents, also needs to plan his future and integrate those plans with life insurance protection. The principal item in many estates is life insurance. Many would die without resources, or even go bankrupt, but for the life estate created immediately with the purchase of life insurance.

The Needs. For any given family, needs may be divided into (*a*) necessities and (*b*) amenities. Through a conference or a series of conferences, the life insurance agent develops an outline of all

[3]Life insurance programing may also include the broader aspects of estate programing, which includes consideration of all assets available to the estate. Cash, investments, and other valuable rights are coordinated with life insurance proceeds. Also to be considered are the problems of recommending legal advice for drawing of appropriate wills and trusts to carry out estate objectives.

the needs of the individual or family, presenting them to the applicant in the light of their relative importance. The initial step in programing is to establish a priority of needs that must be met to satisfy minimum requirements. The necessities for living, food, shelter, and clothing, of course, come first. The amenities come next. Then consideration may be given to raising the minimums and providing for new requirements.

For necessities, the logical priority is: (*a*) last expenses, (*b*) readjustment income for a year or more, and emergency funds, (*c*) dependency income, during the family-raising period, (*d*) life income thereafter for wife, and (*e*) mortgage payment. Next in the order of priority come: (*f*) educational funds, and (*g*) special funds, such as charitable bequests, or for a dowry, or to set up a child in business, and (*h*) retirement income, if the husband lives to retirement age. If the estate is large and resources are available, consideration may next be given to such items as (*i*) life income for children, (*j*) postgraduate work in college, and (*k*) special bequests, such, for example, as an annual payment on a wedding or birthday anniversary or at Christmas time.

The Method. Two steps must be taken before recommending any program: (*a*) gathering all necessary factual data and (*b*) analyzing the data as they apply to the applicant's estate objectives. Information required will include: (*a*) the names and the relationship of all who are to benefit from the estate, (*b*) all the assets and inheritances of beneficiaries from other sources, (*c*) property held jointly, (*d*) life insurance protection, (*e*) all pertinent information touching upon business interests and plans and (*f*) the amount and nature of all debts or other obligations. In short, the intelligent program requires a complete picture of all personal and business resources of the person whose estate is being planned.

The trained insurance agent will require complete information on all factors bearing on the particular case. These will include: the sex and age of the individual; his general condition of health; the age, sex, and number of his dependents; his personal and present wealth; the tax obligations; the applicant's income; any independent income the wife may have; present insurance owned; and assets other than life insurance. It may be found that there are several insurance policies each issued at different dates and each with features that must be considered in the integration of all insurance protection in a unified plan. Requiring special consideration will be such items as social security benefits, group insurance with employer, and retirement pensions with a refund at death. The instances cited illustrate the point that with insurance programing the problem is largely one of dovetailing any present insurance into the needs of the insured and supplementing where additional protection is needed. It will be necessary to determnie whether or not there are any outstanding loans against policies or dividend accumulations that may be utilized for the repayment of loans or to help finance the selected program. Finally, if the applicant is a war veteran, his rights and those of his dependents to either veterans' insurance benefits or benefits under the United States Government Life Insurance or the National Service Life Insurance program must be considered.

After the data have been assembled and carefully analyzed, the prospect is then invited to outline what, in his opinion, will be his minimum requirements to provide for his family if he should die immediately. When the needs have been established, it is essential to determine: (*a*) the amount of capital required to accomplish the objective and (*b*) the methods for providing the amount at the time it is needed.

With the data summarized on a form, the problem then resolves itself into determining (*a*) whether the needs indicated are feasible, (*b*) to what extent existing resources will supply the necessary capital to satisfy the requirements, (*c*) additional insurance required, if any, and (*d*) the most effective manner of distributing existing and new insurance between cash payments and income.

When requirements have been reviewed and excessive estimates cut down to reasonable minimums, existing resources are then considered to determine to what extent assets are available to meet minimum requirements. Consideration will be given to social security, retirement plans, availability of savings in the form of cash or investments, and finally, the availability of present insurance.

The social security benefits are apportioned to show what would happen for the wife and children should the insured die immediately. The retirement benefits for the insured himself are integrated with any pension plan available. If there are any veterans' benefits, they are utilized in the program.

Assets other than life insurance are studied to determine: (*a*) their money value and (*b*) the monthly income these money assets will produce. Assets of every sort are integrated in the program. An individual without capital has no assurance that he will live to accumulate investments to provide an income for minimum requirements. This being the case, life insurance, particularly where means are limited, forms the basis of the estate program. Investments and other resources may be utilized to build from the foundation established by the life insurance program.

Insurance policies are studied with a view to determining the maximum policy-paying power. Using the various modes of settlement to the maximum advantage may increase the potential paying power of the insurance as much as 50 percent. The summation value of periodic payments represents a substantial increase over the total face value of the insurance. Since income is one of the major requirements of any program, it is important to determine the paying power of the available insurance rather than simply to list the face amount of the various policies. After the social security, pension, or veterans' income facilities have been utilized to their maximum effectiveness, it becomes necessary then to determine the amount of new insurance essential to meet the objectives established in the statement of minimum needs.

The living values of life insurance contracts, that is, the retirement benefits which may be obtained at age sixty-two or sixty-five are combined with estimated benefits from social security and any company pension plan. These living values may be taken partly in cash, partly in paid-up insurance, and partly in income if desired. The insured, at retirement age, might have resources from savings, from a bequest, or from a military disability pension and would prefer to utilize his insurance under a plan other than retirement income.

Integration with Social Security Benefits. The federal Old Age, Survivors', and Disability Insurance system (O.A.S.D.I.), operated by the United States government, is strictly contributory insurance. That is, it limits benefits to those who have earned wages on jobs covered by the law, and these payments are not predicated upon need. Beneficiaries of the law have right to these benefits regardless of financial need. There is nothing in the nature of poor relief or assistance to the needy in the system.[4]

The original Social Security Act in 1935 provided old-age insurance for wage earners only; but the 1939 amendment extended old-age insurance to include survivorship benefits to the wage earner's family after his death. In 1956, disability income benefits for total and permanent disability were added. Thus, social security benefits are of three types: (*a*) retirement benefits to elderly covered workers and their families, (*b*) death benefits to survivors of deceased covered workers, and (*c*) disability income benefits.

It is essential that the full impact of these benefits receive consideration in the life insurance program as part of the planned estate. The process of integrating life insurance with other assets and sources of income is apparent, too, but the universality and size of O.A.S.D.I. benefits is such that special attention is justified here. More than nine out of ten persons in the working population are now included. The substantial size of the benefits, equivalent to

---

[4]An individual or his dependents and survivors are entitled to social security benefits only if an individual has been paid wages up to a stated minimum for work in covered employment.

more than $40,000 of life insurance and over $20,000 of retirement benefits, are indicated in further detail in Chapter 8, "Social Insurance," and in the following Figure 15.

Figure 15 shows the substantial contribution of O.A.S.D.I. benefits to the needs of a family. The diagram illustrates the income which the family (based on assumptions of age, income, and property owned as shown in "A Review of Personal Insurance Needs and Costs" on page 862) would receive from O.A.S.D.I. if the husband died at the widow's age twenty-five. Maximum benefits would be $254 a month for the widow until her two twin boys reached age eighteen. No further O.A.S.D.I. benefits would be received until her age sixty-two, when $104.80 per month becomes payable.

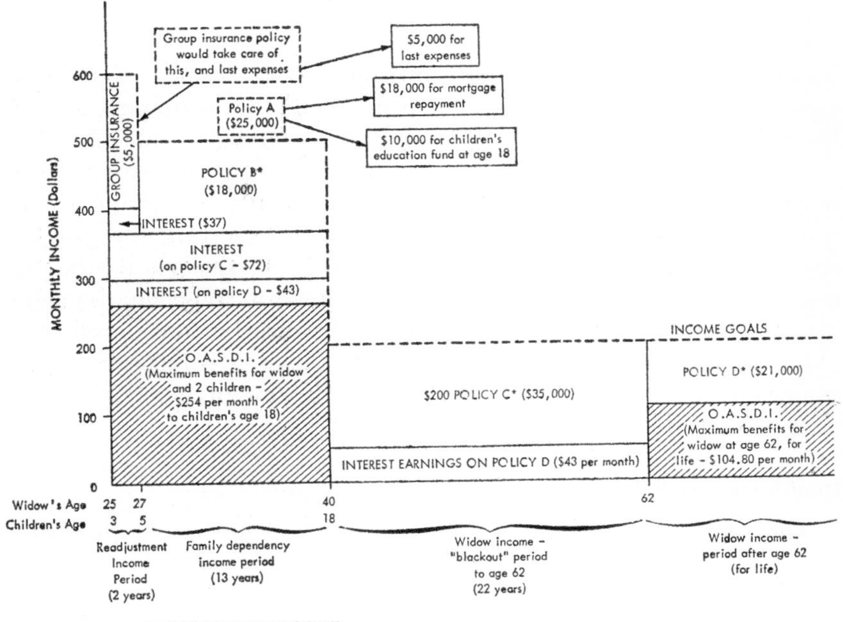

FIGURE 15. Integration of Social Security Benefits with Personal Life Insurance Program

Group life insurance, normally providing about one and a half times annual salary, would be about $10,800. This would be sufficient to take care of the $5,000 of last expenses (taxes, burial, etc.) and a portion of the needed income for the two-year readjustment period.

The other established goals are: (1) $600 per month for two years, (2) $500 a month for thirteen years of family dependency,

(3) $200 a month for life of the widow thereafter, (4) $18,000 for redemption of the mortgage, and (5) $10,000 for an education fund for the children at age eighteen. Based on these objectives, the following individual life insurance policies would be needed:

Policy D—for income after widow's age sixty-two	$21,000
Policy C—for income between age forty and sixty-two, less interest earned on Policy D	35,000
Policy B—for income from age twenty-seven to forty, less interest on Policies C and D	18,000
Policy A—for $18,000 of immediate mortgage redemption, and $7,000 for providing $10,000 educational fund for children at age eighteen	25,000
Total	$99,000

Particularly important to note in Figure 15 is the use of interest earnings on policy contracts which are held for future use in the life insurance program. Also, the need for keeping income goals at a reasonable but minimum level should be recognized. Each $100 per month of income desired at age forty for life, for example, requires over $22,000 more of life insurance. In setting the goal in the diagram at $200 per month after age forty, the possibilities of remarriage of the widow, or her retraining for some employment (if her health and education then permits) must be considered.

For further analysis of this simple personal life insurance program and its costs, see page 862 for "A Review of Personal Insurance Needs and Costs."

Health Insurance Programing

The same technique of planning as used in life estate programming is useful for choosing health insurance coverages. In fact, it is becoming more and more recognized by life and health agents and brokers that both life and health insurance plans must be integrated for successful long-range protection for the policyholder and his family.

Unless proper health insurance is purchased, the life insurance program is threatened by inability of the insured to carry out his estate objectives. A serious injury or illness, without adequate health insurance, may cause (1) extra expenses (or a drain on assets) for medical treatment or (2) loss of income which may prevent the policyholder from keeping life insurance in force.

Medical care coverages should have the following priority: (1) provision for hospital bills, (2) provision for surgical fees, (3) provision for medical care not requiring surgery, (4) X-ray fees and the like, and (5) ordinary home and office medical care. Where the amount available for premiums is limited, as it almost always is, some such ranking of importance to the buyer of various health insurance coverages is essential.

Equally significant for most policyholders is *major* medical coverage on a "blanket" medical care basis. Many insureds, if they have other assets with which to take care of relatively normal medical costs (up to several hundred dollars, perhaps) may need a major medical contract more than they do a hospital-surgical policy for the more frequent kind of losses. Medical expenses of several thousand dollars can be a crippling blow to most family budgets, and these catastrophic types of health losses should be insured.

One example of the need for coordination of life and health insurance programs is seen in the provision in estate plans for "last expenses." Sometimes these expenses include, in addition to taxes and funeral and cemetery costs, the costs of prolonged and expensive medical care preceding death. If these costs are covered by a long-term major medical contract, it is unnecessary to duplicate the coverage in the life insurance estate plan.

The loss of income due to injury or illness is a major area of need for coordination between life and health insurance. Part of the loss-of-income problem can be alleviated by waiver-of-premium or disability income "riders" (see Chapter 24) to life insurance contracts. However, it must be remembered that these features are optional and not included in all such contracts. Also very important is the fact that they provide benefits only for *total and permanent* (normally, over six months) disability, and not for partial or temporary inability to earn an income due to injury or sickness. There remains a pronounced but oftentimes neglected need for more complete protection against loss of income by having an "accident and health" policy (see Chapter 26) for permanent-partial or temporary-total disabilities. These income benefits should be related to the normal earnings of the insured (perhaps between 50-75 percent), rather than be related to the amount of life insurance in force, as the disability income in life insurance riders must be.

The income benefits of individual and group insurance, and the rights under the federal O.A.S.D.I. program should be coordinated in a diagram similar to Figure 15. With objectives set in terms of monthly or yearly income necessary to support the family when the breadwinner is disabled, the Social Security benefits (for total and permanent disability only) provide a minimum base. Then the group and individual health policies for loss of income should supplement the program to reach toward the established goals throughout the years following a disability.

Home and Automobile Insurance Planning

The need for answering the question "How much insurance should I buy?" is not as apparent in purchasing home and automobile insurance as in the life and health insurance fields. Usually, the goal is fairly obvious. In terms of the value of the property insured, it is reasonably close to the full value of the home or automobile. The values, though sometimes requiring appraisal in unusual or larger properties, certainly do not present the difficulties of estimation that are found in placing an economic value on a human life for the purpose of life insurance.

There is planning, however, which is necessary in choosing the proper limits for liability insurance coverage in the Homeowner's Policy and the Family Automobile Policy. Also, the optional features of these contracts, as discussed in Chapters 19 and 16, should be analyzed and fitted to the needs of the policyholder. Much higher than standard liability limits are usually needed, especially in urban areas and territories with a record of high jury verdicts. The broader Homeowner's Policy forms should be considered essential for most homes in the medium to higher-priced categories. Medical payments coverage in the Family Automobile Policy may be considered more essential if the insured and his family have inadequate health insurance protection. The uninsured motorists endorsement may be more important in states having a low proportion of insured cars. Choices among different deductibles in both policies should be based upon the financial status and other objectives of the insured. In all, the comparison of needs and analysis of coverages should involve careful, consistent planning to provide the most important protection and services to the policyholder.

A Review of Personal Insurance Needs and Costs

As an illustration of how life, health, home, and automobile insurance might be brought together in a short survey of personal insurance needs and costs, assume the following:

Assumptions:

Family ages: husband (28), wife (25), two twin boys (age 3)
Income: $7,200 per year, or $600 per month
Property owned: home—valued at $25,000 (including $3,000 lot), with a $18,000 20-year mortgage
car—valued at $2,000
cash savings—$500
investments—$1,000 of stock and mutual funds

Proposed Coverages:

I. LIFE INSURANCE

A. Estimate of Needs:

1. Last expenses (taxes, funeral, etc.)	$ 5,000
2. Mortgage repayment	18,000
3. Education fund for children ($5,000 each)	10,000
4. Readjustment income ($7,200 a year for 2 years)	14,400
5. Family dependency income ($6,000 a year to children's age 18, or 13 years)	78,000
6. Widow income to age 62 ($2,400 a year after wife's age 40 for 22 years)	52,800

I. LIFE INSURANCE—*Cont.*

7. Widow life income after age 62 ($2,400 a year for life expectancy of 18 years) $43,200

Total gross needs $221,400

B. Insurance Coverages:

1. O.A.S.D.I. "Social Security" would provide maximums:
   a. Death benefit .... $ 255
   b. Survivorship dependency income ($3,048 a year, or $254 a month, for 15 years) 45,720
   c. Widow income after age 62 ($1,258 a year, or $104.80 a month, for life. Life expectancy is 18 years) 22,625

   Total $68,600

2. Group life insurance might provide: At normal face value of about 1½ times annual salary 10,800 79,400

Total net needs from individual life insurance $142,000

3. Present value equivalent of net needs:
   a. $70,000 of the total net needs will occur during the next 15 years after widow's age 25 (including the above needs, A. 1., 2., 3., 4., 5., not provided for by O.A.S.D.I. or group life insurance. See Figure 15, also). Present value equivalent of these benefits, estimated at .85 for average of 7 years hence at 2½ percent, is 59,500
   b. $52,800 of the total net needs will occur during the years between the widow's age 40 and 62 (A. 6. in above estimate of needs). Present value equivalent is approximately .53, for average of 26 years hence at 2½ percent. 28,000
   c. $21,000 of the total net needs will occur after age 62 (A. 7. above). Present value equivalent is about .32, for an average of 46 years hence, or 7,000

   Total individual life insurance actually needed $94,500*

4. Individual life insurance of $99,000 might be provided:† — *Estimated Annual Cost*
   a. 15-year term insurance (for mortgage, education, part of readjustment income, and family dependency income, as shown in Figure 15 as Policies A and B). Needed is $43,000, at about $6 per year at age 28 for each $1,000 .. $ 258.00
   b. Guaranteed insurability option rider‡ (for the widow income to age 62, as in Figure 15, Policy C). Needed is $35,000, at about $2 per year at age 28 for each $1,000 .... 70.00
   c. Permanent whole life insurance (for widow's income after age 62, as in Figure 15, Policy D). Needed is $21,000, at about $16 per year for each $1,000 .... 336.00

   Total life insurance annual cost .... $ 664.00

In comparing this total with the sum of Policies A-D in Figure 15 ($99,000), the estimates of average present value discounts used above would have to be recalculated on a year-to-year basis to make the totals correspond.

†Note that these amounts and types of coverage are merely an illustration, and suitability for any particular family would depend on many other factors. Waiver of premium should be included in all these policies.

‡This option would permit the young family man to purchase, without a medical exam, the additional amounts of permanent life insurance at 3-year intervals during the next 15 years.

II. HEALTH INSURANCE

A. Hospitalization and Surgical Contract (for family, with about $20 per day, 120 days, $300 surgical schedule coverage) $100.00

B. Major Medical Contract (for family, $15,000 maximum, with $500 deductible and 80 percent coinsurance) 50.00

C. Accident and Health Contract (for husband's loss of income, non-cancellable, $300 a month, sickness benefits for 2 years, with 50 percent of benefits thereafter) 100.00

Total health insurance annual cost .... $ 250.00

III. HOME INSURANCE

A. Homeowner's Policy (For Form #2, or Forms #3 and #4 Combined):
$22,000 on house
2,200 on garage
8,800 on contents and personal property
4,400 additional living expenses
25,000 comprehensive personal liability limits
Total home insurance annual cost .... $ 60.00

IV. AUTOMOBILE INSURANCE

A. Liability Coverage:
   1. Bodily injury—(at least) $25,000 per person, $50,000 per occurrence
   2. Property damage—(at least) $10,000 per occurrence

B. Medical Payments—$2,000 per person

C. Comprehensive Physical Damage—value of car

D. Collision—value of car, less $100 deductible

E. Uninsured Motorists Endorsement

Total automobile insurance annual cost .... $ 150.00

V. SUMMARY OF APPROXIMATE ANNUAL COST

	Amount §	*Percent of Total*
A. Life Insurance	$ 664.00	59
B. Health Insurance	250.00	22
C. Home Insurance	60.00	6
D. Automobile Insurance	150.00	13
Total	$1,124.00	100

The place of the total insurance costs in the family budget should be considered. The above example might include the following approximate breakdown of family finances:

	Percent of Total Income of $7,200
1. Housing	25
2. Food	20
3. Clothing, entertainment, and miscellaneous	15
4. Insurance	15
5. Automobile and transportation	10
6. Taxes	10
7. Savings	5
	100

§Total annual costs for all of these coverages may vary widely, according to the particular insurers and the provisions in the contracts. Life and health costs assume normal health and occupation. Home and automobile insurance assume average territory, construction, and driving record.

Naturally, these estimates would be subject to many individual differences. The greatest variation in the insurance costs, as a percent of total income, would be in the life insurance section. Here the total might be substantially less, depending on how much is budgeted for other savings media. The permanent life insurance contracts are a combination, it should be noted, of both insurance protection and savings.

The personal insurance review example is an illustration of an *insurance survey* on a family basis. The next section of this chapter analyzes the survey technique as applied to business. While risks with which the individual is personally concerned are limited, they vary with occupation or profession, ownership of real estate, habits, pleasures, and diversions. The personal survey brings all of these to light. Again, while cost is of importance in every insurance program, its distribution may be of especial interest to the individual. It sometimes happens that heavy premium payments fall due about the same time that taxes, notes, or other extraordinary expenses are payable. If the insured is operating on a budget system, he may secure a plan for the readjustment of premium payments to fit his financial planning. If budgeting is not followed, insurance may be rearranged so that the heaviest premium payments fall due at a time when some particular income is received, or in any manner that will prove most convenient to the insured.

BUSINESS INSURANCE PLANNING

Business Life Insurance

Good insurance planning is not only useful in personal estate programing, but in many business situations as well. The objective of business life insurance is either maintaining a business as a going concern or retaining the values of the business interest for the benefit of an owner's estate following his death. This form of insurance is used also to protect surviving members of a business where the loss of (*a*) a partner, (*b*) a stockholder, or (*c*) a key employee could (1) adversely affect control, (2) dissolve the business, or (3) adversely affect its value.

In a closely held business enterprise, numerous relationships must be considered in the event of death. The death of the owner in an individual proprietorship, one of the owners where two or more are associated, or a key employee calls for financial adjustments; without adequate funds the estate of the deceased or the position of survivors, or both, may be adversely affected. Careful planning, combined with the skillful use of life insurance, may preserve for surviving members of a concern or for the estate of a deceased member values that might otherwise be completely lost.

"Buy-and-Sell Agreements." Business life insurance to protect the interest of a deceased member and at the same time to protect the interest of surviving members may be arranged in connection with a purchase-and-sale agreement which provides a sure market for the interest of the deceased and a guarantee to survivors of its purchase at a reasonable price with the funds available for payment.

The details of the *"buy-and-sell agreement,"* known also as a purchase-and-sale agreement, not only must fit the needs of the parties but, as well, must vary with the type of business organization. Certain characteristics of all such agreements fall, within limits, into a broad pattern.

The names of the parties appear in the agreement, and the purpose is detailed. Either the purchasing price will be included or a formula by which it may be determined. All parties commit themselves to the plan for the purchase of the interest of the deceased associate. The method of financing by the use of life insurance is set forth; and provision is made for changing the amounts of insurance, if necessary, from time to time. To establish a guaranteed minimum, it is usual to provide that the sale price will never be less than insurance for the purpose. If a valuation formula is used and the amount of insurance proves inadequate, a time payment plan is set up for the balance. Beneficiary arrangements determine whether the proceeds are to be payable to a trustee who will carry out the transfer or payable directly to the person who, under the agreement, must acquire the business interest of the deceased.

There are numerous other details, such as the debts of a proprietorship or a partnership, and the rights of termination, withdrawal, or amendment. The agreement, properly drawn, is binding and enforceable at law upon heirs, successors, or assigns.

A schedule of the life insurance policies is set forth, and the policies are filed with the agreement. Details are given as to the disposition of the insurance on the life of the surviving associates. The premium payment plan is covered, as well as the conditions upon which rights and privileges under the policies may be exercised during the lifetime of the insured.

The carefully drawn purchase-and-sale agreement, implemented with life insurance, precludes misunderstanding, affords each business associate the knowledge of a definite market for his interest at a fair price, and affords each associate the knowledge that he may acquire the interest of a deceased associate at a fair price and that facilities for such acquisition will be forthcoming from life insurance.

Key Man Life Insurance. The principles underlying *key man life insurance* for one or more individuals held to be of particular value to a business are essentially the same, regardless of the form under which the business is organized. There are some modifications as to procedure set up by the limitations of the business itself.

The objective of key man insurance is to provide adequate compensation for the loss of services by death of a vital employee and to provide resources with which to secure, in a competitive market, the services of a successor.

There can be little doubt of the right of a business organization to insure its president, manager, or other valued employees. It sometimes happens that a business invests large sums in experimental work of such a nature that the investment would be largely, if not entirely, lost by the death of the person entrusted with the work. The risk may be covered by life insurance, payable to, and paid for by, the business itself. Other key employees can likewise be covered—an old and experienced sales manager; a leading salesman with a wide personal following; a specialist such as an engineer or a chemist who carries, through his own personal efforts, an important load for the firm; or a man whose management inspires the confidence of financial backers. The list could be expanded to include many other such persons.

In addition to using key man insurance to reimburse the business for the loss of the services of a particular individual, the plan has been used as a means for attracting and holding such personnel. Because of the tax situation, an offer of an increase in salary is much less attractive than a plan to provide, for the dependents of an employee, a continuation of his salary for a number of years following his death. Key man insurance may work into the program of any business establishment as a means for stabilizing employment in the higher levels. Frequently, a combination of coverages is provided: indemnity to the business for loss of the employee and salary continuation for his dependents. It is a valuable and frequently overlooked use of life insurance in the business field.

The Business Risk and Insurance Survey

Closely akin to the life insurance program is the *insurance survey* made by the underwriter in the property insurance field to outline property insurance needs for a given business establishment. Although most often used in business situations, the term is also appropriate in the individual or personal area, too, as in the preceding section on the personal insurance plan or survey.

Nature. The surveys are known under a variety of names. They are called insurance *plans*, insurance *abstracts*, insurance *analyses*, insurance *audits, fact-finders,* and other such names.[5] In practice all are essentially the same, and all are designed to identify the risks and perils, and then plan for providing insurance or other

[5]For an example, see the general "Risk Analysis" form published by the Insurance Division of the American Management Association.

methods for meeting them. They also may uncover points of weakness in existing insurance programs. A suggested rearrangement of insurance amounts and coverages is then presented. The plans should indicate risks that the insured himself may carry, losses that may be prevented, and where insurance is, therefore, not needed.

The Need. The risk and insurance survey is particularly adapted to the needs of a trustee who, entrusted with new and unfamiliar responsibilities, is disturbed by many perplexing problems. State and city officials, corporation directors, guardians, executors, and trutsees are subjecting themselves to grave criticism if not direct personal liability if without verification they are satisfied that the insurance programs of their predecessors are sufficient. Frequently men who are otherwise qualified for a position, such as that of a trustee of a church or college, have but the vaguest idea of the risks that threaten the institutions under their care. Verbal recommendations or suggestions may be misunderstood or misinterpreted. The carefully prepared insurance program presents a logical solution of the problem.[6]

The risk and insurance plan, while of special interest and value to large business undertakings and to institutions, is by no means limited in value to large enterprises. Many medium and smaller-sized businesses need a good risk and insurance survey equally as much as the larger firms.[7] It is the smaller businesses, in fact, that are particularly vulnerable to financial ruin as a result of a mistake or omission in good insurance protection. They also must plan to take advantage of all insurance cost reductions which are economically advisable. Otherwise, small profit margins can turn into business losses. The lack of full-time, or even part-time, "risk managers" (as might be found in the larger business firms) also emphasizes the need for organized and systematic action by small businesses.

The Method. The risk and insurance survey involves: (*a*) risk detection and analysis and (*b*) insurance planning. The insurance agent or broker can do the planning and may, to a large degree, be able to prepare the risk analysis. The work of the analysis, however, will require the cooperation of the applicant for insurance.

The risk analysis, if properly made, will give no consideration to costs. All insurance exposures will be carefully searched out. A chart may be drawn, sometimes known as an "exposure survey chart."

---

[6]For a thought-provoking article on the importance of the life agent and property agent working together (if one agency or broker is not well versed in all lines of insurance), see Ben S. McGiveran and Digby B. Whitman, "The Ghost of the Estate Plan," *C. L. U. Journal*, Vol. XVIII, No. 1 (Winter, 1964), p. 5. The concept is particularly applicable to persons working as professional counselors, such as those with the designation of C.L.U. or C.P.C.U.

[7]See Mark Greene, *Insurance and Risk Management for the Small Business* (Washington, D.C.: U.S. Government Printing Office, 1964).

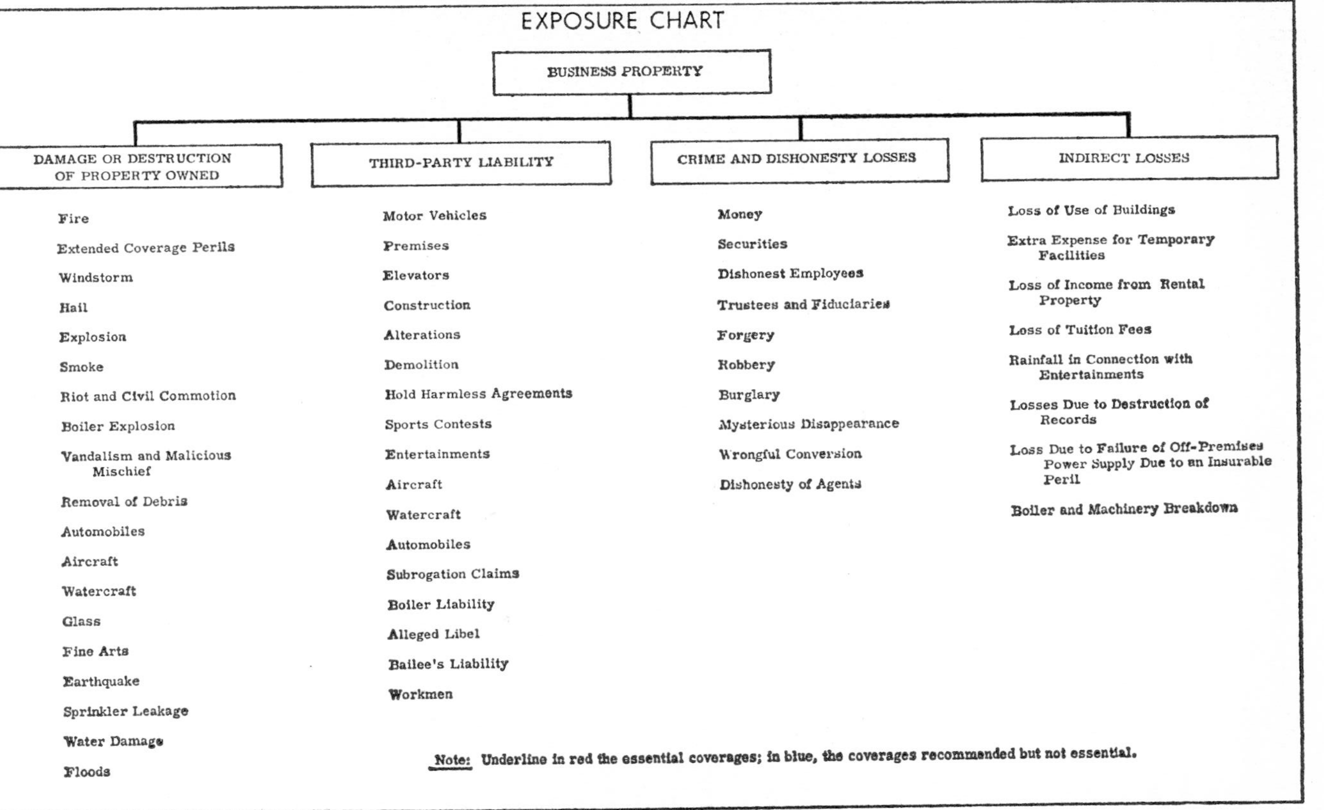

FIGURE 16. Exposure Chart Accompanying Risk and Insurance Survey

With such a chart in complete form (see Figure 16) it is then possible to select the perils that are to be covered by insurance based upon company policy or individual needs. It is at this point that costs are evaluated in terms of balancing benefits against the costs involved in the recommended insurance.

Elaborate survey charts have been prepared to meet the needs of different types of business establishments. Survey forms have been prepared by insurance companies for the use of their representatives. Insurance consultants have advocated several different but effective methods of risk analysis, such as (1) working from the financial statements, (2) analyzing perils, and (3) evaluating exceptions in the contracts.[8] All of these alternative solutions are of value as checks against possible exposures, but none of them will replace the technical knowledge of the insurance underwriter augmented by the specialized information to be derived from the insured's risk analysis. An organized risk and insurance survey is considerably more than the completion of a check list or the arbitrary insertion of recommendations in a set of blank forms. It includes (1) perils analysis, (2) diagnosing current coverage, and (3) program planning.[9] An impressive looking survey delivered by one not fully competent to make it can be a danger in that it may give a sense of security not warranted in the circumstances.

Protection during Negotiations. When an applicant for insurance is discussing possible coverage with an agent it is wise, in so far as it is possible, to secure a binder providing adequate coverage during the period of negotiations. Life insurance protection is not bound, and ordinarily the protection becomes effective with the payment of the first premium and the delivery of the policy while the applicant is in good health. Coverage may be expedited if the premium is paid at the time application is made and a conditional receipt issued to the applicant. This procedure makes insurance effective as soon as the insurability of the applicant has been determined. In the case of property insurance, binders may be issued by the agent providing coverage from the exact time the binder is issued until the binder is canceled or expires or is completed by the delivery of a policy.

During negotiations, failure to determine definitely whether or not the insurance company has assumed liability may result in disappointment and even litigation. In order that there may be no mis-

---

[8]See A. H. Criddle, Henry K. Duke, and Jason Crain, respectively, in "A Case Study in Risk Analysis: Alternative Solutions," *Proceedings of the Twelfth Annual Insurance Conference* (Columbus, Ohio: Ohio State University Publications, College of Commerce Conference Series–Number C-143, March 9–10, 1961), pp. 127–46.

[9]Edwin S. Overman, *ibid.*, "Introduction to the Insurance Survey Technique—A Synopsis," p. 103.

understanding, the binder should be reduced to writing. This need be no formal binder but may be evidenced in the form of a letter, telegram, or other written evidence. Some agents who are particularly punctilious, after reaching an agreement to issue a binder, expecially if large values are involved, sometimes dictate a telegram either to the insured or to their own office, which makes an immediate record of the transaction. This procedure is not necessary but some agents find it to be a desirable practice. If the line is an unusually large one, the agent may notify by telegram the companies to be bound. A situation calling for such a binder might develop where an insured has a new building in the process of construction. He is uncertain whether or not he will carry a reporting builder's risk form or a completed value form. He wishes to discuss the matter with his architect or contractor. In the meantime construction work is getting under way. The agent should bind coverage subject to a final determination as to the form to be use. A similar situation might develop where a reappraisal is being made with the intention of placing new insurance. A generous estimate of the new value should be made and insurance bound with the understanding that the final amount is to be adjusted when the appraisal is completed. To wait until after the appraisal will leave the insured with a substantial uninsured exposure; and, if a loss develops during the period of negotiation, the consequences could be embarrassing and possibly quite serious.

In this respect it may be noted that the agent has a serious responsibility to provide coverage when insurance is ordered. If an applicant for insurance orders coverage and at the same time raises questions with respect to rates, form of policy, term, or method of payment of premium, full protection should be bound and the details adjusted by conference or correspondence. The agent who fails to effect cover when ordered may find himself personally liable for damages. It has been held that the agent or company owes the applicant for insurance what amounts to a legal obligation to act with reasonable promptness on his application. The applicant must either be provided the desired coverage or be notified of the rejection of the risk. Unless the insured is given this notice he has the right to feel that he is protected and in the circumstances takes no steps to seek protection elsewhere. As has been stated: "Those engaged in the insurance business understand perfectly the peculiar urgency of the need for prompt action in these matters."[10]

---

[10]*Coffee* v. *Polimeni,* U.S. Court of Appeals, 9th Circuit, 1951. In this case a letter ordering $6,000 insurance was misplaced and not answered. Not having received a reply to his letter after several weeks, the applicant for insurance wrote to the agent again. During the intervening correspondence period, the property burned. The facts in the case resulted in a verdict of $9,200 against the agent.

Insurance cases, involving delay, are recognized as unlike ordinary commercial or business dealings. This is so since failure of insurance protection may result in a catastrophic loss to the individual.

A Case Study for Business Risk Management

The following example may be useful to the student in reviewing the technique of business risk management. From the facts given, a risk and insurance survey for the shopping center owner can be developed to aid in determining the answers to the kinds of questions which are raised at the end of the case study information.

THE RISKEE SHOPPING CENTER

The Facts:

Mr. I. M. Sure is the developer and chief financier of a new shopping center to be located on the outskirts of a fast-growing residential suburb near a major metropolitan city. He has organized the enterprise under the legal title of Success, Inc., and though construction has not yet begun, he is asking your advice in regard to the risks and insurance he should consider necessary during the developmental and the operating stages of his business venture.

The purchase of property has just been completed, which will provide 88,000 square feet of store space in the center. An architect has been retained and begun plans for a slanted L-shaped line of stores set at an angle to an important traffic route.

Preliminary arrangements have been made for space to be leased to a large supermarket chain, a branch department store, a well-known national restaurant, a theater, a variety store, and several other auxiliary service-type merchants including a barber shop, dry cleaner, branch bank, and insurance agency.

Twenty-four tenants in all shall occupy the premises under 15-year leases which stipulate a minimum rental plus a sliding percentage of sales agreement. The lease relieves the tenant of liability for rent if the premises are substantially damaged by fire.

The flat-roof building itself shall be of "fire-resistive" construction, the largest section of which is the 18,000 square feet of open space for the supermarket store. The heating equipment is designed to be placed at the rear of the main building, and shall provide steam heat for all the stores in the center.

Eighty thousand square feet of macadam parking space are to be provided, with painted 45° parking stalls estimated for 400 cars. Floodlights on aluminum pylons, and attendants for the parking lot were considered but decided against.

Storage space is to be kept at a minimum in order to provide maximum selling space. Each tenant is to be responsible under his lease for his own (1) snow removal, (2) trash removal, (3) repair of fire damage to the building, (4) air conditioners, if the tenant desires them, and (5) fire extinguishers.

A small rental and maintenance office is to be maintained in the shopping center, and ten office and service employees will be employed.

Some Questions for Case Study:

1. What risks does Mr. I. M. Sure have at the present time, while owning the vacant land to be used as the shopping center site? Are these "speculative" or "pure" risks? Should he have some form of insurance to meet these risks?

2. After construction is underway, what risks does Mr. Sure face? What insurance should be considered?
3. Assuming the shopping center to be complete, make a hypothetical risk analysis for Mr. Sure. What risks does the locational factor alone suggest? Are there any life and health risks?
4. Complete the risk and insurance survey that might be performed by a risk manager for Mr. Sure by outlining, with brief explanations, a business insurance survey for the Riskee Shopping Center. Include the following:
   a) Possible risks which Mr. Sure might avoid. Give specific examples.
   b) Possible risks which Mr. Sure might ignore. Give specific examples.
   c) Possible risks which Mr. Sure might retain, and try to prevent losses from occurring. Give examples.
   d) Possible risks which Mr. Sure might "self-insure."
   e) An insurance proposal in detail as to the coverages, including social insurance, you would recommend to Mr. Sure. Separate the essential, desirable, and available coverages.
5. Now, assuming the shopping center complete, and tenants moved in, discuss the exposures and special insurance problems which each of the following tenants might have:
   a) The department store
   b) The supermarket
   c) The restaurant
   d) The branch bank
   e) The dry-cleaner
   f) The insurance agency
6. Would any of the newer multiple-line, package-type insurance contracts be applicable to the businesses in Question 5? What suggestions would you make in regard to using them?

SUMMARY

The objective of risk management (including insurance) is the proper *coordination* of the programs designed for meeting risks. It is necessary that the different *methods,* such as avoiding risk, ignoring risk, retaining risk, loss prevention, and risk transfer, be evaluated and often used in conjunction with one another. Particularly, it is essential that the risks which are best met with insurance be coordinated. The process of buying insurance should be based upon extensive planning, in which the alternatives to insurance, and the alternatives among the many types and forms of insurance coverage, are carefully analyzed.

The final chapter of this text reviews the decision-making process involved in coordinating risk and insurance programs, with special attention to those features pertaining to insurance protection and services. After a choice has been made in regard to the method of treating risk, if insurance is selected as the best technique, then the insurance consumer must choose (1) the right insurer and (2) the right agent or broker. Criteria are outlined for the insurance buyer in his difficult but extremely important task in making the best selections in a broad and diverse *insurance market.* Financial strength, service, and costs are fundamental criteria for selecting insurance companies. Agents and brokers should be chosen on the basis of knowledge, ability, willingness, integrity, character, and representation of the best insurers for the needs of the insurance buyer.

The need for using *specialists* of professional caliber is recognized in modern insurance management. Since each person or business has individualized needs, it is often imperative to have trained experts provide the solutions. Not only are specialists used by the insurance companies, but the newer concept of insurance or "risk managers" (who are employees of the consumer, usually for medium and larger-sized businesses) is increasing cognizance of the growing specialization of this important business function.

Risk and insurance *planning* makes use of the same basic techniques for both personal (or family) situations and the more complex business risk situations. The steps include (1) identification and classification, (2) analysis and evaluation, and (3) treatment of risks. In life and health insurance planning the process is usually referred to as *programing*. In property and liability insurance planning the term *survey* is often used. When referring to all-lines insurance planning, either term may be used.

Personal life estate *programing* is a significant part of family financial planning and budgeting. Through an evaluation of cash and income needs after the death of the husband, specific goals are established. Then social security (O.A.S.D.I.) benefits, group life insurance, and individual life insurance are integrated in a plan which provides the necessary capital and future income for the family. Health insurance may be programed on the same basis. Many families have neglected the need for sufficient income for disability income, especially for long-term sickness and serious injuries which cuts off a family's income for an extended period.

The home and automobile insurance requirements for a family are reviewed in a simple illustration of personal insurance needs and costs, including life and health insurance. The total picture is one which often surprises a person who has not stopped to outline his entire insurance program. The extent of insurance coverage, its purposes and its costs can only be seen in such a complete review.

Business insurance planning also necessitates proper fact-finding, analysis, and choice of protection and service. The advantages of using business life insurance in "buy-and-sell agreements" and "key man" life insurance are discussed. The business risk and insurance *survey* technique is proposed as the logical method for purchasing business insurance. It is only through such a process that the businessman can make rational choices among alternatives, fitting his needs together in a coordinated plan of action.

A case study of a modern shopping center is offered as a final review of the planning and buying phase of insurance. The facts given and the questions posed are an illustration of the business risk management process by which a coordinated insurance program can be developed for the intelligent insurance buyer.

FOR REVIEW

1. Refer to "Case Study for Business Risk Management," near the end of Chapter 28, and have a different group of students consider Questions 1 through 6. Have the class as a whole discuss the proposed answers from each group.
2. Assume you are employed in a small firm of 50 employees and, as a result of your business education background, have been asked by the president of the company for your advice. If the business is a manufacturing concern with several small retail outlets, how would you outline for the president the insurable *risks* which should be considered in a proper risk management analysis. Indicate for each risk the type of *insurance* which might be appropriate.
3. A friend of your comes to you for advice, knowing that you have just completed a course in risk and insurance. He has the necessary home and automobile insurance, but is very confused by the many contracts of life and health insurance available. Making whatever assumptions are necessary, what recommendations would you give him in regard to the following questions?
   a) How should he estimate his life insurance needs, and how much life insurance does he need? Show your method of explanation to him, as well as approximate amounts calculated.
   b) What *riders* to the contracts would you suggest or not suggest? *Justify* your recommendations for (or against) at least three riders which are commonly available with life insurance.
   c) Explain the basic health insurance needs he must consider for his family, and how you recommend they be met by insurance.
   d) How might group insurance provide part of the solution to his life and health protection requirements?
4. *a*) Suppose your parents are both approaching age 62 and have asked you for advice about insurance. What would you advise them about their home insurance, assuming they own their own $30,000 home? Be specific as to contracts, forms, and approximate limits.
   b) What features of their automobile contract would you have them check?
   c) What kind of health insurance would you recommend? Why?
   d) What would you tell them about their O.A.S.D.I. old age benefits and costs?
5. Mr. I. M. Secure is 25 years old and has been working for two years after graduating from college. He has a wife, two small children, and is employed at an annual salary of $8,000. He has just purchased a modest home and a new car. The only life insurance he owns is $10,000 of group life through his employer, and a $15,000 twenty-payment life policy he took out ten years ago. Making whatever assumptions you consider realistic and appropriate, discuss, with reasons for your opinions,
   a) The types of property and liability insurance he should have for his family's protection (outline form is appropriate).
   b) His needs and the types of contracts he should consider in order that his family have proper life and disability insurance (outline form).
   c) The relationship of Social Security to his insurance program.

6. You have just had an estate program completed by a qualified Chartered Life Underwriter (C.L.U.) who has made a number of suggestions for the improvement of your life and health insurance program.
   a) Assuming you have about $50,000 of life insurance, what uses would probably be made of the settlement options in your life insurance contracts? Why?
   b) How could he suggest coordinating your life and health insurance with your savings and investment objectives?
   c) Diagram the relationship of Social Security (O.A.S.D.I.), benefits to you and your family, as he probably would do in explaining a typical family life insurance estate program.
7. What programing benefits can you summarize to a new father, Mr. Z, who has just asked about his basic *health* insurance needs? What insurance plans would you recommend? Do you think the "risk manager" at the plant where Mr. Z works could suggest any part of the solutions to his health protection needs?
8. Suppose you are a merchant, just beginning a new drivein restaurant. You own the building and several vehicles, and have 30 employees.
   a) What property and liability risks would you think most important to insure? (Rank in order of importance, along with brief reasons.)
   b) What kinds of coverage would you recommend that you purchase in order to meet the risks you describe in (*b*)?
   c) Does such a small businessman have any *business* life and health risks which should be protected by insurance? Discuss the basic kinds of insurance contracts which he should consider to obtain proper protection for these risks.
9. In learning about risk and insurance, principles or basic ideas should be stressed. What are the two most significant ideas which you believe will be of lasting value to you as a consumer of insurance in each of the following areas:
   a) The purposes of insurance?
   b) The analysis of risk?
   c) The marketing of insurance?
   d) Insurance contracts?
   e) Auto, home, life and health insurance (one idea from each)?
10. Indicate some of the responsibilities of the professional insurance buyer (or "risk manager") and the services he is able to render to his employer.
11. After an analysis has been made of the risk problems with respect to any given business there are several ways in which the different risks may be handled. One method is not adopted to the exclusion of others, but each may be most useful for particular risks. Explain.
12. Of what importance are risk managers in the development of new insurance contracts? Insurance regulation?
13. The risk manager, in programing insurance, is faced with the question as to which risks to insure. Why is it that identical properties will be treated differently with respect to insurance, depending upon the ownership?
14. How do the insurance problems of a municipality differ from those of an individual.
15. List the insurance coverages that you would suggest to cover (*a*) the office, contents, and operations of a business office; (*b*) a financial institution, such as a bank or a savings and loan association, and (*c*) the professional risks of a doctor or a dentist.
16. Outline the objectives to be accomplished by an insurance survey. The X corporation has placed its business for years with a number of local agents

in the community. One of the agents has offered to make a survey. What can such a survey be expected to bring to light if management is now satisfied with its present coverage?

17. Insurance surveys sometimes recommend coverages as (*a*) essential, (*b*) desirable, and (*c*) available. Discuss the significance of each. Particularly, why should the person making a survey invite attention to coverages which he feels are not essential to the insured?
18. In rearranging insurance it is the custom, in some instances, to resort to oral binders pending delivery of the policy. If the agent has the authority to bind a risk, this procedure is entirely in order. Indicate some of the dangers against which insurance buyers should guard with respect to oral binders.
19. If an insurance agent makes a survey for a client and the client adopts the program in its entirety, as recommended, what is the position of the agent if a loss develops that proves not to be fully covered by insurance?

APPENDIXES

Appendix A

A HISTORY OF INSURANCE

Insurance seeks to reduce the uncertain consequences of a known peril, so that the cost of losses as they affect individuals will be certain, or at least relatively certain. "People want decent homes to live in; they want to locate them where they can engage in productive work, and they want some safeguard against misfortune which cannot be wholly eliminated in this man-made world of ours."[1] In the process of providing safeguards against hazards the insurance idea has developed.

Entirely aside from its economic connotations, the business of insurance in this country, with its many ramifications and divisions, is a powerful social force[2] that can live and grow only in an atmosphere of free enterprise safeguarded by democratic institutions. Because it is an enterprise of major importance, touching the economic and social welfare of the entire population, it is vested with a public interest that distinguishes it from many other types of business enterprise. Its essential attributes are (*a*) private management, (*b*) competition, and (*c*) regulation. Bearing in mind the significance of the past as it affects the present and future of the business, it is pertinent now to view briefly the development of the insurance idea from its inception.

Commercial Insurance a Recent Development. The development of the insurance idea to an institution of the size and importance it is today is the outgrowth of a long period of evolution.[3] Its beginnings were simple and development was gradual. It was not the result of any

---

[1]Message of the President to Congress, June 8, 1934, *Economic Security Act, Hearings Before Committee on Ways and Means, House of Representatives* (74th Cong., 1st sess.), on H. R. 4120 (Washington, D.C.: U.S. Government Printing Office, 1935), p. 17.

[2]Josiah Royce, the eminent writer, teacher, and philosopher, has said, ". . . the insurance principle comes to be more and more used and useful in modern affairs. Not only does it serve the ends of individuals, or of special groups of individuals. It tends more and more both to pervade and to transform our modern social order. It brings into new syntheses not merely pure and applied science, but private and public interests, individual prudence, and a large regard for the general welfare, thrift, and charity. It discourages recklessness and gambling. It contributes to the sense of stability. It quiets fears and encourages faithfulness." *War and Insurance* (New York: Macmillan Co., 1914), p. 2. Dr. Carleton Thomas Lewis says, "It [insurance] has done more than all the gifts of impulsive charity to foster a sense of human brotherhood and of common interests. It has done more than all repressive legislation to destroy the gambling spirit. It is impossible to conceive of our civilization in its full vigor and progressive power without this principle, which unites the fundamental law of practical economy, that he best serves humanity who best serves himself, with the golden rule of religion, 'Bear ye one another's burdens.' " C. T. Lewis, "Insurance," *Encyclopaedia Britannica* (11th ed.; 1910), Vol. XIV, p. 658.

[3]W. W. McClench, *Betterment of Life Insurance Service* (New York: Association of Life Insurance Presidents, 1919), p. 5.

legislative action.[4] Its history is part of the history of commerce and navigation.[5] It has been described as the last term in the evolution of various legal devices invented to provide against the risks of the sea.[6] The origin of the idea is not easily located. It probably made its appearance with the earliest development of commerce, although not until comparatively recent years did the institution become of great commercial importance.

According to extant records, loans of the type known during the Middle Ages by the terms "bottomry" and "respondentia" served as the earliest means in general commercial use to effect a shifting of the burden of risk. Evidence from Babylon, by no means conclusive, warrants a presumption that a contract similar to bottomry was known to the merchants of that country and may have originated with their commercial expansion as early as 4000–3000 B.C.[7] The evidence from India that bottomry was practiced by the Hindus in 600 B.C. or earlier intimates that the insurance feature of the contract was understood.[8] It is well established that the contract was understood in ancient Greece as early as the fourth century before the Christian Era, and was used in connection with maritime loans.[9] The same form of loan agreement was adopted by the Romans in their commercial practice and, following them, by the maritime nations of Europe during the Middle Ages. Maritime interest furnished a most profitable source of income to the money lenders of ancient Greece, and a bottomry contract developed that in its essentials corresponded to the contract of moderns times.[10] A well-defined procedure for effecting a bottomry agreement was developed. Contracts were formed by drawing up articles of agreement and depositing a record of them with a money

---

[4]W. S. Holdsworth, *The Early History of the Contract of Insurance,* 17 Columbia Law Review 85.

[5]F. L. Hoffman, *Insurance Science and Economics* (New York: Spectator Co., 1911), p. 144.

[6]Holdsworth, *op. cit.,* quoting from Lefort's introduction to Bensa's work on insurance: "Le contrat d'assurance maritime n'est pas dû au génie d'un legislateur; c'est le dernier terme d'une série d'évolutions par lasquelles s'est manifestée l'idée de prévoyance dans la lutte contre les fortunes de mer, lutte qui devait être d'autant plus vive que de jour en jour augmentait l'importance des vies et des intérêts confiés aux caprices des flots" (Bensa, E., *Historie du Contrat d'Assurance au Moyen Age,* translated from the Italian by J. Valery [Paris, 1897], p. vi).

[7]C. F. Trennery, *The Origin and Early History of Insurance, Including the Contract of Bottomry* (London: P. S. King & Son, Ltd., 1926), pp. 5ff.

[8]C. Walford, *Insurance Cyclopedia* (London: Charles and Edwin Layton, 1871–78), Vol. I, p. 334.

[9]Trennery, *op. cit.,* chap. v.

[10]The insurance element in this type of loans agreement is to be found in the provision that, if the security upon which the money is advanced is lost or destroyed, then the debt is canceled. Thus, if a cargo of grain were to be shipped from one port to another, the owner of the grain could borrow its value from a money lender, paying a rate in excess of the current interest rate. If the cargo is lost, its owner is indemnified because he need not repay the loans, and the loss rests upon the money lender. According to the custom developed by the ancient Greeks, the ship or the cargo was made the security for the money lent. There is a possibility that the money received from passage and freight was likewise pledged as security. Loans were made, so far as can be determined, most frequently upon the cargo, less frequently upon the ship, and least often, if at all, upon the money received for passage or freight. Because the lender assumed the risk of loss, the borrower, besides securing capital for use in his undertakings, enjoyed the benefits of a contract that in fact provided insurance protection.

changer.[11] These agreements represented the seed of the modern insurance contract.[12] They were widely and extensively used by the ancient Romans[13] and recognized in Roman law.[14] The contract, as used by the Romans, was utilized by wealthy families as an investment outlet.[15]

The forerunner of fraternal benefit societies' and hence life insurance, also came from ancient Rome. The *collegia tenuiorum*, a guild organization of free wage earners and slaves, provided a fund for the burial of its members.[16] A principal source of income for the society was a system of monthly dues.[17] There is no evidence that these societies rendered assistance in time of sickness or other need.[18] They are believed, however, to have influenced the guilds of the Middle Ages,[19] although these organizations do not trace their origin to any single source.[20] Whatever the origin the guilds gave impetus to the development of the insurance idea. Besides concerning themselves with almsgiving and the care and burial of the dead they established insurance funds for the benefit of the members.[21] This insurance feature was usually made effective through regular payments by members into a common fund out of which disbursements were made to those suffering losses from certain specified disasters. The more common of these included fire, flood, or robbery, though the guild system

---

[11]A. Boeckh, *The Public Economy of the Athenians*, translated by A. Lamb (Boston: Little, Brown & Co., 1857), chap. xxiii.

[12]The question naturally presents itself as to whether any of the ancient peoples had provided themselves with means of indemnification in the event of loss by fire. Relying upon a paper read before the Insurance and Actuarial Society of Glasgow in 1881, quoted by Relton in his excellent work on the history of fire insurance in Great Britain during the seventeenth and eighteenth centuries, the statement is frequently made that the beginning of fire insurance is to be found in the towns and districts of Assyria and the East more than 2,500 years ago. Since its appearance in Relton's book, either through further quotation, or the repetition of the subject matter in subsequent works, the statement has had a wide circulation. It is used as a basis for the assertion now frequently made that a form of mutual fire insurance, through compulsory assessment, was in operation in Assyria at this early date.

Notwithstanding the frequency with which this statement is met in insurance literature, reference to the large number of business documents from Babylonia and Assyria furnishes no evidence of any kind of insurance, and makes inevitable the conclusion that the statement as orginally made was based upon faulty information. The improbability of the correctness of the original conclusion is emphasized when it is recalled that in 1881, when the statement originally appeared, the deciphering of Assyrian cuneiform had not progressed far enough to make possible with any degree of certainty the conclusion at that time presented. Until further information is forthcoming, therefore, the statement, frequently met, that mutual fire insurance in the form of compulsory assessments was known and practiced by the early Assyrians should be recognized as extremely doubtful.

[13]J. Duer, *The Law and Practice of Marine Insurance* (New York: John S. Voohies, 1845), Vol. I, pp. 20–22.

[14]H. J. Roby, *Roman Private Law* (Cambridge: University Press, 1902), Vol. II, p. 75.

[15]Trennery, *op. cit.*, p. 95.

[16]M. A. Rostovtzeff, *The Social and Economic History of the Roman Empire* (Oxford: Clarendon Press, 1926), p. 178.

[17]F. F. Abbott, *Common People of Ancient Rome* (New York: Charles Scribner's Sons, 1912), p. 225.

[18]J. P. Waltzing, *Etude Historique sur les Corporations chez les Romans* (Louvain: Charles Peters, 1895), pp. 301, 303, 321.

[19]Walford, *op. cit.*, Vol. V, p. 342.

[20]E. R. A. Seligman, "Mediaeval Guilds of England," *Publications of the American Economic Association*, Vol. XI (1887-88), p. 9.

[21]T. Smith, *English Gilds* (London: N. Trubner & Co., 1870), p. xxxvi.

of indemnity was eventually extended to cover most of the risks which attached to the enterprises of the time.[22]

There seems to be no evidence that the guilds in England developed into distinct insurance associations, or that any fire insurance association, following the decline of the guilds, had become well established previous to the London fire of 1666. During the Middle Ages bottomry continued to serve as the vehicle for effecting marine insurance.

The Advent of Commercial Insurance. Just when the insurance contract, as we understand it today, first made its appearance is not clear. Ordinances of Barcelona dealing specifically with the subject are found as early as 1436.[23] They were followed by others, and it is clear that in the fifteenth century marine insurance became an established institution.[24] Decrees from Venice antedate the earliest recorded ordinances of Barcelona. The Venetian decrees, while not strictly insurance regulations, in the sense of making provisions regulating the contract, are nevertheless concerned with the subject matter of insurance and demonstrate beyond a doubt the existence of an insurance system among the Venetians at the dawn of the fifteenth century.[25]

The practice of insurance was not limited to the Mediterranean. A mercantile practice of Venice was certain to find its way to England because the Italians, or "Lombards," as they were known, had already secured a strong foothold in England and were competing commercially with the powerful Hanseatic League of the North.[26] Three great centers of

---

[22]Relief not unlike the accident and health insurance of modern times was provided in the event of need in old age, at the loss of sight or limb, upon becoming deaf, dumb, or becoming afflicted with a serious malady such as leprosy. There were guilds which rendered assistance to those who lost cattle, or for the fall of a house. Others provided relief in the case of shipwreck, in the case of imprisonment, or for the legal defense of members who became involved with the law. Sometimes provision was made for gifts to the young people so that they could get started in the world, and dowries were provided for young women. Assistance was frequently rendered in pecuniary difficulties, sometimes as special instances, and in others as a regular feature of the guild benefits. In short, the insurance feature of the guilds was expanded to meet the needs of the times, and the manner of accomplishment cannot but excite admiration.

[23]Duer, *op. cit.*, Vol. I, p. 41.

[24]F. Martin, *The History of Lloyds* (London: Macmillan & Co., Ltd., 1876), Vol. I, p. 35.

[25]M. Hopkins, *A Manual of Marine Insurance* (Philadelphia: J. B. Lippincott & Co., 1867), p. 20.

[26]While the date of the introduction of the insurance contract cannot be accurately fixed, the hypothesis that it originated in Italy deserves attention. During the Middle Ages the spread of commercial institutions was from the south to the north. As early as the twelfth century, papal emissaries had penetrated the remote parts of northwestern Europe and were instrumental in disseminating the financial ideas of the south. Italian merchants followed the traveling markets or fairs of northern France, Germany, and England; and they were accompanied by Lombard money changers. Expanding their operations throughout the Continent during the thirteenth century, the Lombards became powerful financiers, and their influence was great. In the hands of their colony in London rested the foreign trade of the kingdom, and to them tradition ascribes the introduction of insurance to England.

Added to tradition is a powerful argument from etymology. The word "policy" which is used today to designate the name of the written instrument containing the contract comes from the Italian. The word in the English language, or in any other language than the Italian, has no meaning save that arbitrarily ascribed to it. *Polizza*, the Italian word from which "policy" is derived, is used as the name of a contract in writing that furnishes evidence of or creates a legal obligation. Hence its application

trade during the period were Lübeck on the Baltic, a center of the Hanseatic League activities; Florence, with trade extending from the great Italian cities to London; and Venice, with an extensive trade in the Near East. The Italian banking families carried on trading activities throughout Europe and maintained branches in the northern cities. Business methods had develped to a point where joint stock companies were organized. Double-entry bookkeeping was an established practice and bankers received deposits, cashed checks, and made loans on much the same basis as such transactions are carried on today. Shippers formed partnerships and joint stock companies, and by this time marine insurance had spread through the lanes of commerce and was well known and commonly used by the merchants and shipowners throughout the whole of continental Europe. The more cumbersome bottomry contract had been supplanted by the contract of indemnity.[27]

The Individual Underwriter. The arrival of the sixteenth century found the practice of marine insurance general and its principles well understood in the maritime nations. For many years after the turn of the century, insurance underwriting was not a specialized business but was carried on by merchants who, from time to time, committed themselves to risks by subscribing to policies as a side line to their other affairs. The policies were written not by companies but by individuals or groups of

---

to the insurance contract by the Italians was perfectly correct, though its use was by no means limited to such contracts. The term has been carried out of the Italian as a name for the insurance contract and leads to the presumption that the insurance idea was introduced by the Italians and the contract designated by them a *polizza.*

[27]The oldest treatise in a modern language dealing with the subject matter of insurance is that entitled *Le Guidon de la Mer,* published in 1671 by Cleirac, a learned French jurist, in the second part of his work on the uses and customs of the sea (*Us et Coutumes de la Mer*). No account is given by Cleirac of the author or origin of the work. Cleirac, in his commentary upon the first article of *Le Guidon,* gives us the earliest statement in any work on insurance concerning its origin. He asserts that insurance was invented by the Jews when they were expelled from France by Philip Augustus in 1182 and sought and found refuge in Italy. This opinion is founded, he states, upon a statement in the universal history of Giovanni Villani, who according to Dr. Duer died at an advanced age in 1348, "the most justly celebrated of the early Florentine historians." It is the theory that the Jews made payments called presents to insurers who assumed, as far as the shipments were concerned, all the risks of the voyage. The Lombards, who were spectators of the transactions, are believed to have preserved the forms of the instruments used and afterwards adapted them to their own commercial transactions.

Another hypothesis was advanced by Vilagut, a doctor of law, in his treatise *De Usuris* published in Venice in 1589. The *Corpus juris canonici* prohibited interest, though certain exceptions were permitted. Such was the situation in bottomry loans where the lender assumed the risks of the venture. In 1243 a decree was promulgated by Pope Gregory IX declaring such loans prohibited as usurious. Aluzet, a French writer, commenting upon this decree, states that while some grammatical doubts were at first raised as to its true interpretation, it was soon understood to be a total prohibition of loans on bottomry and respondentia as usurious; and he adds that it was for the purpose of evading this prohibition, by separating the assumption of the risk from the loan of money, that the contract of insurance was invented. Aluzet states, however, that soon after publication, by reference to the context of the entire document, it was apparent that the true meaning intended was *usurarius non est censendus,* the important word *non* having been omitted by mistake. It was during the period of doubt that insurance was invented.

Insurance historians have commented at some length upon both hypotheses, and by no means agree in their evaluations.

individuals who undertook to assume the risks for a profit. The security thus provided was only as strong as the individual or individuals providing the insurance.

In England the early policies were issued in this manner; and, just as the insurers were merchants, so the business of insurance was in the hands of the sworn brokers who acted as agents for the merchants in buying and selling goods. It was the custom, though not followed in every instance, to have the policies drawn up and attested by a notary.[28] Lombard Street seems to have been the headquarters for merchants engaged in taking marine risks, though there appears to have been no particular control or centralization of facilities.[29]

The "Handmaiden of Commerce." The presumption that a contract similar to bottomry was understood and practiced in ancient Babylon has already been noticed. The use of the contract has been attributed particularly to the period marked by the reign of Hammurabi.[30] The path of development that brings the contract to the Mediterranean countries is not clear. Recalling the commercial prestige of Babylon, it would not be an unexpected development to find the bottomry relationship that appeared in the Mediterranean countries to have stemmed from the Babylonian contracts. In Babylon the principal hazard that concerned merchants was the possible robbery of the caravans. In seagoing ventures the perils that concerned merchants were those of the sea. In each instance the principle involved was identical. The insurance idea in some form seems to appear with the development of commercial activity. It is indeed "the handmaiden of commerce."

Because of the paucity of evidence, we have no means of knowing exactly when the contract developed in ancient Greece. Neither do we know the route by which it arrived there. There is a suggestion that it may have found its way to Greece through India.[31] Whatever the route, when we meet with the contract in Greece, we find it to be a well-established business practice. It was also known and practiced by other of the maritime nations in commercial contract with Greece. Legislation regarding the contract was incorporated in the Laws of Rhodes.[32] While the contract

---

[28]C. Wright and E. Fayle, *A History of Lloyds* (London: Macmillan & Co., Ltd., 1928), p. 35.

[29]The first English statute relating to the subject of insurance is the famous 43 Eliz., c. 12 of 1601, which has for its purpose the establishment of a tribunal, before which disputes arising out of the insurance contract might be settled. The preamble of the act refers to insurance as a well-established business stating "it has bene tyme out of mynde an usage amongste merchants. . . ."

The first case upon insurance to be found in any book of reports was mentioned by Lord Coke in Dowdale's case decided in 1588. In the course of the action the defendants contended that because the loss arose out of the realm the case could not be tried in London. It was held that: "Where as well the contract as the performance of it is wholly made or to be done beyond the sea, it is not triable under our law, but if the promise be made in England it shall be tried." It seems at the time to have been the prevailing idea, however, that disputes arising out of the contract of insurance should be settled by special tribunals rather than by appeal to the courts.

[30]Circa 2123-2081 B.C.

[31]Walford, *op. cit.*, Vol. I, p. 334. See also *Laws of Manu*, viii, 157. *Manava Dharma Castra. Les Lois de Manu.* Traduitus du Sancrit per J. Strehly. Annales du Musee Guimet, Tomo deuixeme (Paris: Ernest Lerous, 1893).

[32]Boeckh, *op. cit.*, p. 184-85.

was known outside of Greece during the Homeric age, there was little commercial activity in the country itself. The Homeric nobles satisfied their simple requirements with the products of their own land, their riches consisting chiefly in flocks, herds, and slaves. Luxuries they imported, securing them from traders of other countries who stopped to dispose of their cargoes. The Phoenicians provided most of the articles imported during this early period, and they in turn secured them by journeying to the far corners of the known world. Wherever there was a prospect of gain, these shrewd traders were to be found; their voyages reached from Britain on the west to India on the east.[33] That the Phoenicians may have been the intermediary by which a knowledge of the practice of bottomry was carried from the more ancient civilization to the Greeks seems very probable. With the advent of the period marked by the great commercial expansion of Greek commerce—which includes the rise to commercial supremacy of the city of Rhodes—great trade routes were established between Greece and the far corners of the world. Rhodes was founded in 408 B.C. The first reference to bottomry in Greece occurs around 350 B.C. To be sure, the contract when we meet it in Greece had been perfected and evidenced a long period of development. At this time the Greeks had established a great line of trade from Hellas, past Rhodes and Cyprus, along the coast of Phoenicia to Egypt. Over this route the Greeks secured the products of the Far East, India, Arabia, and Babylon. It is quite probable that the bottomry contract was introduced into Greece during this period of commercial activity, when the influence of Phoenicia upon Greece was on the wane.

Bottomry with the Romans was in its essentials the same contract as that developed by the Greeks. *Trajeticia pecunia*, the term applied in Roman law to money lent on bottomry, referred to money lent for mercantile adventure beyond the sea, with repayment conditional upon the safe arrival of the security at its destination.[34]

The insurance element in the agreement was clearly defined in Rome. The risk assumed by the creditor was considered a sufficient reason to warrant a higher rate than the usual rate of interest. Contrary to the situation that existed in Greece, however, the *naticum fenus* or *usurae maritimae* could be charged not for the time the borrower held the money but only for the time over which the creditor's risk in the voyage extended. The utility of the contract as a vehicle for risk bearing, and therefore as a means for effecting insurance, was recognized by the Romans; and they extended its use to other than marine undertakings.[35] Whether the contract of insurance was known to the Romans, however, aside from the

---

[33]P. Gardner and F. B. Jevons, *A Manual of Greek Antiquities* (New York: Charles Scribner's Sons, 1895), p. 388.

[34]Roby, *op. cit.*, Vol. II, p. 75.

[35]There is, for example, an instance cited of a loan made to a fisherman for the purpose of purchasing apparatus, repayment of the loan depending upon the catch of fish. This was an instance where the borrower was insured against loss arising out of disbursements, in preparation for an undertaking that might turn out unsatisfactorily. There is another case, where money was lent to an athlete for training purposes, repayment to be made in the event he won at the contests. From these instances it may be seen that the Romans used the conditional loan agreement as a means for shifting the burden of risk in widely different fields and did not, therefore, limit themselves in its application to the field of marine undertakings. Roby, *op. cit.*, p. 76.

insurance element to be found in the bottomry agreement, will, until further information comes to light, remain a matter of speculation.[36]

With the decline of the Roman influence, there is little recorded evidence to throw light upon the development of marine insurance until the revival of commerce in the Middle Ages. It is not easy to believe, however, that an insurance institution such as bottomry—so widely known and so useful in the commercial world—should fall into disuse without a substitute taking its place. It is easier to believe the records as lacking than to believe the great shipping centers carried on their business without insurance protection.

Under the feudal system there were trade organizations of cities and of separate callings that may have furnished some form of marine insurance, and marine risks were among those covered by certain of the guilds. Even though some protection was afforded by these sources, recalling the extent of the diffusion of Roman influence particularly through the incorporation of Roman laws into later codes, it is not to be presumed that bottomry was unknown or fell into disuse only to be revived again at a later time.[37] Certainly, at the close of the thirteenth and early in the fourteenth century, with the activities of the Hanseatic League, the language of the law left no room for doubt as to the use of bottomry as a commercial practice; and reference is made in such a way as to permit the inference that it has

---

[36]There are in the writings of the classical authors four passages, upon which have been centered the attention of writers on insurance, and which have been held forth as proof that insurance not only was known to the Romans but also was a common commereial practice. The passages in question include two references in Livy (*Ad Urbe Condita*, xxiii, c. 49) dated around 215 B.C., another from a private letter of Cicero (*Epistolae ad C. Sallust*) dated 49 B.C., and a final instance from Suetonius (*De Vita Caesarum*, v. 18) dated at A.D. 58. The Livy references have to do with a government assurance to merchants against loss for supplies shipped to military forces operating in Spain. Cicero refers to guarantees to protect public monies against possible loss while in transit. The reference in Suetonius is to a guarantee to owners of corn against loss while being shipped to Rome. The guarantee was made to encourage the import of corn during a period of severe famine. Writers have by no means agreed in their interpretation of these passages in the light of their proving a reference to a contract of insurance. They do, however, afford evidence that the insurance idea was utilized in times of necessity.

[37]The period from the fifth to the eleventh century is extremely poor in documentary evidence, and records of business transactions or mercantile practices that might throw light upon the field of insurance are lacking. It may be supposed, however, that the practice of bottomry continued uninterrupted down to the ninth century, for in the *Basilica*, a compilation of laws made by the Byzantine Emperor Basilius in A.D. 867-80, there are to be found regulations regarding the practice that follow in all important particulars those that appear in the *Digest of Justinian*. The *Jus Navale Rhodeorum*, a Greek compilation whose date is placed earlier than A.D. 1167, likewise contains regulations regarding loans on bottomry essentially the same as those to be found in the earlier *Digest*. At this point, however, we come to a break, for the two important marine codes governing the European nations are conspicuously silent regarding either bottomry or marine insurance. The famous *Consolatio del Mare*, in force as early as the eleventh century, and the *Roles D'Oleron*, known as the "laws or judgments of Oleron," published in the thirteenth century make no mention of either bottomry or insurance. The danger of concluding, however, that bottomry was no longer used in commercial practice and that insurance was unknown, solely because affirmative evidence is lacking in legislative expression, is easily demonstrable. Practices common to merchants have existed for long periods before regulations concerning them were incorporated in the legal system. Experience shows that in the case of insurance, it has existed probably in every country for a long time as a practice among merchants before the subject became a matter of law.

long been in use as a commercial custom.[38] Bottomry during the Middle Ages furnishes no new contribution to the science of insurance but remains in its essentials the same contract as practiced in ancient Greece, 1,500 years earlier.

Insurance Becomes Specialized Business. By the beginning of the eighteenth century the business of insurance brokerage had become a specialized occupation. As the system developed, two marked defects eventually forced themselves to the attention of the commercial community and were instrumental in effecting the evolution of the business. While the business of insurance had centered in the hands of specialists, a shortcoming was to be found in the lack of any kind of a financial guarantee of stability on the part of the underwriters.[39] They committed themselves as individuals to a part of the risk insured under the various policies. And a number of these individuals were interested as insurers of each risk. The second defect was that there was no recognized center for carrying on the business, and the brokers who had policies to complete were obliged to go from office to office in order to secure sufficient insurers.

Without any concerted action or preconceived design on the part of any group, underwriters and brokers with common interests and no other places to meet begin to assemble in the coffeehouses, which seemed admirably designed to serve their needs. There seems to have been no effort on the part of the coffeehouse managers to limit their patronage to any given class; anyone who desired might be served. But it was natural that patrons with common interests should be attracted to each other, and specialization in the coffeehouses was the result.[40]

The business was at the outset confined to marine risks. It was carried on by merchants, and the brokers had to go from office to coffeehouse in the course of completing policies. There was, up to the close of the seventeenth century, no centralization of the business; and so far as specialization was concerned, it was at this time limited to the brokers.

Fire Insurance Lags. The development of the insurance of buildings and goods against loss by fire followed by many centuries the custom of insuring marine risks. It is generally conceded that the great fire of London in 1666 brought the world face to face with the fire menace and directed the attention of insurance underwriters to the possibility of insuring the risk.[41] While the lag in the development of fire insurance may, to a degree,

---

[38]Duer, *op. cit.*, Vol. I, p. 41.

[39]Wright and Fayle, *op. cit.*, p. 40.

[40]The first coffeehouse of which there is a record opened in 1652. Within a very short time these coffeehouses had become the popular resort of merchants who patronized them for business purposes. While not the first of these, the coffeehouse of Edward Lloyd has become inseparately associated with insurance underwriting. It was destined to become famous in insurance history. Recognizing the value of supplying business news, Lloyd seized an initiative that enabled his coffeehouse to outdistance its competitors. From the coffeehouses of the day, and particularly from Lloyd's, it may fairly be said that the great present-day insurance institution known as "Lloyd's" traces its beginning.

[41]There are some isolated references to earlier attempts to provide fire insurance protection. There is a reference that would indicate the practice of fire insurance in Scotland early in the fifteenth century. The information is vague and furnishes no evidence as to the form in which the insurance was effected. It is stated that in 1437 an act was passed in the Seventh Parliament of King James I, of Scotland which bore the title, "The leave to Merchants to sure their gudes." The act itself is now lost, and information concerning its details are wanting. Such knowledge as we have of the legislation

(Continued on next page)

be attributable to the custom of neighbors helping when a fire loss occurs as well as to the fire insurance feature of guild membership, it is also true that lack of initiative in the development of fire insurance may be attributable to a characteristic of human nature.

There is a tendency on the part of individuals to disregard risks to which they have become conditioned. They become entirely unconscious of their existence. Because of the tendency to disregard customary risks in the early days, frequently no steps were taken to effect insurance where the need was greatest. It is to be noticed that the loss of a ship or cargo involved substantial amounts of capital and was a loss suffered by some and not by others. On the other hand, fire losses were frequently made good by the contributions from families, neighbors, or guild benefits. It is not surprising that a plan for sharing marine losses should develop while fire losses were ignored. As individuals separated themselves from the family group, the concept of individual rights and individual property developed. As time went by, with the increase in individual wealth, the need for some form of protection against loss by reason of unforeseen eventualities became intensified. As the family gave way to more and more individualistic operation, the guilds afforded protection—sometimes very limited—to its members. Nevertheless, the protection thus afforded was unquestionably an inhibiting influence to the development of a modern insurance system not limited to classes or groups. That the guilds had less influence in the case of marine insurance than in other fields has been attributed to the fact that marine ventures were in the hands of the wealthy and the influence of the guilds was felt less upon them than upon the poorer groups. In any case, as time went on, with reactions against the concept of "mercantilism," the principle of *laissez faire* inaugurated a new age of individualism. A natural concomitant was an intensified development of private insurance ventures.

Such was the relationship between the hazards of fire and those of the sea. Buildings, merchandise, furniture, and the like were familiar possessions. The individual became conditioned to the risks to which they were subjected. The human tendency to do things as they have always been done manifested itself, and current custom and methods as a matter of habit were accepted as good enough. Not so with marine ventures; here a choice must be made. The unconscious acceptance of risk changes to the conscious assumption. When a risk is consiciously assumed, the person assuming it establishes the conditions. To minimize the burden of such risks marine insurance was devised. With respect to land and merchandise, as cities grew and hazards increased, there was no conscious assumption of risk but a tendency to ignore the hazards of fire. The stark disaster represented by the fire of 1666 changed this.[42]

---

of James dealing with the subject of fire concerns itself with fire protection and not with the matter of insurance. The shred of evidence found in the title of the foregoing act furnished us little information that is of value, although we may conclude from this title of the law that some form of fire insurance was known to the merchants and used by them (F. S. Relton, *An Account of the Fire Insurance Companies, Associations, Institutions, Projects, and Schemes, Established and Projected in Great Britain and Ireland during the 17th and 18th Centuries, including the Sun Fire Office, also of Charles Povey* [London: Sonnershein and Company, 1893] p. 8).

[42]So great was the calamity, that the anniversary of the fire was observed as a fast day for over a hundred years. The fire burned for four days and nights, and its destruction spread over 436 acres of the city's area. Over 85 per cent of the buildings of the city were estimated destroyed, with a property loss estimated at £ 10,000,000. The blow

The Bubble Period. The second decade of the eighteenth century will always be remembered as an era of stark speculative madness. Strange as it may seem, when the bubbles had burst and the wreckage had cleared away, the business of insurance was in the final stages of the development that carried it to the threshold of modern times. In fact, if a date can be named that marks the beginning of insurance as practiced today, that date may be fixed at the close of the "bubble" period, with the granting of Royal Charters to two groups of insurers who became the first of the chartered insurance companies.

Speculation during the period centered around the stock of the South Sea Company organized in 1711 by the Earl of Oxford with an important trading monopoly. When the speculative fever had commenced its work, the soaring market for South Sea stock soon carried it out of reach of thousands who were unable to purchase the coveted security. Rich and poor alike began a scramble for stocks, and swindlers and rogues were not lacking to supply the demand. Other companies sprang up, and opportunities to subscribe for their stock were offered to a gullible public. In the midst of this orgy of speculation and the organization of get-rich-quick undertakings, it was not to be expected that the business of insurance would be slighted, nor was it. During the period of the "bubble" mania, there were brought forth about a hundred schemes concerned with insurance, most of them fraudulent or at least impracticable.[43] Strange as it may seem, in this period noted particularly for its frauds and cheats, two great insurance companies were organized that have enjoyed an uninterrupted business from that day to this—a span of over two centuries —and they rank today among the leaders in the field.

When the speculative crash came, it was complete. Consternation and rage were everywhere, and the credit of the country was shaken to its very foundations. Parliament was hastily summoned; and upon investigation, frauds were uncovered in which members of the government were involved. The scandal was terrific. In striking the death blow to the bubbles of the period, an important insurance development was effected. A turning point was marked with the establishment of the first chartered companies.

On May 31, 1720, the now famous Bubble Act passed the Commons by 123 votes to 22, passed the Lords soon after, and received royal approval

---

staggered the city and the kingdom, and it is not surprising that the attention of business interests was then drawn to fire insurance. Immediately following the fire, it is reported that mutual insurance groups were formed to effect fire insurance. In 1667 an office was opened by Dr. Nicholas Barbon that merged in 1680 into the "Fire Office." Barbon was the first projector of fire insurance in England who succeeded in bringing his scheme to maturity. Other offices followed, notably the Hand in Hand organized in 1696 and the Sun Fire Office organized in 1710 as a partnership and changed to a joint stock company in 1726. The Sun marks the permanent inauguration of fire underwriting by a nonmutual company.

[43]Besides companies for insuring houses and goods from fire, as well as ships and merchandise at sea, there were companies organized to insure "horses dying natural deaths, stolen, or disabled," and "Masters and Mistresses against losses they shall sustain against servants' thefts, etc." There was insurance for "Insuring and Increasing Children's Fortunes"; for "Insurance from death by drinking Geneva"; for "Assurance from lying"; for "Insurance from Housebreakers"; for "Rum Insurance"; for "Insurance from Highwaymen"; for "Insurance Against Divorce"; and numerous others. The extent to which the absurdity was carried may be estimated from the organization of "A project to insure uniformity amongst Protestant dissenters"; and "Another to insure it amongst the Orthodox" (Martin, *op. cit.*, p. 89).

under date of June 10. Petitions of two companies for charters were pending, and under the terms of the act the king was authorized to grant the two charters for marine insurance and all other corporations were expressly prohibited from entering this business. The right was still reserved for individual underwriters to continue in the business, and this provision exerted a powerful force in shaping the trend of insurance business.

On June 22, 1720, Royal Charters were granted both companies. The first was chartered under the name of the "London Assurance Corporation," and the other was called the "Royal Exchange Assurance Corporation." While it was apparently the intent of the organizers of these companies to write marine business at the beginning, for which purpose their charters were granted, the following year both merged fire insurance offices that had already been established and were granted charters that permitted the writing of fire and life business.[44]

Beginning of Modern Insurance Business. With the granting of the Royal Charters to the London Assurance Corporation and the Royal Exchange Assurance Corporation, we are brought down to the early days of the modern business of insurance. Both of these companies have been continually in business from the date of their incorporation. Under the terms of the Bubble Act, individual underwriters were still permitted to do business, and the Act served as a great stimulus to the business of the individual underwriters, because under its terms all insurance that was not placed with the two chartered companies fell to them. It was the further association of these individual underwriters that gave rise to the development of Lloyd's, from whose method of doing business has grown not only the great organization in England that bears the name but also the considerable number of similar groups of individual underwriters, whose business is located in different parts of the world, and who are known as Lloyd's Groups. The individual underwriters continued for a considerable period as a dominating factor.

First American Insurance Covered Marine Risks. The first policies issued in this country were marine coverages, issued in part by agents of English companies, and in part by American interests. Records dated as early as 1682 indicate that the vessels plying between England and the colonies carried insurance; and an insurance office in Philadelphia was advertising in newspapers as early as 1721.[45] Within the next 50 years numerous offices were established, but the business was confined primarily to the writing of marine risks.

With the growth of American shipping, marine insurance attained a position of considerable importance. This was particularly the case in New England, where shipbuilding and ocean transportation were leading forms of business activity. The first major setback came with the War of 1812. American shipping was in a state of demoralization, and many marine underwriters failed.[46]

First American Company. With the growth of cities on the Atlantic

---

[44]G. S. Street, *The London Assurance, 1720-1920* (printed for private circulation, London, 1920), p. 21.

[45]S. Huebner, "The Development and Present Status of Marine Insurance in the United States," *Annals of the American Academy of Political and Social Science,* Vol. XXVI, No. 2 (September, 1905), p. 432.

[46]F. C. Oviatt, "Historical Study of Fire Insurance in the United States," *Annals of the American Academy of Political and Social Science,* Vol. XXVI, No. 2 (September, 1905), p. 336.

seaboard and the gradual increase in capital invested in buildings, the problem of fire became of increasing importance. Marine insurance had been written for a considerable period before any effort was made to adapt the principle of insurance to buildings. The earliest efforts to meet the fire problem resulted in the establishment of fire-fighting companies. The first of these was organized by Benjamin Franklin in Philadelphia during the winter of 1730. It was over two decades later, in 1752, that Franklin organized the first incorporated fire insurance company in America.[47] This company is a mutual organization and has the distinction of being the oldest insurance company now in business.[48] Underwriting continued, in the colonial period, largely in the hands of individual underwriters. There was little supervision over their activities, and their facilities were extremely limited. They were powerful enough, however, to bring formidable opposition to bear when a charter was sought for a stock insurance company. The first such charter was granted to the Insurance Company of North America in 1794, two years after the company was organized for business. The company was organized to do a marine business but extended its activities to fire lines during its first year. The Insurance Company of North America is the oldest American joint stock insurance corporation and occupies today an important place in the business of insurance.[49] By the close of the century, ten mutuals and four stock companies were formed; and by 1820 there were 17 stock companies in New York alone, with numerous other companies along the Atlantic seaboard.

First Life Insurance. The Presbyterian Ministers' Fund was granted a charter from the Province of Pennsylvania in 1759. This company was the first permanent life insurance organization to be established in this country. For a considerable period, the company specialized in the writing of annuities and, for a period prior to 1875, was known as the "Presbyterian Annuity Company." After 1875 the company assumed a position of con-

---

[47]Franklin had written a great deal on the subject of fire protection in his *Pennsylvania Gazette,* and it is not unnatural that he should have turned his attention to fire insurance. It was not, however, until 1752 that a fire insurance company was actually formed. Following an advertisement inserted in the *Gazette,* a group of citizens organized the Philadelphia Contributionship, patterned after the Amicable Contributionship of London. Both companies designated the buildings they insured with a mark designed as two clasped hands, and because of this both companies became known as the "Hand in Hand". Franklin was one of the first to subscribe to the new company and was chosen its first director. John Morton and Robert Morris, signers of the Declaration of Ind ependence, were among the founders and among the first to whom policies were issued.

[48]Fire insurance business in the colonies was stimulated by the fact that the London insurance companies were unable, because of charter limitations, to write fire insurance in America. Applications for such insurance were, therefore, rejected. Local insurance companies were formed, and it is generally believed that the first of these, "The Friendly Society," dates from November, 1735, and was founded in Charleston, South Carolina. The great fire of November 18-20, 1740, apparently put the company out of business. Franklin's company was, therefore, not the first fire insurance company organized but is believed to be the first incorporated company in America and certainly the oldest in business today.

[49]For a complete history of the Insurance Company of North America see Marquis James, *Biography of Business 1792-1942* (Indianapolis: Bobbs-Merrill Company, 1942). Since the Insurance Company of North America parallels in its development the history of property insurance in the United States, this work is a valuable case study of insurance history.

siderable importance in the life insurance field, writing life insurance for clergymen.[50]

Ten years after the founding of the Presbyterian Company, other companies were organized along similar lines in New York, New Jersey, and Pennsylvania for the benefit of Episcopal clergymen. After the Revolution, the Episcopal companies became generally inactive, with the exception of the Pennsylvania company, which enjoyed a long period of usefulness but confined its activities to insuring only Episcopal clergymen. These organizations, however, together with the Presbyterian Company, mark the transition from policies issued by individual underwriters to those issued by incorporated organizations.

The need for greater security and stability of life underwriters was answered by the organization of life insurance companies with large sums in the form of paid-in capital. A number of the early ventures failed. No small contributing factor to the early difficulties was to be found in the extreme fluctuations in the death rate. Epidemics of smallpox, diphtheria, and other diseases swept through the cities bringing death to abnormally large numbers. However, during this period stock life insurance companies made a start; and the companies successfully organized marked the inauguration of life insurance in the United States as a business institution.

The first of the companies, the Pennsylvania Company for the Insurance on Lives, was organized in 1809 and introduced numerous innovations in this country, notably: the requirement of an application and medical examination and premium charges based upon the age of the applicant. The New York Life Insurance and Trust Company was chartered in 1830 and from the first was active in writing life insurance business. The total volume of business written by these companies was small, and they eventually abandoned the business but continued to do a banking and trust business in the communities where they were chartered.

By 1800 there were not more than a hundred policyholders in the country. There was little demand for life insurance because it was little understood and there was considerable prejudice against the idea. Following the turn of the century a few life companies were organized in America, but the business expanded rapidly abroad. The period was marked by many failures. Bubble companies were organized, and frauds were practiced upon the companies by criminals. Control and supervision were lacking, and the business was unstable and widely regarded with suspicion.

Period of Expansion. The period immediately following 1835 was one of great expansion. It has been referred to as the "period of trial and error." With the rapid development of transportation and communication facilities, an outstanding effect upon the business of insurance was the tendency to eliminate small local companies. The business tended to gravitate into the hands of the more substantial organizations doing business over a wide territory. Competition between the companies continued keen, often to the detriment of the business.

It will be remembered that prior to the War between the States industrial activity in this country was largely in the handicraft stage. Business was largely carried on by merchants who operated one- or two-man enterprises. Commercial enterprises were local in their operations. Transportation of merchandise was effected either by ocean steamships or by riverboats or canalboats.

---

[50]The Insurance Company of North America, whose organization has already been noticed, was authorized to write life insurance. By 1799 only a few policies were issued, and within a very few years the company discontinued its life insurance business.

During this period the New England Mutual Life Insurance Company commenced business. The charter was granted in 1836, but the company did not begin to write insurance until 1844. The Mutual Life Insurance Company of New York had in the meantime been chartered and had written its first business in 1843. The organization of these companies marks the advent of a new era in American life insurance. So long as the agrarian economy was the predominant one and individual security was a family and neighborhood problem, the need for life insurance was less apparent than was the case in a later period of development with the concentration of population in cities. Nevertheless, in the period between 1843 and 1850, 12 important companies entered the field and the basis for a sound life insurance was established.[51] Accident and health insurance made its appearance but was sold in small volume.

The business of fire insurance continued to develop. The necesssity for a wide geographical distribution of risk became increasingly apparent. This prompted the development of the American agency system as a feeder for companies that might otherwide be local in their operations. The business responded to meet the needs of shipping, finance, and trade; and because of the increase in economic activity, insurance, of necessity, expanded to meet the need.

Period of Growing Pains. The years immediately following the War between the States were marked by great industrial activity. As the years of the postwar depression passed, whole new industries made their appearance. Mass-production techniques were followed by expanding commerce and increased property values. Merchants' stocks reached hitherto unheard-of values, and population tended to gravitate to urban areas. The development of the fire insurance business was inhibited by the lack of fire-fighting equipment. This drawback was overcome by the replacement of volunteer firemen and handpumps with professional companies and steam fire engines. Construction yielded less readily to fire-prevention requirements, but building codes began to make their appearance with requirements oriented in the direction of fire prevention. Nevertheless, flimsy construction persisted in many areas; and, when disastrous conflagrations made their appearance, the need of the fire insurance companies for adequate reserves as well as geographical distribution of risks became recognizable as a paramount requirement of sound fire insurance underwriting. Rate cutting, incendiarism, disastrous competition, and hostile legislation—all contributed to the problems of the period.[52]

---

[51]During this period a table of mortality based upon American data was drawn up, and level premium policies were made available. Adequate reserve plans were developed, and dividends were distributed on a scientific basis. Physical impairments as well as occupational hazards were given consideration as underwriting factors. State regulation of insurance companies became a factor in the business, and the agency system for marketing the insurance developed.

[52]Two great fires severely tested the fire insurance business: the Chicago fire of 1871 with a property loss estimated in excess of $153 million and an insurance loss of over $96.5 million, and the Boston fire of 1872 with a property loss of $75 million and an insurance loss of $56 million. Many companies were unable to meet their obligations and failed as a result of the Chicago fire. The Boston disaster in the year following the Chicago catastrophe brought a stunning blow to the insurance companies. Within 24 hours, 65 acres were burned over, with the destruction of 776 buildings. Other destructive fires, before these two, occurred in New Orleans in 1854; Troy, New York, in 1862; and Portland, Maine, in 1866. It was the Boston and Chicago fires, however, that brought real consternation to the fire insurance underwriters and demonstrated once and for all that failure to secure geographical distribution of risks invited disaster.

During this period we find three lasting developments of importance: (1) As a result of expansion, companies began to appoint agents. (2) In large centers they began to pay brokers for business. (3) It became necessary to provide for the inspection of risks and the adjustment of losses at points distant from the home office. Hence, we have the appearance of the *local agent*, the *broker*, and the *field man*.

Life insurance, during the period, enjoyed a phenomenal growth. This business, too, suffered serious failures. Business quadrupled from the end of the War between the States to the panic of 1872-73. In the period immediately following the outbreak of the war, many of the British companies withdrew their operations from this country. New companies were organized here and, with supervision in its infancy, the practices of the companies were not always in line with prudence, sound judgment, or even honesty. The economic depression that followed the panic resulted in reducing the number of companies by one half.

Inception of State Regulation. Regulation is generally recognized to be one of the important contributing factors to the soundness of the present-day system of insurance. Regulation does not create high ethical standards, but it seems to control or eliminate those who would subvert the business to unethical ends. Regulation, as we understand the term today, was a long time in coming. The first vestiges made their appearance about a century ago. In New Hampshire, legislation was enacted establishing the first board of insurance commissioners in 1851.[53] Massachusetts followed in 1852,[54] and Rhode Island in 1856.[55] However, legislation regulatory in nature made its appearance far earlier. The first regulatory statutes in the United States were the legislative enactments chartering the early stock insurance companies.[56] The Insurance Company of North America, the first such company to be incorporated in the United States, received its charter from Pennsylvania April 14, 1794. By statute, limitations were placed upon the investments of the company, the real estate it could hold, and the depository of its funds; and provision was made for a reserve for losses. The action of Pennsylvania was followed in other states, and it became customary in granting charters to insurance companies to make provisions to provide for the solvency of the company.[57] The business of insurance soon attracted the attention of taxing authorities as a source of revenue.[58] When licenses were issued, it became the custom to secure evidence of financial responsibility. The conception that insurers had a responsibility to the public, in which the governing authority had an interest, made its appearance almost coincident with the development of the insurance idea as a business institution.[59] In this country, the serious regulation of the business as a state function began with the establishment of the state insurance departments.

[53]N.H. L. 1851, c. 1111.

[54]Mass. L. 1852, c. 231.

[55]R.I. L. 1854, sec. 17.

[56]E. W. Patterson, *The Insurance Commissioner in the United States* (Cambridge: Harvard University Press, 1927), p. 523.

[57]*Ibid.* It has already been noticed that the Insurance Company of North America was organized for business in 1792. In December, 1792, the General Assembly of Pennsylvania was petitioned for permission to incorporate the company. It was not until April 14, 1794, that the incorporation of the company was actually authorized.

[58]*Ibid.*, p. 524, citing Pa. L., 1809-10, c. 59, p. 81.

[59]It is an interesting commentary on insurance regulation that the earliest known statutes dealing with the subject of insurance treat of insurance regulation. These were the Barcelona Statutes of 1458, 1461, and 1484.

The Insurance Department. Toward the middle of the nineteenth century the insurance business began to reach a size and importance that gave continued emphasis to a public interest. The recognition on the part of legislative authority to the cooperative nature of the business, together with the disastrous experience of failures growing out of rate wars and other unhealthy competitive practices, made it increasingly apparent that regulation, far more reaching in its operation than had previously been in vogue, would be imperative if the business of insurance was to retain public confidence—in fact, if the business were indeed to survive.

The first state insurance department was organized by Massachusetts in 1855, followed by New York in 1859. The first officials appointed for supervision in Massachusetts were the secretary, treasurer, and auditor of the commonwealth. These officials were appointed in 1852 to constitute a board of insurance commissioners. It was not until 1855 that an independent insurance department was created. As early as 1851 the state of New York required life insurance companies to deposit with it a fixed sum in approved securities as a condition precedent to securing authority to do a life insurance business in that state. Prior to 1859, other laws were enacted setting forth the conditions required for the organization or operation of an insurance company. There were, however, many failures—some tainted with fraud, others the outgrowth of inefficiency or unscientific management—and the necessity for actual supervision was indicated. In due course, other states followed Massachusetts and New York in establishing insurance departments—Connecticut in 1865, Ohio in 1867—until eventually the business of insurance was under the direct supervision of state authorities in every state in the Union.[60]

Early in the course of development of regulation it was recognized that the insurance business, as it was developing, tended to become interstate in its operations. Those most intimately associated with the business and the development of regulation saw the possiblities of confusion arising from state control and were, from the earliest days, advocates of federal regulation. Probably the first formal recommendation looking toward federal regulation was that made in 1865 by Elizur Wright, whose name will remain inseparably associated with the development of insurance regulation.[61] A graduate of Yale, his family expressed the wish that he become a Presbyterian clergyman. Feeling that his vocation was not in the ministry, Wright became a professor of mathematics and, in the course of his studies and research, interested himself in the mathematical aspects of life insurance.

On a visit to England in 1844, Wright recognized that much of the English business was issued on an unsound basis. Of 300 life insurance companies formed in a quarter of a century in England, 250 failed. While

[60]As early as 1837 the General Court of Massachusetts passed a law that required insurance companies to maintain a fund adequate to reinsure all outstanding contracts. This was the forerunner of the now universally required unearned premium fund. By virtue of such a fund an insurance company may at any time turn over outstanding risks to another company on a fully insured basis, should it elect to retire from business.

[61]Following Wright's recommendations, a bill designed to effect federal control was introduced in Congress but failed of adoption. From time to time, other bills have been introduced for the same purpose but in every instance failed to be enacted into law. An amendment to the Constitution designed to bring insurance under the regulation of the federal government was proposed to Congress in 1914; but the movement was without effect until the S.E.U.A. decision in 1944, and even here the congressional delegation of regulation to the states with the passage of Public Law 15 established the continued regulation of insurance by the states.

there was suspicion that dishonesty may have been involved in some of the failures, it was apparent to Wright that much of the difficulty grew out of a lack of a fundamental mathematical knowledge essential to carry on the business on a sound basis. He was one of the prime movers in urging the establishment of the Massachusetts insurance department and served for eight years as one of the two commissioners of insurance. He calculated tables of reserves that were adopted as legal standards by Massachusetts in 1850, to be followed in subsequent years by other states. During his period as commissioner, Wright set new standards for the conduct of the business. Insurance companies were required to make detailed reports showing that necessary reserves were maintained for each policy. Such reserves guaranteed that the company was solvent and was in a position to fulfill its obligations as policies matured. The standard thus established by Massachusetts tended to give direction to the business throughout the country. The high standards were applicable not only to Massachusetts companies but to companies chartered in other states if they expected to carry on a business in Massachusetts.[62]

In attempting to protect the solvency of insurance companies in the field of property insurance and to establish rate making on a sound basis, various regional organizations entrusted with the responsibility of rate making were established. This generated a hostility on the part of the public to insurance cooperation. Opposition was voiced on the ground that cooperative action was monopoistic and contrary to the public interest. As the outgrowth of this opposition various state legislatures undertook to prohibit cooperative rate making by the enactment of bills that came to be known as "anticompact laws." In the belief that the public would be served best by unrestricted competition, 22 states enacted statutes prohibiting combinations between insurers for the joint fixing of rates. As time went on it became apparent that unlimited competition, far from being in the public interest, could, on the contrary, be injurious. The tide began to turn when insurance commissioners realized the importance of safeguarding the solvency of the companies and ending the practice of rate discrimination. Laws were then enacted authorizing the association of companies in the making of rates.

With the failure of anticompact legislation, it was found that insurance companies could be protected from the disastrous consequences of unrestricted competition through the organization of rating bureaus, whose promulgated rates would be predicated upon statistical information ac-

---

[62]Wright's activities were not limited solely to protecting the solvency of companies so that they might meet the obligation of matured policies but, as well, were concerned with the equitable treatment of policyholders who were unable to carry their policies to maturity. Prior to Wright's time, life insurance policies had no surrender value. It is true that some companies made provision for payment to policyholders in the event of lapse, but in the ordinary instance there was no legal obligation to do so. This being the case companies viewed lapses as profitable transactions. It is reported that some companies attempted to encourage lapses. There are even instances where rumors of the insolvency of a company were circulated by the company itself in order to start a panic among policyholders so that they would discontinue the payment of premimums. It was due to Wright's persistence that the Massachusetts Legislature, in 1861, passed the first nonforfeiture law. Wright so forcibly presented his views to the Legislature that he was able to secure passage of some of the most important of the laws now in effect that have put the business of life insurance on a sound and equitable basis. See the *Bible of Life Insurance*, a photographic reprint of the original studies and official reports of Elizur Wright (Chicago: American Insurance Digest, Inc., 1932).

cumulated from all available sources and upon the loss experiences of member companies.

Growth of Industrial Activity. The last quarter of the nineteenth century was a period of industrial expansion. The financial panic of 1873 brought with it a trail of consternation and business failures. Labor troubles developed and troops were called out in an effort to maintain order. Many insurance companies failed, both in America and abroad. A declining American merchant marine had an adverse effect upon the marine business. The depression reached its low point in 1878.

The period of business revival that followed was marked by the organization of pools and trusts. These in turn tended to create monopolies and in opposition to monopolies antitrust laws were enacted. During this period the steel mills produced steel rails for such roads as the Union Pacific, the Santa Fe, and the Northern Pacific which extended their lines and connected sections of the country that were previously virtually inaccessible. New industries made their appearance with the development of mass-production techniques. Boiler insurance made its appearance with the machine age; and development continued to the end that, as years passed, broader coverages were offered including engine breakdown insurance and forms of electrical insurance. With the continued industrial expansion, accidental injuries increased in number. Demand for public liability insurance increased with the result that contractors, manufacturers, landlords, and professional men sought coverage to protect them against legal liability claims for injury suffered by the public for which they might be held responsible. At first bodily injury liability was the principal coverage; property damage liability was a natural sequence, although it did not make its appearance until around 1920. During the entire period new inventions led to new industry. Many of the social and economic changes were revolutionary in their nature. Through policies covering against direct loss or damage to physical properties, liability policies providing protection for legal liability for injuries, surety bonds indemnifying for loss or failure to complete an undertaking, and policies paying income to injured workmen and their families, the insurance industry contributed to the scheme of things in this period of expansion and development. It was in this period that the concept of liability without negligence for industrial accidents appeared.[63] The advent of workmen's compensation laws developed the necessity for workmen's compensation insurance.

The Armstrong Investigation. The period of expansion that cul-

---

[63]The compensation idea had its inception in the Bismarck socialistic era. Workmen's compensation acts were passed in Germany in 1884 and in England in 1897. The first compensation laws enacted in the United States made their appearance at a considerably later date—Maryland in 1902, Montana in 1909, and New York in 1910. The American acts followed the pattern set by the British Parliament when in 1897 it passed an act obligating the employer to furnish compensation to employees injured in the course of their employment. Not everyone realizes the significance of this idea. The British workmen's compensation acts, by permitting a private insurance carrier to insure the hazard, made it possible for an important social policy sponsored by the government to be carried out by private commercial enterprise and initiative. Although the early acts in this country were declared unconstitutional, the idea became established with the New York law of 1911. This law marks the inauguration of workmen's compensation in the United States. Other states followed the lead, and within a very short time the compensation principle for industrial accidents became generally accepted throughout the country. The germ of the idea, however, made its appearance in the closing years of the nineteenth century.

minated with the end of the nineteenth century saw in many forms of business not only consolidation and expansion but also competition tainted with business transactions that were unscrupulous if not actually fraudulent. Antagonism developed toward business enterprises where minority interests were without influence and where stock ownership and interlocking directorates enabled individuals to manipulate corporations to their personal advantage. Life insurance companies did not escape. Following the turn of the century there was a growing feeling of antagonism and distrust toward the life insurance business that led to the New York investigation of 1905. In that year the New York Legislature appointed a joint committee to make a comprehensive inquiry into every phase of the life insurance business. Senator William W. Armstrong was named as chairman, and from him the investigation gets its name. Charles Evans Hughes, later to become Governor of the state of New York and Chief Justice of the United States, headed counsel retained to conduct the proceedings.

The inquiry searched into all phases of the business. Included within its scope were investigation of allegations of mismanagement, the question of insurance company investments, the relation of company officers to investment transactions, the relation of life insurance companies to subsidiary corporations, as well as a consideration of the problems of government control, the relationship between policyholders and the company, the cost of life insurance, and company expense costs.

The result of the work of this committee was to bring to light many abuses. The life insurance business had not been conducted in many instances in the best interest of the policyholders. On the other hand, many of the evils complained of either were exaggerated or were limited to a few companies. It was, nevertheless, true that policyholders were deeply interested in the safety of the insurance business in general and the solvency of the companies writing their own policies. Much important legislation was at that time enacted. Some of the laws passed under the pressure of excitement have since been held to be drastic and unwise, and others have been substituted. The investigation marked a turning point in life insurance history.[64]

The Merritt Committee. With the enactment of legislation following the report of the Armstrong Committee, life insurance started out with a clean bill of health. The situation was not quite the same in the field of property insurance. The Armstrong investigation had directed the attention of legislators to the field of insurance, and during the next decade investigations of fire insurance were carried on in at least ten states.

The San Francisco fire of 1906 rocked the fire insurance business to its foundation. Immediately following, there was a general increase in fire rates throughout the country. Because of the fire there was little or no concerted opposition to these rate increases at the time. However, as time went by, the fact that companies were quoting uniform rates began to be a matter of concern. Likewise, the practice of companies settling losses on an indemnity basis created some opposition. Complaints were registered that companies were making tremendous profits, and so-called "anticom-

---

[64]For a contemporary report of the Armstrong Investigation see G. A. Henderson, *History of the Insurance Investigation* (New York: Legislative Reporting Co., 1906); reprinted in the *Insurance Examiner* for January, 1936.

pact laws" were filed with the legislatures. Valued policy bills were filed designed to make the face of the policy the amount the companies would be obliged to pay in the event of a total loss.

An investigation, made by the Superintendent of Insurance in New York in the spring of 1910, concerning the legislative activities of fire insurance companies brought into prominence the fact that at nearly every session of the legislature anticompact and valued policy bills were filed and always opposed by the insurance companies. A joint committee of the Senate and Assembly was appointed pursuant to a resolution adopted May 24, 1910. The Committee taking its name from the chairman, Hon. Edwin A. Merritt, Jr., is known as the "Merritt Committee." Among other things, the Committee was directed to investigate the subject of fire insurance with the hope that the problems surrounding the contested legislation could be solved and grounds could be found either for passing or rejecting the measures.

The public hearings on fire insurance began on November 22, 1910, and ended on January 6, 1911. The investigation was comprehensive and far-reaching, and witnesses from every interested source were heard. Leaders in specialty fields throughout the country were examined, and conditions in the state of New York were compared with those existing in a number of other important states. The Committee published its report in 1911.[65] It went on record as opposing anticompact laws and also the arbitary regulation of fire insurance by the states. It urged, however, that rating bureaus established by the companies be recognized and regulated by the states. This report is far-reaching in its effect because it definitely reversed the established trend which had previously regarded fire insurance companies that combined to make or maintain rates as forming trusts and, hence, as antisocial. The investigation tended to clarify misunderstandings based upon misapprehensions regarding unduly large profits and clarified the atmosphere in the matter of premium charges and rating organizations by pointing out that unrestricted competition frequently led to inability to pay losses and, hence, to company failures. Legislation following the report of the Merritt Committee did much the same for the fire insurance business that legislation following the Armstrong Report did for the life insurance business. Both tended to renew public confidence and enhance the prestige of the insurance business.

The Period of Maturity. The period following the investigations may be termed the "period of maturity." There were changes in supervision, with the intensification of the trustee concept, which unquestionably accelerated the expansion that marked the period immediately preceding. Services were extended and contracts were developed to meet every conceivable insurance need.

The turn of the century evidenced a turning away from the economic doctrine of *laissez faire* heretofore welcomed by industrial leaders and accepted as a dominant policy of government. The feeling that uncontrolled *laissez faire* benefited only a limited group of the more wealthy led to more vigorous regulation in the field of business. Insurance, therefore, was not

---

[65]*Report of the Joint Committee of the Senate and Assembly of the State of New York Appointed to Investigate Corrupt Practices in Connection with Legislation, and the Affairs of Insurance Companies, Other than Those Doing Life Insurance Business*, Assembly No. 30, transmitted to the Legislature February 1, 1911 (Albany, N. Y.: J. B. Lyon Co., 1911).

singled out for more intensive regulation but participated in the general movement.[66] This more intensive control took its point of departure from the investigations already noticed.

The increasing use of the automobile was one of the outstanding developments of the period. Legal precedents were studied and accident statistics were accumulated to a point that complete automobile coverage could be made available by the insurance industry. This extended to include not only private passenger cars but also commercial trucks and the cargoes they transported. With the advent of the automobile, casualty insurance entered upon a period of expansion.[67] Industrial expansion definitely established the need for casualty insurance.[68] Following World War I commercial aviation made its appearance. Casualty and fire insurance carriers investigated the hazards and needs and undertook to provide insurance facilities for aviation risks.

During this period new inventions led to new industry. Many of the social and economic changes were revolutionary in their nature. Policies against direct loss of or damage to physical properties, liability policies providing protection for legal liability or injuries, surety bonds indemnifying for losses due to dishonesty or failure to complete an undertaking, policies paying income to injured workmen and their families, accident and health insurance, plate glass insurance, steam boiler and flywheel insurance—all were part of the scheme of things in this period of expansion and development and became established lines in the field of property insurance.

In the field of life insurance, policy contracts continued to be liberalized and new forms developed to meet competition. The use of the optional modes of settlement came into increasing use as part of life insurance programing. Perhaps one of the outstanding developments was the ex-

---

[66]Reflecting the changing attitude, the Interstate Commerce Act of 1887 and the Sherman Antitrust Act of 1890 were enacted. For a considerable period they were without much effect. After the turn of the century further railroad legislation increased the power of the Interstate Commerce Commission. The Clayton Act of 1914 dealing with combinations in restraint of trade and the Federal Pure Food Law of 1906 were indicative of the trend that evidenced itself. During the first decade of the century social legislation dealing with public utilities, rate regulation, taxation, child labor, and minimum hours and wages for women and children made its appearance. In some instances because of a conflict of authority between the federal government and states, the states instituted regulatory measures where the federal government failed. This was the case with insurance. Early efforts to bring insurance under federal control failed. The effect of the Paul decision in 1868 tended to keep regulation of insurance in the hands of the states and this was the situation until the S.E.U.A. decision in 1944. In the hands of the states, regulation as it developed contributed to the stability of the business and inspired confidence in its integrity.

[67]Casualty insurance may be said to date from 1863 when the Travellers Insurance Company was organized to write travel accident insurance. Other companies were formed in this early period, although little business was written and in most instances the companies were organized to handle one specialized line. Public liability insurance is said to date from around 1890 and was first written as a supplementary coverage to employers' liability insurance. Both coverages were ordinarily provided in a single policy.

[68]It is reported that in 1912 the Missouri Commissioner of Insurance ordered all companies writing automobile and bodily injury liability insurance to leave the state. The insurance commissioner is reported to have felt that insurance made joy riders careless. This was so because in the event of an accident the companies undertook to protect them. It was the commissioner's opinion that, if a car was driven over 25 miles an hour, this evidenced lack of care (Clarke J. Fitzpatrick and Elliott Buse, *Fifty Years of Suretyship and Insurance* [Baltimore, Maryland: United States Fidelity & Guaranty Company, 1946] p. 82).

tension of group insurance, group annuities for pension plans, and the various types of group disability and hospital expense covers. During the period great strides were made in the field of impaired risk protection and life insurance facilities were extended to protect business organizations or associates against loss occasioned by death.[69]

The period was marked by a continued extension of a money economy accompanied by an improved standard of living. There was a marked recession in business activity in 1903 with a "panic" in 1907. There were other business dislocations, notably in 1914 with the outbreak of World War I and in 1919 with the postwar recession.[70] Recovery which began in the

---

[69]Present-day methods of selection are a far cry from the early days when companies discriminated against residence in certain of the southern states, California, and foreign countries, and against persons going on sea voyages and those in military service. One company at one time used as a basis for physical selection an individual rated as ideal as a physician specimen. It is stated that those whose applications had been rejected because of physical deficiencies were sometimes taken in to see the ideal specimen. (Richard Hooker, *Aetna Life Insurance Company, Its First Hundred Years* [Hartford, Connecticut: Aetna Life Insurance Company, 1936] p. 85). As a result of continuous study of the effects of health and occupational hazards on mortality and life expectancy together with advances in medical knowledge and treatment, improvements in job safety, and the use of policies where a higher premium is charged to cover above-average risks, only a very few applicants for life insurance now are not accepted. Disability insurance is said to date from 1848 when the Railway Passenger Assurance Corporation of London was chartered by the British Parliament. Railway travel at the time was thought by many to be hazardous, just as aviation travel was viewed with some apprehension with the introduction of passenger airlines. Accident insurance was promoted by railroad interests to encourage train travel. In 1864, the Travellers Insurance Company was founded in the United States and successfully introduced accident insurance in this country. Other companies followed. In the period of expansion and competition immediately following the Civil War there were failures in this field as in others, though many of the companies founded in that period are in existence today. Health insurance dates from about 1890, although it was not until 1910 that coverage akin to that now available was offered. The depression years following the first World War gave emphasis to the need for more complete coverage; and the medical, hospital and surgical forms were developed. In the meantime the labor movement was making itself felt and the inauguration of workmen's compensation insurance intensified the need for nonindustrial accident and sickness protection. The development of group benefits ultimately brought group disability coverages into the field of wage negotiations. Growth has continued at a phenomental rate and according to the Health Insurance Council (*13th Annual Survey, August 1959*) the American people through voluntary health insurance had greater security for themselves in 1958 against the costs of illness and injury than ever before. By the end of that year over 123 million persons were protected by some form of voluntary health insurance.

[70]Perhaps the outstanding contribution in the field of insurance during the first World War was the establishment of the principle that certain hazards were beyond the capacity of private industry and should be handled by the government. Marine insurance for a time was impossible to secure; or when rates were quoted, they were prohibitive. In August of 1914, in response to the appeal of business interests, and upon recommendation of Secretary of the Treasury McAdoo, a bill creating the Bureau of War Risk Insurance was placed before Congress. This bill became a law on September 2; and Insurance was offered on American vessels, their freight, cargo, and passenger money whenever this coverage was unobtainable elsewhere at reasonable rates. Life insurance likewise became faced with a war-risks problem. Obviously, life insurance companies had no experience upon which to predicate insurance policies for soldiers engaged in combat. Under an act of Congress approved October 6, 1917, members of the military forces of the United States, in addition to other privileges, were given the right to take out life insurance with the government. The insurance industry made available to the government its actuarial facilities and the services of its experts to facilitate and encourage the establishment of the war-risks projects.

fall of 1921 culminated in the stock market crash in 1929 and the severe depression years that followed. In addition to financial dislocations and wars, the catastrophe, a great threat of former days, was almost continuously in evidence. In 1906 the San Francisco fire brought about the destruction of 28,000 buildings with a property loss of approximately $350 million. Recalling the failures following the Chicago fire of 1871, the financial world in general and immediately interested parties in particular waited in apprehension to learn whether the fire insurance industry could survive. The treatment of insureds at this fire established for all time confidence and stability in the insurance business. In the first 60 years of this century, property values amounting to many millions of dollars were destroyed and thousands of lives were lost.[71] Catastrophes are not limited, however, to fire. Windstorm losses have been tremendous. Within recent memory are the New England hurricane of 1938 and the hurricane of somewhat lesser severity that made itself felt along the North Atlantic coast in 1944. The windstorm of November, 1950, is estimated to have damaged a million structures.[72] Including losses other than building losses, the total number of claims is estimated to have exceeded 1.5 million.[73] This is said to be the greatest number of insurance claims ever to result from a single occurrence. There were more insurance losses in one day, as the outgrowth of the storm, than were reported for the entire year 1950 throughout the United States; and the paid loss was exceeded on only two other occasions: the San Francisco fire and the Chicago fire.[74] Stock companies alone are reported to have paid in excess of $150 million. The South Amboy explosion of 1950 resulted in the death of 31 persons, injured more than 350 persons, and caused property damage of approximately $10 million.[75] More disastrous was the explosion of the Liberty ship "Grand Camp" in the harbor of Texas City, Texas, on April 17, 1947. Over 500 persons were reported killed or missing, and over 3,000 were injured; property loss was estimated at $60 million. The property, liability, and life insurance claims paid in connection with catastrophes, year in and year out, represent astronomical sums. The business today takes them in its stride, and no one has any anxiety concerning the stability of his insurance. Catastrophe losses today are paid as part of the day's business—there is never a hint of fear that the companies are in danger and there is every confidence that reserves and reinsurances are ample to meet any contingency.

---

[71]According to the National Fire Protection Association, in the first 60 years of the twentieth century, 1,278 lives were lost and approximately 40,430 buildings and other property valued at $816 million were destroyed in United States and Canadian conflagrations alone. The Association points out that, based upon 1961 appraisal values, the dollar loss would be much larger (National Fire Protection Association, *NFPA Handbook of Fire Protection* [12th ed.; Boston: 1961])

[72]Prentiss B. Reed, *The Windstorm of November 24th, 25th, and 26th, 1950* (New York: The author, 1951), p. 1.

[73]National Board of Fire Underwriters, *Fire Insurance Facts and Trends*, Vol. VII, No. 6 (December, 1951), p. 1.

[74]General Adjustment Bureau, Inc., *A Report of the Great Storm, November 25, 1950* (New York: 1951), p. 1.

[75]General Adjustment Bureau, Inc., *A Report on Adjusting Operations After the South Amboy Explosion* (New York: 1950), p. 1.

Appendix B

FIRE INSURANCE RATING NOTES

N. B. F. U. Grading Schedule for Cities and Towns

Class	*Points of Deficiency*
First	0– 500
Second	501–1,000
Third	1,001–1,500
Fourth	1,501–2,000
Fifth	2,001–2,500
Sixth	2,501–3,000
Seventh	3,001–3,500
Eighth	3,501–4,000
Ninth	4,001–4,500
Tenth	A city or town receiving more than 4,500 points; or without a water supply and having a fire department grading tenth class; or with a water supply and no fire department; or with no fire protection.

In preparing the schedule, the National Board of Fire Underwriters has taken into consideration the effect of climatic conditions upon fire losses. It is recognized that in cold climates there is a heating hazard as well as a hazard growing out of the difficulty of fire apparatus to respond quickly and operate efficiently in cold weather. In hot, dry climates there is increased combustibility, and fires may be readily spread by high winds. Likewise, earthquakes, tornadoes, hurricanes, cyclones, blizzards, floods, and other unusual conditions contribute to the conflagration hazard. However, for those weather conditions that are more or less common to the whole country, there is no deficiency provided in the schedule. When climatic conditions are abnormal in these sections, an additional deficiency is applied, based on available data of the United States Weather Bureau. Additional deficiencies are applied when there is a danger that forest fires may spread to destroy a city or when tornadoes, hurricanes, and cyclones are common and may result in numerous fires or the interruption of fire service. Blizzards and severe snowstorms which impede operation of the fire department; earthquakes of such intensity as to injure buildings, water mains, and cause numerous fires; mine cave-ins affecting extensive areas; and floods which cover part of the district considered or cause wide detours of fire apparatus—all warrant the application of an additional deficiency. The additional deficiency is added to the deficiency determined by appli-

Standard Mercantile Building Schedule (U. M. S.)

No.	Item		Charges and Credits
	STANDARD RISK (Building in Bangor, Maine) .45		
1	FRAME		.60
2	HEIGHT. For each story over four, as follows, viz:—		
	(*a*) For five-story building, charge		.15
	(*b*) For six-story building, charge		.50
	(*c*) For seven-story building, charge		1.00
3	AREA. For each 1,000 feet or fraction thereof over 5,000 feet on all floors and basements	.01	
	NOTE.—See Rule for exceptions.		
4	ROOF. (*a*) Shingle, Wood or Paper		.10
	(*b*) Mansard with Wooden Frame, each side	.05	
5	SKYLIGHTS. Other than Standard		.10
6	CORNICES. (*a*) Other than Standard, each side	.05	
	(*b*) If metal clad and stopped every 20 feet each side	.02	
7	INTERIOR FINISH. (*a*) Plastered or sheathed		.10
	(*b*) If Sheathing is oiled or varnished, add		.05
8	STAIRWAYS. Other than Standard		.10
9	WELL HOLES. Other than Standard		.15
10	ELEVATORS. Dumb Waiters, etc.		
	(*a*) Open or in wooden wells		.20
	(*b*) If Elevator is in tin-lined well with *Standard* doors		.05
	(*c*) If Dumb Waiter is tin-lined metal-clad doors		.05
	NOTE.—When Stairways and elevators are together or in same well hole, make the higher charge only. No charge for No. 8 above 1st story in buildings not over 4 stories high, occupied only for offices and dwellings above first floor.		
11	HEAT. Other than Standard		.10
12	LIGHTING. Other than Standard		.10
13	POWER. Steam Boiler not Standard		.10
14	OCCUPANCY. (*a*) Each mercantile occupant, over two (see (*b*) for exception)	.05	
	(*b*) If milliners, tailors, dentists and similar small mercantile occupants above grade floor	.02	
	(*c*) Manufacturing or mechanical or hazardous occupancy not less than		.15
15	EXPOSURE. N. S. E. W.		
	Deduct for exposure protection, side,		
	Total		
16	*Deduct.* For Watchman and Clock or approved equipment of Thermostats	.10	
17	For A.D.T. System for Watchman, additional	.05	
18	For Thermostats in stores and basements only	.05	
19	For Approved Fire Extinguishers	.10	
20	For exceptional good features		
	Total		
21	For ELECTRICAL DEFECTS, add not less than		.25
22	For exceptional bad features, add as per rule		
	Net Flat Rate		

OCCUPANCIES

cation of the schedule proper. It is apparent, therefore, that weather is an important factor in determining basis rates and, more than this, it is a factor over which the insured can exercise no control. The introduction of the weather factor, however, is evidence of the care exercised in grading cities and towns.

PRINCIPLE OF RELATIVITY IN THE DEAN ANALYTIC SCHEDULE

The Analytic System makes use of the principle of relativity with respect to (*a*) the risk itself, (*b*) place, and (*c*) time.

With respect to the risk itself, assuming a large number of buildings of a given construction, occupancy, and protection, a loss ratio will develop during a given period. It is assumed under the law of averages that with respect to any risk the relativity between the whole and its part does not change, and the relativity between its parts is constant. In 100,000 buildings of like construction it may be assumed that nonstandard heat, elevators nonstandard well holes, cornices, and the different types of occupancies will each make a proportionate contribution to the total loss cost. The charge for each, therefore, is not a flat charge but a proportion of the whole. This has led in the analytic schedule to the practice of making charges and credits percentages of the basis rate. This is illustrated as follows: Assume a frame building in a fifth-class Maine community. We might develop the following building rate:

	Charges	
Basis rate		$0.61
Height	10%	
Basement	15	
Area	10	
Roof	20	
Interior finish	20	
Open stairway	20	
Occupancy	100	
Total percentage charges	195%	
	1.95 × $0.61 =	1.19
		$1.80
Less fire extinguisher credit, 5%		0.09
Individual building rate		$1.71

Since all charges in the schedule become percentages of the basis rate and since all factors that contribute to a risk are relative, the schedule adapts itself as well to one location as to another. If it is found that the loss ratio in one state differs from that of another, the corresponding difference in rate required can be effected by a change in the basis rate. Thus we have relativity of place. For example, to increase the rates in a given state 25 per cent, it is only necessary to increase the basis rate by that amount. Since the individual charges and credit are percentages of the basis rate, the entire rate structure moves proportionately as the basis rate is changed. Like a ship that moves up and down with the tide as a complete unit, the entire rating structure in the Analytic System may be moved in one direction or the other by an adjustment in the basis rate. Assume in a given state rates were to be increased 25 percent over those used in the area for the computation of the $1.71 rate just noted. No charge need be made in the charges and credits. The basis rate is increased 25 percent from 0.61 to 0.76. Now our problem works out as follows:

	Charges	
Basis rate		$0.76
Height	10%	
Basement	15	
Area	10	
Roof	20	
Interior finish	20	
Open stairway	20	
Occupancy	100	
Total percentage charges	195%	
	1.95 × $0.76 =	1.48
		$2.24
Less fire extinguisher credit, 5%		0.11
Individual building rate		$2.13

The rate structure is increased by increasing the basis rate, and this increase is reflected in new rates on the basis of charges and credits attributable to the risk at the time the new rate is made.[1]

The same relationship may be applied with respect to time. A substantial change in loss cost from the period on which the rates are based may require an increase or decrease in premium income. As before, this can be effected by a change in the basis rate. A movement of the basis rate one way or the other provides for an adjustment of premium income without any distortion of the relative contribution to the total made by each hazard of every risk. It makes no difference whether the necessity for a change in rate level grows out of different loss costs developed in different geographical areas or different loss costs that develop in the same area but in different periods of time. Because of the operation of the principle of relativity, the procedure for adjusting premium income levels is the same. In other words, by moving the basis rate in one direction or the other, the entire rate structure may be adjusted upward or downward without in any way affecting the relativity established by the system with respect to the risk itself.

MASTER BASIS TABLES FOR THE DEAN SCHEDULES

The following table is a Master Basis Table for A buildings designed as a medium for the derivation of standard basis tables. These are the tables necessary to produce the level of rates deserved for any given territory and are obtained by taking ratios of the Master Basis Table:[2]

---

[1]This calculation is based on the New England edition of the Analytic System which is different in several respects from the edition used in the Middle West. The system used in New England is a modification of the older and parent system developed by Mr. Dean.

[2]This table, as well as others used in this appendix, is reproduced from the *Analytic System for the Measurement of Relative Fire Hazard.* Definitions, as well as other explanatory matter, such, for example, as the Combustibility and Damageability Classifications, are drawn directly from the same source. This material, copyrighted by R. D. Hobbs, General Manager, Western Actuarial Bureau, is used with permission.

Master Basis Table, A Construction

Class of Exterior Fire Protection	1	2	3	4	5	6	7	8	9	10
With no starred occupancies	0.4989	0.5039	0.5090	0.5142	0.5194	0.5246	0.5299	0.5520	0.9200	1.0000
With starred occupancies	0.6101	0.6147	0.6194	0.6240	0.6287	0.6335	0.6383	0.6580	0.9400	1.0000

At this point it is necessary to note the impact of occupancies on the Master Basis Table. Occupancies are divided into two classes: (*a*) ordinary, and (*b*) starred. All occupancies not classified as starred are considered as ordinary. Starred occupancies, sometimes known as "starred risks," are those having rapidly burning qualities so that for these risks the value of municipal protection is relatively less than is the case with ordinary risks.

It is axiomatic with fire fighters that the first five minutes may determine the extent of the loss. Obviously, fires in certain risks will get beyond control in a much shorter time than others. In those risks where combustion is so rapid that fire may be expected to assume large proportion before the arrival of a fire apparatus, damage, once a fire starts, may be expected to be extensive. Thus, in those risks where the fire department can hardly be expected to reach the fire while it is still in the incipient stages, credit for municipal protection is less than is the case with the ordinary risk. The rate adjustment for starred risks is effected by the use of higher basis rates. The basis rate in the tenth class is 1.0000 for both classes of occupancy. This means that for starred risks the value of exterior fire protection is relatively less than for other risks and this decreased value has been recognized by increases in the basis rate under all classes of exterior fire protection except Class 10. Thus, while the basis rate in the first class with no starred occupancies is 50 percent of the tenth class rate, with starred occupancies it becomes 61 percent. Starred occupancies are indicated in the Alphabetical Occupancy List with an asterisk (*), and it is from this marking that the named "starred risk" is derived. As has already been indicated, the principal point of difference between the tenth-class rates for A buildings with or without starred occupancies is to be found in the effect of exterior fire protection. Thus, when exterior fire protection is of recognizable value (first-ninth classes), there is a difference in the basis rate. Under the tenth class, however, the basis rates are the same, since the exterior fire protection is not of recognizable value to any occupancy.

The Master Basis Tables for A, B, and D construction differ in make-up. The A basis table makes no reference to height, and the D basis table makes no deduction for lack of basement nor does it make any additional charge for subbasement. It is necessary, however, in giving consideration to the construction of the Master Basis Table for B building to notice not only the height of buildings but also the basements. Basis rates in the case of B and D buildings are increased for each additional story over one. If there is no basement, the basis rate is reduced in the case of B buildings but increased for subbasement. A table thus derived giving consideration to height of buildings and the presence or absence of basements is reproduced below.

The Master Basis Table thus derived is called the 100 table. This grows out of the fact that $1.00 is the point of departure in the tenth-class town. It is called the Master Table because it is from this table that others are derived. Derived tables are designated by the percentage of the 100 table that they represent. Thus we may have a 95 table or a 60 table or any other table, depending upon the percentage of the Master Table used for its derivation.

Master Basis Table, B Construction

Class of Exterior Fire Protection	*1*	*2*	*3*	*4*	*5*	*6*	*7*	*8*	*9*	*10*
Height:										
1 story	0.5428	0.578	0.6133	0.6532	0.6931	0.7381	0.7831	0.8628	0.9425	1.00
2 stories	0.5699	0.6069	0.644	0.6858	0.7277	0.775	0.8223	0.906	0.9896	1.05
3 "	0.597	0.6358	0.6747	0.7185	0.7624	0.8119	0.8615	0.9491	1.0367	1.10
4 "	0.635	0.6763	0.7176	0.7642	0.8109	0.8636	0.9163	1.0095	1.1027	1.17
5 "	0.6898	0.7346	0.7795	0.8302	0.8809	0.9586				
6 "	0.7598	0.8296								
Add for each additional story	0.12	0.12	0.12	0.12	0.12	0.12	0.12	0.12	0.12	0.12
Subtract if no basement	0.0271	0.0289	0.0307	0.0326	0.0346	0.0369	0.0391	0.0431	0.0471	0.05
Add for each subbasement	0.0271	0.0289	0.0307	0.0326	0.0346	0.0369	0.0391	0.0431	0.0471	0.05

Appendix C

PREPAID TERM RATES, CANCELLATION TABLE, AND DEFERRED PREMIUMS

CONVERSION TABLE
ANNUAL RATE TO DEFERRED PREMIUM PAYMENT RATE

Ann.	*DPP*	*Ann.*	*DPP*	*Ann.*	*DPP*
.10	.094	.40	.38	.70	.66
.11	.105	.41	.39	.71	.67
.12	.112	.42	.39	.72	.68
.13	.122	.43	.41	.73	.69
.14	.133	.44	.42	.74	.70
.15	.14	.45	.42	.75	.71
.16	.15	.46	.43	.76	.72
.17	.161	.47	.44	.77	.73
.18	.171	.48	.45	.78	.74
.19	.178	.49	.46	.79	.74
.20	.189	.50	.47	.80	.76
.21	.199	.51	.48	.81	.77
.22	.21	.52	.49	.82	.77
.23	.22	.53	.50	.83	.78
.24	.23	.54	.51	.84	.79
.25	.23	.55	.52	.85	.80
.26	.24	.56	.53	.86	.81
.27	.25	.57	.54	.87	.82
.28	.27	.58	.55	.88	.83
.29	.27	.59	.56	.89	.84
.30	.28	.60	.57	.90	.85
.31	.29	.61	.58	.91	.86
.32	.30	.62	.58	.92	.87
.33	.31	.63	.59	.93	.88
.34	.32	.64	.60	.94	.89
.35	.33	.65	.61	.95	.90
.36	.34	.66	.62	.96	.91
.37	.35	.67	.63	.97	.92
.38	.36	.68	.64	.98	.93
.39	.37	.69	.65	.99	.93
				1.00	.94

Rates for Prepaid Term Insurance

1 yr.	2 yrs.	3 yrs.	4 yrs.	5 yrs.	1 yr.	2 yrs.	3 yrs.	4 yrs.	5 yrs.
.06	.11	.16	.21	.26	.61	1.13	1.65	2.16	2.68
.07	.13	.19	.25	.31	.62	1.15	1.67	2.20	2.73
.08	.15	.22	.28	.35	.63	1.16	1.70	2.24	2.77
.09	.17	.24	.32	.40	.64	1.18	1.73	2.27	2.82
.10	.18	.27	.35	.44	.65	1.20	1.75	2.31	2.86
.11	.20	.30	.39	.48	.66	1.22	1.78	2.34	2.90
.12	.22	.32	.43	.53	.67	1.24	1.81	2.38	2.95
.13	.24	.35	.46	.57	.68	1.26	1.84	2.41	2.99
.14	.26	.38	.50	.62	.69	1.28	1.86	2.45	3.04
.15	.28	.40	.53	.66	.70	1.29	1.89	2.48	3.08
.16	.30	.43	.57	.70	.71	1.31	1.92	2.52	3.12
.17	.31	.46	.60	.75	.72	1.33	1.94	2.56	3.17
.18	.33	.49	.64	.79	.73	1.35	1.97	2.59	3.21
.19	.35	.51	.67	.84	.74	1.37	2.00	2.63	3.26
.20	.37	.54	.71	.88	.75	1.39	2.02	2.66	3.30
.21	.39	.57	.74	.92	.76	1.41	2.05	2.70	3.34
.22	.41	.59	.78	.97	.77	1.42	2.08	2.73	3.39
.23	.42	.62	.82	1.01	.78	1.44	2.11	2.77	3.43
.24	.44	.65	.85	1.06	.79	1.46	2.13	2.80	3.48
.25	.46	.67	.89	1.10	.80	1.48	2.16	2.84	3.52
.26	.48	.70	.92	1.14	.81	1.50	2.19	2.87	3.56
.27	.50	.73	.96	1.19	.82	1.52	2.21	2.91	3.61
.28	.52	.76	.99	1.23	.83	1.53	2.24	2.95	3.65
.29	.54	.78	1.03	1.28	.84	1.55	2.27	2.98	3.70
.30	.55	.81	1.06	1.32	.85	1.57	2.29	3.02	3.74
.31	.57	.84	1.10	1.36	.86	1.59	2.32	3.05	3.78
.32	.59	.86	1.14	1.41	.87	1.61	2.35	3.09	3.83
.33	.61	.89	1.17	1.45	.88	1.63	2.38	3.12	3.87
.34	.63	.92	1.21	1.50	.89	1.65	2.40	3.16	3.92
.35	.65	.94	1.24	1.54	.90	1.66	2.43	3.19	3.96
.36	.67	.97	1.28	1.58	.91	1.68	2.46	3.23	4.00
.37	.68	1.00	1.31	1.63	.92	1.70	2.48	3.27	4.05
.38	.70	1.03	1.35	1.67	.93	1.72	2.51	3.30	4.09
.39	.72	1.05	1.38	1.72	.94	1.74	2.54	3.34	4.14
.40	.74	1.08	1.42	1.76	.95	1.76	2.56	3.37	4.18
.41	.76	1.11	1.45	1.80	.96	1.78	2.59	3.41	4.22
.42	.78	1.13	1.49	1.85	.97	1.79	2.62	3.44	4.27
.43	.79	1.16	1.53	1.89	.98	1.81	2.65	3.48	4.31
.44	.81	1.19	1.56	1.94	.99	1.83	2.67	3.51	4.36
.45	.83	1.21	1.60	1.98	1.00	1.85	2.70	3.55	4.40
.46	.85	1.24	1.63	2.02	1.01	1.87	2.73	3.58	4.44
.47	.87	1.27	1.67	2.07	1.02	1.89	2.75	3.62	4.49
.48	.89	1.30	1.70	2.11	1.03	1.90	2.78	3.66	4.53
.49	.91	1.32	1.74	2.16	1.04	1.92	2.81	3.69	4.58
.50	.92	1.35	1.77	2.20	1.05	1.94	2.83	3.73	4.62
.51	.94	1.38	1.81	2.24	1.06	1.96	2.86	3.76	4.66
.52	.96	1.40	1.85	2.29	1.07	1.98	2.89	3.80	4.71
.53	.98	1.43	1.88	2.33	1.08	2.00	2.92	3.83	4.75
.54	1.00	1.46	1.92	2.38	1.09	2.02	2.94	3.87	4.80
.55	1.02	1.48	1.95	2.42	1.10	2.03	2.97	3.90	4.84
.56	1.04	1.51	1.99	2.46	1.11	2.05	3.00	3.94	4.88
.57	1.05	1.54	2.02	2.51	1.12	2.07	3.02	3.98	4.93
.58	1.07	1.57	2.06	2.55	1.13	2.09	3.05	4.01	4.97
.59	1.09	1.59	2.09	2.60	1.14	2.11	3.08	4.05	5.02
.60	1.11	1.62	2.13	2.64	1.15	2.13	3.10	4.08	5.06

Short Rate Cancellation Table for One Year

Policy in Force	Term of Policy					Policy in Force	Term of Policy				
	1 Yr.	2 Yrs.	3 Yrs.	4 Yrs.	5 Yrs.		1 Yr.	2 Yrs.	3 Yrs.	4 Yrs.	5 Yrs.
Days	Per Cent of Premium Earned					Days	Per Cent of Premium Earned				
1	5	2.7	1.9	1.4	1.1	154–156	53	28.6	19.6	14.9	12.
2	6	3.2	2.2	1.7	1.4	157–160	54	29.2	20.	15.2	12.3
3–4	7	3.8	2.6	2.0	1.6	161–164	55	29.7	20.4	15.5	12.5
5–6	8	4.3	3.	2.3	1.8	165–167	56	30.3	20.7	15.8	12.7
7–8	9	4.9	3.3	2.5	2.	168–171	57	30.8	21.1	16.1	13.
9–10	10	5.4	3.7	2.8	2.3	172–175	58	31.4	21.5	16.3	13.2
11–12	11	5.9	4.1	3.1	2.5	176–178	59	31.9	21.9	16.6	13.4
13–14	12	6.5	4.4	3.4	2.7	179–182	60	32.4	22.2	16.9	13.6
15–16	13	7.	4.8	3.7	3.	183–187	61	33.	22.6	17.2	13.9
17–18	14	7.6	5.2	3.9	3.2	188–191	62	33.5	23.	17.5	14.1
19–20	15	8.1	5.6	4.2	3.4	192–196	63	34.1	23.3	17.7	14.3
21–22	16	8.6	5.9	4.5	3.6	197–200	64	34.6	23.7	18.	14.5
23–25	17	9.2	6.3	4.8	3.9	201–205	65	35.1	24.1	18.3	14.8
26–29	18	9.7	6.7	5.1	4.1	206–209	66	35.7	24.4	18.6	15.
30–32	19	10.3	7.	5.4	4.3	210–214	67	36.2	24.8	18.9	15.2
33–36	20	10.8	7.4	5.6	4.5	215–218	68	36.8	25.2	19.2	15.5
37–40	21	11.4	7.8	5.9	4.8	219–223	69	37.3	25.6	19.4	15.7
41–43	22	11.9	8.1	6.2	5.	224–228	70	37.8	25.9	19.7	15.9
44–47	23	12.4	8.5	6.5	5.2	229–232	71	38.4	26.3	20.	16.1
48–51	24	13.	8.9	6.8	5.5	233–237	72	38.9	26.7	20.3	16.4
52–54	25	13.5	9.3	7.	5.7	238–241	73	39.5	27.	20.6	16.9
55–58	26	14.1	9.6	7.3	5.9	242–246	74	40.	27.4	20.8	16.8
59–62	27	14.6	10.	7.6	6.1	247–250	75	40.5	27.8	21.1	17.
63–65	28	15.1	10.4	7.9	6.4	251–255	76	41.1	28.1	21.4	17.3
66–69	29	15.7	10.7	8.2	6.6	256–260	77	41.6	28.5	21.7	17.5
70–73	30	16.2	11.1	8.5	6.8	261–264	78	42.2	28.9	22.	17.7
74–76	31	16.8	11.5	8.7	7.	265–269	79	42.7	29.3	22.3	18.
77–80	32	17.3	11.9	9.	7.3	270–273	80	43.2	29.6	22.5	18.2
81–83	33	17.8	12.2	9.3	7.5	274–278	81	43.8	30.	22.8	18.4
84–87	34	18.4	12.6	9.6	7.7	279–282	82	44.3	30.4	23.1	18.6
88–91	35	18.9	13.	9.9	8.	283–287	83	44.9	30.7	23.4	18.9
92–94	36	19.5	13.3	10.1	8.2	288–291	84	45.4	31.1	23.7	19.1
95–98	37	20.	13.7	10.4	8.4	292–296	85	45.9	31.5	23.9	19.3
99–102	38	20.5	14.1	10.7	8.6	297–301	86	46.5	31.9	24.2	19.5
103–105	39	21.1	14.4	11.	8.9	302–305	87	47.	32.2	24.5	19.8
106–109	40	21.6	14.8	11.3	9.1	306–310	88	47.6	32.6	24.8	20.
110–113	41	22.2	15.2	11.5	9.3	311–314	89	48.1	33.	25.1	20.2
114–116	42	22.7	15.6	11.8	9.5	315–319	90	48.6	33.3	25.4	20.5
117–120	43	23.2	15.9	12.1	9.8	320–323	91	49.2	33.7	25.6	20.7
121–124	44	23.8	16.3	12.4	10.	324–328	92	49.7	34.1	25.9	20.9
125–127	45	24.3	16.7	12.7	10.2	329–332	93	50.3	34.4	26.2	21.1
128–131	46	24.9	17.	13.	10.5	333–337	94	50.8	34.8	26.5	21.4
132–135	47	25.4	17.4	13.2	10.7	338–342	95	51.4	35.2	26.8	21.6
136–138	48	25.9	17.8	13.5	10.9	343–346	96	51.9	35.6	27.	21.8
139–142	49	26.5	18.1	13.8	11.1	347–351	97	52.4	35.9	27.3	22.
143–146	50	27.	18.5	14.1	11.4	352–355	98	53.	36.3	27.6	22.3
147–149	51	27.6	18.9	14.4	11.6	356–360	99	53.5	36.7	27.9	22.5
150–153	52	28.1	19.3	14.6	11.8	361–365	100	54.1	37.	28.2	22.7

Appendix D

FORMS, CLAUSES, AND ENDORSEMENTS

PAGE 2 OF DWELLING PROPERTY FORM

SECTION X

Other Provisions

(A) **Mortgage Clause:** (Applies to building items only and is effective only when policy is made payable to a named mortgagee or trustee.)

Loss, if any, under this policy, shall be payable to the aforesaid as mortgagee (or trustee) as interest may appear under all present or future mortgages upon the property herein described in which the aforesaid may have an interest as mortgagee (or trustee), in order of precedence of said mortgages, and this insurance, as to the interest of the mortgagee (or trustee) only therein, shall not be invalidated by any act or neglect of the mortgagor or owner of the within described property, nor by any foreclosure or other proceedings or notice of sale relating to the property, nor by any change in the title or ownership of the property, nor by the occupation of the premises for purposes more hazardous than are permitted by this policy; provided, that in case the mortgagor or owner shall neglect to pay any premium due under this policy, the mortgagee (or trustee) shall, on demand, pay the same.

Provided, also, that the mortgagee (or trustee) shall notify this Company of any change of ownership or occupancy or increase of hazard which shall come to the knowledge of said mortgagee (or trustee) and, unless permitted by this policy, it shall be noted thereon and the mortgagee (or trustee) shall, on demand, pay the premium for such increased hazard for the term of the use thereof; otherwise this policy shall be null and void.

This Company reserves the right to cancel this policy at any time as provided by its terms, but in such case this policy shall continue in force for the benefit only of the mortgagee (or trustee) for 10 days after notice to the mortgagee (or trustee) of such cancellation and shall then cease, and this Company shall have the right, on like notice, to cancel this agreement.

Whenever this Company shall pay the mortgagee (or trustee) any sum for loss under this policy and shall claim that, as to the mortgagor or owner, no liability therefor existed, this Company shall, to the extent of such payment, be thereupon legally subrogated to all the rights of the party to whom such payment shall be made, under all securities held as collateral to the mortgage debt, or may, at its option, pay to the mortgagee (or trustee) the whole principal due or to grow due on the mortgage with interest, and shall thereupon receive a full assignment and transfer of the mortgage and of all such other securities; but no subrogation shall impair the right of the mortgagee (or trustee) to recover the full amount of said mortgagee's (or trustee's) claim.

(B) **Alterations and Repairs:** Permission granted to make alterations, additions and repairs, and to complete structures in course of construction.

(C) **Control of Property:** This insurance shall not be prejudiced by any act or neglect of any person (other than the named Insured), when such act or neglect is not within the control of the named Insured.

(D) **Debris Removal Clause:** This insurance covers expenses incurred in the removal of all debris of the property covered hereunder which may be occasioned by loss caused by any of the perils insured against in this policy. However, the total liability under this policy for both loss to property and removal of debris shall not exceed the amount of insurance applying under this policy to the property damaged or destroyed. This Company shall not be liable for more than the proportion of such debris removal expense as the amount of insurance under this policy bears to the total amount of insurance on the property covered hereunder, whether or not all such insurance includes this clause.

Unless liability is otherwise specifically assumed by endorsement attached hereto, this Company shall not be liable for debris removal expense occasioned by the enforcement of any state or municipal law or ordinance which necessitates the demolition of any portion of a building covered hereunder which has or has not suffered damage by any of the perils insured against.

Debris removal expense shall not be considered in the determination of actual cash value in the application of the Coinsurance Clause, if any, made a part of this policy.

(E) **Electrical Apparatus Clause:** This Company shall not be liable for any loss resulting from any electrical injury or disturbance to electrical appliances, devices, fixtures or wiring caused by electrical currents artifically generated unless fire ensues and, if fire does ensue, this Company shall be liable only for its proportion of loss caused by such ensuing fire.

With respect only to electrical appliances, devices, fixtures and wiring covered under this policy and only as to loss caused by lightning, this Company shall be liable only when such loss exceeds $50.00 in any one occurrence and then only for its proportion of such excess.

(F) **Inherent Explosion Clause:** This policy shall insure against direct loss to the property covered caused by explosion occurring in the described dwelling or appurtenant private structures or in any structure containing property covered hereunder from hazards inherent therein.

Loss by explosion shall include direct loss resulting from the explosion of accumulated gases or unconsumed fuel within the firebox (or combustion chamber) of any fired vessel or within the flues or passages which conduct the gases of combustion therefrom.

This Company shall not be liable for loss by explosion of steam boilers, steam pipes, steam turbines or steam engines, if owned by, leased by or operated under the control of the Insured.

The following are not explosions within the intent or meaning of these provisions: (a) Electric arcing, (b) Rupture or bursting of rotating or moving parts of machinery caused by centrifugal force or mechanical breakdown, (c) Water hammer, (d) Rupture or bursting of water pipes, (e) Rupture, bursting or operation of pressure relief devices.

Loss by nuclear reaction or nuclear radiation or radioactive contamination, all whether controlled or uncontrolled, or due to any act or condition incident to any of the foregoing, is not insured against under this clause, whether such loss be direct or indirect, proximate or remote, or be in whole or in part caused by, contributed to, or aggravated by Inherent Explosion; and nuclear reaction or nuclear radiation or radioactive contamination, all whether controlled or uncontrolled, is not "Inherent Explosion."

(G) **Liberalization Clause:** If during the period that insurance is in force under this policy, or within 45 days prior to the inception date thereof, on behalf of this Company there be adopted, or filed with and approved or accepted by the insurance supervisory authorities, all in conformity with law, any changes in the form attached to this policy by which this form of insurance could be extended or broadened without increased premium charge by endorsement or substitution of form, then such extended or broadened insurance shall inure to the benefit of the Insured hereunder as though such endorsement or substitution of form had been made.

(H) **Nuclear Clause:** The word "fire" in this policy or endorsements attached hereto is not intended to and does not embrace nuclear reaction or nuclear radiation or radioactive contamination, all whether controlled or uncontrolled, and loss by nuclear reaction or nuclear radiation or radioactive contamination is not intended to be and is not insured against by this policy or said endorsements, whether such loss be direct or indirect, proximate or remote, or be in whole or in part caused by, contributed to, or aggravated by "fire" or any other perils insured against by this policy or said endorsements; however, subject to the foregoing and all provisions of this policy, direct loss by "fire" resulting from nuclear reaction or nuclear radiation or radioactive contamination is insured against by this policy.

(I) **Prorata Clause:** If this policy covers on two or more items for which specific amounts are shown, the amount of this policy applies to each item in the proportion that the specific amount shown for each item bears to the sum of all items.

(J) **Subrogation Clause:** This insurance shall not be invalidated should the Insured waive in writing prior to a loss any or all right of recovery against any party for loss occurring to the described property.

(K) **Vacancy or Unoccupancy:** Permission granted for vacancy or unoccupancy without limit of time, except as provided in any endorsement attached to this policy. A building in process of construction shall not be deemed vacant.

PAGE 2 AND 3, DWELLING PROPERTY FORM

SECTION XI—EXTENDED COVERAGE ENDORSEMENT

(Perils of Windstorm and Hail [$50 Deductible Applicable], Explosion, Riot, Riot Attending a Strike, Civil Commotion, Aircraft, Vehicles and Smoke)

Effective only when rate and premium for Extended Coverage is inserted in the space provided on the first page of this policy, or endorsed hereon after the effective date of this policy.

THIS POLICY IS EXTENDED TO INSURE AGAINST DIRECT LOSS BY WINDSTORM, HAIL, EXPLOSION, RIOT, RIOT ATTENDING A STRIKE, CIVIL COMMOTION, AIRCRAFT, VEHICLES, AND SMOKE, EXCEPT AS HEREINAFTER PROVIDED.

Deductible: The sum of $50 shall be deducted from the amount of loss resulting from each windstorm or hailstorm. This deductible shall apply separately to each building or structure and separately to all personal property in the open. This deductible does not apply to contents in any building.

This Deductible Clause shall not apply to insurance covering Business Interruption, Tuition Fees, Extra Expense, Additional Living Expense, Rent or Rental Value or Leasehold Interest.

Provisions Applicable only to Windstorm and Hail: This Company shall not be liable for loss caused directly or indirectly by frost or cold weather, or ice (other than hail), snow or sleet, whether driven by wind or not.

This Company shall not be liable for loss to the interior of the building(s) or the property covered therein caused: (a) by rain, snow, sand or dust, whether driven by wind or not, unless the building(s) covered or containing the property covered shall first sustain an actual damage to roof or walls by the direct action of wind or hail and then shall be liable for loss to the interior of the building(s) or the property covered therein as may be caused by rain, snow, sand or dust entering the building(s) through openings in the roof or walls made by direct action of wind or hail; or (b) by water from sprinkler equipment or from other piping, unless such equipment or piping be damaged as a direct result of wind or hail.

Unless liability therefor is assumed in the form attached to this policy, or by endorsement hereon, this Company shall not be liable for damage to the following property: (a) grain, hay, straw or other crops outside of buildings; or (b) windmills, windpumps or their towers; or (c) crop silos (or their contents); or (d) metal smokestacks or, when outside of buildings, cloth awnings, signs, radio or television antennas including their lead-in wiring, masts or towers; or (e) lawns, trees, shrubs or plants.

Provisions Applicable Only to Explosion: Loss by explosion shall include direct loss resulting from the explosion of accumulated gases or unconsumed fuel within the firebox (or combustion chamber) of any fired vessel or within the flues or passages which conduct the gases of combustion therefrom.

This Company shall not be liable for loss by explosion of steam boilers, steam pipes, steam turbines or steam engines, if owned by, leased by or operated under the control of the Insured.

The following are not explosions within the intent or meaning of these provisions:

(a) Shock waves caused by aircraft, generally known as "sonic boom,"
(b) Electric arcing,
(c) Rupture or bursting of rotating or moving parts of machinery caused by centrifugal force or mechanical breakdown,
(d) Water hammer,
(e) Rupture or bursting of water pipes,
(f) Rupture or bursting due to expansion or swelling of the contents of any building or structure, caused by or resulting from water,
(g) Rupture, bursting or operation of pressure relief devices.

Any other explosion clause made a part of this policy is superseded by this endorsement.

Provisions Applicable Only to Riot, Riot Attending a Strike and Civil Commotion: Loss by riot, riot attending a strike or civil commotion shall include direct loss by acts of striking employees of the owner or tenant(s) of the described building(s) while occupied by said striking employees and shall also include direct loss from pillage and looting occurring during and at the immediate place of a riot, riot attending a strike or civil commotion. Unless specifically endorsed hereon, this Company shall not be liable for loss resulting from damage to or destruction of the described property due to change in temperature or humidity or interruption of operations whether or not such loss is covered by this policy as to other perils.

Provisions Applicable Only to Loss by Aircraft and Vehicles: The term "vehicles," as used in this endorsement, means vehicles running on land or tracks but not aircraft. Loss by aircraft or by vehicles shall include only direct loss resulting from actual physical contact of an aircraft or a vehicle with the property covered hereunder or with the building(s) containing the property covered hereunder, except that loss by aircraft includes direct loss by objects falling therefrom. This Company shall not be liable for loss: (a) by any vehicle owned or operated by an Insured or by any tenant of the described premises; (b) by any vehicle to fences, driveways, walks or lawns, trees, shrubs or plants; (c) to any aircraft or vehicle including contents thereof other than stocks of aircraft or vehicles in process of manufacture or for sale.

Provisions Applicable Only to Smoke: The term "smoke" as used in this endorsement means only smoke due to a sudden, unusual and faulty operation of any heating or cooking unit, only when such unit is connected to a chimney by a smoke pipe or vent pipe, and while in or on the described premises but not smoke from fireplaces or industrial apparatus.

Nuclear Exclusion: Loss by nuclear reaction or nuclear radiation or radioactive contamination, all whether controlled or uncontrolled, or due to any act or condition incident to any of the foregoing, is not insured against by this Extended Coverage Endorsement, whether such loss be direct or indirect, proximate or remote, or be in whole or in part caused by, contributed to, or aggravated by windstorm, hail, explosion, riot, riot attending a strike, civil commotion, aircraft, vehicles or smoke; and nuclear reaction or nuclear radiation or radioactive contamination, all whether controlled or uncontrolled, is not "explosion" or "smoke."

War Risk Exclusion: This Company shall not be liable for loss caused directly or indirectly by (a) hostile or warlike action in time of peace or war, including action in hindering, combating or defending against an actual, impending or expected attack, (1) by any government or soverign power (de jure or de facto), or by any authority maintaining or using military, naval or air forces; or (2) by military, naval or air forces; or (3) by an agent of any such government, power, authority or forces, it being understood that any discharge, explosion or use of any weapon of war employing nuclear fission or fusion shall be conclusively presumed to be such a hostile or warlike action by such government, power, authority or forces; (b) insurrection, rebellion, revolution, civil war, usurped power, or action taken by governmental authority in hindering, combating or defending against such an occurrence.

Water Exclusion: This Company shall not be liable for loss caused by, resulting from, contributed to or aggravated by any of the following—

(a) flood, surface water, waves, tidal water or tidal wave, overflow of streams or other bodies of water, or spray from any of the foregoing, all whether driven by wind or not;
(b) water which backs up through sewers or drains;
(c) water below the surface of the ground including that which exerts pressure on

or flows, seeps or leaks through sidewalks, driveways, foundations, walls, basement or other floors, or through doors, windows or any other openings in such sidewalks, driveways, foundations, walls or floors;

unless loss by explosion as insured against hereunder ensues, and then this Company shall be liable for only such ensuing loss.

Other Provisions:

A claim for loss by any peril insured against by this endorsement shall not be barred because of change of occupancy, nor because of vacancy or unoccupancy.

This endorsement does not increase the amount(s) of insurance provided in this policy.

If this policy covers on two or more items, the provisions of this endorsement shall apply to each item separately.

Apportionment: This Company shall not be liable for a greater proportion of any loss less the amount of deductible, if any, from any peril or perils included in this endorsement than (1) the amount of insurance under this policy bears to the whole amount of fire insurance covering the property, or which would have covered the property except for the existence of this insurance, whether collectible or not, and whether or not such other fire insurance covers against the additional peril or perils insured hereunder, nor (2) for a greater proportion of any loss less the amount of deductible, if any, than the amount hereby insured bears to all insurance whether collectible or not, covering in any manner such loss, or which would have covered such loss except for the existence of this insurance; except if any type of insurance other than fire extended to cover additional perils or windstorm insurance applies to any loss to which this insurance also applies, or would have applied to any such loss except for the existence of this insurance, the limit of liability of each type of insurance for such loss, hereby designated as "joint loss," shall first be determined as if it were the only insurance, and this type of insurance shall be liable for no greater proportion of joint loss than the limit of its liability for such loss bears to the sum of all such limits. The liability of this Company (under this endorsement) for such joint loss shall be limited to its proportionate part of the aggregate limit of this and all other insurance of the same type. The words "joint loss," as used in the foregoing, mean that portion of the loss in excess of the highest deductible, if any, to which this endorsement and other types of insurance above referred to both apply.

Provisions Applicable Only When This Endorsement is Attached to a Policy Covering Business Interruption, Tuition Fees, Extra Expense, Additional Living Expense, Rent or Rental Value, Leasehold Interest or Other Consequential Loss: The term "direct," as applied to loss, means loss, as limited and conditioned in such policy, resulting from direct loss to described property from the peril(s) insured against; and while the business of the owner or tenant(s) of the described building(s) is interrupted by a strike at the described location, this Company shall not be liable for any loss due to interference by any person(s) with rebuilding, repairing or replacing the property damaged or destroyed or with the resumption or continuation of business.

CAUTION

WHEN THIS ENDORSEMENT IS ATTACHED TO ONE FIRE POLICY, THE INSURED SHOULD SECURE LIKE COVERAGE ON ALL FIRE POLICIES COVERING THE SAME PROPERTY.

MANUFACTURING FORM—BUILDING AND CONTENTS—BLANKET

Tariff Page............. **UNSPRINKLERED OR SPRINKLERED RISKS**
Risk No................ (FOR USE IN MAINE, VERMONT, RHODE ISLAND AND CONNECTICUT)

The following, subject to the conditions and provisions printed hereon, is attached to and forms part of

Policy No. of the NAME OF INSURANCE COMPANY

issued at its Agency. Dated 19

$

(Continued on next page)

(*Continued from preceding page*)

On the building and additions structurally attached and communicating, occupied as and for purposes incident thereto, including foundations (except as hereinafter specifically excluded), vaults, stacks, elevators, hoists, chutes and their appurtenances; engines, boilers, pumps, their settings and appurtenances; heating, lighting and ventilating equipment; piping and plumbing of every description; electrical wiring for lighting and power service; landlord's storm and screen doors, storm windows, screens and awnings, whether in place or stored in said building; also on machines and machinery of every description incident to the business; electrical appliances and devices of any kind, including wiring; machinery parts and supplies, implements and tools; models and dies in use; furniture and fixtures, signs, manuscripts; equipment and supplies usual to the business; wearing apparel owned by the Insured; stock, merchandise and material, raw, in process or finished, including packages, labels, packing materials and supplies for same, the property of the Insured; all while contained in the above described building and additions structurally attached and communicating, situated

Loss, if any, on real estate payable to the following mortgagee or mortgagees as the interests of the below named mortgagee or mortgagees may appear in order of their priority, under any present or future mortgage or mortgages of the within described real eastate (but in no event to exceed the amount of insurance named in the within policy): Mortgagee: Address:

It is understood and agreed and made a condition of this contract, that any notice relative thereto, that is delivered to the address herein set forth for any of the mortgagees herein mentioned shall be considered as being in full compliance with any and all requisites relative to the delivery of such notice.

Reduced Rate Contribution Clause: In consideration of the reduced rate and (or) form under which this policy is written, it is expressly stipulated and made a condition of this contract that in the event of loss this Company shall be liable for no greater proportion thereof than the amount hereby insured bears to ninety (90) per cent of the actual cash value of the property described herein at the time when such loss shall happen, nor for more than the proportion which this policy bears to the total insurance thereon.

In the event that the aggregate claim for any loss is both less than Ten Thousand Dollars ($10,000) and less than five per cent (5%) of the total amount of insurance upon the property described herein at the time such loss occurs, no special inventory or appraisement of the undamaged property shall be required.

If this policy be divided into two or more items, the foregoing shall apply to each item separately.

Automatic Sprinkler Clauses Nos. 1 or 2 as printed apply only when specifically referred to. Subject to Clause No.........................

This policy covers property described belonging to the Insured or sold but not removed; also on the Insured's interest in and/or legal liability for similar property held by the Insured as follows, viz.: in trust or on commission, or on joint account with others, or on storage or for repairs.

This policy covers also property similar to that hereby insured while (a) in cars on switches or sidetracks when such cars are on premises described or within 100 feet of buildings described in policy; (b) on platforms in contact with buildings described in policy; (c) on sidewalks, streets, alleys or detached platforms, when within 50 feet of buildings described in policy; (d) while temporarily in the open on premises.

Property Not Covered: This policy does not cover cost of excavations; brick, stone or concrete foundations, piers, or other supports which are below the under-surface of the lowest basement floor, or, where there is no basement, which are below the surface of the ground; underground flues, pipes or drains. This policy does not cover the Insured's interest in personal property in which parties other than the Insured also have an insurable interest when the Insured's interest in said property is otherwise covered. This policy does not cover automobiles, including all self-propelled vehicles and machines using gasoline.

Electrical Apparatus Clause A: If electrical appliances or devices of any kind, including wiring, are covered under this policy, this Company shall not be liable for any electrical injury or disturbance to the said electrical appliances, devices or wiring from artificial causes.

Alterations and Repairs Permit: Permission granted during the life of this policy to employ mechanics to make alterations, additions and repairs, and this policy (so far as it applies to building) shall also cover in accordance with its conditions such alterations or additions and all materials and supplies therein or therefor adjacent thereto, and (so far as it applies to contents of said building) shall extend to cover such additions.

If the building is equipped with automatic sprinklers the following Alterations and Repairs Permit applies in place of the foregoing permit: Permission granted during the life of this policy to employ mechanics to make alterations or repairs, and this policy (so far as it applies to the building being altered or repaired) shall also cover in accordance with its conditions all such alterations, materials and supplies therein or therefor adjacent thereto, but this shall not be held to include the reconstruction or the enlargement of any building herein described. This permission does not waive or modify any of the terms or conditions of the automatic sprinkler clause attached to this policy.

Cease Operations: Permission is hereby granted, without charge, to cease operations for sixty (60) consecutive days after the period permitted by the Standard Policy Conditions, at any one time during the term of this contract; but, in consideration of the fact that no additional premium is charged, it is made a condition of this insurance that all fire extinguishing appliances and apparatus, installed on the premises described in this policy, shall be maintained in complete working order and that one or more watchmen shall be continuously on duty day and night during the cessation of operations under this permit and be required to make hourly rounds of inspection, recording same on an approved recording station or watch clock.

Automatic Reinstatement of Losses: The amount of insurance hereunder involved in a loss payment of not more than One Hundred Dollars ($100) under this policy shall be automatically reinstated.

Work and Materials Clause: Permission is hereby granted for such use of the premises as is usual and incidental to the occupancy as herein described and to keep and use all such appliances, devices, articles and materials (including such materials as are prohibited by the printed conditions of this policy) in such quantities as are usual and incidental to such occupancy.

Warranty Endorsements: This policy shall not be affected by failure to comply with any of the warranties endorsed hereon in any portion of the premises over which the Insured has no control.

OPERATION OF THE PRORATA DISTRIBUTION CLAUSE

The prorata distribution clause has the effect of making a blanket policy specific. It has the effect of dividing the whole amount at risk to cover proportionately, in each specific location, an amount based upon the value of each location relative to the total value of all locations.

For example, a manufacturing plant has four warehouses located in different parts of a city. As goods are completed, they are removed to one or the other of the warehouses to await shipment as orders come in. While values fluctuate in the different buildings, the aggregate remains reasonably constant. If the total values in the four warehouses aggregate $50,000 and the total insurance carried is $30,000, blanket with the distribution clause, with inventories distributed as indicated below, the insurance would cover at each location as shown:

	Inventory	*Proportion*	*Coverage*
Warehouse A	$ 5,000	5/50	$ 3,000
Warehouse B	10,000	10/50	6,000
Warehouse C	15,000	15/50	9,000
Warehouse D	20,000	20/50	12,000
Total	$50,000	50/50	$30,000

Now let us suppose that during the following month new goods as manufactured are added to Warehouse A, where there is the greatest amount of room, and shipments are made from Warehouse D. At the end of the month we have:

	Inventory	*Proportion*	*Coverage*
Warehouse A	$15,000	15/50	$ 9,000
Warehouse B	10,000	10/50	6,000
Warehouse C	15,000	15/50	9,000
Warehouse D	10,000	10/50	6,000
Total	$50,000	50/50	$30,000

The point to emphasize in the foregoing examples is that the coverage automatically shifts with the inventory changes without any endorsement or change in the insurance policies. If any warning is necessary in connection with the use of the clause, it concerns itself with the necessity for an adequate total amount of insurance to value.

When the prorata distribution clause is used in connection with a coinsurance clause, the amount of insurance that covers on each location is allocated first, and then the procedure so far as the co-insurance clause is concerned is the same as if the insurance had been specific. It is apparent, however, that if the percentage of insurance to value required by the coinsurance clause is maintained as to total insurance to total values, there will be no difficulty in the specific application of the coverage. The following apportionment illustrates inadequate insurance with the 80 percent coinsurance clause:

Location	*Inventory*	*Proportion*	*Coverage*	*Required for 80 Per cent Clause*	*Insurance Pays*
Warehouse A	$ 20,000	20/100	$ 8,000	$16,000	½ loss
Warehouse B	30,000	30/100	12,000	24,000	½ loss
Warehouse C	50,000	50/100	20,000	40,000	½ loss
Total	$100,000	100/100	$40,000	$80,000	

Appendix E

SPECIAL AND ALLIED FIRE LINES

Nature of Collateral and Special Coverages. There are a number of risks that involve neither extensions of the standard contract nor the insurance of consequential hazards. They are, however, so closely associated with the fire business that inclusion of the lines in the general field of fire insurance was probably inevitable. For example, the writing of a sprinkler leakage insurance is a natural accompaniment of fire insurance. Water damage insurance has no immediate relationship to fire coverage but, having included the water damage from sprinkler leakage within the scope of the fire business, it was a logical step to the writing of a straight water damage policy. The sprinkler leakage policy, rain insurance contracts, and the like fall within the category of allied lines.

Sprinkler Leakage Insurance. The automatic sprinkler system is a device designed to make fire, itself, a watchman. A building protected with a sprinkler system is piped throughout in accordance with rating specifications, and, at given intervals, "heads" are set. These heads are designed to open if the temperature rises to a predetermined point. Thus, when a fire occurs in the vicinity of a sprinkler head, the head is opened and water released on the fire. Water damage caused by the opening of sprinkler heads to extinguish an accidental and unfriendly fire is covered under the property damage fire policy.

It occasionally happens, however, that water is discharged from the sprinkler system when no fire is involved. In such an instance the fire policies do not cover the damage, and to supply the needed protection, the sprinkler leakage contract is written. This policy provides indemnity against direct property loss or damage caused by the discharge or leakage of water or other substances from within an automatic sprinkler system. In addition to damage from water from the heads, the coverage extends to leakage from valves, pumps, pipes, tanks, and supply mains, as well as direct property loss or damage caused by the collapse or fall of tanks forming part of the system. Outside sprinkler systems, or water curtains when supplied from the sprinkler system may be included in the policy. The sprinkler policy may be written to cover buildings or their contents or both. Manufacturing, mercantile, residential, or other occupancies are insurable. The policy insures against loss due to leakage, discharge, or precipitation from within any automatic sprinkler system when no fire has occurred. The policy also covers, without additional charge, leakage from nonautomatic sprinklers, hydrants, standpipes, and base outlets. The policy does not cover leakage from nonautomatic systems independent of a sprinkler system, and if insurance of loss from this source is required, a water damage policy will satisfy the need. Damage caused by the collapse or fall of tanks, or the component parts or supports thereof, which form a part of the sprinkler system is regarded as a sprinkler leakage loss. This is a very important coverage, since water tanks located on the roof of manufacturing plants have been known to cause terrific loss when the supports collapsed.

The sprinkler leakage policy does not cover damage caused directly or indirectly by seepage or leakage of water through building walls, foundations, sidewalks, or sidewalk lights unless the loss is caused specifically by sprinkler leakage. Nor does the policy cover for loss caused by condensation of deposits on the sprinkler system itself. Loss by flows, inundation, or backing up of sewers or drains, or by water from any source other than from the sprinkler system is excluded, as well as loss caused by hazards for which special insurance forms are provided and specifically mentioned in the form, including hazards of fire, lightning, cyclone, tornado, windstorm, earthquake, explosion, including explosion or rupture of steam boilers and flywheels, blasting, invasion, insurrection, riot, civil war, and commotion. Likewise excluded are losses occasioned by usurped power or by order of any civil authority. There is no coverage for accounts, bills, currency, deeds, evidences of debt, money, or securities. Unless specifically assumed, bullion or manuscrips are not covered. Theft losses are not covered. Neither are losses which are the outgrowth of negligence on the part of the insured to use reasonable care to save and preserve the property. Losses caused directly or indirectly by aircraft, aircraft equipment, and objects falling or descending from aircraft are excluded. Damage to the sprinkler system itself is covered in some forms, but it is best to check the policy carefully to see that it is specifically included. Loss by sprinkler leakage or by collapse or the fall of a tank caused directly or indirectly by fire, lightning, windstorm, earthquake, blasting, explosion, rupture of a steam boiler, flywheel explosion, riot, civil commotion, or any water damage except from within the automatic sprinkler system are all excluded. These last-mentioned exclusions are all insurable under other forms and to include them in the sprinkler leakage policy would constitute duplication.

Not only may sprinkler leakage insurance be written to cover direct damage but it may also cover all of the consequential losses for which fire insurance is written.

Rates are based upon the susceptibility of the subject of the insurance to water damage, with charges for any element peculiar to the risk that might increase the hazard, such as: inadequate heating, alarm system, water supply, care and supervision; infrequent tests; and ineffective type of sprinkler and installation.

Policies may be written for a year or for a longer term. Though companies usually require at least a 10 percent coinsurance, a lesser or greater percentage may be used, 25 percent being customary. Rates are reduced so sharply as the percentage in the coinsurance clause is increased that the insured will do well to consider carefully the advisability of a high amount of insurance with a high coinsurance clause. In mercantile risks, furniture and fixtures may be insured at the building rate, plus 50 percent. Because the building rate is less than the contents rate, to exclude fixtures from the contents policy and cover this item specifically will result in a material saving in premium.

Sprinkler Leakage Liability. The installation of a sprinkler system in a building may, because of an accident to the system, result in serious loss or damage to the property of others, and if any element of negligence can be shown on the part of the owner of the system he may be held legally liable for the damage. One of the most frequent causes of sprinkler leakage loss is freezing. There are numerous other causes of accident which may introduce the element of liability. It may be contended that the system has not been properly maintained, that parts are faulty, or that the construction, particularly of parts bearing great weights, such as the support of tanks, was unsafe.

In all sprinkler leakage policies covering contents items there is a limited legal liability protection. This covers the interest of the insured in and his legal liability for loss to property similar to his own and held by him in trust or on commission, or on joint account with others, or sold but not removed, or in storage or for repair. This is similar to the commission clause found in fire insurance policies. If the insured wishes to protect himself for claims of a tenant or others, attributable to sprinkler leakage, he must secure a policy covering liability imposed by law. This policy excludes liability assumed by the insured. If there is any assumed liability, there is a special form by which the risk is assumed.

Water Damage Insurance. The sprinkler leakage policy excludes liability for water damage losses except for water leaking from inside the sprinkler system. To provide complete water damage insurance, the water damage policy is essential. The policy covers direct loss or damage caused by the accidental discharge, leakage, or overflow of water or steam from plumbing systems, tanks, heating systems, elevator tanks and cylinders, standpipes for fire hose, industrial and domestic appliances, and refrigerating systems and air-conditioning systems. The policy also covers loss or damage caused by rain or snow admitted directly to the interior of the building through defective roofs, leaders, or downspouts, or by open or defective windows, show windows, transoms, ventilators, or skylights.

The coverage is fairly comprehensive. Except in special situations the policy does not cover seepage, leakage, or influx of water through building walls, foundations, lowest basement floors, sidewalks, or the like. Losses attributable to aircraft, aircraft equipment, or to gases, fumes, or vapors also are not covered. Losses attributable to fire, lightning, windstorm, earthquake, and explosion are not covered. Such losses are expected to be covered by the policies written to cover loss against these perils. Theft losses are not covered, and losses due to failure of the insured to use all reasonable means to protect property after damage are excluded. Unless covered by endorsement, leakage from underground mains or leakage of refrigerants is not covered. There is no coverage to any part of a sprinkler system, since this is covered by the sprinkler leakage policy. Direct damage caused by the water leakage is covered, but there is no coverage for damage to the system, tank, or other source of the water damage loss.

There are three additional coverages available for the payment of an additional premium. These are coverage for (*a*) leakage from street water supply mains or hydrants, (*b*) leakage of refrigerants, (*c*) damage caused by aircraft. The policy contains clauses providing coverage for the first of these two items on an optional basis. Protection is provided if a premium is inserted in the blank clause. Aircraft damage may be inserted in the policy as a separate item for the payment of an additional premium.

Water Damage Liability Forms. As in the case of sprinkler leakage, there are three forms of water damage liability protection: (*a*) limited protection under property damage form, (*b*) liability imposed by law, and (*c*) assumed liability.

a) *Protection under Property Damage Form.* The extent of the protection of the property of others afforded under the standard fire property damage form is identical to that provided by the sprinkler leakage property damage contract. Legal liability of the insured for property similar to his own held in trust or on commission in storage or the like is covered with a contents item.

b) *Liability Imposed by Law.* This form protects the insured for liability obligations imposed by law for loss of or damage to property of others caused by water damage. As in the case of the sprinkler leakage, policy liability for loss or damage to property in the portion of the building occupied by the insured is excluded. It is important to notice that while the loss must originate as the result of ownership or occupancy of premises described in the policy, liability is not limited to property damaged on these premises.

c) *Assumed Liability.* Liability assumed by contract must be insured as a coverage in addition to the policy providing protection for liability imposed by law. This coverage follows the pattern of the sprinkler leakage form. It must be recalled, therefore, that in a situation where a lessee assumes responsibility under a lease for damage to the premises in which he is a tenant, only a policy covering assumed liability will afford him protection for a water damage loss.

Tenant's Improvements and Betterments. It is customary for a tenant planning a business establishment to lease real estate in a condition unsuitable to his needs. After the lease has been obtained upon suitable terms, the property may be partly or entirely renovated and reconstructed, involving substantial expenditure of money. Actually, however, to have an insurable interest in improvements or betterments, it is not necessary that the tenant have a written lease nor is it necessary that the improvements be installed during the term of the lease in force at the time of the loss. To constitute tenant's improvements or betterments, it is required that they be installed at the expense of the tenant who is the insured and that after installation the tenant has no legal right to remove them.

Insurable tenant's improvements, therefore, are of a nature that make them a part of the building and, hence, are absorbed into the realty. In such an instance, they cease to be the property of the lessee and instead are the property of the owner of the building. Nevertheless, they represent a substantial outlay on the part of the tenant, and the outlay is made in contemplation of their use over the period of his tenancy. They are within his control and available for his use so long as the rental agreement remains effective, and the loss of their use would represent a substantial loss indeed. It is this use interest in the improvements that the tenant's improvements and betterments policy undertakes to cover.

Nature of Improvements and Betterments Coverage. It is not always possible to work out an equitable or satisfactory agreement with the owner of the real estate in which a business is located with respect to loss of or damage to improvements and betterments. Insurance is now written frequently as an endorsement to the fire insurance contract to include improvements and betterments in the contents item of the fire insurance coverage. This permits recovery by the tenant entirely independent and apart from recovery by the owner of the real estate. Improvements and betterments provide that in the event improvements and betterments are damaged or destroyed during the policy term by the perils insured against, liability of the company shall be determined as follows:

a) If repaired or replaced at the expense of the insured within a reasonable time after such loss, the actual cash value of the damaged or destroyed improvement or betterments.

b) If not repaired or replaced within a reasonable time after such loss, that proportion of the original cost of the damaged or destroyed improvements and betterments which the unexpired term of the lease at the time of loss bears to the period(s) from the date(s) such improvements and betterments were made to the expiration date of the lease.

c) If repaired or replaced at the expense of others for the use of the insured, there shall be no liability hereunder.

d) If cloth awnings, signs and metal smokestacks, which qualify as improvements and betterments, are damaged or destroyed by windstorm or hail, there shall be no liability therefor unless the 80 percent or higher coinsurance clause applies.

e) If radio and television equipment on the outside of the building is damaged or destroyed by windstorm or hail, there shall be no liability therefor.

There is coverage under this form for two situations: (*a*) where the landlord refuses to restore but the lease is not canceled, and (*b*) where the lease is canceled.

a) *Landlord Refuses to Restore.* If the landlord in rebuilding the damaged premises restores the improvements at his own expense, it is apparent that the tenant has suffered no loss. The landlord secures title to the improvements once they become part of the real estate, and it is entirely in order for him to insure them. Actually, he is required to give consideration to their value if his insurance is written with a coinsurance clause. If the landlord restores the improvements without cost to the tenant, then there is no liability on the part of the tenant's improvements and betterments policy. On the other hand, if the landlord refuses to replace the betterments, whether or not he collects insurance for them, and the tenant replaces them at his expense, then his policy covers. Settlement is made on an actual cash value basis of the damaged improvements or betterments.

b) *Where the Lease Is Canceled.* There are two situations with respect to improvements and betterments where the lease is canceled under a fire clause. The improvements and betterments may be damaged or destroyed, or they may be uninjured or only partly injured. If the premises, however, are sufficiently damaged to warrant cancellation of the lease, then from the standpoint of the insured the betterments are a total loss. If the lease is canceled, it follows that the betterments cannot be repaired or replaced within a reasonable time after the loss. In these dircumstances, settlement is made by determining how much longer the lease has to run from the time of the loss. The loss is settled then by paying the insured prorata for the unexpired term of the lease based on the original cost of the improvements. In contrast to the situation where the improvements and betterments are replaced at the expense of the tenant and adjustment made on an actual cash value basis, when the lease is canceled original cost is the basis of adjustment. No consideration is given to either depreciation or increased costs. The prorata cost of the improvements determined by the unexpired term of the lease is the sole criterion.

Deferred Payment Insurance. Many types of business have large amounts of merchandise in which they have an interest located in widely different sections of a territory. These are items that have been sold on a partial payment basis. In this category are washing machines, radios, vacuum cleaners, refrigerators, pianos, fur coats, and many other different types of merchandise. Since regular payments are a part of the sales agreement, the interest in each item of merchandise differs from month to month. The problem of specifically insuring the interest at the various locations is complicated and cumbersome. To provide adequate coverage, a form has been devised that insures merchants who sell goods on a partial payment plan against loss of their interest in the goods while in the hands of customers. In addition to fire, the usual allied fire coverages, such as tornado, earthquake, explosion, and the like, are written.

The policy is written under three forms: (*a*) dual- or multiple-interest form, (*b*) the unpaid-balance form, and (*c*) the single-interest form. The first two forms cover the interest of the seller and the purchaser. The third form covers only the interest of the seller.

a) *Dual- or Multiple-Interest Form.* This form covers the interest of the seller and the purchaser for the actual value of the merchandise until it is paid for. If the transaction is financed, the interest of the finance company is covered. Certificates of insurance are available and may be supplied by the insured to the purchaser in connection with the installment sales transaction.

b) *Unpaid-Balance Form.* This form, like the foregoing form, covers both the interest of the seller, or, as the case may be, the finance company, and the purchaser. It covers, however, only for the unpaid balance due the merchant or the finance company at the time of the loss. It may be written to exclude unpaid balances that are past due. When so written it is usual to provide that the portion of unpaid balances 120 days past due are not covered.

c) *Single-Interest Form.* This form is written to cover only the interest of the seller or the finance company. As in the case of the unpaid-balance form, the company is liable only for the amount of the balance due at the time of the loss. It is usually written to exclude liability for unpaid balances more than 120 days past due. The form provides no protection for the purchaser. It is intended to reimburse the insured only in the event he is unable to collect a balance due him because of the loss of the item sold. The insured is required to make every reasonable effort to collect the account or repossess the damaged merchandise before the company is liable. The insured, however, is not required to bring suit.

Deferred payment insurance is what is known as "excess" coverage. Thus, if a purchaser of the article has, himself, placed specific insurance, the deferred payment policy will not cover until the amount of the specific insurance has been exhausted. Deferred payment policies do not, of course, cover failure of the merchant to secure payments as set forth in the contract. Nor do they cover against any losses other than those growing out of the perils specifically set forth in the agreement.[1]

Yard Improvements Insurance. Unless specifically insured or included by endorsement in the fire, windstorm, or other hazard contract, policies on buildings do not include damage to trees, hedges, shrubs, plants, fences, pergolas, arbors, ornamental steps, bridges, bird baths, seats, benches, or permanent yard betterments of any sort. Special coverage is available to indemnify the insured in the event of loss or damage to yard improvements.

The policy is ordinarily written by attaching a form to the fire policy.

---

[1]The policy provides insurance against loss or damage caused by fire and may be written to provide protection against extended cover perils. The policy never covers the perils of transportation. An inland marine form may be written on a named-perils basis and include transportation coverage which provides insurance while the goods are in transit from the store or warehouse of the seller to the location on the premises of the buyer. Such forms ordinarily cover interests of both the vendor and the vendee, though the single-interest coverage may be written on an inland marine form if required.

The scope of the coverage may be extended to include certain of the hazards covered by the extended cover endorsement. Notable in this category are the hazards of loss to property from falling aircraft, as well as explosion, riot, and windstorm. A usual exclusion is loss or damage caused by sleet or freezing, as well as loss or damage to any tree unless the trunk or main branch is destroyed, and a limit of $100 is placed for each tree. In some jurisdictions, a prorata distribution clause or a coinsurance clause is mandatory. In other jurisdictions, such a clause is optional.

Some forms limit the coverage to an area within a designated number of feet, usually 250, of the main building insured by the policy. Forms also frequently provide a clause limiting the loss or damage under the policy in question to such proportion of the loss or damage as the amount of insurance to which the form is attached bears to the total insurance of the same kind and nature. This is the usual contribution clause and makes essential, when the coverage is endorsed on a fire or other hazard policy, that all other identical policies be likewise endorsed. Not to do so will result in incomplete coverage.

The property description in the dwelling form is usually written to include coverage not only for the buildings but, as well, for outdoor equipment pertaining to the services of the premises but excluding "trees, shrubs and plants." Trees, shrubs, and plants may be specifically covered under a separate clause. Some forms limit the liability of the insurance, company to $300 on any one tree, $25 on any one shrub, and $5.00 on any one plant. Other forms do not print a limitation in the form but provide a blank so that limitations may be inserted consistent with the circumstances. It is the general custom, however, to place a definite limitation on each tree, plant, or shrub.

Coinsurance Deficiency Insurance. In some jurisdictions insurance is obtainable which is devised to protect the insured against becoming a coinsurer because of fluctuating values covered under specific or blanket insurance. The policy protects the insured against loss if his values increase to a degree that makes him a coinsurer. The coinsurance deficiency policy does not contribute to the loss, but if the insured is a coinsurer under his specific insurance, the deficiency coverage makes up what would otherwise be the insured's contribution. The deficiency coverage is limited to not more than 10 percent of the total value of the merchandise insured and is issued in the usual course only with insurance having a 90 percent reduced-rate contribution clause.

Automatic Builder's Risk. A building in the process of construction presents a situation in which values are constantly changing. If insurance is placed at infrequent intervals, it follows that there will be periods of overinsurance and others in which the insurance is inadequate. To eliminate such a situation and at the same time provide an equitable insurance plan, the automatic builder's risk form has been devised.

When the contractor is prepared to commence construction, a binder is issued, and as soon as there is any insurable property on the location a policy is issued for a period of a year covering this value. The form covers not only the building under construction but also temporary or permanent buildings, sheds, fences, tool houses, builder's machinery, tools, implements, apparatus, supplies, and materials of every description used in connection with the construction of the insured building if located on the premises or adjacent thereto.

The insured is required on the first day of each month to furnish the company with a statement setting forth the insurable value of the property as of the last day of the previous month. Upon receipt of the statement, an endorsement is attached to the policy showing the increase in the insurable value of the property and charging an additional premium therefor. Upon receipt of subsequent reports, the insurance is increased to meet the new values reported. The policy undertakes to protect the insured automatically against loss or damage by fire as the value at risk increases, pending the attachment of the monthly endorsements. This form provides the insured with full protection during the process of construction of a building up to the limit stated in the policy. To illustrate its operation: If at the time of the last report values were $50,000 and just before time for the next report they had increased to $55,000 and a fire occurs, the policy covers for the full value of $55,000, even though this amount is not endorsed on the policy. The 100 percent coinsurance clause is mandatory. The interest of the contractor or owner, or both, may be covered under the policy, and the usual extended cover hazards may be included in addition to the regular fire coverage.

Completed Value Builder's Risk. A form is now offered in some jurisdictions designed to provide automatic coverage and at the same time eliminate the necessity of monthly reports. This form provides for placing insurance equal to the completed value of the property at the commencement of construction. As in the case of the reporting form, full insurance to value is required. To compensate for the fact that more insurance than is required is carried at the inception of construction, the rate charged is 55 percent of the 100 percent coinsurance builder's risk rate. Coverage under this policy terminates when the building has been completed. It is ordinarily written for a year, but if the building is not completed within the period, the policy term may be extended by endorsement. The loss is paid in full if fire occurs during construction.

Supplemental Mortgage Interest. In communities where it is not customary to carry property insurance against windstorm, earthquake, explosion, or riot, lending institutions may protect their interests against loss or damage from these sources by a supplemental coverage written in the name of the lending institution.

The blanket supplemental policy, as written to cover the mortgage interest of financial institutions, furnishes no protection whatever to the property owner, and there can be no payment in any instance of an amount greater than the mortgage interest of the insured in the damaged property, regardless of the extent of the damage or the value of the property. Nor can the insured collect under the policy until the security has been so impaired that the loan is no longer adequately protected.

The policy is written to cover only on dwellings and mercantile properties. Farms and manufacturing properties are excluded, although coverage may be added at a special rate. A coinsurance clause calls for insurance in amount equal to 25 percent of the loans outstanding. Thus, a bank with $4,000,000 in real estate loans secured by mortgage would require a $1,000,000 policy in order to avoid becoming a coinsurer in the event of loss.

Blanket Tornado and Windstorm Mortgage Interest. It is not often that a blanket mortgage interest coverage as broad as the contract mentioned in the foregoing section is deemed necessary. Scientific information concerning the formation of the earth's structure permits a more dependable prediction of the probability of a disastrous earthquake than is possible in the case of tornado and windstorm.

For this reason, it is sometimes only from windstorm or tornado that an unforeseen and unexpected catastrophe is considered even remotely probable. Where the earthquake hazard can seemingly safely be ignored and where the loss from riot or explosion would not reach the proportions of a catastrophe, the blanket mortgage interest can be written, protecting the financial institution against losses due to impairment of the security because of tornado and windstorm damage.

This type of policy is not in demand in the areas where windstorm or earthquake insurance is usually written as a specific coverage, for in such areas the financial institution would require the borrower to furnish the protection under his specific policies when he negotiated the loan.

Contract of Supply Insurance. This contract is designed to provide protection for a favorable contract for material or goods. If, for example, a manufacturing plant is receiving raw material at a favorable price that cannot be duplicated either because of an advance in market prices or because, if bought elsewhere, freight and other charges would advance the price, the loss that would accrue because of the interruption or delay, if the interruption is caused by an insurable hazard, may be made the subject of an insurance contract. The usual hazards covered by policies as issued include fire, windstorm, explosion, and riot. The risk of riot is covered if it is felt that the strike hazard is a serious one.

The contract of supply policy takes for granted that the raw material or goods will be readily obtainable in the open market but obtainable only at a higher price than that being paid under the present contract. The policy is a direct-loss cover and is to be distinguished from the consequential loss contract that pays for the interruption of business due to inability to get the raw material or goods.

Flood Insurance. Insurance against rising water is to be distinguished from insurance against leakage or rain. The term "flood insurance" is applied to forms covering against direct loss by flood, such as, for example, the overflow of a river or a tidal wave. The statement is frequently made that flood insurance is unobtainable in this country. As a matter of fact, loss or damage caused by floods is covered under fire and marine contracts, but the protection is usually incidental to a more comprehensive coverage. Straight flood insurance, if obtainable at all, is very rare coverage. Such risks as insurance companies are willing to accept are carefully underwritten with respect to the nature of the contents of buildings insured as well as the structure of the buildings. They usually require warranties covering storage and make the insured a participant in every loss through the use of high deductibles.

The usual marine policies covering the perils of transportation include loss or damage from the rising of navigable waters, and flood losses are covered under the all-risks transportation floaters. Baled cotton in the Mississippi flood area has been insured successfully against flood loss, the risk at times being pooled and carried by an association of companies. Policies covering on bridges and their approaches may include, among other hazards, flood loss. Insurance against loss to growing crops, buildings, or land is not commonly written.[2]

---

[2]The difficulty attendant upon writing flood insurance is based upon the impossibility of getting a sufficient distribution of risks. In places subject to flood only at long intervals, the demand for coverage appears when the flood starts, and during other periods, when the risk is remote and the insurers might be enabled to accumulate a reserve, there is a reluctance on the part of property owners to pay the premiums. In any case, such demand as there is for flood insurance comes from localities where the

(Continued on next page)

Crop Insurance. Among the numerous hazards that threaten the destruction of crops are unfavorable weather conditions, hail, floods, insects, and disease. The distress resulting from widespread crop failure and the urgent necessity for relief have focused the attention of agricultural interests upon the necessity for crop insurance as a social measure.

Policies, as written, become effective at the date agreed upon when the application is filed, and the application ordinarily provides that the coverage will be effective provisionally 24 hours after the application has been received by the company. Within that 24-hour period, the company has an opportunity to decline the business if it wishes to do so. When the crop is harvested, the insurance terminates and is reduced prorata as harvesting progresses. In any case, the insurance terminates with the expiration of the limit set forth in the contract.

If the policy covers tree fruits, bush fruits, beans, grapes, or strawberries, no liability is assumed for loss or damage resulting in injury to trees, vines, leaves, bushes, plants, blooms, or blossoms. In the case of beans, vine vegetable crops, and the like, there is no liability for damage to blooms or blossoms or for damage to vines, plants, bushes, or leaves unless it can definitely be shown that such damage was caused by hail causing a loss to the product itself. There is liability in this case only to the extent that the product itself has been affected. In the case of corn, insurance does not take effect until at least 75 percent of the plants have formed the second joint above the ground, and there is no liability for loss or damage to leaves unless the grain product has been affected. Like limitations are set for other crops with a view definitely to limiting the liability of the insurer to situations in which a real risk has developed. It is usual to provide a limit of liability per acre, and policies may include a clause similar to the memorandum clause found in marine policies setting forth that there shall be no liability on the part of the insurance company unless the crop

---

flood record is already high. Any distribution of coverage, such as the fire companies obtain, is impossible. Under such circumstances, flood insurance can be effected, if at all, on property subjected to frequent flood losses only at a rate that seems prohibitive to the prospective insured. For a statement of the position of the insurance industry with respect to flood insurance, see *Report on Floods and Flood Damage,* Insurance Executives Association (New York, 1952). The report is divided into two sections. Section I treats with the insurance aspects of flood damage to property. Section II is made up of a report prepared for Insurance Executives Association by the New York engineering firms of Parsons, Brinkerhoff, Hall & Macdonald, entitled "Report on Floods and Flood Damage" and dated April, 1952, and treats primarily with the technical engineering aspects of flood damage. Following the August, 1955, floods in the northeast, this firm was again retained to study the problems of floods and flood damage and to review the 1952 report. The study was under way and was extended to include the October, 1955, floods. Based on the findings of the report American insurers here found no reason for changing the conclusion based on the original report that "insurance against the peril of flood cannot successfully be written." Numerous flood-disaster insurance or reinsurance measures have from time to time been proposed for congressional enactment. A bill termed an "indemnity bill" was finally passed and signed by President Eisenhower, August, 1956. The act calls for a five-year, $5 million government insurance and reinsurance system against flood losses, plus a program of government guaranteed loans. "This new program is a venture into an untested field of risk protection, and is admittedly experimental," President Eisenhower stated. He went on to say: "It does not propose putting the Federal Government permanently into a flood insurance business. On the contrary, it provides for the government to lead the way on a basis that will enable this field of responsibility to be absorbed into our private system as quickly as possible."

is damaged more than a certain designated percentage—5 percent is a figure frequently used. If the crop can be reset or reseeded, the liability of the company is limited to actual cost of these operations. The policy specifically provides that there shall be no abandonment to the company of any insured crop.

Underwriting insurance on growing crops presents numerous difficulties. At the planting season it is impossible to known what the market will be at the time of harvest. A solution that has seemed to be equitable provides that, if there is a loss covered by the policy, the insurance company will pay the farmer on the basis of his decreased yield. This plan provides indemnity to the insured for a partial loss, even though he is able to sell as much of the crop as may be salvaged and show a profit for the year's operation.

Frost and freeze coverages are written for owners of orchards or growing citrus fruits or those engaged in marketing crops that are particularly susceptible to frost damage. One of the major difficulties in connection with writing this form of insurance is to be found in the effects that serious frost losses have upon the market price of the balance of the crop. If the frost losses throughout a wide territory are severe enough to reduce the entire crop seriously, then part of the loss is regained by the increased value in the part of the crop that is marketable. This increased value is, of course, of no assistance to the orchard owner whose entire crop is destroyed. If, however, he is able to salvage part of his crop, the scarcity reflects to his benefit. Attempts have been made to take this factor into consideration by providing for only a partial settlement at the time the damage occurs and a final settlement based upon the income received when the salable crop has been marketed.

Crop-hail insurance is a popular form of crop coverage and as usually written utilizes the so-called "annual percentage form." The contract provides indemnity for the percentage of physical damage resulting from hail. Windstorm damage may be included for some crops susceptible to windstorm losses. There is coverage only, however, if the wind is accompanied by hail, and to establish a loss it must be shown that the actual hail damage equalled or exceeded 5 percent of the loss. Crops are usually insured on a "specific amount per acre" basis. The amount of insurance usually represents the cost of production though in some instances it may be increased to include a portion of the expected profit from the crops. Insurance may range from $10 per acre on grain in the West to as high as $2,500 an acre on shade-grown tobacco in the Connecticut Valley. In a few areas a "bushel policy" has been made available. Under this form the insurance guarantees a price per bushel for the actual bushels per acre destroyed or damaged by hail.

In some instance crop insurance is written on a named-peril basis. When written on tobacco it may include in addition to the perils while the crop is in the field coverage while the harvested crop is in the barn. Coverage during storage may include the usual fire and extended coverage perils.

All-Risks Crop Insurance. Crop insurance written on an all-risks basis and designed to cover, among others, such perils as blight, insect pests, drought, and the like is written on a limited basis by some private insurers in conjunction with crop-hail coverage.

All-risks crop insurance differs from other forms of crop insurance in that it is virtually a crop guarantee. Instead of determining the amount of loss or damage attributable to an insured peril, the insurance company is obligated to pay to the insured any difference between the coverage and the amount of the crop actually produced. If there is no production because the crop fails to grow, the loss is total. Unfavorable weather may result in a loss either in the quality of production or in the quantity.

One reason, among others, that private insurers are reluctant to offer all-risks crop insurance is to be found in the element of moral hazard. The policyholder, knowing that his insurance will indemnify him fully if his crop fails, may tend to neglect the crop by failing to take the necessary precautions to minimize the loss. Efforts have been made to eliminate the moral hazard by reducing the amount of insurance to a percentage of the average yield. Three fourths of the yield has been a widely accepted maximum in the past, and such a contract leaves the farmer a coinsurer for one fourth of any loss.[3]

Automatic and Open Binders. Automatic binders are available for banks and trust companies acting in the capacity of executor, administrator, trustee, guardian, or conservator. The insured is automatically covered for an amount up to a stipulated limit against loss or damage by fire to any property passing into its control in any of the previously mentioned capacities.

The insured is obligated within the 60-day period to ascertain the insurance in effect upon the property, and any deficiency is to be written in the company writing the automatic binder. By means of this coverage, continuous fire protection is provided from the time the property passes into the control of the financial institution, making good any deficiency pending the insured's having an opportunity to check the existing coverage.

An open binder is issued to a bank and is designed to indemnify it against loss sustained through the impairment of its mortgage interest because of fire when such loss is covered by specific insurance in an insolvent company. The company issuing the binder automatically covers the insured for a period of 30 days when a company placing specific insurance on the mortgage interest of the insured becomes insolvent. Within 30 days the insured is obligated to replace the insurance in the insolvent company with a like amount of insurance in the binding company. A nominal premium of $1.00 is charged for the binders.

Multiple-Location Contracts. The trend of business has been in the direction of larger and larger organizations, each controlling subsidiaries or branches, frequently with property values distributed among many locations. To simplify the problem of providing complete and ade-

---

[3]The insurance of crops has been effected over the past 22 years by the Federal Crop Insurance Corporation, an agency of the United States Department of Agriculture. This insurance covers essentially all natural causes of loss, including drought, flood, hail, wind, frost, winter kill, lightning, fire, excessive rain, snow, wildlife, hurricane, tornado, insect infestation, plant diseases, and such other unavoidable causes as it is determined by the board of directors of the Corporation to cover. It does not cover such causes of loss as neglect, poor farming practices, or theft, nor does it cover the risk of financial loss due to low prices. Tree crops are insured for only a few named perils. Federal crop insurance is not available in all counties and in most of the counties where it is offered it is made available only on one crop. The insurance is effected by guaranteeing the farmer a certain amount of production and if the production amounts to less than that, he is indemnified for the shortage. For a comprehensive presentation of the experiences of the government in the field of crop insurance, see *Report to Congress*, Federal Crop Insurance Corporation, U.S. Department of Agriculture (Annual). For a history and description of the operations of the Federal Crop Insurance Corporation see *Federal Crop Insurance—A Description*, 4th revision (Washington, D.C.: Government Printing Office, 1959).

quate protection for insureds having contents at a number of locations and with fluctuating values over the year, the multiple-location forms have been prepared, whereby all locations may be covered by a single policy, with automatic coverage for new locations. Property suitable for coverage under the multiple-location forms includes contents only and excludes buildings. Insurable items include merchandise, machinery, supplies, furniture, fixtures, and the insured's interest in betterments. Furniture and fixtures, machinery, and the like can be written only in connection with merchandise. For this reason, risks, such as banks with numerous branches, barber shop chains, theater chains, beauty shops, hotels, farms, theaters, grain risks, oil risks and other similar lines, cannot be written on a reporting form.[4] The reason for this is obvious when it is recognized that the forms are designed to take care of fluctuating classes of merchandise where an automatic coverage following values is desirable.

A prime objective of the multiple-location idea was the development of reporting and automatic pickup forms to eliminate the necessity of canceling and rewriting or endorsing policies where the values at various locations fluctuate.

Present rating laws forbid the charging or fixing of rates for any class or risk that is excessive, discriminatory, inadequate, or unreasonable. While not all insurers were in agreement as to the exact nature of the credits to be allowed in rating large multiple-location risks, there was a general agreement on the proposition that the risks did show savings that should be reflected in the rate structure. The chief point of disagreement centered over the allowance of experience debits or credits. It was argued that the basic principle of fire rate making required the measurement in advance of fire hazards and other contributing hazards against a predetermined standard. To allow credits or debits on the basis of the experience of an individual risk amounts to superimposing such credits or debits upon a specific rate which has already measured the risk.[5] There is no point of disagreement, however, with the contention that multiple-location underwriting would affect savings that in turn should be handed on to the insured. Commissions are generally lower on this class of business. Savings are reported in administration. For example, it is less expensive to write one policy for from 100 to 2,000 or more locations than it would be to write a separate policy for each location. Comparable economies have been noted in accounting, statistical maintenance, collection expense, credit reports, and underwriting. There are some additional expenses such as the establishment of a special department, but it has been conceded that the net result

---

[4]There are special forms for grain, cotton, petroleum, and tobacco in auction warehouses.

[5]It has been argued that because casualty companies have successfully developed experience rating that the idea may be carried into the field of fire insurance. Those who oppose the idea contend there is a fundamental difference. It is pointed out that experience-rated casualty coverages bear the common characteristic of small but frequent general losses that may be reduced by prevention activities. The fire business, it is argued, offers no such assurance. Amounts at risk may be very large and loss may originate from hazards over which the insured has no control. On the other hand, experience shows there are certain risks that consistently develop better loss records over the years than do other risks in all respects similar from an underwriting standpoint. It is argued that management, good housekeeping, and other factors where (*a*) overall management is unified and (*b*) there is a sizable premium and a spread of risks between locations will permit an application of experience credits to the particular risks.

of multiple-location underwriting is a savings. This savings is reflected in the rating plans.[6]

Multiple-location rate adjustments apply only to that portion of the basic annual premium which is in excess of $1,000. By preserving the first $1,000 of premium without discount, (*a*) there is no area for comparison between insureds with multiple-location coverage and those without it, and (*b*) it commences the application of rate adjustment at a point where economies in handling the business commence to make themselves felt. Not all multiple-location risks are large enough to reflect inherent characteristics so as to warrant premium credits from the basic annual premium produced by the application of specific rates. In the case of some of the reporting forms with a limited number of locations the premium is based upon the limits of liability computed at the full tariff coinsurance rate applying to each location and not upon average values and averate rates. The convenience of the single contract covering each location with insurance automatically following values and automatically extending to newly acquired locations is the appeal to the insured.

Multiple-location rating is held not to be unfairly discriminatory as against individual risks. It is held that various insureds comprising a group possess sufficient similarity to be grouped together for rating purposes with differences from insureds noneligible under the plan. One of the purposes of insurance rating is to provide discrimination as to classes. It is only unfair discrimination that is forbidden.[7] On the other hand, to withhold a merited discount from a sizable group of policyholders, it is pointed out, is tantamount to maintaining an excessive rate level.[8]

Property Eligible for Coverage. Since the multiple-location forms are designed to provide protection for fluctuating values, they do not lend themselves to the insurance of buildings. Coverage is provided for merchandise and materials, though betterments and improvements to buildings may be covered in the same policy. This is an important feature, since chain stores frequently make long-term leases followed by extensive improvements. The improvements are regarded not in the category of real estate owned but rather as an investment to be amortized over the term of the lease. It simplifies the entire insurance problem to allow betterments values to be covered under the same contract that covers other values of the business.

Generally speaking, stocks, materials, and supplies including packages, as well as patterns and dies, may be covered. Consigned stocks, wherever located, are insurable. The same is true with respect to furniture and fixtures when covered in the same policy with the stock. Leased machinery

[6]There are two plans that have met with general approval. The multiple-location service office plan, sometimes referred to as the "credit and debit plan" or the "Escott plan," takes into consideration loss experience. The independent plan is a competitive filing that recognizes multiple-location economics but does not recognize individual loss experience.

[7]State of New York Insurance Department, *Decision: In the Matter of Appeal by members of the American Four Group; members of the Loyalty Group; members of the Aetna Life Group; members of the Hartford Group; and the New York Underwriters Insurance Company, from a decision of the New York Fire Insurance Rating Organization, under Section 184, Par 11, of the New York Insurance Law; and Proceedings for review of a decision of the New York Superintendent of Insurance, under Section 186-B, of the New York Insurance Law; and Proceedings to review Rate Filing, under Section 186, Par 3, of the New York Insurance Law*, p. 39.

[8]*Ibid*, p. 40.

or other machinery incidental to a business operation may be covered in the same policy with the stock. This does not apply to machinery located on the premises of a manufacturing plant owned or controlled by the insured. Machinery in this last-named category is expected to be insured specifically like the real estate. There are certain classes of risk that might appear to be eligible for coverage by a multiple-location contract that may not be so covered because of existing rules. Certain of these either have values sufficiently stabilized or other forms have been provided for their needs. The rule provides that banks, barber shops, beauty shops and beauty parlors, cotton risks, grain risks, hotels, laundries, shoe repairing shops, and theater furniture, fixtures, and betterments may not be covered under a multiple-location form.

Multiple-Location Forms. Insurance is written under two general types of coverage: (1) reporting and (2) coinsurance. There are five available forms. One form may cover as a multiple-location form, but it may also cover fluctuating values in a single location. The forms differ with respect to the number of locations required and whether or not they are reporting forms. There are also differences with respect to rating plans and requirements for minimum premiums.

Features Common to All Multiple-Location Reporting Forms. It is the intent of reporting forms to follow fluctuating values so that whenever a loss occurs full insurance to value will be provided. The insurance company obligates itself in this respect, but to make the contract effective there are certain obligations which the insured must meet, and to do this it is important that he have a full comprehension of the features that distinguish the reporting forms from specific insurance. It is particularly important to notice: (*a*) the reporting requirement, (*b*) penalties for noncompliance, (*c*) provisional amount of insurance, (*d*) liability limits, (*e*) effect of specific insurance, and (*f*) premium adjustment.

a) *Reporting Requirement.* The value reporting clause obligates the insured to report in writing to the company not later than 30 days after the last day of each calendar month: (1) the exact location of all property covered, (2) the total actual cash value of insured property at each location, and (3) specific insurance in force.

b) *Penalties for Noncompliance.* Failure on the part of the insured to make the required report limits the obligation of the company for no more than the amounts included in the last report filed prior to a loss less specific insurance. If the insured neglects to make a report, he must abide by the values of his last report. The form also contains an "honesty clause" similar to that found in certain of the inland marine contracts. This clause provides that if the last reported value prior to a loss is less than the actual cash value at the time the report is made, then the company is liable for any loss only in the proportion that the value reported bears to the actual value. If an insured reports a $50,000 value where there is $100,000 actual value and sustains a $10,000 loss, the company is liable only for $5,000. The insured reported 50 percent of actual values, so the company pays 50 percent of a loss subject to policy limits.

c) *Provisional Amount of Insurance.* Since it cannot be known at the outset the full amount of insurance coverage that the policy will provide, the forms are written with a provisional amount of insurance and a deposit premium is collected at the time by applying the rate to the provisional amount. The minimum provisional amount is determined by taking the total of the average values at all locations less the amount of specific insurance to be permitted by endorsement. The premium for all forms is adjusted at the end of the policy term on the bais of actual values reported.

d) Liability Limits. Reporting forms provide a limit of liability which is to be distinguished from the provisional amount of insurance. It is the intention of the policy to cover fluctuating values, but in order to exercise some underwriting control the company establishes a limit to its liability. Where two or more locations are involved, a separate limit is established for each location. The limit of liability applies not with respect to each policy but to all contributing insurance. If reports are made showing values in excess of liability limits, premiums are collected for the full values reported, but if the values exceed the liability limits established, they remain the limit of recovery. Hence, if values are ever determined to be in excess of liability limits, steps should be taken immediately to have the limits increased. It is not common practice to forestall this necessity to write the coverage with liability limits established considerably higher than actual anticipated requirements.

e) Effect of Specific Insurance. Where specific insurance is written and is considered in the computation of the final premium, the insured is obligated either to continue specific insurance in force upon expiration or to increase the limit of liability immediately under the reporting form if the values require it. Multiple-location coverages are always excess over specific insurance payments. Limits of liability for multiple-location coverages are always determined by subtracting specific insurance from peak values. It follows, therefore, that if substantial amounts of specific insurance are allowed to expire without a corresponding increase in the limits of liability, the insured may find himself with inadequate protection.

f) Premium Adjustment. In effecting the final premium adjustment, three factors are considered: (*a*) total monthly values reported, (*b*) specific insurance, and (*c*) minimum premiums. An average of the total monthly values reported for the term of the policy is determined, and if the premium on this average at the applicable rate exceeds the provisional premium, the insured is required to pay for the excess. If the premium is less than the provisional premium, the insurance company is obligated to return any excess paid. In calculating total monthly values, permitted specific insurance at any location, if reported, is deducted from the value reported at that location and the remaining value is considered. The final adjusted premium in any case must equal the minimum premium.

Charges for Fire Apparatus. Many valuable properties are situated outside the limits of towns or cities where fire departments are located. Summer residences particularly, located on isolated islands, in the woods or mountains, frequently involve many thousands of dollars in value that could be saved when fire threatens by calling for the assistance of the fire department of a neighboring community. Country estates, farms, isolated filling stations, stores, and other types of secluded property all fall in the same category. Forest fires, grass burning, or a fire breaking out in a neighboring property may each be the occasion for summoning help. If the neighboring fire department is called in time, it may succeed in warding the fire from the threatened premises, save the owner his property and the insurance companies from paying a total loss. This expense, however, regardless of the fact that insurance companies may be beneficiaries of the action, is not covered in the policy unless the risk is specifically assumed.[9] Fire insurance companies will endorse a fire policy to indemnify

[9]Fire departments are supported by the taxpayers of the community in which they

the insured for fire apparatus charges when the coverage is deemed desirable.[10]

Standing Timber Insurance. The insurance of standing timber is, from the standpoint of underwriting, a highly specialized form of cover. A fire involving serious loss, from the point of view of the insurance underwriter in all probability, is liable to develop into a catastrophe. The demand for this form of insurance made its appearance when tracts of standing timber were included in the security offered lending institutions in connection with the negotiation of loans.

Standing timber insurance contemplates two types of risk: (1) merchantable lumber and (2) reforestation plantation. The merchantable lumber classification includes timberlands containing a growth of a size that permits profitable operation for saw logs. Reforestation plantations include trees planted by hand, in contrast to second growth that has developed from seed. In the case of merchantable lumber, in the ordinary course, companies tend to limit their commitments to $25,000 subject to one fire; and in the case of a reforestation plantation the limitation is fixed at the actual outlay for trees and labor plus interest at 5 per cent from the date of planting, compounded annually.

Whereas the policy is written on an annual basis, the major fire hazard exists during the summer months. For this reason, the companies regard the months from April to November as the dry season and make for that period what is known as a "dry season charge." If the policy is in force during any part of the dry season, the dry season charge is regarded as fully earned, and no return premium for any part of it is allowed. This charge represents 80 percent of the annual premium.

---

are located and expect and demand remuneration if called to assist neighboring property owners. Sometimes the selectmen of the town will assume the responsibility for sending for help in case of fire, and the bill will become a public charge. This, however, is frequently not the case, and the expense must be paid by the property owner who sends for the help and whose property is threatened. The cost ranges from $25 or $50 in some communities to several hundred dollars a day in others. In one instance where fire apparatus and men were transported by steamer to an island off the Maine coast to help control a fire, the charge was nearly $1,000. Twenty-five dollars an hour for a motor pumper and an hourly charge for each man is not unusual.

[10]The policy definitely places an obligation upon the insured to use all reasonable means to save the insured property when threatened by fire. Because of its inclusion, the clause is held to impose no additional liability upon the insured, since such a duty is said to arise from the nature of the insurance contract. The extent to which an individual is bound to go is that prompted by reason. For example, it has been held that if the duty of caring for a family or saving a life prevents the care of threatened property, the insured is not to be charged with negligence in devoting his entire attention to the former at the expense of the property. However, an insured may not sit complacently by and watch his property burn without expending such effort as in the circumstances seems reasonable. Authorities agree that under the New York policy the insurer is not liable for expenses incurred either in protecting property from threatened fire or even in putting the fire out when discovered.

Appendix F

OTHER SPECIAL FEATURES OF MARINE INSURANCE CONTRACTS

War Risks. The practice now in vogue in this country is to insure marine perils and war risks under separate contract. War perils are dropped from the perils clause of cargo policies, but in connection with hull risks the clause continues to include the war perils. There is an F.C. & S. ("free-of-capture and seizure") clause printed on the form. This clause states that unless the clause is physically deleted by the underwriters, it shall be paramount and supersede and nullify any contrary provision of the policy.

The ocean marine policy covering perils of the sea includes such perils as sinking, collision, damage, stranding, damage from storms, and fire damage. These particular hazards are increased during wartime because of the necessity to run without lights, removal of guides to navigation, danger of collision in convoys, and the like. Even though the increase in hazard was due to war, for many years it was held that such increase was not to be regarded as war risks within the meaning of ocean marine war-risks insurance. War risks included only cover against losses caused by acts of an enemy such as torpedoing, bombing, and damage from shell fire. More recently, the war-perils clause has been enlarged to include certain losses resulting from wartime conditions, such as collision in convoy, collision resulting from vessels running without lights, stranding occasioned by removal of lights, buoys or other aids to navigation, or by navigating without a pilot. Simultaneously, these perils were excluded from the marine policy by the revised F.C. & S. clause.

On the basis of a noted English case growing out of a seizure during World War I, it was held that underwriters covering under the usual war-risks clause which included "restraint of princes" as a peril were liable in case of loss of voyage or frustration of voyage if it could not be completed because of the orders of government authority.[1] It was held that not only the thing that insured but the voyage for which it is insured together formed the subject matter of the insurance and, therefore, the insurance covered against loss by frustration of the voyage. Because of this, when insurers are prepared to cover war perils but do not wish to cover losses which amount to loss of market owing to inability to complete the voyage, the policy is endorsed with the so-called *frustration clause*. This clause

[1]*British and Foreign Marine Insurance Company* v. *Sanday* (1916), 1 App. Cas. 650; 85 L.J.K.B. 550; 114 L.T. 521; 32 T.I.R. 266; 60 Sol. Jo. 253; 21 Com. Cas. 154; 29 Digest 276, 2236.

has the effect of eliminating losses based upon failure to complete the voyage due to the orders of government authority.

Limitations to Perils Clause. The marine insurance contract undertakes to cover only losses that are accidental and beyond the control of the insured. This being the case, the underwriters are not liable for loss to the subject of insurance growing out of inherent vice or improper methods of shipment. Hence, losses that are the outgrowth of decay, leakage, or evaporation do not come within the scope of the perils clause. More particularly, the policy does not cover wear and tear due to packing and unpacking or the vibration of the vessel. The test as to whether there is liability under the policy is to be found in determining whether the cause of the loss is a fortuitous happening of an extraordinary and abnormal nature. If the cause of the loss is a normal and customary incident of the voyage that might reasonably have been foreseen, the underwriters are not liable.

"***Lost or Not Lost.***" The phrase "To be insured lost or not lost" appeared in the early marine policies when, among other reasons, because of limited communication facilities, it was impossible to know the exact status of the subject of the insurance when the policy was written. Under the terms of the clause, the insured is protected if the thing insured is lost before the insurance becomes effective. The phrase continues in modern contracts of marine insurance and is particularly useful to the merchant importing stocks of merchandise. Upon receipt of notice that a consignment has been made to him, he can provide insurance immediately, and if by chance the merchandise is damaged prior to the time the policy attaches, the underwriters are liable for the damage. An important condition in connection with the operation of this clause is the requirement that the underwriter be acquainted with all information available.

"***At and From.***" Policies usually provide that the insurance shall cover "at and from." For example, a policy may read: "At and from London to New York" or "At and from Liverpool to New York and Baltimore, via New York." The word "at" in the policy provides protection for the risk *in* the port of departure, whereas "from" covers the risk only after sailing. The combination of both terms has the effect of covering the risk not only in the port of departure but on the voyage as well. The omission of the word "at" requires that the ship must have sailed upon the voyage before the insurance attaches. The policy, if written for a single voyage, usually provides that the insurance "shall continue and endure until the said merchandise shall be safely landed." In the case of an "at and from" policy or a policy written "from" covering on a hull, the insurance terminates 24 hours after the arrival and safe mooring of the vessel at her destination.

Strikes, Riots, and Civil Commotions. The marine policy as ordinarily written does not include strikes, riots, or civil commotion in the scope of the contract. To avoid any possible confusion of including losses from this source within the war-risks covers, it is usual to incorporate a clause, known as the "S.R. & C.C. clause," which provides as follows: "Warranted free of loss or damage caused by strikers, locked out workmen, or persons taking part in labor disturbances, or riots, or civil commotions."

As in the case of goods in storage on land, the riot and civil commotion hazard is a very real one. This hazard, of course, exists entirely apart from the war-risks hazard. In time of peace, when goods may be shipped insured under policies which contain the warehouse-to-warehouse clause, it is quite possible that losses might develop resulting from the action of strikers, locked-out workmen, or other persons involved in riots or civil conflicts. The marine policy does not cover this hazard, but the risk may be written when specifically accepted by the underwriter and made part of a special agreement incorporated in the contract.

Janson Clause. Under the terms of the various F.P.A. clauses, the damage is paid without deduction in case of loss provided the loss equals the percentage stipulated in the clause. Under the terms of the Janson clause, a proportion of the loss falls upon the insured in any case. The clause is so written that only the excess of loss upon the stipulated percentage shall be paid by the underwriters. Thus, in the case of a valuation of $5,000, with the use of the 5 percent Janson clause a loss of $300 would obligate the underwriters to a payment of but $50. This is true because, under the terms of the clause, 5 percent of the value is deductible from any loss.

Cancellation and Premium Credits. Because of the nature of marine insurance, it is held that in the ordinary course to provide for cancellation of a policy and the return of a part of the premium inequitable situations might frequently develop. For example, if the underwriter for a given premium assumes the risk of a voyage and the ship sets forth and the policy attaches, the full premium is held to be earned. If the ship shortly after departure is lost and the cause of the loss is not one of the perils insured against, the underwriters are obligated neither to make a payment under the policy nor to return any part of the premium. In the case of transfer of ownership, the same general rule applies and underwriters are not obligated to make a return of premium. On the other hand, the insurer may not cancel once the insurance attaches. It can readily be seen that if the underwriters learned of the development of hazardous conditions and could cancel the insurance on notice, the owner of the ship or goods insured might be left in a position in which new insurance would not be obtainable or, if obtainable at all, at a prohibitive cost. Indicative of the extent to which the rule is carried, if a policy is issued and, unknown to the parties at the time, the voyage had successfully terminated, no return premium is due the policyholder. It is of course true that if the insurer should accept a premium knowing the voyage had successfully terminated, he would be perpetrating a fraud and in such circumstances could not retain the premium.

While the foregoing is the basic rule, as a matter of practice, clauses have been incorporated into policies providing for its modification. For example, it is sometimes provided that, in case of the sale of a ship, a return premium will be allowed at an established rate per month. It is also frequently provided that in case of a lay-up for repairs or if for any reason the vessel is out of service, there shall be a return premium for each 15 or 30 consecutive days in port. A delay in port while the ship is in commission is not a lay-up warranting a return premium. To come within the meaning of the clause, the ship must be deliberately taken out of commission for a definite reason, as for overhauling or lack of business.

Express Warranties. Express warranties are written into policies to cover particular situations and operate in the case of marine insurance as in other forms of coverage. Express warranties are rarely found in marine contracts covering on goods. Occasionally an underwriter, in order to limit his liability under an open policy, may provide for a limitation in the following terms: "Warranted not more than $10,000 by any one steamer." In the case of hull policies, however, the use of express warranties is common. A warranty must be literally complied with, and, in the event of a breach of warranty, the insurer is discharged of all liability from the date of the breach but not from liability incurred before that date. Warranties frequently found in policies have to do with the date of sailing, the position of the ship, and the number of the crew, and in time of war it is usual to warrant that vessels shall sail under the protection of an armed convoy. Likewise, warranties of nationality and neutrality are frequently met with in wartime.

A warranty sometimes used when the insurer wishes the insured to bear a part of the loss provides: "Warranted $ .... uninsured." For example, in the case of a cargo valued at $10,000 insured under a cargo policy with the clause attached providing "Warranted $2,500 uninsured," the insurance company knows that the insured will bear 25 percent of any loss. If the insured were to purchase a policy covering the full value of the cargo, this would be a breach of the warranty and the entire insurance would cease to cover.

To constitute an express warranty it is not necessary in every instance that the word "warranty" be used. For example, a simple statement in the policy with respect to the nationality or construction of the ship constitutes a warranty. On the other hand, the clause in the policy which reads "warranted free of particular average unless 3 percent" is not in the true sense a warranty but rather a stipulation indicating a limitation of the liability of the underwriter. Actually there is no limitation with respect to subject matter covered by a warranty. It is only required that it be a matter concerning which the underwriters demand a warranty and concerning which the assured is willing to warrant. There are, however, certain areas in which it is customary to provide limitations by means of expressed warranties. Few insureds would be willing to accept a policy containing warranties over which the had no control. This being the case underwriters ordinarily limit warranties to matters within the control of the insured.

Certain warranties are known as "trading warranties." For example, certain vessels that are build to operate in a particular area are not always safe for worldwide operations. A case in point is to be found in vessels constructed for operations on the Great Lakes. When policies are issued on such vessels, it is usual to designate definitely the geographical areas in which they will operate. Because of weather conditions, as in the case of the Great Lakes operations, policies may contain a warranty that the vessels will operate only in the open season of navigation.[2] Another group of warranties are known as "loading warranties." These concern the nature of the cargo to be handled. In the case of extra heavy cargo, such as lead, coal, iron, or the like, the policy will contain a warranty that the vessel will not load in excess of registered under-deck capacity. Other loading warranties concern themselves with cargoes that are inherently dangerous.

Special Clauses for Merchandise Insurance. Frequently the bill of lading grants to the carrier certain liberties with respect to the voyage that ordinarily might unfavorably affect the rights of the insured under a marine policy. Likewise, bill-of-lading conditions exempt the carrier from liability for loss or damage caused by negligence of master or mariners, as

---

[2]The American Institute of Marine Underwriters has promulgated a number of trading warranties. These concern themselves with areas in which navigation is particularly hazardous. Insured vessels, for instance, are prohibited from entering Greenland waters and the North Atlantic coast of North America. These warranties also have to do with the northern part of the Pacific Coast, Baltic seas, Bering Sea, and northern Asiatic waters, to mention but a few.

well as from latent defects in the hull or machinery of the vessel. The policy may be written to give the insured permission to ship under such bills of lading.

The implied warranties concerning deviation and seaworthiness and all of the other implied warranties except that warranting the legal conduct of the voyage may be waived by agreement. Obviously, in most instances the insured has no control over the management or the condition of the vessel in which his goods are shipped, and insistence upon compliance with these warranties would tend to make the insured uncertain as to the effectiveness of his coverage. In connection with the implied warranty of seaworthiness there is a warranty of seaworthiness of the vessel, but not of the cargo. Therefore, the shipper of a cargo may presume the vessel to be seaworthy and have no reason to believe otherwise. So that his insurance may not be voided by a condition over which he has no control and of which he has no knowledge, he may have his policy endorsed: "Seaworthiness of the vessel as between the assured and the underwriter is hereby admitted."

In the case of deviation, the deviation clause provides that the policy shall not be voided by deviation of the vessel, change of voyage, over-carriage, or any error or unintentional omission in the description of interest, vessel, or voyage. The insured, however, must communicate the information of the deviation or defect to the company as soon as the information comes to him and, if required to do so, pay an additional premium.

Appendix G

PARTIAL PROSPECT LIST FOR MARINE, INLAND MARINE, AND "ALL RISKS" LINES*

Army, Navy and Diplomatic Service Personnel

Insurable Property	*Form of Policy*
Household and Personal Effects	Government Service

Art Collectors
Art Dealers
Art Galleries

Paintings, Works of Art Antiques and objects of art or historical value	Fine Arts

Armories

Flags and Paraphernalia	Special Floater
Musical Instruments	Musical Instrument Floater
Privately owned Saddle Horses	Livestock Floater
Paintings, Trophies and objects of historical value	Fine Arts

Banks

Customers' Furs for Storage	Furriers' Customers
Electric Signs	Neon Sign
Financed Installment Accounts	Installment Floater
Fine Arts	Fine Arts
Securities, Currency	Armored Car and Messenger Registered Mail
Floor Plan Accounts	Floor Plan

Book Binders and Printers

Property of others in custody	Bailees' Customers

Breweries and Beverage Distributors

Barrels, Cases and Containers	Transportation—Location Motor Truck Merchandise Floater
Beer	Marine Cargo Policy Transportation
Horses and Wagons	Horse and Wagon Floater

Bridge Owners and Mortgagees

Insurable Property	*Form of Policy*
Bridges	Bridge Property Damage Bridge Use and Occupancy

Broadcasting Stations

Radio Towers	Individually Drawn

Caterers

Movable Equipment	Special Floater

Cemeteries

Power lawn mowers, chapel tents, lowering devices, and covers, cocoa matting, artificial grass and other tools and equipment	Special Floater

Churches and Chapels

Paintings, Works of Art and Stained Glass Windows	Fine Arts
Projection Machines	Camera
Religious Articles and Vestments	Special Floater

Clinics

Murals and Paintings	Fine Arts
Radium	Radium Floater
Scientific Instruments	Phys. & Surg. Fl.

Clubs

Guns	Special Floater
Horses and Saddlery	Livestock Floater
Paintings, Works of Art and Stained Glass Windows	Fine Arts
Paraphernalia	Special Floater
Power Lawn Mowers	Special Floater
Projection Machines	Camera
Property on Exhibition	Exhibition (Transportation—Location)
Theatrical Scenery, Costumes and "props"	Theatrical Floater

*Reprinted by permission of the Royal Liverpool Insurance Group.

Colleges and Schools

Insurable Property	*Form of Policy*
Athletic Equipment	Special Floater
Bandsmen's Uniforms	Special Floater
Guns	Special Floater
Horses and Saddlery	Livestock Floater
Musical Instruments	Musical Instrument Floater
Paintings, Works of Art, Rare Books, Manuscripts and Art Glass Windows	Fine Arts
Paraphernalia	Special Floater
Projection Machines	Camera
Property on Exhibition	Exhibition (Transportation—Location)
Scientific Instruments	Special Floater
Theatrical Scenery, Costumes and "props"	Theatrical Floater
Tickets (for Athletic events sent by Mail)	Individually Drawn
Trophies (Possessing quality of Fine Arts)	Fine Arts

Contractors

Equipment	Contractors' Equipment Floater
Machinery, Tanks, etc.	Installation (Transportation—Location)

Dairies

Cans, cases and bottles	Transportation—Location
Dairy Products	Transportation
Dispensing units	Individually Drawn
Horses and Wagons	Horse and Wagon Floater

Decorators

Flags, Lighting, Sound Equipment and similar paraphernalia	Special Floater

Department Stores

Customers' Furs for Storage	Furriers' Customers
Electric Signs	Neon Sign
Fur Stock	Furriers' Block
Jewelry Stock	Jewelers' Block
Paintings, Pictures, etc.	Fine Arts
Merchandise	Department Store Floater
	Exhibition (Transportation—Location)
	Installation (Transportation—Location)
	Installment Floater
	Motor Truck Merchandise Floater
	Marine Cargo Policy
	Parcel Post
	Transportation

Doctors

Medical Lamps	Phys. & Surg. Fl.
Radium	Radium Floater
Surgical and Scientific Instruments and Apparatus	Phys. & Surg. Fl.

Dyers and Cleaners

Insurable Property	*Form of Policy*
Customers' Furs for Storage	Furriers' Customers
Customers' Goods	Dyers and Cleaners
Horses and Wagons	Horse and Wagon Floater

Engineering Concerns

Equipment	Equipment Floater
Surveying Instruments	Special Floater

Exhibitors

Property on Exhibition	Exhibition (Transportation—Location)
Works of Art	Fine Arts

Exporters

General Merchandise	Marine Cargo Policy
	Transportation—Location

Farmers

Livestock	Livestock Floater
Mobile Agricultural Machinery and Equipment	Mobile Agricultural Machinery and Equipment Floater
Horses and Wagons	Livestock Floater

Foundries

Patterns (Property of Others)	Transportation—Location

Furniture Stores

Furniture, Radios, Pianos, Refrigerators, etc.	Installment Floater and Transportation

Furriers and Fur Storage Concerns

Customers' Furs	Furriers' Customers
Furs on Exhibition	Exhibition (Transportation—Location)
Skins, furs, coats, etc. in transit	Transportation
Trimmings, cloth, etc.	Parcel Post

Golf Clubs

Paintings	Fine Arts
Power Lawn Mowers	Special Floater
Trophies	Exhibition (Transportation—Location)

Governments (Town, City, County and State)

Bridges	Bridge Property Damage
	Bridge Use and Occupancy
Musical Instruments	Musical Instrument Floater
Power Lawn Mowers	Special Floater
Road Machinery and Equipment	Contractors' Equipment
Securities, etc.	Registered Mail
Surveyors' Instruments	Special Floater
Tunnels (Vehicular and Rail)	Property Damage

Government (Town, City, County and State)—Continued

Insurable Property	*Form of Policy*
	Use and Occupancy
Voting Machines	Voting Machine
Works of Art	Fine Arts

Hospitals and Clinics

Cameras and Projection Machines	Camera
Paintings, etc.	Fine Arts
Radium	Radium Floater
Scientific Instruments	Special Floater
Surgical Instruments	Special Floater

Hotels

Paintings and objects of Art	Fine Arts

Importers

General Merchandise	Ocean Marine Cargo Transportation—Location

Individuals

Cameras and Projection Machines	Camera
Coin Collection	Coin Collection
Furs	Jewelry-Fur Floater
Gold and Silverware	Silverware
Golfers' Equipment	Golfers' Equipment
Guns	Special Floater
Jewelry	Jewelry-Fur Floater
Model Railroads	Special Floater
Musical Instruments	Musical Instrument Floater
Outboard Motor Boats and Motors	Outboard Motor Boat
Paintings, Tapestries, Rare Books, Valuable Rugs and other objects of art	Fine Arts
Personal Effects	Personal Effects Floater
Personal Property	Personal Property Floater Form Trip Transit
Power Lawn Mowers	Special Floater
Private Railroad Cars and Equipment	Individually Drawn
Riding Horses, Saddlery and Equipment	Livestock Floater
Scientific Instruments	Special Floater
Ship Models	Special Floater
Stamp Collections	Stamp Collection Floater
Trophies (possessing qualities of Fine Arts)	Fine Arts
Wedding Presents	Wedding Presents
Yachts and Motor Boats	Yacht

Investment Houses and Stock Brokers

Securities, Currency, etc.	Armored Car and Messenger Registered Mail

Jewelers

Electric Signs	Neon Sign
Jewelers' stock	Jewelers' Block
Parcel Post shipments	Parcel Post
Street Clocks	Neon Sign

Laundries

Insurable Property	*Form of Policy*
Customers' Furs for Storage	Furriers' Customers
Customers' Goods	Laundry Form
Horses and Wagons	Horse and Wagon Floater

Libraries

Books (while loaned, leased or rented)	Transportation—Location
Paintings, Works of Art	Fine Arts
Property on Exhibition	Exhibition (Transportation—Location)
Rare Books and Manuscripts	Fine Arts
Stained Glass Windows	Fine Arts

Linen Supply Concerns

Office Coats, Aprons, Smocks, etc.	Transportation—Location

Lithographers

Paintings (Property of others)	Fine Arts

Lodges, Fraternal Organizations and Legion Posts

Musical Instruments	Musical Instrument Floater
Paraphernalia, Flags	Special Floater
Projection Machines	Camera
Stained Glass Windows	Fine Arts
Trophies (possessing qualities of Fine Arts)	Fine Arts
Works of Art	Fine Arts

Manufacturers, Distributors, Wholesalers and Retailers

Electric Signs	Neon Sign
Exhibitions	Exhibition (Transportation—Location)
General Merchandise	Installation (Transportation—Location) Installment (Transportation—Location) Motor Truck Merchandise Floater Marine Cargo Policy Parcel Post Salesmen's Floater Transportation Trip Transit
Horses and Wagons	Horse and Wagon Floater
Ladies' and Men's Wear	Garment Contractors' Floater
Patterns	Transportation—Location
Privately owned rolling stock and locomotives	Individually Drawn

Milk Distributors

Horses and Wagons	Horse and Wagon Floater
Milk and Dairy Products	Transportation

Mobile Agricultural and Construction Equipment Dealers

Insurable Property	*Form of Policy*
Agricultural and Construction Equipment	Equipment Dealers' Form Installment Floater

Museums

Paintings, Rare Books, Manuscripts, objects of art of historical and scientific value	Fine Arts

Musicians, Bands and Orchestras

Musical Instruments and Orchestrations	Musical Instrument floater
Bandsmen's Uniforms	Special Floater

Newspapers

Newsprint Paper	Transportation—Location

Photographers

Cameras and Equipment	Camera
Photographic Supplies	Parcel Post
Property of others	Bailees' Customers

Processors

Customers' Goods for Processing	Transportation—Location

Publishers and Printers

Insurable Property	*Form of Policy*
Books, Magazines, etc.	Parcel Post
Property out for processing	Transportation—Location

Railroads

Bridges and Tunnels	Bridge Property Damage Bridge Use and Occupancy
Models of Engines and Rolling Stock	Special Floater
Rolling Stock	Individually Drawn

Surveyors

Scientific Instruments	Special Floater

Theatrical Producers

Scenery and Costumes	Theatrical Floater

Truckmen

General Merchandise	Motor Truck Merchandise Floater

Undertakers

Morticians' Equipment	Morticians' Equipment

Veterinarians

Surgical Instruments	Physicians and Surgeons

Warehousemen

Customers' Furs for Storage	Furriers' Customers
Household Goods and General Merchandise	Motor Truck Merchandise Floater Transportation Floater

Appendix H

SPECIAL CRIME INSURANCE AND BONDS

BURGLARY AND ROBBERY INSURANCE FOR FINANCIAL INSTITUTIONS

Bank Burglary and Robbery Insurance. Since the greatest concentration of money and securities is in banks and other financial institutions, it is natural that these institutions should early have been a target for burglary and holdup. The risk was readily apparent; and because of this, bank burglary and robbery insurance was one of the first forms of this type of coverage to be written. Institutions carrying blanket bond coverage are protected for burglary and robbery losses. The individual burglary and robbery policy is still used (*a*) for institutions that do not require the broad protection furnished by a blanket bond or do not elect to pay the premium for such a bond, and (*b*) as excess cover for large institutions that require more burglary and robbery insurance than the blanket bond provides.

The standard bank burglary and robbery policy provides four distinct coverages: (1) burglary, (2) robbery, (3) property damage caused by either burglary or robbery, and (4) property damage caused by vandalism or malicious mischief.[1]

Burglary and robbery, together with the attendant property damage, may be covered under a single policy. It is possible, however, to cover losses from either burglary or robbery with attendant property damage. When burglary and robbery are carried together, a separate limit of liability is designated in the policy for each hazard, and property damage losses

---

[1]The standard form in use has passed through a considerable period of evolution. The form now in use was developed in cooperation with the American Bankers Association and was known as the "American Bankers Association Standard Form Bank Burglary and Robbery Policy." The original form was drawn to furnish adequate and satisfactory protection to banking institutions. Over the years it has been considerably modified and broadened as experience evidenced the need for modifications. The form because of the nature of the protection is a long one. It is copyrighted by the American Bankers Association and differs in pattern from the policies already noticed. It is divided into four sections: (*a*) declarations, (*b*) insuring clauses, (*c*) exclusions, and (*d*) conditions. Companies using the form are licensed to do so by the Association.

The policy defines the term "robbery" as follows: "Robbery, as used in this policy, shall mean a felonious and forcible taking of property: (1) by violence inflicted upon the person or persons having the actual care and custody of the property; (2) by putting such person or persons in fear of violence; or (3) by an overt felonious act committed in the presence of such person or persons and of which such person or persons were actually cognizant."

from either hazard are subject to the policy limit designated for that particular hazard.

Burglary. The burglary protection furnishes indemnity for loss of money or securities by burglary of safes or vaults. In order to establish the liability of the insuring company one must prove that entry was made by force. This is to be demonstrated by the presence of marks caused by the use of tools, explosives, electricity, gas, or other chemicals. Money, securities, and other property taken from safes while open are not covered. If the vault is forced open and a money box or safe carried away and opened off the premises, the burglary coverage is effective.

Robbery. The robbery coverage provides indemnity for loss of money or securities by robbery from within any part of the premises occupied exclusively by the insured or his officers or employees.

Property Damage. The property damage feature provides indemnity for loss sustained as the result of damage to money and securities or to the premises, furniture, fixtures, vaults, safes, money boxes, or the like when caused by burglary or robbery or any attempt thereat. Vandalism and malicious mischief coverage takes within its scope any intentional wrongful injury to money or securities or the fixtures of the insured. Providing protection for vandalism losses eliminates the possibility of a dispute as to whether the damage in a particular case is actually an attempted burglary. In the property damage coverages, loss caused either by burglary, robbery, vandalism, or malicious mischief, or by fire damage to money and securities is not excluded. There is no fire damage exclusion here because damage to money and securities is not covered under the fire policy. However, fire losses to premises, furniture, fixtures, and the like are never covered under the bank burglary and robbery insurance policy regardless of how the fire loss is caused.

The policy provides that there is no liability on the part of the company for loss or damage to securities unless the insured takes active steps and exercises due diligence in preventing negotiation, sale, or retirement. It is also mandatory for an insured to keep adequate records so that the amount of any loss can be accurately determined. There is no loss under a burglary policy if the vault is left unlocked or if it is opened through a manipulation of the combination. The policy does not cover transit risks or property stolen away from the premises of the bank. Neither are the contents of safe-deposit boxes covered unless the loss involves the contents of a specified vault for which a record is maintained. Unobserved sneak-thief losses are not covered, nor are losses due to mysterious disappearance. Losses that are the outgrowth of dishonest, fraudulent, or criminal acts of employees of the bank are excluded, except in the instances when an employee is an active participant in a burglary or robbery.

Bank burglary and robbery rates are computed separately. Burglary coverage is based upon a classification of safes and vaults. A rate is quoted, and the premium is determined by multiplying the rate by the thousands of dollars of insurance to be carried. From this sum certain deductions are allowable. Discounts are based upon: (*a*) the use of an approved alarm system, (*b*) watchman service, (*c*) the division of insurance so that not more than 50 or 75 per cent applies to any one safe or vault at any one place, and (*d*) the limitation of policy to cover securities only or securities and subsidiary coin only. A discount is allowed for the use of certain designated locks and for insurance if written for a term.

Bank robbery rates include discounts for (*a*) daytime guard or watchman, (*b*) daytime burglar alarm, and (*c*) limitation of insurance to securities, silver, and subsidiary coin.

Safe-Deposit Boxes Insurance. In the absence of negligence it has been generally held that there is no liability on the part of a bank for loss to the contents of rented safe-deposit boxes. In those cases in which the decisions of the courts have held the banks liable, the question has been presented as to whether the bank had furnished the holders of safe-deposit boxes the same protection as the bank gave its own property. With the question of liability to this extent uncertain, the owners of securities or other valuables in rented boxes are interested in providing insurance against loss of the contents. Banks are likewise interested in providing the same insurance protection for property in boxes as they provide for their own property. Two forms of burglary and robbery policies are offered: (1) to the bank that wishes to insure all the boxes, and (2) to the individual who wishes to insure his own box only.

Bank Forms. Insurance written for the bank is the combination safe depository policy. It covers against the risks of loss of property in customers' safe-deposit boxes through burglary or robbery. The policy also covers damage or destruction caused by these hazards or attempts thereat, as well as that caused by vandalism or malicious mischief. All property is covered, including money in the customers' safe-deposit boxes. Damage to the premises, safes, vaults, and other furnishings of the insured institution are covered. The measure of loss is the pecuniary loss. This precludes making a claim based upon a sentimental value.

Damage to the premises, equipment, or furnishings of the lending institution is paid for first, and the balance of the insurance is prorated among the boxes. While this contract is not a legal liability form and the interest of box renters is covered regardless of the liability of the bank, the protection afforded may be limited to legal liability by endorsement. The policy then covers, for a reduced rate, legal liability for burglary and robbery losses only.

The combination safe-depository policy issued to banks also covers the legal liability of the insured for loss to the property of a lessee. There are no restrictions as to how the loss or damage must occur, nor is there any limitation as to the amount applicable to each box.

Lessee Form. This form issued to individual lessees undertakes to indemnify the insured for loss or damage to his own property or to property for which he is liable. The burglary coverage is effective while such property is contained in leased or rented boxes in a designated vault. The robbery feature provides coverage inside the premises of the bank while at least one officer or employee of the bank is on the premises.

The most popular form is an all-risks securities safe-deposit form. This form is issued to lessees and provides protection against all risks of loss, damage, or destruction caused by burglary and robbery only, and only securities are covered. In addition, the policy provides insurance against any form of theft or larceny and includes within its protection the unexplainable disappearance or misplacement of securities. Losses originating through dishonesty or the criminal act of an agent of the insured would fall in the fidelity category and are not covered, although the policy does extend to cover losses occasioned by carelessness or negligence. This form is particularly desirable for the use of institutions that have large security holdings.

Church Coverage Form. This is a comprehensive coverage written for churches only.[2] The protection afforded is very broad, covering all theft. Property coverage not only includes money, securities, and such valuable items as chalices, ciboria, and other sacred vessels but also extends to other furnishings used in a church edifice, including musical instruments and vestments.

The theft features of the coverage apply both to the church structure itself and to the parish house, rectory, parsonage, or other residence occupied by the administrative officer of the church. If the church owns or leases other buildings used in connection with its activities, the coverage extends to these properties. The robbery coverage includes holdup and protects the insured against loss of church property, including money or securities outside its buildings. While the policy is usually written as a blanket coverage, it is sometimes advisable to insure special valuables specifically.

Money or securities stolen from "poor boxes" constitute the only exclusion under the policy. In contrast to the usual coverage under burglary and robbery policies, under this form there is no exclusion of losses due to the collusion of employees of the insured, nor is there exclusion of burglary or robbery losses caused by them.

If the church customarily has on hand unusually large sums of money on particular days, such as Christmas, Easter, or other days when special offerings are taken up, larger amounts of insurance may be written to apply to these particular days.

FIDELITY BONDS

Blanket Fidelity Bonds. There are three classes of blanket bonds: (*a*) blanket commercial bonds, (*b*) blanket bonds for financial institutions, and (*c*) public official blanket bonds. There are a number of different forms under the blanket commercial classification. These include: (1) primary commercial blanket bond and (2) blanket position bond, both of which are designed for a wide number of commercial or industrial enter-enterprises. There are, as well, limited forms designed for special types of business enterprises. In this category are the insurance company blanket bond and the railroad blanket bond. Public official blanket bonds are patterned after the primary commercial blanket bond and the blanket position bond.

Several of the bonds have features in addition to the fidelity protection. The fidelity feature of the comprehensive dishonesty, disappearance, and destruction policy (the 3-D policy) is a blanket commercial fidelity cover; but the policy is in fact a combination of coverages that may be purchased as separate contracts. Only the first insuring clause provides fidelity cover. The blanket commercial forms are fidelity coverages; but the blanket bonds for financial institutions contain, in addition to the fidelity feature, a number of other forms of protection written originally as separate insurance contracts. Additional coverages are afforded, as well, with the insurance company blanket bond.[3]

---

[2]This policy covers only the hazards of burglary, robbery, theft, larceny, or property damage caused by any of these hazards. It may be written, however, for such amounts as the insured may elect.

[3]The blanket coverage for financial institutions appeared first and takes its point of departure from a form first offered by English underwriters that undertook in a single instrument to provide fidelity coverage on all of the bank's officers and employees as well as to furnish burglary, robbery, theft, and transit insurance protection. The blanket

Insurance Company Blanket Bond. This form is written to provide blanket protection for insurance companies similar to the blanket bond protection available for banks. There is a special form for life insurance companies which is extended to indemnify the insured against the dishonest acts of general agents, soliciting agents, and servicing agents.

The form of the bond has been arranged to harmonize with the bankers' blanket type of bond and contains six insuring clauses: (*a*) dishonesty of employees, (*b*) on-premises hazards, (*c*) intransit hazards, (*d*) forgery or alteration, (*e*) securities coverage, and (*f*) counterfeit currency. The insuring clauses providing forgery and securities protection may be deleted by endorsement. Coverage provided in the premises insuring clause of the life insurance company bond may be extended by endorsement to cover loss of property while within the premises of agents. The policy may be written to exclude one or more of the designated classes of agents or to limit the amount of coverage on one or more designated classes to an amount less than the bond amount.[4]

Dishonesty of Employees. Under this clause the insured is indemnified against loss, sustained during the term of the bond, which is the result of dishonesty or fraud on the part of employees. The protection is similar to that afforded by the primary commercial blanket bond.

On-Premises Coverage. This clause provides coverage against loss of property as defined in the contract through robbery, larceny, burglary, theft, false pretenses, holdup, misplacement, mischievous unexplainable disappearance, damage, or destruction. The loss is covered even though attridutable to negligence of employees. Loss of subscription, conversion, redemption, or other like privileges is covered if attributable to the loss of property insured under this section, such as warrants, interim certificates, rights, or other securities needful for exercise of such privileges. Loss to property, such as furnishings, fixtures, and equipment, is covered if the damage is attributable to attempted larceny, theft, or burglary, robbery, or holdup. Fire losses are not covered.

---

bond idea was predicated on the proposition that banks attempting to protect their exposure to loss through the purchase of a number of separate contracts frequently purchased coverages that either overlapped or were inadequate in that they left gaps between the coverages. The blanket bond for financial institutions undertook to provide integration of the various coverages and offer them in a single contract.

Not until 1915 did the American companies undertake to follow the lead set abroad. Since the first blanket bonds were offered, a large number of forms have been prepared to meet specific needs. Many of them have long since become obsolete. It was not until 1925 that the idea of writing blanket bonds for commercial accounts was given sufficient attention to result in the development of a form. In 1926 the commercial blanket forms were first made available. These forms contain none of the additional insurance coverages to be found in the blanket forms written for financial institutions. They are strictly fidelity coverages, and the term "blanket" is probably derived from the fact that they provide group protection. Blanket fidelity coverages are now included in forms containing features other than strict fidelity features.

[4]At first thought the protection under this form might appear to be identical with that of the 3-D policy but tailored to fit the needs of an insurance company. Upon consideration it will be noted that this is not the case. Under the first insuring clause of both, employee dishonesty is covered. Under the 3-D policy, the other exposures may or may not be included at the option of the insured and the amount of protection under the different exposures may differ. Under the insurance company blanket bond, one aggregate penalty covers not only all employees but all the various hazards included within the bond. The limit of the liability of the company is the amount of the penalty which is applicable to all exposures included within the scope of the protection

Off-Premises Coverage. This clause provides protection for the insured for property in transit in the custody of his messenger. It includes protection for loss caused by robbery, larceny, theft, holdup, misplacement, mischievous unexplained disappearance, damage, destruction, negligence on the part of the transporting messenger, or any other cause whatsoever. This clause provides much the same coverage outside the premises that the foregoing clause provides within the premises.

Forgery. This is the first of the two optional coverages and provides protection for the insured against loss arising from forgery or alteration. The coverage is similar to that provided under the depositors' forgery policy.

Securities Coverage. This is an optional clause and provides protection for the insured, whether acting for himself or for others with respect to dealings in securities. He is protected against loss with respect to instruments which may have been counterfeited, forged, altered in any respect, lost, or stolen. Protection is provided under this clause as well for loss through receipt by the insured of counterfeited or altered United States paper currency or coin. Because of the needs of the particular type of business and to avoid any question of doubt, the property covered is defined in the policy in considerable detail. It includes money in all forms, postage and revenue stamps, precious metals and gems as well as articles made therefrom, securities, evidences of debt, life insurance policies, and all similar instruments and valuable papers and documents.

Counterfeit Currency. This clause protects the insured against loss through the receipt in good faith of counterfeited or altered United States paper currencies or coin.

The bond undertakes to indemnify the insured against court costs at reasonable attorney's fees in defending any suit or legal proceedings designed to establish liability on the part of the insured which, if established, would constitute a loss under the bond. The section providing for court costs and attorney's fees is, therefore, applicable to all insuring clauses; and by its terms such costs and fees are not deductible from the amount of the bond applicable to pay claims.

Railroad Blanket Bond. This is another special form of commercial fidelity bond designed to meet the need of a particular type of business. It protects the insured against loss of money or other property owned or held by the insured in any capacity resulting from fraud or dishonest act. It provides a further protection not to be found in the other commercial blanket bonds in that losses attributable to gross carelessness are covered. "Gross carelessness" is defined to mean the careless performance or an omission of duties or the deliberate assumption of risks by an employee in violation of written instructions, rules, or regulations of the insured. Losses resulting from mistakes or errors of judgment are not covered. Losses which are the outgrowth of a misinterpretation of a rate table and a resulting improper classification are not included, nor are mathematical errors that result in mistakes in computing flat or other charges. The bond is designed to provide a very broad fidelity protection.

Blanket Bonds for Financial Institutions. There are twenty-four forms of blanket bonds designed to meet the needs of financial institutions. The figure at first seems formidable, but many of the forms have become obsolete and are discontinued due to the development of newer forms that have superseded them. In other instances, the need for which a form was devised has passed, and, therefore, the bond is no longer in use. There are but three forms in general use for commercial banks—one form for savings institutions, and two forms for building and loan associations. In addition, there are two forms in general use for private bankers and stock brokers and a form for credit unions.

The adoption of the blanket bond idea was the outgrowth of a demand among bankers for a comprehensive protection designed to cover not only the fidelity risks of the bank but also other theft hazards, such as holdups, burglary, robbery, and the like. Prior to the development of the blanket bond, lending institutions were obliged to buy separate policies covering the fidelity of employees and the risk of burglary and robbery, both against the risk of loss on the premises and the in-transit risk of money and securities shipped or in the hands of messengers. Forgery coverages were purchased separately, as well as insurance protection involving safe-deposit boxes. The chief concern of the officer responsible for placing insurance was always the possibility of leaving a "tendon of Achilles" in the form of an uninsured gap between coverages. Not of equally serious import, but serious enough, was the ever-present possibility of excess payment of premiums in the form of overlapping coverages. To meet the need of financial institutions for a complete and comprehensive coverage in a single contract, the blanket forms were developed.

The bankers' blanket bond in form consists of three major divisions: (*a*) the insuring clauses which indicate the risks covered; (*b*) the exclusions indicating risks not insured or to what degree the coverages are modified; and (*c*) the discovery period which covers such features as notice requirements in event of loss, the reinstatement provisions, and the like. It is the intent of the bond to provide as complete coverage as possible against all risks due to criminal acts such as embezzlement, burglary, robbery, theft, larceny, and forgery. The bond is not in actual fact an all-risks cover in that, from an underwriting standpoint, it has not been found feasible to cover losses due to clerical errors, carelessness, and incompetence. The coverage, however, is very broad and is as near to an all-risks form as good insurance practice could devise. In addition to the hazards noted, the bond covers indemnity for loss of property through damage, destruction, misplacement, and mysterious disappearance. Property losses, when covered, are primarily losses associated with a criminal act such as, for example, property destroyed or lost through robbery, theft, burglary, or holdup. Misplacement and mysterious unexplainable disappearances are covered even though there is no criminal implication.

Insuring Clauses. There are four insuring clauses in the bond which indicate the classes of risk which the company is willing to assume. Insuring Clause A is the fidelity coverage and provides protection against dishonest acts of employees. Insuring Clause B provides the on-premises protection, insuring against loss caused by burglary, robbery, holdup, theft, larceny, misplacement, mysterious unexplainable disappearance, and damage (except by fire) to the insured's offices, safes, vaults, equipment, or other property. Insuring Clause C provides the in-transit coverage which includes insurance against losses due to larceny, robbery, holdup, misplacement, or mysterious unexplainable disappearance, damage or destruction, and negligence of employees or of employees of armored mortor-vehicle companies. It also provides a misplacement coverage for interim certificates, warrants, rights, and other securities. Insuring Clause D provides a broad forgery coverage.

Exclusions. Exclusions vary with the form of the bond. Typical are losses due to hurricane, cyclone, tornado, earthquake, volcanic eruption, or similar disturbances of nature. It is likewise customary to exclude losses from military, naval, or usurped power; insurrections; or riot and civil commotion. The transit coverage of the policy applies in such instances, however, if, when the transit was initiated, there was no knowledge of such war risk or riot and civil commotion hazard on the part of any party who acted for the insured in initiating such transit. Some bonds will cover transit losses due to outbreaks of nature if the conditions laid down in the transit insurance clause are satisfied. It is also customary to exclude loss recoverable from an armored motor-vehicle company, its insurer, or from any other insurance carried by the motor-vehicle company for its benefit. In other words, the bond covers only in excess of the amount that may be recovered from other insurance. It is also customary to exclude losses from customers' safe-deposit boxes unless the loss is occasioned through the dishonest act of an employee under circumstances making the insured legally liable. The exclusions are generally limited, but each individual bond should be studied to determine the exclusions peculiar to that instrument.

Discovery Period. The final section of the bond has to do with the discovery period, notice requirements in the event of loss, and reinstatement provisions. It is usual to provide that losses must be discovered by the insured prior to the expiration of 12 months after termination or cancellation of the bond in its entirety. Requirements vary as to filing notice of loss, proof of claim, and suit for enforcing termination of the bonds. In the case of form No. 24, notice is required within a reasonable time after discovery, and proof of claim must be filed within 120 days after discovery. Twenty-four months is allowed as a period within which proceedings may be instituted.

JUDICIAL BONDS

Probate Bonds. The guarantee of a probate bond that the fiduciary will fulfill his trust in accordance with law involves numerous specific obligations, such as the filing of inventories, taking prompt steps to conserve assets, properly investing funds, and properly making distributions where so directed. In addition to the reputation of the principal for honesty, the surety company is interested that he have full knowledge of the responsibilities he assumes and the ability to fulfill the requirements of the trust.

Among the more frequently used probate bonds may be mentioned those required by an administrator, temporary administrator, special administrator, administrator to collect, ancillary administrator, administrator with the will annexed (*cum testamento annexo*), administrator d.b.n. (*de bonis non*), administrator to sell real estate, executor, guardian, guardian *ad litem*, conservator, and testamentary trustee.

When an individual dies without making a will, the person appointed by the court to administer the estate is termed an *administrator*. Fiduciaries appointed to serve as administrators temporarily, pending the making of a permanent appointment, are termed *temporary* or *special* administrators. Sometimes an appointment is made for the purpose of collecting and preserving perishables, pending the initiation of a permanent administration, and such an appointee is known as an *administrator to collect*. An *ancillary administrator* is a fiduciary subordinate to the general administrator. An *administrator with will annexed* is appointed when the decedent has made a will without naming an executor, or when the executor is unable or unwilling to serve. An *administrator d.b.n.* is appointed when the general administrator first appointed has been unable fully to complete the administration because of death, resignation, or removal. An administrator ordinarily has no right to sell the real estate of an estate; and, where such a step is necessary to pay the debts of the estate, a court order is required. In connection with the granting of authority to sell, a bond of an administrator to sell real estate must be filed.

If a will names a person to carry out the instructions of the deceased as set forth in the will, the person so designated is termed an *executor*. A person designated by the court to manage the estate of a minor is termed a *guardian*. Sometimes the term is applied to a fiduciary appointed to handle the estate of an adult incompetent, though in this case the term *conservator* is more usual. A *guardian ad litem* is appointed to represent a minor or incompetent in some litigation in which he has or may have an interest. A *testamentary trustee* is appointed under the terms of a will to carry out the terms of a trust created in the instrument. Such a trustee may be the executor, or he may be another person.

Joint Control. Because of the nature of the guarantee under a probate bond, surety companies are not always willing to assume the risk without retaining for themselves some control over the direction and management of the estate. This has given rise to the writing of bonds under a plan of joint control. Under the plan, a special joint-control agreement is executed at the time application for the bond is made.

When the principal and surety agree to joint control, the principal is required to deposit all funds belonging to the estate in a bank under the name of the estate. Checks then may be drawn on this account by the fiduciary, but before presentment for payment they must be countersigned by a representative of the bonding company. A similar procedure is followed in the event that funds are deposited in a savings bank. After the agreement is made, arrangements are made with the bank that no withdrawals are to be allowed unless a withdrawal slip is countersigned by the bonding company consenting thereto. If the savings bank is unwilling to consent to such an arrangement, joint control is sometimes arranged by placing the bank book in a safety-deposit box and arranging for joint control of the box. When securities are involved, they are to be kept in a safety-deposit box in the name of the estate and arrangements are made so that access to the box may be had only in the presence of a representative of the surety company.

Applicants for fidelity bonds frequently resent the request of surety companies for joint control. There is a tendency on the part of those not fully informed to feel that such a request in some way carries a reflection upon their honesty. A careful scrutiny of the entire problem will show the case to be otherwise. The obligations placed by law upon the fiduciary are not always simple matters to those unacquainted with the duties of the position to which they have been appointed. A fiduciary, by some improper act, though committed with the best intention, or by the failure to act through carelessness or inadvertence, may bring upon himself huge personal losses. Through cooperating with a surety company and permitting the exercise of joint control, the fiduciary has nothing whatever to lose and stands in a position to gain through the experience and wide knowledge of company respresentatives. Obviously, persons are sometimes named in a fiduciary capacity—and this is particularly so in the case of executors—who, having no experience or training in the duties of a fiduciary, are entirely incompetent to act without some guidance or direction. In such cases joint control is absolutely essential. On the other hand, it often happens that persons of wealth and wide experience are appointed to such positions. These persons are in the habit of making available to themselves the best legal advice. In such cases joint control may sometimes be waived by the surety company.

Sometimes in large estates, as a means of simplifying the handling of detail, a special account termed a "free-working account" is set up. This account is not subject to the joint control but is supplied with funds from time to time from a joint-control account. Otherwise, the balance of the estate is subject to joint control. It is a policy of surety companies never to waive joint control entirely on the basis of the excellence of the reputation and the standing of the fiduciary in the community. Sometimes, however, circumstances are such that joint control is not absolutely essential. This is the case when the estate is small or when it is in such shape that a final distribution will be promptly made under the direction and advice of a competent attorney.

Special Probate Bonds. Frequently, in probate affairs, bonds are required that are essentially financial guarantees. Such a bond is a *refunding bond.* If a beneficiary or heir desires to receive all or part of his share of the estate before distribution may properly be made by the administrator or executor, the fiduciary will require a surety bond to protect him from loss. Sometimes, when personal property is insufficient to pay the debts of the deceased, and the heirs wish to save the real estate from sale, they may file a bond guaranteeing the payment of the debts. On the other hand, heirs who may wish to sell real estate before the estate has been settled are required by the purchaser to file a bond guaranteeing him against loss if the personal property proves insufficient to meet the decedent's debts.

Fiduciaries Other than Probate. Into this classification fall fiduciaries appointed in the district, county, circuit, and state courts other than probate. They are appointed to handle an estate or to manage a business when there are a number of conflicting interests; and an impartial person in charge will safegard the interests of all and ultimately effect an equitable distribution of assets.

In this group are to be found: (*a*) conservators, trustees, custodians, or others, under whatever title, appointed to conserve the assets of closed state or national banks; (*b*) receivers or liquidators of closed state banks or building and loan associations; (*c*) receivers appointed in all state courts and receivers in federal courts; (*d*) assignees or trustees for the benefit of creditors, under state laws; (*e*) masters, referees, trustees, or commissioners for the sale of real estate or other property in partition, foreclosure, reorganization, winding up proceedings, or other litigation where the duties do not require conservation or investment of assets or any duties of administration other than a sale with the distribution of the proceeds; (*f*) receivers, trustees, liquidators, or others managing or liquidating property on which mortgages are in default; (*g*) receivers or trustees in bankruptcy appointed solely to close the business, marshal the assets, and distribute prorata to creditors; (*h*) custodians, receivers, or trustees, whether temporary or permanent, authorized or empowered to conduct a business as a going concern, for any period pending reorganization under the Federal Bankruptcy Act or the Corporate Bankruptcy Act.

Monetary Obligations. This category includes all bonds filed in behalf of litigants in connection with judicial proceedings in the courts. The bond finds its usefulness in permitting the principal thereunder to maintain an action when damages are required if the action is unsuccessful, and when the court requires a surety to protect the other party from loss in the event that the action brought is unsuccessful. Liability under the bond, therefore, is not contingent upon the honesty of the principal or his ability to fulfill a trust. The obligation assumed by the bonding company is the payment of money in the event that the action brought, for which the bond is given, comes to an unfavorable termination from the point to view of the principal. It is this feature of the bond that gives rise to the term "monetary obligation."

Plaintiffs' Bonds. A creditor, living outside the state in which he brings an action against a debtor to recover, is required to file a bond guaranteeing the payment of the costs of the suit. In the event that property of a defendant is held as a means for satisfying a claim if the action is successful, the plaintiff will be required to file a bond guaranteeing the defendant against loss through having his property so tied up. Again, if a plaintiff undertakes to compel a defendant to do or refrain from doing certain things, a bond is required to save the defendant against loss if the plaintiff is unsuccessful in sustaining his position. Bonds of this type are termed *plaintiffs' bonds.*

Since the action in such cases is initiated by the plaintiff and the bond is given by him so that he may proceed with his action, such bonds are termed *voluntary bonds* by underwriters.

Defendants' Bonds. It often happens that because of the nature of the action it is necessary or convenient for the defendant to file a bond. For example, when property has been tied up pending the outcome of an action, the defendant may release the property and secure to himself the use of it by filing a bond. Again, when the court has ordered a defendant to temporarily refrain from some action, unless unusual features make the procedure inequitable, the defendant may be permitted to proceed with the act enjoined by filing a bond to indemnify the plaintiff if the case is decided against the defendant.

Bonds in this category are *compulsory bonds,* since the defendant is obliged to file the bond if he would protect his position or continue the action in his own interest.

Collateral Requirement. Since the principal on a court bond, if the case is decided against him, is liable for damages suffered by the party opposing him in his action, and the obligation of the bond is the payment of money, the surety will undertake to satisfy itself that, if unsuccessful, the principal is in a position to meet his obligations.

Surety companies regard bonds of this class as particularly hazardous. Unless the applicant for such a bond is in a strong financial position and his ability to pay is beyond doubt, the company asked to be surety will require that the bond be fully secured by suitable collateral.

The question is sometimes asked how a surety company in supplying a bond can justify charging a premium for the bond and at the same time secure itself against any possibility of loss by requiring the deposit of full collateral to cover the risk. A comparison is made between the procedure of a bank and that followed by a surety company. The bank lends money and charges interest, yet only in unusual cases in which the borrower's position is particularly strong will the bank lend without the deposit of collateral to secure the loan. So with the bonding company. By supplying a bond for a court action, the surety company lends its credit, which is closely akin to money, and will therefore waive the requirement for collateral only under conditions much the same as those warranting a bank to lend on an unsecured note. Bonds executed in behalf of plaintiffs are regarded by underwriters as less hazardous than those issued for defendants, and for this reason companies have a tendency to be more lenient with their collateral requirements for bonds of the voluntary or plaintiff group.

Frequently Used Forms. The use of certain of the bonds of the monetary obligation group is a matter of everyday routine in the courts. Some of the more widely used forms include:

a) *Attachment Bonds.* This type of bond is issued on behalf of the plaintiff when provisional seizure is made of the defendant's property which is held by the sheriff as security for the payment of any judgment obtained. If the plaintiff loses his case, the bond protects the defendant for damages sustained as a result of the action.

b) *Discharge of Attachment Bonds.* These bonds are filed to make possible the release of attached property. They are filed by a defendant and are regarded as extremely hazardous from an underwriting standpoint.

c) *Injunction Bonds.* When one party wishes to prevent another from doing a certain act or following a certain procedure claimed to be inequitable, he may appeal to a chancery court for a restraining order or injunction. Pending a final hearing, the plaintiff must file a bond to indemnify the defendant if the case is not sustained.

d) *Replevin Bonds.* An action to secure possession of personal property by its alleged owner is instituted by filing a replevin suit. The question of title is settled by the suit, but in the meantime the defendant is deprived of the possession of the property in question. This is a plaintiff's bond to indemnify the defendant if the suit is decided in his favor.

e) *Bonds Given to Sheriff or Marshal.* These bonds guarantee to protect the sheriff or marshal to whom they are given against damage suits growing out of the seizure of property.

f) *Appeal Bonds.* If an unsuccessful litigant desires to appeal his case to a higher court, he is required to file a bond in the court from which the appeal is taken. The bond guarantees payment of the judgment, plus interest and cost, if the appeal is not maintained successfully.

g) *Bail Bonds.* These bonds are given to secure the release of an individual who is under arrest. The bond guarantees that the person released will appear when required by the court; and, in the event of his failure to appear, the amount of the bond is forfeited.

Sufficient examples are here given to indicate the nature of court bonds. The bonds used in other court actions are in principle essentially the same as those in one or the other of the examples mentioned.

Construction Contract Bonds. Contractors undertaking the construction of public works or public buildings are, as a rule, required by law to furnish a bond. The advantages of the surety bond in guaranteeing the faithful performance of the contract have proved attractive to private enterprise, so that this type of bond is also widely used in connection with private undertakings.

The guarantee under a construction bond obligates the surety to indemnify the owner in the event that the contractor fails to complete the undertaking. To make the owner whole in the event of default on the part of the contractor, the surety is faced with the choice of undertaking to finish the work and pay any difference in cost occasioned by the change or of allowing the owner to proceed with the work to completion and reimbursing him for the cost in excess of the original contract price.

In addition to the foregoing, most contract bonds, particularly in the case of public contracts, guarantee that the contractor will pay all labor and material bills incurred. The surety is likewise required to indemnify the owners for the loss occasioned by injury either to employees or to the public. This risk is, or course, usually insured by the contractor under the proper public liability and workmen's compensation forms.

Some element of maintenance may be incorporated in construction contracts and, when so incorporated, forms part of the risk covered by the bond. This element is usually limited to a guarantee to the owner that he will suffer no loss through incompetent workmanship or the use of defective materials. The time for the discovery of defects is limited ordinarily to a year. Surety underwriters scrutinize construction contracts carefully to determine the extent of the maintenance risk.

Bid Bonds. Bid bonds, sometimes termed "proposal bonds," form an important subdivision of the construction and supply contract group. Bid bonds are filed before the contract is awarded and usually accompany the bid. The purpose of the bid bond is to guarantee that the contractor bidding, if he is awarded the contract, will sign the contract, supply such bond as is required, and proceed to carry on the work to a satisfactory conclusion.

Bid bonds fall into three main groups. Under the first type, if the contractor should fail to sign the contract and furnish a satisfactory *final bond*, the surety would be liable for an additional cost to the owner because of his being obliged to relet the contract. A second type of proposal obligation is known as a *bid letter*, *surety's consent*, or *surety's agreement*. This is a communication addressed to the owner by the surety company, in which the company agrees to execute the final contract bond if the bidder named therein is awarded the contract. The third type of proposal bond is known as an *automatic bid bond* and in itself operates as the final bond if the bidder is successful and is awarded the contract.

Frequently owners offer to bidders the option of filing either a bid bond or a certified check. The amount of the bond or check is usually placed at about 5 to 10 percent of the contract price. In the case of automatic bonds the face will equal that required in the case of final bonds.

Mortgagors' Completion Bonds. By the terms of this bond, the surety guarantees the lender of money that the owner will complete the building described in a contract in accordance with its terms and deliver it free of liens. Bonds of this class are, strictly speaking, not contract bonds; but they are noticed at this point because they find their use in connection with the financing of construction projects.

The construction contract bond guarantees that, if the owner keeps his part of the agreement, which among other things is to make payments to the contractor as they become due, the contractor will faithfully complete the work. A failure to make payments when due relieves the contractor of the obligation to finish, and there is no obligation on the part of the bonding company on the contractor's construction bond to proceed with the work since there has been no default by the contractor. A bank or other lender, in such circumstances, might find a partially completed building on its hands heavily encumbered with liens. To obviate any such happening, the completion bond is written.

The completion bond is given by the owner, not the contractor, to the lender of money. It guarantees to the lender that the borrower will fulfill his part of the lending agreement and his obligations to the construction contractor to the end that no act or default of the borrower, who is the owner of the property, will give grounds for failure on the part of the contractor to complete the building.

Relationship of Bid, Final, and Completion Bonds. A brief illustration will indicate the use of each of the three bonds mentioned in a construction operation. Assume a group of persons with a valuable piece of land and a sum of money. They decide to erect a hotel but need $1 million more funds to use their land profitably. They bring their plans to a group of investment bankers, together with an estimated operating statement. The bankers feel that an issue of first mortgage bonds will sell readily but wish to be assured that the building costs will remain within estimates and that a completed and unencumbered building will be available as security for the mortgage.

The promoters of the hotel enterprise, when they advertise for bids, will require a bid bond of all bidders. This will guarantee that the successful bidder will undertake the work or indemnify the owners for any loss occasioned by his failure to do so. When the job is let, the contractor will furnish the owners a construction bond, which guarantees that the contractor will fulfill the terms and conditions of the agreement. The lenders of the money will require of the owners of the property, who are the borrowers, a completion bond, which guarantees that they will administer the funds in the manner agreed and advance their own share so that the building will be completed unencumbered by liens.

There is no confusion of risks assumed by the different bonds and, in order that the lender be completely protected from the beginning of the negotiations to the completion of the transaction, all three bonds or their equivalents are essential.

Supply Contract Bonds. As the term indicates, a "supply contract" is an agreement to furnish and deliver supplies; but, for the purposes of surety underwriting, supply contract bonds are those guaranteeing the faithful performance of contracts for furnishing supplies and material when such materials do not become part of the realty or attach thereto, at least until after the contract in question has been completed.

Supply contract bonds are required by the federal government, as well as by state, county, and municipal governments. The surety is liable for any loss sustained by the obligee through failure to secure the supplies in accordance with the conditions of the contract. This includes any additional expense attendant upon securing substitute supplies and may include loss or damage occasioned by delay.

Indicative of the types of supplies and material for which contracts covered by bonds are made are the following: ammunition, arms, automobile parts, fire hose, fuel, rolling stock, pipe, office furniture, filing cases, books, desks, seats, printed matter, electric current, railroad ties, and water softener. Contracts for furnishing engines, boilers, printing presses, electrical machinery, pumps, and other machinery are regarded as supply contracts if the machinery is built complete for sale at the factory or premises of the seller.

Maintenance Bonds. These bonds are given to guarantee that the principal will maintain in good condition all or some part of a construction project. The bonds are also used in connection with supply contracts when performance of the material sold is guaranteed by the seller.

The maintenance bond finds frequent use in connection with highway construction work for federal, state, borough, township, and municipal governments.

In connection with building contracts, the element of maintenance is most often found in a guarantee, for example, that a roof will last without leaks or the development of other defects for a stated period of years. Such guarantees are sometimes made in connection with the use of materials manufactured for special purposes, such as waterproofing, insulating material, or paints. Maintenance in connection with supply is found when the contract guarantees performance of the material, as is frequently the case in contracts for sale of oil for use as a dust palliative.

Miscellaneous Contract Bonds. A number of bonds are written for contractors that do not fall into the category of construction, maintenance, or supply. Among these may be included bonds guaranteeing the fulfillment of charter parties, bonds to the state for the lease and hire of state convicts, bonds given in connection with draying and hauling contracts, stevedoring contracts, contracts for the transportation of school children, bonds guaranteeing payment of general average adjustment, bonds required by state or public commissions guaranteeing the completion of an irrigation project, bonds guaranteeing payment of rent or the performance of other covenants in a lease except convenants to build, bonds guaranteeing against infringement of patents, bonds given by printers to the controllers of patented paper covering the use of such paper for specific purpose, bonds guaranteeing to replace property in its original condition, and bonds given by realty operators to a county guaranteeing to construct or finance improvements.

In this category are to be found deficiency judgment and demolition bonds. A deficiency judgment bond is given in favor of lenders furnishing money to finance the cost of a building improvement. The bond guarantees payment of the mortgage or any deficiency judgment on foreclosure. Demolition bonds guarantee to indemnify the holder of an existing mortgage or other lien on a property against impairment of security by the demolition of existing buildings for the purpose of making other improvements.

Other bonds in the miscellaneous group are those given in connection with United States mail contracts, for city delivery and collection service, pneumatic-tube service, and carriage of the mail between post offices in rural districts under star route contracts.

Special Provisions and Exclusions. Bond forms are by no means uniform. Frequently the obligee supplies his own form, incorporating his own terms and conditions. Surety companies supply printed forms that are widely used, and certain stipulations are found in most bonds of this kind.

The surety requires prompt notice of any failure on the part of the principal that may involve the surety. The surety usually reserves the right to complete the contract upon default of the contractor and is to be subrogated to all of the rights of the contractor under the contract. The surety excludes liability for loss or damage resulting from strikes or other labor difficulties, mobs, riots, fire, the elements, or acts of God such as tornadoes, cyclones, earthquakes, and the like. No change is allowed in the plans, specifications, or terms of the contract if the change increases the price beyond a stipulated percentage of the contract price, unless consented to by the surety. The owner is required to retain a percentage of the contract price until after the work has been completed and accepted.

A construction contract bond is automatically canceled with the completion and acceptance of the work free of all liens. There is no provision in the bond that permits the surety to cancel before the work covered by the bond is completed, and the surety has no power to terminate its liability once it is assumed pending completion of the work. The same rule applies to supply and maintenance bonds. Each is automatically terminated with the fulfillment of the conditions of the contract by the principal, and the surety has no means for terminating liability through cancellation.

Agent's Authority. Few agents have authority to bind or in any way commit a surety company on a contract bond. When the agent possesses a power of attorney from the home office of the company, properly executed by duly authorized officers of the company, his authority is strictly limited by the terms of this document. In no case does the local agent possess the broad powers to bind risks which are enjoyed by the agent of a fire company, though owners familiar with the customs and practices of fire agents have sometimes assumed that the same authority is given surety agents.

An agent without authority cannot bind his principal unless the principal conducts himself in such a manner as to lead third parties to believe that agency exists. Architects and contractors know of the limitations of the authority of local agents to execute contract bonds. For this reason it is considered an excellent practice to insist that to every contract bond there be attached a duly authenticated copy of the agent's power of attorney to execute the bond. This is neither an unusual nor an unreasonable request, and most bonding companies anticipate it by having forms specially prepared for the purpose.

OTHER SURETY BONDS

Surety Bonds Other than Contract. A number of bonds that involve financial guarantees are included in the surety classification but are not included in the contract group. The following three classifications have already been noticed: (1) depository and miscellaneous, (2) license and permit, and (3) federal. Many of these forms have become standardized to comply with statutory requirements or the needs of private enterprise.

Depository and Miscellaneous Bonds. Depository bonds guarantee that a bank in which funds are deposited will pay the funds so deposited on demand. The bond is a guarantee of the continued solvency of the bank during the period the bank serves as a depository for the principal's funds. These bonds were to a large degree required for the protection of public money. With recent changes in banking legislation and the advent of Federal Deposit Insurance, the need for depository bonds has largely passed; and such bonds are rarely required today.

In the miscellaneous category are to be found public warehouse and grain-elevator bonds guaranteeing that merchandise described in storage receipts shall be delivered on presentation of the receipt and in accordance with its terms. Auctioneer bonds guarantee to the owner of property entrusted to an auctioneer for sale that the auctioneer will faithfully account for the proceeds. Owners of property entrusted to others in the form of a loan frequently require a bond guaranteeing the safe return of the loaned property. The bond is known as a "leased or borrowed property bond." Lost securities bonds guarantee that when a valuable instrument is lost, the person to whom a duplicate is issued will reimburse the issuing party for any loss or expense suffered should a claim subsequently be made under the original instrument. Insurance companies, in order to operate in a state other than that in which they are organized, are required to meet with certain legal formalities. In some instances this may require a deposit of securities in an amount specified by the statutes. In others the insurance company is permitted to file a bond in a sum prescribed by the statutes which guarantees the payment of any liability incurred under policies issued in the state. In those states where laws have been enacted governing the selling of securities, the statutes frequently require investment companies, firms, or corporations engaged in selling securities or their agents or representatives to file a bond guaranteeing compliance with its requirements. The list might be carried on indefinitely, but the foregoing examples are sufficient to illustrate the nature of bonds included in the miscellaneous category.

State and Municipal License and Permit Bonds. License and permit bonds are required by state, county, city, town, village, or other political subdivisions to guarantee to the public authority that the licensee or permittee will comply with the terms of the license or permit. In some instances bonds are required to extend indemnity to third parties who may be injured. The following list, while by no means complete, is indicative of the class of enterprise for which licenses or permits are granted and for which bonds are required: abattoirs, blasting operations, building operations, boarding houses, cigarette dealers, collection agencies, abstractors, assayers, contractors, detectives, electrical contractors, electricians, employment agencies, dealers in explosives, fumigators, funeral directors, game dealers, garage and filling station operators, hack or taxi drivers, hunters, house movers, junk dealers, loan companies, nurserymen, pawnbrokers, peddlers, pilots, plumbers, public accountants, public movers, second hand dealers, ticket brokers, and travel bureau operators.

Federal Bonds. The federal government requires the filing of bonds in a wide number of situations. Before a permit is granted to manufacture and distribute certain articles subject to an internal revenue tax, a bond is filed which guarantees that the principal shall comply with the regulations of the government and pay all taxes in the manner required. Such bonds are filed by manufacturers and distributors of intoxicating liquors. Bonds are required in connection with a permit to operate an industrial alcohol plant, to establish a bonded warehouse, or to operate a plant to manufacture denature alcohol. In connection with the manufacture of cigars, cigarettes, and snuff, four bonds are written as follows: (1) tobacco manufacturers', (2) cigar and cigarette manufactuers', (3) leaf tobacco dealers', and (4) tobacco peddlers'.

Articles upon which an internal revenue tax is required if consumed domestically are free from tax if exported. Such articles if destined for export may be shipped free of tax, but with the permit necessary to allow such shipments the government requires a bond guaranteeing the amount of the tax and providing for a penalty in the event that the goods are not actually exported or if, after export, they fraudulently re-enter the country.

Under the federal immigration laws, aliens not otherwise eligible for admission may be temporarily admitted for medical care or as students, tourists, or visitors. When so admitted, they assume an obligation to leave the country within an agreed period and file a bond guaranteeing departure. In some instances a bond is required guaranteeing that the alien shall not become a public charge. Hospitals providing for the treatment of aliens may file a single bond covering a definite or indefinite number of alien patients.

Customhouse bonds are required when permits are obtained for the temporary importation of dutiable items. These bonds are used particularly in connection with exhibits but are likewise used to cover property of troupes and amusement companies, works of art, models, and samples that are temporarily imported. Importers may store dutiable goods in a bonded warehouse under a permit which requires no duty until the goods have been withdawn. If the goods are re-exported, no duty is required. In connection with such a permit, a bond is required guaranteeing that the goods will be withdrawn within three years and the duty paid or that they will be re-exported within the period.

Appendix I

SUPPLEMENTARY INFORMATION ON MISCELLANEOUS PROPERTY AND LIABILITY INSURANCE

AVIATION INSURANCE

Development of Aviation Insurance. Under the pressure of wartime needs, aerial navigation made tremendous forward strides, and with the termination of World War I the wartime accomplishments were consolidated. This marked the beginning of a period of public interest in aircraft both for private and commercial use.

With the development of the airplane for use in commercial transportation and the private ownership of planes for business or pleasure came the problem of insuring the attendant risks. There is a record that an aviation policy was written as early as 1912 through Lloyd's. At the beginning of hostilities in 1914, Lloyd's continued to write the business until the volume became so large that its facilities were taxed, and to meet the growing need the English government entered the field. At the close of the war, the government withdrew from underwriting, leaving the business in the hands of private enterprise.

The Hull Contract. Hull risks use the same policy form regardless of the perils covered. The insuring clause indicates that, in consideration of the premium stated and subject to the stipulations and general conditions included in the policy, insurance is granted, in respect to the aircraft listed in the schedule of particulars, against direct loss or damage from the perils defined in the schedule of coverage. The insuring clause further states that the policy itself embodies all agreements between the insurer and the insured. The schedule is attached in the form of a rider and indicates the perils against which the insurance is written. Immediately following the schedule of coverages is a schedule of particulars which describes the make, model of aircraft, and other pertinent data concerning the insured craft, describes the use to which the insured craft is to be put, and lists the pilots who may fly the craft.

In the case of partial loss, the liability of the company is limited to the cost of repairing the damaged property with material of like kind and quality, plus reasonable transportation charges, and less any applicable deductions. The policy provides, however, that the liability of the company in the event of a partial loss shall never exceed the amount due if the loss payable were a total loss. It is further provided that, if the amount payable for partial loss is equal the amount payable as a total loss, any salvage value remaining shall inure to the benefit of the insurer. The policy provides that there shall be no abandonment to the insurer without its consent. Reasonable transportation charges to which reference is made are defined in the policy as the cost of the least expensive method of transporting new or damaged parts, or the aircraft itself, to the place of repair and the return of the repaired aircraft to the place of accident or home airport, whichever is nearer.

There are but few exclusions in the policy. There may be summarized as follows: (*a*) unlawful use; (*b*) operations outside the standard geographical limits provided in the policy; (*c*) war risks, riots or civil commotion, malicious mischief, sabotage, or any intentional injury or destruction or attempt thereat by any person whatsoever; (*d*) wear and tear, deterioration, conversion by a person in lawful possession of the aircraft, mechanical breakage or structural failure (but not excluding damage caused by the perils insured against even though such damage results from mechanical breakage or structural failure); and (*e*) while the insured aircraft is being operated in violation of the regulations of the Federal Aviation Agency applying to acrobatic flying.

Fire Insurance. The fire policy is essentially a ground coverage, though it may be extended to cover under all circumstances or to cover under circumstances specified in the policy. When written as a ground cover, the insured plane is covered against fire from any cause, as well as from explosion and lightning, but not against fire and collision resulting from crash or collision while in flight. The policy also covers damage sustained to the insured plane as the outgrowth of any accident to the conveyance in or upon which the aircraft, when properly dismantled and prepared for shipment, is being transported by land or by water.

The fire peril may be written in connection with any or all of the other named-perils; and, of course, this peril is covered in the all-risks policies. However, a named-perils policy is never written for one or more perils without including the fire peril. Fire coverage is basic and must be included in all hull contracts.

The fire hazard in aviation is particularly great not only because of risk inherent in the construction of the plane itself but also because of the conditions usual to the hangars in which planes are stored. Causes of plane fires, exclusive of hangar hazards, include (*a*) the backfiring of engines, (*b*) short circuits in electrical wiring or other electrical equipment, and (*c*) the development of static electricity in filling or emptying tanks. Hangar hazards are to be found in the accumulation of gasoline fumes in the enclosed structure; in the use of blow torches and welding machines; in carelessness with matches by employees or visitors; and in carelessness with oily rags, grease, or waste.

All airplane fire rates are "loaded" because of the conflagration hazard. It has been demonstrated by experience that a hangar fire, once started, burns furiously and develops a terrific heat. The fire spreads rapidly, often because of gasoline fumes or exploding gasoline tanks, and the chances of saving planes stored in the building are negligible. Fire policies exclude fire following a crash. This is so because it is virtually impossible to determine the value of the plane immediately after the crash and before any fire damage evidences itself. Fire coverage after a crash is available only as part of crash coverage.

Theft Insurance. Airplanes are rarely stolen, and for this reason theft rates are comparatively low. On occasions when planes have been stolen, they have usually been badly damaged, if not entirely wrecked. The pilferage hazard is much greater, and accessories and valuable instruments are frequently stolen. This is particularly the case when a plane has been forced to land in unfrequented territory.

The aviation theft policy covers theft, robbery, or pilferage, including damage done by thieves. The coverage excludes liability for theft, robbery, or pilferage committed by any person in the insured's household, or in the insured's service or employment, as well as wrongful conversion, embezzlement, or secretion by a mortgagee, vendee, or lessee.

Windstorm Insurance. The tornado, cyclone, and windstorm contract is strictly a ground coverage and, therefore, covers no loss whatsoever occasioned by flight or descent. Flight damage from tornado or windstorm is covered under the accidental damage form. The insured machine is covered while in the hangar or in the open. Fire damage is excluded except when fire is the aftermath of the collapse or fall of the building housing the insured plane when the fall is caused by a windstorm. The coverage includes damage caused by hail, storm, rain, sleet, snow, earthquake, flood, or water.

Windstorm insurance is considered an essential coverage for airplanes. In the case of automobiles, the risk is ordinarily very slight; in the case of airplanes, losses are very common. Because of the construction of airplanes, a seemingly harmless breeze may lift the plane and carry it against some object, causing serious damage. Cases are recorded where planes, after being pegged down, tore the pegs from the ground, were carried into the air on a strong wind 1,000 feet or more, and when finally hurled to the ground were completely wrecked.

In addition to the hazard due to the construction of the plane, the hangar further contributes to the risk. An airplane safely housed in its hangar may be seriously damaged by collapse of the hangar or by it partial destruction.

Mooring Damage. This provides insurance against perils of the sea while the insured craft is moored. Seaplanes, amphibians, and flying boats of every class are required on occasion to be moored. While not in use, such craft are usually hauled out of the water and securely housed. Nevertheless, because of the necessity from time to time of mooring, insurance is provided to cover the risk incurred.

The principal hazards are the danger of being struck or run down by another craft and sunk, of being torn away from moorings by a wind, and of being overturned and submerged. Losses occasioned by mooring mishaps can run to very substantial amounts.

Stationary Land Damage. The danger of an airplane of becoming involved in the mishap of another plane or of being otherwise injured while stationary is covered under this form. The insured plane is covered against loss or damage other than damage caused by windstorm while the aircraft is on land but not in flight. Losses caused by collision with another aircraft, vehicle, building, or other object are covered, as are losses by breakage, denting, marring, or scratching while the insured aircraft is in the care and custody of a hangar keeper or a repair or service organization for storage, service, repair, overhaul, or reconstruction and provided the aircraft at the time of loss of damage is not under the control of the insured, his agent, or employee and the loss or damage is not caused by any act or omission on the part of the insured, his agent, or employee. The insurance is usually written with a deductible to provide that a part, at least, of every land damage claim is to be borne by the insured.

Accidental Damage Insurance. This is primarily a coverage against the perils of the air. It is commonly referred to as "crash insurance," and the protection afforded is similar to collision coverage in automobile insurance. The policy covers loss or damage that may occur to the insured aircraft by collision with the ground or with another object arising during flight or any attempt thereat. Loss or damage caused by fire and lightning is excluded, except that the risk of fire while the machine is under its own power, including fire following crash, is covered. Mechanical breakdown is not covered; but if mechanical breakage is the cause of an accident, the resulting damage is covered. The coverage extends to losses due to stranding or sinking or to towing following a forced landing on the water. Salvage charges, if any, are covered. If the aircraft is missing and unreported for 60 days after commencing flight, the plane is presumed to have been lost from one of the perils covered under crash damage.

The rates for this coverage are high. It is the practice, in the interest of a moderate rate, to provide that the owner of the insured ship bear a part of any loss. Policies are written to follow one of two practices. In some instances the policy calls for a deductible of either 5 percent or 10 percent of the amount of the insurance; in other instances a percentage ranging from 20 percent to 33⅓ percent applies to the amount of the loss. Hence, a plane valued at $50,000 and insured against accidental damage at the rate of 8 per cent would require an annual premium of $4,000. A crash resulting in a $6,000 damage, with a 10 percent deductible feature, makes the insurer liable for the difference between the deductible amount of 10 percent of the value of the plane and the amount of the loss, or $1,000. Of course, had the plane been completely demolished, the company's loss would have been $45,000.

Combined Additional Coverages. In order to provide a complete ground coverage, a policy may be written to cover fire insurance with a list of perils in addition that includes virtually every source of injury or loss to a plane not in flight. Included in the list of perils are windstorm, theft, earthquake, flood, collision on the ground, and collapse of hangar. The policy is usually written with a deductible applying to all perils but theft. The policy may be written with fire as a ground coverage or fire in the air. This form provides a complete named-perils coverage with the exception of crash damage in flight.

Products Liability. This form is similar to the products liability forms offered for other classes of business. It provides protection for the insured growing out of the handling, use, or existence of goods or products in any condition that are manufactured, sold, handled or distributed at the premises by the named insured if the accident occurs after the insured has relinquished possession thereof to others and away from premises owned, rented, or controlled by the insured. This protection picks up where the premises liability coverage terminates.

Products liability is ordinarily written to cover personal injury. With respect to aviation insurance both personal injury and property damage liability are important hazards. Defective repair work, misdelivery of gasoline, or the like might cause a serious accident to a plane with resulting personal injuries and heavy property damage.

Cargo Liability. Policies are written covering the legal liability of the carrying plane for loss or damage to cargo or baggage. Cargo liability is written as a separate form and covers the liability of the aircraft owner to shippers for loss or damage to merchandise for which the airline may be legally liable. Passenger baggage liability covers aircraft owners' liability for loss or damage to passengers' baggage.

Both of these forms are third-party, or liability, coverages and are to be distinguished from the inland marine cargo cover written for the account of merchandise owners against loss or damage caused by agreed perils of air transportation.

Hangar Keepers' Liability. Hangars are frequently owned or leased by airlines, flying services, aviation schools, and aircraft and engine manufacturers. In the course of business operations, aircraft belonging to others is taken in for storage or repair. The hangar keepers' liability policy covers the legal liability of the hangar owner or lessee for loss or damage to aircraft in his custody and not owned by him. The perils insured against are fire and such other perils as may be agreed upon. It is strictly a legal liability form and affords essentially the same protection as the garage keepers' legal liability form. The policy covers the liability imposed by law upon the insured for damage or destruction of any aircraft, including resultant loss of use, which is the property of others and which at the time of the loss is in the custody of the insured for storage, repair, or safekeeping in the premises set forth in the declarations.

The policy is written with two limits. It is provided that at each of the listed premises the liability of the insured shall not exceed the limit established (*a*) in respect to any one aircraft and (*b*) in respect to a casualty or disaster or loss or series of losses arising out of one event involving a number of aircraft. The lower of the two limits, therefore, establishes the maximum liability of the insured for any one aircraft. The second, and higher limit, establishes the maximum liability for any one loss. Hence, in writing a policy the company must be supplied with information giving the highest valued aircraft for which the insured may be held responsible during the policy year. Then the company must have a figure that represents the total value of all aircraft that may at any one time be placed in the care and custody of the insured.

Fixed-Base Liability Policy. This form covers risks that are usually classified as commercial and operate out of one airport. It is purchased by insureds that charter, rent, and instruct in aircraft that operate from a fixed base. The policy provides the same liability coverages that are found in the usual aircraft liability contracts. The contract is unique in that it is a package policy and provides in a single contract the following coverages:

Aircraft Third-Party Liability. The coverage is to insure against losses for liability imposed by law (other than passenger) due to ownership, maintenance, or use of any insured aircraft.

Property Damage Liability. This coverage is to insure against losses for liability imposed by law for damages and loss of use to property caused by the maintenance, use, and ownership of any insured aircraft.

Passenger Liability. This coverage is to insure against losses for liability imposed by law due to the use and operation of an insured aircraft.

Premises Operations. This coverage is to insure against losses due to ownership maintenance and use of the premises. This is the coverage generally referred to as "airport liability."

Alterations and Repairs. This coverage is to provide insurance against loss caused by the airport operator's employees and independent contractors for extraordinary alterations, such as repairing or extending runways and the like.

Contractual. This would insure gainst losses due to liability assumed by the insured.

Products. This would insure against losses due to the handling, use, or the existence of any condition in goods manufactured or handled or distributed by the insured in connection with operations.

Hangar Keepers' Liability. This coverage is to insure against loss caused by liability imposed by law or for loss or damage to aircraft which are the property of others and in the custody of the insured for storage and repairs.

In addition to the foregoing coverages included in the contract, baggage liability may be included by endorsement.

Airport Liability. This coverage has many of the characteristics of the owners', landlords', and tenants' liability policy; but because the risk is peculiar to the business of aviation, it is usually written by insurers specializing in aviation risks.

Airports, whether individually owned, the property of private corporations, or under municipal management or ownership, may be insured under this form. The policy covers the insured's liability for bodily injury and may likewise be written to include property damage. The coverage protects the insured not only for his liability for loss to persons or property of vistors to the airport and patrons but also for claims if planes using the airport meet with accidents that may be attributed to his negligence or that of his employees.

In airport liability insurance, an application is required in the case of each risk, and the insurer willing to assume the risk bases his premium charge upon the data supplied in each individual case. The following data are required before fixing a rate: (1) area of the airport in acres; (2) number of lineal feet on highway; (3) how fenced; (4) average number of aircraft located at airport; (5) automobile parking space and whether or not charge is made for parking; (6) list and description of all buildings on the airport; (7) whether or not there is student instruction; (8) approximate population within ten-mile radius of airport; (9) effective landing length in four directions; (10) description of bleachers or group-seating structures on the airport; (11) system of air traffic control; (12) number of daily stops made by scheduled airlines; (13) whether or not repair work is done by insured; and (14) estimated total dollar-amount of sales, and description of all products sold. A plan or sketch may be required showing all pertinent features of the airport.

The airport liability policy is designed to meet primarily the aviation hazards incidental to the operation of an airport. Coverage for air meets for which an admission charge is made is excluded in the policy, but a special form of contract to cover this risk is issued by the aviation companies after making appraisal of the hazard involved.

The airport liability policy may be written to cover both bodily injury and property damage liability claims. This follows the pattern of the usual owners', landlords', and tenants' liability form. The basic limits in both contracts are the same. The bodily injury limits are $5,000 for each person and, subject to the same limit, $10,000 for each accident. The standard limit for property damage is $1,000. These limits are likely to be misleading since the liability for loss in connection with the operation of an airport may run to several times the standard limits. An accident that results in the complete demolition of a sizable airplane with death or injury to a number of passengers could develop claims that would aggregate many thousands of dollars. Insurance advisers suggest the estimated total of claims that a single accident could produce as the minimum limits for this type of insurance.

The airport liability policy may be written to include incidental liability hazards other than those strictly associated with aviation. These include, in addition to the premises coverage which provides liability protection for claims growing out of the maintenance, ownership, or use of the premises, the following: (*a*) elevators, (*b*) alterations, (*c*) products, and (*d*) contractual liability. Any or all of these coverages may be written in a single contract. Hangar keepers' legal liability may be written as an endorsement to the airport liability contract.[1]

Employer's Aviation Indemnity. This policy provides insurance coverage to reimburse insureds for payments made to employees or their survivors for death or dismemberment while traveling on planes in the interests of an employer. Coverage may be provided for executives, salesmen, and others who use schedued airlines on their employer's business.

The contract is a form of contractual liability partaking of the nature of accident insurance. It is issued, however, to cover only named employees. Additional employees may be covered by endorsement. When additional employees are to be included, the coverage is effective from the time their names are mailed or telegraphed to the company.

The insurance covers loss occasioned by death or dismemberment sustained through accidental means by any named employee: (*a*) while as a passenger, boarding, riding in, or alighting from an aircraft operated on a regular schedule by an airline holding an airline certificate from the Civil Aeronautics Administration; (*b*) if while a passenger, either at regular airports or at a place of forced landing, the employee is struck by any aircraft or propeller; and (*c*) while awaiting rescue following the forced landing of an aircraft in which the employee was a passenger.

The policy undertakes to indemnify the insured for payments made as the outgrowth of a voluntary agreement to employees so injured or to the legal representatives of deceased employees. Policies as now written provide coverage in the United States, Canada, and Mexico. The policy does not extend to cover: (*a*) suicide, or any attempt thereat by any employee, sane or insane, or death or injury suffered by any employee while insane or intoxicated or while violating law, resisting arrest, or fleeing from justice, or death from disease in any form; or (*b*) death or injury directly or indirectly the result of war, invasion, strike, insurrection, riot, civil commotion, naval, or usurped power.

In some instances, particularly in the case of corporations owning industrial airplanes, group indemnity policies are written covering executives, salesmen, or other employees in the habit of using airplanes in connection with their business activities. Group policies are flexible and protection may be written to fit any particular situation or to meet the needs of any employer. In some instances all employees are covered for identical amounts, while in others the amount of insurance may vary with the position of the employee or the amount of his salary. Insurance may be paid to a named beneficiary who is designated by the employee, or the employer may be designated beneficiary, thereby reimbursing himself for commitments made to employees or their beneficiaries with respect to accidental deaths.

---

[1]Airport liability insurance is big business. With the advent of jet planes and larger airport crowds bringing increased frequency in exposure to accidents, airport liability premiums have reached sizable sums. For a $10 million three-year general liability policy covering its jet field San Francisco is reported to pay $249,000, an increase from $59,000. Chicago is reported to have appropriated $129,000 for airport insurance for 1960, compared with the $31,850 spent for this coverage in 1959.

Workmen's Compensation and Personal Accident. Because of the nature of the employment of those connected with the aviation industry, personal accident and workmen's compensation coverages for members of this group are sometimes classed as aviation coverages.

In addition to those actually engaged in flying, the aviation industry employs large numbers of workers engaged in many forms of ground work. Compensation insurance is written in accordance with the requirements of each particular state.

Personal accident policies are available, but they are issued only after careful underwriting. Policies issued to cover pilots are more acceptable to the insurance companies than are those required by passengers who do not wish to be subject to any restrictions as to the type of flying to be covered. Many personal accident policies today cover the risk of travel on domestic scheduled airlines. However, pilots, students, and passengers, in private or nonscheduled aircraft as well as those flying on established lines, secure accident insurance coverage in the aviation insurance market, and the coverages are regarded as aviation lines.

Trip-Ticket Personal Accident Policy. Insurance covering personal injury due to accidents is offered to passengers in licensed planes piloted by duly licensed pilots. The coverage is issued in two forms and covers the flying, day by day. The first form covers the perils of death and dismemberment only, while the second form provides the same coverage as the first, plus a weekly indemnity feature for accidental injuries. Rates for this insurance vary with the coverage, and the charge is made for each day of flying.

Manufacturers' Risks. Aircraft in production are insured under a blanket policy, and the coverage attaches automatically to each plane as it comes at risk. The policy is written on a reporting form. Premiums are collected on a flying-hour basis for the flight risks and on a per diem basis for the ground risks.

In the case of a new model, before it has completed its test and received its approval certificate from the Inspection Department of the Civil Aeronautics Administration, special premiums are fixed governing the trial period. A manufacturer may have an enormous investment in a model plane that will not reflect in subsequent like models once the plane is in production. The perils during the test period involve great uncertainty, and insurance covering the replacement cost of the model is of paramount importance to the manufacturer. Crash risks and liability coverages on such planes are usually written to cover for a specific number of flying hours with provision for an additional charge at a predetermined rate for additional hours. The ground coverages are written on a per diem basis. Before a policy is written covering a test risk, a complete survey is made of all the factors that may bear upon the situation and the rate is determined on the basis of this survey.

PATENT PROTECTION INSURANCE

Patent protection policies are designed to protect patentees against infringement of their patents and to defend suits against patentees for alleged infringements of the patents of others. There are two forms of contracts issued: (1) protective contracts and (2) defensive contracts.

The protective contract covers legal expenses of suits brought by the policyholder against infringers of his patent or trademark. The insured has a claim under the policy whenever he discovers an infringement of his patent. Upon notice to the insurance company, a settlement is attempted on a basis that will satisfy the policyholder but in the event that this proves impossible, the policyholder is authorized to secure an attorney approved by the insurance company and enter suit against the infringer. The costs of the suit up to the face of the policy are paid by the insurance company.

Defensive contracts cover legal expenses of defense of suits brought against the insured for alleged infringements of patents or trademarks of others and also pay damages if any are awarded against the policyholder. Such a policy may be extended to cover not only the policyholder but also his customers and any others who may be liable to suit by reason of the use of the patent or trademark owned by the policyholder. A certificate of protection is issued by the insurance company to each customer named in the policy. Policies also may be written covering damages only by excluding legal expenses.

The underwriting of patent insurance is similar to some degree to that followed in a real estate title search. The underwriting company requires that a comprehensive investigation be made by a competent patent counsel and a written opinion rendered before the company passes on the risk. Upon request of the party desiring protection, the company obtains in advance an estimate of the cost of the required legal opinion from patent counsel. When the application for insurance is filed, the applicant deposits a check to cover the cost of the infringement opinion. If the opinion indicates the risk to be an insurable one, it is customary to allow a credit of 15 percent on the annual premium to apply against the cost of the opinion. If the opinion indicates the risk is not an insurable one, the applicant is charged the exact cost of obtaining infringement opinion from patent counsel, and he is furnished with a copy. The owner of the patent, therefore, has the benefit of expert opinion if the policy is issued to the effect that the patent was in all respects legally granted and the patentee holds a valid claim to its benefits.

Defense contracts for product and process protection may be written. The product or process policy is issued to manufactures and merchants and defends them against loss growing out of the charges of infringement of patents because of the manufacture, sale, or use of the protected product or process.

A valuable feature of the defense contract is found in the fact that it may be written to cover decrees, judgments, or awards but excluding legal expenses, even after the manufacturer has been notified of an alleged infringement of patents. This is particularly valuable because the business of a manufacturer might be all but destroyed if his customers learned that suits were pending against him, the outgrowth of threats of competitors. In such an instance, the insurance company would not, of course, obligate itself to assume the expenses of litigation, because this would represent a sure loss. It is willing, after due investigation, to assume the responsibility to pay damages which may be awarded against the policyholder. The protection may be written not only to cover the policyholder but, as in the case of other defense contracts, his customers as well.

Among the more important conditions of the patent contract is the requirement that the insured forward by registered mail any charge of infringement made against the insured and give the insurance company all information available touching upon the charge of infringements, as well as all information with respect to the party claiming infringement. The insurer has the right to negotiate with the party alleging infringement in an effort to compromise or settle the claim, but no final agreement may be entered into that is not satisfactory to the insured. In the event of suit, the insured is obligated to turn over to the insurance company or its designated counsel every notice, demand, summons, subpoena, pleading, or other papers filed in such suit immediately upon receipt by the insured. He, moreover, must turn over to the company complete control of the defense of the suit to the extent of the limit of liability. The insured may, if he elects to do so, select patent counsel, but this must be with the consent and approval of the insurance company. In the event that the insured is charged with infringement, even though no suit has actually been filed, the insured is obligated upon request to supply to the company all cooperation and assistance that may enable it to defend or settle any claim for infringement. The insured may not negotiate with any party making a claim for infringement, looking to the settlement of a claim; nor may the insured agree or attempt to agree to any settlement of such claim prior to a final decree in the court of last resort having jurisdiction of the cause of action without the written consent of the insurance company. Nor may the company settle in like circumstances without the written consent of the insured.

LIVESTOCK INSURANCE

Livestock insurance is written only by a limited number of commercial companies. The problem of moral hazard has created the major difficulty to underwriting this class of risk. Insurance is obtainable to protect against loss by death resulting from fire, lightning, windstorm, disease, and accidental death. This type of insurance is a form of term life insurance and does not indemnify for depreciation in value, loss of services, theft, or disappearance. Since the policy covers death resulting from disease or accident, coverage extends to death from any causes except intentional slaughter without the consent of the company.[2] Generally, the coverage of the livestock policy is broader than that afforded by the animal floaters and are adopted to cover either on an individual or group basis particularly valuable animals such as race horses, polo ponies, and the like.

The following policies are issued: (1) general livestock policy, (2) mortality floater policy, (3) floater coverage, (4) limited coverage, and (5) trip-transit policies. The general livestock policy provides protection against loss by death resulting from disease, accidental injury, fire, lightning, and windstorm covering while the animal or animals are on the premises of the insured or while temporarily in the vicinity thereof.

The mortality floater policy provides protection against loss by death

---

[2]The Hartford Live Stock Insurance Company lists among insurable risks the following: race horses, trotters, pacers and thoroughbred runners, saddlers and drivers, show horses, hunters, jumpers, polo horses, stallions and mares used for breeding purposes, farm and work horses, farm and work mules, commercial draft horses and mules, commercial dairy cattle, dairy and beef cattle used for breeding purposes, show cattle, family milk cows, calf clubs, and cattle and horses sold at public auction or private treaty but not belonging to, or in the hands of, dealers.

Prohibited risks include: chronic indigestion or colicers, cryptorchids or ridglings, blind animals, nerved animals, extremely aged animals, wild animals, fur-bearing animals, circus and rodeo animals, contractor-owned horses and mules used for excavating and construction purposes, horses and mules used for logging, junk dealer horses, dogs, sheep, goats, hogs, vicious animals, females within ten days of parturition, animals owned by dealers, range cattle, horses in public riding clubs (rented to the public), and jacks.

resulting directly from disease, accidental injury, fire, and lightning, including while in transit by rail, ferry, air, or properly equipped motor vehicle in the United States and Canada. No mention is made in the policy of windstorm as a hazard, but since death caused by windstorm is construed as a loss by accident, such a loss comes within the protection of the policy. The floater coverage is provided by extending the general livestock policy by endorsement to include the hazards of transportation anywhere within the limits of the United States or Canada. The coverage is broad, and the policy has a wide appeal.

Limited coverage provides insurance against death caused by specifically named hazards. The policy is issued primarily to exhibitors and breeders. There are two principal forms: Proposition No. 1 provides insurance against the hazards of fire, lightning, and tornado, while proposition No. 2 is broadened to include accidental death, "meaning death resulting from external, accidental, and violent means only."

A herd policy is available covering all the insurable animals of a given kind when there are ten or more animals in a herd. This contract is written to cover commercial dairy herds and breeding herds of either pure breed or grade cattle. Horses also may be covered under the form. Cattle being fed for market and slaughter are not insurable.

The trip-transit policy is a special form designed to cover valuable stock while in transport only. The coverage becomes effective when the animals are loaded on the cars for shipment in good condition and expires when the cars are unloaded. This policy is a form of inland marine insurance, although the coverage is largely written by specialists covering livestock risks.

CAREER COVERAGES

Numerous special contracts are available which provide an indemnity in the event of the happening of an accident that would terminate the career of the insured. The policies are of the nature of a personal accident policy but differ from the policy ordinarily written in that they are designed to protect one particular feature or physical characteristic that is an important factor in the career of the insured.

It is reported that a well-known novelist insured her hand. It was her contention that she was unable to produce fiction on a typewriter and was unable to dictate successfully. She, therefore, obtained a policy covering her right hand, contending that her occupation would be terminated if she were unable to write in longhand. A dancer insured her feet for $100,000. A few years ago, a radio actor sought a $100,000 policy against loss of his British accent, including the loss of his voice or change in its tone. An actress insured her film career through a clause attached to a life and accident policy which guaranteed her earnings to be $125,000 a year for a period of three years. A well-known skater obtained a policy providing that any accident or injury to her legs which would prevent her from skating made the insurance company liable for $5,000 weekly for 52 weeks. Perhaps one of the most unusual policies ever written was that obtained by Prince Sukhodava. When he was King Prajadhipok of Siam (1925-35) he is said to have taken out insurance against the risk of loss of this throne. In 1935 the first payments were made by French and British firms. Under the terms of the policy, he was to receive about $40,000 a year for the rest of his life. He died in 1941.

For underwriting purposes, policies of this class fall in the same category as that of insurance written against isolated contingencies. The amount of insurance are ordinarily high and involve a risk usually peculiar to itself. There is no group experience available as a basis for determining rates, and the underwriter is forced to rely upon his best judgment. A severe loss in a classification where the number of risks is limited requires the company to draw on the business as a whole to meet its payment. In accepting such risks the underwriter, to use a Lloyd's phrase, underwrites "against the pot."

LIBEL LIABILITY

This policy is offered to publishers and undertakes to indemnify the insured for loss occasioned by the settlement of libel claims.

The risk covered is something more than the liability due to negligence which is assumed by the usual liability form. A publisher who holds a person up to scorn, contempt, or ridicule may find himself liable for heavy damages. Damages must be paid when a damaging untrue statement is published maliciously. The law recognizes two classes of malice. When there is a deliberate desire to injure, there is malice in fact. A careless disregard for another's rights constitutes malice in law. Absence of intent to libel does not constitute a defense. Publication of a retraction is not a complete defense and serves only to mitigate damages.

There is no standardized form of policy covering the libel risk. A form that has made an appeal to publishers is written as an excess policy to cover the insured against large losses. The policy covers not only the liability that may develop as a result of errors but also any losses that may develop even if the published statement is held to be malicious.

Premiums for this coverage are based on the average circulation and the nature of the publication. The insurance company requires an application form which supplies all pertinent data. Particularly, the company wishes to know whether or not the paper has in past years been sued for libel and whether or not judgments were rendered. It wishes to know whether or not the relations of the publisher with other publications in the territory are friendly and the nature of the community served—whether metropolitan, small town, or rural. With these data, a specific rate is quoted for each individual risk.

Policies may be written to include coverage for slander as well as libel. When so written, the policy protects the insured against claims for both written and spoken defamation of character. Libel is written defamation, and slander is spoken defamation. The slander feature appeals to radio broadcasting stations as well as to credit bureaus and associations that make verbal reports to subscribers by telephone or otherwise.[3]

In addition to libel and slander, which concern reputation, an insured may become involved in claims for damages when privacy is violated. This is particularly the case with a newspaper or broadcasting station. The right of privacy concerns the peace of mind of the individual. Every person has the right to demand that his private personal affairs should not be commented upon or scrutinized in public without his consent. Truth is not a

[3]Closely akin to the libel and slander protection is the advertisers' liability policy, which indemnifies an insured advertiser against loss from the liability imposed upon him by law or assumed under contract and resulting from judgments for infringements such as would involve copyrights, property or contract rights, piracy, or violation of the rights of privacy committed or alleged to have been committed in the conduct of the insured's advertising activities. Policies providing the same protection are issued to advertising agencies and radio producers.

defense to an action for the infringement of the right of privacy.[4] For this reason libel liability policies are written to include protection against claims based not only upon slander but also upon invasion of privacy.[5] Policies also may be written to cover claims based upon plagiarism and violation of copyright.[6]

Libel insurance is usually written on an excess coverage basis to cover the risk. Small losses up to a designated sum are met by the publisher. A usual deductible is $2,500 or upwards. The insurance, however, may be written on a full-cover basis. Or it may be written so that the insured bears a percentage of the loss instead of a predetermined deductible. Insurance with a substantial deductible carries the lowest premium.

In the adjusting and settling with claimants, the libel policy introduces a provision radically different from the usual liability form. The insured is required to conduct his own defense and pay all attorney's fees and other costs of litigation, the company having the right, if it wishes to exercise it, of participating in the defense at its own expense. The company is not required to appear until the amount actually to be paid to the claimant has been determined, and then it is liable to the insured for the excess stipulated in the policy.

CONTINGENCY COVERAGES

The practice of issuing policies providing for the payment of loss in the event of the happening of some isolated contingency has proved fascinating to the layman, and the coverages have frequently been the source of misunderstanding. Numerous examples are to be found and, because many of the policies have been issued by Lloyd's of London, the popular notion has developed that Lloyd's are writing insurance policies covering any conceivable risk. This is not the case. Insurance policies issued by Lloyd's or any other reputable insurance carrier involving the payment of loss in the event of the happening of some particular contingency require a condition precedent that the insured shall be placed in such a position by the happening of the contingency that financial loss will follow.

Several examples may be appropriate. When war threatens, policies are issued covering the hazard and paying an indemnity if war does, in

---

[4]*Carson v. Baskin*, 155 Fla. 198; 20 So. (2d) 243; *Barber v. Time*, 348 Mo. 1199; 159 S.W. (2d) 291.

[5]In *Themo v. New England Newspaper Publishing Company* (306 Mass. 54; 27 N.E. [2d] 753), a leading case decided in 1949, it is stated: "Modern cases have made it possible to reach certain indecent violations of privacy by means of the law of libel that discredits the plaintiff in the minds of any considerable and respectable class in the community though no wrongdoing or bad character is imputed to him." The case goes on to say: "Great difficulty exists in defining a right of privacy that will protect individuals against abuse and yet will not infringe the rights of the public and the press to discuss personalities."

[6]Suits against newspapers amounting to hundreds of thousands and millions of dollars are not at all uncommon. A record of actual judgments indicates that publishers constantly face a very real risk of loss through libel claims. A verdict of $290,000 was reported in 1948 based upon the invasion of privacy when a moving picture was made without the plaintiff's consent. William E. Mooney. "The Right of Privacy in Insurance." *Insurance Law Journal*, No. 313 (February, 1949), p. 105. In 1963 a much publicized suit by a football coach at a southern university resulted in a $3 million judgment against *The Saturday Evening Post*, for a libelous story which claimed that the coach had given a rival college team its football plays. The case was settled before retrial for less than one sixth the original verdict.

fact, break out within the term and between the countries specified in the contract. Prior to the advent of the second World War, policies were issued by Lloyd's insuring the income of businessmen who were reservists against the possibility of being called to the colors. The premiums on such policies ranged from 5 to 10 percent of their face value. The premium depended upon the age and nationality of the applicant for the insurance. In 1935, an American insurance company is reported to have paid an indemnity of approximately $300,000 to the national organization of the Boy Scouts of America which had taken out a policy of $400,000 against the cancellation of the Jamboree scheduled that year in Washington. The Jamboree was, in fact, canceled because of the prevalence of infantile paralysis. According to the report, the Scouts had been able to cancel $100,000 of contracts for foodstuff and equipment, and the loss represented primarily expenses incurred in preparing the camp site on a 400-acre tract in the city of Washington. Policies have been issued on an athletic event covering training expenses to pay an indemnity if the insured loses the event. A manufacturer, paying a royalty to the Canadian government for the privilege of manufacturing dolls resembling the Dionne quintuplets, secured a policy from Lloyd's which undertook to pay him the face amount of the policy in the event that any one of the quintuplets should die during the period of 12 months covered by the contract.

Immediately preceding the death of King George V, policies were issued covering against his death. As his condition became more critical, rates increased from 25 per cent to 60 percent, and policies were issued to trades which would suffer from a long period of official mourning. A period of court mourning in England affects unfavorably the business of hotels, theaters, caterers, dress shops, and the like. Some of these institutions regularly purchase annual policies protecting against the death of any member of the royal family which would have the effect of interrupting social activities. In the ordinary course, when no serious illness threatens, rates for this type of coverage vary from 10 to 12 percent.

When King Edward VIII selected May 12, 1937, as the date of his coronation, there developed three contingencies: (*a*) marriage, (*b*) postponement, and (*c*) abandonment due to death or other causes. Developments indicated that placing insurance covering these hazards was not without reason, for losses were paid when the abdication of Edward VIII became effective. Other policies were taken out covering simply the postponement of the coronation. Such policies insured the owners of grandstands put up along the line of march of the procession and other like concessions. George VI was crowned on the day scheduled for Edward VIII, and, therefore, there was no postponement of the coronation and no losses were paid. The question of marriage or possible abdication did not present itself in connection with the coronation of Queen Elizabeth II set for June 2, 1953. Policies were, however, issued on her life. There were hundreds of such contracts. As it developed, no losses were paid.

In this country, insurance is frequently effected when there are heavy advanced reservations for the appearance of a particular star performer. Should anything happen that would require a cancellation of the performance, the promoters would be heavy losers because of expenses incurred. In 1933, policies were issued on the theory that President Roosevelt's death would have an adverse effect on the stock market. In 1937, a musical comedy entitled "I'd Rather Be Right" mimicked important public personages, and among those burlesqued were President Roosevelt, his family, his cabinet, and the Supreme Court. The burlesque had a tremendous appeal, and the play drew capacity audiences. It was recognized, however, that the death of the President or any serious misfortune to any member of his family would have been disastrous and terminated the play's run. The producers were said to have insured against this contingency. In England, policies have been issued paying an indemnity if taxes are increased.

1941 CSO MC

Age	Number Living	Deaths Each Year	Deaths per 1,000	Expectancy, Years	Per Cent Living to 65						
1	1,000,000	5,770	5.77	62.76	57.79	51					
2	994,230	4,116	4.14	62.12	58.12	52					
3	990,114	3,347	3.38	61.37	58.37	53					
4	986,767	2,950	2.99	60.58	58.56	54					
5	983,817	2,715	2.76	59.76	58.74	55					
6	981,102	2,561	2.61	58.92	58.90	56	74				
7	978,541	2,417	2.47	58.08	59.05	57	72				
8	976,124	2,255	2.31	57.22	59.20	58	710,				
9	973,869	2,065	2.12	56.35	59.34	59	694,				
10	971,804	1,914	1.97	55.47	59.46	60	677,7				
11	969,890	1,852	1.91	54.58	59.58	61	659,74				
12	968,038	1,859	1.92	53.68	59.70	62	640,761				
13	966,179	1,913	1.98	52.78	59.81	63	620,782				
14	964,266	1,996	2.07	51.89	59.93	64	599,824				
15	962,270	2,069	2.15	50.99	60.05	65	577,882	2			
16	960,201	2,103	2.19	50.10	60.18	66	554,975	23,			
17	958,089	2,156	2.25	49.21	60.32	67	531,133	24,			
18	955,942	2,199	2.30	48.32	60.45	68	506,403	25,5			
19	953,743	2,260	2.37	47.43	60.59	69	480,850	26,30			
20	951,483	2,312	2.43	46.54	60.73	70	454,548	26,95			
21	949,171	2,382	2.51	45.66	60.88	71	427,593	27,481			
22	946,789	2,452	2.59	44.77	61.04	72	400,112	27,872			
23	944,337	2,531	2.68	43.88	61.19	73	372,240	28,104			
24	941,806	2,609	2.77	43.00	61.36	74	344,136	28,154			
25	939,197	2,705	2.88	42.12	61.53	75	315,982	28,009	8		
26	936,492	2,800	2.99	41.24	61.71	76	287,973	27,651	96		
27	933,692	2,904	3.11	40.36	61.89	77	260,322	27,071	103.		
28	930,788	3,025	3.25	39.49	62.09	78	233,251	26,262	112.5		
29	927,763	3,154	3.40	38.61	62.29	79	206,989	25,224	121.8		
30	924,609	3,292	3.56	37.74	62.50	80	181,765	23,966	131.85		
31	921,317	3,437	3.73	36.88	62.72	81	157,799	22,502	142.60		
32	917,880	3,598	3.92	36.01	62.96	82	135,297	20,857	154.16		
33	914,282	3,767	4.12	35.15	63.21	83	114,440	19,062	166.57		
34	910,515	3,961	4.35	34.29	63.47	84	95,378	17,157	179.88		
35	906,554	4,161	4.59	33.44	63.74	85	78,221	15,185	194.13	3	
36	902,393	4,386	4.86	32.59	64.04	86	63,036	13,198	209.37	3.	
37	898,007	4,625	5.15	31.75	64.35	87	49,838	11,245	225.63	3.1	
38	893,382	4,878	5.46	30.91	64.68	88	38,593	9,378	243.00	2.98	
39	888,504	5,162	5.81	30.08	65.04	89	29,215	7,638	261.44	2.77	
40	883,342	5,459	6.18	29.25	65.42	90	21,577	6,063	280.99	2.58	
41	877,883	5,785	6.59	28.43	65.83	91	15,514	4,681	301.73	2.39	..
42	872,098	6,131	7.03	27.62	66.26	92	10,833	3,506	323.64	2.21	..
43	865,967	6,503	7.51	26.81	66.73	93	7,327	2,540	346.66	2.03	...
44	859,464	6,910	8.04	26.01	67.24	94	4,787	1,776	371.00	1.84	....
45	852,554	7,340	8.61	25.21	67.78	95	3,011	1,193	396.21	1.63	....
46	845,214	7,801	9.23	24.43	68.37	96	1,818	813	447.19	1.37	.....
47	837,413	8,299	9.91	23.65	69.01	97	1,005	551	548.26	1.08	.....
48	829,114	8,822	10.64	22.88	69.70	98	454	329	724.67	.78	.....
49	820,292	9,392	11.45	22.12	70.45	99	125	125	1,000.00	.50	.....
50	810,900	9,990	12.32	21.37	71.26	..	.....	....	....	....	.....

Indexes

AUTHORS AND CASES CITED*

*Not including those in Appendixes.

INDEX

S

T

U

V

W

This book has been set on the Linotype in 11 and 9 point Caledonia leaded 1 point. Chapter numbers are in 18 point Deepdene italic cap and lower case and chapter titles in 18 point Deepdene roman caps. The size of the type page is 27 by 47 picas.

fact, break out within the term and between the countries specified in the contract. Prior to the advent of the second World War, policies were issued by Lloyd's insuring the income of businessmen who were reservists against the possibility of being called to the colors. The premiums on such policies ranged from 5 to 10 percent of their face value. The premium depended upon the age and nationality of the applicant for the insurance. In 1935, an American insurance company is reported to have paid an indemnity of approximately $300,000 to the national organization of the Boy Scouts of America which had taken out a policy of $400,000 against the cancellation of the Jamboree scheduled that year in Washington. The Jamboree was, in fact, canceled because of the prevalence of infantile paralysis. According to the report, the Scouts had been able to cancel $100,000 of contracts for foodstuff and equipment, and the loss represented primarily expenses incurred in preparing the camp site on a 400-acre tract in the city of Washington. Policies have been issued on an athletic event covering training expenses to pay an indemnity if the insured loses the event. A manufacturer, paying a royalty to the Canadian government for the privilege of manufacturing dolls resembling the Dionne quintuplets, secured a policy from Lloyd's which undertook to pay him the face amount of the policy in the event that any one of the quintuplets should die during the period of 12 months covered by the contract.

Immediately preceding the death of King George V, policies were issued covering against his death. As his condition became more critical, rates increased from 25 per cent to 60 percent, and policies were issued to trades which would suffer from a long period of official mourning. A period of court mourning in England affects unfavorably the business of hotels, theaters, caterers, dress shops, and the like. Some of these institutions regularly purchase annual policies protecting against the death of any member of the royal family which would have the effect of interrupting social activities. In the ordinary course, when no serious illness threatens, rates for this type of coverage vary from 10 to 12 percent.

When King Edward VIII selected May 12, 1937, as the date of his coronation, there developed three contingencies: (*a*) marriage, (*b*) postponement, and (*c*) abandonment due to death or other causes. Developments indicated that placing insurance covering these hazards was not without reason, for losses were paid when the abdication of Edward VIII became effective. Other policies were taken out covering simply the postponement of the coronation. Such policies insured the owners of grandstands put up along the line of march of the procession and other like concessions. George VI was crowned on the day scheduled for Edward VIII, and, therefore, there was no postponement of the coronation and no losses were paid. The question of marriage or possible abdication did not present itself in connection with the coronation of Queen Elizabeth II set for June 2, 1953. Policies were, however, issued on her life. There were hundreds of such contracts. As it developed, no losses were paid.

In this country, insurance is frequently effected when there are heavy advanced reservations for the appearance of a particular star performer. Should anything happen that would require a cancellation of the performance, the promoters would be heavy losers because of expenses incurred. In 1933, policies were issued on the theory that President Roosevelt's death would have an adverse effect on the stock market. In 1937, a musical comedy entitled "I'd Rather Be Right" mimicked important public personages, and among those burlesqued were President Roosevelt, his family, his cabinet, and the Supreme Court. The burlesque had a tremendous appeal, and the play drew capacity audiences. It was recognized, however, that the death of the President or any serious misfortune to any member of his family would have been disastrous and terminated the play's run. The producers were said to have insured against this contingency. In England, policies have been issued paying an indemnity if taxes are increased.

Appendix J

1941 CSO MORTALITY TABLE

Age	Number Living	Deaths Each Year	Deaths per 1,000	Expectancy, Years	Per Cent Living to 65	Age	Number Living	Deaths Each Year	Deaths per 1,000	Expectancy, Years	Per Cent Living to 65
1	1,000,000	5,770	5.77	62.76	57.79	51	800,910	10,628	13.27	20.64	72.15
2	994,230	4,116	4.14	62.12	58.12	52	790,282	11,301	14.30	19.91	73.12
3	990,114	3,347	3.38	61.37	58.37	53	778,981	12,020	15.43	19.19	74.18
4	986,767	2,950	2.99	60.58	58.56	54	766,961	12,770	16.65	18.48	75.35
5	983,817	2,715	2.76	59.76	58.74	55	754,191	13,560	17.98	17.78	76.62
6	981,102	2,561	2.61	58.92	58.90	56	740,631	14,390	19.43	17.10	78.03
7	978,541	2,417	2.47	58.08	59.05	57	726,241	15,251	21.00	16.43	79.57
8	976,124	2,255	2.31	57.22	59.20	58	710,990	16,147	22.71	15.77	81.28
9	973,869	2,065	2.12	56.35	59.34	59	694,843	17,072	24.57	15.13	83.17
10	971,804	1,914	1.97	55.47	59.46	60	677,771	18,022	26.59	14.50	85.26
11	969,890	1,852	1.91	54.58	59.58	61	659,749	18,988	28.78	13.88	87.59
12	968,038	1,859	1.92	53.68	59.70	62	640,761	19,979	31.18	13.27	90.19
13	966,179	1,913	1.98	52.78	59.81	63	620,782	20,958	33.79	12.69	93.09
14	964,266	1,996	2.07	51.89	59.93	64	599,824	21,942	36.58	12.11	96.34
15	962,270	2,069	2.15	50.99	60.05	65	577,882	22,907	39.64	11.55	100.00
16	960,201	2,103	2.19	50.10	60.18	66	554,975	23,842	42.96	11.01	.....
17	958,089	2,156	2.25	49.21	60.32	67	531,133	24,730	46.56	10.48	.....
18	955,942	2,199	2.30	48.32	60.45	68	506,403	25,553	50.46	9.97	.....
19	953,743	2,260	2.37	47.43	60.59	69	480,850	26,302	54.70	9.47	.....
20	951,483	2,312	2.43	46.54	60.73	70	454,548	26,955	59.30	8.99	.....
21	949,171	2,382	2.51	45.66	60.88	71	427,593	27,481	64.27	8.52	.....
22	946,789	2,452	2.59	44.77	61.04	72	400,112	27,872	69.66	8.08	.....
23	944,337	2,531	2.68	43.88	61.19	73	372,240	28,104	75.50	7.64	.....
24	941,806	2,609	2.77	43.00	61.36	74	344,136	28,154	81.81	7.23	.....
25	939,197	2,705	2.88	42.12	61.53	75	315,982	28,009	88.64	6.82	.....
26	936,492	2,800	2.99	41.24	61.71	76	287,973	27,651	96.02	6.44	.....
27	933,692	2,904	3.11	40.36	61.89	77	260,322	27,071	103.99	6.07	.....
28	930,788	3,025	3.25	39.49	62.09	78	233,251	26,262	112.59	5.72	.....
29	927,763	3,154	3.40	38.61	62.29	79	206,989	25,224	121.86	5.38	.....
30	924,609	3,292	3.56	37.74	62.50	80	181,765	23,966	131.85	5.06	.....
31	921,317	3,437	3.73	36.88	62.72	81	157,799	22,502	142.60	4.75	.....
32	917,880	3,598	3.92	36.01	62.96	82	135,297	20,857	154.16	4.46	.....
33	914,282	3,767	4.12	35.15	63.21	83	114,440	19,062	166.57	4.18	.....
34	910,515	3,961	4.35	34.29	63.47	84	95,378	17,157	179.88	3.91	.....
35	906,554	4,161	4.59	33.44	63.74	85	78,221	15,185	194.13	3.66	.....
36	902,393	4,386	4.86	32.59	64.04	86	63,036	13,198	209.37	3.42	.....
37	898,007	4,625	5.15	31.75	64.35	87	49,838	11,245	225.63	3.19	.....
38	893,382	4,878	5.46	30.91	64.68	88	38,593	9,378	243.00	2.98	.....
39	888,504	5,162	5.81	30.08	65.04	89	29,215	7,638	261.44	2.77	.....
40	883,342	5,459	6.18	29.25	65.42	90	21,577	6,063	280.99	2.58	.....
41	877,883	5,785	6.59	28.43	65.83	91	15,514	4,681	301.73	2.39	.....
42	872,098	6,131	7.03	27.62	66.26	92	10,833	3,506	323.64	2.21	.....
43	865,967	6,503	7.51	26.81	66.73	93	7,327	2,540	346.66	2.03	.....
44	859,464	6,910	8.04	26.01	67.24	94	4,787	1,776	371.00	1.84	.....
45	852,554	7,340	8.61	25.21	67.78	95	3,011	1,193	396.21	1.63	.....
46	845,214	7,801	9.23	24.43	68.37	96	1,818	813	447.19	1.37	.....
47	837,413	8,299	9.91	23.65	69.01	97	1,005	551	548.26	1.08	.....
48	829,114	8,822	10.64	22.88	69.70	98	454	329	724.67	.78	.....
49	820,292	9,392	11.45	22.12	70.45	99	125	125	1,000.00	.50	.....
50	810,900	9,990	12.32	21.37	71.26	..	.....	....	....	....	.....